Guide to Gale Literary Criticism Series

For criticism on	Consult these Gale series
Authors now living or who died after December 31, 1999	*CONTEMPORARY LITERARY CRITICISM (CLC)*
Authors who died between 1900 and 1999	*TWENTIETH-CENTURY LITERARY CRITICISM (TCLC)*
Authors who died between 1800 and 1899	*NINETEENTH-CENTURY LITERATURE CRITICISM (NCLC)*
Authors who died between 1400 and 1799	*LITERATURE CRITICISM FROM 1400 TO 1800 (LC)* *SHAKESPEAREAN CRITICISM (SC)*
Authors who died before 1400	*CLASSICAL AND MEDIEVAL LITERATURE CRITICISM (CMLC)*
Authors of books for children and young adults	*CHILDREN'S LITERATURE REVIEW (CLR)*
Dramatists	*DRAMA CRITICISM (DC)*
Poets	*POETRY CRITICISM (PC)*
Short story writers	*SHORT STORY CRITICISM (SSC)*
Literary topics and movements	*HARLEM RENAISSANCE: A GALE CRITICAL COMPANION (HR)* *THE BEAT GENERATION: A GALE CRITICAL COMPANION (BG)*
Asian American writers of the last two hundred years	*ASIAN AMERICAN LITERATURE (AAL)*
Black writers of the past two hundred years	*BLACK LITERATURE CRITICISM (BLC)* *BLACK LITERATURE CRITICISM SUPPLEMENT (BLCS)*
Hispanic writers of the late nineteenth and twentieth centuries	*HISPANIC LITERATURE CRITICISM (HLC)* *HISPANIC LITERATURE CRITICISM SUPPLEMENT (HLCS)*
Native North American writers and orators of the eighteenth, nineteenth, and twentieth centuries	*NATIVE NORTH AMERICAN LITERATURE (NNAL)*
Major authors from the Renaissance to the present	*WORLD LITERATURE CRITICISM, 1500 TO THE PRESENT (WLC)* *WORLD LITERATURE CRITICISM SUPPLEMENT (WLCS)*

ISSN 1056-4349

DRAMA
CRITICISM

Criticism of the Most Significant and Widely Studied
Dramatic Works from All the World's Literatures

VOLUME 27

Jelena O. Krstović
Project Editor

THOMSON
—★—
GALE

Detroit • New York • San Francisco • San Diego • New Haven, Conn. • Waterville, Maine • London • Munich

THOMSON

—✦— ™

GALE

Drama Criticism, Vol. 27

Project Editor
Jelena O. Krstović

Editorial
Jessica Bomarito, Kathy D. Darrow, Jeffrey W. Hunter, Michelle Lee, Rachelle Mucha, Thomas J. Schoenberg, Lawrence J. Trudeau, Russel Whitaker

Data Capture
Francis Monroe, Gwen Tucker

Indexing Services
Laurie Andriot

Rights Acquisitions and Management
Edna Hedblad, Jacqueline Key, Lisa Kincade, Kim Smilay

Imaging and Multimedia
Dean Dauphinais, Leitha Etheridge-Sims, Lezlie Light, Mike Logusz, Dan Newell, Christine O'Bryan, Kelly A. Quin, Denay Wilding, Robyn Young

Composition and Electronic Capture
Amy Darga

Manufacturing
Rhonda Williams

Product Manager
Marc Cormier

LIBRARY OF CONGRESS CATALOG CARD NUMBER 76-46132

ISBN 0-7876-8111-3
ISSN 1056-4349

Printed in the United States of America
10 9 8 7 6 5 4 3 2 1

Contents

Preface vii

Acknowledgments xi

Literary Criticism Series Advisory Board xiii

Preface

*D*rama Criticism (*DC*) is principally intended for beginning students of literature and theater as well as the average playgoer. The series is therefore designed to introduce readers to the most frequently studied playwrights of all time periods and nationalities and to present discerning commentary on dramatic works of enduring interest. Furthermore, *DC* seeks to acquaint the reader with the uses and functions of criticism itself. Selected from a diverse body of commentary, the essays in *DC* offer insights into the authors and their works but do not require that the reader possess a wide background in literary studies. Where appropriate, reviews of important productions of the plays discussed are also included to give students a heightened awareness of drama as a dynamic art form, one that many claim is fully realized only in performance.

DC was created in response to suggestions by the staffs of high school, college, and public libraries. These librarians observed a need for a series that assembles critical commentary on the world's most renowned dramatists in the same manner as Thomson Gale's *Short Story Criticism* (*SSC*) and *Poetry Criticism* (*PC*), which present material on writers of short fiction and poetry. Although playwrights are covered in such Thomson Gale literary criticism series as *Contemporary Literary Criticism* (*CLC*), *Twentieth-Century Literary Criticism* (*TCLC*), *Nineteenth-Century Literature Criticism* (*NCLC*), *Literature Criticism from 1400 to 1800* (*LC*), and *Classical and Medieval Literature Criticism* (*CMLC*), *DC* directs more concentrated attention on individual dramatists than is possible in the broader, survey-oriented entries in these Thomson Gale series. Commentary on the works of William Shakespeare may be found in *Shakespearean Criticism* (*SC*).

Scope of the Series

By collecting and organizing commentary on dramatists, *DC* assists students in their efforts to gain insight into literature, achieve better understanding of the texts, and formulate ideas for papers and assignments. A variety of interpretations and assessments is offered, allowing students to pursue their own interests and promoting awareness that literature is dynamic and responsive to many different opinions.

Approximately five to ten authors are included in each volume, and each entry presents a historical survey of the critical response to that playwright's work. The length of an entry is intended to reflect the amount of critical attention the author has received from critics writing in English and from foreign critics in translation. Every attempt has been made to identify and include the most significant essays on each author's work. In order to provide these important critical pieces, the editors sometimes reprint essays that have appeared elsewhere in Thomson Gale's literary criticism series. Such duplication, however, never exceeds twenty percent of a *DC* volume.

Organization of the Book

A *DC* entry consists of the following elements:

- The **Author Heading** consists of the playwright's most commonly used name, followed by birth and death dates. If an author consistently wrote under a pseudonym, the pseudonym is listed in the author heading and the real name given in parentheses on the first line of the introduction. Also located at the beginning of the introduction are any name variations under which the dramatist wrote, including transliterated forms of the names of authors whose languages use nonroman alphabets.

- The **Introduction** contains background information that introduces the reader to the author and the critical debates surrounding his or her work.

- A **Portrait of the Author** is included when available.

- The list of **Principal Works** is divided into two sections. The first section contains the author's dramatic pieces and is organized chronologically by date of first performance. If this has not been conclusively determined, the composition or publication date is used. The second section provides information on the author's major works in other genres.

- Essays offering **overviews and general studies of the dramatist's entire literary career** give the student broad perspectives on the writer's artistic development, themes, and concerns that recur in several of his or her works, the author's place in literary history, and other wide-ranging topics.

- **Criticism** of individual plays offers the reader in-depth discussions of a select number of the author's most important works. In some cases, the criticism is divided into two sections, each arranged chronologically. When a significant performance of a play can be identified (typically, the premier of a twentieth-century work), the first section of criticism will feature **production reviews** of this staging. Most entries include sections devoted to **critical commentary** that assesses the literary merit of the selected plays. When necessary, essays are carefully excerpted to focus on the work under consideration; often, however, essays and reviews are reprinted in their entirety. Footnotes are reprinted at the end of each essay or excerpt. In the case of excerpted criticism, only those footnotes that pertain to the excerpted texts are included.

- Critical essays are prefaced by brief **Annotations** explicating each piece.

- A complete **Bibliographic Citation,** designed to help the interested reader locate the original essay or book, precedes each piece of criticism. Source citations in the Literary Criticism Series follow University of Chicago Press style, as outlined in *The Chicago Manual of Style,* 14th ed. (Chicago: The University of Chicago Press, 1993).

- An annotated bibliography of **Further Reading** appears at the end of each entry and suggests resources for additional study. In some cases, significant essays for which the editors could not obtain reprint rights are included here. Boxed material following the further reading list provides references to other biographical and critical sources on the author in series published by Thomson Gale.

Cumulative Indexes

A **Cumulative Author Index** lists all of the authors that appear in a wide variety of reference sources published by Thomson Gale, including *DC.* A complete list of these sources is found facing the first page of the Author Index. The index also includes birth and death dates and cross references between pseudonyms and actual names.

A **Cumulative Nationality Index** lists all authors featured in *DC* by nationality, followed by the number of the *DC* volume in which their entry appears.

A **Cumulative Title Index** lists in alphabetical order the individual plays discussed in the criticism contained in *DC.* Each title is followed by the author's last name and corresponding volume and page numbers where commentary on the work is located. English-language translations of original foreign-language titles are cross-referenced to the foreign titles so that all references to discussion of a work are combined in one listing.

Citing *Drama Criticism*

When citing criticism reprinted in the Literary Criticism Series, students should provide complete bibliographic information so that the cited essay can be located in the original print or electronic source. Students who quote directly from reprinted criticism may use any accepted bibliographic format, such as University of Chicago Press style or Modern Language Association (MLA) style. Both the MLA and the University of Chicago formats are acceptable and recognized as being the current standards for citations. It is important, however, to choose one format for all citations; do not mix the two formats within a list of citations.

The examples below follow recommendations for preparing a bibliography set forth in *The Chicago Manual of Style,* 14th ed. (Chicago: The University of Chicago Press, 1993); the first example pertains to material drawn from periodicals, the second to material reprinted from books:

Morrison, Jago. "Narration and Unease in Ian McEwan's Later Fiction." *Critique* 42, no. 3 (spring 2001): 253-68. Reprinted in *Drama Criticism.* Vol. 20, edited by Janet Witalec, 212-20. Detroit: Gale, 2003.

Brossard, Nicole. "Poetic Politics." In *The Politics of Poetic Form: Poetry and Public Policy,* edited by Charles Bernstein, 73-82. New York: Roof Books, 1990. Reprinted in *Drama Criticism.* Vol. 20, edited by Janet Witalec, 3-8. Detroit: Gale, 2003.

The examples below follow recommendations for preparing a works cited list set forth in the *MLA Handbook for Writers of Research Papers,* 5th ed. (New York: The Modern Language Association of America, 1999); the first example pertains to material drawn from periodicals, the second to material reprinted from books:

Morrison, Jago. "Narration and Unease in Ian McEwan's Later Fiction." *Critique* 42.3 (spring 2001): 253-68. Reprinted in *Drama Criticism.* Ed. Janet Witalec. Vol. 20. Detroit: Gale, 2003. 212-20.

Brossard, Nicole. "Poetic Politics." *The Politics of Poetic Form: Poetry and Public Policy.* Ed. Charles Bernstein. New York: Roof Books, 1990. 73-82. Reprinted in *Drama Criticism.* Ed. Janet Witalec. Vol. 20. Detroit: Gale, 2003. 3-8.

Suggestions are Welcome

Readers who wish to suggest new features, topics, or authors to appear in future volumes, or who have other suggestions or comments are cordially invited to call, write, or fax the Product Manager:

Product Manager, Literary Criticism Series
Thomson Gale
27500 Drake Road
Farmington Hills, MI 48331-3535
1-800-347-4253 (GALE)
Fax: 248-699-8054

Acknowledgments

The editors wish to thank the copyright holders of the excerpted criticism included in this volume and the permissions managers of many book and magazine publishing companies for assisting us in securing reproduction rights. We are also grateful to the staffs of the Detroit Public Library, the Library of Congress, the University of Detroit Mercy Library, Wayne State University Purdy/Kresge Library Complex, and the University of Michigan Libraries for making their resources available to us. Following is a list of the copyright holders who have granted us permission to reproduce material in this volume of *DC*. Every effort has been made to trace copyright, but if omissions have been made, please let us know.

COPYRIGHTED MATERIAL IN *DC*, VOLUME 27, WAS REPRODUCED FROM THE FOLLOWING PERIODICALS:

American Scientist, v. 90, November-December, 2002. © 2002 by Sigma Xi, The Scientific Research Society, Inc. Reproduced by permission.—*American Theatre,* v. 12, March, 1995 for "The Muses of Terrence McNally: Music and Mortality are His Consuming Themes" by Toby Zinman; v. 15, December, 1998 for "The Last Temptation of MTC" by Charles McNulty. Copyright © 1995, 1998, Theatre Communications Group. All rights reserved. Both reproduced by permission of the respective authors.—*Anglia: Zeitschrift fur Englische Philologie,* v. 105, 1987 for "Captain Thomas Stukeley: The Man, the Theatrical Record, and the Origins of Tudor Biographical Drama" by Joseph Candido. Copyright © Max Niemeyer Tubingen 1987. Reproduced by permission of the author.—*ANQ,* v. 17, winter, 2004. Copyright © 2004 by Helen Dwight Reid Educational Foundation. Reproduced with permission of the Helen Dwight Reid Educational Foundation, published by Heldref Publications, 1319 18th Street, NW, Washington, DC 20036-1802.—*The Atlantic Monthly,* v. 280, October, 1997 for "Maria, Not Callas" by Matthew Gurewitsch. Copyright © 1997 by The Atlantic Monthly Company. Reproduced by permission of the author.—*Cahiers Elisabéthains,* April, 1983 for "Elizabethan Epideictic Drama: Praise and Blame in the Plays of Peele and Lyly" by R. Headlam Wells. Reproduced by permission of the publisher.—*CLA Journal,* v. 30, June, 1987. Copyright, 1987 by The College Language Association. Used by permission of The College Language Association.—*Educational Theatre Journal,* v. 22, October, 1970. Copyright © 1970 The Johns Hopkins University Press. Reproduced by permission.—*ELH,* v. 47, fall, 1980. Copyright © 1980 The Johns Hopkins University Press. Reproduced by permission.—*The Explicator,* v. 48, fall, 1989; v. 61, summer, 2003. Copyright © 1989, 2003 by Helen Dwight Reid Educational Foundation. Both reproduced with permission of the Helen Dwight Reid Educational Foundation, published by Heldref Publications, 1319 18th Street, NW, Washington, DC 20036-1802.—*The French Review,* v. 32, April, 1959; v. 36, January, 1963; v. 40, October, 1966; v. 43, February, 1970; v. 52, April, 1979; v. 53, December, 1979; v. 58, May, 1985; v. 65, February, 1992. Copyright © 1959, 1963, 1966, 1970, 1979, 1985, 1992 by the American Association of Teachers of French. All reproduced by permission.—*Hungarian Journal of English and American Studies,* v. 6, spring, 2000. Copyright © by *Hungarian Journal of English and American Studies.* Reproduced by permission.—*Journal of American Folklore,* v. 94, October-December, 1981. Copyright © 1981 by the American Folklore Society. Republished with permission of the American Folklore Society, conveyed through Copyright Clearance Center, Inc.—*Journal of Dramatic Theory and Criticism,* v. 2, 2002 for "The Scientist as Byronic Hero: Michael Frayn's *Copenhagen*" by August W. Staub. Reproduced by permission of the author.—*Journal of Evolutionary Psychology,* v. 4, August, 1983. Copyright 1983 by the Institute for Evolutionary Psychology. Reproduced by permission.—*Kentucky Romance Quarterly,* v. 32, 1985. Copyright © 1985 by Helen Dwight Reid Educational Foundation. Reproduced with permission of the Helen Dwight Reid Educational Foundation, published by Heldref Publications, 1319 18th Street, NW, Washington, DC 20036-1802.—*The Massachusetts Review,* v. 42, summer, 2001. Copyright © 2001. Reprinted by permission from *The Massachusetts Review.*—*Modern Drama,* v. 36, December, 1993. Copyright © 1993 by the University of Toronto, Graduate Centre for Study of Drama. Reproduced by permission.—*Nineteenth-Century French Studies,* v. 20, fall-winter, 1991-1992; v. 31, spring-summer, 2003. Copyright © 1991-1992, 2003 by the University of Nebraska Press. Both reproduced by permission.—*Partisan Review,* v. 70, winter, 2003 for "'Two Wings of the Same Breathing Creature': Fictionalizing History" by Cushing Strout. Reproduced by permission of the author.—*Philological Quarterly,* v. 65, winter, 1986. Copyright 1986 by The University of Iowa. Reproduced by permission.—*Physics World,* June, 1998. Reproduced by permission.—*PMLA,* v. 55, June, 1940. Copyright © 1940 by the Modern Language Association of America. Reprinted by permission of the Modern Language Association of America.—*Queen's Quarterly,* v. 110, spring, 2003 for "The Uncertainty about Heisenberg" by Michael Posner. Reproduced by permission of the author.—*Renaissance Drama,* v. 8, 1965; v. 1, 1968. Copyright © 1965, 1968 by Northwestern University Press. Both reproduced by permission.—*Romance Notes,* v. 24, fall, 1983; v. 28, spring, 1988; v. 38, fall, 1997; v. 44, fall, 2003. All reproduced by permission.—*Studia Anglica Posnaniensia,* v. 11, 1979. Reproduced by permission.—*Studies in English Literature, 1500-1900,* v. 21, spring, 1981. Copyright © 1981

The Johns Hopkins University Press. Reproduced by permission.—*Theatre Journal,* v. 49, May, 1997; v. 51, May, 1999. Copyright © 1997, 1999 The Johns Hopkins University Press. Both reproduced by permission.

COPYRIGHTED MATERIAL IN *DC*, VOLUME 27, WAS REPRODUCED FROM THE FOLLOWING BOOKS:

Drukman, Steven. From "Terrance McNally," in *Speaking on Stage: Interviews with Contemporary American Playwrights.* Edited by Philip C. Kolin and Colby H. Kullman. The University of Alabama Press, 1996. Copyright © 1996 The University of Alabama Press. All rights reserved. Reproduced by permission of the author.—Free, Mary G. From *Renaissance Papers 1983.* The Southeastern Renaissance Conference, 1984. Reproduced by permission.—Frontain, Raymond-Jean. From "'All Men Are Divine': Religious Mystery and Homosexual Identity in Terrence McNally's *Corpus Christi,*" in *Reclaiming the Sacred: The Bible in Gay and Lesbian Culture.* Edited by Raymond-Jean Frontain. New York: Harrington Park Press, 2003. Copyright © 2003 by The Haworth Press, Inc. All rights reserved. Reproduced by permission.— Gochberg, Herbert S. From *Stage of Dreams: The Dramatic Art of Alfred de Musset.* Librairie Droz S.A., 1967. © 1967 by Librairie Droz S.A. Reproduced by permission.—Harrell, Wade. From "When the Parody Parodies Itself: The Problem with Michael Frayn's *Noises Off,*" in *From the Bard to Broadway.* Edited by Karelisa Hartigan. University Press of America, 1987. Copyright © 1987 by University Press of America, Inc. All rights reserved. Reproduced by permission of Karelisa Hartigan.—MacInnes, John W. From "*Lorenzaccio* and the Drama of Narration," in *Text and Presentation: The University of Florida Department of Classics Comparative Drama Conference Papers, Volume VIII.* Edited by Karelisa Hartigan. University Press of America, 1988. Copyright © 1988 by University Press of America, Inc. All rights reserved. Reproduced by permission of Karelisa Hartigan.—Mazer, Cary M. From "*Master Class* and the Paradox of the Diva," in *Modern Dramatists: A Casebook of Major British, Irish, and American Playwrights.* Edited by Kimball King. Routledge, 2001. Copyright © 2001 by Kimball King. All rights reserved. Reproduced by permission of Routledge/Taylor & Francis Group, LLC, and the author.—Román, David. From "Negative Identifications: HIV-Negative Gay Men in Representation and Performance," in *Queer Representations: Reading Lives, Reading Cultures.* Edited by Martin Duberman. New York University Press, 1997. Copyright © 1997 by New York University. All rights reserved. Reproduced by permission of the author.—Savran, David. From *The Playwright's Voice: American Dramatists on Memory, Writing, and the Politics of Culture.* Theatre Communications Group, 1999. Copyright © 1999, Theatre Communications Group. All rights reserved. Reproduced by permission.—Sices, David. From *Theater of Solitude: The Drama of Alfred de Musset.* The University Press of New England, 1974. © 1974 University Press of New England, Hanover, NH. All rights reserved. Reproduced by permission.—Soto-Morettini, Donna. From "'Disturbing the Spirits of the Past': The Uncertainty Principal in Michael Frayn's *Copenhagen,*" in *Crucible of Cultures: Anglophone Drama at the Dawn of a New Millennium.* Edited by Marc Maufort and Franca Ballarsi. P.I.E.-Peter Lang, 2002. © P.I.E.-Peter Lang S.A. Reproduced by permission.—Whitney-Brown, Carolyn. From "'A Farre More Worthy Wombe': Reproduction Anxiety in Peele's *David and Bethsabe,*" in *In Another Country: Feminist Perspectives on Renaissance Drama.* Edited by Dorothea Kehler and Susan Baker. The Scarecrow Press, Inc., 1991. Copyright © 1991 by Scarecrow Press. All rights reserved. Reproduced by permission.

PHOTOGRAPHS APPEARING IN *DC*, VOLUME 27, WERE RECEIVED FROM THE FOLLOWING SOURCES:

de Musset, Alfred, engraving. The Library of Congress.—Frayn, Michael, holding the American Theatre Wing's 2000 Tony Award, photograph by Brad Rickerby. © Reuters NewMedia Inc./Corbis.—McNally, Terrence, photograph. Ron Galella/ WireImage.com.

Thomson Gale Literature Product Advisory Board

The members of the Thomson Gale Literature Product Advisory Board—reference librarians from public and academic library systems—represent a cross-section of our customer base and offer a variety of informed perspectives on both the presentation and content of our literature products. Advisory board members assess and define such quality issues as the relevance, currency, and usefulness of the author coverage, critical content, and literary topics included in our series; evaluate the layout, presentation, and general quality of our printed volumes; provide feedback on the criteria used for selecting authors and topics covered in our series; provide suggestions for potential enhancements to our series; identify any gaps in our coverage of authors or literary topics, recommending authors or topics for inclusion; analyze the appropriateness of our content and presentation for various user audiences, such as high school students, undergraduates, graduate students, librarians, and educators; and offer feedback on any proposed changes/enhancements to our series. We wish to thank the following advisors for their advice throughout the year.

Michael Frayn
1933-

English playwright, novelist, and translator.

INTRODUCTION

A prolific writer, Frayn has tackled novels, plays, nonfiction books, and screenplays during his lengthy career. To date, four of Frayn's plays have been filmed for British television and two plays have been made into motion pictures. A thoughtful writer with a deeply philosophical mind, Frayn carefully shows his audience the possibilities inherent in any situation he puts on stage. He has turned the theater around on itself with the ground-breaking parody *Noises Off* (1982) and he has given audiences a chance to ponder the what-ifs of the history of the birth of atomic energy in his surprise international hit *Copenhagen* (1998).

BIOGRAPHICAL INFORMATION

Frayn was born in London on September 8, 1933. He grew up in the suburb of Ewell and attended public school during his teenage years. Upon graduating, Frayn spent two years doing National Service. During this time, he learned the Russian language and worked as an interpreter. He later put these language skills to use translating several of Anton Chekhov's plays. Upon leaving the military, Frayn went to Emmanuel College, Cambridge; he graduated in 1957 with a degree in "moral sciences." His first years out of college were spent working as a journalist, first for the *Guardian* and then the *Observer.* While working for these newspapers, Frayn also began writing novels. His first novel, *The Tin Men* (1965), won the 1966 Somerset Maugham Award—the first of many such awards Frayn was to receive for his writing. Frayn is married to Clare Tomalin, who is also a noted writer.

MAJOR DRAMATIC WORKS

Most of Frayn's dramatic works have been solid, well-received plays. Some stand out from the rest, however. Several positively reviewed plays written in the 1970s, including *Donkeys' Years* (1976), established Frayn as a comic writer to be reckoned with. *Noises Off,* first presented in 1982, broke new ground with its twist on the play within the play and its focus on backstage

mayhem. His 1984 play *Benefactors* received critical acclaim and an Antoinette Perry Award (more commonly known as a Tony Award). But by far the play that has gained Frayn the most critical attention is his stark drama, *Copenhagen.* The plot centers on the recollections of three characters: Werner Heisenberg, a German physicist working on the atomic energy project for the Nazis; his former colleague, the Danish physicist, Nils Bohr; and Bohr's wife, Margrethe. In 1941 Heisenberg made a now-famous visit to his former mentor, Bohr, in German-occupied Copenhagen. By then, they were on opposite sides of the war, though they were apparently not personally enemies. The conversations that took place between the two men during this visit are a matter of much speculation. Frayn does not seek to settle what happened; rather, he examines the possibilities of what might have been discussed, what likely was discussed, and the possible repercussions of decisions made by both world-class physicists who were on the cutting edge of atomic physics during World War II. The play made ripples in theater and science circles alike because of its highly technical subject matter wrapped around powerful human emotions. *Copenhagen* won the Critics' Circle Award for Best New Play in 1998, the Evening Standard Award for Best Play of the Year in 1998, the Prix Molière for Best New Play in 1999, and a Tony Award in 2000.

CRITICAL RECEPTION

The very first play Frayn wrote, a one-act, was rejected for performance. Frayn responded by writing a full-length play, *The Two of Us,* which premiered in 1970 to not entirely favorable reviews. Some critics were deeply offended by the onstage changing of a baby's diaper. This willingness to take risks and push the envelope regarding what the theater can be is a common thread that runs through Frayn's dramatic writing. His next production, *Noises Off,* showed audiences the behind-the-scenes drama that happens during a play's production. Many critics felt the play was uneven; the solid first and second acts were followed by a weak, meandering third act. Not all critics or readers felt that way, however. This parody of theater itself won three major awards: the Evening Standard Award for Best Comedy of the Year in 1982, the Laurence Olivier Award for Best Comedy that same year, and a Tony Award in 1984 for the Broadway production. A later play, *Look, Look* (1989), entailed the audience seeing itself watching the production. Critics panned it and the play did not do well. Frayn wrote a few pieces in the years after, but it was not until 1998 that his reputation as a dramatist rebounded on the release of his deeply thoughtful drama, *Copenhagen.* Like *Noises Off, Copenhagen* came under fire for presenting a strong first act and then a less compelling concluding act. Some critics also suggested that the play only raised difficult philosophical questions, but left the audience dangling without answers. Others praised the open-ended format in which Frayn presented several recollections of past events from the viewpoints of different characters and then let the audience draw their own final conclusions about what really happened. Regardless of some critics' objections to the play's philosophical structure, the play became an international success.

PRINCIPAL WORKS

Plays

The Two of Us 1970
Alphabetical Order 1975
Clouds 1976

Donkeys' Years 1976
The Cherry Orchard [translator; from *The Cherry Orchard,* by Anton Chekhov] 1978
Make or Break 1980
Noises Off 1982
The Three Sisters [translator; from *The Three Sisters,* by Anton Chekhov] 1983
Benefactors 1984
Wild Honey [translator; from *Wild Honey,* by Anton Chekhov] 1984
Uncle Vanya [translator; from *Uncle Vanya,* by Anton Chekhov] 1988
Look Look 1989
Here 1993
Alarms and Excursions: More Plays than One 1998
Copenhagen 1998

Other Major Works

The Tin Men (novel) 1965
The Russian Interpreter (novel) 1966
Towards the End of the Morning (novel) 1967
A Very Private Life (novel) 1968
Clockwise (screenplay) 1986
First and Last (screenplay) 1987
A Landing on the Sun (novel) 1991
Headlong (novel) 1999
Spies (novel) 2001
Democracy (novel) 2003

NOISES OFF (1982)

CRITICAL COMMENTARY

Wade Harrell (essay date 1987)

SOURCE: Harrell, Wade. "When the Parody Parodies Itself: The Problem with Michael Frayn's *Noises Off.*" In *From the Bard to Broadway,* edited by Karelisa V. Hartigan, The University of Florida Department of Classics Comparative Drama Conference Papers, Vol. 7, pp. 87-93. Lanham, Md.: University Press of America, 1987.

[*In the following essay, Harrell evaluates Frayn's* Noises Off, *focusing on the third act and on the idea of the parody of a parody.*]

After successful runs in London, New York, and other cities with a touring company across the U.S. in 1985, *Noises Off* probably has garnered a great deal more critical acclaim than it deserves. Jack Tinker of the *Daily Mail* calls it "Mr. Frayn's brilliant and best work" (Reprinted in *Noises Off,* np). To the theatre-goer, however, the play is very uneven comically, the first two acts being much funnier and more tantalizing than the third act. The first two acts satisfy our conventional notions of what good parody is, while the third act deteriorates into a muddle of confusion onstage. To the drama critic, the play raises an interesting set of problems concerning the quality of the play itself, and its placement within the genre. In short, it is hard to decide just exactly what kind of play it is—parody? travesty? improvisation?

An analysis of the play first requires a familiarity with some basic literary definitions. Hugh Holman, in *A Handbook of Literature,* offers the standard but perhaps obsolete definition of travesty. He says the travesty is "writing which by its incongruity of style or treatment ridicules a subject inherently noble or dignified." This definition is unsatisfying because it is too closely related to that of parody which he defines as "a composition burlesquing or imitating another, usually serious, piece of work. It is designed to ridicule . . ." Enoch Brater, in an essay about parody in Tom Stoppard's plays, attempts a much needed distinction between parody and travesty. He says that "while both parody and travesty closely imitate the style of an author or work for comic effect or ridicule, only the former employs this strategy to make some critical commentary on the original. Travesty, on the other hand, makes no such evaluative claim and harbors no such analytical pretension" (Brater, 1981, 119). This distinction so far seems somewhat inadequate since ridiculing something is in fact making a critical commentary on it. But what Brater goes on to say is probably more important for differentiating the two: "A travesty is merely a burlesque whose tactics are gross distortion and incongruity for their own sake" (Brater, 1981, 119). Linda Hutcheon, (1985) in her exhaustive study of parody arrives at a broad but satisfying definition of parody as "repetition with difference" (101). She goes on to assert that "any codified form, can, theoretically, be treated in terms of repetition with critical distance" (18). It is clear from these definitions, that *Noises Off* is two-thirds well conceived parody which draws upon well-known codes, that is, props, plot twists, character types, etc., while the last act is clearly nonsensical travesty in which there are no readable codes for the audience and whose exaggerated action on stage is there for its own sake and as a way of compensating for other weaknesses in the plot.

Noises Off is not a well-made play, but the first two acts are made very well. Act I is exposition. Frayn teases us with a rehearsal for what we know will be a very funny parody of English comedy, with all the conventional codes: a fragile vase placed precariously on a small table, a box of important documents, a flight bag, telephones and newspapers, a plate of sardines, and a row of doors leading to various rooms in a deserted country estate. Add to this two couples who enter the house each thinking they will be alone. As the play opens we see the actors rehearsing *Nothing On,* a farce in one act. As the actors enter and attempt to rehearse, the audience learns what is supposed to happen during the play. The rehearsal does not go smoothly, however. Lloyd, the director, keeps interrupting to reprimand the actors, one of the actresses disrupts the rehearsal by losing a contact lens, and one actor is nowhere to be found. All of this Frayn handles very well. Rather than presenting us with a complete version of *Nothing On,* he shows us only what we know to be the familiar props and a few of the events in a type of drama that we are already familiar with. What is funniest in Act One is what is left unsaid and undone, because the audience already knows what to expect. In short, Frayn has presented us a with clearly defined set of codes for the parody of a parody.

In Act Two, in the rising action, Frayn breaks those codes. In a clever twist, the audience is taken behind the stage during a production of *Nothing On* one month later and sees how the personal affairs, arguments, and actions of the crew and cast affect what happens on stage. The familiar props and situations that the audience expects in *Nothing On* never materialize. For example, we learn in the first act that at one point Belinda, who plays Flavia in *Nothing On,* is supposed to carry a dress on stage. What actually happens is that Lloyd, the director, sends Tim, the stage hand, to buy flowers for Brooke, who has the role of the dumb blonde in both plays and is his lover. Tim enters the backstage area with the flowers. Belinda enters and tells Tim that Selsdon, a fading and alcoholic star, has locked himself in his room. Tim gives the flowers to Belinda and goes in search of Selsdon. She in turn gives the flowers to Frederick, another actor, and grabs an axe in order to help Tim. Poppy enters to inform Belinda that she has an entrance; Belinda hands the axe to Brooke, another actress, so that she can make her entrance. Garry, a goodlooking but also dumb younger actor, enters and eyes Frederick's flowers suspiciously because the two men are both in love with Dotty, another actress. Frederick gives the flowers to Garry and exits the backstage area. Brooke comes down the stairs and Garry and Brooke exchange the flowers and axe, Garry intending to hit Frederick with the axe when he enters again. Belinda enters, grabs the flowers from Brooke, sends her after Selsdon, sees Garry, and runs to take the axe from him. Her cue comes, and she almost misses it, runs up the stairs, desperately grabs at a dress, misses, and enters the stage of *Nothing On* with flowers instead of a dress. We hear her exclaim, "Darling, I never had a dress, or rather a bunch of flowers like this, did I?" (90). Clearly, as its title suggests, much of the action of

Noises Off happens offstage, as in the ancient Greek plays where much of the violence and bloodletting happens offstage. Again Frayn's understatement makes for a successful parody. The audience does not have to see every action on the stage of *Nothing On* because it can guess at the ramifications of what is happening backstage.

What the audience does see backstage are the codes of a serious parody being broken. The actors and actresses are misplacing props and nearly missing cues, throwing off the comic timing of the play within the play. Clearly, Frayn is breaking the codes of his parody of a parody, *Nothing On,* and is replacing them with new ones. That is, a dress becomes a bouquet of flowers. Certainly parody can parody itself, as long as the acceptable code is there and recognized by the audience. For example, Stoppard in *Travesties* parodies Joyce's *Ulysses,* which is of course itself a parody. Unfortunately, in Act Two, Frayn's new set of codes, the action that is now occurring on stage does not become familiar enough to us so that in the third act we will be able to realize, see, understand, or remember how the action is being modified. The problem may be that there is not enough time for what Hutcheon has described as the "critical distance," the time to decode and look at a work objectively.

In the third act, which is definitely the climax—there is no resolution to *Noises Off*—we become an audience to a production of *Nothing On* twelve weeks into its run. As the audience quickly guesses, the play has deteriorated. Unfortunately, as the play within the play has worsened, so has the quality of Frayn's own play. By this time the personal conflicts behind stage have to become so heated that they are not influencing what happens in *Nothing On,* rather they are dictating the action. And this action is chaos. As the title of the play within the play suggests, nothing of importance is happening onstage. The action has become far from what we know from the first act should be happening, and since all of our rules for what to expect have been broken, clearly anything could happen. It makes no difference whether Brooke enters with a dress, an axe, flowers, or even a dog. What is happening on stage is what Peter Kemp terms "an undermining" of the traditional formula for farce (Reprinted in *Noises Off,* np). I would argue that this undermining has already occurred in Act Two. As Hutcheon writes, "The parodic text is granted a special license to transgress the limit of convention, but, . . . it can do so only temporarily and only within the controlled confines authorized by the text parodied—that is quite simply, within the confines dictated by 'recognizability'" (Hutcheon, 1985, 75). Clearly, in Act Three Frayn has lost that control and the audience no longer recognizes codes of what he is parodying. What we are left with in Act Three is simply travesty, where the actions are distorted and

grotesque for no apparent reason. For example, *Nothing On* contains the conventional telephone, which of course will ring at the wrong time or be answered by the wrong people. In the third act, however, the phone is useless except to be torn to pieces. Consequently, the actors throw the phone to the floor, pull it by the cord, rip the receiver from it, and carry it all over the stage from room to room. Such an exaggerated emphasis on the phone as a prop, for no apparent reason, does not, I think, suggest that Act Three is very well-conceived drama. At another point a burglar is supposed to enter the villa, but in the final version of *Nothing On,* three burglars enter. This alone would be an acceptable variation on the familiar motif of having a masked intruder, except that one burglar is played by the director, another by the stage hand, and another by Selsdon, the actor who is supposed to play him. Again we have no information about why the director or the stage hand has gotten on stage. We only know they are not supposed to be there. As one might imagine, the third act resembles improvisation more than drama.

What is intriguing about the first two acts is what Frayn doesn't tell us or show us, but what we can speculate about. What makes Act Three less interesting is that while we can no longer see the actions backstage which are dictating the action on stage, we are also not in the least interested in speculating about them. The main reason for this is that there has been so little character development thus far. Somehow it seems important to know the backstage hijinks since the whole second act is devoted to them. However, we quickly forget about the actors and their personal affairs in Act Three, and they suddenly seem unimportant to Frayn, who separates us from them.

Robert Corrigan (1973) writes that often directors will seek to compensate for this lack of character development or lack of significance in the script with an exploitation of the action in an effort to achieve novelty and uniqueness (68). Corrigan says that "rapidity of pace is seen . . . as a means of compensating for the script's obvious insignificance" (68). He goes on to warn that taken to the extreme, pacing can be detrimental because when everything is speeded up, what "has been created is not art at all, only confusion" (67). It is clear that this is what has happened in Frayn's comedy in Act Three. Frayn has relied on stage directions calling for a rapid pace and much movement to compensate for a weak script and character development. The funniest parts of the play are in the first two acts when the action is centered on the comic action of only one person or on all the characters who are in turn concentrating on only one action, as when Brooke loses her contact lens and everyone must look for it. In Act Three there is so much divided action, with people entering and exiting and doors opening and closing, that the result is chaos for an audience who is probably looking for order. The disconcerting fact is that the order in Act Three is difficult to discern, and seems to be, in fact, non-existent.

Ironically, Frayn defended the weak second act of Chekhov's *The Cherry Orchard* in a 1978 essay by suggesting that the "difficulties with Act Two throw into even greater relief the sound structure of the rest of the play" (Frayn, 1978, xix). Clearly, this weak argument does not hold up for Frayn's own play or any other since certainly not all good plays must have weak spots for us to appreciate the rest of the structure. Rather, the best playwrights sustain a play's strengths throughout its duration, something that Frayn in *Noises Off* is unable to do.

But the value in *Noises Off* is that it helps to define and solidify through example the difference between parody and travesty. The first two acts, which are very clever and succeed well enough, illustrate that preconceived notions, rules, or codes are necessary to an understanding and appreciation of good parody, whose aim may be to ridicule. But the sheerly nonsensical third act just as clearly shows that when there is no preconceived idea of what to expect, drama may seem to lack order and turn into improvisation, while art itself turns into chaos.

References

Brater, 1981: Enoch Brater, "Parody, Travesty, and Politics in the Plays of Tom Stoppard," *Essays on Contemporary British Drama,* ed. Hedwig Bock and Albert Wertheim (Max Hueber Verlag) 117-130.

Corrigan, 1973: Robert W. Corrigan, *The Theatre in Search of a Fix* (New York: Delacorte Press).

Frayn, 1983: Michael Frayn, *Noises Off.* (London: Methuen).

———, 1978: Introduction to *The Cherry Orchard* by Anton Chekhov (London: Methuen).

Holman, 1979: Hugh Holman, *A Handbook of Literature.* "Parody" and "Travesty."

Hutcheon, 1985: Linda Hutcheon, *A Theory of Parody.* (New York: Methuen).

COPENHAGEN (1998)

PRODUCTION REVIEWS

John Ziman (review date June 1998)

SOURCE: Ziman, John. "An Evening with the Bohrs." *Physics World* (June 1998): n.p.

[*In the following review, Ziman considers the scientific aspects of Frayn's play.*]

There is a new play by Michael Frayn, best known for his humorous writings, about the famous visit of Werner Heisenberg to Niels Bohr in *Copenhagen* in the autumn of 1941. Those who dismiss the work as likely to be yet another populist mishmash of half-understood physics, personality stereotyping and political mystery-mongering would be wrong. An enquiry into the events of a particular evening in Bohr's home becomes a wise and perfectly informed journey to the core of the scientific enterprise.

It is also brilliant theatre. The three characters—Bohr, Heisenberg and Bohr's wife Margrethe—are on stage nearly all of the time. Notionally, they are in the Bohrs' house, with three chairs as their only props. But they grip us continually with words, tones, gestures, movement and lights. The professional magic of the Royal National Theatre, embodied in David Burke [Bohr], Sara Kestelman [Margrethe] and Matthew Marsh [Heisenberg], is mediated by the refined direction of Michael Blakemore. But Frayn's sharp, spare script is the score for an intricate contrapuntal trio, played briskly back and forth in crisp sentences that merge into a sparkling stream of conversation, confrontation and debate among three old friends.

Historically, of course, Bohr was notoriously woolly in speech, and Margrethe was probably much gentler. Sometimes Heisenberg interpolates comments into a conversation about himself from which he is supposedly absent, or Margrethe plays Greek chorus to the other two. But this is not an exercise in factitious reconstruction. In any case, they are all ghosts, trying to work out in an after-life what really happened, re-enacting various versions of that brief encounter or recalling other times together. With unostentatious skill, these chunks of memory and afterthought are woven seamlessly into the fabric of the conversation. Nothing is unclear—except what was actually said between two people in a few fateful minutes.

And that uncertainty—the physics metaphor is much used throughout—is genuine. It was a very secret, undated conversation, of which the participants gave changing and conflicting accounts in later years. On stage, the actors are as much in the dark as the many historians who have studied the two physicists' lives and times. The actors must also infer the facts from the surrounding circumstances, with only the advantage of fallible emotional memories and empathic insights. Stepping out of that frame, we see how the author has built into his drama as much as he can find out about two highly complex individuals and about the extremely tense world in which they lived. Alas for the recent death of Charles Frank (*Physics World* June p43), who interrogated many German scientists at the end of the Second World War and edited the "Farm Hall" transcripts, in which Heisenberg unwittingly revealed some of his thoughts when he heard of Hiroshima. Not being an expert on this subject, I can only assume that Michael Frayn has pretty fairly represented what is now publicly known.

The question is: in which of many contexts should the visit be best interpreted? The political context is obvious. But it is deeply fissured and riddled with secret caverns. Heisenberg was involved in a German nuclear weapons project. He suspected that there was a parallel Anglo-American project, and might have been fishing for information about it from Bohr. Or was he trying to tell the Americans, through Bohr, that the German project was not likely to be fruitful? Or perhaps it was just a subtle move in Heisenberg's campaign to retain control of his project inside the Nazi bureaucratic jungle.

The patriotic context seems clearer, yet makes no sense. Heisenberg was a sentimental German. His country was his beloved home: its people were his people. It must continue to shine among nations for its science, he felt. In 1941 the ultimate national disaster was not obvious. Even though Hitler was a homicidal maniac, it would probably come out all right in the end, he possibly thought. In visiting the Bohrs, Heisenberg tries clumsily to play a card of potential protection for Bohr, who is half-Jewish. They love him, but are affronted by his disregard for their Danish patriotism. Could he really have expected to enlist Bohr in the Nazi cause?

Hindsight makes the immediate scientific context too credible. Was a Uranium-235 fission bomb feasible? Conveniently for his conscience, Heisenberg had grossly overestimated the required critical mass of such a bomb, and was only trying to build a power reactor. But even if Bohr would not help directly, his confirmation of the estimate would have been reassuring. Indeed, in retrospect, one can imagine a fearful alternative universe opening up, in which Bohr suggests to Heisenberg that he should check his calculation, the Germans make the bomb, and eventually London replaces Hiroshima as the first nuked city.

All physicists know of the communal context. Just fifteen years earlier, Bohr and Heisenberg had tirelessly walked and talked themselves into the "Copenhagen interpretation" of quantum mechanics. Advised by Balazs Gyorffy, formerly professor of theoretical physics at Bristol University, Frayn has made a witty attempt to present this in lay terms, although I cannot guess how successfully. The main point is that Bohr and Heisenberg were at the centre of a truly international "invisible college" in which the new theoretical physics was being created. Perhaps Heisenberg was moved by the fragmentation of that community under the hammers of anti-Semitism and war, and was seeking vaguely to regenerate it.

It could be, of course, that Heisenberg, who had worked as a brilliant young man with Bohr back in the 1920s, has returned years later to show himself off to his former patron as a power in the great world. I doubt it. Certainly, the intellectual rivalry with Schrödinger spilled into their professional careers, but that was all past. Much more likely was a deeper personal context, in which Bohr plays father figure to the clever but insecure younger man. Was Heisenberg desperately seeking moral reassurance? Was he asking for absolution for the sin of plunging pure physics into the pitch-pot of war? But then, didn't he realize that there could be no forgiveness for putting the diabolic power of the atom into human hands, especially the hands of such demons as the Hitler gang? Did even Niels Bohr understand then what is now all too clear?

It is impossible to answer these questions, for nobody can know what happened that evening in Copenhagen. The contexts and dimensions are too complex and contradictory. But these are also the contexts and dimensions of the great world of physics. They can no more be reconciled or resolved in the large than in the small. *Copenhagen* rehearses in microcosm the indeterminacy of all our lives and works. It is a fable for our times, a Greek tragedy where fate itself is shrouded in mystery and uncertainty. Go and see it, for sure.

Peter B. Young (review date May 1999)

SOURCE: Young, Peter B. Review of *Copenhagen,* by Michael Frayn. *Theatre Journal* 51, no. 2 (May 1999): 218-19.

[*In the following review, Young positively assesses the Royal National Theatre production of Frayn's* Copenhagen, *singling out its staging, performances, and thematic emphasis on the motivations of the three characters in the drama.*]

Michael Frayn's new play **Copenhagen** explores the puzzling trip German physicist Werner Heisenberg took to Copenhagen in 1941 to see his Danish counterpart Niels Bohr. That the meeting of these two old friends took place is historical fact, but what they said to each other is not, despite the best efforts of colleagues and British intelligence to find out during and after the war. Why did the German physicist, who was not a Nazi even though he worked on atomic energy research for his government, go to see Bohr, his half-Jewish friend and mentor then on the opposite side and working in occupied Denmark? The Gestapo was watching both men. Whatever they said to each other made Bohr deeply angry. He later gave one version of their meeting, Heisenberg another, further clouding matters.

How does one get an audience interested in such questions, and even heighten their involvement while having three characters discuss atomic physics? This problem was solved admirably by Frayn's eminently playable script and by director Michael Blakemore and his cast, creating a riveting and theatrically intense production in this première of the play at the Royal National's Cottesloe Theatre. The play works because Frayn is a competent dramatist who is able to keep his own voice from intruding upon that of his characters. They are each complete, independent creations and believable agents of the play's events. Although Frayn is best known for his comic writings, *Copenhagen* should come as no surprise to anyone familiar with such works as *Benefactors, Here,* or the novel *A Landing on the Sun.*

Frayn's beautifully crafted play is not about the ethics of developing the atomic bomb, although it could be read that way. More fundamentally, the play concerns motivations for human actions and the uncertainty of even individuals knowing why they do what they do. As he said in a "Dialogue" presentation with Blakemore at the National Theatre on 1 June, "I thought what was said in 1941 might have some relation to uncertainty, at least in the theoretical limits on what we can know about human thought." Characteristically, Frayn does not solve the puzzle for the audience. He merely explores the situation in several permutations. The play is, in a way, a philosophical construction of another human attempt to make order and sense out of the world in which we find ourselves. Frayn's Cambridge degree is in moral sciences, now known as philosophy, and he has frequently said that all his plays have a philosophical basis to them.

The theatrical device framing the action is that, now dead, all three characters, Heisenberg, Bohr, and Bohr's wife Margarethe, have gathered one more time to determine just what happened and why. *Copenhagen* explores the multiple memories and versions of what may have actually happened, much as his *Benefactors* examines the manifold aspects of benefaction. As in the earlier play, here Frayn frequently has his characters address the audience directly from their post-life presence, setting the stage for us as they move to their several re-enactments of the 1941 meeting, like variations on a theme. This technique is always made to seem perfectly natural in both Frayn's writing and the actors' portrayals.

Peter J. Davison's design is appropriately simple. He provides an arena setting at the center of which a large white circle with markings suggests a flattened and abstracted globe of the earth. At the rear is a steeply raised bank of four rows of seats, looking like either a lecture hall or an operating theatre. The sole entrance to the stage area, which thrusts into the globe design by means of a pointed wedge painted on the floor, bisects the bank. Three dark aluminum chairs, ironically designed for use on the Hindenburg dirigible, are the only other props. The result is that all emphasis and attention is rightly directed to the actors and the text. Michael Blakemore's direction, his sixth collaboration with Frayn, reveals a solid concept at work. Movement patterns, for example, seem entirely natural because they are integral to the action, yet they also subtly illustrate and clarify it. Mark Henderson's lighting complements Blakemore's staging perfectly, keeping clear the transitions between characters' direct address to the audience and their reliving and enacting of the past. He accomplishes this with an economical selection of sources, angles, and a restrained but evocative use of color.

Matthew Marsh convincingly combines the Teutonic reserve and correctness of Heisenberg with his boyish desire to be accepted by Bohr as he was before the war. He shows us Heisenberg's complex mix of elusiveness and ambiguity, combined with a quickness of mind and precision of understanding. David Burke's Bohr is the opposite, a genial and fatherly sort given to methodically working through each step of a problem. Sarah Kestelman creates Bohr's wife Margarethe as a strong and gracious woman who is clearly Bohr's partner in discussions of physics and other matters, yet who maintains and asserts her own independence as occasions arise.

This production is a fine ensemble mounting of what may be Michael Frayn's best play to date. Setting, lighting, direction and acting combine smoothly to do what only the theatre can do so well: present the living semblance of an action unfolding before us.

Michael Posner (review date spring 2003)

SOURCE: Posner, Michael. "The Uncertainty about Heisenberg." *Queen's Quarterly* 110, no. 1 (spring 2003): 87-92.

[*In the following review, Posner discusses the mystery surrounding the actual events that inspired Frayn's drama.*]

At the height of World War II a secret meeting took place in German-occupied Denmark between Danish physicist Niels Bohr and a former student and colleague, the German physicist Werner Heisenberg. Did Heisenberg set up the meeting in order to spy on Bohr's nuclear research on behalf of the Nazis, or was he trying to assist the Allies by passing on information about Germany's progress toward building a nuclear bomb? Six decades after the event, a new play by Michael Frayn is recreating the drama and suspense of the wartime encounter, posing a series of challenging questions, not yet resolved.

Copenhagen, directed by Diana Leblanc; starring Michael Ball, Martha Henry, Jim Mezon; NAC English Theatre/Neptune Theatre (Halifax)

* * *

In September 1941, Werner Heisenberg, Germany's most illustrious physicist, and his close friend Carl von Weizsäcker visited Copenhagen under the aegis of the Nazi cultural propaganda authority, which organized similar trips to other parts of occupied Europe. In Copenhagen, the main purpose of the visit was to enable Heisenberg to meet with his friend and mentor Niels Bohr.

The importance of the meeting has made the Copenhagen encounter the stuff of history. There is Bohr, the founder of atomic physics—like Einstein, not merely a great physicist but also a great man. Then there is Heisenberg, the formulator of the famous Uncertainty Principle, and also von Weizsäcker, son of the top diplomat in Hitler's foreign ministry, and a promising theoretical physicist himself, who had the same kind of surrogate relationship to Heisenberg as Heisenberg had to Bohr.

* * *

Werner Heisenberg's Uncertainty Principle stipulates that the position and momentum of an atomic particle cannot be simultaneously and definitively known. The more precise the measurement of one, the more uncertain the other becomes. But reduced to its essence, the theory speaks to the ultimate mystery of life itself—position and momentum, time and energy—the mystery of forces that play not only upon the natural world, but on human behaviour.

Michael Frayn's award-winning play *Copenhagen,* which recently made its long-awaited Canadian debut at Halifax's Neptune Theatre and then moved on to Ottawa's National Arts Centre, demonstrates the power of the Uncertainty Principle on two levels.

The first, of course, is the content of the play itself, which deals with Heisenberg's 1941 visit to his mentor, who was half-Jewish, in occupied Copenhagen. Heisenberg made the journey at a critical moment. Nazi Germany was at its zenith, occupying most of continental Europe. The United States had not yet entered the war. But on both sides, elite communities of physicists were wrestling with the theory and practice of the atomic bomb: what mathematical formulas would, on paper, yield the possibility of such a weapon, and could it actually be built?

What remains undetermined—and highly controversial—is how much Heisenberg knew about the theory of the bomb and whether, knowing its destructive power, his objective was to thwart its production. Was he trying to enlist Bohr in an honourable pact to block development of the A-bomb? Or was he trying to pick Bohr's brain, and see how far scientists on the other side had taken their research?

More than 60 years later, there are still no certain answers to these questions about why Heisenberg, then head of Germany's atomic research program, undertook the mission, what he hoped to achieve, or what was said. Frayn's three-hander (Bohr's wife, Margrethe, also appears) is a speculative reconstruction of what might have been said. The characters are essentially ghosts, moving in orbit around the nuclear core of their discussions of six decades ago, trying to grapple with what was *really* said and what was *really* meant.

The second, unintended, application of the principle was the reception the play received. When he wrote it in 1998, Frayn thought it was unlikely even to be produced, let alone become a celebrated international hit. After all, exchanges about quantum mechanics and subatomic particle physics do not the stuff of contemporary theatre typically make.

"It was a total surprise," Frayn, now 72, recalled. "I was passionately interested in the subject, but I began to think it was really just of interest to me. I thought it might get on radio or into a small theatre, but the idea of [Britain's] National Theatre never penetrated."

Nor, presumably, did he imagine the shower of awards that would follow its productions in London and New York, or the scholarly seminars of historians and physicists who continue to debate the issues it raises.

On the key questions posed by *Copenhagen,* Frayn—a prolific playwright, novelist, and screenwriter best known for the comedy *Noises Off* (1982) and his Booker Prize nominated novel *Headlong* (1999)—remains appropriately agnostic. *Heisenberg's War,* the Thomas Powers book that inspired the play, argues that the German did understand the theoretical physics of the bomb and, more important, deliberately concealed them from his Nazi masters. "It's extremely difficult to know," says Frayn, reformulating the Uncertainty Principle yet again.

> There is evidence to support Powers' view—that the Germans did have a grasp of the theoretical physics of the bomb, but the evidence is ambiguous. They may not have had, in 1941, a practical understanding. And I don't agree Heisenberg concocted a false version to fool the Nazis, because in 1941 he thought it would be technically impossible [to build it] and he didn't do the crucial calculations of critical mass.

The tantalizing question, then, becomes why Heisenberg, known as an aggressive researcher, didn't do those calculations. "There is no knowable answer," Frayn insists.

Maybe he thought it was something better not looked into, and therefore there was no moral decision to make. But it was rather convenient for them to go on thinking it was absolutely impossible, and it is striking that the physicists on the Allied side did do the calculations on critical mass and felt justified in working on atomic weapons. You can't help suspecting that if Heisenberg and his colleagues had felt the same sense of justifica- tion, they might have looked at it differently.

It is precisely these mysteries that the play explores in a discussion fuelled by Bohr's and Heisenberg's conflict- ing memories of the visit. Bohr fled Denmark in 1943 for Sweden, England, and finally America, where he worked on the Manhattan Project. It is clear from Bo- hr's draft letters to Heisenberg—which were never sent and were only recently released by his estate—that he was even angrier than the play depicts him in recollect- ing the encounter.

More intriguing still, says Frayn, is that it is clear from these letters that Heisenberg was risking his career simply by making the trip and, while under surveillance by the Gestapo, disclosing in a roundabout way to the fervently anti-Nazi Bohr that there was a German bomb program and that Heisenberg was working on it. "I find this absolutely astonishing. It goes some way to sup- porting Heisenberg's suggestion that what he hoped would come out of the conversation was that [he and] Bohr would come to some understanding that scientists on both sides would advise their governments it was too expensive and impractical to build the bomb."

Although Heisenberg himself was not a Nazi sympa- thizer, he was a German nationalist, thought the war was at least partly justified, and predicted a German victory. At the same time, he said years later that the purpose of his trip to Copenhagen was to pose to Bohr the question: does one as a physicist have the moral right to work on the practical exploitation of atomic energy?

There may be more fallout to come. The Heisenberg family will soon release the contents of a letter he wrote to his wife while in Copenhagen in 1941. What it makes clear, says Frayn, is that Heisenberg went to Bohr's house on three occasions—so they remained on cordial terms even after the explosive events of the second evening.

* * *

Today, Heisenberg and von Weizsäcker are still seen in Germany as heroes of German science. What may be less well known, at least on this side of the Atlantic, is that they are also revered on the German left as leading lights of the postwar anti-nuclear weapons movement. In 1957, when the United States was preparing to place tactical nuclear weapons on German soil, 18 scientists issued a manifesto, the Göttingen Appeal, in which they protested the deployment of such weapons and opposed any effort to make Germany a nuclear armed state. The principal author of the appeal was von Weizsäcker, and probably the most distinguished co-signatory was Heisenberg. But did the two scientists experience a genuine or an expedient change of heart? The signatures only compound our uncertainty, and underscore the mysteries of human affairs that lie beyond the reach of science.

CRITICAL COMMENTARY

Nicholas Ruddick (essay date spring 2000)

SOURCE: Ruddick, Nicholas. "The Search for a Quantum Ethics: Michael Frayn's *Copenhagen* and Other Recent British Science Plays." *Hungarian Journal of English and American Studies* 6, no. 1 (spring 2000): 119-37.

[*In the following essay, Ruddick examines the interplay between ethics and science as well as questions of motivation and its knowability in* Copenhagen.]

BOHR:

Heisenberg, I have to say—if people are to be measured strictly in terms of observable quantities . . .

HEISENBERG:

Then we should need a strange new quantum ethics.

—Michael Frayn

In 1893, T. H. Huxley, the most notable and eloquent Victorian proponent of Darwinian evolutionary theory, delivered the famous lecture "Evolution and Ethics" at Oxford. His aim was at once to affirm that he had no doubt that evolution was an amoral cosmic process to which all life on earth, including mankind, was subject, and to propose that human beings had an innate ethical sense which they had the responsibility to attempt to apply in their dealings in the world: "Social progress means a checking of the cosmic process at every step and the substitution for it of another, which may be called the ethical process" (81). The issues raised by Huxley's evolutionary ethics inspired the flowering of fin-de-siècle scientific romance at the hands of his most notable pupil, H. G. Wells.[1] Surely science fiction, which owes its descent and much of its literary credibility to Wellsian scientific romance, ought to have as one of its primary functions the engagement through metaphor of a scientifically-determined worldview with the intention of humanizing, or at least struggling to make humanly comprehensible, a universe that might otherwise seem bewilderingly indifferent to human concerns? As Brian Aldiss has put it, "sf is an ideal negotiator between the two hemispheres of the brain, the rational cognitive—i.e., 'scientific'-left and the intuitive, i.e., 'literary-artistic'-right" (1-2).

Yet contemporary science fiction has, one fears, largely abandoned such a lofty goal. Since the success of the *Star Wars* movies from 1977 on, sf has quickly been subsumed into sci-fi, a popular-cultural phenomenon dominated by Hollywood and characterized by the subordination of textual to visual values, of extrapolation to extravagance, of speculation to special effects. Hollywood economies of scale now determine the criteria according to which a successful work of sf is measured, and the financial rewards of the tie-in for the aspiring sf writer are so great that it is not surprising that there has been a gradual decline in the literary ambitions of sf since the heady days of the New Wave. However, that ability, specified by Aldiss, of good sf to mediate between the cerebral hemispheres is as important as ever in a contemporary world in which the most powerful cultural dynamic is everaccelerating technological change. Though contemporary sci-fi may be neglecting Huxley's challenge to apply humane ethics to the scientifically-conceived universe, the task has been taken up elsewhere in the literary field.

* * *

Michael Frayn's **Copenhagen** (1998) is the latest of a number of notable "science plays" to have graced the British stage at the end of the second millennium.[2] The unexpected box-office success of **Copenhagen,** a play that is in some ways the complete antithesis of the Hollywood scifi blockbuster, suggests that the theater-going public is prepared to respond with enthusiasm to a serious, uncompromising attempt to explore ethical issues raised by scientific developments. Though not science fiction by any usual modern definition of this term, the science play—primarily realistic, though capable of incorporating fantastic elements—functions in a similar way to Wellsian scientific romance a century ago. *The Time Machine* (1895) and *The Island of Doctor Moreau* (1896) raised, without sentimentality, sometimes brutally, the necessary question of how to formulate an evolutionary ethics; **Copenhagen** and the other four plays dealt with here point the way to an equally necessary quantum ethics.

Three of these science plays dramatize aspects of the lives of famous scientists: Alan Turing in Hugh Whitemore's *Breaking the Code* (1987), Charles Darwin in Timberlake Wertenbaker's *After Darwin* (1998), Niels Bohr and Werner Heisenberg in Michael Frayn's **Copenhagen** (1998). One of the most ambitious and complex plays of the 1990s, Tom Stoppard's *Arcadia* (1993) explores the human implications of scientific ideas—in

particular thermodynamics, chaos theory, and fractal geometry.[3] Stephen Poliakoff's *Blinded by the Sun* (1996) deals with how cultural pressures affect contemporary scientific research. Yet behind the obvious differences between these five notable plays are many points of similarity. For example, Stoppard and Wertenbaker both contrast nineteenth-century certitude with twentieth-century indeterminacy, both Stoppard and Poliakoff deal with the ambiguous phenomenon of the researcher co-opted (and corrupted) by the media, while Whitemore, Poliakoff, and Frayn all explore the ironic contrast between the reputed precision of science and the haze surrounding human motivation. It will be suggested here that one theme that links all these plays is the contemporary need of a quantum ethics, that is, an ethics that will serve in a world in which science, an epistemological instrument of unmatched precision, nevertheless must concede that there is a "final core of uncertainty at the heart of things" (Frayn 96). More specifically, these plays are concerned to show that there remains a right and wrong way for people—including scientists—to act, even though the structure of physical reality, not to mention mathematical reality, has been revealed to be fundamentally indeterminate.

At the risk of over-simplification, one may venture that the revolution in quantum physics as it relates to the plays under examination here had as its twin foci Werner Heisenberg's Uncertainty or Indeterminacy Principle[4] (1927) and Niels Bohr's Complementarity Principle (1928), the "two central tenets of the Copenhagen Interpretation of Quantum Mechanics" (Frayn 72-73). The former principle allowed an observer to ascertain either the position or velocity of a particle but not both at once; the latter treated physical objects at the atomic level as if they were simultaneously constituted of waves and particles, two different and apparently incompatible orders of phenomena. In the quantum realm, the observer determines what is observed, and reality is always a subjective construct. As the idea of scriptural or divine authority had been dealt a series of blows by late nineteenth-century biology and early twentieth-century relativity, it seemed no great leap of daring in the later twentieth century to apply the quantum model to the ethical sphere. Without transcendental authority or perspective, each person is his or her own measure. As Frayn's Bohr puts it, the Copenhagen Interpretation placed the individual "back at the centre of the universe" (73). But if the line between good and evil is thereby rendered subjective, can moral categories really be said to exist at all? May not modern science be said to endorse a view of the world as an ethical vacuumin which scientists, be they nuclear physicists building weapons or biochemists manipulating genes, may do anything they like because it is possible (and especially if it is lucrative)?

Early in Hugh Whitemore's *Breaking the Code,* the protagonist, the mathematician Alan Turing, confesses that another major statement of indeterminacy, Gödel's First Incompleteness Theorem (1931)—which asserts that in all mathematical systems which are consistent there is a formula which can neither be proved or disproved—"is the most beautiful thing I know" (27). Yet even if there is a liberating sense of freedom and possibility in the idea that there is ultimately no telling a correct from an incorrect mathematical solution (26), that does not mean that the mathematician is freed from the strictures of right and wrong at the ethical level. Turing's crucial involvement in the Allied code-breaking program during the Second World War was the result of a difficult moral decision (24) to break with his 1930s pacifism. The loss of lives caused by Turing's decryption of the German Enigma code was in his view a "necessary evil" (25) to be measured against the greater evil of Nazism. Evil may be relativized, but it is not thereby made immensurable or meaningless.

Turing tries to extend the theory of mathematical unde-cidability to moral issues as an argument against the law's determination to prosecute him for gross inde-cency (i.e., homosexual activity), as in this speech to Detective-Sergeant Ross:

> Even in mathematics there's no infallible rule for prov-ing what is right and what is wrong. Each problem—each decision—requires fresh ideas, fresh thought. And if that's the case in m-m-mathematics—the most reli-able body of knowledge that mankind has created—surely it might also apply in other, less certain, areas?
>
> (64)

To this, Ross replies that the idea may work in theory but does not in real life, where the law, trancendentally embodied by himself, is all there is to help people decide between right and wrong. But when Ross then, as a token consolatory gesture for prosecuting him, tells Turing, "I understand how you must feel," the mathema-tician replies, "No you don't. How can you?" (64). This seems to be an allusion to the two men's apparently ir-reconcilable sexual perspectives but, when Ross concedes, "You're right, I don't. I can't" (64), it becomes at the same time an assertion of the ultimate subjectivity of quantum reality.

Whitemore's play is also interested in the indetermin-ability of Turing's motive for his suicide. Turing was certainly a victim of both society's prejudice and his own honesty when he was convicted for homosexual acts that he had confessed to the police in the course of reporting a robbery. He was not jailed like Oscar Wilde, but put on estrogen to kill his illegitimate sexual urges. Wildean tragedy seems to repeat itself as farce when Turing ruefully wonders whether, as a result of the drug regime, he is going to have to wear a bra (66). However,

someone who can joke about such a humiliation seems an unlikely candidate for self-destruction, raising a larger question about his fate as dramatized. Whitemore accounts for Turing's suicide in a number of ways. Pos-sibly he was driven to it by a recurrent nightmare of be-ing "trapped inside an enormous mechanical brain" (33); or by a romantic desire to be reunited with his schoolboy love object, Christopher Morcom (38-39, 78); or by a loss in dismal postwar Manchester of the self-integration that he felt at Bletchley Park during the war (73); or by his desire to go to the ultimate length to learn whether the mind can exist without the body (80). Suicide as a result of any or all these factors would make Turing a self-involved idealist. But Whitemore's Alan Turing is pragmatic, humorously self-deprecating, and capable of inspiring warmth and admiration in all those he comes into contact with, even the police. It is difficult to gainsay his mother, who, unable to accept the coroner's verdict of suicide, concludes defiantly, "He had everything to live for" (80). Indeed, by not rejecting him upon his revelation of homosexuality, she had clearly strengthened his confidence in his ability to be loved for who he was.

Turing muses enigmatically toward the end of the play, "In the long run [. . .] it's not breaking the code that matters—it's where you go from there" (78).[5] But where Turing goes is suicide, and thereby the play, presenting a terminal act of self-destruction that is out of character, suggests that it is not merely difficult, but impossible to determine why people do what they do. Thus Turing's fate, which was comprehensible to his mother only as an absurd waste of a life, must be interpreted likewise by the audience. Yet given Turing's strong ethical sense, his self-destruction ought to be invested with a dimen-sion that is less contingent, more driven by necessity, more tragic in the traditional sense. To speak of the often excessive complexity of human motivation—of its overdetermined quality in psychoanalytic terms—is not the same as to say that motivation is ultimately impenetrable and all actions consequently absurd. To draw this important distinction is one of the many achievements of Frayn's *Copenhagen.*

A major success by a contemporary master-dramatist, and a much more complex play both structurally and thematically than *Breaking the Code,* Tom Stoppard's *Arcadia* is not about historical scientists, but it is about the problems of research in both the sciences and the humanities. The play also stands as a dramatic metaphor for the complex nature of quantum reality.[6] In 1809, a young lady of aristocratic background and mathematical bent, Thomasina Coverly, anticipates chaos theory, frac-tal geometry, quantum theory, and the implications of the second law of thermodynamics, before losing her life on the night before her seventeenth birthday in a fire at her ancestral mansion, Sidley Park. Quasi-simultaneously, in the present day, a group of researchers convene in the same mansion, each confronted by a problem of making reality conform to his or her own agenda. The social historian Hannah Jarvis is writing a history of the garden that will support her thesis about "the decline from thinking to feeling" between the Enlightenment and the Romantic period (27); the mathematical biologist Valentine Coverly tries to discover laws in the apparently randomly fluctuating population of grouse at Sidley Park, and use them to draw "pictures of turbulence—growth—change—creation" (47). The literary historian Bernard Nightingale attempts to promote his idea that Lord Byron was involved in a sensational duel at Sidley Park, in the hope of getting his name in the papers and achieving his desired status as "Media Don" (56).

As Heinz Antor has well noted, *Arcadia* deals with the transition from "a classical belief in regularity, order, finite linear teleology and the existence of well-structured patterns to a postmodern and poststructuralist scepticism about these things and an awareness of irregularity, chaos, non-linearity, infinity and unstructured patternlessness or complexity" (328-29). For Valentine Coverly, as with Alan Turing, the sheer unpredictability and unknowability of nature makes the present "the best possible time to be alive, when almost everything you thought you knew is wrong" (48). To Valentine, "What matters" is not the personality of the scientist but "the calculus. Scientific progress. Knowledge" (61). This assertion echoes that of his ancestor Thomasina (37), who shares an incipient romance with her tutor, the young mathematician and naturalist Septimus Hodge. Septimus consoles Thomasina, who has been mourning the cultural losses wrought by time, thus: "We shed as we pick up, like travellers who must carry everything in their arms, and what we let fall will be picked up by those behind. The procession is very long and life is very short. We die on the march. But there is nothing outside the march so nothing can be lost to it" (38). Yet Septimus's consoling vision works only in a world in which there is an unquestioned belief in linear temporality and teleology—a world which has now gone forever. Thomasina's insights were impossible to verify using the mathematics of her time (93), and her life is absurdly cut short by a heat-death, not precisely the one she foresaw. Septimus, maddened by both her loss and the vertiginous scientific vistas she evoked for him, becomes a hermit, attempting vainly to perform a mathematical operation involving an iterated algorithm in an age when there "weren't enough *pencils*" or paper to perform it (51; see also Melbourne 566).

Yet if the quantum reality this play cunningly encrypts allows no providential reward for Thomasina or Septimus, *Arcadia* still manages emphatically to affirm an ethical position. The execrable Bernard views himself as a defender of the humanities against the sciences, the poets against the physicists. He has no time for modern science, claiming to prefer Aristotle's cosmos to whatever came after and dismissing the findings of post-Newtonian physics as trivial: "Quarks, quasars—big bangs, black holes—who gives a shit?" (61). Yet he is the only researcher in the play whose conclusions are, in the traditional sense, absolutely incorrect, and his wrongness also has a clear moral dimension. His evidence for the duel between Byron and Chater eventually becomes too overwhelmingly non-existent for him to manipulate to his advantage; meanwhile his motives for research are revealed to have always been purely self-centered. He is a shallow egoist whose humanism is false, a degenerate "parody" (Melbourne 567) of his nineteenth-century counterpart Byron, possessing all the negative qualities of his hero and none of the genius. But *Arcadia* does not attack the humanities through Bernard; it suggests instead that the science of contemporary quantum reality *is* one of the humanities, and those who deny it are themselves likely to be lacking in humanity. Bernard's fate is to be justly expelled from Sidley Park, an arcadian locus where what is of value in the past is miraculously preserved for the future, and which forms an exception to the general rule of chaos.[7]

Stephen Poliakoff's *Blinded by the Sun* centers on a scientific fraud perpetrated by a member of a chemistry department at a university in Northern England. The play's plot is offered as a subjective framed narrative presented by its protagonist Al Golfar, a mediocre chemist but "born administrator" (10), and it charts his rise via the chair of his department to fame as the author of "pop-science best sellers" (99) and ubiquitous media don. By the end of the play Al has dissolved the department he was appointed to rejuvenate, and the chemistry building itself has been turned over to media studies. Early in act 1, in a scene reminiscent of the Fleischmann and Pons cold fusion announcement of 1989, Christopher Lathwell, the academic star of the department, claims to have invented a "Sun Battery" (30), an efficient means of extracting hydrogen from water using solar power. Al becomes instrumental in exposing Christopher's fraud, while at the same time cleverly protecting his colleague from the media backlash. Meanwhile, Elinor Brickman, the "pure" scientist admired by Al as the "most scrupulous" (65) member of his department, becomes tainted in Al's eyes when she tries to persuade him not to expose the fraud (61). Indeed, Al himself later suggests that his subsequent dismantling of the department resulted from his disillusionment with Elinor (112).

As Christopher's star falls, Al's rises, until this scientific hack has become a darling of the media. The play seems to suggest that in the contemporary world, the pressures on scientists to produce financially lucrative research (or at least to generate good public relations) are so great that unethical practices are almost inevitable and purely scientific achievement, which involves a long and exhausting struggle in a "dark tunnel" (116), almost impossible. The play ends with a ceremony honoring Elinor's contribution to science, but it seems clear that the mysterious research that she has been jealously guarding for years was a kind of confidence trick, in that her posthumous legacy was no more than a set of indecipherable handwritten notes (120). But then Al himself, exposer of the Sun Battery fraud, feels that he too is an imposter (66); after all, of the members of his department he is one of the least academically qualified to hold the Chair.

Blinded by the Sun raises questions of indeterminacy through the device of Al's obsessive habit of collecting in plastic bags objects relating to specific moments in his life that he will use to attempt to structure a retrospective, self-justifying narrative. Towards the end of the play, Elinor, picking up one of Al's bags at random, notes to him: "Don't you see, [. . .] none of this is the real pattern of what happened. The *only* shape we can be definite about is this . . ." (i.e., the bag itself as physical object) (118). The objects in the bag are real, but the truth of what "really" happened, of which the objects are mementos, is a perpetually-changing construct of a quite different order of reality (114). (The parallel here with the objects from both time-scales that accumulate on the table at the end of *Arcadia* is unmistakable.) The play results from an ordering of the objects by Al, and thus is a consciously subjective interpretation of what happened by one character, not an authoritative last word.

But ultimately the contribution of *Blinded by the Sun* to the formulation of a new quantum ethics is a little disappointing. We get not enough insight into Christopher's character to stir our interest in the undoubtedly complex, overdetermined motives impelling a brilliant scientist to perpetrate a sleazy fraud using baking powder. Al, whose point of view determines the action, suggests that motives such as greed and the desire for celebrity were minor compared with the "real" reason, which is that Christopher did not have the stamina to endure the "hell of creating something" (116). For Al himself has had a "Eureka moment" (77) when he thought up a project to extract fuel from household waste, only to discover that he did not have the intellectual toughness to get the plan from the theoretical to the practical stage. The play insists that "pure" scientific research should exist, but that it has become impossible in a late twentieth-century academic environment. Such insistence works against the idea that the action is merely one subjective version of reality, and Al seems too much the mouthpiece of a playwright with a jaundiced view of the ability of university science departments to resist the pressures of contemporary media culture.

Timberlake Wertenbaker's *After Darwin*, like *Arcadia*, cuts between the nineteenth century (in this case the years 1831 to 1865) and the present, and she, like Whitemore and Frayn, presents her theme through a gloss on the life of a great scientist. A play by Lawrence, a black American playwright, is being mounted in London about the Victorian conflict between the agnostic, whiggish Charles Darwin and Robert FitzRoy, the Tory, religiously orthodox captain of the *Beagle*. The latter came to feel that he was personally responsible for unleashing the faith-destroying Darwinian revolution upon the world and killed himself. Meanwhile, the actors playing FitzRoy and Darwin, their director and the playwright are involved in a modern ethical conflict that has its roots in the Darwinian challenge to Victorian orthodoxy.

The divided temporal structure of *After Darwin* functions, as it does in *Arcadia,* to subvert traditional linearity, causality, and teleology, while the play's main quantum theme is that nineteenth-century ethical certainty can never be fully recovered in the modern world—indeed, one "cannot be tragic after Darwin" (65). At the same time (and here Wertenbaker extends the search for a quantum ethics backwards to the aftermath of the *Origin of Species*), natural selection does not in the end endorse human selfishness or greed, any more than it endorsed the suicide of FitzRoy. As the director Millie puts it, as she tries to impose her vision of the play upon Ian, the emotionally repressed old-style actor playing FitzRoy, "I want light and tenderness. It is thought tenderness gave mammals an evolutionary advantage" (9).

Meanwhile, we learn that there are ethically dubious motives, supposedly justified by the Darwinian struggle for existence, behind the actions of both Millie and Tom, the new-style actor playing Darwin. Millie, an expatriate of Turkish background who has known oppression in her homeland of Bulgaria, struggles to establish herself in the British theater so that she will not be sent home. Her survival depends upon the success of Lawrence's play, but she has concealed the truth about her background and motivations from the cast until a crisis forces her to confess it. As she puts it, "The truth is not a good survival tool. It makes you vulnerable [. . .]" (51). Tom, gay, narcissistic, and hiding behind a "camouflage of idiocy" (46) when it comes to researching his character, is prepared to destroy the whole production to further his career by decamping to join the cast of a trashy movie. When Ian remonstrates with him, Tom justifies himself in crude Darwinian terms, "I'm hungry, Ian, I want to go where there's lots of food" (45).

IAN:

You're not some animal foraging for food.

TOM:

That's what Darwin's saying here, isn't it?

(45)

Ian is not immune to the struggle for existence. He feels that his "ornate skills," those of the classically-trained actor (44), have become like the cumbersome antlers of the vanished Irish elk. He is being superseded by actors like Tom, for whom moral self-questioning is "an overspecialized refinement that leads rapidly to extinction" (54). Having fallen for Millie, so that his survival, hers, and that of Lawrence's play become inextricably bound, Ian sabotages Tom's attempted defection by spreading the false rumor that Tom is HIV positive (66). But Lawrence cannot endorse Ian's act, for a necessary evil is still an evil. Having been brought up by a mother who made enormous sacrifices to educate him well, Lawrence knows that "I am responsible for my own integrity" (68), and that the production of his play would be "contaminated" (69) if allowed to continue on such terms. The production ceases, but Millie and Ian find love, while Lawrence affirms that Darwinism's true legacy is "empathy" (73) in that it connects mankind to all other creatures on earth. Yet though the play is an intriguing work, its resolution relies in the end too much on a traditional ethical absolutism to resolve satisfactorily the questions of uncertainty raised by the divided action. Unlike Stoppard in *Arcadia,* Wertenbaker cannot maintain the fine equilibrium between two time-scales, and the modern conflict overshadows the nineteenth-century one to the detriment of unity of dramatic effect.

The popular success of Michael Frayn's ***Copenhagen,*** in both London and New York seems to have taken everyone by surprise, including the playwright himself. Frayn, perhaps best known to playgoers as a brilliant farceur,[8] has noted almost apologetically that ***Copenhagen,*** a play about a controversial meeting between the great physicists Niels Bohr and Werner Heisenberg in Nazi-occupied Denmark in 1941 was "written entirely for my own benefit" (Wroe 8) and is "entirely joke-free, I am afraid" (Davidson 1). The *New York Times,* wondering if anyone understood the play, asked some members of the audience after a production if they could explain Heisenberg's Uncertainty Principle, with mixed results (see Marin 2). In fact, ***Copenhagen,*** though intellectually challenging, is a less complex work than *Arcadia.* However, Frayn's play is perhaps the greater dramatic tour de force, especially given its rejection of spectacle and its refusal to ingratiate itself with its audience. At the same time ***Copenhagen*** offers perhaps a more coherent integration of scientific theory and aesthetic form than any contemporary science play.

At first glance the play seems an unlikely box office hit. Though running for more than two hours, it has only three roles—Bohr, his wife Margrethe, and Bohr's former friend and colleague the German physicist Werner Heisenberg. In the playtext no setting is described nor are there any stage directions. The play in London and New York was performed in a circular space of Beckett-like austerity, with chairs as the only props. The three characters, perpetually onstage, move realistically, but the setting is so abstract that, as John Lahr put it, they seem to "collide, separate, realign themselves like so many neutrons and protons" (219). They have the ontological status of revenants, though they dress realistically and behave onstage as if they were still alive. Frayn's purpose in summoning these ghosts is so that they can revisit the vexed question—one that has exercised historians for years—of why Heisenberg in 1941, then working for Hitler's war effort and under Gestapo surveillance, should have taken the trouble to pay a visit to Bohr in Nazi-occupied Copenhagen. Clearly the play's title does not refer to a real city in historical time and space, but alludes to Frayn's more abstract concern: to offer an interpretation of what happened in Copenhagen in 1941 from a perspective has been determined—or made indeterminate—by the Copenhagen Interpretation.

Frayn has indicated that he is interested in the epistemological questions raised by people's actions—in particular "how one knows why one does what one does" (Dickson 3; see also Davidson 1). Indeed, he seems to feel that in a quantum universe in which there is "a final core of uncertainty at the heart of things," the questions of motive are ultimately unanswerable. However, he is commendably aware that the behavior of people is a different order of phenomenon from the behavior of elementary particles, and in his lengthy "Postscript" to the play he explains carefully why one may serve as a coherent metaphor for the other:

> The idea [of uncertainty] as introduced by Heisenberg into quantum mechanics was precise and technical. It didn't suggest that everything about the behaviour of particles was unknowable, or hazy. What it limited was the simultaneous measurement of "canonically conjugate variables," such as position and momentum [. . .]. None of this, plainly, applies directly to our observations of thought and intention [. . .]. What the uncertainty of thoughts does have in common with the uncertainty of particles is that the difficulty is not just a practical one, but a systematic limitation which cannot even in theory be circumvented [. . .]. And since, as the Copenhagen Interpretation establishes, the whole possibility of saying or thinking anything about the world [. . .] depends upon human observation; and is subject to the limitations which the human mind imposes, this uncertainty in our thinking is also fundamental to the nature of the world.
>
> (100-01)

This awareness allows Frayn to structure ***Copenhagen*** "around the interchange between metaphor used to explain science and science itself used as a metaphor to explain action" (Stewart 302), with the result that there is an unusually close and fruitful connection between the scientific and emotional content of the play.

As the play unfolds, the characters, restlessly orbiting each other, struggle towards an understanding of what happened in 1941. We learn that Heisenberg came to Copenhagen for some, or all, of the following reasons: to talk with Bohr about physics (3, 10); to deliver a lecture at the German Cultural Institute (6); to ask Bohr to come to Germany (16); to receive the love of Bohr as his surrogate father (17); to offer Bohr, a half-Jew, the protection of the German embassy (20); to ask Bohr if he thinks that a physicist has the moral right to work on atomic energy (36); to ask him if one can build atomic bombs if one has built a nuclear reactor (37-38); (possibly, at least in the Bohrs' view) to recruit Bohr to the Nazi nuclear program (38); to gain "absolution" from Bohr as the "Pope" of nuclear physics (39); to tell Bohr that he, Heisenberg, has an important voice in the funding of the Nazi nuclear program, so that the two of them might be able to stop all nuclear research by a joint refusal (41, 44); to pick Bohr's brain about the Allied nuclear program (42); to present himself as an emotional replacement for the Bohrs' drowned son Christian (52); or simply to show off as the citizen of a once-humiliated, now victorious nation (76).

The gradual exposure of Heisenberg's motives, some of them contradictory, all of them to a greater or lesser extent credible, is fascinating, but this process alone is not what makes ***Copenhagen*** a compelling dramatic experience. What grips the audience is its growing realization of the underlying importance of what at first seemed an abstruse academic question, namely, *why* it is so important to try to establish what happened in Copenhagen. The question's significance remains almost under repression until it is enforced by the third of only three sound effects in the Broadway production, "a roar and rumbling that shakes the gut of every playgoer with stunning intensity" (Powers 6). Did Heisenberg know, as Bohr did, that only a few kilograms, and not tons, of Uranium 235 were required to make an atomic bomb? If so, why didn't he take the news back to Germany? The fate of the world hung on this meeting in Copenhagen, for it takes little imagination to figure out how history may have unfolded differently had Hitler been provided by Heisenberg with the means to make an atomic bomb in 1941.

Copenhagen is a retrospective play, in that these three ghosts look back on their younger selves from an indeterminate time after 1945. They know, as we do, that Hitler never had the Bomb. The real question for the Bohrs, and for the audience (who almost certainly did not realize how close Hitler was to getting a bomb[9]), is: if Heisenberg potentially understood how to make one, why wasn't one made? If the answer lies in what happened in Copenhagen, then what certainly did happen there—a falling out between Bohr and Heisenberg—may seem likelier to have actually hastened the development of a Nazi bomb. To this problem, Frayn's play provides a tentative solution. Heisenberg, whatever his initial motivation for meeting with Bohr in Copen-

hagen, and despite the "terrible offense" given there "which could never be recalled" (Powers 4), was influenced perhaps unconsciously by the positive moral qualities of his former mentor not only not to make a bomb, but actually to conceal from his Nazi masters the ease with which a bomb might be made. Had Bohr and Margrethe been less morally steadfast, more pliant, less outraged, the outcome might have been different; but in their angry reaction to Heisenberg (they unquestionably suspected him, with good reason, of the dubious motives he may very well have started out with) Heisenberg was brought to mind of "a strange new quantum ethics" in a world in which there often seems to be no good action possible, only actions of lesser or greater evil.[10]

Frayn resists making a hero of Heisenberg, suggesting that his ethics may have been unconscious: he kept the knowledge of how little U-235 was needed to produce a bomb "not to himself but from himself" (112). Powers suggests that "Heisenberg is not a hero of the resistance, but something more disturbing—a scientist asked to build a bomb who raised the question whether it was right" (7).[11] Strictly, however, Heisenberg, under Gestapo surveillance, did not and could not *raise* the question at all in 1941. But he was in a position to change the world for better or worse, and consciously or not, for whatever ultimately indeterminable reason, he did what in retrospect can with some certainty be considered the right thing—or, more precisely, he did not do the wrong thing. If there is indeed a quantum ethics, his mode of inaction may serve as a model for a strange new quantum heroics.

* * *

If these science plays have a function similar to that of good sf in the Wellsian tradition, is there not a case to be made for their inclusion in the genre of sf? As Joseph Krupnik has shown (197-219), there exists a considerable body of sf drama, even if it is little-known, indicating that sf on the stage is by no means a contradiction in terms. Moreover, the two most successful of these science plays, *Arcadia* and ***Copenhagen,*** are the least bound by realistic conventions: Stoppard develops two parallel temporalities, which he ultimately blends in a manner that is literally impossible, while Frayn's revenants inhabit a spatio-temporal limbo, a blank space in which history can perpetually be restaged in an attempt to attain an always elusive final truth. Both plays certainly fit Patrick D. Murphy's description of a postmodernist fantastic drama that resists closure and "question[s] consensual reality rather than simply producing alternative realities" (4). Yet in spite of what Veronica Hollinger terms a "new valorization of the fantastic" (186), it seems that sf defined generically will continue to serve as "postmodernism's noncanonized or 'low art' double" (B. McHale qtd. in Hollinger 186) for the foreseeable future. For the cultural dominance of Hollywood sci-fi, so dependent for its generic self-definition upon pulp motifs, reduces the likelihood that sf will any time soon come to be defined functionally in accordance with Aldiss's proposition, let alone come to be viewed as one of the finest flowerings of the postmodernist era. In short, the old (reversible) adage, "if it's good, it can't be sf," continues to hold sway both in literary circles and among the consumers of sci-fi, with the consequence that a good science play, no matter how fantastic, cannot be part of sf as currently conceived.

Why should the *stage* have become, at millennium's end, the arena of serious negotiation between the sciences and humanities about a quantum ethics? The answer may lie in what makes a play different from a movie. Julius Kagarlitski has proposed that theater is a conditional art whose power depends on something immediate and unrepeatable, as opposed to film in which everything represented "has, as it were, already happened" (qtd. in Krupnik 198); this may suggest why the older art remains a more suitable medium for engaging quantum reality. Furthermore, in relation to **Copenhagen,** it has been suggested that the unrepeatability of a theatrical performance is particularly compatible with the play's theme of uncertainty (Stewart 303). Extrapolating from these two ideas, one may propose that the theater remains a place in which the live unfolding drama retains, from the audience's perspective, a measure of unmediated authenticity that is precious in an otherwise highly mediated culture. At the same time the audience reciprocally affects, be it ever so slightly, the quality, tone, or atmosphere of the production in a way impossible in the movie theater. In this way the complex and variable interactions between the individual playgoer, the audience of which he or she is a part, and the living actors on the stage dramatize the perpetually indeterminate quality of quantum reality.

In one of a series of interviews with contemporary playwrights under the rubric *A Search for a Postmodern Theater* (1991), Timberlake Wertenbaker notes that absurdist drama now seems passé and "It's time to try to make sense of the world" (DiGaetani 269). If the contemporary world is one in which the abbreviation A.D. might stand more appropriately for After Darwin, and if modernism saw a deepening of the gulf between the arts and the sciences, then who could argue that one of the necessary aims of a postmodernist theater should be to make sense of the world after Darwin, Copenhagen, Los Alamos, and Hiroshima? Of the five science plays under scrutiny here, two in particular, *Arcadia* and **Copenhagen,** would seem in their different ways to serve as models for a postmodernist drama that seeks to reconcile the arts and the sciences (see Antor 327). They assert the immensely liberating possibilities of the idea that the individual is back at the center of the quantum universe, while affirming that right action is possible, necessary, and effective, even if it may take an unconventional form.

Notes

1. See Hillegas 18-21 and ff. for a discussion of the relation between Huxley's cosmic pessimism and Wellsian scientific romance.

2. The fin-de-millennium science play is not an exclusively British phenomenon. Myers 7, 34 lists a number of American examples in production or development in late 1999.

3. Of the five plays dealt with here, *Arcadia* seems the least evidently a science play, yet it was reviewed very favorably as such in *Scientific American* (see Beardsley 1-2).

4. In his "Postscript" to *Copenhagen,* Frayn discusses the various translations of the German *Unbestimmtheit,* giving convincing reasons for preferring *indeterminacy* or *indeterminability* to *uncertainty* (101-02).

5. Andrew Hodges, biographer of Turing, suggests that this final speech is "wrong and in fact ridiculous [in biographical terms]. But I'm sympathetic because I think Hugh Whitemore had a good sense that there should be something dramatic to say about uncomputability" (3).

6. I use this phrase as a convenient term for a world characterized by the epistemological acceptance of fundamental indeterminacy. Strictly, as Stoppard himself has pointed out (see Gussow 84), the important scientific metaphors in *Arcadia* are drawn from chaos mathematics, while quantum theory (in particular the wave-particle duality) is a central metaphor in his earlier and rather less successful play *Hapgood* (1988). For Stoppard and the use of chaos theory in modern drama, see Demastes, "Re-Inspecting" 252-53. For a succinct analysis of what *Arcadia* owes to chaos theory, see Kramer 3-5.

7. A key to understanding Sidley Park's immunity to entropy is provided by Melbourne: "*Arcadia* is not a natural but a self-consciously created aesthetic object, which succeeds in conveying the coherent and timeless aesthetic pleasure we glimpse only in fragmentary moments of beauty, complexity, and mystery in the natural world" (571).

8. Frayn's most popular successes were *Donkeys' Years* (1976) and *Noises Off* (1982)—the latter of which has been described as the "King Lear of farces" (qtd. in Demastes, *British* 149)—as well as the movie *Clockwise* (1986), to which he wrote the screenplay.

9. There is a received idea that science could not flourish in Nazi Germany because of its expulsion of Jewish scientists or its totalitarian ethos, but John Cornwell has recently noted: "In fact, science and technology prospered in the Third Reich after 1933. Jet propulsion, guided missiles, electronic computers and calculators, the electron microscope and data processing, were all first developed in Germany during the period, or at least brought to fruition," and there were advances in nuclear fission, hormone and vitamin research, pharmacology, synthetic gasoline and rubber, chemical warfare agents, and television (9.36).

10. Ironically, Bohr himself actually had a small role in developing at Los Alamos the trigger for the atomic bomb dropped on Nagasaki (Frayn 47; Powers 7), a catastrophe often justified, and perhaps only justifiable, as a lesser evil to prevent a greater one (the potential loss of lives of American soldiers undertaking a Japanese invasion).

11. In a recent exchange in the *New York Review of Books,* Powers, replying to the charge that Heisenberg's failure to produce an atomic bomb was simply the result of incompetence, notes: "I think that in fact Heisenberg did find a way to say no—by stressing the expense and difficulty—that made a difference, thereby demonstrating that scientists everywhere, then and since, have the power to decide for themselves" (Rose 66).

Works Cited

Aldiss, Brian. *Science Fiction as Science Fiction.* Frome, UK: Bran's Head, 1978.

Antor, Heinz. "The Arts, the Sciences, and the Making of Meaning: Tom Stoppard's *Arcadia* as a Post-Structuralist Play." *Anglia* 116.3 (1998): 326-54.

Beardsley, Tim. "Sex and Complexity." Rev. of *Arcadia* by Tom Stoppard. *Scientific American* (July 1997). <www.sciam.com/0797issue/0797review1.html>. 2 pp.

Cornwell, John. "The Battle of Science." Rev. of *Hitler's Gift: Scientists Who Fled Nazi Germany* by Jean Medawar and David Pyke, and *Einstein's German World* by Fritz Stern. *Sunday Times* 13 Aug. 2000: 9.35-36.

Davidson, Max. "The Master of Self-Effacement." Interview with Michael Frayn. *Daily Telegraph* 30 May 1998. <www.telegraph.co.uk:80/et?ac=0001...mo=99999999& pg=/et/98/5/30/btfray30.html>. 3pp.

Demastes, William W., ed. *British Playwrights 1956-1995: A Research and Production Sourcebook.* Westport: Greenwood, 1996.

———. "Re-Inspecting the Crack in the Chimney: Chaos Theory from Ibsen to Stoppard." *New Theatre Quarterly* 10 (August 1994): 242-54.

Dickson, E. Jane. "An Old Master's New Trick." Interview with Michael Frayn. *Daily Telegraph* 31 Aug. 1999. <www.telegraph.co.uk:...mo=99999999& pg=/et/99/8/31/btfray31.html>. 4pp.

DiGaetani, John L. *A Search for a Postmodern Theater: Interviews with Contemporary Playwrights.* New York: Greenwood, 1991.

Frayn, Michael. *Copenhagen.* [1st perf. 21 May 1998.] London: Methuen, 1998.

———. Interview. See Davidson.

———. Interview. See Dickson.

Gussow, Mel. *Conversations with Stoppard.* New York: Limelight, 1995.

Hillegas, Mark R. *The Future as Nightmare: H. G. Wells and the Anti-Utopians.* New York: Oxford UP, 1967.

Hodges, Andrew. "The Alan Turing Internet Scrapbook: Breaking the Code: Alan Turing on Stage and Screen." <www.turing.org.uk/turing/scrapbook/btc.html>. 7pp.

Hollinger, Veronica. "Playing at the End of the World: Postmodern Theater." Murphy 182-96.

Huxley, Thomas H. "Evolution and Ethics" [The Romanes Lecture, 1893.] *Collected Essays.* Vol. 9. *Evolution and Ethics and Other Essays.* New York: Appleton, 1902. 46-116.

Kramer, Prapassaree and Jeffrey. "Stoppard's *Arcadia:* Research, Time, Loss." *Modern Drama* 40 (1997): 1-10.

Krupnik, Joseph. "'Infinity in a Cigar Box': The Problem of Science Fiction on the Stage." Murphy 197-219.

Lahr, John. "Bombs and Qualms." Rev. of *Copenhagen* by Michael Frayn. *New Yorker* 24 Apr.-1 May 2000: 219-20.

Marin, Rick. "Enjoy the Show. Test Will Follow." *New York Times* 14 May 2000: WK2.

Melbourne, Lucy. "'Plotting the Apple of Knowledge': Tom Stoppard's *Arcadia* as Iterated Theatrical Algorithm." *Modern Drama* 41 (1998): 557-72.

Murphy, Patrick D., ed. *Staging the Impossible: The Fantastic Mode in Modern Drama.* Westport: Greenwood, 1992.

Myers, Robert. "Science, Infiltrating the Stage, Puts Life Under the Microscope." *New York Times* 5 Dec. 1999: AR7, 34.

Poliakoff, Stephen. *Blinded by the Sun.* [1st perf. 28 Aug. 1996.] *Blinded by the Sun* and *Sweet Panic.* London: Methuen, 1996. 1-122.

Powers, Thomas. "The Unanswered Question." Rev. of *Copenhagen* by Michael Frayn. *New York Review of Books* 25 May 2000: 4, 6-7.

Rose, Paul Lawrence, and Thomas Powers. "Heisenberg in Copenhagen." An Exchange of Letters to the Editor. *New York Review of Books* 19 Oct. 2000: 65-66.

Stewart, Victoria. "A Theatre of Uncertainties: Science and History in Michael Frayn's *Copenhagen*." *New Theatre Quarterly* 15.4 (1999): 301-07.

Stoppard, Tom. *Arcadia*. [1st perf. 13 Apr. 1993.] London: Faber, 1993.

——. *Hapgood*. 1988. London: Faber, 1994.

Wertenbaker, Timberlake. *After Darwin*. [1st perf. 8 July 1998.] London: Faber, 1998.

Whitemore, Hugh. *Breaking the Code*. [1st perf. 15 Sept. 1986.] Oxford: Amber Lane, 1987.

Wroe, Nicholas. "A Serious Kind of Joker." Profile of Michael Frayn. *Guardian* 14 Aug. 1999. <www.guardianunlimited.co.uk/Archive/Article/0,4273,3892233,00.html>. 9 pp.

Robert L. King (essay date summer 2001)

SOURCE: King, Robert L. "The Play of Uncertain Ideas." *The Massachusetts Review* 42, no. 2 (summer 2001): 165-75.

[*In the following essay, King explores* Copenhagen *as a play about uncertainty and morality, noting that Heisenberg craves the ability to make decisions even when he has no way of knowing the results of those decisions.*]

Early reviewers appreciated the staging of Michael Frayn's **Copenhagen** as a dramatic rendering of its theoretical physics. The play's lighting and blocking display human interactions as parallels to the waves and particles of matter, simultaneously interdependent and isolated. The first time I saw the play, the circles of light in and through which its three characters move struck me as welcome illustrations of how bodies in space have clear and shifting positions simultaneously, by turns fully visible, stationary, in motion, or in partial light. In conventional staging, where characters stand determines what they see and how they are seen by others, the audience included. We expect directors to block characters' movements to illuminate a playwright's vision, and spare properties often direct an audience's attention to the play of words. So, straining to focus on pools of light, and expecting, mistakenly, scientific exposition, I gave into jet lag for a dozing moment. But soon my head was snapped erect by the realization that beneath the simplicity of the staging and of much of the dialogue, Frayn was presenting, not clarity, but how muddled our ways of knowing inevitably are and how foolish our attempts to apply abstract "truths" to human affairs. Even in the pursuit of pure scientific knowledge, our affections and affectations, our prejudices and preconceptions, intrude.

Two of **Copenhagen**'s three characters, Niels Bohr and Werner Heisenberg, in fact made revolutionary discoveries in physical theory; they did so in competitive cooperation, but mutual respect and friendship never fully suppressed their conflicting egos, as the third character, Margrethe Bohr, testifies. In a program note—all one needs to follow the play's discussion of physics—Heisenberg's uncertainty principle is summarized: "The more accurately you know a particle's position, the less accurately you know its velocity, and vice versa." Or, in its human application: One form of accurate knowledge creates doubt about another. Bohr further complicated the theory with his principle of complimentary; in the words Frayn gives him: "Particles are things, complete in themselves. Waves are disturbances in something else." As a consequence, we must choose one of the two ways of seeing, but "as soon as we do we can't know everything about them." So the two insights, crucial to making the atomic bomb, are revolutionary discoveries that end in paradox, an often mysterious, discomforting form of knowledge that Frayn extends to his portrayals of character:

HEISENBERG:

> *(to Bohr)* We can't completely understand your behaviour without seeing it both ways at once, and that's impossible, because the two ways are mutually incompatible.

How we know each other, then, makes full human understanding impossible, and like **Copenhagen**'s discussions of physical theory, imperfect character relationships are suggested by the play's staging. The technical achievement of the production has, however, diverted attention from a greater artistic one, for **Copenhagen** takes the play of ideas well beyond the theoretical limits set by Shaw and Brecht, the two modern playwrights clearly committed to the principle that drama provoke its audience to rational thought as prelude to a new social awareness or action. Unlike the thesis play which directs an enlightened conclusion or pits conflicting positions against one another, **Copenhagen** presents, as only a drama can, the intellectual excitement and emotional burden of uncertain or incomplete knowledge, and it does so without taking moral refuge in an indeterminacy with no practical consequences.

Shaw was explicit about his own purpose: "My plays are built to induce . . . intellectual interest." He admired Ibsen and Strindberg for their "attack[s] all along the front of refined society," and he endorsed the "problem" play for its "remorseless logic and iron framework of fact." To Brecht, the theorist of alienation,

Shaw practiced what he praised: "The reason why Shaw's own dramatic works dwarf those of his contemporaries is that they so unhesitatingly appealed to reason." Shaw's "Quintessence of Ibsenism" elevates his didactic commitment to the level of a formal theory in which the "unraveling in the third [act]" of a "well-made play" is replaced by a "discussion and its development." Shaw discovered this "technical novelty" empirically; even today, the climactic discussion of *A Doll's House* remains the prime example of his new dramatic form. The discussion that Shaw admires does not tie up the loose ends of a plot to the audience's satisfaction; instead, it settles a question in dispute and so has the decisiveness of a formal debate. It is climactic because all that can be said has been said, and the audience is left to choose one of two positions, one of which is obviously preferable. In its dialogue as well as its form, Ibsen's last act also exemplifies techniques of debate in which Nora controls the discussion and directs its resolution. Like a disputant, Nora distinguishes her opponent's meanings: when Torvald says "loved," she replies, "You never loved me. You've thought it fun to be in love with me"; when he calls her "incompetent," she turns his word back upon him, "I must learn to be competent." When Torvald asserts as a fact that "no one gives up honor for love," Nora responds with a strategy taught to Renaissance men, the direct denial: "Millions of women have done just that." Her slamming the door puts a triumphant exclamation point to her victory as debater. The discussion has a clear winner, a resolution similar to the intellectual satisfaction an audience gets when plot complications are resolved. Likewise, although Brecht claims that his dramatic form frees the audience to "think for itself," his political lessons come through with unmistakable clarity. At the end of *Copenhagen,* however, the character who most strongly wants the others to understand him is resigned, as the audience must be, to accept an inconclusive ending, one which leaves ideas in play, jostling against one another, mutually uninforming.

Frayn's imagined conversations take place after the deaths of *Copenhagen*'s three characters. The premise frees him to create arguments that the German physicist, Werner Heisenberg, might have used to justify his Nazi-sponsored research to his early mentor, Niels Bohr, in meetings that took place in 1941 and 1947. Heisenberg did in fact go to Copenhagen early in the war and returned after it, both times to talk to Bohr. Beyond that, the record of what they actually said is blank; historians rely, reasonably enough, on circumstantial evidence to argue contrary conclusions: that Heisenberg willingly tried to develop the atomic bomb for Hitler or that he deliberately obstructed efforts to make one; that he was indifferent to the destruction of Jews or that he went to Copenhagen to save Bohr and thousands of others. Frayn seems to be offering a resolution of such opposing positions when he attributes a debater's

proposition to Heisenberg as he drives to recover a certain account of his conversation with Bohr: "I chose my words very carefully. I simply asked you if as a physicist one had the moral right to work on the practical exploitation of atomic energy." But Bohr's reply prevents a Shavian discussion or a Brechtian lesson: "I don't recall." In Frayn's view, answering that question Yes or No would only comfort us with smug certainty imposed from an impersonal historical distance. A better proposition, one that would be a witty paradox in other hands, comes in the play's opening minutes when Heisenberg alludes to his theoretical achievement as a physicist: "Everyone understands uncertainty." He quickly qualifies that absolute ("Or thinks he does") and in a sharp antithesis locates abstract knowledge in its confused human context: "No one understands my trip to Copenhagen."

In the play's structure, theoretical physics is subordinated to character; what we think we know is only one part of what makes us human. Frayn delays his most complete explanation of the uncertainty principle until well into the second of *Copenhagen*'s two acts when Heisenberg, in one of many artful lines that ambiguously combine the idiomatic and the esoteric, says, "That's when I did uncertainty." He talks about taking a walk and realizes that if he could be seen through a distant telescope, he would appear as a series of "glimpses" to the spectator, not as someone on a continuous path. This insight told him that fellow scientists view "what we see in a cloud chamber," not as a fixed reality observable for and in itself but as something conditioned by their point of view and by their laboratory techniques. Whenever we observe—the unstated analogy to the theatre audience is a constant—we introduce "some new element into the situation" which allows us to measure its effects but which also makes that measurement less than absolutely accurate. Bohr confirms this point in his summary of Einstein: "Measurement . . . is not an impersonal event that occurs with impartial universality. It's a human act, carried out from a specific point of view in time and space, from one particular viewpoint of a possible observer." This comment also comes late in the play, long after Bohr has advocated logical calculation as a step toward deciding whether to welcome Heisenberg to his home; early in Act I, he meets his wife's objection to the visit with, "Let's add up the arguments on either side in a reasonably scientific way." His first reason, though, is based on *ethos* not *logos,* "Heisenberg is a friend," and it argues for the priority of human values over scientific ones in weighing arguments.

Throughout *Copenhagen,* scientific problems and procedures are silently subordinated to questions of character and motivation even as the dialogue recounts the physicists' thinking in precise detail. An audience need not follow discussion of isotopes and neutrons, of

U-238 and U-235, to appreciate Frayn's point about the worth of certain ideas in an uncertain world. Theoretical abstractions and laboratory experiments, once proved to work, can no more be isolated from their effects than physics can be removed from politics, for as Heisenberg says of the latter pair, "The two are sometimes painfully difficult to keep apart." As dramatic and thematic preliminary to such observations, Frayn has the men recount their first meeting when Heisenberg, a "cheeky young pup" as Bohr remembers him, publicly questions the mathematics in the older man's lecture. Although Heisenberg was not only cheeky but correct, the men became friends, the human relation more important than the mathematics. Later, when Bohr wonders if he could have "miscalculated" absorption rates of neutrons in their first conversation, each of the three characters in close sequence asks what "exactly" was said. To come to terms with the past they want an exact historical record, a way of knowing as comforting in its way as mathematical certainty but more of a false fire because it relies on memory which, even in the pursuit of truth, has a capacity to deceive. Frayn himself creates a drama based on the recollections of his three characters, but he cautions his audience on memory's reliability when Margrethe corrects her husband's recollection, and he defends himself by calling memory "a curious sort of diary."

In contrast, Heisenberg's faith in mathematical certainty can be absolute. He recalls being excited by a vision of "a world of pure mathematical structures," and disputing with Bohr, he declares, "What something means is what it means in mathematics." But when Frayn obliges him to account for the Bohrs' working partnership, Heisenberg must qualify his pure belief: "Mathematics becomes very odd when you apply it to people. One plus one can add up to so many different sums," and his voice then trails off. Logic offers no firmer ground for clear resolutions; the steps to its conclusions are taken by flawed human beings. Both Bohr and Heisenberg warn and are warned against "jump[ing] to conclusions" about each other. Although Heisenberg's theory "lays waste to the idea of causality" as a physical force, prejudice as a moral and social cause had profound practical effects for the Nazi atomic project. Heisenberg says that the men who "should have been making their calculations for us" were in England, and Margrethe gives the reason, "Because they were Jews." Hitler saw the Jewish scientists as less than human, their science too relativistic, so he lost the men who did the calculations necessary to solve the diffusion equation. Heisenberg's reaction to Margrethe, completely in character, compresses uncertainty and certainty with unconscious irony: "There's something almost mathematically elegant about that." In many lines like these, *Copenhagen* argues, outside of logic, that human concerns—the very stuff of much drama—inform all our actions and that the formal structures of our thinking are

inevitably qualified in practice by uncertain "somethings" and "almosts."

Countering Heisenberg's drive for certainty, Bohr can delight in paradox, the trope that turns in on itself and, so, leaves ideas in suspension, unresolved, perhaps mysterious. In a subtle undercurrent, Frayn introduces paradox and its natural partner, ambiguity, in simple language; they are his stylistic renderings of a certain uncertainty. Besides the early "Everyone understands uncertainty," we get a critique of the play's dialogue: "Each time he explained, it became more obscure." A pun on "chilly" questions the bond between the men: "A little chilly tonight, perhaps for strolling." Margrethe speaks of "the questions that haunt us still," and the last word can be either adjective or adverb—both meaningful in context. Recalling the Bohrs' lost children, Heisenberg sees them both as "simultaneously alive and dead in our memories," an observation that applies to the characters themselves in the dramatic exchanges Frayn creates. Like them, a responsive theatre audience lives in paradoxical time with present and past alive and dead simultaneously, and what Heisenberg says later applies to them as well, "All we possess is the present, and the present endlessly dissolves into the past." These insights belie Heisenberg's judgment on the pleasure Bohr takes in scientific mysteries:

HEISENBERG:

> You actually loved the paradoxes, that's your problem. You revelled in the contradictions.

BOHR:

> Yes, and you've never been able to understand the suggestiveness of paradox and contradiction. That's *your* problem. You live and breathe paradox and contradiction, but you can no more see the beauty of them than the fish can see the beauty of water.

From the first word of **Copenhagen,** Frayn locates the audience in the ambiguous space between Heisenberg certainty and Bohr suggestiveness; we are teased into thought without following Brechtian signposts or Shavian deductions. That first word, "But," is the conjunction that doesn't quite connect, that qualifies what comes before. Not only does silence precede it, Margrethe also wants to know a reason: "But why?" The last words of the play are similarly unsettling—sentence fragments delivered by Heisenberg, the character who most strongly wants to be understood but who can conclude only to "that final core of uncertainty at the heart of things." Early critics could disagree whether Nora did the right thing precisely because *A Doll's House* so openly argues to a dramatized conclusion. Her worth may be debated after the curtain goes down, but Ibsen closes the door on his case as forcefully as she slams it on her marriage. Mother Courage's wagon may go around in stage circles, but Brecht directs the audience to follow his straightforward thinking about war and survival. No such quasi-logical finality resolves the human ambiguities and theoretical paradoxes in *Copenhagen.* Had Frayn put Heisenberg's last words in axiomatic form—Be certain of uncertainty—the assertion would teach us only to be guarded in thought and action.

This final stasis is a satisfying ending to a non-linear play that relies almost exclusively on the dramatic present, an immediate present that subsumes stage presence, the historical present and the past all at once. The three characters remain in view throughout; when Bohr and Heisenberg go for a walk, they circle the edges of the playing space, bare except for a few straight chairs and Margrethe. Imagined as dead by the playwright, the three can examine their motives before and after the speeches they recreate, and Margrethe can speak directly to us from an apparently dispassionate point of view. Her first words echo Bohr's second line in the play, "Now we're all dead and gone." The men have yet to meet at the point, but Frayn's staging has put Heisenberg before us as a way of insisting on the theatrical present through his repeated "Now": "The more I've explained the deeper the uncertainty has become. Well, I shall be happy to make one more attempt. Now we're all dead and gone. Now no one can be hurt, now no one can be betrayed." Characters and their ethos, Heisenberg suggests, can be abstracted from the circumstances of historical time, and a truth may emerge. Frayn's staging seems to collaborate with Heisenberg: a minimal use of props, pools of light from above, and bland period costumes. The paucity of stage effects, those circumstances that can direct an audience to judge, narrows and sharpens *Copenhagen*'s focus. Beyond the words of its resurrected characters, the play offers no theatrical signs to convey sure meaning—no symbolic seagulls, no vulgar *Paycock* furniture. As a result, the immediate present acquires a dominance even as the characters reconsider their versions of the past.

Much as Frayn summons the past into that present, he finds the significant in the transient and the essential in the accidental. What Heisenberg says of social contacts opposes the permanent ("essential") and the fleeting ("circumstances") and ironically modifies them with antithetical qualifiers: "Essential perhaps, in certain circumstances." What we try to fix as permanent truth is similarly qualified by our angle of vision as spectators, for Frayn has situated the theatregoer in a position analogous to the physicist's. Not only must we choose how to listen—to lines and speeches either as convincing in themselves or as parts of dialogue (as waves or particles)—but we must also evaluate the characters' speeches as choices made under a major constraint. Early in the play, Margrethe acknowledges the historical and dramatic pressures that prevent full disclosures: "What can any of us say in the present circumstances?"

Ordinarily, stage entrances make characters "present" and give promise of something to come, an action to unfold plot or dialogue to develop relationships. In a departure from the norm, Heisenberg does not enter a scene without first appearing on stage, and his entrances, such as they are, circle back to the constant "Now" of his opening speech. This formal pattern of recurrence undermines any expectations of chronological or logical progression that the audience might have. The "Here" in "Here I am" refers to the actor's place on stage and to several distinct places which—absent scenery—must be imagined both by actor and audience. Heisenberg speaks the line to himself as he walks toward the Bohr house, and yet again, "But now here I am," much later in dialogue with Bohr who, positioning himself to recreate a conversation, resigns himself to follow Heisenberg's prompting, "Very well. Here I am walking very slowly." At three important times, Heisenberg prefaces his entrance to the house with "I crunch over the familiar gravel"—near the beginning and end of Act I and near the end of the play. The lines signaling these returns sound like creative variations on Brecht's rehearsal prompts:

Three aids . . . may help to alienate the actions and remarks of the characters being portrayed:

1) Transposition into the third person.

2) Transposition into the past.

3) Speaking the stage directions out loud.

Speaking in the first person, as actual performance dictates, and in the present tense, Frayn's characters retain their immediacy and gain emotional distance at the same time. Like the repeated "crunch," the men's greeting—a version of hundreds of conventional entrances—is reenacted at the close of the first act:

HEISENBERG:

   My dear Bohr!

BOHR:

   Come in, come in . . .

These textual and thematic returns are realized theatrically in the characters' movements and gestures, and the pattern argues subtly about our ability to know. For, although the three characters have applied singular talents and intelligence to understand themselves and each other, their discussions, explanations, reconstructions and reminiscences do not make connected sense of the past. At best, they "glimpse" discrete points in a loop, but to their credit they labor hard to make their circular journey and finally they learn to cherish the moment that they glimpse. Journeying with them, the audience is led to evaluate modes of thinking from the privileged position of intellectual voyeurs and at the same time to fill out the empty space imaginatively.

Copenhagen, like many other plays, stands squarely in the tradition dominated by *Waiting for Godot.* Its minimal setting and its non-linear form connect Frayn to Beckett, while the questions that Heisenberg and Bohr raise have profound political and social implications. They are heirs of Didi and Gogo, but they do not play roles to pass the empty time; rather, along with Margrethe, they play them as reenactments of actual events, as present recreations of discussions and of their historical contexts. At times, the Brecht and Beckett traditions merge, as in one passage when the characters resemble actors in rehearsal trying to get inside their roles. Since the roles are the selves they would study, however, the playacting teaches a form of objectivity:

MARGRETHE:

I watch the two smiles in the room . . .

BOHR:

I glance at Margrethe . . .

HEISENBERG:

I look at the two of them looking at me . . .

BOHR:

I look at him looking at me . . .

Their limited self-awareness authorizes interpretations of the others' acting; Bohr, addressing the audience, uses language that calls attention to Heisenberg's practiced delivery and, so, to his sincerity: "With careful casualness he begins to ask the questions he's prepared." And Heisenberg, in turn, cues a response to Bohr: "He gazes at me, horrified." A few lines later, Bohr tries to engage the historical past with a form of theatrical improvisation: "Let's suppose for a moment that instead I remember the paternal role I'm supposed to play. Let's see what happens if I stop, and control my anger, and turn to him. And ask him why." Watch them watching themselves closely, Frayn seems to advise, and see how proper sight can lead to insight for the audience as well as the characters. So, we learn with Margrethe that the past, laden with emotional weight, resists rounded, causally finished accounts: "What I see isn't a story! It's confusion and rage and jealousy and tears." We sympathize with Bohr, his memory burdened by the loss of children and his role in developing the Bomb: "Before we can glimpse who or what we are, we're gone and laid to dust." At the very end, we are aligned with Heisenberg who wanted mathematical certainty but must, too, be content—richly content at that—with fragments:

HEISENBERG:

In the meanwhile, in this most precious meanwhile, there it is. . . . Our children and our children's children. Preserved, just possibly, by that one short moment in Copenhagen. By some event that will never quite be located or defined. By that final core of uncertainty at the heart of things.

Copenhagen also entertains the weighty questions of man's place in the universe, of ultimate responsibility for unintended consequences and of evil. Frayn roots these and other moral abstractions in flawed human beings; the imperfect truths they earn survive their social and theatrical roles. And, for me, Frayn's truths survive performance, for the second time I saw *Copenhagen,* having read the text and knowing what to expect, I left the theatre shaking my head at the wisdom of the play's inconclusiveness. If it has a Shavian lesson, it's something like Relish the Moment, always remembering that we can never really know if we got the moment right.

August W. Staub (essay date spring 2002)

SOURCE: Staub, August W. "The Scientist as Byronic Hero: Michael Frayn's *Copenhagen.*" *Journal of Dramatic Theory and Criticism* 16, no. 2 (spring 2002): 133-41.

[*In the following essay, Staub suggests that Heisenberg emerges as a Byronic hero operating in a postmodern ethos framed by uncertainty.*]

It is both strange and exciting in a postmodern world to find science and scientists becoming the touchstone of popular culture. There was a time when the movies featured various "mad scientists" such as Dr. Frankenstein, or there were romantic biographies of heroes of science such as Madame Curie or Louis Pasteur journeying to truth, or brilliant servants of progress like Alexander Graham Bell with the popular singer Don Ameche in appropriate period costume. Fifty years ago science was amusing and tolerable; it was far enough in the past or made your milk safer to drink or gave you a telephone. Later there were mad science works in the form of science fiction where in films like *2001, A Space Odyssey* the mad scientist becomes a mad computer. But of late science has become more real, more mainstream as it were. Oh, I know there have been odd instances of the phenomenon in the past such as the WPA Theatre's production of $E=MC^2$ and the ultimate canonization of St. Einstein, and all that pop romance quality of the NASA program. But now science is truly a metaphor for human life, or—as the playwright Michael Frayn and others are now confounding the two—the state of being human and the scientific method have now become inseparable so that great scientists like great poets can suffer as Byronic heroes trapped in their own human condition.

Not that scientists are entirely enamored with the idea. There is still the ideal of the scientist as passionate puritan, a person so devoted to intellectual ideals and "the truth" that no mere humanist concern could swerve the scientist from his righteous path. While most of my colleagues in the sciences would publicly deny being attracted to such a mantle, it is there for the wearing and that is another issue which Frayn deals with in his play, *Copenhagen.*

Copenhagen opened over three years ago in London to enormous critical acclaim and strong audience interest. It premiered on Broadway in April of 2000 to equal critical and audience excitement. When one realizes that Broadway is usually occupied by musicals and light comedies, Frayn's achievement becomes all the more impressive. And when we realize that the subject matter of *Copenhagen* is a visit between two theoretical physicists the achievement is astonishing.

The play is set in September, 1941 when Werner Heisenberg, the articulator of the "uncertainty principle," came to visit his mentor, Neils Bohr, the propagator of the so-called Copenhagen Interpretation. World War Two was in its second year, and the two men were on opposite sides. The meeting was fraught with danger and embarrassment. It ended abruptly, and even to this day there are heated discussions of what actually transpired. Several books and many articles have considered what might have been discussed.[1] At the center of the debate is the atomic bomb. Heisenberg was working on German projects in atomic fission. Whether he was working on an atomic bomb is not clear even to this day. After the war, in order to save his reputation as a scientist-hero and to put the best face on his relation to the NAZI's, Heisenberg always argued that he had miscalculated the critical mass of U235 needed to construct a bomb. Though never actually saying so, he let stand the assumption that he deliberately miscalculated in order not to provide the bomb to the NAZI's. Some have argued that so great a mathematician could hardly have miscalculated. Others, pointing out the failure of other great physicists, including Neils Bohr, to arrive at a correct calculation, argue that Heisenberg may well be telling it the way it was. Frayn comes now, a half century later, to explore this issue among others.

Like science itself, the play does not allow extraneous matter on the bench. There are only three characters: Heisenberg, Neils Bohr and Bohr's wife, Margrethe. The stage is bare except for three chairs. The play takes place in the present, after all three characters are dead. They return to re-live the events and they re-live them not once but several times, in several different fields as in an Einsteinian universe, and in several forms of relationships between the three as in a quantum universe. What is intriguing is Frayn's manner of structuring the play itself as a model of the famous two-slit experiment or even, since the characters are already dead, as a working example of Shrodinger's famous cat in a lead box.

At the opening Bohr and his wife speculate about why Heisenberg had asked for a visit, and why, after all these many years of being dead, the visit or what was said matters to them. It matters, of course, because of the issue of the scientist as contemporary hero and of the scientist as passionate puritan. Even as they talk, Heisenberg chats with the audience.

> . . . there are only two things the world remembers about me. One is the uncertainty principle and the other is my mysterious visit to Neils Bohr in Copenhagen in 1931. Everyone understands uncertainty or thinks he does. No one understands my trip to Copenhagen. Time and again I've explained it. To Bohr himself and Margrethe. To interrogators and intelligence officers, to journalists and historians. The more I've explained it, the deeper the uncertainty has become. Well, I shall be happy to make one more attempt. Now we're all dead and gone . . . so what was Bohr? . . . the father of us all. Modern atomic physics began when Bohr realized that quantum theory applied to matter as well as energy.

Inside the house Bohr chats with his wife.

BOHR:

> When you think that he first came to work with me in 1924 . . . and in just over a year he had invented quantum mechanics.

MARGRETHE:

> It came out of his work with you.

BOHR:

> Another year or so and he'd got uncertainty.

MARGRETHE:

> And you'd done complementarity.

BOHR:

> We'd argued them both out together.

HEISENBERG:

> *(outside the house)* We did most of our best work together.

BOHR:

> Heisenberg usually led the way.

HEISENBERG:

> Bohr made sense out of it.

BOHR:

We operated like a business.

HESIENBERG:

Chairman and managing director.

MARGRETHE:

Father and son.

Exposition is taken care of, and it is done so in what I might call a "subatomic" manner, in that each of the nuclei on stage is demonstrating an entirely different spin. Nils and Margrethe are dead but spinning in the Denmark of 1941, even though they are disagreeing and thus have antagonistic spins. Heisenberg, on the other hand, is spinning in the universe also inhabited by the audience of the 21st century. This is what is exciting about Frayn's play. First Bohr and his wife list some of the scientific problems he and Heisenberg had worked on together, and then Heisenberg demonstrates the thought process behind "uncertainty" and the "measurement issue."

HEISENBERG:

First of all there is the official visit to Bohr's work place, The Institute of Theoretical Physics, with an awkward lunch in the old familiar canteen. No chance to talk to Bohr, of course. Is he even present? There's Rosenthal . . . Peterson, I think . . . Christian Moller, almost certainly. It's like being in a dream. At the head of the table—is that Bohr? I turn to look, and it's Bohr, it's Rosenthal, it's Moller, it's whomever I appoint to be there . . .

This is the first wave function of Heisenberg-in-the-ghost-house-of-the-Bohr's. That wave function collapses and another function follows almost immediately as Heisenberg announces to the audience that he is approaching the Bohr residence.

HEISENBERG:

What am I feeling? Fear, certainly—the touch of fear that one always feels for a teacher, an employer, a parent. Much worse, fear about what I have to say. About how to express it. How to broach it in the first place. Worse fears about what will happen if I fail.

MARGRETHE:

It's not something to do with the war?

BOHR:

Heisenberg is a theoretical physicist. I don't think anyone yet has discovered a way you can use theoretical physics to kill people.

MARGRETHE:

It couldn't be something about fission?

BOHR:

Fission? Why should he want to talk to me about fission?

MARGRETHE:

Because you're working on it.

BOHR:

Heisenberg isn't.

MARGRETHE:

Isn't he? Everyone else in the world seems to be and you are the acknowledged authority.

BOHR:

He hasn't published on fission.

MARGRETHE:

But if the Germans were developing some kind of weapon based on nuclear fission—

BOHR:

My love, no one is going to develop a weapon based on nuclear fission.

MARGRETHE:

But if the Germans were trying to, Heisenberg would be involved.

BOHR:

There's no shortage of good German physicists.

MARGRETHE:

There's no shortage of good German physicists in America.

BOHR:

The Jews have gone obviously.

Then Heisenberg makes his public proposition.

HEISENBERG:

I don't suppose you could ever come to Germany?

MARGRETHE:

The boy's an idiot.

HEISENBERG:

I was simply going to say that I have my old ski hut at Bayrischell. So if by chance . . .

BOHR:

Perhaps Margrethe would be kind enough to sew a yellow star on my old ski jacket.

Heisenberg apologizes and the two physicists go on to discuss Germany's lack of cyclotrons, and then Bohr observes that the Germans always turned their backs on theoretical physics because so many of its practitioners were Jewish. Margrethe cautions them to talk about physics, not politics to which Bohr replies: "The two are sometimes difficult to keep apart." Enter the first hint of Byronic agony.

As they argue the old camaraderie of colleagues who respect one another and who do not resent an intellectual jab fest begins to emerge. Heisenberg recalls their ski trips. "What about those games of poker in the ski-hut . . . you once cleaned us all out! . . . with a non-existent straight! We're all mathematicians—we're all counting the cards—we're 90% certain he hasn't got anything. But he goes on raising us. This insane confidence. Until our faith in mathematical probability begins to waiver, and one by one we all throw our cards in." Bohr laughs and says: "I thought I had a straight. I misread the cards. I bluffed myself."

Heisenberg is also laughing. "You were insanely competitive." Bohr observes that Heisenberg engaged in his own competitiveness. Everything Heisenberg did, even skiing down to get provisions became a contest. "You were down in ten minutes of course . . . At the speed you were going you were up against the uncertainty relationship. If you knew where you were when you got down, you didn't know how fast you'd got there. If you knew how fast you were going, you didn't know you were down." "I certainly didn't stop to think about it," replies Heisenberg. Bohr quickly retorts: "not to criticize, but that's what might be criticized about your science." "I usually got there all the same," says Heisenberg. Bohr reminds him that "you never cared what you destroyed on the way though. As long as the mathematics worked out you were satisfied." Heisenberg shrugs. "if something works it works." "But," says Bohr, "the question is always, what does the mathematics mean in plain language? What are the philosophical implications?" Heisenberg chuckles. "I always knew you'd be picking your way step-by-step down the slope behind me, digging all the capsized meanings and implications out of the snow."

MARGRETHE:

The faster you ski the sooner you're across the cracks and crevasses.

HEISENBERG:

The faster you ski the better you think.

BOHR:

Not to disagree but that is most . . . most interesting.

HEISENBERG:

By which you mean it's nonsense. But it's not nonsense. Decisions make themselves when you're coming downhill at 70 kilometers an hour. Suddenly there's the edge of nothingness in front of you. Swerve left? Swerve right? Or think about it and die. In your head you swerve both ways. . . .

MARGRETHE:

Like that particle . . . the one you said goes through two slits at the same time . . . Or Schroedinger's wretched cat.

HEISENBERG:

That's alive and dead at the same time.

Until the experiment is over, this is the point, until the sealed chamber is open, the abyss detoured; and it turns out the particle has met itself again, the cat's dead.

MARGRETHE:

And you're alive.

HEISENBERG:

The swerve itself was the decision.

Now we have thoroughly mixed the issues of the scientist as hero, as passionate pilgrim and the scientist as humanist, and Frayn has us hooked. And then finally the scientist-humanist as agonized soul. "I was formed by nature to be a mathematically curious entity," remarks Bohr. "Not one but half of two." To which Heisenberg adds, "Mathematics becomes very odd when you apply it to people. One plus one can add up to so many different sums . . ."

Ah ha, now we will entertain the question of just what Heisenberg is up to—saving his country or like Pasteur saving the "good guys." To save his country he need only remain a "pure scientist, "but to save the "good guys" he will have to become a humanist. In which role will he emerge as the scientist-hero? He asks Neils to take a walk with him as they once did when they worked out the Cophenhagen Interpretation.

They leave the stage, but quickly they are back. Bohr is obviously upset. Heisenberg leaves, the field dissolves. Neils and Margrethe, once again ghosts, review the problems of the play. Heisenberg re-enters the field.

MARGRETHE:

What did Heisenberg tell Neils—what did Neils reply? The person who wanted to know most of all was Heisenberg himself.

BOHR:

The conversation went wrong almost as it did before.

MARGRETHE:

You couldn't even agree on where you walked that night.

HEISENBERG:

Faelled Park, of course. Where we went so often in the old days . . . I can still see the drift of autumn leaves under the street lamps.

BOHR:

Yes because you remember it as October!

MARGRETHE:

And it was September.

BOHR:

No fallen leaves.

MARGRETHE:

And it was 1941. No street lamps.

BOHR:

I thought we got no further than my study.

HEISENBERG:

We must have been outside! What I was going to say was treasonable. If I'd been overheard, I'd have been executed. I remember it absolutely clearly because my life was at stake. I chose my words very carefully. I simply asked you if as a physicist one had the moral right to work on the practical application of atomic energy. Yes?

BOHR:

I don't recall.

HEISENBERG:

You don't recall because you immediately became alarmed.

BOHR:

I was horrified.

HEISENBERG:

. . . and you jumped to the conclusion that I was trying to provide Hitler with nuclear weapons.

BOHR:

And you were.

HEISENBERG:

No, a reactor . . . to generate electricity, to drive ships!

BOHR:

But then I asked you if you actually thought that uranium fission could be used for the construction of weapons.

HEISENBERG:

I said that I now knew it could be.

BOHR:

That is what really horrified me.

HEISENBERG:

If we could build a reactor we could build bombs. That's what brought me to Copenhagen. But none of this could I say. At this point you stopped listening. The bomb had already gone off inside your head . . . Our one chance to talk was gone forever.

The act then ends with another reliving of the 1941 meeting—seemingly as proof that it did happen, but the meeting this time will have other aspects, just as the scientist at his bench repeats his experiment and adds other variables. But unlike science, these variables turn to the humanities for an answer. Heisenberg argues that Germany is his country, and he must help his country. He points out that his love of his country is not unlike Bohr's love of Denmark for whom he aided the Americans to create a bomb. What is right and what is wrong? When does patriotism go too far, when does it become treason? The first act ends with Margrethe's observation: "From these two heads the future will emerge. Which cities will be destroyed, and which will survive. Who will die and who will live. Which world will go down to obliteration and which will triumph."

As the second act begins, we have introduced the variable of the early relationship of Bohr to Heisenberg. This time the German scientist comes to Copenhagen as a graduate student in 1924. Bohr and Heisenberg relive the student-mentor relationship as they go through the discoveries they made together working in Bohr's lab. Suddenly, as it is with a master teacher and his or her best graduate student, they were friends and colleagues. Bohr exclaims, "three years of bracing, northern springtime . . . At the end of which we had uncertainty . . . we had complementarity . . . we had the whole Copenhagen Interpretation." But Heisenberg had his problems. He protests he had trouble understanding matrix calculus. He says that he was betrayed by Bohr, who at one point rejected Schroedinger and wave mechanics and then "turned coat." Bohr went on a skiing vacation and Heisenberg remained in Copenhagen and perfected the uncertainty principle, which I best understand as the universe is composed of the world of potential and the world of actuality, with the two joined by the act of measurement, so that the measurer and the thing measured form a unified whole in which there is no certainty of boundaries.[2] Now we have the full and complex issue of the play: If Bohr measures or evaluates what a German scientist did it will contain uncertainties, and if the German scientist, Heisenberg, measures what he did, that measurement will contain other uncertainties. Bohr makes this point but it is Margrethe who draws the ultimate conclusion: If it's Heisenberg at the center of the universe then the one bit of the universe he can't see is Heisenberg . . . So it's no good asking him why he came to Copenhagen in 1941. He doesn't know." Or as David Merman puts it: "The moon really isn't there if you don't look at it."[3]

Margrethe, however, is willing to look at the moon. She points out that the Uncertainty Principle and its Copenhagen Interpretation—that says that all measurement must be seen in the context of the measurement situation (complementarity) and that all measurement is done by a human measurer so that the universe, as far as quantum phsycis is concerned, is anthrocentric—is entirely humanist in quality. There is no room for a believer in a contextual universe to adhere to universal principles such as those proclaimed the NAZI's. And so much for the concept of the scientist as passionate puritan. The Copenhagen interpretation has returned us to classical Greek humanism, put the human at the center of the universe where man is the measure (and measurer) of all things.

It is at this point that Heisenberg as humanist puts the question: does one as a physicist have the moral right to work on the exploitation of energy? Bohr, still the puritan, is horrified and dashes off into the night, collapsing the wave function for the two. Margrethe sums it up: "That was the last and greatest demand Heisenberg made upon his friendship with you. To be understood when he couldn't understand himself. And that was the last and greatest act of friendship for Heisenberg that you performed in return. To leave him misunderstood."

But there is yet one more reliving, one more *pas de trois* for the trio to perform in an altered field. In this final field Bohr proposes "to see what happens if I do not go flying off into the night."

HEISENBERG:

> Meanwhile you were going on from Sweden to Los Alamos.

BOHR:

> To play my small part in the deaths of a hundred thousand people . . . whereas you, my dear Heisenberg, never managed to contribute to the death of a single solitary person in all your life. Heisenberg, I have to say that if people are measured strictly in terms of observable quantities—

HEISENBERG:

> Then we would have a strange new quantum ethics. There would be a place in heaven for me and another for the SS man I met on the way home.

Now we have it: a postmodern ethic that confounds science with humanism, that makes of Heisenberg as much a hero of science, albeit something of a Byronic hero,

as Bohr. For all things must be understood as complementary, as uncertain even as we evaluate them. Goodbye to the passionate puritan, the scientist as shining hero, and even the "mad scientist". Hello to the postmodern condition. The moon isn't there if YOU don't look at it.

Notes

1. Quite a body of literature deals with the Heisenberg-Bohr issue. Among the more interesting are: Jeremy Bernstein, *Hitler's Uranium Club, The Secret Recordings at Farm Hall* (Woodbury, New York: American Institute of Physics, 1996); David Cassidy, *The Life and Science of Werner Heisenberg* (New York: Knof, 1996); Werner Heisenberg, *Physics and Philosophy* (New York: Penguin, 1958); Paul Lawrence Rose, *Heisenberg and the Atomic Bomb Project* (Berkeley: U of California P, 1998). It should be noted here that the Bohr family became concerned about the talk and controversy surrounding the play that they released in early February, 2002, 11 unpublished documents that related to the Bohr-Heisenberg meeting. In an interview in the *New York Times,* February 9, 2002, Michael Frayn discussed the documents, but stated that they were not sufficiently informative enough for him to consider changing anything in his play. Several conferences on the play have been held in Denmark and throughout the world. There is a very popular web site for the play.

2. Several popular studies of late have made the whole issue of quantum mechanics more accessible to the educated non-scientist. Among the more informative are: John Casti, *Paradigms Lost* (New York: Avon Books, 1989); Murrray Glenn-Mann, *The Quark and The Jaguar* (New York: Freeman, 1994); Brian Green, *The Elegant Universe* (New York: Random House, Inc., 1999); Stephen W. Hawkins, *A Brief History of Time* (New York: Bantam Books, 1988).

3. David Merman, quoted in John L. Casti, *Paradigms Lost* (New York: Avon Books, 1989) 433.

Harry Lustig and Kirsten Shepherd-Barr (essay date November-December 2002)

SOURCE: Lustig, Harry and Kirsten Shepherd-Barr. "Science as Theater." *American Scientist* 90, no. 6 (November-December 2002): 550-55.

[*In the following essay, Lustig and Shepherd-Barr examine science as a theme in several contemporary plays, including* Copenhagen.]

Two thousand million people in the world, and the one who has to decide their fate is the only one who's always hidden from me. . . .

On a bare stage, actor Hank Stratton, playing the role of Werner Heisenberg in Michael Frayn's acclaimed play **Copenhagen,** muses on the impossibility of self-knowledge. The fictional Heisenberg is agonizing over his role in the Nazi effort to build an atomic bomb and finds himself unsure of his own motivations.

For four years on the London stage, two years on Broadway, and in cities across Europe and America, **Copenhagen** has defied the conventional wisdom that science and art cannot co-exist. Despite or perhaps because of its heady mix of quantum physics and moral dilemmas, it has been popular with critics and audiences alike; it won the Tony Award for Best New Play in 2000 and was filmed for presentation this fall to U.S. public-television audiences. As *New York Times* critic Ben Brantley put it, "Who would have ever thought that three dead, long-winded people talking about atomic physics would be such electrifying companions?"

Yet the success of **Copenhagen** has not been an isolated phenomenon. In recent years, science has become a surprisingly popular subject for playwrights. According to our best count, more than 20 plays on a scientific theme have opened in a professional production over the last five years, although none has yet matched **Copenhagen**'s popular success. At the very least, science is in vogue on stage as it has never been before. The best of these plays go far beyond using science as an ornament or a plot device. They seriously embrace scientific ideas and grapple with their implications. In an era when traditional dramatic subjects such as dysfunctional families have become tired, playwrights have found the lives and discoveries of real scientists to be full of dramatic possibilities and thought-provoking metaphors.

In his famous 1959 essay on "the two cultures," C. P. Snow lamented the widening gulf between science on one side and the arts and humanities on the other, and expressed his hope for a "third culture" of art that would "be on speaking terms with the scientific one." A number of recent science plays show how effective this conversation can be, and suggest that the "third culture" that Snow envisioned may actually be arriving in the intersection between science and the theater.

ANXIETY AND DISTRUST

"Science plays" have a long history and a distinguished provenance, starting with Christopher Marlowe's *Dr. Faustus,* published in 1604. Although it does not deal with specific scientific concepts, the play features a scientist who strikes a bargain with the Devil and meets a horrible demise as a result of his lust for knowledge.

Marlowe's distrust of the motives of scientists set the tone for many future plays in the genre. Other playwrights expressed this distrust in more comedic form. Ben Jonson's *The Alchemist* (1610) lampooned both the practitioners of this ancient pseudo-science, unmasked by Jonson as jargon-babbling rogues, and their willing dupes. When Jonson's sly alchemist, Subtle, quizzes his accomplice, Face, Jonson has great fun with the terminology of Renaissance science:

SUBTLE:

> Name the vexations, and the
>   martyrisations
> Of metals, in the work.

FACE:

> Sir, putrefaction,
> Solution, ablution, sublimation,
> Cohobation, calcinations,
>   ceration and
> Fixation.

SUBTLE:

> This is heathen Greek,
>   to you, now?
> And when comes vivification?

FACE:

> After mortification.

Later, George Bernard Shaw's *The Doctor's Dilemma* (1906) made fun of a passel of medical charlatans with such famous lines as "Stimulate the phagocytes!" But the play also shows that Shaw has genuinely investigated the biochemistry that the doctors discuss.

Bertolt Brecht's *Galileo,* with its portrayal of actual scientists in historical situations, marked a turning point in the history of scientific plays. In a version of the play published in 1939 (but not translated, and therefore not widely known), Brecht took a very positive view of his protagonist; but in later revisions, which were strongly influenced by Hiroshima and Nagasaki, he portrayed Galileo as an antihero. The revised play, published in 1947, is the Brecht *Galileo* most widely used and read around the world.

Several other playwrights also saw the bomb in Faustian terms. Friedrich Dürrenmatt, in *The Physicists* (1962), warned of the apocalyptic results of modern physics put into the wrong hands. The play uses the Möbius strip as a central image and is one of the first modern plays to integrate science formally as well as thematically. Another remarkable science play that warns of the dangerous potential of physics, while actually discussing scientific ideas, is Hallie Flanagan Davis's $E = mc^2$ (1948). This play is part allegory and part documentary, as it features a character called Atom and a Professor who explains the physics that the audience needs to know. Much of the play's dialogue is taken directly from transcripts of hearings of the Atomic Energy Commission and contemporary news sources. Davis leaves the fate of the Earth in the audience's hands, pleading with us to choose the right path in our use of atomic energy.

MEMORY AND DUALITY

Even as they retain some elements of skepticism toward science, contemporary science plays explore a broader range of attitudes and, as in $E = mc^2$, have frequently drawn their themes from science itself. No play illustrates this better than the masterpiece of the genre, **Copenhagen.**

Michael Frayn's play, familiar by now to many *American Scientist* readers, re-enacts the 1941 visit of Werner Heisenberg to his mentor and friend Niels Bohr, in Nazi-occupied Denmark. The third "long-winded" character is Bohr's wife Margrethe, who in this play (although probably not in reality) was present for the first part of the conversation. The action takes place outside chronological time, as the three deceased characters struggle, with the hindsight of 60 years of history, to make sense of what happened that afternoon.

From 1939 until Germany's defeat in 1945, Heisenberg was in charge of the most important part of the country's uranium project. As a result of the visit to Copenhagen, the friendship between the two men cooled abruptly. Something had happened, but neither ever explained definitively what it was. Frayn explores the mystery with three alternative scenarios, or "drafts" as the characters call them, each with different outcomes. No concrete answers are provided in the text. Even the characters' own memories of the events prove unreliable.

The questions begin with the very opening lines from Margrethe to her husband: "Why did he [Heisenberg] come to Copenhagen? . . . What was he trying to tell you?" They continue: Did Heisenberg say to Bohr what he had intended? If not, why not? What was Bohr's reaction? What was Heisenberg's? And inevitably, why did the Germans not achieve an atomic bomb, and why, under Heisenberg, did they not even try—or did they? Did Heisenberg deliberately slow down the bomb effort for moral reasons? Was it Heisenberg's or his fellow German scientists' incompetence? Had he made an incorrect calculation, or no calculation at all, of the critical mass required for an explosive chain reaction?

In the script, Frayn dives right into the physics, going far beyond what most theatergoers can be expected to know. The level of sophistication makes the characters believable, and it also conveys crucial plot points. First, the characters explain why they both thought, in 1939, that an atomic bomb could never be produced:

BOHR:

What all this means is that an explosive reaction will never occur in natural uranium. To make an explosion you will have to separate pure [uranium-]235. And to make the chain long enough for a large explosion . . .

HEISENBERG:

Eighty generations, let's say . . .

BOHR:

. . . you would need many tons of it. And it's extremely difficult to separate.

HEISENBERG:

Tantalisingly difficult.

BOHR:

Mercifully difficult. The best estimates, when I was in America in 1939, were that to produce even one gram of U-235 would take 26,000 years. By which time, surely, this war will be over.

Later we find out what they had missed:

HEISENBERG:

Because you'd always been confident that weapons would need 235 and that we could never separate enough of it. [. . .]

HEISENBERG:

What we'd realised, though, was that if we could once get the reactor going . . .

BOHR:

The 238 in the natural uranium would absorb the fast neutrons . . .

HEISENBERG:

[. . .] And would be transformed by them into a new element altogether.

BOHR:

Neptunium. Which would decay in its turn into another new element . . .

HEISENBERG:

At least as fissile as the 235 that we couldn't separate . . .

MARGRETHE:

Plutonium.

HEISENBERG:

Plutonium.

HEISENBERG:

[. . .] If we could build a reactor we could build bombs. That's what had brought me to Copenhagen.

Scientifically, the first passage is not completely accurate, but it is basically correct about what Bohr and Heisenberg had thought at one time. The second passage is scientifically correct, and moreover it is thematically crucial. Heisenberg says he wanted to ask if it was morally right to go on working on the reactor project in light of this apocalyptic discovery; Bohr thinks Heisenberg came to ask for his blessing—or, even worse, for his help.

Copenhagen is built out of such dual, and dueling, interpretations. The title itself does double duty, as the location of the action but also as the name of the famous "Copenhagen interpretation" of quantum mechanics developed by Bohr and Heisenberg in the mid-1920s. In this interpretation, the state of a quantum particle is not determined until the act of observation puts it into a definite state. Even then, complementary attributes such as a particle's position and momentum obey an uncertainty relation: The more precisely the observer (who may be a machine) measures one, the less precisely can the other be measured. Quantum-mechanical objects and light behave, to use classical language, sometimes as waves and sometimes as particles. The principle of complementarity states that these two attributes can never be demonstrated in the same experiment or observation.

The uncertainty principle and complementarity are grist for the playwright's mill. The characters cannot agree on anything that happened—not even when and where the conversation took place. The staging of the play reinforces the scientific ideas. In the Broadway and London productions, the stage was round and bare, and the actors' motions around it called to mind the electrons, protons and neutrons moving in an atom. Some of the audience sat in a tribunal at the back of the stage, watching and "judging" the action in stark marble stalls. They were in turn watched by the rest of the audience—the observers observed.

Many philosophers of science have questioned the application of the Copenhagen interpretation to the macroscopic world of human beings, finding it impermissibly reductive. In spite of the fact that this extrapolation is the very premise of the play, in one of his two copious "postscripts" Frayn has said he doesn't take it literally. "The concept of uncertainty is one of those scientific notions that has become common coinage, and generalized to the point of losing much of its original meaning," he writes. Clearly his intent is not to debase the coinage any more. Instead, he uses uncertainty as a metaphor (always part of the artist's license) for the inherent unfathomability of memory, "a systematic limitation which cannot even in theory be circumvented."

Copenhagen has, in its own way, created an observer effect, leading to a reexamination of the historical record

that it scrutinizes. In February, a decade ahead of their stated schedule, the Bohr family unsealed, for publication, some letters to Heisenberg that Bohr drafted in the 1950s but never sent. They cast serious doubt on one of the suggestions in the play: that Heisenberg might have been reluctant to work on the bomb for moral reasons. But the new revelations do little to settle the uncertainties in the play and nothing to alter Frayn's essential points about uncertainty. In fact, some lines of Bohr's letters, such as his repeated statement "I am greatly amazed to see how much your memory has deceived you," read as if they could have been written by Frayn.

The Slip of the Screwdriver

On May 21, 1946, Louis Slotin, a Canadian physicist at Los Alamos, repeated a "criticality test" that he had done many times before. He slipped the pieces of a plutonium bomb closer together and farther apart, "flirting" (as Dennis Overbye has written in the *New York Times*) "with the moment when the assembly would be tight enough to achieve critical mass." He had chosen an extraordinarily dangerous partner to flirt with. Richard Feynman once called such experiments "tickling the dragon's tail."

Ordinarily, wooden spacers separated the two halves of the bomb and prevented a chain reaction from getting started. But for the test, Slotin had removed the spacers and was using the blade of a screwdriver to keep the shells apart. The screwdriver slipped, and the assembly clicked together. A blue glow enveloped the room. Slotin pulled the bomb apart instantly, but there was no way to undo the lethal dose of radiation he had received. Seven other men who were in the chamber with him received smaller doses and survived, because they had been shielded by Slotin's body, but he died after nine days of increasing agony at the Los Alamos hospital.

Playwright Paul Mullin has turned this terrible accident into what could be one of the most provocative science plays since *Copenhagen,* called *Louis Slotin Sonata.* (Like several other recent science-based dramas, this play received funding from the Alfred P. Sloan Foundation through a program that encourages playwrights and artists to take on scientific and technological themes.) Where *Copenhagen* is spare and cerebral, *Louis Slotin Sonata* is flamboyant and emotional. In the play, Slotin suffers hallucinations during his final days, giving Mullin a chance to bring on some unlikely characters. J. Robert Oppenheimer is there, repeating his line from the *Bhagavad-Gita:* "I am become death, shatterer of worlds." Einstein shows up—you guessed it—playing dice, and God himself puts in an appearance, dressed in a pinstripe suit and fedora and bearing an uncanny resemblance, as Overbye points out, to Harry S. Truman. Obviously the playwright is giving the audience some strong hints about human beings playing God.

In one of the hallucinations, Josef Mengele, the sadistic Nazi death camp doctor, arrives in Hiroshima to watch the scientists achieve in milliseconds "what took us years to do in stinking, filth-filled camps." To critic Bruce Weber, writing in *The New York Times,* the scene seemed too contrived: "It feels motivated by theatricality rather than drama, especially when Mengele leads the show's weirdest sequence, a parody of a vaudeville chorus line, with scientists singing doggerel about thermodynamics. Like a lot of elements in the play, the scene is ornamental and distracting, presented by the playwright not because he should but because he can."

Louis Slotin Sonata succeeded in provoking a symposium at Los Alamos after a special reading of the play. (The postperformance symposium seems to be turning into a new science / art form; **Copenhagen** has also given rise to several of them.) Many of the Manhattan Project veterans complained bitterly about the antiscientific bias of the play. But the play's excesses do not hide the fact that Mullin has done his homework; as he told Overbye, he plowed through a three-inch-thick file at Los Alamos on the Slotin case. "I vowed to tell it like it was," he said. "Anything less would be grave digging." It seems to us that the playwright has every right to question whether the atomic scientists were heroes or irresponsible "cowboys," playing around with the dragon when there were safer ways to test the bomb assembly. He is also entitled to the conclusion that the bomb should not have been dropped on Hiroshima and Nagasaki, although one might have wished for a more balanced presentation of the argument.

Still, the "two cultures dichotomy dies hard. Curt Dempster, the artistic director of the Ensemble Studio Theatre, told Overbye after the symposium: "They were running into us, the illusionists. We were running into the reality." **Copenhagen** has decisively undermined the old argument. Illusion and reality do not have to run into each other, if both are treated with respect.

Evolution and Betrayal

In recent years most "science plays" have been physics plays, perhaps because the bomb brought the consequences of modern physics so forcefully to the public's attention, raising powerful ethical and historical issues that science itself could not solve. But biology has taken its own turn on the stage. One example is Timberlake Wertenbaker's play *After Darwin,* dramatizing another explosive scientific topic: the theory of natural selection.

After Darwin borrows a metatheatrical technique from Tom Stoppard's mathematics play *Arcadia,* with scenes alternating between two historical periods. The present-day characters are actors, Tom and Ian, putting on a play about Charles Darwin (played by Tom) and Robert FitzRoy (Ian), the captain of the *Beagle.* The scenes alternate between this historical costume drama and the present, in which Tom and Ian talk with the Bulgarian director, Millie, and the African-American playwright, Lawrence.

As the play progresses, the tension builds in each time frame. Darwin and FitzRoy become estranged, as the very religious captain feels increasingly threatened by the implications of Darwin's discoveries. FitzRoy even threatens his former friend with a pistol. Ian feels threatened, too, when Tom confides to him that he has been hired to appear in a movie and will have to quit the play in order to do so. That would close down the production. In order to save his job, Ian betrays Tom by secretly emailing the film director and telling him (falsely) that Tom is HIV-positive.

Where does evolution by natural selection come in? Wertenbaker relies on the somewhat shopworn parallel between biological Darwinism and social Darwinism, which seems to be defined here as people being incredibly selfish in order to survive. Tom defends his defection to the film project by citing adaptation and survival, and Ian justifies his betrayal in the same terms: "I don't want another two years without work. I want to survive, I want Millie to survive, I want this to survive." Just as FitzRoy wants his faith to remain intact, Ian wants the play to go on; but both of them know in their hearts that Darwin/Tom's decisions are irrevocable. They object to the way that Darwin and Tom "play God," but they fail to see their own interventions in the same hubristic light.

The play's subplots strengthen the scientific metaphors. The stories of Millie and Lawrence, who are both transplants of a sort, provide different "takes" on adaptation and the losses and compromises it entails. A second subplot involves Ian's "babysitting" a Tamagotchi toy for his niece. The toy is constantly beeping and interrupting him to demand virtual nourishment, which he must provide speedily lest the creature die. The attention he gives to the virtual pet while betraying his flesh-and-blood colleague sends a bleak message about technology as a dehumanizing force.

After Darwin, which was produced at the Hampstead Theater in London, received mixed reviews. On the one hand, the London-based critic Benedict Nightingale noted that Wertenbaker "bangs away at her theme a bit relentlessly." But on the other hand, Nightingale wrote, "the dramatic brew is rich and mentally nourishing, embracing as it does questions of God and godlessness, determinism and free will, biology and ethics." It remains to be seen whether *After Darwin* presages a lasting subgenre of "biology plays," but it is the first serious attempt to integrate evolutionary theory with the theater both thematically and formally. (As an aside, we would like to note one very worthy successor, Tom McGrath's *Safe Delivery,* a play about gene therapy inspired by the research of the writer's daughter. This play was sponsored by the Wellcome Trust, which has mounted in England a program comparable to the Sloan Foundation's support of U.S. plays about science.)

We hope that the three plays we have chosen to discuss—out of the many that we could have chosen—give some flavor of the variety of treatments of scientific themes in contemporary plays. The infusion of scientific ideas has invigorated a theatrical scene that, as recently as 15 years ago, was criticized by the prominent theater critic and scholar Martin Esslin for the banality of its subject matter and its refusal to treat topics "outside the narrow range of family squabbles." Clearly, science works as theater. And theater can work at conveying the ideas of science. In an article he prepared for the symposium "The Copenhagen Interpretation: Science and History on Stage," physicist John Marburger wrote, "Many stories can be told of [science's] struggles and their consequences, but I doubt that many will rise to the standard set by Frayn's ***Copenhagen.*** I will end by thanking Michael Frayn for bringing the core issues of this beautiful aspect of science to such a large audience." We hope that other playwrights will take up the challenge.

Bibliography

Bernstein, J. 2001. *Hitler's Uranium Club, the Secret Recordings of Farm Hall.* New York: Copernicus Books.

Bethe, H. A. 2000. The German uranium project. *Physics Today* 53:34-36.

Bohr, N. 1957-1962. Unsent drafts of letters to Heisenberg and memoranda about the 1941 meeting. Released by the Niels Bohr Archive, February 6, 2002. *Naturens Verden* 84(8-9); http://www.nbi.dk/NBA/papers/docs/cover.html

Brantley, B. 2000. "Copenhagen": A fiery power in the behavior of particles and humans. *The New York Times,* April 12:E-1.

Carpenter, C. A. 1999. *Dramatists and the Bomb: American and British Playwrights Confront the Nuclear Age, 1945-1964.* Westport, Conn.: Greenwood Press.

Cassidy, D. In press. New light on *Copenhagen* and the German nuclear project. *Physics in Perspective.*

Frayn, M. 2000. *Copenhagen.* New York: Anchor Books.

Frayn, M. 2002. Post-postscript. http://web.gc.cuny.edu/ashp/nml/artsci/frayn.htm

Haynes, R. D. 1994. *From Faust to Strangelove: Representations of the Scientist in Western Literature.* Baltimore: Johns Hopkins University Press.

Jonson, B. 1987. *The Alchemist* (ed. Peter Bement). London, New York: Methuen.

Logan, J. 2000. "A strange new quantum ethics." *American Scientist* 88:356-359.

Marburger, J. H., III. 2002. On the Copenhagen interpretation of quantum mechanics. http://web.gc.cuny.edu/ashp/nml/artsci/marburger.htm

Overbye, D. 2001. Theatrical elegy recalls a victim of nuclear age. *The New York Times* (April 3):F-4.

Pais, A., and M. Frayn. 2000. What happened in Copenhagen? A physicist's view and the playwright's response. *Hudson Review* 53:2.

Powers, T. 2000. The unanswered question. *New York Review of Books,* May 25.

Rhodes, R. 1995. *The Making of the Atomic Bomb.* New York: Touchstone Books.

Rose, P. L. 2000. Frayn's "Copenhagen" plays well at history's expense. *The Chronicle of Higher Education* (May 5):B4-6.

Ruddick, N. 2001. The search for a quantum ethics: Michael Frayn's "Copenhagen" and other recent British science plays. *Journal of the Fantastic in the Arts* 11:415-29.

Shepherd-Barr, Kirsten. In press. "Copenhagen" and beyond: The "rich and mentally nourishing" interplay between science and theatre. *Gramma.*

Snow, C. P. 1993. *The Two Cultures.* Cambridge, U.K.: Cambridge University Press.

Weber, B. 2001. "Louis Slotin Sonata": A scientist's tragic hubris attains critical mass onstage. *The New York Times* (April 10):E-1.

Wertenbaker, T. 1998. *After Darwin.* London: Faber.

Donna Soto-Morettini (essay date 2002)

SOURCE: Soto-Morettini, Donna. "'Disturbing the Spirits of the Past': The Uncertainty Principle in Michael Frayn's *Copenhagen.*" In *Crucible of Cultures: Anglophone Drama at the Dawn of a New Millennium,* edited by Marc Maufort and Franca Bellarsi, pp. 69-78. New York: P.I.E.-Peter Lang, 2002.

[*In the following essay, Soto-Morettini approaches* Copenhagen *as humanist history, suggesting that Frayn tries to see events through the eyes and thoughts of his characters.*]

In 1941, an historic but undocumented meeting took place in Copenhagen between two giants of twentieth-century physics, Werner Heisenberg and Niels Bohr.

The tantalising lack of certainty about why the German went to Denmark at this particularly crucial historical time has puzzled scientists and historians ever since—after all, Heisenberg was working under the Nazi regime, while Bohr's country, Denmark, was under German occupation. Michael Frayn's play offers an extended examination of the possible answers to the questions that have surrounded this mysterious meeting, of which no record remains. As Frayn's postscript to *Copenhagen* makes clear "[Heisenberg] almost certainly went to dinner at the Bohr's house, and the two men almost certainly went for a walk to escape from any possible microphones, although there is some dispute about even these simple matters. The question about what they said to each other has been even more dispute [. . .]" (97).

Structurally, *Copenhagen* is a series of repetitions. The actual moment of Heisenberg approaching the door, the Bohrs answering and welcoming him into their home, the ensuing awkward moments are played out a number of times for the audience. The three characters, Heisenberg, Bohr, and his wife, Margarethe, attempt to test their memories against each other's in each staged recollection—as they all try to puzzle out the answer to the recurring questions of the play: what was the meeting about? What had Heisenberg come to say? Why did he put himself and the Bohrs at risk in this way? What was at stake? Frayn places this central public concern within a deeper, more personal replay of memory: at points the Bohrs recall the tragic death of their son, who is swept away by the sea in sight of his helpless father. The memory reoccurs to all three characters, who speak their thoughts out loud in the silence as Heisenberg first appears:

MARGARETHE:

All the things that come into our heads out of nowhere.

BOHR:

Our private consolations. Our private agonies.

HEISENBERG:

Silence. And of course they're thinking about their children again. [. . .]

BOHR:

She's thinking about Christian and Harald.

HEISENBERG:

The two lost boys. [. . .]

BOHR:

And once again I see those same few moments that I see every day.

HEISENBERG:

Those short moments on the boat, when the tiller slams over in the heavy sea and Christian is falling.

BOHR:

If I hadn't let him take the helm . . .

HEISENBERG:

Those long moments in the water.

BOHR:

Those endless moments in the water. [. . .]

MARGARETHE:

I'm at Tisvilde. I look up from my work. There's Niels in the doorway, silently watching me. He turns his head away, and I know at once what's happened.

(29, 30)

As Frayn notes in his postscript to the play, the mystery surrounding the Copenhagen meeting was one that haunted Heisenberg, who actually attempted to discuss the memories of that night with Bohr years later, but reached no conclusion: "We both came to feel that it would be better to stop disturbing the spirits of the past" (97). If Heisenberg's memoirs are unhelpful in providing any conclusive evidence about the meeting that Frayn reconstructs, there is still something for a playwright to admire about the centrality which Heisenberg gives to dialogue in his recollections—a perhaps unexpected demonstration of interest in human exchange on the part of a theoretical physicist. As Frayn points out, in the actual memoirs written by Heisenberg, "dialogue plays an important part [. . .] because he [Heisenberg] 'hopes to demonstrate that science is rooted in conversations'" (98). This section from the postscript sums up the sophistication of the argument that Frayn's play seems to be putting forth about the relationship between science, history, and memory.

The implication ventured by *Copenhagen* suggests that—like Heisenberg's particular brand of theoretical physics—the "science" of the historian is one which hinges crucially upon including a kind of "calculated" uncertainty within the act of apprehension. This uncertainty inhabits the spaces between language, text and memory. (That "calculation," of course, can never be represented in mathematical terms beyond being expressed as an "X" factor—but its intrinsic *value* is less significant in this context than the effect of its indeterminate *presence*.) Frayn's dramatic license triggers yet more uncertainties—questions about the value of histories, and about the ways in which we invest histories with an authority that would cause even those making them to feel uncomfortable; and questions about the status of history-as-knowledge altogether, which oscillates in its narrative structure somewhere between what we represent to ourselves as certain and the manifestly uncertain fragments of the past.

Frayn refashions time itself into a repetitive scientific experiment; he incorporates the imaginative in a plethora of possible reasons, excuses, motivations, and associations that tenuously fix and then radically unhinge historical representation in his replaying of the past; he explores the unconscious through continually revealed mistakes in memory, and in the shifting of the roles of Heisenberg and Bohr: as father and son, as brothers, as Others.

A number of things make Frayn's play distinct from earlier British ones dealing with political histories and science, but perhaps it will be most immediately compared to Bertolt Brecht's *Galileo*—with its similar meditations on the relationship between science and ethics, and its questions about ideas of scientific "heroism." If so, the comparison can only emphasise the great distance between the clean bright weapons of Brecht's historical materialism and the more oblique ones available to those writing after the loss of such grand meta-narratives as Marxist theory. Brecht's episodic journey was meant somehow to fracture time and to jolt us out of our ease in the presence of classical narrative structure. Our "surprise" did not come from finding out that Galileo was no hero, but from discovering that we had been lulled somehow into *expecting* scientists to be heroes.

For Frayn, time is not fractured so much as it is inescapably circular. He structures his play like a controlled-observation experiment: conditions surrounding the eve of Heisenberg's visit are carefully set up and played out a number of times, then behaviours and reactions are carefully recorded. Each time, data is analysed, questioned, and the characters become more detached, and more observant of themselves. But their scientific method is not adequate to the task of answering the fundamental question: why did Heisenberg come? What was it he had to say? And in the wake of the scientific disasters of the Twentieth Century, perhaps our "surprise" as viewers is to realise that from our historical perspective no one expects science and heroism to inhabit the same places.

FRAYN'S "IDEA OF HISTORY"

Any number of reviews of the play centred on Frayn's ability to conflate the difficulties of accurately observing the physical matter of the universe and the difficulties of accurately observing human behaviour, or intuiting motives—either our own or others'. And where this approach leads straight into the territory of human psychology, it does so only in the sense that Frayn's disposition as a historian is also squarely focused there. In the postscript to the play, Frayn declares that as far as he could, he attempted to follow "the original protagonists' train of thought." "But," he writes, "how far is it possible to know what their train of thought was? This is where I have departed from established historical record—from any possible historical record. The great challenge facing the storyteller and the

historian alike is to get inside people's heads, to stand where they stood and see the world as they saw it, to make some informed estimate of their motives and intentions [. . .]" (98-99).

Here Frayn, for all the postmodern sophistication of his characters' debates in *Copenhagen,* harks back to a historiographical tradition as old as Thucydides—and perhaps best framed in our times by R. G. Collingwood in his seminal "The Idea of History." Collingwood attempted to elucidate a method whereby the historian could comprehend the seemingly incomprehensible: the thought processes of historical agents. And despite the objections that have come his way—from those which emphasise history as a totality of mutually conditioning structural and conscious processes, to those which displace subjectivity or agency altogether—here we find Frayn at the end of the century sounding remarkably like Collingwood himself: "The history of thought, and therefore all history, is the re-enactment of past thought, in the historian's own mind" (Collingwood 215).

Collingwood's point, like Frayn's, turns out to be less simple than it appears, since he is keen to make it clear that the historian's own mind is specifically grounded in a contemporary context. But perhaps the most interesting parallel between Frayn and Collingwood occurs when the latter defends history from those who would conceive its discipline as some kind of science. Collingwood saw a major difference between the two fields in that for the "scientific observer nature is always merely a phenomenon presented to his intelligent observation; whereas the events of history are never mere phenomena, [. . .] but things which the historian looks, not at, but through, to discern the thought within them." (214). Frayn is more wary of apprehending the natural phenomena observed through quantum mechanics as brute or static, but he sees that the more dialectical approach suggested by Collingwood toward human subjects applies to physics as well. Nor does Frayn follow Collingwood down the road of attempting to objectify the process of understanding itself—for throughout his play, there is little objective ground, even when the issues of historical evidence are brought up.

Still, for both Collingwood and Frayn, the historian's primary interest seems to be ferreting out the secrets of intention manifested in the historical act. As Collingwood's critics have pointed out, even if he fails to take into account the larger picture of socio-structural determinants in history, he does so on humanist grounds, and his fundamental project aims to elucidate his assertion that history constitutes above all a "humanistic" discipline with a specific and progressive function. The sting in the comparison is in the tail of this last sentence: one must work hard to find the evidence of a "progressive function" in Frayn's history, although it remains a deeply humanistic approach in the telling.

HISTORY AND PHYSICS

The fundamental question of **Copenhagen** is voiced over and over again by its characters: "[. . .] what exactly had Heisenberg said?" (34). Margarethe suggests that "The person who wanted to know most of all was Heisenberg himself" (35); and Bohr, stymied by the same inability to recall his own words confesses: "Heaven knows what I said" (39). At one level, the play appears to be about the ways in which historical inquiry at many points becomes an almost metaphysical inquiry—one which beavers away at uncovering the tomes of what Louis O. Mink once called the "omniscient chronicler" (see Louis O. Mink). In fact, Mink could be suggesting what Frayn's fictional Niels Bohr character states: "Heaven knows." Heaven: the presumed domicile of the omniscient chronicler—that ideal scribe who knew, who recorded the WAY IT WAS, but never publishes, leaving the lesser mortal historians to endlessly scratch away, trying to fill in the details of a Platonic historical form.

"Did these things really happen to me?" asks Heisenberg. "We wait," he says, "for the point of it all to be revealed to us" (46). In another time, of course, another kind of historian—Collingwood, for one—would have seen this grand act of narrating events from a distance to be charged precisely with this purpose: to reveal the point of it all. In Frayn's play, the physicists come to realise that quantum mechanics—in a sense—returns man to the centre of the universe by insisting that the physicist's perception of the universe will always be inextricably linked to the knowing subject. But once they reach this conclusion, they simultaneously realise that the man at the centre of the universe can see absolutely everything except himself.

BOHR:

> We put man back at the centre of the universe. Throughout history we keep finding ourselves displaced. We keep exiling ourselves to the periphery of things. First we turn ourselves into a mere adjunct of God's unknowable purposes, tiny figures kneeling in the great cathedral of creation. And no sooner have we recovered ourselves in the Renaissance, no sooner has man become, as Protagoras proclaimed him, the measure of all things, than we're pushed aside again by the products of our own reasoning! [. . .] Then, here in Copenhagen in [. . .] [the] [. . .] mid-twenties we discover that there is no precisely determinable objective universe. That the universe exists only as a series of approximations. Only within the limits determined by our relationship with it. Only through the understanding lodged inside the human head.

MARGARETHE:

> So this man you've put at the centre of the universe—is it you, or is it Heisenberg? [. . .] If it's Heisenberg at the centre of the universe, then the one bit of the universe that he can't see is Heisenberg. (73-74)

And this dilemma—the historical agent with a panoptical blindness—is for that aforementioned historian the very problem that drives his vocation: the idea that from a distance, discrete events in the historical field ultimately converge into patterns, into shapes that reveal some significance. Which of course is why when Heisenberg and Bohr are debating the ontology of matter (are we talking ultimately about particles, which Bohr calls "things, complete in themselves"? (71) or are we talking about waves, which he describes as "disturbances in something else" (71), they could just as easily be describing the historian's difficulty in apprehending what s/he see in the historical field. Does the historian discern "things, complete in themselves"— perhaps easily identifiable agents of historical change—or does the historian see "waves," disturbances that shape something else such as historical agents? The latter could be said to fairly describe a kind of "structuralist" approach to history that seeks perhaps to write history without a subject. The former could maybe describe pre-structuralist histories—Collingwood's history. The extraordinary thing about **Copenhagen** is that its conclusion argues vigorously for the validity of "complementarity" in physics—which asserts that matter is both wave and particle. And once through the piece, it becomes difficult not to think that what Frayn is putting forth, knowingly or not, is that the validity of any historical understanding may also, crucially, depend on its ability to adopt an approach of "complementarity." In other words, history is both structure and subject; its ontological status oscillates; and it is both and neither.

But Frayn's physicists go on to make another deeply problematic point about complementarity in the field of quantum mechanics—which is that oscillation does not yield a viable point of view. Indeed, as the fictional Niels Bohr exposes, he cannot understand Heisenberg because to do that he must treat him "not just as a particle, but as a wave. I have to use not only your particle mechanics, I have to use the Schroedinger wave function." (71). But as he goes on to explain, the smallest bits of matter are "either one thing or another. They can't be both—we have to choose one way of seeing them or the other. But as soon as we do, we can't know everything about them." In other words, if we try to translate this into an historiographical problem, when we view the historical field, we know that it contains both particles (subject/agents) and waves (structures: linguistic, cultural, political etc.). We can intellectually appreciate that to apprehend historical motion in any kind of totality, we must be continually oscillating our point of view between particle and wave, but if Bohr is correct, ultimately we must choose. Because to align oneself theoretically with one is, perforce, to deny the other. And yet, to position one's method of apprehension from only one point of view entails forever living with partial sight. Here, ultimately, lies the fundamental paradox of postmodern physics, postmodern thought, and postmodern history—uncoupled from certainty the questions begin to oscillate from the one extreme to the other: if there are no answers, then any answer will do.

QUIETLY COLLAPSING HISTORY

From the point of view of the historical subject on the ground, we know that this final paradox is simply one clever conundrum too far. If any answer will do, we are left with no ground on which to pitch a moral argument—and in the end, Frayn's play remains a deeply moral piece of work. His characters stay centred around the moral dilemma of the physicist working in Hitler's pay. For all the sophistication of their arguments, the final moments of the play are given over to questions of good and bad, right and wrong:

BOHR:

So perhaps I should thank you.

HEISENBERG:

For what?

BOHR:

My life. All our lives.

HEISENBERG:

Nothing to do with me by that time. I regret to say.

BOHR:

But after I'd gone you came back to Copenhagen.

HEISENBERG:

To make sure that our people didn't take over the Institute in your absence.

BOHR:

I've never thanked you for that, either.

HEISENBERG:

You know they offered me your cyclotron?

BOHR:

You could have separated a little 235 with it.

HEISENBERG:

Meanwhile you were going on from Sweden to Los Alamos.

BOHR:

To play my small but helpful part in the deaths of a hundred thousand people.

MARGARETHE:

Niels, you did nothing wrong!

BOHR:

Didn't I?

HEISENBERG:

Of course not. You were a good man, from first to last, and no one could ever say otherwise. Whereas I . . .

BOHR:

Whereas you, my dear Heisenberg, never managed to contribute to the death of one single solitary person in all your life.

(93)

A simple—rather disturbingly simple—place in which to leave this highly sophisticated meditation on the ways in which lived experience and survival so often prevents one from the practical exercise of moral and ethical reason and certainty.

On one level, this is where Frayn's drama brings us squarely before what Keith Jenkins calls the linguistic contradictions between "life" and the "writing up of life." The context in which Heisenberg and Bohr made their choices was one in which the deductive or syllogistic logic driving moral decisions could not apply. The very specific context in which the physicists made their choices therefore yielded a terrain on which their conclusions about good or bad were quite startlingly incongruent. As Hayden White has pointed out: "[. . .] you need another kind of logic to talk about practical affairs, a logic of praxis. The logic of praxis cannot follow the logic of identity and non-contradiction [. . .]. Society creates situations in which you must act in contradiction [. . .] you need a theory of the representation of life lived in contradiction. That would allow you to account for the syntax of real lives" (quoted in Jenkins 122). Frayn's play does not provide this "logic of praxis," but it does throw the contradiction of which White speaks into a strange relief. Hayden White's point is also made eloquently by the fictional Heisenberg:

Complementarity, once again. I'm your enemy; I'm also your friend. I'm a danger to mankind; I'm also your guest. I'm a particle; I'm also a wave. We have one set of obligations to the world in general, and we have other sets, never to be reconciled, to our fellow-countrymen, to our neighbours, to our friends, to our family, to our children. [. . .] All we can do is to look afterwards, and see what happened.

(79-80)

Comparatively, where other modern and postmodern dramatists—Brecht, Trevor Griffiths, Caryl Churchill, for example—write plays and characters reminding us that history is in the eye of those living it, and that a single event is recalled in myriad ways, they do so to complicate history, to raise unbridgeable gaps. But they do not, in the end, suggest what Frayn's uncertain characters do: which is to put forth that the contradiction between logic and a "narrated memory" is unresolvable. *Copenhagen* questions the breach between ethical language and socio/practical language and behaviour, but, of course, in its tropological structure (in which Bohr's lost son and his own helplessness in watching that loss become a metaphor for Bohr's relationship with Heisenberg), the play goes much further. It concludes, ironically, by collapsing its own historical specificity and transforming a particular moment into an ongoing universal tragedy of the human condition. In the final moments before Heisenberg departs, the characters once again voice their thoughts aloud, in an exchange much like one earlier in the play:

MARGARETHE:

Silence. The silence we always in the end return to.

HEISENBERG:

And of course I know what they're thinking about.

MARGARETHE:

All those lost children on the road.

BOHR:

Heisenberg wandering the world like a lost child himself.

MARGARETHE:

Our own lost children.

HEISENBERG:

And over goes the tiller once again.

BOHR:

So near, so near! So slight a thing!

MARGARETHE:

He stands in the doorway watching me, then he turns his head away . . .

HEISENBERG:

And once again, away he goes into the dark waters.

(95-96)

But if Bohr and Heisenberg metaphorically represent Bohr and son, then they are both, in their turn, figurative emblems of a greater "transhistorical" tragedy: the tragedy in which those on the firm ground of a world apprehension based on the syntax of logical deduction/identity/non-contradiction will always be condemned to witness the loss of their certainties in the maelstrom of socio/political praxis, whether that loss is sustained in the context of the Third Reich or the Manhattan Project.

This collapse of history, ultimately, allows Frayn to rescue an older, simpler notion of morality from an arguably "deconstructive" approach to historiography.

By the end of the play, we have watched his characters drag a barely breathing moral "body" out of the burning buildings on the postmodern landscape, which leaves us with many questions about the play's ideological implications. Hayden White's idea of a language able to accommodate "lived contradiction" remains no more than a theoretical sketch. And in the place of an ethical theory elegant enough to match the grace and complexity of quantum physics, a play like *Copenhagen* must inevitably, perhaps, make way for the concluding judgements that operate under the yet-to-be-replaced metanarratives of Marxism or Christianity, whose baseline guidance in questions of right or wrong still hold tenuous sway amidst the particles and the waves.

Works Cited

Collingwood, R. G. *The Idea of History.* Oxford: Clarendon Press, 1946.

Frayn, Michael. *Cophenhagen.* London: Methuen, 1988.

Jenkins, Keith. *Why History.* London: Routledge, 1999.

Mink, Louis O. "Narrative as Cognitive Instrument." *The Writing of History.* Ed. Robert H. Canary and Henry Kozicki. Madison: University of Wisconsin Press, 1978.

Cushing Strout (essay date winter 2003)

SOURCE: Strout, Cushing. "'Two Wings of the Same Breathing Creature': Fictionalizing History." *Partisan Review* 70, no. 1 (winter 2003): 93-105.

[*In the following essay, Strout examines Freyn's attempt to portray his characters realistically, focusing on the differences between history and drama.*]

"Calliope and Clio are not identical twins," Wallace Stegner pointed out, "but they *are* sisters." For that reason the actual can be transposed into the fictional by a novelist whose imagination has been stimulated by real events and persons, or the fictional can be transposed into the actual by a historical novelist, writing about a particular time and place. "There is a whole middle ground between fiction and history," Stegner argues in his essay "On the Writing of History" (1965); and he has often made it his own territory, whether working as a novelist or a historian. In either role a writer can present material in generalizing, expositional form or in particularizing, dramatic form, often in some combination of both. "There are respectable books all across the spectrum," Stegner observes, "but it is important that they be called what they are, and do not pretend to be what they are not." His account in *The Preacher and the Slave* of the life and death of the IWW martyr Joe Hill, for example, was based on as much research as he would have done had he intended to write a biography. Nevertheless, he took pains in a foreword "to label it an act of the imagination," which is what he wanted it to be so that he could "invent characters, scenes, motivations, dialogue," taking a "novel's liberties."

An influential French theorist of literature, Gerard Genette, in *Fiction & Diction* (1993) acknowledges that most of the theoretical work on narratives, including his own, has been on fictional rather than factual narratives. Trying to avoid this omission, he asserts that factual narratives are characterized by having "the obligation to report only what one knows—but at the same time everything that one knows, to provide all the relevant information—and to state how one has come by that knowledge." By the end of his difficult and abstract chapter, however, he comes to attenuate his distinction by conceding that in practice "there is no such thing as pure fiction and no such thing as history so rigorous that it abjures any 'emplotting' and any use of novelistic techniques." If narrative forms "readily cross the borderline between fiction and nonfiction, it is no less urgent, rather it is all the more urgent, for narratology to follow their example." Catching up, in effect, with a position that Stegner had articulated several decades earlier, Genette fails to consider, however, the case of historical fiction (whether as novel, play, or poem), which has always had to cross this borderline and to use both fictional and historical techniques.

John Updike confessed that in thinking about doing historical fiction about an actual person, James Buchanan, his "imagination was frozen by the theoretical discoverability of *everything*. An actual man, Buchanan, had done this and this, exactly so, once, and no other way. There was no air." Georg Lukács's *The Historical Novel* (1962) dealt with the problem of respecting the singularity of historical persons and events by having the novelist focus instead on the general milieu, make protagonists fictional, view actual historical persons through the eyes of other people, and avoid dealing with well-known episodes in the careers of historical figures.

Cynthia Ozick has sharply formulated the issue in *Quarrel & Quandry* (2000). As a novelist, she would like to believe that "imagination owes nothing to what we call reality; it owes nothing to history." By definition "a work of fiction cannot betray history." Yet the point of her title is that "there are certain difficulties." Notable among them is her objection that in the popular Broadway version of Anne Frank's story, "history was transcended, enobled, rarefied," leaving out or diluting not only its grimness but also her "consciousness of Jewish fate and faith." She also objects to William Styron's *Sophie's Choice* and Bernhard Schlink's *The Reader* because their protagonists (a Polish Catholic and an illiterate Gestapo agent, respectively) deflect from the historical fact that Jews were the specific target of Hitler's genocidal racism; and middle-class and educated Germans were complicit with the atrocious crimes committed in his name. Typicality is not the obligation of a novelist, as she says, yet in these two cases it is the historical importance of the Holocaust that makes the books targets of her criticism. That is the quandry.

Her way out of it is to conclude that history has its rightful claims on a novel when the fiction is "directed consciously toward history." She suspects both authors of attempting to deflect their readers away from the more typical Jewish victims of the Holocaust. Yet she acknowledges that both authors recognize the atypicality of their protagonists. Why shouldn't that entitle them to more artistic freedom than she is willing to give them? Anyway, the question of the intentions of both authors is a historical one, requiring more evidence and argument than she presents. But her crucial point is that poetic license is not always immune to criticism. A reading of historical fiction is not a matter of wholesale response any more than a reading of a historian's work need be.

An excellent current example of the use—not the abuse—of poetic license is Tracy Chevalier's *Girl with a Pearl Earring* (2000). She invents a maid to the painter Johannes Vermeer in the seventeenth-century Dutch Republic. We see everything from her point of view, a Protestant young woman who, out of economic necessity, becomes a maid to a higher-class Catholic family. She has an artistic eye, as the painter realizes, so she finally enjoys the high privilege of sitting for the portrait that has become known as "Girl with a Pearl Earring." Most women in Vermeer's paintings are engaged in domestic actions and are seen in relation to the interiors of the rooms they inhabit. Two figures have only a black background, and one of these is dramatically distinguished by looking over her shoulder at the viewer, her lips parted expectantly, as if she is responding to a voice and is about to speak. It fits the novel's depiction of a sexual undercurrent sometimes running between the artist and his model, though it never results in action that would violate the social barriers between them.

The point of the novel is not to answer the question, "Who sat for this intriguing portrait?" Perhaps no one ever did. We shall never know. The success of the novel is that its story about the genesis of the painting fits the social context of the Dutch Republic and the style of Vermeer's artistry, by making something eloquent, restrained, and moving about ordinary domestic life. The novel does not aim to fill in a gap in the historical record. It enhances our response to Vermeer's portrait.

In the 1930s John Dos Passos invented a complex border-crossing technique in his trilogy, *USA,* that covered several decades, involved fictional stories, an authorial stream-of-consciousness ("Camera Eye"), newspaper headlines, and biographical sketches of famous persons with whom the fictional stories are emotionally resonant. Some of the biographies (Thorstein Veblen, Sacco and Vanzetti, Frank Lloyd Wright) are icons whom Dos Passos celebrates. Historical persons, however, are not intermingled with fictional ones, for Dos Passos had the traditional sense that the line between the fictional and the historical, though it could be crossed, should not be eradicated or entirely confused. In 1941, at a time of international crisis, he turned to writing history himself. It was the sort of Whig history that searches for a useful past to provide a "a sense of continuity with generations gone before" by finding "what kind of firm ground other men, belonging to generations before us, have found to stand on." He used his novelist's sense for narrative and the humanly significant detail; but he was writing a kind of history in *The Ground We Stand On* that was consistent with his literary talents by being primarily a series of biographical sketches of several influential American figures, most of whom lived in the eighteenth century.

Since Dos Passos's time, the border crossings have become more frequent and more complex. Max Byrd's historical novel, *Grant* (2000), is in many ways a descendant of Dos Passos's trilogy in attempting to portray the Gilded Age on a canvas much broader than its title suggests. Byrd creates a fictional memoir based on an actual one written by a Chicago reporter, newspaper accounts of Grant, and extracts from his notes and letters. Byrd's novel, however, follows Lukács's principle in that Grant is mainly seen from the point of view of the surrounding characters. The historical characters are all connected to Grant in important ways: Sylvanus Cadwallader, a reporter who wrote *Three Years with Grant;* Henry Adams, who investigated the scandals in the Grant administrations and satirized him in *Democracy;* Senator James Donald Cameron, who managed Grant's unsuccessful third-term campaign; and Mark Twain, who irreverently joked about him in a speech at a Union veterans banquet, idolized him, and published Grant's memoirs.

Grant goes beyond Dos Passos's technique, however, by seamlessly mingling fictional persons and real persons and events. His crossing of the literary with the historical can be multilayered. Byrd prints a newspaper review, supposedly written by the fictional Nicholas Trist, of Adams's actual novel *Democracy*. Later on, Byrd presents, as an extract from Trist's notebook, a passage directly quoting word for word a page of Adams's novel *Esther*, which he wrote under a pseudonym.

Grant was called "the American Sphinx" and has seemed to be a mystery to his biographers, even to himself. Brooks D. Simpson has recently declared that

"there are no single threads that hold everything together." He finds Grant to be an enigma: "How to explain both the depths of defeat and the heights of triumph?" He thus makes a good subject for a novelistic treatment in which he can be seen obliquely and through many different lenses.

Byrd's interpretation of Grant's extraordinary hold over the emotions of Americans after the war is expressed by Cadwallader: Grant's generous terms at Appomattox were "the first great step toward national reconciliation and forgiveness." As his friend and heir, Grant was "the country's last true connection to the martyred Abraham Lincoln." "The two of them had walked side by side down the smoking streets of Richmond in 1865, the tall and the short of it, as Lincoln had joked." Byrd also recognizes that Grant and Twain have an affinity as self-invented men who have risen from obscurity to eminence, and that as writers, they have (as Trist puts it) "cleared the arabesques out of American prose." Interviewing Grant in his last days, Trist concludes that in writing his memoirs Grant was exhibiting "the old qualities of his generalship, which had seemed to vanish during the dark days of his presidency—utter clarity, complete mastery of detail, singleness of purpose, a will that could apparently defy the fierce rebellion even of his own body." Byrd appropriately concludes the section on Grant's death with the dying Grant's poetic insight into himself, written in a letter to his doctor: "The fact is I think I am a verb instead of a personal pronoun. A verb is anything that signifies to be; to do; or to suffer. I signify all three."

The novelist Diane Johnson, in reviewing Gore Vidal's *The Golden Age,* recognizes that "the historical novel has a sort of implied contract with truth," but she goes on to claim that "on faith, we must decide whether it is all made up or true." For all his mingling of fact with fiction, Byrd's sense of his contract with the reader includes explaining how much he has fictionalized fact. In a note at the end of it he explains that the wounded journalist Nicholas Trist is an invented character, though his romance with Elizabeth Cameron is "loosely based on her real-life affair with the poet Joseph Trumbull Stickney." Historical characters, however, "do and say here pretty much what they actually did and said. . . . Whenever possible I have taken dialogue verbatim from letters, books, diaries, etc."

Byrd admits that his version of Clover Adams's dismayed discovery that her husband wrote *Esther* is "speculative, but not inconsistent with the facts," because there is "no evidence whatsoever" that she "knew all along about the authorship," as most scholars assume. In Byrd's novel she comes upon her husband's letters, which lead her to see *Esther* as referring obliquely to their marriage—such as when a character says that "being half-married must be the worst torture."

Byrd appropriately has Trist, a wounded veteran in the disastrous battle of Cold Harbor, find a bond with the witty, artistic, childless Clover, who has a morbid preoccupation with death and a fear of insanity as a family curse. Trist comes to the conclusion that *Esther* is an "angry, frustrated book" that obliquely "sought to cause pain" to Clover Adams and was "as terrible and deadly to her in the end as cyanide." Trist's harsh judgment is consistent with his persistent dislike of Adams as a disdainful patrician, and Byrd could cite Gore Vidal's view that the historical novelist is justified in using fictional characters to speculate about the motives of historical persons, though it is "dangerous territory for historians." But no biographer of Adams would support Trist's interpretation.

To see just how controversial Byrd's treatment is one can compare it to, at the other end of the spectrum, Edward Chalfant's biography of Adams, *Better in Darkness* (1994). He asserts that reading the novel in the light of Clover's suicide is "egregiously mistaken, as well as lugubrious." He sees it as a book written by "a happily married person for another happily married person." In Chalfant's view, after reading George Eliot's *Middlemarch* and Hawthorne's *The Scarlet Letter,* Adams and Clover were "in a position to imagine his writing a novel truly Clover's" that would show an American woman rejecting a self-centered clergyman because of her agnostic lack of Christian belief. Chalfant insists, moreover, that though it was "written with her knowledge" and "was designed to express her thoughts and feelings" as an agnostic, the novel's heroine must be seen as "exclusively and only" the fictional Esther, not the actual Clover. This claim is excessive, but it is at least true that whatever the private subtext of the novel may have been, its public text was a novel of ideas in which the characters (loosely linked to actual persons whom Adams knew) are engaged in discussions about science, religion, and art. Neither Byrd nor Chalfant, however, make anything out of that.

In 1911 Adams told Clover's niece that he was the author of *Esther,* and Chalfant cites her plausible belief that she didn't see how Adams could have written it without his wife knowing about it. She had, after all, participated in the secret of his authorship of *Democracy.* Chalfant has no evidence, however, for his dogmatic claim that Adams and Clover conceived the novel together, nor can he so clearly separate the heroine from Clover. Esther's devotion to her father and her depression after his death can be paired with Clover's attachment to her own father, whose death precipitated her clinically severe depression. (Perhaps a genetic trait was involved, for her sister, shortly afterwards, also committed suicide.) Trist's subtext for *Esther* is supported in *Grant* when Elizabeth Cameron points out to him that Clover and her father are inseparable: "It's a wonder Henry isn't jealous." Rather than being jealous, however, he may have been perceptive enough to foresee in his novel the psychological danger of her dependence on her father.

Adams's friend Clarence King told him that Esther should have jumped into Niagra when she visited the Falls, given the conflict between her love for the minister and her refusal to pretend to a faith she did not have. King reported that Adams said, "Certainly she would but I could not suggest it." Chalfant, as if he were telepathic, interprets this reply as a "half assent" that conceals an actual "disagreement in fact." Nor does he cite Adams's own statement, made a year after Clover's death, that the novel was "written in one's heart's blood." It is not surprising that Adams too would look back on his novel, as critics have done, with grim hindsight.

The novel's Catherine Brooke is as beautiful as Elizabeth Cameron, Esther is as plain and troubled as Clover Adams, and Adams did later develop a platonic love affair with Mrs. Cameron. Trist's reading of *Esther* as maliciously directed at Clover is consistent with his affection for her and his hostility to her husband; nevertheless, it is a melodramatic stretch of poetic license on Byrd's part. Have I put myself in a quandry by giving Byrd so much freedom already that I am no longer in a position to criticize his treatment of Adams? Is it arbitrary to draw the line at this point?

It is not as irrelevant as it may seem that Trist makes a mistake by assuming that the characters in *Democracy* congregated to visit Monticello, when actually they did so in order to visit Mount Vernon. There is nothing to indicate that Byrd knows Trist is wrong. For Adams the response of his characters to Mount Vernon was a measure of their worth. He would not consider it a trivial mistake, because he was a tenacious critic of Jefferson and an ardent admirer of George Washington, a "pole star" who, Adams remarked in his autobiography, "alone remained steady, in the mind of Henry Adams, to the end." Trist's view of Adams as a prejudiced disdainful patrician blots out the patriot, reformer, and great historian.

Byrd has conceded that his exercise of poetic license is "speculative," and he is right that there is no evidence to settle the question decisively of when Clover knew about Adams's authorship of *Esther.* Trist's lurid version of Adams's maliciousness, however, is hard to reconcile with the abundant evidence for Henry and Clover's mutual love. An afterword from Byrd about Trist's prejudice, or a way of dramatizing his unreliability on *Esther,* would make the story more subtle and complex.

Uncertainty has become a modern theme, especially in postmodern literary theory in which "undecidability" has become something of a critical refrain. In some influential extreme versions there is a dogmatic skepticism about the ability of either fiction or history to get into referential relationship to anything outside our own imagination. Michael Frayn's play, *Copenhagen* (1998), might seem to fall into this category. It uses the indeterminacy principle in quantum mechanics as a metaphor to explore the historical and moral uncertainties about Werner Heisenberg, its discoverer, who was head of the German nuclear program during World War II. Yet Frayn is historically very well informed about his subject, discusses the issues in a lengthy postscript, and even comes to some firm conclusions about them. He denies that he is imposing ambiguity, for "where there's ambiguity in the play about what happened, it's because there is in the recollections of the participants."

In an interview Stegner once defended his extensive use of the letters of an actual Eastern woman (Mary Hallock Foote) who had gone West with her husband as the basis for making a novel about such a transition (*Angle of Repose,* 1971). But he also has cautioned that "if you are writing about what might be called public events, historical events that are almost everybody's property—conspiracy of Pontiac, Montcalm and Wolfe—then I think you had better be very, very careful about changing anything or inserting anything which is too personal or speculative."

Frayn faced this difficulty at once, because all three of his characters in the play are historical persons, two of them well-known internationally as great physicists. In his postscript Frayn acknowledges that "where a work of fiction features historical characters and historical events, it's reasonable to want to know how much of it is fiction and how much of it is history." While he has invented the speeches of his characters, he has done so according to the Thucydidean principle of following "in so far as possible the original protagonists' train of thought." Like Stegner, Frayn believes that the historian and the fictional storyteller occupy some common ground because "the great challenge" facing both of them is "to get into people's heads, to stand where they stood and see the world as they saw it, to make some informed estimate of their motives and intentions."

Frayn asserts, however, that recordable history cannot reach motives and intentions, so "the only way into the protagonists' heads is through the imagination." This distinction is meant to justify his departures from the historical record, but it ignores the fact that historians often do deal with motives and intentions: Did Lincoln intend to have the South fire upon Fort Sumter when he reinforced it? Did Franklin Roosevelt plot to bring America into the war by provoking the Japanese to bomb Pearl Harbor? In both cases historians have used evidence and reasoning to deal with such controversies, distinguishing, for example, between an agent's willingness to risk an enemy's military response, while hoping

and expecting to avoid it, and an agent's intention to bring about that result. Frayn himself discusses and assesses the historical evidence about Heisenberg's motives and purposes just as historians have had to do.

Questions have arisen because of the claim made by some German scientists after the war that they had deliberately slowed work on the atomic bomb because of their fear of what Hitler might do with it. The argument had the advantage of making them look better than the Allied scientists, who not only had produced the bomb but had dropped it on two Japanese cities, killing thousands of civilians. Frayn's play is in no way an apology for the German scientists, but it does provide an opportunity for an audience to hear Heisenberg's version of what he was trying to do when he headed the German nuclear program and in particular what his purpose might have been in his wartime visit to Copenhagen, where he talked with Niels Bohr, his former teacher, scientific collaborator, and friend.

"Why did he come to Copenhagen?" is the question, asked by Margrethe Bohr, that opens the play. As it unfolds, the play enables the audience to think about Heisenberg's visit not only through his explanations but also through the critical responses of Bohr and his wife, who were strong opponents of fascism. It is a fascinating mystery to unravel. Frayn audaciously obtains imaginative freedom for exploring it by having the principals discuss the problem posthumously in the hope of arguing "until they achieved a little more understanding of what was going on, just as they had so many times when they were alive with the intractable difficulties presented by the internal workings of the atom." The time frame shifts back and forth to recollections of earlier meetings in 1924 and a later one in 1947. At times the characters replay a past moment in their history as if it were happening again. Conventional realism is further rejected by having Heisenberg and Margrethe speak thoughts that are heard by the audience rather than by the other characters.

The play requires the audience to understand something about quantum mechanics and the historical situation of the time, while it also dramatizes the emotional currents that animate the characters, who are on opposite sides in the war at a time when the Germans have already occupied Denmark. Moreover, Bohr had lost his eldest son in a drowning accident when they were sailing together, and his pupil Heisenberg is in part a surrogate; while the German feels especially drawn to Bohr as a father-figure with the memory of their collaboration in creating the new physics. Heisenberg is also under the strain of working for a brutal regime for which he has no ideological sympathy, while still having strong patriotic feelings about his country. (These feelings kept him from accepting handsome offers of professorships in America.)

In the play, looking back on the meeting of 1941, Heisenberg says that what brought him to Copenhagen was knowing that "if we could build a reactor we could build a bomb." Therefore he asks Bohr if physicists have the right to work on the military application of atomic energy. Heisenberg remembers Bohr "muttering something about everyone in wartime being obliged to do his best for his own country." Yet governments would have to come to the scientists to find out if there was any hope of producing the weapons in time for them to be used in the war. "We are the ones who will have to advise them to go ahead or not," Heisenberg says.

Both men believed it would be extremely difficult practically to produce a bomb, therefore it would have been possible for both of them to tell their governments "the simple discouraging truth." Nine months later, Heisenberg asked for so little money from Albert Speer to keep the reactor program going that the Nazi high command did not take the project seriously. Heisenberg claims that his strategy worked: "And that is the end of the German atomic bomb."

It is not, however, the end of questions about the visit in 1941. Heisenberg's reactor had almost reached a critical mass, and if he had more time and more uranium, he tells Bohr proudly in the play, "it would have been German physics that achieved the world's first self-sustaining chain reaction." (Bohr points out, however, that it would have killed Heisenberg's team because the device had no control rods.) His boast fits Margrethe's charge that he came to Copenhagen because he wanted to show that he was important enough to have been given the chance "to save the honor of German science." If he didn't tell Speer that the reactor could produce plutonium (and therefore a bomb), it was, she says, because he was afraid of what might happen to him if the Nazis committed huge resources to a project that he could not bring to fruition. Moreover, she has an even simpler explanation for his not building a bomb: "You didn't understand the physics."

Bohr realizes in the play that Heisenberg had spent the war believing that it would take a ton or more of plutonium to create a critical mass, when actually it would take only kilograms, as the Allied project proved. He had not done the essential calculation that would have kept him from his error, and it bolstered his belief that the bomb could not be made in time to be used in the war. Bohr speculates that if he had asked him if he had made the calculation, instead of angrily ending their talk, Heisenberg might have seen that he needed to make it and then "suddenly a very different and very terrible new world begins to take shape." Instead, Bohr reflects ruefully, he went on to Los Alamos "to play my small but helpful part in the deaths of a hundred thousand people." Perhaps, Heisenberg suggests in the play's last lines, the present world was "preserved, just possibly, by that one short moment in Copenhagen. By some event that will never quite be located or defined." We have come full circle with the play's analogy between uncertainty in physics and uncertainty in history.

The play's speculation is more appropriate to a historical drama than it is to a history, because we know so little about it. There are no documents, only conflicting and incomplete recollections. It is possible, however, as Heisenberg's scrupulously judicious biographer, David C. Cassidy, has suggested, that Heisenberg was in 1941 trying to avert an Allied crash program for a bomb that might be used on his country by telling Bohr that the Germans were "a long way from constructing an explosive." That hypothesis would fit the point of a drawing that Heisenberg gave to Bohr in their 1941 meeting, who passed it on to the Los Alamos scientists when he joined their project. They judged it to be the sketch of a reactor, not a design for a bomb. The drawing cannot now be found. Neither the biographer nor the play mentions it, but Frayn discusses it in his postscript, wondering why Heisenberg didn't refer to it in order to bolster his interpretation of what he was trying to tell Bohr.

Heisenberg had not convinced Bohr of his sincerity, as Richard Rhodes points out in his authoritative history, *The Making of the Atomic Bomb* (1986), "nor in any way begun a dialogue to avert possible catastrophe." Instead, he had only "managed potentially to alarm Germany's most powerful enemy further with news of progress in approaching the chain reaction. That news must necessarily accelerate Allied efforts to build a bomb." Not surprisingly, J. Robert Oppenheimer concluded that Heisenberg wanted "to see if Bohr knew anything that they did not; I believe it was a standoff."

As soon as Heisenberg heard of the Allied success in making the bomb, he said to his scientific colleagues, in a discussion which was secretly taped by their captors at Farm Hall in England, "At the bottom of my heart I was really glad that it was an engine [a reactor] and not a bomb." Yet a reactor using natural uranium can produce plutonium, and it can be extracted by chemical means and used as an explosive. The German scientists knew of this method and in 1942 Heisenberg told the Nazi leaders about it, though he cautioned against expecting quick results and emphasized the technical difficulties that remained to be solved. Heisenberg also had another reason for visiting Copenhagen, as Frayn's play suggests. He participated in a lecture series sponsored by the German cultural propaganda institute. It would help to prove his reliability to Gestapo officials, who had long been suspicious of him; it would therefore give him more freedom to develop atomic physics in Germany, for he had often tried, as he put it, "to make warfare serve physics by demonstrating how physics could serve warfare."

Margrethe's charge in the play that Heisenberg didn't "understand the physics" is supported by Jeremy Bernstein's thorough analysis in his edition of the Farm Hall documents, *Hitler's Uranium Club* (1996). Frayn in his play's postscript comes to the same "inescapable" conclusion that is "beyond a reasonable doubt": Heisenberg did not do the necessary and correct calculation of what would be needed for a critical mass. He therefore thought that the technical problems of making the bomb would be much too difficult to solve during the war. "The effects of real enthusiasm and real determination are incalculable," Frayn points out, but they are "sometimes decisive." Ironically, the Allied project had these qualities in large part because of a reasonable fear that German scientists might make the bomb, which Hitler would then surely use with devastating effect.

Plays seldom create a stir among scientists, but *Copenhagen* has done that. As a result the Bohr family decided to release, much earlier than had been planned, eleven documents on Bohr's drafts of letters to Heisenberg, which he never sent, about their controversial meeting in Copenhagen. Bohr was responding sixteen years later to Heisenberg's account of it as reported in Robert Jungk's *Brighter than a Thousand Suns* (1957). A letter to Heisenberg on the issue was found in Bohr's personal copy of the book. He maintained that Heisenberg had given him the impression, though he spoke in "vague terms," that "Germany was participating vigorously in a race to be the first with atomic weapons" and "I did not sense even the slightest hint that you and your friends were making efforts in another direction."

Bohr claimed to have remembered "every word" of their conversation, though in another draft he acknowledged more credibly "how difficult it is to form an accurate impression of events in which many have taken part." Heisenberg is surely believable when he wrote of their attempt in 1947 to reconstruct what had been said in 1941: "we noticed that both our memories had become blurred." Bohr's drafts of his letters of 1957 cannot and have not settled the issue. Distinguished scientists still take contrasting views of the episode. Some think he was possibly trying to get Bohr "to be a messenger of conscience, and wanted Bohr to persuade

the Allied scientists also to refrain from working on a bomb," as Hans A. Bethe, a Cornell University physicist and Nobel Prize winner, has put it. This view is also endorsed by Klaus Gottstein of the Max Planck Institute for Physics in Munich, who worked under Heisenberg when he was director from 1950-1971. Cassidy, the biographer of Heisenberg, thinks he wanted Bohr to use his influence to prevent the Allies from building a bomb that could be used against Germany. Other scientists think Heisenberg was doing a little espionage, just trying to find out what Bohr knew. From this point of view, as Bernstein has argued, "Heisenberg may not be the 'complex figure of the play,'" but a person who is easier to understand.

I would argue on the contrary that Frayn's complex view is all the more pertinent, given the mysteries that still surround the meeting. Why did Bohr never send his letter? Why did he wait until 1957 to explain what he thought Heisenberg had said? Why did Heisenberg give Bohr a rough sketch of the German reactor, which Bohr drew from memory for the Los Alamos scientists? Was it a message that Germany was a long way from making a bomb? Unlike the silence of the dog that helpfully did not bark in the night, the silence of both Bohr and Heisenberg about this sketch leaves their meeting fraught with ambiguity. It is this historical uncertainty that justifies Frayn's exploration of the possibilities with their psychological and moral implications. Our sense of being at terrible risk in a nuclear world and our concern about the way dedication to technological prowess can blunt our moral sensitivities have given *Copenhagen* attentive and enthusiastic audiences for its dramatizing of a historical moment of what might seem at first to be only an obscure and transitory meeting between arcane scientists.

As fictionalizers of history, Tracy Chevalier, Max Byrd, and Michael Frayn have in their own ways exercised with artistic effect a good deal of poetic license, but they also have the merit of not treating that license as a blank check. A reviewer of a current historical novel in the *New York Times* complains about its author's long afterword, telling us which characters are imaginary and which real. "We read fiction with our disbelief suspended," the reviewer insists, "and most of us like to leave it that way." The historical imagination, however, is not something the literary imagination can ignore in fictionalizing history, because modern minds care about both. Only the best practitioners know how to solve the difficult problem of reconciling and integrating them. It is their artistic practice, rather than any critical generalizations, that in the end can bring to life the point of Benedetto Croce's elegant aphorism: "Poetry and history are, then, the two wings of the same breathing creature, the two linked moments of the knowing mind."

FURTHER READING

Criticism

Feingold, Michael. "Not-Right Triangles." *Village Voice* (12-18 April 2000): n.p.

> Feingold looks at the unequal triangles that form the basis of Frayn's *Copenhagen* and Arthur Miller's *The Ride down Mt. Morgan* in two contemporary New York productions of the plays.

Frayn, Michael and Ursula Canton. "Interviews: Michael Frayn." In *Theatre Archive Project,* edited by Dominic Shellard, pp. 1-15. Sheffield, U.K.: The British Library and the University of Sheffield, 2004.

> Frayn discusses how he began writing for theatre, some of his early influences, and current British plays and playwrights.

Lukacs, John. "The Conversation: *Copenhagen* by Michael Frayn." *Los Angeles Times* (21 May 2006): 6.

> Provides a somewhat detailed juxtaposition of the play and what we know of the history of the events on which *Copenhagen* is based.

Worth, Katherine, "Farce and Michael Frayn." *Modern Drama* 26, no. 1 (May 1983): 47-53.

> Examines Frayn's *Noises Off* as a dramatic farce.

Additional coverage of Frayn's life and career is contained in the following sources published by Thomson Gale: *British Writers: The Classics,* **Vol. 2;** *British Writers Supplement,* **Vol. 7;** *Contemporary Authors,* **Vols. 5-8R;** *Contemporary Authors New Revision Series,* **Vols. 30, 69, 114, 133;** *Contemporary British Dramatists; Contemporary Dramatists,* **Eds. 5, 6;** *Contemporary Literary Criticism,* **Vols. 3, 7, 31, 47, 176;** *Contemporary Novelists,* **Eds. 1-7;** *Dictionary of Literary Biography,* **Vols. 13, 14, 194, 245,** *DISCovering Authors Modules: Dramatists and Novelists Editions; Drama for Students,* **Vol. 22;** *Literature Resource Center; Major 20th-Century Writers,* **Eds. 1, 2;** *Major 21st-Century Writers,* **Ed. 2005;** *St. James Guide to Fantasy Writers;* **and** *St. James Guide to Science Fiction Writers,* **Ed. 4.**

Terrence McNally
1939-

American playwright.

INTRODUCTION

McNally is an openly gay American playwright known to critics and theatergoers for plays that are often funny and sad at the same time. His works frequently feature gay characters and dwell on themes that resonate with homosexual audiences, but are universal. *Love! Valour! Compassion!* (1994) was one such play; it won a Tony Award for Best Play. Today McNally is a driving force in the theater industry. Many critics consider him the successor to Tennessee Williams as one of the most important playwrights in America.

BIOGRAPHICAL INFORMATION

McNally was born on November 3, 1939, in St. Petersburg, Florida, son of Hubert Arthur and Dorothy Katharine (Rapp) McNally. He grew up in Corpus Christi, Texas—a lonely child who enjoyed listening to radio dramas and live opera broadcasts. He became deeply enamored of the theater and received encouragement from his parents, native New Yorkers. McNally moved to New York City in 1956 to attend Columbia University, where he majored in journalism. He graduated Phi Beta Kappa in 1960 with a B.A. in English. McNally then spent six months in Mexico on a creative writing scholarship and worked on his writing. Not long afterwards, McNally submitted a play to the Actors Studio in New York. Although the play was not accepted, the Studio saw promise in McNally and offered him a job as stage manager. Through this job, McNally learned about the practical aspects of running a theater.

And Things That Go Bump in the Night (1964) was McNally's first play to be produced; he was only 25 years old. It received scandalized reviews in part because of its frank portrayal of a homosexual character. Disappointed, McNally worked as an editor for several years until a friend convinced him to return to playwriting. He won a Guggenheim Fellowship in 1966 to support his writing. After the critical and commercial success of his one-act play *Next* (1969), McNally won a second Guggenheim Fellowship that same year. He received an Achievement in Playwriting citation from the American Academy of Arts and Letters in 1975, the

same year that his hit farce *The Ritz* was staged. McNally's career suffered in the early 1980s after one of his plays failed to complete its run and make it to Broadway, but he eventually achieved even greater success. *Frankie and Johnny in the Clair de Lune* (1987) was a hit, spawning a movie adaptation (with a screenplay written by McNally) starring Al Pacino and Michelle Pfeiffer, as well as a London production of the play.

McNally's preferred form is the one-act play. He won an Emmy Award in 1990 for his television adaptation of the one-act *Andre's Mother* (1990). With the rise of AIDS awareness and a wider acceptance of homosexuality, McNally garnered further attention for his work. In the 1990s he won four Tony Awards: for best book of a musical in 1993 for *Kiss of the Spider Woman* (1992); for best play in 1995 for *Love! Valour! Compassion!*; again for best play in 1996 for *Master Class* (1995); and for best book of a musical in 1997 for *Ragtime* (1996). *A Perfect Ganesh* (1993) was nominated for a

Pulitzer Prize in Drama in 1994. McNally has been a member of the Dramatists' Guild since 1970, serving as vice-president in the 1980s, and is currently on its elected Council. In his forty years as a playwright, McNally has written over forty-five plays, librettos, adaptations, television scripts, and movie scripts. In 2004 McNally was awarded the prestigious Helen Hayes Tribute for his enormous contribution to American theater.

MAJOR DRAMATIC WORKS

Critics have often noted that McNally's skill as a playwright has continued to improve over the course of his career. His early works were dark but comic and, over time, critics found parts of these plays that they liked. His later works are more life-affirming and compassionate, but still funny. Many of these plays have been lauded, adapted, and are considered significant works in American theater of the late twentieth and early twenty-first centuries.

From his very first Broadway play, *And Things That Go Bump in the Night,* homosexuality has been an important part of McNally's plays. Sometimes he explores such aspects of gay culture as bathhouses in the farcical *The Ritz* (1975), or the isolation of Mendy and Stephen in *The Lisbon Traviata* (1985). In his controversial play *Corpus Christi* (1998), McNally depicts Jesus and his apostles as gay men living in Corpus Christi, Texas, McNally's childhood hometown. In this play he brings the story of Christ into the context of gay life, often ostracized by religious groups. As the concluding line of the play puts it: "He belongs to us as well as you."

AIDS awareness and its impact on gay men has also been an important theme for McNally. For example, in *Lips together, Teeth apart* (1992), a woman inherits her brother's beach house after he dies from AIDS. While vacationing there with her husband, sister-in-law, and sister-in-law's husband, she must confront her prejudices against homosexuality and AIDS. In *The Perfect Ganesh,* two women travel to India after losing their sons, one to AIDS and the other to a reckless driver. *Love! Valour! Compassion!* is the story of eight gay men who take several holidays together. One of them has lost his brother to AIDS.

Music is perhaps McNally's favorite feature to include in his plays and his love for it goes back to his childhood, when he listened to operas on the radio. *The Lisbon Traviata* is about two gay men who are opera fanatics, one of them obsessed with a recording of Maria Callas's *La Traviata* performance in Lisbon, Portugal. McNally returns to Maria Callas in *Master Class,* where he brings a partially fictional version of Callas to larger than life proportions. The play's plot draws on a series of master classes that Callas conducted at the Julliard

School in the 1970s. McNally has also been involved in writing librettos for musicals. *Kiss of the Spider Woman,* originally a novel by Manuel Puig, was McNally's first successful musical adaptation. This musical tells the story of two gay men in a Latin American prison and their fascination with a movie musical star known as the Spider Woman. McNally's libretto for the musical *Ragtime* is an adaptation of E. L. Doctorow's novel, which tells the story of three families in America around 1900. McNally also wrote the libretto for *The Full Monty* (2000), a staged musical adaptation of the hit movie by the same name.

CRITICAL RECEPTION

McNally has been writing plays for more than forty years. He achieved commercial success early in his career, but critical appreciation came much later. Although his plays are sometimes contentious, McNally is not an experimentalist. His first Broadway production, *And Things That Go Bump in the Night,* was a flop, with critics deriding McNally as a poor disciple of Edward Albee and absurdism. But the flurry of comedic, antiwar, socially conscious one-acts that followed drew more positive appraisals from critics and audiences. *Next* (1969), about a middle-aged, out-of-shape man who is mistakenly drafted into the Army, charmed reviewers; it remains one of McNally's most performed one-act plays. When his next few full-length productions flopped, critics thought McNally would only be successful writing short plays. But critics also acknowledged that McNally had developed his own style.

The Ritz was McNally's first full-length success. Reviews of the show were positive and complementary; critics enjoyed the humor and were not put off by the play being set in a gay bathhouse. McNally's next successful production, *Frankie and Johnny in the Clair de Lune,* a play about a one night stand between a waitress and short-order cook, garnered even better reviews, with some critics stating it was his best work so far. By the early 1990s McNally's success with critics was well ensured. Subject matter was no longer a barrier and his writing talent had matured. Critics compared McNally with Tennessee Williams and Anton Chekhov in reviewing *A Perfect Ganesh. Love! Valour! Compassion!* received excellent reviews and was an extremely successful play, although a few reviewers felt distanced from the action because of the play's exclusive focus on gay men. *Master Class* was a little less well liked by critics. Some found it too long, and some were unsettled by McNally's characterization of Callas, purposefully portrayed as larger than life. David Shengold, for example, regarded McNally's script as "trashily reductive commentary" in his *Theatre Journal* performance review. Examining subsequent productions, critic Matthew Gurewitsch wrote in *The Atlantic Monthly* that McNally's "purposes . . . are only incidentally documentary. Above all the play is a highly personal, deeply perceptive meditation on the wellsprings and the consequences of supremacy in art." The play that polarized audiences and critics alike was *Corpus Christi.* There were protests, bomb threats, and scathing editorials before the play even opened. Early reviews were unfavorable but later ones, such as those written by Charles McNulty in *American Theatre* and Sharon Green in *Theatre Journal,* have held that *Corpus Christi* holds an important place in contemporary American culture. While *Corpus Christi* is not considered McNally's best work, it has had a significant impact on opinions concerning freedom of speech. As McNally put it himself in a speech later published in *American Theatre* (see Further Reading), "[A]bove all, theatre is the oldest way we have of trying to tell the truth about who we are."

PRINCIPAL WORKS

Plays

The Roller Coaster 1960
This Side of the Door 1962
And Things That Go Bump in the Night 1964
Botticelli 1968
¡Cuba Sí! 1968
Sweet Eros 1968
Witness 1968
Bringing It All back Home 1969
Next 1969
Bad Habits 1971
Where Has Tommy Flowers Gone? 1971
Whiskey 1973
The Ritz 1975
It's Only a Play 1982
The Lisbon Traviata 1985
Frankie and Johnny in the Clair de Lune 1987
Andre's Mother 1990
Kiss of the Spider Woman [adaptor] 1992
Lips together, Teeth apart 1992
A Perfect Ganesh 1993
Love! Valour! Compassion! 1994
Master Class 1995
Ragtime [adaptor] 1996
Corpus Christi 1998
The Full Monty [adaptor] 2000
Dedication or The Stuff of Dreams 2005

Other Major Works

The Ritz (screenplay) 1977
Frankie and Johnny (screenplay) 1987

Andre's Mother (television play) 1990
Love! Valour! Compassion! (screenplay) 1994

OVERVIEW

Toby Silverman Zinman (essay date March 1995)

SOURCE: Zinman, Toby Silverman. "The Muses of Terrence McNally: Music and Mortality Are His Consuming Themes." *American Theatre* 12, no. 3 (March 1995): 12-7.

[*In the following essay, Zinman provides an overview of McNally's life and work.*]

Terrence McNally sits patiently, helping the photographer pick white fuzzies, residue from a stripped-off sweatshirt, from the shoulders of his dark green shirt. The Manhattan Theatre Club rehearsal room is backlit by the fading light of a December afternoon, and McNally's good-natured forbearance seems a measure of the man. MTC, he'll tell you, is his theatrical home: "My life is in this building—they've done eight of my plays in ten years."

His life in the American theatre began 31 years ago when the then-25-year-old playwright's first play, ***And Things that Go Bump in the Night,*** landed on Broadway—to hilariously scandalized, resoundingly disapproving reviews. Remarkably, that bumpy start has led to this golden moment: As 1994 spun to a close, McNally could count among his Christmas blessings MTC's critically acclaimed, sold-out Off-Broadway production of his intensely personal play ***Love! Valour! Compassion!;*** a long-running Broadway musical, ***Kiss of the Spider Woman,*** for which he won a Tony award as book-writer in 1993; and the auspicious launching of his newest play, ***Master Class,*** at the Philadelphia Theatre Company, with Zoe Caldwell in the central role of Maria Callas. If that show moves to Broadway as is hoped, with ***L!V!C!*** [***Love! Valour! Compassion!***] already transferred (under the auspices of the Broadway Alliance) to Broadway's Walter Kerr Theatre, he may have three shows on the Great White Way simultaneously—what may well be a world record, especially since two of them will be dramas, the most fragile of Broadway commodities.

Small wonder McNally refuses to get aggravated over the fuzzies or the picky photographer. From this playwright's perspective, life is looking good, and hard work is the key.

Is there another American playwright who could use the word "valor" (with or without the "u") and mean it? In these cynical, undercutting times, is there another author who actually *means* his exclamation points? McNally is not and has never been on theatre's experimental frontier, its cutting edge (although his *Sweet Eros* brought nudity to Off Broadway in 1969, well before the more sensational *Ché!* and *Oh! Calcutta!*). He is a solid, prolific writer who has stayed the course, a playwright who knows his Shakespeare, who values technique, who considers the term "craftsman" a compliment—and his plays have grown steadily over the years in scope as well as depth.

The most recent plays (beginning with the eccentric 1987 romance *Frankie and Johnny in the Clair de Lune*) are celebrations of love between people in the face of emotional danger—damaged, neurotic people whose capacity to love is almost always increased in the course of the drama.

"I suppose I have to grit my teeth and refer to my plays as 'comedies,'" McNally says ruefully, "because people do like handles. I agree that there's laughter in my plays, and that I have a comic sensibility. But *I* don't think I write comedies."

* * *

McNally is certainly right about his early one-acts. They are manifestly products of their times: The anti-Vietnam war plays, like *Botticelli* (1968) and *Bringing It All Back Home* (1969), and the anti-establishment protest plays, like *Next* (1967), *¡Cuba Si!* (1968) and *Witness* (1968), all suggest that McNally is not at heart a political playwright. "I think our generation of writers went through a period of being overpraised for anything we wrote," he says today. "In the '60s, if you wrote a play and you were under 30, you could get it done in New York. The result was that a lot of young American writers never developed a sufficient technique in playwriting."

Nevertheless, McNally hasn't relinquished his affection for the one-act. *Prelude and Liebestod* (1989), a theatrical aria that is simultaneously hilarious and horrifying, and *Andre's Mother* (1988), a tender and wrenching drama about lives affected by AIDS (which was subsequently revised for television and for which McNally won a 1990 Emmy award), show how his skill with the short form has grown.

Comedy, the playwright's disclaimers aside, became something of an obsession in a second stage of McNally's career. His writing in the early '70s was devoted to farce—particularly sex farce—and the theme of homosexuality which had lurked in the earliest plays moved downstage, but not in ways that aimed at

conveying gay life authentically for a straight audience. Farce is farce, after all, and plays like *Whiskey* (1973), *Bad Habits* (1974) and *The Ritz* (1975, subsequently made into a movie with McNally's screenplay and F. Murray Abraham, Rita Moreno and Jerry Stiller reprising their stage roles) are funny, but retreat from the intimacy and compassion that now seem to be keynotes of McNally's best work.

Whatever handle audiences and critics attached to them, from the start McNally's plays have been death-haunted and music-vitalized.

If music is for McNally a redemptive, life-giving force, death is always the fact, the point of a play's departure—that which makes not only the action of the play but the writing of the play necessary. In *Lips Together, Teeth Apart* (1992), it is the death of her brother that brings Sally and three companions to a beach house on Fire Island for the July 4th holiday, and, accordingly, the play begins with a farewell (the "farewell trio" from Mozart's *Cosi fan tutte*). The plot of *A Perfect Ganesh* (1993) is generated by two women's secret sorrow over the deaths of their sons, and their grief, however obliquely, motivates the trip to India which is the action of the play. (McNally is currently working on a screenplay of *Ganesh* for Merchant Ivory Productions, although he has no say about casting or final approval of the screenplay. "They could read mine, think it was terrible, and say, let's give it to Sam Shepard to rewrite," he quips.)

Love! Valour! Compassion! takes the playwright's twin preoccupations to new heights: the play is death-soaked and music-redeemed. Its account of the long-term friendships of eight gay men who holiday at an upstate New York country house culminates in a powerful final sequence of scenes: Six of the men perform *Swan Lake* in drag, hilariously; there follows a gently presentational litany of the characters' future deaths; then, in a shimmering, Eakins-like tableaux behind a scrim, all join in an a capella rendition of "Harvest Moon" as they jump naked into moonlit water.

"I don't think *Love! Valour! Compassion!* is particularly shocking—people discuss the nudity in it, but what I'm really proud of is that everyone has tolerated and accepted an enormous amount of affection and tenderness between men," McNally reasons. "The most common comment I get is that by the end of act 1 the person has forgotten that the play is about gay men, and just thinks about them as human beings they can identify with—and I take that as a compliment."

Despite general approbation, the play has elicited some remarks that no one could construe as complimentary. Commentators in the gay press have objected to the generic quality of the characters, with their stereotypical attachments to artistic pursuits, bitchy repartee and sex. *Variety* critic Jeremy Gerard created a minor tempest when he wrote that the play's world, being "exclusively gay and unabashedly in-your-face about it," made him, as a heterosexual man, feel as though he were from Mars.

McNally places more store in what he hears from audiences, one-on-one. "People tell me, 'I was moved by these people. I wasn't threatened by them, I wasn't harangued by them, they didn't seem so exotic to me—I *know* these people.' There's a humanity going back and forth between the actors and the audience—you can feel it in the theatre."

* * *

Talking about this play elicits many stories about McNally's gratitude to his collaborators—lighting designer Brian MacDevitt, who enlivened the mock ballet with purple footlights; costume designer Jess Goldstein, who created the little headdresses the men remove when they recount their future deaths; and actor Nathan Lane, whose reading of his character Buzz's lines, wickedly comic or otherwise, McNally characterizes as "genius."

"I work with really good people. People say, where do you find them? I go to the theatre about three times a week—so many theatre people only go to see hits. Six months ago people were asking me, who's Joe Mantello? Now it's too late to get Joe Mantello—I'd seen three plays the man directed. I believe that being a playwright is being 100 percent responsible for what's on stage, and that means acknowledging how people have amplified your vision."

Edward Albee phoned McNally recently, having read something the latter had said about the importance of collaboration. McNally recounts the conversation wryly. "Albee said, 'You're such a goody-two-shoes. Do you really believe all that bullshit?' And I said, 'I really do. And you really don't, do you?' And he said, 'No, I really don't.'"

Borrowings from Shakespeare are sprinkled throughout McNally's plays (like the exclamation "O for a Muse of fire!" in **A Perfect Ganesh,** which Katherine turns into "Offamof!" for short), but it is perhaps the use in **L!V!C!** of Hamlet's phrase "We defy augury" by the AIDS-afflicted James that seems the most resonant. The line stands alone, and the famous speech about death and timing ("there's a special providence in the fall of a sparrow . . . the readiness is all") is never spoken, merely invoked. This is McNally's oblique declaration of "the courage, the valor" required in the age of AIDS. "Give a play a title that makes you write up to it," he adds gamely.

"Death is a fact—it's always present," he says of his plays' emphasis on the subject. "I think I was once more frightened of it than I am now. I don't see death now as punitive. In the early plays it's more terrible, the worst thing that can happen to you; now it's part of the process of being alive."

As is music. There's always music in a McNally play, whether it's classical, musical comedy songs, folk music or opera. If he were a composer, McNally told me, he'd write opera, but in point of fact he cannot sing or play an instrument. That has not stopped him from delving deep into the subject, however, and his expertise is frequently put to use introducing the Metropolitan Opera broadcasts.

McNally's very earliest play was a 1963 adaptation of *The Lady of the Camellias* (which is, of course, the Dumas story Verdi used for *La Traviata*); the characters in **Bump** are named for operatic figures; **Frankie and Johnny** opens with Bach, closes with Debussy; the opening stage directions of **Lips Together, Teeth Apart** indicate that as Mozart's trio progresses, "the stage and the actors will slowly come to 'life.'"

It is as though for McNally music is the life force, that which precedes the theatrical givens of speech and gesture. In fact, the playwright told me, "Music can articulate feelings in a more examined way than words—sometimes dance and music make me feel inarticulate. Dance is the most beautiful expression of sensual love; in theatre, that's the hardest thing to convey."

With opera legend Maria Callas as its lead character and the celebrated master classes she held at Juilliard in the early 1970s the circumstance of its action, the new play **Master Class** makes music a central issue—and an apt metaphor for the redemptive power of art. **Master Class** is, of course, not McNally's first play about Callas—the opera-queen characters in **Lisbon Traviata** (written in 1985 and revised in 1989) are fixated on a pirated recording of her performance of *La Traviata* in Lisbon. When he wrote the play, McNally says, no such recording existed; it surfaced after the play appeared. (Only half-joking, he adds that if recordings of all the Callas performances could be magically elicited, he would gladly write a play to procure each one.)

It was Callas's voice McNally fell in love with, he assures me firmly, not the glamorous/tragic Callas myth that has inspired her cult. "I don't consider myself an opera queen. I approach Callas totally as sound." Elsewhere he has called her, a "great singing shark devouring every note in a score" who "sings meaning" when other singers sing only notes.

Master Class presents Callas at the end of her career, when her voice was gone. The audience is, in effect, the class, and her first lines are, "No applause. We're here

to work. You're not in a theatre. This is a classroom."
(My quotations come from an early typescript which
may be considerably revised, since McNally does a
great deal of work during rehearsals.) Out of the "audience" come, in turn, three student singers—two
sopranos and a tenor—to perform for the great diva.
They are nervous and intimidated, and we soon learn
why: McNally's Callas is a demanding, rigorous,
temperamental teacher. She is a bitter, broken creature,
but one who is also self-aware ("I bark quite a bit actually, but I don't bite").

The play's most crucial concern is, finally, the making
of art—art of any kind—and the enormous thrill and
responsibility of that enterprise. "*Master Class* is about
the need for art, and what we do with our enormous
feelings, and how we can keep some sanity," the
playwright ventures. Does it take an art form, like opera,
with a lavish and extravagant take on life to contain
and convey these "enormous feelings"?

"Well, I believe that my plays *are* lavish and extreme,"
McNally assures me. "They are my attempt to make
sense of what it's like to be alive, or to be in love, or to
experience joy. That, by definition, is what art is."

AUTHOR COMMENTARY

**Terrence McNally and Steven Drukman (interview
date 1996)**

SOURCE: McNally, Terrence and Steven Drukman.
"Terrance McNally." In *Speaking on Stage: Interviews
with Contemporary American Playwrights,* edited by
Philip C. Kolin and Colby H. Kullman, pp. 332-45.
Tuscaloosa, Ala.: The University of Alabama Press,
1996.

[*In the following interview, Drukman and McNally
discuss several key themes in McNally's work.*]

Terrence McNally was born in St. Petersburg, Florida,
on 3 November 1939, was raised in Corpus Cristi,
Texas, and received his bachelor's degree in English
from Columbia University in 1960. His most recent
plays are *A Perfect Ganesh* (1992), *Lips Together,
Teeth Apart* (1991), and *Frankie and Johnny in the
Claire de Lune* (1987). *Lips Together* has been
produced in a record-breaking number of regional
theatres throughout the United States, including the
recent controversial staging in Marietta, Georgia, where
conservatives, in a mind-boggling mixture of illogic
and ignorance, boycotted the production because of its
threat to "traditional family values." McNally won the

1993 Tony award for best book of a musical for his
adaptation of Manuel Puig's *Kiss of the Spider Woman,*
which is still playing to sold-out houses on Broadway.
Other plays include *The Lisbon Traviata* (1985), *The
Ritz* (1975), *Bad Habits* (1973), *Where Has Tommy
Flowers Gone?* (1971), and *Next* (1967). McNally won
an Emmy award for *Andre's Mother* (1990, for
American Playhouse) and has received two Guggenheim fellowships, a Rockefeller grant, and a citation
from the American Academy of Arts and Letters. He
has been vice-president of the Dramatists Guild since
1981.

It was my good fortune to meet and talk with McNally
in his Chelsea brownstone in late October 1993. I could
hardly be unaware of the timeliness of this interview.
After having won the Tony the previous June, McNally
was perhaps the "hottest" dramatist in New York at the
moment (*Time* magazine had recently dubbed him "the
height of hot"). At the time of the interview, he had not
one but two eagerly awaited world premieres coming
up: *L'Age d'Or* at Circle Repertory and *Love! Valor!
Compassion!* at Manhattan Theatre Club. He was busily
making the lecture circuit while in the preliminary
stages of writing a biography of Tennessee Williams.
He teaches playwriting at Juilliard and has also taught
at New York University.

What's more, McNally seems at present to be in a
period of creative regeneration and artistic maturation.
Ever since *The Lisbon Traviata* in 1985 (although, in
this interview, McNally marks the turning point as 1982,
with *It's Only a Play*), his voice has become more serious. His incursions into his characters' psyches seem
richer now, and he has learned to orchestrate their
discordant souls to produce sonorous, and often unsettling, drama. All these later plays have shared the same
dramatic motif: despite yearning for intimacy, human
beings have myriad ways of building barriers between
one another, denying and evading emotion, and keeping
their distance. "Only connect," E. M. Forster's oft-
quoted dictum, hangs onimously, unheeded, in the salt
air of *Lips Together, Teeth Apart,* so, too, in *The Lisbon Traviata, Andre's Mother,* and *A Perfect Ganesh.*

This is not to give short shrift to his early satires. Plays
like *Whiskey, Bad Habits,* and *It's Only a Play* drew
up scathing parodies of American theatre folk, in the
tradition of Noël Coward. Still, McNally is very much a
"man of the theatre," as demonstrated in this interview.
He was most passionate in his musings about the practical side of the business—the prohibitive economics of
New York theatre and the "suburbanization" of its audience—rather than the vagaries of literary analyses of
his drama. It was refreshing to hear a playwright calling
for *more* critics (to diffuse the power of the *New York
Times* as sole arbiter) as well as his concern for actively
rebuilding the atrophied young audience in the theatre.

Finally these two themes that I have chosen to extract—
the world of the theatre and the complicated negotiations of intimacy—sadly make the subject of AIDS

almost an inevitability in McNally's work. AIDS has, of course, robbed our community in so many ways, and McNally's plays (since **Frankie and Johnny**) have responded in kind. He spoke of the issue candidly in this interview.

* * *

[*Drukman*]: *First of all, congratulations are in order for your Tony award. I'm wondering if these awards mean that much to you.*

[McNally]: Oh, yes, of course. They're dessert, they're icing on the dessert even, but they're very nice. I don't think you write things to win Tony awards, but it's nice to have that kind of acknowledgment, and there are days when you wonder if your work means anything to anybody. That's what an award means to me: an affirmation that you've been heard, as opposed to "you are better than" anybody else. I don't see them as contests in that way. I see them as kind of recognitions, and I think anybody who wins any kind of prize, it's also for what's come before it. It's not *just* for **Spider Woman,** it's for a body of work.

Although it's not surprising that you did win for **Spider Woman,** *a musical, because music seems to play such a major role, both thematically and structurally, in your plays. I'm wondering how that translates into compositional strategies. Do you "score" a play? Do you hear the music or the rhythms of certain characters and try to get that down first?*

Well, you're right, music *is* important in my work. I'm not a trained musician, and I don't read music or play an instrument, so it's kind of intuitive, and most of my plays have a musical tonality to them. Often when I write a play, I will play the works of a composer all the time, even while I'm *writing* sometimes, and it's sort of a subliminal influence. For example, when I wrote **The Ritz,** I played only Rossini overtures, and when I wrote the second act of **Lisbon Traviata,** I remember I played *Pagliacci* and *Cavelleria Rusticana* and other verismo operas a lot. I forget what I played when I wrote the first act of **Lisbon Traviata**—I think maybe Maria Callas.

But I think listening to music without being able to talk about it technically has given me a sense of structure. But it's very hard to talk about it; it's something I *feel* more than I can define how I do it. But I do know about creating themes, developing themes, bringing them all together, resolution, and I think listening to chamber music is obviously very helpful there. The characters also obviously have their own musicality. That's sort of a separate issue, though. That's really in building a character, learning to listen to how they really speak and express themselves, so that your characters don't sound like each other, which I think is terribly important.

There the best example, I think, is Shakespeare. Hamlet never once sounds like Othello, who never once sounds like Lear, who never once sounds like Ariel. So Shakespeare is the real model there, when you want to be reminded how important it is that characters have their own rhythm, vocabulary, accent, tonality.

One of your more musical characters, Googie Gomez, first appears in **Bad Habits,** *only to reappear as a major character in* **The Ritz.** *Have you ever created characters that you thought either so exemplary or so appealing that you wanted to write other plays around them, something along the lines of Lanford Wilson's Talley plays?*

It hasn't occurred to me yet. The only character I'd like to do another play about is Mendy in *Lisbon Traviata.* Audiences love him, I love him, and I want to call it *Mendy in Love,* which I think is a wonderful title. But to answer your question, "Do I want to write a bunch of plays where people are connected?" I don't know, that was kind of an "in" joke, the Googie Gomez. It's funny you ask that. I've already tried some cross-referencing of characters once or twice, and usually it goes out in previews because it's so self-conscious. It's like you're nudging the audience: "Remember **Bad Habits?** Remember **The Ritz?**" I think in all these Lanford Wilson plays people really related, and they're about the same people. But I do want to write *Mendy in Love.*

Speaking of Mendy, you're known around town as an opera aficionado. Would you ever like to write a libretto?

No, because I think librettos are really the work of poets. I think opera needs really strong plot, and I'm very minimalist when it comes to plot, so I think that would be a very bad combination. But I don't know why contemporary composers don't go to playwrights and people who have a sense of drama to write librettos. Most of these librettos are written by people who are *not* of the theatre, and I think you have to be of the theatre to write a really strong libretto.

What about directing one of your plays?

No, no interest, none. Because I don't have the patience or concentration to direct. You really have to be at every rehearsal, and you have to care about everything: the acting, the script, the lighting, what color shoes the leading lady is wearing. I like to go to rehearsal when I'm working on the script. I don't enjoy rehearsals unless I'm really fixing a scene.

And yet you have clearly made a home for yourself in the New York theatre. In fact a list of your plays' dedications reads like a who's who of American theatre. Leonard Melfi, Lynne Meadow, Elaine May, James Coco—

Well, Elaine May directed my first successful play, which was a play I wrote for Jimmy Coco. They weren't "Elaine May" and "James Coco" then, if you know what I mean. Elaine was somebody who was trying to figure out what to do with her life after the breakup of Nichols and May. She was a very successful comic performer, but this was her first directing that I know of—I think she might have done some things when they were students in Chicago—but Elaine hadn't directed in a long while.

Of course I don't dedicate them to well-known people just to flatter them!

Oh, no, I'm not suggesting that. In fact your plays don't always draw the most flattering renderings of theatre people. Does this reflect an ambivalence about the community of which you've been such an important part for decades?

Actually, I think that the main play I've written about "the theatre," *It's Only a Play,* is a very positive piece. When people talk about it as bitchy comedy about the theatre, I really don't think they've understood what the play's about. People in the theatre say desperate and bitchy things just like anybody does. *It's Only a Play* is a very positive portrait of the theatre. I think the only negative theatre people I've invented are the Pitts in *Bad Habits,* that overweening-ego kind of couple, which was a, perhaps not so affectionate, jibe at Ron Leibman and Linda Lavin. It was no secret that that's who that couple was based on. They weren't terribly thrilled. I thought it was more affectionate than they did, so they were kind of unhappy with me for a while. But we've made it up, and we've all gone on to other things.

Still, all my characters are me as much as they're anybody else, so I also have the same ego as the Pitts in *Bad Habits.* I never make up a character one hundred percent. I don't believe you can write a character unless you've experienced the emotion that that character portrays. So everything that is petty and desperate and ambitious about the Pitts has to be in me too, or I couldn't have written it. Just as everything that's loving and tender in another character has to be in there. I don't think you can write feelings you've never had. So, to say that those characters were based *only* on "real people" is a little false. It's not *really* about Ron and Linda; I didn't know them that well. But I think you write about characters you recognize yourself in, elements of yourself. And then you perhaps build that up.

But I think in my work a character is usually about thirty-three percent me, thirty-three percent somebody else I've observed, and thirty-three percent by the grace of God, or inspiration or creativity. I'm not of the school

of playwriting where you list ten characteristic traits about each person so that they're different. That's for an actor—to chew gum or play with his ear, or stutter—let *him* characterize. The playwright must simply *listen* to how they talk, and *see* what they're doing. That's the main thing Elaine May taught me. She'd say, "What are your characters doing? I don't care what they're saying." And I still fall into the same trap. I write a thirty-page scene, it's brilliant writing, but no one's *doing* anything. That's the biggest problem I find, in my own work still (I'm fifty-four), and from my students at Juilliard who are in their twenties. They are writing reams of dialogue, but no one's doing anything. It's the hardest thing to get through our heads: *playwriting is recording behavior, not dialogue.* Dialogue is something people do while they're doing something. You talk a different way when the turkey's burning in the oven than you do sitting in a hammock on a cool summer day. So that's what I got from Elaine, which is why you dedicate a play to someone like Elaine. She taught me more about playwriting than anyone. I'm also a self-taught playwright. I did not take any playwriting courses in college. I was an English major.

Right. At Columbia?

Yes.

And after graduation you took off for Mexico to write the Great American Novel.

(*Laughs*) Ah, well.

So how did you drift into the theatre?

Well, I'd always liked it, and when I came to Columbia, I started going to the theatre practically every night. And then when I was off in Mexico, I wrote this play called *This Side of the Door.* I don't even think I still have a copy of it! It was autobiographical in a way that made me uncomfortable, and I thought, "If you can't enjoy watching your own plays, that's not good." But I sent it off to Actors' Studio, and I was asked to join the playwrights' unit and also to work there as a stage manager, by Mollie Kazan, who ran it. So I learned a lot by observing other actors and directors, and I saw some very exciting projects done there for the first time. *Zoo Story* was done there for the first time! *Night of the Iguana* was done there for the first time! It was kind of the height of the studio. It was wall-to-wall famous actors doing scenes, and Marilyn Monroe was sitting there with no makeup, and Olivier was doing Beckett. It was a very intense place to be.

My favorite of your plays from this period is the absurdist **Bringing It All Back Home.** *Handy comparisons of this play can be made to Edward Albee's* American Dream. *Was he one of your major influences?*

Oh, he was an influence on any writer of my generation. Had to be. His stories were this startling explosion
of language. The only performance of **Bringing It All
Back Home** I've ever seen was given on the back of a
truck in Central Park at a Vietnam demonstration, and
you couldn't hear any dialogue. It was written for
Vietnam moratorium day, one of those events. But
Edward certainly was an influence on **Things That Go
Bump in the Night.** I think one way Edward influenced
a lot of writers is just by subject matter. In comparison
to what was going on, the norm in Edward's theatre
seemed rude and impolite. Because Tennessee Williams
did always seem gothic and southern and somewhat
poetic, whereas Edward's voice was, "This is how we're
living in New York City right now." As much as I revere
Tennessee Williams, there's that feeling of watching a
poem, and that kind of wasn't *really* about life on the
IRT and Morningside Heights and all that. Whereas
Edward's work, I think, had that kind of energy. Tennessee Williams is kind of a dead end as a stylistic
writer. It's southern, and he's pretty much cornered that
territory, and I think you'd have to be very foolhardy to
get into that milieu after he's been there.

What about **Cuba Si** *[1968]?*

Wow, yes, that was another very specific piece, in terms
of intention. That was written for a benefit reading for
Melina Mercouri to do at Madison Square Garden. They
were raising money for the Greek junta. A lot of Greeks,
she and [Irene] Papas, they were all living here in exile.
And then it was picked up by Viveca Lindfors, who did
it quite a bit.

Cuba Si *can almost be thought of as a proto-***Perfect
Ganesh,** *in its tackling the issue of white bourgeois
complacency. Of course 1968 was a very different time.*

It's funny, you're talking about some of my work that I
really have forgotten. You're right about that. I had
hoped to expand it, and maybe I did, in a sense, through
Ganesh. But what I remember best about that play is
Melina. She had that kind of larger-than-life style,
which *I* respond to. I was never *totally* at home with
Actors' Studio style of acting. I mean, I'll take Olivier
over Marlon Brando any day, or Zoe Caldwell over
Kim Stanley. It's just my taste.

*Although your work became more concerned with the
psychological in* **Bad Habits,** *a play about two different
paths to fulfillment and ways of forming a cohesive
"identity." Act one in Ravenswood presents a hedonistic,
follow-your-bliss approach, and act two in Dunelawn
prescribes a self-abnegating, fasting from pleasure. Any
new thoughts on this topic, in the age of AIDS?*

That's very interesting, but a hard question to answer. I
think people will always follow the anything-you-do-is-
okay route, even in the age of AIDS. And the second

approach, that vigorous self-abnegation, starving
yourself, well, we know people still pursue that.
Consider the millions of people just battling with their
waistlines—that becomes so important, that they be
able to wear a size six or four dress. It will never go
away, this "we're not good enough." In both plays
people really aren't accepting who they are. But I think
our bad habits, you could also say, define who we are.
Everybody would end up all the same if all the bad
habits in the world were eradicated. AIDS hasn't
changed that.

But I think that play is more properly understood as my
having fun with psychotherapy, which seemed to be
very, very big twenty years ago, and maybe a little annoying, since all my friends were busy being analyzed
more than anything else. Some were of the school of
therapy "I'm OK, you're OK," and others were "Let's
go back and look at everything" and discover where our
personalities went "askew." I think **Bad Habits** is probably the blackest play I've ever written. I think it's *very*
negative about what it says about human change and
endeavor. In act one, the woman has totally changed
her life by the end, and the man still doesn't love her,
and her only recourse is a kind of sedation. In the
second act, I think the couples accept that we often end
up with partners because nobody else in the world
would put up with our particular foibles. So I don't
think either message is *positive,* and I think it's pes-
simistic about true change. Not like my later plays.

*AIDS, as you know, has had a tremendous impact in the
theatre community, and so many of your plays seem a
well-considered response to this. While other playwrights, for example, Larry Kramer, have written
polemical works around the subject, your work again
documents the private and often agonizing responses to
a plague in late twentieth-century America. It's intriguing that AIDS, as the acronym, as the word, isn't even
really mentioned in* **Lisbon Traviata**—*I think Stephen
refers to it obliquely. I don't know if you mention it at
all in* **Andre's Mother** . . . *once, maybe.*

I don't know either, but it's pretty clear . . . I think
actually the word is there once, I'm not sure; I'd have
to look at the text. I think AIDS affects everything we
do, in this part of the twentieth century. We don't talk
about it all the time, but it's like something sitting there
on the table. The men in **Lisbon Traviata** don't *have* to
talk about AIDS. They allude to it, certainly, but, you're
absolutely right, I don't think the word AIDS is said
there, but it's everywhere. Certainly it permeates **Lips
Together.** And I guess it's in **Ganesh,** too. I don't see
how you can write a play today—if you're writing about
contemporary life—and, if not mention it, have it as a
subtext in the play. It was certainly a subtext in **Frankie
and Johnny** without ever discussing it overtly. And
even if you're writing a period play today, I think it

would still somehow get into it—it'd be like a time when it was easier, freer, or there wasn't a specter hanging over people. Any writer who's really seriously dealing with our society must contend with AIDS. I'm trying to think of serious plays that don't, and I guess I'd be hard-pressed. In a play like **Lips,** it's a response to the situation that would never have been created without AIDS. If her brother hadn't died, they wouldn't be in that house. So, it's the way it's affected everybody's lives. And the mother in *Ganesh* who dreads her son calling to say, "I have AIDS"—the biggest fear of her life—instead gets a call that he's been murdered, sacrificed to another kind of homophobia. In fact, one of the plays I'm writing right now, **Love! Valor! Compassion!,** is about seven gay men—they're not talking about AIDS so far, but it's there. It's there if you say, "Were you at so-and-so's memorial?" There's a line in **Lips** when Sally, calling across from the deck, asks, "Were you there? Yes, wasn't it lovely?" I'm sure everyone in the audience knows she means her brother's memorial service. You don't have to *say,* "AIDS." That's what I mean, that it permeates everything.

Well, it certainly does permeate **Lips Together, Teeth Apart,** *a play about the demarcations drawn between ourselves and other people, as well as our inner and outer selves. This makes the response in Cobb County, Georgia, all the more ironic, doesn't it? Does all this controversy around this play surprise you?*

Yes, mainly because the play has been done so many times without even a ripple. As usual, of course, the man that started all of this hasn't even seen the play, only heard about it. I think it's somebody who's looking to make an issue down there, heard there was a gay play, and decided to make the issue without even bothering to see the play. And you know, he's getting support. But it's such a misreading of the play that it's bizarre. Ironically, some gay critics have accused the play of being homophobic, because it's about four uneasy people. The people in that play are homophobic, but I don't think they go around in the streets yelling, "Faggot," and loosening goon squads out to beat up gay men and women. No, they're homophobic the way I think a lot of people are. It's in that when-they-see-something-they-don't-like, under-their-breath way. But when his wife says, "John's been terrific—there's somebody on the faculty with AIDS," I believe that. I think he's probably been wonderful, despite his uneasiness. So homophobia is like a virus in them that bubbles up sometimes, and that's what I'm dealing with. I would never want to write a play about four homophobic people; that wouldn't interest me. The people who are doing this in Cobb County, I wouldn't know *how* to write a play about them, because I would hate them so much, and you can't really write characters you hate. So, to answer your question, it's a crazy play to cause

this commotion. If they were doing **Lisbon Traviata,** I would've certainly disagreed with the issues at large, but I would've understood it. This seems bizarre, to accuse this play of promoting a gay lifestyle. I just don't get it. But, as I said, the guy hadn't seen the play, so he's really a jerk in my opinion.

This theme—building barriers through granting people the status of the "other"—is carried over into **A Perfect Ganesh,** *and again the terror of AIDS is shown to evoke this response from "civilized" people. That telling line, something like, "You held an angel, and you didn't even know it."*

Yes, her own son, yes. And she's also holding an Indian child at that point. "Foolish woman," I think it was, "you held a god in your arms, and you didn't know it." I do believe there is a divinity in all of us, and we all are perfect in a way. It's such a change from what I wrote about in **Bad Habits.** I think we all are divine and perfect, but we set up so many rules. I talk about that a lot in **Frankie and Johnny.** Because give me another five minutes and I'll think of a million things I don't like about you, the way you hold a pencil, the way you cross your legs. It's so *easy* to find what separates us, and we're so frightened of what connects us, and it's so easy to say, "He's a Jew, he's a faggot, he's a nigger." I think it's out of terror of one another and of intimacy that we become racist and homophobic and sexist and all these things. Likewise I think men are terrified of the intimacy women seem to want to offer them, so they relegate them and keep them apart.

It's really become a very big theme in my writing, which I wasn't aware of, but now you're having me look back, and it's in all the plays. When Margaret has a chance in **Ganesh** to reveal that she also has lost an infant, and she *doesn't,* some people have pointed out that they didn't understand *why* she didn't. In fact, one fellow playwright said, "You must rewrite one scene, then you've got a big hit: that scene on the train when she says, 'Well, there's one thing that we'll never have in common; I lost a son.' And the other one has the chance where she can tell her that *she too lost a son,* and then they become friends." He completely missed the point of what I was trying to do, that Margaret respected the other woman's grief and privacy too much to sort of one-up her. I think maybe one day she does tell her, when they get back to Connecticut, but to have told her there would have been on the order of, "Oh, you think you have a bad life!" That was what was so wonderful about Margaret. She didn't have the need at that point to *top* her. She's allowing Catherine her grief.

I think that that issue, the barriers between people, and why they stay there, will always interest me. I don't know what AIDS, being fifty-four, this society, have to do with it all. I think so many forces impinge on us and make us write the things we do. And I think it's after the work is done that people start tracing themes in your writing. I know there are writers who start out with "themes." My plays usually begin about people that interest me, and a journey, and I've gotten more and more interested in using the theatre. I thought it was very *theatrical* of me not to have the gay men on-stage—I could've put them on so easily—and then to read that the play is homophobic, when the gays are reduced to offstage characters, it *completely* misses the point of what I was trying to do. In **Ganesh** I suddenly got interested in masks and more of an expressionistic kind of play, and I feel less and less need for scenery. I like more of an acting space to work in.

A lot of my early plays are either satirical or have an element of satire in them. That interests me very little at the moment, because satire always implies a certain kind of condescension to your characters, as in **Bad Habits.** I think the turning point play for me, in terms of where I am now, was **It's Only a Play,** which is part satiric and part heartfelt. And that's the intention. I've seen productions of it where the balance was not captured, and there should be some really touching moments in **It's Only a Play,** if it's done well, and that's what I intended. And I have seen some productions where it was just silly all evening.

In **It's Only a Play,** *a producer, director, actress, playwright are all awaiting Frank Rich's verdict in the* New York Times. *Now that Rich is handing over the reins—and one might say "reign"—to someone else, would you care to comment on his role in the development of New York, and, by extension, American, theatre in the past decade?*

I would feel free to even if he weren't. It's very hard to talk . . . because you end up talking about Frank Rich, and the issue is that we have one newspaper, and somehow, through tradition, people worry about what New York papers say about a play. They don't worry about what New York papers say about a movie or a TV show. Thousands of movies become big hits without the approval of the *New York Times.* TV shows that the *New York Times* hated entertain fifty million people every night. But when I first came to New York, there were about eight daily newspapers, so we're really not talking about Frank Rich, we're talking about the *Times.* I think we've got to find a way to change that.

If we found a way to develop dialogue about theatre so it wasn't just, "What did Frank Rich say?" . . . we're all very aware when Frank Rich does not give you an enthusiastic review. For a play like **Ganesh,** his less-than-enthusiastic review made it very hard for us. Every performance was like a victory! But we can't blame the

New York Times. It's our fault! We have empowered that paper. If they give us a good review, we take a full-page ad out. If every producer in New York said, "We're never going to advertise in the *New York Times,*" signed a solid pact, and the only way you could find out even when a play began or what was opening that week was to buy an independent journal, and [if the journal were to] hire twenty critics, twenty opinions on each play, and it costs fifty cents a week or a dollar a week, I think people would buy that paper. I think there should be *more* newspapers, *more* critics! Everybody's a critic, after all.

It's not going to change overnight. But we have done this to ourselves. And we have not done anything to develop theatregoing as a habit in which you go to hear various and opposed viewpoints about the way we live today expressed. To me that's what a theatre is; it's a public forum for what's going on in our society. And it's become like the flavor of the month, "This is the hit, that's the hit," and it's like there's only room for one hit at a time. And I think we should do one performance a week free for anyone under eighteen, just to see what happens. Maybe no one would even show up, which is really scary, because they're all at the movies or playing video games. There aren't many young "stage-struck" people, the way I was. Theatre is something their parents or people my age do. Theatre sounds boring to most young people.

You're teaching young people now. Do you find that many of them want to start writing for film and television?

Well, if they do, they wouldn't dare tell me, because that's a no-no of the class. You're supposed to be committed to being a playwright. But it is obviously what's happening. A lot of gifted writers are quickly snatched up by Hollywood. I think maybe they say, "How'm I ever gonna get produced or get established in New York?"

So I say to all my students at Juilliard, "Start your own theatres; it's the only way you're gonna have a theatre." You know, Caffe Cino and La Mama have been romanticized a lot. But it was really hard working in those theatres in the sixties. People forget that these plays by Lanford Wilson and John Guare, Sam Shepard—plays now regarded as contemporary classics—*all* started this way. It was hard. It was fun, but it was hard. Now La Mama's sort of a big deal, with a budget and international prestige and everything. It wasn't then. When I was getting started, *anyone* could have their work done at La Mama. That's not true now. Practically everyone they do now is an established writer.

Yes, but critics have a hand in establishing these writers. Given the power of the critical apparatus of the

New York Times, *how has Frank Rich—considering his taste, his critical prejudices as well as his insights— shaped American drama for the last ten years?*

I actually think Frank Rich, who has been good and bad to me, all told, has been a positive critic for the new writers, and I think he cares about theatre. I think he's stage-struck and really cares about it. Sure, I wished he liked **Ganesh** more, but he loved **Lips Together** and **Frankie and Johnny.** I just wish, at this stage in my life, there were enough people who would be interested in any play I wrote that I wouldn't have to go through that again, that there was like a McNally audience. You know, by the time Tennessee Williams died, there wasn't even a Tennessee Williams audience left, and that's kind of a sad comment on the falling-off of the loyal theatregoers.

Tell me about this biography of Tennesse Williams you will be working on.

Marty Duberman has been asked to publish and edit a series of books written for young readers, ages fourteen to eighteen, presenting gay people in a style accessible to a young gay audience. My contribution is more a long essay on Tennessee Williams, what he's meant to me, and why I think his work is so important and lasting. And I hope that a young person will read this and feel encouraged. For a whole generation such as mine, there were no positive gay role models. Even Oscar Wilde, in my high school, you didn't know who he was. I think this is potentially a very important series. It's an appreciation of Tennessee Williams, written from the viewpoint of another gay playwright. And things have changed, obviously, about being "out" since he worked. Whenever I hear young people critical of Tennessee Williams for not being "out," I just think, "Well, you're too young, you don't know what it was like, and he was pretty terrific, what he did." His plays were really considered shocking in their day, and it's hard, I guess, for someone who's twenty-five to know that *Cat on a Hot Tin Roof* was considered shocking, or in *Suddenly Last Summer,* that homosexuality was even *acknowledged* as a subject. And Tennessee Williams wrote some gay characters in the last few plays of his life, and the plays were not very successful. They were done Off-Off-Off-Broadway, and many people have never even *heard* of them, but they were done. Most people think of them nowadays as never having been performed, because he had sort of really fallen out of favor. People just weren't interested in his work anymore. *Not interested in Tennessee Williams!* And I don't know how that can happen to an artist that's given so much.

Well, I look forward to your book.

(*Laughs*) Me, too. But I'm a *long way* from writing it, and all I can think of is my new play at the moment. So, we'll just wait and see when it happens.

Terrence McNally and David Savran (interview date 23 June 1998)

SOURCE: McNally, Terrence and David Savran. "Terrence McNally." In *The Playwright's Voice: American Dramatists on Memory, Writing, and the Politics of Culture,* pp. 123-38. New York: Theatre Communications Group, 1999.

[*In the following interview, conducted June 23, 1998, Savran asks McNally about how his start in theater, the importance of risky elements in his works, and the increasing prevalence of homosexuality in American theater.*]

[*Savran*]: *You could start by telling me how you got interested in theatre.*

[McNally]: Got interested in theatre as opposed to just enjoying it—I've always enjoyed theatre. My very early memories as a child involve theatre. Right after the war we lived for a while in Port Chester, New York, and I remember watching *Kukla, Fran and Ollie* and *Howdy Doody* on television. And I didn't care for *Howdy Doody,* because I thought he was too real, with the strings and mouth moving. But I loved *Kukla, Fran and Ollie,* which took place on a little stage within a stage— the interaction between Fran Allison and these archetypes. That stage was very real to me, and I made my own theatre down in the basement. I had copies of Kukla and Ollie. Once I read an interview in which Edward Albee talked about no one ever detecting the great influence of Kukla and Ollie in his work, especially the early plays like *American Dream.* And then when I was really young, my parents took me to see *Annie Get Your Gun,* which was the first play I guess I saw. This would have been about 1944 or '45 when I was six or seven years old, and that had an enormous impact on me. When we moved to Texas, Corpus Christi had no television station. Even all through high school, it only had kinescope television, so I didn't get to see those very popular shows that most of my generation loved—we were still watching the old kinescopes of *Kukla, Fran and Ollie.*

So even through high school I still listened to radio, *Masterpiece Theatre, the Shadow, the Phantom* and comic book versions of *Treasure Island, The Prince and the Pauper,* those kinds of things. That was a great appeal to my imagination, and also by that age I had fallen madly in love with opera. When I was in the sixth grade a nun played some recordings for us and I just liked it instantly. I didn't have to learn to like it. I listened to the Metropolitan broadcasts and I made a stage, and I would stage *Aida* and *Rigoletto* while they were broadcasting. Most of my stages weren't very original, I would just copy the pictures in *Opera News* magazine. These were also places my mind wandered.

I started buying a lot of show albums. My parents were native New Yorkers and came up to New York at least once a year and would always come back with programs. My father liked shows like *South Pacific* and *Kiss Me, Kate,* and Edith Piaf, whom he played a lot, which I think developed my taste for rather eccentric, rather identifiable voices like Callas rather than a generic soprano sound like Tebaldi or Sutherland. There was no theatre in my high school. The only play I remember seeing was *Picnic,* because this sad spinster teacher was playing Rosemary, and we just wanted to see her go to pieces and rip the guy's shirt off just like in the movie. And for all the wrong reasons, that's about the only play I remember seeing in Corpus Christi. Opera was as much an influence on me as theatre. For a period we moved to Dallas and they had this huge theatre for operettas, Starlight Operettas, they were called. They had a reputation for getting stars to do shows they never would have done on Broadway, or developing shows that went on to Broadway. They had to compete with june bugs, big beetles that fly around and are particularly attracted to light. And there was a famous night when one flew down the front of June Havoc's dress and she literally went berserk on stage. She was on the floor, she had little convulsions, she was so upset at the idea of some beetle crawling around in her cleavage and brassiere, whereas most of us were used to these flying bugs and batted them away. This was before we had air-conditioning, so the only bearable theatre would have been outdoors.

When we moved to Corpus Christi, opera was more accessible than theatre, the San Antonio Opera, the Metropolitan Opera toured to Dallas. A bunch of us who liked opera conned one of our mothers into driving us up to Dallas on the weekend to see three operas in two days. Opera was a form of theatre, but theatre was *Annie Get Your Gun.* When we lived in Dallas, stage shows would come through periodically. I remember Mary Martin in *Annie Get Your Gun* and Carol Channing in *Gentlemen Prefer Blondes* and other Broadway shows, but also *Red Mill, Naughty Marietta, Rose Marie.* This was long before I thought of becoming a playwright. I remember once I said something terrible to my brother, and my punishment was not going to see *Paint Your Wagon,* and I was really, really upset. I remember I couldn't believe it when my parents took off to see it without me—that was like capital punishment.

So, obviously the theatre spoke to me on some deep emotional level and I still don't know what it is. It's like Boy Scouts sitting around the campfire and the scoutmaster tells you a story and you get open-mouthed, wide-eyed. I don't think I considered writing for theatre until sometime after college. When I was at Columbia I wrote the varsity show my senior year, but that was more of a lark. I still thought I was going to be a journalist, and that seemed more appropriate for a pre-journalism major because it was a spoof. It was about a lot of the celebrities of the day. There was a film company that went to Africa where they were making this film and exploiting the natives, but what they didn't know was that the natives were cannibals. And one by one they were eating the crew until only the ingenue and juvenile were alive at the curtain call. Evil people from Western capitalism had been destroyed, and Ed Kleban, who wrote the lyrics for *A Chorus Line,* wrote the music and lyrics, and Michael Kahn directed it. I was always involved with writing. In grade school I was writing puns and stories, and in high school I was the editor of my school newspaper and founded a literary magazine.

The summer of my junior year in high school I went to Northwestern. There's a famous program where they choose twenty-five outstanding students from around the country, and you go there free and pretend you're a real journalist for six weeks, and it's the first time I'd really been away from home and it was very exciting. My roommate was Jerry Rubin. It was fun when he became Jerry Rubin. I have one friend, a poet, to whom I've stayed close all these years. I had wonderful influences and opportunities as a young man to explore the feelings I had for the arts. My parents were probably as supportive as they could be, even though their idea of becoming a writer was probably writing for *Time* magazine. They thought anyone who wrote independently was asking for poverty. It was certainly not the nineteenth century, "You will become a doctor," or something like that. And there were always playbills on the table. I remember them talking about *Death of a Salesman* and *Streetcar,* they saw shows I think all of America saw, when Broadway was still where you went for intelligent writing. Movies were kind of a stepchild.

There were always people to point the way, a teacher in high school in Texas who cared about the English language and taught us the glories of Shakespeare. I'm one person who was not traumatized by her introduction of Shakespeare. Quite the opposite, she had such a humane and simple approach to him, she taught him as a playwright and not a poet. I'm just so grateful. I read Shakespeare a lot and he's such a profound force in my life, and so many bright friends of mine can't stand Shakespeare—and these are very good playwrights who read *Hamlet* or *Macbeth* in high school. I spent a lot of time at Columbia with him, the whole works and then a seminar just in *King Lear* for a year.

Coming to New York was very fortuitous. I applied to Harvard, Yale and Columbia, and I needed a scholarship and Harvard didn't give me a scholarship, and Yale and Columbia gave me the same scholarship. My best friend and I flipped a coin, because we thought it was silly to go to the same school. He got Yale and I got Columbia, and as it turned out, part of my education became being in New York. I got here in the fall of '56, the tail end of the "golden age" of Broadway, plays by Tennessee Williams and Arthur Miller, and musicals by Rodgers and Hammerstein, and Frank Loesser were still happening with some regularity. You couldn't see all the shows in a season unless you were a critic. It's like Off-Off-Broadway now, there's so much product. I saw a lot of shows. I also went to the opera and the ballet a lot. It was a great day for Balanchine at the City Ballet, and at City Opera Beverly Sills was fabulous and no one knew who she was yet. And the debut of Callas— all those things I would have been denied had I been stuck up in New Haven.

I've never studied playwriting but I've seen a lot of plays and I took some courses in theatre at Columbia. Eric Bentley had a course in modern drama which was pretty much his paperback volumes in modern Italian, French and German theatre. Other than the Shakespeare, I think that was the only theatre course I took. Besides New York, Columbia didn't have a lot. Theatre was totally extracurricular. Michael [Kahn], with all of his work, was extracurricular. The only time I've ever acted was at Columbia when Michael directed a production of *The Little Prince,* and I was taking a lot of French courses and he encouraged me to be in it, saying it would help me lose my inhibition of speaking French in public. Everyone else in the cast was a native Frenchman, and coming backstage, I only understood enough to hear them say, "It was wonderful except for that terrible American with that horrible accent playing the fox." Skipping ahead, the only other time I did act was in a little workshop at Actors Studio, and I was physically ill on the day we did it. I knew everyone in the audience. It was like I was hurled out onto a Broadway stage. My knees literally shook, and I had uncontrollable twitches in my face, and I think I threw up a few times before the play began and it was so horrible. That cliché, you could see his knees trembling through his slacks—you literally could.

How did you get involved in Off-Off-Broadway?

I wrote a one-act after college called *This Side of the Door* [1961], which I sent to Actors Studio. And because of that I got a job as stage manager at Playwright's Union despite the fact that I had no practical knowledge of theatre. I had no idea how a director worked with actors or anything like that. But Molly Kazan, Elia Kazan's wife, said, "There's a job here as stage manager and I think you'll learn a lot about how a play's put together, how actors work, how directors work." So I did that for two years and learned a lot.

And then Barr-Wilder-Albee did *This Side of the Door.* That was the first time I ever heard my lines spoken by professional actors. Estelle Parsons—she was magnificent—played the lead. It was done at the Cherry Lane for two weekends. And that was not even considered Off-Off-Broadway in those days, it was considered a workshop because Off-Broadway was very healthy. There were many more theatres and it was when Beckett, Albee, Ionesco and a whole generation of American writers, Jack Richardson, Arthur Kopit, Jack Gelber, were all being done Off-Broadway. You could be at the Cherry Lane or the Actor's Playhouse or the Provincetown because these theatres were so small.

So Off-Off-Broadway came out of Off-Broadway facing the same economic problems that Broadway was to face in the seventies and eighties. But in the sixties, Off-Broadway was very fertile—hundreds of theatres and lots of activity. This was the height of Circle in the Square reestablishing O'Neill as a writer, the Brecht-Weill evenings, *Brecht on Brecht* and *Threepenny Opera.* It was seen as an alternative to Broadway, and the difference in ticket prices was enormous. Everyone forgets. Right now, to go to the Manhattan Theatre Club costs five to ten dollars less than to see *Art* or whatever play happens to be on Broadway. It used to be, if a Broadway play was twenty dollars, Off-Broadway was five. Now, no one goes to Off-Broadway because it's cheaper. It was the only way to see all this great surrogate European drama, the Theatre of the Absurd, Genet and people like that. Those plays were not being done on Broadway. So the question is really how did I get involved with Off-Broadway, because my first play was on Broadway. In many ways, everything's changed and nothing's changed.

My first play that I put in the credits, ***Things That Go Bump in the Night,*** was a very long one-act, an hour and a half, three scenes, and it was too on-the-nose autobiographically and emotionally. Too much airing of family business. I didn't enjoy watching it. I thought, That's not the purpose of theatre. I should be able to watch the play with the normal discomfort of seeing my work up there as opposed to, Would this upset my mother and father and brother if they saw this? It just seems an inappropriate use of theatre. While I was at Actors Studio, I wrote ***Things That Go Bump in the Night,*** which we did there with minimal sets and props and a very good cast. Then in Minneapolis we had a full production and a new cast. So in a way, I did a workshop, an out-of-town tryout, and then New York. Which is what happened with ***Ragtime*** [1996] or ***Master Class,*** which we did originally in the town of Big Fork, Montana, then at a little theatre in Philadelphia, then at the Taper, then the Kennedy Center. So things are the same but they're wildly, wildly different, too.

Reading your work and hearing you talk about opera and theatre, I've noticed that your plays are so self-

consciously about the theatre and dramatic literature. I'm thinking about the highly theatricalized relationship between Steven and Michael in **The Lisbon Traviata;** *or* **Lips Together, Teeth Apart** *[1991], a comedy of infidelity with its references to* Cosi fan tutte, *another comedy of infidelity; and of course* **Master Class,** *with Maria looking back at her different roles. How conscious are you of that in your writing?*

Maybe not as conscious as you think. For example, I never thought of *Cosi* as a comedy about infidelity until you just said it. But **Lips Together** is a play very much about fidelity and infidelity. I chose that music because that trio to me is a prayer for safe passage. In the context of that play, life is very fragile and it's a moment of prayer. Going back to *Kukla, Fran and Ollie,* I'm not interested in naturalism, my plays are always plays, and the actors I work with most successfully are not internal, Actors Studio method actors. They enjoy being in a play and you know they are acting for you and it gives them great pleasure. That doesn't mean they are any less honest than the method actor who loses himself and it's all about truth, truth, truth. "This is exactly how I felt when my mother died." I would rather see that theatricalized, made into a little larger gesture. Almost every actor I've worked with I've learned from enormously. If you look at people like Zoë Caldwell, Nathan Lane, Christine Baranski, actors I really admire, they're aware the audience is there. I like that dialogue. I like being welcomed to the theatre. Lately I've started using narrative more, but always think, We know you, the audience, are here, let's find out what connects us. When I write a play, I don't write the truth, a documentary, a proto-real experience, I write a play by Terrence McNally. I like the devices of Shakespeare. I have asides, monologues, soliloquies in my plays. I like the devices of opera: arias, trios, cabalettas.

Usually actors say it's very easy to learn my dialogue. The only play where they had trouble was **Lips Together,** because there are a lot of trios, quartets, four people with different conversations, under the house talking to people on the deck, talking to people in the bedroom, behind the screen. I was trying consciously to work like music there. In the last act, after John goes into the pool, it becomes a verbal quartet. I don't know if it really works, but I wanted a canon, overlapped dialogue, four people doing interior monologues. In real life people do not verbalize four monologues in a situation and then freeze—so I would say my theatre is theatrical. My art is painterly realism, and my theatre is very real to me, but it's theatre and a different reality from you and me sitting here. That seems who I am. I never wanted to write a fourth-wall play. Or totally didactic theatre—I'm not terribly drawn to the works of Brecht. I feel I'm being lectured, and things are being demonstrated to me. You see three or four plays as a child, you listen to two operas, you have this high

school English teacher, you go to Columbia, and that all adds up and you write this sort of play.

If I have any sort of artistic credo, I would say it's almost entirely **Master Class.** That's in many ways the most autobiographical play I've written, and I just put all these outrageous thoughts about art into Maria Callas's mouth. I honestly believe she probably wouldn't have said them but would have agreed with them. She wasn't known for her articulation about the world of art. But it's a very autobiographical play of my feelings. I went through a terrible period after I wrote it, after seeing it. I thought I would never write another play. It seemed very valedictory to me. But that passed, and I moved on to other projects. I like writing, I like being in rehearsal. Almost everything else about theatre has gotten very unpleasant. The commerce of it, the business, the fact that a show has to become an institutional hit, run for twenty years, to be considered successful. That's not a new story. People don't want to see a new play by a good writer, it has to become a media frenzy. *Corpus Christi* has become a "story," and that's totally the doing of an irresponsible journalist at the *Post.* It's not something we welcome or love.

I'm interested to hear you talk about the importance of a theatre that acknowledges its theatricality because you sometimes seem intent on bringing up things that are difficult to articulate in other ways. And I've noticed a change in your writing. Your plays of the past few years strike me as more risky, both in terms of form and subject matter, than most of your earlier work.

I'm not sure I would agree with that. I think they're less judgmental of the characters. I'm less conspicuous than I was in my early work. You could divide my work into that which promotes my opinion of the characters and that which tries to let the characters be themselves. There's a big difference. Friends even say, "Your work used to be so much riskier." They always point to **Tommy Flowers** [**Where Has Tommy Flowers Gone?,** 1971] as being so risky and experimental. Those are exactly the kinds of things, one, I don't think about and, two, it's bad to think about, because you get writer's block. "Is this play risky enough?" That's for critics, people like you. **Master Class** is really not a play. The program said, "A Master Class with Maria Callas in the Singer's Program at Juilliard." The play's taking place in real time. Certainly, **Corpus Christi** is very theatrical, and **Ragtime.** The first line is to the audience and in the first number they all sing about who they are in the third person. These are all techniques, maybe I'll discard them. The next couple plays I have in mind are plays where there is actually a fourth wall. So maybe I'm going back to something.

There are only two plays I wrote overnight, *Next,* the play that got me out of journalism and earning a living as a playwright, and **Master Class,** where I just had a vision. I knew the first line, "No applause," and the last line, "Well, that's that." I was at a benefit dinner writing on a program. I think about most of my plays, like **Corpus Christi,** for two or three years minimum, and then I wait and turn on the computer when I feel like I'm not just going to sit there and think, Now wait, how am I going to write a play called **Corpus Christi**? How do I write this play about Christ? I don't think, This should be more theatrical. This play's not going to have monologues, but address the audience instead. This play's going to have audience participation. Every so often I do. In **Master Class** she talked to the audience quite a bit, and in the original draft of **Love! Valour!** there's much more of that. I think they were self-conscious. I like the *idea* of talking to the audience, but in reality I hate it. I hate it when an actor addresses me, especially when he wants a response from me, so it's especially sadistic of me to put it in my own plays. There's four or five passages from **Love! Valour!** that didn't make it to the first preview.

So there's writing that comes easily emotionally to you, that's maybe just a technical thing. And there's making the play work. Basically you want to keep the audience in their chairs for two to three hours. That's the primary goal and everything else is just talk. There's nothing worse than seeing a play and sensing that massive indifference, that absolute void of nonenergy between stage and performance. I think that's the most horrible sound of silence in the world. There's also the very painful thing of seeing audiences leave at intermission. Lately, I've done two three-act plays where you have two chances to lose them. So much of rehearsal is about how do we keep this alive and interesting, not intellectual conversations about meaning. You never discuss meaning with a director and an actor, you discuss why a line doesn't work, why an audience is restless at a certain point. Theatre is incredibly tactical, and it's the only art form where you are so involved with other people. It is a collaboration.

I don't know exactly what percentage of the draft that goes into rehearsal becomes the final product. I sometimes think it's not much more than fifty percent. When you go to **Master Class,** you experience the set, the lighting, the contributions of Zoë Caldwell, Michael McGarty, Lenny Foglia. It's not all me. If **Master Class** had been done with a different director, designer and actress, it would have been a very different experience. I've been very good lately about getting what I want on a stage, that's why I write for specific actors. I know the directors I want to work with, and the designers. John Guare and I were teaching playwriting for a year at Juilliard and our theme was: be responsible for who does your sets and costumes. I don't design the sets and costumes, but I have a stake in it. It's difficult working with really good people that share a vision. So many playwrights get passive when it comes to production.

"They're giving my play to Peter Brook. They're letting Martha Graham do the choreography." Well, maybe Peter Brook and Martha Graham are not the right people to do *Pal Joey.* You've got to say, "No, I don't think this work is in their vocabulary."

People talk about the theatre as if the text were everything. I think it's just a part. I don't think you can talk about a play without talking about the production. When you talk about *Streetcar,* you're talking about Marlon Brando and Vivien Leigh and that movie. How can you erase these memories? It's not this flat, two-dimensional thing that we read. That's what's special about theatre. *Moby-Dick* is in two dimensions, but when you experience *Hamlet* you experience him in three dimensions, and it seems to me you cannot separate notions of what Hamlet looks like or is about from Gielgud, Burton, Olivier, Kevin Kline. It makes it a very special art form. I think you can interview Ernest Hemingway and get the essence of anything by Ernest Hemingway. I don't think you can talk to me about theatre without talking to a thousand other people that contributed to what I consider to be theatre.

I'm thinking of **A Perfect Ganesh,** *for example, and how crucial the lighting is in producing a sense of the sublime.*

Lighting is very, very important to me. Only recently have I started to get the lighting I want. That was an example of being disappointed in the lighting, but not speaking up, thinking, That's technical. Now I feel that a lighting designer is a collaborator and I'm much more eager to hear his impressions of the text, how lighting could enhance it, but also to give him my ideas for it. Brian MacDevitt did my last play and Jules Fisher and Peggy Eisenhauer did **Ragtime.** It's extraordinary work. I used to work with a lot of different people who said, "Here are your lights. Good-bye." Now these designers are there through previews, when the critics come in. I want to work with people who care 101 percent and I know that's obvious, but a lot of people don't. I've gotten in trouble when my own aims are 101 percent. It takes enormous effort on everyone's part. Nothing is good enough in the theatre, unless it's right. You can't be almost right.

Sound is very important to me. I sometimes have to say, "There should be a dog barking here." "Was that important to you?" "Yes, or I wouldn't have put it in." I have no stage directions, I never write, "Crying through her tears sardonically." I never write those kinds of descriptions. When I write, "A dog barks," and it's the only sound effect in the entire act, I want to hear it. I think Lee Strasberg did a terrible disservice. I hope his influence is starting to fade, because I remember him saying to actors and directors, "The first thing to do is to cross out all the playwright's directions, including set descriptions and indications to the actor." And maybe that's where the barking dog gets overlooked, or the lights rise to a blinding intensity. Lee Strasberg was always contemptuous towards playwrights' punctuation. To me, it's the same as reading a Mozart score: that's a quarter note, that's an eighth note. If you make them both eighth notes, it's not the same melody. Zoë Caldwell said to me, "You're very easy to act, I just follow your punctuation." Nathan Lane, another actor with whom I've worked very well, just says every word as I wrote it. The actor needs just to show up and say it. You don't need to embellish it with "oh," "ah," "I mean," mucking about it. In the cast of **Ragtime,** no one adds a comma to the script. When actors add all this other music, suddenly it's not me anymore. I get so crazy about that. I think it's sloppy. The music of a play is there. You try to find people who say, "You've given me all I have, the script, the words, the music, let me sing it to you." As opposed to actors who say, "This is your script, let me make it mine." That's the kind of actor I don't work very happily with.

A lot of actors and directors don't look at the basic stage directions. It's really unimportant whether a character is standing or sitting. Playwrights who still write "crossing downstage right" are wasting time. Who cares? That's not what makes a scene work. The actors will find a place to be if the scene is well written. These other details are part of what I consider the score of the music and the lighting. I'm not very good at describing things, which is maybe why I'm a playwright, not a novelist. I couldn't look around and describe this apartment, but I could have a drunken divorcee in her early fifties who's thinking about having a facelift describe it, or a teenage boy describe his apartment. I write dialogue as opposed to a more objective observation, so I try to give an indication in my first stage direction of the style of the play. I remember the beginning of ***Love! Valour! Compassion!*** was nothing like what Joe [Mantello] and Loy [Arcenas] came up with. But they could tell I did not want a realistic set. Before Joe was going to direct it, I'd spoken to directors who said, "We're going to need two turntables." I said, "The first stage direction makes it so clear that I don't want realistic scenery. A chair becomes a car." They just didn't get what I wanted. So a stage direction is a description of the kind of set which is a way of saying, "This is the kind of designer I think is right for this show." The first thing an audience sees is the set. The psychology of scenery and colors and light—there's no getting around that. A stunning example of that would be ***The Ritz.*** We did it in Washington, and it got very, very few laughs. We thought it was hysterical. Someone came to see it and they said, "The set is three stories tall and battleship gray, it looks so foreboding." The producer ordered a paint call, and stayed up all night and painted the whole thing red. The next night, with no other changes at all, the laughs started right away. I thought, You can write

five hundred plays and never know that the battleship gray set will not be conducive to a sex farce.

So much of this is about taking the audience on a ride, and your job is to engineer that in every way, including working with designers.

It's our job, yes. Every play has different rules. Writing **Love! Valour! Compassion!** only helps you write *Love! Valour! Compassion! II*, not **Master Class** or **Corpus Christi.** Actors can create a persona and do it for ten movies and get away with it, but playwrights can't. Everyone talks differently. If you read Shakespeare, you may not know a passage is specifically from *Othello*, but you know it's not *Hamlet*. They're all different sound worlds. You make that a goal: how do I create this world through my words? It's got to be in the text, if everyone talks the same from play to play, it won't work.

And there are other elements that also produce the unique character of a play. I was thinking about how the nudity in **Love! Valour! Compassion!** *is so important in producing an almost transcendent, sublime vision of sexuality.*

The design helped. Randy [Becker]'s nice ass to look at up there. The lights just go and the crickets chirp louder. Joe and Brian really worked to give me what I wanted. I didn't even write the stage direction, and I've seen other productions where the lights just stay the same through act two. There's not that moment where they're struck dumb by nature. It also comes during that speech about Alaska and the glacier and there's this incredible silence. In other productions that moment doesn't exist. It's supposed to be nonverbal for a moment or two. Silence is very important in my work. It's there, I can't make a director do it. They did a production of **Lips Together** up in Providence, and at the end of the play, the actors saw the shooting stars and then Mozart comes on and then the lights come up in the audience just as they do on stage. It was a very good production, the music plays, and they're frozen, and the lights start coming up in the auditorium and three and a half, four minutes later, we're all in the same room, in the same light, and then everything went out. It was thrilling. They didn't do that in New York. I said to the director, "Why did you do that?" He said, "It's in your script." It was in the published version, and I'd forgotten I'd left it in. It's so interesting to see someone do what I actually wanted, and I thought it worked. It's pretty scary to stand there for three and a half, four minutes, but it worked. You've just got to take risks. I think a gesture like that says, "This play's about you, these are human beings groping through marriage, fidelity, infidelity, mortality, homophobia, all the things that trouble these people. They're not actors, they've just been tap-dancing out here all night. Let's all listen to this sublime piece of Mozart together. We're all in this thing called life together."

The theme of **Lisbon Traviata** is people trying to connect and failing. I think there's some real connection between people in **Love! Valour!** There's virtually none in **Master Class**—she's trapped in a world of art, as much as Mendy is in **Lisbon Traviata.** There's a world of beauty and wholeness when she sings, but when she's Maria Callas she's as fucked-up as anybody who ever lived. She's a terrible teacher in trying to communicate what she has that made her great. It's her secret, and she can't give it away because she doesn't know what it is. So she gets very angry, "I want some of your genius, your fire. I'm not here to give tips." It's like when I'm teaching playwriting. "How do you get an agent? How do you get your play produced?" No, let's talk about why your scene doesn't work. Frustrating. I don't think it's impossible to communicate with another person, but I think it's difficult. That's really important to me. I find theatre very visceral and very central. I want theatre that has the immediacy of a good lasagna or an exquisite wine. To me you can feel it and taste it, the theatre is not a place to exercise your mind. I want the theatre to introduce me to people I would not meet in my own life, shock me, startle me, but I don't want it to tell me what I should be thinking.

It should seduce.

Yes, theatre is very sensual. And ballet is a form of theatre I'm very drawn to. I go to ballet quite a bit. My favorite painters have a very strong dramatic sense, like Giotto, who is an incredibly dramatic painter. And the relationships between people, how do you get to that moment of the Judas kiss? Writing **Corpus Christi,** I'm very aware of that moment in the Giotto fresco of the life of Christ. The paintings are well staged, he is a masterful director. The angle he chooses, his point of view towards the material is dramatic and useful to me as a playwright. Every playwright has to go his own road, and maybe there are very good playwrights who don't go to the museum or the ballet. I have a lot of friends who are excellent playwrights who don't go to the theatre much. I happen to enjoy going to the theatre, and also that's where you find the Lenny Foglias and Joe Mantellos of tomorrow, by going to workshop productions. If you wait until they're on Broadway and being nominated and winning Tony awards, then everybody wants them and they're not going to go to Big Fork, Montana, to work on **Master Class** with you.

It seems to me that in the years you've been writing, the American theatre has really become much more explicitly gay. It's almost as if it's coming round to you rather than the other way around.

I don't know if I agree. People happen to be out and there are a lot of damned good playwrights who happen to be gay. I don't think that American theatre is becoming gayer. Even ten or fifteen years ago, Paula Vogel's play [*How I Learned to Drive*] would have been done and she would probably have been out. I just think there's a lot of really good playwrights now who happen to be gay, I don't see theatre getting gayer. There's always been a very significant number of great actors, writers, directors who have been gay.

I agree that there've always been a lot of gay men and lesbians active in theatre. But it seems to me that people are more out now than they were a decade ago, and also there's a certain sexual frankness that's more permissible.

Unquestionably.

You couldn't have written some of the characters and events in your recent plays twenty years ago.

My very first play, **And Things That Go Bump in the Night,** was considered really shocking because there were two gay men in it. In a way, I feel I've even been punished for it. That certainly wasn't a masterpiece, but people were really shocked by the relationship between the two men. I think people have stopped being shocked by gay characters. Now it has to be a good play. Additionally, they've stopped saying, "Mr. McNally's homosexual and the women characters are inauthentic." I think a gay playwright can write gay or heterosexual characters without that kind of comment. I'd like to believe that. Anne Heche has opened in a romantic comedy without anyone going hysterical about it. I really think the climate I grew up in has changed. You remember about Tennessee Williams and Edward Albee, the horrible, horrible homophobic critics. I'm so glad they can't get away with that anymore. They either like *Tiny Alice* or they don't. I just think that's terrific. I'm all for everything that's happened in terms of frankness in writing about sex. I'm surprised heterosexuals haven't been quite as frank in writing about sexual relationships. Sex is very important in my work. And then there are other writers for whom sex never seems to be of interest. It's the difference between apples and oranges.

The only criticism of, say, **Love! Valour!** that offended me was that the nudity was gratuitous or it was an attempt to please a gay audience. That really angered me, it just wasn't true. The nudity is an incredible part of **Love! Valour!** I'm saying these people have dicks— just like you—some of them have flabby asses and some don't—just like you. When a theatre says, "We'd love to do **Love! Valour!** but we can't have nudity," I say, "Don't do the play then." If it can't be a spontaneous, "Hey, let's go swimming!" Now if someone comes out nude or in a jockstrap and starts erotic dancing to turn the audience on, that is a very different use of the naked body than skinny-dipping, which is the most innocent pastime—that's when we all become children, we rip our clothes off and jump in the lake. I've had theatres say, "We'd love to do your play, but there's too many four-letter words, can we take them out?" I say, "Don't do my play." That's like saying, "We're gonna show the *David* here, but we're gonna put pants on him," then you're not showing the *David*. I have no problem if you don't want to do **Love! Valour! Compassion!** because of the nudity and the four-letter words, and the physical contact between men. I'm sorry you have that problem in your community. You should aspire to resolve these problems, but don't do the play with bathing suits and the men never kissing or touching each other and someone not saying, "Fuck you." Then it's not my play. Do my play or don't do it—don't do a bowdlerized version.

So, I don't think there's gay theatre anymore. I think there's less now than there was fifteen years or so ago. We begin with *Boys in the Band*. I think people say whether plays are good or bad. People say, "Is yours a good play? It's about three lesbians. It's about eight gay men." Not, "Let's go see it, there's naked men, these cute guys take their clothes off." The whole gay community has changed. In the sixties we used to go to restaurants because they were gay and the food was horrible, but we thought it was so important that two openly gay men could sit in the middle of the restaurant on X Street. Now, we're too integrated, a gay restaurant has to be as good as a straight restaurant. A gay play has to be not as good as a "straight play" but as good as a play should be. There's no more special favors. I can't say I feel there's a backlash, like, "We're so sick of gays in theatre." Someone told me about the night **Kiss of the Spiderwoman** and *Angels* both won Tony Awards—the parents of a playwright that didn't win said, "What have they got against normal people?" I think that kind of thinking is gone, too. I think we're very fortunate to have so many good writers around. And so what if some of them are gay? To say that gay works are not of interest to anybody but gay men and gay women is absurd. **Love! Valour!** would not have had the life it did if it interested just gay men. If **Master Class** were only of interest to opera queens, it would have run three weeks.

So it's very healthy and it's great that so many gay people have taken that big step out of the closet. We still have a way to go in that department. In theatre it's gotten pretty good, there's one or two people who, even if they don't speak openly about their sexualities in public, don't deny it in interviews anymore. We're so over it at the Tonys. Everyone who's gay is there with a partner of their sex, you don't have to invite girls or guys so that when the CBS cameras are on you you look okay. There are a lot of gay people kissing their partners on the Tony Awards now, too. Why gay people have found a life in the theatre is another issue. That's for psychologists. I like to write plays, I don't like to psychoanalyze myself. I have a few patterns I'm not terribly proud of. I'm in therapy. But the crucial thing is not, "Why am I drawn to the world of theatre?" Because it's fun, I always learn from it.

When theatre works, I find it deeply moving, it can be very funny, very bold, very dramatic, touching, you feel connected to people around you in a way. Whether there are ninety-nine seats or fifteen hundred, when a play works well, there's a sense of community and you feel connected to your fellow humans. That's how it should be. You don't have that experience when you're home alone reading a novel. You can be moved, but you don't say, "I'm in this with all these people around me." If a play's really good, people talk going up the aisle, "Didn't you enjoy that?" "Wasn't that moving?" "God, that was funny, wasn't it?" "I really got a lot out of this, didn't you?" When a play doesn't work, we don't talk to each other. Some connection has failed. I think we go to the theatre out of a very basic need to be instructed, enthralled, to learn something. There's a reason the scout master tells little boys these stories. There's a little learning in all of that. That's why we go to see something live at night. Even a very unsophisticated person knows it's not just like a movie, that unlike *Gone with the Wind*, they can't reopen it on Friday with a restored print. There's more theatre in New York now than when I came in the sixties. Broadway has shrunk, but Off-Off-Broadway didn't exist. Off-Broadway really meant the Theatre de Lys, twelve theatres in the West Village, one or two in the East Village, one or two on the Upper East Side, Circle in the Square, and that was the extent of it. About twenty Broadway theatres have been taken down since I came to New York, but a lot of those theatres that were considered Off-Broadway in the sixties and seventies are gone because they're considered impractical. So you have the really small, letter-of-agreement, Equity, 99-seat venues that didn't even exist ten years ago, a lot of them happening in Chelsea right now. But they can only run so long.

So it's important to you that theatre be free, uncensored. And it will be supported, one way or the other, because the kind of communication they facilitate is so essential.

I thought you meant free—no ticket price—that would be nice, too. The cost of production in New York is truly frightening and also, as you get older, it's less possible to work for no money. A twenty year old out of NYU or Juilliard is more inclined to do a workshop production for no pay than someone who's got a family. As you get older, you have more responsibilities financially, and it's very hard. But I think the cost of putting on shows now is so out of hand. It's so disproportionate. I know that prices have increased incredibly, but not like it has in the theatre. When I came to New York, the best seats for *My Fair Lady* were $7 or $8.95. That's not comparable to the $85 for musicals now. I saw a lot of plays on Broadway and $2.90 was the going price for the balcony. Now the cheapest balcony seat for a play is $45 and it's $50-75 for the orchestra. That does not reflect the inflation in the rest of our society.

With the NEA slowly fading away, theatres get very conservative. "Let's keep our subscribers happy." People didn't make enough of a protest about losing Circle Rep. It was terrible to lose that theatre. We just can't afford any loss. We should be welcoming the Vineyard at the same time we're celebrating Circle Rep's twenty-fifth anniversary, not its closing. The Manhattan Theatre Club has certainly gotten more conservative. Any subscription theatre is conservative, because young people don't say, "I want to see a play September 12th and May 11th, and here's the hundred dollars to do that." They make their plans that week. You get the old crowd there. It's sad, these are middle-aged audiences. I certainly don't want Lincoln Center, Manhattan Theatre Club, or the City Ballet to go under. But if you took away the subscriber base, all those companies would really be out of business, including the Met and the Philharmonic. The person who knows they're going to see *Tosca* on January 1st is always less excited than the one who says, "Cool, they're doing *Tosca* with Pavarotti, I've always wanted to see it," and stands in a line for ten minutes or two hours. At the Manhattan Theatre Club, the audiences just aren't as thrilled to be there. But I couldn't have been allowed to produce *A Perfect Ganesh* or *Love! Valour!* at the level to which I've grown accustomed, with that quality of actors, designers and directors, if we didn't have that subscriber base. You don't get Joe Mantello and Brian McDevitt to work at a little loft in Chelsea for fifty dollars. You just have to accept that. So that's the biggest change, subscription didn't exist then. Good plays used to open on Broadway. All of Arthur Miller, all of Tennessee Williams, most of Edward Albee after the sixties opened on Broadway.

LIPS TOGETHER, TEETH APART (1992)

CRITICAL COMMENTARY

Benilde Montgomery (essay date December 1993)

SOURCE: Montgomery, Benilde. "*Lips together, Teeth apart:* Another Version of Pastoral." *Modern Drama* 36, no. 4 (December 1993): 547-55.

[*In the following essay, Montgomery examines pastoral themes in McNally's* Lips together, Teeth apart.]

When Robert Brustein pigeonholes Terrence McNally's *Lips Together, Teeth Apart,* as yet another instance of "Yuppie Realism," he fails to notice that, unlike some other plays which he consigns to this genre, McNally's play does indeed reach past the idiosyncratic and into the "public dimension" that Brustein wishes it might. Rather than write a play as "self-regarding, as self-enclosed, as unanchored as the society it depicts,"[1] McNally has anchored his play securely in a quite public and ancient literary tradition—the pastoral. Moreover, McNally's use of traditional pastoral materials and his arrangement of them into what Thomas Greene might call "heuristic imitation"[2] gives the play a voice that is unique in McNally's canon and rescues it from the "desultory" social thematics that Brustein abhors.

"Pastoral" is, of course, a notoriously eely term. In its broadest sense, "pastoral" here will name that mode of the tradition which "maintains its identity through an awareness of its mainspring in the bucolic poems of Theocritus and Virgil."[3] In a more restrictive sense "pastoral" will denote that dimension of the tradition which posits that

> there exists somewhere (in remote places such as the mountains of Sicily or Arcadia) a society of herdsmen and shepherds who live in harmony with each other, and with the world of nature, its scenery, animals, and gods. These herdsmen combine a life of rustic simplicity (and simplicity of thought and emotion) with the desire and skill to express this simplicity in music. . . . Their happiness is sometimes disrupted by sadness. . . . But this too is converted into song, and the beauty of the song somehow restores the sense of pastoral harmony.[4]

One critic goes so far as to say that "in Virgil Arcadia is hardly more than a 'sound of music.'"[5] Perhaps this interdependence of music and pastoral is what first led McNally to explore the possibilities of writing a play which evokes the mood and conventions of the classic genre. His extensive knowledge of opera, whose origins in sixteenth-century pastoral drama are well documented,[6] and his frequent dramatic use of it and other musical forms suggest both a source for his interest and an awareness of its theatrical potential. McNally's television adaptation of his own short play, *Andre's Mother* (March, 1990), for example, uses as its musical theme the aria "L'amero, saro costante" from Mozart's *Il Re Pastore*. In the opera, this aria is sung by the shepherd Aminta, a character borrowed by Metastasio from its most popular incarnation in Tasso, but who as Amyntas appears first in Theocritus's *Idyll 7* and throughout the subsequent tradition. Produced one year after *Andre's Mother, Lips Together, Teeth Apart* (May, 1991) uses Mozart's trio "Soave sia il vento" in a similar way.

In addition, two aspects of the history of the pastoral tradition converge in McNally's play: the frequent appropriation of pastoral by the "homosexual literary tradition"[7] and its popularity during times of cultural crisis. Beginning with Virgil's *Eclogue 2* and ending with Gore Vidal's *The City and the Pillar*, Byrne Fone has shown how "Arcadia" has entered into the "gay sensibility" as a metaphor which, among other things, validates certain myths prevalent in homosexual life, namely, that there is a place where it is "safe to be gay," and that "homosexuality is superior to heterosexuality and is a divinely sanctioned means to an understanding of the good and the beautiful."[8] Moreover, in calling "war" the ultimate "anti-pastoral," Paul Fussell, citing Northrop Frye, calls our attention to the fact that not only is the pastoral world the model "by which the [war's] demonism is measured"[9] but also in Western literature it frequently becomes the model against which all social crisis is measured. While Fussell reminds us that Wilfred Owen spent his free time during the First World War reading Barbusse's *Under Fire* as well as the idylls of Theocritus, Bion, and Moschus, we ought not to forget that Virgil's *Eclogues* themselves were written during the political crisis following the assassination of Julius Caesar and that Milton's *Lycidas* begins with a note about the "ruin of our corrupted clergy then in their height." It should not be surprising then that when McNally chose to write a play about AIDS, he chose the pastoral form in which both of these aspects of the pastoral tradition converge.

The most obvious place to begin a discussion of pastoral is with setting. McNally's "Arcadia" is not on the island of Sicily or in the remote mountains of Greece, but rather on New York's Fire Island and, implicitly, in the affluent gay community on the Island called "The Pines." Like Virgil's Arcadia of the first *Eclogue*, caught as it is between Rome and the marshes, Fire Island also has two vulnerable borders: one separates it from the formed, civilized mainland; the other separates it from the unformed, natural sea. It thus becomes an instance of what Leo Marx calls the "ideal pasture," a mediating place which classically makes possible a resolution between the apparent opposites of nature and art.[10] The more specific location in "The Pines" helps also to recall that the pine tree is sacred both to Pan, the mythic guardian of the flocks (the very "deus Arcadiae," according to Virgil),[11] and to Attis, the dispassionate shepherd loved by Cybele. In Virgil, the pines call to Tityrus (1), and it is on the "sacred pine" that Corydon hangs his "tuneful pipe" (7); in Ovid's Golden Age, Pan appears to Syrinx "in a crown of sharp pine needles"; and in some versions, the shepherd Attis metamorphoses into the same pine trees beneath which he mutilated himself.[12]

Moreover, McNally sets his play on the Fourth of July weekend, and on the deck of his summer house, he asks that there be an "outdoor shower" and a "swimming pool."[13] During Act Three, the pool, in fact, becomes "*the main source of light*" (71). Again, McNally evokes pastoral convention, but in this case with the particularly

American version embodied in Thoreau's *Walden,* a work whose "serious affinity" with the Virgilian mode Leo Marx has demonstrated at length.[14] Walden is Arcadia in suburban Massachusetts, and like the classical ideal pasture, it mediates the lawlessness of the frontier and the corruptions of civilized Concord with the temporary experience of independence and personal freedom. Central to both American and classic versions of Arcadia is the transformative power of purifying water. Theocritus's *Idyll 13,* for example, tells how Hylas, lured from his lover, Heracles, topples into a pool "like a star that shoots from sky to sea" (an image which McNally exploits with some irony at the conclusion of his play) and thereby achieves immortality.[15] Similarly, *Idyll 15* associates the death of Adonis and his subsequent immortality with the sea. Virgil's Arcadia, needless to say, is also dotted with sacred fountains, Pierian springs, and "leaping streams of sweet water" (5). The most popular modern appropriation of this trope is, of course, Milton's *Lycidas,* but it has been exploited in similar ways, for example, in Whitman's images of boys and soldiers bathing and even in Tadzio's final summons to Aschenbach in Mann's *Death in Venice.*[16] The uses to which McNally puts this will be discussed below.

In the design of pastoral, the idealized, "Arcadian" order is juxtaposed to a more "realistic," a "more complicated order of experience."[17] Virgil's Meliboeus is dispossessed by land reform, for example; Corydon loses his lover Alexis to a rich, urban suitor; the railroad comes to Concord. The ideal pastoral life of McNally's Fire Island is also juxtaposed to the more realistic life of the four protagonists who arrive from the mainland: Sam and Sally Truman, who have inherited the summer house; and Chloe and John Haddock (Sam's sister and her husband). This city-country relationship, typical of pastoral, is immediately apparent in the tension between these two "straight," transient couples and the more permanent gay community of The Pines. In the course of the play, each of the "realistic," straight characters develops a unique relationship to the idealized gay community which surrounds them. From the outset, Chloe, whose name McNally borrows directly from the tradition and which means, by the way, "the first green shoot of a plant in spring," responds to her neighbours positively and seems to be the first among the visitors to have some inkling of where she is: "And look at Manhattan. I don't care what anyone says. This is paradise. . . . Sally, it's heaven. The house, the setting, I am green" (5). Chloe reminds the others of the irrelevance of time to the Island (7) and claims to understand the resident gays because of her connection with amateur musicals. While the music she prefers is different in quality from her neighbours', it provides her with the most obvious link to the world around her. Like Chloe, Sally, an amateur painter, also appreciates music but is more knowledgeable about the particular music that she hears. She tries to get others to listen to it, and at the conclusion of Act One, identifies an aria from Gluck's *Orfeo* as a "description of Paradise. Where the Happy Shades go" (50). Sally's primary connection to her neighbours and to the place, however, is through her brother David (named, of course, for the biblical shepherd king), who now dead from AIDS has left her his house. Sally has brought the others here to decide if she should keep the house for herself and thereby, like the urbanites in Virgil, deprive David's lover of a home that, sentimentally at least, seems more properly his.

On the other hand, the male characters seem less comfortable on the Island. Even though John Haddock's cancer might have made him more sympathetic to David's death and the sufferings of the gay community, the gays remain "goddamed fairies" (41) to him, as he hides his illness and only at the end reluctantly discusses it out loud. Although Sam, Chloe's brother, resents being called "puerile" (71), he has the kind of boyish simplicity which connects him to the eternal adolescence of pastoral. He even has an onstage shower scene which suggests an allusion to the Daphnis of myth whose nakedness before the mythic Chloe causes her to think that "the music must be the cause of his beauty."[18] When Sam's sister, another Chloe, intrudes on his shower, she is impressed with the size of his penis. Sam, however, remains steadfastly homophobic, even while he literally kills the hidden snake that threatens to destroy this ideal pasture and his intense curiosity about his gay neighbours causes him to study two men making love beside the house and to wonder, "Is that what we look like when we make love?" (124).

The tension between the visitors from the mainland and the resident community is complicated for the audience because, like Chekhov's cherry orchard, the gay community is never seen. Its dramatic function as the "ideal" world is made possible by its presence as the "sound of music" rather than as physical bodies. The ideal community, consequently, is revealed to us largely through the perceptions of others. We know, among other things, and significantly in contrast to what we observe of the others, that the gay community is open and welcoming; that they dance; that they make love; that they are attractive and wealthy; that they are comfortable with their bodies. While we only imagine the gay community and know them through their effects, we know them somewhat objectively, however, through their music. Unlike Chloe's show music, which she knows only superficially (she confuses *Annie* with *Gypsy* and finds *Carousel* and jazz "too deep") and which has no significance for her other than the diversionary, the music of the gay community clearly makes them like Virgil's Arcadians, "soli cantare periti" (*Ecloque 10*). Their music not only expresses their cohesiveness as a group but is also intimately connected with the place. As in the world of the classical

shepherds, nature and art find a harmony in the gay community, a harmony that the visitors obviously lack, fail to recognize, and consequently never find.

Indeed, McNally's isle, like Caliban's, is "full of noises." Here, Chloe's incessant prattle, sprinkled with phrases from musical comedy ("Gray skies are going to clear up, put on a happy face!" [10]; "So sue me. Sue me. Shoot bullets through me" [27]), the cassette recording of her child's *"clumsy piano playing"* (100), and the *a cappella* quartet of visitors singing "America the Beautiful" (129) contrast sharply with the opera and jazz of their neighbours. This contrast not only makes clear a division of taste and sexual orientation but also embodies the fracture between nature and art that is preserved among the visitors but is not present among the idealized residents. Chloe's songs are all in her head, a distraction for her and an annoyance to the others; the group's patriotic quartet is only reluctantly sung (Sam wonders what he is "supposed to do" on the Fourth of July [127]). The music of the resident neighbours, however, is rooted in the pastoral nature of the place, helps name it, and makes obvious the possibilities that the echoing woods of pastoral traditionally offers us: that nature and art can exist in a reciprocal relationship; that music can transform nature, even death, into something "rich and strange"; that people need not live in isolation from one another and the world. Sam allows David's gold ring to fall into the water and sees no relationship between this event and Wagnerian opera. He kills the snake, not because he wishes to preserve a mythic Eden but because, as he says, "I hate nature. I like New Jersey" (78). When the gay neighbours' stereo blasts forth Jussi Björling's version of Meyerbeer's "O Paradiso" ("Hail beauteous garden, a paradise on earth art thou!") onto his deck, he recognizes no connection between the music, the place where he is, the "Garden State" he comes from, and his own mythic acts. He merely protests, "what have these people got against Tony Bennett?" (78). In addition, although John's next speech describes him as a golden-haired child "holding an apple" (79), he too remains disconnected from the music and any myth of primal innocence. Earlier, while he wondered whether his affair with Sally would continue, he failed to understand that when Orpheus's question was sung across the deck, it was his own question: "Shall I indeed find my loved one here?" (50). Sam, predictably, asks, "Gluck? Gluck who? Who's Gluck? Where do we know about Gluck from?" (51). That the harmony between nature and art is something that the visitors crave, some consciously, some intuitively, is clear in Sally's "pathetic" (28) attempts to capture the ocean on canvas. Yet, when Sam, cuckolded husband of a childless wife, observes two of his gay neighbours in an act of love, he describes a scene which embodies a pastoral ideal. Private act and public event, music and nature, the sky and the earth converge in an image of almost universal harmony:

"They still don't move. They lie in each other's arms on the sand, in the poison ivy, under a full July moon, the sound of the Atlantic Ocean and Ella Fitzgerald wondering 'How High the Moon.' And now I hear it. I hear 'I love you.'" The stage directions note that "*there is a burst of color in the night sky above them. The Fourth of July fireworks have begun*" (125).

While both groups are experiencing crises, or what Chloe and Sally agree are "difficult times" (84), each group approaches the difficulties quite differently. Faced with AIDS, the gay community clings to its music and one another. "Look next door," John says, "Everybody's dancing." Chloe responds, "Thank God they still can" (140). When Sam asks Sally to dance, however, she refuses, and as the play draws to a close, Sam, a bit incestuously perhaps, dances with his sister while Sally confides in John, the brother-in-law/lover with whom she will never sleep again.

Sally's refusal is consistent with the whole group's refusal (Chloe waffles) to accept the invitation of the gay community to join in celebrating Independence Day. Like Shylock and Malvolio, other "refusers of the feast," the visitors remain passive observers of an idealized pastoral world. While, like pastoral shepherds, the gay community delights in dance and music, the visitors, as a typically pastoral evening falls, remain self-enclosed, inactive and silent, finding solace in the "zap" of a machine killing the bugs that dare to crawl into their unacknowledged garden. The title, ***Lips Together, Teeth Apart,*** describes a dentist's treatment for Sam's anxiety: a physical act designed to keep him silent. We witness this silence in grotesque form at the conclusion of Act II when Chloe, forbidden to make noise, practises her dance routine and only apes her words in silence to the tape of the clumsy piano. We see it later when, at the height of the surrounding festival, the visitors play charades. Moreover, only the anonymity in the characters' internal dialogues, heard only by the audience, allows them to confide to strangers what they fear to say to one another. When Chloe says that she "cannot hear through walls or screens or whatever they are! Partitions!" (118), she expresses her own alienation, and that of her group, and also calls attention to the architectural arrangement of the summer house, a series of areas divided from each other by blinds and sliding glass/screen doors; I don't think it goes too far to say that the house is a series of "closets" into which each of the visitors can escape, from neighbours, companions, and self.

This alienation is no more clearly manifest than in each realistic character's failure to reconcile "truth" and "love." After the Independence Day fireworks, each remains locked in a secret life—Sally is pregnant, but will not tell her husband; Sam doesn't want children, but, with Chloe's encouragement, will not tell Sally;

Chloe and Sam will not speak of their spouses' infidelity; John's illness inadvertently becomes public, but is contextualized only in the clichés of pop psychology; Sally has assisted in her brother's death, but will tell only John. Ironically, the "straight" characters remain in closets; that is, they persist in thinking, perhaps correctly, that silence will preserve their private illusions and assist them in their unrelieved confusion of sincerity and truth. For them, "real" life remains performance. When the clock starts ticking at the end of the play to signal the resumption of their game of charades, when they try to identify a title and keep repeating the refrain "There's no business like show business," they are in fact telling us something about the sterility of the lives they will resume once they leave this ideal pasture.

This unresolved conflict between the groups of the city and of the country suggests, of course, something about McNally's relationship to the pastoral tradition that he is imitating. In Virgil, when Meliboeus, before his dispossession, accepts an evening in Tityrus's home, he receives some strength for his future. Corydon's complaint about Alexis leads to a dimension of self-knowledge that is restorative. Thoreau's stay at Walden helps transform him into the defender of civil disobedience. The virtually ineffective presence of the pastoral ideal in McNally's play speaks not only about the inaccessibility to the visitors of all but pop cultural categories (Chloe gives *Guys and Dolls* its full title, "A Musical Fable" [86]), names it a "classic," and calls Sondheim a "devil" [27], but also about the impotence and evanescence of the pastoral ideal itself, an ideal here embodied in a dying and invisible community which alone has access to the myths and categories that have sustained, for better or for worse, the Western tradition. So that while McNally evokes a genre from that same tradition, he also questions its present effectiveness and its future existence. As Susan Sontag's "Notes on Camp" gives way to *AIDS and its Metaphors,* so the ideal pasture that has sustained so much gay literature in the past shows itself as no longer capable of completing the echo between nature and art: the ivy upon which the ideal lovers lie is indeed poison. Rather than engaging in a "reverent rewriting" of classical tropes, McNally has written what Greene calls a "heuristic imitation" of pastoral: "Heuristic imitations come to us advertising their derivation from the subtexts they carry with them, but having done that, they proceed to *distance themselves* from the subtexts and force us to recognize the poetic distance traversed."[19]

That distance between traditional forms and contemporary experience is made clear in many ways, but especially in the swimmer Sally watches throughout the first two acts of the play. Sally tells us that he was young and beautiful and naked when he entered the water (17) and when his body is washed ashore, she exclaims, "Oh my God. Drowned" (101). These as-

sociations link the dead swimmer to the dying and rising gods that preside over Theocritus's *Idylls,* especially
with the Adonis of *Idyll 15.* There, as the crops wither
in the heat of summer, the death of Adonis is celebrated
at a festival during which his image ("our handsome
prince of love . . . cheeks touched with down . . . our
darling on earth and in Acheron") is flung into the sea
with the sure knowledge that as the crops will return
next year, so will Adonis: "You alone / Cross back to
this world over Acheron . . . You bestow / Your presence on us, year by year, and bless us now." McNally's
modern Adonis is, as in Theocritus, a symbol for the
untimely death of youth and beauty. Now, however,
Adonis is a god that will no longer rise; he is a young
suicide, a despairing victim of AIDS, and neither the
object of worship nor a source of hope. Beachcombers
steal the clothing he left behind, and when Sally wants
to tell his story to her nephew ("He was very young.
Even though his features were swollen from the water,
he was very handsome. Nobody wanted to look at him
like this, but I made myself" (109), Chloe and John
forbid her, and she's left speaking her new version of
an old myth only in silence: "Oh children . . . such
perils await you, such pain and no one to protect us"
(110).

Then, too, all the transformative rituals which traditional
pastoral associates with a "purification by water to
prepare for an eternity of blissful habitation in the
garden"[20] are absent: the very water seems poisoned.
While Milton's Lycidas, another symbol of destroyed
youth, becomes the "genius of the shore" and is good
"to all that wander in that perilous flood," McNally's
Adonis, bloated and inert, is the anonymous prey of
vandals. While bathing is the cause of the mythic Daphnis's beauty, Sam is burnt in a shower that is "very hot.
Scalding" (86). Sally has always been frightened of the
ocean because her father once threw her off a pier to
see if she could swim (89). While Chloe says that she
feels "so fucking liberated" (128) by the ocean she is
still trapped in a cage of words. The pool, too, to which
Thoreau journeyed on another Independence Day, is
here filled with Sam's chlorine but, nonetheless, unused:
David swam here, not the shepherd king, but Sally's
brother, and the contamination of his disease might still
linger. When Sally drinks from the pool and John dunks
his head into it, we have a celebration of death, a
contemporary "black" baptism, the "ceremony of innocence" drowned in a flood of suicidal guilt and self-
pity.

Like traditional pastoral, the design of ***Lips Together,
Teeth Apart*** allows us to see the ideal world as an
alternative to the one in which we must live. As Andrew
Ettin points out, that kind of comparison lets us see our
"faults more clearly and imagine what it would be like
to live without them."[21] If, for a modernist imagination
like Eliot's, the solution to human isolation was a

reintegration of private life with public myths, a postmodernist like McNally cannot offer such an easy
alternative. If, as his play suggests, contemporary
experience is satisfied with sincerity rather than truth
and construes love as a self-pitying solipsism; and if we
understand these faults more clearly now because of
McNally's positing them against the cohesiveness and
generosity of an Arcadian ideal, the truth is that that
ideal is carried in fragile vessels. If the "realistic" world
is cut off from its sustaining myths, the last stronghold
of those myths is under mortal siege: the death that
stalked even Virgil's Arcadia has now polluted the very
waters that once were able to transform it.

Notes

1. Robert Brustein, "Yuppie Realism, Continued,"
   New Republic, 21 October 1991, 28, 29.

2. Thomas M. Greene, *The Light in Troy: Imitation
   and Discovery in Renaissance Poetry* (New
   Haven, 1982), 40.

3. E. Kegel-Brinkgreve, *The Echoing Woods: Bucolic
   and Pastoral from Theocritus to Wordsworth*
   (Amsterdam, 1990), 1.

4. Longus, "Daphnis and Chloe," ed. and trans.,
   Christopher Gill, *Collected Ancient Greek Novels,*
   ed. B. P. Reardon (Berkeley, 1989), 285.

5. Kegel-Brinkgreve, 127.

6. See, for example, Ellen T. Harris, *Handel and the
   Pastoral Tradition* (London, 1980).

7. Byrne Fone, "The Other Eden: Arcadia and the
   Homosexual Imagination," *Essays on Gay Literature,* ed. Stuart Kellogg (Binghamton, 1985), 13.

8. Ibid.

9. Paul Fussell, *The Great War and Modern Memory*
   (London, 1975), 231.

10. Leo Marx, *The Machine in the Garden: Technol-
    ogy and the Pastoral Ideal in America* (New York,
    1964), 22.

11. Virgil, *The Eclogues,* trans. Guy Lee (London,
    1984). Citations to eclogue number are made
    within the body of the text.

12. See Ovid, *Metamorphosis,* especially books 1, 2,
    11, and J. G. Frazer, *The Golden Bough,* abridged
    edition (New York, 1960) chapters 34-36.

13. Terrence McNally, *Lips Together, Teeth Apart*
    (Garden City, NY, 1992), x. All other citations to
    the play are made within the body of the text.

14. Marx, 244.

15. Theocritus, *The Idylls,* trans. Robert Wells
    (London, 1989). Citations to idylls are made by
    number within the body of the text.

16. Fone, 25-29.

17. Marx, 25.

18. Gill, 294.

19. Greene, 40.

20. Fone, 13.

21. Andrew V. Ettin, *Literature and the Pastoral* (New Haven, 1984) 30.

LOVE! VALOUR! COMPASSION! (1994)

CRITICAL COMMENTARY

David Román (essay date 1997)

SOURCE: Román, David. "Negative Identifications: HIV-Negative Gay Men in Representation and Performance." In *Queer Representations: Reading Lives, Reading Cultures,* edited by Martin Duberman, pp. 162-76. New York: New York University Press, 1997.

[*In the following essay, Román explores McNally's treatment of self-identification and creation of identity, in this case HIV-positive and HIV-negative, in* Love! Valour! Compassion!.]

Seronegativity has remained an unmarked category, the unexamined term in the HIV-negative/HIV-positive binarism. "HIV-negative" has not been adequately addressed by AIDS activists; therefore the category has been vulnerable to a series of inscriptions by both dominant culture and queer culture. For uninfected gay men, these markings remained uncontested and, as a result, normalized as the experience of all HIV-negatives. The origins of this problem can be traced back to the introduction of the HIV antibody test in 1985.[1] Previously gay men not diagnosed with AIDS had no way of knowing our relationship to AIDS other than through symptoms associated with the early stages of AIDS, what was then termed AIDS Related Complex (ARC), or through our own conjectures. The reactionary politics of homophobic and/or AIDS-phobic public figures in the mid-eighties who advocated quarantines, mandatory testing, and legislations designed to discriminate against people testing HIV-positive or diagnosed with AIDS, accentuated the separatist politics already in place within and among gay men. Once armed with HIV-negative test results, many gay men defined themselves in opposition to, and at the expense of, gay men testing positive. One of the first means by which HIV-negative gay men defined themselves *as* HIV-negative gay men was through the formation of HIV-positive gay men as Other.

Progressive and radical activists provisionally advocating for, or at times hesitantly endorsing, anonymous testing in some ways exacerbated the problem by inadvertently introducing the concept of the secret.[2] Out to eliminate the possibility of discrimination directed toward HIV-positives, progressive activists advised gay men to keep our test results private. To announce one's seronegativity was constructed as insensitive, politically suspect, and ultimately complicit in maintaining a binary between HIV-negatives and HIV-positives, a divisive gesture understood to be at the expense of people living with HIV.

The introduction of the HIV antibody test also put forward the myth that to test HIV-negative is to be immune to HIV. Some gay men who tested negative assumed incorrectly that they were naturally immune to HIV and therefore could continue the very sexual practices that put them at risk for HIV in the first place.[3] The HIV antibody test launched a cultural binarism between HIV-negatives and HIV-positives and introduced the idea of having a "status." Binary systems rely on an interdependent relationship between the two terms in opposition. In the HIV-negative/HIV-positive opposition, HIV-negative is rendered not only the preferred position, but—given its relation to HIV—the moral one as well. Indeed, as William Johnston, the author of *HIV-Negative: How the Uninfected Are Affected by AIDS,* explains, "HIV status" as a term itself is laden with ideological meanings. "In one sense," Johnston points out, "the word 'status' implies a rigid social or moral hierarchy like caste . . . HIV-negative status is portrayed as better than—rather than merely different from—HIV-positive status. In another sense, the word 'status' implies a state of being that is mutable, like a status report" (120). Walt Odets, the Bay Area clinical psychologist, while concurring with Johnston's ideas, problematizes the use of the term "status" when he writes that "in daily life antibody status is usually tacitly acknowledged as an important difference between positive and negative [gay] men, even when we do not quite know what it means—either medically or humanly."[4] That we are not quite sure "what it means" suggests that, to some degree, we (and others) can put forth interpretations on these very specific clinical terms: HIV-negative, HIV-positive, and HIV status.

The effects of these competing and sometimes contradictory meanings of the term "HIV status," while operating as politically unmarked but understood as signifying certain unarticulated social positions for gay men, allow for the divisive potential among us. The very term "HIV status" engenders the complex psychosocial responses to the specific results of the HIV antibody test among gay men. Simon Watney agrees with this idea when he claims that "[i]t is not sufficiently recognised that HIV antibody testing involves ways of thinking about ourselves, and one another, that have the profoundest implications for everyone."[5] AIDS educators and activists have not carefully examined the effects of this social process or the "implications for everyone." While the goal of activists was to protect HIV-positives from potential discrimination, one of the ironic and unfortunate results of obfuscating gay men's specific serostatus was the emergence of an imagined social binary opposition between HIV-negatives and HIV-positives, even if this binary based on the results of the HIV antibody test did not enter fully into public culture and debate. Despite the efforts to shelter HIV-positives from public discriminations, the social practice of privatizing the serostatus of all gay men allowed for the social binary and its moral underpinnings to take shape in the subaltern world of gay male culture.

Odets argues that the culture of AIDS—from HIV testing to AIDS education campaigns—inadvertently contributes to the unconscious belief that eventually all gay men will seroconvert. Concerned with the emotional health of HIV-negative gay men, Odets points out the underlying homophobic and moralizing rhetoric of the very prevention programs that are meant to save gay men's lives.[6] The power of this pervasive logic of inevitable seroconversion—not *if* but *when*—set forth by both reactionary political forces and AIDS prevention programs, while different in intent and in experience, converges in the individual and cultural psyche of HIV-negative gay men as a primary means of understanding and experiencing seronegativity. The cultural logic of inevitability, in other words, begins to define what it means to be HIV-negative. Within this system, HIV-negativity is considered a tentative status or a temporal condition located on a trajectory leading to eventual seroconversion.[7]

The grassroots organizing of early lesbian and gay community-based AIDS activism, which was based less on the model of compassionate volunteerism and more on the model of political resistance, was replaced in the cultural imaginary by nonprofit altruism, the result of cuts in federal funding under the presidency of Ronald Reagan. Rather than focusing on the collective resistance of people infected and affected by HIV, dominant culture individuated AIDS and thus, as Cindy Patton observes, inscribed "a rigid role structure which constructed 'victims,' 'experts,' and 'volunteers' as the *dramatis personae* in its story of AIDS" (*Inventing AIDS,* 20). HIV-negative gay men working from the position of "volunteer" were sometimes absorbed under the rubric of "victim," a cultural forecasting of the projected conversion of roles for gay men fighting the epidemic. Within the gay community, post-HIV antibody

testing volunteerism was founded on the political model of pre-HIV testing, that is, as a community-driven and community-organized response to AIDS. If earlier community organizing did not have the means to differentiate activists on the basis of their HIV status, later community-based AIDS organizing did, but chose not to make much of it. HIV-negative gay men, unmarked and undifferentiated, failed to politicize their AIDS involvement *as* the politicized work of HIV-negative gay men; this failure led HIV-negative gay men to see themselves as singular entities in the growing AIDS service industries rather than as communal participants in a tactic of shared political resistance.[8]

While dominant culture positioned HIV-negative gay male volunteers within a trope of redemption, the culture of AIDS activism made room for negative gay male AIDS Service Organization volunteers to enter into public AIDS discourse as responsible and compassionate. The formation of the HIV-negative gay man as caregiver was evident in independent gay film, gay literature, and gay politics throughout the mid-eighties.[9] Caregiving, a valued and necessary contribution in the fight against AIDS,[10] emerged as the primary means for HIV-negative gay men to identify as HIV-negative gay men in a manner valorized by the culture of AIDS. And yet even within this system, HIV-negative gay men did not mark their serostatus. The unexamined social roles of HIV-negative gay men—*as* HIV-negative gay men—as AIDS volunteers and caregivers unwittingly domesticated the origins of political communal resistance from which these social practices emerged. Before the HIV antibody test, AIDS volunteerism and caregiving were understood within lesbian and gay culture as a direct form of AIDS activism, a product of the long-standing community-based resistance to social oppression. Volunteerism, as Cindy Patton observes, which began at "grassroots organizations in which unpaid labor was seen as a contribution to community self-determination and liberation," shifted by 1986 to "an acceptable vehicle for the New Altruism promoted by Reaganism" (21).

With the arrival of ACT UP in 1987, HIV-negative gay men participated in a public culture that reimagined AIDS activism and challenged, among other things, the trope of the volunteer. ACT UP intervened in the logic of inevitability and the trope of the good son by agitating the forces of power sustaining AIDS. AIDS was not inevitable, ACT UP demonstrated, but negotiable and preventable. Yet HIV-negative gay men in ACT UP rarely spoke publicly about their seronegativity or about the issues specific to HIV-negative gay men. Instead they subscribed to the Diamanda Galás ethos that "we are all HIV-positive."

The distortion of the experiences of HIV-negatives—as "we are all HIV-positive"—while designed to serve the interests of the infected, ends up obscuring the specific experiences of those who are living with HIV and the specific experiences of those who are not. So for whom does this performative utterance ultimately operate and to what effect? As a public stance of communal identification and solidarity, the HIV-negative's political insistence that "we are all HIV-positive" intervenes in the potential divisions between HIV-negatives and HIV-positives and puts pressure on HIV-negatives to get involved in AIDS activism "as if your life depended on it." But the phrase also plays into the majoritarian hysteria of associative contagion, on the one hand, and the conflation of HIV with gay men on the other. When spoken by HIV-negative gay men, the phrase invests in an unconscious logic that presumes seroconversion. Unlike the earlier AIDS activist acts of surrogacy and identification—the public performatives of the lesbian and gay community between 1982 and 1984 and before the HIV antibody test—where people unsure of their own relationship to AIDS publicly performed an identification with people who had died of AIDS, the new activist identification with HIV-positives, in light of the HIV antibody test that makes HIV status knowable, contributes to the idea that gay male life is intrinsically linked with "being positive." Politically, it runs the risk of locating HIV-negative gay male experience not merely in solidarity with people with AIDS, but rather as symbiotically dependent on people with AIDS. In other words, HIV-negatives are imaginable only if linked inextricably with a person with AIDS.

Such was the case throughout the late 1980s and early 1990s when HIV-negative gay men entered public representation as "AIDS widows" and as partners in "magnetic" relationships. The terms "AIDS widow" and "magnetic relationship" are gay male vernaculars for the surviving partner of a person who has died from AIDS complications and for couples where one partner is HIV-positive and the other is HIV-negative.[11] In both the media and art forms of the dominant culture and of the gay subculture, HIV-negative gay men were marked as HIV-negative in direct relation to someone who was either HIV-positive or who had died from AIDS complications. Brought into public culture on the coattails of the person with HIV or AIDS, the HIV-negative gay man could enter into public representation and discourse as an HIV-negative gay man only through his relationship to someone on the other side of the HIV binary pole. Public culture licensed HIV-negative gay men to speak and be heard as HIV-negative gay men based on these relationships, a perpetuation that fetishized the person with AIDS as having the authentic experience of AIDS.

But what if you were not an AIDS widow or involved with someone HIV-positive? HIV-negative gay men could speak as HIV-negative gay men if they adhered to two primary discourses: quantitative and qualitative. The quantitative discourse allows the HIV-negative gay man to identify as such when he prefaces his identification with a catalogue of the number of friends buried and friends ill. According to the logic of this discourse, the more AIDS fatalities accumulated, the more legitimate the HIV-negative's voice. Often this quantitative discourse is accompanied by, or leads to, the qualitative discourse, which proceeds to account for the poor quality of the HIV-negative gay man's life in the midst of AIDS. The qualitative discourse has its origins in survivor guilt, but it goes further: life is now meaningless and empty. The public circulation of these two limited discourses—quantitative and qualitative—participates in the distortion of HIV-negative gay men's lives. Although many of us are AIDS widows or partners in magnetic relationships, and many of us have buried countless friends and care for many who are ill, and although we may also suffer severe bouts of depression and anxiety regarding our lives given the context of AIDS, these are not our only experiences of AIDS. Rather, these are the experiences and discourses permitted to enter into public consciousness, and their circulation, moreover, begins to construe what it means to be HIV-negative.

How might the public discourses available for HIV-negative gay men have something to do with the rising rates of seroconversion? All the ways HIV-negatives are represented in public culture are extremely depressing and, consequently, offer little incentive to imagine a life worth living. One effect of this situation is that HIV-negative gay men have begun to overidentify with the new culture of HIV-positives; another effect is the occasional fantasy of seroconversion.[12] While the culture of HIV-positives—which includes periodicals, 'zines, films, documentaries, support groups, and socials—is a direct result of the PWA self-empowerment movement founded in 1983, it is also often constructed by dominant media as *the* experience of gay life in the 1990s. If earlier conflations of AIDS and homosexuality were based on the logic of inevitability (that is, homosexuality and AIDS were not only associative but interchangeable), the current variation on this theme anchors gay men's ontology in a narrative of sequential "coming out" occasions—as gay, as positive—into a culture of positivity. In this sense, the sociocultural support systems of, by, and for HIV-positive gay men become urban gay culture. This translation, from a subcultural process within the larger lesbian and gay culture to the majoritarian understanding of what gay life is in the 1990s, domesticates the political necessity of seropositive gay men who must create and sustain social and institutional structures for their survival. Moreover, the conflation of HIV-positive culture with gay male culture ignores the specific needs of HIV-negative gay men in the midst of AIDS. Given these conditions, as Odets has argued, HIV-negative gay men sometimes embark on fantasies of seroconversion. In response to a culture that systematically denies their identity and experience, some HIV-negative gay men assume that seroconversion will bring meaning to their lives and attention and love.

HIV-negative gay men's desire to test positive results from the anxiety associated with the logic of inevitability, but it is also motivated by the desire to be seen and heard. The current proliferation of HIV-negative gay men's unprotected sex stories is symptomatic of these interrelated (but not interdependent) desires.[13] HIV-negative gay men can now enter into the public sphere as HIV-negative gay men through confessional discourse. Despite the many stories HIV-negative gay men have to tell about our experiences as HIV-negative gay men, the unprotected sex confession seems to be the preferred narrative of our times. The failure of AIDS activists and educators since 1985 to establish primary prevention efforts specific to HIV-negative gay men was symptomatic of a larger political need to address the lives of the new category of those who were infected but not diagnosed with AIDS: "HIV-positive." Moreover, the sociopolitical effects of this inadvertent neglect of HIV-negatives extended beyond the specific practices of HIV prevention and into gay male culture. AIDS plays and performances participated in this neglect, offering their audiences not only undifferentiated AIDS pedagogies, but undifferentiated spectatorial positions as well. Undifferentiated AIDS pedagogies fail to acknowledge and address the differences between HIV-negatives, HIV-positives, and people with AIDS. For this reason "undifferentiated" can also be understood as "unmarked." Undifferentiated primary HIV prevention efforts for uninfected gay men fail to mark HIV-negatives as the only outcome population. This failure to mark seronegativity within the address of primary prevention campaigns contributes to the rising rates of seroconversion among this outcome population. AIDS plays, although not necessarily designed as sites of HIV prevention pedagogies, nonetheless participate in the ways that AIDS is understood.

HIV-negative gay men are prominent in Terrence McNally's 1995 Tony award-winning drama, *Love! Valour! Compassion!* Unlike Paul Rudnick's earlier play *Jeffrey*, McNally's work does not present any serodiscordant couples in the four sets of lovers in the play, nor is McNally interested in exploring the comic hero's journey into the social world. Instead *Love! Valour! Compassion!* dramatizes the social world as it already is understood. Seronegativity is not the topic of *Love! Valour! Compassion!* Still, the prominence of HIV-negative gay men, even if for the most part they are inconspicuous as HIV-negative gay men, provides a glimpse into the ways that HIV-negative gay men interact with one another and with gay men living with HIV. In the play's most explicit scene addressing the distinct experiences of HIV-negatives and people living with HIV, two couples are canoeing separately on the

lake. In one canoe, Arthur and Perry question their survival. In the other canoe, Buzz and James contend with health matters. The image of these seroconcordant couples—an HIV-negative pair, an HIV-positive pair—canoeing on the lake becomes a metaphor for these men's relationship to AIDS. Although they are "paddling" through the same waters, they are not in the same boat. Their experiences of AIDS—as HIV-negative gay men, as gay men living with HIV—bring forth separate issues and specific concerns. While Buzz and James must deal with the often random physical effects of their compromised immune systems, Arthur and Perry discuss the emotional effects of AIDS on the uninfected. The HIV-negative couple are represented in this scene neither in competition with the couple with HIV nor to set up the couple with HIV as more dramatic.[14] Instead, the scene stages the two couples as undergoing a shared but distinct experience. Still it is peculiar that in a play about the lives and kinship structures of eight urban gay men, where the concerns of people living with HIV are explicitly accommodated, the HIV-negative couple must retreat, from a summer house already troped as pastoral, in order to give voice to their experiences of AIDS *as* uninfected gay men. Their conversation occurs outside the walls of Gregory's home and in the private "green world" of the lake, unheard by anyone else. Moreover, it seems implausible that Arthur and Perry, two gay men whose fourteen-year relationship began before AIDS, have never had such a conversation—"We've never really talked about this."

Perry and Arthur, affluent and professional white HIV-negative gay men, bear the mark of privilege in the play. Their interchangeability, moreover, seems necessitated. In many ways, their similarity, rather than obscuring their identity, actually pushes it forward. Unlike the other gay men in the play, Arthur and Perry become representative of a generational norm that the other characters are positioned against. "We're role models," Perry says to James after explaining that he's been with Arthur for fourteen years. "It's very stressful" (84). Perry's self-reflexive comment, while somewhat ironic, seems to refer to the position he and Arthur inadvertently hold as partners in a long-term relationship, a concept already laden with various moral values—fidelity, commitment, maturity—that they rehearse for each other and the others throughout the play. But since they also represent a generational norm and are presented as self-identifying uninfected gay men, this notion of the role model takes on an added embedded meaning. As older uninfected gay men who have lived through fourteen years of AIDS and all that this entails, Arthur and Perry are positioned uniquely to be role models for a younger generation of gay men determined to remain uninfected. Unfortunately, they do not do so. Arthur and Perry are barely capable of discussing their seronegativity among themselves—

"We've never really talked about this"—let alone introducing the topic to others. Their occasional encounters with the younger gay men are awkward and strained. There is no "role modeling" on remaining uninfected on their behalf. In fact, the older generation of uninfected gay men—Arthur, Perry, Gregory, and John—have little to offer the younger generation—Bobby, Ramon—on their experiences of AIDS, nor do they even seem all that interested in this possibility.

I raise this issue of role modeling and its effects on younger HIV-negative gay men in order to pursue a line of questioning that unveils the ideological effects of the play's pedagogy around HIV and AIDS. Uninfected gay men of all ages experience confused identifications with HIV. For older gay men like Arthur and Perry (whose personal history with the epidemic spans over a decade), sexually active before AIDS and before knowing their HIV antibody test results, the confused identification begins with the possibility of having been infected and not knowing it. Once aware of their status, they experience survivor's guilt. Younger gay men like Bobby and Ramon come out into a public world already informed by AIDS. Gay identity and gay community are already linked with AIDS; because of this, as Walt Odets explains, "younger men . . . may experience confused identifications with HIV" ("Why We Stopped Doing Primary Prevention for Gay Men," 21). Odets is concerned with the possible disenfranchisement of younger HIV-negative gay men from gay communities because of this confused identification—that AIDS is inevitable, that HIV-positive culture is gay culture—and the relationship between these feelings and the rising rates of seroconversion.

Love! Valour! Compassion! could be said to be a play that produces confusion for its characters and for its audiences around what it means to be HIV-negative. In part this confusion is a result of the play's undifferentiated address and its inconsistent demarcation of serostatus. The inability of an older generation of uninfected gay men to mentor a younger generation of gay men who might want "role models" for remaining uninfected further confuses the play's purported interest in this very notion of mentoring and teaching expressed by Arthur, Perry, and Gregory. This same confusion, paradoxically and unfortunately (from a prevention standpoint), is what sustains the ideology of confusion *and* confused HIV ideology that characterize the play. This seemingly circuitous practice, where confusion is both an underlying theme in the play and an experience of the spectator, is the very force of the play's AIDS politics. Such a politics of confusion and such a confused politics compound the relationship between representation and spectatorial identification. The question of identification, so central to Odets's notion of prevention, moreover, is obscured by the HIV-negative characters' unmarked serostatus. Unmarked, from this

perspective, converges with undifferentiated; the result is that the spectator now too experiences confused identifications around HIV and AIDS. This confusion is only heightened by the ambiguity of the play's conclusion.

McNally ends *Love! Valour! Compassion!* with each character speaking to the audience and fast-forwarding to his death. The couples with marked serostatus speak first: Arthur and Perry live long lives and die quiet deaths; Buzz dies sooner than the others and "sooner than I thought, even"; James commits suicide (137). The circumstances of the characters' deaths are shaped by their HIV status. Those with a marked serostatus die deaths that confirm that HIV status; those with unmarked serostatus—who, at the time of the play, are presumably HIV-negative—die deaths whose relation to HIV remains unclear. Ramon dies in a plane crash, although we do not know when in his life this crash will occur. Bobby does not want to know about his death or does not want to tell. The deaths of the younger generation continue the concealment of their HIV status. In other words, there is no suggestion that they seroconverted and no suggestion that their deaths are unrelated to AIDS. John and Gregory's deaths are similarly unmarked. The conflation of all these deaths replaces the primacy of the notion that for gay men AIDS is inevitable with the cliché that death is inevitable. By the end of the play, the reality of AIDS is eclipsed by the banality of death. No one—regardless of HIV status—can escape death.

In the year and a half between *Jeffrey* and *Love! Valour! Compassion!* a shift in the theater's representations of HIV-negative gay men begins to emerge. The move from unmarked status to marked status signals a discursive opening where seronegativity can be more forcefully addressed. This address will need to maximize comedy's potential to present the lived experiences of HIV-negative gay men in the public sphere. Questions of dramatic form and audience reception figure in this reconceptualization of the representation of HIV-negative gay men in the theater. One spot where this investigation is being pursued is solo performance. Solo performance, unlike conventional theater, deflects the constraints of dramatic form and, in the process, may provide audiences a more efficacious investigation of seronegativity. Because performance is already understood as not being a "play," the formal conventions of theater and drama can be suspended. Moreover, since solo performance, especially community-based solo performance, allows for the autobiographical, HIV-negative gay men may find their AIDS stories welcome in this format. In *Naked Breath* (1994), for example, solo performer Tim Miller, who identifies as HIV-negative in the performance, refuses to allow the impulse of tragedy to override the story of his relationship with Andrew, a "boyfriend" who is HIV-positive.

Miller asks gay men to find their own stories and bring these stories into the public world. The stories are framed by a communal ritual in which the performer breathes in the energy circulating within the performance space. *Naked Breath* includes recorded songs from Michael Callen's *Legacy*. The stripped-down theatricality of *Naked Breath* enables Miller to shift the focus from the theatrical and dramatic conventions associated with AIDS performance to a more direct community-based and community-specific social performative.

Miller explains that with *Naked Breath* he intended to "make a leap into a topic that carries a lot of tension in my community of queer men: sexual intimacy between HIV-negative and HIV-positive men. . . . It became clear to me that my own deepest need to claim sexual connection in the face of the AIDS crisis was a necessary subject both for me and my tribe. This called the piece forward."[15] *Naked Breath* sets out to speak to an undifferentiated gay male spectator. The performance, however, calls for HIV-negative gay men to bring their emotional responses to the AIDS crisis into the public sphere. Miller demonstrates that this public assertion need not be at the expense of people with HIV. Speaking out as an HIV-negative gay man involved in serodiscordant relationships, Miller opens up the possibility of representing the support that both HIV-negative and HIV-positive gay men should have in maintaining a sexual life.

HIV-negative gay men have only recently been the topic of gay theater and performance. As this brief historical trajectory demonstrates, gay male playwrights and performers have been reluctant to explore the issues of HIV-negative gay men in the theater for a number of reasons. Some of these reasons, I have argued, are based on a progressive political concern to focus attention on the distinct needs and experiences of gay men living with HIV and a desire to avoid a divisive politics between HIV-negative and HIV-positive gay men. Other reasons are based on dramatic conventions and generic constraints. Tragedy and comedy each pose specific challenges to gay playwrights interested in portraying HIV-negative characters. Solo performance faces it own constraints, including, in particular, the limited referential field of the solo performer's body. Solo performers run the risk of having their work individuated, interpreted as the rarified experience of the sole body on stage. Despite these limitations, gay playwrights and performers have begun the necessary task of exploring seronegativity in their work. These recent attempts to mark seronegativity in theatrical representation have opened up a new set of questions and possibilities for gay men. Perhaps the most pressing question raised by these recent explorations is whether or not to mark seronegativity as such. In other words, what are the effects—political, artistic, psychological—of naming HIV-

negativity? And relatedly, what are the effects—political, artistic, psychological—of leaving HIV-negativity unmarked?

HIV-negative gay men need to expand the means by which HIV-negativity is rendered intelligible in public culture. HIV-negative gay men must create space in public culture for new means of understanding seronegativity outside, or in relation to, the primary means now in place. The force of the proliferation of diverse representations of HIV-negatives will unleash new identificatory possibilities for HIV-negatives. HIV-negative gay men need to be public not only about their serostatus but more urgently about how it is that we have remained uninfected. Moreover, such an identificatory politics, where an HIV-negative gay man begins to identify with other HIV-negatives who are public about their serostatus and their means of staying uninfected, needs to account for the problem of individuation that accompanies identification. In other words, HIV-negative gay men do not simply need a new private imaginary; we need a new structure for the private and public imaginaries—nothing short of a new political culture. This new political culture will need to address without blame or abjection the conscious and unconscious desires all gay men may share for unprotected sex. Gay men committed to reducing the rates of seroconversion must encourage HIV-negative gay men to come out about their status and share their experience of being HIV-negative with others, and not simply with other HIV-negatives; the combined energies of HIV-negatives and HIV-positives in reducing seroconversion can be the public force of the social magnetic relations between us. Such a political project will also need to account for the force of the HIV-negative/HIV-positive binarism that now exists. HIV-negative gay men need to challenge more forcefully the logic of the HIV-negative/HIV-positive binary and our investments in this binary system. We can begin to understand what it means to be HIV-negative only by first interrogating the ways we have been led to understand our serostatus. And one of the primary means of understanding seronegativity we have left unexplored is the very force and logic of the HIV-negative/HIV-positive binary construction.

Gay men have accepted the logic of the binary and as a result have sustained the force of the HIV-negative/HIV-positive division. Gay men often imagine, and at times even enforce, the idea that the HIV-negative/HIV-positive system is homologous to other social binarisms based on identity factors such as race, gender, and sexuality. In these binaries—white/black, male/female, heterosexual/homosexual—one of the terms of the binary assumes a dominant position—white, male, heterosexual—and that term circulates as unmarked. Within the specific logic of these social binarisms, one of the terms must emerge as unmarked, as the alleged norm. In this regard, unmarked translates as normative; marked translates as deviant. Feminist, antiracist, and queer theory, along with the activism behind these intellectual movements, have gone to great lengths to denaturalize the cultural logic that positions unmarked categories as normative. "Whiteness," "masculinity," and "heterosexuality" have thus emerged as sites of contestation and denaturalization. These various cultural theorists have demonstrated new ways of seeing the terms of these binaries. Moreover, feminists, antiracists, and queer theorists have unsettled the myth that these binary systems work in culture as monolithic structures.

AIDS cultural theorists have consistently argued against the monolithic structure that has forced HIV-negative and HIV-positive into a simple binary. This important project has been played out primarily in critiques of the systems of power—government, science, media, for example—that promote the concept of a general population versus an abject population. Dominant culture, as various AIDS theorists have argued, presumes itself HIV-negative; the threat of HIV is imagined through the cultural abject: homosexuals, intravenous drug users, and people of color. In this system, all gay men regardless of our status are implicated as embodiments of HIV. The either/or logic of the HIV antibody test—either one has HIV antibodies in the bloodstream or one does not—allows for only two test results: HIV-negative or HIV-positive.[16] Within dominant culture, these test results were molded into a binary structure. The binary established around HIV-negative and HIV-positive positioned HIV-positive as the abject term. The unmarked term—HIV-negative—has assumed the position of power, the status of natural.[17]

In general, HIV-negative gay men do not set out to oppress HIV-positive gay men. But insofar as HIV-negative gay men have accepted the structure and language of the HIV-positive/HIV-negative binary, we have accepted the power accompanying the logic of HIV-negative as the natural status. The fact that these characteristics accompany the logic of the binary—normative/abject, natural/unnatural—functions as an oppressive force for infected gay men. By marking seronegativity, HIV-negative gay men begin the process of denaturalizing HIV-negative as the natural condition. The effect of this denaturalization will remind us that HIV-negative is itself an "unnatural" act, that HIV-negative is a process of being associated with a medical procedure and not the assumed normative, permanent status.[18] The logic of the HIV antibody test sets up the assumed binary between HIV-positive and HIV-negative, but these test results only obscure the more precise binary between its related terms—infected and uninfected—through the official language of biomedical science. In other words, the terms "HIV-positive" and "HIV-negative," although related to the terms "infected" and "uninfected," are neither interchangeable nor coterminous. By marking seronegativity as a constructed category and by contextualizing HIV-negative within a larger, more official ideological system concerning HIV and AIDS, we can begin to unpack what it means to be HIV-negative. And by marking seronegativity in this way, we may actually help keep the "category" of HIV-negative alive. Since we have not adequately addressed what it means to be HIV-negative or what it means to be uninfected, we have allowed the force of the binary to take shape and the terms "HIV-negative" and "uninfected" to be conflated. For infected men, the effects of this binary have led to the establishment of necessary social and political structures of support, under the rubric of HIV-positive or Person With AIDS. For uninfected gay men, the effects of this binary system have primarily perpetuated our anxieties about, and perhaps even our desires for, seroconversion. But this need not remain the case. This enterprise of denaturalizing "HIV-negative" will demand that we address our experience as either uninfected or HIV-negative gay men in public culture, small groups, and among our friends. These discussions, moreover, will need to address the ways that we are imagined and constructed in dominant culture, including the actual HIV-negative/HIV-positive binary system that makes our status intelligible in the first place.

Gay men living with HIV have already demonstrated to the world the possibilities of this practice by revising the cultural psyche around our understanding of what it means to be positive or living with AIDS. It is time now for uninfected gay men to begin to intervene in the limited understanding of what it means to be HIV-negative. The current means we have of understanding seronegativity do not adequately reflect the actual lived experiences of uninfected gay men. Representations and discourse, of course, do not transmit HIV, but they do transmit meanings, and these meanings have their effect on our understanding of who and what we are and, to a great extent, what we do. The first step in intervening in the systems that make us intelligible to ourselves and to others is to interrogate the means by which uninfected men are understood and heard in public culture. The challenge set before us is to construct a public culture for all of us—infected and uninfected—in which we can love one another and survive.

Notes

This essay is part of a longer chapter from my book on AIDS and performance. I wrote most of the chapter in the spring of 1995 while living in New York City in the midst of a very heated public debate on AIDS prevention. Many friends have helped shape these ideas. Thanks to Michael Warner, Paul Sutherland, Carolyn Dinshaw, Marty Duberman, and John Fall for reading earlier versions of this work, and especially to Richard Meyer for his continuous support and engagement with my work.

1. The ELISA test first became available in the spring of 1985. The ELISA and Western blot tests detect the presence of antibodies to HIV, rather than HIV itself.

2. Initially most AIDS activists were strongly against gay men testing. See Cindy Patton, *Sex and Germs: The Politics of AIDS* (Boston: South End Press, 1985). She writes that "[a]lmost immediately, influential members of the AIDS activist community came out strongly against the test and discouraged gay men from getting it. They argued that the test placed seropositive men under undue mental stress and endangered them should the test results be obtained by an employer or insurance company" (35). Moreover, in 1985 there was no available treatments for people testing positive. Others, however, advised gay men to take the test at anonymous sites, hoping that the test would promote behavior change. The debates over testing are discussed by Patton in *Inventing AIDS* New York: Routledge, 1990).

3. See the personal testimonies of HIV-negative gay men in William I. Johnston, *HIV-Negative: How the Uninfected Are Affected by AIDS* (New York: Insight Books, 1995).

4. Walt Odets, *In the Shadow of the Epidemic: Being HIV-Negative in the Age of AIDS* (Durham: Duke University Press, 1995), 146-47.

5. Simon Watney, "Perspectives on Treatment," in *Practices of Freedom: Selected Writings on HIV/AIDS* (Durham: Duke University Press, 1994), 194.

6. Walt Odets, "AIDS Education and Harm Reduction for Gay Men: Psychological Approaches to the 21st Century," *AIDS & Public Policy Journal* (1994) 9:1, 1-16.

7. I want to call attention to what is meant by "seroconversion" throughout this essay. "Seroconversion" is often used interchangeably with "HIV infection," but they are not necessarily the same. According to William Johnston, who provides a useful distinction in *HIV-Negative: How the Uninfected Are Affected by AIDS*, "'seroconversion' refers not to HIV infection but to a biological event made evident by two HIV tests: the movement from the absence to the presence of HIV antibodies in the blood stream. In popular usage, 'seroconversion' often refers to the psychological event of learning one is HIV-positive after learning one was HIV-negative" (318).

8. The structure of volunteer-based emotional support systems for people with AIDS contributed to this individuation. "Buddies," for example, are paired up with a "client." The nature of these relations was confidential. Buddies and other emotional support volunteers were unable to discuss their volunteer work and the issues around it, except with others "Buddies" in official shared support meetings.

9. See, for example, Arthur J. Bressan Jr.'s 1985 film *Buddies.*

10. See Phillip M. Kayal, *Bearing Witness: Gay Men's Health Crisis and the Politics of AIDS* (Boulder. Westview Press, 1993) for a detailed discussion of AIDS volunteerism and activism based on the history of GMHC in New York City.

11. On AIDS widows, see Paul Monette, *Borrowed Time: An AIDS Memoir* (New York: Harcourt, Brace, Jovanovich, 1988) and *Afterlife.* On "magnetic relations," see Mark Schoofs, "Love Stories in the Age of AIDS," *Village Voice,* August 16, 1994.

12. See Walt Odets, *In the Shadow of the Epidemic,* and William Johnston on gay men's desire to test HIV-positive.

13. See Michaelangelo Signorile, "Out in America," *Out Magazine* 16 (1994); and Michael Warner, "Why Gay Men Are Having Risky Sex," *Village Voice,* January 31, 1995, 33.

14. McNally inserts an interesting commentary to this idea of competition. At one point, Perry spots Buzz and James in the canoe and challenges them to race to shore; Perry to Buzz and James: "You want to race?" (122). Arthur immediately scolds his lover. Buzz, preoccupied with his lover's discomfort and already in a hurry to get back to the shore, mishears Perry; Buzz to James: "Grace. I thought he said something about grace." Terrence McNally, Love! Valour! Compassion! *and* A Perfect Ganesh: *Two Plays* (New York: Plume, 1995), 123.

15. Tim Miller and David Román, "Preaching to the Converted," *Theatre Journal* 47 (1995): 181.

16. The possibility of a false-negative or false-positive test result still confirms that a retesting will eventually determine either an HIV-negative or an HIV-positive test result.

17. In part, this cultural phenomenon results from the conflation of HIV-negative/HIV-positive with two other terms, which set up a related binary: infected and uninfected. The terms "infected" and "uninfected" do not circulate culturally as terms to describe gay men primarily because as descriptives they can enter into official culture only through the mediated power of biomedical science, which translates these terms into "HIV-positive" and "HIV-negative." "Infected" and "uninfected" are intelligible only if they convey the nature of an infection. Before the discovery of HIV as the agent of infection that leads to what we know as AIDS, "infected" and "uninfected"

were the terms gay men used to describe their presumed relation to the unfolding epidemic of disease and death. This presumption was verifiable only through the set of diseases associated with the epidemic. Uninfected gay men, on the other hand, had no way to verify their relationship. It was not until the availability of the HIV-antibody test in 1985 that uninfected gay men who were and remained sexually active could verify that they had not been exposed to the virus that allegedly can lead to AIDS. With this new means to determine one's relation to HIV, infected and uninfected gay men adopted the language of biomedical science—HIV-negative and HIV-positive—and began to forge identities around these two terms of medical discourse. Uninfected gay men were finally able to divest from the possibility of their eventual progression to AIDS under the newly established category of HIV-negative. See also Ruth Finkelstein, "Gay Men Have Worked It All Out? Entering the Fray over Safe Sex Practices," *Gay Community News,* spring 1995, 10-11, 21.

18. I feel compelled to point out that simply replacing "HIV-positive" and "HIV-negative" with "infected" and "uninfected" does not defuse the force of the binary and its associated characteristics. Infected and uninfected are no more "natural" than HIV-positive and HIV-negative. The point here is that HIV-negative is "unnatural" in so far as it emerges from the official practice of biomedical science. One could also argue that infected and uninfected are the more "natural" terms in that they do not inflect the ideological weight of biomedical science. But this too would be a mistake. Infected and uninfected, while ostensibly the more "pure" conditions of the body before the intrusion of the practice of HIV antibody testing, nonetheless are absorbed into the logic of a binary through their oppositional pairing, through the logic of the either/or. As such, infected and uninfected are thus positioned to be located along the hierarchical power system inherent in all binary structures.

MASTER CLASS (1995)

PRODUCTION REVIEWS

David Shengold (review date May 1997)

SOURCE: Shengold, David. Review of *Master Class,* by Terrence McNally. *Theatre Journal* 49, no. 2 (May 1997): 225-27.

[*In the following review of a production of* Master Class *at the Golden Theatre in New York, Shengold praises the performers and staging but is less positive in his assessment of the script.*]

Upon her death in 1977, the Greek-American soprano Maria Callas joined the ranks of those bruised icons (Dean, Monroe, Garland) whose unhappy lives have fueled posthumously the further depredations of cult industries of cultural production. Her relatives, colleagues, admirers, and recording companies have packaged and repackaged the biographical and artistic legacy of Callas endlessly, and often heedlessly, collectively fashioning a romantic narrative of an artist who suffered for love ever further from, and more obscuring of, Callas's actual achievements as a startlingly vivid and innovative singing actress.

Terrence McNally has drawn on this composite Callas before, as the patron saint of the sad Mendy in *The Lisbon Traviata.* The duplicity of that play's premise—that Callas's 1957 Lisbon Violetta was a kind of Lost Grail for her fans, when in fact it had circulated widely on readily available pirate recordings—pales before that on display in *Master Class,* seen at the Philadelphia Theatre Company and The Mark Taper Forum before opening on Broadway in November 1995.

In a program note, McNally avers that when Callas sings, she tells us her secrets, and we tell ours right back. Indeed, *Master Class,* with its repeated bromides about misunderstood artists and their courage and discipline in the face of a brutal world, would seem an especially nasty authorial fantasy of what it means to be a diva. Certainly the unprofessional behavior and remarks McNally's Callas indulges in here derive more from a generalized (and misogynist) showbiz narrative about life at the top than from Callas's career or indeed her well-documented master classes. Drawing loosely on the transcripts and tapes of the classes Callas gave at Juilliard in 1971 and 1972, McNally has fashioned a generic egotistical monster who largely ignores her students, dispenses mordant one-liners and seems to relate to music only insofar as it expresses facets of her pop psychologized and often inaccurately rendered personal biography.

The play transpires in part in "real time," with the audience treated as the master class audience and a pianist (the excellent David Loud) who enters, warms up, and gestures to an imaginary friend in the auditorium. Other Thornton Wilder touches run to a doubled program and an onstage technician with whom Callas has a running dialogue.

Zoe Caldwell, resplendent in a black Chanel suit, makes a star entrance and gives a tour-de-force performance of wit and steely charm. It remains for subsequent Marias, Patti Lupone and Faye Dunaway (who has acquired the film rights), to capture more precisely the vulgarity inherent in the role as written. The three students function chiefly as victims of Callas's (or rather McNally's) one-liners; their personal qualities are generic and obvious, and the lines placed in their mouths stretch all credulity. Nevertheless they are very well embodied by Karen Kay Cody (the awkward one), Jay Hunter Morris (the overconfident one), and Audra McDonald (the truly talented one who talks back to Callas). The standard of singing is fairly high, though one worries for the future of McDonald's lovely lyric voice after being put through Lady Macbeth's punishing Letter Scene night after night.

The fine direction by Leonard Foglia mirrors the simplicity and elegance of the single set by Michael McGarty. Brian MacDevitt's lighting comes to the fore in two reverie sequences in which Callas relives past triumphs instead of listening to her young charges. As the lighting eerily evokes La Scala's auditorium and Callas's recordings of *La Sonnambula* and *Macbeth* resound through the theatre, Caldwell delivers with considerable bravura monologues explicitly and facilely linking the music to Callas's life (Amina for betrayal and Lady Macbeth for ambition). Striking in themselves, these experiments in classical *mélodrame* highlight a major weakness of the play: those familiar with Callas's voice will scarcely want to listen to these sublime and harrowing recordings with the distraction of McNally's trashily reductive commentary, whereas operatic neophytes will merely be confused.

As boulevard entertainment, *Master Class* makes an effective star vehicle for Zoe Caldwell; as biography, or as exploration of genius and its relation to the transmission of performance tradition, it falls flat. Better five minutes of Maria Callas's recordings than two hours of the meretricious malice with which McNally seeks to "honor" her memory.

Matthew Gurewitsch (review date October 1997)

SOURCE: Gurewitsch, Matthew. "Maria, Not Callas." *The Atlantic Monthly* 280, no. 4 (October 1997): 102-07.

[*In the following review, Gurewitsch contrasts McNally's character with the real Maria Callas and evaluates various performances of* Master Class.]

"Art is domination. It's making people think that for that precise moment in time there is only one way, one voice. Yours."

So says Maria Callas in Terrence McNally's play *Master Class,* exposing the bold hoax that none but the most exceptional practitioners are able to pull off. When Zoe Caldwell introduced the play on Broadway, nearly two years ago, she herself perpetrated that hoax, for which

she was rewarded, quite deservedly, with the fourth Tony Award of her career. Whatever one's view of the play (and lasting sentiment for and against the late diva ensured that judgments would be fierce), the role of Maria was Caldwell's property. She was a python, humorless and stern, mesmerizing in her refusal to countenance any form of compromise. Her reading was definitive, pre-emptive, exhausting all possibilities. When she departed the vehicle, it would surely fall apart.

Or so it seemed, which is exactly what would spur an ambitious actress to try to impose her own way. What is performance history, after all, but the endlessly self-renewing saga of dethronement? Caldwell left *Master Class* on June 29, 1996, at just the time of year when all but the hardiest Broadway shows wither and die, yet the New York production continued to play to good houses until this past June 28, chalking up more than 600 performances. Beyond Broadway the play has had some forty productions abroad, as far afield as Argentina, Australia, Brazil, Croatia, Estonia, France, Greece, Hungary, Israel, Italy, Japan, Korea, Mexico, New Zealand, Scandinavia, Turkey, and Yugoslavia, not to mention nine in Germany alone. Never mind the slew of productions by American regional, stock, and amateur companies, which could soon number in the dozens.

Since Caldwell, stars true and false have been stalking *Master Class* the way ballerians do *Swan Lake,* and what at first seemed fixed now proves to be fluid. Textual variants have been creeping in: St. Patrick's is bumped for Notre Dame, Pavarotti anachronistically for Richard Tucker. No harm is done. This is the process by which classics are born.

Of the many second-generation Marias I have seen five: Patti LuPone, who took over from Caldwell on Broadway; Dixie Carter, who succeeded LuPone; Faye Dunaway, making the national tour with the movie rights in her pocket, hitting Boston, Chicago, Philadelphia, Seattle, Dayton, Houston, Fort Lauderdale, Palm Beach, Detroit, Los Angeles, San Francisco, and a score of other cities; the Fellini protégée Rossella Falk, in Milan; and Truffaut's muse Fanny Ardant, in Paris. Of all the actresses it is Ardant who yields not an inch to Caldwell, and she has the added advantage of Roman Polanski's stylish, psychologically richer production. Patti LuPone runs Caldwell and Ardant a close second, with Carter a respectable third. Falk and Dunaway are nowhere in sight, yet even they have light to shed on the role's multifarious—though not unlimited—possibilities.

"Art is domination." As the example of the historic Callas teaches us, great performers do not inherit. They take charge; therein lies whatever authority they have. Known to legions of worshippers as La Divina, Callas embodied an astonishing variety of tragic heroines, from the bel canto period through verismo, with such conviction that her readings remain touchstones even now—twenty years after her death, more than thirty years since her last theatrical appearance, and forty years since her heyday. Remastered and repackaged over and over (currently in a commemorative twenty-volume set from EMI), her albums remain best sellers while those of other divas, contemporary and past, come and go. Many listeners recognize her timbre and intensity of expression from a single recorded note; at least one critic asserts, perfectly credibly, that in certain cases Callas can be identified by a single intake of breath. Her charisma, onstage and off, blazes in photographs, too, as exhibits and books have proved time and again. And we should not discount the buzz of her tempestuous personal life—crowned by an adulterous romance with Aristotle Onassis, who entertained her, her husband, the Winston Churchills, and the Gianni Agnellis on his yacht in the presence of the apparently unruffled first Mrs. Onassis. When Jacqueline Kennedy became the second Mrs. Onassis, Callas was cut loose. The recent coffee-table volume *Callas: Images of a Legend* is chockablock with photographs as deeply branded in the memory of music lovers as those of the Kennedy assassination, the first landing on the moon, and the little Vietnamese girl burned by napalm.

Can such a personality, so much larger than life, be encompassed in a play? By some lights McNally is riding on the real-life diva's notoriety, and should more properly have invented a diva whose place in the firmament he would have been at liberty to define. But can one invent the North Star? No less a judge than Leonard Bernstein pronounced Callas the world's greatest artist. The reality of her achievement is a point of reference impossible to make up. The character that McNally calls Maria (as shall I) shares most biographical particulars with the historical diva (whom I shall continue to call Callas). But McNally's purposes in **Master Class** are only incidentally documentary. Above all the play is a highly personal, deeply perceptive meditation on the wellsprings and the consequences of supremacy in art. Without the real-life example McNally would in effect have been writing science fiction.

* * *

Since Aeschylus dreamed up *The Persians,* playwrights beyond number have spun fantasies about historic figures. Why should performers be exempt? On stage and at the movies we have seen actors play Edith Piaf, Billie Holiday, Lon Chaney, Charlie Chaplin, Isadora Duncan, and Vaslav Nijinsky, to name just a few. The resurrection usually incorporates an anthology of the artist's greatest moments—frequently the whole point of the exercise, affording the actor a shortcut to an ersatz glory. McNally gives the actress playing Maria

no such break. "No one can sing like Maria Callas," Maria declares, speaking for her creator. McNally drives the point home with authentic Callas recordings, using the inimitable voice as a soundscape for two bravura monologues. In these passages the actress gets to show what she can do, impersonating a raft of absent characters: Callas's unromantic, doggedly devoted husband, the brick-factory owner Giovanni Battista Meneghini, nearly thirty years her senior; her coarse, sensualist lover, Aristotle Onassis; Elvira de Hidalgo, the teacher whose approval she craved; and assorted snotty backstage personnel.

McNally gives Maria a single line to sing, and that with strategic, destructive intent. The opera scene she is demonstrating to a student begins, strikingly and quite exceptionally, with speech: it is the entrance of Verdi's Lady Macbeth, who reads her husband's letter about the witches before launching into song, as Maria does in the heat of the moment. *"Ambizioso spirto tu sei, Macbetto"* is the line: "Ambitious thou art, Macbeth." "What comes out is a cracked and broken thing," McNally writes in the stage direction. "A voice in ruins. It is a terrible moment." Yes—though a spectator in the theater, not privy to the editorializing, might well think it terrible for a different reason. In the original production Caldwell's voice was flatly incredible as the cracked and broken instrument of someone who had at any time been a singer.

* * *

Callas, of course, actually did conduct a famous series of twenty-three master classes, with twenty-five students, at Juilliard in 1971. People who were there (I was not) remember the classes as the sensation of the musical season, though they cannot possibly have been of much interest to readers of gossip columns. Unlike Maria, who is constantly wallowing in self-serving reminiscence and resentfully spilling beans, Callas was thoroughly prepared, rigorously technical, demanding, and relentlessly focused on the job at hand. Her concerns were breath control, diction, accents, phrasing, tempo, scales, trills. Anyone who went hoping for dish would soon have fled.

The classes were taped, and *Maria Callas at Juilliard* (EMI), a three-CD compilation (interspersed with arias culled from the extensive Callas discography), is available. The scholar John Ardoin published a more inclusive, expertly assembled book of transcripts, *Callas at Juilliard,* which is rich in musical examples. Neither source is anything like the play. On the tapes we hear a lot of singing, both from the students and from Callas; hers is seldom dulcet but always authoritative. There is not much talking, and Callas does most of that, limiting herself in the main to concise technical corrections. In the book the students vanish almost completely.

The displays of temperament, personal revelations, and lordly putdowns of the students that make McNally's script so playable are mostly pure invention. So, actually, are the musical and dramatic analyses. Of Maria's three "victims" only the tenor comes in with an aria represented on the Juilliard syllabus. Callas was especially brief and clinical on the subject of this aria, but it moves Maria to the brink of tears. With the Callas specialties brought in by the play's two sopranos, McNally is working on a clean slate.

Master Class, then, is virtually pure fabrication, for all its harping on the theme of authenticity—and purposely so. McNally might have included, but did not, Callas's frequent injunction to let emotion register on the face while singing a phrase, *and even before;* this is hard-won theatrical wisdom that audiences would instantly understand. But giving an aesthetic education of this sort is not McNally's concern. One rare passage in which Maria does quote Callas is perfectly in character: she is telling a student to wear a longer skirt, or slacks, because "the public that looks at you from down there sees a little more of you than you might want." "Eh?" she continues. "It's no use now. You should have thought of it before." On a more solemn note, Callas's spare farewell to the students is also preserved essentially intact.

> Whether I continue singing or not doesn't matter. *Besides, it's all there in the recordings.* What matters is that you use whatever you have learned wisely. Think of the expression of the words, of good diction, and of your own deep feelings. The only thanks I ask is that you sing properly and honestly. If you do this, I will feel repaid. *Well, that's that.*

Except for the two sentences in italics, this passage from the play matches Ardoin's transcript word for word. The remark about the recordings is also authentic, although interpolated. As for the exit line, untranscribed by Ardoin, it is heard on the CD, followed by explosive applause.

McNally is in search of a seamless imaginative truth. On the face of it, not much "happens" in *Master Class.* Maria arrives, vamps the audience (we have a role to play as auditors), and eventually settles down to the business at hand. There is some byplay with the rehearsal pianist and with a stagehand. Otherwise, for the entire first act Maria torments a timid soprano who tries her luck with Amina's heartbroken lament from Bellini's *La Sonnambula,* a celebrated Callas vehicle. The second act is split between a cocky tenor, who after a clownish beginning unexpectedly touches a chord in Maria with "Recondita armonia," from Puccini's *Tosca;* and a second soprano, this one bold and overdressed, who comes in with the letter scene from Verdi's *Macbeth,* another Callas specialty. Between volleys of sarcasm, condescension, and criticism, very seldom leavened with encouragement, Maria frequently digresses, revisiting her life and career. Toward the end of each act she has a tremendous monologue; the room vanishes as the music plunges her into a violent malestrom of memory.

The failure of Maria's first victim to bring a pencil to class prompts a reminiscence of all but epiphanic force.

MARIA:

> At the conservatory Madame de Hidalgo never once had to ask me if I had a pencil. And this was during the war, when a pencil wasn't something you just picked up at the five and ten. Oh no, no, no, no. A pencil meant something. It was a choice over something else. You either had a pencil or an orange. I always had a pencil. I never had an orange. And I love oranges. I knew one day I would have all the oranges I could want, but that didn't make the wanting them any less.
>
> Have you ever been hungry?

SOPRANO:

> Not like that.

MARIA:

> It's. It's something you remember. Always. In some part of you.

In the second act, in the context of *Macbeth,* Maria asks the other soprano, "Is there anything you would kill for, Sharon? . . . A man, a career?" (Sharon doesn't think so.) Hunger and willingness to kill: these are what make Maria who she is. Hunger, for more than oranges, fueled her art. What has destroyed her life is a love great enough to kill for. As the second grand monologue reveals, Maria *has* killed, not for her career but for a man: for Onassis, the love of her life, who has rebuffed her tenderness, saying he gives love only to his children. "Have a child of mine," he scoffs, "and I will love him." When she conceives, Onassis tells her to have an abortion. To keep him, she complies. He dumps her anyway.

The importance of the pregnancy in McNally's scheme is paramount, forging the link to the character with whom Maria most identifies, both as a woman and as an artist: Medea.

> "Ho dato tutto a te." Medea sings that to Jason when she learns he's abandoning her for another woman. A younger woman. A woman of importance. A princess. "Ho dato tutto a te." "I gave everything for you. Everything." That's what we artists do for people.

Though not exact, the parallels are close enough. Medea, we recall, murdered her brother for love of Jason, and later killed her own children for revenge on Jason. The princess, of course, is Jacqueline Kennedy. And Maria's climactic line in her second monologue, following her desperate cry to Onassis to marry her, is none other than Medea's: "Ho dato tutto a te." Earlier in *Master Class,* Maria has used those words to make another point: "Anyone's feelings can be hurt. Only an artist can say 'Ho dato tutto a te' center stage at La Scala and even Leonard Bernstein forgets he's Leonard Bernstein and listens to you." Unconditional devotion, unconditional sacrifice: these are the core of her life and her art. How hard it is to distinguish the two.

* * *

"Ho dato tutto a te." Few plays hinge on a line as *Master Class* does on this one. Indeed, it is in the trajectory to the final utterance of this line, and in the reading of the line when it comes, that every actress I have seen in the part of Maria has proved (or not) her worth. Leonard Foglia, who has directed all the Broadway casts and Dunaway's touring ensemble as well, has given his actresses considerable latitude to succeed or fail on their own terms. The keynote of Caldwell's performance, struck ringingly in that line, was towering, contemptuous, ice-cold rage. LuPone, Broadway's original Evita, came to Maria a diva burned by her ouster from *Sunset Boulevard*—a real-life humiliation that may have accounted in part for her pervasive attitude of plucky defiance. A younger, more flirtatious Maria, she brought forth in the climactic cry a blaze of despair and loss. Ardant's reading was at once the most enigmatic and the most haunting: she shed tears, yet her features were open, beaming, with the same lonely, Vestal-like rapture that suffused her both when her Maria spoke of her art and also—to unexpected yet utterly convincing effect—in her assessments of colleagues and students. She was crushing in her kindness. To Ardant's advantage, Polanski conceived of the students as real people rather than cartoonish foils for the star. (Foglia's inadequacy in this regard grows more glaring with each change of cast.)

Carter, best known as Julia Sugarbaker in the CBS Series *Designing Women,* was the most girlish of the five Marias I saw, mischievously aware of her power to entertain and gratified when her jokes got a laugh. In the main, though, her moods seemed affected rather than spontaneous. In Milan, Rossella Falk portrayed a star-struck, little-me Cinderella, back at the fireplace reminiscing about a night at the ball that didn't pan out. It wasn't a viable choice.

But Falk's failure pales in significance beside Dunaway's, since Dunaway's Maria is the one destined to achieve immortality of sorts on the screen. Dunaway has a movie star's ability to turn on pathos as one switches on a light, and the effect when she does so as the heartbroken sleepwalker Amina is fairly breathtaking. Otherwise she is still playing Bonnie Parker: winsome, hungry for life, cheerful, insecure, and more than

a little dim. With the students Dunaway's Maria pulls punches, which renders especially false the awkward scene toward the end when the *Macbeth* soprano rounds on Maria and tells her off. (In my experience, only Polanski's cast makes this believable.)

Maybe by the time Dunaway takes her performance into the film studio, she, too, will have succeeded in making the role her own. Maybe she will team up with a director who can help her find the way. Word is that she was hoping for Franco Zeffirelli—an intimate of Callas's who directed the diva in historic productions of *La Traviata, Tosca,* and *Norma*—but that he, citing loyalty, declined. Maybe Polanski will prove amenable. It will be a pity if the movie puts an end to the burgeoning gallery of Marias.

"You must try to characterize the person you will play, decide what sort of individual she is, what her background is, what her attitudes must be," Callas said at Juilliard. "This you will get from the music, not from history. History has its Anne Boleyn, for instance, and she is quite different from the Anna Bolena of Donizetti." Whatever clues future actresses may glean from Callas's life and recordings, the text they must master is McNally's.

CRITICAL COMMENTARY

Cary M. Mazer (essay date 2001)

SOURCE: Mazer, Cary M. "*Master Class* and the Paradox of the Diva." In *Modern Dramatists: A Casebook of Major British, Irish, and American Playwrights,* edited by Kimball King, pp. 153-65. New York: Routledge, 2001.

[*In the following essay, Mazer discusses McNally's handling of the "diva" theme in* Master Class.]

Master Class begins with a double untruth. Maria Callas (or, more accurately, the actress playing Maria Callas) strides on stage, almost certainly to the accompaniment of the audience's applause, looks directly at the audience, and announces, "No applause. We're here to work. You're not in a theatre. This is a classroom" (1).

The first untruth is the statement that we are not in a theatre, since we in fact are in a theatre, both outside of and within the fictional world of the play.[1] In *Master Class,* the stage of the theatre represents the stage of a theatre—the recital hall at the Juilliard School, where Maria Callas gave a series of master classes in 1971 and 1972 before a full house of students and spectators.

In the theatre, when *Master Class* is performed, it is, of course, not really 1971 but the present; it is not Juilliard but (for the play's Broadway run) the Golden Theatre; and the audience is comprised of paying theatregoers, not advanced voice students. But the audience is *there,* as an audience, in both the reality of the theatrical event and the fiction of the play. The actor may be (in the original production) Zoe Caldwell and not the "real" Maria Callas, but the response of the audience to Caldwell—applause—is the same response that the 1971 Juilliard audience (the fictional audience that the real audience pretends to be) has for Callas. For Caldwell/Callas to tell us that we are not in a theatre flies in the face of what we know to be true, both in life and in the fiction of the play.

The other untruth is that Maria Callas does not want applause. Maria Callas, we soon see, lives for applause, and thrives on having an audience, alternately revealing and concealing herself from it, pandering for its affection and sympathy and holding it in contempt. Later in the play (60) she will even deny that she had asked the audience not to applaud. Maria's attitude and her philosophical pronouncements are filled with such contradictions: that we cannot know what she suffered in Greece during the war and that we have to know it; that one can only create art if one has suffered and that one must not bring one's private suffering to one's art; that singers sing for the sheer joy of it and that singers must never give away their talent except for sufficient pay, etc., etc. The paradox of the audience's simultaneous presence and absence, of the fiction's theatricality and non-theatricality, is mirrored by Maria Callas's opinions—at best paradoxical and at worst contradictory and mutually exclusive—about life, art, performance, and their relationship. And at the heart of these paradoxes is the real subject of the play, what one might call "the Paradox of the Diva."

Terrence McNally has dramatized the phenomenology of the diva before, most notably in what might be considered the ultimate play about "opera queens," *The Lisbon Traviata.* But there the focus is not on the diva but on her fans, the homosexual protagonists who project onto the diva their own identity, desires, and suffering. In *The Lisbon Traviata* the opera queen's identification is both with the singer and with the operatic role she plays: both with Maria Callas, the self-consuming performer who makes her private suffering transcendently public through her performances, and with Violetta, the consumptive courtesan in *La Traviata,* who sacrifices her happiness and her health for love.

McNally is not interested in the phenomenon of the opera queen in *Master Class* (though in one of the flashback sequences, Maria ventriloquizes the voice of her lover Aristotle Onassis, who observes "The fags just want to be you" [26]). Instead he shifts his focus to the object of the opera queen's emulation, the diva herself. But the way he views the diva is clearly in line with the paradoxes and contradictions in the way opera queens admire and emulate the diva, a phenomenon most recently articulated in Wayne Koestenbaum's autobiographical polemic, *The Queen's Throat: Opera, Homosexuality, and the Mystery of Desire.* The opera queen, Koestenbaum argues, admires both the diva's persona—her arrogance, grandeur, and self-fashioned hauteur and sublime bitchiness—and the roles that the diva plays. Indeed, the opera queen's identification with the roles the diva plays magnifies the opera queen's emulation of the diva, for the diva, the opera queen believes, identifies with the character even more closely than the opera queen ever can and so becomes the opera queen's emotionally expressive, sacrificial surrogate. As Stephen, one of the two opera queens in *The Lisbon Traviata,* explains, "Opera is about us, our life-and-death passions—we all love, we're all going to die. Maria understood that. That's where the voice came from, the heart, the soul, I'm tempted to say from some even more intimate place" (61). At the end of the play, Stephen, having failed to enact Don Jose to his departing lover's Carmen, throws his head back in a silent scream of heartbreak while Callas's Violetta plays on the stereo, the diva's voice expressing a pain that is simultaneously the singer's, the character's, and the listener's.[2]

The diva, the subject of the opera queen's emulation, is simultaneously present and absent, playing a distilled and self-fashioned version of herself in every role she plays and dissolving herself into the music and the dramatic situation of the character she acts and sings, rendering herself transparent to the character and the composer (and librettist) behind the character. The difference between the actor and the character she is playing is erased in the eyes of the opera queen: the diva is both transcendently herself and transubstantially the character; indeed, that is to a great extent the source of her glory.

But the relation of an actor to the character he or she is playing is, in the theatre as well as in opera, much more complicated and more paradoxical than the opera queen imagines. And this complicated relationship of actor to role—the paradoxical complementarity of the consummately self-effacing actor and the transcendently-herself diva—is the real subject of *Master Class,* a play in which the opera-singer-as-lecturer is not "in character" ("You're not in a theatre. This is a classroom") and yet is never, strictly speaking, "out" of character, in which theatrical performances draw upon the performer's true "self" and yet the "self" is itself always performative.

The salient biographical facts about Maria Callas's life are all made reference to in *Master Class* her American and Greek upbringing, her training, the patronage of

Battista Meneghini, her debut, her radical physical transformation and weight loss, her affair with Onassis, her conflicts with tenors, managers, directors, and rival sopranos, the hirings and firings, and the precipitate decay of her voice. But the play is less a biography of the artist than it is a play about the nature of artistry, the relation of a particular artist's life to her art. The paradoxes of this relationship are both the play's subject and dictate the play's form, and these paradoxes ultimately lead to a shift in the play's focus that muddies the play's focus and, as we shall see, finally undoes the play's otherwise pristine structure.

The play's action, such as it is, consists of three consecutive coaching sessions in real time: Sophie de Palma, a soprano, who sings Adina's "Ah, non credea mirarti" from Bellini's *La Somnambula;* Anthony Candolino, a tenor, who sings "Ricondita armonia" from Puccini's *Tosca;* and soprano Sharon Graham, who is driven from the stage by Callas's brow-beating but returns to be coached in Lady Macbeth's entrance aria, "Vieni! t'afretta" from Verdi's *Macbeth.* In each of these sessions, Callas is rude, condescending, dismissive, and egocentric. And in all three sessions she is a brilliant teacher. And there emerges from her teaching, however obnoxious, a coherent, if complex, philosophical position about the relationship of the singing actor to the operatic role.

Callas interrupts the first note that Sophie de Palma sings in the Bellini aria: "I want to talk to you about your 'Oh!'" The student answers, "I sang it, didn't I?" Callas explains:

> That's just it. You sang it. You didn't feel it. It's not a note we're after here. It's a sob of pain. The pain of loss. Surely you understand loss. If not of another person, then maybe a pet. A puppy. A goldfish.
>
> (13)

Mixed with Callas's patronizing examples ("a puppy. A goldfish") is a stereotypical "Stanislavski Method" acting exercise—Lee Strasberg's "emotional memory"—in which the actor substitutes an experience from his or her own life to generate an emotional response equivalent to the emotions of the character that are called for in the dramatic situation of the script. Callas repeatedly rejects "just singing" ("You were *just* singing," she tells the tenor, "which equals nothing" [40]). Instead she calls for acting, in the twentieth-century Stanislavskian tradition: feeling "real" emotions based on the "given circumstances" of the script and embellished or translated in the imagination of the actor (when the tenor complains that "It doesn't say anything about ten A.M. or spring or Tosca's body in the score," Callas responds, "It should say it in your imagination. Otherwise you have notes, nothing but notes" [43]).

The emotions that Callas calls for are not "realistic"; they are channeled through the artifice of the operatic medium ("Anyone can walk in their sleep," she tells Sophie, singing a somnambulist's aria; "Very few people can weep in song" [11]). Each successive level of expression in opera is more artificial: speech is more active and demands more actively channeled emotional energy and a more intense revelation of one's own more intense emotions than silence; recitative calls for more energy and emotion than speech ("When you can no longer bear to speak, when the words aren't enough, that's when he [Bellini] asks you to sing" [18]); aria more than recitative; and a cabaletta more than its preceding aria.

"This is not a film studio," she explains, "where anyone can get up there and act. I hate that word. 'Act.' No! Feel. Be. That's what we're doing here" (16). And she later tells Sharon, helping her "make an entrance" for her Lady Macbeth entrance aria, "This is opera, not a voice recital. Anyone can stand there and sing. An artist enters and *is*" (35). What Callas means by "be" and "is" is clearly something more than passive existence or inexpressive emotion and is rather a grand, artificial, projected distillation of one's identity and emotional truth: as she tells Sophie, "This is the theatre, darling. We wear our hearts on our sleeves here" (11). When she tells Sophie "I'm not getting any juice from you, Sophie. I want juice. I want passion. I want you" (16), she clearly means that the "you" that an opera singer needs to "be," the being that breathes and feels and sings on stage, is something grand, extreme, distilled, and directed. Callas doubts whether Sophie has that magnitude of experience or the magnitude of expressiveness: "He's broken her heart. Have you ever had your heart broken?" she asks. When Sophie answers, "Yes," Callas adds, snidely, "You could have fooled me" (11); and Sophie herself concludes, ruefully, "I'm not that sort of singer. . . . I'm not that sort of person either" (16).

What "sort of person" does it take to be an opera singer? Here again there are both paradoxes and contradictions in what Callas teaches. On the one hand, she claims on her first entrance, the diva must practice complete self-effacement: "If you want to have a career, as I did—and I'm not boasting now, I am not one to boast—you must be willing to subjugate yourself—is that a word?—subjugate yourself to music" (2). But, paradoxically, the singer both erases herself and is completely herself. For subjugation involves sacrifice, and what is being sacrificed is the singer's own self. The diva must be a supreme egotist in order to make the supreme sacrifice of her ego to her audiences. And, she argues, you must be well paid for your pains. "Never give anything away. There's no more where it came from. We give the audience everything and when it's gone, *c'est ca, c'est tout. Basta, finito.* We're the ones who end up empty" (32). She invokes Medea's line to Jason in Cherubini's *Medea*—"I gave everything for you. Everything"—to explain this: "That's what we artists do for people. Where would you be without us? Eh? Think about that. Just think about it while you're counting your millions or leading your boring lives with your boring wives" (32). The sacrifice of the self is too great to be wasted on psychotherapy: "Feelings like Sharon's"—who has run off stage to vomit and has not yet returned—"We use them. We don't give them away on some voodoo witch doctor's couch" (40). Instead, they should be saved for the stage, where they are distilled and delivered, at great personal pain, to the audience.

Callas's relation to her audience—both the audience of her operatic past and the current audience in the classroom/recital hall—is fraught with contradictions. "The audience is the enemy," she says, quoting Medea's line to Jason; "Dominate them. . . . Art is domination. It's making people think for that precise moment in time there is only one way, one voice. Yours. Eh?" (37). At times (including the flashback sequences, in which Callas recalls singing only for Meneghini or only for Onassis), the audience is worthy of the singer's self-immolation and sacrifice. At other times the audience is passive, unappreciative, and unworthy: she talks scornfully of an acquaintance whose favorite part of the operas are the intervals; and we see her hold in contempt the stagehand in the recital hall, who neither knows nor cares about the art being created on the stage within earshot.

McNally best dramatizes the capacity of an audience to be moved by the artificially distilled expressive powers of the singer's voice and emotions channeled through the composer's music when Callas herself listens to Tony Candolino sing "Ricondita armonia." To the tenor's disappointment, after he has finished singing, she says only "That was beautiful. I have nothing more to say. That was beautiful" (44). Being an audience member, being the recipient of the imagined emotions of Cavaradossi for Tosca as channeled through the voice and soul of the tenor as she never was when she played Tosca herself ("I was always backstage preparing for my entrance" [45]), Callas is, for one of the rare moments in the play, left speechless. And she stumbles awkwardly from that moment—a moment that demonstrates why, from an audience's point of view, the singer's art is worthwhile—to the unexpected admission that "It's a terrible career, actually. I don't know why I bothered" (45).

Through her pedagogical encounters with Sophie and Tony, Callas teaches both the students and the audience what it takes to become an effective singing actor. One must have suffered sufficiently to provide the emotional raw material for embodying the character's emotion. One must be willing to reexperience the most difficult times of one's life over and over again, with all of the focused and distilled intensity of the first experience.

One must be willing to display one's most private feelings and experiences in public, both to an uncaring and ungrateful audience (personified, in **Master Class,** by the stagehand) and to an attentive and appreciative public that demands that each performance be yet another self-consuming and self-consumed display of reexperienced emotional agonies. And, finally, becoming a singing actor requires the singer to turn him- or herself into an artificial being, in part because the medium of musical and theatrical expression is so highly conventionalized and artificial and in part because of the cutthroat world of the operatic profession. One must, in short, play the part of the diva to be a diva; one must become a monster of egotism, selfishness, competitiveness, and vindictiveness, capable of cutting a swathe for oneself in the world of managers, conductors, directors, claques, and other divas, in order to get the opportunity to practice one's art. And, by practicing one's art, by dredging up every life experience and emotion in the service of the drama, and the dramatic character, and the music, one self-destructs, consuming irreversibly the raw material of the art in the very act of making the art. Becoming the diva leaves little more than dry tinder; singing sets the tinder alight, burning with a brilliant flame before the audience, until all that is left are ashes, thorns, and nails.

And so we see Maria Callas through the play: a brilliant actress still, still wearing her all-too-public life's pain on her sleeve, still grabbing the spotlight, indulging her ego, destroying with a glance or a quip everyone around her. And when she finally sings, the stage directions record, "What comes out is a cracked and broken thing" (47).[3]

By the middle of the second act, after Callas has coached two singers and driven a third from the stage, we have learned about the paradoxes of acting contained within the diva's craft, and we have come to some understanding of how this craft calls upon the singer to create a particular performative persona and to put that persona to the service of the self-consuming art of singing. Callas, in her roundabout and often contradictory way, explains these principles to us as she coaches Sophie and Tony, and she demonstrates, in her abominably egotistical behavior, what she has become in service of this art. But it not until the final third of the play, when she coaches Sharon Graham, that we see the means by which a younger singer can put these principles into practice, that we see a singer who can become, potentially at least, another Callas and, in this instance, chooses not to.

Sharon has returned to the recital stage after vomiting in fear and humiliation, determined now to prove herself. Callas humiliates her and browbeats her into acting and not just singing the aria, as she did with Sophie and Tony. But here, as we watch, the Stanislavskian exercises and the Strasbergian emotional memory substitutions begin to work. Callas insists that everything be concrete, specific: the letter from Macbeth that Lady Macbeth reads, in unsung speech before the recitative, must be real, and not imagined ("I don't want pretending. You're not good enough. I want truth [46]); the news of Duncan's imminent arrival comes not from 'someone' but from 'a servant'" (51). When Sharon hesitates between the recitative and the aria, Callas, swept up in the flow of the drama and encouraging Sharon to be swept up too, insists "don't even think of stopping! You are Lady Macbeth!" (48). After the aria, with the news of Duncan's arrival, the emotional identification of Sharon with Lady Macbeth is, with Callas's coaching, nearly complete:

MARIA:

How does that make her feel?

SOPRANO:

Happy?

MARIA:

Don't keep looking at me for answers, Sharon. Tell me, show me. Vite, vite!

SOPRANO:

Really happy.

MARIA:

Love happy? Christmas morning happy?

SOPRANO:

Murder happy!

MARIA:

Ah! And what is she going to do about it?

SOPRANO:

She's going to sing a cabaletta!

MARIA:

She's going to kill the king! Do you know what that means?

SOPRANO:

Yes, it's terrible.

MARIA:

Not to her! Do you believe women can have balls, Sharon?

SOPRANO:

Some women. Yes, I do!

MARIA:

Verdi is daring you to show us yours, Sharon. Will you do it?

SOPRANO:

Yes.

(51-52)

The stakes of the scene, the stakes of the act of performing itself, have become, for Sharon, nearly like those for Callas. "This isn't just an opera. This is your life," Callas insists (50). "Is there anything you would kill for, Sharon," she asks her, suggesting "A man, a career?" (53). "You have to listen to something in yourself to sing this difficult music," she insists, suggesting that the characters she has sung, and the characters of the classical tragedies of her native Greece—Medea, Electra, Klytemnestra—were real people, to whom she has a real connection:

MARIA:

These people really existed. Medea, Lady Macbeth. Or don't you believe that? Eh? This is all make-believe to you?

SOPRANO:

I've never really thought about it.

MARIA:

That's because you're young. You will. In time. Know how much suffering there can be in store for a woman.

(53)

As Sharon sings, she feels in her soul, her body, and her voice the connection that Callas insists is the true art of the diva. And she is told, and undoubtedly understands, the life, emotions, and experience to which the singing actor's art must be connected: one in which she is capable of feeling that she *could* kill for a man or a career, where in time she will know how much suffering is in store for her, where she can not only believe in Medea or Lady Macbeth but can feel so strong a kinship with them that she can *become* them, emotionally and viscerally. Sharon, unlike Sophie and Tony, is capable of learning the lessons that Callas has to teach.

After Sharon finishes singing the complete aria and cabaletta, Callas, coming out of her reverie/flashback sequence, dismisses Sharon's professional prospects, damning her with the faint praise:

I think you should work on something more appropriate for your limitations. Mimi or Micaela maybe. But Lady Macbeth, Norma, I don't think so. These roles require something else. Something. How shall I say this? Something special. Something that can't be taught or passed on or copied or even talked about. Genius. Inspiration. A gift of god. Some recompense for everything else.

(61)

Sharon, in tears, responds:

I wish I'd never done this. I don't like you. You can't sing anymore and you're envious of anyone younger who can. You just want us to sing like you, recklessly, and lose our voices in ten years like you did. Well, I

won't do it. I don't want to. I don't want to sing like
you. I hate people like you. You want to make the world
dangerous for everyone just because it was for you.

(61)

Sharon clearly wants to get back at Callas for her
condescension. But there is more to her response than
this. Sharon sees in Callas's cruelty the more important
truth of the diva's art: that this type of art exacts too
high a price, that one would not wish upon oneself the
experiences and suffering that could generate such art,
and that creating art from such personal and emotional
raw materials is self-consuming, and ultimately destroys
the medium of the art—the singer's voice. Sharon
leaves the stage; Callas brushes off the confrontation,
withdraws into the shell of her professional persona, utters a few platitudes about art and, saying "well, that's
that" (62), brings both the master class and *Master
Class* to a close.

Throughout the play, McNally has been putting forth as
his hypothesis the myth of Callas the diva: she so channel, her own life and emotions into her singing and acting; she so fully becomes a conduit for her own sor-
rows and the object of projection for the fantasies and
emotions of her audiences that she has ruined her voice
and withered into a cruel and egotistical if magnificent
monster, a *monstre sacre*. Sharon's defection at the end
only confirms the hypothesis and elevates the diva to an
even-greater level: a figure of sublime loneliness,
shunned as a pariah, so monstrous that she can be
watched in awe but is too horrifying to be emulated.

The dramaturgical mastery of *Master Class* lies in its
twin strategies for representing Callas as a dramatic
character. For, in watching her teach, we see the monster
she has become; and in learning *what* she teaches—the
practices of personal, emotional-based acting that she
teaches unsuccessfully to Sophie and Tony and successfully if Pyrrhically to Sharon—we learn how she has
become that person. We see less the genuine person and
more the persona that Callas has created for herself and
that has been created for her: the diva. From the moment that Callas singles out a member of the audience
to demonstrate how "It's important to have a look" (3),
we see the theatricality, the performativity of the diva's
persona. "This isn't a freak show. I'm not a performing
seal," she tells Sophie, explaining that her fabled fieriness is not a performance but an ingrained part of her
identity: "My fire comes from here, Sophie. It's mine.
It's not for sale. It's not for me to give away. Even if I
could, I wouldn't. It's who I am. Find out who you are.
That's what this is all about. Eh?" (8). And yet Callas *is*
a freak, a performing seal.[4] Within Callas's talents as a
self-creator, within the persona that she has forged from
her status as diva ("Never miss an opportunity to theat-
ricalize," she tells Sharon [35]), everything is a
performance. Acting, even when acting means sur-

rendering to a character and effectively becoming that
character, never entails the loss of self; indeed, it is
where the performative self is created and articulated.
As the stage director Visconti tells her (in the first-act
flashback sequence), "You are not a village girl. You
are Maria Callas playing a village girl" (24). Callas's
"performance" as teacher of a master class *is* Callas.
The diva uses herself to perform; consequently she only
is when she performs.

And so it is—or should be—with McNally's drama: We
see what she has become and we learn the process by
which she became this way. But this is, of course, not
the entire play, nor is the master class, despite the plays
title, the only narrative and dramaturgical means by
which the playwright shows us Callas's character. Mc-
Nally has demonstrated for us what she has become and
taught us the process of acting that has made her this
way—one that demands that she wear her emotions on
her sleeve and transmit her own life and suffering into
her performances through her body and voice on stage.
What we do not know—and what opera queens cannot
know about a diva, except through gossip columns and
the fanciful projections of their own imaginations—is
the life lived, the nature of the actual sufferings that the
singer transmutes into her performances.

The genius of *Master Class* is that, once we have seen
what Callas has become and learned how she used (and
used up) her life to get this way, we don't actually *need*
to know the life that she lived. But this is precisely
what McNally gives us, in the most theatrically stunning sequences of the play: the flashback fantasy
sequences, to the accompaniment of Callas's live
recordings of the arias that the student singers are singing. These sequences—brilliant as they are in performance, affording an opportunity for the actor to jump
back and forth between Callas's student years and her
triumphant debuts and between her public and private
lives—belong to two other genres of play entirely. One
genre is the autobiographical one-hander (such as the
Lillian Hellman vehicle that Zoe Caldwell played a few
years before she created the role of Callas in *Master
Class*), in which the historical figure, through some
theatrical pretense (Emily Dickinson inviting us in as
neighbors to share her recipes, Truman Capote speaking
into a tape recorder for the benefit of a journalist) retells
and relives formative events from his or her life.

The other genre to which the flashback sequences of
Master Class belongs is, arguably, the largest segment
of American twentieth-century dramatic writing, what
might best be called the "psychotherapeutic whodunit."
In such plays, a protagonist's tragic agony or a family's
crippling dysfunction can be traced, as in the Freudian
psychoanalytical model, to a single, traumatic event,
real or imagined, that is concealed from several of the
characters and the audience until late in the play: Biff

sees Willy with a prostitute in a cheap hotel in Boston; Mary Tyrone regresses to a point in her life before she discovered her husband to be an alcoholic and, more significantly, before the infant Eugene died of the infection given to him by his older brother Jamie; George and Martha "kill off" the child which the audience and Nick discover to have been invented by them; Dodge and Bradley narrate the story of the child buried in the backyard.

The flashback sequences in **Master Class** satisfy the whodunit energies generated by the theories of acting taught and practiced by Callas in the real-time framework of the play. If Callas is indeed transforming her real-life suffering, to which she casually alludes repeatedly in her teaching, then the audience naturally desires to learn more about these traumatic experiences: Callas proving herself to her teacher, Callas's La Scala debut, her final performances at La Scala in defiance of the general manager who was firing her, the patronage of Battista Meneghini, and her abusive relationship with Onassis. Moreover, the flashback sequences confirm the ways that Callas's personal emotions—shame, desire, vindictiveness, revenge—are channeled into her singing. Just as Lady Macbeth invites the unholy spirit to enter her body, Callas invites the voices of her own life to enter her, through Verdi's "infernal music," to "Come, fill me with your malevolence" (55). As the house lights in La Scala come up as Callas finishes her *La Somnambula* aria on the stage of La Scala, she is able to reverse the audience's vampiric gaze, to see the eyes of the viewers devouring her performance, and can declare, "My revenge, my triumph are complete" (29).

The logic of the standard American dramaturgical master narrative demands that the audience know the biographical causes of characterological effects. For an audience, to understand the formative traumas is to know the character; for a character, to face the cause is to begin to heal; and, for character and audience alike, theatrically reliving these traumas is both a form of purgation and a fulfillment of the plays dramaturgical logic. In **Master Class,** the traumatic event to which the whodunit logic of the play points turns out to be a familiar one in American drama: Callas, having been told by Onassis that the greatest gift she can give him is a child, announces that she is pregnant and is now told by him that she must get rid of the child. As in *Long Day's Journey into Night, Desire Under the Elms, Who's Afraid of Virginia Woolf, The American Dream, Buried Child, Talley's Folly,* and countless lesser American plays, the central hidden trauma of the play turns out to be female fertility; the missing center of the play discover that Callas, the object of the opera queen's emulation and envy, is herself consumed with envy; and the object of her envy is something common both to American drama and to the mythology of male homosexuality: the womb.[4]

In exploring the phenomenon of the diva, the play's own logic asks us to resist such easy answers. Callas was willing to create art from the material of her life at great cost. We learn how she did so, and we see the cost. If **Master Class** is indeed about art and its making out of life, then, ironically, we need to see the life *only* through the art. But in the flashback sequences and in their reversion to the traditional dead-baby trope, the playwright gives us too much. The sequences are arguably more than just a violation of the playwright's own metatheatrical fiction and more than just a deviation from his chosen dramaturgical structure in favor of a return to the more traditional structural conventions of the psychotherapeutic whodunit: they are a violation of the theories of art explored in the play. The flashbacks effectively turn the playwright, and the audience, into opera queens: they not only allow us, like the opera queen, to imagine that the person's real pain can be heard in the diva's voice; they materially confirm that the pain and its origins is everything we imagine it to be. In narrating and reenacting her life to sounds of her own voice singing Adina or Lady Macbeth on a recording, Callas is effectively lip-synching her own life, just as Stephen lip-synchs to Callas's Violetta at the end of **The Lisbon Traviata.** Callas not only fulfills the opera queen's myth of the diva; in **Master Class** the queen of opera demonstrably becomes an opera queen herself.

Notes

1. Virtually every conventional twentieth-century play asks an audience to efface its existence, to pretend that it is not in a theatre: to pretend that the stage is not a stage but is an estate in Russia, a tenement in Brooklyn, or an apartment in New Orleans; and to pretend that the audience itself is invisible and incorporeal, voyeurs to the fiction of a life unfolding on the stage. Even in Pirandello's Six Characters in Search of an Author, which dispenses with one layer of fiction (the stage represents a stage and the auditorium represents an auditorium), the audience present in that auditorium must pretend that they are not there, that the auditorium is empty, that the performance they are attending is actually a rehearsal before empty seats.

2. The phenomenon of homosexual identification with the performer is dramatized in The Kiss of the Spider Woman, McNally's adaptation of Manuel Puig's novel for the musical stage. Molina, the homosexual pederast and movie buff, displaces his artistic expressiveness onto his fantasy film actress just as the opera queen displaces his own emotional expressiveness into the throat of the diva. While Aurora performs her song-and-dance numbers (in Molina's fantasy projections) down-

stage, Molina, seated upstage in his jail cell, moves his lips and silently gestures, mirroring Aurora's words and gestures.

3. In this, McNally has cleverly found a way to compensate for the impossibility of casting an actress who can actually sing like Callas; the role was written for an actress—Zoe Caldwell—who is not a singer.

4. And she demonstrates repeatedly (and demonstrated only a few seconds before) that fieriness and temperamentality are character traits only insofar as they put into action, and that a diva can put them into action at will. Sophie has boasted that her own Greek and Italian heritage has given her a fiery temperament Callas asks:

MARIA:

Do something fiery.

SOPRANO:

I can't Not just like that. No one can.

MARIA:

WHERE IS MY FOOTSTOOL?

SOPRANO:

Well, I guess some people can.

(8)

5. It is not unusual for male playwrights, of whatever sexual orientation, to turn to issues of fertility when they invent formative traumas for their female characters. A key example is the South African playwright Athol Fugard: in *The Road to Mecca*, his first (and to date only) play with two principal female characters and only a subsidiary male role, he needed to invent a biographical source for Elsa's dramatic crisis (the other principal female character, Helen, was drawn from life), and chose to have her reveal to Helen, in the play's final moments, that she had just had an abortion.

Works Cited

Koestenbaum, Wayne. *The Queen's Throat: Opera, Homosexuality, and the Mystery of Desire.* New York: Poseidon Press, 1993.

McNally, Terrence. *Master Class.* New York: Penguin Books, 1995.

Three Plays by Terrence McNally: The Lisbon Traviata, Frankie and Johnny in the Clair de Lune, It's Only a Play. New York: Penguin Books, 1990.

CORPUS CHRISTI (1998)

PRODUCTION REVIEW

Charles McNulty (review date December 1998)

SOURCE: McNulty, Charles. "The Last Temptation of MTC." *American Theatre* 15, no. 10 (December 1998): 64-7.

[*In the following review, McNulty examines the controversy surrounding McNally's* Corpus Christi.]

The swirl of controversy that attended Manhattan Theatre Club's off-again, on-again production of Terrence McNally's **Corpus Christi** culminated in an opening night standoff between First Amendment activists and members of various Christian groups led by the Catholic League for Religious and Civil Rights. Outside MTC's City Center home on West 55th Street, nearly 2,000 dueling protestors waved signs with messages like "Excommunicate McNally!" and "Free Speech Not Only Lives—It Rocks!" To avoid any potential violence, the police divided the block into two heavily patrolled halves, voices of support on one side, voices of condemnation on the other. Despite the bitter recriminations of both parties, the evening translated into a resounding affirmation of the First Amendment— **Corpus Christi** maintained its right to be seen in the face of telephoned bomb threats, while those who felt strongly either for or against the production were free to peacefully air their views.

This victory in the battle over free speech, however, was neither easy nor completely reassuring. The case of **Corpus Christi** is indicative of the current cultural climate of intolerance and intimidation that threaten one of the most persecuted minorities in America—gays and lesbians. The conservative agenda has aggressively stepped up its tactics of exploiting the unpopularity of this group—in effect using them as scapegoats to consolidate their own increasingly nervous constituency. What better way to galvanize their voting troops than to campaign against the NEA and all those tax dollars going to support "elitist" (i.e., illicit) art catering to the warped values of the unconverted homosexual?

Early inflammatory accounts in the *New York Post* egged on the Religious Right by referring to McNally's then work-in-progress as the "Gay Jesus play," and falsely claiming that the story features a Christ-like character named Joshua who has gay sex with his 12 disciples. The firestorm of outrage that ensued against this presumed wickedness mixed legitimate protest with criminal menace, leaving MTC officials in the no-win situation of having to decide between issues of censorship and public safety.

In a regrettable moment of genuine fear and confusion, MTC artistic director Lynne Meadow announced last May that she could not move forward with *Corpus Christi,* citing, in addition to numerous death threats that McNally had received, one anonymous caller's vow "to exterminate the author, the staff and our audiences, and burn the building to the ground." That decision led to a fierce show of solidarity from the theatre community in support of McNally and in opposition to any form of censorship. Less than three days later Meadow reinstated the play, explaining that she had been given reasonable assurance by police commissioner Howard Safir regarding security measures that would enable her to produce the play "responsibly and safely."

Certainly no one was taking any chances on opening night. A tremor of fear could be felt as ticketholders for *Corpus Christi* made their way through the metal detectors and past the security agents, while members of the Catholic League cried "shame, shame, shame." The evening's protest began with a rallying oration from William A. Donohue, the Catholic League's president, a fiery man whose white hair and oversized glasses had many in his camp confusing him with the former talk show host with the same last name. Amid the frenzy of bobbing crucifixes and prayerful murmuring, Donohue denounced the play as "deliberate blasphemy," calling it a form of "hate speech" that the liberal community is simply too hypocritical to recognize.

"The play is saying that the Catholic religion is a joke," one demonstrator said. "It's ridiculous to claim that Jesus Christ was a homosexual. There's absolutely no respect involved." Donohue claims his organization is not challenging the legal right to insult his religion, but the moral right. The distinction, however, between the two categories became superfluous when he later shouted into his bullhorn, "Keep it clean when you deal with our religion, or get out of town."

The well-attended if more subdued rally organized by the People for the American Way Foundation and several other free-speech groups was distinctly more Apollonian in its approach than Donohue's Dionysiac ritual. No eyes-closed, hallucinatory chanting for these demonstrators, who held signs with quotes from Voltaire and Adlai Stevenson. Most defended the right of the Catholic League to publicly express their views, though a vocal minority obviously wanted to silence the opposition.

Tony Kushner, Wallace Shawn, Robert MacNeil and Norman Lear were in attendance, as was Diane Torr, a performance artist with a painted mustache and picket sign that read "Jesus Christ—Get Over It." An elderly tourist from California wondered what the phrase implied. "This is about who owns Jesus," Torr explained to the woman. "Everyone has the right to write about him. You can define him as gay or straight—he's a mythological character, like Zeus or Hercules." Her questioner looked skeptical.

The two sides rarely had such opportunities to address each other's arguments directly, though Kushner challenged the Catholic League's appropriation of the term "hate speech," which he sees as another instance of "the Reaganite tactic of co-opting the language of genuinely endangered minorities to further their own oppressive agenda." The designer Ming Cho Lee, who personally invited students from Yale, NYU and Columbia to join him in the protest, explained his position: "We are at a crossroads right now. This is no time to bicker among ourselves. We deal with ambiguity—they deal with fundamentalism. The other side is not timid at all. We have to defend every square inch of our freedom." Shawn looked puzzled when asked for his thoughts about the public's reaction to a play that most hadn't yet seen. "If you really believe in free speech, you don't need to have seen it," he replied. "If you're outraged, then you probably should have gone."

The reviews haven't been exactly favorable. Neither the *New York Times*' Ben Brantley nor the *New Yorker*'s Nancy Franklin could resist the joke that the theatrical fun stops right after the metal detectors. But *Corpus Christi* isn't the embarrassment most critics would have us believe. And while objectionable to those who hold the literal word of the New Testament as sacred, it is not intended as an assault on Catholic values. *Corpus Christi* is, in fact, an earnest reckoning with the Christ story's contemporary resonance, which, far from trying to shock, wears its good intentions on its sleeve. It represents the playwright operating in a new, more self-consciously didactic vein (enhanced by director Joe Mantello's graceful, neo-Brechtian staging). For those who adore the humorous poignancy of McNally's portraits of characters trapped in lonely prisons of their own bad habits (is there anything in contemporary gay writing more comically sublime than the first act of *The Lisbon Traviata*?), the play may very well disappoint. But for its courage to relate the deeper significance of a 2,000-year-old story to a community traditionally excluded from its potentially healing message, *Corpus Christi* deserves our attention. The current media storm may have unfairly raised our expectations, but no doubt the play, modest as it is, will outlast its sensationalized headlines.

Sharon L. Green (review date May 1999)

SOURCE: Green, Sharon L. "Performance Review: *Corpus Christi.*" *Theatre Journal* 51, no. 2 (May 1999): 194-96.

[*In the following review, Green gives* Corpus Christi *a lukewarm reception, applauding the performers and the production, but finding the script bland.*]

On May 23, 1998, the *New York Times* announced that the Manhattan Theatre Club would be canceling its scheduled production of playwright Terrence McNally's newest play, *Corpus Christi,* due to bomb and death threats made against the theatre, its personnel, and the playwright. The Catholic League for Religious and Civil Rights disavowed responsibility for the threats but did publicly applaud the decision, calling the play "blasphemous." A week later, after counter-demonstrations by a roster of well-known contemporary playwrights, the play was reinstated at MTC. Although the Catholic League's president had not read the play, reports claiming that it depicted a gay Jesus-like figure who has sex with his apostles was enough to ignite a series of events that captured the attention of New Yorkers, theatre artists and others, perhaps to a greater extent than McNally's play itself.

On opening night, two separate demonstrations took place concurrently on opposite ends of the block outside the theater. Play protesters assembled at one end with placards declaring McNally's play a lie and homosexuality a sin, as well as demanding the play be censored. At the other end of the block, supporters of the play, who were participating in a "silent march" organized by the People for the American Way, carried small white placards with quotes from various notable individuals on the importance of freedom of expression. Hundreds of New York City police officers and dozens of news reporters rounded out the outdoor cast. Throughout the play's run, as a precautionary measure, all audience members passed through a metal detector, and the city stationed a police officer outside the theatre.

Corpus Christi is presumably a reclamation of the story of Christ's life for gay men. Within its metatheatrical structure, the thirteen male actors assembled onstage to announce their intentions of retelling "an old and familiar story." The actors were then transformed into their characters by the actor playing John, who symbolically baptized each of them. The theatre had been stripped bare to expose its backstage areas and lighting equipment. The actors changed into their costumes—khaki pants, white shirts and bare feet—at the rear of the space, in full view of the audience. Most of the play's action then took place on the large wooden stage in the center of the space, but exposure of the backstage areas meant that the actors remained in view of the audience for most of the performance.

The story begins with Mary giving birth to Joshua, the Jesus-like figure, in a motel in Corpus Christi, Texas. McNally's script is peppered with comic giveaway lines, such as Joseph's sexually frustrated acknowledgment of Mary's virginity. The story follows Joshua as he grows up feeling different from his classmates, although the reasons for his difference are vague: is it because he hears the voice of God speaking to him constantly, or is it because he is gay? As the play progressed, his flustered high school prom date discovered him sharing his first stolen kiss with Judas, played by Josh Lucas. After their kiss the lights faded out and when they came back up the two were leaning against each other in a tired familiar way, fully clothed, smoking cigarettes, implying the two had sex. While Joshua later performed a marriage between two of his disciples, this was the extent of the sexually explicit content that had sparked controversy. Joshua hitchhiked out of Corpus Christi shortly after the prom to begin his predictable journey, perform the expected miracles, and amass a following of young disciples.

Much of what McNally points out—such as the hypocrisy of the Church's persecution of homosexuals in light of Christ's teachings of love and tolerance—is obvious. Parallels that both he and director Joe Mantello make between the persecution of Joshua and contemporary oppressions are hardly original. Of course, the protesters outside the theatre are a poignant reminder that even the obvious oftentimes needs to be restated. However, McNally's script does not come close to the searing critique of such hypocrisy in, for example, the 1989 French-Canadian film, *Jesus of Montreal.*

What rescued the production were the performances by the thirteen actors and the sometimes evocative direction by Joe Mantello. The ease, compassion and tenderness with which male bodies interacted onstage was rare, and for that, the production is notable. (However, they were all young bodies and, with the exception of James Leung, who played James the Less, all appeared to be white). The interaction of those bodies was certainly erotic, but not gratuitously vulgar as protesters imagined. The characters touched and held one another with tenderness and love, though, perhaps, that was what the protesters imagined and refused to accept. Anson Mount as Joshua captured the character's adolescent naiveté and confusion regarding his own destiny, both of which mature into immense, though not infinite, compassion for others. Joshua is human, and also exhibited moments of fear and impatience. He did not go unquestioningly to his death: he asked God if the nails would hurt as they pierced his skin and wondered, as he looked over his disciples, if they were worth suffering and dying for.

At the beginning of the performance, one actor declared the play's intention to take its audience somewhere "thrilling." *Corpus Christi* is ultimately disappointing for its failure to do so and its lack of originality and provocation, making the vehemence of the protests against its content come more sharply into focus as displaced homophobic anxiety. I wished McNally had told a bolder, more interesting story. And yet, there is also something powerful and moving in McNally's intention to reclaim this "old and familiar" story and the sheer presence of these bodies onstage trying to make it their own. In the context of recent debates over decency in artwork, the importance of this staging of *Corpus Christi* extends beyond the play's literary significance.

CRITICAL COMMENTARY

Raymond-Jean Frontain (essay date 2003)

SOURCE: Frontain, Raymond-Jean. "'All Men Are Divine': Religious Mystery and Homosexual Identity in Terrence McNally's *Corpus Christi*." In *Reclaiming the Sacred: The Bible in Gay and Lesbian Culture,* edited by Raymond-Jean Frontain, pp. 231-57. New York: Harrington Park Press, 2003.

[*In the following essay, Frontain explores the motif of Christianity in McNally's* Corpus Christi.]

At the heart of Terrence McNally's *Corpus Christi* is the performance of radical religious unorthodoxy. The play hinges upon the paradox that what has developed as historical Christianity, and is guarded as orthodox teaching by the most vocal and firmly established Christian sects, betrays the essence of Jesus' teachings. There is an expansive quality to religion, as to comedy; both enlarge the human spirit and strengthen it against the threat of existential diminishment that characterizes the profane life, which is generally the subject of tragedy.[1] In his preface to the printed text of his play, McNally anticipates the contradiction between true religion and facile pietism that he will develop within the play, distinguishing between worship of a sectarian idol and worship of a genuinely religious deity.

> If a divinity does not belong to all people, if He is not created in our image as much as we are created in His, then He is less a true divinity for all men to believe in than He is a particular religion's secular definition of what a divinity should be for the needs of its followers. Such a God is no God at all because He is exclusive to His members.
>
> (*Corpus Christi* v)

True religion is inclusive, guaranteeing enhancement of life for everyone, not just for a chosen few. "I am come that they [his sheep] might have life, and that they might have it more abundantly," explains Jesus, the Good Shepherd who unhesitatingly abandons the obedient members of his flock to rescue the lamb that has gone astray (John 10: 10, KJV).

Sects, conversely, are exclusive, propping up their members' spiritual and social confidence by degrading all nonmembers. Because their identity is so heavily invested in their need to believe that they are the elect or chosen of God, members of sects are driven not to love others but to make scapegoats of them, in effect perverting the very nature of religion. As an example of a sect's diminishing by coopting a broader, originally more inclusive religious system, McNally cites Roman Catholicism's re-creation of the Gospels' compassionate and deeply loving Jesus in the homophobic image of its ecclesiastical hierarchy, and the consequent reaffirmation of that "narrow-minded" belief in and by the Roman Catholic laity. Sectarianism—the conviction that one belongs to the minority that alone properly understands the teaching of the Scriptures and, thus, is deserving of salvation—creates a hell on earth rather than a New Jerusalem. At the heart of religious experience for McNally, conversely, are those qualities of "love! valour! compassion!" that figure in the title of his most successful play to date.

In *Corpus Christi,* McNally seeks to save the Bible from those who pervert it by trying, ironically, to safeguard its most limited and exclusionary meaning. The play, however, is the more extraordinary for alluding in its title to the "mystery" or "Corpus Christi" cycle plays designed to inculcate orthodoxy in the Middle Ages by arousing in their audience the desire to renounce the fleeting pleasures of this world and to share with God the eternal, purely spiritual bliss of the next. Rather than asking its audience to renounce its sinful humanity, however, *Corpus Christi* attempts to demonstrate that "all men are divine" (*Corpus Christi* 20), that paradoxically "We're each special. We're each ordinary. We're each divine" (*Corpus Christi* 50). In a maneuver that is typical of parodic satire but, significantly, that carries no satiric force in *Corpus Christi,* McNally reverses the traditional poles of expectation, showing the self-righteous people who are quick to judge others to be the real blasphemers against religion and life, and the marginalized and seemingly unorthodox to be the genuinely blessed. This is not a "queering" of biblical Judeo-Christianity, which McNally implies can be as hateful and perverse a behavior as that practiced by ardent religionists,[2] but an acceptance of (homo) sex as grace, and a sharing of grace through the salvific ritual that is theater.

Fellatio as Salvation

Corpus Christi retells the life of Jesus in terms of the 1950s coming of age of a gay teenager in the American "Bible belt," and his subsequent ministry during the post-Stonewall era of sexual license. The play's title phrase "Corpus Christi" engages multiple fields of reference, each of which indicates one of the oftentimes conflicting value schemes that operate in McNally's drama.

Most obviously, Corpus Christi is the name of protagonist Joshua's home town, the Texas city in which the play's action begins, and as such suggests a contradictory and ultimately self-destructive set of socially conservative values. Unable to accept the existence of a world larger than the local one, the "redneck" mind-set represented by the town's denizens elevates parochial values into universal absolutes, which consequently renders automatically suspect anyone who deviates from the local norm or who exists on its margins. Particularly suspect is anyone who engages in art or who is perceived as being "sensitive," for art challenges narrow-minded parochialism by asking a person to look beyond the protective hedge of comfortable, familiar, local values and see what one shares with others in the broadest sense. Teenaged Joshua is, thus, disparaged by his classmates for the decorations that he contributes to the senior prom ("Love that feminine touch, Joshua," *Corpus Christi* 29), and even by his mother, both for his seemingly unmanly participation in high school musicals (23-24) and for his friendship with a female teacher with whom he shares a love of poetry, opera, and chess (25-27).

It naturally follows that a community that is suspicious of artistic creativity is incapable as well of seeing the creative potential of human sexuality. Sex in the community of Corpus Christi is reduced to the exploitation, oftentimes violent, of women and queers. On the night of Joshua's nativity, for example, the audience hears (coming from the motel room next to Joseph and Mary's) first the "sounds of a couple making wild, uninhibited love":

WOMAN NEXT DOOR:

    Fuck me, fuck me, fuck me.

MAN NEXT DOOR:

    That's what I'm doing, you damn woman. I'm fucking you, I'm fucking you, I'm fucking you.

                       (*Corpus Christi* 14)

At the end of the scene, however, two other voices sound:

ANGRY MAN:

    You stupid piece of shit. You fucking cow.

FRIGHTENED WOMAN:

    I'm sorry. Just don't hit me again.

ANGRY MAN:

    Just don't (*sounds of a hit*) you again? Is that what you said? Just don't fucking (*sounds of a hit*) hit you again? Is that what you (*sounds of a hit, sounds of a hit, sounds of a hit*) fucking said to me? . . . Now what? You just gonna lie there like that? Fuck this shit. (*Sounds of a door slamming.*)

                       (*Corpus Christi* 19)

Males are privileged in Corpus Christi society, as is suggested by the motel manager's response to Mary's giving birth to a boy: "I like boys. Boys are best" (*Corpus Christi* 12). But from the start, boys are taught to understand their masculinity in terms of competition so fierce that it borders on violence. Upon first seeing Mary's newborn son, Joseph exults: "It's a boy. Hey, little fella. You gonna grow up and be an All-American halfback?" (*Corpus Christi* 14). In adolescence, however, Joshua's preference for music and poetry puts him at odds with his society. Even his parish priest, who is called upon by his religion to display love and kindness to a boy perceptibly weaker than others on the playground, torments him for not playing football, and turns a simple game into a clash of male wills or, even, ritualized emasculation (21-22).

When boys are taught to channel their physical energies so aggressively, it is little wonder that sex is reduced to a means by which men abuse those who are physically weaker than themselves. Teenaged Joshua's male classmates do not simply "score" sexually with girls, but they "keep score" among themselves of the girls they have shared, sex proving as competitive an arena as the football field. Not surprisingly, one of the high school classmates who attempts to humiliate Joshua sexually (32-33) is revealed later in life to still be repressing his sexual desire for the boy derisively voted by their class "Most Likely to Take It Up the Hershey Highway" (*Corpus Christi* 30, 38-39).

On its first level of signification, then, "Corpus Christi" represents a mind-set which has no sense of where sex fits into the divine scheme of things. Significantly, Corpus Christi—described by Joshua as "the armpit of Western civilization" (*Corpus Christi* 26)—is the Texas city in which McNally himself was raised, and which he left in order to live as a gay man and creative artist in New York City.

But "Corpus Christi" also refers to a feast in the Roman Catholic church calendar which celebrates the body of Christ. At the heart of Catholic ritual is the belief that at the moment of consecration, bread and wine (recalling those served by Jesus to his disciples during the Last Supper) miraculously become the body and blood of Christ, to be ritually consumed by the faithful.[3] This is the salvific mystery that is at the heart of Christian belief, that Jesus sacrificed his body and blood to redeem humankind from original sin. But whereas Protestant belief asserts that the Eucharist represents a figural process, the bread and wine being only a symbol of Jesus' actual flesh and blood, Roman Catholic teaching insists that the communicant literally consumes the savior's flesh.[4]

On its second level of signification, then, "Corpus Christi" suggests a redemptive sharing of one's body with those whom one loves; it points to the religious mystery by which the sharing of one's flesh and bodily fluid provides others with a transcendent happiness that they will in turn share with others and, thus, extend peace and harmony into the world. Essential to Catholic celebration of the Feast of Corpus Christi is the procession of a crucifix and a consecrated host through the city; the naked body of the lover-redeemer is placed on display for all to see and worship. This, essentially, is what one finds in a highly homoeroticized form in McNally's play. As in *Love! Valour! Compassion!,* male nudity is on display throughout *Corpus Christi.* The actors change on stage from their street clothes into their uniform khaki trousers and white shirts as the play begins (1), the hustler Philip advertises his availability by dancing high above the others as "a go-go boy" in the bar scene (53-55), and Joshua himself strips to white jockey shorts in the crucifixion scene. The cover photograph on the printed edition suggests the extent to which, in the original production, the actor's beauty was offered as a sexual gift to the audience.[5]

Indeed, at the heart of the play is McNally's representation of sex as a form of grace, the body of Christ offered for the redemption of others figuring as the "more loving one['s]" gift of his own body in the sacrament of sex.[6] "[A] good part of our humanity is expressed *through* our sexuality and is not exclusive of it," McNally argues in his preface to the printed text of the play (*Corpus Christi* v), challenging the widespread fundamentalist argument that sexuality is inherently sinful and that Jesus could not have indulged in anything so shameful as sex while living on earth. Yet when charging Joshua with his mission, God the Father himself insists that sexual pleasure is one of the great joys of life which no one should be denied, at the same time cautioning that humans must learn that there is more to love than genital gratification (19-20). The play suggests that gays are as open to the charge of violating the sacrament of sex as the heterosexual couple in the motel room whose violent sex noises punctuate Joshua's nativity. Joshua institutes gay marriage as a sacrament (61-62), but is pursued sexually by the libidinous Judas whom Joshua must warn: "You can come no closer to Me than My body. Everything else you will never touch. Everything important is hidden from you" (*Corpus Christi* 37). Significantly, when Joshua discusses Shakespeare's *Sonnets* with his high school English teacher, McNally calls particular attention to Sonnet 129,

"Th'expense of spirit," a poem which maps the physical and psychological degradations of lust (27).[7]

Gay relationships, Joshua tells the sexually predatory Judas, must include kindness, love, and respect for the other person. When they do, as Joshua tries later to explain to Philip, sex is capable of healing the wounds that every gay man carries, as opposed to inflicting a new wound such as the HIV infection (54-55). Joshua heals Philip by refusing to allow the hustler to treat him as just another "faggot" who wants to "suck my dick" (*Corpus Christi* 55); offering one's body for someone else's pleasure should be an act of generosity, not an attempted humiliation. The most controversial aspect of the original production of *Corpus Christi* was its assertion that Jesus had sex with all twelve of his male apostles (69), picketers outside the theater nightly betraying by their outrage the very disregard for the sacramental potential of all human sexuality that Joshua is ordained to preach. When Joshua offers his body and blood for the salvation of humankind, he is teaching "another way" of sex, "the way of love and generosity and self-peace" (*Corpus Christi* 19), not of lust, exploitation of others, and resulting self-disgust.

The title phrase "Corpus Christi" identifies, thus, the two antithetical value systems that operate within the play. On the one hand is the bigoted denial of someone else's worth that leads to antigay violence in general, to the crucifixion of Joshua in particular, and, most unsettlingly, to the contemporary event to which McNally refers in his preface, the murder of gay college student Matthew Shepard.[8] "All who do not love all men are against Me!" Joshua proclaims after striking the homophobic High Priest (*Corpus Christi* 63), and throughout the play emphasis is upon Joshua's ability to love everyone, male and female. But, on the other hand, "Corpus Christi" suggests, as the antidote to that poisonous first value system, a recognition of sex as a form of grace. Promoting an understanding of the redemptive potential of human sexuality, the play is a proclamation of the mystery of fellatio as salvation, as it were.[9]

Thus, even as the first use of "Corpus Christi" (to indicate a bigoted mind-set) suggests a perversion of the Christian Bible, McNally's second use of "Corpus Christi" (to indicate sex as a form of grace) suggests that in his play McNally is creating an alternative gospel. "No one has ever told this story right," Judas comments at the opening of the play, dismissing earlier versions of the Jesus story including, presumably, the canonical Gospels; "even when they get the facts right, the feeling is wrong" (*Corpus Christi* 8). Similarly, as the actors leave the stage at the conclusion of the play, The Actor Playing Thaddeus comments, "Maybe other people have told His story better. Other actors. This was *our* way" (*Corpus Christi* 81, emphasis added).

The power of myth, and the reason why all religions are grounded in a network of myths, is that the narrative contained therein touches on so many important truths that it bears retelling over the centuries and is so expansive as to allow, maybe even provoke, multiple interpretations. By asserting the legitimacy of "our way" of telling Jesus/Joshua's story, McNally calls attention to how often people interpret the Bible for their own purposes. For example, capitalists rationalize that token tithing to the church satisfies Jesus' command that following him means selling all that one has and giving it to the poor. Therefore, as McNally says in the passage quoted at the outset of this chapter, a god must be created in the image of *all* of his or her followers. If Africans and African Americans are allowed a black Jesus with whom they can identify, as opposed to the blond-haired, blue-eyed Jesus popularized in Italian Renaissance art, then gays should be free to identify with those parts of the Jesus story which speak most deeply to them. Some believers may not even call him Jesus, but Joshua ("That was *our* name for him," Andrew explains; *Corpus Christi* 2, emphasis added). The myth of Jesus is expansive enough to meet the needs of gay believers as well as those of other Christian groups.

Even more provocatively, McNally seems to see in the Christian Gospels evidence of Jesus *as* homosexual. The facts of Jesus' life are indeed suggestive: his love for women was never romantic or sexual; he was an outsider, rejecting the orthodox and socially powerful while ministering to the vulnerable and socially marginalized; he preached tolerance and forgiveness; and he not only created a homosocial community among the twelve men whom he called to follow him, but had a special relationship with one disciple in particular which enjoyed some physical expression. The Bible itself invites a homoerotic interpretation of the character and actions of Jesus, proving the best counterargument to fundamentalists who, unable to find their homophobia supported by the Gospels, must rely upon the Pauline epistles to defame and persecute gays. But rather than claiming that McNally is offering a new or alternative gospel, perhaps it is more accurate to say that he is recovering the Gospels for gays who feel dispossessed by institutionalized Christianity when in reality the Bible has a great deal to teach them, especially about the difference between lust and love.

McNally's gospel of the divinity of all men, far from being a radical departure in *Corpus Christi,* is the inevitable conclusion to be drawn from the religious humanism that is developed elsewhere in his canon.[10]

McNALLY'S RELIGIOUS HUMANISM

Unlike Pirandello, Brecht, Beckett, and Albee,[11] the representative figures of modern drama, McNally is concerned not with alienation, distancing effects, and the disintegration of meaning, but with communion. What brings audiences to the theater is "the expectation that the miracle of communication will take place" (373), explains the Last Subscriber to the board of a city arts complex in *Hidden Agendas* (1994), a one-act play that McNally wrote in response to the Robert Mapplethorpe controversy. "Words, sounds, gestures, feelings, thoughts! The things that connect us and make us human. The hope for that connection!" (in *Fifteen Short Plays* 373). McNally aims to create community through theater by challenging the modern anxiety and insecurity that replace "love! valour! compassion!" (those qualities which sustain relationships) with the hatred, cowardice, and solipsism that disrupt social ties. His is a theater that practices rather than preaches acceptance. Like Chekhov, McNally makes it impossible for his audience not to smile at his characters' foibles, and, in the process, celebrate our shared humanity, however imperfect. McNally writes comedy in its richest, most religious sense.

It is that humanizing "hope for . . . connection" which dominates McNally's theater, farcically, in *The Ritz* (1975) as Chris wanders in and out of bathhouse cubicles looking for sexual contact, but more poignantly in the later plays. McNally's earliest produced play, *And Things That Go Bump in the Night* (1964; New York production 1965) analyzes the fear of some unspecified threat that drives Ruby and her family to promote their own sense of security by demeaning other people. "The only issue of *passionate* concern in this family . . . the only one any of us really care about . . . is who's going to get who: where, when, and how" (*Collected Plays* 55). By ritually humiliating, then sacrificing, a scapegoat whom they lure into their bunkerlike home, Ruby teaches her children that "if we are without charity, we suckle the bitter root of its absence . . . wherefrom we shall draw the sustenance to destroy" others (*Collected Plays* 25).

The victim sacrificed on the night dramatized in *And Things That Go Bump* is a sweet, ineffectual young gay man named Clarence. Ruby's doctrine proves McNally's first attempt to analyze the operation of homophobia. Similarly, a horrible gay bashing is enacted in *A Perfect Ganesh,* but which, the victim makes clear, was nowhere near as painful as his mother's rejection of him because of his sexuality. In *Love! Valour! Compassion!* Perry and Arthur debate the peculiar satisfaction that comes from using hate words. Little wonder that, after witnessing an incident of antigay violence on the news in *Love!,* Buzz can only despair: "They hate us. They fucking hate us. They've always hated us. It never ends, the fucking hatred" (*Love!* 107).

The psychology and consequences of homophobia are treated most fully in *Lips Together, Teeth Apart* (1991), in which two heterosexual couples spend the Fourth of

July weekend at the Fire Island home that one woman has inherited from her brother, who has recently died of an AIDS-related illness. They not only hold aloof from their gay neighbors but from one another, each revealing only in soliloquy some private wound that he or she cannot share with his or her partner, or some desire upon which they do not know how to act. The self-destructiveness of such isolation—of repressed emotion and unarticulated anxiety—is comically rendered by the tendency of both men to grind their teeth in their sleep. The paralyzing homophobia of all four adults, however, is revealed by their recurring refusal to use the pool on the deck of where the action is played out. "We all think it's infected. We all think it's polluted. We all think we'll get AIDS and die if we go in," Sally admits at the climax of the play (*Lips Together* 80). An invisible threat lies in the pool of our common humanity against which individuals attempt to erect barriers of resistance and mistrust, talking about anything but what concerns us most, and listening to, but without hearing, what others may be struggling to say. For McNally, homophobia is but one aspect of a greater problem: the fear that one's precarious sense of self will be compromised or contaminated by contact with others.

The result of such resistence is death, McNally makes clear in play after play. "We gotta connect. We just have to. Or we die," Johnny tells Frankie in *Frankie and Johnny in the Clair de Lune* (1987; 136). The characters in *Lips Together* are first seen occupying separate quadrants of the stage, to all appearances acting together as an ensemble, but in actuality deeply isolated emotionally. After spending the play talking at cross purposes with her husband, brother, and sister-in-law, however, Chloe insists that her husband speak to her directly: "If you have something to say to me, John, come in here and say it. I cannot hear through walls or screens or whatever they are! Partitions!" (*Lips Together* 80-81). McNally's theater examines both this lack of communication—the walls, screens, and partitions that people defensively erect—and the heroic attempt to break through them. The breakthrough can be positively guttural, as when in *Love!* Gregory struggles to speak despite an inhibiting stutter and Bobby breaks into an inhuman howl of pain upon receiving word of his sister's death. Such attempts to communicate one's deepest feelings to another person are to be valued, no matter how spastic and unsettling they may be to others. The only sin in McNally's world, rather, is to refuse to listen. Andre's Mother does not speak a single word in her eponymous drama (*Fifteen Short Plays* 347-351), remaining as silent at her son's funeral as she was distant to him during his life because she could not accept his homosexuality. At the memorial service her difficulty in letting go of the white balloon that Cal says represents Andre's soul mirrors her inability throughout

her son's life to let him discover and develop his intrinsic self. Now that she has lost him permanently, all she can utter is a silent cry of grief.

The thrust of McNally's drama is toward the moment of communication when one partner can sympathetically hear what the other is saying. This is the extraordinary movement of *Frankie and Johnny,* as Johnny describes it: "This wall of disparity between us, Frankie, we gotta break it down. So the only space left between us is just us" (*Frankie and Johnny* 112). The scars that Frankie and Johnny discover on each other's body, like the scars that Gregory's friends are allowed to inspect on the dancer-choreographer's body in *Love!,* suggest the emotional scars that every person carries: reminders of the things that one is ashamed of, evidence of ways in which one has been hurt by relationships in the past, the residue of past struggles to communicate. Such scars may leave one feeling uncertain of one's attractiveness to another person or worthiness to enter into a new relationship. McNally insists that we break through the walls that divide us, not with baseball bats (as the fag bashers do when murdering Walter in *Perfect Ganesh,* 25-26), but with the compassion and understanding that Johnny shows Frankie. Communication that issues from kindness makes the moment of connection all the more extraordinary: "This is the only chance we have to really come together, I'm convinced of it. People are given one moment to connect. Not two, not three, one!" (*Frankie* 121). Such moments McNally terms "grace."[12]

Indeed, the glory of McNally's theater is that it enacts so movingly those moments of grace when an understanding is reached, "seeing somebody for what they really are and still wanting them warts and all" (*Frankie* 127). Thus, the importance of nudity which is present in several of McNally's plays, not for titillation, but as a sign of both the exposure of one's own, and acceptance of another person's full humanity, "warts and all." The men in *Love!,* whose nudity in the original Broadway production proved so controversial, reveal their own, and accept each other's, intrinsic self in the course of the three holiday weekends that they share together. Only John, the most guarded and manipulative of the gathered company, remains fully clothed throughout. McNally's book for the musical *The Full Monty* (2000) addresses in comic terms contemporary American males' inability to expose themselves, whether physically or emotionally. Actions of robing and disrobing similarly occur as Johnny tears down Frankie's wall of resistance in *Frankie and Johnny.* Margaret's revealing to Katherine in *A Perfect Ganesh* the lump in her breast that she had discovered at the outset of their journey but has kept to herself until this moment is the gesture that seals their friendship and allows a communion that deeply affects both women.

Only acceptance of another person's difference allows community, and only in community, McNally repeatedly emphasizes, lies salvation from the threat of things that go bump in the night. Fear of addressing one's own painful isolation, or refusal to reduce, simply by acknowledging, another person's despair, will hurt oneself as well as the other person. In *Lips Together,* Sally is devastated to understand that the lone swimmer whom earlier that morning she was uneasy to watch swim out to sea has indeed drowned himself. She faults herself for sitting quietly and, thus, tacitly encouraging him in his despair.

> My eyes didn't say "Stay—life is worth living." They said "Go, Godspeed, God bless." My wave didn't say "Hurry back, young man, happiness awaits you ashore." It said "Goodbye, I know where you're going. I've wanted to go there too." I knew his secret, and he knew mine. Even from a great distance we know so much about each other but spend our lives pretending we don't.
>
> *(Lips Together,* 75)

"No one should be out that far alone," she had worried earlier (11). But, she also recognizes, "No one wants to listen to who we really are. Know somebody really" (*Lips Together* 30), which is what prevented her from attempting to dissuade the swimmer from suicide: his pain was too real for her to bear. The potential for connection is always present; only the strength to acknowledge our shared humanity is lacking, because acknowledging someone else's "secret" means having to admit one's own. The play intimates that the fear which kept Sally from being anything more than a silent witness to the stranger's suicide also allowed her to stand quietly by when in childhood her father bullied her younger brother David (58); as, later, David constructed his adult life as a gay man apart from his biological family; and, finally, as he lay dying of AIDS.

McNally proposes, rather, that we participate in each other's pain, lessening the burden by sharing it. The need is most beautifully explored in *A Perfect Ganesh,* which records not one, but two such moments of grace. In the first, Katherine reminds Margaret of an afternoon when, vacationing years earlier with their husbands, they and others on a beach were startled to hear a single-engine plane suddenly stall in the sky overhead. "No one moved. It was terrifying. That little plane just floating there. No sound. No sound at all. Like a kite without a string, without a wind" (*A Perfect Ganesh* 17). The pilot, however, was finally able to restart his engine, leaving Katherine to reflect:

> But what kept that plane up there? God? A God? Some Benevolence? Prayer? Our prayers? I think everyone on that beach was praying that morning in their particular way. So maybe we aren't so helpless. Maybe we are responsible. Maybe it is our fault what happens.
>
> *(A Perfect Ganesh* 17)

This scene is the antithesis to that in which Sally watches the lone swimmer head out from shore, for here a community shares, if only for a moment, in

someone else's desperate, panicked, potentially fatal isolation. McNally does not suggest that the onlookers' collective prayer miraculously averted the tragedy; rather, that simply by being conscious of another's distress, humans can lessen each other's agony and hold each other aloft. The word "responsibility," catechist Florence Michels emphasizes, indicates one's "ability to respond in a completely human manner" to "love's demand" (23, 11). To avoid making the response that one full well knows the situation demands, she says, is to dehumanize oneself (23).

The fruits of such response-ability are illustrated in the play's second moment of grace. Standing on a shared hotel balcony with a fellow tourist in Bombay, Margaret is pained to recall the death many years earlier of her young son Gabriel, who impetuously had run out into the street and fallen under the wheels of a passing car. At the emotionally contained Episcopalian funeral service, she and her family are startled to hear a low moan of song, which Margaret at first mistakes for the church organ.

> It was the Negro woman whose car had struck my son. . . . She was just humming but the sound was so rich, so full, no wonder I'd thought it was the organ. The minister tried to continue but eventually he stopped and we all just turned and listened to her. Her eyes were closed. Tears were streaming down her cheeks. Such a vibrant, comforting sound it was! Her voice rose, higher and higher, loud now, magnificent, like a bright shining sword.
>
> *(A Perfect Ganesh* 51)

Margaret's attempt to contain her grief and maintain her proverbial WASP stiff upper lip is subverted by the black woman's generous willingness to share and celebrate Margaret's loss. The song's expression of their common pain brought everyone in the congregation together, if only for the moment of her singing.

Significantly, Margaret's telling the story so many years later becomes the occasion for an additional act of grace. When she sees that Margaret is shivering in the cool night air from the recollected emotion of telling her story, the Japanese tourist to whom she is speaking spontaneously wraps a beautiful kimono around Margaret's shoulders, which she insists that Margaret keep. "It's not warranted, such kindness," Margaret protests, deeply moved by the stranger's consideration (*A Perfect Ganesh* 52). Margaret's willingness to share her pain, to expose the most vulnerable part of herself, is rewarded by kindness that is as freely given as it is undeserved; she is rewarded by grace.

Thus, all of McNally's theater illustrates the paradoxical message in *Corpus Christi* that Joshua is sent to preach: "We're each special. We're each ordinary. We're each divine" (*Corpus Christi* 50). Humanity is not to be divided into sheep and goats, some persons feeling more special than everyone else because they are confident that they have been elected to salvation whereas other people are to be damned for eternity; such, as was noted at the outset of this essay, is a sectarian, rather than a truly religious, approach to life. Rather, every person is ordinary and special at once, simultaneously human and divine: ordinary in that the sacred is not a rare, transcendent force but inheres in every person, making everyone special, worthy of respect, and even worship. Every "ordinary" person is divine as well in that he or she possesses Joshua's power to heal others; one need only tear down the partitions, speak honestly, acknowledge what others are saying, and accept their difference, celebrating the fact that they are as paradoxically special and ordinary as oneself. In the prologue to *Corpus Christi* John the Baptist blesses the actors, including Joshua, calling upon each to "recognize your divinity as a human being" (2-7). The baptisms infuse the seriousness of the situation with comic levity as the apostles introduce themselves variously as doctor, hustler, hairdresser, etc., the very ordinariness of their professions initially keeping both the audience and themselves from recognizing their inherent divinity.

Acceptance of the paradox that everyone is simultaneously human and divine makes for what in *Corpus Christi* McNally calls "a perfect, defining moment." The radical nature of the community that Joshua creates among his followers becomes clear to them only at the Last Supper.

JAMES:

> Josh, there's a woman outside who says she is Your mother.

JOSHUA:

> Tell her I have no mother. You are My mother and father and brothers and sisters. You are My family now. We are all mother, father, brothers, and sisters, to each other. Now do you understand?

ANDREW:

> We looked at each other and we did.

PHILIP:

> It was breathtaking.

JAMES THE LESS:

> A perfect moment.

BARTHOLOMEW:

> A defining one.
>
> (68)

The perfect, defining moment occurs when one accepts one's shared humanity, worshiping others "warts and all" as divine. Such acceptance has particular meaning

for gays, too many of whom, as Ramon says in *Love!* (in a powerful dramatic quotation of Mart Crowley's *The Boys in the Band* [1968]), do not know how to love either themselves or one another (54), for it is difficult not to demean or exploit others in turn when one is oneself irrationally despised by society at large. Recognition of one another's simultaneous ordinariness and divinity shapes the twelve apostles into a family in *Corpus Christi* which, unlike the gay men's biological families, supports and affirms them spiritually.[13]

Joshua's teaching in *Corpus Christi* that one needs to accept even the most ordinary person as divine translates into Christian narrative terms the message previously delivered in a Hindu context in *A Perfect Ganesh.* This parallel suggests that, for McNally, the insight that "all men are divine" is essential to religion, whatever the tradition. The Hindu god Ganesha appears throughout his play in the most ordinary of guises—as an airline clerk, a hotel chambermaid, a stranger whom one meets in a tourist hotel, or a child in a foreign land whose language one cannot understand. Katherine's search for a perfect image of the god is useless, Ganesha himself tells her, for "They're all perfect, Katharine" (*A Perfect Ganesh* 106). Similarly, acceptance that they are each ordinary, each divine—that even though it is their differences which make them each special, they have more in common than either suspects—allows Margaret to break down the wall that has always existed between herself and Katherine, and attempt to comfort her friend in a moment of terrible self-doubt:

> You're not alone, Kitty. I'm here. Another person, another woman, is here. Right here. Breathing the same air. Riding the same train. Looking out the window at the same timeless landscape. You are not alone. Even in your agony.
>
> (*A Perfect Ganesh* 85)

As they travel in a small skiff down the Ganges to Varanasi, the sacred city of the dead, Margaret and Katherine are at first revolted by the corpses that float by and knock against their boat, but learn finally that "We all have a place here. Nothing is right, nothing is wrong. Allow. Accept. Be" (*A Perfect Ganesh* 101).

Katherine and Margaret's river travel is part of a powerful thematic motif in McNally's work: the need of individuals to enter the pool of our shared humanity, however contaminated it may at first appear. If the heterosexual couples in *Lips Together* will not go into the dead brother's pool for fear that they contract AIDS, Margaret and Katherine learn from the Ganges to accept the most unsettling aspects of human existence. *Love!* concludes with all the men but John undressing and slipping into the lake, a symbol of their acceptance of their shared mortality and their willingness to confront together the things that go bump in the night.

In the stillness of the country night, Perry remarks that "We could be the last eight people on earth." This would be a frightening thought, James replies, if one were not "with the right eight people" (*Love!* 88). The apocalyptic threat of AIDS can be faced in *Love!*—one can withstand the threat of things that go bump in the night—only if one bonds in community.

Just as Gregory's weekends in the country create the occasion for his eight friends to join as a community, it is Joshua's nature ("Kindness . . . Love . . . Respect for others," 37) which enables him to create community and renders him a savior in *Corpus Christi.* Both men prove the antitheses of Ruby's response to apocalyptic threat in *And Things That Go Bump.* After all twelve apostles are finally assembled in *Corpus Christi,* the stage direction notes that "The DISCIPLES come together, happily embracing each other. Music. Laughter" (*Corpus Christi* 57). The men called by Joshua are taught by his example to interact in a loving way, their gladness in coming together creating a perfect, defining moment, whatever their differences. This comes in large part from their growing acceptance of their own and each other's divinity, from their accepting sex as communion rather than as exploitation; "Respect the divinity in your partner," Joshua tells James and Bartholomew when instituting the gay marriage ritual (*Corpus Christi* 62). The perfect, defining moment of Joshua's ministry that occurs during the Last Supper is similar dramatically to the luminous moment of acceptance and joy that McNally creates in the penultimate scene of *Love!,* as eight men clad in tutus join hands and dance joyously in the face of death. The ensemble camps madly, their rehearsal of the *Swan Lake* "Pas des Cygnes" becoming a parody of the medieval Dance of Death, and one by one each steps forward and narrates to the audience the circumstances of his eventual demise. Even after an electrical blackout reduces their dance space to candle-lighted darkness, the dying swans continue to dance, hand over hand, joined as a community, each ordinary and special, able to ward off the threat of things that go bump in the night if only for this moment of grace.[14]

Corpus Christi as Religious Ritual

Finally, in addition to designating both the south Texas town representative of Bible-belt homophobia and sexual violence, and the eroticized body of Christ that is shared in the sacrament of sexuality to heal and redeem others, the phrase "Corpus Christi" recalls the medieval cycle of plays that were traditionally performed as part of the annual Corpus Christi Sunday festival. McNally's title thus acknowledges his attempt to create a modern drama that functions as religious ritual, one that leads the audience to its own perfect defining moment of illumination, acceptance, and grace.

A complex relationship exists between the medieval mystery plays and the broken, naked body of the crucified Christ that is celebrated on the Feast of Corpus Christi. Theater historians conclude that the processions, which grew increasingly elaborate over the years, eventually included the performance of plays supported by the craft guilds that offered instruction in salvation history from creation to doomsday for the illiterate. As William Tydeman notes, "their authors' primary business was to instruct the populace in those truths essential for their salvation by rendering them accessible, and to alert men and women to those cosmic battles being waged over the fate of their own immortal and individual souls" (18). The plays, which were performed in England from around 1378 until the later half of the sixteenth century, possessed a distinct evangelizing purpose, intended as they were to function as "vehicles designed to bring home to the people their spiritual potentialities and responsibilities," particularly those suggested by the Easter miracle (Tydeman 20). At the conclusion of a play cycle, notes Jerome Taylor, "the faithful are invited to live and to preach the consequences of Christ's redemptive death, continued in the Eucharist, which the Feast and its plays were instituted to honor" (155). In the medieval Corpus Christi plays, theater approximates the function of the Eucharist, the culture's most sacred ritual, but does so in the vernacular, making more accessible to the average person the mass's mysterious Latin rite.

Corpus Christi "is more a religious ritual than a play," McNally observes in the preface to the printed text.

> A play teaches us a new insight into the human condition. A ritual is an action we perform over and over because we *have* to. Otherwise, we are in danger of forgetting the meaning of that ritual, in this case that we must love one another or die. Christ died for all of our sins because He loved each and every one of us. When we do not remember His great sacrifice, we condemn ourselves to repeating its terrible consequences.
>
> (*Corpus Christi* vii)

When they forget that "*all* men are divine"—that Christ "died for *all* of our sins because He loved *each and every one of us*" (emphasis added)—Christians permit and even encourage discrimination against homosexuals in the name of religion and, thus, ensure that Christ's crucifixion is repeated in the form of the brutal murder of gay college student Matthew Shepard. As McNally writes in his preface,

> Beaten senseless and tied to a split-rail fence in near-zero weather, arms akimbo in a grotesque crucifixion, [Matthew Shepard] died as agonizing a death as another young man who had been tortured and nailed to a wooden cross at a desolate spot outside Jerusalem known as Golgotha some 1,998 years earlier. They died, as they lived, as brothers.
>
> (*Corpus Christi* vi)

Medieval drama, Taylor points out, is figural, "an early episode finding its complete significance in a later one which it foreshadows and adumbrates" (154). Although

McNally's play shows how Christ's crucifixion anticipates the passion play that every gay man must live out, his description of Matthew Shepard's death underscores the horror of the type's most recent fulfillment. Homophobia is un-Christian; that it should be supported and encouraged by fundamentalist Christians (as in the case of a popular bumper sticker urging people to "Kill a Queer for Christ" during the 1970s Anita Bryant controversy, or the Christian Family Coalition's advocating the 1996 antigay Defense of Marriage Act) is sacrilege. Any religious leader or church which is unable to accept that *all* persons, including gay persons, are divine ritually repeats through their exclusionary politics the crucifixion of the god in whose name they supposedly act.

In *Corpus Christi,* McNally seeks to stimulate his audience's "love! valour! compassion!" through their shared horror at Joshua's death. It is unsettling for an audience to hear Pilate condemn Joshua not because he claims to be King of the Jews, but because he's "queer" (*Corpus Christi* 75), the distant words of the biblical Passion story taking on a startling new resonance when placed in an all-too-familiar contemporary context. Likewise, when given the choice of securing the release of one man from prison, the crowd privileges the thief over the queer (75), so many parts of contemporary American society still more easily outraged by homosexuality than by dishonesty. In McNally's drama, the Roman soldiers who scourge Jesus and nail him to the cross double as the fag baiters who tormented Joshua in high school, both groups reinforcing their own insecure masculinity, or attempting to repress their own homoerotic yearnings, by viciously beating and killing a gay man. Even the biblical story of Peter's betrayal of Christ takes on a sharper edge when McNally's Peter rationalizes his failure to come to Joshua's aid by protesting "I had no choice! They would have killed us all" (*Corpus Christi* 77), the fear of so many gay men to come out of the closet being one of the primary reasons why gays who are out front remain such easy targets of homophobic violence. The shock of witnessing a viciously enacted hate killing on stage has a doubly strong impact on sensitive audience members when it is presented in terms of Christ's passion and crucifixion, ensuring that they consider the relation of organized religion to socially sanctioned homophobia. McNally is using theater to evangelize his audience, sending them out to preach a new gospel of tolerance: the gospel that *all* men are divine.

Throughout his canon, McNally is interested in theater's potential moral agency, but even more importantly, with theater's ability to recreate its audience. McNally's oeuvre, in fact, may be read as a sustained meditation upon the power of art, but most especially theater, to confront prejudice, break down resistance, and effect reconciliation—that is, to create "love! valour! compassion!" "The world can and will go on without us," Maria Callas acknowledges at the conclusion of her *Master Class*

(1995), "but I have to think that we have made this world a better place. That we have left it richer, wiser than had we not chosen the way of art" (61-62). In *Frankie and Johnny,* Frankie and Johnny's relationship is sealed by two pieces of music that they hear on the radio. In *The Lisbon Traviata* (1985; revised production 1989) Stephen and Mendy live for and through the operas of Maria Callas (much as Buzz does through musical comedy in *Love!*); opera expands their lives, allowing them a broader, richer, more emotionally satisfying existence. And, while supposedly addressing her master class at Julliard, the actress playing Maria Callas speaks directly to McNally's audience, her comments on how an artist lives and performs becoming McNally's encouragement to his audience to allow art to enlarge their lives. Even *It's Only a Play* (1985), a seemingly light-hearted farce, shows how theater creates a community that in turn creates a new work of art. Art crystallizes the "defining moment" that characters in every McNally play must experience if they are to find their way to acceptance of others and redemption of themselves. McNally's is, finally, a tragicomic theater of "reconciliation, renewal and re-birth" in which, as he puts it in *A Perfect Ganesh,* opposites are able to exist peacefully side by side and "a tiny leap [can be made] across the void between two people" (*A Perfect Ganesh* 89, 92).

"In India we participate in theatre. We don't sit back, arms folded and say 'Show me,'" the puppeteer tells Katherine in *A Perfect Ganesh* (87). His story of how Ganesha's mother was partially responsible for his decapitation comes closer than Katherine can bear to the story of how her rejection of her homosexual son Walter destroyed him as surely as the roving gang of gay bashers who smashed in his skull (*A Perfect Ganesh* 87). The puppet play that Katherine witnesses in India holds up her pained relationship with her gay son for her examination, the puppeteer drawing her into the play in a way that, although terrifying, is ultimately redemptive. Similarly, in *Corpus Christi,* the actors who enter through the auditorium as though entering from the street, and who change into their costumes on stage before the audience, erase the boundary between audience and players, demonstrating quite literally how one's identity can be transformed by theater, and implicating the audience (who, like the players, have only just entered the theater from the street) in the transformative action that follows. For just as Katherine finds something deeply personal in the puppeteer's story of Ganesha, the audience finds the comfortably familiar biblical story enacted in *Corpus Christi* only too painfully real when retold in terms of a contemporary hate crime. The Christian audience member's identity is necessarily challenged, for how can one claim to love Christ when one hates his or her gay children? The play makes the audience aware of the Ruby-like night-mare that they are caught up in, Christ re-crucified daily in countless acts of homophobic violence. One way of breaking that cycle of violence, McNally suggests, is by the ritual-like performance of his play.[15]

Conclusion: The Playgoer as Evangelist

Mapping the place of the medieval cycle plays within the shift from Romanesque and Byzantine to Gothic culture, theater historian David Bevington places the Corpus Christi plays firmly within Gothic tradition:

> Above all, Gothic artists were drawn to Christ's suffering as a poignant demonstration of his compassion for mankind. The Corpus Christi cycles, with their tender depictions of Christ's birth amidst poverty and cold, and their gruesomely vivid renditions of the Crucifixion, abundantly reveal this Gothic emphasis on Christ's humanity.

(234)[16]

This is probably what McNally likewise aims to do in *Corpus Christi*: to enhance his audience's recognition of gay men as human beings who, like themselves, are simultaneously ordinary and divine. "I'm a playwright, not a theologian," McNally acknowledges at the start of his "Preface" (*Corpus Christi* v), which goes on to distinguish between how different groups may read the Bible, and between how he himself "sounds" as a homosexual and as a human being. *Corpus Christi* is his attempt not to "queer" the Christian gospels, but to humanize his audience's interpretation of them. Seeking to unite a divided community rather than to prove that gays are superior to straights, McNally refuses as much to be coopted as "queer" as to be dismissed by religious ideologues.

In its evangelization of acceptance *Corpus Christi* can be seen as forming a diptych with *A Perfect Ganesh*. In the earlier play, Ganesha calls attention to the fact that he, part elephant, is traditionally depicted riding on the back of a mouse. "This demonstrates the concept—so important to me!—that opposites—an elephant and a mouse—can live together happily. . . . In fact, I prove that the world is full of opposites which exist peacefully side by side" (*A Perfect Ganesh* 69). *A Perfect Ganesh* offers a vision of acceptance, as much as *Corpus Christi* demonstrates the violence that comes of not accepting differences, of opposites being unable to exist peacefully side by side. Like the authors of the medieval cycle plays, McNally sends his audience from the theater to evangelize—that is, to preach the danger of what occurs when individuals cannot accept that *all* men are divine.

Clearly, it is a message with which audiences have had difficulty. Gay theater historian John Clum, for example, misses McNally's point completely when he objects that

> even I, a secular humanist, was bothered by the notion that Christ was crucified primarily because he was gay and that the most revolutionary thing he did was

perform a gay marriage. . . . Gayness does not make us inferior, but it sure as hell does not make us divine (not literally, anyway).

(282)

McNally never claims, as Clum further adduces, that gays are "the Sons of God. The poor, unhappy brutal heterosexual, humping away in Texas motel rooms or stuck in unhappy marriages[,] should want to kill us. We've got it all. *And we* can work miracles" (283, Clum's emphasis). Rather, McNally asserts that all persons, heterosexual as well as homosexual, are divine, making it sacrilege to deny any person his or her dignity and richness of humanity. Violence against any person is profanation, as when the heterosexual woman is beaten by her lover in the adjoining motel room during Joshua's nativity. But violence against another person that is authorized by religion—as is the case of so much recent American homophobia—is sacrilege. McNally's play is not an idealization of homosexuality, but a decryal of prejudice, most especially that which is religiously enjoined.

Indeed, in *Corpus Christi,* McNally challenges the very same simplistic gay political correctness that Clum mistakenly ascribes to him. Joshua is betrayed, not by a homophobe, but by another gay man who covets his body. The members of the Religious Right who would silence his pro-gay message are assisted in their task by cowardly gays who fear to speak out against another gay man's beating lest they call attention to themselves. Joshua's particular ministry is to gays who are unable to see the sanctity of all human sexuality; betrayal of one's partner leads to one's own death, Judas learns. As St. Augustine observes, "Men come to recognize the body of Christ, the Corpus Christi, if they do not disregard their *being* the body of Christ" (quoted in Taylor 152). One must find Christ in oneself, in one's own sexuality, as much as in being able to accept another person and his or her variant sexuality as divine.

This is the mystery—theologically of the body of Christ, and theatrically of gay identity—in McNally's *Corpus Christi.*

Notes

1. For me, the aim of festive comedy is neatly summarized in the toast with which Lotte concludes Peter Shaffer's *Lettice and Lovage* (1990): "Enlargement for shrunken souls—Enlivenment for dying spirits—Enlightenment for dim, prosaic eyes" (98). I develop a theory of the religious basis of festive comedy in "Anatomizing" and "Perfect Foolishness."

2. I am not aware of any comment made by McNally concerning ACT UP's disruption of services conducted by the late Cardinal John O'Connor in New York City's St. Patrick's Cathedral (see "Stop the Church Action"), but I suspect that he would

disavow them, for any action which denies the integrity of Roman Catholic belief or ritual is easily as bigoted as the attempts of American Catholicism's formerly most visible homophobe to deny the integrity of gay and lesbian lives.

3. The doctrine of transubstantiation was not promulgated until 1215. Although, as a way of popularizing the doctrine, Pope Urban IV proclaimed the Feast of Corpus Christi in 1264, it was not formally implemented until the Council of Vienne in 1311. I discuss the historical relation of the Feast of Corpus Christi to the performance of the medieval mystery cycle plays more fully as follows.

   On the historical development of both the Feast of Corpus Christi and the medieval Corpus Christi cycle plays, I have relied upon Bevington, Taylor, and Tydeman.

4. On the imagery of feasting or consumption of bodily nourishment that dominates early discussions of the Corpus Christi celebration, see Taylor 150-151. For example, by the sacrament of the Eucharist, John Chrysostom notes, "our Shepherd feeds us; in it we are made one body of Christ, one flesh" (qtd. in Taylor 152).

5. John Clum, in a brief but dismissive reading of the play, compares *Corpus Christi*'s "erotically charged" picture "of Christ as a beautiful young man, crucified in his white jockey briefs (the image adorns the cover of the published text of the play)" to Renaissance paintings of Saint Sebastian, in which "a semi-nude, beautiful young man is being penetrated by arrows." "Martyrdom can also be sexy," Clum argues (281), later implying that at least part of McNally's purpose in dramatizing a gay man's crucifixion is to gratify McNally's own desire in middle age to look upon a younger man's naked form, theatrical scopophilia being a major consideration of Clum's book.

6. The phrase is, of course, W. H. Auden's in "The More Loving One" (line 8). (On Auden's conviction that *agape* is the antidote to the modern poison of self-love, see Summers.) By using the phrase, I do not mean to suggest that McNally was in any way influenced by Auden or that McNally's play may serve as a commentary upon Auden's poem. The poem, however, has proven popular among gay men of a certain age. David Leavitt uses another phrase from the same couplet in the title of his novel, *Equal Affections* (1989). The phrase seems to articulate the concern of gay men who came of age around Stonewall with finding an alternative to the narcissistic self-indulgence and sensation seeking that reduced potential partners to "meat" on a "rack," an attitude devastatingly skewered by Larry Kramer in *Faggots* (1978). I return to this debate in the section on McNally's religious humanism, as follows.

7. Curiously, McNally misnumbers the sonnet as 64, which is one of the sonnets deploring Time's destruction of Beauty.

8. Dominating the American news media the week that *Corpus Christi* opened at the Manhattan Theater Club were stories of gay college student Matthew Shepard's murder. He had been tied to a fence in a Colorado [sic] field and left to die in sub-zero temperatures after being severely beaten (see, for example, Chua-Eoan and Lacayo). I return in my Conclusion to McNally's parallels between the Shepard tragedy and Joshua's crucifixion.

9. Unfortunately, more attention has been paid to the destructive aspects of gay "consumption" of one's partner's flesh; see, for example, Bergman on cannibalism in gay literature, most famously Sebastian being literally devoured by the Mexican boys whose flesh he exploited in Tennessee Williams's *Suddenly Last Summer* (1958). Bakhtin's influential analysis of the body as feast in carnivalesque literature like Rabelais' *Gargantua and Pantagruel* has yet to be systematically applied to gay texts, yet the possibilities are rich and various. On Allen Ginsberg, for example, see Frontain, "Sweet boy."

10. Curiously, the essays collected in Zinman, which remains the only book publication on McNally's theater, ignore his religious humanism entirely.

11. Albee, significantly, was McNally's mentor and lover, their relationship having begun shortly after McNally's arrival in New York City and lasting approximately five years; see Gussow 107-108 and passim. Presumably, neither McNally nor Albee were willing to speak in detail with Albee's biographer about their relationship, as Gussow offers little insight into its dynamic. Even more frustrating is Gussow's failure to speculate about the possible influence of McNally's *And Things That Go Bump in the Night* (1965) upon Albee's *A Delicate Balance* (1966), or of veteran Albee upon novice McNally's early writing.

12. The word is introduced in *Frankie and Johnny* (95), but see also the references to "this one particular and special moment" in *A Perfect Ganesh* (31), to "that moment to speak the truth" in *Lips Together* (43), and to Buzz's glorious misprision in *Love!*, when he and James are paddling in a canoe and are asked by the men in another boat if they want to race ("Grace. I thought he said something about grace," 123). Such moments are similar to the climactic moments in Tony Kushner's *Angels in America,* as when in *Millennium Approaches,* Belize can smell "Softness, compliance, forgiveness, grace" in the air (100), and Prior offers the blessing of *"More life"* as he sends the audience to begin "The Great Work" at the conclusion of *Perestroika* (148).

13. That McNally should challenge the American norm of the family, suggesting that alternate ways of structuring interpersonal relationships may be more supportive of individual spiritual growth, is not surprising; after Gaetano is marked for death by his father- and brother-in-law in *Ritz*, for example, he is saved only the madcap intervention of promiscuous Chris and chubby-chasing Claude. But McNally's recurring figuration of the silence that divides, of the partition that is erected, in terms of the relations between mothers and their gay sons, or a sister and her gay brother, is unusual. In *A Perfect Ganesh*, Katherine is unable to accept her son Walter's homosexuality; Andre's Mother had exiled Andre to stony silence while he was alive, which leaves her unable to speak to anyone at his memorial service; in *Lips Together* Sally did not know how to talk with her brother David while he was alive, or with his lover after David's death; and, far from being the divine mother of Michelangelo's Pietà, Mary in *Corpus Christi* is a lower-class East Texas girl who got knocked up and is disappointed with her resulting son's effeminacy. Unlike American theater of the 1940s and 1950s, which focused upon a gay son's self-assertion before a powerful father figure (e.g., Robert Anderson's *Tea and Sympathy* [1953], or Arthur Miller's *A View from the Bridge* [1955]), or that sees a mother and her gay son as natural allies ("We were a famous couple. People didn't speak of Sebastian and his mother or Mrs. Venable and her son, they said 'Sebastian and Violet, Violet and Sebastian . . .'"; Tennessee Williams, *Suddenly Last Summer* 111), McNally's theater concentrates upon the female who fails to nurture her child or dependent. It is the mother's betrayal of her son that is unnatural in McNally, not her son's homosexuality.

14. The loving testimonies to his actors, directors, and the management of The Manhattan Theater Club that McNally makes both in interviews and in the prefaces to his printed texts suggest the extent to which McNally enjoys theater as community. The Manhattan Theater Club's loyalty to McNally and his work is equally impressive. I am not aware of any other contemporary playwright who enjoys or is able to create such community.

15. McNally intimates through his epigraph from Chekhov's *The Seagull* how he hopes his theater will operate. Looking at the outdoor stage erected on a Russian country estate for the performance of his play, Constantine Treplev exclaims: "There's a theatre for you. Just a curtain, two wings, and then open space. Not a bit of scenery. A view straight onto the lake and the far horizon. We'll raise the curtain at half past eight, exactly, when the moon rises" (xiii). Theater, McNally suggests by using this statement, should be the most natural thing in the world, which he demonstrates by hav-

ing his actors enter through the theater in their street clothes and change before the audience's eyes prior to being baptized and renamed by John. Theater is ritual which should lead the actors as well as the audience to an awareness of their deeper selves; one should be reborn through theater. Like his contemporary Peter Shaffer, McNally reconceives theater as religious ritual, restoring to modern drama the religious element that disappeared in the Renaissance.

16. Tydeman likewise places the Corpus Christi plays within the twelfth century's "fresh assertion of Christ's significance as the type of vulnerable and suffering humanity" (19-20).

Works Cited

Auden, W. H. "The More Loving One." *Collected Poems.* Ed. Edward Mendelson. New York: Random House, 1976. 445.

Bakhtin, Mikhail. *Rabelais and His World.* Trans. Helene Iswolsky. Cambridge: MIT P, 1968.

Bergman, David. "Cannibals and Queers." *Gaiety Transfigured: Gay Self-Representation in American Literature.* Madison: U of Wisconsin P, 1991. 139-162.

Bevington, David. *Medieval Drama.* Boston: Houghton Mifflin, 1975.

Chua-Eoan, Howard. "That's Not a Scarecrow." *Time* (October 19, 1998): 72.

Clum, John M. *Still Acting Gay: Male Homosexuality in Modern Drama.* New York: St. Martin's P, 2000.

Frontain, Raymond-Jean. "Anatomizing Boccaccio's Sexual Festivity." *Approaches to Teaching Boccaccio's "Decameron."* Ed. James H. S. McGregor. New York: Modern Language Association, 2000. 95-102.

———. "Perfect Foolishness: Rabelais' Christian Wisdom." *PAPA: Publications of the Arkansas Philological Association* 17 (Spring 1991): 23-44.

———. "'Sweet boy, gimme yr ass': Allen Ginsberg and the Open Body of the Beat Revolution." *CEA Critic* 61, 2-3 (Winter and Summer 1999): 83-98.

Gussow, Mel. *Edward Albee: A Singular Journey.* New York: Simon and Schuster, 1999.

Kushner, Tony. *Angels in America. Part One: Millennium Approaches.* New York: Theatre Communications Group, 1993. *Part Two: Perestroika.* New York: Theatre Communications Group, 1994.

Lacayo, Richard. "The New Gay Struggle." *Time* (October 26, 1998): 32-40.

McNally, Terrence. *Collected Plays, Vol. II: "And Things That Go Bump in the Night" and "Where Has Tommy Flowers Gone?"* Lyme, NH: Smith and Kraus, 1996.

———. *Corpus Christi: A Play.* New York: Grove, 1998.

———. *Fifteen Short Plays.* Lyme, NH: Smith and Kraus, 1994.

———. *Lips Together, Teeth Apart.* New York: Plume, 1992.

———. *Love! Valour! Compassion!* Garden City, NY: Fireside Theatre, 1995.

———. *Master Class.* New York: Plume, 1995.

———. *A Perfect Ganesh.* Garden City, NY: Fireside Theatre, 1993.

———. *Three Plays: "The Lisbon Traviata," "Frankie and Johnny in the Clair de Lune," and "It's Only a Play."* New York: Plume, 1990.

Michels, Florence, O.L.V.M. *Faces of Freedom.* Westminster, MD: Newman P, 1968.

Shaffer, Peter. *Lettice and Lovage: A Comedy.* New York: Harper and Row, 1990.

Summers, Claude J. "'Or One Could Weep because Another Wept': The Counterplot of Auden's 'The Shield of Achilles.'" *Journal of English and Germanic Philology* 83 (1984): 214-232.

"Stop the Church Action." Available online <http://www.actupny.org/YELL/stopchurch99.html>.

Taylor, Jerome. "The Dramatic Structure of the Middle English Corpus Christi, or Cycle, Plays." 1964. Rpt. in *Medieval English Drama: Essays Critical and Contextual.* Ed. Jerome Taylor and Alan H. Nelson. Chicago: U of Chicago P, 1972. 148-156.

Tydeman, William. "An Introduction to Medieval English Theatre." In *The Cambridge Companion to Medieval English Theatre.* Ed. Richard Beadle. Cambridge: Cambridge UP, 1994. 1-36.

Williams, Tennessee. "Suddenly Last Summer." In *Plays 1957-1980.* New York: Library of America, 2000. 99-148.

Zinman, Toby Silverman, Ed. *Terrence McNally: A Casebook.* New York: Garland, 1997.

FURTHER READING

Criticism

McNally, Terrence. "What I Know about Being a Playwright." *American Theatre* 15, no. 9 (November 1998): 25-6.

> Adapted from a speech delivered at a New Dramatists luncheon; McNally shares personal, sometimes tongue-in-cheek advice drawn from his experience working in theater.

Román, David and Alberto Sandoval. "Caught in the Web: Latinidad, AIDS, and Allegory in *Kiss of the Spider Woman, the Musical.*" *American Literature* 67, no. 3 (September 1995): 553-85.

> Román and Sandoval examine perceptions of homosexual and Latino identities in light of McNally's *Kiss of the Spider Woman.*

Savran, David. "Terrence McNally." In *The Playwright's Voice: American Dramatists on Memory, Writing, and the Politics of Culture,* pp. 119-21. New York: Theatre Communications Group, 1999.

> Provides a brief overview of McNally's life, major works, themes, characters, and preoccupations.

Simon, John. "The Tell-Tale Art" *New York Magazine* (1 March 2004): n.p.

> Scathing review of McNally's *The Stendahl Syndrome* focusing on characterization and treatment of sex.

Additional coverage of McNally's life and career is contained in the following sources published by Thomson Gale: *American Writers Supplement,* **Vol. 13;** *Authors and Artists for Young Adults,* **Vol. 62;** *Contemporary American Dramatists; Contemporary Authors,* **Vols. 45-48;** *Contemporary Authors New Revision Series,* **Vols. 2, 56, 116;** *Contemporary Dramatists,* **Eds. 5, 6;** *Contemporary Literary Criticism,* **Vols. 4, 7, 41, 91;** *Dictionary of Literary Biography,* **Vols. 7, 249;** *DISCovering Authors 3.0; DISCovering Authors Modules: Drama Edition; Drama for Students,* **Vol. 16, 19;** *Encyclopedia of World Literature in the 20th Century,* **Ed. 3;** *Gay & Lesbian Literature,* **Ed. 1;** *Literature Resource Center; Major 20th-Century Writers,* **Ed. 2; and** *Major 21st-Century Writers: eBook Edition.*

Alfred de Musset
1810-1857

(Full name Louis-Charles-Alfred de Musset) French playwright, poet, and novelist.

INTRODUCTION

Unappreciated in his lifetime, Musset is now considered one of the greatest playwrights of nineteenth-century French theater. He still remains relatively unknown outside his native country, though his writing has influenced subsequent generations of French writers, dramatists, and filmmakers. Musset also wrote several volumes of poetry. Like his plays, his poems focus primarily on human drama. It was not until after Musset's death that most of his plays were performed, and then the reception was quite favorable. Today, Musset's works are nearly as popular in France as those of such better-known authors as Jean Racine and Molière.

BIOGRAPHICAL INFORMATION

Born on December 11, 1810, Musset was raised in Paris. Both of his parents came from wealthy old families. His father, Victor de Musset, was a writer known for his work on the philosopher Jean-Jacques Rousseau. Musset grew up with a brother, Paul, who later wrote a biography about him. Musset entered the Collèe Henry IV and won second prize for an essay in the summer of 1827. By 1828, however, he abandoned previous plans for a career in medicine and focused all his attention on writing. He was fortunate enough to make the acquaintance of such literary giants as Victor Hugo, Alfred de Vigny, and Charles-Augustin Sainte-Beuve. It is quite likely Hugo influenced Musset to start writing for the theater. In 1833 Musset met the novelist George Sand and they became romantically involved. A ragged end to the love affair in 1834 occurred just prior to Musset beginning what would become his greatest works—*On ne badine pas avec l'amour* (1834; *No Trifling with Love*), *Lorenzaccio* (1834), and *Fantasio* (1834). Musset's 1835 *La Confession d'un Enfant de Siècle,* (*The Confession of a Child of the Century*) gives a fictional account of their affair. The book is laced with a deep sense of disillusionment about the future. The next 22 years of Musset's life were characterized by a broken engagement, fleeting affairs, and a slow decline in his literary output and talent. He died of heart failure in Paris on May 2, 1857, at the age of 47.

MAJOR DRAMATIC WORKS

After a chilly reception to his first staged play, *La Nuit Vénitienne* (1830; *A Venetian Night*), Musset began to write for a reading audience rather than a theater audience. He called his *Un Spectacle dans un Fauteuil* (1832; *A Spectacle in an Armchair*) and subsequent plays *théatre du fauteuil,* or "armchair theater." Because he was no longer concerned with the technical aspects of staging the plays, Musset allowed his imagination to soar when concocting scenes, plot twists, and situations. His plays focus almost entirely on the characters—their desires, frustrations, cares, and woes—who drive the plot forward into humorous but also tragic circumstances. Very often in Musset's dramas, serious themes are contrasted with light-hearted dialogue; most of his plays have ambivalent protagonists who are driven by their passions to make both comic and tragic mistakes. The most famous of Musset's plays are the comedies *Les Caprices de Marianne* (1833; *The Follies of Marianne*), *No Trifling with Love, Fantasio, Le Chande-*

lier (1840; *The Candlestick*), and *Il ne faut jurer de rien* (1840; *You Can't Be Sure of Anything*). These and the tragedy *Lorenzaccio* remain popular with French audiences today at such venues as the Comédie Française and the Odéon.

CRITICAL RECEPTION

Musset's first work written for the theater, *A Venitian Night,* debuted in 1830. The play received a less-than-favorable critical reception—some biographers have called it hostile—that caused the young playwright to withdraw from the theater scene in Paris. Musset continued to write poetry, prose, and drama, however, and his self-imposed exile, historians and critics now believe, proved to be of great importance in enabling Musset to hone his craft without outside influences. Many critics also assert that Musset was ahead of his time; his drama was the prototype of a dramatic tradition that did not really take hold in France until the end of the nineteenth century. It was then that his ironic and self-mocking anti-heros began to appeal to theatrical audiences. The 1957 centenary of Musset's death sparked a re-evaluation of his works and their influence on French drama. Many critics focused more attention on Musset's work, perhaps for the first time, and found many things to praise, especially his unusual use of imagery: Musset relied on imagery only to further plot or reveal character traits; unlike his contemporaries, he did not use flowery imagery for its own sake. Many critics find that Musset's plays are a study in human emotions permeated with a richly-laid symbolist language that has yet to be fully explored.

PRINCIPAL WORKS

Plays

La Nuit vénitienne [*A Venitian Night*] 1830
*Un Spectacle dans un Fauteuil [Spectacle in an Arm-chair] 1833-34
†Comédies et Proverbes par Alfred de Musset 1840; revised 1853
La Nuit de décembre [*A December Night*] 1910

Other Major Works

L'Anglais Mangeur d'Opium [translator; from *Confessions of an English Opium Eater,* by Thomas De Quincey] (novel) 1828
Contes d'Espaigne et d'Italie [*Tales of Spain and Italy*] (prose and poetry) 1830

La Confession d'un Enfant de Siècle [*The Confession of a Child of the Century*] (novel) 1836
Premières Poésies Nouvelles [*First Poems*] (poetry) 1852
Poésies Nouvelles [*New Poetry*] (poetry) 1852
Œuvres complètes. 2 vols. (poetry and plays) 1968

*The 1833 volume comprises *La Coupe et les lèvres* [*The Cup and the Lips*], *A quoi rêvent les jeunes filles* [*Of What Young Maidens Dream*], and *Namouna.* The 1834 volume comprises *Lorenzaccio, Les Caprices de Marianne* [*The Follies of Marianne*], *André del Sarto, Fantasio, On ne badine pas avec l'amour* [*No Trifling with Love*], and *La Nuit vénitienne.*

†This work is comprised of *La Nuit vénitienne, André del Sarto, Les Caprices de Marianne, Fantasio, On ne badine pas avec l'amour, Lorenzaccio, La Quenouille de Barberine, Le Chandelier* [*The Candlestick*], *Il ne faut jurer de rien* [*You Can't Be Sure of Anything*], and *Un Caprice.* The revised 1853 edition also contains *Il faut qu'une porte soit ouverte ou fermée* [*The Door Must Be Either Open or Shut*], *Louison, On ne saurait penser à tout* [*One Cannot Think of Everything*], *Carmosine,* and *Bettine.*

OVERVIEWS

George Ross Ridge (essay date April 1959)

SOURCE: Ridge, George Ross. "The Anti-Hero in Musset's Drama." *The French Review* 32, no. 5 (April 1959): 428-34.

[*In the following essay, Ridge discusses Musset's use of anti-heros rather than standard romantic heros in his plays.*]

It is strange that Alfred de Musset early sets himself against the kind of romantic hero which he himself personifies so much. But he writes in "La Coupe et les lèvres" (*Premières poésies*):

> Mais je hais les pleurards, les rêveurs à nacelles,
> Les amants de la nuit, des lacs, des cascatelles,
> Cette engeance sans nom, qui ne peut faire un pas
> Sans s'inonder de vers, de pleurs et d'agendas.
> La Nature, sans doute, est comme on veut la prendre.
> Il se peut, après tout, qu'ils sachent la comprendre;
> Mais eux, certainement, je ne les comprends pas.

Musset ridicules the romantic hero, whose eyes flash mysteriously throughout romantic fiction, and criticizes him for wallowing in emotion. The gage is down. Even while he draws his inspiration from romanticism, Musset will continue to attack the romantic hero. And this attack, explicit in "La Coupe et les lèvres," becomes implicit in his drama with the formulation of a unique kind of romantic hero—the anti-hero.

There is no better term than *anti-hero* for Musset's dramatic protagonist, for he represents the other side of the coin. He is the antithesis of the romantic hero in every respect. The anti-hero is weak, vacillating, often absurd; he is the hero of what might have been but never in fact became. Yet his roots are the same as the romantic hero's. Both are the products of romantic self-consciousness and hypersensibility; both are potentially titans of thought, action, feeling. But whereas the romantic hero becomes in fact a "titan," the anti-hero fails because he turns an ironic, debilitating analysis upon himself. The anti-hero is abortive. He is abortive because he is too sophisticated to be a romantic hero or because he is a weakling who cannot act though he retains an immense capacity to feel. In either case the anti-hero is a pathetic figure who despises his weakness. He is no more satisfactory, at length, than his antipode, the romantic hero.

Razetta is an anti-hero in **La Nuit vénitienne.** He feels a romantic grand passion for Laurette, and when she rejects him he exclaims effusively: "Laurette! Laurette! Ah! je me sens plus lâche qu'une femme. Mon désespoir me tue; il faut que je pleure." (I, 1) His romantic despair amuses the young sophisticates of Venice, who look upon him as a naive young fool. They cynically ridicule him while enjoying their own casual liaisons. Appearance notwithstanding, Razetta is to this point a romantic hero, but he does not appear to be because he is a ridiculous figure.

Razetta's foil is the supreme sophisticate, Prince Eysenach, whose wife Laurette, has been Razetta's mistress. Eysenach is unperturbed when he discovers her infidelity; he is neither angry nor jealous. He casually discusses love and society even after learning that Laurette has agreed to murder him, for he sees himself part of a universal comedy. He takes nothing seriously. His sophistication overwhelms Laurette, and she renounces Razetta. She walks off with her husband at the appointed hour of assassination.

Razetta is overwhelmed. He does not know whether he ought to scale the walls and kill Eysenach, like a romantic hero, or commit suicide in despair. Just then the sophisticated young Venetians pass and taunt him for his naïveté:

> Veux-tu tuer ton rival, ou te noyer? Laisse ces idées communes au vulgaire des amants; souviens-toi de toi-même, et ne donne pas le mauvais exemple. Demain matin les femmes seront inabordables, si on apprend cette nuit que Razetta s'est noyé. Encore une fois, viens souper avec nous.

(I, 3)

Razetta rejects suicide and accepts their laughing invitation. Thus he changes, in a moment, from a romantic hero to a sophisticate—a man who wryly comments on his own passion; and in that moment he becomes the anti-hero. For there can be no sophisticated romantic heroes.

Perdican is the sophisticate of **On ne badine pas avec l'amour.** He falls in love with Camille, a romantic heroine, but their love is star-crossed because they are basically unlike. Camille asks, for instance:

> Lève la tête, Perdican! quel est l'homme qui ne croit à rien?

PERDICAN:

> En voilà un; je ne crois pas à la vie immortelle.—Ma sœur chérie, les religieuses t'ont donné leur expérience; mais, crois-moi, ce n'est pas la tienne; tu ne mourras pas sans aimer.

(II, 5)

Perdican is a blasé sophisticate who has enjoyed his mistresses. He might take another after their marriage, he says, if their love should die, and in that case he would not mind her taking a lover. And love, he adds, so frequently dies. Camille is profoundly hurt, but Perdican, not unfeelingly, scoffs at her romanticism:

> Adieu, Camille, retourne à ton couvent, et lorsqu'on te fera de ces récits hideux qui t'ont empoisonnée, réponds de ce que je vais te dire: Tous les hommes sont menteurs, inconstants, faux, bavards, hypocrites, orgueilleux ou lâches, méprisables et sensuels; toutes les femmes sont perfides, artificielles, vaniteuses, curieuses et dépravées; mais il y a au monde une chose sainte et sublime, c'est l'union de deux de ces êtres si imparfaits et si affreux. On est souvent trompé en amour, souvent blessé et souvent malheureux; mais on aime, et, quand on est sur le bord de sa tombe, on se retourne pour regarder en arrière, et on se dit: J'ai souffert souvent, je me suis trompé quelquefois, mais j'ai aimé. C'est moi qui ai vécu, et non pas un être factice créé par mon orgueil et mon ennui.

(II, 5)

A romantic hero could never be so cynically sophisticated. Perdican and Camille never consummate their love, for their separation is of course inevitable. Perdican, the sophisticate, the anti-hero, cannot understand the romantic Camille.

The anti-hero may be a weakling rather than a sophisticate. Of course the sophisticate is a kind of weakling, but his cynicism and wit are formidable weapons in dealing with society. Without sophistication the anti-hero loses his last trace of "titanism," and he more clearly emerges as the romantic hero's antipode.

Célio and Octave are weaklings in **Les Caprices de Marianne.** Célio is too shy to express his love to Marianne, Claudio's wife, and asks his friend, Octave, to serve as go-between. Octave, as a kinsman, has access to Claudio's home. Marianne scoffs when she hears about Célio, but she falls in love with Octave. In the meantime Claudio becomes suspicious and plots Célio's death. Believing that Octave has betrayed him with Marianne, Célio walks calmly into Claudio's trap. He turns to suicide because he is too impotent to face life.

Now Célio and Octave, as men of deep feeling, have romantic sensibility, but they are never heroic or "titanic." Rather they are weak and their actions abortive; both men are cowards. Célio cannot speak for himself, and Octave is no romantic hero scaling the walls to flee with his gasping beloved in the night. He, too, cannot act. Yet his abulia is not the collapse of a great soul; it is simply weakness.

Both men whimper in their weakness. Célio describes himself:

> Pourquoi donc suis-je ainsi? pourquoi ne saurais-je aimer cette femme comme toi, Octave, tu l'aimerais, ou comme j'en aimerais une autre? Qui pourrait dire?
>
> (I, 4)

Octave simpers when he learns of Célio's death:

> Célio m'aurait vengé, si j'étais mort pour lui comme il est mort pour moi. Son tombeau m'appartient; c'est moi qu'ils ont étendu dans cette sombre allée; c'est pour moi qu'ils avaient aiguisé leurs épées; c'est pour moi qu'ils ont tué!
>
> (II, 20)

Yet he does nothing as he confesses: "Je ne suis qu'un débauché sans cœur." (II, 20) Now while the romantic hero may indeed have faults, they are always titanic, i.e., bigger than life, and charged with emotion. But the anti-hero comments wryly upon his weakness, which becomes a petty thing.

André del Sarto, in the drama of the same name, is Musset's completest portrayal of the anti-hero as a weakling. Prompted by his wife, Lucrèce, Del Sarto steals money from King Francis and flees France. He is repaid with flagrant cuckoldom. Consequently he loses all self-respect:

> Que faisait-elle de mal en me demandant ce qui lui plaisait? Et moi, je lui donnais parce qu'elle me le demandait, rien de plus; faiblesse maudite! pas une réflexion! . . . à quoi tient donc l'honneur?
>
> (I, 8)

The great artist fawns pathetically before Lucrèce:

> Les instants que nous passons ensemble sont si courts et si rares! et ils me sont si chers! . . . Vous seule au monde, Lucrèce, me consolez du chagrin qui m'obsède. . . . Ah! si je vous perdais! . . . tout mon courage, toute ma philosophie est dans vos yeux.
>
> (I, 12)

Lucrèce mocks him in his spinelessness, and when she deserts him for her lover, Del Sarto commits suicide. He wallows in despair as he dies:

> C'est un cordial puissant. Approche-le de tes lèvres, et tu seras guéri, quel que soit le mal dont tu souffres. Vos mains, et adieu, chers amis. . . . Oh, combien je l'aimais!
>
> (II, 10)

Del Sarto never shows any degree of strength in the entire play. The tragedy consists in the fact that such strength and weakness coexist in one man—the strength of creative genius (romantic hero), but with all the weakness of the anti-hero.

Yet if the anti-hero is defined as a protagonist antipodal to the romantic hero *in every respect,* then Célio and Del Sarto are not the purest examples. Célio has some potentiality, and Del Sarto is a genius. They simply cannot express a latent strength and hence may be accounted romantic heroes *manqués.* Musset's Fantasio, on the other hand, lacks every trace of heroism. He is the archetypal anti-hero.

Although Musset published *Fantasio* in 1834 during the apogee of French romanticism, Fantasio is foreign to the romantic spirit. He is no hero at all. He is neither a poet-prophet guiding his people, nor Promethean rebel suffering for mankind, nor wanderer engaged on a romantic quest, nor pathological nor titan in any respect. Fantasio is an intelligent, sensitive scoundrel who acts apart from his fellows but never towers above them. He has an earthy sense of camaraderie for Spark, Hartmann, Facio, and is no romantic solitary brooding apart in grand isolation. Now the romantic hero often substitutes emotion for mind, but Fantasio dulls both with excessive drinking: "Il faut que je me grise," he explains (II, 3). It is drunkenness for its own sake.

This does not mean that the anti-hero is an ordinary man. Although Fantasio is never heroic, he has emotional sensitivity and is prey to cynicism and despair. He speaks nostalgically of his penchant for art when he was a boy; the next moment he makes a quip. He is an acute observer, with much psychological insight, who distrusts the intellect because he does not want to be victimized by his rationalizations. He observes, for instance, in the romantic tradition:

> Hélas! tout ce que les hommes se disent entre eux se ressemble; les idées qu'ils échangent sont presque toujours les mêmes dans toutes leurs conversations; mais, dans l'intérieur de toutes ces machines isolées, quels replis, quels compartiments secrets! C'est tout un monde que chacun porte en lui! un monde ignoré qui naît et qui meurt en silence!
>
> (I, 2)

His frustration and despair are evident. But while he suffers he quips in the same breath that his only real worry is how to evade his creditors. Once more he turns to wine.

Fantasio is a scamp who sometimes yearns for what might have been. Indeed, his actions are antithetical to what a romantic hero would have done, and he knows this. He is whimsical and his struggle to escape the creditors farcical. There is no real romantic fire in him, and he even refers to himself as a "vieille cheminée sans feu." (I, 2) The image contrasts sharply with that of the *volcanic* romantic hero.

Consider for example the romantic motif of flight. Fantasio disguises himself as the dead jester, Saint-Jean, in order to evade his creditors by hiding in the King's court. He does not commit a crime, turn to violence, defiance, or even disdain; he simply runs away from society. Contrast this with the familiar romantic motif of flight to the wilderness, to the Alps, to the lonely places where the soul communes with itself. Fantasio even compromises with the world on its own terms, symbolically, when he puts on the fool's garb. The romantic hero never compromises. Fantasio strips himself of identity whereas the romantic hero egomaniacally asserts his identity.

Fantasio assumes that man is a ludicrous ass and exclaims:

> Quelle misérable chose que l'homme! ne pas pouvoir seulement sauter par sa fenêtre sans se casser les jambes! être obligé de jouer du violon dix ans pour devenir un musicien passable! Apprendre pour être peintre, pour être palefrenier! Apprendre pour faire une omelette!
>
> (I, 2)

Man is utterly helpless. Whereas the romantic hero says that man can be grand even in helplessness, Fantasio argues that he is merely ludicrous. There are no heroes. No superman thunders from the peak, and no inexplicable passion impels a hero on strange quests. Man is a simple animal, not a poet or prophet or seer. Man, Fantasio would say, has to study to be a good ostler. And when the idea of romantic genius is precluded, then obviously the romantic hero goes. Only the anti-hero remains.

Thus Fantasio's sensitivity results in cynical weakness, not heroism:

> L'amour n'existe plus, mon cher ami. La religion, sa nourrice, a les mamelles pendantes comme une vieille bourse au fond de laquelle il y a un gros sou.
>
> (I, 2)

Fantasio never tries to replace the Prince of Mantoue as Elsbeth's suitor. Love does not exist, nor are there any other passions. There is only wine, which brings forgetfulness, and that, again, is weakness.

Now if he had so wished, Musset could have changed the plot to have Fantasio, disguised as a jester, slip into the King's court, woo the beautiful Princess, and slay the wicked and foppish Prince. Such a plot would be in the romantic mainstream. But since Fantasio is an anti-hero, the plot is exactly reversed. It is a parody of the romantic plot, and the cynical Fantasio continues to pun rather than act in the grand manner:

> Un calembour console de bien des chagrins; et jouer avec les mots est un moyen comme un autre de jouer avec les pensées, les actions et les êtres. Tout est calembour ici-bas, et il est aussi difficile de comprendre le regard d'un enfant de quatre ans, que le galimatias de trois drames modernes.

Life is absurd and there are no heroes.

Fantasio is consistently anti-heroic. While the romantic hero often commits, or feels he commits, great crimes, Fantasio's "crime" is no more than a caprice. He snatches the wig from the Prince's head. The page recounts the incident to Elsbeth:

> La perruque s'est enlevée en l'air au bout d'un hameçon. Nous l'avons retrouvée dans l'office, à côté d'une bouteille cassée; on ignore qui a fait cette plaisanterie. Mais le duc n'est pas moins furieux, et il a juré que, si l'auteur n'en est pas puni de mort, il déclarera la guerre au roi votre père, et mettra tout à feu et à sang.
>
> (II, 5)

There could be no greater contrast with the romantic hero. Musset, ironically, has the Prince demand the death-penalty for this supreme affront, while the good King finds the crime heinous enough only for a stiff prison sentence.

There is no room for the romantic hero in an absurd world, for he would then become—as Musset shows—a laughable figure. Thus the romantic hero is replaced by the anti-hero, like Fantasio, who is no less absurd than life itself. And Fantasio describes himself while in prison: "En vérité, lorsque je suis gris, je crois que j'ai quelque chose de surhumain." (II, 7) The demise of the romantic hero is complete. Fantasio renounces even the desire for heroism or action as he turns in upon himself.

A final note is instructive. Fantasio is almost but not quite a part of his society, the court, which is a ludicrous microcosm of life. When Elsbeth offers him a position as court-fool, Fantasio declines:

> Fantasio, veux-tu rester le bouffon de mon père? Je te paye tes vingt mille écus.

FANTASIO:

> Je le voudrais de grand cœur; mais, en vérité, si j'y étais forcé, je sauterais par la fenêtre pour me sauver un de ces jours.
>
> (II, 7)

This comment comes at the end of a parody on the romantic hero, and it leaves the reader momentarily uncertain about Fantasio. Perhaps it is that the persona breaks and reveals the face of the anti-hero. Would, *could,* Fantasio have been different in another society, one which was not absurd? Would the anti-hero then become the romantic hero? The reader is not quite sure, and romantic irony consists in the reader's uncertainty as to what Fantasio, i.e., the anti-hero, really is. Since Fantasio does not know himself and never reveals himself—if there is such a persona—then the reader can never know him. The final element of doubt is ticklish.

But this is certain: Musset rejects the romantic hero as an absurd figure and replaces him with the *anti-hero,* a protagonist who meets life on far different terms. As such he may be a sophisticate with the cutting weapons of wit, irony, cynicism. Lacking such sophistication, he will fail. But in success or failure the anti-hero remains the antipode of his brother, the romantic hero.

Margaret A. Rees (essay date January 1963)

SOURCE: Rees, Margaret A. "Imagery in the Plays of Alfred de Musset." *The French Review* 36, no. 3 (January 1963): 245-54.

[*In the following essay, Rees examines the ways in which the imagery used by Musset in his plays differs from that of his contemporaries.*]

> Tandis qu'il me parlait, il me passait devant les yeux des tableaux délicieux; sa parole donnait la vie, comme par enchantement, aux choses les plus étranges.

These words are spoken by Elspeth, the Bavarian princess in *Fantasio,* of the court fool (Act II, sc.i); but in this as in many other ways Fantasio's qualities are those of his creator, and Elspeth's feeling that she is under the spell of a magician in imagery must have been shared by many a spectator of this arm-chair theater.

Nowadays, to admit to such a reaction to Musset's prose tends to be unfashionable. Indeed, asked to predict the characteristics of his imagery in the *Comédies et Proverbes,* scoffers at Romanticism would probably open the list with cloying sentimentality, followed by a glut of themes dear to the Romantics—such as moonlit nights, ghostly ruins, pallid lovers, the passionate South—and of their typical and often exaggerated moods—melancholy, despair, emotional fervor, and exaltation. One might certainly expect images of such a nature to prevail in Musset's plays and also, although dramatic

prose is inherently less given to original metaphor than poetry, to appear more often and in brighter colors than in the works of a more sober literary age.

Yet when one turns to the *Comédies et Proverbes,* one finds images used with a surprising economy. Indeed, in many plays there are scarcely any except those which have passed into everyday life as part of the small change of conversation. The absence of striking imagery in those pieces which are chiefly comedies of polished wit set in a brilliant society—for instance, *Il faut qu'une porte soit ouverte ou fermée, Il ne faut jurer de rien,* and *Un Caprice*—points to an interesting conclusion about Musset's use of such imagery as a dramatist. It is not settings and situations in which superficial sparkle predominates that act as tinder to his flashes of poetic comparison. Brilliant and witty as some of his images may be, they do not occur primarily as demonstrations of verbal or mental agility.

At first sight it seems surprising to find imagery rare in *La Nuit vénitienne* also. Surely, since this was an early play, an attempt by a young frequenter of Hugo's group at storming the Parisian stage, the dialogue might be expected to display sparkling and colorful word-pictures. Yet practically the only metaphor to be developed at any length is the musical one in scene ii. *La Nuit vénitienne* indicates that in the *Comédies et Proverbes,* images will not be chiefly baubles to serve as ornament any more than they are merely an opportunity for wit. This view of their function is borne out by later plays, including those where intense feeling prevails and where poetic outbursts might have been expected. In *André del Sarto,* where the passions of love, jealousy and grief run high, only three images that are new can be found in the space of two acts, and these are fairly short. (Two of these occur in speeches by Cordiani in Act I, Scene iii, and the third is a simile in lines spoken by André del Sarto in Act II, Scene vi.) Each of these three represents, as we shall see later, a theme recurring like a leitmotiv in these plays—love, disillusion and hallucination. All three are closely bound to the subject of the piece, and no superfluous play of comparison is allowed to impede the action. Even in *Carmosine,* where the subject might easily have led a lesser writer to indulge in a flood of sentimental images, there are only two which are striking. The first is the down-to-earth metaphor of the pharmacist, Maître Bernard, provoked by his daughter's oafish suitor into asking: "Qu'est-ce qu'un âne peut faire d'une rose?" (I, i); and in the second this same suitor, Ser Vespasiano, employs metaphors so banal that they help to increase his stature as a monument of ridiculousness in our eyes (Act I, sc. vii).

Images which have lost their impact through frequent use, such as "comme l'aiguille aimantée attire le fer"

(*Les Caprices de Marianne,* I, iv), and "cette fraîche aurore de jeunesse, dans cette rosée céleste de la vie" (*ibid.,* II, xi) occur as a matter of course throughout the *Comédies et Proverbes,* but to find more than a sparse sprinkling of original comparisons we must turn to a small number of plays—*Fantasio, Lorenzaccio, On ne badine pas avec l'amour,* and, above all, *Les Caprices de Marianne.*

Even here, every act or scene does not always yield a greater crop of images than those of, say, *Le Chandelier* or *Barberine.* Rather, there often seem to be sudden volcanic eruptions of image-making, of which one of the most striking is found in *Lorenzaccio.* The early scenes of this play have little to offer in new comparisons, bright with color though the dialogue may be. Yet in a scene which is perhaps, even more than that showing the accomplishment of Lorenzo's mission of murder, the crux of the play, images start cascading. This passage forms part of Act III, Scene ii, during the interview with Philippe Strozzi in which Lorenzo, an enigmatic figure until this point, drops his mask, stirred by Philippe's state of mind to reveal the secret of his life, the transformation which took an idealistic, studious young man and made him the cynical, debauched weakling of the earlier scenes. Here, as he speaks of the purpose which dominates him and for which he has already paid a high price, Lorenzaccio launches into a whole series of images, so that within the space of a few pages there are at least four developed at length, in addition to many shorter ones.

Philippe, on the verge of taking desperate revolutionary action, is warned that he is being tempted by a demon more fair than Gabriel.

> La liberté, la patrie, le bonheur des hommes, tous ces mots résonnent à son approche comme les cordes d'une lyre; c'est le bruit des écailles d'argent de ses ailes flamboyantes. Les larmes de ses yeux fécondent la terre, et il tient à la main la palme des martyrs. Ses paroles épurent l'air autour de ses lèvres; son vol est si rapide que nul ne peut dire où il va. . . .

After this figure reminiscent of Milton's Lucifer, the tyrant Alexandre is represented as a buffalo brought to the ground by the huntsman with all his apparatus of nets and ropes. Then, still intent on showing Philippe the dangers he runs if despair draws him to revolt, Lorenzo takes up an image bringing to mind lines spoken by Fantasio in Act I, Scene ii of the play bearing his name. Philippe, the philosopher, has lived like a lighthouse rising above the ocean, seeing in the water only the reflection of its own brightness, admiring both sea and skies and knowing nothing of the wrecks and scattered bones on the sea-bed that are seen by the diver who plunges deep into this sea of life.

Close on this image there follows a second which is similar to one evoked by Fantasio in his café-table conversation with Spark (Act I, sc.ii). Life, says Lorenzo, is a city where one can spend fifty or sixty years seeing no other aspect than the broad avenues and palaces, but a city with its low quarters to be shunned. Finally there comes a picture showing Musset's absorption into the world of his play, Renaissance Italy with the pageantry of its processions. "Quand j'ai commencé à jouer mon rôle de Brutus moderne, je marchais dans mes habits neufs de la grande confrérie du vice, comme un enfant de dix ans dans l'armure d'un géant de la fable. . . . Le vice a été pour moi un vêtement, maintenant il est collé à ma peau." With the ending of this peak scene of self-revelation, the frequency of the imagery falls back to its former level. Similarly it is at a moment of crisis, in a state of wild exaltation before his planned elopement with his master's wife that Cordiani in *André del Sarto* conjures up a mental vision of a supernatural figure not unlike Lorenzo's demon, although this fallen angel is not the spirit of evil but the spirit of love, "qui, après la création, ne voulut pas quitter la terre, et tandis que ses frères remontaient au ciel, laissa tomber ses ailes d'or en poudre, aux pieds de la beauté qu'il avait créée" (I, iii).

It is worth noting that, although imagery flowers in Musset's theater at moments of intensity, these peaks do not always coincide with the climax of the plot, but rather with one in the emotions of a leading character. It is not the murder scene in *Lorenzaccio* which is especially rich in comparison, but the interview mentioned above, empty of physical action but supremely important for the light it throws on the hero's motives and mental state. In the same way, Fantasio, always ready for verbal conjuring, is particularly quick to draw imaginative parallels at times when the dialogue touches on matters which concern him deeply. In the café scene already mentioned Hartman, with his comment "Tu as le mois de mai sur les joues," provokes Fantasio's description of his state of disillusionment and boredom:

> C'est vrai; et le mois de janvier dans le cœur. Ma tête est comme une vieille cheminée sans feu: il n'y a que du vent et des cendres. Que cela m'ennuie que tout le monde s'amuse! Je voudrais que ce grand ciel si lourd fût un immense bonnet de coton, pour envelopper jusqu'aux oreilles cette sotte ville et ses sots habitants!

Later, in a prolonged image, Fantasio compares his mind to a town whose every feature is familiar to the point of boredom.

Once he has entered the Court as royal jester, it is during his conversations with the princess, whose approaching marriage of convenience to a princely dolt has stirred him to indignation, that the most striking and highly developed images occur. The palace flower garden lends its tulips to provide a comparison with the princess's marriage contract, and its roses as figures of the ladies of the Court. One of the most extended images equates the princess with a glittering toy which brings to mind the shop-windows of the rue Saint-Honoré:

> . . . un joli petit serin empaillé, qui chante comme un rossignol. . . . C'est un serin de Cour; il y a beaucoup de petites filles très bien élevées qui n'ont pas d'autres procédés que celui-là. Elles ont un petit ressort sous le bras gauche, un joli petit ressort en diamant fin, comme la montre d'un petit-maître. Le gouverneur ou la gouvernante fait jouer le ressort, et vous voyez aussitôt les lèvres s'ouvrir avec le sourire le plus gracieux, une charmante cascatelle de paroles mielleuses sort avec le plus doux murmure, et toutes les convenances sociales, pareilles à des nymphes légères, se mettent aussitôt à dansoter sur la pointe du pied autour de la fontaine merveilleuse. Le prétendu ouvre des yeux ébahis; l'assistance chuchote avec indulgence, et le père, rempli d'un secret contentement, regarde avec orgueil les boucles d'or de ses souliers.
>
> (II, 5)

Clustering at such points in the plays, Musset's images are clearly not merely ornament or rhetoric. Rather their function is one which C. Day Lewis has pointed out as typical of the Romantics' use of comparison[1]—to probe more deeply thoughts and emotions, here those of the principal characters and often, through them, those of the writer himself.

This is not the sole function of imagery in the *Comédies et Proverbes,* since Musset was too gifted a dramatist to rivet his eyes entirely on those figures in whom he could see reflections of himself and his own problems. Often images used by or of a character are effective additional touches to the picture which is being drawn of his personality. So Claudio, the humourless, stupid judge in *Les Caprices de Marianne,* describes his wife as "un trésor de pureté" (I, viii), a conventional phrase typical of the pompous dullness Musset saw in him, as in many of the bourgeois in his plays. In the same way, Ser Vespasiano in *Carmosine* helps to ridicule himself through overblown stereotypes: "Que vois-je! La perle de mon âme à demi privée de sentiment! Ses yeux d'azur presque fermés à la lumière, et les lis remplaçant les roses" (I, vii)!

Again, both comedy and characterisation gain from the chorus's well-known greeting first to Maître Blazius and then to Dame Pluche early in *On ne badine pas avec l'amour.* "Comme un poupon sur l'oreiller, il se ballotte sur son ventre rebondi. . . . Vous arrivez au temps de la vendange, pareil à une amphore antique. . . . Bonjour donc, dame Pluche, vous arrivez

comme la fièvre, avec le vent qui fait jaunir les bois." Here, in one short passage, the reader has a vivid mental picture of the bulging form of the cleric and the parched, arid appearance of the governess, and already has the key to their natures.

Nor is it only in the gallery of grotesques that the impression of a character is strengthened through imagery. In *Les Caprices de Marianne* neither Cœlio nor Octave has been on stage for long before the words of each have summoned up a scene representative of his own personality. Cœlio evokes a picture at the same time melancholy, solitary and fatalistic:

> Malheur à celui qui . . . s'abandonne à un amour sans espoir! Mollement couché dans une barque, il s'éloigne peu à peu de la rive; il aperçoit au loin des plaines enchantées, de vertes prairies, et le mirage léger de son Eldorado. Les flots l'entraînent en silence, et quand la Réalité le réveille, il est aussi loin du but où il aspire que du rivage qu'il a quitté. Il ne peut plus ni poursuivre sa route ni revenir sur ses pas.
>
> (I, iii)

Shortly afterwards, it is a bustling fair-scene, full of defiant and reckless gaiety which Octave presents with the comment: "Voilà ma vie, mon cher ami; c'est ma fidèle image que tu vois (I, iv).

Imagery, then, helps the patron of this "spectacle dans un fauteuil" to form his visual impression of Blazius and Dame Pluche, and in a drama whose spectacle exists only in the imagination of the reader it is often valuable too in summoning up a picture of the setting against which the action is taking place. Musset has little of Hugo's fondness for prefacing each change of stage set with a luxuriantly detailed description, but when Fantasio has finished drawing his parallel between human beings and the flowers among which he and the princess are standing, a vision of the palace flower garden is as clear to us as though we had been given an account of its exact layout. We have already noticed Lorenzaccio using an image drawn from Italian carnival and, in *Les Caprices de Marianne,* Octave, sitting at a café table in Florence and comparing the wine before him to a woman less remote than Marianne, brings before us a vivid glimpse of Italian hillsides:

> Combien de temps pensez-vous qu'il faille faire la cour à la bouteille que vous voyez pour obtenir d'elle un accueil favorable? . . . Dieu n'en a pas caché la source au sommet d'un pic inabordable, au fond d'une caverne profonde; il l'a suspendue en grappes dorées sur nos brillants coteaux. Elle est, il est vrai, rare et précieuse, mais elle ne défend pas qu'on l'approche. Elle se laisse voir aux rayons du soleil, et toute une cour d'abeilles et de frelons murmure autour d'elle matin et soir. Le voyageur dévoré de soif peut se reposer sous ses rameaux verts; jamais elle ne l'a laissé languir, jamais elle ne lui a refusé les douces larmes dont son cœur est plein.
>
> (II, viii)

It would be a strange prose which did not make use of traditional comparisons such as "pâle comme la neige," but the more one reads of the **Comédies et Proverbes,** the more striking appears the high proportion of original images, which yet are never so obtrusive as to hinder or detract from the dramatic purpose of the passage where they are found. Most of the examples quoted here have been of comparisons developed at some length, but many of those which merely present an image without elaboration are equally vivid, as, for instance, the Chevalier's advice on courtship given in **Barberine**: "Que toutes vos façons près d'elles ressemblent à ces valets polis qui sont couverts de livrées splendides (I, iv). Among the slightly longer images, freshness of treatment and sensitivity of perception are the rule. A dealer in trite similes, depicting a lover seeing his beloved as a huntsman catching sight of a doe, would not have spared the reader a mention of the creature's liquid eyes and grace, but Musset creates an unhackneyed and attractive picture almost exclusively in sound and silence:

> C'est ainsi qu'au fond des forêts, lorsqu'une biche avance à petits pieds sur les feuilles sèches, et que le chasseur entend les bruyères glisser sur ses flancs inquiets, comme le frôlement d'une robe légère, les battements de cœur le prennent malgré lui; il soulève son arme en silence, sans faire un pas, sans respirer.
>
> (I, iv)

Whether the images have the softness of sound and delicacy of suggested colour of this last image, or the warmth and splendour of **Barberine**'s liveried valets, they are usually arresting in their pictorial charm. Scarcely ever could they be judged insipid and sentimental. It is also surprisingly rare to come upon an image whose material might be classified as "typically Romantic," formed of the themes which were in danger of becoming clichés in the writings of the period. There are a few of this kind, such as Fantasio's vision of a girl who might have stepped from the ballet routine of *Les Sylphides,* "quelque chose de doux comme le vent d'ouest, de pâle comme les rayons de la lune" (I, ii); but this type of comparison is not necessarily less appealing because it is expected.

Strangely lacking in Romantic stereotypes, Musset's imagery has a surprise in store too for those who hold the view that nature plays a far smaller part in the works of this Parisian dandy than in those of most of his contemporaries. It is true, as we have seen, that many of his metaphors and similes have their source in city life—in the circus scene to which Octave compares his life, in the vistas of streets which seem to Lorenzaccio and Fantasio to represent existence, or around the gaming tables as in the line from **Les Caprices de Marianne**: "Qu'importe comment la bille d'ivoire tombe sur le numéro que nous avons appelé" (II, xvii)! Yet that type occurs no more frequently than others such as Octave's woodland picture of the doe, or Cœlio's evocation of a boating scene which might so easily belong to the banks of the Seine. City-dweller though he might be, Musset knew too from his childhood the scenery around his grandfather's country house, apart from the landscapes with which he became familiar in later life, and the dialogue of his plays makes it clear that he had a store of mental pictures of the countryside on which he drew readily.

Since imagery is said to be a key which may open the way to the inner recesses of a writer's mind, it is interesting to note certain themes and traits recurring in the plays. We have seen how both Lorenzaccio and Fantasio use a town as a symbol for the human mind or life, and how Lorenzaccio and Cordiani imagine the principal moral forces in their lives—in the former, desire for heroic action, in the latter, love for a woman—in the form of a brilliant supernatural figure. It is rare for Musset to repeat a particular image, but there is one characteristic which is frequent enough in his metaphors and similes to attract attention. Sometimes, as we read a passage of sustained comparison, we are overtaken by a sense of hallucination. Of two of the examples of imagery taken from **Les Caprices de Marianne** which have already been mentioned, Cœlio's picture of the man whose love is not returned and Octave's image of his own precarious mode of life, the first begins as a boating scene whose setting might be anywhere in France. Then it acquires a touch of the unreal with the phrase "le mirage léger de son Eldorado" and the final sentence plunges into nightmare helplessness.

Again, Octave's metaphor begins with a sight ordinary enough—the tight-rope walker suspended between heaven and earth. Then we are in a nightmare once more, for a crowd reminiscent of a Hieronymus Bosch painting throngs round the performer: ". . . de vieilles petites figures racornies, de maigres et pâles fantômes, des créanciers agiles, des parents et des courtisanes, toute une légion de monstres se suspendent à son manteau et le tiraillent de tous côtés pour lui faire perdre l'équilibre." These caricatures of some of those who peopled Musset's own experience are joined by even more fantastic creatures, by terrifying personification: "De grands mots enchâssés cavalcadent autour de lui; une nuée de prédictions sinistres l'aveugle de ses ailes noires."

A little later in the same scene there is a direct reference, illustrated by metaphor, to a sense of unreality:

> La réalité n'est qu'une ombre. Appelle imagination ou folie ce qui la divinise. Alors la folie est la beauté elle-même. Chaque homme marche enveloppé d'un réseau transparent qui le couvre de la tête aux pieds; il croit

voir des bois et des fleuves, des visages divins, et l'universelle nature se teint sous ses regards des nuances infinies du tissu magique.

It is well known that hallucinatory figures play a part in Musset's works—the brother-like phantom in *La Nuit de décembre,* the spectre that appears to Marie Soderini of her son Lorenzo as he was in his youth (*Lorenzaccio,* Act II, sc.iv). We are told that Musset himself knew what it was to be in the grip of hallucination, and certainly more than one of the images in his plays suggests that he was familiar at times with a nightmarish feeling of haunted unreality.

Musset's biography makes imagery on the theme of human love easily predictable in the *Comédies et Proverbes,* and indeed this probably overshadows all other subjects of his comparisons. Occasionally love is shown in the pose which one would expect of a Romantic writer—high on a pedestal and draped with an air of fatality and melodrama. To see love idealized, there is no need to look further than Perdican's famous speech in *On ne badine pas avec l'amour,* where the world is depicted as "un égout sans fond où les phoques les plus informes rampent et se tordent sur des montagnes de fange" and in which love between two human beings is the one thing of importance and beauty (II, v).

Surprisingly, it is the cynical Octave who puts into imagery the melancholy and melodrama of Romantic love, describing it as:

> un mal le plus cruel de tous, car c'est un mal sans espérance; le plus terrible, car c'est un mal qui se chérit lui-même et repousse la coupe salutaire jusque dans la main de l'amitié; un mal qui fait pâlir les lèvres sous des poisons plus doux que l'ambroisie et qui fond en une pluie de larmes le cœur le plus dur, comme la perle de Cléopâtre; un mal que tous les aromates, toute la science humaine ne sauraient soulager, et qui se nourrit du vent qui passe, du parfum d'une rose fanée, du refrain d'une chanson, et qui puise l'éternel aliment de ses souffrances dans tout ce qui l'entoure, comme une abeille son miel dans tous les buissons du jardin.

(I, v)

Again, it would be easy to foretell in these plays the presence of imagery showing the Romantic sanctification of love, as in the comparison Fantasio makes with a sacramental wafer which must be divided before an altar and both halves swallowed in a kiss. The same attitude can be seen in Cordiani's vision of love as an angel, fallen but still superb. Yet even here on this holy ground of the Romantics Musset's sense of comic reality is too strong to be prevented from breaking in, and in *Le Chandelier* Clavaroche declares: "En vérité, on représente l'Amour avec des ailes et un carquois; on ferait mieux de nous le peindre comme un chasseur de canards sauvages, avec une veste imperméable et une perruque de laine frisée pour lui garantir l'occiput" (II, ii).

This group of comparisons dealing with love seems to conform far more closely to what might generally be expected, or feared, of Romantic imagery than is typical of Musset in his theater. Certainly samples of what was prevalent at this period can be found in the *Comédies et Proverbes,* both in subject matter and in mood. Yet, among those images which are not merely a part of everyday speech, these are rare, outnumbered by imagery which is the result of an original mind. Above all, the keenness and delicacy of perception are those of a poet who couples with the powerful imagination and powerful feelings capable of conjuring up in his metaphors worlds in which the reader is completely absorbed for their duration, the restraint which never allows a passage of imagery to slow down the action of a play. Indeed, a study of the images in his dialogue intensifies admiration for Musset's workmanship as a dramatist. Never obtruding themselves for their own sake, never appearing merely as decorative tinsel, his metaphors and similes help the lines of the dialogue to delineate more firmly and vividly the background characters, and to penetrate more incisively into the mind of the main characters. Even more important for us, while delighting our ear and imagination, they reveal a little more of the mind of Musset himself.

Note

1. C. Day Lewis, *The Poetic Image* (London, 1947), pp. 58-59.

John Kenneth Simon (lecture date May 1965)

SOURCE: Simon, John Kenneth. "The Presence of Musset in Modern French Drama." *The French Review* 40, no. 1 (October 1966): 27-38.

[*In the following essay, originally presented as a lecture in May, 1965, Simon evaluates the impact Musset has had on modern French theatre.*]

That we are still involved in a profoundly romantic era few will contest. Many "moderns" have been recognized in the first generations of Romantics: Constant, Stendhal, Nerval. . . . But Musset, doubtlessly judged on his nondramatic writings alone, has been considered at antipodes with the modern spirit, serving as a foil for all subsequent movements and generations. Following Baudelaire, Lautréamont and Rimbaud, men of letters like Valéry and Mauriac have seen the author of "Les Nuits" as "un garçon coiffeur qui a dans son cœur une belle boîte à musique," or worse.[1] While the centenary for the poet in 1957 provided a potential forum for a new interpretation, matters of biography and sources have remained the principal preoccupation of scholars. Few have sought, in more than a general, vague way, to relate the child of *that* century to this one.[2]

Nevertheless, the theatre of Musset, in particular, creates an impression that seems singularly contemporary.[3] It is true that, like the poems, various elements of *Fantasio* are outmoded: a so-called socio-political plot, the pale suggestion of republicanism in the royal milieu; the exaggerated poses of Elsbeth and Fantasio himself; above all perhaps the complacency with which the princess' garden is figuratively sanctified like a private refuge of the heart. Similarly, in *Les Caprices de Marianne,* the Byronic figure of Célio is disconcertingly two-dimensional. Between the dual figures of lyricism and cynicism, the former has such a conventional expression that we find it difficult to keep the equilibrium. Octave alone is our hero.[4] And the pose that he assumes at the end of the play, like Fantasio's, propounds a moral too sentimentally, didactically. Yet, the confrontation between cynical realism and a desperate insistence upon purity has a modern appeal. In the less schematic worlds of such plays as *On ne badine pas avec l'amour* and *Lorenzaccio,* a dramatic tension is created which, in its deliberately stylized form, suggests precise parallels with the French theatre of the 1930's and 1940's.

I

In *On ne badine pas avec l'amour,* the three characters of *Les Caprices* have been fused into two: Camille and Perdican, cousins who were brought up—separately—to be married to one another. Their antithetical dialogue opposes not only Romantic perspectives on love (the absolute and the natural), but on the sexes as well. A balance between the two characters is held in check by their common vanity and egotism, the guilt which they share at the end of the play. Their victim, Rosette, has the natural purity and innocence of Célio, the victim in *Les Caprices,* but, unlike Célio, Rosette is not a principal character. While symbolically at the center of the play, she is not asked to express too many embarrassingly simple truths. She is only used by the two protagonists, and she dies off-stage. The interest lies in the stalemate and fated separation of the lovers.

The stylized symmetry of the play is not merely a comic artifice. It creates the uncertain tension in the atmosphere: the balance between comedy and pathos, the equilibrium between the positions of the two cousins. At the start of the play the entrance of Blazius and Dame Pluche, their contrast, prefigures that of the two main characters in the following scene. Another symmetrical duo, Blazius and Bridaine, and the somewhat ridiculous figure of the baron himself parallel and undercut the main action by their worldly preoccupations with food, drink and money, their mockery of the children. Perdican's pathetic nostalgia and dejection are shadowed by Bridaine's apostrophe to the *bonne chère* of the baron's table, by Blazius' lament at his impending exile. The spying and lack of comprehension on the

part of all the comic secondary characters are an ironic commentary on these same failings in the lovers.

The form which emerges, while artificial like a libretto, bears comparison, in one respect, with the classical theatre; it consists of a series of meetings between Camille and Perdican. The important one occurs at the end of the second of three acts, in the woods beside a fountain which recalls their innocent childhood. The exchange, planned as a formal adieu on Camille's part, is underscored by pride and cruel flirtation. Vicariously, through stories that have been told to her in the convent, Camille has learned that life in the world, marriage and love in particular, hold no promise of perfection. Similarly, Perdican will not give her *absolute* answers to her questions. Rather, believing in the relative happiness of the heart, in nature, he denounces the ideal of purity as a convent-bred illusion. Love is defined two ways. Perdican complains that Camille, for whom it is all or nothing, does not believe in it . . .

CAMILLE:

> Y croyez-vous, vous qui parlez? Vous voilà courbé près de moi avec des genoux qui se sont usés sur les tapis de vos maîtresses, et vous n'en savez plus le nom. Vous avez pleuré des larmes de joie et des larmes de désespoir; mais vous saviez que l'eau des sources est plus constante que vos larmes, et qu'elle serait toujours là pour laver vos paupières gonflées. Vous faites votre métier de jeune homme, et vous souriez quand on vous parle de femmes désolées; vous ne croyez pas qu'on puisse mourir d'amour, vous qui vivez et qui avez aimé. Qu'est-ce donc que le monde? Il me semble que vous devez cordialement mépriser les femmes qui vous prennent tel que vous êtes, et qui chassent leur dernier amant pour vous attirer dans leurs bras avec les baisers d'un autre sur les lèvres. Je vous demandais tout à l'heure si vous aviez aimé; vous m'avez répondu comme un voyageur à qui l'on demanderait s'il a été en Italie ou en Allemagne, et qui dirait: Oui, j'y ai été; puis qui penserait à aller en Suisse, ou dans le premier pays venu. Est-ce donc une monnaie que votre amour, pour qu'il puisse passer ainsi de mains en mains jusqu'à la mort? Non, ce n'est pas même une monnaie; car la plus mince pièce d'or vaut mieux que vous, et dans quelques mains qu'elle passe, elle garde son effigie.

Continuing the stylized symmetry of the entire play, the first half of the central scene at the fountain is Camille's; the latter half is given over to Perdican. When his cousin had spoken, he had answered her insistent, rhetorical questions with short defensive replies. Now he responds in like anger taking up her same terms and framing his apology for the limited form of human love in corresponding rhetoric:

PERDICAN:

> Adieu, Camille, retourne à ton couvent, et lorsqu'on te fera de ces récits hideux qui t'ont empoisonnée réponds ce que je vais te dire: Tous les hommes sont menteurs,

inconstants, faux, bavards, hypocrites, orgueilleux ou lâches, méprisables et sensuels; toutes les femmes sont perfides, artificieuses, vaniteuses, curieuses et dépravées; le monde n'est qu'un égout sans fond où les phoques les plus informes rampent et se tordent sur des montagnes de fange; mais il y a au monde une chose sainte et sublime, c'est l'union de deux de ces êtres si imparfaits et si affreux. On est souvent trompé en amour, souvent blessé et souvent malheureux; mais on aime, et quand on est sur le bord de sa tombe, on se retourne pour regarder en arrière: et on se dit: J'ai souffert souvent, je me suis trompé quelquefois, mais j'ai aimé. C'est moi qui ai vécu, et non pas un être factice créé par mon orgueil et mon ennui.[5]

When Perdican has finished, his exit closes Act II; the Romantic paradox of purity and cynicism has been allowed to express itself in parallel arias and conclusively.

It would be wrong to presume that the emotions of this scene find their origin only in Musset's liaison with George Sand (begun the year before, in 1833). The kind of "feminine mystique," expressed in Camille's absolutism, like Perdican's rejoinder, has its predecessors in French literature. When Musset's heroine says, "Je veux aimer, mais je ne veux pas souffrir; je veux aimer d'un amour éternel, et faire des serments qui ne se violent pas," she is offering a new variation on a theme created at the time of classicism.

The fear of being betrayed, combined with an irrepressible need for love, had characterized the Princess of Clèves. Confronting M. de Nemours after her husband's death, she pronounced the same catechism. Marivaux's Sylvia also proudly hesitates before bowing to the finitude of human passion. The shadow side of her eighteenth-century game of love evokes the sadness which would prevail if the moment of recognition came too late or not at all, if the mask were real.

There is a subtle mixture of coquetry and egoism in each of these ladies as she puts her lover to the test of perfection. Always, in one form or another, the doors of the convent stand open as a refuge. It is there, usually, that the heroine was schooled in the ways of the absolute. In time, however, the ideal has become more philosophical or metaphysical; the classical need for calm, *repos,* has turned into "enlightened" rationalism and finally become a Romantic conception of pure grace.

Musset's originality, that of the period in general, comes of permitting this feminine voice to express itself in counterpoint with a balanced statement of the libertine ways of the world. In classical tragedy, the "higher" good is always a source of pride and admiration; M. de Nemours, in awe, can only retire, himself, in the end. In comedy, fable and satire, Molière, La Fontaine, and Marivaux—not to mention Laclos—make sure that the puritanical precious or prude gets her due and gives in.

It is only in such distinctly Romantic works as *Adolphe* or Musset's plays that an irreconcilable balance is struck, a stalemate between the world and an absolute.

Rosette's melodramatic death at the end of the play, as she overhears Camille's and Perdican's last encounter, extends this paradox. Rosette gives in to her heart in spite of knowing that Perdican's love is false; by succumbing—It is fortunate that, even from his armchair, Musset had this scene, at least, take place behind an altar!—she proves, in an absolute act, that one can die for love. Both points of view are validated—the human and the ideal—while the inexorable failure to make them work and to secure happiness is reaffirmed. At the center of the stage: Rosette, like a broken toy; to each side, Perdican and Camille, separating forever.

* * *

Our intention is not to speak about the *influence* of Musset, precisely, not to study him as a *source*. It is rather that the theme, the pattern and the style of a play by Giraudoux or Anouilh follows analogous lines.[6] The meeting between Camille and Perdican, in particular, suggests a prototype in the manner of a dramatic tradition.

It is not that in Giraudoux there is consistently a series of meetings between boy and girl in the same circumstances, beside a fountain recalling the idyllic innocence of their childhood. Such *is* the case in Anouilh's plays of the decade 1931-1941, in the first collections of *Pièces noires* and *Pièces roses,* and more recent plays have not departed essentially from that formula. One after another, Anouilh's heroines, legendary or Parisian, seek an impossible purity, associated with an expectation from the past; they refuse to barter with the cynical present, eluding the common happiness offered by the helpless young man. In a reverse form of *marivaudage,* similar to the cruel caprices of Musset's heroine, the game comes of flirting, not with tragedy, but with a happy ending which will never come to pass. Even, Musset's prose anticipates the flat, bittersweet exchanges of *Eurydice, L'Hermine, La Sauvage* or *Colombe.* Certain of the expressions suggest Anouilh's vulgar effects, his preoccupation with the soiled, worn and impure nature of things, particularly money, the hopeless image of the immaculate that might have been.

A Giraudoux drama is less of a one-sided thesis. Taking a legend, or, in its personal form, a character in search of an absolute, the playwright is more inclined to debate, to write—a little like George Bernard Shaw, in this sense—a "problem play." Love or a woman may be at the basis of every human event, but Hélène, Lucrèce, Electre, Ondine, Alcmène and Judith by no means stand alone at the center of their plays. While the argument, evenly pursued, is often between the sexes, with the side of perfection invariably feminine in mode, more often the choice is between two complementary spokesmen, rival suitors or the child and adult. There may be a *conclusion* in that the war of Troy *does* take place, or on the basis of dramatic necessity, but there is no *resolution*. Rather, in accordance with the precious style of Giraudoux, the curtain falls on a pun-like image or spectacle: the definition of dawn at the end of *Electre,* the ambiguous "saintliness" of Judith.

In spite of the hundred-year interval that separates them, the artifice of Musset and the self-conscious theatricality of Giraudoux have a comparable aim: to make the audience accept, through artful sophistication, a rather banal paradox, namely, that man both aspires to the purity of abstractions and remains satisfied with the limited pleasures of earth. Like Rosette's death in *On ne badine pas avec l'amour,* the crucial scenes in Giraudoux are constantly grazing sentimentality, which he avoids with a grace which, for all its modern self-consciousness, is not dissimilar from that of Musset.

Giraudoux' taste for antithesis has been traced to a split personality.[7] And, in fact, with his usual charm, he has projected this schism on a national scale. Writing about "Bellac [his tiny, provincial birthplace] et la tragédie," in an essay which forms a pendant to his play *Intermezzo,* he writes:

> Qu'est-ce que la tragédie? C'est l'affirmation d'un lien horrible entre l'humanité et un destin plus grand que le destin humain; c'est l'homme arraché à sa position horizontale de quadrupède par une laisse qui le retient debout, mais dont il sait toute la tyrannie et dont il ignore la volonté.
>
> Qu'est-ce que la France? C'est l'affirmation d'une vérité humaine et qui ne comporte aucune adhérence avec les survérités et les supermensonges. La tragédie suppose l'existence d'une horreur en soi, d'une menace immanente, d'une stratosphère surpeuplée. La France suppose au dessus d'elle une couche d'air agréable à respirer et dont la densité va s'atténuant avec les progrès de l'altitude.
>
> Qu'est-ce que le héros tragique? C'est un être particulièrement résigné à la cohabitation avec toutes les formes et tous les monstres de la fatalité.
>
> Qu'est-ce que le Français, bellachon ou non bellachon? C'est un être peu accueillant déjà pour les étrangers, qui l'est encore moins pour l'étrange et dont la langue et le vocabulaire, par leur netteté et leur clarté, déclinent toute traduction de l'inhumain.[8]

By biographical reference, his studies and diplomatic career, one could show the same opposition between nationalism and cosmopolitanism in Giraudoux that characterized many Romantics. It is not insignificant that one of his first successes, his first dramatic success in fact, *Siegfried,* made use of the Franco-German antithesis famous since the beginnings of Romanticism.

For Giraudoux' *dédoublement* is a literary contrivance, not a serious psychological obsession. Like Célio and Octave in *Les Caprices de Marianne,* like Perdican and Camille, it represents a device with which to improvise a dialogue. It can be a full-scale parliamentary debate, surrounded by the pomp and augury of legend, though wittily conscious of its artifice, as between Electre and Egisthe, Hector and Ulysse. Or else it can be the more familiar charm of *Intermezzo,* where the favor of the young maiden Isabelle is disputed between the ordinary *contrôleur* and the specter from the abstract kingdom of death. While the latter gives up his bounty to the prospect of human happiness, he cannot resist saying, as he leaves:

> Adieu, Isabelle. Ton contrôleur a raison. Ce qu'aiment les hommes, ce que tu aimes, ce n'est pas connaître, ce n'est pas savoir, c'est osciller entre deux vérités ou deux mensonges, entre Gap et Bressuire. Je te laisse sur l'escarpolette où la main de ton fiancé te balancera pour le plaisir de ses yeux entre tes deux idées de la mort, entre l'enfer d'ombres muettes et l'enfer bruissant, entre la poix et le néant. Je ne te dirai plus rien. Et même pas le nom de la fleur charmante et commune qui pique notre gazon, dont le parfum m'a reçu aux portes de la mort et dont je soufflerai le nom dans quinze ans aux oreilles de tes filles.[9]

The image of the swing recalls Musset's predilection for similar evocations of uncertain equilibrium, Fantasio's and Octave's parapets, dancers, and tightrope-walkers. As with similar double emblems in Giraudoux, twice in *On ne badine pas avec l'amour* Camille and Perdican contemplate antithetical images (the painting of a saintly ancestor and a pot of flowers; the painting of a scholar-monk with a goat-herd dancing in front of an Italian *locanda* outside).

This is the mode of Romantic juxtaposition, and it resurges with World War I in the concept of the adolescent, refusing to enter the world of compromise. It is prevalent in the magic charm of *la jeune fille,*[10] that impossible creature who exists, by definition, only in the fragile limbo of nostalgic fantasy where she can murmur "All or nothing" until the moment of choice.

II

With the coming of World War II, we pass from a time of theorizing to one of action; for France, from a period of abstract complicity to the ugly realities of the Occupation. By deliberately leaving Giraudoux and Anouilh for Camus and Sartre, it is possible to suggest a parallel movement in drama. In terms of Musset, the presence of *On ne badine pas avec l'amour* is replaced by that of *Lorenzaccio.*[11]

The search for purity is no longer phrased in terms of the *badinage* of love or in a proverbial context with dialogues between opposing factions. The equilibrium is broken. The individual continues his quest for absolutes, but, called upon to translate them into moral extremes of good and evil and to transpose them into acts within a world of relativity, he cannot avoid the judgment of public consequence. It is this distinction which Sartre makes in a more philosophical sense when he writes an analysis of Giraudoux' style in 1940.[12] The latter is accused of reverting to the medieval Aristotelian belief in absolute substantial forms, in the poetic dialogue between superlatives. Sartre admits at the beginning of his essay that his intention is to take Giraudoux seriously, and his findings, in these terms, are accurate. On the other hand, Giraudoux' conscious use of language demands, above all, *not* to be taken seriously; his theatricality, like Anouilh's, comes from a classical tradition relayed in the nineteenth century by way of Musset's armchair. Sartre's own dramatic works in their flashiest moments occasionally recall Giraudoux: the adaptation of Dumas' *Kean,* for example, or the equally theatrical dialogues of *Le Diable et le bon dieu.*[13] One could attribute this similarity to the two authors' common schooling at the Ecole Normale Supérieure, to a common use of actors trained in the intellectual and witty manner of Louis Jouvet, or to a common, deeper heritage of drama, a heritage which Sartre seeks to deny at every opportunity. In any case, a shared tradition exists, even if traced back only to Musset. The difference lies in a change of emphasis.

It is common by now to contrast Sartre's and Giraudoux' versions of the *Oresteia.* Compared to the Argos of *Les Mouches,* Giraudoux' city resembles some remote abstract Troy, just as, to take a detail, his depiction of the Furies as a group of adolescent girls growing into their fateful period of revenge seems precious and effete beside the constant presence of the flies with their realistic pestilential implications, their sound and smell. While one may oppose the different ways characters are constructed in the two plays—the deterministic sense of destiny in Giraudoux, the choice of *becoming* in Sartre—one could also stress a still simpler difference which, in some sense, implies the others: the change from female to male hero.

One of the reasons that *Anouilh's* plays of this period are so grating is due to his obsessive reliance upon heroines. While trying to write a play which would be, not about abstract concepts of purity, but about action, he was able only to recreate his *sauvage,* his ermine, in a more patriotic arena. The coy and gawkish sentimentality which makes these plays so one-sided is in great part due to the feminine charm that Antigone or Joan the lark exercises upon the dramatist.

Giraudoux remained a 1930's dramatist in this sense. His Judith exists always in counterpoint with Holopherne, his Electre with Egisthe. In *Sodome et Gomorrhe,* the voices that are heard in the black chaos of the world's end are male and female both, and their dispute will never be resolved. In fact, as in an analogous oratorio, some sort of artifice is always required to resolve a Giraudoux play thematically—the theatrical magic of a *homo ex machina:* the gardener in *Electre,* the drunken guard in *Judith.* At the basis of each human event—war, sex, daily life—there is, not just a woman, a *femme à histoires,* but a scene pitting against one another two spokesmen from different camps: man and woman, man and god, living and dead, reason and passion. The influence of a familiar school exercise, the theme (imagine a meeting between Ulysses and Hector . . .), is still there, a precious *jeu de société* as well, the long-awaited joust of words between the principals in a classical play.

In Camus and Sartre, however—in Montherlant, as well—the irremediable is part of the dramatic situation. While a similar conflict arises between idealism and compromise, the latter ultimately prevails and crushes the protagonist. The male hero—in Sartre's *Huis clos,* the most lucid of the three inhabitants of hell, Inès, is, significantly enough, a lesbian—may seek an impossible absolute, but it is in the form of *action,* not a *state* of purity. The evil acts which are performed—assassination in *Caligula Les Mains sales* for example— never attain their ideal goal, because the world is one of corrupt half-measures. **Lorenzaccio** is in some measure the model for certain scenes of these plays, and this under the farther off ægis of Shakespeare.

* * *

Like Musset's, in a similar time of crisis and corruption, Sartre's or Camus' hero feels himself weak and inadequate. He seeks desperately, futilely, in the end, to kill as a test or purge, a way to attain the absolute within the real. There are of course a certain number of comparisons which would apply to the more general description of the Romantic hero: his origin as an intellectual, often a frustrated scholar; his loneliness and the way he is contrasted with other, ordinary beings; his ambiguous attitude toward women—his mother, sister or mistress from whom he no longer derives comfort or pleasure; his situation in a position of power, his ability to perform abstract, gratuitous acts of evil or good; his sadistic, but basically masochistic need to corrupt others, himself and his ideal; the equivocal feelings he has toward his potential victim; the relief with which he finally greets his annihilation as a sort of self-driven purge; the ironic superfluity of the crime to which his whole existence, absurdly, has been sacrificed; and so on. However, once again, our intention is not to bear down heavily upon matters which are best left in the form of a broad outline. Briefly, in a merely suggestive way, we wish to show how two modern scenes in particular reveal the presence of **Lorenzaccio:** specifically, the meeting with the youthful, pure artist; and the drunken monologue preparatory to murder. Indeed, one reason for the brevity of our final comments is the fact that the evocation of Musset seems so self-evident.[14]

When Caligula, wanting the moon, but satisfying himself with the abstract power of embodying chance, decrees life and death in increasingly self-destructive ceremonies, he is following, quite deliberately, the itinerary of Lorenzaccio. At a certain point, he too turns to a youth in a parallel scene of confession. Tebaldeo in Musset's play, the young Scipion in Camus' are both young artists—painter and poet—suffering in the present corrupt state but still believing in pure ideals: dreams, nature, humanity, freedom, and most urgently, the magic power of art. Caligula and Lorenzaccio see themselves as they once were and gain pleasure—one might even say a rather ambiguously intimate one—from hearing a recital of those beliefs which no longer touch them and which they feel impelled to mock cruelly. Caligula speaks the spare, hard language of his abstractly conceived kingdom, but the ironic use to which he puts young Scipion, the foil which he makes of his own former self, the mixture of nostalgia and contempt which he feels, above all, for art and its relation to a higher "nature," these are elements which make one think of the comparable role played by the scene with Tebaldeo in *Lorenzaccio.*

Rather than a metaphysician, Hugo, the hero of *Les Mains sales,* is a bourgeois intellectual. Like Lorenzaccio, he is trying merely to learn the science of assassination. Through this act, which he envisions as a pure and clear abstraction, as he had hoped his commitment to the Communist party would be, he thinks to escape the confusion and relativity of his contradictory thoughts. Although the drunken speeches which come at the end of the fourth tableau in Sartre's play are carried on—dangerously—in front of several characters, taken in context they form a monologue which parallels that of Lorenzaccio the night he murders the Duke of Florence. Specifically alluding to Hamlet's soliloquy, Hugo retraces familiar themes: illusion and reality, life as a comedy, an impatience with words, exhaustion and the desire to give it all up, to destroy himself in a holocaust, an envy of ordinary mortals who act without thinking, etc. Strangely, Lorenzaccio, like Hugo, is attracted by his victim and even compares his murderous act with a wedding. When Hugo finally kills Hœderer in *Les Mains sales*—later in the play, since the drunken speeches end only in ridiculous collapse—it is an impulsive act of jealousy, equally ambiguous. Both Hœderer and the Duke of Florence represent manliness, and a refusal to accept abstractions in any form. Theirs is a world of human compromise, and their death, in one way or another, is meant to restore purity. The circumstances of the murders, however, obviously take them out of the realm of abstraction. The world returns to its normal corrupt state. On the other hand, the dif-

ference between Lorenzaccio's and Hugo's victims is essential and may furnish us with our conclusion. Simply enough, the Duke of Florence is a corrupt villain; Hœderer, on the contrary, has the heroic qualities of a man who has come to quietly accept the compromises of the world, who, for the sake of practical results, believes in half-measures.

In modern times, the search for the absolute and the way that it is depicted have many similarities with Romantic aspirations. The failure is just as final. But the spirit of compromise which had, in a past era, all the pejorative connotations of corruption is no longer so evil. The lesson to be learned in Sartre and Camus is basically humanistic, that we must dirty our hands. *Lorenzaccio* was not so didactic; its "message"—the significance of the hero's death, the use to which it could be put in a political sphere—was not so clear. Like so many other revivals, however, its rediscovery can be said to have typified, with astonishing clarity, a period of climax. As with certain modern-dress versions of Shakespeare, the feeling of anachronism, in spite of all the Florentine local color, is relatively insignificant. Lorenzaccio too—the character at least—has become a twentieth-century hero.

Notes

This paper was read at the Modern Drama Conference of the Midwest Modern Language Association meeting in May 1965.

1. Cited, with his own qualification, by Gide in the *Journal* (*1939-1959*) and *Si le grain ne meurt* (Pléiade edition, Paris, 1954), pp. 323, 472. Baudelaire, more contemptuous still, describes Musset as though he were the Paul Géraldy of his day: "On le trouve maintenant chez les filles, entre les chiens de verre filé, le chansonnier du Caveau et les porcelaines gagnées aux loteries d'Asnières.—Croque-mort langoureux" (*Notes posthumes,* 1865, quoted, with some relish, by Mauriac, "Fidèle à Musset?" *Le Figaro Littéraire,* XII, No. 567, March 2, 1957, p. 1.)

2. See, especially, Henri Guillemin, "Notes sur Musset," *Les Temps Modernes,* XVIII (February, 1963), 1447-1483. Aragon pleads for a "modern" look at certain works and scattered verses, *Les Lettres Françaises,* No 667 (April 18-24, 1957), pp. 1, 2. In a brief note, Dussane points specifically at the plays, "Un Théâtre de la jeunesse," in a special hommage, "Musset cent ans après," *Les Nouvelles Littéraires,* No 1549 (May 9, 1957), p. 10.

3. The revival of Musset's dramatic works began in the 1920's. Jacques Copeau produced *Un Caprice* in 1921 and Pitoëff and the others of the Cartel

put on his plays. Among the Romantics which the Comédie Française began trying to resurrect in 1927 (Hugo, Dumas, Vigny), Musset alone caught on successfully. Gaston Baty produced famous controversial performances of *Les Caprices de Marianne* during the 1935-36 season, and then *Lorenzaccio* and *Le Chandelier* (1937). See Jacques Copeau, "Le Théâtre d'Alfred de Musset," *Revue Universelle,* XLVII (October, 1931), 1-24; Dussane, *op. cit.*

4. It might be mentioned that the same flaw carries over into "Les Règles du jeu," Jean Renoir's pre-war, cinematographic variation on the play. While *modern* rules of the game continue to be fatal to the innocent and naive, they also make us identify with the eccentric, lucid hero from the beginning. Renoir underestimated the amount of importance that the spectator would attach to his "Octave." The role, which the director himself portrayed, thus does not have sufficient weight, is not sketched, from the beginning, with sufficient detail.

5. *Théâtre complet* (Pléiade edition, Paris, 1958), pp. 361-362, 364-365.

6. Giraudoux has seldom singled out Musset for comment. He was once to have written a preface for an edition of *Contes et Nouvelles,* but, although it often is included in bibliographies, apparently it never appeared. Anouilh, while paying tribute to Giraudoux, did not share the latter's acceptance of the *anciens* as masters; the author of *La Répétition* thinks of himself as more modern and writes, "Musset, Marivaux reread a thousand times? They were too far off. They were from an era already fabulous in which spoken French still had periods and commas, from an era in which the very sentences danced." ("To Jean Giraudoux," *Tulane Drama Review,* III [May 1959], 3.)

7. Most explicitly in Will L. McLendon, "Giraudoux and the Split Personality," *PMLA,* LXXIII (1958), 573-584.

8. *Littérature* (Paris, 1941), pp. 246-247.

9. *Intermezzo* (Paris, 1933), pp. 195-196.

10. It is senseless to choose among Giraudoux' myriad statements about the gentle sex. One remark, however, containing a historical and sociological context may be particularly relevant: "Un autre élément de réussite, conséquence indirecte de la guerre, ce fut la prépondérance croissante du public féminin: les femmes qui n'avaient pas subi—ou moins que les hommes, en tout cas—le dressage pseudo-classique, nous offraient des esprits neufs. Elles étaient aussi plus aptes, par nature, à aimer les éléments nouveaux que nous avions introduits dans le roman: la fantaisie, le rêve, l'arbitraire. [Women provided a public] vivant, frémissant, travaillé par une irritation agréable qui est la 'nervosité de l'intelligence.'" (Interview for *Comœdia,* recorded by Simone Ratel, *Dialogues à une seule voix,* Le Tambourin, 1930, p. 13).

11. See Dussane, *op. cit.;* Robert Kemp, "Importance et actualité de 'Lorenzaccio'", *Erasme,* I (1946), 53-55. The relationship between *Lorenzaccio* and the preceding plays in Musset himself is treated by Philippe van Tieghem in "L'Evolution de Musset des débuts à *Lorenzaccio,*" *Revue d'Histoire du Théâtre,* IX (1957), 261-275, but with some confusion. Van Tieghem's seems a wilful effort to suppose moral development in Musset, which even if true, does not help in an understanding of the plays themselves. The separation made between *Lorenzaccio* and the others, within the context of Musset's own preoccupation with impurity, seems artificial. In fact, van Tieghem may well be influenced by our modern distinction, somewhat false and tendentious, between the themes of love and action.

12. *NRF,* LIV (1940), 339-354, also in *Situations I* (Paris, 1947), pp. 82-98. Sartre's article, "M. Jean Giraudoux et la philosophie d'Aristote," while it emphasizes Giraudoux' novels, and *Choix des élues* in particular, applies to the drama as well, even though few examples from Giraudoux' plays are given.

13. In Sartre, there are similarities, too, with Anouilh—the pathetic fatalism of the bourgeois who can never be poor, of the man, free from suffering, unable to be accepted by those who have suffered.

14. Another reason is that, while no one has taken up the subject in a general way from the point of view of Musset, others have already noted the possibility of comparisons: see Roger Quilliot, *La Mer et les prisons: essai sur Albert Camus* (Paris, 1956), pp. 68n, 73; Dussane, *op. cit.*

David Sices (essay date 1974)

SOURCE: Sices, David. Introduction to *Theater of Solitude: The Drama of Alfred de Musset,* pp. 1-12. Hanover, N.H.: The University Press of New England, 1974.

[*In the following excerpt, Sices offers an overview of the reception of Musset's work, of its resistance to translation, and of the evolution of Musset's style.*]

> *"Quelles solitudes que tous ces corps humains!"*
>
> (*Fantasio,* I, 2)

The most imaginative, "contemporary," and, by general consensus, significant playwright of the nineteenth century in France is, paradoxically, one whose work is virtually unknown on the American stage. Alfred de Musset's literary reputation in this country is based principally upon a somewhat faded collection of lyrics which were once in vogue with young ladies and French teachers—the celebrated "Nuits"—and a lachrymose autobiographical novel aptly entitled *Confession.* Both of these appear to justify one American critic's typical lumping of him with Vigny, Sainte-Beuve, and "other sad young men of the nineteenth century."[1] But the stereotype, if it may be applied more or less exactly to Musset's distressingly humorless Romantic compatriots, seems inapt to a man noted by contemporaries for his flashing wit and verve. It is all the more unsuitable if we think that he is the author of five or six of the most delightful comedies ever to grace the French stage, not to mention what has come to be considered the finest example of French Romantic historical drama. A poet who has accomplished a feat of this magnitude by the age of twenty-five, after making a brilliant début at nineteen with a volume of hyper-Romantic (and in good part ironic) narrative verse, merits consideration as more than a "sad young man." Concealed behind the stereotype is a complex and inventive literary personality, whose dramatic works harbor a rich vein of material largely unexplored outside of France. Yet they can speak to us now more fully, more insistently, than they did to Musset's contemporaries, and their dramatic technique has begun to be fully exploited only through the expanding stage resources of the past twenty or thirty years.

The comedies—*Les Caprices de Marianne, Fantasio, On ne badine pas avec l'amour, Le Chandelier, Il ne faut jurer de rien,* to mention the most important—and the historical drama *Lorenzaccio,* have become standard French classical repertory at the Comédie-Française and the Odéon. Moreover, they have inspired independent directors like Jacques Copeau, Gaston Baty, René Clair, and Otomar Krejca to mount them in imaginative experimental stagings. *Marianne, On ne badine pas avec l'amour,* and *Lorenzaccio* provided Gérard Philipe with three of his finest roles, and Jean Vilar with some of his most exciting productions, at the Théâtre National Populaire. Yet Musset's stage works are little known by theater people outside of France. In Germany, where the poet's direct influence on so vital a dramatist as Georg Büchner might be expected to promote his reputation, little attention has been paid to his plays.[2] As for the English-speaking world, only specialists in French literature—and by no means all of them—seem to be aware of Musset's importance in the theater, and of the original, delightful quality of his works.

Why this should be so is difficult to pin down. Many of Musset's compatriots have found a place on the American stage: Molière, Beaumarchais, Dumas fils,

Feydeau, Rostand, Giraudoux, Anouilh, Sartre, Ionesco, Genet. Only one or two of these have made a contribution to their national theater equal to Musset's, or represent dramatic talent of comparable stature. Victor Hugo and Alexandre Dumas père, who reigned together over the Paris theater of the 1830's in the brief but intense moment of Romantic glory, achieved considerable success in its belated extension to the American stage, whereas Musset seems hardly to have been noticed.[3] Of course, several of Musset's most illustrious countrymen are victims of similar neglect. Corneille, Racine, and Marivaux have never succeeded in transplanting their peculiar appeal to the English-speaking theater. At first glance there would seem to be no basis of comparison between the first two and Musset. Their inexorably regular alexandrine verse in relentless heroic couplets appears untranslatable into English idiom without generating an excruciating monotony; and the *diktat* of neoclassical doctrine does not hold sway beyond the sphere of the cultural brainwashing which inculcates it into French *lycéens.* Musset, like the other Romantics with whom he is lumped, was trying to break the neoclassical order, to introduce a more Shakespearean drama into the French theater. Nonetheless, the problem with Musset, as with the neoclassics, seems in great part one of translation, to judge by the evidence of published texts.[4] Not for lack of prosodic equivalents, since his best work is written in prose; but, like Marivaux's subtle and elegant language, Musset's has a peculiarly Gallic balance which seems to resist efforts to English it. In the hands of journeyman translators, the passion of *On ne badine pas avec l'amour* becomes bombast; the sallies of *Fantasio* evaporate, or degenerate into heavy-handed puns; and the political tirades of *Lorenzaccio* are transformed into awkward, tiresome moralizing—none of which is true of the original. Yet is should be possible for a sensitive writer to find an English equivalent of this alert prose, which Théophile Gautier wittily labeled "pure French dialect."

If Musset's theater has been so long in finding receptive audiences in the non-French world, that is also explainable in part by its difficult history in France itself. The poet's isolation from the theater of his time was consecrated by a tragicomic stage debut, the ignominious fiasco of his one-act play, *La Nuit Vénitienne* in 1830. That work, whatever its intrinsic merits (it is somewhat less than halfway between Musset's earlier pastiche Romanticism and his mature style), today seems too slight to justify the hostile reception accorded it. Even without the legendary encounter between the heroine's white dress and a freshly painted green trellis, the "Cabale" seems to have been ready to inflict humiliation on this young upstart whose wit had offended Romantics and classics alike.[5] Out of this defeat, it is true, emerged the "armchair theater" which permitted the young author to explore a drama freed from the practical imperatives of the contemporary stage. But it was also the start of a long series of delays and misunderstandings which were to keep most of Musset's best plays from reaching the stage until after his death—in the case of **Lorenzaccio,** some fifty years afterward. And then they were so adapted and restructured, either by the author himself or by tinkerers, as to lose a great deal of their freshness and originality. It was not until well into this century that all of Musset's plays finally had been produced in their authentic text and according to the original stage directions. As for **Lorenzaccio,** the first productions respectful of the poet's dramatic intentions took place only in 1945 and 1952, at the Théâtre Montparnasse and the Théâtre National Populaire.

When Musset experienced such difficulty at home, it is not so surprising that he was unable to establish himself on foreign stages. Despite the belated success which Paris first granted several of his minor plays in 1847-48—more than a decade after the publication of his major stage works—Musset's theatrical career can be categorized as a resounding failure, one which goes beyond the limits of his personal life and fortunes and extends over the French stage itself. For Musset could have revitalized a theatrical tradition that was in a sad state of decay and remained so for most of his century. In the words of Jean Vilar, "It is significant, I think, that Musset's theater, which might after 1830 have provoked a wholesome dispute, was of use to no one under Louis-Philippe's know-nothing monarchy and under the Empire, not even to Musset himself."[6] Not to Musset himself, for when it came time to stage his works during the last decade of his life, he rejected the innovations he had made in his earlier plays, either adapting and regularizing them (as was the case with **Marianne** in 1851) or creating trivial new ones which no longer followed his original system. It was not until the latter years of the century, with the Symbolists, Maeterlinck, and Claudel, that drama so imaginative and adventurous, so close to the real sources of the theater, was to replace the bourgeois comedies and melodramas, the post-Romantic spectacles, the realist thesis-plays that inhibited theatrical renewal. Even then the new productions of Musset's plays remained timid compared with the freedom and fantasy inherent in their original texts. For many years it seemed as if an anonymous reviewer of **La Nuit Vénitienne** might in fact be right: "I believe . . . I heard the name of Monsieur Alfred de Musset pronounced [at the curtain]. That is a name which will never emerge from its obscurity."[7] Despite the insistent pleas of such contemporary admirers as Gautier, we are confronted in Musset's work with the paradox of a writer who is without doubt the greatest French dramatist of his century, yet who had little influence on its theatrical practice and traditions.

To understand this failure and, at the same time, the tremendous distinction of Musset's dramatic creation, it is useful to view it in the context of the theater of his time. If the author withdrew from the stage and devoted himself to a literary drama, divorced from the cares—and the triumphs—of production, it was evidently because that stage and his concept of theater had little in common. Musset was thus free to create without concern for theatrical "possibility." The experience had both advantages and drawbacks. To quote another theatrical innovator, Jacques Copeau: "The greatest dramatic authors are those who have lived on the stage, provided they were its masters. But when the stage is in the hands of poor craftsmen, it is better for the poet to stand aside, to create his world apart, provided he has an intuition of the laws which govern a play.—Musset had it."[8] Musset did not have the opportunity, like Shakespeare or Molière, to experiment with staging, to play his roles himself and to experience their effect, to evolve through the dialectic of creation and production a constantly refined definition of theatrical art—and thereby to modify the givens of stage practice in his time. In any case, his aristocratic temperament and his impatience with the necessities of practical life would never have permitted him such a career (unlike his contemporary Dumas). What he did, he did in isolation, and he never had the pleasure of seeing his best works realized in suitable productions.

When we examine the milieu in which Musset's dramas were written, it is difficult not to be struck by two conflicting facts: the intense theatrical activity of Paris in the second quarter of the nineteenth century, and the pitifully small number of contemporary plays that have survived the passage of time. No doubt the latter is true of most periods of theater history: we tend to ignore the immense quantity of trivia and hackwork produced by the contemporaries of Shakespeare, Lope de Vega, Molière, or Tchekhov, and think of their ages as fertile in works of genius thanks to their presence. Perhaps Musset's period is disappointing because there were so many treatises and manifestos promising a "new" theater and such violent polemics in the journals of the time. When we follow the debate, and read of the Romantics' noisy battle to capture the Comédie-Française, it is hard not to wonder that so much sound and fury produced so remarkably little in the way of enduring results. A good deal of theoretical literature, of course: Stendhal's *Racine and Shakespeare,* Hugo's Preface to *Cromwell,* Vigny's "Dernière nuit de travail" and his "Lettre à Lord * * *." But the dramatic works corresponding to these statements seldom come close to living up to their promises. The ferment in which the French theater was involved during this period should have given birth to an unusually rich repertory of stage works. In the words of an English critic, "Much of the romantic theoretical writing tended to become divorced from the theater . . . It might almost be said that, for the only development of romantic theory which is intimately related to practical theater affairs, we must turn to the controversy which was excited in Paris by the production of Victor Hugo's *Cromwell* in 1827. It was at this time that the romantic concept of the dramatic 'grotesque' was evolved. In England and in Italy the public theaters pursued their own melodramatic course, the poets turned out their dull bookish verse-plays, and criticism more and more remained 'literary'."[9]

But somewhat as Romantic poetic theory, despite the enormous profusion of lyrical works in France at the movement's height, only finally achieved its real summits with Baudelaire and Rimbaud, so the theater, which was even more central to the movement's ambitions, does not appear to have then reached the promised level of achievement. It is not until our century that the liberation called for by the Romantic publicists can be said to have taken effect. Examined objectively from the vantage point of history, the Romantic theater seems strangely hollow despite the great names it invoked for its inspiration: Sophocles, Shakespeare, Schiller. "The life of Romantic drama? It is not to be found in its paradoxical themes, with their deliberate 'immorality,' nor in its historical tableaux which too willingly evoke mere tintype images, nor in its oversimplified psychology, nor in its artificial structure, cluttered with misunderstandings, mistaken identities, fatal quiproquos and final recognitions . . . It is no more to be found in its settings' claim to local color . . . The life of romantic drama is contained in the inner tremor, the bursts of lyricism, the generous inspiration which animate it. Once that inspiration falls, there remains nothing but puppets in paste-board buildings."[10] A good deal of that "inspiration" seems to have been in the atmosphere surrounding production, rather than in the plays themselves. Contemporary accounts evoke a frenetic emotional climate generated by the great triumphs of the Romantic theater: Dumas' *Henri III et sa cour* and *Antony,* Hugo's *Hernani,* Vigny's *Chatterton.* Reading the plays today, it is difficult not to be surprised at the vehemence of both their partisans and their opponents. Dumas' vulgar grandiloquence and "immorality" and Hugo's prosodic virtuosity and air of dark mystery thinly mask a remarkable degree of theatrical conservatism. The atmosphere of their premieres can be judged from reports like Gautier's in *Les Jeunes-France,* which have become part of literary legend. The actors themselves, even at the august Comédie-Française, entered into the hysteria fomented by the young Romantics in the balconies. Inspired by recent Paris productions of Shakespeare by Kemble, they attempted to regenerate classical tradition by massive injections of primordial quaking and bellowing. "Alongside Firmin (Hernani) who, according to Madame Dorval's quip, gave 'the impression of a man being tickled standing up,' adopting 'a febrile nervousness which was his substitute for warmth' and which made people take him for an epileptic, Mademoiselle Mars went so far in the last act as to 'imitate the frightful convulsions of a lengthy death-agony' in the English manner so decried by the 'tribe of the beardless' (the classics)."[11] Dispassionate reading of these works leaves many modern readers with the feeling that standards of judgment had been impaired by the prevalent "enthusiasm" which Mme. de Staël had brought into fashion.[12]

Even *Chatterton,* which reflects its author's intellectual soberness and his disdain for vulgar publicity, seems to have benefited from a powerful current of emotion from its first audiences, as well as a sensational performance by Vigny's leading lady (and mistress) Marie Dorval. In typical Romantic theater fashion, she triggered the premiere's success by her unrehearsed (but long-meditated) fall down a flight of stairs, at the climactic moment when Kitty Bell learns of the hero's suicide by poison. It is ironic that the "philosopher" Vigny's painfully serious social treatise should have been acclaimed in large part on the basis of this stunt. The frenzy of enthusiasm which Madame Dorval aroused is a measure of the peculiar blend of cynicism and naïveté which reigned in the Paris theater of 1835. The theatrical demands and aspirations of a Musset were of a different nature.

The odd combination of enthusiasm and charlatanry which characterizes the Romantic drama as a whole is reflected on all levels and in all facets of its construction. For classical tragedy's subtle, overrefined prosody it substituted the superficial brilliance of *Hernani*'s or *Ruy Blas*'s alexandrines (though they were still alexandrines), or the brutal vulgarity of Dumas' prose. On the level of social commentary, its heroes were accursed Byronic outcasts (Hernani); bastards and other nonquintessential pariahs (Antony); disguised valets who became prime ministers of Spain (Ruy Blas), poets hounded by a pitiless society, their genius condemned as a sickness (Chatterton); regal libertines and hunch-backed jesters (in *Le Roi s'amuse*): exceptional types meant to cast a gauntlet in the face of the bourgeois public, which applauded these dramas as it might applaud adventure stories or fairy tales. The taste for antithesis and paradox personified by Victor Hugo was especially remarkable in the reigning psychology: beside the dark-souled, haunted heroes stood lily-white heroines like Kitty Bell, or the Queen of Spain (in *Ruy Blas*), loyal to their persecuted lovers despite the villains' machinations, preserved in innocence by ignorance even when poised on the brink of adultery. The "realistic" experiments in local color, historical verity, and the mixture of genres often seem to be merely spice for familiar dramatic recipes.

Nowhere was the prevailing bad taste more evident than in the staging. This was the age of panoramas and dioramas (cf. the joyous play on the suffix "rama" in Balzac's *Père Goriot*), the mammouth pseudo-historical "mimodramas" of the Cirque-Olympique (half theater, half circus), the spectacular machinery which had begun to take top billing in Paris toward the end of the eighteenth century and reached its climax in the 1830's.[13] The storms, fires, floods, and other forms of violent transformation which had constituted a major attraction of Paris' boulevard theaters finally got a foothold on the austere stage of the Comédie-Française at the same time as the Romantics, when Baron Taylor's administration hired the celebrated Ciceri to do the sets for Dumas' *Henri III et sa cour,* Vigny's translation of *Othello,* and Hugo's *Hernani.* The exaggerated taste for mechanical spectaculars which found its true home in the Opéra has remained a constant of the Paris stage for better or worse until the present, in the splashy shows familiar to tourists. So, at the other end of the spectrum, have the machine-made comedies of Scribe, whose unimaginative *mise en scène,* formulistic plot-construction, and facile, cynical "realism" are still very much alive in the boulevard theater.

Musset's noisy rejection by the public which acclaimed all this gimcrack merchandise would be worthy of the term "symbolic" if *La Nuit Vénitienne* were not such an imperfect play. In the circumstances we may see it only as a stroke of good fortune. It is difficult to imagine what the poet's evolution as playwright might have been if his first venture in the theater had been a success. It seems evident, however, that Musset's wonderful plays written for the reading public would have been a very different affair if he had intended them for immediate production. This is not merely matter for conjecture: we have only to look at his revisions of plays for production after 1847 and the plays written for the stage during that period to see the effect of the practical theater on his literary creation. (These revisions, and some of the later plays, will be examined in subsequent chapters.) The important thing is that Musset, hurt and angered by the public humiliation his talent had received, devoted himself during a particularly fruitful period of his literary life to the creation of a free, "ideal" theater, responsible only to the dictates of his imagination and his intelligence.

Musset's dramatic message was expressed with startling rapidity and density; not in one of the innumerable prefaces on which the Romantics lavished their creative energies, but in four masterful, varied, and elegant plays which, written in the space of less than two years (1833-34) by a very young author, have become pillars of the French classical repertory. In the next chapter, I will deal briefly with the period of Musset's apprenticeship in the drama, during which some of the foundations for his great works were being laid.[14] In four subsequent chapters of this study—on *Marianne, Fantasio, Lorenzaccio,* and *On ne badine pas avec l'amour*—I will analyze some of the structural, thematic, and linguistic elements that contribute to the artistic integrity of these works. In two succeeding chapters I examine more

briefly two plays dating from the years immediately following this precocious flowering: *Le Chandelier* (1835) and *Il ne faut jurer de rien* (1836). My analyses seek to illuminate both the considerable strengths of these latter comedies and the symptoms of Musset's premature decline which pervade them. Although the emotional climate in which all these plays were created was an intensely pathetic and fascinating one, my observations are restricted for the most part to internal and aesthetic questions: a large body of Musset biography already deals in sufficient detail with the "drame de Venise" and the poet's Muses. Rather, I hope to show from the evidence of the plays themselves—their moral basis as well as their dramatic technique—how the particular set of values and aesthetic aims which was fused into the remarkable artistic whole of Musset's greatest dramas deteriorated in the works of subsequent years and, after his astonishingly rapid accession to artistic maturity, succumbed to his premature decline and senility. In a final chapter I examine one of the author's last plays—*Carmosine* (1850)—in which, although Musset experienced a brief resurgence of his creative energy, we sense a spiritual lethargy, an abdication of revolt, which makes this bourgeois fairy tale doubly pathetic.[15]

Notes

1. Maurice Shroder, *Icarus: The Image of the Artist in French Romanticism* (Cambridge, Mass., 1961), p. 152.

2. Cf. Werner Bahner, *Alfred de Mussets Werk. Ein Verneinung der bürgerlichen Lebensform seiner Zeit* (Halle, 1960), p. 9; Maurice Gravier, "Georg Büchner et Alfred de Musset," *Orbis litterarum,* 9 (1954), 29-44; Henri Plard, "A Propos de 'Leonce et Lena,' Musset et Büchner," *Etudes Germaniques,* 9 (1954), 26-36.

3. Except for French-language productions in New Orleans. See Charles M. Lombard, "French Romanticism on the American Stage," *Revue de Littérature Comparée,* 43 (1969), 161-72.

4. The list includes translations by Raoul Pelissier, E. B. Thompson and M. H. Dey of the Comedies in *The Complete Works of Alfred de Musset* (New York, 1905); *A Caprice,* translated by Anne Grace Wirt (Boston, 1922); the versions of *Fantasio* and *Lorenzaccio* in Eric R. Bentley's *The Modern Theater* (Garden City, N. Y., 1955-60), translated by Jacques Barzun and Renaud C. Bruce; *Il faut qu'une porte soit ouverte ou fermée* in Bentley's *From the Modern Repertoire,* series three (Bloomington, 1956), translated by Barzun; George Graveley's translations of *Un Caprice, Il faut qu'une porte soit ouverte ou fermée* and *On ne saurait penser à tout* in *A Comedy and Two Proverbs* (London, New York, 1957); and *Seven Plays,* translation and introduction by Peter Meyer (New York, 1962).

5. See Henry Lyonnet, *Les "Premières" d'Alfred de Musset* (Paris, 1927), p. 7.

6. *De la Tradition théâtrale* (Paris, 1955), p. 15.

7. *Courrier des Théâtres* (December 3, 1830), cited by Lyonnet, p. 8.

8. *Comédies et Proverbes,* with an introduction by Jacques Copeau (Paris, 1931), p. x.

9. Allardyce Nicoll, *The Theater and Dramatic Theory* (London, 1962), p. 208. Hugo's play, the celebrated preface of which appeared in 1827, was not produced and is generally considered to be unproducible.

10. Gaston Baty and René Chavance, *La Vie de l'art théâtral des origines à nos jours* (Paris, 1932), pp. 238-39. Cf. also Charles Affron, *A Stage for Poets: Studies in the Theater of Hugo and Musset* (Princeton, 1971), p. 10 and passim, for a discussion of Hugo's verse drama as "opera."

11. Quotations from *Les Jeunes-France* cited by Marie-Antoinette Allevy, *La Mise en scène en France dans la première moitié du dixneuvième siècle* (Paris, 1938), p. 95.

12. Eugene Ionesco's reaction to the Romantics' splashiest theatrical triumph, while exaggerated, represents one significant modern evaluation of its theatrical viability: "As for Hugo, he is ridiculous . . . When I attended a performance of *Hernani* they had to eject me from the theater because I was laughing too hard . . ." Quoted in *Le Figaro* (May 28, 1970), p. 30. (Could *Hernani* be one of the sources of the theater of the absurd?)

13. See Nicole Decugis and Suzanne Reymond, *Le Decor de théâtre en France du Moyen Age à 1925* (Paris, 1953), p. 141; Allevy, passim.

14. For a detailed study of this formative period, cf. Herbert S. Gochberg, *Stage of Dreams* (Geneva, 1967).

15. Among the most familiar plays of Musset are his one-act "proverbs" *Un Caprice* (1837) and *Il faut qu'une porte soit ouverte ou fermée* (1845), which are frequently performed at the Comédie-Française as curtain-raisers. If I have chosen, somewhat arbitrarily, to eliminate them from consideration in this work, it is because they seem to me to belong to another genre than the plays I study, equally subtle and perfected, no doubt, but more limited in its imaginative and moral scope by the salon origins from which it sprang. Another proverb, *On ne saurait penser à tout* (1849), owes so considerable a debt to *Le Distrait* of Carmontelle that it would not bear study as an authentic Musset work, even if it were a better play.

David Sices (essay date 1974)

SOURCE: Sices, David. "The Originality of Musset's Theater." In *Theater of Solitude: The Drama of Alfred de Musset,* pp. 241-52. Hanover, N.H.: The University Press of New England, 1974.

[*In the following excerpt, Sices dicusses the reasons Musset's work was misunderstood in his own day, but celebrated in later times.*]

The distance separating **Carmosine** from the great plays of 1833-34, sixteen years in time, but light-years in terms of force and vision, is thus paradigmatic of Musset's artistic decline. It is, of course, no consolation to find in this descending curve the mythic fulfillment of the author's familiar themes. Musset's biography is a pathetic tale, devoid of redeeming heroism or tragic catharsis. All of his contemporaries—friends, lovers, and enemies alike—testify volubly to the disintegration of his public and private personality which accompanied an artistic decline no less poignant for the former dandy's vain attempts to keep up appearances.

But his contemporaries, with rare exceptions like Gautier and Paul de Musset, were unaware of the significance to the theater of what Alfred had created in his brief period of greatness. No one could foresee that six or seven of his plays would become staples of the Comédie-Française; more significantly, no one could have imagined that a work like **Lorenzaccio,** judged simply unplayable in its original form, would be an important part of that theatrical renascence known as the Théâtre National Populaire, or the hit of the 1970 Prague theater season; or that the fluid, shifting perspectives of **Les Caprices de Marianne** would provide a dramatic base for the film technique of Jean Renoir's *La Règle du jeu.* The "cinematic" quality of Musset's drama, which was noted as early as the 1920's, makes it apparent that the motion picture was not so much a device which revolutionized the concept of dramatic structure as the necessary realization of an evolving theatrical vision in search of its technological means. The works of a Musset or a Büchner are part of a historical becoming whose results are now being felt fully in the contemporary flowering of the cinema.

Musset's biography as a creator thus transcends the disappointments of his life and his self-fulfilling myth of failure. The importance of his dramatic work has gradually been appreciated and analyzed by critics over the past fifty years. Its originality, which makes it one of the first examples of what can be termed "avant-garde" theater, can finally be assessed in the context of a stage and screen that have come of age. But that originality is not so easy to define. Our continually increasing body of information concerning the environment and the traditions in which the artistic figures of the past evolved their peculiar style or vision makes it a far less simple matter today to isolate that original "genius" which Musset's own, more innocent Romantic generation found in predecessors like Sophocles, Dante, or Shakespeare. It is all the more difficult in dealing with so young an author: the precocious, although they tend to proclaim their individuality louder than their elders, inevitably bear deeper marks of their spiritual and artistic nurturing than do the Goethes, Beethovens, and Matisses. Even the boy genius Rimbaud spent a relatively long apprenticeship with Baudelaire and Banville. Musset's theatrical personality is further complicated by his desire to adapt Shakespearean dramatic practice to the ways of the French stage, and by his expressed admiration for Schiller, for Molière, for Racine. The direct lineage between Musset's comedies and Marivaux's, also, with perhaps a collateral link via Beaumarchais, has been frequently cited, although the bonds between specific plays, themes, and techniques have not been clearly delineated. The influence of Richardson and, particularly, of Byron on the character of Musset's heroes has received thorough study. The sources and spirit of a peculiarly German fantasy which Musset (with Gérard de Nerval) translated more authentically than any of his compatriots, especially in *Fantasio,* before he passed it back to Büchner, have interested French Germanists like Jean Giraud and Albert Béguin. Italian and Spanish sources and alternative influences for everything have been exhaustively documented over the past century or more. Little remains to be studied or said in this domain, beyond the inevitable "further notes" which strew every great artist's path.[1]

And yet the artistic originality of Musset's plays shines through all this impressively cluttered scaffolding. It can first be felt as a vague "distinctiveness," as a divergence from the particular models he admitted to following. If, for René Clair, who mounted *On ne badine pas avec l'amour* at the TNP in 1958, "Musset is a Shakespeare who might have known Marivaux,"[2] the philosopher Alain found in his theater a radical "un-Shakespeareanism": "If I ever went so far as to compare Musset and Shakespeare (as many are tempted to do), I would on the contrary oppose them to each other."[3] For his turn-of-the-century appreciator Jules Lemaître, the spirit of Musset's dramas was foreign to both Shakespeare and Marivaux: "Neither Shakespeare's nor Marivaux's theater could give us an idea of Musset's theater, if it did not exist: for there is really something more there, something absolutely original and irreducible, an intellectual consistency, a certain *quality* of vision, sentiment and expression which is only his, and which is all of him."[4] This seems subjective or impressionistic. But it evidences a conviction among readers of discernment which bears further analysis.

Certainly a factor which radically distinguishes Musset from Shakespeare (or from Marivaux or Molière) is the remarkable youthfulness which radiates from his best dramas. This is not true in the same way that Musset's lyrics are now considered poetry for adolescents, whose pathos and grandiloquence fade once the age of indulgent self-interest is outgrown: that is the Musset of Heinrich Heine's untranslateable quip: "un jeune homme de beaucoup de passé," or Lamartine's cruel portrait: "Blondhaired child, waxen-hearted young man, / Poetic plaything of soft poesy . . . / You who take your vague whim for passion . . ."[5] Unlike his lyrics, Musset's plays succeed in objectifying the "youthful condition," the eternally repeated drama of the young—their anguished fear of adulthood and its inevitable betrayal of youth's instinctive, generous passions; the sense of impotence and rage at the contradiction between ideal, or dream, and reality. This anxiety is one that seems to be captured by those who flower prematurely—a Musset or a Jarry, a Rimbaud or a Radiguet. Few have produced so complete a body of work as Musset, however, during their brief period of vision. That is what constitutes his drama's enduring dialogue with the young, at the same time that the aesthetic perfection of these works renders them continuingly accessible to those beyond the generation gap. In Leclerc's words, "It is he who most luminously reflected the state of mind of the younger generation in the first half of the nineteenth century, and who retains to our day the most amazingly modern appeal."[6] Despite the outmoded sound of some of Musset's Romantic rhetoric and of his terminology (Lorenzo's lost "virtue," for example, or the convent-bred compunctions of his heroines), the delicate balance of sentiment and irony, idealism and cynicism, which imbues his heroes, their thirst for experience and their fear of failure, their exaltation of love at the expense of morality and wisdom—all remain a unique representation in traditional literature of the permanent drama of youth. The slogan of Coelio and Octave, those marvelous alter-egos whose unselfish friendship is as modern as their opposing forms of inebriation, might well be "Make love, not law," in the face of their antagonist, the middle-aged judge Claudio, just as Fantasio's disdain for the Establishment leads him to flight into the irrational, the unorganized, and Lorenzo's profound sense of betrayal goes beyond political violence into cosmic despair and self-destruction.

The intense air of "relevance" is perhaps unexpected in an author who was one of his generation's principal antirealists, whose *Fantasio* has typically been qualified as the "dreamiest of dreams." But in an age when social and political commentary has been inextricably mingled with psychedelic fantasy, this may not seem so paradoxical as it once did. The uneasy marriage of drugs and commitment, of dropping out and protest, has accustomed our generation to forms which the nineteenth century suspected only in certain privileged moments (often, as in the case of Musset and Rimbaud, associated with abuse of alcohol, sex, and drugs). But this is precisely what constitutes another facet of Musset's original theatrical personality, the coupling of relevance with fantasy which has permitted his works, in that acid test (if the expression may be permitted) of artistic universality, to be interpreted as "critical realism" (as it is by the Marxists,)[7] or as philosophical and psychological documentation of the profoundest sort,[8] or pure "theater," divorced from the realm of reality by the sheer poetry of its language and dramatic technique.[9] *Lorenzaccio* is both a well-documented recreation of Florence in 1536, with its political factions and social struggles, and a highly personal expression of the hero's—and Musset's—internal spiritual conflict *Fantasio* is both a satirical commentary on marriages and the reason of state—Princess Louise's wedding to Leopold of Belgium—and a lyrical, inebriated paean to freedom and chaos. *On ne badine pas avec l'amour* begins as a stylized comedy, with grotesques and chorus, and ends as something like Romantic melodrama. *Les Caprices de Marianne* blends elements of Renaissance Italian comedy with observations on the captivity of woman in nineteenth-century society and a hymn to the "new" morality. Whether we call this eclecticism or elusiveness, one of the chief traits of Musset's originality is the indefinability of his theater according to traditional genres, definitions, or viewpoints. No better example of Musset's complexity in these respects can be cited than the production of *Lorenzaccio* by the Za Branou Theater of Prague, in which the poignant relevance of the author's political ideas to the reality of post-1968 Czechoslovakia was intensified by a highly stylized, intensely modern staging employing masks, semiabstract sets, disciplined mass movement, and electronic audiovisual devices.[10]

This suggests a further aspect of Musset's theatrical personality: this literary drama, written in defiance of the contemporary theater and freed from the practical requirements of the stage as his time and tradition conceived it, is eminently, essentially playable, as succeeding generations in the theater have come to realize. In this respect it differs significantly from enterprises like Ludovic Vitet's *Scènes historiques* and Renan's *Drames philosophiques,* or even the later Hugo's *Théâtre en liberté.* Theatrically, Musset's armchair shows are far freer than Hugo's, whose *liberté* is mainly verbal and political. Yet Hugo's dramatic scenes were imagined as "unplayable theater," which "could not be presented on our stage such as it exists."[11] But Musset's works have demonstrated their practicability in a wide range of theatrical contexts. For his freedom somehow remained subject to theatrical principles, even if they were not those observed by the contemporary stage. Aside from his normal playgoing, Musset had seen Shakespeare done by Kemble's troupe; he had taken

part in family and society theatricals. These limited experiences seem to have confirmed a stage instinct which he possessed beyond any of his contemporaries in the theater. Dumas' and Scribe's involvement in the day-to-day problems of producing their plays—Scribe's clever engineering of his comedies to the observed reactions of his audiences, Dumas' protean activities as writer, director, publicist, actor, costumer, set-designer and machinist, even Hugo's need to provide sketches of costumes and sets for *Marion de Lorme* and *Hernani,* contrast sharply with Musset's *pudeur,* his hesitation even in later years to take an active part in production of his works.[12] Yet he was the most professional of them all, because his instinct transcended the narrow limits which the nineteenth-century French stage set to its ambitions and its definition of theater. No one is more qualified to speak of this than Jacques Copeau:

> Musset said verses marvelously, a supreme art among poets when they master it . . . His gift for imitation goes so far as to reproduce with his body the expression, the walk, the age and the physical habits of the people he observes. It is this actor's instinct which proclaims any born dramatist.
>
> Musset has a sense of acting. See his reflections on a certain "exit" of Mlle Pressy in the *Barber of Seville;* they denote a man who sees what goes on on the stage, an uncommon gift. He is interested in production. See his review of *Gustave III,* March 14, 1833 . . . But he does not underestimate the importance of their art . . . And he understands their problems . . . He admires Rachel, for the right reasons, which he expresses well . . . Finally, he takes an interest in the material conditions of performance, in the dimensions of the stage, its "layout" as we say today, and he lingers with Voltaire to determine what influence the theatrical customs of his time might have had on Racine's tragedies.[13]

Musset's instinctive sympathy for Shakespeare (which did not turn him automatically and arbitrarily against Racine, as Romantic dogma willed) let him see that there was a deeper theatrical logic to be found than that of the unities. Shakespeare's stage, more flexible than the contemporary French proscenium stage, had greater potential for the dramatic imagination: it offered Musset possibilities beyond the linear structure and the Cartesian rationalism that governed even the Romantics' attempts at liberation. He saw that stage reality might and should be other than a reasonable transposition from "real life" and evolved a principle of elliptical development and allusive dialogue, the music and rhythm of scenic organization, which the Symbolists were much later and only gradually to bring (or restore, after the "realist heresy") to the theater. In the words of Copeau, "He possesses the secret of light composition. I do not mean something mawkish or weak by that. But an agility, a joyousness. True power in art is delicate and explosive. It abolishes real duration at one stroke. At one stroke the poet has entered his own world. There he is in command of everything. An image, an allusion, a passage, a break, a balancing of scenes or speeches, and perhaps even less, is enough for him to stir up the powers of illusion, to awaken a desire in the imagination and to satisfy it at the same moment."[14] No doubt Musset's sense of dramatic composition resulted from the theatricality which his family and friends all remarked in his character, and which made him don a great yellow overcoat and lie chanting on the floor of his room during spells of remorse for his misspent youth, or illuminate his room with candles and torches when he was expecting the "visit of the Muse," as when he wrote the "Nuit de mai."[15] He felt that theater is not the illusion of reality but illusion itself, as a function and need of the human spirit. His dramatic structures, his dialogue, his rapidly shifting settings all speak to that need rather than to the need to be reassured about probabilities and logic. Without overstepping the boundary of whimsy, wish fulfillment, or fairy tale in his major works, he had the instinctive *métier* to create a world firmly governed by its own invincible logic, peopled by characters who, on a variety of levels, are theatrical beings, difficult to imagine in real life (as are their settings) yet inevitable and true on the stage.

Part of the reason for this resides in their language, which succeeds in being natural in its context, and unreal at the same time. Nobody we know speaks Musset's poetic prose.[16] Yet its balance and rhythm, its music, make it remarkably speakable; it "lies well in the voice." Musset's ear for dialogue (which incidentally makes his verse also so deceptively casual when he wishes it) has nothing to do with the imitative realism, the ear for the vernacular, of a Courteline. But an actor with a sensitive ear and a sense of style—that which actor-poet Jules Truffin termed a "lilac voice"—can make it sound as true and unforced as any theater language written.[17] For Musset had the good sense to root his *enfants du siècle* in the solid linguistic tradition of the Enlightenment to which his taste naturally drew him. Auguste Brun says: "The language we hear in the **Comédies** . . . is easy to identify: it is that which characterizes the 18th century in France. But at times romanticism slips in with its rhetoric, its phraseology, its poetical images . . ."[18] This mixture is typical of Musset's personality. His images, however, are not merely decorative, as they would have been in eighteenth-century usage and as they remained even in much of the Romantics' theatrical dialogue (the current which leads to the poetry of *Cyrano*). They are the very basis of his logic. All of Musset's characters, even his minor figures and his grotesques—who have been characterized as "clods of genius"—utter their ideas metaphorically or allusively. This gives the sequence of his dialogue a peculiar elliptical quality all its own, analogous to the elliptical progress of his scenes. Boissy referred to this as Musset's "indirect language," and asserted that he was alone among French dramatists in using it. Thus Marianne talks of precious and cheap wine

to Octave when she is really opening the dialogue of seduction (**Marianne,** II, 1); Fantasio speaks of blue tulips, and of mechanical dolls, to Princess Elsbeth, in opposition to her impending marriage (**Fantasio,** II, 1 and 5); Camille asks Perdican about a picture in a gallery when she wants to be persuaded not to join a religious order (***On ne badine pas avec l'amour,*** II, 5). The examples could be multiplied at will. Even the sense of prosaic boredom to which Musset's heroes are subject tends to find a symbolic expression: a cotton nightcap covering the city of Munich; counting from one to infinity; deploring a botched sunset; sitting in the sun staring at one's new suit or watching one's wig grow . . . But a witty eighteenth-century critical spirit is never far behind the Romantic *Weltschmerz*.

Here again we find the unmistakable echo of Musset's voice: this "mixture of wit and sentiment, of pathos and comedy, of fantasy and truth, of passion and irony, of sadness and buffoonery, an inimitable and unique blend which constitutes the charm, the originality, the secret and the miracle of Musset comedy."[19] Musset alone among French Romantic dramatists possessed the mastery that enabled him to avoid the temptations of sentimentality, facile virtuosity, bombast, exoticism, diabolism, Byronism—all the *isms* to which the Romantic flesh was heir. The tendencies are all latently present: Musset was not a shy recluse from his times. But every tendency has its corrective, with the result that we are constantly being surprised yet at the same time feel a reassuring sense that he is not going to betray us by lapses into the maudlin, sensational, or excessive.

Beyond the unique voice, the elliptical structure; the balance of emotion, intelligence, and taste; the sense of true theater; the rare expression of youthful passions and anxieties—beyond all these the theater of Alfred de Musset possesses for us today a virtue we may seek in vain in French drama of his century: its expression of deep and insistent ethical preoccupations of our day. Behind its lightness, its wit, its amorous sentiment, his theater is uncommonly serious. In the words of one of his most perceptive commentators, Bernard Masson, "An entire dialectic of personal existence is sketched out in this singular theater, which formerly passed for one of fantasy and laughter."[20] But it took almost a century, and painstaking examination of the texts and of Musset's life, to discover this. We take it for granted, in an era when metaphysical anguish can be represented by clowns and tramps, that seriousness has its derisive or destructive laughter. But the literary climate of Musset's century did not favor such an appreciation of his part-time buffoon, Fantasio; his pasty-faced, effeminate jester-assassin, Lorenzo; or his grotesque caricatures of the aging and conformist, the *fantoches*.

It took the efforts of Léon Lafoscade, Jean Giraud, and above all Pierre Gastinel to reveal the truth about this "waxen-hearted young man."[21] More than any of his literary contemporaries who paid extensive lip service to German thought and letters, Musset had read and understood the German artists and philosophers. He knew Shakespeare, he translated DeQuincy, he read widely in modern English literature. He spoke less Italian, perhaps, than George Sand, as she discovered in their celebrated escapade to Venice, but he read Dante, Boccaccio, Bandello, and Leopardi (whom he admired intensely, a revealing taste at a time when Leopardi was almost unknown in France). By a duality worthy of his best comedies, which reveals the roots of his literary creation in the depths of his personality, Musset took pains to hide under the mask of the handsome playboy this other Musset, intellectually solid, preoccupied with the pervasive human problems of his and our day: the complex nature of love, the painful difficulty of communication, the temptation of conformity, the conflict between the individual and society, the idealist's simultaneous aspiration toward fulfillment and toward death, the struggle and incomprehension between generations, the inexorable conquest of man by time.

The quotation from **Fantasio** which opens this study is a fitting epigraph to Musset's theater: the theater of solitude. No body of dramatic work of his time or nation—indeed few *oeuvres* of any time—better express the dilemma of modern man, caught between the defense of his own dignity and the collective needs of mankind. No one foresaw or felt more clearly, more intimately, than he the incomprehension between generations and peoples which has come to be a predominant concern today. Nor has anyone better expressed the comical incongruity, the tragic absurdity of the struggle pitting man against himself, across the barricade of time and space, in a battle of incomprehension and dogmatism which prevents its participants from seeing that the face glimpsed through the smoke and blood is their own, distorted by the enemy within us all who will one day claim each of us as his victim. The thirst for love to break down the barrier of the body's isolation, and love's paradoxical obligation to use that body, the locus of our solitude, for its expression is what gives their terrible poignancy to Musset's lovers and heroes: to Coelio, Octave, and Marianne; to Perdican and Camille; to Lorenzo, Philip Strozzi, and Ricciarda Cibo; even to Fantasio, the cosmic jester in the Princess' garden, who utters the magic formula amid the quips and paradoxes inspired by his ennui: "Quelles solitudes que tous ces corps humains!"

Notes

1. For all these "influences" cf. Léon Lafoscade, *Le Théâtre d'Alfred de Musset*. See also, in particular, Pierre Nordon, "Alfred de Musset et l'Angleterre," *Les Lettres Romanes* (1966-67); and Jean Giraud, "Alfred de Musset et trois romantiques allemands," *Revue d'Histoire Littéraire* (1911-12).

2. Cited by Guy Leclerc, *Les Grandes Aventures du théâtre* (Paris, 1965), p. 248.

3. "Marivaux-Musset," *Mercure de France*, 50 (1950), 582.

4. *Théâtre d'Alfred de Musset*, I, v.

5. Cited by Gastinel, *Le Romantisme*, p. 590. Cf. Jacques Copeau's penetrating remark about this other Musset, whose deceptive "sincerity" dominates many of the lyrics, but especially the *Confession*: "He lavishes at once all that is noblest and all that is basest in his nature: 'I have never put my knee to the ground without putting my heart in it.' It is this perversion of 'sincerity,' this collusion of the flesh with the soul, which is the fatal poison of his debauchery. This suffering libertine could never worship anything but purity . . . Musset was never able to recover from his youth. Despite his forced marches, he could never cross and leave behind him that region of life where 'knowing nothing in the world, desiring everything, the young man feels the seed of all the passions at once.'" "Le Théâtre d'Alfred de Musset," p. 21.

6. *Les Grandes Aventures du Théâtre*, p. 247.

7. See, for example, Henri Lefebvre, *Alfred de Musset dramaturge;* and Werner Bahner, *Alfred de Mussets Werk*.

8. Bernard Masson, *Lorenzaccio ou la difficulté d'être;* Joachim-Claude Merlant, *Le Moment de "Lorenzaccio" dans le destin de Musset*.

9. Louis Jouvet, *Tragédie classique et théâtre du XIXᵉ siècle;* Jacques Copeau, "Le Théâtre d'Alfred de Musset."

10. Under the direction of Otomar Krejca, in a Czech translation by Karel Kraus, at the Odéon-Théâtre des Nations, Paris, May 11-16, 1970.

11. Quotation from Hugo's preface cited by Georges Ascoli, *Le Théâtre romantique*, p. 172.

12. Cf. Allevy, *La Mise en scène*, pp. 117-18.

13. Alfred de Musset, *Comédies et Proverbes*, introduction by Jacques Copeau (Paris, 1931) I, v.

14. Ibid., p. xviii.

15. Paul de Musset, *Biographie*, in *Oeuvres complètes*, "l'Intégrale," pp. 23, 31.

16. For an examination of Musset's dramatic language, see Auguste Brun, *Deux Proses de théâtre: Drame romantique, Comédies et Proverbes*.

17. Barbey d'Aurevilly referred to Musset's theater as "a lilac struck by lightning." Both quoted by Gabriel Boissy, *Le Figaro* (April 9, 1920).

18. Brun, *Deux Proses*, p. 59.

19. Maurice Donnay, "Les Comédies de Musset," *Revue française* (June 22, 1924), 682.

20. *Lorenzaccio ou la difficulté d'être*, p. 51.

21. *Le Théâtre d'Alfred de Musset;* "Alfred de Musset et trois romantiques allemands"; *Le Romantisme d'Alfred de Musset.*

Rachel L. Wright (essay date February 1992)

SOURCE: Wright, Rachel L. "Male Reflectors in the Drama of Alfred de Musset." *The French Review* 65, no. 3 (February 1992): 393-401.

[*In the following essay, Wright explores the roles of male characters in Musset's works.*]

Musset would have been amused to hear himself described as a didactic writer, and few would think of his plays as *pièces à thèse*. However, the volume of social commentary in his theatrical creations, chiefly directed against convention, conventional attitudes, and patterns of behavior, is undeniable. He avoids clumsy didacticism by casting his sermons as demonstrations rather than direct statements. In a theater where the spotlight is most frequently on the woman at grips with convention, the male character is a major instrument in the process of demonstration.

While Musset does not appear to question the validity of convention as a necessary social phenomenon, his criticism is directed toward the habitually constricting and deforming interpretations and practices which become inimical to the flowering of the human personality. His most frequent targets are the education provided for young women in contemporary religious institutions, revered religious guidance, marriage, and parental sanctions. Again and again there is proof of their inefficacy in the face of intelligent youthful reappraisal. The later plays, notably *Il ne faut jurer de rien,* testify to the successful revaluation, if not the complete overthrow of these conventional forces. The female protagonist is the chief victim of their tentacles which so embarrass and hamper her development that she is trapped physically and morally, with no apparent escape route. Musset sees the primacy of the man's role in this impasse. To begin with, the mother figure has little relevance except as a point of reference. A virtual minor in society herself, she is largely ineffectual. Confused, preoccupied, even selfish, she usually proves unequal to her daughter's needs. The father figure tends to pale into insignificance after Laerte of *A quoi rêvent les jeunes filles,* to be represented by fathers who are variously remote, panic-stricken, sympathetic but wary and retiring, or incorrigibly egotistic. Thus, by obscuring the parent figure, Musset highlights the male peer who is, in effect, most involved in the girl's natural and conventional existence for the greater part of her life. Furthermore, the male-female relationship being the most fundamental of all human states, what more natural situation could be used to explode the myth of convention's traditional dominance of human behavior and destiny?

By the natural order of things, the adolescent girl relates with increasing confidence to men as her consciousness of them and their influence grows. The opportunities offered by this situation can therefore be exploited to strengthen and develop her psychologically rather than confuse, stultify, or destroy her as conventional education and religion have obviously done. At the same time, the male-female relationship is equally conventional, hence the paraphernalia of procedures attending courtship, marriage, and adultery. All Musset's men except Fantasio are also basically conventional types. Nothing could be more authentic and natural. This is why, with the thrust of irony, Musset's commentary takes for granted the dual nature of the male role within which convention is, as it were, used against itself to throw the natural into relief.

With typical Romantic zest for the natural, Musset pronounces his truth through Fantasio's elucidating moral lesson to Elsbeth, where the image of a flower dramatizes the belief that the purpose of life and education is to harness and nurture the natural, not to disfigure and destroy it: "mais une fleur ne peut en devenir une autre: ainsi qu'importe à la nature? on ne la change pas, on l'embellit ou on la tue" (*Théâtre* 302). Reflections are crucial to Musset's view of the world and of life. The man, usually shedding his conventional cloak, stands poised between nature and the dehumanizing forces of convention, continually mirroring the latter to the advantage of the former, for the lifelong benefit of the beleaguered, often tormented girl. The purpose of his exercise is to achieve the embellishment of her personality, thus improving her chances of successful living. Four plays will be examined: *La Nuit vénitienne* (1830), *Les Caprices de Marianne* (1833), *Fantasio* (1833), and *Il ne faut jurer de rien* (1836).

The very notion of Musset as a commentator on social issues has been open to question. Doumic has denied him a social conscience on the grounds of his egoism and the limitation of his intellectual and moral curiosity (934). Campos remarks:

> Musset remains aloof from the preoccupations of a socially conscious writer like Hugo or Eugène Sue whose protests against society's abuses helped the growth of a general social conscience in their day.
>
> (74)

Rees suggests that Musset's social awareness was expressed in his short stories more clearly than in his other work (47-48). It is true that at a primary level, the short stories reveal truths about the plight of underprivileged women—the "grisettes" and their kind, but Musset may have contributed to this output on a popular contemporary social issue for financial reasons or out of a desire to follow fashion. However, Cabani comments perceptively: "On peut regretter que la vérité de Musset soit restée cachée sous un voile de bonne compagnie" (7). What is this truth? A vital part of it is that the social interest is present, though often veiled in the plays. It is therefore unfair to minimize their testimony to Musset's social commitment. It is also essential in this regard to distinguish between mere statement through demonstration and overt didacticism with direct reforming aims as exemplified by the contemporary writers quoted by Campos. It is true that Musset deliberately posed as the dissolute playboy and was at pains to exaggerate his boredom with trite contemporary preoccupations: "Je ne me suis pas fait écrivain politique / N'étant pas amoureux de la place publique / D'abord il n'entre pas dans mes prétentions / D'être l'homme du siècle et de ses passions" (*Poésie* 155). We have only to turn to the plays to realize the misleading nature of such a statement.

Conventional norms are epitomized in the situation of the arranged marriage. Whether already within marriage or on the verge of it, every major female character in Musset's theater pits her personal desires and loyalty to herself against the almost impregnable mass of conventional procedures. Every play adds its details to the prescribed limits imposed by conventional notions of marriage or adultery. The constant opposition between the individual and conventional norms is therefore frequently the center of the struggle, the internal action which replaces "intrigue" as practiced by Hugo or Dumas *père*, the setting being the woman's mind and her psychological response to social stimuli. Of paramount importance in provoking a response is the role of the man as father, lover, friend, or mentor: for the man often focuses the essence of the young woman's problem and leads her to an intelligent understanding of her position.

Convention has entrenched her in the arranged marriage which presupposes the complicity of husbands and parents. Society has conditioned her to accept her insignificance, her husband's unassailable position and the stronghold of her marital home. Powerless, enslaved, a social plaything, she is superbly characterized by the counterfeit clown Fantasio, in the prolonged metaphor of the "serin de Cour":

> C'est un serin de Cour; il y a beaucoup de petites filles très bien élevées qui n'ont pas d'autres procédés que celui-là. Elles ont un petit ressort sous le bras gauche, un joli petit ressort, en diamant fin, comme la montre d'un petitmaître. Le gouverneur ou la gouvernante fait jouer le ressort et vous voyez aussitôt les lèvres s'ouvrir avec le sourire le plus gracieux, une cascatelle de paroles mielleuses sort avec le plus doux murmure, et toutes les convenances sociales, pareilles à des nymphes légères se mettent aussitôt à dansoter sur la pointe du pied autour de la fontaine merveilleuse. Le prétendu ouvre des yeux ébahis, l'assistance chuchote avec indulgence, et le père rempli d'un secret contentement, regarde avec orgueil, les boucles d'or de ses souliers.

> (***Théâtre*** 311)

This comparison heightens the enigma of the woman's situation, thus commenting incisively on the basic artificiality surrounding marriage. More significant still is the role of Fantasio in helping Elsbeth to fuller self-knowledge. The aptness of his image, the thrust of his satire, sharpen the indictment against a system which bedevils a girl's chance of happiness. Biting sarcasm castigates the participants in this almost ritualistic transformation of something natural and lovely into an object operated by a spring. This image echoes throughout Musset's drama with extensions and variations such as the roles of the "Fantoches" in *On ne badine pas avec l'amour,* and the muttering doll of *Les Caprices de Marianne,* together with the images of the statue and the plaster cast. It is essential to see the technique of commentary through imagery on the one hand, and on the other, the power of the male counterpart, himself the ultimate image, the poet, the man of vision who sees the problem clearly and finds a perfect expression of it that will move the woman to self-discovery and a sense of personal dignity.

The man is usually himself an actor, someone playing a part within the play either in full disguise (e.g. Fantasio, the Prince d'Eysenach of *La Nuit vénitienne,* Laerte, the father of Ninon and Ninette in *A quoi rêvent les jeunes filles,* Valentin of *Il ne faut jurer de rien*) or partially (like Perdican who briefly acts a part watched by Camille). Lefebvre stresses the strong link between art and disguise and the revelation of truth (68), a principle which Musset is known to have shared with Marivaux. The truth can emerge more freely when conventional barriers that normally entrap or separate people are removed. The logical impact of the device in criticizing conventional attitudes, a sensitive issue, is all the more eloquent. Thus the actor-partner engages the heroine in polemic, helping her see herself. Not only do his words project the truth of her status, but more impressively, his whole personality and outlook can incarnate his vision. He holds the mirror up to nature thereby assuming the attributes of a reflector.

Musset's complex approach to social criticism in the plays does not always exclude direct invective. What is innovative against the background of Romantic didacticism is the frequent transposition of invective or criticism to the lips of the male figure. It is true that Marianne protests personally against the treatment she receives from callous male indiscretion as does Vigny's Kitty Bell. However, Musset's more provocative technique of social commentary often dispenses first and foremost with convention in the characterization of the man so that he can fully represent fulfillment of the yearnings of the woman and the freedoms she is denied. She is thus attracted to see various facets of herself through his eyes. For example, Marianne's temptation to revolt is set in motion, not by the conventionally romanesque, love-lorn Célio, but by his friend and emissary Octave, who is detached, critical, almost hostile. With one stroke, the wine-drinking, whoremongering Octave storms the barriers of pious prudery with which Marianne has involuntarily armed herself. He symbolizes the freedom to indulge in sexual and other pleasures for which her spirit yearns. She sees an urge in herself which the restrictions of traditional marriage and the imperfect preparation of convent education have failed to satisfy. The sadness of her discovery recalls that of Camille faced with Perdican's criticism of her foolish self-denial: "O Perdican! ne raillez pas; tout cela est triste à mourir" (362). Secondly, the reflector and his object are well matched. Octave's exchanges with Marianne show clearly that they have several characteristics in common: intelligence, impetuosity, daring, a sense of humor, wit, consciousness of beauty. By his mirroring and his almost ribald teasing he disarms and unmasks her. We see her writhing under the sting of self-discovery. Célio's love for her becomes "un pauvre enfant à la mamelle" left by a careless nurse to fall head first on the ground (253). The brutally earth-bound stress of her metaphor betrays in physical terms her irrepressible longing for Octave's love rather than Célio's. Before we meet Marianne, we have heard her described as "un dragon de vertu dans toute la ville" (231), an evocation carrying all the appurtenances of Fantasio's image of a stuffed canary. Now, stimulated by Octave, the lifeless, mechanical thing warms up and, instead of emitting a flow of ready-prepared "paroles mielleuses" in response to the conventionally directed advances of an acceptable admirer, explodes into a volley of invective aimed at those very conventions which dominate a woman's life. "Am I not free to choose even my own lover?" she asks. Stunned by the shocking aptness of Octave's description of her indifference to the realities of life—the "milk" of convention that still drips into all her speech, with the result that she knows neither how to love nor to hate, and is "comme les roses du Bengale . . . sans épine et sans parfum" (253)—, Marianne reacts by admitting a woman's powerlessness in the hands of convention.

In the case of the unmarried Laurette of ***La Nuit vénitienne,*** contempt for or distress at her fate is never expressed in lachrymose vein by the heroine herself but is transferred to the lips of the wounded lover whose rantings clearly label the chief characteristics of the girl's position, the inhumanity and indifference of her legal owners, again reminiscent of Fantasio's image:

> Et toi, ton cœur, ta tête, ta vie marchandée par entremetteurs, tout a été vendu au plus offrant, une couronne de reine t'a faite esclave pour jamais; et cependant ton fiancé enseveli dans les délices d'une cour attend nonchalamment.
>
> (394)

In an earlier remark, Razetta has reminded Laurette of her status in relation to the Prince who is now to be her "second père" (393), thus punctuating the truth of her habits of dependence and timid aquiescence to male authority now merely transferred to her new role as wife. Razetta's reflection and the urge toward "the easy way" which he represents, evoke an immediate response in Laurette whom common sense obliges to shrink from the latent irresponsibility of his way of life and the obvious threat to standards of decorum to which she chooses to remain a disturbed adherent. Having recognized herself with some alarm, she pleads with him to refrain from further inroads into the security of her position.

Her accepted suitor, the Prince d'Eysenach, mirrors her situation in a more stylized way. He carries a portrait of her which he discovers does not measure up to her real beauty. A conventional reproduction cannot do justice to the beauty with which nature has endowed her. Then he is himself of "un caractère le plus fantasque, la paresse personnifiée" (402), who, like Octave, is detached from all conventional norms. The Prince and Laurette are again matched in their youthful intelligence, their idealism, and sense of insecurity. The Prince's opposition to convention, which reflects the main element of what could be Laurette's struggle, springs from fundamental immaturity. He clings to childhood habits—"j'ai toujours des joujoux de poupée dans mes poches" (410)—and an inordinate lust for adventure. His reflection of the freedom she might desire is exaggerated and distorted, for she will be monarch of "une atmosphère de despotisme et de tyrannie" (413). She is obviously destined to be just another of his playthings. Disillusioned and chastened, she revaluates her position and seeks contentment in conventional marriage which, she knows, can never be ideal. Thus the remarks and personalities of the two men reflect the essence of the heroine's problem, stimulate her thinking and lead her to a solution. Their role as reflectors and catalysts is essential in the process of rethinking to which the woman is subjected. This is reminiscent of the experience of the Marquise in ***Lorenzaccio*** who is ringed by three men: her religious adviser, the Cardinal; the head of state, Alexandre, whose mistress she has been; and her husband. All these men throw back images of her and of her life, which remind her of her posturing. Disappointed but enlightened, she reverts to normal marriage.

The reflector technique finds its richest expression in *Fantasio.* Even before Elsbeth appears, there is a network of images heralding her situation, pronounced by her father the king, Fantasio, and the young courtiers. The king's metaphor of the "pauvres mouches mutilés," victims of the spider's web of "la politique" (278), sums up the infirmity of the girl, victim of convention. Hartman's stress on the necessity to make a show of conventional enthusiasm for a national event to which he is personally quite indifferent is a discreet shadow of the tearful princess preparing herself for an outward show of conformity with her conventional marriage. Fantasio's "mois de janvier dans le cœur" in response to Hartman's suggestion that he has "le mois de mai sur les joues" (282) sets the seal for the unity of feeling between Fantasio and Elsbeth which will effect the perfect mirror of her state of mind as Fantasio is to present it, and lead her to discovery of and reconciliation with herself and her position. Fantasio's wish to change places with someone—"Si je pouvais être ce monsieur qui passe" (284)—has in fact been granted through his impersonation of the dead clown, and he is in a position to understand and express the intensity of Elsbeth's loneliness. He seems to jump the boundaries of their separate personalities and act for her. He mirrors her youthful gaiety, her pensiveness, her recurrent depression. In order to do this satisfactorily he is divested of all conventional characteristics: professional respectability, class, sexual attraction. Drunken, nameless, deformed, penniless, a debtor, a vagrant impostor masquerading as a dead clown, he is the perfect epitome of everything that a conventional figure is not. A totally liberated spirit, he declares:

> Je suis un des animaux domestiques du roi de Bavière et si je veux, tant que je garderai ma bosse et ma perruque, on me laissera vivre jusqu'à ma mort entre un épagneul et une pintade.
>
> (306)

He views Elsbeth, lying on a carpet and through a window pane. Musset's veiled sarcasm directed against the pious pronouncements of direct criticism is easily recognizable in Fantasio's satisfaction at not being "un écolier de rhétorique" when he comments sparingly "Pauvre petite!" and hastens to add that the princess is quite unaware of his presence and that he is a totally indifferent observer. The intensity of Musset's artifice for the protection of the distant, objective social commentator cannot be missed. Fantasio ridicules the pretensions of a writer who might have described Elsbeth as a pink-ribboned lamb being led to the slaughter, and, without embellishment, pronounces the truth of her position and that of the contemporary girl: "Cette petite fille est sans doute romanesque, il lui est cruel d'épouser un homme qu'elle ne connaît pas" (306).

The case for the girl against convention in all its apparent playfulness, could not be more soberly put. He comments with equal moderation and poignant simplicity on her silent sacrifice and the capriciousness of chance. His summing-up explains clearly his role as catalyst, agent of discovery, holder of the mirror up to nature, poet, and seer, an important role which reaches its climax in this play:

> Il faut que je me grise, que je rencontre l'enterrement de Saint-Jean, que je prenne son costume et sa place, que je fasse enfin la plus grande folie de la terre, pour venir voir tomber à travers cette glace, les deux seules larmes que cette enfant versera peut-être sur son triste voile de fiancée.
>
> (306-07)

Valentin and Cécile of *Il ne faut jurer de rien* are similar on several levels. Mutual attraction exists already. Class, sophistication, means, parallel intelligence, so typical of Musset's thinking: every prospect augurs well for their union. Again, moreover, the male who mirrors the possible reaction of the woman to convention, is himself unconventional in outlook, even though by class, orientation, and social expectation, he is, in fact, a conventional suitor. Somewhat reminiscent of the Prince d'Eysenach, he cherishes an ideal, but not of beauty or any exaggerated absolute. Rather, his mirror picks out the qualities and propensities of a totally unconventional, non-romanesque, illusion-free young woman, entirely removed from the constricted stereotype of a Camille. He describes his ideal woman as someone face to face with stark reality, involved in some of its ugliness, who is thereby revitalized so that she can face the vicissitudes of marriage with stability and resilience; and he adds in response to a question from his astounded uncle Van Buck: "Non, mais je voudrais qu'une fille fût une herbe dans un bois et non une plante dans une caisse (557) Unconventional in his ideal, he is equally daring in his determination to arrive at firsthand knowledge of his bride by unconventional means. Flouting all notions of propriety, he enters her home uninvited and finally entices her to a nocturnal rendez-vous in the most outrageously compromising circumstances. Iconoclasm about convention is his motive force. Even his letter to Cécile deposes the traditional notion of respect for age and parenthood when these are justifiably irresponsible. There could be no better mirror of Cécile's rebellion to convention were she disposed to it. In fact, the reality of her existence comes very close to Valentin's ideal image, for she has been nurtured in a manner that has freed her from inherited stereotypes. Even the characterisation of her absent-minded mother is an aid in this direction. Again, the truth about the young woman is to emerge in a situation of disguise. Also, the pleasure of following her self-revelation and the matching of the hero's dream to the true picture of her is reminiscent of the effect produced by Marivaux's plays.

In Musset's plays, however, perspectives are constantly shifted. Whereas we discover a discrepancy both between the Prince d'Eysenach's original portrait of Laurette and her real beauty, and between his exaggerated image of the freedom she may desire and what she knows real life will offer, whereas in several other plays, however, a similar discrepancy exists which either leads to tragic confrontation as in *Les Caprices de Marianne* and *On ne badine pas avec l'amour* or has to be contained through subtle reconciliation as in *Fantasio*; the dimensions of Valentin's image and the reality of Cécile's presence are perfectly matched. More naturally down-to-earth than Elsbeth, this heroine, taken from contemporary French life with the play's direct references to its house parties, charities, pastimes, modes of travelling, domestic activities and food, needs no mirror of herself to convert her to a sensible view of life. Cécile's bourgeois values have been amply discussed by critics, notably Sices who sees in her a disappointing counterpart of the earlier heroines whose reaction to convention appears more vital (217). The reduction in tension embodied by the heroine's outlook and demands is also seen by Masson as a sign of decline in Musset, who now shows a tendency to extol conformity (551). Rather, it is necessary to see Cécile as the ultimate symbol of a woman in whom discrepant elements between her expectations and the potential offered by the conditions of contemporary life have been removed. Intelligent adaptation and initiative dominate her thinking so that the threat of confrontation disappears. The plays move from the uneasy acceptance of Laurette, through Marianne's and Camille's escapism, to Elsbeth's refined resignation, which has to be learned, and end with Cécile's natural, good-humored integration with life, innate in her thinking and strong enough to influence that of her male partner, who discovers and applauds her values: "Tendre enfant! je devine ton cœur. Tu fais la charité n'est-ce pas?" (602). The loss of dramatic tension, unavoidable as it is, should be seen positively in relation to the strength of Musset's commitment to the female problem and his final word on its solution.

Men are, in effect, the key figures in the woman's dilemma. Women, traditionally minors in their society, cannot be blamed for their position. Through his technique of reflections Musset suggests how interrelated are the destinies of the two sexes, the initiative being taken by the man as sympathetic observer and catalyst of change. The interaction, a kind of twinning of their powers, is enhanced by the reflecting device, which largely suppresses direct statement by the female protagonist, and relies on careful demonstration and skillful use of imagery. Conventional notions of male supremacy are manifestly played down. The man's strength is portrayed as setting in motion the consciousness and liberating forces that will lead to fulfillment for both sexes. The emphasis seems to be on the light of lucid thinking and responsible action.

Thus, tongue-in-cheek, within the self-imposed limits of his armchair theater, Musset achieved, apparently without effort, the perfect expression of the Romantic ideal of commitment to social change. Octave's declaration "Je me sens moi-même une autre Marianne (249) is central in Musset's method of expressing his message.

Works Cited

Cabani, José. "Dr. Jekyll ou Mr. Hyde?" *Les Nouvelles Littéraires 2261.* (21 janvier 1971): 7.

Campos, Christophe. "Social Romanticism." *The Early Nineteenth Century. French Literature and its Background.* Ed. J. Cruickshank. Oxford UP, 1969.

Doumic, René. "Le Classicisme d'Alfred de Musset." *Revue des Deux Mondes* (15 juin 1907): 923-34.

Lefebvre, Henri. *Musset.* Paris: L'Arche, 1970.

Masson, Bernard. "Le Masque, le double et la personne dans quelques comédies et proverbes." *Revue des Sciences Humaines* 108 (Oct.-Dec. 1962): 551-71.

Musset, Alfred de. *Œuvres complètes.* Vol. 1: *Poésie complète.* Vol. 2: *Théâtre complet.* Bibliothèque de la Pléiade. Paris: Gallimard, 1968.

Rees, Margaret. *Alfred de Musset.* New York: Twayne, 1971.

Sices, David. *Theater of Solitude: The Drama of Alfred de Musset.* Hanover, NH: UP of New England, 1974.

Yifen Beus (essay date spring-summer 2003)

SOURCE: Beus, Yifen. "Alfred de Musset's Romantic Irony." *Nineteenth-Century French Studies* 31, nos. 3-4 (spring-summer 2003): 197-209.

[*In the following essay, Beus analyzes Musset use of romantic irony in his plays.*]

The year of 1797, though somewhat arbitrary in terms of historical significance in German and French drama, marks German philosopher and theorist Friedrich Schlegel's initial efforts to establish irony as a philosophical as well as literary concept. The concept of irony was then being rediscovered and redefined by the early Romantics and is now considered by scholars of Romanticism essential to the understanding of the Romantic doctrines. As Friedrich and his brother August Wilhelm Schlegel drew inspiration from the early (Shakespeare and Cervantes) as well as the contemporary moderns (Sterne, Diderot, and Goethe) in analyzing and theorizing modern art and literature, the French also noticed the dominance of Shakespeare in English and German literary criticism as well as of eighteenth-century sentimentality. Sterne's *A Sentimental Journey* and *Tristram Shandy* were widely read in France and gave him a near celebrity status during his visits to numerous literary salons in Paris. Diderot deliberately copied Sterne's model when writing his *Jacques le fataliste* and prompted the French literary circles to reflect on the use of humor and the role of the author in the creative process and the relation to his work and audience. The transition from the classic to the modern is most notably fostered by Mme de Staël and her group at Coppet. Under the impact of eighteenth-century sentimentality, the promotion of German literary theory by the Coppet Group as well as the anti-classicist sentiment developed within the French literary circle, a number of writers, such as Hugo, Stendhal, Musset, and Vigny, produced works that recognize the merits of the new Romantic ideals and advocate what their German counterparts had done decades before. In this article, I will examine the dramatic works of Musset in the light of Romantic irony, an irony that synthesizes conflicting forces to produce a universal type of poetry and reveals the nature of artistic creation by a self-critical writing process of the author while preserving the art work's function to describe the author's duty to the society and to reflect his own time.

Among the French Romantic dramatists, the theories of Hugo, Vigny, and Musset on "modern drama" and the role of the author bear most striking resemblance to that of Friedrich Schlegel. This is in no way accidental. The Schlegels' discussions of humor, irony, and poetry are not unfamiliar in the French literary circle thanks to translations of the Schlegel brothers' works, the Schlegels' debates with the French literary and publishing circles about the Romantic/classic contrast, and the publications, Staël's *De l'Allemagne* in particular, and literary discussions of the Coppet group. Nor has the subject gone altogether unnoticed.

At the time when Hugo and Vigny were primarily poets, the younger Musset also started his career writing poetry. However, he found himself lacking passion as a poet, and after the indifferent reception of his first staged play, **La Nuit vénitienne** in 1830, he also lost enthusiasm for writing plays for the stage. Instead, as the title of **Un Spectacle dans un fauteuil** (1832) indicates, he went on to write plays for reading. Most of these were not meant to be performed at the time of their writing, though they were staged later, thanks to the advancement of stage technology. Quite ironically, his place as one of the greatest dramatists of his time was established through these then unstageable works. These works, along with those of Hugo and Vigny, are generally considered the best exemplars of Romantic irony in nineteenth-century French drama.

Some personal traits of Musset group him with Hugo and Vigny, while others distinguish him from the latter. On one hand, Musset belongs to a younger generation of the French Romantics (with Gautier, Nerval, and others) than that of Hugo and Vigny (who are his seniors by eight and thirteen years respectively). Yet, though only in his twenties, he produced, contemporaneously with them and all in the short span of two years (1833-34), such brilliant dramatic works as **Les Caprices de Marianne, Fantasio, On ne badine pas avec l'amour** and **Lorenzaccio.** Secondly, his affair with George Sand, though brief, had a profound impact upon his view on the nature of the poet and his creative process, one that made several of his poetry collections and prose writings (*Les Nuits, Le Poète déchu,* and *Le Fils du Titien*) more intensely biographical than theirs. Thirdly, despite their ideal to bring forth a harmonious yet critical synthesis of the duality of their personal life and their experience as poets and dramatists, Hugo and Vigny fell short of realizing their theories—Hugo often had to compromise his ideals to accommodate the contemporary stage and audience,[1] and Vigny practically withdrew from the theatre after *Chatterton,* the only dramatic work that reflects a real attempt to use the stage to advocate his criticism and to attack a society responsible for stifling poetic genius. Musset also turned away from the contemporary theatre after the failure of **La Nuit vénitienne** in 1830, only to create the closest French exemplars of Romantic irony in drama in the Schlegelian sense. His armchair drama literally freed him from the restraints and demand of contemporary theatrical conventions and practice. The power of his poetic imagination and youthful passion overflows in his plays, an exalted creative state which he was not able to reach in his earlier poetry.

The modernity of Musset's dramas was not to be recognized until the twentieth century when they could be produced in their original versions without the modifications dictated previously by the limits of nineteenth-century stage, where such techniques and design as swift scene changes and poetically colorful landscape were not possible. Inspired by Musset's comedies, Jacques Copeau, one of France's most innovative directors in the 1920s and 30s, published a manifesto for a new theatre where the director's duty is to faithfully translate the dramatist's work into a "poetry of the theatre," using complex composition of lighting and stagecraft to convey such an effect. In an introduction to an edition of Musset's **Comédies et Proverbes** (Paris, 1931), he describes the playwright as one of the greatest of dramatic authors who have an intuition of the laws that govern a play. Speaking of Musset's craftsmanship as a dramatist, Copeau writes:

> He possesses the secret of light composition. I do not mean something mawkish or weak by that. But an agility, a joyousness. True power in art is delicate and explosive. It abolishes real duration at one stroke. . . . There he [Musset] is in command of everything. An image, an allusion, a passage, a break, a balancing of scenes or speeches, and perhaps even less, is enough

for him to stir up the powers of illusion, to awaken a desire in the imagination and to satisfy it at the same moment.

(qtd. in Sices 241-42)

Musset's comedies have also been referred to as "cinematic":

The "cinematic" quality of Musset's drama, which was noted as early as the 1920's, makes it apparent that motion picture was not so much a device which revolutionized the concept of dramatic structure as the necessary realization of an evolving theatrical vision in search of its technological means.

(Sices 241-42)

Thus the shifting perspectives of **Les Caprices de Marianne** provided a dramatic base for Jean Renoir's film technique in *La Règle du jeu*. These distinct qualities of his dramas are ahead of their time in terms of dramaturgy and audience appeal, for the nineteenth-century stage was not equipped to manage the shift of perspectives within a short time, and such changes often created inconsistency in the plot and thus disoriented the audience. "His mind leaps from idea to idea, image to image almost too quickly to provide his reader with the logical links between," comments Margaret Rees (128). Only a modern stage or else the cinema, where advanced machinery and technology are available, can match the speed of Musset's mind at work to realize the visions expressed in his plays.

Though Musset is considered one of the most important figures of the French Romantics, his attitude towards the practice, particularly in drama, of his contemporaries is more suspicious than readily agreeing. Musset's fundamental attitude toward the contemporary Classical and Romantic debate appears to be an ironic one in that Musset mocks both the haughty self-important posture of cultural superiority of the French with their pride in their classicism and the Romantics' idealistic yet naive attempt to revolutionize the literary tradition with its expressive lyricism; notwithstanding, both classicism and the new Romantic development gave inspiration to Musset's own youthful eccentricities. This attitude is reflected in his own dramatic style, which interestingly combines the wit and cynicism of seventeenth-century French classicism with Shakespeare's method of describing characters, settings, and costumes through dialogue rather than detailed stage directions at the beginning of each scene, as is common in nineteenth-century drama. Uncompromising in his views of a theatre that concentrates on the development of the characters' minds and motives as well as revealing the playwright's idealistic yet cynical attitude toward his work, Musset was not a popular success as a dramatist like Dumas or Hugo, who, despite their attempt to realize the ideals of the new genre "drame," often suc-

cumbed to stage conventions of exotic local color, ornate setting, and melodramatic manipulation of emotions. Many critics[2] agree that Musset's dramas come closest among their peers to the realization of the ideals developed, in the Romantic manifesto "Preface to Cromwell," by the poet who had served him as a mentor and introduced him into the Romantic circle. Unlike Hugo and Dumas, who enjoyed a great degree of popularity but, at the same time, needed to constantly deal with theatre managers, scene/costume artists, technical staff, and cast during productions, Musset, after giving up writing for the stage, had greater freedom to realize the poetic ideals fostered by the Romantics.

Musset had always been concerned with defining the role of poetry and the poet. A number of his poems and prose writings reveal this concern. *Les Nuits* (1835) consists of dialogue-like stanzas between the Poet and the Muse. *Le Poète déchu*, a fragmentary narrative written in 1839, can be read like a *Bildungsroman* or portrait of a young artist who discovers the true poet's function after going through mental trials and suffering—a biographical overtone of his wrenching relationship with George Sand. I. G. Daemmrich summarizes Musset's conception of the poet:

He must have suffered an emotional crisis which reveals to him the fundamental importance of genuine feeling for his creativity; he must sacrifice his most intimate feelings to his art; he must renounce political activism in order to concentrate on the general human condition; and his work must touch his readers. In order to create truly significant poetry, he should attain both a state of exaltation and one of detachment from his emotions. Finally, he should face the bitter reality that his high calling will lead to his rejection by a materialistic and politically oriented society.

(5-10)

The end of Musset's relationship with George Sand produces the "emotional suffering" for him to mature as a poet, argues Daemmrich. This experience also becomes the raw material for his poetry. But while expressing such emotional agony in his writing, Musset treats his works with a certain degree of detachment. In order to achieve this, it would be necessary for him to become isolated from his society, to free himself from social, political, and even personal concerns. This detachment will serve the true poet as a purifying stage leading to the state of spiritual "exaltation." But, this antagonistic view towards society often leads him to a state of complete self-absorption and to a self-isolation with no escape, like that described in Vigny's *Chatterton*.

Musset's ironic affection for and detachment from his work are reflected through a juxtaposition of sarcastic and comic attitudes. A central aspect of the Schlegelian irony, the author's overall tone of being serious while at the same time appearing comic and critical, is thus also present in Musset's "comédie." Most of the heroes and situations in his plays clearly embody such irony—the seriousness of Musset's attitude is often conveyed with and disguised in laughter, and a surprising tragic denouement is common in his "comedies." This Shakespearean mixture of tragic/comic (as in *Lear* and *Hamlet*) and Socratic irony expressed through seeming lightness make his aesthetic practice closer to the Schlegelian aesthetic than that of his peer dramatists. The striking resemblance between Musset's own philosophy of art and poetry and his love affairs and those of his protagonists/antagonists reflects his commitment to the poet's personal experience as the subject matter for poetry. And yet, this identification with his hero is often juxtaposed with an attitude of critical cynicism toward him. Using "Namouna," one of Musset's longest poems, which exhibits a "curious mixture of irony-at-the-expense-of romanticism and romantic irony," Lloyd Bishop points out this general characteristic of Musset's irony. In dealing with Musset's irony, he says, we must bear in mind that

> romantic irony is a double irony, it works in two opposite directions at once: the poet will declare himself alienated from his hero, but this alienation itself is also ironic—it masks the author's limited but genuinely sympathetic identification. Romantic irony commits itself to what it criticizes.
>
> (98)

Musset's hero often speaks in elegant classical style with lyrical images to express ideas, emotions, and desires in serious situations when such mannerism seems comically out of place. As Célio, for example, expresses his frustration in courting the heroine of *Les Caprices de Marianne,* his pitiful lovesickness makes his metaphors trite and Octave's unsympathetic response sarcastic and yet reasonable:

CÉLIO:

> Qui pourrait dire: ceci est gai ou triste? La réalité n'est qu'une ombre. Appelle imagination ou folie ce qui la divinise. Alors la folie est beauté elle-même. Chaque homme marche enveloppé d'un réseau transparent qui le couvre de la tête aux pieds; il croit voir des bois et des fleuves, des visages divins, et l'universelle nature se teint sous ses regards des nuances infinies du tissu magique. Octave! Octave! Viens à mon secours! . . . Fais ce que tu voudras, mais ne me trompe pas, je t'en conjure. Il est aisé de me tromper; je ne sais pas me défier d'une action que je ne voudrais pas faire moi-même.

OCTAVE:

> Si tu escaladais les murs?

CÉLIO:

> A quoi bon, si elle ne m'aime pas?

OCTAVE:

> Si tu lui écrivais?

CÉLIO:

> Elle déchire mes lettres ou me les renvoie.

OCTAVE:

> Si tu en aimais une autre?
>
> (I: iv)

This dialogue displays a typical dichotomy between two protagonists—one appears strong and rational while the other is weak and sentimental. In this plaint from Célio, Musset presents his agony in a poetic statement full of symbolism and at the same time as a comic result of Célio's hopeless cowardice. Octave's simple suggestions only make Célio's lovesickness an apparent theme for a love comedy and occludes the tragic element through Octave's ironically comic indifference toward the heroine. However, this jest-like tone turns out to be antithetical to the tragic development of the story. The Schlegelian irony of seriousness and jest at the same time is manifested here in Musset's detached humor and cynicism toward his protagonist.

Although his sarcastic attitude toward his contemporary Romantics distinguishes his manner from that of other French Romantics, Musset shares the characteristic of a socially detached Romantic hero in his profession as a dramatist/poet. Goethe's *Werther* was the first German work that expressed the developing "mal du siècle" pessimism through its suicidal theme and attracted immense popularity in France. Ever since, suicide, one of the many forms of the Romantic hero's agony of alienation, became a common motif in Romantic literature, and many Romantics expressed this alienation complex in their own lives by remaining silent or by softening their critical tone. Their choice of silence or conciliation led to withdrawal (in the case of Vigny), or to compromising their ideals in order to conform with public taste and maintain popularity (Dumas, a typical and very successful example, and Hugo, to a lesser degree). In Musset's case, his silence and ceasing to be an active dramatist for the contemporary stage takes a different turn—he becomes a voice for his own youthful zeal and imagination by liberating them from social concerns and by producing works that require tremendous imaginary participation on the reader's part. He turns the reader's closet into a world of imagination and jest, often setting his plays in foreign lands and at times without any chronological reference (such as Naples in *Les Caprices de Marianne,* Florence in *André del Sarto,* Munich in *Fantasio,* and Venice in *La Nuit vénitienne*), creating incoherent story lines (a potential love interest begins in *Fantasio,* but ends without any result, or a war is declared without particular effects) providing anti-dramatic denouements (Octave refuses the love of Marianne in *Les Caprices de Marianne*), using disguised identities of characters (Fantasio disguises himself as a jester, and the prince as his own aide-de-camp) to confound theatrical reality. All these devices that draw the spectator's attention to an intentional "break of theatrical illusion" are essential to create an irony that highlights the self-reflexivity and fictionalization of the work itself.

Musset's techniques of irony can be broken down into the following areas, all of which in fact are interwoven with each other in the structure of the play to contribute to the total ironic effect of the work: using dialogues for lyrical yet humorous descriptions of set, costume, and characters, use of disguise (personification, masks, etc.) to manipulate the ambiguities of reality and illusion, and finally, perception of love as the overarching theme of his drama. Writing for the closet without all the production-related hassles and by embedding these techniques of irony in his work, Musset was able to rely on his lyricism and the reader's imagination to create dramas at his will.

Les Caprices de Marianne, ironically the only major play performed during Musset's lifetime, can best represent his youthful burst of poetry and freedom of imagination. All of his techniques interwoven to create an irony can be seen in this comic-tragedy. The plot turns around Célio's desire to gain Marianne's love. Célio, a shy, timid, and good-natured young man, is frustrated by his failure in courting Marianne, wife of judge Claudio. He asks the brave and outspoken Octave to win her heart in his behalf. As Octave stirs up Marianne's passion, he also arouses jealousy in her husband. Claudio issues a warning that whoever steps into their garden to meet with Marianne will be killed. As Célio hastens to the rendezvous arranged by Octave, Marianne's note to Octave about the trap comes too late to Célio, who consequently dies believing that Octave has betrayed him. At Célio's grave site, Marianne confesses her love for Octave, but the latter reveals the truth to her: "Je ne vous aime pas, Marianne; c'était Célio qui vous aimait" (274).

At the beginning of *Les Caprices de Marianne,* the only description of the two men, Octave and Célio, both dressed up in carnival attires is through their dialogue, which also contrasts the two personalities by their costumes:

OCTAVE:

> Comment se porte, mon bon monsieur, cette gracieuse mélancolie?

CÉLIO:

> Octave! . . . O fou que tu es! Tu as un pied de rouge sur les joues. D'où te vient cet accoutrement? N'as-tu pas de honte, en plein jour?

OCTAVE:

> O Célio! O fou que tu es! tu as un pied de blanc sur les joues. D'où te vient ce large habit noir? N'as-tu pas de honte, en plein carnaval?

(I: iv)

As the characters ask each other what their costumes mean, the reader is shown this contrast between the two characters, though the contrast is quite obvious—an aspect common in Musset's comic irony and a sort of mocking attitude of Musset toward the audience's ability to interpret the play. The polarization of the characters (Octave: lively, daring, and outspoken; Célio: reserved, timid, and passive), emphasized by the use of repetition and symmetry, in fact underlines the spiritual kinship between Octave and Célio and their structural relationship in the play—they are sort of mirror images that reflect each other and two sides of the same soul—indeed, Musset's own—in reaction to the world (Sices 35).

In another conversation between Octave and his cousin Claudio, Musset's reliance on wordplay rather than acting and stage movement, displays an ironic twist:

OCTAVE:

> Ah! Cousin Claudio, vous êtes un beau juge; où allez-vous si vite?

CLAUDIO:

> Ou entendez-vous par là, seigneur Octave?

OCTAVE:

> I entends que vous êtes un podestat qui a de belles formes.

CLAUDIO:

> De langage ou de complexion?

OCTAVE:

> De langage, de langage. Votre robe est pleine d'éloquence, et vos bras sont deux charmantes parenthèses.

(II, vi)

As in the scene describing the traits of Octave and Célio, the humor and irony arise from the play of metaphor and meaning during the dialogue. Characterization as well as the plot are developed through such play of language—by Musset as well as characters in the play. Octave uses his witty and symbolic language to court Marianne in Célio's behalf, acting as the double of the latter, while this intrigue and illusion in fact produce comic effects, but also lead to the play's tragic ending. The duplicity of the signifying process reveals the fictionality of the play itself—it's a product of the author's wordplay. This irony is further complicated by the contrast of the use of language between male and female characters. While buffoonery and wit appear in conversations among male characters, lyricism typifies expressions of views of love and the admiration/criticism of the heroine in these two passages by Octave addressed to Marianne at different times:

> Vous êtes comme les roses du Bengale, Marianne, sans épine et sans parfum. . . . Qu'y trouvez-vous qui puisse vous blesser? Une fleur sans parfum n'en est pas moins belle; bien au contraire, ce sont les plus belles que Dieu a faites ainsi. . . .
>
> (II: iv)

> Elle n'en vaut ni plus ni moins. Elle sait qu'elle est bonne à boire et qu'elle est faite pour être bue. Dieu n'en a pas caché la source au sommet d'un pic inabordable, au fond d'une caverne profonde; il l'a suspendue en grappes dorées sur nos brillants coteaux. Elle est, il est vrai, rare et précieuse, mais elle ne défend pas qu'on l'approche. Elle se laisse voir aux rayons du soleil, et toute une cour d'abeilles et de frelons murmure autour d'elle matin et soir. Le voyageur dévoré de soif peut se reposer sous ses rameaux verts; jamais elle ne l'a laissé languir, jamais elle ne lui a refusé les douces larmes dont son cœur est plein. Ah! Marianne! C'est un don fatal que la beauté . . . puisse Célio vous oublier!
>
> (II: viii)

In the first passage, Octave uses a simple metaphor (roses of Bengal) to describe Marianne's beauty and indifferent attitude (without hate or love), while in the next, he not only uses much more complex and suggestive images, hinting at a contrast between the unapproachable Marianne and easily accessible good wine that quenches any thirsty and fatigued travelers, but he also presents bitter criticism of her beauty and indifference as a fatal attraction to Célio. On one hand, his descriptions flip back and forth between ambiguous compliments (without thorns/without perfume; nonetheless beautiful) and vigorous criticism (unlike thirst-quenching wine), for he only intends to court her on Célio's behalf, but his metaphors appear double-edged and even embarrassing, yet honest to Marianne. On the other hand, he also senses a potentially tragic outcome that will spring from their plot and genuinely hopes that Célio will simply forget her. The mixture of sensuality in his words and indifference in his intention produces a near comic oddity in a tragic triangular relationship between Célio, Marianne, and Octave. These images also disturb the flow of the plot, for their power of symbolism overshadows the story and heightens the contrast between Octave's strength and the passiveness of Marianne and Célio.

As with characterization, the treatment of love—the main theme in most of Musset's dramas—is in the same manner of wit and sarcasm. Some contemporaries might have viewed his treatment of love affairs as a cliché for the Romantic poetic ideal. However, the fact that he

wrote most of his plays in his early twenties when youthful passion and free imagination would dominate his writing distinguishes his style from that of the other Romantics. In fact, love relationships became the very source of his creativity and originality during this prolific period.[3] Shakespeare also served as an obvious inspiration for using love themes (intrigues, betrayals, and mismatches) combined with humor to create comic irony. However, Musset's love stories are never an *All's Well That Ends Well*. The audience's expectation of a happy ending in comedies is subverted by the bitter, even tragic denouement and the non-resolution of the plot: Célio dies believing that Octave has betrayed him, and the latter rejects Marianne's love only to confess to her that it was Célio who loved her; Fantasio's life is spared and freedom regained, but the ending is not the happy and predictable one of a romance between Fantasio and Esbeth; Lorenzo succeeds in assassinating Alexander, but falls victim to a hired killer; after an apparent reunion of Camille and Perdican in *On ne badine pas avec l'amour,* Camille abruptly bids farewell to Perdican upon Rosette's death. Musset toys with the very concept of comedy, using it as an antithetical term to undermine theatrical conventions and definition of the genre. Like most Romantic dramas, Musset's "comedies" are also full of intrigues, themes of revenge and betrayal, disguise or exchange of identities, but the subject of love is neither sublime nor trifling; instead, it is Musset's source of irony and illusion, for man's grotesque nature is brought forth in its forms of duplicity (jest, disguise, and concealment of intention) when man is trapped in love.

Musset's use of intrigue and disguise to confound dramatic illusion and reality complements the apparently superficial themes of love and complicates the fictive reality in the reader's reading process. The pride of Perdican and Camille conceals their true feelings for each other and motivates their role-playing in order to make the other suffer. Perdican delights in making others believe what is other than his true intention as he expresses to Rosette his determination to marry her against the wishes of his family and all the townspeople: "Je trouve plaisant qu'on dise que je ne t'aime pas quand je t'épouse" (III: vii). The irony of this statement lies in the fact that what Perdican is telling Rosette is but an intrigue to punish Camille, while the townspeople are right about his pretending to love Rosette. His initial satisfaction of misleading Camille and eventually his agony of losing her affection originate from this role-playing that not only conceals his true intention from others, but also confounds himself. Only toward the end does he realize that it is his pride that has led to all the pretense and misunderstanding between him and Camille:

> Orgueil, le plus fatal des conseillers humains, qu'es-tu venu faire entre cette fille et moi? . . . Elle aurait pu

m'aimer, et nous étions nés l'un pour l'autre; qu'es-tu venu faire sur nos lèvres, orgueil, lorsque nos mains allaient se joindre?

(III: viii)

However, as Perdican has always believed (or been tricked into believing by his pride?), he justifies vanity, revenge, and pride as but human nature: "Il a bien fallu que nous nous fissions du mal, car nous sommes des hommes" (387). Musset uses "pride" as the deciding factor to set up the role-playing parallel for both protagonists in developing the plot and to manipulate characterization. He turns it into a disguise to create a double illusion for the audience, making the role-playing a drama within the drama.

Another instance of disguise appears in the double-natured court jester in **Fantasio.** The intricate mixture of comic and serious elements in the fool's character provides the author a convenient means for manipulating the dramatic illusion through sporting with the meaning of words and appearances. While *The Arabian Nights* signifies to Fantasio magical transportation to fantasy lands to elude reality, he longs to discover interior reality of individuals concealed under their appearances:

Quelle admirable chose que les Mille et Une Nuits! Ô Spark! Mon cher Spark, si tu pouvais me transporter en Chine! Si je pouvais seulement sortir de ma peau pendant une heure ou deux! Si je pouvais être ce monsieur qui passe! . . . Je suis sûr que cet homme-là a dans la tête un millier d'idées qui me sont absolument étrangères; son essence lui est particulière. Hélas! Tout ce que les hommes se disent entre eux se ressemble; les idées qu'ils échangent sont presque toujours les mêmes dans toutes leurs conversations; mais, dans l'intérieur de toutes ces machines isolées, quels replis, quels compartiments secrets! C'est tout un monde que chacun porte en lui! Un monde ignoré qui naît et qui meurt en silence!

(I: ii)

Fantasio's desire to uncover what is truly inside every man's head is materialized through the ironic concealment of his own identity by disguising himself as the jester. The character of jester prescribes a double nature in his words and deeds and thus obscures others' vision in seeing his true intention: can he be only joking, or can he be serious? And in fact, most likely, the jester reveals truth through his jokes; thus the role of jester serves as a natural disguise of truth, and at the same time a means to discover truth. Fantasio provides an omniscient perspective in the development of the story and allows the reader/spectator to see the dramatic irony created through this very character.

Fantasio's playing the fool also raises a question about the act of representation for the character as well as for the author:

Quel métier délicieux que celui de bouffon! J'étais gris, je crois, hier soir, lorsque j'ai pris ce costume et que je me suis présenté au palais; mais, en vérité, jamais la saine raison ne m'a rien inspiré qui valût cet acte de folie.

(II: iii)

Is this monologue speaking only for Fantasio, or for the author as well? That is the question. Since most of Musset's plays were not staged till much later, this technique addresses the reader and his imaginative ability to paint a picture of the two realities—the fictional and the one disguised within the fictional. Like the fool in *King Lear,* Fantasio has the liberty to speak truth through jest or to joke in order to deceive. This self-reflexive disguise invites the audience/reader to investigate the nature of the narrative, or the illusion on the stage. It turns the play into a meta-theatre for the theatre, questioning the art of drama as a form of representation and expression through the character's very act of acting.

This (con)fusion of characters and realities leads further to a philosophical question about truth, about reason, and unreason. As in *King Lear,* the intermingling of truth and untruth, sanity and madness, reality and illusion, is presented through the character of the fool, whose profession as master of sarcastic wordplay and double identity as the king's jester and confidant best suit Musset's artistic intention in creating Romantic irony. Musset's use of disguised personalities (Octave acting on Célio's behalf as Marianne's suitor in order to win her hand for Célio, Fantasio as the clown to conceal his love for Elsbeth, Lorenzo in **Lorenzaccio** concealing his true self in order to gain the trust of the Duke— and even various male leads in his plays being played by actresses)[4]—reveals to the reader the very nature of theatre: reality depends on the manipulation of perspectives by the author as well as the reader's imaginative involvement in the viewing process. It is a technique of authorial control similar to that of the German ironist Ludwig Tieck. And as with Tieck, Musset's only option to create such drama is to free the dramatist from the physical restraints of the theatre. Only thus can drama express the self-reflexivity of Romantic irony to its fullest.

Notes

1. Lloyd Bishop comments that Hugo's heroes appear to be "mere antithesis, not ambivalence or paradox" as the dialectic prescribed in the "Preface" hoped to achieve (94).

2. W. D. Howarth points out that there is usually cynicism and idealism united in handling the dramatic situation with a bitter intensity that "seems to belie the label 'comédie' in Musset (Charlton 235-38). David Sices recounts the

numerous Romantic theoretical treatises and manifestos that call for a new theatre (Stendhal's *Racine et Shakespeare,* Hugo's "Preface to Cromwell," and Vigny's "Dernière nuit de travail"), and argues hat the dramatic works corresponding to these statements seldom live up to their promises due to practical theatre affairs. Lloyd Bishop criticizes Hugo's characters for lacking psychological depth in terms of his ideal of the grotesque/sublime paradox.

3. For instance, Octave's descriptions and praises of Marianne have an overtone of Musset's view of George Sand.

4. Although not prescribed by Musset, these male leads played by actresses became standard at the Comédie. Madame R. Debrou played Fortunio in the 1848 *Le Chandelier* at the Théâtre Historique, while in 1916 Mlle Piérat revived the tradition of the female Fortunio and became Comédie Française's first female Lorenzaccio. See Sices, 180.

Works Cited

Bishop, Lloyd. *Romantic Hero and His Heirs in French Literature.* New York: Peter Lang, 1984.

———. *The Poetry of Alfred de Musset: Styles and Genres.* New York: Peter Lang, 1987.

Charlton, D. G., ed. *The French Romantics.* Cambridge: Cambridge UP, 1984.

Daemmrich, I. G. "Alfred de Musset's View of the Poet." *Revue des Langues Vivantes* 39.1 (1973): 5-10.

Musset, Alfred de. *Théâtre complet.* Paris: Gallimard, 1958.

———. *Œuvres complètes en prose.* Paris: Gallimard, 1960.

Rees, Margaret A. *Alfred de Musset.* New York: Twayne, 1971.

Sices, David. *Theater of Solitude: the Drama of Alfred de Musset.* Hanover, NH.: UP of New England, 1974.

LES CAPRICES DE MARIANNE (1833)

CRITICAL COMMENTARY

Albert B. Smith (essay date fall-winter 1991-92)

SOURCE: Smith, Albert B. "Musset's *Les Caprices de Marianne:* A Romantic Adaptation of a Traditional Comic Structure." *Nineteenth-Century French Studies* 20, nos. 1-2 (fall-winter 1991-92): 53-64.

[*In the following essay, Smith discusses the ways in which the structure of Musset's play differs from that of traditional drama.*]

"The spontaneous loves of the Young, traversed by the Old, are aided and abetted by the Servants." Such is the formula by which E. J. H. Greene sums up one of the most common situations in comic drama since ancient times.[1] The situation was especially popular among French dramatists of the seventeenth and eighteenth centuries. Numerous authors of comedies played variations on the theme of the young couple in love forced to circumvent obstacles to their union posed by one of their elders. A frequent usage, as Greene amply emphasizes, has the young couple enlisting the aid of resourceful servants in order to gain their ends.

According to Greene, use of the tripartite formula died out in France toward the end of the eighteenth century, the role of the servants having lost its appeal (153). The traditional formulation of the comic conflict may indeed have ceased to be broadly popular, but this does not mean that French playwrights abandoned the structure altogether. A number of Romantic dramatists built plays on a conflict between old man and young lovers and not infrequently introduced characters who assumed the role of the wily servant: Dumas, in *Antony;* Hugo, in *Hernani,* and in the short play from *Théâtre en liberté, Mangeront-ils?* Gautier, in his little *commedia, Le Tricorne enchanté;* and Musset in **Les Caprices de Marianne.** These authors found in the structure an intertext that they could profitably exploit to express their particular perspectives on human relations. It is my intention here to study Alfred de Musset's use of the formula in **Les Caprices de Marianne.**[2]

The situation that Musset posits falls squarely into line with the comic structure studied by Greene. The older generation is represented by Claudio, the husband, cast in one of the conventional roles, that of a judge; the young are played by Claudio's wife, Marianne, and by Coelio. That Marianne has no interest in the overtures of a suitor might appear to be a retreat from the traditional formula, but it is not without precedent: Lucrezia, the young wife in Machiavelli's *La Mandragola,* is depicted at the beginning of the comedy as faithful and devout, much like Marianne. Nor is the assignment of the servant's role to Coelio's friend Octave an aberration. Menander, in his comedy *Dyskolos,* gives the responsibility for organizing the amorous strategy to the new-found friend of the young lover.

The dramatic situation that Musset presents thus takes its place in a long line of comedies exemplifying the standard tripartite comic structure. Indeed, all of the elements which Musset brings into play inform us that *Les Caprices de Marianne* will be a comedy like numerous others in the European repertory. The title suggests that at the very least the play will be light and frothy. The setting in "Naples," with the events of the first scene occurring in "une rue devant la maison de Claudio," could be the locale of any conventional Italianate comedy. Also signaling comedy is the hint that we are in the season of Carnival (I, i, 56). The names of certain characters also evoke the Italian comic tradition. Claudio and its augmentative Claudione are frequent names given in scenarios of the *commedia dell'arte* to older men on the verge of being cuckolded. Likewise, Octave is a common appellation assigned to young lovers in Italian comedy.[3] The role of Ciuta, the procuress in Musset's play, reinforces yet further the impression of comedy, and of coarse comedy to boot. Her name is the same as that of an ugly servant woman in a scurrilous story by Boccaccio (*Decameron* VIII, 4).[4]

Musset adds a turn of the screw by giving other characters names that recall comedies belonging to a different tradition, that of Shakespeare.[5] A young woman named Hermia figures in *A Midsummer Night's Dream*. A certain Malvolio appears in *Twelfth Night*. (Interestingly, he and Musset's character have similar roles and personalities; each is a sort of major domo, and each takes a dim view of what he considers inappropriate conduct in those around him.) Shakespeare introduces a Mariana in two of his comedies, *All's Well That Ends Well* and *Measure for Measure*. Orsini, the unhappy suitor in Hermia's *récit* of her youth, recalls another forlorn lover in Shakespeare, the Orsino of *Twelfth Night*. Even the prostitute whom Octave summons in II, i (75) has a namesake in Shakespeare: Rosalinde, the off-stage presence in *Les Caprices de Marianne,* is also the name of one of the principal female roles in Shakespeare's comedy *As You Like It.*

The dialogues which make up the early action of *Les Caprices de Marianne* confirm the impression of comedy. The flippancy of Octave's initial words to Coelio (I, i, 56) establish a humorous tone; while his mocking self-characterization as a social tightrope walker, nimbly managing his perilous role between creditors, disapproving relatives, and women of easy virtue (I, i, 57), can be seen at first as only frivolous. The exchange between Claudio and his valet Tibia at the beginning of the play (I, i, 54-55) reads much like those of any number of older comedies representing married men threatened with cuckoldry: Claudio, like his predecessors, talks of impudent serenades and the violent punishment of imagined lovers, while Tibia attempts to reassure him as to the virtuousness of Marianne (I, i 54-55).[6]

Even Coelio's expressions of melancholy and despair, which have led some readers to consider Musset's play

to be serious from the very beginning, are not without precedent in the comic tradition. Numerous lovers in Italianate comedy exaggeratedly detail their suffering and bemoan their sense of helplessness when forced to contemplate actually facing the object of their infatuation.[7]

A principal effect of Musset's initial treatment of his subject is thus to create in the reader the expectation that *Les Caprices de Marianne* will end in comedy just as it begins. The action, we believe, will proceed to a denouement typical of comedies participating in the traditional formula. Coelio will conquer his paralysis and, with the help of Octave, overcome the virtuous reserve of the young wife. He and Marianne will then at last be united, probably without the husband's knowledge, perhaps even like Machiavelli's lovers in *La Mandragola,* with his naive blessing.

Yet Musset shatters our expectations by having Coelio die a violent death at the hands of the husband's hired thugs and by leaving Octave empty and remorseful and Marianne facing a future of religious, social, and personal solitude. Why should the author have inflected the action of his "comedy" so that it veers to catastrophe and then to tragedy?

By and large, critics have interpreted *Les Caprices de Marianne,* despite its inclusion among the *Comédies et proverbes,* as a serious, if not "tragic," drama. They are undoubtedly correct in this view.[8] Yet attention to the problems of genre and of genre integrity posed by Musset's shift promises a clarification of the denouement essential for a full understanding of the play.[9]

Musset stands at the head of a group of Romantics who, disenchanted with the dramatic and theatrical usages of their time, attempted to renew French dramaturgy along lines which ran diametrically counter to prevailing contemporary practices, not only in tragedy and comedy but also in the *drame* and the *vaudeville.*[10] To offer an alternative to the ever greater prosaism that they considered was stifling the French theater, they sought inspiration in the comedies of Shakespeare, the *comédies romanesques* of French Baroque playwrights, and the *commedia dell'arte* and its French progeny.

It was Théophile Gautier who, shortly after the publication of Musset's first *spectacles dans un fauteuil,* articulated the new dramaturgy. In his novel, *Mademoiselle de Maupin,* and in his theater reviews for *La Presse,* Gautier promoted a type of drama that he called the *comédie romanesque,* far removed from the forms common in his day.[11] The *comédie romanesque* seeks full freedom from all conventions imposed by concern for realism or verisimilitude. Settings have no association with any place in the world, present or past, near or far. Costumes are thoroughly fanciful, evoking no recognizable historical or local dress. Sets and stage effects make no attempt to reproduce reality. Authors willfully transgress against geographical integrity and natural law. Characters have nothing of the individuality that would establish them as inhabitants of a particular country at a specific time. They represent types, drawn from the world of romance: lovers, maidens, kindly kings and nobles, simple peasants and servants.

Comédies romanesques break all of the conventional rules of plot development. The dramatic action displays little if any unity. Multiple plots, digressions, and loose structure are the rule. Superfluous characters are frequent, entering and exiting without motivation. The principle of cause and effect, that cornerstone of European dramaturgy, is abandoned. No attempt is made to organize the action in view of a reasonable denouement.

Gautier justifies the *théâtre romanesque* on the grounds that it represents fundamental truths of human nature. The characters and the events in which they participate symbolize the author's inner life; in them, he personifies, in Gautier's words, "sa joie, sa mélancolie, son amour et son rêve le plus intime."[12] But the *comédie romanesque* is not merely another exercise in Romantic solipsism. Every individual, according to Gautier, is a microcosm of all mankind: "Tout homme renferme en lui l'humanité entière; et, en écrivant ce qui lui vient à la tête, il réussit mieux qu'en copiant à la loupe les objets placés en dehors de lui" (*Mademoiselle de Maupin* 2: 102-103). The author's symbolic representation of his psyche will thus have universal applicability. It will, moreover, have infinitely greater value than any work whose interest stops at the prosaic surface of objects and of people.

The dramatic work which serves Gautier as the model of the *théâtre romanesque* is Shakespeare's comedy, *As You Like It,* a play in which French critics, steeped in tradition, found a certain charm, but major offenses to form and plausibility.[13] As for Musset, Gautier admired his early plays and recognized that they coincided perfectly with the concept of a *comédie romanesque.* He says of **Les Caprices de Marianne** that the play was conceived "dans la liberté toute Shakspearienne de la comédie romanesque; elle court où sa fantaisie l'emporte . . ."[14] Oddly enough—or perhaps not so oddly after all—in addition to similarities between Musset's play and the tri-partite comic formula, there is close resemblance between **Les Caprices de Marianne** and the comedy by Shakespeare that Gautier saw as the archetype of the *théâtre romanesque.* Along with a number of material parallels—ahistorical dramatic world, inverisimilitudes, unmotivated turns in the action—*As You Like It* and **Les Caprices de Marianne** share a common theme. It is this theme that I wish to address.

As You Like It has a multiplicity of plots, all of which turn on a single subject, love, represented in a variety of forms. Orlando's inspired passion for Rosalind goes side by side with Touchstone's sexual attraction to the country girl Audrey. Rosalind and Celia share a strong sisterly devotion; Orlando and the old servant Adam display a generous affection for one another that derives from long sufferings together; the friendship between the banished duke and his companions is warm and close; and the mutual love of Rosalind and her father never flags.

Love is the central motif in most of the speeches in *As You Like It.* Shakespeare has his characters evoke the different forms and phases of love, and he devotes considerable space to characterizations of love and its effects. We witness the birth of love in Orlando and Rosalind, the amorous suffering of the shepherd Silvius, forced to endure the repeated rebuffs of the frivolous Phebe, and Phebe's sudden pain when she herself comes to experience rejection. Rosalind reports on Celia's and Oliver's sudden love, giving a vivid characterization of the classic *coup de foudre.*

Love is shown as producing a diversity of reactions. The lover pining for his beloved avoids company, neglects his person and his dress, and goes about, as Jaques ironically puts it, "Sighing like a furnace, with a woeful ballad / Made to his mistress' eyebrow" (II, vii). The influence of hopeless love on Orlando is well known to readers of Shakespeare: the distraught youth spends his time carving Rosalind's name on the trees of the forest and writing poems of praise to her which he hangs on the branches. At the same time, he displays a love for his cruel brother Oliver that can only be termed heroic: he generously risks his life to protect the very person who has driven him from the family home and even sought to have him killed.

Orlando's act in fact epitomizes a lesson of love that is at the very base of *As You Like It:* love is essentially charitable. Even that love which appears selfish in demanding reciprocation—the love between man and woman—displays a strong element of generosity. Among the numerous characteristics of love that he calls up, Silvius, a sort of spokesman for Eros, includes faith and service (V, ii). He himself displays these very traits in his willingness to deliver a love letter from his beloved Phebe to Ganymede, the one person who appears to threaten his ever hopeful passion.

That all is not well in the dramatic world at the beginning of the play is due to the absence of generous love in some of the characters. The old duke lives in banishment cruelly ordered by his younger brother Frederick, who has usurped the ducal power. Rosalind lives on at the court, forcibly separated from her father; Duke Frederick harshly banishes her, too, thus threatening to separate her also from her beloved cousin Celia. Orlando must endure wretched material circumstances and the constant verbal abuse of his brother Oliver, who has selfishly defied the terms of their father's will and seized Orlando's share of the estate. Without love in some of the personages, disharmony characterizes the world of the play.

Comic harmony can come into being only when all of the characters join in a generosity guaranteed by true love. This requires a change of heart in some of the characters. Oliver undergoes a full moral metamorphosis on recognizing that he owes his life to Orlando. In gratitude uncommon in his character, he surrenders to his brother the entire family estate. Duke Frederick, on his way to the Forest of Arden to kill the banished duke and his companions, has a sudden religious experience that teaches him the value of charity, renounces his selfish ways, and restores the dukedom to its rightful ruler. With the resolution of the unhappy relations between the sets of brothers and the union of the different pairs of lovers, *As You Like It* takes its natural course to the traditional festive wedding of comedy, which represents the establishment of harmony in the dramatic world (Frye 163).

Though it might be considered redundant to emphasize that love is the theme also of **Les Caprices de Marianne,** we should not be too hasty in closing discussion on the subject. Critics are clearly justified in having concentrated on different forms of love among the main characters in the play; but their focus has prevented their seeing that Musset's perspective on love, like Shakespeare's, goes much farther than one or two associations. Some type of love is at the base of practically all the relations in **Les Caprices de Marianne.** Coelio's exalted passion for Marianne causes him to suffer suicidal despair when she rejects his overtures (I, i, 58-59, 60; II, i, 72; II, ii, 82-83) The close friendship between Coelio and Octave is comparable to few cases in literature. Each cares for the well-being of the other, and Octave especially is firm in his commitment to his friend (I, i, 61, 62; II, i, 71; II, iii, 89; II, vi, 94-95). Octave has other affections, also; and these represent yet another face of love. As a thoroughgoing rake, he pursues amorous relations that are purely materialistic transitory, and based on principles that can best be termed commercial (I, i, 60; II, i, 75). Claudio's relationship with his young wife is strictly proprietary. He shows no affection for Marianne, his chief concern being to protect his chattel and his honor (I, i, 54; I, iii, 70; II, iii, 84). Musset portrays Tibia and Malvolio as faithful and devoted to the interests of their respective employers, Claudio and Hermia. In Hermia, Musset represents a case of maternal love, peculiar for the strong incestuous note that one perceives in it (I, ii, 64-65)

Marianne's love is by far the most complex of all the forms represented in the play. As depicted at the beginning, she appears as more or less contented in the conjugal relationship that society has imposed upon her. It is impossible at first to determine whether she has any true affection for her husband (I, i, 63). Whether she does or not, she nevertheless accepts the situation that marriage to Claudio entails and she dutifully— perhaps even willingly—spurns the advances of would-be suitors (I, i, 63; I, iii, 69). Musset then shows the gradual development of her interest in Octave until, in not so veiled terms, she invites him to a rendezvous (II, iii, 88-89).

As in Shakespeare's play, so in Musset's, the factor that initially prevents harmony in the dramatic world is egoism. Egoism in **Les Caprices de Marianne** is universal. All of Musset's characters are motivated by the desire for self-satisfaction. We view Hermia as egoistic, wishing to maintain an intimate relation with her son, apparently more for her own pleasure than for his. Coelio, at bottom, cares for no one but himself. Nothing is so important as his desire, not even his sincere friendship for Octave. Indeed, he will use his relationship with Octave primarily as a means for gaining access to Marianne. Though one may sympathize with Marianne as regards her social situation—she is no more than chattel—one nevertheless is led to view her as egoistic, too. When she at last understands just what her conjugal— and social—position is (II, iii, 84-85) she decides to spite her husband by taking a lover. Whoever the lover may be is of small concern (II, iii, 86). If he happens to be attractive and witty, like Octave, so much the better. In the final analysis, he will be no more than an instrument. We understand that that kind of generosity in love which Shakespeare proposes in *As You Like It* is absent in Marianne. Even at the end of the play, when her interest in Octave has had time to grow, it is still in terms of her own happiness that she expresses herself: "Ne serait-elle point heureuse, Octave, la femme qui t'aimerait?" (II, vi, 94). The most openly egoistic character in **Les Caprices de Marianne** is Claudio. Like the traditional old man of comedy, with his enormous fear of what damage cuckoldry will cause to his public image, he makes clear that he will do whatever is necessary to protect his honor no matter the cost to others (II, iii, 84; II, vi, 91-93). Octave's character is less clear-cut. His relationship with Coelio is of course governed by generosity; on the other hand, he is proud. Even though he may wish to serve Coelio, at the same time he considers his task a challenge to his ingenuity and his powers of persuasion (II, i, 71-72). In serving Coelio, he is serving his own pride. In his relationships with women, Octave is thoroughly callous, considering them only as material for male gratification. Rosalinde, he says, *serves* him as a mistress (II, i, 79). His well known comparison of woman with a bottle of wine— even one of outstanding quality—further reveals his egoism. He conceives that the bottle holds a substance created to give momentary pleasure to the drinker who, having consumed the contents, sees no more value in the container (II, i, 81). Woman also is a vessel that promises pleasure. She has value only as a means for satisfying the man's desire. Having served her purpose, she may be cast away, while the man seeks another object of gratification.

These characters are, moreover, so set in their egoism that they cannot—or will not—change. This is a major point in Musset's play. In *As You Like It,* Shakespeare demonstrates how change in favor of generosity in love brings about the universally happy resolution of the dramatic action and the establishment of comic harmony. Such change appears as impossible for any of the characters in **Les Caprices de Marianne.** The unexpected denouement is indeed tragic and inevitable.

Though Musset might have chosen another dramatic configuration by which to represent questions of love, the traditional tripartite comic formula was a particularly happy discovery. With its basic form, the structure allowed him to treat a network of relationships embodied by Claudio, Coelio, and Marianne. Giving Octave the role of the resourceful servant enabled him to add further dimension to his study, here, of love in the form of friendship between the two young men. The extraordinary introduction of Hermia permitted him to represent yet another type of intimate relationship, one with which we are all familiar.

The formula also presented a perfect structure for a message only part of which has been recognized. We may easily agree with all of those readers who find the tragic denouement plausible; and we may readily find the cause of the tragedy in pride or selfishness, which render the conflict unresolvable. Yet we need to recognize the additional dimension inhering in the action of the play: the meaning that resides in Musset's use of the traditional comic structure and in his implicit invitation to recall the comedies of Shakespeare. That the initial situation in **Les Caprices de Marianne** is comic tells us that the action of the play is amenable to a happy resolution. As we learn from *As You Like It*— from most comedies, for that matter—such an outcome would require a change of temperament in the characters, each adopting a more charitable outlook toward the others. Musset's play also, then, leads us to recognize the desirability of unselfishness in human relations. It suggests what degree of social harmony could be achieved if the characters—representative of all humankind, as Gautier indicated—were willing and able to change.

Musset, as a man of his time, wrote a great deal on the subject of change. A sudden shift in outlook in the protagonist permits the happy ending of **La Nuit véniti-**

enne. The question of political progress is at the very heart of **Lorenzaccio.** A major concern in the series of poems, "Les Nuits," is the personal maturation of the "poet." In these and other works, change in the direction of generosity may be recognized as eminently desirable. Musset's fundamental pessimism—not unlike that of Shakespeare's Jaques—caused him to view the question usually in a negative perspective, emphasizing that beneficial change was unlikely and representing, as in **Les Caprices de Marianne,** cases in which failure to change leads to catastrophe.

Notes

1. *Menander to Marivaux: The History of a Comic Structure* (Edmonton: University of Alberta Press, 1977) 2. Greene takes his cue from Northrop Frye, who calls attention to the origin of the structure in Greek New Comedy and suggests that it forms the basis for most comedy. See *Anatomy of Criticism* (Princeton: Princteon University Press, 1957) 163.

2. I use the edition prepared by P.-G. Castex (Paris: CDU/SEDES, 1978). Castex reproduces the text published in *Comédies et proverbes* (Paris: Charpentier, 1840), which follows almost to the letter the original of May 5, 1833, in the *Revue des Deux Mondes.* I agree with Castex that this early version is preferable to the recasting that Musset effected for the production of *Les Caprices* in 1851. The reworking contains changes that reduce the pungency of the play, to make it compatible with the rigors of contemporary censorship and the requirements of contemporary staging.

3. For parallels, see François et Claude Parfaict, *Histoire de l'ancien théâtre italien depuis son origine en France jusqu'à sa suppression en 1697* (Paris: Rozet, 1767; rpt. New York: AMS Press, 1978) 55-56, 132; and *Scenarios of the Commedia dell'Arte: Flaminio Scala's "Il Teatro delle favole rappresentative,"* tr. Henry F. Salerno, foreword by Kenneth McKee (New York: New York University Press, London: University of London Press, Ltd., 1967) 249-257, 275.

4. Some of these associations—and others—have been emphasized by scholars since Léon Lafoscade first traced influences on Musset. See Lafoscade, *Le Théâtre d'Alfred de Musset* (Paris: Hachette, 1901; rpt. Paris: Nizet, 1966), and Simon Jeune, "Souffles étrangers et inspiration personnelle dans *Les Caprices de Marianne,*" *RSH* 121 (janvier-mars 1966): 81-96, to cite only those principally concerned with sources. Others note recollections of traditional comedy in *Les Caprices,* but make no point of their function. See Herbert S. Gochberg, *Stage of Dreams: The Dramatic Art of Alfred de Musset (1828-1834)* (Genève: Droz, 1967) 136; David Sices, *Theater*

of Solitude: The Drama of Alfred de Musset (Hanover, N.H.: University Press of New England, 1974) 27, 57.

Ruth Amossy et Elisheva Rosen (*Carnaval et comédie dans "Les Caprices de Marianne" de Musset,* Archives des Lettres Modernes, 173 [Paris: Minard, 1977], 21) relate *Les Caprices* particularly to the *commedia dell'arte* and, more generally, to Carnival, which institutionalized the belief in social regeneration through general licence and riot. Musset's use of the *commedia* structure, for these readers, is not gratuitous, as will become clear below.

5. Lafoscade (72) and Jeune (82) point to a number of Shakespearean reminiscences in *Les Caprices de Marianne,* some of which I note here. Cecil Malthus, in a posthumously published book, argues that many situations, speeches, and characterizations in *Les Caprices* have more than coincidental parallels in Shakespeare. See *Musset et Shakespeare: étude analytique de l'influence de Shakespeare sur le théâtre d'Alfred de Musset,* ed. Rex A. Barrell. American University Studies, Series II: Romance Languages and Literature, Vol. 62 (New York, Bern, Frankfurt am Main, Paris: Peter Lang, 1988): 137-150, 185-195, 240-243. Malthus shows no interest in structural or genre questions, so is of little interest for my ultimate purposes here.

6. For an example of an earlier comedy, see in *Scenarios of the Commedia dell'Arte* "The Jealous Old Man," 47-54.

7. See Parfaict, *Ancien théâtre italien,* 132. The example is from the *commedia* scenario entitled "La Double Jalousie," of 1667. Margaret A. Rees's suggestion that *Les Caprices de Marianne* is of a single serious piece from the opening scene and thus displays perfect dramatic unity fails to take into consideration Musset's invitation to view the play at first as a comedy. Her view of the play is possible only when one considers the action retrospectively. See her *Alfred de Musset* (New York: Twayne, 1971) 101. It should be clear that I am approaching the play from the opposite direction.

8. For some, *Les Caprices de Marianne* represents an indictment of an inflexible social order, which defeats any individual attempt at freedom and fulfillment. Others find the tragedy in a failure of communication among individuals governed by pride and selfishness. Still others see in the play a regretful comment on modern men's ability to achieve a unified personality.

To the first group belong Gochberg, *Stage of Dreams;* Eric L. Gans, *Musset et le "drame tragique": essai d'analyse paradoxale* (Paris: Corti, 1974); Amossy and Rosen, *Carnaval et*

comédie; and Bernard Masson, "Le Masque, le double et la personne dans quelques *Comédies et proverbes,*" *RSH* 108 (octobre-décembre 1962): 551-571.

The second group of critics includes Gustave Michaut, *Pascal, Molière, Musset: essais de critique et de psychologie* (Paris: Alsatia [1942] after original publication in 1908) 200-216; Sices, *Theater of Solitude,* 52-53 (Sices also discusses the attack on social structures in the play); W. D. Howarth, "Comedy," in *Comic Drama: The European Heritage* (New York: St. Martin's Press, 1978) 117.

The third group of critics is represented by Maurice Allem, ed., *Théâtre complet,* Bibliothèque de la Pléiade (Paris: Gallimard, 1958) 1321; Rees, *Alfred de Musset,* 120; René Bourgeois et Jean Mallion, eds., *Le Théâtre au XIXe siècle* (Paris: Masson, 1971) 117; and Andreas Forrer, "Zwei Ausdrucksformen der romantischen Seele in *Les Caprices de Marianne,*" in his *Spaltung und Doppelung: Momente eines literarischen Motives* (Zürich: Juris Druck, 1977) 83-89.

9. In what dramatic genre to situate the play has naturally interested critics, but the problem remains unresolved—probably unresolvable. See Michaut, *Pascal, Molière, Musset;* Lafoscade, *Le Théâtre d'Alfred de Musset;* Arthur Tilley, *Three French Dramatists: Racine, Marivaux, Musset* (Cambridge: Cambridge University Press, 1933); Maurice Allem, *Alfred de Musset,* éd. revue et corrigée (Grenoble et Paris: Arthaud, 1947), and notes to his edition of Musset's *Théâtre complet,* 1321; Rees, *Alfred de Musset;* Bourgeois et Mallion, eds., *Le Théâtre au XIXe siècle;* Lucienne Ngoué, "Pour une étude dramatique des *Caprices de Marianne,*" *Annales de la Faculté des Lettres et Sciences Humaines de l'Université de Yaoundé* 2.5 (1973): 59; Gans, *Musset et le "drame tragique;"* and Sices, *Theater of Solitude.*

Amossy and Rosen, as already mentioned in note 4, recognize that the structure of Musset's play has a number of parallels with that of the *commedia dell'arte.* They recognize further, as I do, that the play's divergence from the model is unusual. Their article, "La Comédie 'romantique' et le carnaval: *La Nuit des rois* et *Les Caprices de Marianne,*" *Littérature* 16 (décembre 1974): 37-49, encapsulates their view. Musset's play resembles the comic form which Northrop Frye identifies as a representation of social renewal through carnivalesque licence and confusion. Traditional comedy depicts the transformation of a rigid, repressive society into a new, harmonious social order through the unrestrained action of carnivalesque characters. Such is the case in Shakespeare's *Twelfth Night.* Amossy and Rosen interpret Musset's deviation from this tradition thus:

Musset is reaffirming his hopelessness in regard to social change. The alienating social order ends by suppressing all attempts to effect change. I agree, of course, that Musset breaks with tradition; and I find Amossy and Rosen's explanation plausible. That my perspective and reading differ from theirs simply confirms the rich signifying potential of *Les Caprices de Marianne.*

10. The following statement by Musset gives a fair idea of his attitude toward the dramatic production of his day: "Je conviendrais tant qu'on voudra qu'on trouvera aujourd'hui sur la scène les événements les plus invraisemblables . . . un luxe de décoration inouï et inutile, des acteurs qui crient à tue-tête, un bruit d'orchestre infernal, en un mot—des efforts monstrueux, désespérés, pour éveiller notre indifférence et qui n'y peuvent réussir." Cited by Amossy and Rosen in *Carnaval et comédie,* 69.

11. Gautier uses both *romanesque* and *fantasque* to qualify the type of theater which he favors. *Fantasque* is the more general term, including the *romanesque* and examples of the *commedia dell'arte.* For a full treatment of the genre, see my articles, "*Mademoiselle de Maupin,* Chapter XI: Plot, Character, Literary Theory," *KRQ* 25 (1978): 250-252; and "Fantasque: A Romantic Dramaturgy of Fantasy," *RQ* 34 (1987): 443-453.

12. *Mademoiselle de Maupin* (Paris: Renduel, 1835-1836) 2: 102-103.

13. See, for example, François Guizot, *Shakespeare et son temps: étude littéraire* (Paris: Didier, 1852) 74-92; George Sand, letter to M. Régnier of the Comédie Française, dated April 10, 1856, and published at the head of her adaptation of Shakespeare, *Comme il vous plaira, Théâtre complet* (Paris: Calmann-Lévy, 1876) 5: 111-122. Sand emphasizes that, though she found great charm in the play, she considered herself obliged to reorganize the "untidy" action so as to make Shakespeare's vision accessible to French *raison* (119).

14. *Histoire de l'art dramatique en France depuis vingt-cinq ans* (Bruxelles: Hetzel, 1858-1859) 6: 240-241. Gautier's statement appeared originally in a theater review published in *La Presse* in 1851.

FANTASIO (1834)

CRITICAL COMMENTARY

Herbert S. Gochberg (essay date 1967)

SOURCE: Gochberg, Herbert S. "*Spectacle dans un Fauteuil,* Act III. *Fantasio.*" In *Stage of Dreams: The Dramatic Art of Alfred de Musset,* pp. 149-67. Geneva, Switzerland: Librairie Droz S.A., 1967.

[*In the following excerpt, Gochberg presents the context of Musset's writing of* Fantasio.]

There is an interval of almost nine months between the publication of **Les Caprices de Marianne** (May 15, 1833) and that of **Fantasio** (January 1, 1834). The gap corresponds neatly to a change in Musset's personal life, for it was shortly after the publication of **Les Caprices de Marianne** that Musset first met George Sand. By the time **Fantasio** appeared in the *Revue des Deux Mondes,* Musset and his mistress were in Venice, nearing the end of the happy phase of their romance. The exact time and circumstances of the execution of **Fantasio** are not known, and the best guess is that it was written toward the end of 1833.

While the play's origin remains uncertain,[1] it is still possible to account for its creation in a period which is otherwise marked by a cessation of professional activity. The only work which Musset published between **Les Caprices de Marianne** and **Fantasio** is the long narrative poem *Rolla* (*Revue des Deux Mondes,* August 15, 1833). His only other work is a group of about a dozen poems, all published posthumously.[2] These poems are either expressions of his love for George Sand, or comic vehicles dealing with diverse Romantic personalities. Both types were intended initially for the private enjoyment of the two principals. Thus, to any one who might, in 1833, have been following Musset's career, it would have seemed that he had become distinctly less prolific, with *Rolla* serving as an isolated interruption of an otherwise sustained period of silence. What actually happened, as the evidence indicates, was that Musset withdrew provisionally and voluntarily from the theater of his dreams in order to celebrate the happy actuality of his liaison.

Rolla can be readily linked to the previous narrative and dramatic works, as well as to **Fantasio.** It was begun shortly after **Les Caprices de Marianne,** and was probably completed before Musset's involvement with George Sand, although the date of publication follows by a few weeks the consummation of their relationship. The morbid tone of *Rolla* negates the likelihood that any part of it could have been conceived in the bliss of Musset's first serious commitment to love. *Rolla* presents the reader with a strange amalgam, having at its heart the story of a *débauché* who, after exhausting the family fortune, purchases with his last bit of cash a night of *ivresse* in the bed of a youthful prostitute (Marion *alias* Marie) and then fulfils an earlier threat of suicide by swallowing poison. The narrative winds deviously through patches of effusion, regrets of time past, and bouts of *mal du siècle.* The poem enshrines futility, even to the point of the hero's suicide. At the same time, the work is a repository for old images and ideas: absence of God, awakening to reality, love leading to death, specters and phantoms, the disgust felt for habit and convention, the mask worn by the living, the salute to liberty, the apotheosis of true love, and the impossibility of changing the course of destiny.

While the brooding darkness of *Rolla* clashes vividly with the fragile gaiety of **Fantasio,** it is not difficult to isolate the trait which binds the two works. Like Rafael, Razetta, and Octave before him, Rolla belongs to the class of "mauvais sujets," for he is described as "le plus grand débauché" of Paris. He is impatient, easily bored, a drinker and a gambler, a creature living for the moment, following the dictates of whim and passion. In rounding out his description, Musset writes:

> Il avait de son bien mangé plus de moitié.
> En sorte que Rolla, par un beau soir d'automne,
> Se vit à dix-neuf ans maître de sa personne,—
> Et n'ayant dans la main ni talent ni métier.
> Il eût trouvé d'ailleurs tout travail impossible;
> Un gagne-pain quelconque, un métier de valet,
> Soulevait sur sa lèvre une rire inextinguible.
>
> [*Poésies*, p. 276.]

Like Rolla, Fantasio is bored and disoriented. His friend Spark calls him a "désœuvré," and Fantasio himself realizes that "Il n'y a point de maître d'armes mélancolique" (**Théâtre,** p. 285). Fantasio lives from one moment to the next on his wits and on his imagination. Nothing is planned; his every act is an improvisation. Society nags at him in the guise of creditors who demand his imprisonment, but Fantasio, merely by being himself, succeeds in finding an escape, and even manages to bring the established social order to a complete halt, creating "good" out of his uselessness.

Fantasio has no real problems of his own to resolve. In fact, the entire play is characterized by the absence of the kinds of problems which have dominated the earlier works. There are no characters who have to face their destinies, no love, no jealousy, no vengeance, no death, and, finally, no meaningful attempt to rebel against society. The fantasy world of **Fantasio** is pointless by conventional standards, but it is also a place of gaiety and contentment, and its unique conflicts are easily resolved according to criteria which exist nowhere but within the play. In this sense, the play is definitely singular in conception. The absence of conventional dramatic or artistic problems, however, is not remarkable when we regard **Fantasio** as a manifestation of Musset's *état d'âme*. At no other time in his life was Musset so happy as he was when he wrote **Fantasio.** At a time when he had apparently found the fulfillment of his ideals of love and destiny, there was naturally no motivation to elaborate in his work problems which had seemingly ceased to exist. **Fantasio** is a light-hearted comedy-dream, in which, for once, everything works out for the best, in which there are no barriers to stop dreams from being realized.

In spite of the singularity of **Fantasio,** in spite of its lack of typical problems, it is still a comedy, with a perceptible dramatic organization. Musset re-employs, in fact, the two-act format which worked so successfully for **Les Caprices de Marianne.** The play is set in Munich, but once again the geographical background is unimportant. The action is so fanciful that it could have been set anywhere, or for that matter, nowhere at all. As in **Les Caprices de Marianne,** the first act deploys the various characters as they *are,* and the second act serves as a medium for the shaping of an event brought about by interlocking *actions* or *acting.* The principal character of **Les Caprices de Marianne,** namely Octave, assumes a role which is partially in conflict with his given character, contributing thereby to the unhappy dénouement. Fantasio assumes a role which is fully consistent with his known character, and *because* he behaves like himself, he brings about a happy outcome.

The comedy of **Fantasio** springs first of all from the character of the same name. The restless, debt-ridden "mauvais sujet" plays the role of a jaded youth who appears to have run out of tricks. His wit and his drinking insulate him against despair. Normally, he would resolve the problems of his creditors by avoiding his own doorstep. Toward the end of the first act, however, a passing burial party serves to remind Fantasio and his clique that the court jester Saint-Jean has expired and that his post is vacant. Fantasio quickly arranges things so that he can replace Saint-Jean, thereby finding a refuge from his creditors and providing himself, at the same time, with a self-made invitation to the wedding of the princess Elspeth and the crown prince of Mantua. To fit himself out as the new *bouffon,* Fantasio has a tailor manufacture for him a wig of red hair and a hump for his back, both emblematic of the late Saint-Jean. Once accepted inside the palace, Fantasio learns that the princess is secretly miserable about her forthcoming marriage. The marriage has been arranged to satisfy the needs of state and to put an end to the war between the king of Bavaria (Elspeth's father) and the Mantuan prince. Elspeth is dutiful, but sad, because it has been rumored that the prince is stupid and unattractive, whereas she has been brought up by her *gouvernante* to expect from life a kind of Prince Charming. Fantasio gets drunk in a pantry, and as the prince's entourage passes by outside, he fishes up the prince's ceremonial wig. The insulted prince cancels the wedding, leaves the palace, and goes off to resume the war. Fantasio is rewarded with a cash gift and with the unlimited opportunity to return to the palace whenever he has the urge to flee his creditors. The king is happy because his wish for his daughter's happiness is fulfilled. Elspeth is happy because she can continue to dream on about an unreal prince. Fantasio is happy because he has earned a perpetual escape from the normally inescapable realities of his "worthless" existence. The requirements of the social order—satisfaction of debts, marriage of convenience, negotiations for truce—are obviously jettisoned to lighten the burden of reality. For once, the dreamers are the winners.

When we examine more carefully the principal role, we realize that the assumption of a disguise is not accompanied by any shift in character. To be sure, Fantasio adopts the external marks of Saint-Jean, but this neither alters him nor does it fool any one, for the court knows that Saint-Jean is dead. More significant, however, is the fact that Fantasio was himself a *bouffon* long before he assumed the disguise. Throughout the first act, Fantasio's behavior is precisely that of a fool or jester. His conversation moves wittily, and often incoherently, from one trivial subject to another, providing a stream of cerebral amusement for his companions (Spark, Facio, and Hartman). When he dons the garb of Saint-Jean, he is merely moving from one milieu (the street) to another (the royal court), adopting in the transfer a suitable symbol of his character, as it already *is*. Since he is already a clown, he assumes the one and only *métier* which suits him perfectly. As Fantasio, his horizons are limited by the harassment of reality. Fantasio-Saint-Jean, however, is endowed with unlimited freedom and with the power to make dreams come true.

Musset enriches the action with the contrapuntal development of the prince and his aide, Marinoni. Just before reaching the palace, the prince decides to switch roles with his aide, in order to observe furtively his future wife. The prince indicates that he has been nursing this dream for a long time. Unfortunately, the prince is not a dreamer. He is clumsy, inept, snobbish, and unimaginative. He is incapable of playing the role of an aide and, "loup devenu berger," continues to act like a conventional prince. Marinoni, on the other hand, plays his assigned role rather well and is accepted by the Bavarians as the prince. In fact, the prince's ineptness is itself a contributing cause of the broken marriage contract, for as an *aide de camp,* he behaves in such an obnoxious manner as to make the king uncomfortable about the whole affair. When Fantasio adds the final touch of filching the prince's wig, it is actually the wig worn by the masquerading Marinoni which flies into the air. It is the prince, however, who feels the insult, for it might have been *his* wig. The difference between the disguise of Fantasio and that of the prince is at the heart of Musset's counterpoint. Fantasio succeeds because he is perfectly cast in his second role; the prince fails because he has miscast himself. Even the two wigs are embodied symbolically within the texture of the play. The lifting of the prince's wig leads to the unmasking of its owner and to his decision to leave the inhospitable atmosphere of the palace. For the sake of form, the wig-pincher Fantasio spends a moment or two in a prison cell, for the king had to convince the prince that there would be some punishment for the malefac-

tor. When Elspeth learns that the counterfeit Saint-Jean has been imprisoned, she and her *gouvernante* pay him a visit. They find him asleep, with his disguise removed. For a moment, as the two dreamy women gaze upon the countenance of young Fantasio, they are convinced that he is the real prince of Mantua, for they had learned a few minutes earlier of the prince's masquerade. The removal of Fantasio's wig results not in an immediate revelation of identity, but in a supreme fugue of fantasy, during which the romantic imaginations of the two ladies run wild. Fantasio wakes up, and quickly disabuses the dreamers. The very idea of being taken for a prince frightens him. He wants only to be himself, and, in the end, his desire will be fulfilled. The gift of the princess frees him from having to worry about his lack of profession. He insists, however, on preserving his state of perpetual indebtedness:

Fantasio:

> J'aime ce métier plus que tout autre; mais je ne puis faire aucun métier. Si vous trouvez que cela vaille vingt mille écus de vous avoir débarrassée du prince de Mantoue, donnez-les-moi, et ne payez pas mes dettes. Un gentilhomme sans dettes ne saurait où se présenter. Il ne m'est jamais venu à l'esprit de me trouver sans dettes.

Elspeth:

> Eh bien! je te les donne; mais prends la clef de mon jardin: le jour où tu t'ennuieras d'être poursuivi par tes créanciers, viens te cacher dans les bluets où je t'ai trouvé ce matin; aie soin de prendre ta perruque et ton habit bariolé; ne parais pas devant moi sans cette taille contrefaite et ces grelots d'argent; car c'est ainsi que tu m'as plu: tu redeviendras mon bouffon pour le temps qu'il te plaira de l'être, et puis tu iras à tes affaires. Maintenant tu peux t'en aller, la porte est ouverte.

> [Pp. 322-323.]

Thus, Fantasio will be perpetually able to glide between two realms, having nothing to fear from either. If his reality bores or harasses him, he need only open the gate to the palace garden and pass instantly into the freedom of fantasy.

The possibility of the happy, but asocial ending of the play is very carefully planted from the very beginning. The reader learns immediately of the princess' imminent marriage, and more significantly, of her father's concern for her emotional well-being. When the king asks his secretary, Rutten, to tell him how Elspeth feels, Rutten replies: "Il m'a paru que le visage de la princesse était voilé de quelque mélancolie. Quelle est la jeune fille qui ne rêve pas la veille de ses noces? La mort de Saint-Jean l'a contrariée" (p. 278). Subsequent developments will reveal that the princess is indeed dreaming, but not for the reasons suggested by Rutten. The alleged sadness over the death of the jester will be dissipated later, along with all other sadnesses, as Saint-Jean returns to "life," in the form of Fantasio.

The king cannot understand how the death of the infirm Saint-Jean can possibly inspire sadness. Rutten affirms simply that the princess "l'aimait." This cursory testimony and the fanciful interlude in which Elspeth mistakes Fantasio for the prince are the only elements of the play in which we encounter anything remotely definable as a love interest. In neither instance is the love "real," nor does it resemble the relationships which have flourished (and usually failed) in Musset's other works. Elspeth's fondness for Saint-Jean derives from his *bouffonerie*. Although he is dead, his image lives on forever in the character of Fantasio, and Elspeth's attachment to her *bouffon* becomes a sustaining device throughout the play. When Elspeth sees the real countenance and form of Fantasio, and attributes nobility to them, she is merely perceiving according to the dictates of her fancy, which, along with her novel-reading *gouvernante,* has prepared her for the advent of an "Amadis" or a "Lindor." The fact that these two aspects of love follow the Saint-Jean-Fantasio thread of the plot is suggestive, for it points at once to the confusion as well as to the separateness of Fantasio's role. He is Saint-Jean, whom Elspeth loved and he is Fantasio, who resembles the ideal prince whom Elspeth has loved in her dreams. In the second act, Elspeth declares that her fondness for Saint-Jean was due to his "perpétuelle moquerie de mes idées romanesques" (p. 298). It is only when Fantasio removes his disguise that he becomes, for an instant, a part of these "idées romanesques." As soon as Elspeth has been disabused, she thanks Fantasio for having kept her little world intact, but will welcome him back only on condition that he inhabit it as Saint-Jean. The "prince" Fantasio must not intrude.

As the first scene continues to take shape, the king questions his secretary about the appearance and character of his prospective son-in-law, whom he has not yet met. Rutten fails to provide a direct response to the king's questions, and the king becomes concerned, at this late date, about the rightness of his choice. When all Rutten can say is "le prince passe pour le meilleur des rois," the king condemns politics, and elevates personal happiness above all else: "La politique est une fine toile d'araignée, dans laquelle se débattent bien des pauvres mouches mutilées; je ne sacrifierai le bonheur de ma fille à aucun intérêt" (p. 278). In the initial dialogue of the play, therefore, the reader-spectator has before him the contours of the situation into which Fantasio is going to stumble. Saint-Jean is dead, the princess is unhappy, something is wrong in Mantua, and the king is at heart an unstatesmanlike hedonist.

The second scene begins with Spark, Hartman, and Facio, drinking at a streetside table, within sight of the palace. They are awaiting Fantasio, so that the four of them can go off into the night and celebrate the wedding of the princess. Their idea of amusement is to "éteindre quelques lampions sur de bonnes têtes de bourgeois" (p. 279). An officer of the palace approaches them and asks them to muffle their revelry, for the princess is taking a breath of air on her balcony, and it would not be seemly for the noise to intrude upon her royal meditations. Hartman and Facio protest, but Spark observes: "Si elle ne veut pas qu'on rie, c'est qu'elle est triste, ou qu'elle chante; laissons-la en repos" (p. 280). At this very moment, Fantasio's cronies are interrupted by Marinoni, who has been sent out among the townspeople to record opinions about the princess. Marinoni's inquiries parallel those of the king in the preceding scene. Here, however, the situation is farcical, as the following exchange demonstrates:

MARINONI:

Ah! ah! c'est une belle femme, à ce que je présume?

HARTMAN:

Comme vous êtes un bel homme, vous l'avez dit.

MARINONI:

Aimée de son peuple, si j'ose dire, car il me paraît que tout es illuminé.

HARTMAN:

Tu ne te trompes pas, brave étranger, tous ces lampions allumés que tu vois, comme tu l'as remarqué sagement, ne sont pas autre chose qu'une illumination.

MARINONI:

Je voulais demander par là si la princesse est la cause de ces signes de joie.

HARTMAN:

L'unique cause, puissant rhéteur. Nous aurions beau nous marier tous, il n'y aurait aucune espèce de joie dans cette ville ingrate.

MARINONI:

Heureuse la princesse qui sait se faire aimer de son peuple!

HARTMAN:

Des lampions ne font pas le bonheur d'un peuple, cher homme primitif. Cela n'empêche pas la susdite princesse d'être fantasque comme une bergeronnette.

MARINONI:

En vérité! vous avez dit fantasque?

HARTMAN:

Je l'ai dit, cher inconnu, je me suis servi de ce mot.

[Pp. 280-281.]

Marinoni's feeling of satisfaction is broken by the word "fantasque," just as the king's contentment is shattered by the reticence of his secretary. Within Hartman's sharp retorts, one can see the denial of any relationship between the state and the happiness of the princess. This denial is appropriate, for it corresponds to the reversal of social values which characterizes the entire play.[3]

Finally, the eagerly awaited leader, Fantasio, makes his entrance. His friends are positive that there is "quelque lubie" ripening in his brain. They are wrong, for Fantasio appears to be completely disoriented and has no desire to partake in the frolics of his companions. The key to Fantasio's behavior is boredom: "Ma tête est comme une vieille cheminée sans feu: il n'y a que du vent et des cendres. Ouf! (*Il s'assoit.*) Que cela m'ennuie que tout le monde s'amuse!" (p. 282). Fantasio makes a counter-suggestion: ". . . restons un peu ici à parler de choses et d'autres, en regardant nos habits neufs" (p. 283). Facio and Hartman are not attracted by the lacklustre idea, and go off on their own, leaving Spark to keep Fantasio company. Fantasio flits in his conversation from one subject to another, often not even responding directly to Spark's cues. First, he is disappointed in the sunset; then, he tells Spark that his company is tiresome; then, he starts, with no apparent stimulus, to praise the *Thousand and One Nights*. "Si je pouvais seulement sortir de ma peau pendant une heure ou deux!" (p. 284). Here, at least, there is a dramatic responsiveness, for Fantasio's craving for a world of fantasy will be realized in short order. Spark listens patiently, all the while urging Fantasio to keep drinking. Fantasio mentions his creditors and the threat of imprisonment. Again, there is preparation at work, for Fantasio will in fact end up in a jail cell, if only temporarily. When Spark offers money to his friend, he receives this response: "Imbécile! si je n'avais pas d'argent, je n'aurais pas de dettes" (p. 285). This is the essentially same kind of response with which he will greet Elspeth's offer to discharge his indebtedness.

At this point in the exchange between Spark and Fantasio, the latter states gratuitously that he would like to "prendre pour maîtresse une fille d'opéra." Spark assures his friend that such an enterprise would only bore him "à périr." Fantasio contradicts the assertion: "Pas du tout; mon imagination se remplira de pirouettes et de souliers de satin blanc; il y aura un gant à moi sur la banquette du balcon depuis le premier janvier jusqu'à la Saint-Sylvestre, et je fredonnerai des solos de clarinette dans mes rêves, en attendant que je meure d'une indigestion de fraises dans les bras de ma bien-aimée" (p. 285). Fantasio is not verbalizing his desire as such, but is demonstrating that his boredom is related to the lack of a medium in which his imagination can flourish. It is not a "fille d'opéra" which he craves, but the free play of musings and imaginings which would color the reality of a relationship. Fantasio jumps from his "indigestion de fraises" to the observation that he and Spark have no "état," no professional affiliation, and

that "Il n'y a point de maître d'armes mélancolique." Spark pinpoints Fantasio's boredom by observing: "Tu me fais l'effet d'être revenu de tout." Fantasio's reply: "Ah! pour être revenu de tout, mon ami, il faut être allé dans bien des endroits" (p. 286). Fantasio then expresses the thought that there is or seems to be nothing left for him to explore. He is bored with the physical world around him, but more poignantly bored with his knowledge of self: ". . . eh bien, mon cher ami, cette ville n'est rien auprès de ma cervelle. Tous les recoins m'en sont cent fois plus connus; toutes les rues, tous les trous de mon imagination sont cent fois plus fatigués; je m'y suis promené en cent fois plus de sens, dans cette cervelle délabrée, moi son seul habitant! . . ." (p. 286). Fantasio's inner boredom draws from Spark the confession that he cannot fathom Fantasio's self-imposed "travail perpétuel." Spark offers his own solution: ". . . moi, quand je fume, par exemple, ma pensée se fait fumée de tabac; quand je bois, elle se fait vin d'Espagne ou bière de Flandre . . ." (p. 286). What is striking here is that in a matter of moments, Fantasio and Spark have each reversed course. Fantasio has already displayed his imagination at work in the exchange over the "fille d'opéra," thus denying Spark's allegations of prospective boredom. Spark, in his turn, does exactly the same thing when Fantasio affirms that he is bored with his "cervelle." This reversal parallels all the other reversals, of roles as well as of values, which characterize *Fantasio.* It also underlines the nature of Fantasio's "mélancolie," which is not a deep, constant agony of boredom, but rather a lighthearted impatience, revealing an ebullient imagination waiting for events to grace it with a theater and an audience.

Fantasio's next inspiration is to suggest killing time at the casino. Spark rejects the suggestion on the grounds that they would end up losing their money. Fantasio: "Ah! mon Dieu! qu'est-ce que tu vas imaginer là! Tu ne sais quoi inventer pour te torturer l'esprit. Tu vois donc tout en noir, misérable! tu n'as donc dans le cœur ni foi en Dieu ni espérance? tu es donc un athée épouvantable, capable de me dessécher le cœur et de me désabuser de tout, moi qui suis plein de sève et de jeunesse?" (p. 287). Fantasio is once again affirming the ascendancy of his imagination, as he accuses Spark of having an uninventive mind, in other words, of being too practical. By adding to this the allegation that Spark has lost his faith in God and in hope, by calling him an "athée," Fantasio is also indulging in the *jeu* of reversing values. To place God on the side of rakes and gamblers is not merely anti-traditional. It is also a contradiction of the God-society equation which, in Musset's armchair world, frustrates the Franks and the Octaves. Here, in *Fantasio,* God and hope are to be marshalled in the service of dreamers. Spark is therefore an "athée," because his conventional objection to gambling is a "sacrilegious" intrusion of the social order into the inviolable realm of fantasy. Spark's retort: "En réalité, il y a de certains moments où je ne jurerais pas que tu n'es pas fou" (p. 287), responds appropriately to the momentary caprice of Fantasio, and prefigures the confusion of the *fou* Fantasio and the *bouffon* Saint-Jean.

Spark advises Fantasio to become a journalist or a writer, assuring him that this will be the most effective way to "amortir l'imagination." In one sense, Spark is merely telling Fantasio that if he immerses himself in the routine of a *métier*, he will no longer have to worry about the nagging of his boundless imagination. In another sense, he is expressing Musset's ongoing contempt, already manifest in the *Revues fantastiques*, in "Les Vœux stériles," and in **La Coupe et les lèvres**, for the journalists and professionals who, according to Musset, had compromised art, fiction, and imagination. Fantasio responds to Spark's suggestion by indicating his desire for a lobster, a *grisette*, a class of minerals, and a house for two, in that order. Spark then urges: "Pourquoi n'écris-tu pas tout ce que tu rêves? cela ferait un joli recueil" (p. 288). Fantasio's response, "Un sonnet vaut mieux qu'un long poème, et un verre de vin vaut mieux qu'un sonnet," affirms, on one level, Fantasio's abhorrence of professional identification, his inveterate laziness, his preference for living out his dreams rather than committing them to written formulation. One may also see in Fantasio's remarks a reflection of Musset's attitudes toward his work during the period in which **Fantasio** was created. Spark's remark and Fantasio's retort contain still other possibilities of personal reference, for Musset had already "written" his dreams, not in one "joli recueil," but in two: *Contes d'Espagne et d'Italie* and **Un Spectacle dans un fauteuil**, part I. Since neither was greeted by any real public acclaim, Fantasio's retort may well represent the writer's awareness that, for the moment at least, he has found in his personal life the pleasure of recognition which had eluded him as an artist. If we respond to the implicit invitation to see Musset in Fantasio, then Fantasio's rejection of writing his dreams is in itself a kind of gay contradiction of reality, for the play **Fantasio** is in fact a written dream, and Fantasio the character is denying what Musset the author is actually doing. By this time, the reader of **Fantasio** begins to sense that Musset is using Fantasio to poke fun at himself, and that he is enjoying every moment of it.

Spark tries to suggest other ways to avoid boredom. He starts with travel, but when Fantasio rejects every country named, Spark becomes exasperated and shouts: "Va donc au diable, alors!" Fantasio, however, takes even this in stride, giving to Spark's exclamation a seriousness which was not intended, and playing with expletives just as Musset himself did in his earlier dramas: "Oh! s'il y avait un diable dans le ciel! s'il y avait un enfer, comme je me brûlerais la cervelle pour aller voir tout ça! Quelle misérable chose que l'homme! ne pas pouvoir seulement sauter par sa fenêtre sans se

casser les jambes! être obligé de jouer du violon dix ans pour devenir un musicien passable! Apprendre pour être peintre, pour être palefrenier! Apprendre pour faire une omelette! . . ." (p. 289). The increasing incoherence of Fantasio's chain of associations is due in part to his given character and in part to gradual inebriation. Fantasio starts to sing a song, and is inspired to remark that the song in question always makes him want to love some one. When Spark asks whether Fantasio has any specific lady in mind, Fantasio replies: "Qui? Je n'en sais rien; quelque belle fille toute ronde comme les femmes de Miéris . . ." (p. 189). Fantasio then plunges into a vivid verbal reproduction of a Flemish painting. Spark tries to pick up the thread of the conversation by suggesting to Fantasio: "Si tu étais amoureux, tu serais le plus heureux des hommes." Fantasio replies: "L'amour n'existe plus, mon cher ami. La religion, sa nourrice, a les mamelles pendantes comme une vieille bourse au fond de laquelle il y a un gros sou. L'amour est une hostie qu'il faut briser en deux au pied d'un autel et avaler ensemble dans un baiser; il n'y a plus d'autel, il n'y a plus d'amour. Vive la nature! il y a encore du vin" (p. 290). After affirming that a Portuguese romance makes him want to love a Flemish woman, he turns around and denies the existence of love, at least of that variety of human love which has traditionally been sanctioned by religious ceremony. The curious aspect of the dialogue is that Spark puts in the conditional tense what in Musset's life was a *fait accompli:* he was in love at the time he wrote the play. His denial of conjugal love and his "Vive la nature'" become, in this light, part of his celebration of happiness. This very felicity, at the moment it is being expressed, runs distinctly counter to the prevailing fate of the profane and adulterous lovers who populate the works of Alfred de Musset. It corresponds perfectly, however, to the pattern of value-reversals which marks the entire conception of **Fantasio.**

As Fantasio's intoxication becomes more and more pronounced, his retorts to Spark become accordingly more and more unresponsive and immaterial. The exchange is soon interrupted by Saint-Jean's funeral procession. Fantasio exchanges light sarcasms with the bearers of Saint-Jean's remains, and when one of them indicates that there is now a vacancy at court, Fantasio instantly accepts the opportunity. "Puisque je ne puis coucher chez moi, je veux me donner la représentation de cette royale comédie qui se jouera demain, et de la loge du roi lui-même" (p. 292). The immediate reference to Elspeth's wedding is enriched by the expression "cette royale comédie," because it is an apt description of the second act, in which Fantasio, the royal clown, and the prince of Mantua, also royal and also a clown, do their best to undermine a royal marriage. As the long second scene comes to an end, Fantasio awakens the royal haberdasher in order to be outfitted à la Saint-Jean, and the stage is left vacant for the oncoming prince of Mantua.

The brief third scene is set in an inn, to which Marinoni has returned to report that the princess is "Mélancolique, fantasque, d'une joie folle, soumise à son père, aimant beaucoup les pois verts" (p. 293). The prince asks him to put his report in writing, because he can understand clearly only "les écritures moulées en bâtarde." As Marinoni starts to write, he also starts to repeat aloud his earlier statement. The prince interrupts him: "Ecris à voix basse; je rêve à un projet d'importance depuis mon dîner" (p. 293). We can see from Marinoni's description that the princess and Fantasio have, apparently, a great deal in common: "Mélancolique, fantasque, d'une joie folle." This serves as a further reinforcement of Elspeth's alleged closeness to the late Saint-Jean and her willingness to tolerate the masquerading Fantasio. The coincidence of attributes is important because it supports the joining of Fantasio and Elspeth in a fantasy world in which the prince of Mantua is an alien. Elspeth's dutiful exterior, reported by Marinoni, is of course indicative of her relationship to her father (but not to him as king), whereas her fondness for green peas is no more consequential than Fantasio's longing for lobster.

As for the prince, it is apparent from the moment he opens his royal mouth that he is a fool. He claims that he is a dreamer ("je rêve à un projet d'importance . . ."), but he is obviously both stupid and unimaginative, thoroughly incapable of pretending to be other than what he is. In the same breath, he "appoints" Marinoni his "ami intime," and asks him to be seated "à quelque distance" (p. 293). The prince then deigns to inform Marinoni of his "dream," to wit, that he is going to disguise himself. Marinoni makes the appropriate gestures of subordinate incredulity, but the prince assures him that he, the prince of Mantua, "est le plus romanesque des hommes." The significance of the prince's delusion is now clear, for if any one in the first act is "romanesque," it is Fantasio, and no one else. Marinoni points out humbly what appears to be a flaw in the prince's scheme: "L'idée d'un tel travestissement ne pouvait appartenir qu'au prince glorieux qui nous gouverne. Mais si mon gracieux souverain est confondu parmi l'état-major, à qui le roi de Bavière fera-t-il les honneurs d'un festin splendide qui doit avoir lieu dans la galerie?" (p. 295). The prince concludes, therefore, that his dreams of disguise have been frustrated. Why? In his own words: "Je puis bien abaisser la dignité princière jusqu'au grade de colonel; mais comment peux-tu croire que je consentirais à élever jusqu'à mon rang un homme quelconque?" (p. 295). The prince's basic discomfort in his self-assigned role as *aide de camp* will constantly prevent him from play-acting. The fear inspired by rigidity of character is given additional value because of the prince's concern over what his father-in-law would think of such a trick. Marinoni assures his master that the king is regarded as "un homme de beaucoup de sens et d'esprit, avec une humeur agréable." This observation helps the prince overcome his scruples, and he and Marinoni exchange identities.

The curtain of the second act opens on Elspeth and her *gouvernante*, who are in the process of discussing two unhappy events: the death of Saint-Jean and the royal wedding. Because of this, the scene functions initially as a reinforcement of what has already been established, by action or implication, in the preceding act. Elspeth's fondness for Saint-Jean and her qualms about the wedding are competing for her tears. When the *gouvernante* advises Elspeth of the rumor that the prince is an "Amadis," Elspeth replies: "Que dis-tu là, ma chère! Il est horrible et idiot, tout le monde le sait déjà ici" (p. 296). It seems then that every one but the king is familiar with the true character of the prospective son-in-law. This knowledge has already been transferred to the audience, so that, even though Elspeth does not appear in a speaking role in Act I, there is a strong bond of sympathy between audience and character. The mention of Amadis places Elspeth and her *gouvernante* squarely in the realm of fantasy. Elspeth knows that the prince is not cut from the cloth of dreams and romances, and that he corresponds in no way to what she has been led to anticipate. She confesses that she is "une pauvre rêveuse," attributing some of the blame to her companion, who has raised her on a diet of fiction. Nevertheless, she is dutiful to her father and responsive to the needs of the state.

As tears of woe begin to dampen the eyes of the two interlocutors, the *gouvernante* tries to cheer her mistress: "Si le prince de Mantoue est tel que vous le dites, Dieu ne laissera pas cette affaire-là s'arranger, j'en suis sûre." Elspeth responds: "Tu crois! Dieu laisse faire les hommes, ma pauvre amie, et il ne fait guère plus de cas de nos plaintes que du bêlement d'un mouton" (p. 297). This exchange holds our attention, because we are once again faced with a reversal of values. Measured in terms of the function which Musset has usually assigned to the heavenly power, Elspeth's view is correct, for the divinity imagined earlier by Musset has either not interfered with the affairs of happiness-seekers, or it has been identified with the established social order which rejects and punishes those who seek happiness outside of it. In *Fantasio,* however, the God-man relationship will be effectively and fancifully turned around. Elspeth's denial of possible divine intervention is merely another way of expressing her willingness to face a marriage of state convenience. When, in the first act, Spark tried to be practical, he was berated by Fantasio, who called him an unbeliever. Elspeth, in parallel fashion, is stating a practicality which violates the prevailing mood of the play. Within the context of *Fantasio,* it is the *gouvernante* who is "right."

The conversation comes back to Saint-Jean, and both ladies seem to feel that somehow things would be more bearable if only the jester were there. The key to Saint-Jean's influence seems to be expressed in the words of the princess: "C'était un homme bizarre; tandis qu'il me parlait, il me passait devant les yeux des tableaux délicieux; sa parole donnait la vie, comme par enchantement, aux choses les plus étranges" (p. 298). Elspeth's description provides still another link between the two acts, for her portrait of Saint-Jean is also a portrait, and a faithful one, of Fantasio, who is indeed bizarre, who is able to paint pictures with words, and whose language is animated and captivating. Moreover, his predilection for the *Arabian Nights* puts him on an equal footing with those who have found enchantment in romances of chivalry.

Elspeth, resigned to the inevitable, finally asks her companion to leave her alone, for, as she says, "je n'ai plus longtemps à rêver." This gives the *gouvernante* a chance to address an entreaty to God, praying for the non-realization of the wedding. It is at this moment that Elspeth sees in the garden a figure which she first records as the "fantôme de mon pauvre bouffon." Fantasio slides easily into his assumed role as Saint-Jean's replacement. He tells Elspeth that he has been gathering flowers "en attendant qu'il me vienne de l'esprit" (p. 300). He affirms that he is only interested in being well-fed and that all he intends to do is to watch his shadow "pour voir si ma perruque pousse." Elspeth expresses mild annoyance at Fantasio's costume, for it reminds her of Saint-Jean, but she accepts him as the new *bouffon* because he looks and talks like one. There is one early exchange of sarcasms which is arresting in substance as well as in form:

ELSPETH:

> Pauvre homme! quel métier tu entreprends! faire de l'esprit à tant par heure! N'as-tu ni bras ni jambes, et ne ferais-tu pas mieux de laborurer la terre que ta propre cervelle?

FANTASIO:

> Pauvre petite! quel métier vous entreprenez! épouser un sot que vous n'avez jamais vu!—N'avez-vous ni cœur ni tête, et ne feriez-vous pas mieux de vendre vos robes que votre corps?

[Pp. 300-301.]

Elspeth's suggestion that some kind of *real* work is more desirable than trying to live by one's wits recalls Fantasio's earlier recognition that part of his boredom stemmed from a lack of *métier*. Fantasio, however, is actually working as he speaks, doing the only thing of which he is capable, responding to the only calling which is fully appropriate to his known character. Fantasio's clever, but insolent retort, is in keeping with his character as well as with his assumed role, for the king's jester is merely a fool, and therefore enjoys a license denied to ordinary courtiers. Elspeth chides him for his

audacity, but at the same time, appears to enjoy talking with the new Saint-Jean. It is clear that as Fantasio talks to her, even about her most intimate sorrow, a part of her burden is lightened.

As the initial encounter between Fantasio and Elspeth comes to an end, Fantasio sees the king walking toward them, accompanied by the prince and Marinoni, each playing his new role. Fantasio exits, and Elspeth steps forward to greet her father. Marinoni asks for the pleasure of kissing Elspeth's hand. She declines, suggesting that the occasion is not appropriate, and takes her leave. The prince, unable to contain himself, remarks: "La princesse a raison; voilà une divine pudeur" (p. 304). The king is visibly annoyed at the insolence of the "aide," and asks Marinoni to dismiss him. Before Marinoni can act, however, the prince, again forgetting his role, turns to Marinoni and compliments him: "C'est fort adroit de ta part de lui avoir persuadé de m'éloigner; je vais tâcher de joindre la princesse et de lui toucher quelques mots délicats sans faire semblant de rien!" (p. 304). As the counterfeit aide turns to leave, the king tells Marinoni that his subordinate is an imbecile. Contrasting Fantasio's insolence with that of the prince, we are brought back directly to the fundamental distinction between the two principal operating characters. Mantua's insolence is regal in origin; it stems from his basic role, and cannot be hidden beneath his disguise. Fantasio's insolence is largely derivative of his earlier asocial temperament, as manifested, for example, by his behavior toward the royal pallbearers. Having slipped into the garb of Saint-Jean, he can be even more insolent, without threat of punishment. His audacity is accepted by Elspeth, whereas that of the prince is completely out of place, and is therefore censured by the king.

The second scene of the act begins with the prince alone on stage. His monologue is a masterpiece of self-deception: "Mon déguisement me réussit à merveille; j'observe et je me fais aimer. Jusqu'ici tout va au gré de mes souhaits; le père me paraît un grand roi, quoique trop sans façon, et je m'étonnerais si je ne lui avais plu tout d'abord. J'aperçois la princesse qui rentre au palais; le hasard me favorise singulièrement" (p. 304). Every statement of the prince, with the exception of his seeing Elspeth walking back into the palace, contradicts what is actually happening in the play. The disguise is obviously not working; the prince is not observing, as he puts it, because he is inherently unable to keep from talking; he is certainly getting nowhere in his quest for love. He is wrong when he sees Elspeth's father as a "grand roi," but ironically correct in noting that he appears to be "trop sans façon." The important motivation in the case of the king is not that he is a monarch, but that he is a father, for he is more concerned for his daughter's welfare than he is for the welfare of the state. As for having pleased the king, it is already perfectly clear that the king finds the prince obnoxious, and that he has made no attempt to keep his feelings private.

He approaches Elspeth, and speaks to her in the guise of "un fidèle serviteur" of her bridegroom. He praises the noble heart which is fortunate enough to win Elspeth, and then launches into a fictional description of his own fate, which is at once amusing and absurd: ". . . je suis d'une naissance obscure; je n'ai pour tout bien qu'un nom redoutable à l'ennemi—un cœur pur et sans tache bat sous ce modeste uniforme—je suis un pauvre soldat criblé de balles des pieds à la tête—je n'ai pas un ducat—je suis solitaire et exilé de ma terre natale comme de ma patrie céleste, c'est-à-dire du paradis de mes rêves; je n'ai pas un cœur de femme à presser sur mon cœur; je suis maudit et silencieux" (p. 305). One senses here that Musset is allowing the half-disguised prince to parody the Musset hero. The words are similar to those of Coelio, Frank, Dalti, Octave, Cordiani, *et al.,* but because his little fiction is betrayed by his character, everything he says rings false. Elspeth listens to the prince's sad story, and then inquires: "Etes-vous fou, ou demandez-vous l'aumône?" (p. 305). The prince seems not to hear her, and continues to spout away regally. Elspeth is obliged to turn her back on him, and she leaves him alone on the stage.

The following scene, a long monologue delivered by Fantasio lying on the floor, is set off in sharp contrast with the *jeu* of the prince. The anguished rigidity of the Mantuan suitor is replaced by the gay comfort of the clown, who is perfectly at home. "Quel métier délicieux que celui du bouffon! J'étais gris, je crois, hier soir, lorsque j'ai pris ce costume et que je me suis présenté au palais; mais, en vérité, jamais la saine raison ne m'a rien inspiré qui valût cet acte de folie." Fantasio accepts his *métier,* not because it involves work but because it is "délicieux." He now remembers that his "acte de folie" was inspired by drunkenness, and not by deliberation. His sudden urge to be the court jester is an "acte de folie" when evaluated in the light of "la saine raison," but it is also the act of a *fou,* which Fantasio is, as well as the act of a *bouffon,* which Fantasio has become. Fantasio's folly, however, will be the instrument of the prince's ultimate exasperation, and of Elspeth's ultimate salvation. His behavior and character are dramatically "reasonable," for it is the prince, and no one else, who is really foolish. As Fantasio continues to ruminate, he observes: "Dieu merci, voilà ma cervelle à l'aise, je puis faire toutes les balivernes possibles sans qu'on me dise rien pour m'en empêcher . . ." (p. 306). In other words, he has escaped from all his problems, real or imagined, and can now literally be himself. "En attendant, mes créanciers peuvent se casser le nez contre ma porte tout à leur aise. Je suis aussi bien en sûreté ici, sous cette perruqe, que dans les Indes occidentales" (p. 306). Here again, Fantasio's thoughts reflect the basic difference of role between clown and prince. Fantasio feels perfectly secure in his disguise, because it blends smoothly with his caracter. The prince, on the other hand, is uncomfortable from the very beginning. He wriggles insecurely beneath his wig and is reluctant to give Marinoni the freedom to emote from beneath the royal hairpiece.

In the next episode, the prince is beginning to believe that the way he has been treated is not suitable to his dignity. His irritation is loosed against Marinoni, whom the master calls "sot," "butor," and "maraud," terms which suit only the prince himself. Marinoni senses this when he objects: "Votre Altesse se trompe sur mon compte de la manière la plus pénible" (p. 307). The prince's anger centers on the fact that Marinoni, playing his role properly, has dared to call the prince "un impertinent en présence de toute la Cour," and has in general been acting too imperially. Marinoni points out patiently that "il faut cependant que je sois le prince ou que je sois l'aide de camp" (p. 307), and "Songez donc, Altesse, que ce mauvais compliment s'adressait à l'aide de camp et non au prince. Prétendez-vous qu'on vous respecte sous ce déguisement?" (p. 308). The prince fails to recognize the à-propos of his aide's reasoning, and asks for the surrender of his royal apparel. As Marinoni starts to obey, the prince is stricken again with uncertainty. He decides provisionally to continue the masquerade, because the obsession with carrying out his scheme has blinded him to the truth of the situation: "La princesse ne paraît pas répondre indifféremment aux mots à double entente dont je ne cesse de la poursuivre. Déjà je suis parvenu deux ou trois fois à lui dire à l'oreille des choses incroyables" (p. 308). It is true that the princess has not been indifferent; she has been overtly annoyed. As for words with double meanings, they exist only within the role of Fantasio.

The fifth scene begins with a brief exchange between the king and Elspeth. The king is trying to find out how his daughter feels about her impending marriage, and he gives her ample opportunity to state frankly that she is not happy. The princess remains dutiful and evades the question, concluding with the words: "Je pense donc que je l'épouserai, et que la guerre sera finie" (p. 309). The king, however, is not ready for an irrevocable commitment, and decides to postpone the celebration for a few days, alleging that he cannot bear the sadness in Elspeth's eyes.

The scene continues, as the king is replaced on stage by Fantasio. Elspeth's earlier suspicion has been completely dissipated, and she accepts Fantasio as a regular fixture of the court. The beginning of their conversation is cordial and open:

ELSPETH:

Te voilà, pauvre garçon! comment te plais-tu ici?

FANTASIO:

Comme un oiseau en liberté.

ELSPETH:

Tu aurais mieux répondu, si tu avais dit comme un oiseau en cage. Ce palais en est une assez belle; cependant c'en est une.

FANTASIO:

La dimension d'un palais ou d'une chambre ne fait pas l'homme plus ou moins libre. Le corps se remue où il peut; l'imagination ouvre quelquefois des ailes grandes comme le ciel dans un cachot grand comme la main.

ELSPETH:

Ainsi donc, tu es un heureux fou?

FANTASIO:

Très heureux. . . .

[Pp. 309-310.]

The *jeu* at this point is obviously a contrast between Elspeth's sadness and sense of confinement and Fantasio's feeling of complete freedom. At the same time, Fantasio's homage to liberated imagination plants the idea of possible redemption for Elspeth, for imagination is given wings of divine proportions. Fantasio turns the discussion away from himself and gradually returns to his provocative questioning of Elspeth's choice of bridegroom. Elspeth does not know that Fantasio had been an eyewitness to her private weeping, and cannot imagine how he has been able to penetrate her most intimate thoughts. "Je croirais volontiers que tu épies mes actions et mes paroles." To this Fantasio says: "Dieu le sait. Que vous importe?" (p. 312). Fantasio's little retort serves to tighten the link between God and the cause of happiness. The *gouvernante* has already sent an appeal for heavenly intervention, whereas Fantasio's remark about winged imagination has established a rapport between what is divine and what is freely imagined. Fantasio's offhand words, "Dieu le sait," are clearly part of the same pattern. The bond between Fantasio and Elspeth is cemented when the princess remarks: "Tu me parles sous la forme d'un homme que j'ai aimé, voilà pourquoi je t'écoute malgré moi. Mes yeux croient voir Saint-Jean . . ." (p. 312). The exchange ends shortly thereafter as Fantasio sees the *gouvernante* coming and bows out, indicating that he is heading for the pantry, "pour manger une aile de pluvier que le majordome a mise de côté pour sa femme" (p. 313).

The good companion of Elspeth brings the news that the real prince is running around in disguise. The *gouvernante* classifies the discovery as a "vrai conte de fées," Marinoni has been properly identified as an aide, but the identity of the prince remains a mystery, for it occurs to no one that the obnoxious aide might be a head of state. As the princess is trying to adjust to the news, a page enters, and in a brief *récit,* reports the lifting of the prince's wig. She says: "Viens écouter toute cette histoire, ma chère. Mon sérieux commence à m'abandonner" (p. 315). The only real obstacle to the fulfillment of happiness—the princess herself—is cleared away, as Elspeth's capacity for laughter is restored. Another page enters to report that the royal jester has been clapped in prison, for it was he who authored the flight of the wig. Elspeth indicates an immediate desire to visit Fantasio in his cell.

The beginning of the sixth scene is given over to the prince and Marinoni. As in their previous exchange, the prince is furious at the latest insult to his royal dignity, and is ready to unmask himself. He is hurt not only by having seen the hairpiece dangling at the end of a hook, but also by the reaction of the king, who began to laugh "en voyant la perruque de son gendre voler dans les airs!" (p. 316). Following this, the prince affirms: "Ah! il y a une providence; lorsque Dieu m'a envoyé tout d'un coup l'idée de me travestir; lorsque cet éclair a traversé ma pensée: 'Il faut que je me travestisse,' ce fatal événement était prévu par le destin. C'est lui qui a sauvé de l'affront le plus intolérable la tête qui gouverne mes peuples" (p. 316). As furious as the king is, he is at least thankful that it was Marinoni's head, and not his own, which was laid bare by Fantasio's gesture. Ironically, he attributes his relative good fortune to the intervention of Providence. In spite of his initial reaction, he lets Marinoni persuade him that there is still a chance for success. The disguises remain in place, absurdly, for the game is already up.

In the final scene, Fantasio's first words pick up the motif of destiny introduced by the prince: "Je ne sais s'il y a une providence, mais c'est amusent d'y croire." Fantasio enjoys thoroughly what has been happening, and is willing to give due recognition to chance, as long as it is amusing. "Il y avait dans tout cela la fortune de deux royaumes, la tranquillité de deux peuples; et il faut que j'imagine de me déguiser en bossu, pour venir me griser derechef dans l'office de notre bon roi, et pour pêcher au bout d'une ficelle la perruque de son cher allié! En vérité, lorsque je suis gris, je crois que j'ai quelque chose de surhumain. Voilà le mariage manqué et tout remis en question" (pp. 317-318). Fantasio recognizes that his prank was conceived in a moment of inebriation, as was his desire to become Saint-Jean. The moment of unbridled, drunken folly is likened to something "surhumain," beyond the normal capacities of mere mortals, so that Fantasio is tempted to relate his unmotivated conduct to some mirthful, but divine guidance. Toward the end of the monologue, Fantasio sighs: "Ah! si j'étais poète, comme je peindrais la scène de cette perruque voltigeant dans les airs! Mais celui qui est capable de faire de pareilles choses dédaigne de les écrire. Ainsi la postérité s'en passera" (p. 318). Here, we have still another instance in which Musset appears to be making fun of himself. The description of the wig dancing in the air has already been given by the exasperated prince. As for the expressed disdain for realizing imagination in words, the character is merely denying what the author has accomplished by creating the character and the dramatic medium in which he functions.

Fantasio falls asleep. Elspeth and her *gouvernante* enter at this point and make their mistaken identification of the wigless, humpless youth. Fantasio wakes up after a few moments, and has considerable difficulty persuading the ladies that he is not of royal blood. He is even led to remark: "Suis-je donc un prince, par hasard? Concevrait-on quelque soupçon sur l'honneur de ma mère?" (p. 320). He finally manages to identify himself as Fantasio, a burgher of Munich. When the mystified princess asks him, "Qui vous a poussé à cette action?" he can only reply: "Je ne puis dire le motif qui m'a conduit ici" (p. 320). The exchange is somewhat cryptic because of Fantasio's evasiveness. It is only when Elspeth alters the question, demanding an explanation for the disguise, that Fantasio finally answers, alluding to his debts. Although Fantasio cannot explain his wig-fishing escapade, the "rightness" of it, in terms of the play's dramatic problem, is unmistakable. Folly and imagination, aided and abetted by a smiling providence, bring happiness to Elspeth and to the king. The fact that war has been re-declared seems to bother no one, for the social realities have no meaning in the very private dream-world of **Fantasio**.

Notes

1. There is no known source, in the strict sense, for *Fantasio*. It may have been inspired in part by the marriage of Louis-Philippe's daughter or by one of Hoffman's *Tales*. (See Jean Giraud's article, "Mariage de princesse. Vérité et fantaisie dans une comédie de Musset," *Revue de Paris*, March 1, 1913, pp. 32-46.) Certain elements of *Fantasio* appear to derive from Musset's fragmentary novella *Le Roman par lettres*, which is set in a royal court and which includes a character named Spark. Consult the notes of Maurice Allem, *Prose*, pp. 1087-1093.

2. These poems were included in the Second Part of *Poésies posthumes*. They appear in the Pléiade edition, pp. 512-525.

3. The witty exchange provides a link to *Les Caprices de Marianne*, for Hartman's retorts and epithets follow the pattern established in Act II, Scene I of *Les Caprices de Marianne*, where Octave and Claudio engage in a sarcastic battle of wits (ed. Gastinel, pp. 152-154).

Vivien L. Rubin (essay date April 1979)

SOURCE: Rubin, Vivien L. "The Idea of the Clown in Musset's *Fantasio*." *The French Review* 52, no. 5 (April 1979): 724-30.

[*In the following essay, Rubin examines the influence of the character of the dead jester on the action of* Fantasio.]

As[1] David Sices has commented, "**Fantasio** is a play that seems to generate misunderstandings."[2] One misunderstanding which persists and which is shared by a number of distinguished commentators is, I believe, a crucial one. It is, to put it briefly, the belief that, alone among the plays of Musset's most creative dramatic period, **Fantasio** is a work "in which for once everything works out for the best."[3] To read **Fantasio** in this way is to fail to recognize fully the use that Musset makes here of the idea of the clown and hence is to miss one of the fundamental ironies of a play which proposes as hero the figure of the court jester.

Let us look first at the picture that we are given of Saint-Jean, the dead jester whose place at court Fantasio briefly fills, for Saint-Jean is essential to the play, even though we never meet him. We are alerted at once to his importance for he is first spoken of in the very opening exchange of the play where, in a conversation between the king and his secretary, we learn both that the buffoon is dead and that his death has caused the princess sorrow. The strength and unexpectedness of the princess's attachment are underlined by the king's blunt expression of surprise:

RUTTEN:

La mort de Saint-Jean l'a contrariée.

LE ROI:

Y penses-tu? la mort de mon bouffon? d'un plaisant de cour bossu et presque aveugle?

RUTTEN:

La Princesse l'aimait.[4]

It is, of course, the death of Saint-Jean which provides the occasion for Fantasio's escapade and hence for the play itself. Moreover, in a play concerned with a brief meeting or two and a few insignificant events, where we know next to nothing of the past lives of the characters and, when we leave them, nothing specific of what their future will be, the memory of Saint-Jean has the effect of opening a shadowy door into the past, just as the deliberately inconclusive ending invites us to peer at the dim forms of what is yet to be. More important, however, is the fact that the personality of the dead Saint-Jean, his relationship with the princess and the affection which she felt for him, help to determine the quality and tone of the relationship which is established between Elsbeth and Fantasio. No doubt Fantasio's own wit and charm count for much, but we are not allowed to forget Saint-Jean. The princess herself says at one point: "Tu me parles sous la forme d'un homme que j'ai aimé, voilà pourquoi je t'écoute malgré moi. Mes yeux croient voir Saint-Jean" (II, 5). Finally, and very important in a play in which pairing, both contrasting and complementary, is an essential feature of the structure, much of the complexity and suggestiveness of *Fantasio* is expressed through the identifications and oppositions which Musset establishes between Saint-Jean as he is revealed to us by those who knew him, and Fantasio himself. The evocation of the dead clown gives us a sharper perception of the living one.

Saint-Jean is clearly intended to represent the natural, not merely the professional, fool, for he possessed both the sharp wit and the physical deformities so often associated with the idea of the buffoon. But however physically deformed he may have been, his spirit was whole. His gaiety made his hearers forget his ugliness so that, as Elsbeth's governess recalls, "les yeux le cherchaient toujours en dépit d'eux-mêmes!" (II, 1). Faced with the prospect of the princess's marriage to a foolish prince, both Elsbeth and her governess feel his lack sorely: "Si Saint-Jean était là!" laments the governess, while Elsbeth sighs, "Ah! Saint-Jean, Saint-Jean!" He loved the princess and she admired and loved him in return. Elsbeth speaks of him, in this same conversation with her governess, as having been "un diamant d'esprit" and confesses that "son esprit m'attachait à lui avec des fils imperceptibles qui semblaient venir de mon cœur." She recalls how much she appreciated his bracing reaction to her own romantic inclinations and muses, "Sa perpétuelle moquerie de mes idées romanesques me plaisait à l'excès, tandis que je ne puis supporter qu'avec peine bien des gens qui abondent dans mon sens." Deformed and nearly blind though he was, his position was a secure and established one, accepted without question by all. But there was more to Saint-Jean than a witty jester who teased the princess with grace and warmth: there was also Saint-Jean, the man of creative imagination. This nearly blind man could make others see. The princess is still speaking: "C'était un homme bizarre; tandis qu'il me parlait, il me passait devant les yeux des tableaux délicieux; sa parole donnait la vie, comme par enchantement, aux choses les plus étranges." Thus, in this retrospective evocation of Saint-Jean, Musset proposes the image of an ideal fool type whose station, though lowly, was secure, who loved and inspired love, and who was creative as well as sharply perceptive: a poet as well as a punster.[5]

If we now take a look at Fantasio himself as he first appears to us in the long second scene of act one, we shall discover, as other commentators have noted, that Fantasio is also a fool, even before he assumes the dead jester's wig and hump.[6] But the dissimilarities between Fantasio and Saint-Jean are, it becomes clear, as significant as the resemblances. For Fantasio is a modern fool. He is the fool who has no roots, no settled, accepted place in the world. He wears no livery and has no physical deformity, but he is nonetheless a prisoner of his role, for his ailment is spiritual.

As soon as we meet Fantasio, it becomes apparent that, like the court jester, his main occupation is the exercise of his wit upon every subject which catches his attention. His conversation, in colorful and picturesque language, moves with facility from one subject to another as he passes in rapid review the major questions which are wont to exercise man's mind and feelings. Contrary to Gochberg's assertion that Fantasio speaks on frivolous topics, Fantasio in fact trivializes the serious.[7] For, whereas we understand that Saint-Jean's wit sprang from a certain mental and spiritual health, Fantasio's is symptomatic of a pervasive malaise. Fantasio is not merely mocking the ways of the world but is expressing his own disenchantment, his sense of the emptiness of life, while transposing his distress into an acceptably frivolous key. Fantasio is as disenchanted with himself as with the world around him and the holiday mood serves only to bring into relief his sense of alienation from himself and others: "Que cela m'ennuie que tout le monde s'amuse." His constant introspection has made him unutterably weary of himself. Life, whether it be of the senses, the emotions or the intellect, has lost its savor. Lacking the discipline or dedication which would enable him to apply himself to some purpose, he sees man in terms of limitations rather than potentialities: "Quelle misérable chose que l'homme! ne pas pouvoir seulement sauter par sa fenêtre sans se casser les jambes!" The sense of the uniqueness of the individual is felt by Fantasio but turns easily into a sense of his isolation: "Quelles solitudes que tous ces corps humains!" Fantasio casts around for some escape from his ennui: if only he could *do* something, if only he could feel some enthusiasm, if but for superficial pleasures; if only he could be someone else, be somewhere else; if only death held out some prospect of interest: "Oh, s'il y avait un diable dans le ciel! S'il y avait un enfer, comme je me brûlerais la cervelle pour aller voir tout ça!" If only he could achieve complete mental and emotional surcease: "Tiens, Spark, il me prend des envies de m'asseoir sur un parapet, de regarder couler la rivière et de me mettre à compter un, deux, trois, quatre, cinq, six, sept, et ainsi de suite jusqu'au jour de ma mort."

In his chapter on *Fantasio,* Gochberg defines Fantasio's melancholy as "not a deep, constant agony of boredom, but rather a light-hearted impatience, revealing an ebullient imagination waiting for events to grace it with a theater and an audience" (p. 157). Certainly, to use Starobinski's expression, Fantasio still has wings.[8] His verbal brilliance and command of imagery reveal that he, too, represents the poetic imagination. Like Saint-

Jean, he has the poet's touch and can play magically with words. But "play" is the operative term: ideas, feelings, actions are become for him a mere game of words in a world without true meaning. In his conversation with Spark, his restless review of impossible alternatives serves only to underline how incapable he is of constructive action. His sallies, however colorful and witty, harp insistently on the same themes: the empty weariness of life, the futility of effort.

The same sense of isolation and impotent desire for something different informs the long and important passage in which Fantasio imagines the scene of a woman offering a stirrup cup to a stranger at her door. In the course of his conversation with Spark, and with a characteristic non-sequitur, Fantasio breaks into a Portuguese love song, declaring that when he hears it, it always makes him want to fall in love. When Spark asks with whom, Fantasio replies airily that he has not the faintest idea and, in order to answer the question, launches into an evocation of a type of woman found in the works of a Flemish painter, thereby removing the question of falling in love from the realm of life and possibilities into that of art and the ideal. This evocation of an ideal type then develops into a more detailed description. The image of the woman is progressively intensified in terms of feeling, charity, responsibility, as she also grows older. She begins as "quelque belle fille toute ronde," then becomes "quelque chose de pensif comme ces petites servantes d'auberge"; midway she is "une jeune femme sur le pas de la porte," with the fire alight within, supper ready and the children asleep; and finally she is "la bonne femme," who watches for a moment the lonely traveler as he pursues his journey and who, as she returns to her hearth, lets fall "cette sublime aumône du pauvre: 'Que Dieu le protège!'" A lesser but similar intensification takes place with the figure of the rider. By the end of the passage, Fantasio is gazing not so much at the mental picture of an ideal woman with whom he could fall in love, but at that of a kind of reality into which he cannot enter. For both the man and the woman symbolize participation and commitment, the woman with her domestic ties and responsibilities, who can yet still offer up a compassionate prayer for a stranger and the rider who, already having traveled far, is still pressing on through a long and hazardous night. Fantasio, meanwhile, has no commitments and his adventures, all in the imagination, have apparently been only self-destructive, for he already feels too overcome by lassitude to wish to continue. True, in this at least, to the essential nature of the buffoon, he remains an observer, uncommitted—except to self-indulgence of an irresponsible and frivolous kind.

It is just such an irresponsible self-indulgence which leads Fantasio to take the place of the royal jester. When he appears at court we see him entering gleefully into his role, declaring: "Quel métier délicieux que celui du bouffon!" (II, 3). As Starobinski comments, Fantasio represents the mind which, bored with itself, recovers a certain temporary vitality by assuming a disguise, playing a masquerade (p. 271). Fantasio appears, almost miraculously, to have solved several of his problems. Characteristically, he does not content himself with just any suitable jester costume, but needs must have a replica of the livery that Saint-Jean had worn, complete with hump and large red wig; he does not contemplate creating an entirely new personage, but depends on the tangible props of another's life to give himself the illusion of leaving his own.

The external transformation which Fantasio now undergoes not only dramatizes his tendency to escape from responsibility but also illustrates the question of the contrast between appearance and reality. We have already spoken of the glaring contrast between Saint-Jean's outwardly deformed person and his clear spirit, between Fantasio's youth and inventive wit and his sense of imaginative death, to give but two examples. Fantasio himself is ever conscious of the disparity between appearance and reality and strikes this note early on: "Tu as le mois de mai sur les joues," cries a friend, while Fantasio retorts, "C'est vrai et le mois de janvier dans le cœur." The play is compact with ironic disparities and dualities of this kind. Now, the handsome godchild of the dead Queen becomes the ugly jester, while the Prince of Mantua will shortly don his aide-de-camp's "simple frac olive," as Marinoni prepares to array himself in the glorious uniform of his prince. These different exchanges of costume all warn against accepting appearance for reality and they are, also, examples of that process of man-made metamorphosis which can compound the deceptive nature of appearances. For while appearances may be misleading by their very nature, at times they are so because, as Fantasio explains to Elsbeth, "le monde entier se métamorphose sous la main de l'homme" (II, 1). Yet the problem is further complicated by the fact that, though many artful transformations may be wrought by the hand and mind of man, these metamorphoses may be doubly illusion. In the two most glaring examples of metamorphosis in the play, that of Fantasio into fool and the prince into aide-de-camp, the change of costume has in fact the effect of bringing into clear relief existing aspects of their characters: the prince's ineptitude declares itself more clearly and immediately than might otherwise have been the case, while for Fantasio the adoption of the jester's wig confirms how at home he is in the part.

Fantasio's transformation then is, as Gochberg noted, more apparent than real. However, when he moves into the court, he is moving into a context where the role of the buffoon is legitimate, even necessary: "Il nous faudra absolument un bouffon," says Elsbeth in the final scene. Fantasio suddenly finds himself with a certain harmony established between himself and his context. Nothing will be asked of him and he need ask nothing of himself. As a result, we are conscious of a change of emphasis or of mood, to use Sice's word. Fantasio's conversation is no longer recording an absence, an undefined but strongly felt desire for something different; instead, he speaks of the pleasures of his situation. Whereas before he had complained of the wearisome limitations imposed by the town and, more effectively, by his own ennui, he now chides the princess for comparing the castle to a gilded cage. And he who had earlier been tantalized by the illusory promises of metamorphosis, whatever the form it might take, now warns the princess that not all such changes are equally felicitous and attacks her, however charmingly, for accepting her forthcoming marriage. Finally, because he has inherited, along with the costume, the dead jester's legitimacy and therefore also the creative possibilities of the role, Fantasio is able by a curious dispensation to achieve a positive good.[9] Having adopted his disguise to serve his own purposes, he is able by chance to serve another, as he perpetrates the practical joke which quite unexpectedly brings all plans for the wedding to an end.

Yet, after all, Fantasio is *not* the admirable Saint-Jean; he is not the legitimate poet-jester, at one with his role and therefore fulfilled by it. Just as he underwent no essential change when he donned his jester's costume, so will this brief interlude in his life bring no change when his charade is discovered. Once outside the context of the court and without the suggestive powers of the legitimate role, he will return to his former condition where buffoonery is both an expression of his isolation and a substitute for something more positively creative of which he is incapable. Starobinski comments, "Fantasio . . . n'a pas d'avenir et ne veut pas en avoir. Musset nous le montre courant à sa propre perte dans un bruit de flacons et de grelots . . ." (p. 275). Fantasio is aware of the incapacitating effects of his ennui. He rejects every proposal, whether his own or someone else's; he rejects, however humorously, the notion of composing a comic poem on the events of the day; and he also refuses the princess's offer of the jester's job, in revealing terms: "J'aime ce métier plus que tout autre, mais je ne puis faire aucun métier." The fact that the part of the buffoon is a veritable metaphor for his own personality means that, with the discovery by the princess of his true identity, the element of impersonation or masquerade, already slim enough, would be reduced to the vanishing point, if he stayed, and he would no longer be playing Saint-Jean, but himself. Inevitably, he would soon be saying restlessly, "Si je

pouvais seulement sortir de ma peau pendant une heure ou deux! si je pouvais être ce monsieur qui passe!" When his impersonation is over, we are conscious of a subtle dispersion of the magic and authority which he had generated in his buffoon's coat and wig. Having been wittily and delicately on the offensive, he now becomes rather absurdly, almost awkwardly, on the defensive. Thanks to the princess's generosity, he will return to the aimless life of a young man who on principle never pays his debts. The futility of the existence that he is contemplating is underlined anew in this, his last speech in the play: "Si vous trouvez que cela vaille vingt mille écus de vous avoir débarrassée du prince de Mantoue, donnez-lesmoi, et ne payez pas mes dettes. Un gentilhomme sans dettes ne saurait où se présenter. Il ne m'est jamais venu à l'esprit de me trouver sans dettes."

What of Elsbeth's present of the key and her invitation to him to retreat to the garden whenever the pressures of the world weigh too heavily? Does this represent a solution to Fantasio's existential difficulties, as Sices suggests (pp. 87-88)? Significantly, Elsbeth receives from Fantasio no response to this invitation. Just as Fantasio cannot remain, so he could surely not return, and for the same reasons. Besides, the castle is now known to him. How could this creature of whim, for whom the spontaneous, unpremeditated act represents a temporary escape from himself and his ennui, choose to return to this now familiar place? How could he contemplate a repeat performance? This short play is full of parallels and contrasts, echoes and reverberations, and here, at the end, Elsbeth and Fantasio act out a variation on the scene which Fantasio had imagined earlier, of the woman at the inn offering a benediction for the traveler bound for the unknown. Elsbeth, secure in her castle and her garden, holds out to Fantasio a helping hand, while Fantasio, who has stopped only for a moment's respite, moves on. For him, also, we must feel, "la nuit est profonde là-bas, le temps menaçant, la forêt dangereuse" (I, 2).

Thus, Musset's originality in **Fantasio** lies not only in his wit and inventive fantasy but also, in part, in the use that he makes of the idea of the clown to explore that state of "disenchantment" which he saw as new and critical and which he was to describe so eloquently in the second chapter of his *Confession d'un enfant du siècle*. Musset is also the first to make that identification of clown and poet which, as Starobinski points out, was soon to become familiar and which already expresses here the poet's sense of loss and isolation (pp. 270-71). Through his brilliantly suggestive use of pairing and juxtaposition, Musset creates in this play a nostalgic perspective which suggests a past in which the poet, though often no doubt perceived as a strange and lowly creature, yet had an accepted and creative place in society; now, however, the poet is a prisoner of his premature disillusionment and no longer feels that he has a legitimate—and necessary—part to play. Saint-Jean, however grotesque his appearance, remained whole to the end. It is the handsome Fantasio who is deformed and it is he who succumbs to the temptations of inertia and self-destruction. And so, in this supposedly light-hearted comedy, Musset in fact develops themes of alienation and failure which, in various guises, inform his other major plays and which, though typical of the Romantic period, still have meaning for us today.

Notes

1. A version of this article was read at the Colloquium in Nineteenth-Century French Studies, 12-14 October 1978, at Michigan State University.

2. *Theater of Solitude: The Drama of Alfred de Musset* (Hanover: University Press of New England, 1974), p. 66.

3. Herbert S. Gochberg, *Stage of Dreams: The Dramatic Art of Alfred de Musset (1828-1834)* (Geneva: Librairie Droz, 1967), p. 151.

4. All quotations from Musset's play are taken from his *Œuvres complètes,* edited by Philippe Van Tieghem (Paris: Editions du Seuil, 1965).

5. Charles Affron, in *A Stage for Poets: Studies in the Theatre of Hugo and Musset* (Princeton: Princeton University Press, 1971), p. 161, sees Saint-Jean as "a metaphor for art, the particular art of Musset."

6. See, for example, Henri Lefebvre, *Musset,* 2nd ed. (1955; rpt. Paris: L'Arche, 1970), p. 68; Gochberg, p. 152.

7. "His conversation moves wittily and often incoherently from one trivial subject to another" (p. 152).

8. Jean Starobinski, "Note sur le bouffon romantique," *Cahiers du Sud,* 61 (1966), 271.

9. Starobinski comments, "Derrière la modernité romantique du caractère de Fantasio, nous voyons subsister l'une des fonctions archétypales du clown: il fait tourner, presque innocemment, la roue de fortune" (p. 274). It should perhaps be noted that the positive good which Fantasio achieves is an immediate, personal one for the princess. From the larger view, and granted that any alliance with the Prince of Mantua would seem to be of dubious long-term benefit, the resumption of the war, which is spoken of in the last scene, can hardly be considered an altogether happy outcome.

LORENZACCIO (1834)

CRITICAL COMMENTARY

Herbert S. Gochberg (essay date 1967)

SOURCE: Gochberg, Herbert S. "*Spectacle dans un Fauteuil,* Act IV. *Lorenzaccio.*" In *Stage of Dreams: The Dramatic Art of Alfred de Musset,* pp. 169-99. Geneva, Switzerland: Librairie Droz S.A., 1967.

[*In the following excerpt, Gochberg discusses the writing of Musset's play* Lorenzaccio.]

If *Fantasio* appears to draw its gay animation from the encounter with George Sand, then we must look to the same cause for a possible motivation of *Lorenzaccio.* What surprised us in *Fantasio* was the unexpected affirmation of *bonheur,* a state of being which had been repeatedly idealized, without fulfillment, in Musset's previous works. The uniqueness of *Lorenzaccio* is its sudden grandeur. It is well over three times longer than any of its predecessors, and the creations which follow it shrink back to the typical shorter formats. It also sinks deep roots into historical reality, for it dramatizes a recorded moment in the story of Renaissance Florence. This is not the first time that Musset has chosen characters from the inventory of Renaissance history (*André del Sarto,* for example), but it is the first and only time that he has actually *used* history as a source.

The genesis of *Lorenzaccio* begins shortly after the liaison with George Sand, whose then-unpublished "scène historique," *Une Conjuration en 1537,*[1] was made available to Musset, thus giving him the initial impetus to adapt and magnify the circumstances leading to the death of Alessandro de Medici. In addition Musset consulted chronicled versions of the event, notably Benedetto Varchi's *Storia fiorentina.*[2] The only other certainty about the composition of *Lorenzaccio* was that it was written between the summer of 1833, the initial phase of the George Sand interlude, and the autumn of 1834, when the play was published. Scholars agree that the play was written in stages and that a substantial part of it must have been written before the lovers' excursion to Italy, December 1833. The rest of it is placed, in varying proportions, partly in the brief happy period in Venice, and partly in the sick and lonely atmosphere of Musset's return to Paris.[3] The failure to isolate *Lorenzaccio* derives in part from the difficulty of dissociating its creation from that of the other works which date from the same period. Knowing that *Fantasio* was written before the trip to Venice, that *On ne badine pas avec l'amour* was completed before July, 1834, and that Musset was ill and despondent during the winter and early spring of 1834, scholars have naturally been intrigued by the appearance of a monumental work under circumstances which appear to have left little time for its execution. The feat is not so incredible as it may at first seem, for if Musset was able to write *Les Caprices de Marianne,* a finished play, in six weeks, he certainly could have brought *Lorenzaccio* to fulfillment in three or four months.

To identify *Lorenzaccio,* its action, its characters, and its language, it is hardly enough to disengage merely those traits associated with the circumstances of conception and realization. The closing acts of *Un Spectacle dans un fauteuil* are artistic as well as personal fulfillments, for they are the crowning of a growth, the roots of which go all the way back to Musset's apprenticeship, to a series of manifestations during which the existence of a George Sand was at best a dream. If it is true that he could not have written his major dramatic works without the reality of George Sand, then it is just as true that he could not have written them without the reality of his acquired literary experience.

We look in vain among the earlier works for a clue to the dimensions of *Lorenzaccio,* for it is a full-blooded five-act drama, whose performance requires a multitude of players. The lead role is obviously that of Lorenzo de Medici, *alias* Lorenzaccio, Renzinaccio, Renzo, Lorenzino, Renzino, Lorenzetta, and "mignon." Even the proliferation of names is meaningful, for it is a way of posing the play's crucial problem, namely the identification of the hero and the attribution of motive to his actions. To the citizens of Florence, he is Lorenzaccio, witty, but cowardly and depraved cousin of the reigning duke, Alexander, whom he serves as buffoon and procurer. To his mother, he is usually Renzo, a name corresponding to the maternal recollection of the uncorrupted son. To the duke, he is also Renzo, and the name here connotes the affection of a particular relationship, ranging from amused tolerance to the close ties of debauchery. Lorenzo becomes Lorenzetta when he swoons at the sight of a drawn sword. Only Philippe Strozzi, noble scholar, *père de famille,* and patriot, knows Lorenzo, but even so, he cannot understand him.

Besides the major supporting roles already mentioned (Lorenzo's mother, the duke Alexander and Philippe Strozzi), the cast includes Pierre Strozzi, hot-tempered son of Philippe, Julien Salviati, a lecher who makes his prey available to the duke, Tebaldeo, a painter, Scoronconcolo, a *spadassin* in the service of Lorenzo, Giomo, bodyguard to the duke, Catherine Ginori, youthful aunt of Lorenzo, Louise Strozzi, daughter of Philippe, and, finally, Cardinal Cibo and his sister-in-law the Marquise Cibo. There are also two roles without names, but which are none the less significant: a merchant and a goldsmith[4] who represent differing reactions to the courtly and political events which they witness as citizens of Florence.

The only major character whom Lorenzo does not encounter in the course of the play is the Marquise Cibo, who surrenders her body to Alexander in the vain hope of trying to persuade him to redeem Florence from the clutches of Rome and of "César," the Emperor of Germany. The fact that Lorenzo and la Cibo do not meet on the stage is not a flaw. In fact, the contrast between her role and that of Lorenzo is most effective. She corrupts herself, hoping thereby to breathe patriotism into the soul of her ruler. At the same time, Lorenzo, who is already corrupt, is planning to murder the duke for reasons which have nothing to do with patriotism.

Lorenzaccio demonstrates that virtue and *honnêteté* are either swallowed up by corruption, as in the case of la Cibo, or they are powerless, as in the case of Philippe Strozzi. Lorenzo, the one character who acts, does so for purely private reasons, and although his action opens wide the gates of political change, no one crosses the threshold. His murderous act is completely without political consequence. He derives from it a brief, supreme moment of fulfillment, but soon becomes a hunted man and suffers a swift but horrible death, the only possible social retribution for an act of treason.

Lorenzo's role as *meneur* is fulfilled at the end of Act IV, when the aim of his private conspiracy is realized. The *meneur* of the fifth act is Cardinal Cibo, an ambitious emissary of the Pope and of the Emperor, who delays the public announcement of the duke's death, tyrannizes the leaders who are presumably responsible for running the state, and handpicks the docile Cosimo de Medici as the new duke. The only resistance to the cardinal's will is a vote of abstention cast by Palla Ruccellai. The abstention is, of course, as futile as all the other patriotic gestures of the play. Lorenzo's cynical views on politics and society are therefore vindicated by what follows in the wake of his act.

Contrasting with Lorenzo's solitary plot and with the cardinal's tyrannical perpetuation of *status quo,* is the republican conspiracy which centers around the two Strozzi, the father Philippe and the son Pierre. The older Strozzi longs for and works for the ultimate liberation of the city, but his conduct is basically temperate. Even under the heel of despotism, the philosopher-patriot is unwilling to be committed to treasonable violence. The son, however, is volatile and ambitious. When Julien Salviati attempts to dishonor the reputation of his sister Louise, he strikes back in immediate reprisal, unstayed by the moderation of his father. When Pierre is in turn arrested, Philippe loses his earlier patience, and cries vengeance. Lorenzo tries to stop the elder Strozzi, but his eloquence falls, and the patriot goes off to round up his family. He is no longer a patriot, however, for his libertarian motivation has been compounded by the desire for vengeance. When Louise is poisoned by a

Salviati hireling, the shocked father abandons the vendetta. He withdraws to Venice, leaving militancy to younger and hotter heads. Philippe's patriotism, like that of Marquise Cibo, is ineffectual as an instrument of political upheaval.

The significance of Philippe's role goes far beyond his failures as a patriot, as a philosopher, or as a father, for he is the only character in the play who receives any kind of direct revelation of Lorenzo's inner or former self. He is the only Florentine who welcomes Lorenzo into his home and who knows him as anything other than "Lorenzaccio." He is the first character to whom Lorenzo reveals his long-nurtured plan of murder. Lorenzo's access to the Strozzi circle serves a double purpose. It allows Lorenzo to play out his role as Lorenzaccio, for he reports much of the republican unrest to the duke, who promptly arranges for the banishment of offending individuals. Lorenzo's presence in the Strozzi house is therefore part of his disguise, for as the duke's informer his association with Strozzi is beyond suspicion. Lorenzo also has a personal relationship with the older Strozzi. The philosopher accepts Lorenzo on faith, so to speak, on the naked assurance that behind Lorenzaccio there lives a Lorenzo, and that this Lorenzo shares a common aim with other patriots. In order to understand the relationship, we must see Philippe as a matured image of the Lorenzo who might have been, of the Lorenzo who had started out to be a scholar. Had he not corrupted himself while constructing his plot against Alexander, he would have developed into, something very much like Philippe Strozzi. As Lorenzo and Philippe meet again and again on stage, there is a striking interplay between the wisdom of virtue (Philippe) and the wisdom of corruption (Lorenzo-Lorenzaccio). Ironically, it is the latter wisdom which leads to Lorenzo's act, while the wisdom of Strozzi remains inactive. Lorenzo believes that it is not enough to distinguish good from bad, virtue from vice, purity from corruption. He is convinced from his experience as Lorenzaccio that corruption is largely self-perpetuating and resistant to virtue. Corruption, in other words, contaminates most of those who are surrounded by it. Those who would fight tyranny and depravity find that their weapons are "hommes sans bras," ineffectual abstractions such as virtue, honor, liberty, patriotism, and republicanism.

As for Lorenzo's deed, he performs it in spite of his conviction that it will contribute not one whit to the restoration of free Florence. The only real beneficiary of Lorenzo's act is Lorenzo himself, and since he dies as he has anticipated, stigmatized as a traitor, it is important to isolate his motivation. His doing and dying cannot ultimately be equated with religious or political martyrdom.[5] The only person who regards him as a political hero is Philippe Strozzi, with whom Lorenzo takes refuge after the murder. To Philippe, Lorenzo's

act is equivalent to Lucius Junius Brutus' overthrow of Tarquin, an event which led to the establishment of a republic. The resemblance is sharpened by the fact that Brutus had also to assume a role (that of madman) in order to bring his plot to fruition. The closing events of the play, however, make it perfectly clear that the analogy is misleading, and even Philippe is finally disabused.

The question of motivation is partially obscured by the ambiguous nature of Lorenzo's first desire to kill. This urge, fixed outside the play, is discussed by Lorenzo in one of his scenes with Philippe (III, iii). The latter, incensed over the arrest of his sons, has asked Lorenzo to commit himself, to stop playing at being Lorenzaccio, and to join the republican cause. Lorenzo remarks: "Tel que tu me vois, j'ai été honnête. J'ai cru à la vertu, à la grandeur humaine, comme un martyr croit à son Dieu. J'ai, versé plus de larmes sur la pauvre Italie, que Niobé sur ses filles" (*Theatre*, p. 133). It is clear that Lorenzo is not describing himself as he *is*, but only as he once was. Prodded by the mystified Philippe, Lorenzo continues: "Ma jeunesse a été pure comme l'or. Pendant vingt ans de silence, la foudre s'est amoncelée dans ma poitrine; et il faut que je sois réellement une étincelle de tonnerre, car tout à coup, une certaine nuit que j'étais assis dans les ruines du Colisée antique, je ne sais pourquoi je me levai; je tendis vers le ciel mes bras trempés de rosée, et je jurai qu'un des tyrans de ma patrie mourrait de ma main. J'étais un étudiant paisible, et je ne m'occupais alors que des arts et des sciences, et il m'est impossible de dire comment cet étrange serment s'est fait en moi. Peut-être est-ce là ce qu'on éprouve quand on devient amoureux" (p. 133). The purity of Lorenzo's youth was interrupted, suddenly and inexplicably, by an inner "étincelle de tonnerre." The inspiration to kill reduces itself to a "je ne sais quoi," for Lorenzo describes his youthful purity as a state of being rather than as a cause. Lorenzo himself can attribute no inner motive to the sudden urge. The gesture toward "le ciel" raises the possibility of divine inspiration, but it does not explain the human factor. The last sentence of the quoted passage is perhaps the most meaningful, for it is there that Lorenzo establishes a conscious link between his own exaltation and that of a fever-stricken "amoureux."

Philippe does not comprehend and Lorenzo elaborates as follows: "J'étais heureux alors, j'avais le cœur et les mains tranquilles; mon nom m'appelait au trône, et je n'avais qu'à laisser le soleil se lever et se coucher pour voir fleurir autour de moi toutes les espérances humaines. Les hommes ne m'avaient fait ni bien ni mal, mais j'étais bon, et pour mon malheur éternel, j'ai voulu être grand. Il faut que je l'avoue, si la Providence m'a poussé à la résolution de tuer un tyran, quel qu'il fût, l'orgueil m'y a poussé aussi. Que te dirais-je de plus? tous les Césars du monde me faisaient penser à Brutus"[6] (pp. 133-134). Providence is invoked as an inspiring force, thus repeating the suggestion that the original "étincelle" is of superhuman origin. To this, Lorenzo adds pride as the associated human element. Within the temporal structure of the play, however, Lorenzo has already been transformed into Lorenzaccio, whose actions are no longer related to pride and Providence. The *desire* to kill a tyrant, any tyrant, has a different motivation from the *plan* to kill Alexander. While Lorenzo's first urge may be associated with divine inspiration, Lorenzaccio's final act is an entirely human project.

The initial choice of victim was Pope Clement VII. Unfortunately, Lorenzo had to flee Rome after having insulted the Pope by decapitating the statues of the Arch of Constantine. He took refuge with his cousin Alexander. Lorenzo explains to Philippe that living with the idea of killing a tyrant became an obsession. Killing Alexander, however, was not something which could be done on the spur of the moment. The duke was well-protected, especially by Giomo, and by a light, but impervious shirt of mail, which he never took off. In order to kill, Lorenzo had to plan carefully. He had to gain his cousin's confidence, and it was for this reason that he began to play the role of Lorenzaccio. Corruption worked its way into Lorenzo's character, and there was nothing he could do to erase it and go back to what he had once been. What sustained him was the fond anticipation of killing. During the gradual erosion of virtue, the political aspect of the obsession faded away. It is not Alexander the *tyrant* whom he kills, but the man Alexander, with whom he had come to share a sordid existence. Just before he commits the act, he realizes that he is not an assassin. He even acknowledges that Alexander, in his own peculiar way, has been kind to him. The murder becomes, therefore, an act for its own sake, motivated primarily by the desire for satisfaction, by the urge to realize an obsession. For Lorenzo, it is an ecstasy.

Lorenzaccio's inability to resume his former identity is a variation of the pattern of destiny-failure. The hero of *La Coupe et les lèvres,* corrupted by false values, found himself unable to return to the life and love which he had abandoned. Frank wanted to "revenir sur ses pas," but was frustrated by forces beyond his control. Lorenzaccio, on the other hand, remembers the Lorenzo of old, but realizes from the very beginning that there is no hope of return. The impossibility of taking the backward step toward restoration of character has also appeared in *Les Caprices de Marianne,* in *André del Sarto,* and in *Les Marrons du feu.* The *dédoublement* and the role-playing associated with the Lorenzo-Lorenzaccio transformation are also variants of an old theme. There are two Razettas and two Franks, just as there will be two Perdicans. In other instances, the *dédoublement* is expressed by the juxtaposition of two characters: André and Cordiani, Octave and Coelio.

Questions of fate and identity, of what is real and what is illusory, have all been repeatedly posed in the works preceding *Lorenzaccio.* Even the strangely inverted world of *Fantasio* may be appropriately recalled, for Fantasio and Lorenzo have something in common: the urge to seek pleasure from acts which appear to be gratuitous. Here, the resemblance stops, for while Fantasio glided into his role as jester in a moment of drunken caprice, retaining completely his original character, the pure Lorenzo becomes the corrupt Lorenzaccio in order to satisfy a consuming state of will. It is evident, then, that part of Lorenzo's ancestry is traceable; his family tree goes at least as far back as *Les Marrons du feu.* Still, the complexity of his character and the rich medium in which he functions, make his ancestors appear pale and monolithic. The casting of his body into the sea duplicates the watery demise of Rafael Garuci, but between these two seemingly twin dramatic events there is a gulf of dreamed, written, and lived experience.

The detailed discussion of the text must begin with a scene which Musset decided to suppress in the transfer from manuscript to print. The scene in question was originally intended to serve as the first scene of the play. It dramatizes the visit of Benvenuto Cellini to the sleeping quarters shared by Alexander and Lorenzo.[7] The purpose of the visit is to show the duke the obverse of a medal which Cellini has just struck. The discussion centers initially on the problem of designing the reverse of the medal, for Cellini is obliged to leave Florence and must turn the job over to some one else. The duke attempts to seduce the artist into his service, but his rhetoric has no effect, and the independent Cellini exits, leaving the duke somewhat piqued. The closing dialogue of the scene reveals that the duke is already bored with his affair with la Cibo, and is ready to take on Lorenzo's young aunt Catherine. Lorenzo agrees to bring the matter to Catherine's attention, but he is somber and distracted. The probable reason for the omission of this scene can be easily inferred, for the episode would have revealed, in too obvious and too premature a manner, the salient threads of the action: the strange relationship between Alexander and Lorenzo and the fact that there is more to Lorenzaccio than there appears to be. The suggestivity of the setting, revealing the cousins who have been sleeping in the same room, is heightened by the appellation "mignon" which Alexander bestows on Lorenzo. A hint of Lorenzo's plot springs from the conversation about the medal. He assures Cellini and Alexander: "N'en doute pas, Benvenuto; je ferai un revers à la médaille du duc," and "J'en ferai tel que le monde n'en a point encore vu" (*Théâtre*, p. 218). Cellini himself was no doubt intended to function as a spokesman for the artist who has maintained professional integrity. His refusal of Alexander's patronage affirms his independence. Although the character was suppressed, the function remains intact in the published version, for it was merely transferred to the role of the painter Tebaldeo.

The beginning of the play reveals Alexander, accompanied by Lorenzo and Giomo, waiting for a maiden whom Lorenzo has procured for him. Lorenzo entertains them with a description of his procuring activities, a recital into which he plunges with obvious relish: "Voir dans un enfant de quinze ans la rouée à venir; étudier, ensemencer, infiltrer paternellement le filon mystérieux du vice dans un conseil d'ami, dans une caresse au menton—tout dire et ne rien dire, selon le caractère des parents—habituer doucement l'imagination qui se développe à donner des corps à ses fantômes, à toucher ce qui l'effraye, à mépriser ce qui la protège! Cela va plus vite qu'on ne pense; le vrai mérite est de frapper juste" (p. 52). Lorenzo's words furnish a clue to the nature of his still-hidden obsession, for they suggest the process through which he has corrupted himself, and through which he has gained the intimacy of the duke. The allusion to "donner des corps à ses fantômes" recalls all the earlier spectral patterns of Musset's work. The echo is immediately intensified by the introduction of Maffio, the girl's brother. "Il me semblait dans mon rêve voir ma sœur traverser notre jardin, tenant une lanterne sourde, et couverte de pierreries. Je me suis éveillé en sursaut. Dieu sait que ce n'est qu'une illusion trop forte pour que le sommeil ne s'enfuie pas devant elle" (p. 53). When Maffio realizes that what he thought was a dream is actually happening, he rushes out, sword in hand, to defend the family honor. When Giomo disarms him, Maffio cries out: "O honte! ô excès de misère! S'il y a des lois à Florence, si quelque justice vit encore sur la terre, par ce qu'il y a de vrai et de sacré au monde, je me jetterai aux pieds du duc, et il vous fera pendre tous les deux" (p. 54). The duke then appears in person and arranges for Maffio to be paid a few ducats, in exchange for his silence. The question of justice is clearly raised at the very beginning of the play, and it emerges from an atmosphere of corruption, but Maffio, and those like him, who have been outraged by the captivity of Florence, demonstrate by their ultimate inaction that Lorenzo's corruptly acquired wisdom is dramatically sound.

The second scene enlarges the initial portrait of vice. It is daybreak, and two shopkeepers, the merchant and the goldsmith, are in the process of opening their establishments. Across the way, the Florentine aristocracy is beginning to emerge from an all-night wedding celebration. The merchant is chained to his business and has yielded long ago to the corruption around him. In fact, he doesn't even recognize it as evil, and is openly indulgent about the decadence before his eyes. The *orfèvre*, on the other hand, is clear-sighted. He sees Florence as a victim, yoked fast to the joint despotism of Rome and Germany. He cites Philippe Strozzi, a known patriot, as "le plus brave homme de Florence." He asserts that Alexander holds power only thanks to the German garrison. "C'est en vertu des hallebardes qui se promènent sur la plate-forme qu'un bâtard, une moitié de Médicis, un butor que le ciel avait fait pour être garçon boucher ou valet de charrue, couche dans le lit de nos filles, boit nos bouteilles, casse nos vitres, et encore le paye-t-on pour cela" (pp. 58-59). As perceptive as the goldsmith is, he too fails to act in the end. In terms of Lorenzo's insight, what the artisan does not realize is that the German garrison is only part of the story. The rest is that corruption thrives because it contaminates, in one way or another, those who would fight it.

Masked men and women are seen leaving the wedding celebration. Alexander and Julien Salviati emerge, dressed as nuns, a *travestissement* which is visually decadent, but which Cardinal Cibo will later justify as not *intentionally* reprehensible. As the *provéditeur* of Florence is mounting his horse, he is struck by a broken bottle. The official, unhurt, looks up to locate the culprit, who turns out to be Lorenzaccio, also costumed as a nun. The *provéditeur* lashes out verbally at Lorenzo, calling him a drunk and a juvenile prankster. Lorenzo is indulging in the sordid game which is necessary to his scheme, for he must be sure that he will be fully accredited as Lorenzaccio. The scene ends as Julien Salviati makes unwholesome advances to Louise Strozzi, who rebuffs him and rides off.

The next episode begins as a tender leavetaking between the marquise Cibo and her husband, who is about to go off and visit his estates. The natural beauty of the region which the marquis will be inspecting is associated with honor in love and marriage. After the marquis' exit, Cardinal Cibo begins to talk about the duke, for he knows, through intercepted messages, that Alexander has been trying to win la Cibo. The mention of the duke arouses la Cibo's patriotic ardor. She repeats, for the benefit of the cardinal, the same theme already elaborated by the goldsmith: Florence is in the grip of monsters. Her solution is to induce Alexander to break the grip of tyranny. Later, she will yield to Alexander, thinking that she can imbue him with the right kind of spirit. She will destroy in vain the honor of her marriage for the sake of a political ideal. The only gain will be still another corruption to add to the vast catalog.

The fourth scene places us in the ducal courtyard, where Alexander, Cardinal Valori (the official papal emissary to Florence), and Sire Maurice, are discussing Lorenzo. Valori, with a little help from Sire Maurice, advises the duke that Pope Paul III claims Lorenzo as a fugitive from justice. Alexander's first response is characteristic: "De sa justice? Il n'a jamais offensé de pape, à ma connaissance, que Clément VII, feu mon cousin, qui, à cette heure, est en enfer" (p. 69). Sire Maurice points out that Lorenzo is an atheist who respects nothing, and that the government of Florence must have an aura of respectability. He adds to the indictment the fact that the people call Lorenzo "Lorenzaccio," because of his direction of the royal sex life. The duke, becoming more serious, reminds the courtiers that Lorenzo is his cousin. At this moment, Cardinal Cibo enters and reports that "Messire Francesco Molza vient de débiter à l'Académie romaine une harangue en latin contre le mutilateur de l'arc de Constantin" (p. 69). The duke begins to lose his composure: "Allons donc, vous me mettriez en colère! Renzo, un homme à craindre! le plus fieffé poltron! une femmelette, l'ombre d'un ruffian énervé! un rêveur qui marche nuit et jour sans épée, de peur d'en apercevoir l'ombre à son côté! d'ailleurs un philosophe, un gratteur de papier, un méchant poète qui ne sait seulement pas faire un sonnet!" (p. 70). The harangue ends as Alexander affirms: "J'aime Lorenzo, moi, et, par la mort de Dieu! il restera ici." Thus, the duke rounds out the portrait of Lorenzo-Lorenzaccio: he is an effeminate coward, a would-be intellectual, the last person in Florence capable of inspiring fear. In spite of what Alexander attributes to Lorenzo, he likes him or loves him, as the case may be. The Cardinal points out that if Lorenzo poses a threat, it is to the duke himself. Alexander quells this rejoinder by reminding the assembled leaders that Lorenzo has been helping him by serving as an informer. As Lorenzo is glimpsed below, Alexander provides a word-picture to accompany his cousin's ascent of the stairway: "Regardez-moi ce petit corps maigre, ce lendemain d'orgie ambulant. Regardez-moi ces yeux plombés, ces mains fluettes et maladives, à peine assez fermes pour soutenir un éventail, ce visage morne, qui sourit quelquefois, mais qui n'a pas la force de rire. C'est là un homme à craindre?" (p. 70).

Shortly after Lorenzo appears, his witty barbs irritate Sire Maurice, who draws his sword. Teasingly, the duke allows the *jeu* to continue by offering to serve as Lorenzo's second. Pages are sent to bring Lorenzo a sword, for the Medici honor is at stake. Lorenzo quivers and shakes and faints away in a heap, to the great amusement of the duke, who shouts exultantly: "Quand je le disais! personne ne le sait mieux que moi; la seule vue d'une épée le fait trouver mal. Allons, chère Lorenzetta, fais-toi emporter chez ta mère" (p. 73). While Cardinal Valori, the official emissary of Rome, shows compassion toward Lorenzaccio ("Pauvre jeune homme!"), Cardinal Cibo asks Alexander: "Vous croyez à cela, monseigneur?" The duke does, indeed, believe that Lorenzo's pattern of behavior is perfectly credible, for he has seen him behave similarly on other occasions. Lorenzo has clearly done a good job of habituating Alexander to Lorenzaccio. The Cardinal, on the other hand, finds Lorenzo's swooning cowardice hard to swallow. In the end, the Cardinal is the only person at court

who begins to suspect what Lorenzo has in mind. Consequently, he is the only political character who gains from Lorenzo's act.

The setting of the fifth scene is out of doors, "devant l'église de Saint-Miniato, à Montolivet." A crowd of unnamed characters, representing the upper and middle classes, is already stationed in the plaza as an even larger group of worshipers emerges from the church. The merchant and the goldsmith of the second scene reappear, and serve as links to the preceding action. The goldsmith still voices his patriotic bitterness at the fate which has overtaken Florence; the merchant is still concerned only with selling goods to the aristocrats. A *cavalier* overhears the goldsmith and asks him whether "la haine de la tyrannie fait encore trembler tes doigts sur tes ciselures précieuses" (p. 74). The response: "C'est vrai, Excellence. Si j'étais un grand artiste, j'aimerais les princes, parce qu'eux seuls peuvent faire entreprendre de grands travaux. Les grands artistes n'ont pas de patrie. Moi, je fais des saints ciboires et des poignées d'épée" (pp. 74-75). The *orfèvre*'s words are somewhat cryptic, because he seems to be saying that he is able to hate tyranny because he is not a great artist. If he were a great artist, the question of tyranny would be purely academic, because as a great artist, he would need the help of princes, who alone are capable of subsidizing great works. The great artist, however, is independent of political situations, for he has no *patrie* except his work. He deals with the prince as patron, and has no need to make distinctions based on social or political criteria. The mediocre artist is by nature committed to his times and is susceptible of being corrupted by political considerations. Therefore, he can indulge in the luxury of hating tyranny. The contrast between the purity of great art and the prostituting of mediocre art has already been seen in earlier works such as "Les Vœux stériles" and the "Dédicace" *of* **La Coupe et les lèvres.** The goldsmith's response also gives us added insight into some of the internal relationships which abound in **Lorenzaccio.** The painter Tebaldeo, for example, has views which contrast with those of the goldsmith. Finally, the response of the *orfèvre* suggests that Lorenzo's enterprise may itself be a work of art, for Lorenzaccio, like the great artist, is a man without a country, steadfastly refusing to allow his project to be contaminated by politics.

As the scene continues, a patriotic burgher speaks out about the "malheurs" of Florence: "Le pape et l'empereur sont accouchés d'un bâtard qui a droit de vie et de mort sur nos enfants, et qui ne pourrait pas nommer sa mère" (p. 75). Soon, the prior of Capua, a son of Philippe Strozzi, emerges from the throng. He is on stage to receive the insults of Julien Salviati, who, knowing that the prior is Louise's brother, insists loudly that he and Louise are to sleep together "au premier jour." As the churchman turns his back and walks away, the depraved Salviati remarks: "J'aime beaucoup ce brave prieur, à qui un propos sur sa sœur a fait oublier le reste de son argent. Ne dirait-on pas que toute la vertu de Florence s'est réfugiée chez ces Strozzi? Le voilà qui se retourne. Ecarquille les yeux tant que tu voudras, tu ne me feras pas peur" (p. 79). Salviati's words are a foreboding of things to come, for corruption has nothing to fear from the innocuous gestures of virtue and patriotism.

The closing scene of the first act is set along the banks of the Arno, where Marie Soderini, Lorenzo's mother, and Catherine Ginori, his aunt, have gone for a stroll. Already ashamed of her son, Marie now must add to her burden the news of Lorenzo's latest act of cowardice: his fainting at the sight of a sword. Catherine tries to avoid making judgments, but soon points out that the worst thing of all is that Lorenzo is not an *honnête homme*. She also observes that there was another Lorenzo: "Ah! cette Florence! c'est là qu'on l'a perdu! N'ai-je pas vu briller quelquefois dans ses yeux le feu d'une noble ambition? Sa jeunesse n'a-t-elle pas été l'aurore d'un soleil levant? Et souvent encore auojurd'hui il me semble qu'un éclair rapide. . . . Je me dis malgré moi que tout n'est pas mort en lui" (p. 80). Catherine is obviously not convinced that Lorenzo is thoroughly corrupt, and she attributes to him a residue of goodness. Marie's response to this ray of hope is outwardly negative, but in the course of elaborating her despair, she remembers Lorenzo as a student, when he used to admire Plutarch (the Brutus motif) and when "un saint amour de la vérité brillait sur ses lèvres et dans ses yeux noirs" (p. 81). The irony here is that the one thing Lorenzo does not lose in his metamorphosis is his love for truth, for he finds in his corruption an order of truth the existence of which he never would have discovered otherwise. It is this truth which makes him skeptical of the power of virtue and which convinces him that his act of murder will be politically and morally meaningless.

Marie affirms that "la souillure de son cœur est montée au visage" (p. 81). Here we have dramatic proof that Lorenzo has had to hide his intentions even from those who are closest to him, for Marie's judgment of her son is actually the reverse of the prevailing situation. The corruption did not begin in Lorenzo's heart, and spread from there throughout his body, until it reached his countenance. The role of Lorenzaccio began with his *face;* it started as a pose. The borrowed mask of corruption soon became a part of him, and the infection spread into his entire being. Marie, bitter and sorrowful, ends by chastising herself: "Ah! Cattina, pour dormir tranquille, il faut n'avoir jamais fait certains rêves. Cela est trop cruel d'avoir vécu dans un palais de fées, où murmuraient les cantiques des anges, de s'y être endormie, bercée par son fils, et de se réveiller dans une masure ensanglantée, pleine de débris d'orgie et de restes hu-

mains, dans les bras d'un spectre hideux qui vous tue en vous appelant encore du nom de mère" (p. 81). Marie's outburst picks up the threads of dreaming and waking which were first woven into the words of Maffio in the first scene. Also, the image of being in the embrace of a *spectre hideux* is a familiar one, which can be traced back to Musset's first poems and to his struggles with translation. Finally, the reappearance of Maffio adds an effective touch to the structure of the entire act, for having one dreamer encounter another embellishes the dramatic frame of Lorenzaccio's first portrait.

The end of the scene is devoted to Maffio and the *bannis,* whom the two women have glimpsed and heard in the twilight. They talk about awaiting orders from Philippe Strozzi, the last hope of liberty. Then they bid Florence an accursed farewell:

LE PREMIER:

> Adieu, Florence, peste de l'Italie; adieu, mère stérile, qui n'as plus de lait pour tes enfants.

LE SECOND:

> Adieu, Florence la bâtarde, spectre hideux de l'antique Florence; adieu, fange sans nom.

TOUS LES BANNIS:

> Adieu, Florence! maudites soient les mamelles de tes femmes! maudits soient tes sanglots; maudites les prières de tes églises, le pain de tes blés, l'air de tes rues! Malédiction sur la dernière goutte de ton sang corrompu!

> [P. 84.]

The curses of the *bannis* are not gratuitous, for the language in which they are couched is linked in several ways to the action. The motherchild relationship between Florence and her citizens is reiterated by the artist Tebaldeo, who regards the city as his mother. The maternal quality of Florence suggests also that there may be significant parallels emerging from the Marie-Lorenzo and from the Philippe-Pierre and Philippe-Lorenzo sets, for they are all, in fact or in essence, relationships of parent to offspring. The image of sterility contrasts videly with the closing words of Act IV, Scene V, when Lorenzo, contemplating his crime, remarks: "Eh bien! j'ai commis bien des crimes, et si ma vie est jamais dans la balance d'un juge quelconque, il y aura d'un côté une montagne de sanglots; mais il y aura peut-être de l'autre une goutte de lait pur tombée du sein de Catherine, et qui aura nourri d'honnêtes enfants" (p. 168).[8] The word "bâtarde" stigmatizes the city ruled by the bastard duke Alexander. The "spectre hideux" follows by a few moments the similar description of Lorenzo given by Marie, so that Lorenzaccio is associated with Alexander in the corruption of Florence.

The closing malediction is, on the other hand, not integral to the action. It is rather an echo of Frank's curse, at the beginning of *La Coupe et les lèvres.*

In the monologue which begins the second act, Philippe meditates over the destiny of Florence. He wonders whether corruption is a natural law, whether virtue is merely a mask which people don on Sunday. In his moment of pessimism, he puts himself in the class of "nous autres vieux rêveurs," who can accomplish all sorts of wondrous things in their *cabinet d'étude.* He finds it difficult to believe that "le bonheur des hommes ne soit qu'un rêve." In fact, he rejects the idea at the end of his musings: "Allons-y donc plus hardiment! la république, il nous faut ce mot-là. Et quand ce ne serait qu'un mot, c'est quelque chose, puisque les peuples se lèvent quand il traverse l'air . . ." (p. 85). Philippe is not ready to accept Lorenzo's truth. He takes comfort from the word "Republic," and attributes to this abstraction the power to move the populace.

In the next scene, Cardinal Valori and Lorenzo are standing before a church. Valori listens to the sounds coming from within and reveals his deep love for the "pompes magnifiques" of Catholic worship. His words bring together into a harmonious unity the music of the organ, the texture and color of the tapestries, the paintings of the early masters, the fragrance of incense, and the sweet sounds of the choir. He concludes: "Rien n'est plus beau, selon moi, qu'une religion qui se fait aimer par de pareils moyens. Pourquoi les prêtres voudraient-ils servir un Dieu jaloux? La religion n'est pas un oiseau de proie; c'est une colombe compatissante qui plane doucement sur tous les rêves et sur tous les amours" (pp. 87-88). Tebaldeo, who has been in the background, overhears Valori. He steps forward eagerly, for he shares Valori's feelings, and is especially grateful because he knows that Valori is an *honnête homme* whose opinions are respectable. Tebaldeo tells of his apprenticeship, spent largely in churches. He sees in the religious art of Raphael and Michelangelo "la gloire de l'artiste." The conversation between Valori and Tebaldeo reiterates the ideas on art and religion which Musset voiced in "Les Vœux stériles" and in *La Coupe et les lèvres,* and which he dramatized in *André del Sarto.* Valori's homage to a harmonious religion, not dependent on the idea of a jealous divinity, is an idealization, just as Philippe Strozzi's hopes for human happiness are also on the ideal side of the line separating dream from reality. Valori, an *honnête homme* like Strozzi, is the same Valori who was moved by compassion to say of the swooning Lorenzo: "Pauvre jeune homme!" He is the same Valori who serves ineffectually as official papal delegate, while Cardinal Cibo pulls the strings in the background. He is dreaming when he claims that religion is not a bird of prey, for the characterization of Cardinal Cibo, who *succeeds* in the reality of the drama, stands out sharply in contradiction.

Valori offers Tebaldeo a chance to paint for him. At this point, Lorenzo intervenes, for he notices that the artist is carrying a *cadre,* and suggests that it is as good a moment as any to accept Valori's commission. Tebaldeo, who insists throughout the discussion that he is mediocre, is reticent in his reply: "C'est une esquisse bien pauvre d'un rêve magnifique." Lorenzo's retort is outwardly flippant: "Vous faites le portrait de vos rêves? Je ferai poser pour vous quelques-uns des miens" (p. 89). The response is meaningful, for Lorenzo will in fact end by using Tebaldeo as an unwitting accessory. It will be while Alexander is posing half-naked for Tebaldeo that Lorenzo will steal and secrete the ubiquitous coat of mail, thereby rendering the duke vulnerable to the sword. Since Lorenzo's obsession with killing Alexander is in the order of a dream, his casual remark to Tebaldeo will be fulfilled in the course of the drama. Tebaldeo at first ignores Lorenzo's jibes and continues to theorize in earnest: "Réaliser des rêves, voilà la vie du peintre." He develops his theme by comparing the imaginations of great artists to "un orbre plein de sève." The process of moving, in art, from imagination to realization, is similar to the ways of nature: the tree produces buds, flowers, and fruit beneath the growth-inspiring warmth of the sun. The dreams of the artist reach fruition under the aegis of divine inspiration (p. 89). The theme is an old one for Musset, and we have seen it in many forms in virtually all of his early work. Within the play, the happy marriage of the Cibo has already been linked with the unsullied beauties of nature. True love and true art are born and mature by a process which duplicates that of nature. Can the growth of Lorenzo's obsession be likened to the course of love and art? Can the act of murder, for all its corruption, be at the same time an act of love and a work of art?

Lorenzo continues to badger Tebaldeo by offering him the golden opportunity to paint "la Mazzafirra toute nue." Tebaldeo replies: "Je ne puis faire le portrait d'une courtisane" (p. 90). Lorenzo then asks Tebaldeo whether he would be willing to do a landscape of Florence. Tebaldeo responds affirmatively, and a brief discussion ensues as to the best vantage point for such a study. Lorenzo, having put Tebaldeo at his ease, suddenly reaches his rhetorical objective: "Pourquoi donc ne peux-tu pas peindre une courtisane, si tu peux peindre un mauvais lieu?" (p. 91). Tebaldeo is shocked: "On ne m'a point encore appris à parler ainsi de ma mère." Lorenzo snaps back: "Alors, tu n'est qu'un bâtard, car ta mère n'est qu'une catin." Tebaldeo takes the provocation in stride, answering calmly and with conviction: "Une blessure sanglante peut engendrer la corruption dans le corps le plus sain. Mais des gouttes précieuses du sang de ma mère sort une plante odorante qui guérit tous les maux. L'art, cette fleur divine, a quelquefois besoin du fumier pour engraisser le sol et le féconder (p. 91). Tebaldeo does not mean that art can cure social and political ills, but that it can exist and even thrive in a decayed environment. His words also apply to Lorenzo, who started out as a "corps sain," and who became corrupt. The work of art which emerges from his corruption is the murder of Alexander. Tebaldeo explains in the continuing exchange that there is no conflict between his views on art and his religious devotion. "Je ne ris point du malheur des familles; je dis que la poésie est la plus douce des souffrances, et qu'elle aime ses sœurs. Je plains les peuples malheureux, mais je crois en effet qu'ils font les grands artistes" (p. 92). The artist can sympathize with the sufferings born of political corruption, but he does not act to alleviate it, for the simple reason that art is above and beyond sociopolitical commitments. This idea is reinforced by Tebaldeo's response to Lorenzo's invitation to become his protégé: "Je n'appartiens à personne. Quand la pensée veut être libre, le corps doit l'être aussi" (p. 92).

Lorenzo continues to provoke Tebaldeo. He tells him that he must be either "boiteux" or "fou" to remain in Florence, where "en l'honneur de tes idées de liberté, le premier valet d'un Médicis peut t'assommer sans qu'on y trouve à redire" (p. 93). Tebaldeo indicates that he stays only because he loves his "mother," and adds, in response to still another jibe, that he would kill the duke if attacked by him. Finally, Lorenzo asks him whether he is a republican or a monarchist. Tebaldeo's response, "Je suis artiste; j'aime ma mère et ma maîtresse," appears to satisfy Lorenzo who ends the scene by inviting Tebaldeo to the palace: ". . . je veux te faire faire un tableau d'importance pour le jour de mes noces" (p. 93). When the entire exchange between Tebaldeo and Lorenzo is reviewed in the light of subsequent events, it is evident that Lorenzo's insulting behavior is designed to test Tebaldeo's integrity. The artist passes the test because he maintains his professional independence, refuses to take political sides, and reveals in his responses that his decision to remain in Florence (when others had left) has nothing to do with the patriotism of which Lorenzo has such a low opinion. Thus, Tebaldeo establishes himself as a character whom Lorenzo can use in the elaboration of his murder plot. Lorenzo's parting words about a "tableau d'importance" refer to what will take place in Scene VI, when Lorenzo brings about the disappearance of the coat of mail. The second part of Lorenzo's invitation, the mystifying "pour le jour de mes noces," means nothing to Tebaldeo, but clearly reveals the sexual nature of the murder.

The third scene of Act II conveys the reader to the palazzo of the Cibo family. The cardinal is alone at first, waiting to confess his sister-in-law. His monologue reveals that he has a secret ambition to seize power for himself and that he would like to use the marquise as a pawn in his plan to check Alexander. The marquise's confession is a routine matter until she admits having read a letter inviting her to break her marriage vows. At this point, the cardinal insists on being told who wrote the letter, even though he already knows that it was written by the duke. The marquise refuses to comply, and the cardinal threatens to withhold absolution. She becomes angry, and is on the point of walking out, when the cardinal tries to assure her that he is not so evil as he may appear to be. When asked to clarify his words, he responds: "Qu'un confesseur doit tout savoir, parce qu'il peut tout diriger, et qu'un beau-frère ne doit rien dire, à certaines conditions" (p. 98). He adds suggestively: "Je voulais dire que le duc est puissant, qu'une rupture avec lui peut nuire aux plus riches familles; mais qu'un secret d'importance entre des mains expérimentées peut devenir une source de biens abondante" (p. 98). The marquise, however, is not immediately responsive to the vague words of her brother-in-law, who becomes irritated and storms out of the room. Left to herself, the marquise senses a greater, darker conspiracy, but is not sure of her own intuition. "Cibo ne ferait pas un pareil métier. Non! cela est sûr; je le connais. C'est bon pour un Lorenzaccio; mais lui!" (p. 99). The métier in question is that of *entremetteur.* La Cibo cannot believe that the cardinal would stoop so low as Lorenzaccio. She is, of course, mistaken in her knowledge of her brother-in-law, just as she is deluded in her hopes to instil patriotism into the indifferent soul of Alexander. Her failure is a failure of self-knowledge, whereas Lorenzo will succeed because of acquired wisdom. The cardinal is perfectly capable of being a Lorenzaccio, in his own way. He understands the deviousness of plotters and is able to distinguish the real from the feigned. As the action develops, he will be the only one capable of seeing through Lorenzo's disguise, and of stopping the murder of Alexander. As for the marquise, her closing remarks reinforce her uncertainties, for she cannot tell whether she is attracted to the duke patriotically or sexually: "Que tu es belle, Florence, mais que tu es triste! Il y a là plus d'une maison où Alexandre est entré la nuit, couvert de son manteau; c'est un libertin, je le sais.—Et pourquoi est-ce que tu te mêles à tout cela, toi, Florence? Est-ce donc que j'aime? Est-ce toi? Est-ce lui?" (pp. 99-100).

As the next scene unfolds in the palace of the Soderini, Catherine is about to read aloud a segment of Roman history. Lorenzo interrupts: "Je suis très fort sur l'histoire romaine. Il y avait une fois un gentilhomme nommé Tarquin le fils." Catherine stops him, not wishing to hear what she believes to be an "histoire de sang." Lorenzo replies: "Pas du tout; c'est un conte de fées. Brutus était un fou, un monomane, et rien de plus. Tarquin était un duc plein de sagesse, qui allait voir en pantoufles si les petites filles dormaient bien" (p. 100). The resemblance between Tarquin and Alexander is deliberately striking. More important than this, however, is the way in which Lorenzo plays out his role as Loren-

zaccio even with those dearest to him. Lorenzo's words
serve also as the first of many denials that there is any
similarity between the patriotic Brutus and the solitary
Lorenzo.

The next part of the scene is devoted to another spectral
visitation recounted by Marie and to Lorenzo's bizarre
reactions:

MARIE:

> Ce n'était point un rêve, car je ne dormais pas. J'étais
> seule dans cette grande salle; ma lampe était loin de
> moi, sur cette table auprès de la fenêtre. Je songeais
> aux jours où j'étais heureuse, aux jours de ton enfance,
> mon Lorenzino. Je regardais cette nuit obscure, et je
> me disais: il ne rentrera qu'au jour, lui qui passait au-
> trefois les nuits à travailler. Mes yeux se remplissaient
> de larmes, et je secouais la tête en les sentant couler.
> J'ai entendu tout d'un coup marcher lentement dans la
> galerie; je me suis retournée; un homme vêtu de noir
> venait à moi, un livre sous le bras—c'était toi, Renzo:
> "Comme tu reviens de bonne heure!" me suis-je écriée.
> Mais le spectre s'est assis auprès de la lampe sans me
> répondre; il a ouvert son livre, et j'ai reconnu mon
> Lorenzino d'autrefois.

LORENZO:

> Vous l'avez vu?

MARIE:

> Comme je te vois.

LORENZO:

> Quand s'en est-il allé?

MARIE:

> Quand tu as tiré la cloche ce matin en entrant.

LORENZO:

> Mon spectre, à moi! Et il s'en est allé quand je suis
> rentré?

MARIE:

> Il s'est levé d'un air mélancolique, et s'est effacé
> comme une vapeur du matin.

LORENZO:

> Catherine, Catherine, lis-moi l'histoire de Brutus.

CATHERINE:

> Qu'avez-vous? vous tremblez de la tête aux pieds.

LORENZO:

> Ma mère, asseyez-vous ce soir à la place où vous étiez
> cette nuit, et si mon spectre revient, dites-lui qu'il verra
> bientôt quelque chose qui l'étonnera.

[Pp. 101-102.]

Marie's vision is related in its substance to her earlier
evocations of young Lorenzo and to Catherine's blind
confidence in the possibility of redemption. Lorenzo is
shaken, not because he is superstitious, but because his
mother's hallucinatory experience with the "other"
Lorenzo corresponds to his own recognition of lost self,
a recognition which comes out into the open in his
third-act revelation to Philippe Strozzi. Since Lorenzo
already knows that he is going to carry out the long-
cherished dream of killing a tyrant, he regards Marie's
fantasy as a kind of mystical encouragement. This is
why he changes his attitude toward hearing the story of
Brutus. He remembers, at least for a moment, the days
of his youth, when he too compared himself to his Roman predecessor. Marie's recital reminds him vividly of
his still-secret plot, for the "quelque chose" of which he
speaks is nothing other than the contemplated murder.

The trio is joined on stage by Lorenzo's uncle Bindo
and the *bourgeois* Venturi. Both are patriots, especially
Bindo, who immediately starts berating Lorenzo, urging
him to stop his foolishness and to declare himself for
the republic. Lorenzo responds with facetious insolence,
concluding with a mock confession: "Je suis des vôtres,
mon oncle. Ne voyez-vous pas à ma coiffure que je suis
républicain dans l'âme? Regardez comme ma barbe est
coupée. N'en doutez pas un seul instant; l'amour de la
patrie respire dans mes vêtements les plus caches" (p.
104). The same words which exasperate the uncle summon the reader to seek Lorenzo's true self outside of
the political arena.

The exchange is interrupted by the unexpected visit of
Alexander. Lorenzo introduces Bindo and Venturi, and
before either can utter a word, he secures for each an
unsolicited boon. Instead of protests, the two recipients
of Alexander's largesse murmur protestations of
gratitude. As they exit, their conversation is easily
overheard:

BINDO:

> *(sortant, bas à Venturi)* C'est un tour infâme.

VENTURI:

> *(de même)* Qu'est-ce que vous ferez?

BINDO:

> *(de même)* Que diable voulez-vous que je fasse? Je suis
> nommé.

VENTURI:

> *(de même)* Cela est terrible.

[P. 106.]

The two patriots feel that they have been duped by
Lorenzo, and they are upset because their new al-
legiances will interfere with their patriotic impulses.

Their little dialogue is an eloquent salute to the impotent patriotism which surrounds Lorenzo. Bindo's helplessness is epitomized by the commonplace resignation of "Que diable voulez-vous que je fasse?" Lorenzo, for his part, did more than merely play a trick ("un tour infâme") on his uncle, for his intervention effectively stifled a patriotic impulse which, to Lorenzo, could be healthy neither for Florence nor for the individual. Since the suppression of patriotism at this juncture is accompanied by the favor of the duke, and, for Bindo, a happy and safe exile from Florence, Lorenzo can enjoy the brief satisfaction of having saved two would-be patriots from inevitable disaster.

The closing portion of the scene reveals that Alexander has conquered la Cibo, an event which we have been expecting. It also reveals his interest in having Catherine as one of his bedmates. Lorenzo tries hard to take the duke's mind off Catherine, but he has no success. Even Lorenzo's attempt to get Alexander to think about having his portrait painted fails to distract fully his lecherous attention. There is, finally, one illumination which cannot be ignored. This episode is one of several when Alexander and Lorenzo are alone, when Lorenzo and Alexander address each other as "mignon," revealing an intimacy which is suppressed in the more crowded scenes. The only previous hint of this intimacy occurred in the non-inserted manuscript scene. There will be other "mignons" in the subsequent action, and it will be necessary to relate this suggestive *sobriquet* to the sexual aspects of the murder.

In the fifth scene, a bloodstained Pierre announces to Philippe and Lorenzo that he has disposed of Julien Salviati. There is a brief exchange between the two young men, designed to bring out the fundamental contrast between Lorenzo's detachment from patriotism and Pierre's incapacity to discriminate between what is patriotic and what is vindictive. Philippe, however, is capable of making the distinction, and it emerges effectively from the monologue which he delivers even before Pierre makes his appearance:

> Pauvre ville, où les pères attendent ainsi le retour de leurs enfants! Pauvre patrie! pauvre patrie! Il y en a bien d'autres à cette heure qui ont pris leurs manteaux et leurs épées pour s'enfoncer dans cette nuit obscure—et ceux qui les attendent ne sont pas inquiets—ils savent qu'ils mourront demain de misère, s'ils ne meurent de froid cette nuit. Et nous, dans ces palais somptueux, nous attendons qu'on nous insulte pour tirer nos épées! Le propos d'un ivrogne nous transporte de colère, et disperse dans ces sombres rues nos fils et nos amis! Mais les malheurs publics ne secouent pas la poussière de nos armes. On croit Philippe Strozzi un honnête homme, parce qu'il fait le bien sans empêcher le mal! Et maintenant, moi, père, que ne donnerais-je pas pour qu'il y eût au monde un être capable de me rendre mon fils et de punir juridiquement l'insulte faite à ma fille! Mais pourquoi empêcherait-on le mal qui

> m'arrive, quand je n'ai pas empêché celui qui arrive aux autres, moi qui en avais le pouvoir? Je me suis courbé sur les livres, et j'ai rêvé pour ma patrie ce que j'admirais dans l'antiquité. Les murs criaient vengeance autour de moi, et je me bouchais les oreilles pour m'enfoncer dans mes méditations—il a fallu que la tyrannie vînt me frapper au visage pour me faire dire: Agissons!—et ma vengeance a des cheveux gris.

> [P. 111.]

Philippe discourses bitterly on the gap between thought and action and on the possible shortcomings of being merely an *honnête homme*. He asks himself whether it is really enough to do good when at the same time one does nothing to uproot evil. Philippe's helplessness is compounded by the awareness of age, for even though he is moved to action by the insults and threats to his family, his vengeance "a des cheveux gris." The crucial point of Philippe's meditation is ". . . et j'ai rêvé pour ma patrie ce que j'admirais dans l'antiquité." Since the only aspect of antiquity which is built into *Lorenzaccio* is the story of Brutus and Tarquin (confused with Brutus and Caesar), it is at once apparent that Philippe's dream is the same as Lorenzo's. Philippe, however, remained an *honnête homme,* he continued to dream, whereas Lorenzo was moved to activate his vision, even though he could no longer remain *honnête,* and even though he knew eventually that the political hopes of his dream would remain unfulfilled.

The sixth scene brings us back to the palace, where Tebaldeo is busy painting the duke's portrait. Lorenzo enters and inquires: "Cela avance-t-il? Etes-vous content de mon protégé?" At this point, Lorenzo picks up the *cotte de mailles* from the couch, saying: "Vous avez là une jolie cotte de mailles, mignon! Mais cela doit être bien chaud!" (p. 114). He asks Alexander why he is not wearing it, and the duke indicates that "c'est le peintre qui l'a voulu." Besides, Alexander feels that he is right to pose "le cou découvert," after the fashion of the "antiques." Pretending to be looking for his guitar, Lorenzo walks out of the room. At the same time, Tebaldeo indicates he has finished for the day.[9] Giomo looks out of the window and sees Lorenzo "en contemplation devant le puits qui est au milieu du jardin . . ." (p. 115). Meanwhile, with Tebaldeo gone, Alexander starts to dress, but cannot find his armored garment. Both he and Giomo recall having seen it in Lorenzo's hands. Lorenzo, back from his excursion to the well, insists that he put the *cotte* back where he had found it. He then tries to distract his antagonists by strumming on the guitar which he brought back with him. Giomo suggests, not without sarcasm, that Lorenzo apparently found his guitar in the garden well. Lorenzo testifies that he was merely spitting into the well, in order to "faire des ronds." In spite of Giomo's natural incredulity, Lorenzo gets away with his crude deception. It does not even occur to Alexander that Lorenzo is the culprit. It does occur to Giomo, but he dismisses his suspicions after brief deliberation: "Quitter la compagnie pour aller cracher dans le puits, cela n'est pas naturel. Je voudrais retrouver cette cotte de mailles, pour m'ôter de la tête une vieille idée qui se rouille de temps en temps. Bah! un Lorenzaccio! La cotte est sous quelque fauteuil" (p. 117). All the suspicious Giomo has to do is to inspect the well, but he cannot believe that the Lorenzaccio whom he knows is capable of acting against Alexander.

The third act opens on a frenetic note, as Lorenzo and Scoronconcolo are revealed in a well-rehearsed mock duel. The make-believe struggle takes place in Lorenzo's bedroom, the same room which he plans to use for the murder. His design is to accustom the neighboring residents to the sounds of brawling. To Lorenzo, however, the occasion is more than a mere *jeu de bruit*, for his heated words stress the passionate nature of his murder plot. "Meurs, infâme! Je te saignerai, pourceau, je te saignerai! Au cœur, au cœur! il est éventré.—Crie donc, frappe donc, tue donc! Ouvre-lui les entrailles! Coupons-le par morceaux, et mangeons, mangeons! J'en ai jusqu'au coude. Fouille dans la gorge, roule-le, roule! Mordons, mordons, et mangeons!" (pp. 118-119). Lorenzo falls, exhausted, after this utterance. The bestial ferocity of his words is self-evident, as he anticipates the bloody act. Oblivious of Scoronconcolo's presence, he maintains his climactic pitch, thus bringing into sharper focus the ritual and sexual aspects of his scheme: "O jour de sang, jour de mes noces! O soleil! soleil! il y a assez longtemps que tu es sec comme le plomb; tu te meurs de soif, soleil! son sang t'enivrera" (p. 119). The act of stabbing Alexander will be a consummation.

As Scoronconcolo wonders whether his master has been stricken with delirium, Lorenzo shifts the stress of his exaltation to his own image: "Lâche, lâche—ruffian—le petit maigre, les pères, les filles—des adieux, des adieux sans fin—les rives de l'Arno pleines d'adieux!—Les gamins l'écrivent sur les murs" (p. 119). This is Lorenzo addressing himself to Lorenzaccio, "le petit maigre," whose name is written in shame on the walls of Florence. Thus, the contemplated murder is also an act of self-destruction. The supreme irony of Lorenzo's act is that the principal "good" which results from it is the elimination of the infamous Lorenzaccio.

In the next scene, Pierre and Philippe argue the merits of immediate action against the tyrants. Pierre has considerable difficulty persuading his father that it is time for patriots to take up arms. Philippe holds back, trying to moderate the spirit of revenge. He wants Pierre to grasp the difference between patriotism and vengeance, but he meets a stone wall of resistance. Finally, Philippe decides to cast his lot with his son. "Depuis quand le vieil aigle reste-t-il dans le nid, quand ses aiglons vont à la curée?" (p. 124). His sudden shift

does not imply that he himself has been befuddled by Pierre's rigidity. Earlier, he had concluded a monologue with the words "ma vengeance a des cheveux gris." Now, although he still realizes the distinction between acting for the public good and acting out of personal interest, he is willing to prove that he is not too old to act, that he is capable of seeking redress and of using vindictiveness as a trigger for republican action. Pierre replies: "Venez, mon noble père; nous baiserons le bas de votre robe. Vous êtes notre patriarche, venez voir marcher au soleil les rêves de votre vie. La liberté est mûre; venez, vieux jardinier de Florence, voir sortir de terre la plante que vous aimez" (p. 125). Pierre's words recall Tebaldeo's claim that a fragrant plant may spring from the decayed environment of Florence. Tebaldeo was talking about art, but in the politics of **Lorenzaccio**, the analogy fails to be sustained.

The third scene, which begins with the arrest of Pierre Strozzi, is devoted principally to the long discussion between Philippe and Lorenzo, the same discussion in which Lorenzo drops his mask and reveals himself completely. Philippe is furious now about what is happening to his good name, and is clearly indulging in saber-rattling. Lorenzo can hardly believe that the "paisible" Philippe has adopted "le masque de la colère." Philippe begs Lorenzo to stop playing his "hideuse comédie," his "rôle de boue et de lèpre," and to join him in action. He entreats him to be "honnête," and to help him seek a just revenge. Lorenzo, however, refuses to regard the imprisonment of Pierre as a calamity. As for Philippe's loss of self-control, Lorenzo sees it as a menace, and he urges the old man to leave Florence, assuring him that he, Lorenzo, will take care of everything. Philippe is insulted at the idea of being a *banni*, and keeps insisting that action is the only remedy. Lorenzo elaborates: "Prends-y garde, c'est un démon plus beau que Gabriel. La liberté, la patrie, le bonheur des hommes, tous ces mots résonnent à son approche comme les cordes d'une lyre; c'est le bruit des écailles d'argent de ses ailes flamboyantes. Les larmes de ses yeux fécondent la terre, et il tient à la main la palme des martyrs. . . . Prends-y garde! une fois dans ma vie, je l'ai vu traverser les cieux. J'étais courbé sur mes livres—le toucher de sa main a fait frémir mes cheveux comme une plume légère. Que je l'aie écouté ou non, n'en parlons pas" (pp. 131-132). To Lorenzo, abstractions such as liberty, patriotism, and public felicity are merely manifestations of the most perfect of fallen angels. They are part of a diabolical plot to lure virtue into the snare of corruption. Moved by Philippe's lack of insight, Lorenzo finally surrenders a small parcel of his identity by confessing pointblank that he is going to kill Alexander "demain ou après-demain." The revelation mystifies Philippe even further, for he cannot see how he is wrong to worship liberty when Lorenzo himself is about to strike a blow for the cause. It is here that Lorenzo alludes to his former innocence and virtue, to the unexplained call to strike a blow against tyranny, to his love-like exaltation, and to his living with the idea of being a second Brutus.

As Lorenzo develops the history of his stay in Florence, he makes it clear that he was not moved to start a revolution, but to act alone, to come to grips "corps à corps avec la tyrannie vivante, la tuer, porter mon épée sanglante sur la tribune, et laisser la fumée du sang d'Alexandre monter au nez des harangueurs, pour réchauffer leur cervelle ampoulee" (p. 134). He views his act as an isolation from political tumult, almost as a contradiction of that sort of political activity which can fight only with words. As he continues to unveil himself before Philippe, the sexual undertones of his act are unmistakable: "Pour plaire à mon cousin, il fallait arriver à lui, porté par les larmes des familles; pour devenir son ami, et acquérir sa confiance, il fallait baiser sur ses lèvres épaisses tous les restes de ses orgies" (p. 135). It hurts Lorenzo to think about what he has had to become in order to carry out his plot: "Ce que je suis devenu à cause de cela, n'en parlons pas. Tu dois comprendre ce que j'ai souffert, et il y a des blessures dont on ne lève pas l'appareil impunément. Je suis devenu vicieux, lâche, un objet de honte et d'opprobre . . ." (p. 135). As he speaks, tears come to his eyes, and Philippe mistakes them for the honest weeping of a patriot who is about to see his republican dream become a reality. Philippe insists on seeing along the "route hideuse" a sublime ambition, but Lorenzo is determined to disabuse him: "Je me suis réveillé de mes rêves, rien de plus" (p. 136). Philippe, however, refuses to be similarly awakened to reality. "Je crois à tout ce que tu appelles des rêves; je crois à la vertu, à la pudeur et à la liberté" (p. 137).

Realizing that Philippe has not yet fully comprehended the role of Lorenzaccio, Lorenzo reveals even more of his sordid existence, hoping to prove to Philippe that liberty is a fine dream for the virtuous, but, politically, a lost cause, for the simple reason that enslaved Florence has done absolutely nothing to stop Lorenzaccio from existing:

> Suis-je un Satan? Lumière du ciel! je m'en souviens encore; j'aurais pleuré avec la première fille que j'ai séduite, si elle ne s'était pas mise à rire. Quand j'ai commencé à jouer mon rôle de Brutus moderne, je marchais dans mes habits neufs de la grande confrérie du vice, comme un enfant de dix ans dans l'armure d'un géant de la fable. Je croyais que la corruption était un stigmate, et que les monstres seuls le portaient au front. J'avais commencé à dire tout haut que mes vingt années de vertu étaient un masque étouffant—ô Philippe! j'entrai alors dans la vie, et je vis qu'à mon approche tout le monde en faisait autant que moi; tous les masques tombaient devant mon regard; l'Humanité souleva sa robe, et me montra, comme à un adepte digne d'elle, sa monstrueuse nudité. J'ai vu les hommes tels qu'ils sont, et je me suis dit: pour qui est-ce

donc que je travaille? Lorsque je parcourais les rues de Florence, avec mon fantôme à mes côtés, je regardais autour de moi, je cherchais des visages qui me donnaient du cœur, et je me demandais: Quand j'aurai fait mon coup, celui-là en profitera-t-il?—J'ai vu les républicains dans leurs cabinets, je suis entré dans les boutiques, j'ai écouté et j'ai guetté. J'ai recueilli les discours des gens du peuple, j'ai vu l'effet que produisait sur eux la tyrannie; j'ai bu, dans les banquets patriotiques, le vin qui engendre la métaphore et la prosopopée, j'ai avalé entre deux baisers les larmes les plus vertueuses; j'attendais toujours que l'humanité me laissât voir sur sa face quelque chose d'honnête. J'observais . . . comme un amant observe sa fiancée, en attendant le jour des noces! . . .

[Pp. 137-138.]

Lorenzo's account of evil clarifies his outlook on man and society, and also brings together in a single outburst the several strands of the action. We find in it the false analogy between Brutus and Lorenzo; the one-way street into which man is led by tyranny and decay; the procurer Lorenzo who finds that a whole populace is earger to sell its body; the corrupt Lorenzaccio who is accompanied everywhere by the ghost of Lorenzo; the political insignificance of his plot. The "républicains dans leurs cabinets" are epitomized by Philippe himself. The reference to "boutiques" recalls the *orfèvre* and the *marchand,* and the general indifferece to tyranny of the middle class. The mention of "banquets patriotiques" and of the wine which engenders "la métaphore et la prosopopée" looks ahead to the convocation of the Strozzi family, who will drink to the death of tyranny at the very moment when Louise Strozzi is being murdered before their eyes. Finally, the idea of a watchful lover, waiting for the day when the bride will be his, reminds us vividly of the act of love and death which Lorenzo is about to commit.

Philippe still fails to see anything more than a disguise which can be easily thrown off after the fact. Although he senses that Lorenzo craves compassionate understanding, he does not realize fully the source of this need. He still sees above Lorenzo's head the halo of virtue. "Pauvre enfant, tu me navres le cœur! Mais si tu es honnête, quand tu auras délivré ta patrie, tu le redeviendras" (pp. 138-139). Lorenzo corrects "tu es honnête" with "j'ai été honnête," indicating that there is no return from the truth which he has discovered. The anguish of knowing can be eased only by "l'Ange du sommeil éternel," by the finality of death. Lorenzo tells Philippe that he has become acclimated to his vicious métier. "Le vice a été pour moi un vêtement, maintenant il est collé à ma peau" (p. 139). He advises Philippe again not to become involved in the futility of patriotic action. He is willing to make with him the very safe bet that there will be no uprising after his coup. Philippe remains unmoved in his convictions, and finally, in sheer exasperation, asks Lorenzo why he wants to kill Alexander if he is not motivated by love of country. Lorenzo exposes himself completely, offering a series of personal rationalizations in defense of his contemplated act. There is first of all the need for self-destruction, the need to destroy the image of Lorenzaccio. There is at the same time the urgent desire to bring to fulfillment the "ombre" of the old Lorenzo. "Songes-tu que ce meurtre, c'est tout ce qui me reste de ma vertu? . . . veux-tu que je laisse mourir en silence l'énigme de ma vie?" (p. 141). It is corruption which drives him: "Oui, cela est certain, si je pouvais revenir à la vertu, si mon apprentissage du vice pouvait s'évanouir, j'épargnerais peut-être ce conducteur de bœufs—mais j'aime le vin, le jeu, et les filles, comprends-tu cela? Si tu honores en moi quelque chose, toi qui me parles, c'est mon meurtre que tu honores, peut-être justement parce que tu ne le ferais pas" (p. 141). Lorenzo is weary of being abused verbally by republicans and patriots who cannot act. There is above all the question of identity, for the world must find out for itself what it is and who Lorenzo-Lorenzaccio really is. Finally, Lorenzo is seeking immortality in his own way; he wants to be remembered for his act, and does not seem to care so much what people will think of him: "Brutus ou Erostrate, il ne me plaît pas qu'ils m'oublient. Ma vie entière est au bout de ma dague, et que la Providence retourne ou non la tête en m'entendant frapper, je jette la nature humaine à pile ou face sur la tombe d'Alexandre—dans deux jours, les hommes comparaîtront devant le tribunal de ma volonté" (p. 142). Lorenzo is putting society on trial. His act will give men the chance to redeem themselves. To all this, the sympathetic but immovable Philippe retorts: "Tu peux avoir raison, mais il faut que j'agisse . . ." (p. 142).

The next major event, in which the marquise tests her rhetoric on Alexander, takes place in Scene VI. To the marquise's opening remarks, the laconic Alexander replies: "Vous rêvez toute éveillée." His companion grasps at this straw and admits that she does indeed have a dream, a dream of independence and glory for Florence, a dream fit for kings and princes, for "toutes les chimères de leurs caprices se transforment en réalités . . ." (p. 145). The interplay of dream and reality is perfectly suited to what has been happening in the play. The dreams of the marquise and of Philippe will remain unrealized; the only dream that counts is Lorenzo's. The duke does not want to listen to the marquise, but she continues unabashed with the revelation of her private visions of public felicity: "Le jour où tu auras pour toi la nation toute entière, où tu seras la tête d'un corps libre, où tu diras: 'Comme le doge de Venise épouse l'Adriatique, ainsi je mets mon anneau d'or au doigt de ma belle Florence, et ses enfants . . .'" (pp. 145-146). The episode focusses attention on Lorenzo himself, for the woman's language, her allusion to a wedding ceremony, serve as a sharp reminder of the emotional basis for Lorenzo's act. The image of the wedding ring, for example, will reappear in the murder episode. The marquise warns Alexander that if he does not act, he will surely be assassinated. "Eh! parbleu, quand tu aurais raison, de qui veux-tu que j'aie peur" (p. 147). The marquise answers: "Tu as tué ou déshonoré des centaines de citoyens, et tu crois avoir tout fait quand tu mets une cotte de mailles sous ton habit" (p. 147). The discussion of an attempt on Alexander's life, his complete lack of fear, and the mention of the *cotte de mailles* are designed obviously to make Lorenzo's act appear all the more remarkable. When the marquise realizes that she has failed, she begins to moan "malheur à moi!" Alexander's response is fascinating: "Pourquoi? Tu as l'air sombre comme l'enfer. Pourquoi diable aussi te mêles-tu de politique? Allons, allons, ton petit rôle de femme, et de vraie femme, te va si bien" (pp. 148-149). The duke's words make us realize that there is a deliberate parallel between this scene and the long conversation between Philippe and Lorenzo. Both Lorenzo and Alexander want their interlocutors to understand the importance of preserving their basic roles, to comprehend the folly of departing from their assigned characters in order to play the vain and dangerous game of politics. The parallel is even more striking, for the interlocutors have already deviated from their original roles. Philippe has abandoned his *honnêteté* and is entangled in the web of republicanism. The same is true of the marquise, who, because of her patriotic dreams, has corrupted herself, leaving behind her role of "vraie femme."

The next tableau is set "chez les Strozzi," where forty members of the clan have gathered to hear Philippe's call to action. He delivers a series of short, fiery speeches, each one supported by encouraging choral responses from the "convives." The climax is reached when Philippe exclaims: "Notre vengeance est une hostie que nous pouvons briser sans crainte, et partager devant Dieu. Je bois à la mort des Médicis!" (p. 151). The Strozzi chorus responds in kind, but at that very moment, the chanting is interrupted by the agonized voice of Louise: "Ah! je vais mourir." The timing of Louise's death is perfect. Philippe has just claimed divine approval of his vengeance, and has toasted the death of the Medicis. Louise's death comes then as a double contradiction: God is not on the side of the patriotic avengers, and it is a Strozzi who dies in response to Philippe's homage to death. The poisoning of Louise redoubles the patriotic ardor of the chorus, which views her as the "nouvelle Lucrèce," just as Philippe looked upon Lorenzo as the new Brutus. The old man, however, has sensed the hand of God awakening him to the reality to which he had been blind in his scene with Lorenzo. "Liberté, vengeance, voyez-vous, tout cela est beau. . . . Je suis vieux, voyez-vous, il est temps que je ferme ma boutique. . . . Je m'en vais de ce pas à Venise" (p. 155). He now realizes that he is miscast as the leader of a conspiracy. As the scene and act come to an end, Philippe's last words are: "Dieu de justice! Dieu de justice! que t'ai-je fait?"

The fourth-act curtain rises, revealing the ducal palace. Alexander and Lorenzo are alone. There are three things on Alexander's mind: news of the manner of Louise's death (which pleases him), concern over his missing coat of mail, and the burning desire to sleep with Catherine. His worrying prompts Lorenzo to suggest: "Méfiez-vous de Giomo; c'est lui qui vous l'a volé" (p. 156). While savoring his private joke, Lorenzo ascertains that Alexander has not replaced the missing garment. He assures his cousin that Catherine is looking forward eagerly to the tryst, which is to take place in Lorenzo's bedroom. The duke exits with a dainty "Bonsoir, mignon," and Lorenzo goes off to prepare the event.

After an intervening scene revealing Pierre Strozzi's release from prison, we catch up with Lorenzo, just as he is giving final instructions to Scoronconcolo. Left alone, Lorenzo is harassed by a sequence of disquieting thoughts. He begins by wondering how he has reached the point at which he finds himself: "De quel tigre a rêvé ma mère enceinte de moi? Quand je pense que j'ai aimé les fleurs, les prairies, et les sonnets de Pétrarque, le spectre de ma jeunesse se lève devant moi en frissonnant" (p. 160). In addition to the struggle for identity, we can see in Lorenzo's words a kind of fulfillment of the good and bad dreams which his mother described earlier, including the "spectre" of the Lorenzo who used to be. He wonders what people will say when they learn of the murder. He is sure that everyone will ask "Pourquoi l'as-tu tué?" He is not certain, however, that he himself can answer the question, for in thinking about Alexander, he recognizes: "Il a fait du mal aux autres, mais il m'a fait du bien, du moins à sa manière" (p. 160). As he plunges more deeply into doubt, it occurs to him that perhaps the motivation of his act lies completely beyond his power: "—Suis-je le bras de Dieu? Y a-t-il une nuée au-dessus de ma tête? Quand j'entrerai dans cette chambre, et que je voudrai tirer mon épée du fourreau, j'ai peur de tirer l'épée flamboyante de l'archange, et de tomber en cendres sur ma proie" (p. 160). This will be Lorenzo's last moment of doubt, the last time he will glimpse the aura of virtue which Philippe wanted to place over his head.

In Scene V, Lorenzo receives a visit from Catherine. She tells him of the duke's proposition, and of the mortal grief which it has inflicted on Marie. Lorenzo dismisses Catherine, and then condemns himself for having been on the verge of corrupting his own family. The brief threat of domestic involvement restores him to his earlier confidence, and the doubts of the preceding monologue are dispelled. Lorenzo affirms both the decision to kill and the awareness of two selves. "Je puis délibérer et choisir, mais non revenir sur mes pas quand j'ai choisi . . . je ne puis ni me retrouver moi-même ni laver les mains, même avec du sang!" (pp. 167-168). Like Frank, Lorenzo cannot turn back and become again what he once was. Unlike Frank, however, he is aware that he cannot efface the corruption within him, and will not attempt to revert to his past. Because he recognizes fully what he is, his act becomes one of pure fulfillment. He has chosen to kill, and there can be no turning away or turning back. His burst of confidence and determination is triggered by Catherine's visit. While he is not acting directly to save his kin from corruption, it is nevertheless the imminence of this corruption which strengthens his resolution. Philippe Strozzi was struck down when he was prompted to act for domestic reasons. He was chastised for having strayed from his own character. Even to the slight degree that Lorenzo may be motivated by love for his aunt, no such punishment is in store for him, for he has already become Lorenzaccio and no power can restore him to his former self.

In the curious seventh scene, Lorenzo goes around knocking on the doors of noble republicans, informing them that he is going to kill Alexander. In each case, his interlocutors believe him to be drunk and refuse to pay any attention to him. He is boldly putting to a final test the long-worn disguise. So convincing is the role of Lorenzaccio that, even if he meant to be taken seriously, even if he was moved at the last minute to help the cause of patriotism, his warning would still have been received with amused incredulity. Lorenzo gives up the game, muttering "Pauvre Florence! pauvre Florence!" (p. 173).

Shortly afterward, Lorenzo, out for a stroll in the Florentine night, begins to act out in his imagination the little things which he will say to put Alexander at his ease. He tries to imagine every possible situation. As he anticipates the moments to come, he dances excitedly around the stage. His closing words bring back the sexual and marital aspects of his crime: "Eh, mignon, eh, mignon! mettez vos gants neufs, un plus bel habit que cela, tra la la! faites-vous beau, la mariée est belle. Mais, je vous le dis à l'oreille, prenez garde à son petit couteau" (pp. 176-177). "Mignon" is Alexander; "la mariée" is Lorenzo.

Lorenzo's warning is reiterated in the next scene. Alexander is having a late supper with Giomo, prior to his rendez-vous with "Catherine." Cardinal Cibo enters and says without ceremony: "Altesse, prenez garde à Lorenzo" (p. 177). The cardinal repeats the warning, for he sees that Alexander did not pay attention the first time. He adds the information that Lorenzo has arranged for transportation out of Florence. Alexander replies regally: "Cela ne se peut pas." When the cardinal assures him that it is true, Alexander becomes impatient: "Allons donc! je vous dis que j'ai de bonnes raisons pour savoir que cela ne se peut pas" (p. 177). It is obvious that Lorenzo, in his role as *entremetteur,* has never disappointed the duke, and that Alexander has therefore no reason to give credence to the cardinal's warning. Admitting finally that the information about Lorenzo's departure from Florence may be true, Alexander sees nothing ominous in it. He even suggests that Lorenzo is probably going to visit his mother in Cafaggiuolo. The cardinal then reports having seen Lorenzo dancing in the plaza "comme un fou." He adds: "Soyez certain qu'il mûrit dans sa tête quelque projet pour cette nuit" (p. 178). The "projet pour cette nuit" merely reinforces Alexander's "knowledge" of Lorenzo's plan to lead him to Catherine. Amused, Alexander retorts: "Et pourquoi ces projets me seraient-ils dangereux?" (p. 178). The cardinal next offers a final scrap of information, which he claims to have withheld to avoid offending Alexander: "Faut-il tout dire, même quand on parle d'un favori? Apprenez qu'il a dit ce soir à deux personnes de ma connaissance, publiquement, sur leur terrasse, qu'il vous tuerait cette nuit" (p. 178). The duke laughs, reminding the cardinal that Lorenzo is usually drunk by sunset. At this juncture, Sire Maurice strides in, alarmed, and repeats the warning: "Altesse, défiez-vous de Lorenzo." Maurice reports that Lorenzo told three of his friends that he was planning to murder the duke. Alexander greets this news exactly as he greeted the report of the cardinal. Lorenzo appears, and after a brief discussion about "gants d'amour" and "gants de guerre," leads Alexander off to meet his destiny. When Sire Maurice asks Cardinal Cibo what he thinks, the churchman answers enigmatically: "Que la volonté de Dieu se fait malgré les hommes" (p. 179). Cardinal Cibo knows that something is amiss, but he makes no attempt, except that required by form, to stop Alexander. The cardinal also knows that if Lorenzo is in fact going to murder Alexander, the event has nothing to do with God's will. His pious words mask his very human thoughts. It is his own "volonté" which will be fulfilled, thanks to Lorenzo. Realization of dream comes to Lorenzo and to Cardinal Cibo as a result of the same act.

The final scene of Act IV dramatizes the murder. Alexander is completely disarmed, physically and psychologically. As he lies in bed awaiting Catherine, Lorenzo strikes and strikes again. Scoronconcolo emerges from his hiding-place to see whether his master needs help. Lorenzo greets him with: "Regarde, il m'a mordu au doigt. Je garderai jusqu'à la mort cette bague sanglante, inestimable diamant" (p. 180). This is the climax of the Lorenzo-Alexander relationship. The bitten finger, the blood, the "bague sanglante" which is at once the mark of a wedding and of a consummation, bring together in a final spasm all those elements which, throughout the course of the play, have touched with passion the brilliant machinations of Lorenzaccio. The completion of the *geste* brings to Scoronconcolo the sudden recogni-

tion that the victim is the duke himself. He urges Lorenzo to flee, but Lorenzo must first escape from his rapturous trance: "Que la nuit est belle! Que l'air du ciel est pur! Respire, respire, cœur navré de joie!" (p. 180). Unmindful of Scoronconcolo's repeated warnings, Lorencio remains ecstatic: "Que le vent du soir est doux et embaumé! Comme les fleurs des prairies s'entr'ouvrent! O nature magnifique, ô éternel repos!" (p. 181). After a final outburst ("Ah! Dieu de bonté! quel moment!"), Lorenzo's emotions subside, and he begins to prepare his escape. The murder of Alexander is clearly a sexual act. The fulfillment which it brings to Lorenzo embellishes both God and nature. In Musset's earlier work, the dream of love fulfilled has regularly been linked to godliness and to the purity of natural beauty. The attempt to realize this dream has regularly led either to the absence of God or to the presence of a vindictive "Dieu de justice," the same divine power to which Philippe attributes the death of his daughter. In *Lorenzaccio,* the very climax of the action is at the same time an ecstatic fulfillment, so that "Dieu de justice" is transformed into "Dieu de bonté," by a character infected with crime and corruption. Lorenzo's post-mortem effusions also simulate the fragrant plant which the artist Tebaldeo saw emerging from the decayed environment of Florence. The naturally beautiful world evoked by Lorenzo's rapture is a product of his own corruption. His act, therefore, is a masterpiece which can be held up to the eyes of the world. As an act of love, it must inevitably subside, but as a work of art, it can survive. Lorenzo's love will end in death, but his artistry will give him the touch of immortality which he seems to have craved in his revelations to Philippe.

The fifth act of *Lorenzaccio* represents the aftermath of Lorenzo's act of murder. The second scene is set in Venice, where Lorenzo has come to seek refuge with Philippe Strozzi. When the old man hears what Lorenzo has done, his hopes for liberty are rekindled. In this sense, their long conversation of Act III merely picks up where it left off. Lorenzo refuses the mantle of Brutus which Philippe insists is fitting. Lorenzo is accused of despising mankind, but he denies this: "Je ne les méprise point, je les connais. Je suis très persuadé qu'il y en a très peu de très méchants, beaucoup de lâches, et un grand nombre d'indifférents" (p. 191). Lorenzo describes in capsule form the whole array of characters, named and nameless, who populate the world of *Lorenzaccio.* Few of the characters are actually evil: Salviati, Cardinal Cibo, Giomo, Alexander, and the *alter ego* of Lorenzo. Most of the remaining seventy-old characters fit into the roles of "lâches" of "indifférents," with the important exceptions of some of the principal roles: Philippe and Pierre Strozzi, the marquise Cibo, and Lorenzo himself. Philippe's brief surge of hope is crushed, as a servant brings in a proclamation offering a handsome reward for the death of the traitor Lorenzo.

The futility of trying to fight corruption is brought out more and more obviously by the continuing events of the fifth act. The marquis and marquise Cibo are seen walking together in Florence as if nothing had happened. Pierre Strozzi is revealed briefly lamenting the lack of armed support. His greatest suffering comes from his bruised amourpropre, for he is angry at Lorenzaccio for having deprived him of his chance for revenge. The merchant and the goldsmith appear. The former is curious only about the astrological significance of Alexander's death. Through the eyes of the *orfèvre*, we learn that the *provéditeur* has offered to turn the citadel over to the republicans. Their response to his offer is merely another fulfillment of Lorenzo's wisdom: "Ah bien oui! on a braillé, bu du vin sacré, et cassé des carreaux; mais la proposition de ce brave homme n'a seulement pas été écoutée. Comme on n'osait pas faire ce qu'il voulait, on a dit qu'on doutait de lui, et qu'on le soupçonnait de fausseté dans ses offres" (p. 197).

As the two burghers leave the stage, two young boys and their tutors appear. One of the lads is a Strozzi and the other a Salviati. There is a double *jeu* in this cynical tableau, for the two children are continually fighting and calling each other names, while the two *précepteurs* are discussing a sonnet which one of them has composed. The two pedants are completely oblivious to the political uneasiness which has followed in the wake of the murder. They are also oblivious to the feuding of the two youngsters, until the scuffling interferes with the reading of the sonnet. Part of the tableau's cynicism derives from the fact that the Strozzi-Salviati scuffle is completely meaningless as a combat between virtue (Strozzi) and corruption (Salviati). This is compounded by the first line of the sonnet (at no point does the would-be sonneteer succeed in uttering more than two lines). The sonnet begins: "Chantons la Liberté, qui refleurit plus âpre . . ." (p. 198). One cannot avoid seeing in the verse a summary of the political aspects of the plot. The sonnet is itself futile; it has no meaning, and it is left unfinished. It salutes the abstraction Liberty, which has been a failure. It describes Liberty as a flowering, thereby evoking the theories of Tebaldeo and the bloody act of Lorenzo. The murder has been a private satisfaction, a personal fruition. Politically, however, nothing happens. Liberty is merely a word; it is not a sweet-smelling flower which blossoms after having been nourished by corruption.

The penultimate scene presente a Lorenzo completely spent after his act: ". . . je suis plus creux et plus vide qu'une statue de fer-blanc" (p. 200). Life seems to have no meaning for him. Philippe tries to persuade him to flee to another country, but Lorenzo is content to await his fate in Venice. Although there have already been several attempts on his life, he insists on going out for a walk. Just as Philippe is instructing one of his servants to follow Lorenzo at a safe, but protective distance, a second servant enters, announcing the murder of Lorenzo. Philippe looks down below and sees a crowd shoving Lorenzo's corpse into the water.[10]

The ironies of the play work their way to the very end. In the last scene, Cardinal Cibo is still masterminding the change in regime. First, the new duke is obliged to swear privately, "sur l'Evangile," that he will be just, that he will obey Charles-Quint, that he will avenge Alexander's death, and that he will see to the care of the bastard children of the late duke. Cosimo responds docilely: "Je le jure à Dieu—et à vous, Cardinal" (p. 203). Then, hand in hand with Cardinal Cibo, Cosimo turns to address the people, promising to keep always uppermost ". . . la crainte de Dieu, l'honnêteté et la justice, et le dessein de n'offenser personne . . ." (p. 203).

The theatrical history of *Lorenzaccio* was itself a dream unrealized for over a hundred years. The first adaptation of the play was made in 1896, when a considerably abridged version was performed, with Sarah Bernhardt in the title role. Other adaptations appeared in 1925, 1927, 1945 (Gaston Baty) and 1952 (*Théâtre National Populaire*). It is the last of these adaptations which comes closest to reproducing the play in its original textual form. The post-World War II performances are doubly significant, because they magnified the reputation of Musset, the dramatist, and, at the same time, caused many spectators to see in a century-old play a reinforcement of political and literary trends prevalent in the forties and fifties. Lorenzo's act and the atmosphere in which it was committed made people think of occupied France, and also of the *littérature engagée* flowing from the pens of existentialist writers. Whatever *Lorenzaccio* is, it is certainly not a play which celebrates liberation from the yoke of tyranny, nor does it exalt the *maquisard* of 1940-1944. The only liberation in *Lorenzaccio* is that of Lorenzo himself and the nearest thing to a resistance movement is the futile gesture of Pierre Strozzi, who "wasn't born to be a bandit leader." There are nevertheless analogies which can be legitimately drawn: Florence and France both occupied by Germans; Alexander serving the emperor Charles and Laval serving Hitler; the "méchants," "lâches," and "indifférents" of two epochs, who collaborate overtly or tacitly with the occupying regime; the *bannis* of Florence and the exile army of De Gaulle; the failure, in both instances, of naked virtue and intellect, when set against armed force and against the habit of living under tyranny.

As for the *engagement* of Lorenzo's act, it must be viewed both individually and politically. There is no analogy whatsoever in the realm of political commitment, for Lorenzo's act cannot be firmly rooted in the soil of politics. The text makes this clear, and the view is supported by Musset's opinions on art and politics.

There is, however, a personal *engagement* which characterizes Lorenzo's conduct. He makes a choice, decides that be must execute it, suffers acutely from the corruption into which he has plunged, but, seeing that there is no turning back, forces himself, after a moment of self-doubt, to finish what he started. While the course of his suffering is obviously an outgrowth of Musset's earlier dramatic commentaries on man and destiny, it does appear to the modern reader to resemble the anguish of choice which is one of the recurrent motifs of existentialist literature. All these analogies are in part children of circumstances, for if Lorenzaccio had been properly staged fifty years earlier, there would have been no analogies to make. The same comparisons, whether successful or not, all fail to take into account the essential emotive force of Lorenzo's act, for as complex as his motivation may appear to be at various stages of the play, there is one factor which remains constant: the murder of Alexander is an act of love, conceived in purity, and nurtured in corruption.

Notes

1. The text of *Une Conjuration en 1537* was first published by Paul Dimoff, *Revue de Paris,* December 15, 1921. He later included it in his major work on Musset, *La Genèse de Lorenzaccio* (Geneva, 1936).

2. Published in Milan, 1803-04, in five volumes. The extent of Musset's dependence on Varchi is examined carefully by Paul Dimoff, *op. cit.*

3. For a summary of views concerning the composition of *Lorenzaccio,* see the notes of Maurice Allem, *Théâtre,* pp. 1243-1249.

4. The goldsmith does in fact have a name ("père Mondella"), but it is used only by the silk merchant as an occasional form of address. The name appears neither in the cast of characters nor in the textual designations of speaking parts.

5. Lorenzo's original impetus to kill a tyrant may, however, be linked with the idea of martyrdom, for Lorenzo's own words betray the possibility: "J'ai cru à la vertu . . . comme un martyr croit à son Dieu" (p. 133).

6. The unfortunate ambiguity of the word "Brutus" arises naturally from the mention of "César."

7. The scene is included in *Théâtre,* pp. 217-220, as an appendix.

8. Lorenzo does not kill Alexander to save his aunt from corruption, but he hopes that the crime will at least have this effect, as a kind of by-product.

9. The timing of Tebaldeo's exit suggests possible collusion between him and Lorenzo, but there is no way of being sure, especially because of Lorenzo's desire to operate independently.

10. The death of Lorenzo, in its dramatic form, marks Musset's most serious deviation from historical fact, for the Lorenzino of history lived on as a fugitive until 1547, when he was finally struck down by agents of Cosimo.

Joseph Lowin (essay date December 1979)

SOURCE: Lowin, Joseph. "The Frames of *Lorenzaccio.*" *The French Review* 53, no. 2 (December 1979): 190-98.

[*In the following essay, Lowin examines Musset's handling of structure to convey maximum meaning in* Lorenzaccio.]

Were one to view a full-length play, not as one observes a stage production, through perception of its temporal, linear development, but, spatially, as one views a painting, with an immediate impression of a static whole, one would perceive the most "important" scene of the play at or near the center of the canvas, receiving the greatest concentration of light. It would be less clear but no less true that the first and last acts of the play would be at or near the margins of the canvas in a subtle play of darkness, shadow, and diffused light. One might find as well, embedded in works of art of considerable technical subtlety and nuance—for example in *Las Meninas* by Velázquez or in *Hamlet*—a structure which, by its mirroring of the whole of the work of art, reveals its unity.

In what ways does the play—as a *literary* text—circumscribe itself so that it may best posit a created world within its limits? How does the play reveal what it is that is going on? If many plays lend themselves to such "frame analysis," few lend themselves to such an analysis more fully than Musset's ***Lorenzaccio.***[1]

The central scene of ***Lorenzaccio,*** the one receiving the greatest concentration of light, is, of course, the enormous third scene of the third act of the play, containing an extended dialogue between Philippe Strozzi and Lorenzo in which Lorenzo realizes and expresses for the first time his true motives for the proposed tyrannicide. The action of the play revolves around this moment of self-revelation and affirmation of consciousness.[2] This essay will focus on the ways the action of the play frames the central scene, making two main points. The first point concerns the correlation between "marginal" characters and structural "marginality." It stresses the significance of formal and thematic symmetry and shows that the margins of the play are not necessarily finite. One finds in the play a recurrent insistence on an "elsewhere" which expands the given space. The second point builds on the first and takes up where the first leaves off. It concerns the more meaningful of the dilations of the scenic space, the ones which are contractions as well as expansions and which are reduced models of the play. Emphasis is placed on the thematics of the frame, which embraces either a *paysage* or a *portrait,* either virtue or corruption, or which conceivably might embrace a void.

The analyses of Hassan el Nouty[3] and Bernard Masson[4] and the *mise en scène* of the director of the Za Branou Theatre in Prague, Otomar Krejca (discussed in Masson, pp. 337-91) pay particular attention to the opening and closing of the play. According to Nouty, although the situation at the beginning and at the end of the play is static in appearance only, there is enough of a similarity between the initial and final situations to allow for the view that the architecture of the piece is circular, even helical; viewed thus, the play has no true ending. Although Nouty's analysis affirms the vagueness of its ending, he seems to deny that Musset's work has any borders. As our analysis will show, they are there and they play an important role in the esthetic wholeness of the work. Bernard Masson analyzes the play with even more attention to detail. He notes that scene for scene and sometimes decor for decor the last act returns us to the point of departure. History is like nature; a tyrant replaces a tyrant the way one night follows another. According to Masson, the fifth act of the Za Branou production of the play, which took place in Prague in 1969, is a complete annihilation of the action of the play. In Krejca's *mise en scene,* according to Masson, "la pièce de Musset n'aura été après tout qu'un long, tumultueux et fertile entracte (Masson, p. 389).

Unclosed circle, spiral, or broad intermezzo, the play, though it may have no ends, does have margins. The first and fifth acts are what permit the viewer to distinguish the play from what is non-play, much as a frame on a painting permits one to distinguish between the painting and the wall. Although a part of the work, the framework is definitely a limit of the work. And it is a limit in a very positive sense.

In *Lorenzaccio,* above all, the first and fifth acts insist on their own marginality. It is evident that the intrigues played out in act I and mirrored in act V are peripheral not only to the main action of the play but also to the political life of the Florence of 1537.

The quarrel between the Strozzi and Salviati families, for example, is a personal one and, finally, has no wider repercussions. One might have thought at the beginning of the play that since the Strozzi name appears to stand for virtue and the Salviati name for vice, this strand would have been woven more prominently into the text. In act V the Strozzi-Salviati quarrel is reduced to a quarrel between children, who fight not only because that is what their families do, but because that is what

children do. By the end of the play as well, Philippe, the only Strozzi who might have been called on to play a central role, has abdicated that position and has placed himself outside even the periphery of the intrigue.

Another pattern which serves as a framework around the main action of the play is that of the episode of the marquis and marquise Cibo. Like Philippe, the marquise, although peripheral, attempts to have some effect on the central action. Like Philippe, she fails abysmally and is relegated finally to the margins of the play where she belongs. She belongs there not at all uselessly but because Musset gave her a role to play which carries with it much of the significance of the structure of the play. More than any of the male characters, she mirrors the essence of Lorenzo's dilemma.

The movement of the scene in which the Cibo couple makes its first appearance is directed outward, away from the main stage. Laurent Cibo takes leave of his wife the marquise to inspect his properties on the outskirts of Florence and will be gone for the duration of the central action of the play. He is totally outside the framework. The marquise is left behind ostensibly to make an attempt at centrality: an adulterous affair with Alexandre will save Florence. Before she plunges in, however, she follows her husband visually, away from the scene, away from Florence. She breaks through the framework of the play by opening a window and seeing, with her mind's eye only, the vast expanses of freedom and purity that are represented by the Cibo domain at Massa, where, we are told, she has spent idyllic hours. What is far away, what is off-stage, what is past, is good.

The window of the marquise represents the first instance in the play of what Masson calls dilation of scenic space. He makes much of the proliferation of windows in *Lorenzaccio*: "Musset suggère un au-delà du décor, qui fait du microcosme scénique la cellule d'un univers plus vaste qui le contient. Tel est le sens premier de ces fenêtres qui ouvrent sur un envers du décor et évoquent un ailleurs où les personnages en scène ne sont pas, mais où ils pourraient être" (Masson, p. 124). It is not only windows, however, which create the possibility of infinite expansion.

In another instance, Catherine, Lorenzo's aunt/cousin/ sister/beloved, and Marie, Lorenzo's mother, are seated on the banks of the Arno. Like the marquise, who "sees" Massa, Marie sees another *locus amoenus,* the Cafaggiuolo of Lorenzo's youth and purity. She sees a mirror of Florence—and its opposite. Again, not only are the bounds of space overcome but those of time as well. For with Marie, we are privileged to gain a glimpse of the *Lorenzino d'autrefois.* Marie's lament presents us with another para-text: the story of a potentially different unfolding of events. Had Lorenzo remained where he belonged by birth, at the center, he would not be today what for Marie has become "un spectre hideux." The marginality of the scene between Marie and Catherine on the banks of the Arno is further emphasized at its conclusion when the two women become witnesses to the departure of citizens who have been banished from Florence by the duke. The movement of the scene is a generalized, structured, impersonal, mannered, almost choral one, away from the center toward the periphery and beyond, leading out of the view of those on stage. This movement away from the center is mirrored in the scene of the reconciliation of the marquis and marquise Cibo in the last act. They have once again become the idyllic lovers of act I, as though the adultery had not taken place. The manner of Musset's presentation of the reconciliation is significant. Not a word is spoken onstage by the lovers. Rather, two anonymous gentlemen, in six simple *répliques,* describe the happy couple, oblivious to the tumult surrounding them, passing hand in hand through the stage. For all their presence contributes to the effect of the scene, they might as well be in the wings.

Probably the most important scene of the first act which is subsequently reduplicated in the last takes place between the silk merchant and the goldsmith. Masson remarks that the scene itself is a "spectacle dans un spectacle: il y a ceux qui se divertissent et ceux qui regardent se divertir" (Masson, p. 188). The people are spectators of their own political and social destiny. But they are more than just spectators; they are witnesses, commentators, critics of the scene they are observing and about which they bear solemn testimony. The stylized language of their testimony is significant. The *orfèvre* delivers a discourse in which the political life of Florence is transformed metaphorically into architectural life. Substance becomes structure; the tableau becomes its framework. The language of the goldsmith is crucial. His speech appears unnatural, contrived, stilted, as though read from a text. To the silk merchant, his interlocutor, it appears to have come from a script: "Vous avez l'air de savoir tout cela par cœur." The formal nature of the goldsmith's speech rises to consciousness in the mind of the merchant and is subjected to analysis or criticism within the play itself.

In the final act of the play, these two peripheral characters, the merchant and the goldsmith, reappear. Their roles now are reversed. Whereas previously it was the goldsmith who indulged in prolixity, he now remains relatively silent, and it is the merchant's turn to be garrulous as he delivers himself of the famous speech of the six Sixes. His language is so contrived as to appear absurd and is dismissed as such by the goldsmith. Abruptly, with almost no transition, the two bourgeois disappear from the scene to be replaced by another couple, the Preceptors, accompanied by the Strozzi and Salviati children. It is as though the bourgeois had dis-

solved into the Preceptors. Even the language remains the same; it is the language of caricature. It is outrageously affected, pedantic, *précieux.* The two Preceptors appear to be influenced neither by the macrocosmic political upheaval which has just taken place nor by its microcosmic reflection which appears before their eyes in the actions of the contentious children. The Preceptors themselves are a mirror, reduced to the absurd, not only of the Cibo couple, but of the artist Tebaldeo. Like Tebaldeo, they are interested only in the work of art that results from the revolution. One of the Preceptors has, in fact, written a sonnet describing the events as he perceives them, and is parading it before his colleague for commentary and appreciation. Because of the scuffling of the scamps only a two-line fragment of the sonnet is recited. These two lines are sufficient to show that we are in the presence of an antiphrastic interior reduplication of the larger work:

> Chantons la liberté qui refleurit plus âpre,
> Sous des soleils plus mûrs et des cieux plus vermeils.
>
> (V, 5, p. 198.)

If the reflowering at the end is more harsh than the situation at the beginning, the liberty of which the poet/pedant speaks is ironic. Liberty is the one thing which is decidedly not the result of the action of the play.

Undramatic language, produced by undramatic, peripheral characters, leads away from the action of the text in the direction of its limits. The structure of repetition constitutes a framework around the main action of **Lorenzaccio.** Grouped in the framework of the play, at its margins, are the spectators, the commentators, and the inefficacious actors. Theme and structure play off against each other in the diffused light as the distinction between the two is blurred at the point of their conjuncture. Paradoxically, by alluding to an "elsewhere," the framework states poetically but clearly that the limits of the text may be transcended, both by expansion and contraction.

It is at the point where expansion and contraction occur simultaneously that Musset's contribution to the poetics of framing is most striking. The notion of simultaneous expansion and contraction is embodied in what is the most peripheral set of *répliques* in the first act. It relates to the non-appearance of Benvenuto Cellini on stage and to his presence as potential story-teller in the wings. The content of Cellini's "bonne histoire" is never recorded in the play and will remain an unknown paratext, an abstract possibility. The peripherality of Cellini, the artist who "appears" in the wings, is reflected by the peripherality of Tebaldeo, the artist who does actually appear on stage.[5]

Of the thirty-eight scenes of **Lorenzaccio,** none is more peripheral than the one in which Tebaldeo appears so prominently. Of the forty-four-odd characters in the play, few are more unnecessary. None of Musset's characters illustrates more forcefully Musset's technique of literary framing.

In act II, scene 2, Lorenzo notices that Tebaldeo is carrying a painting in his hands. He calls attention to it metonymically: "Vous avez, il me semble, un cadre dans les mains" (II,2, p. 89). The ensuing conversation has as its subject the contents of the frame. From Tebaldeo we learn that his painting of the Campo Santo is an "esquisse bien pauvre d'un rêve magnifique." This humble statement provokes a number of assertions by Lorenzo which reveal the true function of Tebaldeo's "frame." What is crucial is not what is on the canvas but *what might be put inside the frame.* "Vous faites," says Lorenzo, "le portrait de vos rêves? Je ferai poser pour vous quelques-uns des miens." Tebaldeo's frame, therefore, serves a function similar to that of the unseen canvas in Velázquez's painting, *Las Meninas.* Not only might it reflect the scene being painted, but it might also reflect a scene *outside* the borders of the work of art.

Lorenzo, in fact, declines to see the painting at all. His taunting remarks, "Estce un paysage ou un portrait? De quel côté faut-il regarder, en long ou en large?" appear to be the tasteless appreciation of a philistine. This blurring of the distinction between a *paysage* and a *portrait* has far-reaching significance, however. The marquise Cibo, when she feels the need to escape from the suffocating atmosphere of her adultery, does not go to a window for relief from the dramatic tension; instead, she contemplates a portrait of her husband. What is crucially important about the picture is that the marquise transforms the *portrait* into a *paysage:* the marquis becomes Massa. She sees in the portrait something that is not there, or rather something that is evoked by it and which results in its expansion. This distortion of the contents of the frame is central to Musset's handling of interior framing, where the reduced model is transformed into a structure even larger than the main body, where concentration leads to expansion.

For Lorenzo, as well, what is in a frame is far less important than *what might be there.* For Lorenzo, Tebaldeo's frame *could* contain the portrait of a courtesan (whom Tebaldeo would decline to paint) or it *could* contain a view of Florence. These two options, the *portrait* and the *paysage,* are qualitatively different microcosmic reflections of Lorenzo's own corruption. Tebaldeo's refusal to paint "la Mazzafirra toute nue" (II,2, p. 90), coupled with his enthusiastic willingness to paint corrupt Florence, appears to irritate Lorenzo keenly. As long as the contents of Tebaldeo's frame do not make a severe distinction between Lorenzo's corruption and that of society, Lorenzo can see himself as a mere reflection of the corrupt society, as a mirror—or as a work of art. As soon as the artist, however

mediocre, insists on a severe distinction between personal and social corruptions, Lorenzo is threatened. Is his criminal life a reflection of the portrait of a lowly courtesan or is it the reflection of a noble city which has become like a whore? "Est-ce un paysage ou un portrait? De quel côté faut-il regarder, en long ou en large?" Tebaldeo's frame is important for what it might contain, the mirror of Lorenzo's moral dilemma. It is *both* a scale model *and* a dilation of the scenic space. The insight provided by the frame applies an unbearable pressure on Lorenzo. The only issue from the abyss represented by the frame is to attempt to corrupt the artist, to make him an accomplice in a political act. After his confrontation with Tebaldeo, Lorenzo is challenged by another incarnation of virtue, Catherine. She proposes to read from a book on Roman history. Lorenzo interrupts and "reads" *his own version of the text:* "Il y avait une fois un jeune gentilhomme nommé Tarquin le fils (II,4, p. 100). Lorenzo changes the "histoire de sang" into a "conte de fées," rewriting the text, as the marquise has repainted the portrait.

Tebaldeo, a reflection of what Lorenzo once was, and Brutus, a model for what he wishes to become, are only two of the many doubles of Lorenzo in the play. In fact, all the male characters in the play who display individuality, with the exception of Cardinal Cibo,[6] mirror Lorenzo. All are virtual incarnations of Lorenzo, either past or future, either probable or at least remotely possible.

The case of Philippe is especially instructive. In the central scene of the play, the one receiving the greatest concentration of light, Philippe challenges Lorenzo directly, the way Tebaldeo had challenged him only obliquely. It is in this scene (III,3) that Lorenzo is led, by a mysterious process which lacks both logical and chronological development, to his self-revelation. The scene itself only seems to lack internal coherence. It is held together in fact by the repeated use of framing metaphors, devices which focus on the surface of things and on the inexorable forces—from both inside and out—which cause a puncturing of the surface.

Philippe, using the metaphor of the container, demands that Lorenzo exhibit its contents. "Que l'homme sorte de l'histrion! Ne m'as-tu pas parlé d'un homme qui s'appelle aussi Lorenzo, et qui se cache derrière le Lorenzo que voilà?" (III,3, pp. 128-29). And then he throws down the gauntlet. "Es-tu au dedans comme au-dehors une vapeur infecte? Toi qui m'as parlé d'une liqueur précieuse *dont tu étais le flacon,* est-ce là ce que tu renfermes?" (III,3, p. 132, my italics). Philippe demands a change of perspective from inside to out.

Lorenzo rises to the challenge with deliberation. His answer is not a direct one, however. He notes that there is a danger in looking beneath the surface, beyond mere reflection, or even beyond a complex system of reflections. Lorenzo sees himself as having once been an admirer of surfaces. He claims to have been able to penetrate the surfaces of things, to reach their essences, and to have found them corrupt. He even uses the architectural metaphor the goldsmith had proposed in describing the political life of Florence, comparing life itself to a city. Lorenzo claims to have looked through the windows of the city, not outwardly to Massa or Caffagiuolo, but inwardly at evil, and, having done so, even though protected by a *cloche de verre,* to have become tainted.

The surfaces, both of the macrocosm represented by the corrupt city whose windows are its limits and of the microcosm represented by the *Lorenzino d'autrefois* who contains virtue's precious liqueur and who is himself contained in a protective bell-jar, have been hopelessly intertwined. As Lorenzo reviews the text and texture of his life, he sees that there have been other surfaces as well, which have been more than mere surfaces. At one time Lorenzo was able to externalize the virtue he knew he contained. He would even walk around with his good *fantôme* at his side. He takes seriously his mother's fantastic vision of the spectre of the *Lorenzino d'autrefois.* He records as well that, in order to execute his "political" plan, he chose still another surface identity, the theatrical mask of vice. Lorenzo fully realizes now that this mask has stuck to his skin. And yet, it is not the interfusing of surfaces which is, finally, important.

What Lorenzo has come to fear is not that the interior of the *flacon* be *infecte,* not that the interior of the frame be vicious, but that it be empty. He is concerned lest the bell-jar house a vacuum. The enigma of Lorenzo's life is not solved by the assassination; it is merely expressed, externalized, exhibited, mirrored in the larger world of the play. Lorenzo has been the scaffolding in which there existed a scale model of the larger-than-life Lorenzo. The expressed Lorenzo is, although not the political savior of Florence, a man of virtue, a witness to virtue—and its prophet. His action is his text, and it is given to be read.

What remains after the writing of the text is a void. In Venice, outside the stage of Florence, Philippe remarks that after all that has taken place, Lorenzo has not changed. Lorenzo concurs, but with one caveat: "Il n'y a de changé en moi qu'une misère—c'est que je suis plus creux et plus vide qu'une statue de fer-blanc" (V,6, p. 200). Lorenzo, in realizing his act, in realizing his mother's dream, has realized at the same time his greatest fear: he has lost his potentiality. Both the "Lorenzaccio" and the "Lorenzino" spectres are now externalized. "Lorenzo," however, remains, metaphorically, an empty frame, a frame that contains neither *paysage* nor *portrait.*

The ending of **Lorenzaccio,** the play, is parallel to the end of Lorenzo the person: it is neither good nor bad; it is neither progress nor change. Côme's inauguration speech is a text read off-stage which renders ambiguous the action which has taken place on stage. Indeed, we may question whether *Lorenzaccio* as a whole is a *portrait* or a *paysage.* "De quel côté faut-il regarder, en long ou en large?" As in the case of Tebaldeo's painting, one can only speculate about what the frame *might* contain. As in the case of Lorenzo, what we actually see is only a frame.

Outer and inner framing are functions of an esthetic system. By the use of a complex network of frames, Musset expands the work of art beyond its material limits. His contribution in **Lorenzaccio** is that he was able to expand the limits without transgressing the strict bounds of the genre in which he wrote. He was able to fashion the frame out of the painting.

Notes

1. A theory of "frame analysis" as an interdisciplinary methodology can be found in Erving Goffman, *Frame Analysis* (New York: Harper & Row, 1974). Among literary critics, see Boris Uspensky, *A Poetics of Composition* (Berkeley: University of California Press, 1973), and Jurij Lotman, *The Structure of the Artistic Text* (Ann Arbor: Michigan Slavic Contributions, 1977).

   All references to *Lorenzaccio* will be taken from the following edition and will be made in the text: Alfred de Musset, *Théâtre complet,* Bibliothèque de la Pléiade (Paris: Gallimard, 1958).

2. Apparently, Anne Ubersfeld (in "Révolution et topique de la cité: *Lorenzaccio,*" *Littérature* 24 (1976), 41 sees the regicide as the center of the play. The present analysis, by its very method, excludes such a perspective. It agrees wholeheartedly, however, with Ubersfeld's general statements concerning the rest of the action: "S'il se passe beaucoup de choses dans la pièce, elles sont toutes marginales par rapport au régicide." Many, she says, "n'ont aucun caractère de nécessité dramatique."

3. Hassan el Nouty, "L'Esthétique de *Lorenzaccio,*" *Revue des Sciences Humaines,* 108 (1962), 589-611.

4. Bernard Masson, *Musset et le théâtre intérieur. Nouvelles recherches sur "Lorenzaccio"* (Paris: Armand Colin, 1974). Subsequent references to this work will be made in the text. One might agree fully with Masson's well-developed argument that for Musset a *spectacle dans un fauteuil* is not so much a *théâtre de lecture* as it is a *théâtre intérieur;* one might insist, however, that it is

interior theatre to the extent that it demands of the spectator, at the theatre or in the armchair, that he look at the work with closer attention to both detail and perspective than a mere reading or stage production permits.

5. Masson comments at length on the central role Cellini was to have played in *Lorenzaccio*. He shows convincingly (pp. 13-31) how Cellini's *Vita*, more than any other work, might have served the function of intertext for the play. Masson also enunciates a hypothesis for Musset's relegation of Cellini to the wings and for his replacement in the text by the non-historical painter Tebaldeo Freccia.

6. The cardinal is neither central nor peripheral to the action of *Lorenzaccio*. At most, he is peripheral to the peripheral story of the marquise, encircling her like a vulture. He is a shadow of a much larger political intrigue, that of the Pope and the emperor, being played elsewhere. He is not merely peripheral to the text; he is foreign to it.

Barbara T. Cooper (essay date fall 1983)

SOURCE: Cooper, Barbara T. "Staging a Revolution: Political Upheaval in *Lorenzaccio* and *Léo Burckart*." *Romance Notes* 24, no. 1 (fall 1983): 23-9.

[*In the following essay, Cooper explores the political overtones of two nineteenth-century plays—Musset's* Lorenzaccio *and Gérard de Nerval's* Léo Burckart.]

During the early decades of the nineteenth century, French dramatists of every aesthetic stripe regularly looked to history to provide them with the raw materials for an ever-increasing number of plays. Today, all but a few of the dramatic works that testify to this widespread enthusiasm for history and to its systematic exploitation have been left to gather dust on library shelves. Indeed, were it not for the work of Charles B. Wicks, Claude Duchet, Hassan El Nouty, and others,[1] we would scarcely be in a position to measure the extent of the early nineteenth-century French playwrights' passion for the past or to notice how frequently they chose to dramatize moments of political upheaval. In the interest of brevity, we cannot here set this predilection for moments of conflict in its contemporary political and cultural context. Nonetheless, it is surely this context, as much as the dramatic potential of the theme of revolution, that explains why Alfred de Musset and Gérard de Nerval, like many of their elders, elected to "stage" a revolution.

Because Musset and Nerval are primarily known for their subjective, lyrical writings, some readers have summarily judged them to be "étrangers à la politique."[2] Yet, as Bernard Masson notes in *Musset et le théâtr intérieur:*

L'intérêt porté par Musset *au* politique plus qu'à *la* politique rend compte ainsi sans peine et des maigres échos suscités dans son œuvre par les événements de son temps et de l'abondance des thèmes politiques qui y sont développés, au premier rang desquels M. Duchet a bien raison de placer "les rapports entre l'individu et la société, et plus précisément l'insertion de l'homme dans la cité, dans une communauté organisée selon des lois".[3]

Like Musset, Nerval may be judged to be indifferent to *la politique* and therefore little inclined to accord a prominent place in his works to current events. He is nonetheless interested in *le politique,* that is to say in the philosophical underpinings of political action and human government; and in *Léo Burckart*—written to some extent with the collaboration of Alexandre Dumas *père*—, Nerval does examine the relationship between men and society, ideology and practical policy. As Jacqueline Lévi-Valensi writes, "Tout le drame, en effet, illustre l'idée que la pureté des théories politiques, la grandeur d'un idéal ne peuvent résister à l'épreuve de la réalité."[4]

Useful as it is, this distinction between *le politique* and *la politique* should not lead us to believe that Musset and Nerval divorced their dramatized reflection on political conflict from the real world. Like Musset, whom Masson describes as a kind of "'Janus bifrons' tourné à la fois du côté de la Florence médicéenne et de la monarchie restaurée,"[5] Nerval, too, must have had one eye turned toward the Germany of 1819 and the other trained on the France of Louis-Philippe when he wrote *Léo Burckart.* Such, at least, was the opinion of the royal censors who reviewed and rejected the first version of the play in 1838.[6]

It should hardly come as a surprise to us that this "double" vision, this layered representation of past and present political upheavals would produce an ironic perspective, an intellectual tension that allows both **Lorenzaccio** and *Léo Burckart* to be read on two levels: first, as a reflection on current events and second, as a statement about the historical process and the human condition. Since, as Bernard Masson writes in *Musset et le théâtre intérieur,* "Dire que le drame de Musset renvoie peut-être à Florence en 1537, mais sûrement à Paris en juillet 1830, c'est à la fois constater une évidence et rester à la surface des choses" (p. 78), in the pages that follow, I shall concentrate on an analysis of what Musset's and Nerval's dramas have to tell us about their conception of the historical process.

In another study, I found it useful to compare the manner in which early nineteenth-century French dramatists represented history to the ways in which early nineteenth-century European historians described the past.[7] On that occasion, I borrowed my description of nineteenth-century historical writing from Hayden White's *Metahistory,* and I shall do so again here.

White tells us that

> The informing presupposition of Contextualism is that events can be explained by being set within the 'context' of their occurrence. Why they occurred as they did is to be explained by the revelation of the specific relationships they bore to other events occurring in their circumambient historical space. [. . .] Insofar as [Contextualism] tacitly invokes rules . . . these rules are not construed as equivalent to the universal laws of cause and effect postulated by the Organicist. [. . .] Contextualist explanatory strategies incline more toward synchronic representations of segments or sections of the [historical] process. . . .[8]

Like the Contextualist historian, Musset and Nerval set the events and efforts their plays describe in a specific spatio-temporal context. As Eric L. Gans reminds us, in *Lorenzaccio* "Le cadre historique n'est pas un prétexte mais une garantie: l'histoire de Florence se porte garant du choix, apparemment inconcevable, de la non-liberté des hommes libres."[9] In *Léo Burckart* Nerval, too, goes to great pains to show the extent to which his protagonists' political actions and ideals are linked to age-old German traditions as well as to the conditions that prevail in 1819. Thus, if these dramatists look back to the "origins" of a given event or forward to its "impact," their perspective is always the fictional "present"—Florence in 1537 and Germany in 1819—and their goal is to describe that moment in all its synchronic richness. Indeed, the very structures of *Lorenzaccio* and *Léo Burckart,* once criticized as being excessively fragmented and today praised as cinematographic, serve as concrete proof of the dramatists' desire to give depth and substance to the historical context in which their characters act and evolve.

As White suggests in his description of Contextualist historical writing, the decision to represent a specific moment in history synchronically is itself suggestive of an implicit rejection of two theoretical perspectives: 1) that history is governed by universal laws and 2) that the historical process advances toward some ultimate goal or end. In terms more familiar to literary scholars, we might say that the contextual approach adopted by Musset and Nerval constitutes a rejection of the neo-classical and Enlightenment world views so often espoused by these dramatists' predecessors and by some of their contemporaries.

To the extent that *Lorenzaccio* and *Léo Burckart* deny the unity and homogeneity of human experience, these works might well be said to "de-mythify" history and to stand as a rejection of the universalist presuppositions which underlie the neo-classical aesthetic. Unlike the "Greece" and "Rome" which serve as a backdrop to the action in so many seventeenth-century plays, "Florence" and "Germany" are not abstract historical fictions meant to serve as microcosmic representations of the whole of human society. Indeed, Lorenzo explicitly rejects the view that the human experience is timeless and unchanging. Challenging Lorenzo's position, Philippe Strozzi declares in Act V, scene two: "Assurément tous les hommes ne sont pas capables de grandes choses, mais tous sont sensibles aux grandes choses; nies-tu l'histoire du monde entier?" To this Lorenzo mordantly replies: "Je ne nie pas l'histoire, mais je n'y étais pas."[10] For him, history is not a common heritage shared by everyone ("tous") everywhere ("le monde entier"), but a contextually-determined set of forces and contingencies. History's status as a unifying myth, Lorenzo seems to be saying, cannot be verified on the level of personal experience and therefore must be rejected.

Despite repeated references to Antiquity and to modern German history, personal experience also forces the characters in *Léo Burckart* to deny the changelessness and communality of history. When Frantz Lewald is chastised by his fellow conspirators for appearing at a court ball dressed in livery, he replies: "Je ne suis pas Romain, mais Allemand; je n'étudie pas la liberté dans les livres, mais dans les faits. Les époques ne sont jamais semblables, et les moyens diffèrent aussi."[11] When a disguised Léo Burckart undertakes to defend Frédéric-Auguste against the accusations of a secret society, he proclaims: "—Eh bien! accusez les coupables selon vous, mais les coupables seulement. Le prince ne vous a rien juré, ni en 1806, ni en 1813; car ce n'était pas lui qui régnait alors" (V iv, 235). Here, as in Musset's text, the characters themselves are cognizant of the ways in which the present differs from the past and prefer to link current events to each other rather than bringing together chronologically distant moments.

If history in *Lorenzaccio* and in *Léo Burckart* is neither immutable nor universal as the neo-classical world view suggests, is history then progress, that is, a path along which society advances toward perfection, as the Enlightenment philosophers and their early nineteenth-century heirs believed it was? With their circular plot-structures and their mocking disparagements of liberal rhetoric and political action, *Lorenzaccio* and *Léo Burckart* appear to reject bourgeois optimism just as surely as they rejected the principle of neo-classical universalism. As Hassan El Nouty notes, "Le devenir historique transposé dans *Lorenzaccio* assimile le mouvement de l'Histoire à une illusion."[12] Indeed, the bitterly ironic lesson of both *Lorenzaccio* and *Léo Burckart* is that revolutionary action ultimately results in a return to the *status quo ante* when it does not actually bring about a worsening of conditions. Early in the play, Léo Burckart chides Frédéric-Auguste when this prince seems to "méconnaître l'éternelle loi du progrès" (I, x, 164). Yet, as the Prince points out to Léo: "Je sais toute la modération de vos principes, toute la légitimité de vos espérances; et pourtant vous avez mis en danger la sûreté d'un grand pays. . . . Vous philosophe, vous écrivain, vous avez ouvert une porte à la guerre et une autre à la révolte . . ." (I, x, 164) When Burckart later becomes an advisor to Frédéric-Auguste—a position which reminds one to some degree of Voltaire's role at the court of Frederick II and of Diderot's at the court of Catherine the Great—the effects of his works continue to belie his intentions. Indeed, Burckart's long absences from the stage and the non-performative nature of his speech acts are clear signs of his political impotence. In the end, Léo's pen becomes an instrument of repression ("Cette plume, madame, cette plume était un sceptre plus réel que [celui du prince] . . . et j'ai peur, en la reprenant, d'en avoir usé le prestige!" (IV, iv, 211) and when Léo finally resigns from the Prince's service, he leaves his country no freer than it was when the play began.

The emptiness of rhetoric and the futility of political action are similarly underscored in **Lorenzaccio.** Lorenzo's mocking comparison of a periodic sentence to a "petite toupie [qui] s'échappe avec un murmure délicieux [et qu'] on pourrait presque [. . .] ramasser dans le creux de la main, comme les enfants des rues" (II, iv, 371) reduces political discourse to a pointless, infantile amusement and is surely the most familiar of the negative characterizations of ideological rhetoric that inform Musset's play. Actions are scarcely more compelling. Neither the Marquise de Cibo's sacrifice of marital fidelity nor Lorenzo's assassination of his cousin the Duke will usher in a new "golden" age of Florentine government. Instead, Alexandre will be replaced by Côme de Médicis, a puppet monarch imposed and clearly manipulated by the Machiavellian Cardinal de Cibo.

What does this failure of language and action mean? What does this rejection of both the progressivist and the universalist views of history imply? Why "stage" a revolution if it is not to be integrated into the flow or timeless fabric of history? The answer, I believe, can only be discovered when Musset's and Nerval's plays are viewed in their original historical context. In **Lorenzaccio** and *Léo Burckart* the failed Revolution of July 1830 has been imaginatively transposed and transported from the streets to the stage. Public and private acts and pronouncements have been transformed into artifacts, ideologies have been made into "suspended objects of esthetic contemplation"—to borrow a phrase from Fredric Jameson.[13] Revolution, then, like drama, appears as pure illusion. Rather than moving one toward a solution, revolution—as the structure and conclusion of these dramas show—is a mere turning of the body politic on its fixed axis. In **Lorenzaccio** and *Léo Burckart,* the Revolution of 1830, set up on the stage, becomes little more than a historicized "media event," distanced from the reader and viewer in both time and space and stripped of all positive political and ideological substance.

Notes

1. Charles B. Wicks, *The Parisian Stage,* University of Alabama Studies, 6 (University, Ala.: University of Alabama Press, 1950); Claude Duchet, "Théâtre, histoire et politique sous la Restauration," pp. 281-302 in *Romantisme et politique, 1815-1851* (Paris: Colin, 1969); Hassan El Nouty, *Théâtre et pré-cinéma* (Paris: Nizet, 1978).

2. The term is borrowed from Pierre Paraf's "Alfred de Musset et la politique," *Europe,* nos. 583-584 (1977), 113-125. This surprising judgment is derived from an examination of Musset's poetry. Dietmar Rieger seems to be one of the few scholars to have considered the political side of Nerval's poetry (see his "Nerval poète politique," *Romanistische Zeitschrift für Literaturgeschichte,* II, 1, 1978, 21-38 which I have been unable to consult personally). More typical is Kurt Shaerer's observation in "La Tentation du drame chez Nerval," *Cahiers Gérard de Nerval* (1980), that "Sa [Nerval's] conception trop subjectiviste du drame l'incitait à s'en servir uniquement comme d'un moyen pour représenter ou incarner ses rêves, ses hantises personnelles, de sorte que le théâtre n'a jamais été pour lui qu'un miroir qui lui renvoyait ses propres images" (p. 5). Shaerer does see *Léo Burckart* as an exception to this general rule.

3. Paris: Colin, 1974, p. 80. Further references to this work will be noted in the text.

4. Jacqueline Lévi-Valensi, "Romantisme et politique dans *Léo Burckart* de Gérard de Nerval et Alexandre Dumas," in *Romantisme et politique, 1815-1851* (Paris: Colin, 1969), p. 365. Further references to this article will be noted in the text.

5. Bernard Masson, "Dans les marges de *Lorenzaccio,*" in *Le Réel et le texte* (Paris: Colin, 1974), p. 220.

6. Jacqueline Lévi-Valensi writes: "La portée politique de *Léo Burckart* est indéniable: elle émut suffisamment la censure pour que celle-ci obligeât Nerval et Dumas à certaines modifications; la version jouée au théâtre de la Porte-Saint-Martin, en 1839, était le résultat d'une 'refonte totale' opérée par Nerval, selon ses propres termes, et qui obéissait à l'injonction gouvernementale d' 'insister sur les idées d'ordre et de pouvoir,' en même temps qu'à la nécessité purement dramatique, mais non moins impérieuse, d'abréger le texte" (p. 359).

7. Barbara T. Cooper, "Master Plots: An Alternate Typology for French Historical Dramas of the Early Nineteenth Century, *Theatre Journal,* in press.

8. Hayden White, *Metahistory* (Baltimore and London: Johns Hopkins University Press, 1975), pp. 17-19.

9. Eric L. Gans, *Musset et le 'drame tragique'* (Paris: Corti, 1974), p. 159.

10. Alfred de Musset, *Théâtre 1,* Texte intégral (Paris: Garnier-Flammarion, 1964), V, ii, p. 434. Further references to this work will be noted in the text.

11. Gérard de Nerval, *Sylvie, suivie de Léo Burckart et de Aurélia,* ed. Henri Clouard (Monaco: Eds. du Rocher, 1946), 3ᵉ journée, scène ii, p. 190. Further references will be noted in the text.

12. Hassan El Nouty, "L'Esthétique de *Lorenzaccio*," *Revue des sciences humaines,* 108 (1962), 603. As will be seen from what follows, I cannot agree with Jean-Marie Piemme, "*Lorenzaccio:* impasse d'une idéologie," *Romantisme* 1-2 (1971), 126, that "Conclure à l'Histoire comme illusion parce que la pièce n'est pas le lieu d'un chargement historique qualitatif, c'est oublier que *Lorenzaccio* ne compte aucun héros positif et que, par conséquent, tous les échecs sont implicitement critiquables." Musset may not have always believed that History is an illusion, but that is certainly what he shows us in this play. As Anne Ubersfeld has pointed out in "Révolution et topique de la cité: *Lorenzaccio*," *Littérature,* 24 (1976), 49, both within the text itself and at the time of its production, "c'est le moment exact où l'optimisme bourgeois, l'universalisme de la Raison bourgeoise se retourne, et où l'on revient à une problématique pessimiste à la Hobbes . . ."

13. "Sartre in Search of Flaubert," *New York Times Book Review,* 27 December 1981, p. 16.

James F. Hamilton (essay date 1985)

SOURCE: Hamilton, James F. "Mimetic Desire in Musset's *Lorenzaccio*." *Kentucky Romance Quarterly* 32, no. 4 (1985): 347-57.

[*In the following essay, Hamilton examines the phychological themes underpinning Musset's play.*]

> "Pour comprendre l'exaltation fiévreuse qui a enfanté en moi le Lorenzo qui te parle, il faudrait que mon cerveau et mes entrailles fussent à nu sous un scalpel."
>
> (III, 3)[1]

In the above passage, the hero challenges us to probe the motives of his obsessive desire. Lorenzo de Médicis dedicates his life to the accomplishment of one feat, the murder of his cousin and constant companion, Alexandre, the Duke of Florence. Musset's insistence upon the sexual exploits of the Medici scions and the underlying tension of their sibling rivalry pushes the text beyond a historical accuracy assured by his travels to Italy and research in Renaissance chronicles. The Lorenzo portrayed by Musset is inspired by a madness akin to the creative impulse of the poet and artist. Lacking ideological conviction, he is not taken seriously as a political assassin.[2] He represents a type of Romantic hero and embodies an aesthetics of action.[3] His denial of convention points not only to a search for identity but to a quest for immortality.[4] However, the contradiction between his "exaltation" and his degenerate conduct invites a psychological analysis; he seems to be driven by an inferiority complex.[5] These insights need to be integrated within a comprehensive theoretical model, one characterized by a broad understanding of myth. From this perspective, the insatiable pride of the Medicis puts them on a par with the ancient Greek house of Atreus.[6] Similarly, the city of Florence is cast as a fallen woman like the decadent Athens, the corrupt Rome, and the whore of Babylon as cited in *Revelations.*

From every angle—historical, psychological, and mythical—the city of Florence constitutes the focus of attention. For example, Emperor Charles V and the Pope intervene militarily and politically in the affairs of Florence, while King Francis I seeks eagerly to find a pretext to do so. The city is viewed as a prize, an object of desire, which is alternately loved and hated by those who compete for its possession. Fallen from its liberty as a republic and bearing a feminine name, Florence embodies the contrary symbolism of mother and harlot. This contradiction imposes an extreme tension upon the psyche of Lorenzo, the originally pure and idealistic student of Florence as a model republic.

The images of republican Florence and his mother, Marie Soderini, merge in Lorenzo's mind. As a child, he absorbs maternal affection and partisan ideology in the same embrace. This subtle indoctrination is confessed by Marie to her younger sister: "Et cette admiration pour les grands hommes de son Plutarque! Catherine Catherine, que de fois je l'ai baisé au front en pensant au père de la patrie" (III, 3). The associated images of mother and city are reciprocal; Marie imagines the accusatory cries of citizens betrayed by Lorenzo: "Tu es la mère de nos malheurs!" (I, 6). A few lines later, the parting curses of exiles reinforce the overlapping identities of Marie, Florence, and mother: "Adieu Florence, peste de l'Italie! Adieu mère stérile, qui n'a plus de lait pour tes enfants!" Sterility in a mother betokens the lack of love for a child. This is the drama of Marie, who identifies herself as a mother but rejects her son. Only an alienated mother can see her son objectively as being ugly, and she dreams of him with revulsion, "dans les bras d'un spectre hideux." In contrast, Catherine rationalizes the cowardice of Lorenzo; she blames Florence for his excesses and defends his essential goodness: "Je me dis malgré moi que tout n'est pas mort en lui."

Without attempting to draw a strict cause/effect relationship between a mother's feelings and a son's behavior, several rather obvious points can be made. First of all, the images of city, mother, and aunt fuse within the mind of Lorenzo. When republicans disregard Lorenzo's nocturnal announcement of his impending assassination of the Duke, he cries out in despair: "Pauvre Florence! pauvre Florence!" (IV, 7). Shortly afterwards, he uses similar language in a reflection that links mother and aunt: "—Pauvre Catherine! Que ma mère mourût de tout cela, ce serait triste" (IV, 9). Contrary to historical fact, Lorenzo receives notice of Marie's death after the failure of his assassination. More important but less easy to prove, the images of Florence, mother, and aunt generalize to all women within a Madonna/prostitute syndrome. His prevailing scorn of women is challenged by Catherine. In reply, he makes only two exceptions to his misanthropy, Catherine and Marie: "Je vous estime, vous et elle. Hors de là, le monde me fait horreur" (II, 4). Hence, from the standpoint of structure, Florence heads the triangular conflict in *Lorenzaccio* and is accompanied at its apex by a number of female surrogates.

The base angles of the triangle are occupied by Lorenzo and Alexandre. In a conventional plot, the two cousins would compete for the attention and favor of a beloved situated graphically in the projection of their desires at the apex of the "eternal" triangle. In fact, a number of conditions place Lorenzo and Alexandre de Médicis in positions of mutual envy, resentment, and admiration. First, the Duke also suffers from a sense of inferiority, as is shown in the duel scene.[7] When Lorenzo faints or pretends to faint at the sight of a naked sword blade, the sibling rivalry and latent antagonism explode on the part of Alexandre: "Fi donc! tu fais honte au nom de Médicis Je ne suis qu'un bâtard, et je le porterais mieux que toi, qui es légitime" (I, 4). Lacking the refinement, education, and imagination of his more noble-minded cousin, Alexandre emphasizes his masculine superiority. He delights in humiliating his effeminate cousin, "une femelette," and calls attention to "ce petit corps maigre," "ces mains fluettes et maladives," etc. Despite such disparaging remarks (provoked partly by jealous courtiers), Alexandre takes a protective stance toward his cousin and shows more loyal affection to him than to any of his mistresses: "J'aime Lorenzo, moi, et, par la mort de Dieu! il restera ici."

The rivalry of Lorenzo and Alexandre does not function according to literary convention, for they are locked in a degrading relationship. Its dynamic of repulsion and attraction constitutes a "mimetic rivalry" which goes to the heart of much human behavior. Basically, the theory of "mimetic rivalry" holds that others' desires teach us what we want. However, the imitative character of desire takes a deviated form in *Lorenzaccio*. Rather than considering Alexandre as an obstacle to the attainment of a prize, a woman, or a mutual ambition,

Lorenzo becomes dependent on him. Lorenzo needs the brute desire of his cousin in order to legitimize and sustain his own desire.[8] For instance, Lorenzo portrays himself as enjoying the women cast aside by Alexandre, "les restes de ses orgies," most of whom he was in the habit of procuring (III, 3). At the same time, he is troubled by the ghost of his pure youth and filled with self-hatred. The destabilizing aspect of this kind of mimetic triangle results from its ambivalence. Desire transfers from the object to its obstacle but is capable of returning to its original orientation. In the case of Lorenzo, he idealizes Florence, is enthralled by the uninhibited sensuality of Alexandre, and intends always to return to the "woman" of his youth. This love of a reflection from a rival feeds upon itself with overtones of a homosexuality permeated with masochism and guilt.[9]

The situation becomes clear if one visualizes a triangle with the object, Florence, at its apex (A) and the rivals, Lorenzo and Alexandre, at its base angles (ABC and ACB). The projection of Lorenzo's desire through Alexandre to the idealized Florence (from B to C to A) becomes dormant. The horizontal plane at the base of the triangle (BC) intensifies to carry the action in reflected images of mutual admiration and disgust. Unlike the traditional love triangle, desire is blocked and turns inward. It becomes incapable of striving upward to attain the ideal in an ennobling quest.

The mimetic triangle in *Lorenzaccio,* with its distinguishing character of sexual ambivalence, takes form in the opening scene of abduction. With Lorenzo and a squire, Alexandre awaits the departure of a maiden from a Florentine home. The darkness of midnight hides corrupt actions which harbor even darker motives in an ambiance of evil. Their shadowy figures mask an ignoble conduct which situates them outside of the law and society. Through the mediation of Lorenzo, the Duke reaches back into time to practice the ancient right of a ruler, "le droit du seigneur," to deflower virgins in his kingdom (III, 3). To be sure, this primordial ritual of fertility has political significance in Renaissance Florence. Alexandre rules the city through force, and the phallus complements the sword to humiliate and to undermine the morale of noble republican families that resist. So, too, seduction as the preference for wealth and pleasure over principle is shown to characterize bourgeois society in the persons of merchants who profit from the Duke's profligate expenditures. More importantly, the opening scene serves to illuminate the peculiar relationship of Lorenzo and Alexandre which is central to the conflict in *Lorenzaccio.*

The triangle of Alexandre, Lorenzo, and the maiden incorporates sexuality, violence, and the metaphysical. These levels of meaning are felt by the maiden's brother, Maffio, who confuses reality and illusion when waking from a dream to surprise the abductors. After being disarmed, he refers to "des lois à Florence" and "ce qu'il y a de sacré au monde" but finds a culprit in the person of Alexandre rather than a defender (I, 2). A more basic confusion of roles occurs between Alexandre and Lorenzo. Little passion is shown by the Duke; his preoccupation with the cold night air and matter-of-fact remark about another social commitment give the impression of performing a princely duty out of habit. His amorous motivation depends upon Lorenzo, who depicts in a long speech the exquisite sensual delight and domination awaiting the Duke in his despoiling of a fifteen-year-old girl. He promises a total possession of body and mind through "le filon mystérieux du vice," and he demeans her as a sexual object with images such as *trésor, chatte, fruits plus rares, exquise odeur.* Verbs of force and penetration convey a vicious violence. The interplay of Lorenzo and Alexandre points to a mimetic mechanism: Lorenzo uses the maiden to excite the Duke, to satisfy his own sexual needs, and to control the behavior of his male superior.

The apex of the mimetic triangle can now be defined with greater comprehension. It represents Florence as an absolute ideal whose profane embodiment, within the rivalry of Lorenzo and Alexandre, includes the maiden in the opening abduction scene as well as Marie and Catherine. So, also, the base angles of the triangle can now be defined vis-à-vis the secondary plots in *Lorenzaccio.* The relationship of Lorenzo with Alexandre as a mimetic rival on plane BC of the triangle degenerates into lust, and it is mirrored on two parallel tiers by competing rivalries. If the sides of the mimetic triangle (AB and AC) are extended for greater complexity, the triangular relationship of Tebaldeo, Alexandre as hero, and Florence (B'C'A) takes shape. Its plane of B'C' operates on the level of art. The third competing rivalry in the extended mimetic triangle includes the Marquise, Alexandre as hero, and Florence (B''C''A). Its plane of B''C'' represents love. Tebaldeo and the Marquise compete with Lorenzo in trying to reveal the republican essence of Florence through idealized images of Alexandre in oil color and in sweet whisperings of grandeur. Artist and mistress seek to immortalize an idealized Florence in the person of Alexandre. Their attempts to incarnate the ideal demonstrate the abstract level of motivation prevailing in the play, and, more importantly, the deviated character of Lorenzo's struggle.

Lorenzo experiences not only the suffering of a mistress in his feeling of self-betrayal but also the more abstract frustrations of an artist. His interrogation of Tebaldeo (the painter who is commissioned to do a portrait of Alexandre) matches the intensity of his heartfelt conversations with Philippe Strozzi. Certain similarities make the bright young men fellow spirits, but one major

difference sets them worlds apart. Each has experienced a vision of the absolute which is referred to by Tebaldeo as "une extase sans égale" (II, 2). and as "l'exaltation fiévreuse" by Lorenzo (III, 3). Each has dedicated his youth to realizing a higher reality of transcendent values through what Tebaldeo describes poetically as "l'enthousiasme sacré" and "ce feu divin" (II, 2). Moreover, each is inspired by an ideal of Florence, which is called "ma mère" by Tebaldeo and "une catin" by the taunting Lorenzo.

The artist and the assassin part company on their vision of the absolute. Whereas descent symbolizes Lorenzo's vision of the sacred, images of ascent in rising organ music, hymns, incense, pale smoke, and perfume characterize Tebaldeo's view of art which serves "la gloire de l'artiste" and that of God (II, 2). Tebaldeo shows himself to be a man of the Renaissance by seeing evil within a humanist perspective ("les terres corrompues engendrent le blé céleste"), and he is able to reconcile his carnal nature with the quest for perfection: "Je suis artiste; j'aime ma mère et ma maîtresse" (II, 2). The psychoanalytic distinction between the creative artist and the compulsive neurotic applies here.[10] By reconciling his conflicts through art, Tebaldeo magnifies his humanity. In contrast, Lorenzo appreciates only the evil in man and seeks through a highly ritualized conduct to elevate a deviation from the norm to the level of art. His dream, born out of despair rather than courage, lacks authenticity and necessarily takes a destructive direction.

The illusory aspect of Lorenzo's creative enterprise is dramatized by another idealist. The Marquise de Cibo seeks to rival the influence of Lorenzo by supplanting him in her role of ideological muse. She also experiences an ambivalence between political ideal and amorous means: "Est-ce que j'aime Alexandre? Non, je ne l'aime pas, non assurément. . . . Pourquoi y a-t-il dans tout cela un aimant, un charme inexplicable qui m'attire? Que tu es belle, Florence, mais que tu es triste!" (II, 4). Her appeals to the heroic imagination of Alexandre ("j'ai de l'ambition, non pas pour moi—mais pour toil toi et ma chère Florence") serve only to cool his ardor, and he abandons her for another woman, Catherine (III, 6). However, failure does not result in tragedy. The Marquise frees herself from an illusory ambition and a degrading role through an act of courage. She confesses everything to her husband in front of her temptor, the Cardinal. Thus, the Marquise reconciles symbolically the dual identity of Florence, mother and woman, when threatened by the loss of her freedom and soul.

The struggle between the flesh and the spirit experienced by the Marquise parallels that of Lorenzo but on a less exalted plane. A metaphysical thrust prevails in his desire from its inception in the Roman Coliseum. This very private moment during Lorenzo's student life in Rome holds the key to his personality transformation, and its confession is provoked by a political incident. The sons of Philippe Strozzi, patriarch of Florentine republicans and father figure to Lorenzo, are arrested. Paternal hysteria and cries of revenge imperil the hero's assassination plan and force him to reveal his secret motives.

The Coliseum scene narrated by Lorrenzo takes place in this emotional context, and his story has a dreamlike quality which further complicates analysis. Nevertheless, a few factual observations can be made. First, having no rational explanation for his experience, Lorenzo pictures himself in a trancelike state of mind: "une certaine nuit que j'étais assis dans les ruines du Colisée, *je ne sais pourquoi* je me levai; je tendis vers le ciel mes bras trempés de rosée, et je jurai qu'un des tyrans de la patrie mourrait de ma main. . . . *il m'est impossible de dire* comment cet étrange serment s'est fait en moi" (III, 3; italics mine). Second, the inspiration takes place in a very special site of heroic grandeur, the Roman Coliseum. Third, a radical change in outlook occurs on the part of Lorenzo, who turns his back on the contemplative life of a scholar and the likelihood, as a Medici, of high office in the Church or the state. Finally, the upheaval is accompanied by a euphoria which Lorenzo likens to the exaltation of falling in love.

The turning point in Lorenzo's life, acted out in a highly symbolic fashion, points to the religious experience of revelation and conversion to a new view of the world. Through a combination of fortuitous circumstances and formative influences, Lorenzo transcends the profane worlds of society and nature to catch a privileged glimpse into the realm of absolute values which promise immortality. This metaphysical level of meaning authorizes the use of myth and ritual. From these interpretative vantage points, Lorenzo's momentary transcendence is facilitated by the Roman Coliseum, which acts as a cosmological point in the planes of time and space where heaven, earth, and hell converge, a "center of the sacred."[11]

Lorenzo undergoes the eternally repeated experience of the *homo religiosus,* an initiation into the sacred, whose various cultural configurations show certain consistent tendencies. Lorenzo's actions deviate from the general pattern of ritual only in their spontaneous occurrence outside of the communal safeguards of tribe, clan, family, or sex group. Traditionally, initiation into the secrets of the sacred takes place upon the reaching of manhood, and the ritual requires the separation of a young man from his mother. This induction into the warrior's group symbolizes the passage from the profane to the sacred worlds, which implies a death and a rebirth into

a higher order of values. The ritualized initiation into manhood and its responsibilities is often followed by a physical trial designed to humiliate the flesh and fortify the spirit.[12]

Because the spiritual character of his adventure defies rational discourse, Lorenzo utilizes the language of metaphor. For example, he compares his vision to "une statue qui descendrait de son piédestal pour marcher parmi les hommes" (III, 3). Through this image (which is reaffirmed subsequently in Lorenzo's beheading of royal statues in the Constantine Arch), he defines himself vis-à-vis the gods and heroes of antiquity.[13] The descent of the statue, comparable to that of Orpheus, is enacted by Lorenzo, who descends symbolically from purity into vice, a hell of his own making, in order to gain immortality.[14] In a mimetic rivalry with the Duke (whose power as a ruler confers automatically the love/hate ambivalence of taboo), Lorenzo immerses himself in carnal pleasure. This perverted ritual of baptism continues his initiation into the sacred by humiliating the flesh through debauchery rather than denial. Political purpose is foresworn by Lorenzo ("Je ne voulais pas soulever les masses"), and he situates his struggle on the allegorical plane of individual combat with "la tyrannie vivante" (III, 3). The tension between his desire to be godlike and his debasing roles as procurer and court jester results in a psychopathological crisis of near madness which, as in the case of shaman priests, verifies mythically his supernatural election.[15]

Lorenzo is caught in "a double bind" between his exalted mission of gaining immortality in the persona of Florence and a blinding fascination for Alexandre.[16] Metaphysically, he is trapped in the initiatory, apprentice stage of the sacred, unable to forget his vision and unable to reverse the effects of his trial by the flesh: "si je pouvais revenir à la vertu, si mon apprentissage du vice pouvait s'évanouir, j'épargnerais peut-être ce conducteur de boeufs. Mais j'aime le vin, le jeu et les filles; comprends-tu cela?" (III, 3). Theoretically, the ambivalence of Lorenzo could have persisted indefinitely. His mimetic rivalry with Alexandre tends to self-perpetuate through the reinforcing of images reflected between cousins. Lacking the Marquise de Cibo's courage and Tebaldeo's humanity, the ability of Lorenzo to break out of an impasse between the dual fascination of an object and its obstacle remains questionable. Paradoxically, the reciprocal character of mimetic rivalry triggers a crisis which, releasing Lorenzo from his ambivalence, allows him to pursue the sacred through an act of violence.

The interaction of Lorenzo and Alexandre undergoes a reversal which casts an ironic light on the ensuing tragedy. For the first time within the dramatized intrigue, Alexandre takes the initiative in a love affair without the help of Lorenzo or someone else such as the

Cardinal. The reversal in procedure (as set in the open- ing abduction scene) is possible within a mimetic rivalry, but the Duke chooses an object of passion repugnant to Lorenzo. Because Lorenzo identifies Catherine with Marie, calling her "la sœur de ma mère," he cannot reflect the lust of Alexandre (III, 3). To be sure, force of habit tempts Lorenzo to repeat his mimetic role as participant in seduction, but he cannot: "J'allais corrompre Catherine; je crois que je corrom- prais ma mère" (III, 3). His impotence reflects more than the taboo of incest prohibition, for Catherine's im- age is elevated to the region of pure ideals. She is pictured by Lorenzo as a mother figure nursing future generations, "une goutte de lait pur tombé du sein de Catherine, et qui aura nourri d'honnêtes enfants" (IV, 6). Hence, the ideal of Florence, the original object of his desire, regains its hold upon Lorenzo. The tension between his initiation into the sacred and his degrading friendship for Alexandre increases to the point of mad- ness and can be released only in a ritual whose action bypasses the conscience to purge aggression through violence as in primitive times.[17]

During the rehearsal of Alexandre's assassination, Lorenzo attains a level of delirium capable of breaking through the civilized barrier of reason. His language transcends politics as he calls for a sacrificial murder which would include eating of human flesh: "Ouvre-lui les entrailles! Coupons-le par morceaux, et mangeons, mangeons!" (III, 1). References to blood, wedding, the sun, arid sterility, and baptism point to the unconscious reenactment of a primordial archetypal pattern of behavior. Pagan rituals required the periodic sacrifice of the king, the king's first son, and then a ram to assure continued fertility.[18] A similar process of transferring evil to an individual or to a group, the scapegoat victim, reappears in the holocaust of modern times.[19]

Lorenzo's murder of the Duke is so immersed in symbolism that the form of his crime overshadows and explains the act itself. First, a complex reversal of sexual roles occurs. Lorenzo takes the place of Cathe- rine, who is supposed to be seduced by the Duke. Pretending to play his habitual role of *entremetteur,* Lorenzo breaks out of his mimetic reflection to identify with Catherine and, indirectly, with Florence. Second, Alexandre is murdered in bed. Symbolically, justice demands that the beast be sacrificed on the altar where so many maidens had yielded their virtue in tribute to his power. The association of nuptials and blood ("jour de sang, jour de mes noces") thus takes on a double meaning. Third, the sword thrust repeatedly into Alex- andre assumes the ironic character of revenge against rule by military and sexual imposition. Fourth, Lorenzo experiences an exaltation of the senses and the spirit, a total release from the contingencies of time and place: "Que le vent du soir est doux et embaumé! comme les fleurs des prairies s'entr'ouvrent! O nature magnifique,

ô éternel repos!" (IV, 11). In the solitude of grandeur, Lorenzo seeks to make known the sacred by spreading chaos. His metaphysical aim of destruction for the purpose of awakening mankind to the truth of his evil places Lorenzo closer to the Caligula of Camus than to Shakespeare's Hamlet.[20]

Lorenzo's murder of the Duke fails politically as an as- sassination and metaphysically as a tragic sacrifice. The citizens of Florence and their foreign allies are not motivated to restore the republic. This failure can be explained mythically by the absence of a valid scapegoat ritual. In order to unite the community against a sacrificial victim, there must be a collective transfer of guilt and a violence carried out anonymously or in the name of widely spread beliefs.[21] To the contrary, Lorenzo imbues the murder with the symbolic signifi- cance of his private world and his personal search for immortality. At most, the murder of Alexandre provokes a political crisis which entails the reenactment of the origins of society in a hypothetical primordial murder.[22] Faced by the fearful prospect of open-ended violence, people opt for the reestablishment of order despite its injustice. Ironically, Lorenzo's murder by a mob carries overtones of scapegoat violence: "Ne voyez-vous pas tout ce monde? Le peuple s'est jeté sur lui. Dieu de miséricorde! on le pousse dans la lagune" (V, 6). The guilt of cowardice for not revolting is transferred to Lorenzo, whose death reestablishes public order.

The failure of Lorenzo is tied to the question of guilt for his death. Who is at fault? Lorenzo? Society? The gods? The bourgeoisie? From the standpoint of mimetic desire, Lorenzo is doomed to failure. Caught in the double fascination for an object and its obstacle, he cannot overcome pride to see his predicament. However, the success of the Marquise in regaining her freedom after degradation makes Lorenzo's status as a tragic hero problematic at best. He dies with his heroic pride apparently intact without understanding his failure and arrogantly defiant until the end. Hence, little catharsis is generated by his fall. Blame is shifted implicitly from a Romantic type of "innocent criminal" to an insensitive society wherein selfish merchants and corrupt politi- cians prevail in a "business as usual" manner. By identifying with the hero's moral superiority and the few university students who did revolt upon Alexan- dre's death, the reader is in his pride also left unchal- lenged and intact.

The Romantic myth of the "misunderstood genius" and his alienation from the ascending bourgeoisie of early nineteenth-century France would seem to blunt the at- tainment of tragic emotion in **Lorenzaccio.** Confronted by the materialistic values which denied the poet's mis- sion, as dramatized in Vigny's *Chatterton* (1835), Romantics could illustrate national history or even play political roles like Lamartine, Balzac, Stendhal, and

Hugo in order to defend their dignity. In contrast, *Lorenzaccio* epitomizes the dangers of a Romantic idealism which confused a personal microcosm and a political macrocosm in the preference for martyrdom over collective action. Lorenzo wrongly identified evil as being primarily a metaphysical question rather than one of actions, and the anonymity of his murder gives the lie to a Romantic's absolute value of differentiation.

The incapacitating disillusionment of Musset's generation is often termed "le mal du siècle." As explained in the opening chapter to *La Confession d'un enfant du siècle* (1836), it arises from the collective despair of failure, that of the Napoleonic Empire and its foundation in the French Revolution. In a frantic attempt to fill the void of lost idealism and boredom, a generation of young men threw itself into libertinage, action without purpose, and materialistic ambition. Disbelief in politics, art, and human nature prevails in Musset's identification of evil as the only remaining source of inspiration: "Au lieu d'avoir l'enthousiasme du mal, nous n'eûmes que l'abnégation du bien; au lieu du désespoir, l'insensibilité."[23] For a generation of Frenchmen, despair is embodied in a historical figure of Renaissance Italy to create not only the most complex hero in the Romantic Theatre of France but also a timeless character whose conflicts are played out in a mythic dimension. The dramatization in *Lorenzaccio* of ritualized violence with heavy sexual overtones strikes chords of universal meaning which yield profound insights into the troubled mind and the origins of motivation.[24]

Notes

1. Musset, *Oeuvres complètes,* ed. Philippe Van Tieghem (Paris: Editions du Seuil, 1963), p. 348. All references to *Lorenzaccio* are taken from this edition and are indicated by act and scene.

2. See Herbert S. Gochberg, *Stage of Dreams* (Genève: Droz, 1967), p. 171, who characterizes the murder as being "completely without political consequence"; David Sices, *Theatre of Solitude* (Hanover, New Hampshire: The University Press of New England, 1974), p. 134, who calls it "a pure act of revenge"; Naomi Schor, "La Pèrodie: Superposition dans *Lorenzaccio,*" *Michigan Romance Studies,* 2 (Winter 1981), 73-86, who theorizes as to an attempted literary parricide of Shakespeare.

3. See Anne Ubersfeld, "Le Portrait du peintre," *RSH,* 42 (1977), 48.

4. See David Baguley, "Le Mythe de Glaucos: l'expression figurée dans *Lorenzaccio* de Musset," *RSH,* 41 (1976), 259-69.

5. See Bernard Masson, *Lorenzaccio ou la difficulté d'être* (Paris: Minard, 1962), pp. 5-19. His psychological thesis is developed further in *Mus-*

set et le théâtre intérieur (Paris: Minard, 1974) and *Musset et son double: Lecture de Lorenzaccio* (Paris: Minard, 1978).

6. The comparison is made by Lorenzo while questioning his motives for killing Alexandre: "Pourquoi cela? Le spectre de mon père me conduisait-il, comme Oreste, vers un nouvel Egisthe? M'avait-il offensé alors?" (III, 3).

7. In his application of Adler's concept of inferiority, Bernard Masson concentrates exclusively on Lorenzo.

8. See René Girard, *"To Double Business Bound": Essays on Literature, Mimesis, and Anthropology* (The Johns Hopkins University Press, 1978), p. 67. While emphasizing Freud's failure to understand the mimetic mechanism, he states, "The subject needs the desire of his rival to sustain and legitimize his own desire."

9. See René Girard, *"To Double Business Bound,"* whose theory on "the mimetic formation of 'neurotic' desire" holds that latent homosexuality and masochism denote a single phenomenon, the rival's predominance over the object and the fascination he exercises (p. 54). The implicit homosexuality in *Lorenzaccio* is verified by a discarded scene involving an audience given to Cellini by the Duke while in bed with Lorenzo. See Paul Dimoff, *La Genèse de Lorenzaccio,* reprint of 1936 edition (Paris: Société des textes français modernes, 1964), p. 169.

10. See Otto Rank, *The Myth of the Birth of the Hero,* ed. Philip Freund (New York: Vintage Books, 1936; rpt. 1964; translation of 1914 text in German), p. 273.

11. See Mircea Eliade, *Images and Symbols* (New York: Sheed & Ward, 1952), p. 75.

12. See Mircea Eliade, *Rites and Symbols of Initiation,* trans. from French (New York: Harper & Row, 1958), pp. 8-9, 96.

13. See David Baguley, "Le Mythe de Glaucos," who compares Lorenzo to the son of Sisyphus who threw himself into the sea to prove his immortality.

14. See Eliade, *Rites and Symbols of Initiation,* p. 125, who asserts: "By assuming such risks of suggested perilous descents to Hell, the Hero pursues the conquest of immortality."

15. See Eliade, *Rites and Symbols of Initiation,* pp. 90-101.

16. See René Girard, *Des choses cachées depuis la fondation du monde* (Paris: Grasset, 1978), p. 358.

17. For the origins of blood rituals, see James G. Frazer, *The Golden Bough. A Study in Magic and Religion* (New York: MacMillan, 1955), I, 329-41, and an opposing view in René Girard's *La Violence et le Sacré* (Paris: Grasset, 1972), pp. 36, 353, 396. For the origins of ritualized conduct, see the summary of research on the brain from an evolutionary perspective in Mary Long, "Ritual and Deceit," *Science Digest,* Nov./Dec. 1980, pp. 87-91, 121. The reptilian part of the brain, the R-complex, controls the unthinking behavior of violence, ritual, and imitation.

18. See Frazer, p. 340.

19. René Girard, *"To Double Business Bound,"* pp. 226-28.

20. The connection is made by Catherine Muder Huebert, "The Quest for Evil: *Lorenzaccio* and *Caligula,"* *Romance Notes,* 18 (Fall 1977), 66-72.

21. René Girard, *"To Double Business Bound,"* pp. 226-28.

22. See Freud's hypothesis as to the slaying of God the Father as the original crime in *The Complete Psychological Works (1917-1919),* ed. James Strachey (London: Hogarth, 1955), 17:261. While Eliade sees the myth of the "murdered divinity" as the basis of ritual, Girard views the original act of violence as a historical reality. See *Myth and Reality* (New York: Harper & Row, 1963), p. 99 and *"To Double Business Bound,"* p. 208.

23. See Musset, *La Confession d'un enfant du siècle,* ed. M. Allem (Paris: Garnier, 1968), p. 16.

24. I should like to thank two colleagues, Professors Richard Grant of the University of Texas and Laurence Porter of the Michigan State University, for their close readings of this study.

Barbara T. Cooper (essay date winter 1986)

SOURCE: Cooper, Barbara T. "Breaking up/down/apart: 'L'Eclatement' as a Unifying Principle in Musset's *Lorenzaccio*." *Philological Quarterly* 65, no. 1 (winter 1986): 103-12.

[*In the following essay, Cooper examines the ways in which Musset crafts a unified play out of disparate elements.*]

In act 3, scene 3 of Musset's **Lorenzaccio,** Lorenzo de Médicis tries to convince Philippe Strozzi that his idealized, optimistic vision of life and humanity is the product of a (self-) delusion—an illusion.

Ah! vous avez vécu tout seul, Philippe [Lorenzo tells his aged friend]. Pareil à un fanal éclatant, vous êtes resté immobile au bord de l'ocean des hommes, et vous avez regardé dans les eaux la réflexion de votre propre lumière. . . . Mais moi, pendant ce temps-là, j'ai plongé; je me suis enfoncé dans cette mer houleuse de la vie; j'en ai parcouru toutes les profondeurs, couvert de ma cloche de verre; tandis que vous admiriez la surface, j'ai vu le débris des naufrages, les ossements et les Léviathans.[1]

Where Philippe sees a smooth, radiant surface, Lorenzo perceives a turbulent sea whose every wave can be counted. While Philippe stands immobile on the banks of the ocean of life, Lorenzo dives to its bottom and explores its murky depths which he finds littered with the debris of ships and bodies and inhabited by not one, but several sea monsters.[2] Lorenzo's vision, then, is of a world that has broken up, broken down, broken apart. Yet from the fragments of men and their ambitions that he has seen, Lorenzo creates a whole: a world view. In the pages that follow, I shall attempt to show how Musset's text, like Lorenzo's underwater vision, is composed of fragments that unite to form a whole. In the end, I hope to be able to demonstrate that the fragmentation of the text, the characters, and their fictional universe makes **Lorenzaccio** a forerunner of many of the twentieth century's most modern dramas.

In recent years, **Lorenzaccio** has been the object of intense critical scrutiny. Practitioners of structuralism, socio-criticism, and semiotics—to name only a few of the theoretical orientations represented in current Musset scholarship—have all contributed to our understanding of the play in some significant way.[3] Yet, as Bernard Masson already predicted in 1974:

Quel que soit, en effet, l'abord choisi, il est frappant que la pièce nous offre à peu près toujours le même visage ambigu: d'une part, la rupture des scènes, les changements de lieux, l'entrecroisement des intrigues, la multiplicité des personnages figurent un univers de la discontinuité . . . mais, dans le même temps, il n'est pas une scène, pas un décor, pas une intrigue, pas un personnage . . . qui ne témoignent, en quelque façon, pour un univers continu, homogène, intelligible, clos sur lui-même et ordonné à sa propre nécessité.[4]

Masson, of course, was right. However one approaches **Lorenzaccio,** one is inevitably struck by the coherence, the underlying unity of this work whose surface is so obviously fragmented. Much has already been written about the temporal and spatial discontinuities and the plural, seemingly disjunctive plot line of the play. The failure of dialogue to convince, to communicate, and to inspire action has also received much attention. I shall not, therefore, repeat those demonstrations here (see note 3). Instead, I shall assume that the breakdown of language, the breaking up of the plot, and the breaking apart of time and space represent a deliberate attempt to create the appearance of a fragmented, disordered, chaotic universe. To go beyond that appearance, to reveal the fundamental unity of Musset's piece, however, one must supplement these analyses of the play's physical components (plot, dialogue, time and space) with an examination of the political, social, and psychological dimensions of the text.

If Florence is a fragmented physical space—and the multiplicity of decors in Musset's drama suggests that it is—it is also a political entity that has broken apart. As the goldsmith tells the silk merchant in act 1, scene 2 (p. 339):

> Florence était encore (il n'y a pas longtemps de cela) une bonne maison bien bâtie; tous ces grands palais, qui sont les logements de nos grandes familles, en était les colonnes. Il n'y en avait pas une, de toutes ces colonnes, qui dépassât les autres d'un pouce; elles soutenaient à elles toutes une vieille voûte bien cimentée, et nous nous promenions là-dessous sans crainte d'une pierre sur la tête.

The harmony, the unity, indeed the very integrity of this political edifice has since been destroyed, the goldsmith goes on to tell his interlocutor. "L'empereur a commencé par entrer par *une assez bonne brèche* dans la susdite maison" and the once protective republican shelter has now become a towering citadel—"un gros pâté informe fait de boue et de crachat"—from which the "bâtard/butor" Alexandre de Médicis and his German troops sweep down on the people of Florence (all quotes p. 339; emphasis mine).[5] Alexandre exercises his illegitimate authority by means of brute, and brutal, force, the goldsmith claims. The city-home has been destroyed and pillaged. While the vandal Duke Alexandre "couche dans le lit de nos filles, boit nos bouteilles [et] casse nos vitres" (p. 339), many of those who once lived in peace, harmony, and safety have been forced to leave the erstwhile republic.

These exiled citizens—"pauvres bourgeois," "pères de famille chassés de leur patrie," republicans reduced to "des ombres silencieuses . . . sur la route" (1.6, p. 335)—stand as further evidence of the fragmentation of the body politic that was Florence. Dispersed to the four corners of Italy (Pisa, Rome, Venice, Ferrara), they curse the motherland from which they have been expelled ("adieu, mère stérile, qui n'as plus de lait pour tes enfants") and which they do not recognize as theirs ("adieu, Florence la bâtarde, spectre hideux de l'antique Florence"—both p. 357). Florence, of course, is no longer theirs. It is Alexandre's, or rather, it is the Holy Roman Emperor's and the Pope's, both of whom seek to manipulate their puppet Duke from behind the screen of Cardinal Cibo's red robes.

Were *Lorenzaccio* a play written in accord with the rules of neo-classical composition, one might expect all of the action to occur in the antechamber to the throne room of the Duke's palace. Even as late as 1825 when Alexandre Soumet wrote his neo-classical tragedy

Jeanne d'Arc, unity of place, although expanded to encompass all of Rouen, nonetheless focussed on conventional sites of power—a prison, a hall of justice, a place of execution. *Lorenzaccio* does not so much break with this dramatic tradition as give shape to a more diffuse, more invasive type of political power that will not be confined or defined by its buildings. The tyranny and debauchery of Alexandre's reign are felt everywhere—in the streets, the marketplaces, the homes of the humble and the palaces of the grand, as well as the Duke's court—and thus all of these spaces are represented in the text. Once united by the ties that link all citizens of a republic to one another, these multiple sites now stand as mute testimony to the shattering, yet perversely binding power of oppression.[6]

Alexandre's rule shatters more than the political unity of Florence, however. It also breaks up families. Mothers sell their daughters (1.1, p. 334 and 3.3, p. 394) and wives sacrifice their honor (2.5, p. 372) to the lustful Duke and his procurers. (See, too, 3.5, p. 398 where Lorenzo's mother accuses her son of trying to prostitute his aunt Catherine and 4.5, p. 416 where Lorenzo declares: "J'allais corrompre Catherine; je crois que je corrompais ma mère, si mon cerveau le prenait à tâche. . . .") On those rare occasions when brothers seek to avenge the insults to their sisters' virtue, they are punished by exile (Maffio) or arrested (Pierre and Thomas Strozzi), thus leaving the family even more fragmented than before.

After his sons ("deux enfants de mes entrailles") have been taken off to prison, Philippe Strozzi assures Lorenzo in 3.3 (p. 389) that "On m'arracherait les bras et les jambes, que, comme le serpent, les morceaux mutilés de Philippe se rejoindraient et se lèveraient pour la vengeance." What his words express is not so much the intensity of his desire for vengeance as the sense of dismemberment, of radical separation from his children that he experiences as a result of their arrest.[7] Clearly, the vigor of his assertion is belied by his drooping posture (he has collapsed on a bench) and his repeated references to his advanced age. Nonetheless, Philippe does soon assemble the Strozzi clan of which he is both the patriarch and the head (see 3.7, p. 404: "Je suis le chef de la famille" which, in addition to its literal meaning, can be read as an extension of the body-family image first advanced in scene 3). He chides his family on its willingness to be dominated by the Médicis and asks the meaning of his sons' arrest. "Est-ce à dire qu'on abattra d'un coup de hache les nobles familles de Florence, et qu'on arrachera de la terre natale des racines aussi vieilles qu'elle?" (p. 404). Yet, when his daughter dies after having drunk poisoned wine, Philippe's spirit breaks down under the weight of his accumulated despair and suffering. Refusing to pursue the revenge he had called down on the Médicis only moments before, Philippe now tells his family:

Liberté, vengeance, voyez-vous, tout cela est beau; j'ai deux fils en prison, et voilà ma fille morte. Si je reste ici, tout va mourir autour de moi. L'important, c'est que je m'en aille, et que vous vous teniez tranquilles. . . . Je m'en vais de ce pas à Venise.

(3.8, p. 407)

Morally "abattu" and physically "arraché de la terre natale," Philippe will never again be able to reconstitute his once-whole being nor his family. Even after he has been reunited with his sons, Philippe discovers that his paternal authority has been eroded and that Pierre no longer treats him with filial respect. (See Pierre's outburst in 4.6, p. 419: "Vieillard obstiné! inexorable faiseur de sentences! vous serez cause de notre perte" which leads Philippe to reflect: "Ton jour est venu, Philippe! tout cela signifie que ton jour est venu."). Thus family solidarity has been fragmented as irremediably as political unity and freedom.

Like the Florentine republic and the Strozzi family, Lorenzo, too, breaks down under the weight of tyranny. He, however, is not so much the victim of Alexandre's rule (Lorenzo notes in 4.3, p. 411 that "[Alexandre] a fait du mal aux autres, mais il m'a fait du bien, du moins à sa manière"), as of his own hubris (3.3, pp. 391-392) and ambition. "Cela est étrange," Lorenzo reflects, "et cependant pour cette action j'ai tout quitté; la seule pensée de ce meurtre a fait *tomber en poussière* les rêves de ma vie; je n'ai plus été qu'une *ruine,* dès que ce meurtre . . . s'est posé sur ma route et m'a appelé à lui" (p. 411, emphasis added). When he thinks back to the time when he loved ". . . les fleurs, les prairies et les sonnets de Pétrarque, le *spectre* de [s]a jeunesse se lève devant [lui] en frissonnant." When he thinks forward to the moment when he will kill Alexandre, ". . . [il a] peur de tirer l'épée flamboyante de l'archange, et de *tomber en cendres* sur [s]a proie" (both p. 411, emphasis added). Clearly, what Lorenzo is risking is both his moral and his physical integrity, the unity and whole(some)ness of his mind and body.

Scholars have already insisted on the importance of the many forms of Lorenzo's name used in Musset's play (see, for example, the articles by Bem and Thomas in note 3). What we need most to derive from their analyses is an awareness that the fragmented signifier Lo/renz/acci/o is not the reflection of a plurality of signifieds, but rather of an absent signified. To prove this point, one need only recall the frequency with which Lorenzo is described as "une ombre" (1.4, p. 347 and 3.3, p. 397), "une fumée malfaisante" (1.6, p. 355), "une vapeur infecte" (3.3, p. 390), "un spectre" (several places, but especially 2.4, p.369), "un fantôme" (3.3, p. 395)—that is, a thing without substance. To give shape to his being, Lorenzo has had to put on "[un] masque de plâtre" (3.3, p. 393) and "[les] habits neufs de la confrérie du vice" (3.3, p 394; 4.5, p. 416). He has

become an effigy—"un homme de cire," "une statue"—an empty shell. The uncertainty of Lorenzo's being and identity is further emphasized by the repeated use of interrogative and conditional sentences. In 2.4 (p. 370), for example, Lorenzo's uncle Bindo asks him: "Etes-vous des nôtres, ou n'en êtes-vous pas? voilà ce qu'il nous faut savoir." In 3.3 (p. 388), Philippe insists: ". . . Si la hideuse comédie que tu joues m'a trouvé impassible et fidèle spectateur, que l'homme sorte de l'histrion. Si tu as jamais été quelque chose d'honnête, sois-le aujourd'hui." In the end, Lorenzo is nothing more than his act (see 4.10, p. 426: "C'est toi, Renzo?— Seigneur, *n'en doutez pas.*" Emphasis added.). It is an act without consequence and thus without duration; it is as ephemeral as it is unsubstantial. Having accomplished his goal, Lorenzo likewise disappears without a trace.

Lorenzo's death (5.6, p. 441) provides a reverse image of the assassination of the Duke. It is an image marked by dispersal. Night becomes day; a closed space is replaced by an open space; a known and seen assassin is replaced by one who is unknown and unseen; and the bed, a place of stillness and repose, is replaced by the lagoon, a place of movement and flux. What is more, Lorenzo's wounds and his watery grave point to his physical disintegration. Set upon by a vicious populace ("des Léviathans"?), Lorenzo is shoved into the lagoon where his body will no doubt be transformed into an "ossement," the anonymous debris of his all too human ambition.

Whereas earlier studies of Musset's play have emphasized the fragmentation of time, space, and the plot line, or the divorce between word and deed, saying and doing, I have tried to show here how the principle of "l'éclatement"—of breaking up/down/apart—operates in the spheres of politics, society, and psychology, on the levels of theme, characterization, and image. One could, of course, multiply the examples given here. A study of the notion of legitimacy would reveal the links among family, state, and psyche that underlie the passages cited above and at the same time would extend our examination of the images of fragmentation even further. Thus when Lorenzo trembles at the sight of a sword in 1.4, the Duke mockingly chides him: "Fi donc! tu fais honte au nom des Médicis. Je ne suis qu'un *bâtard,* et je le porterais mieux que toi, qui es *légitime?*" (p. 348, emphasis added). Alexandre's illegitimacy is more than a fact of his birth, however. "Un bâtard, une moitié de Médicis," as the goldsmith describes him in 1.2 (p. 339), Alexandre is also the illegitimate ruler of Florence. Imposed on the populace by the Emperor and the Pope, he is neither the rightful heir to the throne nor the freely-elected (or consented) choice of "les grandes familles." Lorenzo, on the other hand, might properly have governed the city. "Sa naissance ne l'appelait-elle pas au trône? . . . Ne devais-je pas m'attendre à cela?" asks his mother (1.6, p. 355). But if Lorenzo's youthful beauty and noble ambitions once led Marie Soderini to kiss her son on the forehead "en pensant au *père* de la patrie," she now judges that ". . . il fait tourner à un infâme usage jusqu'à la glorieuse mémoire de ses *aïeux*" (1.6, pp. 354 and 355; emphasis added). Agitated and uncertain as he prepares to assassinate his cousin Alexandre (4.3, p. 411), Lorenzo himself questions the legitimacy of his act ("Que m'avait fait cet homme?"), his motivation ("Le spectre de mon père me conduisait-il, comme Oreste, vers un nouvel Egiste?"), his birth and his humanity ("De quel tigre a rêvé ma mère enceinte de moi? . . . De quelles entrailles fauves, de quels velus embrassements suis-je donc sorti?").[8] The turmoil of his mind is reflected in the repeated use of interrogative sentences and the breakdown of logical progression from one thought to the next. Like these thoughts, illegitimacy is marked by a failure, a breakdown of the principles of succession. It will be recalled that Musset's contemporaries considered this very lack of logical, temporal, and physical succession to be the principal defect of the play. By now, however, it should be obvious that the underlying similarities between the "forme" and the "fond" of the text are in fact the primary source of its aesthetic unity. Having said that, it is time to turn our attention to the broader issue posed by Musset's pervasive use of the themes and techniques of "l'éclatement," that is, to the question of the play's modernity.

In Part 2, chapter 5 of his book *Théâtre et pré-cinéma* (Paris: Nizet, 1978), Hassan El Nouty suggested that *Lorenzaccio,* however disconcerting it might have been for Musset's contemporaries, appeals to the modern reader/viewer because of its cinematographic qualities. Professor El Nouty is right, of course. The cutting and editing techniques, the varied camera angles and distances that are the stock in trade of contemporary filmmakers can all be found in Musset's play. Nonetheless, if we are to discover the connections between *Lorenzaccio* and the modern French theater, we might do well to look beyond these purely technical devices and examine the way Musset's armchair drama casts its "hero" into the world.

Certainly, Musset's alienated, corrupt hero is a product of his age and of the influence of English and German romanticism on his creator. Yet it is also true that Lorenzo resembles those twentieth-century protagonists who have lost touch with or become disconnected from a collectivity (humanity) which they frequently despise. Like them, Lorenzo is both victimizer and victim, director and dupe of the absurdity of existence, the irrationality of evil. His radical Otherness, like theirs, is underscored by logical discontinuities, verbal incongruities, and spatial and temporal disjunctions. More than anything else, perhaps, it is this "éclatement," this

breakdown of causality and personality, of communication and community that makes *Lorenzaccio* a prototype of modern French drama.

In *L'Ecole du spectateur* (Paris: Editions sociales, 1981), Anne Ubersfeld has written at length about the discontinuities that mark the contemporary theater. It seems appropriate, then, to turn to her for a salutary word of caution before arriving at a conclusion. Ubersfeld notes (p. 302) that

> Dans tous les cas la discontinuité n'a pas toujours le même sens ou la même fonction; elle peut: a) donner des images de la dislocation du monde et avoir sur ce point valeur et fonctionnement référentiel; b) montrer chez l'énonciateur la destruction (subjective) d'une vue cohérente du monde, l'impossibilité de penser le monde et surtout de le penser comme représentable; c) elle peut marquer le dégagement par rapport à un *sujet* centralisé, que ce sujet soit l'énonciateur, le personnage ou le comédien

Ubersfeld's distinctions are pertinent to our discussion of the modernity of *Lorenzaccio* precisely because they allow us to perceive the continuities and discontinuities that mark the *Weltanschauung* of nineteenth- and twentieth-century French dramatists. Thus, although Musset's world may have been different from that of, say, Artaud, Ionesco, or Beckett, one can, I think, defend the thesis that *Lorenzaccio,* like their works, stands in part as a referential reflection of the dislocations each dramatist observed in the world around him. (Our readings of Musset's play and, for example, of *Le Rhinocéros* would be as much impoverished by ignoring their referential allusions as by limiting our intepretations of those texts to ideas supported by historical analogies.)

Similarly, Musset may be seen as precursor of modern drama to the extent that his play shows signs of a nascent "dégagement par rapport à un *sujet* centralisé" (emphasis in the original quote, cited above). To be sure, in typical early nineteenth-century fashion, Lorenzaccio gives his name to Musset's piece. Yet Lorenzo is neither the sole nor always the central subject of the drama. As Atle Kittang and others have convincingly shown (note 3, *supra*), Lorenzo shares the actantial role of subject with other protagonists in the play just as, on a thematic level, he shares the title of subject with the city of Florence. Musset, however, does not go as far as his twentieth-century counterparts in exploring the problems of subjective unity or unity of subject. However much his work forecasts our modern preoccupations with these problems, it is nonetheless true that Musset's views are firmly rooted in the romantic literature, philosophy, and psychology of his age.

It is doubtless this same romantic vision of the universe that keeps Musset from sharing twentieth-century dramatists' belief that the world is no longer a coherent whole, that it is impossible "de penser le monde et surtout de le penser représentable" (see quote above). On the contrary, as I argued at the very beginning of this study and as I hope to have shown in the pages that followed, the fragmentation that marks Musset's text does not so much render the dramatized world unrepresentable as differently representable—or as the French might say, "représentable autrement." Just as Lorenzo constructed a unified vision of the world from the underwater debris he poetically equated with humanity and human ambitions, so, too, has Musset created a unified fiction from his fragmented text. As Ubersfeld writes in *L'Ecole du spectateur:* "A travers le discontinu, il y a toujours quelque part le fil de la continuité . . ." (p. 302). To my mind, her statement at once describes Musset's play and its relation to modern French drama.

Notes

1. Alfred De Musset, *Théâtre 1,* Texte intégral (Paris: Garnier-Flammarion, 1964), 3.3, p. 393. Further references to *Lorenzaccio* will be noted in my text. For a recent study of the image of the shipwreck in the nineteenth century, see ch. 10: "Perils of the Deep" in Martin Meisel, *Realizations: Narrative, Pictorial, and Theatrical Arts in Nineteenth-Century England.* (Princeton U. Press, 1983).

2. In her article "Révolution et topique de la cité: *Lorenzaccio,*" *Littérature* 24 (1976): 49, Anne Ubersfeld identifies the Leviathan not with the Biblical monster, but with its Hobbesean descendant, "L'Etat qu'il définit comme le pouvoir de créer et de *casser* toute loi." (This definition of Hobbes's Leviathan is not Ubersfeld's but that of *Le Petit Larousse illustré* [Paris: Larousse, 1982], p. 1466 and the emphasis is mine.) As will be seen, I share her conviction.

3. It would be impossible to list all the recent studies of *Lorenzaccio* here. Some of the most significant for this examination of Musset's play include Jeanne Bem, "*Lorenzaccio* entre l'Histoire et le fantasme," *Poétique* 11, no. 44 (1980): 451-61; Claude Duchet, "Théâtre et sociocritique: La Crise de la parole dans deux pièces de Musset," pp. 147-56 in Duchet et al. eds., *Sociocritique* (Paris: Nathan, 1979); Atle Kittang, "Action et langage dans *Lorenzaccio* d'Alfred Musset," *Revue romane* 10, no. 1 (1975): 33-50; Bernard Masson, *Musset et le théâtre intérieur* (Paris: Colin, 1974); Walter Moser, "*Lorenzaccio:* le Carnaval et le Cardinal," *Romantisme* 19 (1978): 94-108; Jean-Jacques Thomas, "Les Maîtres-mots de Musset: *Peuple* et *pouvoir* dans *Lorenzaccio,*" pp. 179-96 in Michel Glatigny and Jacques Guilhaumou, eds., *Peuple et pouvoir: Etudes de léxicologie politique*

(Lille: Presses Universitaires de Lille, 1981); Anne Ubersfeld, "Le Portrait du peintre," *Revue des sciences humaines* no. 165 (1977): 39-48 and "Le Moi-statue ou le discours auto-réflexif chez Musset," pp. 63-79 in *Journées d'études sur Alfred de Musset* (Clermont-Ferrand: SER Faculté de lettres/ Société des Etudes Romantiques, 1978).

4. In *Musset et le théâtre intérieur,* p. 122.

5. Lorenzo's uncle Bindo Altoviti will take up this image again when he declares in 2.4 (p. 370): "Toutes les grandes familles voient bien que le despotisme des Médicis n'est ni juste ni tolérable. De quel droit laisserions-nous s'élever paisiblement cette maison orgueilleuse sur les *ruines* de nos privilèges?" (emphasis added). On a more personal level, Lorenzo's mother Marie compares her dreams to a fairy palace that has turned into a dilapidated shack. She complains in 1.6 (p. 355): "Cela est trop cruel d'avoir vécu dans un palais de fées, où murmuraient les cantiques des anges, de s'y être endormie, bercée par son fils, et de se réveiller dans une *masure* ensanglantée, pleine de *débris* d'orgie et de *restes* humains, dans les bras d'un *spectre* hideux qui vous tue en vous appelant encore du nom mère" (emphasis added).

6. A similar argument can be made regarding unity of time. Time can be regulated and harmonious like the workings of a benevolent government or it can be as inexorable and unpredictable as tyranny.

7. Writing about a certain type of modern literature in an article entitled "La Déliaison," (*Littérature* 3 [1971]: 48), André Green has suggested that ". . . il s'agit moins de représenter le corps que de le faire vivre en éclats, fragmentés et morcelés." It seems to me that this is precisely the effect achieved by Philippe's words.

8. For a recent analysis of the psychological dimension of the play and the theme of the absent father, see Jules Bedner, "*Lorenzaccio* ou Oedipe à Florence," *Neophilologus* 67, no. 1 (1983): 42-54 and Naomi Schor, "La Pèrodie: Superposition dans *Lorenzaccio,*" pp. 73-86 in Ross Chambers, ed., *Discours et pouvoir* (Dept. of Romance Langs., U. of Michigan, 1982).

Laurie F. Leach (essay date spring 1988)

SOURCE: Leach, Laurie F. "Lorenzo and the Noblest Roman: The Noble Assassins of *Lorenzaccio* and *Julius Caesar.*" *Romance Notes* 28, no. 3 (spring 1988): 241-45.

[*In the following essay, Leach compares the main character in Musset's play to Brutus in William Shakespeare's* Julius Caesar.]

While critics have repeatedly found echoes of Shakespeare's prince of Denmark in Alfred de Musset's Lorenzo de Médicis, making a comparison with *Hamlet* a commonplace of *Lorenzaccio* criticism, this focus has tended to obscure the role of another Shakespearian hero in Musset's formation of Lorenzo's character: Marcus Brutus of *Julius Caesar*.[1] It is only when Lorenzo's aspiration to be another Brutus is considered in the light of the Shakespearian hero that the bitter irony of Musset's tragedy is fully realized.

Although many critics observe in passing that Lorenzo's allusions to Brutus seem to interchange two historical personages: Marcus Brutus, who assassinated Caesar, and Lucius Brutus who ousted Tarquin from Rome, only Jeanne Bem makes a detailed analysis of the figure of Brutus.[2] Bem notes that the character of Lucius Brutus provides a screen on which Musset can project the figure of Hamlet and thus identify Lorenzo with him while avoiding anachronism. In the same manner, the figure of Plutarch's Marcus Brutus enables Musset to link Lorenzo with Shakespeare's hero.

Several scenes in *Lorenzaccio* suggest that Musset was influenced by *Julius Caesar*. When Lorenzo stabs the duke, the latter cries "C'est toi, Renzo?" (IV.xi.25) in an obvious echo of Caesar's stricken realization of Brutus' betrayal: "Et tu, Brute! Then fall Caesar!" (III.i.77). Jeanne Bem notes the allusion but fails to mention that the quotation is not found in Plutarch (454). Lorenzo's expulsion from Rome for decapitating the statues of the emperors (I.iv.41-43) provides a muted echo of the fate of Marullus and Flavius in *Julius Caesar* who "for pulling scarfs off Caesar's images are put to silence" (I.ii.288-290). Shakespeare found this story in Plutarch; however, Marullus' diatribe against the "cruel men of Rome" who unthinkingly "cull out a holiday" and "strew flowers in his way / That comes in triumph over Pompey's blood" (I.i.41, 54-56), is his invention. It bears a strong resemblance to the speech of the Deuxième Bourgeois in the opening act of *Lorenzaccio,* where the citizens of Florence are castigated for receiving the news that the Pope and the emperor are together at Bologna with "une réjouissance publique" (I.v.44). Finally, Pierre Nordon notes "la manière dont, à la scène 10, qui précède le meurtre d'Alexandre, Musset s'est souvenu de celle qui, dans *Jules César* annonce la mort de César (III.1). Dans les deux cas, la victime dédaigne les avertissements qui lui sont adressés" (253). In these scenes, Musset seems to draw deliberately the reader's attention to the similarities between the two plays.

Other references are more subtle. Phillipe's attempts to move Lorenzo to action are reminiscent of Cassius' efforts with Brutus. Cassius urges, "O, you and I have heard our fathers say, / There was a Brutus once that would have brooked / The eternal devil to keep his state in Rome as easily as a King" (I.ii.158-161). While

Cassius urges Brutus to live up to the reputation of his ancestor, Phillipe calls on Lorenzo to fulfill the promise of his youthful self. "Mais, agir, agir, agir! O Lorenzo! le temps est venu . . . Ne m'as-tu pas parlé d'un homme qui s'appelle aussi Lorenzo et qui se couche derrière le Lorenzo qui voilà?" (III.iii.100-102). But Lorenzo feels disconnected from his former self: "je suis vraiment un ruffian" (III.iii.408). Like Brutus he is "with himself at war" (I.ii.46). When his mother attempts to move him by relating her vision of the ghost of his former self, he asks her to give the spirit a message, for it is no longer a part of himself. Tainted by his connection with Alexandre, Lorenzo can no longer make contact with his inner purity. Shakespeare's Brutus has a similar problem. According to Cassius, "it is very much lamented, Brutus, / That you have no such mirrors as will turn / Your hidden worthiness into your eye" (II.i.55-57). Brutus needs Cassius as Lorenzo needs Phillipe and Marie, to recognize and speak to the heroic inner spirit which will rise against the tyrant.

Lorenzaccio is not an imitation but a rewriting of *Julius Caesar,* itself a rewriting of Plutarch. Musset carries the changes Shakespeare made to greater lengths in *Lorenzaccio*. Shakespeare alters Plutarch's version by strengthening the friendship between Brutus and Caesar and permitting Brutus to reveal doubts about his action. The increased intimacy between the men makes the murder more of a betrayal and heightens the tension between public and private obligations. Weighing his decision before the murder, Brutus reflects, "I know no personal cause to spurn at him, / But for the general" (II.i.11-12). To make matters worse, Brutus cannot be sure that the murder is necessary, for he kills Caesar "in the shell," not for what he has done, but for what he might do (II.i.32-34). Musset intensifies these problems in *Lorenzaccio*. Lorenzo is not only Alexandre's friend, but his companion in vice. As he admits, "le vice a été pour moi un vêtement; maintenant il est collé à ma peau" (III.iii.407-408). Furthermore, Lorenzo is thoroughly disillusioned and knows the murder will not change anything, unlike Brutus, who acts in good faith despite his doubts. Thus the tension which makes Brutus hesitate almost paralyzes Lorenzo.

One important difference between the two protagonists is that Lorenzo is corrupted by his association with a tyrant while Brutus is not. Another is that while Brutus maintains his reputation, Lorenzo sacrifices his: "Le peuple appelle Lorenzo Lorenzaccio" (I.iv.35). The distrust between Lorenzo and the people is illustrated dramatically in Act IV, scene vii, when none of the republicans will believe his intention to kill the duke. By contrast, the Romans respect Brutus so highly that they are reluctant to join the conspiracy until he commits himself to it. The gap of mistrust between Lorenzo and the citizens he wants to liberate emphasizes what is perhaps the most important difference between Lorenzo and Brutus. Brutus acts as part of a group, both in committing the murder and in forming the conspiracy. It is not just Cassius' urging, but letters purporting to be from Roman citizens which convince him to act. Thus, he always sees himself as acting on behalf of the people. Lorenzo, on the other hand insists on acting alone. He tells Phillipe, "Je voulais agir seul, sans le secours d'aucun homme" (III.iii.253-254) and cautions Scoronconcolo not to strike the duke even if he misses: "c'est à moi qu'il appartient" (III.i.80). Although he claims to be altruistic ("Je travaillais pour l'humanité"), he really wants to redeem himself by becoming a hero. But this is impossible, not only because, as Bem points out, "un acte de terrorisme individuel ne suffit pas . . . à changer le cours de l'Histoire" but because his motives are not heroic (453). As Brutus proves, one can be a hero without changing the course of history. One cannot be a hero, however, if one knows one's actions to be meaningless.

The sense of meaninglessness at the end of Musset's play distinguishes it from Shakespeare's. As Sices remarks, **Lorenzaccio** is "a work built on a theme of universal disillusionment" (124). The truly heroic is no longer possible; therefore, neither is the truly tragic. While Antony praises Brutus' nobility and Octavius promises him "all respect and rites of burial" (V.v.77). Lorenzo is murdered and thrown into the canal with "pas même un tombeau!" (V.vii.70). Lorenzo is already forgotten by the final scene of the play where the Côme de Médicis becomes the duke of Florence. For Sices, the final oration "consecrates the burial of all the play's ideals under the stifling mediocrity of political reality" (169). He compares the ending to that of *Hamlet* and *MacBeth*, but he might also have compared it to the final scene of *Julius Caesar* which also concludes with a "return to order" marked by a formal speech by one who has assumed power. According to Barbara Cooper, "the bitterly ironic lesson . . . is that revolutionary action ultimately results in a return to the *status quo ante*, when it does not actually bring about a worsening of conditions" (28). Yet, this lesson is already implied in *Julius Caesar*. What is most bitter about **Lorenzaccio** is not the political failure, but the loss of all ideals. While the pain of Brutus' defeat is mitigated by the respect Antony affords him and their shared belief in honor, what Lorenzo and the Côme share is not honor or idealism, but the lack of either. The Côme's promise to uphold justice is as empty of meaning as Lorenzo's murder of the duke. In such a world, where meaning has disappeared, no redemption is possible.

Notes

1. For a discussion of *Lorenzaccio* and *Hamlet*, see Pierre Nordon and David Sices.

2. While Bem's article is the most detailed, see also Ronald Grimsley and Sices (132).

Works Cited

Bem, Jeanne. "*Lorenzaccio* entre l'Histoire et le Fantasme." *Poétique* 11 (1980): 451-461.

Cooper, Barbara. "Staging a Revolution: Political Upheaval in *Lorenzaccio* and *Léo Burckart*." *Romance Notes* 24 (1983): 23-29.

Grimsley, Ronald. "The Character of Lorenzaccio." *French Studies* 11 (1957): 16-27.

Nordon, Pierre. "Alfred de Musset et L'Angleterre: *Lorenzaccio*." *Les Lettres Romanes* 21 (1967): 238-256.

Sices, David. *Theatre of Solitude: The Drama of Alfred de Musset.* Hanover: University Press of New England, 1974.

John W. MacInnes (essay date 1988)

SOURCE: MacInnes, John W. "*Lorenzaccio* and the Drama of Narration." In *Text and Presentation*, edited by Karelisa Hartigan, The University of Florida Department of Classics Comparative Drama Conference Papers, Vol. 8, pp. 137-45. Lanham, Md.: University Press of America, 1988.

[*In the following essay, MacInnes discusses the themes and narrative of* Lorenzaccio.]

For a number of years I read this "armchair" play as a film scenario ahead of its time or as the French say: *avant la lettre*. The thirty-eight scene changes, which sometimes follow upon each other at a staccato pace, result in a stage play that is unwieldy in practice but which at the same time offers the armchair reader of our century a vivid, filmic spectacle to the imagination. To my mind **Lorenzaccio** was a cinema script written, now to distort the French phrase, not so much *avant la lettre* but *avant l'image*. When I learned that a cinematic adaptation of the play had in fact been done in the 1950's, my sense of Musset as a *proto-cinéaste* was only confirmed. But later readings of the play have caused me to reconsider this line of thought. Despite the rapid shifts of setting and the punctuation of the drama by breathless little scenes, **Lorenzaccio** ultimately fails as a film scenario for one fairly obvious reason: too many characters—especially the hero—talk too much. **Lorenzaccio** is no more a scenario awaiting the advent of its proper technology than is *Richard II*, and perhaps—given the bulk of its prose—even less so.

One might, at this point, sigh—thinking of the *récit de Théramène* that bring Racine's *Phèdre* to its end—and conclude that discursive theater is merely an inherit French convention, or even curse. More sympathetically one might point out that **Lorenzaccio** is an historical tragedy whose genre requires a good deal of narrative exposition in order to make clear the setting and conflicts against which the more persona drama of Lorenzo is set. I quite agree with this sympathetic defense of the play's discursivity: the elaborate plotting between the Marquise and the Cardinal, for example, or the heroic call to revolt by the elder Strozzi, need a good deal of explanation in order to be situated in the context of the play. I would call all such passages which function thus first-level narratives. I would not wish to demean them by that categorization; in fact, I am merely reiterating a distinction made by John Dryden in his "Essay of Dramatic Poesy" in 1668. But I want to suggest that these are narratives of contextualization, and can be distinguished from a second level of narration whose source and focus are Lorenzo alone. On this second level, Lorenzo is engaged in narrating himself—in the telling of his self—because, as he puts it: "The world has to know a bit about who I am, and what it is."[1] This second level of narration, this self-presentation and self-representation, constitute as much of Lorenzo's personal drama as do any of his acts on stage: whether or not he kills the Duke is secondary to our appreciation of just who it is who might kill the Duke, and of the ultimate absurdity of that act. It is the telling, not the doing, that gives Lorenzo his fascinating texture, and that makes him less than a mere cinematic *actant* and more, perhaps, and enterprise, as Nietzsche's *Ecce Homo* is an enterprise, to be contemplated from the comfort of an armchair.

Lorenzo must tell himself because he cannot act himself. In order to win the confidence of the Duke whom he wants to assassinate, he must fawn and feign, becoming the Duke's procurer and dissembling his own virility to the point of fainting at the sight of an unsheathed sword. The play opens with a scene at night in a garden, where Lorenzo and the Duke accomplish a rendez-vous with a young Florentine—a tryst that Lorenzo has not only arranged, but over which he now gloats. The scene is interrupted when the girl's brother happens upon the Duke, Lorenzo, and their guards. He decrys the corruption of Florence by the pandemic lascivity which thrives under the Duke's rule. He announces that Florence has become "a forest full of bandits, full of poisoners and dishonored girls" (336), and is about to take his complaint to the Duke when it is revealed to him that the Duke stands before him, disguised in a cloak. The outrage brother can only desist, and the scene ends. This scene is only two pages long and runs only a few minutes, but it evokes a pair of themes that will govern the rest of the play.

First, there is that theme so dear to Neo-classical French theater: the disparity between appearance and being. While they await the girl 's arrival, Lorenzo recounts to the impatient Duke the true character he had espied beneath her appearance or morality:

> Bourgeois mediocrity personified! Moreover, she's the daughter of solid folk, whose lack of wealth has not allowed her a solid upbringing; no depth to her principles, nothing but a thin veneer; but what a violent current of a magnificent river running beneath that layer of thin ice that cracks with each step! Never has a flowering bush promised rarer fruits, never have I sniffed in so childish an air a more exquisite odor of whoredom.

> (334-5)

This theme is echoed visually by the cloaked disguise both Lorenzo and the Duke are wearing, of course, and is further reinscribed in the possible excess of Lorenzo's florid language. We are led to wonder from the start whether this vile procurer, so clearly witty and bright by contrast to his fellows, does not also have some raging torrent hidden beneath his icy amorality.

But this first theme, though evoked with economy and complexity—since it not only calls in to question the truth of the world's appearance but that of our protagonist—is linked to a second one right from the start, which is the decline of patriarchal authority. The rule of the old laws, we are told by the brother, may no longer exist; scoundrels, he says, are cutting the throats of families and dishonoring their daughters; and the brother himself is shown to be impotent in the face of the Duke's armed guards. The danger that has been loosed upon the world of Florence under the reign of Duke Alexandre is clearly not limited to the political decline of a republic toward militarily-enforced tyranny: beyond the question of which form of government might best rule the city lies the issue of the law, the family, and the virtue of maidens, or—in Lacanian terms—the issue of the father's name and its authority. One of the guards announces to the bewildered brother: "*Ta soeur est dénichée . . .*" (336), which we can translate as "your sister has flown off from the nest," or even, to reflect better the brutal level of discourse, "Your sister has flown the coop." Your sister, in other words, is no longer a procreative being under your patriarchal control. Beyond—but not far beyond—the question of equality among men lies the question of the pleasures and powers of women who are no longer under paternal guard. The political institution that is at stake, as numerous allusions and metaphors throughout the play make clear, is not just the republic, but the patriarchal order itself. The alternative to that order is the chaos of harlotry.

Two themes, then, have been evoked in parallel: the theme of appearance versus being, and that of the threat to patriarchal security imposed by *libertinage*. Those themes will not remain in mere parallel, but will ultimately become entwined in Lorenzo's attempt to tell who he is in contrast to who he only appears to be. The height of that telling occurs in the third scene of the third act, in a long conversation between Lorenzo and Philippe Strozzi—the patriarch *sans pareil* in the play.

The scene begins when two of Philippe's sons are arrested and taken to tribunal by a horde of German officers. As the crowd that had been witness to the arrest dissipates, Philippe is left alone, seated on a bench, when Lorenzo suddenly appears to ask with mocking insolence whether Philippe has taken to begging in the street. Philippe replies that he is indeed a beggar—an old man reduced to begging for justice. Musset has recreated, we might note, the scene of *Le Cid* in which Don Diègue must enlist his young son's aid in reestablishing the family's name. Philippe repeats to Lorenzo, in effect, that famous question: "Rodriguez as-tu du coeur?" But he does not receive in return the proud answer of a Rodriguez.

The actual question that Philippe puts to Lorenzo runs:

> You are a Medicis yourself, but only in name; if I know you at all, if the hideous comedy you play has left me an impassive and faithful spectator, then may the man now distinguish himself from the histrion. If you have ever been anything that I deem honest, then be so today. Pierre and Thomas are imprisoned.
>
> (388)

It takes Lorenzo ten pages of text to respond to Philippe's urging. In the course of his response he reveals his secret dream of entering the annals of history by murdering a tyrant, his initial desire to assassinate Clement VII before being bannished from Rome, and his present plunge into debauchery in order to gain the confidence of Duke Alexandre so as to murder him. The entire reply to Philippe forms one of the great document of nineteenth-century French literature, and clearly paves the way to much of the literature off our century that is classed under the rubrics of Existentialism and Absurdity: I do not intend to do it justice in a few minutes here. I would like briefly to focus on its climactic moment however, in which Lorenzo's self-narration gets to the heart of things, reaches its rhetorical apogee, and shows the extent to which the themes of being and of sexual threat have become inextricably intertwined.

In the course of his narration to Philippe, Lorenzo tells of how he conceived a quasi-Sartrian to project for himself one night:

> My youth was as pure as gold. During twenty years of silence thunder piled up in my breast, and I must now in reality be a spark of lightning because, suddenly, one night when I was sitting in the ruins of the Colosseum, I stood up for some unknown reason, I stretched toward the sky my arms soaked with dew, and I swore then that one of the tyrants of my country would die by my hand. I was at the time a peaceful student whose only concern was the arts and sciences, and I cannot tell you how it was that this foreign promise happened within me. Maybe it is the same kind of thing one feels upon falling in love.
>
> (391)

Lorenzo has indeed fallen in love—with an image of himself as a great man in the service of humanity, or what he describes as:

> A statue who would step down from his pedestal to walk among men in the public square is something like what I was the day I began to live with the idea that I had to be another Brutus.
>
> (3902)

But to fulfill this desire, he goes on, he has had to become vile, and yet despite al the viscious acts he has committed to gain the Duke's trust he still walks the streets with impunity His very existence, therefore, has become scandal in which is fellow citizens are implicated by virtue of their approbation.

As he puts it:

> And here I am in the street, me, Lorenzaccio? and children don't toss mud as I pass? The beds of girls are still hot with my sweat and their fathers don't take their knives and brooms to assail me as I walk by? . . . Poor mothers shamefully lift their daughter's veil when I stop at their door; they show me the girl's beauty with a smile more treacherous than Judas' kiss while I, pinching the little one's chin, clench my fist in anger and shuffle in my pocket four of five stinking pieces of gold.
>
> (394)

Lorenzo's project to become a second Brutus has led him, then to observe an aspect of humanity that has shaken his faith in the value of the project itself. His narration continues toward a lurid climax:

> . . . all masks fell before my gaze; humanity lifted its dress and showed me, as it might to an connaisseur worthy of her, its monstrous nudity. I saw men as they are, and I asked my self: for whom, then, am I working?
>
> (394-5)

As I said earlier, the themes of true being and of sexual threat become intricated throughout the play; in this moment of Lorenzo's self-narration they are solidly bound together. That Musset should have Lorenzo formulate his disillusion in this particular way is an event we might well take time to consider. The general metaphorizaiton of truth as nudity appealed to Musset as a general rule. We read in his *Confessions,* for example:

> This baneful idea that truth is nudity came to me in relation to everything. The world, I told myself, calls its make-up paint "virtue," its rosary "religion," its trailing cloak "suitability." . . . It goes to church, to balls, to assemblies; and when evening has come it unknots its dress, and one sees a naked bacchant with a pair of goatfeet.[2]

This is not the occasion to speculate on how "the world" or "le monde," a masculine noun in French, becomes surprisingly transformed into a "bacchant," nor on the additional complexity of the image of a goatfooted celebrant of Bacchus. It is more to the point to note that such problematic confusions of gender disappear from Lorenzo's narration, in which the feminine noun "humanité" lifts her logically consistent skirt to reveal her naked truth to a shocked and frightened Lorenzo. In the dramatic narrative, the scene is simple and consistent: feminine nudity is perceived as monstrous because it is "read," so to speak, as the simultaneous reality and threat of castration. "Humanity" plays the role of the Medusa, as Freud outlined it in his essay in 1922. But Lorenzo, being already a statue who has stepped off his pedestal—and an old mutilator of statues as well, we might recall—is not turned to stone in the face of the Medusa. Whereas Feud had read the stoniness as a phallic erection, to be brandished as a denial of fear and awe, Musset's Lorenzo might be said more to melt or shrivel, when confronted by humanity's truth. if we follow the phantasmatic logic of the narrative's imagery, the truth of humanity appears as the fact of castration, which intervenes to disrupt the project of a narcissistic erection of the self as a reified, statuesque construct.

One might interpret Lorrenzo's narrative sequence in terms that are fairly strictly Lacanian, at this point. That is to say, one might stress the extent to which the sexual-political climate that reigns in Florence under the Duke has raised to the point of verbal intrusion all the anxiety that habitually underlies patriarchal systems—anxieties concerning the mythic, cultural, contingent nature of the forces that determine the Symbolic order. The rule of the Name-of-the Father depends, after all, on a kind of patriarchal stability that has been undermined by Lorenzo in his dealing for the Duke: it is not then surprising to find him reacting with hysterical rhetoric to the collapse of an order upon which his own identity depends. The drama of Lorenzo's self-narration, in this case, would be the story of a man first engaged in a narcissistic infatuation with a phallic representation of the self, but who, in pursuit of that representation, comes to discover in humanity a form of generalized lack in being: the truth behind the appearance would turn out to be what Lacan calls a failure-to-be-there, or a failure to find oneself present, as presence, in the symbolic, patriarchal order of the world. And that reading of Lorenzo's story is certainly justified by the hysterical register of his language, and ought to be taken into consideration.

But there is another, equally compelling, psychoanalytic account of the dynamics of human situations that is lately being foregrounded in the reading of Freud. Recent readings by Derrida, Deleuze, Lacoue-Labarthe, and Borch-Jakobsen have increasingly stressed the role played by identification in the continual formation of any human subjectivity. As Borch-Jakobsen puts it in his book, *Le Sujet freudien,* desire operates at a primary level not as the desire for an object, but as the desire to be or become a subject. Implicated in this desire is the role of a model who is construed as having that mode of subjectivity that the non-subject wants for himself. In Jakobsen's terms:

> We can then reach the following conclusion about the relation between identification and desire. Desire does not work by means of dissimulation, of deformation or dis-placement; it is not a matter of *Entstellung* (Freud's term for dream distortion). To present things in this way would be yet again to suppose that the subject of desire precedes his mask, precedes his phantasmatic places (his *Stellen*). It would be to suppose the subject, the servitor of representation (the *subjectum,* the *hupokeimenon*). And while that supposition would lead us back to the ineradicable problematic of subjectivity itself, it would also satiate once more the ineradicable megalomania of desire—which is nothing less than a desire-to-be-a—subject (a desire-to-be-close-to-oneself, a wanting-to-be-free . . .). And that would be to go on dreaming.[3]

Jakobsen's point is this: the desire of all desire is not to have, for instance an object; it is to be, to experience one's subjectivity as whole and unique. But because being is an object of desire, or we might even say the function of desire, rather than an inherent component of existence, the sense of being must be appropriated through some model—through some double with whom I identify because he appears to *be*. And so I cannot help but live my being in the mode of some other, who serve me a model of subjectivity, which I appropriate as my own "self": a self that is always a duplicate of a "me" that I see elsewhere, and that I want to annihilate and replace by virtue of my identification with him. After all, if he is me then I must come to stand where he now is; the object of identification is always a rival.

This post-Lacanian reading of Freud sheds a clearer light on the dynamics that determine that second-level narration by which Lorenzo tells the truth of his self behind its appearances. The drama of Lorenzo's telling is the revelation of an "abyss,"[4] as Philippe calls it, that is the self. When Lorenzo claims that the lifting of a skirt revealed to him men as they really are, we must take him at his word, but we must also hear him out, for he goes on to say that his play-acting is no longer an act. "Vice, he says, was at first a mere cover; now it is glued to my skin" (396). What he has come to know is the extent to which identity as the murderer of Alexandre is based upon his identification with Duke, or his desire to stand in his place. Lorenzo is, in a sense, the man he abominates; and he hates his double precisely because Alexandre is his double—standing there where he, or they, ought to be.

Lorenzaccio is, then, a play about the tensions inherent in the telling one's real self; in order that "the world know a bit about who I am" I must talk about others, ineluctably, and, finally to prove my point, I must murder them, then die.

Notes

1. *Théatre I,* Garnier-Flammarion, Paris, 1964, p. 397. The translation is my own, as are all other translations from French texts cited. Further references to *Lorenzaccio* will be from this edition of the text, and given in parentheses following the citation.

2. *Confessions d'un enfant du siècle,* Gallimard, 1946, p. 149.

3. Paris, Flammarion, 1982, p. 65.

4. During this crucial attempt to tell his self, Lorenzo elicits a telling response from Philippe Strozzi, who remarks "Quel abîme! que tu m'ouvres!" (397). That is precisely Musset's point, I believe: the attempt to tell one's unicity can only open on to a narrative abyss, an endless soliloquy, and an ontological quicksand, precisely because one cannot "be" oneself without the mediation of others.

Alain Piette (essay date fall 1989)

SOURCE: Piette, Alain. "Musset's *Lorenzaccio.*" *The Explicator* 48, no. 1 (fall 1989): 17-20.

[*In the following essay, Piette compares differing interpretations of Musset's play.*]

Lorenzaccio is usually considered Musset's most original contribution to world literature and drama. Yet, although most critics agree on the play's literary quality, history shows us few successful productions. As was the case with most of his plays, Musset did not write this drama for the stage. Musset's plays are primarily meant to be read, as the title of one of his collections, *Armchair Theatre* (**Un Spectacle dans un fauteuil,** 1832, 1834) indicates. But the trouble with the play lies chiefly in the enigmatic character of its protagonist: the complex, almost obscure motivation for his climactic act is the substance of the play. Lorenzaccio's characterization is a delicately woven texture, whose threads seem to converge toward the murder in act IV, scene 8.[1] Yet the murder does not solve anything: in view of its final result—the immediate coronation of another tyrant—and Lorenzaccio's own indifference, our general comprehension of the play's "hero" is confused, and we are left with more questions than answers.

I would like to suggest that *Lorenzaccio* is not the tragedy of a misunderstood or unappreciated hero: there is little or no evidence in the text that points to a noble motive in Lorenzaccio. The most ambitious, if not completely successful, definitions of Lorenzaccio's character have been thematic and historic. Many critics espouse the optimistic view of the historian F. Schevill,[2] to the effect that Lorenzaccio's murder of Alessandro is designed to free his country from a monstrous tyranny. In this interpretation, Lorenzaccio is a disillusioned young aristocrat fallen from innocence, a man bone-weary of a debauchery to which he had meant only to pretend in order to win Alessandro's confidence. Herbert Hunt[3] and Paul Dimoff[4] adopt a biographical point of view: they see in Lorenzaccio the reflection of Musset's own disgust with society after the failure of the 1830 revolution, which he had wholeheartedly supported, and the deterioration of his relationship with George Sand.

More satisfying perhaps is Robert Denommé's interpretation.[5] He views Lorenzaccio as an early version of what Verlaine called the "poète maudit," the Romantic hero par excellence, who deliberately alienates himself from the society he lives in, and whose predicament puts him above the petty laws of a tedious and hypocritical universe. Inherent in the posture of the Romantic hero is a deep-rooted disgust with the world. In ***Lorenzaccio,*** this feeling takes on ironical overtones, inasmuch as the protagonist, because of his privileged position at court as the Duke's minion and informer, is not only a part of the society he loathes but an instrument of its survival. This irony is the key to Lorenzaccio's character. It elicits an attitude of self-contempt that is present throughout the play, but which becomes prominent in Lorenzaccio's last scene. He is subject to a strong self-destructive impulse, which finally overwhelms him when he willfully surrenders to the blows of his assassin.

Lorenzaccio's tendency toward self-annihilation is a corollary of his predicament as "poète maudit." It arises from his awareness of his own dual nature: unable to reconcile his life of debauchery at the court of Florence with the loftier ideals of his Romantic youth, he chooses to evaporate into nothingness. His murder of Alessandro has no other purpose than itself, and it is nothing short of suicide. On a political level, it achieves nothing. Far from inciting the people of Florence to revolt, as the partisans of the Strozzi would have it at the beginning of the play, it simply reaffirms the rule of the Medici over the city. Lorenzaccio himself is conscious of the gratuitousness of his act from the start. To Filippo Strozzi, who asks him why he is going to commit the murder if he believes it useless, Lorenzaccio replies:

> I'll make a wager with you. I am going to kill Alessandro. Once my deed is accomplished, if the republicans act as they should, it will be easy for them to establish a republic, the finest that ever flourished on this earth. Let's say they may even have the people with them. I wager that neither they nor the people will do anything.
>
> (61)

The murder will not change anything, and Cardinal Cibo knows it; he quotes *The Aeneid:*

> The first golden bough torn down is replaced by another,
> And as quickly there grows a similar branch of a similar metal.

(84)

Alessandro is like one of the statues that Lorenzaccio beheaded at the Arch of Constantine in Rome in a fit of iconoclastic frenzy. Indeed, in his last scene, Lorenzaccio strongly suggests that he himself could be one of them when he confesses to Filippo Strozzi after the murder that "I am hollower than a tin statue" (91). Alessandro's murder is a mere act of vandalism, and, as in vandalism, the emphasis in **Lorenzaccio** is on an individual's act: Musset is concerned only with *what* is done rather than with *why* it is done. The private and public significance of the action are explored, not its motivation.

The murder scene further emphasizes Lorenzaccio's suicidal tendencies. As Marie MacLean noted,[6] it has all the aspects of a tumultuous wedding night; the stabbing has the connotations of a monstrous copulation, whose orgasmic culmination ends in the death of one of the lovers. Ironically, it is Lorenzaccio who is "laid to rest." Transfixed in front of the Duke's dead body, he mutters as Scoronconcolo drags him away: "O magnificent nature! O eternal tranquility!" (82). He realizes that by killing Alessandro he has sealed his own doom. He is not a praying mantis but a wasp, and he has just lost his sting. His actual demise is only a matter of days. By killing the Duke, Lorenzaccio has no other purpose than to realize his own nature, whose essence he tries to explain to Filippo Strozzi in a beautiful moment of shrewd self-definition:

> You ask me why I'm going to kill Alessandro? Do you want me to poison myself or jump in the Arno? . . . Do you realize that this murder is all that's left of my virtue? . . . If you honor anything in me, it is this murder which you honor.

(61-2)

Lorenzaccio *is* this murder.

His own death, which is eagerly called for, is deprived of any tragic dimension: it has nothing to do with tragic retribution. In fact, it occurs almost unobtrusively in a most undramatic scene. Lorenzaccio rushes out on the street despite Filippo Strozzi's warning and almost immediately thereafter is reported dead by one of the servants. The whole takes only a few seconds, and the killing is off-stage. The play closes on the image of the new duke taking the oath of office, and we realize that Lorenzaccio's crime has been useless. As he himself has maintained since the beginning of the play, he is

not invested with a messianic mission. He is merely trapped in a world he cannot call his own. His urge toward self-consumption and the gratuitousness of his act can be seen as Romantic prefiguring of the existentialist cry of the burned-out Meursault in Camus' *Stranger.*

As we see then, Lorenzaccio's murder of his cousin Alessandro de Medici, Duke of Florence, is little else than the culmination of a series of selfish, malevolent acts, the logical outcome of a life of corruption. Lorenzaccio is the Romantic hero par excellence. As Shaw observed in his review of the play in 1897, "In the Romantic school horror was naturally akin to sublimity."[7] Lorenzaccio is a monster whose otherworldliness puts him above the petty laws of a tedious and hypocritical society. The representative of a perversely superior race of giants, as the Medici view themselves, he is an outlaw in the true sense of the term, and his life is governed by a single non-principle: chaos.

Notes

1. Alfred de Musset, "Lorenzaccio," *The Modern Theatre,* vol. 6., ed. Eric Bentley (Gloucester, Mass.: Peter Smith, 1974). Hereafter referred to by page number in the text.

2. Ferdinand Schevill, *The Medici* (New York: Harcourt, Brace, 1949).

3. Herbert J. Hunt, "Alfred de Musset et la Révolution de Juillet: la leçon politique de *Lorenzaccio,*" *Mercure de France* 251: 1934.

4. Paul Dimoff, *La Genèse de Lorenzaccio* (Paris: Droz, 1933).

5. Robert T. Denommé, "The Motif of the 'Poète Maudit' in Musset's *Lorenzaccio,*" *L' Esprit créateur* vol. 5, no. 2 (1965): 138-46.

6. Marie McLean, "The Sword and the Flower: The Sexual Symbolism of *Lorenzaccio,*" *Australian Journal of French Studies* 16 (1979): 166-81.

7. G. B. Shaw, "Lorenzaccio," *Dramatic Opinions and Essays with an Apology by Bernard Shaw* (New York: Brentano's, 1922): 295.

Susan McCready (essay date fall 2003)

SOURCE: McCready, Susan. "Power and Sexual Congress in Alfred de Musset's *Lorenzaccio.*" *Romance Notes* 44, no. 1 (fall 2003): 83-91.

[*In the following essay, McCready examines Musset's use of metaphor in* Lorenzaccio.]

Though born of the Italian fad sweeping the Paris literary scene in the 1830s, Alfred de Musset's 1834 **Lorenzaccio,** which is set in Renaissance Florence, manages not to succumb to it.[1] Rather than simply recycling received myths about Italy to pander to its audience's expectations, the play simultaneously employs and undermines those myths in an interrogation of the process of mythmaking itself.[2] Italy as the land of passion and Italy as the stronghold of patriarchal authority are the main stereotypes that inform the image of Italy in Musset's play. Yet, according to the play, by 1537, that Italy is already in the past. On the throne of Florence sits Alexandre de Medicis, whose lust eclipses all other passion, and whose tyranny displaces patriarchal rule. Out of *Lorenzaccio*'s complicated network of metaphors about passion and patriarchy develops a new image of Renaissance Italy, and not surprisingly, that image may be read as a condemnation of France in the wake of the July Revolution of 1830 (Cooper 23-29). For just as Lorenzo's assassination of the tyrant, itself inspired by the legendary revolutionary acts of the Brutii, will fail to end tyranny, the July Revolution, sometimes called the "stolen revolution," failed to live up to the promise of 1789, and merely replaced one king with another.

In this paper, I will consider at length the network of metaphors I just mentioned, in particular one image to which the play returns almost obsessively: the image of the bride. The bride and wedding imagery in general serve multiple functions over the course of the play, as we will see, but of principal concern to us is the interdependence of this imagery with the myth of Italy as land of passion and patriarchal stronghold. Within this context, the bride becomes more than a static symbol of purity and innocence; she becomes the emblem for what is at stake in the continuing struggle between the patriarchy and tyranny. The wedding becomes more than a spectacle which insures the succession of legitimate heirs and the relegation of passion to one orderly sphere of society; in *Lorenzaccio* it becomes the locus of an interrogation of the very order it purports to uphold.

In the opening scene of *Lorenzaccio* Gabrielle Maffio exchanges her virginity for "un collier brillant," (Musset 139) while her brother seeks out justice in the name of the duke, not knowing that in addressing his sister's seducer he is speaking to the duke, himself. "S'il y a des lois à Florence," he cries, "si quelque justice vit encore sur la terre, par ce qu'il y a de vrai et de sacré au monde, je me jetterai au pieds du duc, et il vous fera pendre," (Musset 140). From this inauspicious beginning, however, we know that there is no justice to be found at the feet of the duke, at least for Maffio. Instead, though he escapes with his life, he receives "quelques ducats" and an order of banishment in exchange for his sister. This opening prefigures a series of scenes which enact both the power of the tyrant and the individual citizen's response to it. Here, as elsewhere in the play, the power of the tyrant finds its expression in sexuality,

in this case, the duke's corruption of the innocent Gabrielle. Here, as elsewhere, the individual's protest is merely discursive, and therefore utterly futile. Maffio's oath is empty language; while the duke's power is embodied quite literally in the body of the girl he now possesses. To Maffio the corruption of his sister precipitates the loss of his home; we see him among the banished at the end of Act One swearing yet another oath, this time against Florence and its "sang corrompu" (*Musset* 163).

In Act II we learn from Philippe Strozzi how common an occurrence this is: "Dix citoyens bannis dans ce quartier-ci seulement! le vieux Galeazzo et le petit Maffio bannis, sa sœur corrompue, devenue une fille publique dans une nuit!" (*Musset* 163). To Philippe, the seduction of girls like Gabrielle is the symptom of a more generalized corruption in Florence itself. The slip from orderly patriarchy to debauched tyranny is reenacted by the duke each time he seduces a young girl and displaces her father's (or brother's) rightful authority. Gabrielle is turned from a virtuous daughter into a commodity for public consumption "in one night." Now a "fille publique," Gabrielle is pointed out to her brother "sortant du spectacle dans une robe comme n'en a pas l'impératrice" (*Musset* 162). Gabrielle herself has become the spectacle, the symbol of the duke's sexual prowess and political dominance and of her brother's complete lack of power, all of which are, perhaps, one and the same. Philippe's response to Gabrielle's seduction is more analytical than Maffio's but no more fruitful. The rhetoric of patriarchy and virtue is, as he recognizes himself, useless against the power of the tyrant and the lure of vice.

The literal prostitution of the women of Florence by the duke reifies Florence's metaphorical prostitution by its rulers: the duke, the pope and the emperor. Early in the play Florence is cursed by the banished Florentines as a "mère sterile" (*Musset* 162) and by Lorenzo as "une catin" (*Musset* 168). Later, Pierre Strozzi says of François I's offer of military aid, "Le roi de France protégeant la liberté de l'Italie, c'est justement comme un voleur protégeant contre un autre voleur une jolie femme en voyage. Il la défend jusqu'à ce qu'il la viole" (*Musset* 245). These gendered metaphors figure Florence as eroticized real estate, to be won and held through sexual force. "C'est en vertu des hallebardes qui se promènent sur la plateforme," explains the jeweler referring to the soldiers of the Citadel, "qu'un bâtard, une moitié de Medicis, un butor que le ciel avait fait pour être garçon boucher . . . couche dans le lit de nos filles" (*Musset* 144). Here the ruling power is represented by the Citadel and the soldiers are metonymically figured as their halberds; the phallic imagery is quite clear. Even the accession of the duke is the result of a metaphoric sexual liaison: "Le pape et l'empereur sont accouchés d'un bâtard qui a droit de vie de mort sur nos enfants, et qui ne pourrait pas nommer sa mère," (*Musset* 156) says the second Bourgeois. This transgressive wedding between pope and emperor produced the illegitimate heir (illegitimate in both the familial and political sense), with the result that the social order of Florence is undermined. A "garçon boucher" is given the power to banish noble fathers and husbands, the power to replace the regulated sexuality of the patriarchy with the sexual whim of the tyrant.

The Marquise de Cibo takes advantage of the duke's lustful nature in order to insinuate herself (not unlike Lorenzo) into a position of influence with him. She submits to the duke's amorous advances only to regale him with republican rhetoric that casts Florence as bride and the duke as bridegroom. She urges him to picture himself as the leader of a Florence freed from the foreign influences of pope and emperor: "Tu diras," she predicts, "'Comme le doge de Venise épouse l'Adriatique, ainsi je mets mon anneau d'or au doigt de ma belle Florence'" (*Musset* 209). In the end, however, it is the Marquise who is taken advantage of by the duke, who has no interest in the public good: "Je me soucie de l'impôt; pourvu qu'on le paye, que m'importe?" (*Musset* 209). The Marquise finds that despite the warmth of her rhetoric, she is unable to assert any control over the duke. His interest in her body, instead of in the high moral and political discourse with which she is trying to sway him is yet another reenactment of the lesson of the opening scene of the play: discourse on the side of the powerless is powerless.

Early in the play, the Marquise declares to the Cardinal, "Ceux qui mettent les mots sur leur enclume, et qui les tordent avec un marteau et une lime, ne réfléchissent pas toujours que ces mots représentent des pensées, et ces pensées des actions" (*Musset* 149). But the connection of word, idea and action only proves solid for those in power in Florence. When Salviati, one of the duke's partisans, insults Louise, the daughter of Philippe Strozzi, *his* words have the power to stain the family. Yet nothing the Strozzi say (or even do) has any effect: Salviati lives on and Louise is unavenged. Later, when Salviati poisons Louise, it seems for a moment as though her body, the body of a beautiful virgin, might be the impetus for a revolution. "Que ta Louise soit notre Lucrèce . . . Nous allons jurer sur son corps de mourir pour la liberté!" (*Musset* 215). Strozzi's guests declare. The rhetoric which attempts to make over Louise as Lucrèce dissolves, however, in Philippe's hesitation. Strozzi and his guests talk at cross purposes of burials and revolutions, but Act III ends only with Philippe's bootless lamentation.

The various dissidents who challenge the tyrant throughout the play are uniformly ineffective; all but the Marquise will eventually be banished. Maffio and the Marquise both attempt to extract justice from the duke through appeals to idealism; Philippe's partisans appeal to the historical-mythic ideal of Lucrece; Pierre goes so far as to try to raise an army, while Philippe analyzes, orates, and laments, but finally fails to act. The discourses of the dissidents vary, but all are essentially nostalgic, as they all refer to a time before Alexandre the tyrant, and in this way they all contribute to the creation of a collective image of the past. The dissidents base their claims against the tyrant in the desire to reinstate what they see as the structured, peaceful, just, even natural order of patriarchy. But Lorenzo's mission, though not without its own brand of nostalgia, works against this rhetoric. Although he uses some of the same images and metaphors (weddings and brides not excepted) to describe his mission, Lorenzo's words and eventually his actions undo the myth of innocence and patriarchal order in which the other characters are so heavily invested.

If the wedding ceremony transgressed is the metaphoric emblem of the patriarchy gone awry, then Lorenzo, the legitimate heir to the throne of Florence is the cuckold bridegroom. Appropriately, his assassination plot plays itself out like a perverse courtship, only to find consummation in the ritual death of the duke in the "marriage bed."[3] Lorenzo's relationship to the duke is characterized throughout the play by a fluidity of gender roles. "Lorenzetta," the "femmelette," faints at the sight of a naked blade, exchanges endearing "mignons" with his cousin the duke, and like his cousin, cross-dresses at the wedding ball in Act I. All the while, as he eventually reveals to Philippe, Lorenzo is plotting the tyrant's death. This elaborate courting/stalking of the duke is thus calculated to culminate in the wedding/murder in Lorenzo's bed. Lorenzo himself speaks of the murder in these terms. In his conversation with the artist Tebaldeo in the second act, he commissions, "un tableau d'importance pour le jour de mes noces" (*Musset* 169). Later, we see that the subject of Tebaldeo's "wedding portrait" is none other than the duke. Moreover, Lorenzo's training session with Scoronconcolo culminates in Lorenzo's apostrophe, "O jour de sang, jour de mes noces!" (*Musset* 188).[4]

In the murder scheme, itself, outlined in Lorenzo's Act IV monologue, he plans to enter the room in place of his aunt Catherine, whom the duke is expecting, and in order to conceal himself he will put out the light, reasoning that "une nouvelle mariée, par exemple, exige cela de son mari pour entrer dans la chambre nuptiale" (*Musset* 231). That same bride, Lorenzo warns, "est belle. Mais je vous le dis à l'oreille, prenez garde à son petit couteau" (*Musset* 233), an image which hints at the phallic potential Lorenzo has yet to reveal. Later, to accomplish the murder, Lorenzo disarms the duke by removing his sword and tying it such that it cannot be removed from its scabbard. This allows Lorenzo, armed at last with his sword, to play the part of the groom, the duke having been made over into the "homme sans epée." Finally, in the struggle that ensues after Lorenzo's first thrust the two roles are conflated as the duke bites Lorenzo's finger, leaving him with a "bague sanglante, inestimable diamant" (*Musset* 235). Presumably, then both the duke and Lorenzo play the part of the virgin bride, leaving blood on the wedding sheets.

The murder scene has convincingly been described by several critics in terms of ritual sacrifice and by others as a "blood wedding" (MacLean 166-181). These are certainly not mutually exclusive options; however, for a sacrifice to be efficacious or for a wedding to be legal, it has to be witnessed; while here, the sacrifice (or the wedding) is self-contained. Since Lorenzo commits the murder in secret and closes the body of the duke in the locked bedroom, he effectively deprives the assassination of any possible effect in the political sphere, where appearances, though sometimes deceiving, are everything. Bernard Masson argues that "la réalité du pouvoir reste entre les mains de l'ordonnateur du spectacle" (Masson 140). The political fate of Florence is sealed in the last scene of the play, as the newly-elected duke is elevated with all the pomp and circumstance that such an occasion requires to declare its authority and legitimacy.

That his revolutionary action fails is no surprise to Lorenzo. In the central scene of the play, the long dialogue with Philippe in Act III, scene iii, Lorenzo reveals that he has long since given up all hope of effecting political change. Here Lorenzo casts the murder explicitly in terms of a wedding; however Lorenzo's bride is not the duke, but all humanity. When he first conceives of his mission Lorenzo likens it to "ce qu'on éprouve quand on devient amoureux" (*Musset* 199). Later, having become the duke's procurer in order to effect his plan, Lorenzo waits for a sign of honesty on the face of humanity: "J'observais comme un amant . . . observe sa fiancée, en attendant le jour de noces!" (*Musset* 202). The sign of honesty of course never manifests itself; instead, explains Lorenzo, "les mères pauvres soulèvent honteusement le voile de leurs filles quand je m'arrête au seuil de leurs portes" (*Musset* 202). While Lorenzo is horrified to admit that "le vice a été pour moi un vêtement; maintenant il est collé à ma peau" (*Musset* 203), humanity, figured as a woman, "souleva sa robe et me montra, comme à un adepte digne d'elle, sa monstrueuse nudité" (*Musset* 202). It is impossible not to notice that within the discourse of sexuality in which Lorenzo has inscribed his mission, all the evils he is fighting are gendered as female. Vice is a lascivious woman; Florence has become a whore. The misogyny of Lorenzo's metaphors is an inevitable extension of his political model: republic declines into tyranny, just as patriarchy declines into debauchery.[5] If this is true, it follows that the degradation of the orderly sexual commerce of patriarchy should result in the sul-

lying of its emblem: feminine virtue. But just as the loss of virginity happens "dans l'espace d'une nuit" (as Gabrielle becomes a courtesan in the space of one night or as Louise goes from healthy to dead in the space of one night), the slip into tyranny is quick and at first imperceptible. According to the jeweler, the Citadel which represents and maintains the tyrant's power, "a poussé comme un champignon de malheur dans l'espace d'une nuit" (*Musset* 144).

Lorenzo is aware all along that his murder will serve neither his country nor himself, as both his virtue and that of Florence are irretrievably lost, and yet he commits the murder anyway. He explains to Philippe that "le seul fil qui rattache mon cœur à quelques fibres de mon cœur d'autrefois" (*Musset* 204) is the desperate attempt to rid the world of a tyrant "quel qu'il fût" (*Musset* 199). This single strand ties him to the past and impels him fatally forward. According to Lorenzo, he passed a point of no return when he looked into the face of humanity: "La main qui a une fois soulevé le voile de la vérité ne peut plus le laisser retomber; elle reste immobile jusqu'à ce que l'Ange du sommeil éternel lui bouche les yeux" (*Musset* 203). In effect, as Lorenzo lifts the veil (as a groom lifts the veil from his bride), he finds himself face to face with the emptiness of his own action. He knows that words like *republic* and *justice* are only as meaningful as the power structure that upholds them is strong. He recognizes that the virtue in which he once believed was as much a mask as is the vice to which he has given himself over. The nostalgia for essential values such as virtue and purity urges Lorenzo toward what is ultimately a nihilistic and self-destructive act.

With the elevation ceremony of the new duke on which the play closes, the forces of tyranny seem only to have tightened their hold on Florence. In the ceremony, Côme de Medicis promises to adopt Alexandre's illegitimate children, thus symbolically incorporating into his own regime the abuses of the previous one. All this takes place before a throng of Florentines who had vaguely wondered what happened to the old duke and why there had not been an official election, but had since been subdued by the carnival atmosphere and the assurances of Les Huit that all was for the best. The deeply-rooted cynicism of this ending reflects political events in France in 1830 when the people's uprising merely removed one king in favor of another. Louis-Philippe's accession to the throne effectively reduced what might have been a new Revolution to a few days' tumult in July.

The nostalgia that drives Musset backward into the history of the Medicis is similar to the nostalgia that compels Lorenzo knowingly toward his own destruction. The collective French fantasies of Italy as a land of passion, of action and of honor, like the collective imaginings of their former republic by the Florentines within the play, embody the same nostalgic impulses toward what is lost, or more accurately, what is *believed* to have been lost. The past is, in fact, unknowable. "Je ne nie pas l'histoire," Lorenzo tells Philippe just before his own death, "mais je n'y étais pas" (*Musset* 243). The fantasy staged in **Lorenzaccio** is, then, a fantasy of return. If only, the play seems to say, we could go back to the source of disorder to find the moment when the fall began, perhaps we will be able recapture some mythic, essential unity between word and action. But in staging the story of a revolution that was not one, the play reveals that the ideals for which revolutions are fought are illusory, and that the source of power lies not in heroism, but in power itself.

Notes

1. For more on the Italian vogue in French romanticism, see Bernard Masson, *Musset et son double: Lecture de Lorenzaccio,* Paris: Librairie Minard, 1978, 17. For more on Italy in the œuvre of Musset, see Donald R. Gamble, "The Image of Italy in the Creative Imagination of Alfred de Musset" in Bauer, Roger (ed.) *Space and Boundaries in Literature,* Munich: Iudicium, 1990, 305-311.

2. To speak of the "audience" and its expectations is slightly misleading since this play, though long considered Musset's masterpiece, was not performed during the author's lifetime. Although the play was written in a form that stagecraft of the 1830s could not accommodate, its theatricality is undeniable, as spectacle becomes (as we shall see) one of the themes of the play. For this reason, I will continue to use theatrical terms, such as *audience,* to speak of the drama.

3. One of the first to speak in these terms of the murder of the duke was Jules Bedner in "Œdipe à Florence," *Neophilologus,* 24:1, 1983, 42-55.

4. Jeanne Bem, in "*Lorenzaccio:* entre l'histoire et le fantasme," *Poétique,* vol. 11, no. 44, November 1980, 451-461, points out an extended pun on the word "noces." While in the play "noces" usually refers explicitly to a wedding ceremony, the word may also mean "dissipation" or "debauchery" as in the expression "faire la noce." So when Lorenzo speaks of his wedding day, "jour de mes noces," we hear the echo of the dissipation in which he has wasted his youth.

5. Of course in *The Republic,* Plato argues that tyranny proceeds rather from democracy.

Works Cited

Bedner, Jules. "Œdipe à Florence," *Neophilologus,* 24:1, 1983, 42-55.

Bem, Jeanne. "*Lorenzaccio:* entre l'histoire et le fantasme," *Poétique,* vol. 11, no. 44, November 1980, 451-461.

Cooper, Barbara. "Staging a Revolution," *Romance Notes,* vol. 24 no. 1, 1983, 23-29.

Gamble, Donald R. "The Image of Italy in the Creative Imagination of Alfred de Musset" in Bauer, Roger (ed.) *Space and Boundaries in Literature,* Munich: Iudicium, 1990, 305-311.

MacLean, Mary. "The Sword and the Flower: The Sexual Symbolism of *Lorenzaccio,*" *Australian Journal of French Studies,* vol. 16, no. 2, 1979, 166-181.

Masson, Bernard. *Musset et son double: Lecture de Lorenzaccio.* Paris: Librarie Minard, 1978.

Musset, Alfred de. *Théâtre complet,* Paris: Gallimard, 1990.

ON NE BADINE PAS AVEC L'AMOUR (1834)

CRITICAL COMMENTARY

David Sices (essay date February 1970)

SOURCE: Sices, David. "Multiplicity and Integrity in *On ne badine pas avec l'amour.*" *The French Review* 43, no. 3 (February 1970): 443-51.

[*In the following essay, Sices discusses the style and construction of Musset's play* On ne badine pas avec l'amour.]

Intriguing parallels between the couples Perdican-Camille and Musset-George Sand have contributed, no doubt, to the disproportionate amount of critical attention paid to the sentimental duel engaged in by the protagonists of **On ne badine pas avec l'amour.** The presence of bits of dialogue obviously drawn from life, fragments of correspondence, and the suggestive polemic between hero and heroine shift the focus of interest away from the play's inner structure, toward external points of reference and toward psychological analysis. The play's apparent regularity, which has contributed to its theatrical success (performance variants are limited almost solely to political and religious bowdlerizings), has further discouraged examination of its construction.[1] As Pierre Gastinel pointed out, **On ne badine pas avec l'amour** is characterized by a curious sort of classical unity, its three acts taking place on successive days about noon.[2] What he did not notice, apparently, is that our awareness of this time-setting is dependent on the grotesque gastronomic jousts of Blazius and Bridaine. I would like to examine the connection between the play's superficial regularity, and one of its essential themes: the protagonists' search for self and personal integrity. I will try to show how the relationships which bind together primary characters and *fantoches,* through the medium of Musset's irony, and the multiple points of view he established toward his protagonists, are an essential element of the play's dramatic structure.[3]

Although Musset makes use of grotesque characters in *Les Caprices de Marianne* and *Fantasio,* he does not bring us so quickly into contact with them, or so forcefully, as in this play. In the two earlier works, we are conscious of a dialogue, an existential dialectic, between *fantoches* and "real" characters. There is more true interaction between the two classes of being than in this play: Marianne's elderly husband Claudio, for all his ridiculousness, is the agent of death for Coelio; and the Prince of Mantua is a real threat to the happiness of both Elsbeth and her kingdom. None of this effective participation of grotesques in the action is to be found in *On ne badine pas avec l'amour.* The Baron, though father and uncle to the protagonists, is essentially a bewildered and frustrated observer of the course of events, signifying his impotence by reiterating after each report that comes in to him, "Cela est impossible" or "Cela est inouï." Blazius and Bridaine, far from exerting any effect on the central dramatic progression, seem to carry out an unrelated action, a burlesque epic sub-plot having to do with the gaining or losing of honors at the Baron's copious table. And Dame Pluche, a dried-out caricature of Camille's devoutness and prudery, is ironically limited in her action to the role of unwilling and ineffectual go-between. Although all these puppet figures spend their time discussing and reporting on the actions of the protagonists, their bewilderment suggests to us that they live in another world, utterly separate from the emotional and spiritual goings-on of the "real" characters.

And yet Musset chooses in this play (unlike *Fantasio* where, oddly enough, the hero and his grotesque "rival" never meet or even share a scene) to have his protagonists and his grotesques hold the stage at the same time, in a variety of combinations and circumstances (Act I, scene 2; Act II, scene 1; Act III, scenes 4, 6 and 7); or else he has them divide a scene alternately (Act I, scene 3; Act III, scenes 1 and 2). In the latter case, by having his two sets of characters share, but separately, the place and time of the action, Musset creates a simultaneous sense of division and unity which is in some ways the most typical sign of his theatrical genius. As critics of the author have pointed out, it is his need to dramatize

the dialectic of his own personality and of the human soul, which lies at the basis of his enduring greatness as a playwright, and his relative decline as a poet. Nowhere is this more clearly realized than in the double incarnation of Musset in *Les Caprices de Marianne,* as Coelio and Octave. But it finds expression as well in *Fantasio*'s existential dilemma and resolution, where the hero has to defeat the mechanism of destiny by evincing his grotesque double, the Prince.

This dialogue of man with himself (with his other self) is worked out in somewhat more complex terms in *On ne badine pas avec l'amour.* The complication is due to the fact that Musset chooses there to embody his psychological and existential problem—unity and integrity of the personality vs. fragmentation and multiplicity—not only in two central characters, but in two sets of characters: Perdican and Camille (the "real" protagonists), and the grotesques. Furthermore, the problem is stated not only in terms of the dialogue between characters and sets of characters, but also in terms of each of the main characters themselves, in time: childhood, maturity and old age. And this time-theme is further complicated by the fact that it is distributed as well between Perdican and a third set of characters, existing on yet another level of literary reality: the Chorus.

It is the Chorus, half caricature and half real character, which makes us aware from the first scene of the play that number—unity vs. duality, and integrity vs. multiplicity—is to be one of the major themes informing the work. Does the Chorus, indeed, speak as one man or several, at once or separately? Conflicting answers have been supplied in production; at any rate, the Chorus seems both humane and anonymous. And it is the Chorus which first reveals to us, through its delightfully artificed introductions of Blazius and Pluche (as well as later on, in its mock-epic account of Blazius' and Bridaine's duel at table) that all "matched pairs" are inherently ridiculous, whether they are matched by polar opposition or by Tweedledee-Tweedledum similarity.

Placed as it is between grotesques and real characters, the Chorus comments from a middle distance on the progress of affairs between Perdican and Camille (Act III, scene 4, for example). It thus establishes a sort of parallel between the ridiculous matched pairs of the *fantoches* and the ill-matched pair of protagonists. This parallelism or ironic echo is not merely incidental, but essential to the structure of the play.

Nowhere else in his dramatic production does Musset make such extensive use of deliberately visible artifice as in this work. His borrowing and adaptation of the Greek chorus is only the first of many palpably "theatrical" and traditional devices in the play. Our entry into the central action—the amorous duel between Perdican and Camille, and its tragic end with the death of Rosette—comes via a series of artificial hurdles which serve, so to speak, as successive frames, creating through the introductory comments of the Chorus, Maitre Blazius, Dame Pluche and the Baron, an effect of aesthetic distancing between the spectator/reader and the "real" action of the protagonists. Despite the intimacy of atmosphere that characterizes this play, one cannot help feeling that the author's irony required this technique of multiple aesthetic frames to reinforce the isolation of his protagonists within their existential framework, and in themselves.

Is this not the real explanation of the fact that much of **On ne badine pas avec l'amour**'s action—the action of its central plot, that is to say—is "narrated" (if so we may term the grotesques' babblings) rather than acted: Perdican walking arm in arm with Rosette, "une gardeuse de dindes!", and making ricochets on the duck-pond; Camille giving her note for Perdican to Dame Pluche, who hops up and down in the grass . . . Of course, the fact that it is Bridaine, in the first case, and Blazius, in the second, who narrate the events in question is of the utmost importance. Both narratives affect the status of the speakers, for better or for worse, in the Baron's bewildered eyes; and both contribute to the latter's sense of confusion and futility in regard to the complex drama that is unfolding under his roof, in spite of his plans. The narratives thus contribute to the development of the trivial sub-plot being acted out by the grotesque characters, in echo to the real drama. But at the same time, they serve an inverse function of distancing in relation to the protagonists. The audience must look at the latter more objectively, see them not only as they themselves, our hearts, and the author's sympathy see them, but also as the indifferent world, the heartless marionettes (thus our wit), and the author's irony perceive them. This technique of multiple vision fulfills the needs of the deeper theme underlying Camille and Perdican's unrequited love: the problem of human integrity or integration.

Jean Pommier notes one aspect of this theme clearly, in speaking of the "duel des caractères" as the central dramatic unity of the play. As he says, "pour Musset l'individu n'est que la moitié mutilée de l'être complet, du couple; et c'est lui pourtant qui dresse ainsi l'un contre l'autre les sexes ennemis."[4] Certainly the joust between the two halves of Aristophanes' primordial jigsaw puzzle is the most evident single manifestation of this theme in the play; as Pommier remarks, it contains within itself the central tragic irony, the struggle between individual integrity and human emotional need. But the problem can be reduced to a lower denominator: that of resolving the conflict between multiplicity and integrity within the individual, what we may call "la *dualité* des caractères."

Seen in this context, the Baron's heartfelt complaint, relayed to Perdican by Maître Blazius—"Le Baron croit remarquer que vos caractères ne s'accordent pas" (II, I, p. 26)—takes on an ironic double meaning. It is not only that the natures of Perdican and Camille do not "match" properly; there exists within the character of each a profound, irreconcilable split which acts to prevent their match. In the case of Camille, it is the "être factice" or "personnage d'emprunt" which Masson astutely sees as her flaw (rather than the traditionally noted pride). Like many of Musset's central characters, she has a combination of immaturity and precocious disillusion: in this case, through the vicarious experience of Sister Louise, her older confidant. Like Fantasio, she has "le mois de mai sur les joues" but "le mois de janvier dans le coeur." It is only at the end of the play that the two halves of her character are momentarily reintegrated.

Perdican, too, is a character in quest of his integrity—even more consciously than Camille. He has returned not so much in search of a bride as in search of his past. Seeking the sweet comfort of "l'oubli de ce qu'on sait," he wishes to reintegrate his present, doctoral and experienced self with the innocent joy of his youth. Perdican seeks a harmonization of all the conflicting forces within him, a unity that will reconcile the contradictions of which his experience in time has made him conscious. That is why, in a significant inversion of the Baron's characteristic formula of intellectual rigidity, Musset has him reply "Cela est possible" to Camille's remark that he has contradicted himself, in the culminating scene of the second act (II, 5, p. 42). Perdican's most ardent desire is to keep for himself the flexibility, the *disponibilité* which will make it possible for all these contradictions to form a unity across time. It is somewhat in the same vein that we have the Chorus' paradox of being both father and son to the returning scholar: this is not just a case of "the child being father to the man."

This desire for flexibility as an antidote to fragmentation and as a principle of personal unity is at the basis of Perdican's curious reply to Camille's question concerning a picture hanging in the castle gallery. Musset here uses the tableau in a characteristic fashion reminiscent of the "stirrup-cup" in **Fantasio**.[5] The painting of a monk and a goatherd suggests that peculiar duality so dear to the author, representing to Camille the dilemma which her pride prevents her from resolving until it is too late: eternity or the present, sacred or profane love. Like Fantasio, she dwells on the source of her perplexity, and cherishes the unreconciled duality which the painting represents. But Perdican rejects the symbol brutally, with a striking affection of incomprehension: the painting represents for him two "flesh and blood" men, "un qui lit, et un autre qui danse"—nothing more. With his fourfold doctorate, Perdican ought at least to perceive the symbolic significance of the painting for Camille. But he refuses to understand, in part because he rejects the spiritual dilemma which she is attempting to resolve, but also because his principle of self-integration is precisely the opposite of what a symbol stands for. He is seeking human integrity within the life-stream, in time; his attempt to harmonize contradictions is inimical to the rationality of the symbol, which emphasizes duality and choice, Camille's idealistic either-or. To see the two figures as standing for distinct and exclusive types, worthy of more or less "esteem" according to a hierarchy of values, would be to reject or to censure one or more of the parts of himself which Perdican is trying to bring into inclusive harmony.

But Perdican's pride, like Camille's, is a self-defeating element in his personality, in so far as self-integration is concerned. His response to the Baron's displeasure at the disaccord between Camille's character and his own has elements of the grotesques' rigidity: "Cela est malheureux; je ne puis refaire le mien" (II, 1, p. 26). The hero seems to be refusing all compromise in his possible adaptation to the emotional needs of the couple; he is also, implicitly and unconsciously, refusing the very principle of flexibility which he later propounds to Camille (II, 5). His unwillingness to bend is the most important element of delay on his part, in the series of amorous manoeuvres, the "duel" through time, which is the principle of action in this play. Here, indeed, we must take cognizance of the dramatic form of *On ne badine pas avec l'amour.* Musset's play is not a polemical comparison between two kinds of life, or two manners of looking at life. The drama of Perdican and Camille is that they are obviously the mutilated parts of one kind of human integrity: the indivisible unity of the human couple. Their tragedy lies in their not being able to realize this integrity "in time." I mean this latter expression in its ambiguity: the couple's ephemeral moment of knowledge and hope, in Act III, scene 8, arrives just before the consequences of their *badinage* across the time of the action, their game of hide and seek, are realized in the death of Rosette. It is there, in the sudden cry of recognition ("Elle est morte. Adieu, Perdican.") that the real force of Musset's innocent-seeming title strikes us. Not only *must* one not "play with love"; one *does* not play with love, it never turns out to be play, in the end.

The profound reason for this has been established within the play, cumulatively, throughout its action: not only in the joust between the protagonists, which has revealed the difficulty of union for a couple composed of powerful (and imperfectly self-integrated) individualities; but also in extensive play with number both among the minor characters and between them and the protagonists. The grotesques' intense consciousness of number is particularly striking, from a thematic point of view, and

typified in the thought and language of the Baron. From the beginning, his highest criterion for recommending Perdican and Camille's union is the six thousand *écus* their education has cost him (I, 2, p. 8). His unhappiness in his solitude at the provincial castle is expressed by the "three months of winter and three months of summer" he must spend there (*ibid.*). Maitre Blazius' description of the scene between Camille and Dame Pluche is transformed by the Baron's obsession, which magnifies grotesquely the numbers in the tableau: "Quelle raison pouvait avoir dame Pluche pour froisser un papier plié en *quatre* en faisant des soubresauts dans *une* luzerne!" (II, 4, p. 35; italics mine). The honor of his family, impugned by Blazius' observations on the protagonists' behavior, is guaranteed in the Baron's eyes by the number of its members: "Savez-vous que nous sommes trentesept mâles, et presque autant de femelles, tant à Paris qu'en province?" (p. 33). We must remember that his severe judgment of Camille's great-aunt was based on her not having contributed to the growth of this number (I, 2, p. 12).

This obsession with numbers, so close to the center of the *fantoches'* nature, is the principle of dehumanization with which Perdican and Camille are struggling. It is not accidental that the Baron uses the animalistic "mâles" and "femelles" in the quotation above. The tragedy of *On ne badine pas avec l'amour* is that time is not to be understood merely in terms of the continuity of human experience. If that were the case, then Camille and Perdican might be expected eventually to achieve union. Time is also, tragically, the accumulation and multiplication of human experiences, which leads to fragmentation of the vital sentimental continuity. It has been noted before that the grotesques in Musset's theater tend to be old, at least of another generation than the protagonists (with the notable exception of the Prince of Mantua). That is not just circumstance, or even, in the traditional sense, a sign of the conflict of generations. The division of nature between younger and older characters is more profound, because it is part of the tragic principle of Musset's theater. Old age, grotesqueness, and mechanical rigidity are synonymous in Musset's world, because passing time brings about the accumulation of sentimental mishaps and failures which eventually leads to fossilization—that hardening of the heart which the author's letters tell us he so feared. Is it not symptomatic of Musset's own decline, in this connection, to see the tempering of his *fantoches* which characterizes *Il ne faut jurer de rien*? That play marks his surrender to the "wisdom" of old age, and a compromise with the tragic force which gives such poignancy to his youthful dramas.

If, in *On ne badine pas avec l'amour,* we see so much of the action through the bewildered, distorting eyes of the grotesques, and if Musset constantly jostles our sensibilities by juxtaposing his protagonists' sentimental struggles with the mechanical absurdities of Blazius, Bridaine, Dame Pluche and the Baron, it is evidently not in order for us to be made more aware of the latter's inanity by comparison with the lovers, which is obvious enough from the beginning. It is true that the grotesques tend to diminish in importance as the play progresses; but that is because their function as aesthetic and spiritual windows—or deforming mirrors—is well established by the middle of the second act; and they remain present, in a diminished way, right up to the penultimate scene of the play. The reason for this narrative importance is rather that the *fantoches* are the deformed and deforming voice of Camille's and Perdican's destiny as suffering beings in a hostile universe, a universe whose principal threat is that of fragmentation and destructive accumulation in the lives of those who seek continuity and unity through the endurance of human sentiment. Perdican is condemned at the end of the play to be the "lover" of the series of mistresses Camille has accused him of having—a series to which she both does and does not now belong, since she is one out of many, but not "the one." Camille, too, is left by destiny without having resolved her dilemma: she will be neither a good nun nor a woman loved, she may very well join the ambiguous group of disappointed women of her convent.

Perdican and Camille thus succumb to their destiny through a double failure. Each fails to achieve harmonization of conflicting forces within his personality: love—pride, altruism—egotism, youthful passion—precocious cynicism. And by this failure they fail to attain that ultimate unity of Musset's romantic vision: the "union de deux de ces êtres si imparfaits et si affreux" which Perdican, in his celebrated moment of clairvoyance at the end of act two, sees as transcending the base material reality of the physical world. In both instances, the essential fault is rigidity, the triumph of the categorical and the mechanical over the fluid and humane. At the end, the *fantoches'* deformed vision of the protagonists has replaced the latter's vision of themselves, for they have been caught in a trap of their own devising. The last-minute realization expressed in Camille's "Adieu, Perdican!" marks the final, total defeat, the end of the couple's brief chance for salvation through love. Its finality is all the more tragic for the implied years of anti-climactic mechanical life which will follow. How far Musset is here from *fin de siècle* optimism, the cyclical historicism with which post-'48, post-Romantic Frenchmen consoled themselves for individual failure! Renan would write in 1885: "Antistius renaitra éternellement pour échouer éternellement, et en définitive, il se trouvera que la totalité de ses échecs vaudra une victoire."[6] But for Musset's protagonists, for Perdican, for Lorenzo, the sum of failures is the defeat of the individual; and nothing beyond that counts. Only Fantasio escapes that law—through a loophole. For his salvation is based on a perpetual juggling act: the avoidance of commitment,

the espousal of chance, and the acceptance of duality, of ambiguity, as the only defense against tragic realization.

In *Fantasio,* Musset underlined this refusal of final unity by his adoption of an open-ended form, the two-act play. Perhaps we can now also see a deeper significance to the action, in Musset's apparent acceptance of classical "unity" and regularity in *On ne badine pas avec l'amour.* The tragedy of Perdican and Camille is symbolized by this reduction of human experience, in all its irregularity and indefinability, to the predictable shape of the traditional comedy. The ironic force of Blazius and Bridaine, that low-comic, mock-epic pair, is that the stroke of noon, echoing in the recesses of their gluttonous stomachs, marking three times the passage of a day in human time, is the death knell of Rosette, and of Camille's and Perdican's love, hope and youth. The sinisterly burlesque machinery of destiny, acting within the mechanism of the human body, has once again claimed a pair of victims for old age and death.

Notes

1. This success gives the lie to the well-known quip that a bill-board advertising a program in honor of Musset should read: "Ce soir, relâche. Lisez chez vous dans un fauteuil *On ne badine pas avec l'amour.*" Cited in Musset, *Comédies et Proverbes,* texte établi et présenté par Pierre et Françoise Gastinel, Paris, 1952, t. 2, p. 331. All references to the text of the play will be from this edition.

2. Pierre Gastinel, *Le Romantisme d'Alfred de Musset,* Paris, 1933, p. 301.

3. Cf. also David Sices, "Musset's *Fantasio:* the Paradise of Chance," *Romanic Review,* LVIII, 23-37; Robert Mauzi, "Les Fantoches d'Alfred de Musset," *Revue d'Histoire Littéraire,* LXVI, 257-282; Bernard Masson, "Le Masque, le double et la personne dans quelques Comédies et Proverbes," *Revue des Sciences Humaines,* fasc. 108, 551-571; Henri Lefebvre, *Alfred de Musset dramaturge,* Paris, 1955, passim.

4. *Variétés sur Alfred de Musset et son théâtre,* Paris, 1944, p. 91.

5. See Sices, pp. 30-32.

6. *Le Prêtre de Nemi, Oeuvres complètes d'Ernest Renan,* Paris, 1863-1926, v. 27, 261.

James F. Hamilton (essay date May 1985)

SOURCE: Hamilton, James F. "From *Ricochets* to *Jeu* in Musset's *On ne badine pas avec l'amour*: A Game Analysis." *The French Review* 58, no. 6 (May 1985): 820-26.

[*In the following essay, Hamilton examines the motifs of games and repetition in Musset's play.*]

Des ricochets! Ma tête s'égare; voilà mes idées qui se
bouleversent. Vous me faites un rapport insensé, Bridaine. Il est inoui qu'un docteur fasse des ricochets.

(1, 5)[1]

Our understanding of Musset's masterpiece on love has
progressed from the study of parallels between the
couples Perdican-Camille and Musset-George Sand to
the examination of conflicting bipolarities, psychological and temporal.[2] To this approach must be added
structural and ideological dimensions capable of
elucidating the play's dramatic mechanism. Only then
can motivation, time, and space be grasped as a dynamic
whole. The generative principle of this expanded
interpretation derives from the verb *badiner* in the title
to Musset's tragi-comedy. The implied motif of *jeu*
goes to the heart of Romantic drama, its psychology
and metaphysics.[3] The complementary image, *ricochets,*
appears four times at the end of Act I and is metaphor-
ized to convey the spontaneous breakdown of order.
Stones are thrown by a university doctor and noble,
Perdican, who courts a peasant girl, Rosette; and, village rascals follow them to the chateau, all to the horror
of the Baron. In short, I contend that the images of
ricochets and *jeu* reflect two contrary modes of
behavior. The first—unreflective, spontaneous, and
natural—characterizes Perdican's conduct up to the
second fountain scene. Here, he joins Camille by operating on the basis of calculation, strategy, and artifice—
the behavioral mode of *jeu.*

"Ricochet" explains repeated movement in the play. It
occurs when Perdican's advances toward Camille are
thwarted. His desires are deflected in the direction of
Rosette where they dissolve in frustration. Then, he
rebounds to Camille and the next "ricochet" takes effect. This dynamics is made apparent upon the reunion
of Perdican and Camille. Rebuffed by his cousin who
refuses a kiss and an invitation to take a walk, Perdican
goes alone to the village. The unreflected quality of
Perdican's "ricochet" from Camille to Rosette is illustrated by his trance-like state of mind the morning
after his argument with Camille on religion: "Où vais-je
donc?—Ah! je vais au village" (3, 1). The kiss intended
for Camille is given to Rosette who is identified by the
chorus: "C'est Rosette, la sœur de lait de votre cousine
Camille" (1, 4). A few lines later, Perdican links the
two women in his inquiry: "Ta sœur Camille est ar-
rivée. L'as-tu vue?" Similarly, Perdican defends his
kisses: "Quel mal y trouves-tu? Je t'embrasserais devant ta mère. N'es-tu pas la sœur de Camille? ne suis-je
pas ton frère comme je suis le sien?" (2, 3). Perdican's
confused images of the two women points to the level
of rich psychological meaning in *On ne badine pas
avec l'amour.*

Structurally, the "ricochet" effect is based upon the
commonplace of a romantic triangle, but it establishes a
trajectory whose terminal points constitute bipolarities.
A confluence of meanings—temporal, spatial, psycho-

logical, and philosophic—is associated with each set of
points. When traumatized by Camille's transformed
personality and her concomitant rejection of him, Perdican is forced to redefine himself. Upon returning to his
country estate after completion of doctoral studies in
Paris, he appears to journey back into time in the search
of enduring values.[4] Perdican finds his emotional roots
among the peasants of the village. There, in spite of his
ten-year absence, he retrieves his ideal self in the eyes
of those who, less corrupted and blinded by prejudice
and social rank, see him both as child and man: "Que
Dieu te bénisse enfant de nos entrailles! Chacun de
nous voudrait te prendre dans ses bras; mais nous sommes vieux, monseigneur, et vous êtes un homme (1, 4).
Moreover, the peasants take joy in the reunion of a
loved one, without regard to his legal status as inheri-
tor, and liken his return to a rebirth: "Votre retour est
un jour plus heureux que votre naissance. Il est plus
doux de retrouver ce qu'on aime que d'embrasser un
nouveau-né."

Chateau and village, present and past, form a temporal-
spatial network around which Perdican careens in his
"ricochets" from Camille to Rosette. Foster sisters,
playmates, beautiful young women, such images overlap
in the troubled mind of Perdican. Rebounding from a
cold, critical Camille, he finds not only Rosette but a
reflection of his cousin in the past. However, on one occasion, the illusion becomes translucent to Perdican. He
is moved by the reflection of his memories in Rosette,
the village folk, and the setting, but he is also disconsolate because of their meaninglessness for Camille. The
contrast strikes a painful emotional chord, and Perdican
mourns the past, as Rosette naively observes: "Regardez donc, voilà une goutte de pluie qui me tombe sur la
main, et cependant le ciel est pur (2, 3). He begs
Rosette's pardon, but she does not understand: "Que
vous ai-je fait, pour que vous pleuriez?". The fault is
not hers but that of Perdican who seeks the impossible,
the unification of the past and the present, the village
and the chateau in the recaptured joy and innocence of
childhood.

The bipolar structure of the plot has a parallel psychological component that provokes Perdican's "ricochets"
and promotes game playing. He sees in himself a
continuum from the past to the present, a child in the
man. However, Maître Bridaine views him as a learned
doctor; the Baron suspects him of seducing "les filles
du village en faisant des ricochets"; Camille regards
him as an experienced man of the world (1, 5). In
confessing a number of love affairs and in rejecting the
sanctity of marriage, Perdican gives evidence of a
double identity. He is a libertine (philosopher-seducer)
and a Romantic hero (lover-child). This principle of
characterization, *dédoublement,* is manifested by oscillation and ambiguity and renders self-knowledge problematic.[5] The same psychological principle motivates
Camille. In addition to being a lover-child, she is a
coquette (casuisttease) in the tradition of Molière's

Célimène but with a premature *pruderie*. Their double identities, libertine/lover and coquette/lover, expose the childlike qualities of Perdican and Camille and verify the extent to which, despite appearances, they are indeed cousins. At crucial moments in the conflict, each doubts not only the sincerity of the other but is unsure also of his own feelings. Because of this inherent instability, psychology in *On ne badine pas avec l'amour* cannot serve as a vantage point from which to elucidate its dramatic structure. The motifs of *ricochets* and *jeu* derive their meaning from the philosophic substance of the play.

Game playing and its preparatory stage of unreflected trajectory, *i.e.*, *ricochets,* along the chateau-village circuit (in its spatial, temporal, and psychological dimensions) can hardly be understood without recourse to ideology in general and to Rousseauist doctrine in particular. Structural bipolarity in *On ne badine pas avec l'amour* corresponds to the ideological opposition between art and nature. Introduced at the opening of the play, it provides the philosophic touchstone upon which all successive actions are judged. The joint arrivals of Maître Blazius and Dame Pluche oppose corpulence, fresh wine, and good cheer to sterility, vinegar, and piety. This opposition of nature and anti-nature, reinforced by stylistic effects, evokes a positive and a negative reaction from the peasant chorus and is continued in the movements of Camille and Perdican. For example, after refusing to kiss Perdican, Camille turns her back to him and focuses on an object which encompasses her values—a portrait of a great aunt devout and never married: "Oh! oui, une sainte! c'est ma grand-tante Isabelle. Comme ce costume religieux lui va bien" (1, 2). In contrast, Perdican lingers before a pot of flowers which he appreciates solely for its beauty and scent and he subsequently waxes lyrical: "Voilà donc ma chère vallée! mes noyers, mes sentiers verts, ma petite fontaine" (1, 4). Not only are the cousins situated in the opposite worlds of nature and art, color symbolism places Rosette and Camille at opposite ends of affectivity. Rosette's name promises passion, fecundity, and spontaniety while Camille's name conveys cold purity, sterility, and contrivance.[6]

Bipolarity—structural, psychological, and philosophic—creates the tension necessary to dramatic conflict and opens the possibility of a reconciliation of opposites in the union of lovers. Steps in this direction are taken in a site where past and present, village and chateau, nature and art converge—"à la petite fontaine." In the first fountain scene, Perdican remains on the "ricochet" projectory of uncalculated movement from chateau to village. Although Camille operates on the level of *jeu* (in the sense that her actions are premeditated, that she wears a mask and has set the stage), the outcome of their meeting still offers hope. Perdican reacts truthfully to her queries, and, in the heat of mutual anger but

heartfelt emotions, she removes her mask to confess a fear of love and its sufferings. The nature principle seems to overcome art, interpreted as deceit and false piety, to promise liberation for her and the possibility of union. However, an event intervenes which removes Perdican from nature and makes him an actor with a mask. Intercepting a secret letter from Camille to Sister Louise, he learns that Camille's conduct had been prearranged so as to deceive him. Feeling victimized by her boasts of having driven him to despair, he promises himself revenge: "je n'ai pas le poignard dans le cœur, et je te le prouverai. Oui, tu sauras que j'en aime une autre avant de partir d'ici" (3, 2).

When pride prevails in Perdican's conduct, he leaves the unmediated level of *ricochets* to compete with Camille on that of *jeu*. The second meeting at the fountain results in the profanation of nature that separates Perdican from the truest part of himself, *l'enfance*, the spiritual source of his being. From the Rousseauist perspective, pride leads to corruption—thought for the purpose of dominance—which makes Perdican liable to evil.[7] Moreover, by imitating Camille's game-playing, he abandons the past, the village, and nature. Morally, Rosette is deserted to become an object of exploitation, the only unmasked and unconscious player of a game which is imposed without her consent.[8] Structurally, the play's bipolar principle becomes so imbalanced in favor of art that any reconciliation of opposites is rendered highly improbable. Resolution of conflict through union would require a miracle.

Once the "game" is set into motion—triggered by fear and unconscious hostility—it escalates through reprisal, denial of aggression through repression, and further emergence in unforseen ways. This spiral of escalating psychological warfare eludes control to threaten the social peace of its community. Two questions emerge from this dilemma, a moral and a pragmatic one: who is at fault and how does one stop the "game"? The first question is broader than the more obvious one: who started the "game"? To this it suffices to reply that the social aspect of games requires that more than one person play. Although Camille is at fault in the first instance, her conduct adheres consistently to the bipolar principles of château and art. Moreover, her free will is severely circumscribed by the negativity of her convent experience. In contrast, Perdican reverses allegiance from nature to art through an apparently free decision, although provoked and made in anger. He defiles the fountain place of his childhood. Although the peasant chorus has nothing positive to say about Camille, its attitude toward Perdican changes from paternal warmth to distrust. The voice of village and nature, a veritable social conscience, sides with Rosette against Perdican who is portrayed no longer as a child returned as a man but as a libertine: "Hélas! la pauvre fille ne sait quel danger elle court en écoutant les discours d'un jeune et galant seigneur" (3, 4).

The theoretical question of culpability and the pragmatic one of stopping the "game" are closely associated. A series of critical moments occurs in the conflict and offers this possibility: Camille's momentary dropping of her mask with the ventilation of anger ("O Perdican! ne raillez pas, tout cela est triste à mourir") which opportunity is thwarted by Perdican's rage (2, 5); the exposure of Perdican's duplicity to Rosette, hidden behind the tapestry, which is misused by Camille to belittle Perdican and to drive him into a marriage which neither wants: "Eh bien! apprends-le de moi, tu m'aimes, entends-tu; mais tu épouseras cette fille, ou tu n'es qu'un lâche!" (3, 6); the meeting of the three in the village where Rosette tries to withdraw by returning her necklace to Perdican. The gesture is accepted by a patronizing Camille but rebuffed by her proud cousin who walks off with Rosette. Shortly thereafter, Camille sends for Perdican but is unable to verbalize her feelings and she retreats: "Non, non—O Seigneur Dieu!" (3, 7). No clear picture of culpability emerges from these missed opportunities. The "game" is out of control.

The failure to stop the "game" serves to elucidate the character traits of Perdican and Camille, but psychoanalysis must yield to philosophy in explaining the improbability of their reconciliation. Three ways of bringing the "game" to a halt come to mind, and two of them apply to the play. They are "return to nature," magnanimous self-sacrifice, and spiritual elevation. Musset adheres faithfully to the Rousseauist inspiration of his thought in **On ne badine pas avec l'amour**. At an abstract level, Perdican and Camille cannot return to the innocent happiness of childhood. They resemble the majority of people in the social state "dont les passions ont détruit pour toujours l'originelle simplicité."[9] In particular, his studies and love affairs in Paris and her indoctrination by forlorn women in the convent condemn the cousins to live in the social state where *paraître,* mask, vanity, and class consciousness prevail.

No synthesis is possible for Perdican between château and village, art and nature, present and past. Camille and Rosette can never become one woman. However, the social state does permit radical reversals in character and conduct. Through the Old Regime system of values propagated by Corneille, a noble person can demonstrate a generosity of such magnitude as to elicit a corresponding self-sacrifice of ego on the part of one's opponent, albeit a lover. Unfortunately, the nobility of Perdican and Camille remains on the level of *orgueil* rather than *fierté.* For example, in their argument on religion and love, Perdican warns Camille: "Tu es une orgueilleuse; prends garde à toi" (2, 5). Likewise, she charges him with pridefulness in the exposure of his lies to Rosette:

"Je m'étais vantée de t'avoir inspiré quelque amour, de te laisser quelque regret. Cela t'a blessé dans ton noble orgueil?" (3, 6). Hence, their noble pride impedes their rising above roles in a childish but fatal game, a microcosm of a corrupt social state.

Since the bipolar world of Perdican does not offer resolution either through a "return to nature" or noble magnanimity, he has no recourse but withdrawal in despair or transcendence of the conflict through spiritual elevation. His communal confession in the chapel of the chateau removes the psychological obstacle to the union of adversaries. He rises above his role: "Orgueil, le plus fatal des conseillers humains, qu'es-tu venu faire entre cette fille et moi?" (3, 7). Tragic irony brings the libertine to his knees in prayer at the end of the play while the would-be nun finds herself unable to pray. The lie of her vocation is made manifest while Perdican's "sentiment de la nature" is shown to have a spiritual foundation, in true Rousseauist fashion. This revelation of truth exacts a price greater than the personal pain of humiliation. Instead of purging their pride through commitment in full responsibility for their actions, Perdican and Camille sacrifice a third party. Rosette witnesses their reconciliation and dies. Separated from village and nature through their game-playing, she is also cut off from the world of the château and art. Deprived of her place in life, she falls prey also to a fictitious temporality, Perdican's desire to unite past and present, and Camille's dissolution of the future through fear.

The question of culpability proceeds to the forefront. Camille is rendered silent before her god and returns to the convent. Her increasing isolation toward the end of the play foretells her fate, the regret of love lost and never enjoyed. At the same time, Perdican imagines blood on his hands. In a patriarchal society where young men are free to be educated and have experiences, while young women are protected, he bears the responsibility of opening up life to Camille with patient persuasion and sensitivity. Unfortunately, he forfeited the possibility of playing the role of preceptor-lover in the manner of Rousseau's Saint-Preux. He takes the initiative in their debate only to overpower Camille by his intellectual, secularized view of the world. The idealism of love ("mais il y a au monde une chose sainte et sublime, c'est l'union de ces êtres si imparfaits et si affreux") is not made accessible to the young novice (2, 5). Perdican makes an ideological point and spurns his would-be student ("Adieu, Camille, retourne à ton couvent") just when she starts to open up: "J'ai eu tort de parler; j'ai ma vie entière sur les lèvres." Literary tradition has Perdican returning to a libertine life in Paris. However, having known love and with a guilt accentuated by an awakened spirituality, he seems destined to be lonely and misunderstood in the world.

The motif of game playing, of consciously assuming a role, culminates in Musset's ***Lorenzaccio*** and reflects the alienation of Romantic writers from postrevolutionary France.[10] The play ends with confessions for sins wrought by "des enfants gâtés" and "deux enfants insensés," an image used in his description of a lost generation, ***La Confession d'un enfant du siècle*** (1836). The pervasive guilt and sense of perdition at the ending to ***On ne badine pas avec l'amour*** would seem to reflect the cosmology of sin without redemption.[11] If institutions and sexual roles constitute secondary factors in social disharmony, its primary cause is found in a human nature made defective by pridefulness, a principle of social fragmentation and self-alienation. However, the images of *jeu* and *ricochets* reflect a dialectic beyond despair. Implicit in ***On ne badine pas avec l'amour*** and explicit in Musset's lyrical poetry, the cure for *orgueil* comes from a commitment to life through love and brave acceptance of suffering in-the-world without transcendence.[12] The interplay of pride and love as a closing and opening to life is set forth by Musset as a Romantic social pact in the final stanza of "La Nuit d'août" (1836):

> Dépouille devant tous l'orgueil qui te dévore,
> Cœur gonflé d'amertume et qui t'es cru fermé.
> Aime, et tu renaîtras; fais-toi fleur pour éclore;
> Après avoir souffert, il faut souffrir encore;
> Il faut aimer sans cesse, après avoir aimé.

Notes

1. Musset, *Théâtre I* (Paris: Garnier-Flammarion, 1964), p. 298. All quotations refer to this edition and are indicated by act and scene.

2. See David Sices, "Multiplicity and Integrity in *On ne badine pas avec l'amour*," *French Review*, 43 (1969-70), 443-51, and Robert Lorris, "Le Côté de Perdican et le côté de Camille," *Australian Journal of French Studies*, 8 (1971), 3-14.

3. See M. Crouzet, "Jeu et sérieux dans le théâtre de Musset," *Journées d'Études sur Alfred de Musset* (Clermont-Ferrand: SER Faculté des Lettres, 1978), p. 35, who characterizes *le jeu* as: "un déchirement manichéen qui est sans doute la métaphysique générale du romantisme. . . . Le jeu est le négatif d'un sérieux absolu, le détour par le néant qui affirme l'absolu de l'homme."

4. See the thesis of David Sices, p. 447.

5. See Jean-Pierre Richard, *Etudes sur le romantisme* (Paris: Editions du Seuil, 1970), p. 208.

6. See Pierre Gastinel, *Le Romantisme d'Alfred de Musset* (Paris: Hachette, 1937), p. 424, who stresses Rosette's incarnation of nature and adds: "Ne reconnaît-on pas là l'influence de Rousseau vers qui Sand a ramené Musset pour un temps?"

7. See Rousseau's "Discours sur l'inégalité" in *Du Contrat social* (Paris: Garnier, 1962), p. 68. Rousseauist pride is not to be confused with the Christian admonition to humility. Rousseau identifies "le premier mouvement d'orgueil" as initiating the separation of man from nature; he sees himself as being superior to other species.

8. Metaphorically, Rosette relives the plight of "natural man" who, upon emergence from nature, is forced into a social pact with prescribed roles, none of his choosing and against his will. See James F. Hamilton, *Rousseau's Theory of Literature: The Poetics of Art and Nature* (York, South Carolina: French Literature Publications Co., 1979), p. 83.

9. See Rousseau, p. 105.

10. For recent studies, see Naomi Schorr, "La Pérodie dans *Lorenzaccio*," *Michigan Romance Studies*, 2 (Winter 1981), 73-86, and James F. Hamilton, "Mimetic Desire in *Lorenzaccio*," *Kentucky Romance Quarterly*, in press.

11. See Richard, p. 208, who characterizes Musset's plays as "psychodrames" and perceives in Musset "un vœu secret d'auto-punition."

12. In the moral landscape of Musset, *l'horizontalité* prevails. Transcendence is limited to "l'éternité de chaque moment de vie." See Georges Poulet, *La Distance intérieure II* (Paris: Plon 1952), p. 248.

UN CAPRICE (1840) AND *LA QUENOUILLE DE BERBÉRINE* (1840)

CRITICAL COMMENTARY

Susan McCready (essay date fall 1997)

SOURCE: McCready, Susan. "Performing Stability: The Problem of Proof in Alfred de Musset's *Un Caprice* and *La Quenouille de Barbérine*." *Romance Notes* 38, no. 1 (fall 1997): 87-95.

[*In the following essay, McCready explores prominent themes in two of Musset's plays.*]

A husband is unsure of his wife's fidelity and hatches a scheme to prove that she is unfaithful; a wife worries that her husband is about to stray and enlists the help of her maid to spy on him; a young man promised in marriage to a young woman wants to test her to prove that she will be faithful before he says "I do." Disguises are worn; letters are intercepted; conversations overheard, but in the end, the lovers always recognize each other's true, essential value and are united. This is a standard comic plot: some sort of conflict (a doubt about fidelity) is introduced into a once-stable system (a happy marriage) and the conflict is resolved through "negotiations," which, in the end, uphold the (slightly altered) status quo.[1] The traditional comic resolution eliminates a sometimes sinister indeterminacy, through a performance of stability—usually the promise of the marriage of the young protagonists to the "correct" partner or the reunion of husband and wife. The lovers in such traditional comedies are exemplary figures whose negotiations about fidelity or marriage can be read in general terms as meditations on the collectively imagined value of love, fidelity and marriage in society. The happy resolution of the conflict is a "making real" (to use Elaine Scarry's term) of these abstract values, which are now anchored for the audience in the theatrical performance and for the characters by some performance *within* the play.

Elaine Scarry shows in *The Body in Pain* how anxieties about indeterminacy (what she calls "unanchored claims"—such as the claim of the realness of God) lead to the complex, collective psychological project of *analogical verification,* which consists of anchoring those claims in a physical body and usually in physical pain. For example, according to Scarry, in the Old Testament, scenes of wounding are meant to substantiate, to "make real" the existence of God; the marks on the bodies of the Israelites are to be read as "proof" of the power of God, who has no body. This process is what "grounds" the claim of God's realness, a claim on which an entire social order is based. We can also see this process at work in the theater, in plays in which the conflict centers on the need to prove something (and in comedies it is often love or fidelity that is in question). The need for *physical* evidence (of love, of fidelity) drives the action of the play until the characters are satisfied, and in plays in the most traditional mode, satisfaction comes only with the happy marriage (performed or renewed) of the protagonists. At the same time, the play itself serves the function of analogical verification for its audience, whose unanchored claims about love and fidelity are embodied in the physical performance of the play.[2]

Many of Musset's plays conform to this basic structure as characters rehearse a variety of strategies to arrive at some sort of "proof." The strategies are the traditional comic devices such as secret, disguise (and recognition), and *dédoublement,* which at first heighten the indeterminacy (and the comic effect). In the end, however, the negotiation of values played out in these strategies reaches a resolution, a collective agreement about

value(s) which (re)stabilizes the system. Thus artificial indeterminacy (disguise, etc.) is a pretext to a performance of stability.[3] In his *Confession d'un enfant du siècle,* Musset as social critic suffers precisely from his "contemporary indeterminacy," a malaise, which according to Musset is endemic to his rudderless generation as it drifts between the past and the future. He describes the situation of the French youth in the 1830s thus:

> . . . derrière eux un passé à jamais détruit, s'agitant encore sur ses ruines, avec tous les fossiles des siècles d'absolutisme; devant eux l'aurore d'un immense horizon, les premières clartés de l'avenir; et entre ces deux mondes . . . quelque chose de semblable à l'Océan qui sépare le vieux continent de la jeune Amérique . . . le siècle présent, en un mot, qui sépare le passé de l'avenir, qui n'est ni l'un ni l'autre et qui ressemble à tous deux à la fois, et où l'on ne sait à chaque pas qu'on fait, si l'on marche sur une semence ou sur un débris.

(Prose 85)

Un Caprice and *La Quenouille de Barbérine,* two comedies from the 1830s are both meditations on this indeterminacy and attempts to establish new exchange values through which the individual and the society might become "grounded" once more.

Both of these plays (and several others in Musset's œuvre) embody concerns about exchange, value, and power, but they do so within a system that presents the value of marriage and fidelity as a given. While the fidelity of specific characters may be put into question in some of these plays, the value of fidelity is always agreed upon in the happy ending which (re)unites husband and wife. Certainly the most well-known of these comedies is *Un Caprice,* a one-act play in eight scenes. First published in 1837, *Un Caprice* had a successful run at the Théâtre-Français beginning in 1847 and has been one of Musset's most performed plays ever since. *Un Caprice* is particularly illuminating as it opens with the proof of conjugal devotion (the purse Mathilde is making for her husband) and the proof of adultery (the *other,* "counterfeit" purse accepted by the husband from another woman). The rest of the play is a series of manipulations that will "set things right" again, negotiating an agreement about the essential value of fidelity.

The opening scene of *Un Caprice* finds Mme Chavigny (Mathilde) placing the finishing touches on a red purse she has made in secret as a surprise for her husband. Urged on by affection for her husband and her fear of losing him to another, Mathilde plans to offer the purse to her husband as a mark of her own fidelity. She has worked in secret, she explains, to avoid the appearance of a reproach: "Cela aurait eu l'air de lui dire: 'Voyez comme je pense à vous' . . . tandis qu'en lui montrant mon petit travail fini, ce sera lui qui se dira que j'ai pensé à lui." (***Théâtre*** 422). She goes on to address an affectionate apostrophe to the purse in which it becomes clear that the real value of the purse is not in any intrinsic worth as an object, but in its offering. "Pauvre petite! tu ne vaux pas grand-chose, on ne te vendrait pas deux louis. Comment se fait-il qu'il me semble triste de me séparer de toi!" (***Théâtre*** 422). In fact, Mathilde has great difficulty in separating herself from the purse. Not only is she already clearly projecting her identity onto the purse, confounding herself psychologically with it,[4] but the act of offering the purse will be physically deferred and finally performed only through the mediation of Mme de Léry.

The first obstacle to offering the purse comes from Mathilde herself, who has not finished it when her husband enters. He proudly (one might say sadistically) displays another purse, a blue purse given to him as a gift. Mathilde's friend and confidante Mme de Léry then enters and immediately identifies the author of the blue purse as a Mme de Blainville, confirming Mathilde's suspicions. Mme de Léry's teasing remarks about the purse show a clear continuity with Mathilde's attitude toward her own purse. That is, here, a purse is not just a purse. "On a mis sept ans à la faire et vous jugez si pendant ce temps-là elle a changé de destination. Elle a appartenu en idée à trois personnes de ma connaissance. C'est un vrai trésor que vous avez là" (***Théâtre*** 426). While the specific item exchanged is not necessarily meaningful, the exchange itself has meaning within the societal context.[5] In this case, the exchange is inscribed in the courtly tradition of the love token, in which accepting a gift or wearing clothing in the lover's color is part of a "code" which signifies the lovers' constancy (or infidelity). Both Mme de Léry and Mathilde (and presumably Mme de Blainville) immediately understand this, but Chavigny refuses to accept the purse's "meaning." He makes much of Mathilde's nonsensical question on first seeing the purse: "De quelle couleur est-elle?" (***Théâtre*** 425). But, in fact, in the context of the courtly code, the color signifies the purse's author and so to ask "What color is it?" is really to ask "Who gave it to you?" Chavigny likewise sees (or claims to see) only nonsense in Mathilde's displeasure that he should display the purse in public, replying "La montrer! Ne dirait-on pas que c'est un trophée?" Of course, that is precisely what it is: the purse represents his (imminent) conquest of Mme de Blainville and his denial of this fact makes his intentions all the more clear. When Mathilde begs Chavigny to give up the blue purse, the subtext is just as clear, but he again refuses, preferring to take everything literally in order to deny its signification.

It is Mme de Léry who, once apprised of the situation between the spouses, is able to turn Chavigny's refusal against him. She has Mathilde's purse presented to him

anonymously, then teases him to guess its author. This time, it is she who remains (at least in appearance) in the realm of the literal as Chavigny (convinced that the purse is a gift from Mme de Léry, herself) attempts to seduce her. In an inversion of his earlier scene with Mathilde, Chavigny begs to know who made the red purse, then gladly exchanges the blue one for it. The exchange made, Mme de Léry reveals that the red purse was made by Mathilde. With this moment of recognition everything falls back into place: Chavigny now understands the true value of Mathilde's love and plans to confess his faults to her and in so doing to restore conjugal felicity.

Musset's 1849 verse play ***Louison*** follows a similar storyline, in which a would-be unfaithful husband is corrected through a series of substitutions, and when the dust settles, rediscovers the true value of his faithful wife. Neither comedy ever puts into serious question the "value" of fidelity; rather in both cases the husband simply needs to be reminded of it. In ***La Quenouille de Barbérine,*** first published in 1835, the *value* of a wife's fidelity is so evident that Ulric wagers "tout ce qu['il] possède sur terre" (***Théâtre*** 313) on Barberine's fidelity. In this case, her fidelity must be (and, of course, is) proven, but its worth is made explicit. In the 1851 play ***Bettine,*** the unfaithful fiancé Steinberg uses the *appearance* of Bettine's infidelity as a pretext to break their engagement, after she has sacrificed all of her belongings to pay his debts. He determines value only in economic terms, and since Bettine is no longer able to support him financially, she is no longer of value to him. Her abandonment leads Bettine in turn to recognize the true worth of the Marquis, her erstwhile suitor, and the play concludes with their happy marriage. Again, value is not put into question; it only needs to be recognized.[6]

In ***Un Caprice,*** the obstacle to Chavigny's recognition of Mathilde's value is his own desire to have it both ways. In refusing to admit that his having accepted a purse from Mme de Blainville "means" anything, he is able to keep both possibilities (fidelity or infidelity) in play. He is able to do this because he himself is not engaged in the exchanges taking place. We have spoken of the purse as an "arbitrary object" in the system of exchange, but in the realm of literature it is anything but arbitrary. As a metonymy for the woman who offers it, the purse has obvious sexual connotations and becomes the object of "analogical verification" of which Elaine Scarry speaks. Not only, as we have seen, do the two purses "make real" certain claims (Mathilde's stands for fidelity, while Mme de Blainville's stands for proof of infidelity), they illustrate the power imbalance inherent in the relationships of the characters. That is, they stand for the radical embodiment of the women as opposed to the un-embodied power of Chavigny who is able to refuse their signification as long as it is convenient because he is not himself embodied in the exchange. Scarry opposes the vulnerable, physical body to the powerful, un-embodied voice, and so it is no surprise if here the power exercised by the un-embodied Chavigny is discursive.

When in her scene iv confrontation with her husband, Mathilde falls on her knees to beg him to give up the blue purse (intending, unbeknownst to Chavigny, to replace it with the red one), the engagement of her body in this action exemplifies the degree to which she is already physically engaged in the exchange of the purses. Chavigny's reply and his immediate exit demonstrate his power; he is able to enforce his will discursively by naming Mathilde's action "un enfantill-age" (***Théâtre*** 430) and physically by cutting off all discussion in leaving. In a way, Chavigny is already absent before his exit as he is not really "in" the negotiation that Mathilde is attempting to operate. In scene viii, the analogous scene between Chavigny and Mme de Léry, the power imbalance is corrected. This time, Mathilde is physically absent from the stage (although metonymically figured in the presence of the red purse) and acting only as her proxy, Mme de Léry is not herself implicated in the exchange she success-fully operates; that is, she is all voice. In contrast, Chav-igny goes through a process of "embodiment" over the course of the scene, as Mme de Léry (by withholding the name of the author of the red purse) is able to reverse the power dynamic of the earlier scene. Chav-igny, himself, begs on bended knee to know the name of his admirer, as Mathilde had done earlier.

When Mme de Léry destroys the blue purse, however, the exchange is not complete, since Chavigny believes that Mme de Léry is the author of the red purse. Another substitution must be made before Chavigny recognizes his error. Significantly, the correction is discursive. As Chavigny had done earlier with Mathilde, after a scene peppered with verbal sparring, Mme de Léry simply states the literal facts: "Si vous trouvez que Mathilde a les yeux rouges, essuyez-les avec cette petite bourse que ses larmes reconnaîtront, car c'est votre bonne, brave et fidèle femme qui a passé quinze jours à la faire" (***Théâtre*** 448). Turning his own discursive strategy against him, Mme de Léry forces Chavigny to recognize the significance of the situation he himself created. The resolution, the return of Mathilde and Chavigny's pledge to tell her of his attempted seduction of her friend, underscores the importance of discourse in this play and in systems of exchange in general. Here word-play can be used to create a sort of indeterminacy (as in the failed seduction of Mme de Léry) or it can be used to diffuse indeterminacy by a cold statement of fact.

La Quenouille de Barbérine presents an even clearer example of the double use of discourse and the power imbalance of embodiedness vs. un-embodiedness. Here a young knight, Rosemberg, wagers that Ulric's wife Barbérine will be unfaithful during his absence. Infuri-ated by this slander and sure of his wife's fidelity, Ulric accepts the wager and Rosemberg journeys to Ulric's chateau to attempt to seduce Barbérine. From the outset, Rosemberg is "all voice"; his only proof of Barbérine's faithlessness is the commonplace "on dit" about the faithlessness of all women. "Je n'ai pas médit d'une femme," he explains, "j'ai exprimé mon opinion sur toutes les femmes en général" (***Théâtre*** 312). But like Chavigny, Rosemberg will undergo an embodying transformation, as the wise Barbérine pretends to be seduced in order to administer a particularly humiliat-ing punishment to Rosemberg: imprisoned in her tower, he is forced to spin to earn his board. "Si vous voulez boire et manger, vous n'avez d'autre moyen que de faire comme les vieilles femmes qui gagnent leur vie en prison, c'est-à-dire de filer. Vous trouverez une que-nouille et un rouet tout préparés dans cette chambre" (***Théâtre*** 322). Barbérine, speaking from off-stage is now all voice and all powerful. At her mercy is Rosem-berg who falls prey to his own bodily need for food and is forced to spin. Foregrounded in this play is, of course, the issue of gender: Rosemberg's punishment is humiliating because he is not only embodied (made vulnerable) but feminized.

While discourse seems to be a sort of double-edged sword, what Scarry refers to as something that is both a tool and a weapon, in this play there is always an external, verifiable truth to which discourse refers. In ***Un Caprice,*** under the watchful eye of Mme de Léry, husband and wife are reunited. The essential superiority of Mathilde is recognized, as is the essential value of fidelity. The same is true of the other plays we have mentioned: they are all about coming "to terms"[7] in dif-ferent relationships, but they all rely on artifice (play-acting, disguise) within the play to arrive successfully at their ends. As we have seen, the *mises en scène* manufactured by the characters within the plays cor-respond narrowly to an essentially unquestioned (though temporarily challenged) "real," which is the value they are "proving" ("embodying," "substantiating," "demonstrating") and whose proof makes its self-perpetuation possible.

Notes

1. This is basically the plot of Marivaux's *L'Epreuve* and *Le Jeu de l'amour et du hasard,* among oth-ers, but it is not limited to comedy. It is also the plot of *A Winter's Tale* and Chaucer's clerk's tale (which is Perrault's "Griselidis") and with the minor variation of an unhappy ending (in which the value of the spouse is recognized too late) becomes the basic plot of *Othello.*

2. Anne Ubersfeld has shown convincingly that the spectator of a theatrical performance does not simply "believe in" the reality of what is enacted

on stage, but undergoes a complex negotiation to discern the referential relationship of *two* real spaces, that of the concrete ("real") space of the stage and that of quotidian reality, "celui où s'exerce son action, celui où il n'est pas spectateur" (Ubersfeld 11).

3. Albert Smith has nonetheless argued convincingly that at least in *Les Caprices de Marianne,* Musset subverts this traditional comic structure, and transforms it into something new and distinctly Romantic precisely by refusing to banish all instability. The same might also be said for other plays in Musset's œuvre, in which comedy and tragedy share the stage, either through comic structure turned tragic, or, as in *La Nuit vénitienne,* tragic conflict diffused into masked comedic gaiety.

4. For example, after failing to present the purse to him, Mathilde is about to throw it on the fire and then stops herself and addressing the purse says: "Mais qu'as-tu fait? . . . Il n'y a pas de ta faute; tu attendais, tu espérais aussi" (*Théâtre* 431). She is clearly projecting her own intentions onto the purse.

5. I follow Marcel Mauss's analysis in his "Essai sur le don," in which the gift's importance lies not in the object itself but in its contextualized function as "total social fact." Of course, in the case of *Un Caprice,* the choice of a purse is not arbitrary, but deeply significant, as we will see.

6. We might compare this to the typical fairy tale, in which virtue is hidden or not recognized (Perrault's "Peau d'âne" is an example) until some especially virtuous prince or king reveals the true identity of the mistreated heroine. As in the plays we are discussing, virtue or value is a "given" but appearance is deceiving (sometimes intentionally so) and it can be mistaken. Usually in fairy tales it is an authority figure who "sets things right." We should remark that in the more "psychologized" theater of Musset, it is often up to the individual to recognize his/her mistake and to make amends.

7. This is perhaps clearest in *Bettine,* which opens with the arrival of the *notaire* with marriage contracts for Bettine and Steinberg ready. By the end of the play, after having been put off on several occasions, he will be invited to stay and preside over the signing of marriage contracts by Bettine and the Marquis.

Works Cited

Mauss, Marcel. "Essai sur le don," in *Sociologie et anthropologie,* Paris: Presses Universitaires Français, 1973.

Musset, Alfred de. *Œuvres complètes en prose,* Paris: Gallimard, 1951.

————. *Théâtre complet,* Paris: Gallimard, 1990.

Scarry, Elaine, *The Body in Pain,* New York: Oxford University Press, 1985.

Smith, Albert. "Musset's *Les Caprices de Marianne:* A Romantic Adaptation of a Traditional Comic Structure," *Nineteenth Century French Studies,* Vol. 20 No. 1-2 (1991-2 Fall-Winter): 53-64.

Ubersfeld, Ane. "Notes sur la dénégation théâtrale," in Régis Durand (ed.) *La Relation théâtrale,* Lille: Presses Universitaires de Lille, 1980.

CARMOSINE (1850)

CRITICAL COMMENTARY

David Sices (essay date 1974)

SOURCE: Sices, David. "*Carmosine*: The Myth Turned Fairy Tale." In *Theater of Solitude: The Drama of Alfred de Musset,* pp. 221-40. Hanover, N.H.: The University Press of New England, 1974.

[*In the following excerpt, Sices examines the mythic quality of Musset's own life and compares it to some of the themes in his dramatic works.*]

The period of Alfred de Musset's life extending from 1836, the date of **Il ne faut jurer de rien,** to 1857, the year of his death, is a rich source of insight into the psychology of the artist—rich particularly in sentimental adventures of striking intensity and number. This is the side of Musset which attracted innumerable biographers for a half-century or more following Musset's death. Even the physical decline of the author has been chronicled by the literary doctors (or men of medical letters) who flourish in France as nowhere else. It is a period of immense interest to those who study the psychopathology of the creative mind. Musset's sentimental adventures, with their invariably unhappy conclusion, are complexly interwoven with his physical ills—the alcoholism and "aortic insufficiency" which led to his premature death at age forty-seven—and the remarkable alteration of his literary talent which, after the initial decline in quality from 1835 to 1838, permitted him to continue producing works of a lesser order until shortly before his death. The pathetic quality of this misspent life remains a source of fascination and conjecture. What might Musset's talents have become had he not squandered the moral resources of his youth?

Yet Musset's life seems unusually "true" in a mythic sense to the themes of his greatest literary works. Coelio, Octave, Perdican, and Lorenzo confront us with the idea of decline as a necessary function of life and human time. Andrea del Sarto, the artist as failure, gave evidence of Musset's precocious fascination with the question asked by Robert Frost's "Oven-Bird": "What to make of a diminished thing?" Musset's short story, "The Son of Titian," took up the theme once again in 1838, and turned it into a symbolic introduction to the poet's declining years. Having produced a perfect portrait of his mistress, Tizianello, second son of the great painter, bids farewell to art for the rest of his life. Musset seems to have found in this legend an idealization of his own obsessions: the praise of laziness, the renunciation of art for love, the premature fruition of a promise never fulfilled thereafter. Details of the plot (for example, an embroidered purse given the artist by his mistress, which also appeared in **Un Caprice**) indicate that this story was intended to some degree as an *apologia* to Aimée d'Alton, the life-long caretaker of his literary estate who, having been Musset's mistress and later his friend, even went so far as to wed the poet's brother Paul in order to continue the task of editing Alfred's works and bringing his plays to production after his death. A suitable conclusion, it might be said, for one of Musset's short stories.

What seemed in the dramatic works of 1833-34 to represent the ultimate pathos of life—the survival of the body following the spirit's death—became daily reality for Musset after 1840. Gustave Flaubert's succinct formula is perhaps the best summation of his life: "Musset will have been a charming youth, and then an old man."[1] The cruel terseness of this remark is deepened by our knowledge of Musset's own feelings. As Pierre Gastinel said, "I know of no adolescent who carried farther than he did the hatred of grey hair and wrinkled faces."[2] Although Musset did not live long enough to grow truly old (he seems to have done everything within his power short of suicide to prevent it), what could the fading of his youthful talent, vigor, and beauty have been for him but premature senility, painfully accentuated by the limp and stiffness, the series of debilitating illnesses, which beset his latter years? From 1840 on, Musset could no longer delude himself about the direction his health was taking. The carefree prodigality with which he had always flung himself into excess began to take a toll on his body and spirit, leaving him exhausted where once he had sprung back. "These failings lead him to ask a painful question: is his youth disappearing? For after all, isn't it one of the signs by which a man recognizes the approach of old age, no longer to be able to commit the follies one used to allow oneself,

to feel ceaselessly one's body protesting, through some ache or pain? The idea haunts Musset's spirit . . . In his eyes, didn't life end with youth?"[3] All his biographers agree that Musset's thirtieth birthday seems to have affected the poet's spirits in the way the fortieth or fiftieth does most men. The poetic texts of the period testify to it—most of all the celebrated sonnet "Tristesse," of 1840. "I have lost my force and my life / And my friends and my joy; / I have even lost the pride / That made men believe in my genius." Even the prose fiction which Musset ground out reluctantly to earn a living contains frequent hints of the author's distress, a bitterness which his dislike of this work unconsciously enhanced. The conclusion Musset gives in his short story "Frédéric et Bernerette" to an affair he had recently passed through is evidence of a frame of mind that rarely left him for long in his latter years: "I have been told that after reading [Bernerette's] letter, Frederick came close to committing a desperate act. I will not speak of it here; the indifferent all too often find reason for ridicule after such acts, when a man survives. The world's judgments are sad on this point; he who attempts to die is laughed at, and he who dies is forgotten." The cruel irony of survival, associated with the indignities of age, was to remain a source of pain to the end of his days.

Yet this period of the author's life was far from sterile in the ordinary sense of the word. He added a considerable number of works to the list of his publications, in practically every genre that he had previously explored: poetry, prose fiction, essay, drama. Musset's legendary *paresse*, which those who loved and respected him kept exhorting him to end, seems to reflect disappointed expectation on their part more than the statistical evidence of his creation. Those who awaited another masterpiece were treated only to rare satisfactions of a lesser order: the poems "Souvenir" (1841) and "Sur trois marches de marbre rose" (1849); two or three of the short stories collected in 1854 under the title *Contes;* the plays **Il faut qu'une porte soit ouverte ou fermée** (1845) and **Carmosine** (1850). The rest is characterized by a deceptive facility—deceptive when we realize how much effort Musset exerted merely to continue producing literary works, for the maintenance of his self-esteem and financial solvency.

These considerations explain to some extent the preoccupation Musset showed for consolidating his literary reputation. The period 1840-57 saw the collection and re-edition of a good part of his works: *Poésies complètes* and **Comédies et Proverbes** in 1840; *Premières poésies* and *Poésies nouvelles* in 1852; the revised **Comédies et Proverbes** in 1854. In 1852, his election to the French Academy presupposes serious campaigning for admission to that august body. If these years did not witness a significant addition to the list of Musset's dramatic works, they were marked by several periods of active theatrical ambition that belied his vow never to return to the scene of his initial fiasco. As early as 1838 he confessed to Aimée d'Alton, then his mistress, a revival of interest in the stage: it may be that the possibility of establishing an enduring bond with her sparked concern for achieving some material success. In 1839 his liaison with the young tragedienne Rachel spurred Musset to begin a regular tragedy in verse, *La Servante du Roi,* which he never terminated, Rachel's initial interest cooling at the same rate as their love affair. It is from this period that his essay "On Tragedy" dates. In it he attempted to define a new basis for the tragic genre, a compromise between the Romantics' rejection of traditional forms and style and the neoclassical tragedy that had stagnated and repeated itself since Racine's time. For his renewal of the genre, he took as epigraph André Chenier's "Sur des pensers nouveaux faisons des vers antiques."[4] Musset's long-standing rebellion against Romantic dogma is evident in these writings. But more than that, his rejection of the original dramatic system which he himself had evolved in his armchair theater is consecrated in them—paradoxically enough because of the theatrical ambition that led to his hope of sharing in the success Rachel momentarily lent to a moribund genre. This hope was rekindled in 1850, when the actress turned briefly back to Musset for a comedy; but nothing concrete emerged from their erratic association.

Musset's absorption by the theater is evident from the series of actresses with whom he was linked during this time by either amorous or professional associations, or both. Madame Allan-Despréaux was the most influential and enduring of these: her correspondence furnishes us with some of the most lucid, sympathetic documentation we have on the poet's mind and actions. This exceptional woman was responsible in great part for Musset's belated success on the stage, since it was she who brought about the production of *Un Caprice* in 1847, at the Comédie-Française, which led to an entire series of successful Musset premieres in the following years. After Madame de Léry, she created the roles of the Marquise in *Il faut qu'une porte soit ouverte ou fermée* (1848), of Jacqueline in the Comédie-Française premiere of *Le Chandelier* (1850), and of the Countess in *On ne saurait penser à tout* (1849). Similarly, the actress Madeleine Brohan was intimately associated with the first production of *Marianne,* in 1851; the role of Lisette in *Louison* (1849), a disappointing verse comedy, was written for her sister, Augustine. An equally ill-advised work, *Bettine,* was written for the young star Rose Chéri; its lack of success seems to have had the side effect of discouraging Rachel from commissioning another comedy from Musset's flagging talent. The concentration of stage works either written or revised for performance between 1848 and 1851, as we can see from the above catalogue, is proof of Musset's surge of hope for his dramatic career. The death of

his ambition can doubtless be traced to the general failure of all his new stage works, as compared with the earlier plays which he had not written for performance.

It is not surprising, given this failure, that the most interesting of Musset's plays from the last period is one he wrote for publication and not for the stage. *Carmosine* was commissioned in 1850 by Louis Véron, publisher of the newspaper *Le Constitutionnel;* it was one of Musset's few important plays not to see the light of day in the *Revue des Deux Mondes.* The circumstances of the writing of *Carmosine* are part of the poet's legend.[5] Véron offered Musset a thousand francs per act for a three- or five-act comedy. The author had already prepared the outline of a play based on Boccaccio's tenth story from the seventh day of the *Decameron.*[6] Since Musset had injured his right hand, he dictated the entire work to his governess, Madame Martellet. Véron was so pleased with it that he insisted on paying for five acts instead of the three Musset wrote; after a contest of generosity, the two men compromised on the figure of four thousand francs. Despite the generous sentiments displayed on both sides, there is something rather depressing about these circumstances which seems in keeping with the qualities of the play itself. No doubt is left in the reader's mind that compared with the great comedies, *Carmosine* is a *pièce de circonstance* that little reflects Musset's deeper emotional or artistic concerns. Despite its sentimentality it has that quality of "objectivity," of dissociation from his life, which Gastinel finds in all Musset's later production:[7] the act of dictation, which gives us one of the poet's only works lacking an autograph manuscript, provides a fittingly symbolic representation of this. Furthermore, Véron's offer, which was far more generous to begin with than any the *Revue des Deux Mondes* had ever been able to make, and his financial surcharge on delivery of the work smack suspiciously of charity, a "benefit performance" for the declining poet. Not a totally disinterested one, of course, since Musset's name still meant something despite the failure of *Louison* and *On ne saurait penser à tout* (an "imitation" of Carmontelle) the previous year, but at least a conscious gesture of solidarity going beyond the normal economic limits of such transactions. Véron is said by Paul de Musset to have been "charmed" by the play Musset handed him. The word is apt for the effect of *Carmosine* on the reader. Certainly no stronger reaction can be generated by the somewhat elaborated adaptation for the stage of Boccaccio's slender original.

The action of the play takes place in Palermo in the thirteenth century. Carmosine, the daughter of Master Bernard, a doctor, and his foolish wife Dame Paque, has fallen in love with Pedro of Aragon, the king of Sicily, whom she saw one day in a tournament. Her father despairs of curing the wasting illness that has since claimed her, and Carmosine is resigned to dying for her impossible love, which she has kept a secret from all around her. Dame Paque is convinced that the girl is pining for Ser Vespasiano, a boastful courtier. Perillo, the young man to whom Carmosine was promised before he left to earn a law degree at Padua, returns from six years' absence to learn of his misfortune. Overhearing the girl's plea to her father not to see him, Perillo sends a letter to Master Bernard freeing him of his obligation: he is going to join the King's armies. Carmosine, feeling death approach, reveals her secret to the troubadour Minuccio and asks him to inform the King of it before she dies. Minuccio meets his old friend Perillo at the palace and decides to help the young couple despite themselves. He tells the King of Carmosine's fatal love, and recites as hers a ballad he has asked the poet Cipolla to compose. Both the King and the Queen are deeply moved. The latter goes to visit Carmosine and speaks in behalf of Perillo, saying that the King desires their marriage. When Pedro himself appears in full regalia, promising to be her knight and wear her colors in exchange for a single kiss, Carmosine accepts Perillo as her husband from his hand.

The plot, it must be admitted, is a bit tenuous—the fault, no doubt, of the even more slender tale from which it is taken. Of course, even Musset's best plays are not particularly distinguished by the richness or originality of their action; that was a quality he willingly left to the journeyman carpenters of the popular theater. But even in its context *Carmosine* is remarkably static and predictable. Once its givens are enunciated, we have a feeling of ceremonial reenactment which goes beyond the fairy-tale atmosphere of its events or the stylization inherent in dramatization of familiar material. Predictability seems to be what the play is about, and the sense of wish fulfillment which dominates its resolution is symptomatic of the moral world in which its characters evolve. Given this atmosphere, the participants in its action have nothing to do but carry out their appointed roles, pending the happy reversal that awaits them. This is particularly true of the two protagonists, whose action in the play is limited to regretting their misfortune and accepting the pain of renunciation until the benevolent forces around them have brought about their union.

It is of course traditional of the fairy-tale genre, to which this play in many ways adheres, that the happy resolution comes from above: not so much from divine or cosmic forces as from the upper strata of the human hierarchy. Here it is the King and the Queen, in their tranquil, elevated harmony, who descend among their subjects to bring health and happiness through union. Musset makes this more than a mere *deus ex machina*: it is part of the moral structure of the entire play. Carmosine has wasted away because of an impossible love, a love aimed far too high even for a girl of her beauty

and character. Her father has tried to cure her with all the art at his command; but he is only a plain-spoken, common man, and medical knowledge is not enough to bring harmony to Carmosine's body and soul. Carmosine's "sin," her departure from the normal aims of a person of her station, has been committed with a good deal of modesty and remorse—indeed, the very source of her ill health is the knowledge of her love's audacity and unreason. But she can be returned to normality only by an intervention from above, which reestablishes her balance by reconciling her with the order of things: a possible love with the King's benediction, and even his promise of token fidelity.

Musset enhances this atmosphere of submissiveness to order imposed from above by attributing the virtues of modesty and resignation to all his sympathetic characters. Master Bernard takes pride in his status as a wealthy physician only to the extent that it permits him to use his riches and science in behalf of his daughter. His failure to accomplish anything for her is a source of mortification, a reminder which he takes very much to heart that he is but an ordinary man. In his eyes, Dame Paque's supreme folly is the social ambition which makes her see Ser Vespasiano, the nobleman who divides his pretentious compliments between mother and daughter, as a possible match for Carmosine. Minuccio, the troubadour, is an interesting example of this process of leveling which affects Musset's characters. It is symptomatic that this "man of art" is nothing so elevated as a poet (even a musician, in the Romantic sense of the term), but rather a minstrel, an amuser. He does not himself set Carmosine's message to the King in verse, but has it done by a professional rimester, Cipolla (who does not appear on stage and is qualified as a pedant). Everything about Minuccio's talent is modest: he finds it impossible to learn the poem by heart in time and renounces his attempt to set it to music, ending by reading the text to the King and Queen (II, 7). His greatest quality, in the judgment of Master Bernard, is not his talent. Replying to Ser Vespasiano's praise of the troubadour's reputation at court (which gives the courtier a pretext for boasting of his own connections), the worthy doctor says:

> Is that so! Well, in my eyes, that is the least of his merits; not that I look down on a good song: nothing goes better at table with a glass of good wine. But more than a clever musician, a troubadour as they say, Minuccio is for me an honest man, a good, old and loyal friend, however young and frivolous he may seem; a devoted friend to our family, the best we have perhaps since the death of Anthony [Perillo's father].
>
> (I, 7)

It appears almost a gesture of self-abasement on Musset's part to treat the artist with such condescension. Implicit in Master Bernard's praise of Minuccio is another surprising rejection of the author's former values: his extolling of the troubadour's "maturity." Minuccio is as worthy as an older man, despite his apparent youth. He has the virtues which the mature prize above all: loyalty, devotion, steadfastness—Master Bernard even goes so far as to say that Minuccio has succeeded to the rank vacated by the death of Perillo's father. This succession is contrary to the deepest tendencies of Musset's youthful theater: virtue there was not something one acceded to in time, it was something time dissolved.

It is this modesty which above all characterizes the two young lovers as well. Carmosine is full of compunction from beginning to end of the play because of her involuntary lack of measure in falling in love with the King. This makes her character sweet and gently appealing, but remarkably monotonous compared with Musset's earlier heroines. Her sending of Minuccio to tell the King of her love is not an attempt at self-satisfaction: Minuccio is supposed merely to inform the monarch, not to accomplish anything more concrete for her. Carmosine goes this far only when convinced of her imminent death, which obviates any vain hope for personal fulfillment. She does not have even that pride, formerly so natural to Musset's heroines, which would make her ridicule Vespasiano's absurd claim to her hand. Instead, she limits herself to paying him no particular attention, emerging from her gentle apathy only enough for an occasional word of cool politeness.

Perillo carries modesty to the point of never actually speaking of his love directly to Carmosine. Despite his appearance as early as the second scene, he refrains from presenting himself to his beloved until the third act; prior to that time he deals entirely through Master Bernard, for fear that his importunity may imperil the girl's health. When the father informs Perillo of Carmosine's illness, he offers to conceal his arrival in the city, to extend the six years' absence which has already seemed so long. When he overhears Carmosine's expression of dismay at the news of his return, he departs with admirable discretion. It is by chance that Carmosine, intercepting Perillo's farewell letter to her father, learns of his despair and his intention to go off to war. Perillo has only one moment, in the second act of the play, in which his self-respect makes him formulate a reproach against his unhappy fate—a fleeting outburst of pride. That comes when he learns from Ser Vespasiano's boasting that he has a rival for Carmosine. But even then his despair is stronger than his anger, and he resigns himself to the absurdity of the courtier's claims:

> Why should I hold it against this stranger, this ridiculous automaton whom God brings across my path? Him or any other, what does it matter? I see in him nothing but Destiny, whose blind instrument he is; I even believe it ought to be so. Yes, it's a most commonplace thing. When a sincere and loyal man is stricken in what he holds most dear, when an irreparable misfortune crushes his force and kills his hopes, when he is mistreated, betrayed, rejected by all around him, almost always, you should note, almost always it is a common lout who deals the final blow, and who, by chance, unwittingly, happening upon the man fallen to the ground, steps on the dagger buried in his heart.

(II, 3)

The rhetoric of these phrases is almost that of Musset's earlier heroes; but in the context it seems ridiculously exaggerated, compared with the moderation displayed by all except the play's one example of overweening pride, Vespasiano. And it must be added that Perillo returns so fully to the paths of modesty that he does not utter a single word in the final scene, when the King and Queen change Carmosine's mind and unite the couple in the bonds of reasonable matrimony.

Perillo's reference to Ser Vespasiano as an automaton, in the speech cited above, immediately raises the question of the *fantoches* in *Carmosine,* as in Musset's earlier comedies. What Perillo has to say about the courtier as a blind instrument of destiny, carrying out the mechanical, unheroic task of destroying the sensitive protagonist, sounds like an abbreviated formulation of what the marionettes stood for: the victory of inhuman fate over human individuals, of the mechanical over the emotional, of time over youth. But there are several elements of this speech and of Vespasiano's function in the play which conflict with what we know of Musset's *fantoches.*

The tone in which Perillo speaks of Ser Vespasiano is something new in the plays we have examined. Although Octave describes Claudio as a "village pedant" (*Marianne,* I, 1) and "an old man who has no more sense, and never had a heart" (II, 3), it is only in passing that he deigns to mention him, as part of his argument in favor of Coelio. Nowhere are the automatons granted such fatal importance by the protagonists as Vespasiano is given by Perillo. This is all the more striking in the light of the courtier's trivial influence in the plot of *Carmosine* compared with *Marianne* or *Fantasio.* Vespasiano, who was invented by Musset to fill out the action of Boccaccio's brief tale, bears a name whose very ludicrousness indicates clearly the sort of character he is. Its echo of the word *vespasienne,* that incongruously pompous title a Roman emperor passed on to the public comfort facilities of Paris, makes it difficult to take him serious as a rival to Perillo.[8] Indeed Perillo's reference to his dire significance has an inverse effect to the one intended: it strikes us as so outlandish, so disproportionate to the simpleton in question, that it makes Perillo himself look rather foolish. We thus have confirmation of our sense that this one hyperemotional speech which Musset puts in the mouth of his moderate, self-effacing hero is meant ironically; it underlines the theme of the beneficial effects of resignation by showing the incongruousness of Perillo's spasmodic revolt.

More than any of Musset's previous grotesques, Vespasiano is evidently intended merely as a comic foil, invented for that purpose. His heavy-handed compliments to Carmosine's addled mother and her ludicrously demure reply are exemplary:

VESPASIANO:

> Would that I might only cleave my heart in two with this dagger, and offer half of it to a person whom I respect . . . I dare not make myself clearer.

DAME PAQUE:

> And I *must* not understand you.

> (I, 7)

The obviousness of Vespasiano's tactics later gives even Carmosine the opportunity to avoid his gallantry with an ironic word: "You are courting my mother, otherwise I was about to ask you to lend me your arm" (III, 2). But all through the play, Vespasiano is the convenient butt of everyone's jokes and insults. When Dame Paque claims that it is he who inspired Carmosine with love at the King's tourney, Master Bernard has an easy time mocking her:

DAME PAQUE:

> Whom would she look for, in the throng, but the people she knows? And what other, amongst our friends, what other than the handsome, the gallant, the invincible Ser Vespasiano?

MASTER BERNARD:

> So much so, that he toppled with his four hooves in the air at the first blow of a lance.

DAME PAQUE:

> It is possible that his horse may have tripped, and his lance was turned aside, I don't deny that; it is possible he may have fallen.

MASTER BERNARD:

> It is most certainly possible; he spun through the air like a top, and he fell, I swear it, just as hard as it is possible.

DAME PAQUE:

> But with what an air he stood up again!

MASTER BERNARD:

> Yes, with the air of a man whose dinner lies heavy on his stomach, and who would much rather remain on the ground. If such a sight is what made my daughter ill, rest assured it wasn't with love.

> (I, 1)

Even the gentle Minuccio turns to ridicule Vespasiano's condescendingly protective attitude toward him by referring to the courtiers as marionettes moved by strings attached to the King's fingers, and including in his enumeration of the puppet figures "the soldiers of fortune, or of chance if you will, whose lance shakes in their hands and whose feet quaver in the stirrups" (I, 8).

Of the *fantoches'* materialism, Vespasiano retains only his interested motives in seeking Carmosine's hand, namely the hope of receiving her considerable dowry and the King's alleged pledge to give him two plots of land on "his wedding-day" (the formula is an obvious way of getting rid of importuners, but Vespasiano has not understood that). Counterbalancing this materialism is the pseudopoetic style that Vespasiano alone cultivates, among all the characters of the play. The courtier's florid eloquence is opposed to Master Bernard's praise of plain language and the simple virtues: it is part of Musset's "de-poetization" of his art, his rejection of the subjective lyricism which characterized his earlier protagonists. In *Carmosine,* poetry is not the matter of vision which the Romantics and their successors believed in. It is strictly a function of that mannerism and cult of form which we associate with a certain stereotype of the medieval court of love: the Sicilian school for example. One of Vespasiano's most exasperating public defeats comes at the hands of the giggling young things who draw him into a typical amorous dispute: "Which is better: the lover who dies of grief at no longer seeing his mistress, or the lover who dies of pleasure on seeing her again?" (II, 6). In the face of their obstinately reiterated shriek—"The one who dies!"—Vespasiano can only sputter his impotent bewilderment and stalk off. Yet it is his pretension to poetic expression that leads him into such humiliations: if he were satisfied to be a simple clod, Musset suggests, there would be nothing seriously wrong with him. *Si tacuisses.* But this is not at all the radical opposition between kinds of life that integrates Musset's earlier puppet figures into their dramatic context. Vespasiano is merely ludicrous, not sinister, alien or menacing. At no time does his suit threaten Perillo's love or the outcome of the play—except perhaps in the young man's mind, and that only for a moment. Vespasiano's function is decorative rather than integral to the action of the play; the mere suggestion that the opposite might be the case is enough to make Perillo ridiculous.

For the real message of *Carmosine* is that everything will turn out for the best, if only we trust to Providence and authority. Vespasiano's mistake, if we were to take him that seriously, would be trying to force that authority by his dogged importunateness, instead of waiting patiently for it to act according to its own superior lights. The mature characters in the play point this out to their impatient or overreaching juniors. Minuccio, who (as we have indicated) is remarkable for his precocious "maturity," illustrates it in his advice to Perillo. Although his words seem at first to reiterate the hymn to passion and suffering in the name of love which Musset sang in his "Nuits," his conclusion is more prudent:

> Your heart has somehow been wounded. Whose has not? I won't tell you to struggle against your grief now, but rather not to attach and chain yourself to it with no hope of return, for a time will come when it will be over. You can't believe that, can you? All right, but remember what I'm going to tell you:—Suffer now if you must, weep if you will, and don't be ashamed of your tears . . . Far from stifling the torment which oppresses you, rend your breast to clear a path for its escape, let it burst forth in sobs, in sighs, in prayers, in threats; but I repeat, do not engage the future! Respect that time which you no longer count on, but which is far wiser than we are, and for a sorrow which must be fleeting, do not prepare the most durable one of all, regret, which renews exhausted suffering and poisons memory!
>
> (II, 2)

In other words, do not do anything rash, which might jeopardize your happiness to come. Play the game of passion for its therapeutic value, but with a calm, appraising eye on your investment in the future. A most reasonable artist this, one who fully justifies Master Bernard's respect! Perillo, who at any rate is a man of law—thus a fairly conservative type at heart—does not go beyond his tirade and his demand of service in the King's armies: a highly indirect form of suicide, which passes through official channels and therefore risks being cut short by official wisdom.

Minuccio's advice is influenced by what he already knows concerning Carmosine's impossible love. He does not underestimate the gravity of her illness, and the serious difficulty which it and its strange cause represent for Perillo's and her happiness. But his "wisdom"—the sagacity born of experience—makes him confident in the outcome of the two lovers' separate appeals to the highest authority, the King. It is true that neither Perillo nor Carmosine approaches him with the intention of resolving their problem by royal fiat, or of receiving direct gratification of their profound desires (which moreover do not coincide): their innate modesty forbids it. But Minuccio, promoting their causes as ambassador to the King, seems to suppose that some such resolution will come, whether or not it takes the form that each of the lovers expects. For as "entrepreneur général" of serenades and "shopkeeper" of love songs (II, 2). Minuccio is a loyal, productive subject who believes completely in his monarch's good offices. Gone are the days when poet and revolutionary were synonymous: this purveyor of lyrics is as solid a bourgeois as any silk merchant or notary.

We are thus immeasurably far from the world of **Lorenzaccio,** both politically and aesthetically. Just as the latter play represents in terms of Florentine history the

political situation of France following the *révolution ratée* of 1830, Carmosine seems to echo in a more dilute and sweetened form the situation of France in 1850 through the Sicily of 1280. Here we have a Pedro of Aragon called to the throne of the Two Sicilies after the Vespers have put an end to the old Angevine monarchy: a dim reflection of the events of 1848 which had deposed the house of Orleans and placed at the head of a short-lived Second Republic that very Louis-Napoleon who was soon to become Emperor Napoleon III. Musset's Pedro seems to be a preshadowing of the latter event—or at least an expression of the poet's desire for it. For Pedro, the recent bloody events (Vespers or Revolution) were intended to restore liberty and internal harmony, not to promote social upheaval. His tirades in the fifth scene of Act II are those of an irate father returning from an absence, to find that his family has been bickering instead of building prosperity:

> Is this unhappy kingdom so accursed of heaven, so inimical to its repose, that it can not keep the peace at home while I carry on war abroad! . . . This one is stirred by pride, that one by greed. They squabble over a privilege, over a jealousy, over a grudge; while all of Sicily calls for our swords, they draw knives over a wheat-field. Is it for this that French blood has been flowing since the Vespers? What was your battle-cry then? Wasn't it liberty and the fatherland? . . . Why did you overthrow a king, if you do not know how to be a people? . . . When a nation has arisen in hatred and in anger, it must lie down again like a lion, in calm and dignity . . . We are all involved, we are all responsible for the bloodbaths of Easter day. We must all be friends, or else risk having committed a crime. I have not come to pluck up Conradin's crown from beneath the scaffold, but to leave my own to a new Sicily . . . If, instead of helping one another, as divine law commands, you disrespect your own laws, by the cross of God I'll remind you of them, and the first one of you who crosses his neighbor's hedge to rob him of a penny, I'll have his head chopped off on the boundary-stone of his field . . .
>
> (II, 5)

Good Queen Constance takes pains to reassure his fearful subjects of Pedro's deep kindness and concern, and to intercede for mercy on their behalf. The King is nonetheless that idol of all bourgeoisies in troubled times, the benevolent despot who will restore order after internal strife, who will consolidate the new liberties for those who can afford to profit by them, by protecting the *status quo* of property and privilege. It is difficult not to see **Carmosine** with the jaundiced eyes of Marxist criticism, so far has Musset departed from that "critical realism" which may be imputed to his earlier works. Here the voice is overwhelmingly *juste-milieu,* middle class and authoritarian-liberal, and justifies one East German critic's despairing commentary on all of Musset's later theater: "It is revealing of the ruling class of the Second French Empire that it quashed the young Musset's 'rebelliousness,' interesting itself in his socially 'uncommitted' plays and giving them its applause."[9] What is true of Musset's successful post-1834 comedies is doubly true of **Carmosine,** which not only turns its back on the poet's earlier revolt, but substitutes a contrary political viewpoint for the one that he abandoned. It would be excessive to say that Pedro of Aragon is a rehabilitation of Cosimo de Medici: the two characters are too different in stature and dramatic significance to justify so facile a comparison. But the political virtues for which Pedro stands in **Carmosine,** and in whose name he exercises a benign and sympathetic influence, are reminiscent of Cosimo's form of "law and order," the praise of harmony as the final aim and the necessary end of revolution.

This political quietism is also reflected on the plane of **Carmosine**'s sentimental action. The young heroine's unreasonable love for her monarch is a sickness that must be cured. If her father's potions are incapable of reestablishing her spiritual and physical order, help must come from above: first from the royal intercessor, the Queen, and then from the ultimate authority, the spirit of sovereignty descended among his common subjects to dispense justice and charity. The religious overtones of this intervention are probably incidental: there is little conscious theological symbolism in Musset's works, and the play is too fragile to support any such interpretation. But the myth of passion in Musset's earlier works is subjected to a curiously inverse dogmatism here: instead of the irresistible power of love which transcends moral and social limits, we find an encroachment of society's norms on the sentimental aspirations of the young hero and, particularly, heroine. Nowhere do we find more than in **Carmosine** the justification of Pierre Gastinel's characterization of the lovers in Musset's later drama: "The sentiment which stirs them is accompanied by such respect that, even when requited, physical desire never speaks loudest; even rejected, they manage to forget themselves . . . They have in common qualities which make us forget their faults: a goodness which would shun playing with another's happiness as a crime, a sincerity which does not hesitate to admit its wrongs; no aggressive pride, no stupid vanity, no selfishness."[10] Gastinel, it is true, considered **Carmosine** to be an exception to the poet's general decline, a return to his earlier manner and vision.[11] Insofar as that vision was intimately related to Musset's emotional viewpoint as formulated by Perdican, however, it does not seem possible to consider the play in this light. Even more than Musset's parlor comedies, **Carmosine** evokes the author's decline, his rejection of the world his youthful ardor had created, *because* it apparently returns to the fantasy and imaginativeness of the earlier works.

In **Carmosine,** the dream of love is resolved by a return to reality. It is the kind and gentle Queen who carries Musset's new message to the lovesick heroine. She cures Carmosine's wasting illness by exposing it to the light of day, taking it out of the realm of mystery (and shame) and transferring it to the plane of the tangible, the everyday:

> Imagine that this prince's sister, or his wife if you will, has been informed of this love, which is the secret of my young friend, and that, far from feeling aversion or jealousy toward her, she has undertaken to console her . . . to take her out of her solitude, to give her a place beside her in the very palace of her husband . . . Suppose that she wants this child who dared to love so great a prince to dare to confess it, so that this love, hidden in unhappy solitude, may be purified in the light of day and ennobled by its very cause.

(III, 8)

The Queen does not intend to yield her royal husband up to her bourgeoise rival. She means, rather, that Carmosine's love will be transformed by a fatherly kiss into a less fatal form, public adoration, and that Carmosine's position relative to the King will be "regularized"—she will join the royal household as maid of honor to the Queen. Once she is absorbed (one is tempted to say "coopted") into the order of things, her love thus normalized into a permissible state, the reasons for Carmosine's illness disappear as if by magic into the reigning harmony of the court of Palermo. She has, it is true, a moment of revolt upon learning that her cherished secret has become common knowledge. But her shame gives way before the onslaught of goodness and assimilation which terminates the play. Her personal will to happiness, out of phase with the general well-being, gives way to an acceptable form of love, a permissible channel to the sentiment which motivated it. And she does this because it is willed from above. As the Queen says, in her final, convincing plea: "Yes, it is the King who wishes first of all that you get well, and that you come back to life; it is he who thinks that it would be a great shame for so beautiful a creature to die of so noble a love—those are his own words . . . It is I who wish that, far from forgetting Pedro, you see him every day; that rather than combatting a penchant for which you ought not to reproach yourself, you should yield to this sincere impulse of your soul toward what is fine, noble and generous . . ." (III, 8).

How well this parallels the political implications of **Carmosine**! Carmosine's love of Pedro is simply the movement of all good subjects toward their monarch's inherent superiority, translated into hyperbolic terms. As all good subjects accept the beneficent will of their ruler, so Carmosine will subordinate her excessive desires to his jurisdiction, accepting a suitable husband from his hand, and thus restoring the sentimental balance of the kingdom! As orthodox religion teaches us that earthly love is the just reflection of divine *caritas,* so Perillo's and Carmosine's marriage will be sanctified by its submission to royal will, its inspiration by the ideal example provided in Carmosine's pure passion for the King.

This is a sad fairy tale. Sad, in its representation of the distance traveled by the Romantic spirit since the 1820's and 1830's, when imagination and revolt were synonymous: here we find the French equivalent of "God's in his heaven, all's right with the world," the Gallic Victorianism that Napoleon the Little was to bring. Sadder still in its testimony to the decline of that fresh, impertinent, and passionate irony that gave Musset's love comedies their peculiarly mordant vigor. Never again would the French theater rediscover this rare combination of sincerity and pose, of poetry and rhetoric, of sentiment and skepticism, which Musset invented and then lost. His imitators and emulators, from Rostand to Anouilh and Giraudoux, have never succeeded in equaling this composition, this equilibrium. A trace too much pose, a slight excess of irony, and the delicate structure loses its stature, slides into the trivial or the mean. The miracle of the young Musset was the degree of dignity, of nobility, which his genius lent to those "imperfect and base creatures" which his wit and his sentiment elevated to the rank of true heroes.

Notes

1. Letter to Louise Colet of June 26, 1852. Gustave Flaubert, *Correspondance,* nouvelle édition augmentée, series 2, 1847-52 (Paris, 1926), p. 447.

2. *Le Romantisme d'Alfred de Musset,* p. 35.

3. Ibid., pp. 568-69.

4. *Oeuvres complètes en prose,* p. 900. "Let us write ancient verses on new ideas."

5. See Paul de Musset, *Biographie,* in *Oeuvres complètes,* "l'Intégrale," pp. 43-44; and Madame Martellet, *Dix Ans chez Alfred de Musset* (Paris, 1899), p. 64.

6. Jean Richer, in Alfred de Musset, *Textes dramatiques inédits,* p. 175, maintains that manuscript

fragments of *Carmosine* in the poet's own hand date from as early as 1833-34.

7. *Le Romantisme d'Alfred de Musset,* p. 636.

8. As Lafoscade points out, Perillo himself is mainly invented by Musset; but his role is at least suggested by the anonymous husband given to Carmosine by the King at the end of Boccaccio's story: *Le Théâtre d'Alfred de Musset,* p. 159.

9. Werner Bahner, *Alfred de Mussets Werk,* p. 85.

10. *Le Romantisme,* p. 627.

11. Ibid., p. 625.

FURTHER READING

Criticism

Denommé, Robert T. "Chatterton, Ruy Blas, Lorenzaccio: Three Tragic Heroes." *Laurels* 61, no. 1 (spring 1990): 55-67.

> Compares and contrasts the tragic heroes in dramatic works by Musset, Alfred de Vigny, and Victor Hugo.

Maclean, Marie. "The Sword and the Flower: The Sexual Symbolism of *Lorenzaccio.*" *Australian Journal of French Studies* 17, no. 2 (January-April 1979): 166-81.

> Examines Musset's use of symbolism to emphasize the action of *Lorenzaccio.*

Rees, Margaret. *Alfred de Musset.* New York: Twayne Publishers, 1971, 141 p.

> General introduction to Musset's life and work, with some critical analysis of works.

Roussetzky, Rémy. "Theater of Anxiety in Shelley's *The Cenci* and Musset's *Lorenzaccio.*" *Criticism* 42, no. 1 (winter 2000): 31–57.

> Contrasts Percy Bysshe Shelley's treatment of inner drama in *The Cenci* with that of Musset in *Lorenzaccio.*

Additional coverage of Musset's life and career is contained in the following sources published by Thomson Gale: *Dictionary of Literary Biography,* **Vols. 192, 217;** *European Writers,* **Vol. 6;** *Guide to French Literature: 1789 to the Present; Literature Resource Center; Nineteenth-Century Literature Criticism,* **Vols. 7, 150;** *Reference Guide to World Literature,* **Eds. 2, 3; and** *Twayne's World Authors.*

George Peele
1556-1596

English dramatist and poet.

INTRODUCTION

Peele was a moderately popular Elizabethan dramatist and poet who was an immediate predecessor to William Shakespeare and Ben Jonson. Although he died young, Peele left behind an sizeable repertoire of plays and poems. His use of different metrical forms and complicated plots testifies to his skill as a writer. In addition, historians are intrigued with Peele's descriptions of Elizabethan culture and his insight into the issues of his day. His plays, which deal with mythological, classical, and historical themes, were uniquely capable of entertaining royalty as well as appealing to the masses.

BIOGRAPHICAL INFORMATION

Peele was born in 1556, the son of James Peele, a successful tradesman, and his first wife, Anne. James Peele was an ambitious man and actively pursued opportunities for his son. George, therefore, first attended school at Christ's Hospital, where his father was a clerk. In 1571, at the age of fourteen, Peele became a student at Christ Church in Oxford, earning his B.A. in 1577 and his M.A. in 1579. He began his writing career while still in school, encouraged by his peers, who enjoyed his work. In 1580 Peele married Ann Cooke and they settled in London by 1581. Records indicate that Peele received a payment of twenty pounds in May, 1583, for providing entertainment to a visiting Polish count—a strong clue that Peele was already an established writer by then, or that this was the event which established him. Peele's next recorded success was the performance of *The Arraignment of Paris* in 1584 for Queen Elizabeth, a key step in his career that was likely brought about by a supporter who had royal ties. Peele also went on to write a number of poems for the Queen, the Lord Mayor of London, and other dignitaries, probably in an effort to solidify his position at court. He composed four more attributable plays over the next decade. At the end of his life, both his finances and his health were suffering. He wrote to Lord Burleigh in 1595 asking for sponsorship and stating that he had been ill for a long time. There is no record that Lord Burleigh responded; the young playwright died on November 9, 1596.

MAJOR DRAMATIC WORKS

Peele's first known play, now lost, probably written while he was still a student, was a translation of Euripides's *Iphigenia*. His *The Arraignment of Paris* is noteworthy as the earliest known example of an English pastoral play. This play appears to have been written especially for its premiere performance at the court of Queen Elizabeth because it is very flattering to the Queen, drawing comparisons between her and various classical goddesses. Peele's subject matter, Troy, was of particular interest to Elizabethan audiences as well. His skill and ingenuity as a writer are exhibited in his use of metrics, which change throughout the play, depending on the subject or characterization. Peele's next play, *The Battle of Alcazar,* was probably begun after the 1588 defeat of the Spanish Armada and eventually performed around 1590. The events of the play are set after a historical battle that took place on August 4, 1578. Thomas Stuckeley, a British national hero and soldier of fortune especially popular with general audiences, is a featured character in the play.

Edward I, performed around 1591, was Peele's least successful play, but is still considered a notable piece. He weaves together multiple plots in an intricate web of activity that is only partially based on history and has been called historical farce by scholars. This play is about King Edward I of England and his wife, Queen Elinor. Edward struggles with the Prince of Wales to maintain his kingdom and to gain Scotland while his wife schemes and torments others. *The Old Wives Tale,* published in 1593, is often designated Peele's most interesting play because of its unique style and structure: it is framed by a presenter who is narrating the story about an abducted Princess. The play is very short, less than 1000 lines, and is written using dramatic techniques that have more in common with modern than with Elizabethan theater.

Peele's final play, *David and Bethsabe,* was performed by 1594 and published posthumously in 1599. It draws on biblical stories of King David and is about the collision between the King's public and private lives. Scholars regard this work as the best example of an Elizabethan play inspired by the Bible.

CRITICAL RECEPTION

Peele's career began strong. He was encouraged as a playwright while still a student and by the age of 28 had one of his plays performed at court for Queen

Elizabeth. Scholars today are divided in opinion concerning Peele's works, however. Some argue that there are too many competing plots in his plays but others assert that he synthesizes these different elements successfully. While *Edward I* has a complicated, convoluted plot, the intricacies of *The Old Wives Tale* are more appealing to modern sensibilities. Some critics consider *Edward I* crude, and beneath Peele's usual quality, while others maintain that there is a kind of consistency and integrity even within the scrambled plot of this play. Despite the popularity of Peele's work during his life, he has slipped into near obscurity four hundred years after his death. None of his plays are performed today, although scholars continue to study his work for its literary and historical merit.

PRINCIPAL WORKS

Plays

Iphigenia [translator, from Euripides's *Iphigenia*] date unknown
The Arraignment of Paris 1584
The Battle of Alcazar c. 1590
Edward I c. 1591
The Hunting of Cupid 1591
The Old Wives Tale c. 1593
David and Bethsabe c. 1594

Other Major Works

The Life and Works of George Peele. 3 vols. [edited by Charles Tyler Prouty] 1952-70

*This play is now lost.

OVERVIEWS

Arthur M. Sampley (essay date September 1936)

SOURCE: Sampley, Arthur M. "Plot Structure in Peele's Plays as a Test of Authorship." *PMLA* 51, no. 3 (September 1936): 689-701.

[*In the following essay, Sampley offers an overview of* The Arraignment of Paris, Edward I, The Old Wives Tale, *and* David and Bethsabe, *pointing to a lack of* unity, use of competing multiple plots, emphasis on minor details, and corresponding inattention to major ones in these works, but praising Peele's use of pageantry.]

Sir Edmund Chambers writes that "Peele's hand has been sought in nearly every masterless play of his epoch."[1] The evidence advanced for such attributions has usually consisted mainly of parallel passages and verbal tests, with the result that plays as different in structure as *The Troublesome Reign of King John* and *King Leir* have been fathered upon Peele by the same critic.[2] Most scholars have been inclined to overlook the importance of structure as a means of determining authorship, though the dramas of Jonson and Shakespeare structure appears to be as much a constant as style or characterization. It is the purpose of this paper to show that Peele's known plays reveal a fairly constant type of structure, and that this type can be used as a determinant in considering the authorship of anonymous plays.

Peele's known plays are:[3] *The Arraignment of Paris, Edward I, The Old Wives Tale,* and *David and Bethsabe.* These plays were written in a period of crude and careless dramas,[4] and have been preserved to us, except for *The Arraignment of Paris,* in garbled texts. Though these conditions undoubtedly make it difficult to analyze the plays, we may judge Peele by the standards of other writers, for his work suffered no more from methods of writing and publishing than did that of Greene, Marlowe, or Kyd.

Very little has been written about Peele's methods of construction. Professor T. M. Parrott writes that Peele "has . . . less sense of plot and structure in his serious work than any playwright of his day,"[5] and Arnold Wynne likewise finds that Peele's plots lack unity and emphasis.[6] Cheffaud states that the dramatist shows an increasing tendency to complexity of action.[7] The critics are at one in regard to *Edward I,* A. H. Bullen,[8] Henry Morley,[9] and Tucker Brooke[10] having found the structure of the play very faulty. *The Arraignment of Paris* has received praise from J. A. Symonds[11] for "its artistic construction." I have found nowhere, however, any full discussion of the structure of Peele's plays.

1.

The Arraignment of Paris, Peele's earliest play, is little more than a succession of pageants and songs bound together by slight threads of plot, and constructed primarily for the purpose of paying an exaggerated compliment to Queen Elizabeth. There are four plots: the love affair between Paris and Œnone; the Colin-Thestylis story; the award of the apple by Paris; and the award of the apple by Diana. In addition there is a long introduction of some 194 lines, which has little bearing on any of these stories. Moreover, vv. 860-886[12] form another digression, while the plethora of songs and of lyric material[13] further detracts from the unity of the work.

Unity is also violated in **The Arraignment** by the poor development of the action and the author's failure to integrate his plots properly. The Paris-Œnone story begins in Act I, Scene ii, and ends in the middle of Act III. The story dealing with Paris' award of the apple begins in Act II and is consummated in Act IV, while the Colin-Thestylis plot is begun and concluded in Act III. The account of Diana's award of the apple starts in the middle of Act IV and continues through the remainder of the play. It is clear, then, that no one plot in the drama runs through more than three acts; one of them appears in only two acts; and the Colin-Thestylis story is taken up and concluded in one division.

In reality, a large portion of the difficulty in the structure of this play comes from the sudden shift of interest in the middle of Act IV. Up to this time attention has been concentrated upon Paris and has been intensified by his dramatic arraignment before the gods. In Act IV, however, Peele had to contrive some scheme for awarding the golden apple to Queen Elizabeth, and Paris could have no part in such a scheme. Nevertheless, this exigency is only partly responsible for the fact that the drama is little more than a series of masques and pageants used to introduce a *grand finale*.

I have referred above to the large number of songs in the play. Closely allied with this lyric quality is an emphasis on pageantry. The storm (vv. 383-384), the separate shows of Juno, Pallas, and Venus (vv. 488-489, 512-514, 534-549), the shepherds bringing in Colin's hearse and singing (vv. 772-780), the concourse of the gods in Act IV, and the appearance and song of the Fates (vv. 1304-19) are really small pageants within the play. Unlike the lyric excrescences, they are dramatically effective and show that Peele was capable of producing stage effects.

An interesting feature of the plot structure of **The Arraignment** is the balancing or contrasting of one plot with another. Thus Peele carefully draws a parallel between Paris' treatment of Œnone and Thestylis' behavior toward Colin. Paris deserts Œnone, who mourns because of his falseness, while Colin bewails the unkindness of Thestylis and dies.

The most outstanding merit of **The Arraignment** from the dramatic point of view is the effective final scene. The compliment to Queen Elizabeth, extravagant though it might be, formed a clever and unconventional *dénouement* to a somewhat hackneyed plot. Nevertheless, **The Arraignment** is a poorly constructed drama. The lack of continuity in the plots, the absence of a main character,

the shift in the course of action in Act IV, and the lyrical digressions throughout the piece all bring out differing phases of one essential fact, namely, that the structure of the play is non-dramatic.

2.

Edward I, from a structural point of view, is one of the worst of Elizabethan plays. It must be remembered, however, that the text is seriously corrupt and probably represents the second or third revision of the original version.[14] But whether or not the play was revised, no one has ever questioned that the drama as it now stands is the work of Peele, and one may fairly expect a playwright in both original composition and revision to construct a play with some semblance of unity and coherence.

Edward I seems at first reading a maze of disconnected incidents; there are besides the main courses of action numerous digressions which impede the progress of the drama. A summary of the separable actions and of the digressions in the play is given below:

Plots in the play:

1. Edward-Lluellen.

2. Queen Elinor's pride and iniquity.

3. Edward-John Baliol.

4. Lluellen-Ellen-Mortimer.

5. Gloster-Jone of Acon.

Scenes and incidents having little or no connection with these plots:

1. Edward's arrival in England and the giving of largess to the wounded crusaders (vv. 1-252).

2. The Friar's combat with Lluellen, and the Harper's prophecy (vv. 342-611).

3. The Robin Hood scenes (vv. 1264-1542; 1908-2132).

4. The Novice's song to the Queen (vv. 1897-1907).

5. The christening of the Prince of Wales (vv. 2133-81).

6. The Friar's hanging of his pikestaff (vv. 2381-96).

7. The procession with David, Mortimer, Friar, and others (vv. 2630-67).

From this summary it appears that the play contains a large number of plots even after all the extraneous incidents have been excluded. The mere number of plots, however, is not so important as the fact that there is no central plot. Among the first three stories, which are the most important, the first seems predominant; yet the pride and iniquity of Queen Elinor is allotted more space in the play and the plot of Edward and Baliol runs a fair third.

Further incoherence is added to the play by the fact that several of the plots do not reach a state of finality. The statement in v. 2945 that Lluellen has rebelled after having been killed before the eyes of the audience may be due to a garbled text, and so may the prediction in v. 2946 that Baliol intends to brave Edward for the second time. In the case of the Mortimer-Lluellen plot, however, we are left in doubt as to whether Mortimer ever won the hand of Ellen. As the play now stands, only two of the five plots reach a solution.

Moreover, the two principal plots, the struggle between Edward and Lluellen, and Queen Elinor's pride and iniquity, are faulty at various stages of their development. The former plot constitutes a sort of enveloping action for the bulk of the play. It is closely connected with, and may be said to include, Lluellen's attempt to free his betrothed wife from Edward's power. The part of the story dealing with the earlier stages of the Welsh war is coherent enough, but the long Robin Hood digression interferes with the progress of the action, and the withdrawal of Edward from Wales weakens the play still further, though it allows Peele to shift the emphasis to the Lluellen-Ellen-Mortimer story. As noted, the Edward-Lluellen plot reaches no satisfactory conclusion.

The plot second in importance and perhaps first in bulk, the story of Queen Elinor's pride and iniquity, really consists of a string of unrelated events, all bringing out the same effect. Her pride in her coronation dress, her jealousy of the Mayoress of London, her complaint at coming into Wales, her boxing Edward on the ear, her scorn at the present offered her son by the Welsh barons, her requests that the men's beards and women's right breasts be cut off, her murder of the Mayoress of London, her sinking and reappearance, and her final confession of her past sins—each of these separate incidents is in turn taken up in order to develop the central theme of the plot, the iniquity of Queen Elinor.[15] Such a mode of development, however, is desultory, and not only fails to give a unified impression, but detracts from the unity of the drama by overburdening it with incidents.

The plots, then, are hopelessly incoherent, but the structure is made infinitely worse by the fact that over one-third of the play, about 1100 lines, has little or no connection with any of the plots mentioned above. Of this extraneous material, all except one hundred lines are in the three main digressions: Edward's arrival in England, the Friar's combat with Lluellen, and the Robin Hood scenes. With no central plot in the play, and since such a large number of plots lack develop-ment and are incoherently arranged, the addition of all this digressive matter turns confusion into chaos.

The play lacks, furthermore, proper distribution of emphasis; so great is this lack that the only distinction that I am able to draw in *Edward I* between plot and digression is that a plot involves a series of connected incidents occurring intermittently throughout the play, whereas a digression consists of an incident or group of incidents which are taken up and finished at once. Thus the Robin Hood scenes are incidents of a discursory character, though they are given much more space than either of the two minor plots.

There is, of course, one unifying character in the play, Edward himself, the drama being a chronicle of a certain portion of the life of this king; and the chronicle play in its earlier development was naturally prone to excrescences and want of regularity. In other chronicle plays of the time, such as *The Contention, The True Tragedy,* and *Edward II,* there are dominant themes even in the midst of much digression. In Peele's play, however, there are such a large number of plots and so great an amount of digression that the reader is lost in a maze of incidents.

Edward I does reveal that the dramatis had a sense of stage effect. One device is the paralleling of one situation with another very similar, a trick which has been noted in the discussion of *The Arraignment.* An example in *Edward I* occurs in Scene xii. Edward and David, disguised, meet Lluellen and Mortimer also in disguise, David having joined Edward, and Mortimer having joined Lluellen under false pretenses. A fight occurs, in which Mortimer takes Edward's part and David helps Lluellen. Edward gets Lluellen down and David overcomes Mortimer, so that the fight ends in a draw. A much slighter parallelism is to be found in the sudden and unplausible death of Jone, which comes as a pendant to the death of Elinor.

Another dramatic trick of Peele is the liberal use of pageantry in the play. *Edward I* is particularly rich in scenic effects, as is witnessed by the stage directions in vv. 46-55, 117-119, 683-686, 1102-6, 1366-69, 1595-99, 2134-37, 2630-32. Closely allied with the pageantry of the play is the use of songs. Six songs were sung in *Edward I,* though only one of them has been preserved in the text.[16]

To such devices as those just discussed and to the abundant use of trumpets, horseplay, and skirmishes must be due the well-attested success of *Edward I.* Overburdened with plots and digressions, badly organized, incoherent in the development of the action, and lacking proper distribution of emphasis, the play, as regards structure, represents Peele at his worst. Though the drama cannot be considered typical of him, a playwright who would fashion such a work must be sadly deficient in the fundamental principles of dramatic construction.

3.

The Old Wives Tale, probably written about the same time as *Edward I,* is infinitely better organized, yet manifests many of the same peculiarities of structure. The play, however, differs sharply from all other plays of the period in the use of the induction. This device was not unknown under Elizabeth, as may be seen by the examples of *James IV* and *The Taming of the Shrew,* but Peele's use of it is unusual in that the characters in the forepiece remain upon the stage throughout the play and are in close relation to the actors and to the plot. The play begins with a story told by Madge, an old woman, to two travelers. She has scarcely begun her tale when the actors appear and begin to act out her story. They proceed with occasional comments from the observers until the end is reached, where it appears that the play was merely the tale told by Madge.

This use of the induction has been highly praised by Gummere, who says that Peele "was the first to blend romantic drama with a realism that turns romance back upon itself, and produces the comedy of subconscious humor."[17] Yet in spite of Gummere's brilliant interpretation, I think Peele's chief purpose in the induction was to give the effect of an old gossip's fairy tale. At any rate, the induction is the one contribution which Peele made to Elizabethan dramatic art.

The Old Wives Tale suffers, just as *Edward I,* from an excessive amount of action. There is, however, this distinction between the two plays: in *The Old Wives Tale* the plots are less numerous and are better integrated. There are four plots in the play:[18]

1. Sacrapant-Delia—the two brothers—Eumenides-Ghost of Jack.

2. Sacrapant-Erestus-Venelia.

3. Sacrapant-Lampriscus-Huanebango-Zantippa.

4. Sacrapant-Lampriscus-Corebus-Celanta.

Four plots are not an unusual number for an Elizabethan play, but it must be remembered that *The Old Wives Tale* contains only 1170 lines, of which nearly two hundred are given to the speakers in the induction. The development of four plots within less than a thousand lines involves, accordingly, an excessive amount of action. This fullness of incident is increased by the fact that the main plot involves six characters and three different actions, the search of the brothers, the quest of Eumenides, and the gratefulness of the Ghost of Jack. The lack of unity in the play is further accentuated by

the presence of Madge and her friends on the stage and their comments during the progress of the play. Finally several digressions detract from the unity of the drama. One is the incident (vv. 441-475) in which the Friar serves Delia with a chine of beef and a pot of wine. Another is the incident at the tavern (vv. 903-959) in which the penniless Eumenides suddenly finds his purse full.

The plots in *The Old Wives Tale* are integrated better than in either *The Arraignment of Paris* or *Edward I.* Sacrapant, the conjurer, who brings about the complications in each of the stories, forms one link connecting all of the plots. In much the same way Erestus, known usually in the play as the Old Man of the Cross, is the chief character in the second plot and appears as adviser to characters in the other three stories. The second plot is further bound to the first by the part that Venelia plays in the overthrow of Sacrapant, and the third and fourth plots are closely linked by a number of unifying factors.

Though the development of the plots is also managed with some attempt at orderly procedure, a distinct structural flaw is the lack of proper emphasis and proportion. This fault may be due in some degree to the corrupt text of the play.[19] However, the fact that several important scenes are treated with the utmost brevity while unimportant incidents are developed fully suggests that Peele himself was also responsible for this weakness.

The *dénouement* illustrates particularly well Peele's disproportionate treatment. In the short space of 160 lines the following actions occur: Eumenides has wool stuffed in his ears and thus escapes the enchantments of Sacrapant; the Ghost of Jack comes in and takes Sacrapant's wreath from his head and his sword from his hand, whereupon Sacrapant dies; then Eumenides, having had the wool extracted from his ears, digs until he comes upon a light, but finally has to wind a horn for assistance; thereupon Venelia enters, breaks the glass, blows out the light, and goes out again; the Ghost of Jack then draws a curtain and shows Delia asleep; Eumenides manages to awaken her and win her hand by the time that the Ghost of Jack is able to cut off the sorcerer's head; then when Eumenides once more winds the horn, Venelia, the two brothers, and Erestus enter; the Ghost of Jack calls for his share in Delia, and Eumenides obligingly offers to cut the lady in two; however, the Ghost of Jack stays him and leaps down into the ground, whereupon all leave.

The development of all this action in 160 lines shows that Peele had not learned the secret of placing emphasis where it is due. The *dénouement* is the most important point in the play; yet the events occurring in it are given no more emphasis than the smallest incidents earlier in the play. On the other hand, the discussion of Wiggen, Corebus, the Churchwarden, the Sexton, and Eumenides concerning the disposition of Jack's body is drawn out to a length of ninety-six lines, and the rather pointless scene involving Eumenides, the Ghost of Jack, and the Hostess contains fifty-six lines. As in *Edward I,* the humorous scenes are rather fully developed at the expense of situations more important to the plot.

The dramatic virtues of *The Old Wives Tale* are much the same as those that have been noted in *The Arraignment of Paris* and *Edward I.* Peele shows a workman-like knowledge of stage effects in the use of the voice and the flame of fire (vv. 670-671), the three appearances of the head at the well (vv. 784-785, 972-973, 983-984), the thunder and lightning (vv. 500-501), and the furies (vv. 503, 773-775). Peele's love of pageantry is shown in the magical appearance of the hostess and her table with fiddlers attending (vv. 916-919) and in the two appearances of the harvest men (vv. 306-311 and 640-650).

Another device of which Peele is fond is the balancing of one plot against another. A striking instance in *The Old Wives Tale* is the nice parallelism between the fortunes of Corebus and of Huanebango. Both seek Delia and are overcome by Sacrapant; but Huanebango is rendered deaf, while Corebus is stricken blind. Huanebango is met at the well by Lampriscus' shrewish daughter, whose tongue cannot offend his ears, while Corebus weds the ugly daughter, whose lack of beauty he cannot perceive.

On the whole, *The Old Wives Tale* is Peele's best constructed play. Its induction marks one real advance in dramaturgy, and the various plots are linked together and developed with some care. On the other hand, one finds in the play a profusion of plots and incidents, a halting and confused continuity of action, and a poor distribution of emphasis. Good scenes appear haphazardly in the play, and songs and pageants are brought forth between flashes of lightning. The play is a medley and a dream, and the paradox of it is that even its confusion seems artistic.

4.

David and Bethsabe, probably the last of the canonical plays of Peele, is a dramatic rendering, with a certain amount of amplification and a smaller proportion of abridgment, of *2 Samuel* XI-XIX. 8, though there is introduced in the last scene the theme of Salomon's succession to the throne, which is taken from *1 Kings* I. 11-31. The structure of the play, accordingly, depends a great deal upon the Scriptures and upon the changes made by Peele in the Biblical narrative. There are four plots in *David and Bethsabe*: the affair between David and Bethsabe, the Ammon-Thamar-Absolon story, the

rebellion of Absolon, and the settlement of the succession to the crown. The first two of these plots take up vv. 25-1002, the third vv. 1003-1719 and 1862-2011, and the fourth vv. 1720-1861.

The number of plots in the play is by no means so confusing as the manner in which they are developed. Thus the first four scenes and the first chorus furnish all the factors necessary for a complete play. We have the exposition, the initial incident in David's summons of Bethsabe, rising action and complicating factors in David's dealing with Urias and in the promise of Urias' death, and the climax, falling action, and *dénouement* sketched in by the chorus. By the end of Scene vi, the David-Bethsabe plot is completed.

The rebellion of Absolon assumes the foreground after the completion of the love *motif.* The initial incident in this plot comes in the return of Absolon from Gesur; then after several scenes of rising action, the climax comes when Absolon prefers the counsel of Cusay to that of Achitophel. The catastrophe is consummated with the death of Absolon, though there are some anticlimactic pendants to it in the last two scenes.

The David-Bethsabe and the David-Absolon plots are complete stories in themselves, and they are developed, as are the stories in *The Arraignment of Paris,* one after another. However, the third plot in order of importance, the revenge of Absolon on Ammon for the defilement of Thamar, is managed somewhat differently. In *2 Samuel* the defilement of Thamar happens two years after the death of Urias, but in the play it is contemporary with David's adultery. The explanation of the change, I think, is that Peele wished to balance the adultery of David and Bethsabe with the incestuous violation of Thamar by Ammon.

A fourth and distinctly minor plot is the settlement of the succession to the throne upon Salomon. It is brought in for no dramatic reason and was probably not in the first version of the play.[20]

The plots in *David and Bethsabe,* then, are not properly merged, and the confusion is heightened by the liberal sprinkling of digressions in the work. The more palpable of these I list below:

1. Vv. 851-875. The capture of Rabath.

2. Vv. 1087-1103. Ithay's devotion to David.

3. Vv. 1330-1415. The cursing of David by Semei.

4. Vv. 1664-1719. Joab's speech after the battle and the strife between the messengers as to who should carry the news to David.

If Peele shows little skill in the management of the play as a whole, he shows no more in the development of the individual plots. In the David-Bethsabe plot the initial incident is David's discovering Bethsabe and sending for her. Then follows a short period of rising action, in which David attempts to conceal his crime by calling Urias home from the war. Up to this point the plot is handled capably. But here, when the rising action has not been completed, Peele throws his story overboard and takes up a new plot. We are told in the chorus:

> Vrias in the forefront of the wars,
> Is murthered by the hateful Heathens sword,
> And Dauid ioies his too deere Bethsabe,
> Suppose this past, and that the child is borne,
> Whose death the Prophet solemly doth mourne.[21]

As the play now stands, the first half of the story is fully depicted, and then at a high point of interest the narrative is suddenly stopped and the author briefly explains the conclusion of the story.

In the same way, the David-Absolon plot is not logically developed. In the first place, there is in this plot little motivation for Absolon's revolt: we are informed in a soliloquy of some fourteen lines that Absolon intends to make himself popular with the people; then we have a lapse in the story, the next scene picturing David in flight from Absolon. The climax of the plot is reached when Abolon prefers the counsel of Cusay to that of Achitophel. Soon after the climax comes the catastrophe in the death of Absolon. Here the story should have ended. The last two scenes, so far as they concern the David-Absolon plot, are in the nature of an anticlimax.

Another characteristic of the structure of *David and Bethsabe* is the liberal use of songs and pageantry. The play opens with one of the finest songs in Elizabethan drama, and stage directions in vv. 745 and 787-788 call for songs now lost. Pageant effects are to be found in vv. 25-27, 740, 787-788, 1020-22, 1160-62, 1536. It is clear from these examples that Peele had a keen sense of stage effect.

David and Bethsabe is probably the last play written by Peele, and it is a significant comment upon his dramatic art that the drama in structure strongly suggests the miracle plays of medieval England. In Peele's use of sources and in the inconsequent development of the plots, *David and Bethsabe* shows distinct likeness to the early cycle plays.

* * *

The four canonical plays of Peele thus show a strong resemblance, particularly in structure. In each is a large number of plots, four stories being used in *The Arraignment of Paris, The Old Wives Tale,* and *David and Bethsabe,* and five in *Edward I.* Moreover, in each there is extraneous material. In much the same way

every play shows structural weakness because the dramatist failed to combine and order his plots to the best advantage. In *The Arraignment* and *David and Bethsabe* the plots are not well integrated because the main threads of action are spliced, not interwoven; one plot ends before another begins, so that each play gives the effect of presenting not one story but several. Though in *Edward I* and *The Old Wives Tale* the merging of the plots is more successful, the plots are developed by fits and jerks so that the effect of a smoothly running story is destroyed. A serious and fundamental lack of unity is characteristic of every play known to be by Peele.

A discursive, haphazard, chronicle type of structure is indeed the norm to which Peele's dramas conform, and a further element of weakness is the incoherent development of the individual plots. In *The Arraignment* the fate of Paris is left in doubt; in *Edward I* the Mortimer-Ellen story and possibly also the Edward-Baliol story lack conclusions; the development of the Erestus-Venelia plot in *The Old Wives Tale* is unsatisfactory; while the David-Bethsabe and the Absolon-David plots in *David and Bethsabe* show various defects in development. In working out even a single story, Peele was apt to burden the action with useless incidents or to arrive at a weak and straggling conclusion.

Closely allied with the incoherent development of the single plots is a faulty proportion in dealing with certain scenes. In *The Arraignment* too much space is allotted to the reception of the goddesses by the rural deities; in the same way excessive emphasis is placed on the Robin Hood scenes in *Edward I. The Old Wives Tale* gives several examples, notably the *dénouement,* in which the action is developed in a very sketchy fashion. On the other hand, humorous scenes are overemphasized. In *David and Bethsabe* the climax of the love affair of David in the death of Urias is related in a chorus, while the scene in which Urias is made drunk is over-elaborated.

To what, then, may we attribute the popularity of Peele's plays in his own day? The answer is that Peele understood the tricks of the stage of his time. Pageant effects appear in all his dramas, and no play contains less than three songs, while *The Arraignment* originally had eleven.

One other characteristic of Peele is his fondness for balancing one plot against another. In *The Arraignment* Paris' desertion of Œnone is balanced by Thestylis' ill-treatment of Colin. In *Edward I* the duel of Edward and Lluellen is balanced by the duel of David and Mortimer. In *The Old Wives Tale* the Huanebango-Zantippa plot is contrasted with the Corebus-Celanta episodes, while in *David and Bethsabe* David's adultery is paralleled by Ammon's incest.

These structural characteristics are to be found in all the plays so far discussed and may be considered typical of Peele.[22] It is not too much to expect, then, that any anonymous play attributed to Peele should show the same structural characteristics if it is to be accepted as a part of the Peele canon. The value of plot structure as a test for authorship is, I think, very strong negatively, but not quite so strong when applied positively. So far as we know, Peele did not write well-constructed plays; on the other hand, he cannot be held responsible for all the poorly constructed anonymous dramas of his period.

Of the numerous plays that have been attributed to Peele, *Titus Andronicus, King Leir,* and *Alphonsus Emperor of Germany* are, on the whole, well constructed.[23] In the light of the evidence presented in this paper, it is hard to understand how Peele could have been responsible for the construction of these plays. In the same way it can be shown that the structure of *Jack Straw*[24] is utterly unlike that of any play known to have been written by Peele. It is worth emphasizing, I believe, that structure is often more important in determining authorship than are parallel passages.

Notes

1. *The Elizabethan Stage* (1923), III, 462.

2. Mr. H. Dugdale Sykes in *Sidelights on Shakespeare* (1919), and *Sidelights on Elizabethan Drama* (1924).

3. I have not included *The Battle of Alcazar* (probably written about 1589) in this discussion mainly because there is no certainty that Peele wrote the play. The ascription of it to him by Malone and Dyce has been followed by all subsequent scholars. The external evidence for this ascription rests on the doubtful and equivocal attributions of *England's Parnassus* (1600), in which six lines from the play are assigned to Peele and one line is attributed to Dekker. Some nineteen parallels have been adduced between Peele's known works and *The Battle of Alcazar,* of which about five are significant. These seem to show either that Peele is the author of the play or that he borrowed from it. The metrical evidence is somewhat adverse to the theory of Peele's authorship, as is also the fact that the play contains no humorous material. On the whole, the ascription to Peele is probably correct.—In note 22 below I have given my general conclusions about the structure of *The Battle of Alcazar.*

4. *The Arraignment of Paris* was published in 1584, but may have been written as early as 1582. See P. H. Cheffaud, *George Peele* (Paris, 1913), pp. 31-33, and Thorlief Larsen, "The Early Years of George Peele, Dramatist, 1558-1588," *Transactions of the Royal Society of Canada,* Section II

(1928), 292-298. Cheffaud assigns *Edward I* to 1590-91, *The Old Wives Tale* to 1591-92, and *David and Bethsabe* to 1592. The last three plays, however, show evidence of revision at later dates.

5. *The Tragedies of George Chapman* (1910), p. 690.

6. *The Growth of English Drama* (Oxford, 1916), pp. 172-173.

7. *George Peele* (Paris, 1913), p. 171.

8. *The Works of George Peele* (1888), I, xxxii.

9. *English Writers* (1893), x, 79.

10. *The Tudor Drama* (1911), p. 338.

11. *Shakespeare's Predecessors in the English Drama* (1881), p. 570.

12. All line references to Peele's plays are to the Malone Society Reprints of the plays.

13. There are eleven songs in the play, nine of which are given in the quarto.

14. A clear indication of the state of the text is given by the fact that vv. 2949-54 are almost surely an older version of vv. 2239-43. Cheffaud, who notes this duplication, thinks that vv. 725-727, 763-784, Sc. xv, and probably also vv. 785-806 show evidence of transposition of scenes. He mentions also the curious error noted by Bullen that in Sc. xiii, vv. 2175-76, Edward addresses David in a friendly fashion, although in a preceding scene David has shown himself to be a traitor. From this fact Cheffaud concludes that all the Robin Hood scenes and the comic passages are later additions made by Peele. One might equally well suppose that the scenes dealing with Queen Elinor's perfidy are a later addition, since vv. 808-832 have no connection with the context and since the Mayoress is first mentioned as being in Wales in v. 1869 although she must have come with Queen Elinor, whose arrival with her train is described in vv. 1102-6. Such a theory would also find support in vv. 2952 ff. as contrasted with vv. 2239-41. If the former passage represents the original version of the play, Elinor did not in that version remain in Wales after the departure of Edward, but went with him into Scotland. In the present text of the play the Mayoress of London is murdered in Wales after Edward leaves for Scotland. A further difficulty not connected with either Queen Elinor or the Robin Hood scenes is to be found in vv. 2354 and 2363, in which Lluellen and David speak of getting "the Bride," who is evidently Lluellen's wife Ellen; but Lluellen had recovered his *fiancée* in Sc. v, some twelve hundred lines earlier.

15. Most incidents in the Queen Elinor plot are also to be found in a ballad of unknown date, "A

Warning-Piece to England against Pride and Wickedness." This ballad is reprinted in *The Works of George Peele,* ed. Bullen, I, 77-83.

16. The song is given in vv. 497-505. Mention of songs is made in vv. 681-682, 1368-69, 1453, 1907, 2393-95.

17. Gayley, Charles Mills, ed., *Representative English Comedies,* I, 341.

18. It is perhaps possible to consider the third and fourth plots as one plot, but inasmuch as two distinct stories are told and as the emphasis is rather upon the two love stories than on Lampriscus, it seems better to consider them two plots.

19. W. W. Greg, who edited *The Old Wives Tale* in the Malone Society Reprints, comments on the bad text of the quarto. See p. ix of the Malone Society Reprint of the play.

20. The quarto text of the play is almost certainly a radical alteration of Peele's original version, as I have tried to show in "The Text of Peele's *David and Bethsabe,*" *PMLA,* XLVI (1931), 659-671. However, since it is pretty clear that the quarto text is Peele's throughout and is therefore a product of his invention, I have not thought it worth while to complicate this study of structure with the intricate and puzzling problem of what constituted the original version of the play.

21. Vv. 591-595.

22. It is here pertinent to ask whether *The Battle of Alcazar* shows the same structural features. This play has three plots, which are well integrated, and originally had five spectacular sets of dumb shows: cf. W. W. Greg, *Two Elizabethan Stage Abridgments: The Battle of Alcazar & Orlando Furioso* (Oxford University Press, 1923). On the other hand, it has much digressive material, and Acts II, III, and IV are weak because of lack of action. There are strong moments at the beginning and at the end of the play, but the intervening acts are almost devoid of interest. In this respect as well as in the general outlines of the main plots, *The Battle of Alcazar* resembles Greene's *Alphonsus, King of Arragon.* The pageantry of the dumb shows, the poor development of the plots, and the faulty distribution of emphasis suggest Peele as the author of *The Battle of Alcazar.* On the other hand, the exceptional unification of the plots and the scantiness of action in the play are not in accord with Peele's habits of play construction. Nor does one find in *The Battle of Alcazar* the trick of balancing one plot or situation against another, a device which occurs in all Peele's known plays. These differences from Peele's known structural methods may be partly explained by the nature of

the material which he was treating, but the fact remains that the play is not in Peele's usual manner. Given the refractory source material of an African battle and asked to concoct hurriedly some sort of dramatic pageant, Peele might have constructed such a play.

23. The chief proponents of the theory that Peele wrote these plays are J. M. Robertson and H. Dugdale Sykes, though Robertson gives Peele only a part in each play. The ascriptions of Robertson are set forth in his *Introduction to the Shakespeare Canon* (1924); Mr. Sykes's attributions are contained in *Sidelights on Shakespeare* (1919) and *Sidelights on Elizabethan Drama* (1924). See my criticism of the verbal evidence of Robertson and Sykes in *StPh,* XXX (1933), 473-496.

24. This play has been attributed to Peele by Fleay, *Biographical Chronicle of the English Drama,* II, 153; Hugo Schütt, *The Life and Death of Jack Straw, Kieler Studien zur englischen Philologie* (Heidelberg, 1901); H. C. Hart, *The Second Part of King Henry the Sixth,* Arden Shakespeare (London, 1909), pp. xxiv-xxix; and J. M. Robertson, *An Introduction to the Shakespeare Canon,* pp. 251-252.

R. Headlam Wells (essay date April 1983)

SOURCE: Wells, R. Headlam. "Elizabethan Epideictic Drama: Praise and Blame in the Plays of Peele and Lyly." *Cahiers Élisabéthains,* no. 23 (April 1983): 15-33.

[*In the following essay, Wells assesses the works of playwrights Peele and Lyly in the context of their handling of literary conventions and expectations of late-sixteenth-century England.*]

There is no topic which illustrates more pointedly the difference between Renaissance and modern poetics than that of praise. For the twentieth-century reader, and indeed many twentieth-century critics, the literature of praise is more or less synonymous with venality. And not without reason. There is, after all, some justice in the fact that Waller, that most representative of neoclassical panegyrists, is remembered chiefly, not for a handful of exquisite lyrics, but for Johnson's acid complaint that

> *It is not possible to read, without some contempt and indignation, poems of the same author, ascribing the highest degree of power and piety to Charles the First, then transferring the same power and piety to Oliver Cromwell, now inviting Oliver to take the Crown, and then congratulating Charles the Second on his recovered right. Neither Cromwell nor Charles could value*

his testimony as the effect of conviction, or receive his praises as effusions of reverence; they could consider them but as the labour of invention, the tribute of dependence.[1]

Time has reversed the judgment of Waller's immediate contemporaries; but if we no longer regard him as one of the greatest poets of the seventeenth century, it cannot be said that Dryden does much to restore our belief in the value of epideictic literature either. Panegyric, it must be admitted, did not inspire the acknowledged master of the age to his greatest efforts.

A century earlier, however, this was not the case. *A prince of poets in his time,* Spenser was also a poet of princes. In an age—indeed the last age—when most people still believed in the concept of an orderly hierarchical universe and when the idea that princes were God's anointed deputies on earth was only just beginning seriously to be questioned, praise was a fundamental article in the credo of the humanist literary critic. Puttenham, for example, in his defence of the dignity of poetry, claims that, second only to poetry composed in praise of the immortal gods, is that which honours *the worthy gests of noble princes.*[2] The task of an author who undertook such a work of praise was *to yeeld a like ratable honour to all such amongst men as most resembled the gods by excellencie of function and had a certaine affinitie with them, by more then humane and ordinarie vertues shewed in their actions here vpon earth* (p. 35). In doing so his object was essentially a moral one. The special nature of the responsibilities assumed by the panegyrist is perhaps best explained by Erasmus in a letter he wrote some twelve years before the composition of his own epideictic treatise on kingship, *The Education of a Christian Prince* (1516). *Those who believe panegyrics are nothing but flattery,* writes Erasmus, *seem to be unaware of the purpose and aim of the extremely far-sighted men who invented this kind of composition, which consists in presenting princes with a pattern of goodness, in such a way as to reform bad rulers, improve the good, educate the boorish, reprove the erring, arouse the indolent, and cause even the hopelessly vicious to feel some inward stirrings of shame.*[3]

Such was the theory of praise which the Renaissance inherited from the rhetoricians of the ancient world.[4] It is true that not every Elizabethan panegyrist is successful in observing Aristotle's important distinction between praise and flattery,[5] that is to say, between the celebration of a moral ideal through the vehicle of a person, a city or an institution and the defence of a particular individual's conduct or policies. (It is one of the chief faults of the fifth book of *The Faerie Queene* that it descends from the former to the latter.) Nevertheless, it was a belief which was fundamental to a didactic theory of literature that, by giving *praise, the reward of vertue, to vertuous acts . . .*[6] the poet might in turn inspire acts of virtue.

In view of the importance of praise in Renaissance poetics it is surprising that Elizabethan epideictic drama has received comparatively little scholarly attention. Indeed, it is remarkable that, in his eloquent and persuasive defence of the Stuart masque, Orgel ignores altogether the Elizabethan forerunners of these royalist extravagazas.[7] In this article I shall consider a group of plays by two underrated Elizabethan playwrights, Peele and Lyly. (In the recent *Revels History of Drama in English,* for example, Peele and Lyly are allocated a mere four pages between them.) It would be foolish to claim that all these plays achieve the status of great art; but though my object is principally to show that their epideictic intention does not necessarily preclude the serious dramatic treatment of moral questions, I suggest that, at their best these Elizabethan plays possess greater intrinsic literary interest than the masques which they in some measure adumbrate.

Peele and Lyly were both members of a group of Oxford graduates living in London in the early 1580s who aspired to positions at court. Both wrote plays which were performed before the Queen by the Children of the Chapel. But whereas Lyly, after the success of his first play, *Campaspe,* went on to write a series of courtly comedies in which royal compliment is barely concealed, Peele appears to have had only one play performed at court. This was **The Arraignment of Paris.**

The Arraignment of Paris incorporates two sixteenth-century traditions—the tradition of royal pageantry and the *debat* tradition of the Tudor expository interlude. A brief account of Peele's debt to the conventions associated with these traditions may help to define his purpose.

Elizabethan royal pageantry was frankly propagandist. Its purpose was to present an image of the perfect prince appointed by providence to rule a chosen people. It employed a variety of means to promote this idea: triumphal arches decorated with emblematic devices, formal orations complimentary verses, songs, tableaux and masques. At the royal entry of 1559 the Queen was addressed as a prince of peace, the symbolic representative of the united houses of Lancaster and York:

> *Therefore as civill warre, and fuede of blood did cease*
> *When these two Houses were united into one,*
> *So now that jarrs shall stint, and quietnes encrease,*
> *We trust, O noble Quene, thou wilt be cause alone.*[8]

As her reign wore on these expressions of pious hope were naturally transformed into confident tributes to Elizabeth's statemanship.

A popular feature of the civic pageant was the use of historical or mythical figures who, acknowledging Elizabeth's superior virtue, gladly resign to her their pre-eminence. For example, in 1578 the city of Norwich offered an entertainment in which five women addressed the Queen in turn from an elaborate stage built in the form of a triple arch. The five figures, of whom *the first was the City of Norwich, the second Debora, the third Judeth, the fourth Esther, the fifth Martia, sometime Queene of England* each complimented the Queen by inviting comparison between their achievements and her own.

These speeches concluded, the Queen was then entertained with a consort song. The song tells of a strife in heaven. The rival claims to supremacy of Juno, Venus, Diana, Ceres, Pallas and Minerva are adjudicated by Jove who resolves the contention by reporting the existence of a *Soveraign Wight* in whom are to be found united the several virtues of the six goddesses. Jove's discovery is greeted with universal approval, and the song ends with a tribute to the Queen.[9]

Although Paris does not appear in the Norwich pageant, the quarrelling goddesses clearly perform precisely the same complimentary function as Peele's deities.[10] However this does not mean that the device should be regarded as a source for *The Arraignment of Paris.* Variations of one kind or another on the Judgment of Paris theme were so frequently employed in sixteenth-century pageantry as a means of flattering royal personages that it is impossible to specify a source for any one particular example of its use.[11] The central device of *The Arraignment of Paris* was traditional.

Traditional also was the *debat* motif used by Peele. In his edition of *The Arraignment of Paris* Benbow traces the development of a new kind of dramatic entertainment in the 1560s and the '70s which grew out of the earlier tradition of expository drama exemplified in the Tudor interludes and moralities. In plays such as Edwardes' *Damon and Pithias* or Farrant's *The Wars of Cyrus* historical or legendary material is used to illustrate an intellectual problem that is discussed and analyzed throughout the play. «The new expository drama», writes Benbow, «is similar to the morality; and the rhetorical debates on love, honour, and friendship recall the tirades and exhortations of the virtues in the moralities. The basic allegorical structure of the morality is disguised by the historical story, and the use of the historical framework is supported by the substitution of concrete characters for the older personifications».[12]

Although the new drama was considerably more sophisticated than the interlude from which it in part derived, its principal concern lay not in the development of character, but in the exposition of a central idea. In *The Wars of Cyrus,* for example, the love-interest, the intrigue against Cyrus' life and the tragic death of Panthea are all subservient to the play's main object, which is to illustrate the nature of true magnanimity. When Araspas confesses to his attempted seduction of Panthea, Cyrus tells him:

> *Araspas, they that would be conquerors*
> *Should chiefly learne to conquer their desire,*
> *Least while they seeke dominion over others*
> *They prove but slaves and bondmen to themselves.*

(IV.3.1276-9)[13]

In presenting a dramatic portrait of the perfect prince *The Wars of Cyrus,* like Lyly's *Campaspe* (which it clearly anticipates), lays great emphasis on sexual self-restraint. Indeed for the Elizabethan court dramatist princely virtue became, for obvious reasons, more or less synonymous with chastity.

Elements of both the *debat* tradition and the tradition of Elizabethan civic pageantry were combined in a masque which Sidney wrote for the Queen's visit to Wanstead in 1578. What slight dramatic structure *The Lady of May* might be said to possess springs from the rivalry between Therion the forester and Espilus the shepherd for the hand of their May queen. However, Sidney's treatment of the debate between these unheroic representatives of the active life and the retired life shows that he was not interested in offering a solution to the problem. His primary object was to entertain the Queen and at the same time to flatter her. Having been 'surprised' in Wanstead gardens by a distraught mother, the Queen is requested to judge between the rival claimants to the daughter's hand. While she listens to the evidence she is entertained first with the songs of the two contenders and then by the malapropisms of Lalus and the inkhorn pedantry of Rhombus. Gracious flattery is provided by the May Lady herself who confesses that *you excel me in that wherein I desire most to excel, and that makes me give this homage unto you, as the beautifullest lady these woods have ever received.*[14] When judgment has been passed Rhombus presents a final compliment in which he claims that Elizabeth surpasses the united virtues of Juno, Venus and Pallas.

The Lady of May is more elaborate than the traditional pageant masque with its stiff allegorical figures and its formal encomiums of the Queen. But although characterization is more fully developed, the piece can scarcely be called a play. It is an entertainment with music and songs designed for a specific situation, and its interest, for the modern reader, lies largely in the verbal comedy of Rhombus, forerunner of many an Elizabethan pedant. Insofar as it combines certain elements of an expository dramatic tradition with the conventions of royal pageantry, it is tempting to see *The Lady of May* as a kind of transitional work forming a link, with *The Arraignment of Paris,* between the pageant masque and the truly dramatic works of a court playwright such as Lyly. Certainly Peele's play has much in common with *The Lady of May:* both employ the device of a debate as a means of drawing the Queen into the action; both make the traditional comparison between Elizabeth and the three classical goddesses; and both use music and song as an essential part of the entertainment. But although the two works are informed by the need to flatter their royal audience, this should not disguise the fact that their dramatic modes are quite different. Sidney's piece is essentially occasional: it was written to meet the needs of a particular royal progress. Peele's was not. Indeed it is because **The Arraignment of Paris** was not actually part of a pageant entertainment that Peele goes out of his way to imitate the setting of a royal progress in the first Act of the play.

The short first scene of **The Arraignment of Paris** is reminiscent of *The Lady of May.* This time the rivals are three in number: a shepherd, a hunter and a woodman. But the object of their rivalry is nothing as serious as the hand of a May queen, and they argue good-humouredly about whose gift will be preferred by the goddesses they are awaiting. After two more scenes in which we see other rustics preparing for the arrival of the Olympians, Pallas, Juno and Venus make their entry to the accompaniment of a song. The three goddesses express their appreciation of the *rare delightes* which have been arranged in their honour, and a welcoming oration is delivered. This done, the rustics present their gifts.

These opening scenes serve a twofold function: first, Peele adumbrates in the rustics' lighthearted banter the more portentous quarrel between the goddesses which Ate provokes in the next Act, and second, he evokes the setting of a provincial progress. By giving his drama a thinly disguised English rural setting and showing a group of local characters making ready for a royal visitation, Peele prepares us for the inevitable entry of the Queen herself. When the play is seen against the background of the pageant conventions it conspicuously imitates, it is impossible to criticize the appearance of Elizabeth in Act V as a violation of dramatic detachment.[15] Nor is it a very pertinent objection to say that Peele fails to give us any resolution of what Benbow sees as the play's central problem, that is the debate concerning the true nature of beauty.[16] Like Sidney, Peele is plainly not interested in the intellectual problem *per se,* only in the occasion it provides for the introduction of Elizabeth as arbiter.

A far more serious criticism of the play is the objection that the tradition within which it was written restricted the dramatist to the presentation of conventional problems in a world removed from reality.[17] There is some truth in this claim. It cannot be denied that there is little intrinsic merit in a tradition of royal panegyric which fostered a national myth for purely propagandist

reasons. However, Peele's play teaches an important political lesson at the same time that it pays a gracious compliment to the Queen. The underlying seriousness of the Paris story is announced in the portentous words of Ate's prologue:

> *Beholde I come in place, and bring beside*
> *The bane of Troie: beholde the fatall frute*
> *Raught from the golden tree of Proserpine.*
> *Proude Troy must fall, so bidde the gods above,*
> *And statelie Iliums loftie towers be racet*
> *By conquering handes of the victorious foe:*
>
> (5-10)

For the Elizabethan, as for the Roman poet, the sack of Troy was quite simply the most important event in the legendary history of the ancient world.[18] Since the achievements of Elizabeth, like those of Augustus, were foreshadowed in the story of Aeneas, any attempt rightly to interpret the significance of the present must begin with its prefigurations in the past. Thus from one point of view Troy could be regarded as the inevitable starting point for a history of Rome (as it was for Livy) and consequently of Britain (as it was for Camden).

From another point of view the story of Troy could be seen as embodying an important moral lesson. If providence had ordained that from this calamity there would follow a long train of events leading ultimately to the founding of two great civilizations, it was believed that their establishment was only made possible through the subjection of passion by the rule of reason. The lesson of Troy, as Golding succintly explains in his commentary on Ovid's *Metamorphoses,* is the dangers of sensuality.

> *The seege of Troy, the death of men, the razing of the*
> *citie,*
> *And slaughter of king Priams stock without remors of*
> *pitie,*
> *Which in the xii. and xiii. bookes bee written, doo*
> *declare*
> *How heynous wilfull perjurie and filthie whoredome*
> *are*
> *In syght of God.*
>
> (Dedicatory *Epistle.* 242-6)[19]

The sack of Troy was the supreme example of a state overthrown by lust. Shakespeare's Thersites reflects the Elizabethan attitude to Troy in his complete identification of *wars and lechery.* As Ralegh laconically puts in in his *History of the World: All writers consent with Homer; that the rape of* Helen *by* Paris *the son of* Priamus, *was the cause of taking armes . . .*[20]

It is important when we read **The Arraignment of Paris** that we keep in mind both the historical and the moral aspects of the Troy story, for in the play itself the two are interwoven with some subtlety. The Trojan myth enjoyed such widespread currency in Elizabethan England that when Ate predicts the sack of Troy in her prologue Peele could be certain of his audience's knowing that from this disorder there would eventually emerge a new order, first under Augustus and then under his 'descendant' Elizabeth. In this way the prologue looks forward directly to Diana's encomium in Act V in which the goddess tells of

> *A kingdome that may well compare with mine.*
> *An auncient seat of kinges, a second Troie,*
> *Ycompast rounde with a commodious sea:*

(V.1.1152-4)

The action of the play is thus timeless: although it appears to be set both immediately before the Trojan war and also in the present time, no attempt is made to give realistic treatment either to the remote past or to present-day England. Indeed Peele deliberately confuses our sense of chronology. On the one hand he characterizes his country gods preparing for their Olympian visitation as English swains, while on the other his evocation of Elizabeth's England reads more like a classical account of the Golden Age.

Although discord is resolved in the general harmony of the play's conclusion, Peele does not allow us to forget that Troy was an historical fact. When Mercury informs Venus that her favourite has been summoned to appear before the court of heaven, she objects:

> *What heere I have, I woone it by deserte:*
> *And heaven and earthe shall bothe confounded bee,*
> *Ere wronge in this be donne to him or me.*

(III.6.772-4)

But Mercury, perceiving the unconscious irony of her words, remarks:

> *This little fruite, yf Mercury can spell,*
> *Will sende I feare a world of soules to hell.*

(III.6.775-6)

Paris appears before the gods and confesses that, being dazzled by Venus's beauty, he had allowed his fancy to rule his judgment. After the arraignment, Jupiter passes sentence and instructs Paris to *take thy way to Troie, and there abide thy fate.* Once again we are reminded what the consequences of Venus's gift will be, for, as Paris leaves the stage, Apollo pronounces the most memorable lines of the play:

> *From Ida woods now wends the shepherds boye,*
> *That in his bosome caries fire to Troy.*

(IV.4.990-1)

The fire that Paris carries in his bosom is, of course, both the fire of love and also the literal flames of Troy: the one is the direct cause of the other. This is the reason

why in *The Arraignment of Paris* love is consistently presented as ignoble and capricious, the cause of suffering and even death. The greater part of Act III is concerned with the unhappy affairs of Colin and Oenone, both betrayed by Venus. Though their complaints are beautiful, their fate is not. Oenone is left to pine away under her poplar tree—symbol of love's inconstancy—while Colin dies of grief. If Colin and Oenone represent the tragic side of love, its grotesque aspect is symbolized by Venus's lecherous and unlovely husband attempting the seduction of one of Diana's nymphs (IV.1).

In the little pastoral world of the play Venus's capacity for mischief and injustice is limited to the disruption of individual lives. But one of the functions of pastoral is to *glaunce greater matters*[21] and if we see in the petty conflicts of the play the historical events which they adumbrate, then it becomes clear that it is Venus, who, as Paris's patron, is ultimately responsible for the Trojan war. The story of Troy, then, contains this important truth: if Elizabeth is Astraea *rediviva* and her London a new Troy, it is only by the disciplined subjection of passion that a repetition of the tragedy can be avoided.

Although Peele treats his material in a light-hearted manner befitting a court entertainment, his play is certainly not, as Benbow suggests, «fundamentally non-serious».[22] *The Arraignment of Paris* performs a dual function: it flatters the Queen in terms of the popular myth which saw her as a Christian Prince inaugurating the new Golden Age prophesied by Virgil; but on another level it employs Elizabeth as a symbolic representative of the justice and order which alone can prevent history repeating itself. Peele presents passionate love as the most powerful threat to civilized order partly, of course, because the woman whom his play was designed to compliment never married, but also because, as a humanist, he believed that civilization depended upon the rule of reason.

The dangers of erotic love is also a prominent theme in Lyly's plays. His most explicit dramatic tributes to Elizabeth are *Sapho and Phao* (c.1582-3) and *Endimion* (c.1585). Like *The Arraignment of Paris,* these plays present idealized portraits of the Queen. But this time she appears not as a miraculous *dea ex machina* graciously condescending to intervene in the disordered affairs of men and gods, but as one of the central characters in the drama. In both plays Elizabeth is portrayed as a queen of love worshipped by an adoring court. *Beleeue me Pandion,* remarks one of Sapho's courtiers to the scholar recently arrived in court, *in Athens you haue but tombs, we in court the bodies, you the pictures of Venus & the wise Goddesses, we the persons & the vertues* (I.2.17-20).[23]

Lyly was not, of course, alone in portraying the Queen as an idealized object of universal quasi-sexual admiration. From the earliest years of her reign Elizabeth's charms had been celebrated by ballad makers commemorating important contemporary events. But in 1579 a precedent was established for depicting her as the object of a poet's love when Spenser included a song of praise to *fayre* Eliza, *Queene of shepheardes all* in the *April* eclogue of *The Shepeardes Calendar.* In the following years Elizabeth was idealized in dozens of lyrics as the very incarnation of feminine beauty and virtue. Constable's address *to the Queene: touching the cruell effects of her perfections* is an example of the way the traditional conceits of literary convention were applied to Elizabeth:

> Most Sacred Prince! why should I thee this prayse
> Which both of sin and sorrow cause hast beene
> Proude hast thow made thy land of such a Queene
> Thy neighboures enviouse of thy happie dayes.
>
> Whoe neuer saw the sunshine of thy rayes,
> An everlasting night this life doth ween
> And he whose eyes thy eyes but once haue seene
> A thowsand signes of burning thoughts bewrayes
>
> Thus sin thou caused envye I mean and pride
> Thus fire and darknesse doe proceed from thee
> The very paynes which men in hell abide
>
> Oh no not hell but purgatorie this
> Whose sowles some say by Angells punish'd be
> For thow art shee from whome this torment is.[24]

In addition to such overt royal tributes as Puttenham's *Partheniades* (1579), Ralegh's *Cynthia* (c.1592), Drayton's *Ideas Mirror* (1594) and Davies' *Hymns of Astraea* (1599) are the numberless sonnets which pay oblique compliments to the Queen while praising the lesser virtues of some other real or imaginary lady.[25] So complete was the popular identification of Elizabeth with an abstract ideal of beauty that when Ralegh wrote his commendatory sonnet on *The Faerie Queene* he claimed that Petrarch's Laura had been deposed from her throne in the temple of fame by Spenser's mistress:

> Me thought I saw the graue, where Laura lay,
> Within that Temple, where the vestall flame,
> Was wont to burne, and passing by that way,
> To see that buried dust of liuing fame,
> Whose tombe faire loue, and fairer vertue kept,
> All suddenly I saw the Faery Queene:
> At whose approch the soule of Petrarke wept,
> And from thenceforth these graces were not seene.
> For they this Queene attended, in whose steed
> Obliuion laid him downe on Lauras herse:
> Hereat the hardest stones were seene to bleed
> And grones of buried ghostes the heauens did perse.
> Where Homers spright did tremble all for griefe,
> And curst th'accesse of that celestiall theife.[26]

It is this tradition of idealizing Elizabeth as a queen of love upon which Lyly is drawing in *Sapho and Phao.* Like her royal audience this queen is *faire by nature, by*

birth royall, learned by education, by gouernment politike, rich by peace: insomuch as it is hard to judge, whether she be more beautifull or wise, vertuous or fortunate (I.2.7-10). Because the parallels between Sapho and Elizabeth are of a fairly explicit nature, Lyly is careful to avoid any imputation of moral weakness by suggesting that her passion for Phao is brought about by means beyond her control. Phao's beauty, the whimsical gift of Venus, is no earthly beauty; and when the humble ferryman appears at court, Sapho, though conscious, like him, of the impropriety of her passion, cannot resist the challenge of a linguistic game. Both are in love, both see through the other's verbal disguise, yet both must sustain the deception for form's sake:

PHAO:

> It were best . . . that your Ladyship giue mee leaue to be gone: for I can but sigh.

SAPHO:

> Nay stay: for now I beginne to sighe, I shall not leaue though you be gone. But what do you thinke best for your sighing to take it away?

PHAO:

> Yew Madame.

SAPHO:

> Mee?

PHAO:

> No Madame, yewe of the tree.

SAPHO:

> Then will I loue yewe the better. And indeed I think it would make mee sleepe too, therfore all other simples set aside, I will simply vse onely yewe.

PHAO:

> Doe madame: for I think nothing in the world so good as yewe.

SAPHO:

> Farewell for this time.

(III.4.72-85)

Princes, it is discovered, are not immune to the passions which afflict lesser mortals. As Alexander says in the earlier play *Campaspe: none can conceiue the torments of a king, vnless hee be a king, whose desires are not inferior to their dignities* (II.2.83-5). But *fancie, thogh it commeth by hazard, is ruled by wisdome* (*Sapho and Phao,* II.4.56). So Sapho renounces her love. Although it is Cupid's dart which causes the cessation of her passion for Phao, we are given to understand that the change is due, in part at least, to Sapho's own moral determination: *Mee thinkes I feele an alteration in my minde*, she tells Cupid, *and as it were a withstanding in my self of mine own affections* (V.2.3-4).

As the embodiment of chaste decorum, Sapho is contrasted with her divine but shameless rival. An ageing coquette who unscrupulously uses her husband for her own irresponsible ends, Venus has much in common with Peele's deity. In both *The Arraignment of Paris* and *Sapho and Phao* it is erotic love which is ultimately responsible for the ironies and confusions which go up to make the comedy. The responsibility of princes in matters of love is an important theme in *Sapho and Phao*. However, Lyly does not develop its political implications. In Peele's play we are never allowed to forget the historical consequences of Paris's irresponsible conduct. But although the immediate effects of Sapho's passion are seen in her whimsical and indecorous conduct (III.3), its social consequences are not stressed. Dramatic emphasis is placed on the unique character of Sapho herself. In reproving Venus for her indiscretions she arrogates Venus's own role and becomes herself a kind of *Goddess of affections* (V.2.64). The final picture of Sapho as a queen of love, leading Venus *in chaines like a captiue* (V.2.66-7) and ruling the fancies of men without allowing herself to become compromised is an overt allusion to Elizabeth's practice of encouraging the amorous attention of her poets and courtiers in what was almost a parody of a medieval court of love.

If *Sapho and Phao* lacks political dimension, this is also true of Lyly's most explicit dramatic tribute to Elizabeth: for the world of *Endimion* is, if anything, more stylized and self-enclosed than that of the earlier play. *Endimion* has much in common with *Sapho and Phao*. Lyly's principal object is to present a dramatic portrait of Elizabeth, and once again we have a plot which concerns the relationship between a queen and her adoring courtier. Unlike Sapho, however, Cynthia is never tempted by love. Although Endimion himself speaks of the difference which heaven has set between them (V.3.168), the question of decorum in sexual choice is not really an important issue in the play.

The dramatic contrast between chastity and erotic love is another motif which Lyly repeats in *Endimion*. In *Sapho and Phao* he had presented a variation on the familiar royal pageant motif of the earthly queen who usurps the place of her divine counterpart. This time the drama deals with the rivalry between two deities, the moon and the earth. In rejecting a topical reading of Lyly's allegory, Bevington has argued that the real subject of *Endimion* is the cosmic struggle between chaste and earthly affection.[27] There is clearly much truth in this suggestion. Both *Sapho and Phao* and *Endimion* exalt chastity over erotic love. But while it is true that any attempt to establish the historical counter-

parts of Lyly's characters is likely to be a distraction from the main point of the plays, it is misleading to describe *Endimion* as a philosophic drama. There is no elaboration in the play of the initial evocation of the two goddesses and their respective spheres of influence (I.2.19-32). Neither does the theme of chastity versus erotic lover ever become the subject of serious debate. The superiority of chaste affection is certainly an important part of the play's meaning; but we are scarcely justified in dignifying such a commonplace of conventional Renaissance thought with the title of philosophy. The real object of the play is not to examine the meaning of Platonic love, but to explore a paradox, the paradox of the Elizabeth of popular myth, that *myracle of Nature, of tyme, of Fortune* (I.4.36-7).

Lyly does not concern himself with the individual personality traits of his central character. Like an Elizabethan portrait painter, he depicts not an individual, but an idea. As a prince Cynthia lacks the humanity of Alexander or even Sapho; as a goddess she has none of the engaging sprightliness of Drayton's Phœbe. She takes little part in the action and she is given none of the ironic dialogue which enlivens *Campaspe* and *Sapho and Phao* and which is seen in its most brilliant form in *Gallathea*. Cynthia's character is evoked through report rather than realized in dialogue or action. A good example of Lyly's technique is Endimion's first apostrophe to his goddess. The speech is a long one, but is best quoted in its entirety, since its effect is cumulative:

> *O fayre* Cynthia, *why doe others terme thee vnconstant,*
> *whom I haue ever found vnmoueable? Iniurious tyme, corrupt*
> *manners, vnkind men, who finding a constancy not to be*
> *matched in my sweete Mistris, haue christned her with the name of wauering, waxing, and waning. Is shee inconstant that keepeth a setled course, which since her*
> *first creation altereth not one minute in her mouing? There is nothing thought more admirable or commendable*
> *in the sea, then the ebbing and flowing; and shall the Moone, from whom the Sea taketh this vertue, be accounted*
> *fickle for encreasing, & decreasing? Flowers in theyr buds are nothing worth till they be blowne, nor blossomes*
> *accounted till they be ripe fruite: and shal we then say*
> *they be changeable, for that they growe from seedes to*
> *leaues, from leaues to buds, from buds to theyr perfection?*
> *then, why be not twigs that become trees, children that*
> *become men, and Mornings that grow to Euenings, termed*
> *wauering, for that they continue not at one stay?*

I, but Cynthia, *being in her fulnes, decayeth, as not
delighting in her greatest beautie, or withering when
she should be most honoured. When mallice cannot
obiect
any thing, folly will, making that a vice, which is the
greatest vertue. What thing (my Mistris excepted) being
in the pride of her beauty, & latter minute of her age,
that waxeth young againe? Tell mee* Eumenides, *what
is
hee that hauing a Mistris of ripe yeeres, & infinite
vertues, great honors, and vnspeakable beauty, but
woulde
wish that shee might grow tender againe? getting
youth
by yeeres, and neuer decaying beauty by time, whose
fayre face, neyther the Summers blase can scorch, nor
Winters blast chappe, nor the numbring of yeeres breed
altering of colours. Such is my sweete* Cynthia, *whom
tyme cannot touch, because she is diuine, nor will
offend because she is delicate. O* Cynthia, *if thou
shouldest alwaies continue at thy fulnes, both Gods
and
men would conspire to rauish thee. But thou to abate
the pride of our affections, dost detract from thy
perfections, thinking it sufficient, if once in a month
we enioy a glymse of thy maiestie, and then, to
encrease our greefes, thou doost decrease thy glemes,
comming out of thy royall robes, wherewith thou da-
zelist
our eyes, downe into thy swath clowtes, beguiling our
eyes,*

(I.1.30-65)

Endimion's speech is a virtuoso performance and a
marvellous piece of Elizabethan invention. Its length is
an essential part of its point, for its effect depends upon
our appreciation of the speaker's skill in discovering so
many points of artful correspondence in a simple analogy. The whole piece is an extended conceit. The speech
is important because it is an index of Lyly's method in
the play as a whole, and it is perhaps a mark of its
weakness as a stage play that *Endimion* is really no
more than a *Labyrinth of Conceits* (Epilogue to *Sapho
and Phao*) expressive of Elizabeth's paradoxical nature.
The play portrays her as the remote idealized object of
men's affections, inspiring noble deeds, condescending
to favour her loyal courtiers with chaste approval, but
never allowing herself to become entangled in amatory
affairs. Cynthia, in short, embodies an ideal of woman-
hood which had been firmly fixed in the European
imagination by two centuries of poets writing in the Petrarchan tradition. Lyly's great gift to the Elizabethan
stage was his unerring dramatic sense. The interminable
flyting and the ponderous humour of the Tudor interludes are gone; and out of the materials of rhetorical
debate Lyly creates truly dramatic dialogue. He is at his
best when evoking the delicate and subtle confusions
which arise when two characters are prevented for social
or political reasons from declaring a mutual passion.
Comedy has come into its own. For all their elegance,
their poise and their stylized sophistication, however, it

must be admitted that *Sapho and Phao* and *Endimion*
are limited by their subject matter. Since their moral
and psychological interest is slight, their principal
importance will always be a technical and historical
one. The same cannot be said of *Campaspe* (1581-2).
Like the two later plays, *Campaspe* represents an idealized portrait of Elizabeth. But in this case, rather than
excluding any independent ethical interest, royal
compliment is actually the vehicle of the play's moral,
as it is in **The Arraignment of Paris.**

Where *Sapho and Phao* and *Endimion* portray Elizabeth
as a chaste queen of love, *Campaspe* depicts her,
through the character of Alexander, as a Renaissance
prince. The duties and accomplishments of the Renaissance prince were well defined. A long tradition of
humanist conduct books dealt with every aspect of the
subject. Among the most popular and influential
sixteenth-century treatises were Castiglione's *Il Libro
del Cortegiano* (1528), translated into English by Sir
Thomas Hoby in 1561, and Sir Thomas Elyot's *The
Boke Named the Governour* (1531). Both these treatises
owed much to Cicero's *De Officiis* and they stimulated,
in their turn, many imitations.[28]

Renaissance humanists were inspired by a wish to create a civilization which would rival the classical
civilizations of the ancient world. The perfect state was
to be ruled by an enlightened prince served by wise and
virtuous counsellors, and it was in order to promote this
ideal that manuals were written prescribing the education, accomplishments and virtues of princes and their
courtiers. The prince is seen as a microcosm of the
state; its virtues are his, and on him depends the well-
being of his court. He is accomplished in all the arts
and social graces; he is comely and decorous in his
speech, his carriage, his dress and his conduct. But his
accomplishments are worth nothing if they are not
devoted to the cause of realizing the humanist ideal of
the just society. It is axiomatic, however, that the man
who governs others must first learn to govern himself.
Thus the cardinal virtues to be observed by a prince or
governor are wisdom, fortitude, justice and temperance.
He must be indifferent to the vicissitudes of fortune; he
must be prepared to undertake arduous tasks in the
public interest; he must exercise impartiality in his judgment of his subjects; and in all his conduct he must
display *mezzura*—the avoidance of excess of any kind.

This traditional body of thought is of particular
importance to a discussion of *Campaspe*, for although
the play is set in antiquity it is clearly a Renaissance
humanist ideal against which Alexander's conduct is
measured. *Campaspe* is a debate play of deceptive
simplicity. Lyly's professed object is to mix *mirth with
counsell, and discipline with delight* (*Prologue at the
Black Fryers*) and he announces his topic of debate in
the opening lines of the play: what is more becoming in

a prince, courage or courtesy? As the action unfolds and Alexander discusses with his general his love for Campaspe we are reminded repeatedly of the issues raised by this question. Campaspe herself knows that *In kinges there can be no loue, but to Queenes: for as neere must they meete in maiestie, as they doe in affection* (IV.4.30-1). It is Alexander who, having finally subdued his passion for his beautiful prisoner, concludes the debate in the play's final speech: *It were a shame* Alexander *should desire to commaund the world, if he could not commaund himselfe* (V.4.150-1). The moral, which is virtually identical with that of *The Wars of Cyrus,* is unequivocal: the cardinal virtue in a humanist prince is self-control.

If *Campaspe* belongs to a clearly-defined *débat* tradition, it also owes something to the pageant conventions which inform **The Arraignment of Paris.** This time, however, pageantry is no more than a dramatic motif in an economically constructed stage play, and *Campaspe* has none of the episodic quality which **The Arraignment of Paris** shares with the royal Progress entertainment.

Like **The Arraignment of Paris,** *Campaspe* begins with a triumphal entry. As the play opens we watch two of Alexander's men discussing their prince and anatomizing his virtues. Their talk is interrupted by a procession of Theban captives accompanied by their guards with other soldiers bearing the spoils of war. As Parmenio and Clito engage in light gallantries with their captives, the tone is immediately set for the drama which is to follow:

PAR:

> *Madame, you neede not doubt, it is* Alexander, *that is the conqueror.*

TIMO:

> Alex. *hath ouercome, not conquered.*

PAR:

> *To bring al vnder his subiection is to conquer.*

TIMO:

> *He cannot subdue that which is diuine.*

PAR:

> *Thebes was not.*

TIMO:

> *Vertue is.*

(I.1.41-7)

This elegant verbal sparring in which serious matters are treated with studied negligence is the very essence of *Campaspe*'s comedy. The interchange is a public

display performed before an audience of minor characters, and Timoclea's witty replies are a necessary device for concealing emotions which she cannot afford to indulge.

When the subject of their debate makes his entry the focus of attention shifts, and Alexander, like a Tudor prince in a provincial progress, acts the part of himself and asks the question which is expected of him and to which he already knows the answer: *Clitus, are these prisoners? of whence these spoiles?* (I.1.58). The question is not a piece of dramatic *gaucherie;* it is part of a script established by custom. As the character of the conversation between Parmenio and Timoclea was determined by its dramatic context, so Alexander's role is fixed by the expectation of his stage audience. What Lyly's opening scene with its formal entries and emblematic displays of power serves to emphasize is the public nature of Alexander's position. He is the focus of his audience's attention because their fate depends on his conduct. As the story develops we discover that this is true of his own court no less than of his prisoners. Ambiguity and confusion arise only when Alexander begins to depart from his script and act out of character—the character, that is, of an enlightened prince.

Act I sees the victorious Alexander turning from military affairs to the art of peaceful government:

> Hephestion, *it resteth now that we haue as great care to*
> *gouerne in peace, as conquer in war: that whilest armes*
> *cease, artes may flourish, and ioyning letters with launces,*
> *we endeuor to be as good Philosophers as soldiers, knowing*
> *it no lesse praise to be wise, then commendable to be valiant.*

(I.1.80-4)

His proposals for the establishment of a humanist court are met with the warmest approval:

> *Your Maiestie therin sheweth that you haue as great desire to rule as to subdue: & needs must that common wealth be fortunate, whose captaine is a Philosopher, and whose Philosopher is a Captaine.*

(I.1.85-8)

Hephaestion's chiasmic reply emphasizes the importance of balancing the rival claims of the active life and the retired life. If philosophy is the servant of virtuous action, scene iii shows the folly of allowing learning to become an end in itself. Alexander's chamberlain summons the philosophers to court. But his first encounter is not a sanguine one:

> *First, I cam to* Crisippus, *a tall leane old man, willing him presently to appeare before* Alexander; *he*

> stoode staring on my face, neither mouing his eies nor
> his body; I vrging him to giue some answer, hee tooke
> vp a booke, sate downe, and saide nothing:
> Melissa his maid told me it was his manner, and that
> oftentimes she was fain to thrust meate into his
> mouth: for that he wold rather starue then ceasse
> studie.
>
> (I.3.2-8)

Lyly's satire is directed not at learning, but its abuse, and later in the same scene we see Alexander reaffirming his humanist proposals:

> sithence my comming from Thebes to Athens, from a
> place
> of conquest to a pallace of quiet, I haue resolued with
> my self in my court to haue as many Philosophers, as
> I had in my camp soldiers. My court shalbe a schole,
> wherein I wil haue vsed as great doctrine in peace, as
> I did in warre discipline.
>
> (I.3.59-63)

However, *Campaspe* tells the story of a court ruled not by reason, but by a passion which affects the lives of prisoner and courtier alike. When Alexander confesses his love for Campaspe, Hephaestion warns him of its impropriety:

> Remember Alexander that thou hast a campe to
> gouerne, not
> a chamber; fall not from the armour of Mars to the
> armes
> of Venus . . . I sighe Alexander that where fortune
> could
> not conquer, folly should ouercome.
>
> (II.2.57-62)

By Act IV Hephaestion's fears have been realized, for instead of an academy of learning Alexander's court has become a Bower of Bliss:

> Sithence Alexander fell from his harde armour to his
> softe robes, beholde the face of his court, youthes
> that were woont to carry deuises of victory in their
> shieldes, engraue now posies of loue in their ringes:
> they
> that were accustomed on trotting horses to charge
> the enimy with a launce, now in easie coches ride
> vp and downe to court Ladies: In steede of sword and
> target to hazard their liues, vse pen and paper to
> paint their loues. Yea, such a feare and faintnes
> is growne in courte, that they wish rather to heare
> the blowing of a horne to hunt, then the sound of a
> trumpet to fight.
>
> (IV.2.11-20)

Eventually Alexander discovers where Campaspe's own affections lie, and, as he graciously resigns all claims on her, Lyly returns to the entry motif of the play's opening scene: *enjoy one an other, I giue her thee franckly,* Appelles. *Thou shalt see that* Alexander *maketh but a toye of loue, and leadeth affection in fetters*

. . . (IV.4.131-3). In renouncing his passion Alexander thus settles the question which the play began with. Self-command is shown to be nobler than military conquest. As Hephaestion remarks: *The conquering of Thebes was not so honourable as the subdueing of these thoughts* (V.4.48-9). But behind the simple debating topic lies a larger issue. The processional image in which Alexander announces his resolve serves to remind us that, like all his deeds, this is a public act with public consequences. If the final scene of the play is a demonstration of courtesy in action, it is not sufficient to define this virtue simply as «graceful self-deprecation».[29] Repeatedly the play has emphasized by dramatic means the dependence of the court on the conduct of its prince. Implied in the debate concerning the nature of true kingliness, therefore, is the question of the nature of the ideal court. For the prince who displays true courtesy is not merely one who knows when to give up gracefully; he is an upholder of humanist values. Courtesy is shown to be synonymous with true courtliness, as the etymological connection suggests.

The prince who graciously resigns personal interests for the higher good is clearly intended to evoke Elizabeth, *that good Pelican that to feede hir people spareth not to rend hir owne personne.*[30] Hunter and Bevington have warned that it is unwise to look for specific court allegory in *Campaspe*.[31] But while it is true that analogies between Elizabeth's court and the world of the play are general and typical rather than precise and particular, the virtues of Lyly's prince are naturally shown to have a special relevance for the royal audience before whom the play was first performed. Praise of great men was traditionally the province of epic and lyric poetry, and Lyly shows a typically Elizabethan disregard for classical precept in his choice of a form associated with the correction of folly rather than the honouring of noble deeds. Nevertheless, his object was essentially epideictic. He was not concerned to dramatize a specific event in the life of the court, still less to admonish Elizabeth for some amatory indiscretion. His purpose, like Spenser's, was to create a pattern of princely virtue both as a model for imitation and also as a tribute to his royal patron; his method was to temper *discipline with delight*.

Campaspe was first performed during the Court celebrations of Christmas 1581-2 when the Queen was at the height of her powers. It was a time when, in the words of Cranmer's sentimental prophecy from *Henry VIII*, Her foes [would] *shake like a field of beaten corn,/ And hang their heads with sorrow* (V.5.31-2). When *Henry VIII* was written the Queen had, of course, already been dead ten years and Shakespeare was obliged to respect the susceptibilities of her successor. So Cranmer prophesies that

> as when
> The bird of wonder dies, the maiden phœnix,

Her ashes now create another heir
As great in admiration as herself,
So shall she leave her blessedness to one
[. . .] Who from the sacred ashes of her honour
Shall star-like rise, as great in fame as she was.

(V.5.39-46)

Although James diligently cultivated the myth of a predestinate monarch appointed by heaven to rule a chosen people,[32] there was no poet of stature comparable with Spenser's to clothe what was already beginning to be seen as an anachronistic fiction; while those theatrical works which did seek to perpetuate the myth were not, in an important sense, truly dramatic.[33] For the Stuart court masque has no meaning outside its immediate topical concerns. Its sole object was glorification of the monarchy. When Orgel invites us to consider the reason for the enormous investment—both financial and artistic—in these prodigal expressions of baroque magnificence, our answer is a simple one. It is precisely that the principles and beliefs which the court masque sought to promote were becoming increasingly remote from contemporary political realities. As Orgel himself admits, the masque provided the monarchy with «an impenetrable insulation against the attitudes of the governed. Year after year designer and poet recreated an ideal commonwealth, all its forces under rational control, its people uniquely happy and endlessly grateful».[34]

Unlike the Stuart court masque, the entertainments of Peele and Lyly were not simply «illusions of power»: these humanist plays were dramatic expressions of a moral and political ideal which, for a brief period, seemed to have become a reality. The balance they achieved between gracious compliment and reverence for a divine principle was a delicate one. When their subject died it was lost.

Notes

1. Samuel Johnson, *Lives of the English Poets,* Everyman edition, 2 vols. (London, n.d.), I, 160.

2. George Puttenham, *The Arte of English Poesie,* edited by Gladys Doidge Willcock and Alice Walker (Cambridge, 1936), p. 24.

3. Letter to Jean Desmarez, *The Correspondence of Erasmus,* translated by R. A. B. Mynors and D. F. S. Thomson, 2 vols. (Toronto, 1975), II, 81.

4. See O. B. Hardison, *The Enduring Monument: A Study of the Idea of Praise in Renaissance Literary Theory and Practice* (Westport, Conn., 1962).

5. *The Art of Rhetoric,* I.9.33.

6. Sir Philip Sidney, *The Defence of Poetry, Miscellaneous Prose of Sir Philip Sidney,* edited by Katherine Duncan-Jones and Jan Van Dorsten (Oxford, 1973), p. 97.

7. Stephen Orgel, *The Illusion of Power: A Political Theater in the English Renaissance* (Berkeley, 1975).

8. *The Progresses and Public Processions of Queen Elizabeth,* edited by John Nichols, 3 vols. (1788-1805; rpt. London, 1823), I, 43.

9. Nichols, II, 145-50.

10. Parallels between the Norwich pageant of 1578 and *The Arraignment of Paris* are noted by Inga-Stina Ekeblad, «On the Background of Peele's *Araygnement of Paris*», *NQ,* 201 (1956), 248.

11. For discussion of the Paris story in sixteenth-century literature see Felix E. Schelling, «The Source of Peele's *Arraignment of Paris*», *MLN,* 8 (1893), 103-4; T. S. Graves, «*The Arraignment of Paris* and Sixteenth Century Flattery», *MLN,* 28 (1913), 48-9; John D. Reeves, «The Judgment of Paris as a Device of Tudor Flattery», *NQ,* 199 (1954), 7-11; Ekeblad, «On the Background of Peele's *Araygnment of Paris*», pp. 246-9.

12. R. Mark Benbow, Introduction to *The Araygnement of Paris, The Life and Works of George Peele,* edited by Charles Tyler Prouty, 3 vols (New Haven, Conn., 1970), III, 36. All quotations from Peele are from this edition.

13. *The Wars of Cyrus,* edited by James Paul Brawner, *Illinois Studies in Language and Literature* (Urbana, Illinois, 1942).

14. *The Lady of May, Miscellaneous Prose of Sir Philip Sidney,* p. 24.

15. See Enid Welsford, *The Court Masque* (Cambridge, 1937), p. 287. Ekeblad («On the Background of Peele's *Araygnement of Paris*», p. 249) and Benbow (Introduction to *The Araygnement of Paris,* pp. 46-7) defend the dramatic propriety of the play's conclusion on grounds similar to those I have adduced. See also Louis Adrian Montrose, «Gifts and Reasons: The Contexts of Peele's *Araygnment of Paris*», *ELH,* 47 (1980), 433-61.

16. Benbow, p. 46.

17. Benbow, p. 13.

18. The significance of Peele's use of the Troy story is discussed by Henry G. Lesnick, «The Structural Significance of Myth and Flattery in Peele's *Arraignment of Paris, SP,* 65 (1968), 163-70.

19. *Shakespeare's Ovid, Being Arthur Golding's Translation of the Metamorphoses,* edited by W. H. D. Rouse (London, 1961), p. 6.

20. *The History of the World* (London, 1614), p. 382.

21. Puttenham, *The Arte of English Poesie,* p. 38.

22. Benbow, p. 49.

23. All quotations from Lyly are from *The Complete Works of John Lyly,* edited by R. Warwick Bond, 3 vols. (1902; rpt. Oxford, 1973).

24. *The Poems of Henry Constable,* edited by Joan Grundy (Liverpool, 1960), p. 138.

25. See Elkin Calhoun Wilson, *England's Eliza,* Harvard Studies in English, XX (1939; rpt. London, 1966), p. 245.

26. *The Poetical Works of Edmund Spenser,* edited by J. C. Smith and E. de Selincourt, one vol. ed. (Oxford, 1924), p. 409.

27. David Bevington, *Tudor Drama and Politics: A Critical Approach to Topical Meaning* (Cambridge, Mass., 1968), p. 181.

28. A bibliography of over nine hundred titles is contained in Ruth Kelso, *The Doctrine of the English Gentleman in the Sixteenth Century,* University of Illinois Studies in Language and Literature, XIV (Urbana, Illinois, 1929), pp. 169-277. See also John E. Mason, *Gentlefolk in the Making; Studies in the History of English Courtesy Literature and Related Topics from 1531-1774* (Philadelphia, 1935) and Sir Ernest Barker, «The Education of the English Gentleman in the Sixteenth Century» in *Traditions of Civility* (Cambridge, 1948).

29. G. K. Hunter, *John Lyly: The Humanist as Courtier* (London, 1962), p. 166.

30. *Euphues' Glass for Europe,* Bond, II, 215.

31. Hunter, pp. 145-52; Bevington, pp. 173-5.

32. See Charles Bowie Millican, *Spenser and the Table Round,* Harvard Studies in Comparative Literature, VIII (Cambridge, Mass., 1932), pp. 127-41 and Glynne Wickham, *Shakespeare's Dramatic Heritage* (London, 1969), pp. 250-8.

33. See Orgel, pp. 37-8. Those Jacobean plays which did incorporate the Tudor myth of an elect nation took the form either of retrospective panegyrics to an apotheosized queen (e.g. Heywood's *If You Know Not Me You Know Nobody* and Dekker's *The Whore of Babylon*) or of historical plays whose purpose was political rather than epideictic (e.g. Rowley's *When You See Me You Know Me* and Dekker and Webster's *Famous History of Sir Thomas Wyat*) (See Judith Doolin Spikes, «The Jacobean History Play and the Myth of the Elect Nation», *Renaissance Drama,* N.S., 8 (1977), 117-49).

34. Orgel, p. 88.

Susan T. Viguers (essay date June 1987)

SOURCE: Viguers, Susan T. "Art and Reality in George Peele's *The Araygnement of Paris* and *David and Bethsabe.*" *CLA Journal* 30, no. 4 (June 1987): 481-500.

[*In the following essay, Viguers presents a detailed analysis of* The Arraignment of Paris *and* David and Bethsabe, *suggesting that Peele deals with art and reality as two different realms.*]

In Robert Greene's *Friar Bacon and Friar Bungay* the sorcerer Bacon invites Prince Edward into his cell to look into his crystal. There, Bacon tells him, he will be able to witness a "comedy" (vi.48).[1] As the "comedy" progresses, Bacon twice has to warn Edward to "sit still" (vi.48,109); the audience must not interfere with the play before it. But finally, in anger at seeing in the glass his friend betray him with Edward's own beloved, the Prince forgets himself. "Gog's wounds, Bacon, they kiss! I'll stab them!" (vi.127), he cries. "Oh, hold your hands, my lord, it is the glass!" (vi.128), exclaims Bacon. The forms Edward sees in the crystal may look like reality, but as he himself the next moment apologetically acknowledges, they are "shadows," not "substances" (vi.130).

Edward's admission that art and reality comprise two different realms is a Renaissance commonplace,[2] nowhere in Renaissance literature more clearly delineated, as the above scene suggests, than in dramatizations of responses to a play-within-a-play. George Peele in his *The Araygnement of Paris* and *David and Bethsabe* makes use of the play-within-the-play to explore that commonplace. Critics have not generally appreciated the rich complexities of those plays,[3] nor have they noted Peele's concern with concepts of art. *The Araygnement of Paris* and *David and Bethsabe* are remarkable examples of plays in which the separation of art and reality is not simply a theme; it creates the dramatic tensions that structure each play. The plays demonstrate how fundamental and resonating the concept can be for a Renaissance artist.

The mechanicals' playmaking in *A Midsummer Night's Dream* and the responses of the Citizen and his Wife to the play presented them in Beaumont's *The Knight of the Burning Pestle* provide well-known illustrations of the confusion of art and reality as a source of considerable humor. In Peele's plays the denial of the separation of art—of the image—and reality is not humorous or even simply lamentable; it is profoundly evil. The word "art" in the Renaissance signifies all of man's efforts to structure and order his life and environment; man's imagination reflects his moral state. In *The Araygnement of Paris* and *David and Bethsabe* the failed imagination leads to tragedy; the healthy imagination leads to the transformation of tragedy into regeneration and salvation.

The scene in *The Araygnement of Paris* which introduces the tension resolved only by the ending of the play is that in which Paris judges who is most beautiful, Juno, Pallas, or Venus. One key to the play is to see that critical scene in terms of the interaction of artist, audience, and artwork. Paris is audience to three masques presented by the goddesses, and both artists and audience demonstrate a failure of the imagination.

What is important is that the goddesses do not present Paris with shows that define themselves as images and fictions, that are, for example, images of those qualities—majesty, wisdom, beauty—that make each deserving in her own way of the title "the fayrest" (l. 358)[4] and thus of the golden apple. Each goddess, rather, presents her show as something that can be part of Paris's world. Their shows are gifts to seduce Paris. And Paris responds in kind. In the climaxing argument in his later defense at his arraignment before the council of the gods, he speaks of being "tempted" (l. 930) and choosing the prize, Helen, "that best did please" him (l. 927), words that imply seduction, not encouragement to judge impartially. The goddesses in presenting shows that seem to be physically possessable, and Paris, in responding as though they are, define and relate to the images in the shows as to reality, which is to deny the separation between audience, or the world of reality, and art. The separation can be maintained, and the artistic experience can be healthy, only if art, images, and shadows are grasped not physically but imaginatively.

Geffrey Witney's famous emblem book, *A Choice of Emblemes* (1586), includes an emblem of the judgment of Paris, and Paris's failure in that emblem suggests Peele's play. Paris is an emblem for Whitney of

> The worldie man, whofe fighte is alwaies dimme,
> Whofe fancie fonde eache pleafure doth entice,
> the fhaddowes, are like fubftance vnto him,
> and tyes more deare, them [sic] thinges of greatest price.[5]

For Peele, too, Paris fails to distinguish between shadow and substance.

Marlowe's *Doctor Faustus* provides a striking analogue to Paris's failure. The fact that Faustus realizes the difference between image and reality is underscored by his emphasis on his audiences' not interfering in the shows he presents. In a scene remarkably similar, both in pattern and language, to the one in *Friar Bacon and Friar Bungay* discussed at the beginning of this article, Faustus stays the German Emperor from embracing the illusion of Alexander and his paramour whom he presents them in a show.[6] Again, when he later conjures up Helen for three scholars, he admonishes them not to address the figure; yet he himself conjures her again, and this

time, explicitly violating the principle of artistic experience which he has previously stressed, he embraces her. In so doing, he embraces an illusion as reality, as "truth," and turns his back on the everlasting truth, the reality, of God's love. The scholars are not hurt by seeing the show of Helen; Faustus *is* hurt, but it is because he steps over the line between audience and illusion, just as Edward in *Friar Bacon and Friar Bungay* starts to do and as Paris in *The Araygnement of Paris* actually does. From the point at which he embraces Helen, Faustus no longer has any hope that his sin will be pardoned, a despair which marks his ultimate pride and damnation.

Paris's failure of imagination, like that of Faustus, reveals a moral failure. In *A Tale of Troy* (Peele's poem, which as Thorlief Larsen observes, "reads in part like a first draft" of *The Araygnement of Paris*[7]) Peele actually suggests that behind Paris's choice of Helen lies his "adulterous pride" (l. 202).[8] The play's emphasis on Oenone and the nature of her love for Paris and the contrasting quality of Helen's love creates a decidedly moral context in which to see Paris's choice. A comparison of the songs each of the women sings reveals the difference between their love. Oenone's is a song of praise to her lover Paris; love exists for her in terms of relationship. In contrast, Helen, singing in praise of herself, celebrates self-love. Paris himself participates in Oenone's song, whereas Helen's is unshared and sung in the linguistically isolating, because foreign, Italian. There is an awareness in the very conception of Oenone's song of the possibility of human failure; the song

> Concludes with Cupids curse:
> They that do chaunge old love for newe,
> Pray Gods they chaunge for worse.
>
> (ll. 300-02)

In contrast, Helen's song is a proclamation of her own invincibility. Hers is a pride that enables her to usurp even the role of Diana:

> To son un Diana dolce e rare
> Che con Le guardi Io posso far guerra
> A Dian' in fern' in cielo, et in terra.
>
> (ll. 506-08)

Prostitution casts out chastity. Helen is a harlot, singing of her powers. As such, she defines love as physical possession—quite different from Oenone's kind of love. Later in the play, using the conceit of Oenone as hunter and Paris as her game, Mercury remarks to the grieving Oenone, "You should have given a deeper wound" (l. 628). Her response reveals a love that was great enough to be restrained, that refused to possess: "I could not that for pity" (l. 628), she says simply. Love, like the healthy imagination, must not, cannot, possess. The mystical union of two lovers is, significantly, a "union," the fusion of two distinct identities, not the possession of one lover by the other. Paris's failure is not only one of the imagination; in choosing Venus and her show, Paris rejects Oenone and chooses lust over real love.

Peele in *The Araygnement of Paris* suggests a connection between a failure of imagination and moral failure, not only in Paris but also in the three goddesses. The Yale editor, R. Mark Benbow, considers the play very differently: he sees it as primarily "an expository play on the theme of beauty,"[9] posing "the academic question of whether majesty, wisdom or love is the most beautiful."[10] Juno, Pallas, and Venus, however, though gracious at the beginning of the play to the country gods and at the end to Diana and Elizabeth, through most of the play hardly seem like great goddesses. The profound philosophical question Benbow poses seems to me to be reduced by Peele to the jealousy and self-pride of three squabbling women. As soon as they appear on the stage alone, they begin bickering. Their talk of the affairs of Jove and Mars and themselves becomes witty and shrewish until Pallas exclaims,

> No more of this, fayre goddesses, unrip not so your shames,
> To stand all naked to the world, that bene such heavenly dames.
>
> (ll. 346-47)

But only fuel is added to the fire. "Nay Pallas," responds Juno, "that's a common tricke with Venus well we knowe, / And all the Gods in heaven have seene her naked, long agoe" (ll. 348-49). And so the match continues. Their arguing as to which one deserves the golden ball that they discover moments later, after a storm, merely continues the kind of interaction they reveal before the storm.

Venus, the most important of the three goddesses for the play, represents and epitomizes a love that is extraordinarily devalued. Venus becomes a harlot, selling herself to Paris in exchange for the golden ball. "And I will give the[e] many a lovelie kysse," she promises him, "And come and play with thee on Ida here" (ll. 488-89). What is most striking in her discussion with Paris about Cupid's power is our feeling that Love has the power to punish, to revenge, to send to hell and torture. Hell, not heaven, is the place Venus talks about. The heavenly rewards of true love, or constant love, are never mentioned. Venus also shows herself as irresponsible, illogical, and inconsistent. She avoids responsibility for the death, from unrequited love, of the young shepherd, Colin (l. 675). She moves from her long discussion of punishment due those who are "false foresworen lovers" (l. 686) to her punishment of the object of Colin's desire, Thestilis, though there is no indication that Thestilis ever plighted her troth in the

first place. And finally, Venus herself is the one who tempts Paris to foreswear his love, Oenone. Love "gives us bane to bring us lowe" (l. 556), says Digon, one of the three shepherds who act as a chorus. That bane is "The bane of Troie" (l. 6), "the fatall frute" (l. 6), of which Ate speks in the prologue to the play. Love, under Venus, becomes a poison. The nature of Helen, Venus's show, reflects Venus herself. For Peele, the deficiency of the three goddesses' art stems from and reveals something more profound.

It is, however, Paris—or human kind—who suffers the consequence of that corruption. In the framework of the play, the scene with the golden apple in idyllic Ida is a reenactment of the original Fall in the Garden of Eden.[11] Before that episode the play is a pastoral idyll, with country gods and images of groves, fields, bubbling brooks, and carpets of flowers. In an Eden-like bower of country beauty, the beautiful unfallen nymph and shepherd, Oenone and Paris, sing of their love. But that is dispelled by Paris's judgment. In the scenes immediately following, all human activity seems doomed, as in the ill-fated love affair of Colin and Thestilis and Oenone's frustrated passion for Paris.[12] The most disastrous result of Paris's judgment is, of course, the fall of Troy. Paris is dismissed from the council of the gods, where he has been arraigned, "that he may know his payne" (p. 979). Apollo's quiet asides underscore the human tragedy that has begun:

> His payne, his payne, his never dying payne,
> A cause to make a many more complaine.
>
> (ll. 980-81)

And ten lines later, even more poignantly:

> From Ida woods now wends the shepherds boye,
> That in his bosome carries fire to Troy.
>
> (ll. 990-91)

The first scene in *David and Bethsabe* has an importance comparable to the judgment scene in *The Araygnement of Paris*. Again, it is presented as a dramatization of an audience involved in the experience of an artwork. The language and action of the Prologue serve to define his role as surrogate artist. He states his intention to "sing" (ll. 1,15)[13] of King David and his son; he speaks of his "yron Pen" (l. 23) and begs help for his "feeble muse" (l. 22). He begins the play proper, the stage directions tell us, by drawing aside curtains, presumably of a pavilion or inner stage, to reveal Bethsabe. As the artist, he is revealing his artwork; the curtain acts as its frame. David, sitting above in his tower, watches: though traditionally he is an artist, a musician, here he is the audience to the Prologue's show of Bethsabe bathing over a stream and singing. Bethsabe is, of course, not simply a vision; she is as real as David. But Peele, in focusing so specifically on the incident as that of an audience viewing a vision of beauty, a work of art, which the Prologue as surrogate artist unveils, metaphorically imports to the scene the dynamics of an experience of art. And as in *The Araygnement of Paris,* that understanding provides a key to the play.

When David first sees Bethsabe, he responds as Faustus and Paris do to the vision of Helen. He does not see Bethsabe as an image of beauty to be grasped imaginatively; he sees her as a woman he can possess—something that is a part of his world. Thus, like Paris, he completely negates the necessary distance between audience and show. We as audience actually see David descend from his "Princely tower" (l. 95) to Bethsabe. That movement is a visual image of both a falling in love and a falling into sin.[14] It is, moreover, a fall that, as in *The Araygnement of Paris,* echoes the original one.[15] Bethsabe's first words after her song are of Eden and Adam (l. 35); and David, enchanted by the lovely Bethsabe, compares her to "Faire Eva plac'd in perfect happinesse" (l. 53). We are reminded that in the Middle Ages and the Renaissance, David and Bathsheba were considered types of Adam and Eve.

In the context of the play, David's lust plunges his house and kingdom into suffering and tragedy. His deed is a poison dropped into a pool that spreads and destroys. His "babe" born of Bethsabe dies because of his sin (ll. 602-03). His own actions become the pattern for those of his sons: David's deception and murder of Ammon, and David's lawless lust for Bethsabe are precedents not only for Ammon's incestuous lust for Thamar, but also for Absolon's rebellion against Israel and his father, a rebellion which is actually spoken of in terms of lust (l. 988). The corruption is in David's house, originating from his sin.

David's sons are frequently aligned with his art; the dynamics of human relationship, as in the first scene of the play, are in part realized in terms of the dynamics of art, extending and enriching our understanding of both. The close connection of David's sons to his art in itself projects a sense of his denying a healthy separation between himself and his sons. His sons are *his* creations of beauty. In sorrow for the illness of his first son by Bethsabe, he cries that he will shatter his lute (ll. 604-05). When he hears that Absolon has killed Ammon, he compares his music to Ammon's life (ll. 875-79). But it is Absolon's life to which David is most tragically bound. And Absolon even more explicitly than his other sons merges into David's musical instruments.

Both Ammon and Joab speak of Absolon's hair as like the strings of David's lute or harp (ll. 747-48, 938-39). Later, after hearing of Absolon's death, David imagines finding a tree, blackened by lightening, under which to mourn Absolon and on which to break his lute and to hang his stringless harp. "There let the winds" (l. 1818), he cries, "Rend up the wretched engine by the roots / That held my dearest Absalon to death" (ll. 1822-23). The tree on which he has hung his harp becomes confused with the one on which Absolon hung, caught by his hair; and in David's following plea, "Then let them tosse my broken Lute to heaven" (l. 1825), that lute becomes one with Absolon himself. Earlier in the play David pays homage to Absolon with the words,

> Faire Absalon, the counterfeit of love,
> Sweet Absalon, the image of content.
>
> (ll. 1683-85)

"Counterfeit" and "image" are striking words. In a sense, Absolon is a work of art—David's art—from which David cannot separate himself.

David's relation to Absolon, as it was to Bethsabe, is self-destructive. Early in the play David sees his "longings tangled in . . . [Bethsabe's] haire" (l. 116), and his love for Absolon in a similar way is symbolized by his delight in the beauty of his son's hair. As with Bethsabe he is metaphorically entangled in Absolon's hair. Thus even when, as one soldier states it, Absolon's "stonie heart did hunt his fathers death" (p. 1561), David admonishes his soldiers,

> . . . touch no haire of him,
> Not that faire haire with which the wonton winds
> Delight to play, and love to make it curle,
> Wherein the Nightingales would build their nests,
> And make sweet bowers in every golden tresse,
> To sing their lover every night asleepe.
>
> (ll. 1401-06)

Absolon's "golden haire" (l. 1533), previously likened to the wires of David's musical instruments, becomes, in a soldier's words, "Cords prepar'd to stop . . . [David's] breath" (l. 1555). His own art, his son, nearly destroys him—because of his failure to distance himself.

David's response to the vision of Bethsabe which the Prologue reveals to him sets the pattern for the play. The whole drama is a working out of the ramification of that first scene; and Peele's particular delineation of that scene renders David's moral failure in terms also of a failure of the imagination. Conversely, David's connecting his sons to his musical instruments suggests that emotional concerns also have aesthetic dimensions.

For both Paris in *The Araygnement of Paris* and David in *David and Bethsabe* the denial of the separation of audience (or artist) and show, of the realm of reality and that of image, results in devastating tragedy, a tragedy that, as in *Doctor Faustus,* figures the fall of man. Peele's two plays, however, go one step further. Both move to dramatize a healthy response to art—one that acknowledges the difference between art and reality; and, as a consequence, the fall becomes a fortunate one. Tragedy and death are transformed into regeneration and salvation.

The movement from fall to redemption in *The Araygnement of Paris* is dependent on the ultimate emergence of an ideal audience, contrasting, of course, to Paris. Time, in that play, does not move in a realistic way. Paris leaves the council of the gods and the tragedy of Troy begins, but we immediately abridge time and that tragedy. After dismissing Paris from its presence and its thoughts, the council turns to solving the three goddesses' quarrel as to which one deserves the golden apple. The solution, worked out by Diana, transports us to a present historical era, to Queen Elizabeth herself, who was audience to the play. It transports us, moreover, to a new Eden, for Diana's solution is to give the golden apple to Elizabeth herself, whom she pictures as combining the virtues of Juno, Pallas, Venus, and Diana: she is the creator and ruler of a glorious and peaceful "seconde Troie" (l. 1153), "Ycompast rounde with a commodious sea" (l. 1154), like the sacred waters surrounding Eden, whose "people are ycleped Angeli" (l. 1155).

"And glad I am," Juno says about Diana's resolving the conflict among the goddesses, "Diana found the art, / Without Offence so well to please desart" (ll. 1194-95); Juno's use of the word "arte" underscores that Diana's conclusion to the play is itself a work of art. As art, like the rest of the play, that conclusion is fictional: in the long speech in which Diana presents her resolution, she creates a figure of Elizabeth, an imaginary realization of a queen who rules over a second Eden. Significantly, the stage direction which comes before Diana's speech about Elizabeth reads, "Diana describeth the Nymphe Eliza a figure of the Queene" (after 1137); she describes "a figure," not the Queen herself. The golden ball, Diana tells Elizabeth, is in

> Praise of the wisedome, beautie and the state,
> That best becomes thy peerless excellencie.

> (ll. 1243-44)

"That best becomes" suggests Diana is not necessarily describing an accomplished fact, but, more likely, a potential or ideal. The play ends with an image that is not exactly the same as the "real" world; it is an image that gains logic and validity only in the context of the play itself. Diana's "arte," unlike that of the other three goddesses, calls attention to itself as an image, separate from the "real" world that defines the audience.

Diana's "arte," moreover, calls for a response from Elizabeth that appreciates that difference. *The Araygnement of Paris* stands in the long tradition of courtly mummings and masques, the purpose of which was to honor the court. We honor someone when we affirm the best in that person; but in so doing we also assert the possibility of that person's further growth, of the realization of that ideal even more fully. It is when we profess that no growth is necessary, that the honoring image is the same as reality, that we flatter or are flattered. What kept courtly mummings and masques from being merely flattery, it seems to me, was not simply convention, but the fact that in those works royalty and nobility watched figures of themselves (as, for example, Katherine of Aragon did in the pageant celebrating her wedding in 1501) or "played" roles, which is quite different from their simply entering the shows as themselves. The reality was not synonymous with the images in the show. The masks traditionally worn by those of the court who participated in such shows insisted on the difference between themselves and the figures they were playing. They were acting not as themselves, but as various symbols or images, images, of course, that reflected honor back on the actors. In 1377 a small play was performed involving the prince (later Richard II) in which several mummers appeared and played dice with him, having previously loaded the dice so Richard would win the gifts they had brought. Though he, of course, did not wear a mask, Richard was essentially "playing" a role: if he had actually believed it was his own nobleness that made the dice fall in his favor, he would hardly have been able to appreciate that he was being honored, and the mumming would have simply flattered him. The knowledge of its fictiveness was necessary for the very purpose of the occasion.[16]

The same demands are made on Elizabeth in her response to *The Araygnement of Paris.* Without seeing the ideal queen depicted by Diana as fiction, Elizabeth would be giving herself no room in which to grow. She would be accepting flattery, not honor, which in itself would belie the play's image of her greatness. In the first act, Juno, Venus, and Pallas accept with considerable graciousness the gifts of the lesser country gods. Juno declares that the welcome they have been given "exceeds these wittes of mine" (l. 187); and Venus, that the delights presented them "pass the banquets of king Jove" (l. 189). The implication is that the welcome is more exceptional than the world of the guests themselves. Since the play defines Elizabeth as outshining those goddesses, she must be fully as gracious in her response to the gift that is honoring *her,* the image with which the play ends. Hers must be a modesty and a generosity that acknowledge that she is being honored, that she has been idealized by Diana. The ending of the play, then, assumes an imaginative experience, on the part of the audience Elizabeth, that is very different from Paris's in the judgment scene. It is an experience that entails an awareness of art (in consisting of images, in being fictive) as separate from reality.

In Philip Sidney's "The Lady of May," written within a few years of *The Araygnement of Paris,* Elizabeth herself was, as in Peele's play, not only the audience, but an actual participant. While visiting the gardens at Wanstead, Elizabeth was accosted by actors who immediately began their masque. The show consists primarily of a contest between shepherds and foresters, which Elizabeth was asked to judge, determining as she did whether the shepherd Espilus or the forester Therion better deserved to wed the May Lady. Elizabeth is implicitly directed to respond in a certain way, to choose the forester over the shepherd. She can make that choice only if she follows the masque's argument and, in so doing, lives up to the wisdom credited her by the characters in the masque. Too much, however, in this instance, was entrusted to the queenly audience. The novelty of the desired choice (the placing of a forester above a shepherd) proved self-defeating, for Elizabeth responded incorrectly. The concluding song, which follows her judgment, in its story of the happy Silvanus and the disappointed Pan, inappropriately celebrates the choice of the forester; her improper response has completely vitiated the coherence of the masque. Sidney's mistake was in part an aesthetic one.[17] He leads Elizabeth into a play, without focusing explicitly enough on the fact that the role in the play is not exactly the same as that of Elizabeth in real life. Peele in *The Araygnement of Paris* is less courageous: he asks Elizabeth to respond in a conventional way. But, also, his play calls attention to the necessary separation of art and reality, the play world versus the real world. Peele makes clear that *The Araygnement of Paris* is honoring, not flattering, Elizabeth.

In Peele's play Elizabeth, in completing Diana's "figure of the Queene," makes possible the play's movement to regeneration. We are not simply dealing with aesthetic response and experience. Elizabeth's audience response is defined by the play as one that affirms her dedication to an ideal and to growth. Indeed, her role as guide and protector of a kingdom implies a moral and spiritual greatness, just as Paris's role as the destroyer of a kingdom suggests his corruption. Elizabeth, a wanderer in "Phoebes groves" (l. 1149), has a purity that aligns her with Diana, a purity juxtaposed to Paris's licentiousness.

The difference between Diana and the other three great goddesses is striking. Although the play takes place in her bower, Diana does not appear on stage until the council of the gods is called. Thus, we think of her as participating in the beauty of the setting, but not in the bickering, comic quarreling of the other goddesses. In the council she does not speak until Jupiter asks her to guide the three goddesses away while the gods decide about the golden apple. When Diana herself is given the apple to award, her manner is eloquent and stately; and the other goddesses' courteous and unified ac-

ceptance of her as judge underscores her dignity. It is through her presence at the end of the play that the majesty of Juno, the wisdom of Pallas, and the beauty of Venus become again noble virtues, which Elizabeth can be seen as embodying. The new Eden with which the play closes is the product of the audience's and artist's healthy imaginations, inseparable from moral health.

The conclusion of *David and Bethsabe* emerges from a comparable development. David does not always respond to art as he does to the vision of the beautiful Bethsabe in the first scene. At three crucial moments in the play, the deaths of each of three sons, someone presents him with a work of art; and his healthy response to those artworks gradually stems the evil let loose in his house. Significantly, each experience of art leads to his accepting the death of one of his sons; and in so doing, David separates himself from them.

On the first occasion, his babe's death, the artwork is the prophet Nathan's tale of the rich man who owns many sheep, yet who robs a poor man of his only lamb; on the second, Ammon's death, it is the Widow from Thecoa's tale of her relatives' intention to kill her only surviving son for the murder of her other son; and on the third, Absolon's death, it is Joab's "tale" (l. 1917) of David's foolishness in turning away from his followers in his grief for Absolon. Quite unlike his earlier reaction to the sight of Bethsabe, David ultimately responds to each "tale" as an artistic structure, apprehending the separation between it and the "actual" world.

First, David takes part in the fictions Nathan and the Widow present him: they each ask him to judge a particular case, and, as king, he does so. But Nathan and the Widow then step back and disclose their stories as fictions. Nathan acknowledges that his tale of the two men and the lamb are not literally true, but a useful fiction, and the Widow, that she was only pretending to be talking about her own sons, only pretending to be begging for her own son's life. By stepping out of those fictions and seeing them as such, David is able to see himself in a new light. In the first case that new light makes him sincerely grieve for his sin of lust and understand the death of his babe as God's justice; and in the second case, his new awareness leads to his recalling Absolon, Ammon's murderer, from banishment, thus signifying his acceptance of Ammon's death.

Joab's "tale" is persuasive rhetoric, but by calling it a "tale" David reveals his awareness of it as a verbal construct, molded and formed by the imagination. David's interaction with Joab's "tale" is similar to his interaction with the other two. He must see the world through the words and images of Joab's rhetoric and then he must step back into his own life and see the relevance of those words and images. Joab's tale makes David leave his pavilion[18] where he has sat sequestered, mourning for Absolon's death. He rises, in Bethsabe's words, "to give honor to" his two captains (ll. 1895-96), one of whom has killed Absolon. That acceptance of Absolon's death provides the final step in David's acknowledging his son Salomon as the heir to his throne. The necessity for Bethsabe and Nathan to petition for Salomon earlier in the scene implies a distance between David and that son that contrasts with the king's previous passionate and disastrous involvements in his sons. That distance and his concomitant ability to separate himself from Absolon suggests David's redemption and triumph for Israel.

Salomon, in embodying the glorious future of David's line, a line that leads to Christ, affirms the play's transformation of David's fall.[19] Significantly, Salomon's speech of ecstasy near the end of the play reminds us in several ways of the Prologue and the first scene. He speaks of himself as an eagle "towring in the aire" (l. 1760), "emboldened / With eies intentive to bedare the sun" (ll. 1763-64), "mounted on the burning wings / Of zeale devine" (ll. 1768-67). The words "towring" and "mounted" bring to mind David in his kingly tower at the beginning of the play. The "burning wings" recall the Prologue's evocation of the image of Icarus, who prays to "devine Adonay" (l. 16) that "The hearers minds" (l. 18) be so guided in their "flight" (l. 19) that "Their mounting feathers scorch not with the fire, / That none can temper but thy holy hand" (ll. 20-21). The Icarus image resonates in the first scene. The song David hears Bethsabe sing while she bathes is of sun, fire, burning, and the tempering sweet air and shrouding shade. Her song is a prayer that her "beauties fire" not "Emflame unstaied desire" (ll. 30-31). That prayer, of course, is not answered and David is brought down from his tower. "[T]hy beautie scorcht my conquerd soule" (l. 134), says David to Bethsabe; he, like Icarus, tumbles headlong from the height of glory.[20] Salomon, however, unlike David, is protected by God. He reverses the *de casibus* tragedy: a transformation of Icarus, he is able to fly toward the sun, like an eagle able to look on the glory above him.

The construction of the first scene of *David and Bethsabe,* that of an audience (David) watching a show (Bethsabe), defines David's possession of Bethsabe as comparable to an audience's failure to see art as separate from nature, from everyday reality. Similarly, Paris sees the show the goddesses present him as possessable, part of his reality. Art perceived in this way, these plays suggest, is destructive, profoundly so because the realm of the imagination and moral health are inextricably connected. The importance of seeing art as separate from nature and of a different order of being is hardly unique to these plays. We have only to think of *The Faerie Queene,* where encampments of

evil—for example the Bower of Bliss, Busyrane's Castle, the false Florimell—are frequently structured by art that seems indistinguishable from nature.

The experience of art, of course, can be beneficial, but for that an audience must ultimately acknowledge the difference (as well as the similarity) between its world and the illusion it is witnessing or in which it has been immersed. In *The Araygnement of Paris,* when Venus presents her show of Helen to Paris, she involves him in a fantasy, an illusion. Similarly, she forces the shepherdess Thestilis into an enchantment when she makes her take part in the second show she presents to Paris. In that play-within-a-play Thestilis is made to fall in love with "A foule croked Churle" who "crabedly refuzeth her" (after l. 721). The destructiveness of Venus's art is evident when we realize there is no evidence that either Paris or Thestilis is ever led out of his or her illusion. Venus's fictions are simply destructive entrapments. In *A Midsummer Night's Dream,* Titania, when she is made to woo the ass Bottom, has a part in a play-within-a-play quite similar to that in which Thestilis is involved; but, unlike Thestilis, Titania is eventually released from that play. Only then is it possible for her experience to be in any way positive. The happy conclusions of both *The Araygnement of Paris* and *David and Bethsabe* depend on the emergence of characters who similarly are led to appreciate the line between art and reality.

William Nelson in his provocative book, *Fact or Fiction,* argues that there was in the Renaissance a pervasive "sense of doubt about the legitimacy and value of fiction."[21] Peele's *The Araygnement of Paris* and *David and Bethsabe,* however, suggest a different attitude: fictiveness, the fact that art is not nature, is not something to be apologized for or dismissed. The value of fiction for Peele—and I also suggest for other Renaissance practitioners such as Shakespeare—lies in the very fact that it is a deviation from truth. Fiction, like a trope, casts a new light on reality: it makes us see with a new perspective, a perspective that depends on appreciating that the vehicle relates to the tenor, yet is not the same as it, that fiction relates to reality, yet is essentially different.

Notes

1. All citations are from the text by Daniel Seltzer, Regents Renaissance Drama Series (Lincoln: Univ. of Nebraska Press, 1963).

2. Sir Thomas Browne's declaration in *Religio Medici* that "Art is the perfection of Nature" (*Works,* ed. Geoffrey Keynes [Chicago: Univ. of Chicago Press, 1964], I, 26) is as typical of the Renaissance as Sir Philip Sidney's opposition of the world of nature, which he calls "essenciall," to that of art, which he calls "imitation or fiction"

(*Defence of Poesie, The Prose Works*, ed. Albert Feuillerat, III [Cambridge: Cambridge Univ. Press, 1968], 8). An understanding of Renaissance aesthetics, it seems to me, must take into consideration the relation of those two contradictory ideas—that the artificial and the natural are ultimately indistinguishable and that art and reality are essentially different. Neither perspective, I believe, must be allowed to subsume the other. In this paper, however, I shall focus more on the separation of the two realms than on their connection.

3. Two notable exceptions are Inga-Stina Ewbanks, "The House of David in Renaissance Drama: A Comparative Study," *Renaissance Drama,* 8 (1965), 3-40, and Henry G. Lesnick, "The Structural Significance of Myth and Flattery in Peele's *Arraignment of Paris,*" *Studies in Philology,* 65 (1968), 163-70. My interpretations of Peele's two plays are consistent in several ways with both of those articles.

4. All citations are to the text by R. Mark Benbow in *The Life and Works of George Peele,* gen. ed. Charles Tyler Prouty, III (New Haven: Yale Univ. Press, 1970).

5. Henry Green, ed. (1586; facsimile rpt. New York: Benjamin Bloom, 1967), p. 83. In Whitney's emblem Paris's choice should have been Pallas. In Peele's play, however, Pallas does not seem significantly better than the other two goddesses.

6. Andrew V. Ettin in his suggestive essay, "Magic into Art: The Magician's Renunciation of Magic in English Renaissance Drama," *Texas Studies in Literature and Language,* 19 (1977), 283, sees the scene in Marlowe's play as simply indicating the fragility of art; but the intensity of the magician's distress, it seems to me, evokes a sense of more profound catastrophe.

7. The Early Years of George Peele," *Proceedings and Transactions of the Royal Society of Canada,* Ser. 3, 20 (1928), Sec. 2, 294. Quoted also by Benbow, *Works of Peele,* III, 15.

8. Line 202, from David H. Horne's text of the poem in *The Life and Minor Works of George Peele,* gen. ed. Charles Tyler Prouty, I (New Haven: Yale Univ. Press, 1952).

9. *Works of Peele,* III, 22.

10. Ibid, p. 46.

11. See Lesnick for a fuller discussion of the tragic-comic patterns in *The Araygnement of Paris.*

12. The play is structured in a way that pushes into the background the logical inference that Colin's unhappiness must have begun before the episode of the golden apple. In our experience of the play, the scene is which Paris responds to the goddesses' shows ushers in tragedy.

13. All citations are to the text by Elmer M. Blistein in *The Life and Works of George Peele,* gen. ed. Prouty, III.

14. It is interesting to compare the first scene of the play with the second. The second scene takes place in Rabath, where David's followers are fighting his war against the enemies of Israel. David's followers, set in motion, ironically, by Bethsabe's husband (not a detail in the Bible), scale and win the "kingly Tower" (line 180) of the city. Suggestively, this tower of Rabath and David's tower in the first scene were likely represented by the same structure on stage. In ascending the tower, David's followers further his kingship; in descending the tower, David undermines that kingship.

15. See Ewbanks' "House of David" for a much fuller discussion than mine of the pattern of the Fall and the effects of David's sin in *David and Bethsabe.*

16. For a different perspective on the show celebrating the marriage of Katherine of Aragon to Prince Arthur and the mumming presented to Prince Richard, see Stephen Orgel, *The Jonsonian Masque* (Cambridge: Harvard Univ. Press, 1965), pp. 19-20, 22-26.

17. There is always the possibility that Sidney's mistake was primarily political, that, as Robert Kimbrough and Philip Murphy argue, Elizabeth understood that Therion represented the Earl of Leicester and, in choosing Epilus, was refusing to give Leicester "a nod of approval" ("The Helmingham Hall Manuscript of Sidney's *The Lady of May:* A Commentary and Transcription," *Renaissance Drama,* N.S. 1 [1968], ed. S. Schoenbaum, p. 105).

18. There are no stage directions saying that he leaves. We are told only that Joab "unfolds the pavillion" (after 1846) and David "riseth up" (after 1896), but obviously rising includes leaving the pavilion, since the final speeches of the play logically must be delivered from a central, opened position on stage.

19. Ewbanks also feels that Peele turns "the love of King David and Fair Bathsheba into a kind of divine comedy" (p. 15). Bethsabe bears to David not only the babe who dies, in retribution for their sin, but also Salomon.

20. Later in the play, the rebelling Absolon, similarly, is spoken of as possessing a "scorched bosome" (line 987).

21. *Fact or Fiction: The Dilemma of the Renaissance Story-Teller* (Cambridge: Harvard Univ. Press, 1973), p. 9.

THE ARRAIGNMENT OF PARIS (1584)

CRITICAL COMMENTARY

Andrew Von Hendy (essay date 1968)

SOURCE: Von Hendy, Andrew. "The Triumph of Chastity: Form and Meaning in *The Arraignment of Paris.*" *Renaissance Drama* n.s. 1 (1968): 87-101.

[*In the following essay, Von Hendy examines* The Arraignment of Paris *as a compliment for Queen Elizabeth, discussing the identification of the Tudors with Troy, the masque, and the reference to Diana.*]

In spite of its charm, *The Arraignment of Paris* is usually dismissed by criticism as either disorganized or trivial.[1] This treatment is understandable if the play is judged by standards appropriate to more mimetic forms of drama. It appears both significant and well-designed, however, if we recognize how strongly it has been affected by the conventions of masques and entertainments. Peele responded to a specific occasion with a beautiful compliment to the Queen. This compliment is the formal intention of his play. He constructs *The Arraignment* to culminate, as masques do, in a scene which will absorb the audience into its imaginary world. The plot inclines us to accept the moral and political ideals with which the climactic moment invests the Queen. When she resolves the pastoral dilemma within the play, we witness a formal "triumph," the triumph of chastity over moral and political subversion.

The resemblance of the play to a masque is indicated on the title page of the 1584 quarto.[2] There *The Arraignment* is called a "pastorall." Our literary historians find the essence of Renaissance pastoral in the self-conscious contrast between the natural and the artificial.[3] The poet withdraws from the world to contemplate the problems of his everyday existence. Spenser and Milton meditated in a form which encouraged the projection of their ideal aspirations. I think both masque and pastoral are species of what Northrop Frye calls "romance," a mood in literature of dreamlike wish fulfillment.[4] Romance moves away from mimetic representation of the "real" world. The unfulfilled wish usually appears as the goal of a quest, and romance plots in general have a way of suggesting allegory. The characters are general types, sometimes clearly fragments of a single personality. Their actions are often absurd or puzzling by realistic standards. A psychologist might call their behavior "compulsive." The setting of romance is nearly always remote in time and space, a magic world where suspension of the natural laws is taken for granted.

Romantic narrative is apt to seem sporadic, since the author is never far from his besetting abstractions. He introduces meditations on matters like fortune and justice or explicit debates, as between love and honor. Finally, to borrow a term from current politics, romance is radically conservative; it contrasts an ideal society that never was or will be to the actual society in which the writer lives.

The Arraignment opens with a prologue best explained, I think, by the political implications of romance. Ate introduces the gold ball which will cause the goddesses' quarrel. But her appearance is in unexplained contrast to the mood of the scenes which follow. Enid Welsford describes the problem in *The Court Masque:* "The appearance of Ate 'from lowest hell' should surely prelude the 'tragedy of Troy,' instead of leading to a piece of extravagant flattery written in pastoral style" (p. 278). This objection seems to me valid if we see no connection between the appearance of Ate and the "extravagant flattery" which follows it. I think we do find such a connection, however, in the political implications of *The Arraignment*'s romantic plot. We can recognize these implications by recalling some commonplaces of Elizabethan literature. First, Tudor history identified Trojan Brute as the founder of England and London as Troynovant. The "tale of Troy" had nationalistic consequences. Second, the poets inherited from antiquity an association of the pastoral world with the Golden Age of Saturn's reign. Third, Elizabeth was frequently identified with Astraea, goddess of justice, who fled the world at the end of the Golden Age. The famous line in Virgil's fourth eclogue, *"iam redit et Virgo, redeunt Saturnia regna,"* is obviously ready for application to the Virgin Queen. Fourth, political unrest was often represented as an anti-Olympian principle of evil. The Titans frequently appear, for example, in the role Ate takes in *The Arraignment.*

These four considerations are associated with each other in various combinations in Peele's nondramatic works, especially in *The Tale of Troy, The Device of the Pageant Borne Before Wolstan Dixi, Descensus Astraeae,* and *Anglorum Feriae.* In the most elaborate grouping, *Descensus Astraeae,* the Lord Mayor's Pageant of 1591, "Astraea with hir sheephook on the top of the pageant" is identified with the Queen.[5] Euphrosyne, guarding Astraea with the other Graces, explains the device:

> Whilom when Saturnes golden raigne did cease,
>   and yron age had kindled cruel warres:
> Envie in wrath, perturbing common peace,
>   engendring cancred hate and bloody jarres:
> Lo then Olympus king, the thundring Jove,
>   raught hence this gracious nymph Astraea faire,
> Now once again he sands hir from above.
>
> (ll. 66-72)

Astraea is threatened by "malecontents" who "strive and cannot strike." Elizabeth is preserved by miracle from the mortal condition. *"In the hinder part of the Pageant did sit a Child, representing Nature, holding in her hand a distaffe, and spinning a Web, which passed through the hand of Fortune and was wheeled up by Time . . ."* (p. 218).

> And Time and Kinde
> Produce hir yeares to make them numberlesse
> While Fortune for hir service and hir sake,
> With golden hands doth strengthen and enrich
> The Web that they for faire Astraea weave.
>
> (ll. 33-37)

Thus, in **The Arraignment,** Ate provokes a whole cycle of war and injustice, but she fails to disturb seriously the order of the gods, and she cannot affect at all a nymph served by the Fates themselves. **The Arraignment** follows the pattern of political myth summarized in Euphrosyne's speech.

The prologue, then, stands in much the same relationship to the scenes which follow it as an antimasque does to the masque proper. That is why Peele considers it decorous to change so abruptly from Ate to an ideal landscape across which the gods move in formal progress. (Their procession resembles a summer pageant greeting the Queen on the grounds of an estate.) Though the reign of Saturn is past, the Iron Age has not yet come and will not come till Ate prevails. Death and unrequited love have already appeared "even in Arcadia," but the natural world still keeps about it some of its unfallen glory. The setting of the first four scenes derives obviously from the *locus amoenus* of medieval dream vision, the earthly paradise just below the moon. The minor deities bring their gifts as Diana's vassals, but these gifts also signify the abundance of nature in the paradisal garden.[6] This traditional mode of symbolism shows most clearly, perhaps, in Flora's lovely catalogue of her jewels (I.iii.17-32). This ordered nature, governed by Diana, will become especially significant in the fifth act.

The procession of minor deities culminates in a spectacular burst of song and dance. A "quier within" responds antiphonally to a choir outside, that is, off stage. The latter is composed of the country gods, whereas the former, we are told, consists of the Muses themselves. This suggests again how far we are from a fallen world. The three goddesses march in "like to the pompe of heaven above" (l. 85), but as they exchange compliments we discover they have a further goal. They leave the stage moving toward a meeting with Diana herself. This procession will not reach its goal, however, until the last act. Its movement is interrupted by the disturbances that comprise the center of the play.

Act I concludes ominously with an interview between Paris and Oenone. The scene is superficially idyllic.

Before the famous roundelay, "Faire and fayre and twise so faire," Paris assures Oenone that their music is "figure of the love that growes twixt thee and me" (I.iii.54). But Oenone is worried. In deciding what he should play, Paris has raised sinister topics:

> How Saturne did devide his kingdome . . .
> How mightie men made foule succesles warre,
> Against the gods and state of Jupiter.
>
> (I.v.19-22)

This catalogue proceeds (as the play does) from political rebellion to "love offence." Peele foreshadows the fate of Paris in terms of Ovid moralized. Paris' repertoire, both political and amatory, consists of tales of infidelity later corrected by justice. Oenone wisely invokes Cupid's curse: "They that do chaunge olde love for new, pray gods they chaunge for worse."

Act II opens *ex abrupto,* as the stage direction has it, with a fight among the goddesses on their way to Diana. Nothing in the first act has prepared us for the low tone and diction of the participants. Discord has invaded even the society of the gods. Its personification, Ate, appears in a thunderstorm and places before the goddesses the fatal apple, to be given "to the fayrest." They agree only to make the next person who appears "umpier in this controversie," and in walks Paris.

His judgment had long been a popular topic for moral allegory. In Montemayor's *Diana,* for example, "Delia and Andronius spend the greater part of a night arguing the question whether Paris gave the apple to the right goddess or not and whether the inscription on it referred to physical or mental beauty."[7] In England the topic had even been applied traditionally to royal compliment. "The Paris story was a common subject of the pageants—for Queen Margaret at Edinburgh in 1503, for the coronation of Anne Boleyn in 1533, and at a marriage masque in 1566."[8] I would guess that the topic was common on such occasions not only because Paris made the most famous pastoral choice but also because of the connection of Troy with the Tudor political myth.

Paris' three temptations are symbolized in the elaborate "shows" with which each goddess accompanies her claim. Juno offers gold and empire, Pallas wisdom and martial glory. Venus offers both herself and Helen, whom she introduces with a significant change of diction as

> A gallant girle, a lustie minion trull,
> That can give sporte to thee thy bellyfull,
> To ravish all thy beating vaines with joye.
>
> (II.ii.75-77)

Helen's song is itself a relevant piece of wit. Its language recalls the great Tuscan celebrators of courtly love, but it is a song against Diana as the personification of chastity. Diana, as Helen sings, is the goddess of a love very different in kind from Helen's. As queen of nymphs and flowers, woodland and forest, Diana deals death to shepherds. But as queen of hell she comforts the damned who died for love, and as queen of heaven she tenders light to weary hearts. She is a goddess of the Platonic ladder. Helen, however, calls herself a "Diana" who can make war with her very glances on this triple goddess of chastity. And Paris gives Venus the ball.

Now, it is quite possible to argue that Paris makes the correct pastoral choice. Paris himself makes this claim in his speech before the Council of the Gods. Hallett Smith summarizes his argument:

> The simplicity of the shepherd's conditions makes for an invulnerability to appeals in the name of wealth or of chivalry. It is only beauty, of the three ideals represented by the goddesses, which has any significant power in a pastoral life.[9]

The structure of the play, however, frames this bold assertion in an ironic moral perspective. Helen's song clarifies the issue. All three of the goddesses represent forms of beauty; Paris chooses the lowest form. At the end of Act II he exits with Venus, but Act III consists almost entirely of choral commentary on his lack of wisdom. At the end of Act II Ate has succeeded in making the goddesses forget their purpose; the Diana against whom Helen sings is the very goal of their progress. From now on, however, the rift widens between gods and men in the post-Saturnian world. After Paris has been arraigned and judged, the gods will remember Diana.

The contrast between "the two loves" determines, I think, Peele's famous plagiarism at the beginning of Act III where he introduces a cast of characters out of *The Shepherd's Calendar*. As Peele conceives their conduct, it resembles the behavior of Lyly's lovers, the behavior Shakespeare remembered with a certain irony in *A Midsummer-Night's Dream* and *As You Like It*. "As all is mortall in nature, so is all nature in love, mortall in folly." Love is midsummer madness, lunacy induced by the elixir of a flower called "Love in idlenesse." Lyly's treatment of the theme in *Endymion* is especially appropriate for comparison with *The Arraignment*; in it, too, the presence of the Queen at the performance actually affects the meaning of the play. And Lyly, as usual, makes his antitheses crystal clear. Cynthia is the Moon, chaste affection, true friendship, and Elizabeth. Tellus is the Earth, physical sex, perfidy, and (perhaps) Mary, Queen of Scots. Eumenides must decide between the two extremes. He must choose between love and honor, attaining his lady, Semele, or freeing Endymion from his fatal sleep. Of course he elects honor: "Vertue shall subdue affections, wisedome

lust, friendship beautie." Eumenides has to make the so-called choice of Hercules prominent in medieval and Renaissance iconography.

Paris' choice in *The Arraignment* is built on a similar dichotomy, although the presence of three alternatives rather obscures the two contraries. Montemayor's characters see the Platonic dualism when they dispute whether the inscription on the apple refers to physical or mental beauty. In his narrative poem, *The Tale of Troy*, Peele himself reduced the three possibilities to two:

> Ah Paris, hadst thou had but equall eyes,
> Indifferent in bestowing of the pryze,
> Thy humaine wits might have discerned well,
> Where the true beautie of the mind did dwell.
> But men must erre, because but men they bee.
> And men with love yblinded may not see.[10]

Act III demonstrates the folly of Paris' blindness to "true beautie of the mind" and the consequences of his erring choice.

It opens with Colin himself exhibiting his famous wares. He sings a medieval "complaint" which will soon be matched by Oenone's venture in the same form. Hobinol, Digon, and Thenot, who succeed Colin on stage, make the connection between his fate and Oenone's. Paris' choice offends all true lovers: "Poore *Colin*, that is ill for thee, that art as true in trust / To thy sweete smerte, as to his Nymphe *Paris* hath bin unjust" (III.iii.19-20). When Mercury enters to summon Paris, Oenone imagines "th'unpertiall skyes" have answered her prayer.[11] She does not realize that he comes at the partial behests of Juno, Pallas, and Vulcan and that injustice seems now to prevail above as below.

This state of affairs is reiterated in the curious scene which follows. A group of shepherds begs Venus for revenge on Thestylis. She has finally murdered Colin by her disdain. Venus promises justice for Paris' sake. She blames her son "that ever love was blinde." Paris has been listening quietly, but now he objects. If Venus would handle Cupid's bow, justice could be done in love. Venus immediately counterattacks by asking Paris if he has ever been in love. In reply to his evasive answer, "Lady, a little once," she seems to insist that true lovers, unlike wantons, will their own condition and cannot be cured by external causes. Paris is worried. Can Venus and Cupid excuse a slight past offence? Venus replies sardonically with a description of the torments false lovers suffer in hell. Paris is astounded: "Is Venus and her sonne so full of justice and severytye" (III.v.31)? The answer sounds even more like something out of a medieval dream vision. Venus explains that her son is not only a boy but also a "mighty god." He is, in fact, the Eros of classical tradition: "His shafts keepe heaven and earth in awe" (l. 38). Paris, however, sees the fallacy (ll. 39-44):

PARIS:

> And hathe he reason to mantayne why Colin died
> for love.

VENUS:

> Yea, reason good I warrant thee, in right it might
> beehove.

PARIS:

> Then be the name of love adored, his bow is full of
> mighte,
> His woundes are all but for desert, his lawes are all
> but right:
> well for this once me lyst apply my speeches to thy
> sense,
> And *Thestilis* shall feele the paine for loves sup-
> posed offence.[12]

Venus' reply is analogous to the traditional Christian explanation of evil as God's will. Cupid's "right" can only seem like "might" to a mere mortal. Venus shrugs off Paris' sarcasm. This one time she will take a position he can understand; she will punish Thestylis according to Paris' standard.

The rest of the scene marks the working of her justice. The chant of the shepherds bearing Colin's hearse is matched by Thestylis' singing of "an olde songe called the woing of Colman" and of the complaint which follows it. The shepherds pick up the refrain of the complaint, "the grace of this song" being, as Peele says in his stage direction, "in the Shepherds Ecco to her verse." In other words, everyone sympathizes with her suffering, even Paris. Or perhaps I should say especially Paris. He has discovered that romantic love is a lord of terrible aspect. There is an undercurrent of threat in Venus' relationship with Paris. When he pities Thestylis aloud, Venus says, "Her fortune not unlyke to his whome cruell thow hast slaine" (l. 57).[13] She had only been toying with him, then, when she asked if he had ever been in love. Paris is already plunged in melancholy when Mercury enters. And when he sees Venus' fury he realizes at last that his folly is an instrument of destiny: "The angrye heavens for this fatall jar, / Name me the instrument of dire and deadly war" (III.vi.39-40).

The scenes of low humor which open Act IV parody in the usual manner the serious plot. Diana's nymph repulses Vulcan who thinks he can "treade awry as well as *Venus* doth" (IV.ii.2). At least this country jig quickly gives way to the Assembly of the Gods. I use Lydgate's title deliberately, to emphasize the medieval tradition behind this scene. The cosmological implications have their sources probably in the late Latin encyclopedists. They were popular in European literature at least from the time of the twelfth-century school of Chartres. The Olympians are not in this scene merely the gods Peele

found in his Latin school texts. They are the planetary powers these deities had come to represent in the Middle Ages. In medieval literature they frequently pass judgment upon changeable men from a realm of changeless values. E. M. W. Tillyard describes this convention in speaking of the descent of the gods in *The Testament of Cresseid:*

> The Middle Ages looked on the stars as an organic part
> of God's creation and as the perpetual instruments and
> diffusers of his will. . . . When Henryson used the
> planets as the instruments of Cresseid's punishment he
> . . . implied that her punishment was by God's will.[14]

Peele's point is no more explicitly Christian, of course, than Henryson's, or Spenser's in the Mutability Cantos. Peele's gods, like Spenser's, convene in a place like the Garden of Eden, an earthly paradise presided over by the goddess Natura, who is called Diana in Peele's play.

The arraignment itself is modeled on the form of the law case, which was nearly as popular for literary analogies as the parliament. Peele probably considered "Paris oration to the Councell of the gods" the major setpiece of the play. It is marked by the specious argument, the handsome elaboration of topics customary in traditional rhetoric. Paris defends himself principally by pleading, as Smith points out, that he made the correct choice for a shepherd. He excuses his moral blindness: "beauties blaze" is physical for him. Peele, however, does not excuse it any more than the Spenser of *Four Hymns* would. After Paris has withdrawn to await the verdict, the gods concur that by his own standards he is innocent. Juno merely pouts, but Pallas comes up with the crucial distinction of the play: "Whether the man be guiltie yea or noe, / That doth not hinder our appeale, I troe" (IV.iv.141-142). The choice of an erring mortal has not decided, and indeed could not decide, which is the greatest sort of beauty.

The sequence of events immediately following the oration has been frequently disregarded. It is crucial, however, to the unity of the plot and to the moral significance of the play. Paris is recalled and dismissed, but the gods do not imagine that in dismissing him they approve his argument. They send him forth to the fate his nature guarantees, to what Apollo calls "his never-dying payne." Paris' choice is its own punishment. Venus will stand by her promise of "luck in love," but Paris is now aware that he has made a tragic error, destined somehow to cause the destruction of his city: "My lucke is losse, howe ere my love do speede" (l. 166). Paris is shut out of the Garden forever. But in the pastoral world of man's fulfilled wish the gods can still triumph. Discord has darkened their counsel, but Apollo, the god of poetry and prophecy, restores them to light. Jurisdiction in the appeal belongs, he says, to Diana, in whose realm the affair took place. As in the Mutability

Cantos, the threat of disorder above the moon is to be handled by the goddess of nature. Apollo recalls the gods to their festal progress toward Diana. As they "rise and goe foorth," the processional movement of the play resumes, proceeding brilliantly now toward a goal off stage.

Act V is a single scene. After Diana receives the goddesses' pledges to support her decision, she *"describeth the Nymphe Eliza a figure of the Queene."* The goddesses agree; Elizabeth combines their wisdom, charm, and majesty. It happens to be the time of year when the Fates, the true "unpartiall dames" of Oenone's world, pay "their yearely due" to Elizabeth. So the goddesses follow them before the Queen, and Diana delivers, amid general acclaim, the ball of gold.

If this scene really strikes us as inconsequential "extravagant flattery," then Peele has failed to lure us sufficiently inside the masquelike mood and structure of the play. By "masque" I mean a spectacular, romantic form of drama which culminates in a dance integrating actors with audience. Masque is spectacular in its use of a full range of auditory and visual effects. It is romantic in plot (what Peele called the "device," Jonson the "hinge"). Its dancing leads to the exaltation of the audience who have been from the beginning the goal of the dancers' processional movement. Both their unmasking and selection of partners are meant to be gestures toward union. The successful masque must somehow incorporate the audience into its imaginary world.[15] The masque usually attempts a compliment which will equate the social harmony of its ideal world with the actual hierarchy of the court. In ***The Arraignment*** Peele wants Elizabeth to share for a golden moment of fantasy the pastoral world of the goddesses. Even granted the Tudor appetite for flattery, a moment of this sort would be indecorous if the mood were not perfect. The mood of an actual dramatic performance is as irrevocable as the mood of a dream, and this is particularly true of a masquelike play written for a specific occasion. But perhaps we can remind ourselves abstractly of the importance of mood in ***The Arraignment*** by considering briefly a masque in which Ben Jonson actually allegorizes the psychology of the revels.

A Vision of Delight opens with the arrival of Delight "accompanied with *Grace, Love, Harmonie, Revell, Sport, Laughter.* WONDER *following*" (ll. 4-6).[16] Delight represents the determination of the court to enjoy itself within the form of the revels. He announces directly (ll. 9-12) that the performance to follow is intended to unite the Christmas festivities of the court with the pastoral atmosphere of the masque. The occasion, even the time of day, must be special. Delight dismisses the clowns of the first antimasque as "all sowre and sullen looks away / that are the servants of the day" (ll. 26-27). He summons up Night instead, "to help the vision of DELIGHT" (l. 31) by keeping "all awake with *Phantomes*" (l. 40). And Night, to accomplish this, conjures up "Phant'sie" while the "Quire" invokes her mood:

> Yet let it like an odour rise
>   to all the Sences here,
> And fall like sleep upon their eies,
>   or musick in their eare.

(ll. 51-54)

These lines express the intention behind the successive regressions from the "real" world. Phant'sie, so to speak, is the audience's willing participation in the "hinge" of the poet. After she first breaks forth with a tumultuous speech, a second antimasque "of Phantasmes" portrays the mental dangers of Night which correspond to the "sowre and sullen looks" of Day. Fancy can be dangerous, even lunatic, if not controlled by the decorum of the occasion. Phant'sie herself dismisses her phantasms and produces a new scene. "The gold-haird *Houre*" descends, to the song of Peace, bringing with her *"the Bower of* Zephyrus." The speech of Wonder which follows praises in descriptive detail this new marvel of Art and Nature. Wonder represents the willingness of the courtiers to exclaim over the spectacular sets. When she concludes, Phant'sie remarks significantly, "How better then they are, are all things made / By WONDER!" (ll. 166-167). Phant'sie, however, immediately surpasses her previous achievement. *"Here (to a loud musicke) the Bower opens, and the Maskers [are] discovered, as the glories of the Spring"* (ll. 170-171). Wonder marvels over the details of this scene as she did the preceding one, concluding, "Whose power is this? what God?" (l. 199). And Phant'sie replies, "Behold a King / Whose presence maketh this perpetuall *Spring*" (ll. 201-202). After the Quire confirms her assertion, the maskers advance, singing and dancing *"their entry"* and *"their maine Dance."* Then *"they Danc'd with Ladies, and the whole Revells followed"* (l. 232). While the "gold-haird Houre" lasts King James does make, in the vision of delight, "perpetuall Spring." But Night and the Moone descend and Aurora appears "to bid you come away." As the maskers dance their *"going off"* the Quire sings, "They yield to Time, and so must all" (l. 244). Only the excited interplay of Phant'sie and Wonder could evoke a vision of a garden court where King James reigns in a timeless world. Our revels now are ended, and the mood melts into air, into thin air.

We can see by comparison that Peele's play is not a proper masque. Its spectacle, though plentiful, is relatively incidental; it does not end in formal dance; and its romantic plot is too rich in action and even in character development. We can also see, however, that it is constructed like a masque to induce the willing suspension of disbelief necessary to the compliment.

Act V of *The Arraignment* is in no sense merely tacked on for the occasion; rather, the occasion shapes the play. The festive social conventions affect the literary ones. To resolve the action Elizabeth must be taken into the pastoral as queen of the triumphing gods.

In the forms of Renaissance romance where a social compliment of this type is intended, political allegory nearly always suggests itself. The works I have mentioned because of their relevance to the conventions of *The Arraignment* all have political implications. Even Spenser's generalized allegory in the Mutability Cantos contains the archetypal pattern of revolt which haunted the Elizabethan mind. Spenser's mythopoeic use of the traditional Platonic cosmology implies a highly conservative politics. The same is true of Johnson's masques, where the favorite themes, as in medieval dream vision, are the triumph of reason over sensuality and of order over disorder. These are the explicit themes, too, of Lyly's *Endymion,* yet Tellus is suspected of being someone like Mary, Queen of Scots in contrast to Cynthia's Elizabeth. One might almost say that the presence of the Queen attracts a political application.

In fact, I believe we can safely reverse the causal relationship and say that where we find this masquelike theme, the presence of the Queen is probable. I have referred, in connection with "Love in idlenesse," to the famous "faire Vestall, throned by the West" passage in *A Midsummer-Night's Dream* (II.i.148-169). The allegory in this passage closely resembles that in both *Endymion* and *The Arraignment,* which we know were affected by the Queen's presence. Cupid, flying between earth and moon, thinks he shoots at an appropriate sublunary target. But the time, the person, and his aim are all misjudged. The song of a mysterious mermaid enraptures nature, and in this brief restoration of the Golden Age the "imperiall Votresse" to Diana walks in a realm apart. Cupid's arrow is analogous to Ate's golden ball. Among fallen mortals it produces the maddening moral blindness called "Love in idlenesse," but Elizabeth is above the sting of sensuality as she is above every assault from below. She passes on, "in maiden meditation, fancy free." Recognition of this theme will not help to resolve the voluminous controversy about the occasion for the first composition of *A Midsummer-Night's Dream* or the occasion alluded to in the passage above, but I think it does support the probability that the play was written for a performance at which the Queen presided.

So in the case of *The Arraignment,* the intention to compliment the Queen seems to draw Peele to a plot with political overtones. He may have chosen the story of Paris for his "device" because it combined with its choice-of-Hercules parable some specific associations with Tudor history. As Tillyard finds in Shakespeare's history plays a kind of secularized mystery cycle, we can find in *The Arraignment* suggestions of a political analogue to the Fall and the Redemption. Paris is the first parent of England. His choice of the lesser good inaugurates a cycle of history in the fallen world which will lead to Brute's settlement of England and to the establishment of the Tudors on the throne after a century of civil broils. Elizabeth's reign in the New Troy restores at last the social harmony and justice which Paris lost. This restoration is symbolized in the play by the course of the golden ball from the hand of Ate to the hand of Elizabeth. Ate first rises at the bidding of Tellus. Whether or not Tellus represents Mary, Queen of Scots as she is sometimes said to do in *Endymion,* Ate does represent the recurrent threat of political chaos in postlapsarian society. But evil is dreamlike in romance. The malcontents are powerless to strike. The revolt of the disordered passions cannot touch a Queen enthroned in the sphere of the moon, changeable like mortals, but changeless like the gods. Peele saw chastity, the predominant virtue of romance, as the symbol not only of the Queen's majesty in general, but of her political stability in particular. And I like to think that by the time the full effect of his beautiful "device" had worked upon her, the old Queen could rest for a moment in the fiction that she *had* restored the order of the world, and deserved the poet's golden ball.

Notes

1. For typical complaints about the play's formlessness see Paul Reyher, *Les Masques anglais* (Paris, 1909), pp. 135-138; Enid Welsford, *The Court Masque* (Cambridge, Eng., 1927), pp. 277-278; Tucker Brooke in *A Literary History of England* (New York, 1948), pp. 455-456. Dismissals of the play as frivolous are generally connected with eighteenth- and nineteenth-century assumptions about the essentially frivolous nature of masque and pastoral. See, for example, W. W. Greg's discussion of the play in *Pastoral Poetry and Pastoral Drama* (London, 1906), pp. 216-224. The only commentary I know which recognizes both the "moral earnestness . . . at all times characteristic of Peele's work" and his "constructive dramatic skill" is Thorleif Larsen's in "The Early Years of George Peele, Dramatist, 1558-1588," *Transactions of the Royal Society of Canada* (1928), pp. 294-311.

2. We have no satisfactory edition of *The Arraignment of Paris.* Except for modernizing spelling for consistency with other editions from which I quote, I have followed throughout the text of the 1584 quarto, ed. H. H. Child (Malone Society Reprints; London, 1910). Child, however, follows previous modern editors in numbering lines according to altered divisions of act and scene. I have consulted for line numbering, therefore, the

edition of the play in *English Drama 1580-1642,* ed. C. F. T. Brooke and H. B. Paradise (New York, 1933), which is unusual in honoring the divisions of the quarto.

3. See, for example, William Empson, *Some Versions of Pastoral* (London, 1935), especially his first two chapters; Frank Kermode's introduction to *English Pastoral Poetry from the Beginnings to Marvell* (London, 1952); Hallett Smith, *Elizabethan Poetry* (Cambridge, Mass., 1952), pp. 1-63; Edward Tayler, *Nature and Art in Renaissance Literature* (New York, 1964).

4. *Anatomy of Criticism* (Princeton, 1957), especially pp. 36-37, 186-203, 304-307. My description of the form is based on Frye but considerably modified by my own opinions. If "romance" is understood in its wide signification, pastoral and masque are species of this kind of narrative fiction.

5. For *Descensus Astraeae* see *The Life and Minor Works of George Peele,* ed. David H. Horne (New Haven, 1952), pp. 214-219. I cite in the text lines as numbered in this edition. The Web in the pageant is a play on the name of the new Lord Mayor, Sir William Webbe.

6. For a good exposition of this symbolism see J. A. W. Bennett, *The Parlement of Foules* (Oxford, 1957), especially pp. 140-142. See also E. R. Curtius, *European Literature and the Latin Middle Ages* (New York, 1953), pp. 183-202. Curtius shows explicitly that this topic was still a commonplace to Shakespeare.

7. Hallett Smith, *Elizabethan Poetry,* p. 6. Smith discusses Peele's play on pp. 3-9, primarily in connection with the significance of Paris' pastoral choice.

8. *Ibid.,* p. 7. Smith follows T. S. Graves, *"The Arraignment of Paris* and Sixteenth Century Flattery," *MLN,* XXVIII (1913), 48-49. As Graves points out, the pageant at Anne's coronation is especially significant, for Elizabeth's mother also received the gold ball from the goddesses. In "The Source of Peele's 'Arraignment of Paris,'" *MLN,* VIII (1893), pp. 206-207, Felix Schelling shows that the topic is applied to Elizabeth in the works of Gascoigne, including an unacted pageant at Kenilworth in 1575. Larsen, in "The Early Years of George Peele," pp. 298-299, adds to the evidence a Latin epigraph addressed to Elizabeth in Lyly's *Euphues His England.* As Larsen observes, it is unlikely that Peele knew none of these allusions.

9. Smith, *Elizabethan Poetry,* p. 8.

10. Horne, *Life and Minor Works,* pp. 187-188. These are ll. 113-118.

11. *Mercu. entr. with Vulcans Cyclops.* The Cyclops have no speaking role. They are apparently an iconographic representation for Peele of Vulcan's jealousy. In the fragment of Peele's *The Hunting of Cupid* anthologized in *Englands Parnassus,* the last two lines read, "Fourth, Jealousie in basest mindes doth dwell,/ This mettall Vulcans Cyclops sent from hell" (Horne, *Life and Minor Works,* p. 208). Within the play, Venus' scornful remark about *"Chimnysweepers"* seems to suggest the same sort of thing (III.vi.29-30).

12. I assume, with modern editors, that ll. 43 and 44 belong to Venus. Does the lower case opening of l. 43 indicate some larger typographical confusion about the beginning of this line?

13. I accept the logic of modern editors who change "his" to "hers," but it is possible that Venus refers not to Oenone but to Colin. The shepherds have pointed out that Paris is unjust to all true lovers, and only Colin at this point is literally dead.

14. E. M. W. Tillyard, *Five Poems 1470-1870* (London, 1948), pp. 20-21. The essay on Henryson's poem contains the best basic exposition I know of "the Assembly of the Gods." See especially pp. 19-22.

15. My attempt to define "masque" owes much to E. K. Chambers' discussion of the form in *The Elizabethan Stage* (Oxford, 1923), I, pp. 149-212, and to Northrop Frye's comments on masque in *The Anatomy of Criticism,* pp. 287-293. For an interpretation of some of Jonson's masques which uses as an aesthetic criterion the success of the "hinge" in joining actors and audience, see Stephen Orgel's *The Jonsonian Masque* (Cambridge, Mass., 1965).

16. For the text of *A Vision of Delight* see Ben Jonson, *Works,* ed. C. H. Herford and P. and E. Simpson, 11 vols. (Oxford, 1925-1952), VII, 463-471.

Louis Adrian Montrose (essay date fall 1980)

SOURCE: Montrose, Louis Adrian. "Gifts and Reasons: The Contexts of Peele's *Araygnement of Paris.*" *ELH* 47, no. 3 (fall 1980): 433-61.

[*In the following essay, Montrose discusses* The Arraignment of Paris *as a "cultural manifestation of the Elizabethan Court."*]

George Peele's ***Araygnement of Paris*** claims attention as a courtly performance and a printed text, an ephemeral social event and a monument of literary history. It has secured a prominent place in the modern canon of Elizabethan literature precisely because it is so characteristic and compendious a production of Elizabethan court culture. The *Araygnement* has been made to exemplify not only hyperbolic royal entertainment but also humble pastoral retirement; it has been interpreted not only as a glorification of power but as a repudiation of ambition. These divergent critical responses point to the ideological complexity of Elizabethan culture and Peele's play. The play's setting is pastoral, its dramaturgy is spectacular, and its royal sentiments are fulsome. Its action repeatedly involves the humble and the great in rites of homage or strategies of coercion. *The Araygnement of Paris* recreates the culture which creates it. Acts of gift-giving and relationships of power within the fiction reproduce basic characteristics of the social world in which the play is written and performed. I shall explore some of the symbolic forms which typify Elizabethan court culture and Peele's play: pastoral conventions, myths of royal power, and acts of prestation. If my exploration of these forms appears as much concerned with the contexts of Peele's play as with the play itself, this is because "text" and "context" define and illuminate each other.

I Pastoral

Hallett Smith opens his historical and critical study of Elizabethan poetry with a seminal chapter on pastoral, in which he takes as his paradigm Peele's *Araygnement of Paris*: "The Elizabethan attitude toward Paris reveals much of the meaning and significance of pastoral in the poetry of the age"; as "the major Elizabethan treatment of the Paris story, George Peele's play . . . is so important as an indication of the significance of pastoral in the Elizabethan mind that it must be discussed" in a study otherwise confined to non-dramatic poetry.[1] Peele's Paris says that he gave the prize to Venus rather than to Juno or Pallas because the only virtue in consideration was beauty; and because, as a shepherd, he is susceptible to the attractions of love and beauty but immune to those of power and riches, chivalry and martial prowess. Smith concludes that

> Paris is the judge precisely because the conditions of the pastoral life provide the greatest independence, the greatest security. The shepherd is not motivated by ambition or greed. Free from these two common passions, he enjoys "content," or the good life. Elizabethan pastoral poetry is essentially a celebration of this ideal of content or *otium*. The contemplative state enjoys a freedom, not only from ambition or greed, but from the vicissitudes of fortune.
>
> (*Elizabethan Poetry,* pp. 8-9)

Thus the "central meaning" of Elizabethan pastoral is defined as "the rejection of the aspiring mind. The shepherd demonstrates that true content is to be found in this renunciation" (p. 10). Smith's questionable though influential thesis invites an antithetical reading of Peele's play; and it provides a basis for fruitful disagreement about "the central meaning" of the Elizabethan pastoral kind.

In the sixteenth century, Paris's meeting with the three goddesses was commonly expounded as a choice among life patterns faced by a young man on the threshold of maturity:

> Hee beginneth nowe to discourse within himselfe, what kinde of life he were best to followe as the most noble in account amongst men: whether that which is grounded uppon knowledge, which the Philosophers were wont to cal a contemplative kind of life: or otherwise, yt which guideth a man that addicteth himself only to worldly matters, which they terme active: or else that which consisteth wholy in pleasure, which they name delightfull.[2]

Smith's argument tends to collapse the threefold Choice of Paris into the prevailing binary oppositions of Renaissance ethics, and to conflate the opposition between *otium* and *negotium* with that between contemplation and action. He turns concupiscible Paris into a philosopher—a lover of flesh into a lover of wisdom. Renaissance moralizers of myth usually opt for Juno or Pallas, or for a Humanist reconciliation of Action and Contemplation; they censure the Venerean alternative which was Paris's choice. Although he makes much of the young man's freedom to choose among all the options, Nenna concludes sternly that "he that is caried away to follow the delightfull kind of life, doth bring unto him selfe unspeakable detriment."

The fable is given an entirely different emphasis in the poetic theology of Florentine Neoplatonism. In a supplement to his commentary on Plato's *Philebus,* Ficino interprets the figure of Paris, tending his flocks on Mount Ida, as an allegory of the soul "nourishing the senses in the disordered matter of the elements."[3] According to Ficino, Paris's choice among the three goddesses is an allegory of the soul's option to pursue wisdom, power, or sensual pleasure. Ficino understands the pursuit of pleasure to be innate in human creatures; his concern is to discriminate among the forms of pleasure. Paris pursues the concupiscible pleasure of the lower senses; Ficino approves the pursuit of a rational pleasure in contemplative tranquility, a pursuit synonymous with Neoplatonic philosophy itself. In a dedicatory proem addressed to Lorenzo de' Medici, Ficino writes that concupiscible Paris, active Hercules, and contemplative Socrates all met with disaster because they were single-minded in the pursuit of sensual pleasure, power, and wisdom, respectively. But "our Lorenzo, having been taught by the oracle of Apollo, has neglected none of the god[desse]s. For he has . . . admired each one for her merits. On this account, he has won wisdom from Pallas and power from Juno and the graces and poetry and music from Venus" (p. 482).

Like the Florentine court philosopher, the Elizabethan court poet turns the Choice of Paris into a lavish compliment for a Renaissance prince precisely by transcending the very act of choice: the point of the compliment is that the prince melds the alternatives into an harmonious *triplex vita.*

Of course, the differences between Peele's transformation of the myth and Ficino's are as important as the resemblances. Indeed, with its stress on a synthesis of pleasure and wisdom and its critique of the active life, Ficino's disquisition on the Judgment of Paris is better fitted to the terms of Smith's argument than is Peele's play. Peele's conceit is true to the prevailing temper of Elizabethan ethics in that it disapproves of the Epicurism and neglects the contemplative and mystical elements that are fundamental to Ficino's philosophy. The most significant innovation in Peele's treatment of the myth is to encompass Diana and the virtue of militant virginity. To proclaim that Elizabeth infolds the excellences of all the goddesses is to perfect the encomium in a manner that is possible only when the prince is a woman. By turning the Choice of Paris into a *Trionfo della Castità,* Peele is skillfully articulating the sexual politics of Elizabethan court culture.[4]

Although he is sometimes treated as a type of the shepherd, Paris is a Trojan prince who has been exiled in a foredoomed attempt to evade the prophecy that he will bring ruin to Troy. Paris's rape of Helen is the fruit of his choice of Venus, and it precipitates the war which destroys his civilization. Peele insists upon this fatal framework by presenting Ate herself as the prologue to his play, to prophesy "the Tragedie of Troie" (l. 29).[5] Paris chooses Venus over Juno and Pallas, and is arraigned by the Olympian gods at the insistence of the disgruntled losers. Diana is called upon to arbitrate because these events have occurred within her territories, and because the harried male gods think it politic for "a woman to be judge amonge her pheeres" (l. 1069). Diana rejudges the contest between the three goddesses; she awards the prize to her own votary, the "peereles nymphe" Eliza, whose country is Elizium and whose people are called Angeli. Eliza is

> In State Queene Junos peere, for power in armes,
> And vertues of the minde Minervaes mate:
> As fayre and lovely as the queene of love:
> As chast as Dian in her chast desires.

(ll. 1170-73)

In the culminating celebration of Elizabeth, fiction is absorbed into actuality and drama is absorbed into rite. Because the queen infolds their separate perfections, the goddesses gladly resign to her; because her virtues are "more than may belong, / By natures lawe to any earthly wight" (ll. 1221-1222), the Fates "lay downe their properties at the Queenes feete."

The play's extravagant compliment to Elizabeth is not an afterthought but a climax. What is significant about Paris is that he chooses wrongly; the movement and meaning of the drama work to discredit his pastoral perspective. Had Paris remained faithful to Oenone, the authentic shepherdess, he would have continued to enjoy the pastoral *otium* of which Smith writes. Paris's abandonment of rustic Oenone for "a face that hath no peere" (l. 490), "a lasse of Venus court" (l. 494), is a Venerean manifestation of the aspiring mind. Paris, as Spenser's Thomalin points out in *The Shepheardes Calender,* is an ironic type of the shepherd, a perverter of pastoral:

> For he was proude, that ill was payd,
>   (no such mought shepheards bee)
> And with lewde lust was overlayd.[6]

Peele's use of the myth of Paris is precisely opposed to Smith's interpretation: pastoral's offer of freedom from ambition, greed, and the vicissitudes of Fortune is an illusion, a deception.

The title page of the 1584 quarto of *The Araygnement of Paris* calls it "A PASTORALL." In Elizabethan literary theory and practice, the pastoral kind is constituted by a complex of formal features—conventions of character, setting, and theme—derived from the material objects and relations of rural life as well as from the traditions of literary history. The flexibility and allusiveness of this complex suit it to a variety of generic combinations and rhetorical strategies. Smith's pastoral formula—authentic contentment found in the renunciation of ambition—is an historical variant of Renato Poggioli's pastoral theory. For Poggioli, "the psychological root of the pastoral is a double longing after innocence and happiness, to be recovered not through conversion or regeneration but merely through a retreat."[7] Smith isolates "the central meaning" of pastoral in an ethical and political *theme;* Poggioli isolates it in the psycho-social *function* of Smith's theme: pastoral "performs with especial intensity the role that Freud assigns to art in general: that of acting as a vicarious compensation for the renunciations imposed by the social order on its individual members, and of reconciling men to the sacrifices they have made in civilization's behalf" (*The Oaten Flute,* p. 31). To mollify civilization's discontents in otiose fictions is to perform what Puttenham characterizes as the recreative function of literature: "the common solace of mankind in all his travails and cares of this transitory life."[8] But Puttenham is describing a function or effect that may be realized by any number of literary forms; it may include but is neither limited to nor wholly characteristic of the pastoral kind. Neither Smith's theme nor Poggioli's function exhausts the meaning of Elizabethan pastoral form.

The "central meaning" of Elizabethan pastoral forms like Peele's is not to be sought in their constitution of a "positive ideal" but in their performance of a social function: courtly pastorals are gracious and intimate cultural mediations of hierarchical political relationships.[9] The play's rustic setting, inhabited by creatures and deities of fields and woods, provides an amenable meeting ground for the humble and the mighty—mortals and goddesses, subjects and their queen. Smith abstracts the Paris-motif from Peele's text and abstracts Peele's text from the context of its performance. Similarly, he abstracts an element of Elizabethan ideology—"the rejection of the aspiring mind"—from its context in the Elizabethan social process. At the heart of orthodox Elizabethan cultural values was a doctrine of divinely appointed, unchanging, hierarchical, and analogical order. This conservative "Elizabethan world picture," however, was very much at odds with the facts of intellectual ferment and social change so evident in the Elizabethan world. "The rejection of the aspiring mind" may have been a requisite avowal of piety but it was only a very partial expression of the spirit of the age.

In his study, *The aspiring mind of the Elizabethan younger generation,* Anthony Esler demonstrates that there were opposing attitudes toward ambition in Elizabethan England, and that the values of Elizabethan gentlemen and courtiers were often ambivalent. He explains this complex and conflict-laden situation in terms of a shift in the collective consciousness—the shared values and experience—of successive generations:

> Two processes seem to have operated simultaneously in the development of this Elizabethan younger generation during the 1570's and early 1580's. First, there was a gradual process of alienation from the ideals of their fathers. Among the consequences of this alienation was an emotional rejection of the older generation's strictures against ambition. Secondly, there was a restless search for new values in a world of new and changing facts. Among the results of this quest for new ideals was the growth of a mood of high aspiration.[10]

The honors, power, and wealth rejected by Paris were ardently pursued by the younger generation of Elizabethan gentleman courtiers; the base-born writers who were their contemporaries and had been educated with them pursued analogous goals within a far more circumscribed range.

The literary sensibilities of these groups were pervasively Ovidian and Petrarchan, and vaguely Neoplatonic; the literature of desire and amorous courtship they created is one of the characteristic expressions of their "mood of high aspiration." Their courtship of Venus shadowed their courtships of Juno and Pallas. This amorous mode must have gained vitality from the fact that the ultimate source of all preferments in Elizabethan society was "a most royall Queene or Empresse . . . a most vertuous and beautiful Lady" (Spenser, "Letter to Ralegh"). The ubiquitous persona of the plaintive and suppliant lover may project the aspiring courtier-poet's response to the impediments he faces: the patriarchal authoritarianism of an older generation who control policy and patronage; the tension between the sober values of Tudor Humanism and new or foreign tastes and values which implicitly challenge or undermine internalized norms; the Crown's severely limited and contracting resources, and its arbitrary bestowal of the rewards at its disposal.

The younger generation of ambitious gentlemen-courtiers and base-born writers aspiring to court patronage were the Elizabethans who most assiduously cultivated the humble pastoral kind. What appears to be a contradiction between ambition and pastoralism, between social value and cultural form, may in fact be a subtle rhetorical strategy. Puttenham dubs allegory "The Courtier or figure of faire semblant" (p. 299): "the Courtly figure *Allegoria* . . . is when we speake one thing and thinke another, and that our wordes and our meanings meete not. The use of this figure is so large, and his vertue of so great efficacie as it is supposed no man can pleasantly utter and perswade without it, but in effect is sure never or very seldome to thrive and prosper in the world, that cannot skilfully put it in use" (p. 186). Puttenham personifies his ironic figure of allegory as a Courtier; and the Elizabethan courtier incarnates such an allegory when he dons the mask of a shepherd. When the courtly poet's pastoral discourse rejects the aspiring mind, the politic shepherd may be speaking one thing and thinking another.

Consider the case of George Peele. A well educated but base-born and socially obscure member of the Elizabethan younger generation creates a lavish compliment to his prince. He is given an opportunity to serve his own interests by serving the Court. "The rejection of the aspiring mind" seems no more applicable to the personal motives of the humble poet than to those of the noble courtier or the prince herself. An expressive and compensatory psychological perspective which sees the function of Elizabethan pastoral as "the solace of mankind in all his travails and cares of this transitorie life" must be complemented by a rhetorical and dialectical social perspective. Such a perspective characterizes the third book of Puttenham's acute treatise on court culture and court conduct: courtly pastorals, like courtiers themselves, "do busily negotiat by coulor of otiation" (pp. 301-302).

II Power

In his discussion of the eclogue, Puttenham makes a fundamental distinction between the pastoral of naive song and the pastoral of "artificiall poesie." In early ages, poetry was a spontaneous expression of actual shepherds, who enjoyed abundant leisure time in which to recreate themselves. Pastoral poets since Vergil, living in complex civilizations, have written artfully and obliquely about great persons and great affairs: "The Poet devised the *Eglogue* . . . not of purpose to counterfait or represent the rusticall manner of loves and communication: but under the vaile of homely persons, and in rude speeches to insinuate and glaunce at greater matters, and such as perchance had not bene safe to have beene disclosed in any other sort" (p. 38). We do not know under what auspices *The Araygnement of Paris* was composed nor under what circumstances it was presented. It is apparent, however, that Peele's play belongs to a corpus of courtly texts and performances which shadowed the controversial issues of royal marriage and succession.[11] Courtly pastorals exemplify Puttenham's "Courtly figure *Allegoria*": in "the rusticall manner of loves and communication," Peele's mythological court pastoral insinuates and glances "at greater matters, and such as perchance had not bene safe to have bene disclosed in any other sort."

By an accident of fortune—or by the inscrutable will of Divine Providence—a profoundly and pervasively patriarchal society came to be governed by a virgin queen. The royal exception proved the patriarchal rule in society at large; even so, most of the men who surrounded the Queen wanted to see her married. There was a deeply felt and loudly voiced need to insure a legitimate succession, upon which the welfare of the whole nation depended. But there seems also to have been a more diffuse and obliquely expressed motivation: the political nation—which was wholly a nation of men—sometimes found it annoying or perturbing to serve a prince who was also a woman, a woman who was unsubjected to a man. Elizabeth was an anomaly. And her political genius manifested itself in her ability to turn to advantage the enormous political handicap of her gender.

Elizabeth's first parliament (1559) urged her to marry. In her reply, she discriminated pointedly between the humble petition of obedient subjects and the "very great presumption" of those who sought "to bind and limit" the sovereign's will—"To take upon you to draw my love to your liking or frame my will to your fantasies; for a guerdon constrained and a gift freely given can never agree together." She concluded that she was content to have as her epitaph "that a Queen, having reigned such a time, lived and died a virgin."[12] When she told her most assiduous suitor, the Earl of Leicester, "I will have here but one Mistress, and no Master,"[13] she was acknowledging the principle by which she retained political authority: the interdependence of her maidenhood and her mastery. The negative examples of her half-sister and her cousin—the fond doting of Mary Tudor, the violent passion of Mary Stuart—taught

Elizabeth that the power of Venus might weaken the woman and corrupt the queen. The psychological factors in Elizabeth's choice of single life were also intrinsically social and political factors. The integrity and strength of the English body politic came to seem mystically dependent upon the integrity and strength—the intactness—of the Queen's body natural. The fantastic cult that celebrated the magical power of royal virginity was grounded in the most basic of socio-sexual realities: in a world otherwise governed by lords, fathers, and husbands, Elizabeth's power over access to her own person was a source of her political power. Her control of the realm was dependent upon her physical and symbolic control of her own body.

Common subjects were considered unfit to hold opinions about affairs of state. Even for courtiers, it was a risky business to offer advice to the prince. From the beginning of the reign, Elizabeth made it clear that she was hostile to discussion of her marital status or the royal succession, the intertwined destinies of her natural and political bodies. And from the beginning of the reign, courtiers and statesmen employed pagan myth to insinuate and glance at these intimate and awesome matters. In March 1565, the Earl of Leicester sponsored a pre-Lenten entertainment at court that included a mythological play. The Spanish ambassador is our witness: "The plot was founded on the question of marriage, discussed between Juno and Diana, Juno advocating marriage and Diana chastity. Jupiter gave the verdict in favour of matrimony. . . . The Queen turned to me and said, 'This is all against me'."[14] The Queen attended an aristocratic wedding in July 1566, at which a masque was performed. The gentleman masquers brought wedding gifts from the gods; Venus sent her golden apple. The presenter acknowledged the royal presence but pointedly bestowed the prize upon the bride. Juno sent word that wedlock was the most honorable state; Diana conceded that it was woman's destiny.[15] To glorify the bride was obliquely to criticize the fair vestal thronèd by the west, the guest of honor.

During the early years of the reign, the Earl of Leicester seems to have thought that Queen Elizabeth's person and the crown itself were within his reach. Although in time Leicester's vision of kingship faded away, the courtship continued until his death. Two of the entertainments he offered to the Queen on progress are of particular interest in connection with *The Araygnement of Paris*: *The Princely Pleasures at Kenelworth Castle* (1575); and *The Lady of May* (1578), a pastoral devised by Leicester's nephew, Philip Sidney, and performed at Wanstead.[16] The *Princely Pleasures* included a mythological show devised by Gascoigne; it was intent on "perswading the Queenes Majestie . . . that she consider all things by proofe, and then shee shall finde much greater cause to followe Juno then Dyana" (p. 107). Diana seeks her nymph, Zabeta, whom she has not seen for seventeen years; Zabeta is said to follow Juno now, though she remains constant to her maiden vows. Diana is a goddess of girlhood chastity, of princesses who live in maiden meditation, fancy-free; Juno is a goddess of womanly majesty, of marriage and matron queens. Zabeta has been a nominal follower of Juno since Elizabeth became Queen in 1558; the intent of the show is to bring the Queen to emulate Juno fully by fulfilling herself in marriage.

One of the most striking features of Gascoigne's text is that it gives full play to the topic of *maistrye*, to the maiden's fear—the maiden queen's fear—that for a woman, marriage means bondage. At the beginning of the play, Diana praises the virgin's estate:

> Rejoysing yet (much more) to drive your dayes,
> In life at large, that yeeldeth calme content,
> Then wilfully to treade the wayward wayes,
> Of wedded state, which is to thraldome bent.
>
> (p. 107)

Castibula, Diana's nymph, fears that Zabeta has been seduced:

> I dread Dame *Juno* with some gorgeous gift,
> Hath layde some snare, hyr fancie to entrap,
> And hopeth so hyr loftie mynde to lyft
> On *Hymens* bed, by height of worldly hap.
>
> (p. 110)

But Mercury reassures Diana and the nymphs:

> For though she finde the skil
> A kingdome for to weelde,
> Yet cannot *Juno* winne her will
> Nor make her once to yeelde
> Unto the wedded life,
> But still she lives at large
> And holdes her neck from any yoke,
> Without controll of charge.
>
> (p. 115)

Diana is led to Elizabeth and praises her splendid fusion of "Princely port" and "Maiden's minde": "I joy with you, and leave it to your choice / What kinde of life you best shall like to holde" (p. 117).

Diana may leave the choice to Elizabeth but Gascoigne concludes his play with a presumptuous attempt to frame the Queen's will to Leicester's fantasy. Iris comes from Juno to discredit Mercury and Diana; she concludes the play with Juno's plea:

> O Queene, O worthy Queene,
> Yet never wight felt perfect blis,
> but such as wedded beene.
>
> (p. 120)

The play "never came to execution," perhaps because the Queen's host thought his servants' efforts would give offence; in any case, the text would soon be in print for all to read.

In Sidney's Wanstead entertainment, Elizabeth is invited to choose a husband—a husband for the May Lady who is said to emulate the Queen. Elizabeth prefers the docile shepherd to the aggressive forester, even though Sidney has deliberately slanted the contest strongly in the forester's favor. Whether or not it pleased her host and his nephew, by her judgment Elizabeth had proved herself "Juno, Venus, Pallas *et profecto plus*" (p. 31). On Leicester's behalf, she was presented with "a chain of round agates something like beads," upon which he faithfully had said his *Ave* Elizabeths. The holy and inviolable virginity of the Queen is acknowledged in a tone of witty sacrilege and self-mockery reflecting a long personal intimacy. The whole entertainment seems to play out a delicately allegorical struggle for sexual and political mastery between a royal mistress and her ardent courtiers.[17]

Courtly entertainments constitute an elaborate sign system, a formation of figurative persons, actions, and topics in which loyal subjects may obliquely consider matters of state and subtly manipulate the royal will. Peele's *Araygnement of Paris* belongs within this tradition but its rhetorical motives are opposed to those which characterize most earlier texts. For example, Peele's play is an obvious antithesis to the 1566 wedding masque, in which the Judgment of Paris was re-judged in favor of the bride rather than the Queen. Entertainments such as those sponsored by the Earl of Leicester at Kenilworth and Wanstead in the 1570's ostensibly offered a choice to the Queen but it was one in which the options were skewed against female independence or dominion. Compared to these, Peele's offering is not "a guerdon constrained" but "a gift freely given." *The Araygnement of Paris* is typical of royal entertainments in its hyperbolic treatment of the royal spectator and her fictional personae. But it differs from many of the entertainments of the previous two decades in that it fully acknowledges and celebrates the Queen's own choice, her complex transcendence of the simplistic oppositions contrived by her courtiers. This Eliza, "whom some Zabeta call" (l. 1176), "is shee, / In whom do mete so manie giftes in One" (ll. 1167-68).

The play begins with Ate's grim prophecy of the fate of Troy, a civilization bound to the cycle of desire and destruction. Diana describes Elizium as "an ancient seat of kinges, a seconde Troie," where Eliza "giveth lawes of justice and of peace" (ll. 1153, 1157). The play ends with the providential Elizabethan fulfillment of Troy's promise, a civilization achieved by the virtuous and gentle discipline of holiness and temperance, chastity and justice. The dynastic and imperial myth which traces Elizabeth's lineage to Aeneas affirms that her state does not merely recapitulate but transcends the glories of Troy and Rome. Lustful Paris and the three covetous, contentious goddesses give way to Diana and Eliza. Like many another Elizabethan text, *The*

Araygnement of Paris is concerned with the establishment and maintenance of order, and with the constant threat of disorder. Paris is the instrument of discord and is subject to the Fates; he is inscribed within a tragic, pagan world. Elizabeth rules the Fates and, like the virgin goddess of Vergil's prophetic fourth eclogue, she redeems history; she masters and harmonizes the contending forces within herself, her court, her realm.[18]

The analogical principle that pervades Elizabethan modes of thought structures Peele's play: order in the body politic depends upon and resembles order in the body natural; ordered selves create ordered states. *The Araygnement of Paris* abounds in examples of ungoverned and destructive passions. Not only does Peele's Venus personify seductive lust but his Juno is ceaselessly jealous and his Pallas is bloody (l. 117). When Paris urges Oenone to sing, she catalogues thirteen classical myths as possible subjects. Almost all of these involve rape or rebellion, violent acts of mastery and illicit desires which incur terrible punishments (ll. 252-77). Peele's double plot concerns the destructiveness of passion: "Poor Colin, that is ill for thee, that art as true in trust / To thy sweete smerte, as to his Nymphe Paris hath bin unjust" (ll. 597-98). The parallel courtships of Oenone and Paris and Colin and Thestylis end tragically, one in desertion and the other in indifference. The Choice of Paris and the Fall of Troy exemplify a cycle of love and death, violence and subversion, in the self and in the state. Elizabeth breaks the cycle; she is "the noble Phoenix of our age" (l. 1235), unique, unmated, and self-renewing. Elizabeth is "As fayre and lovely as the queene of love" but she is also "As chast as Dian in her chast desires" (ll. 1172-73). The play's Epilogue concludes with a simple *credo*: the Queen is "Corpore, mente, libro, doctissima, candida, casta."

A painting of Queen Elizabeth and the three goddesses, formerly attributed to Hans Eworth, gave the prize to the Queen a dozen or more years before Peele's *Araygnement of Paris* was performed.[19] Although this painting has been cited often as an analogue to Peele's play, there has been no comparison of how these two "texts" treat their common subject. The painting is characterized by oppositions, whereas the play achieves overwhelming harmony in the collective worship of the Queen. In royal performance, Elizabeth herself actually became the drama's incarnate resolution; she was the cynosure of both the characters and the audience. Of course, the Queen could only be represented in the painting; she could hardly be present within it. But perhaps the most striking compositional feature of the painting is that the center is occupied by the figure of Juno rather than the representation of Elizabeth. Juno looks toward Elizabeth; for the spectator, however, it is not Elizabeth but Juno who is the painting's cynosure.

Elizabeth and her two ladies-in-waiting are heavily clothed; only their hands and faces are visible. The Queen's black, cross-hatched, and armor-like gown falls heavily in straight lines. It is quite unlike the multicolored finery she wore on state occasions and in most of her portraits, and unlike the simple gowns of vestal white in which she often dressed.[20] The artist seems deliberately to have avoided brilliant effects in his treatment of the royal image. Comparison of the painting with the final pageant of Peele's play suggests that the painting's stylistic and spatial details are at odds with its overt gesture of royal praise.

Juno's position as the focal point of the painting is reinforced by her dynamic pose: the torsion of her body; the swirling and flying of her gown and mantle; the emphatic gesturing of her hands; the intersecting planes formed by her bent and upraised arm, boldly marking the center of the canvas. Juno is equidistant from the Queen of England and the Queen of Love; her head turns back and her eyes fix upon Elizabeth, even as her feet move toward Venus. In the right half of the canvas, Pallas is the mediatory figure in a triad of goddesses; at the center, Juno is the mediatrix between Elizabeth and Venus, the paired and opposed figures on either side of the canvas. Elizabeth stands erect at the top of the stairs; Venus is seated, her feet touching the grass; and Juno stands between them, upon the lowest stair. The glances of these three figures lie in the same plane, which slopes downward across the painting, between Elizabeth and Venus. Venus is appropriately nude but is seated upon what appears to be a white gown. She and Cupid are tenderly embracing, though both look toward Elizabeth. At their feet lie his golden bow and quiver, and a broken arrow that points away from Elizabeth. The artist's treatment of the Goddess of Love is elegant and dignified; the emphasis is decidedly maternal.

The two groups of figures are placed in a sharply contrasted background of enclosed and open spaces, court and country, art and nature. Conspicuously absent are the figures, attributes, and woodland setting of the Diana cult, all of which are essential elements in the iconography of Peele's play. The iconography of the right half of the painting delicately suggests that the flamboyant majesty of Juno is joined to the fecund and protective motherhood of Venus by the heroic wisdom of Pallas. In the absence of Diana, Peele's mediatrix, the goddesses form a reconciled triad in their collective opposition to Elizabeth and her two attendant "nymphs." I am suggesting that the painter equivocates in his handling of the royal theme; and that its equivocations relate the painting to those contemporaneous mythological court entertainments of the 1560's and 1570's which, even as they glorified the Queen, obliquely criticized her obstinate persistence in single blessedness.

The painting of Queen Elizabeth and the Three Goddesses does not provide a visual translation of Peele's play so much as a foil for its unequivocal celebration of the royal virgin cult. The attitude of Peele's play was uncommon in royal entertainments before the 1580's. But by 1582, the prolonged courtship between the Queen and the Duke of Alençon, perhaps her most serious prospect for marriage, was finally at an end. Elizabeth was now entering her sixth decade, and the expectation that she would marry and produce an heir had almost faded away. Peele's play, performed and printed in the early 1580's, is responding to an altered view of the political horizon. His retrial of the Judgment of Paris epitomizes and celebrates a major reorientation in the form of Elizabethan court culture.

III PRESTATION

The central meaning of Peele's play is not to be found in the arraignment of Paris but in the apotheosis of Elizabeth. The presentation of a golden ball to the Queen climaxes a series of courtships involving the offering of gifts. In the first four scenes of the play, the lowly make symbolic offerings to the great. It is good to "give a thing, / A signe of love, unto a mightie person, or a king" (ll. 56-57). Pan, Faunus, and Silvanus—the "poore countrie gods" (l. 69) of shepherds, hunters, and woodsmen—bring votive offerings to their respective goddesses: a lamb for Juno, a faun for Venus, an oaken bough for Minerva. Flora offers an emblematic display of flowers for each goddess. Pomona's offering of apples to all the goddesses balances Ate's demonic gift. The "fatall frute / Raught from the golden tree of Proserpine" (ll. 6-7) is cast among the goddesses in the form of "a ball of golde, a faire and worthie prize" (l. 357). In their competition for Ate's offering, the goddesses themselves offer worthy prizes to a mortal: riches, honors, and sexual favors. Collectively, they invest Paris as their judge; then, individually, they offer bribes to him for his partisanship.

The final offerings and collective act of homage infold and transcend the preceding rites and contests: "This Paragon, this onely this is shee, / In whom do meete so manie giftes in one" (ll. 1166-1167). Accompanying their ritual actions with a solemn Latin chant, the three Fates perform a "sacrifice" (l. 1238) to the Queen; they offer up unto her their distaff, spindle, and fatal knife. Diana offers to Elizabeth "This prize from heaven and heavenly goddesses" (l. 1241). A trio of humble rustic gods pays tribute to a trio of great goddesses, who in turn join a trio of Fates in paying tribute to a figure who is paradoxically human and divine. Peele's scenario suggests an Epiphany scene, in which shepherds and magi bring symbolic gifts to an incarnate deity, a prince of peace.[21] *The Araygnement of Paris* is a gift to the Queen, a rhetorical vehicle of royal courtship, which repeatedly thematizes its own social function.

The gift forms and the motives for giving incorporated into Peele's play recreate characteristic practises of Elizabethan culture. A few examples of Elizabethan prestation will suggest the scope of this dialectic between text and context. Elizabeth's triumphal entry into London on the day before her coronation was conceived and presented as the embodiment of "two gyftes": "blessing tonges, which many a welcome say" and "true hertes, which love thee from their roote."[22] Elizabeth was also presented with material signs of love: "a purse of crimosin sattin richly wrought with gold, wherein the citie gave unto the Quene's majestie a thousand markes in gold . . . The Lord maior, hys brethren, and comminaltie of the citie, to declare their gladnes and good wille towards the Quene's majestie, did present her grace with that gold, desyring her grace to continue their good and gracious Quene, and not to esteme the value of the gift, but the mynd of the gevers" (pp. 26-27).

The Queen received these gifts graciously and requited them liberally; she responded "merveilous pithilie": "I thanke my lord maior, his brethren, and you all. . . . Perswade yourselves, that for the safetie and quietnes of you all, I will not spare, if nede be to spend my blood. God thanke you all" (p. 27). A pageant of Time and Truth culminated in Truth's presentation of the English Bible to Elizabeth. As restorer of the Reformed religion, the Queen herself was *Veritas, filia Temporis*: "Tyme? sayth she, and Tyme hath brought me hether" (p. 26). "She as soone as she had received the booke, kyssed it, and with both her handes held up the same, and so laid it upon her breast, with great thankes to the citie therfore" (pp. 28-29). The pageant following the presentation of the Bible purposed "to put her grace in remembrance of the state of the commonweale, which Time with Truth his doughter doth revele, which Truth also her grace hath received, and therefore cannot but be merciful and careful for the good government thereof" (p. 30). The narrative logic of the pageant conveys the moral coerciveness of the gift. Acceptance of a purse and a bible from the citizens of London puts Elizabeth under obligation to look to their material and spiritual welfare.

The authorized record of the entry, in print within ten days of the event, was an early example of the regime's cultivation of popular opinion. Appended to the narrative were "Certain notes of the quene's majestie's great mercie, clemencie, and wisdom used in this passage." One of them is particularly striking:

> What more famous thing doe we reade in auncient histories of olde time, then that mightye princes have gentlie received presentes offered them by base and low personages. . . . Let me se any writer that in any one prince's life is able to recount so manie presidentes of this vertue, as her grace shewed in that one passage through the citie. How many nosegaies did her grace receive at poore women's handes? how ofttimes staied she her chariot, when she saw any simple body offer to speake to her grace? A branche of Rosemarie given to her grace with supplication by a poore woman about fleetebridge, was sene in her chariot till her grace came to westminster, not without the mervaillous wondering of such as knew the presenter and noted the Quene's most gracious receiving and keping the same.

(p. 38)

The reciprocal actions of the poor woman and the mighty prince introduce touches of calculating improvisation into standardized ritual gestures. The branch offered as a gift is also a symbolic admonition to the petition's recipient: "There's rosemary, that's for remembrance" (*Hamlet*, IV.v.171). Elizabeth showed herself gracefully mindful of the message and the expected response. The episode was a token of "What hope the poore and nedie may looke for at her grace's hande" (p. 38).

"The Quene's Majestie's passage through the citie of London to westminster the daye before her coronacion" was a veritable rite of passage for the new sovereign and for her new subjects. The stations of the journey occasioned a coherent program of allegorical pageants which confirmed the royal succession; affirmed principles of good government and reformed religion; and encouraged the young, female, and virgin ruler with demonstrations of public support and citations of biblical precedent. Like Elizabeth's entry into her capital and her reign, the royal progresses which later took her to aristocratic estates and provincial towns were great social dramas. They repeatedly affirmed the Queen's mystical power, her control over her domains; and they demonstrated the love and devotion of her subjects, both the humble and the great.

The shows performed during royal progresses, M. C. Bradbrook has felicitously called "drama as offering."[23] As in Sidney's *Lady of May,* an integral or culminating feature of these festivities was usually the explicit offering of gifts to the Queen. For example, as the Queen crossed a bridge on her way to the inner court of Kenilworth Castle during the Progress of 1575, she found upon the posts "sundrie presents, and giftes of provi-

sion" (Gascoigne, *Works,* II, 95). These had been left for her by Bacchus, Ceres, Pomona, Neptune, Sylvanus, Phoebus, and Mars. Later in the visit, the gifts were recalled and their significance unfolded in a coy dialogue between a Savage Man and Eccho that was overheard by the Queen (p. 99):

> Gifts? what? sent from the Gods?
>   as presents from above?
> Or pleasures of provision,
>   as tokens of true love?

ECCHO:

>   True love
> And who gave all those gifts?
> I pray thee (*Eccho*) say?
> Was it not he? who (but of late)
>   this building here did lay?

ECCHO:

>   *Dudley*
> O *Dudley,* so me thought:
>   he gave him selfe and all,
> A worthy gift to be received,
>   and so I trust it shall.

ECCHO:

>   It shall

Robert Dudley, Earl of Leicester, who had been offering himself to Elizabeth Tudor for a good many years, gave in order to receive.

The process of prestation was traditionally allegorized in the dancing Graces, "otherwise called Charites, that is thanks. Whom the Poetes . . . make three, to wete, that men first ought to be gracious and bountiful to other freely, then to receive benefits at other mens hands curteously, and thirdly to requite them thankfully: which are three sundry Actions in liberalitye."[24] In the fourth eclogue of *The Shepheardes Calender,* Colin Clout (Spenser's pastoral persona) advances Elisa (Elizabeth's pastoral persona) to be "a fourth grace . . . And reigne with the rest in heaven" ("Aprill," ll. 113, 117). Spenser's Elisa, like Peele's Eliza, is the only She, "in whom do mete so manie giftes in one" (*AP* [*The Araygnement of Paris*], l. 1167). All gifts meet in Elizabeth because her manifold virtues elicit manifold acts of homage; and because, in the symbolic economy of court and monarchy, the Queen is the ultimate source and the ultimate recipient of gifts. This Spenser suggests in the Proem to his Legend of Courtesy:

> Then pardon me, most dreaded Soveraine,
> That from your selfe I do this vertue bring,
> And to your selfe doe it returne againe:
> So from the Ocean all rivers spring,
> And tribute backe repay as to their King.

Right so from you all goodly vertues well
Into the rest, which round about you ring,
Faire Lords and Ladies, which about you dwell,
And doe adorne your Court, where courtesies excell.

                                        (*FQ* [*The Faerie Queene,*], VI.proem.7)

The rhythm of reciprocal giving that was exemplified in such formal rites as the exchange of New Years' gifts at Court also gave symbolic form to the patronage system upon which the Court itself was organized. Where gifts flowed, power flowed.

E. K. Chambers notes that "on New Year's Day it was etiquette for the lords and ladies at Court and many of the officers of the household to present the Queen with New Year gifts . . . while she in turn rewarded the donors with gilt plate from the royal jewel house and distributed largesse amongst her personal attendants and other customary recipients."[25] These exchanges were meticulously inventoried on great rolls signed by the Queen. The Queen's gifts came from magnates and from menials; they ranged from jewels and rich furnishings to finely bound books and fanciful constructions in marzipan. Each gave according to his ability: in 1578/79, for example, Robert Dudley, Earl of Leicester and Master of the Horse, gave "a very fair jewel of gold, being a clock garnished fully with diamonds and rubies," while John Dudley, Sergeant of the Pastry, gave "a very fair pye of quynces."[26] One's vital personal relationship to the sovereign could be renewed symbolically by an exchange of gifts at the threshold between the old court year and the new. But the rite was not without its elements of calculation and cynicism. In his discussion of profit and corruption on "The Elizabethan Political Scene," J. E. Neale remarks that "New Year's gifts were no negligible part of a patron's perquisites—nor, for that matter, of the Queen's." He records that "in December 1595 there was a rumour that the Queen 'will make both councillors and officers of Household.' A courtier was sceptical; 'but,' said he, 'it will increase the Queen's New Year gifts.'"[27] To an office-seeker, giving might bring a return of preferment; to a parsimonious and insolvent monarch, a gift might be less welcome for its sentimental than for its cash value.

In his study of "Place and Patronage in Elizabethan Politics," Wallace T. MacCaffrey explains that, although in theory "all decisions depended ultimately upon the pleasure of the sovereign lady," in fact the Elizabethan regime lacked "coercive power"; "the stability of the system demanded the arduous and constant wooing of the body politic." The monarchy "secured men's loyal service not only by appeals to their moral sense or through the wiles of the royal charmer but also by offering them material advantages. By the expert sharing of those gifts of office, prestige, or wealth at its com-

mand, the government could secure the continuing goodwill of the politically pre-eminent classes."[28] The fruits of patronage were unevenly distributed among great courtiers and government officials; their servingmen and assistants; and a large and heterogeneous group of gentry, professionals, and artisans. Suitors in this last group negotiated their indirect claims on royal munificence with the great courtiers who were not only recipients but sources of patronage.

The workings of an increasingly competitive and corrupt courtly marketplace were imaged in the harmonious order of dance and gift. In practise, the patronage system "produced a host of middlemen of all ranks who stood, hands outstretched for gratuities, between suitors and their goals" (Smith, *Government of Elizabethan England,* p. 63). If Spenser offered an idealized image of the Elizabethan court in the Proem to his Legend of Courtesy, in *Mother Hubberds Tale* he bitterly exposed how sordid and "pitifull" was "Suters state": "To fawne, to crowche, to waite, to ride, to ronne, / To spend, to give, to want, to be undone" (ll. 905-06). A correspondent of Lord Burghley observed that the buying and selling of offices "is winked at, and the mart kept within the Court"; and Michael Hicks, Burghley's secretary and one of the busiest of patronage middlemen, in writing to a friend about possible appointments referred to "us poor bribers here in Court" (Neale, *Essays in Elizabethan History,* pp. 65-67). In a society in which modern bureaucratic and economic structures were in the very process of formation, it was sometimes difficult or undesirable to make precise distinctions between salaries and gifts, between gifts and bribes.[29]

Let us now reconsider the prestation principle formulated at the beginning of ***The Araygnement of Paris***. Pomona asks Faunus if "these goddesses will take our giftes in woorth"; he replies,

> Yea doubtles, for shall tel thee dame, twere better
>   give a thing,
> A signe of love, unto a mightie person, or a king:
> Then to a rude and barbarous swayne but bad and
>   baselie borne,
> For gentlie takes the gentleman that oft the clowne
>   will scorne.

                                                            (ll. 55-59)

The significance of the offering is not in the material value of the gift but in the symbolic value of the act of giving. The material gift is a sign of love, an offering of self and an initiation or reaffirmation of a bond between giver and recipient. Marcel Mauss echoes ancient philosophy in his study of symbolic exchange. He stresses that an act of gift-giving is part of a larger social situation, a dialectical process of prestation which "not only carries with it the obligation to repay gifts received, but implies two others equally important: the obligation to give presents and the obligation to receive them" (*The Gift,* pp. 10-11). As Pierre Bourdieu observes, "the operation of gift exchange presupposes (individual and collective) misrecognition . . . of the objective 'mechanism' of the exchange."[30] E. K. concludes his gloss on Spenser's Graces by noting that they are often represented with "one having her backe toward us, and her face fromwarde, as proceeding from us; the other two toward us, noting double thanke to be due to us for the benefit, we have done." Prestation is a tacitly coercive and vitally interested process predicated on the fiction that it is free and disinterested. Gift-giving is a kind of negotiation "by coulor of otiation."

According to Peele's Faunus, it is far better to give to the great than to the base because the social hierarchy is congruent with the moral hierarchy. In *The Winter's Tale,* this notion leads the ingenuous old shepherd to tell his clownish son, "We must be gentle, now we are gentlemen" (V.ii.152-153). Because gentlemen are gentle, they will accept humble gifts and thus acknowledge a bond to the giver; and because they are "mightie" persons, the signs of love which they return may materially benefit their social inferiors. Such institutionalized forms of giving are gestures in a system of symbolic exchange. Sacrificial offerings open a two-way channel between gods and mortals; and offerings of objects, services, and respects open a two-way channel between lords and subjects, patrons and suitors.

The Araygnement of Paris is an offering to Peele's sovereign that incorporates within it a variety of gifts; it is an epitome of the forms and motives of Elizabethan prestation. At the beginning of the play, the country gods make offerings of homage to the great goddesses; and at the end, the great goddesses in all humility pay tribute to the Queen. The *Araygnement*'s encomium takes the form of an epiphany; its rhetorical motive is simply to acknowledge the Queen's greatness, to worship her. In their offering of tangible signs of loyalty and submission, the Fates and Goddesses stand proxy for all the Queen's subjects. Hierarchical social relationships are ritually defined and affirmed in the offering and acceptance of gifts.

Between the ritual acts of celebration at the beginning and the end is a dramatic action focused upon two contrasting formal scenes of judgment: the Choice of Paris and the Arraignment of Paris. Paris, a mere mortal, is invested as "umpier in [the] controversie" (l. 416) between the goddesses: "Then if you will to avoyde a tedious grudge, / Refer it to the sentence of a judge" (ll. 407-08). At his arraignment, Paris pleads the difficulty of maintaining impartiality under pressure from superiors who possess power to coerce and gifts to corrupt:

> (Yee gods) alas what can a mortall man
> Decerne, betwixt the sacred guiftes of heaven.
> Or, if I may with reverence reason thus:
> Suppose I gave, and judgd corruptly then,
> For hope of that, that best did please my thought,
> This apple not for beauties prayse alone:
> I might offende, sithe I was gardoned,
> And tempted, more than ever creature was,
> With wealth, with beautie and with chivalrie.

(ll. 924-930)

The exchanges between Paris and the goddesses suggest forms of patronage and clientage; they equivocate between gifts and bribes, between praise and flattery. They echo both the social relationships within the Court and Peele's own relationship to his courtly audience.

During a royal performance of *The Araygnement of Paris,* the Queen would have sat in state, perhaps sharing the stage with the actors. The actors always played to her; the others in attendance were not only watching a play but watching the Queen watching a play.[31] Whatever boundary exists between the reality within the fiction and that within the Court dissolves when Diana "delivereth the ball of golde to the Queenes owne hands." The Queen participates in mythic and material worlds simultaneously. The golden ball offered to her is the apple intended "unto the fayrest" (l. 365); it is the golden orb of Christian and British empire; and it is a synecdoche for *The Araygnement of Paris.* The performance offers a cultural form in which Queen and Court may legitimate and celebrate themselves. The negotiations of author, performers, and sponsors for the favor of their superiors and their royal mistress are mediated by the reciprocal wooings of mortals and gods in a pastoral fiction. Although Eliza is Diana's votary, Diana herself is the dramatic agent of Peele's royal compliment. In the world that revolves around Queen Elizabeth, Diana proves to be the exemplary courtier; the ironic fate of Paris and the pathetic fate of Colin exemplify the dangers and the frustrations of courtship.

The Araygnement of Paris manifests those intellectual gifts which recommended George Peele to the Elizabethan regime. Peele, who came from a family of London tradesmen and clerks, prepared to advance himself by a university education and a financially advantageous marriage. A gentleman only by virtue of his Master of Arts degree, he sought the substance of status by writing in hope of Court preferment. In *The Araygnement of Paris,* his first major work, Peele emulates the Vergilian progression by writing a pastoral with epic implications; he emulates Spenser by including a pastoral subplot that makes a conspicuous allusion to the recent *Shepheardes Calender* (1579). In his Epistle to the *Calender,* E. K. remarks that it is the figure of Colin "under whose person the Author selfe is shadowed." The poet begins with pastoral because it allows him to advertise himself to the courtly source of power and reward without violating the decorum of humility and deference required both of social inferiors and of the younger generation. Within the humble pastoral poem which boldly announces his claim to be "our new Poete," Spenser incorporates Colin Clout to project a pattern of failure.[32] Like Spenser's persona, Peele's Colin is a shepherd-poet whose amorous desires are rejected and whose literary gifts are wasted.

Peele himself experienced the social failure which haunted the "University Wits" of his generation. He continued to pen occasional and celebratory courtly poems (often pastoral in form) throughout his short career. But, because he needed a larger audience for his works and a larger market for his wares, he also wrote Lord Mayor's shows for the City of London and bombastic plays for the common stage. By the late 1580's, Peele was in considerable financial difficulty. In 1593, he wrote "The Honour of the Garter" to celebrate the Earl of Northumberland's election to that exclusive order. The prologue begins with lavish praise of the Earl, who had given Peele £3. But it quickly becomes a bitter complaint, on behalf of all Elizabethan poets, against the aristocracy and the courtly culture which Peele is ostensibly celebrating:

> Why goe not all into th'Elisian fieldes,
> And leave this Center, barren of repast,
> Unlesse in hope Augusta will restore,
> The wrongs that learning beares of covetousnes
> And Courts disdaine, the enemie to Arte.
>
>   (ll. 64-68)[33]

In 1596, Peele refurbished a poem from his college days (first printed in 1589) for a desperate offering: "To the r. honorable & woorthie Patrone of Learninge the L. Burleigh L. highe Theasorer of England . . . Georg. Peele mr of Arts Presents ye tale of Troy" (*Life and Minor Works*, p. 105). It was from *The Tale of Troy* that Peele had developed ***The Araygnement of Paris*** at the auspicious beginning of his career. It now made a humble gift indeed for the great minister of Elizabeth's Troynovant. Burghley, who by the 1590's virtually controlled the flow of patronage from the Crown, appears to have had little sympathy for contemporary poetry and poets. His response to Peele's begging letter was to file it "with others from cranks and crackpots, such as . . . 'Austin Metcalf's mad incoherent jargon, addressed to the Queen and Lord Bughley, by way of petition'" (*Life and Minor Works*, p. 108). Peele's gift went unrequited. Within a few months, he was dead.

IV Epilogue

The Araygnement of Paris is a cultural manifestation of the Elizabethan Court; the court itself provides the code in which Peele entertains it. Peele's apparent concern is not to anatomize but to praise and please an audience whose approval and favor he earnestly desires. The courtly pastoral with which Peele began his career makes an apposite contrast to Spenser's Legend of Courtesy, a late pastoral reprise which is markedly analytical and critical in its reproduction of Elizabethan court culture. The tension of values in Book Six of *The Faerie Queene* is epitomized in the contrast of two images of courtship: the heroic poet's courtship of his royal mistress in the proem and the pastoral piper's courtship of his country lass in canto ten. In effect, Spenser establishes two rival courts, the centers of political and poetic power, patronage and love; and the latter emerges late in the poem as the model of grace and courtesy by which courtly culture itself is measured and found wanting.[34] "Of Court it seemes, men Courtesie doe call" (VI.i.1), but Spenser knows not "seemes": "vertues seat is deepe within the mynde. / And not in outward shows, but inward thoughts defynd" (VI.proem.5).

Sir Calidore, the flower of Gloriana's court, sojourns among the shepherds in order to practice his courtship upon Pastorella; like other Elizabethan courtiers, he puts on a pastoral mask:

> That who had seene him then, would have bethought
> On *Phrygian Paris* by *Plexippus* brooke,
> When he the love of fayre *Oenone* sought,
> What time the golden apple was unto him brought.
>
>   (VI.ix.36)

The resonant and ominous simile heralds Spenser's transformation of The Choice of Paris in the following canto. While hunting on a wooded hilltop, the shepherd-knight happens upon a most rare vision: "An hundred naked maidens lilly white, / All raunged in a ring, and dauncing in delight." In the midst of them, the Three Graces dance and sing;

> And in the middest of those same three, was placed
> Another Damzell, as a precious gemme,
> Amidst a ring most richly well enchaced,
> And with her goodly presence all the rest much
>   graced.
>
>   (VI.x.12)

"All gifts of grace" (x.15) emanate in concentric circles from this central figure:

> Another Grace she well deserves to be,
>   In whom so many Graces gathered are,
>   Exceling much the meane of her degree;
>   Divine resemblaunce, beauty soveraine rare,
>   Firme Chastity, that spite ne blemish dare.
>
>   (x.27)

The maiden who infolds all the Graces is both a humble "countrey lasse" and "a goddesse graced / With heavenly gifts from heven first enraced" (x.25); Colin Clout, who plays to her alone (x.15), is both a rustic piper and a hierophant.

"All gracious gifts . . . / Which decke the body or adorne the mynde" are bestowed on men by the Three Graces, whose own powers seem now to emanate from the maiden who has replaced Venus at the center of their dance.

> They teach us, how to each degree and kynde
> We should our selves demeane, to low, to hie;
> To friends, to foes, which skil men call Civility.
>
>   (VI.x.23)

Courtesy makes human society possible, and imposes a civilizing form upon the predatory instincts of the courtier. Spenser's great icon infolds a metaphysics, a politics, and an ethics of reciprocity; it is the "true glorious type" of the Elizabethan court and its patronage system:

> Right so from you all goodly vertues well
> Into the rest, which round about you ring,
> Faire Lords and Ladies, which about you dwell,
> And doe adorne your Court, where courtesies excell.
>
>   (VI.proem.7)

Spenser brings together pastoral conventions, myths of royal power, and acts of prestation to create an encomium conspicuously rivaling his own celebrations of Elisa (*The Shepheardes Calender*, "April") and Gloriana—and rivaling, too, the culminating device of Peele's ***The Araygnement of Paris***. The rustic maiden who replaces Venus as the cynosure of the vision also supplants Elizabeth as the cynosure of the poem. Colin, who has been addressing Calidore within the fiction, turns to address directly the royal reader to whom the poem is ostensibly dedicated. The voice of the heroic poet, heard in the proems, now speaks through the pastoral poet:

> Great *Gloriana*, greatest Majesty,
> Pardon thy shepheard, mongst so many layes,
> As he hath sung of thee in all his dayes,
> To make one minime of thy poore handmayd.
>
>   (x.28)

The shepherd-courtier's very apology is an oblique acknowledgment that Spenser's pastoral mythopoeia subverts the heroic poet's claim that the Queen and the Court are the authentic sources of his inspiration and reward.

In the proem, the weary poet claims scornfully that what now passes for courtesy "is nought but forgerie, / Fashion'd to please the eies of them that pas" (proem.5); and in the last line of the book, the embittered poet cautions his verse to "seeke to please, that now is counted wisemens threasure" (xii.41). The poet must begin and end as an entertainer and celebrant of the Court, as a maker of "fayned shows" for his social betters. But "deepe within the mynd"—within the pastoral fiction that bodies forth "inward thoughts"—the poet

teaches "true courtesie" to the Knight, and celebrates Gloriana's rustic handmaid as the only she in whom do meet so many gifts in one.

Notes

The Oxford English Dictionary defines *prestation* as "the action of paying, in money or service, what is due by law or custom, or in recognition of feudal superiority; a payment or the performance of a service so imposed or exacted; also, the performance of something promised." The earliest usage cited is in the Parliamentary rolls of 1473. The word is obsolete in English, though still current in French. *Prestation* is a central term in Marcel Mauss' ethnological classic, *Essai sur le don* (1925), where it is used of material and symbolic objects given within a network of social exchanges. The translator of the English edition (*The Gift*, trans. Ian Cunnison [New York, 1967]), uses *prestation* for want of an adequate modern English equivalent. I use *prestation* to connote an implicitly obligatory or coercive act of giving.

1. *Elizabethan Poetry* (1952; rpt., Ann Arbor, 1968), pp. 4, 7.

2. *Nennio, or a Treatise of Nobility,* trans. William Jones (London, 1595), sig. H3ᵛ (quoted in Smith, *Elizabethan Poetry,* pp. 5-6, n. 13). I have modified obsolete typographical conventions in quotations from this and other Elizabethan texts. See the discussion of "Virtue reconciled with Pleasure," in Edgar Wind, *Pagan Mysteries in the Renaissance,* rev. ed. (Harmondsworth, 1967), pp. 81-96.

3. *Marsilio Ficino: The* Philebus *Commentary,* ed. and trans. Michael J. B. Allen (Berkeley, 1975), p. 446. I do not imply that Ficino's work is a "source" for Peele's. Other Tudor treatments of the Choice of Paris device are catalogued in John D. Reeves, "The Judgment of Paris as a Device of Tudor Flattery," *N&Q,* N.S. 1 (1954), 7-11; and Inga-Stina Ekeblad, "On the Background of Peele's 'Araygnement of Paris,'" *N&Q,* N.S. 3 (1956), 246-49.

4. On the theme of Chastity in Peele's play (to be discussed more fully below), compare Andrew Von Hendy, "The Triumph of Chastity: Form and Meaning in *The Arraignment of Paris,*" *RenD,* N.S. 1 (1968), 87-101; on the motif of the *trionfo* in Elizabethan iconography, see Frances A. Yates, *Astraea* (London, 1975), pp. 112-20. On Peele's spectacular dramaturgy, see Inga-Stina Ewbank, "'What words, what looks, what wonders?': Language and Spectacle in the Theatre of George Peele," in *The Elizabethan Theatre V,* ed. G. R. Hibbard (Hamden, Conn., 1975), pp. 124-54, esp. pp. 136-41.

5. *The Araygnement of Paris,* ed. R. Mark Benbow, in *The Dramatic Works of George Peele,* C. T.

It is this Stukeley, charismatic and controversial, whose personality lent itself ideally to representation in the newly emerging biographical drama.

III

The first extant English play to deal with Stukeley—and the first to depict the life of a Tudor figure in any detail—is George Peele's **Battle of Alcazar** (1588-89). Perhaps the most striking aspect of Peele's dramatic rendering of the folk-tale and legend that had already gathered around Stukeley's life, is the deftness with which he casts this material into the currently popular heroic vein. Marlowe's *Tamburlaine* (1587-88) preceded **The Battle of Alcazar** by about a year, and throughout Peele's play, especially in the episodes involving Stukeley, high astounding Marlovian terms serve as a major vehicle for developing personality. Stukeley's very first speech in the play, an unabashed defense of his Irish expedition in the presence of both the governor of Lisbon and the Spanish king, reflects fully the expansiveness of spirit that typifies the Marlovian hero at his overweening best:

> As we are Englishmen, so are we men,
> And I am Stukeley so resolvde in all,
> To follow rule, honor and Emperie,
> Not to be bent so strictly to the place,
> Wherein at first I blew the fire of life,
> But that I may at libertie make choise,
> Of all the continents that bounds the world.
>
> (ll. 410-416)

Here is Stukeley the citizen of the world, recklessly overusing the first person pronoun in the royal presence, asserting boldly to anyone who will listen (something in the ebullient manner of Dekker's Simon Eyre) that king is he none, yet is he kingly born. And naturally all are captivated. It is also worth noting, however, that Peele's hero is more than simply the mouthpiece for Marlovian rant. When a drily sententious Irish churchman attempts to justify the invasion as a matter of "conscience and religion" (1. 429), Stukeley has the readiness of wit to pun inventively and irreverently on the prelate's title of Bishop of St. Asaph[6]:

> Well said Bishop, spoken like your selfe,
> The reverent lordly bishop of saint Asses.
>
> (ll. 431-432)

But the reckless adventurer who exults in putting "all conscience into one carouse" (1. 450), is still at his best when speaking (as the true hero in the Marlovian vein inevitably does) of the sweet fruition of an earthly crown:

> There shall no action passe my hand or sword,
> That cannot make a step to gaine a crowne,
> No word shall passe the office of my tong,

> That sounds not of affection to a crowne,
> No thought have being in my lordly brest,
> That workes not everie waie to win a crowne,
> Deeds, wordes and thoughts shall all be as a kings,
> My chiefest companie shall be with kings,
> And my deserts shall counterpoise a kings,
> Why should not I then looke to be a king?
> I am the marques now of Ireland made,
> And will be shortly king of Ireland,
> King of a mole-hill had I rather be,
> Than the richest subject of a monarchie[7],
> Huffe it brave minde, and never cease t'aspire,
> Before thou raigne sole king of thy desire.
>
> (ll. 452-467)

Thus Stukeley's personality, as Peele chooses to depict it, has its origins both in folk-tale and stage convention—its peculiar quality resulting from the grafting of popular details about the adventurer's life onto an established stage type, the Marlovian hero.

It is not surprising that the most revealing insights into Stukeley the man occur when the more individualized, "factual" side of his character resists the confines of its heroic stereotype and comes ineluctably to the surface. Such is the case when young Sebastian undertakes to lecture the experienced soldier on the dangers of invading Ireland in the hope that Stukeley will follow him to Morocco instead. The Portuguese king delivers a lengthy and impassioned encomium of "Irelands Queene" (1. 671), which runs its rhetorical course through every conceivable accolade about Elizabeth and her island paradise, ending with a warning not to "wrong the wonder of the highest God" (1. 700), but instead to "followe me in holy christian warres" (1. 704). Stukeley's reply to Sebastian's show of bravado is both terse and ironically double-edged: "Rather my Lord, let me admire these wordes" (1. 706). The genially sarcastic thrust is one we would never expect to find on the lips of Tamburlaine, yet it is fully consistent with Stukeley's particular brand of blithe and unfettered heroism. Moreover, the same wry practicality that underlies the remark manifests itself on still another occasion. Just after Sebastian delivers another of his impassioned pronouncements, this time metaphorically clapping his hands "for joy" over the promised aid of Philip of Spain (1. 801), a sober and thoroughly politic Stukeley remarks:

> Sit fast Sebastian, and in this worke
> God and good men labor for Portugall,
> For Spaine disguising with a double face,
> Flatters thy youth and forwardness good king,
> . . . . .
> Let Portugall fare as he may or can,
> Spaine meanes to spend no pouder on the moores.
>
> (ll. 806-820)

It hardly seems possible that the same man who only a few moments earlier had resolved to "huffe" his way to kingship could now quietly and thoughtfully ask God to

Prouty, gen. ed. (New Haven, Conn., 1970). My quotations follow the text and lineation of this edition.

6. *Julye*, ll. 149-51. All quotations are from *Spenser: Poetical Works*, ed. J. C. Smith and E. De Selincourt (1912; rpt. Oxford, 1975).

7. Renato Poggioli, *The Oaten Flute* (Cambridge, Mass., 1975), p. 1.

8. George Puttenham, *The Arte of English Poesie* (1589), ed. G. D. Willcock and Alice Walker (Cambridge, 1936), p. 24. All quotations will be from this edition.

9. For a detailed discussion of the politics of royal pastoral, see my study, "'Eliza, Queen of shepheardes' and the Pastoral of Power," forthcoming in *ELR*, 10 (1980).

10. Anthony Esler, *The aspiring mind of the Elizabethan younger generation* (Durham, N.C., 1966), p. 51. Esler's study is provocative and enlightening for students of Elizabethan literary history, even though it overstates its case. Esler pays insufficient attention to occupational and other categories of social status which cut across the generational categories. See Lawrence Stone, "Social Mobility in England, 1500-1700," *Past & Present*, 33 (1966), 16-55, for facts, figures, and a model of social change.

11. This corpus is well discussed in David Bevington, *Tudor Drama and Politics* (Cambridge, Mass., 1968), pp. 141-86; and Marie Axton, *The Queen's Two Bodies* (London, 1977), pp. 38-115.

12. Quoted in J. E. Neale, *Elizabeth I and Her Parliaments 1559-1581* (New York, 1958), p. 49. On the sixteenth century debate about gynarchy, see James E. Phillips, Jr., "The Background of Spenser's Attitude Toward Women Rulers," *HLQ*, 5 (1941-42), 5-32.

13. Sir Robert Nauton, *Fragmenta Regalia* (written ca. 1630; printed 1641), ed. Edward Arber (London, 1870), p. 17.

14. *Calendar of State Papers, Spanish* (1558-67), pp. 404-05; quoted in Axton, *The Queen's Two Bodies*, p. 49.

15. Bodley MS Rawlinson Poet 108. The masque has long been cited in connection with *AP*; it is quoted and discussed in Axton, *The Queen's Two Bodies*, pp. 50-51.

16. I quote the text of the Kenilworth entertainment (first printed 1576) from vol. 2 of *The Complete Works of George Gascoigne*, ed. J. W. Cunliffe, (Cambridge, 1910); and the text of the Wanstead entertainment (first printed 1598) from *Miscellaneous Prose of Sir Philip Sidney*, ed. Katherine Duncan-Jones and Jan Van Dorsten (Oxford, 1973).

17. I have studied this text in greater detail, from the perspective of the author rather than the sponsor, in "Celebration and Insinuation: Sir Philip Sidney and the Motives of Elizabethan Courtship," *RenD*, N.S. 8 (1977), 3-35.

18. Henry G. Lesnick suggests some "historicomythical" elements in "The Structural Significance of Myth and Flattery in Peele's *Arraignment of Paris*," *SP*, 65 (1968), 163-70. The ideology and iconography of the Elizabeth cult are discussed suggestively in Yates, *Astraea*, pp. 29-111; and Roy Strong, *The Cult of Elizabeth* (London, 1977).

19. "Elizabeth I and the Three Goddesses" (formerly at Hampton Court; presently in the collection of The Queen's Pictures, Buckingham Palace), monogrammed "HE" and dated 1569. The painting is catalogued in Roy C. Strong, *Portraits of Queen Elizabeth I* (Oxford, 1963), p. 79, and reproduced as Plate VI; it is reproduced in color, with details, in Roy Strong, *The English Icon* (London, 1969), pp. 143-45. I reproduce the painting by gracious permission of H. M. Queen Elizabeth II.

20. On the Queen's wardrobe, see Neville Williams, *Elizabeth: Queen of England* (London, 1967), pp. 226-27; and Paul Johnson, *Elizabeth I: A Study in Power and Intellect* (London, 1974), p. 197.

21. On the Elizabethan transformation of Nativity pastoral into royal pastoral, see my "'Eliza, Queene of shepheardes' and the Pastoral of Power."

22. *The Queene's Majestie's Passage* (1559), rpt. in *Elizabethan Backgrounds*, ed. Arthur F. Kinney (Hamden, Conn., 1975), pp. 16-17; all quotations will be from this edition. I am indebted to Kinney's Introduction, pp. 7-9; and to Sydney Anglo, *Spectacle, Pageantry, and Early Tudor Policy* (Oxford, 1969), pp. 344-59.

23. See *The Rise of the Common Player* (Cambridge, Mass., 1962), pp. 243-64.

24. E. K.'s gloss on "The Graces," in the "Aprill" eclogue of Spenser's *Shepheardes Calender*. The fundamental iconographic study of the Graces is Wind, *Pagan Mysteries*, pp. 26-52.

25. *The Elizabethan Stage* (Oxford, 1923), I, 19.

26. John Nichols, *The Progresses and Public Processions of Queen Elizabeth* (1823; rpt., New York, 1966), I, xxxviii. In his collection, Nichols prints full rolls for five years of the reign.

27. In Neale, *Essays in Elizabethan History* (London, 1958), p. 71.

28. Wallace T. MacCaffrey, "Place and Patronage in Elizabethan Politics," in *Elizabethan Government and Society*, ed. S. T. Bindoff, J. Hurstfield, and C. H. Williams (London, 1961), pp. 96-97. See also

Lawrence Stone, *The Crisis of the Aristocracy 1558-1641* (Oxford, 1965), pp. 385-504; and, for a good overview, Alan G. R. Smith, *The Government of Elizabethan England* (New York, 1967), pp. 57-69.

29. See Joel Hurstfield, *Freedom, Corruption and Government in Elizabethan England* (London, 1973), pp. 137-62.

30. Pierre Bourdieu, *Outline of a Theory of Practice,* trans. Richard Nice (Cambridge, 1977), pp. 5-6. I have also benefitted from Esther Goody, "'Greeting,' 'begging,' and the presentation of respect," in *The Interpretation of Ritual,* ed. J. S. La Fontaine (London, 1972), pp. 39-71; and Raymond Firth, *Symbols: Public and Private* (Ithaca, 1973), pp. 368-402.

31. See Stephen Orgel, *The Illusion of Power* (Berkeley, 1975), pp. 9-11.

32. I have advanced this interpretation in "'The perfecte paterne of a Poete': The Poetics of Courtship in *The Shepheardes Calender,*" *TSLL,* 21 (1979), 34-67. Also see Richard Helgerson, "The New Poet Presents Himself: Spenser and the Idea of a Literary Career," *PMLA,* 93 (1978), 893-911.

33. Quotations are from the text in David H. Horne, *The Life and Minor Works of George Peele* (New Haven, 1952). Horne's study is the source of biographical information.

34. The introspection, disillusionment, and social criticism of Book Six have received considerable attention in recent studies: See, for example, Michael O'Connell, *Mirror and Veil: The Historical Dimension of Spenser's* Faerie Queene (Chapel Hill, 1977), pp. 161-89; and Daniel Javitch, *Poetry and Courtliness in Renaissance England* (Princeton, 1978), pp. 137-59. I have discussed *FQ,* VI.x from the perspective of Spenser's poetic career, in "'The perfecte paterne of a Poete,'" pp. 55-58.

THE BATTLE OF ALCAZAR (C. 1590)

CRITICAL COMMENTARY

Joseph Candido (essay date 1987)

SOURCE: Candido, Joseph. "Captain Thomas Stukeley: The Man, the Theatrical Record, and the Origins of Tudor 'Biographical' Drama." *Anglia: Zeitschrift für Englische Philologie* 105, no. 1 (1987): 50-68.

[*In the following essay, Candido explores the dramatization of Captain Thomas Stukeley, a popular figure in the sixteenth century, focusing on Peele's* Battle of Alcazar *and other works.*]

I

The literary critic who encounters the word "tragedy" on the title page of "histories" such as Shakespeare's *Richard III* will be duly forewarned of the danger of trying to ascribe precise generic distinctions to the drama of Renaissance England. Yet in discussing the dramatic hybrids of an age which itself failed to insist upon neat artistic categories, he is faced with the unhappy prospect of either making convenient (albeit somewhat arbitrary) generic distinctions, or falling into Polonius-like circumlocutions that reveal nothing specific about the subject at hand. So it is that modern critics of the Elizabethan history play have seen fit to distinguish a sub-genre of the type called the "biographical" drama, similar to the history play in its concern with statecraft, kingship, patriotism, and political morality, yet distinct from it in the sense that its emphasis is not on historical events, but rather on the personalities who both shape and respond to them. This distinction is, of course, often difficult to draw, yet Irving Ribner has made perhaps the most lucid attempt to unravel the difficulty. He points out that

> it is possible to distinguish a group of plays in which the central issue is not so much the life of the state as the life of an individual. The protagonist in such plays is not *Respublica*. But since the heroes are almost always historical figures, their lives touch upon important political problems.[1]

What we have in the biographical drama, then, is the same combination of historical event and historical personality that informs the chronicle-history play, yet with the significant difference that here "history" functions chiefly as the panoramic backdrop against which the life of the central character is brought into salient relief. It is quite simply the setting for the stone, or, to put it another way, the scenery in the portrait: it is never the main subject of the play.

Obviously this distinction is a subtle one, and were it not for the fact that the plays in this biographical mode have other significant features in common, it would be difficult to regard them as a separate dramatic phenomenon. Ribner amplifies his definition of the type by distinguishing its episodic form, and its *de casibus* structure as defining characteristics (p. 195); yet each of these qualities can also be found in any number of history plays. He gets much closer to the essence of biographical drama, however, when he notes its almost exclusive preoccupation with the Tudor personality.

> The heroes of the biographical drama tend further to be drawn from fairly recent history. They are almost always Tudor courtiers, and the plays thus carry on the Italian humanist tradition of history as a mirror of contemporary life.
>
> (p. 195)

Indeed, except for *Sir John Oldcastle* (1599), a play with unmistakable analogies to Tudor politics, every extant play designated by Ribner as "biographical" deals expressly with Tudor figures. Moreover, in the period 1600-1603, which falls squarely in the midst of the vogue for biographical drama, we know of six lost plays on Tudor figures which appear from their titles also to have been in the biographical mode: *Owen Tudor* (1600), *The Life of Cardinal Wolsey* (1601), *The Rising of Cardinal Wolsey* (1601), *Sebastian, King of Portugal* (1601), *Lady Jane* (1602), and *The Earl of Hertford* (1603).[2] When we add to this list the titles of those extant plays of roughly the same period in which Tudor figures either play a prominent role or are the major focus of attention, i. e., **The Battle of Alcazar** (1588-89), *Captain Thomas Stukeley* (c. 1596), *Thomas Lord Cromwell* (c. 1600), *Sir Thomas More* (c. 1600-01), *Sir Thomas Wyatt* (1603-05), *1* and *2 If You Know Not Me, You Know Nobody* (1603-05), *When You See Me, You Know Me* (1604-05), and *The Whore of Babylon* (1605-06)[3], it becomes apparent that around the turn of the century in England there emerged on the public stage a clearly identifiable dramatic type, biographical in nature and "Tudor" in orientation.

It is my purpose in this essay to examine the two earliest extant plays of this "biographical" group, **The Battle of Alcazar** and *Captain Thomas Stukeley,* not only because they share a single biographical purpose, but also because of the unique insight they provide into the artistic genesis of a curious yet much-neglected dramatic genre—the "Tudor" biographical play. I should like to begin by considering very briefly the factual details of the life of a central character in these two plays, Captain Thomas Stukeley, and then move on to a more detailed examination of the significantly "biographical" features of the plays themselves.

II

Few contemporary figures captured more thoroughly the imagination of Elizabethan Englishmen than the flamboyant soldier of fortune Captain Thomas Stukeley. The fragmentary yet colorful details of his life that historians have been able to piece together read like a perpetual gyration on the wheel of fortune.[4] After falling out of favor with the crown because of his involvement in the Duke of Somerset's rebellion in 1551, he fled to France and became a favorite of Henry II; yet when he learned of the French king's plans to invade England, he returned home to inform the Privy Council of the plot—an act of patriotism for which he was unceremoniously jailed. In the midst of this turmoil he found the time to marry Anne Curtis, the daughter of a wealthy alderman, but he soon squandered her inheritance on drink and riotous living.

In an attempt to mend his ruined fortunes he agreed to sail to Terra Florida in the service of the queen, ostensibly to "people" (p. 32) the region, yet actually to plunder French ships on her behalf. He performed his task with such efficiency that his piracies soon became "much railed at" (p. 35) in European courts, and the queen, for form's sake, was forced to sacrifice her adventurer to public opinion by censuring him at home. It was, however, Stukeley's failure to garner large profits by his enterprise, not the queen's embarrassment, that earned him her lasting displeasure.

Following the ill-fated Florida enterprise Stukeley made his way to Ireland where he won the friendship of both the queen's deputy, Sir Henry Sidney, and the rebel leader Shane O'Neill. Yet here he also met with two new misfortunes: the first when Elizabeth maliciously blocked his attempt to purchase valuable lands, and the second when he was jailed for allegedly sympathizing with Irish nationalists. But no jail ever held Stukeley long. He somehow escaped, and on the pretext of sailing for England to make his peace with Elizabeth, he set his course for the court of Philip of Spain. The "Catholic king" and the Catholic exile obviously had much in common, and Stukeley instantly became much celebrated at the Escorial. He was made a knight in the order of Calatrava and given a handsome pension, but again fell out of favor with Philip and Elizabeth made tentative overtures of peace, and the queen specifically demanded that Philip "abandon Stucley" (p. 93).

Once more the English adventurer took to the seas, th[is] time toward Rome, where he was "splendidly received" (p. 93) by Pope Pius V. Here he entered into negoti[a]tions with the Pope to conquer Ireland and free it fr[om] Protestant rule, but was deterred from this enterprise [by] his enforced participation in the Battle of Lepanto [in] 1572, at which his brilliant generalship won him [ad]ditional fame. Yet the self-styled "Marquis of Irela[nd]" still longed to conquer his adopted country for [the] Church of Rome, and at long last obtained from [a] new Pope, Gregory XIII, a meagre force with whic[h to] mount an invasion. On his way to Ireland, howeve[r, he] stopped mysteriously at Lisbon where he was persua[ded] (or forced) by Sebastian of Portugal to accompany [the] young zealot on his holy mission to Alcazar, and th[ere] along with three foreign potentates, he bravely me[t his] death on the field of battle.

Such is most assuredly the stuff that legend is mad[e of,] and the large body of Stukeley material that surviv[es to] this day in ballads, biographies, tracts, and pros[e fic]tion, attests to the hold that this romantic figure h[ad on] the spirit of Renaissance Englishmen. Partic[ularly] informative in this regard is John Yoklavich's app[raisal] of Stukeley's reputation in his own age:

> He may have been a roisterer, but he was certainl[y a] brave captain, beloved by his own soldiers and gen[er]ally esteemed for his military virtues. By some he w[as] called thriftless; by others, magnanimous. It was adr[mit]ted by all that he was extremely generous with ot[her] people's money. Proud he may have been, and am[bi]tious, but never petty. A man of agreeable prese[nce,] aspiring mind, and ready wit, in many ways Tho[mas] Stukeley was a typical child of Renaissance Englan[d.]

intervene on Sebastian's behalf. Yet however irreconcilable the two sentiments may appear (the typical Marlovian hero, it will be remembered, seldom looks to God except to flout Him) the strange presence of self-inflation and Christian concern in Stukeley does at least reflect Peele's rudimentary attempt to convey something of the diversity that was so obviously central to his subject's character. And it is this determination on Peele's part to imbue his stage hero with certain innate tensions and contradictions of personality that marks the first glimmering of an interest in Tudor biography on the English stage. In fact, the explicitly "biographical" aspect of Peele's treatment of Stukeley becomes even more apparent when the adventurer delivers his final speech. Just after he is stabbed by his own Italian mercenaries he turns to the audience, and instead of regaling them with the customary Senecan premonition of hell, he begins to narrate "the story of [his] life" (1. 1326). His speech, some forty-eight lines long, begins with an account of his "yonger carelesse yeeres" (1. 1330), then progresses through his numerous adventures in Ireland, Spain, and Rome, and culminates with the present "hard exigent" in Alcazar (1. 1357), at which point he draws his statement to a close by alluding explicitly to its biographical nature:

> Stukley, the story of thy life is tolde,
> Here breath thy last and bid thy freindes farwell.

> (11. 1365-1366)

By allowing a single character in the play, albeit its most colorful one, to retard the forward movement of the plot by engaging in a long digression on the events of his own life, Peele hardly chooses the most artistically sophisticated way to set the wheels of Tudor dramatic biography in motion. Yet despite the faults of the medium, the message here is important. For the first time in English dramatic history a Tudor character appears on the stage to direct the attention of the audience to his life, exploits, and personality; and with his appearance, despite its artistic imperfections, the seeds of Tudor biographical drama begin to take root.

IV

The only other extant English play to deal with Stukeley, the anonymous *Life and Death of Captain Thomas Stukeley* (c. 1596), is even more thoroughly biographical in technique than is **The Battle of Alcazar.** In its original form the play consisted of five clearly distinguishable acts, each set in a different country and each depicting a separate stage in the flamboyant hero's life; yet the play as we have it today bears the marks of considerable, sometimes imperfect, revision. Richard Simpson notes that the play in its original form was meant "to exhibit five distinct pictures of Stucley's career—in England, Ireland, Spain, Rome, and Africa"[8], but that as a result of the increased interest around the

turn of the century in the claim of Sebastian's cousin Don Antonio to the Portuguese throne, and in that of an imposter claiming to be Sebastian himself, the last two acts were largely replaced by scenes from another play "intended to recommend to the English the claims of Antonio to the crown"(p. 140). And J. Q. Adams, obviously indebted to Simpson's findings, reconstructs a similar history of the text:

> In *Captaine Thomas Stukeley,* then, we have in the main the old play of *Stewtley,* with the entire fourth act and the larger part of the fifth act omitted, and their place supplied by scenes dealing with the Portuguese expedition to Africa, taken from a drama celebrating the career of Antonio.[9]

The textual history of *Captain Thomas Stukeley* is important to our purposes in two respects: first, it illustrates how willingly and conveniently the biographical dramatist of the 1590s could restructure his play to focus upon any figure currently enjoying wide popularity; secondly it underscores how completely his artistic medium emphasizes the individual personality at the expense of any clearly delineated "idea of history". When interest was rekindled in Stukeley, Sebastian, and Antonio as a result of the political machinations of the time, out came the old Stukeley play, somewhat revised, to vivify once more for the playgoing public those personalities who figured so prominently in the events surrounding the settlement at Alcazar.

Captain Thomas Stukeley, in the manner of most biographical plays, is highly episodic in structure; and the multi-faceted personality of its hero is developed slowly, by accretion, as each succeeding incident provides us with fresh and revealing insights into his complex character. The play opens in the home of alderman Thomas Curtis whose daughter has just resolved to forsake her lover Vernon, and to pledge herself instead to Stukeley "the man whom heaven appointed for me" (1. 85). Indeed, even the forlorn Vernon appears only too willing to acknowledge the extraordinary personal qualities of his friend and rival, admitting that Stukeley "is the substance of my shadowed love / I but a cypher in respect of him" (11. 55-56). Yet it is Stukeley himself, basking exuberantly "in the public worlds repute" (1. 88), who most delights in singing his own praise:

> Madam, and kind Sir Thomas, look on me
> Not with disdainful looks, or base contempt.
> I am a gentleman, and well deriv'd
> Equal, I may say, in all true respects,
> With higher fortune than I aim at now.

> (11. 70-74)

This is, of course, the familiar Marlovian mode of expression; yet what is significant about its appearance in *Captain Thomas Stukeley* is the fact that the veracity of its rhetoric is constantly called into question. No sooner does Stukeley make his grand pronouncement than the skeptical Curtis deflates it by noting quite correctly that his future son-in-law is "very wild, a quarreller, a fighter / Aye, and I doubt a spend-good too" (11. 108-109). And when the scene concludes a moment later with Stukeley callously rejoicing over the "love" that brings a rich alderman's "fortune" with it (11. 119-120), his heroic dimensions seem suddenly less splendid than his words. Thus, in the very first scene of the play, the dramatist[10] establishes a pattern of simultaneous praise and blame which he uses repeatedly in drawing the character of Stukeley. One need look only so far as Shakespeare's *Antony and Cleopatra* (or for that matter a later and much more sophisticated Tudor stage biography, Ford's *Perkin Warbeck*) to see the effectiveness of such a technique in depicting the complex and often seemingly contradictory sides of a single personality; and it is worth noting that the same spirit of *discordia concors* that informs the more mature work of Shakespeare and Ford also lies at the heart of one of the earliest English biographical plays.

A similar juxtaposition of the attractive and unattractive aspects of Stukeley's character occurs in the very next scene. The episode opens in charming fashion as Stukeley's father, himself a "fresh and lusty" (1. 140) gentleman of advanced years, determines to go to the Temple[11] "to see my son . . . that unthrifty boy, Tom Stukeley" (11. 149-150). It soon becomes apparent, however, that the elder Stukeley's oft-repeated objections to his son's roistering are really more formal than substantive:

> I hear his courage very much commended,
> But too licentious—that is all I fear.
> But that he doth accommodate with the best,
> In that he shows himself a gentleman;
> And, though perhaps he shall not know so much,
> I do not much mislike that humour in him.
> A gentleman of blood and quality
> To sort himself amongst the noblest spirits
> Shows the true sparks of honourable worth
> And rightly shows in this he is mine own.
> For when I was of young Tom Stukeley's years
> And of the Inns of Court, as he is now,
> I would be conversant still with the best,
> The bravest spirits that were about the town—
>
> (11. 172-185)

In this mood of tolerant disapprobation old Stukeley sets off to observe the behavior of his son; yet what he encounters at the young man's lodgings gradually, but inexorably, tips the balance of his opinion toward a more settled discontent. Instead of finding, as he expects, a lusty yet serious student of the Temple who sorts himself "among the noblest spirits", he discovers a "vild lewd unthrift" (1. 299) who is seldom out of taverns and who spends his generous allowance on sword and buckler rather than on books of law. Yet even these "disordered courses" (1. 287) of Stukeley's,

however intolerable they may appear to his father, are nonetheless a source of entertainment for the audience. We enjoy the frank charm of the young man who can assert outright to his disapproving parent that

> I've done my goodwill, but it will not do.
> John a Nokes and John a Style and I cannot cotton.
> O, this law-French is worse than butter'd-mackerell
> Full o' bones, full o' bones. It sticks here; 't will not down.
> *Aurum potabile* will not get it down.
>
> (11. 289-293)

This is the blunt, lively style that lovers of the "Stukeley myth" both expect and revel in; yet in the midst of our enjoyment the dramatist is quick to remind us that the humor has a darker side. We may be inclined to laugh along with the swashbuckler who can toss aside his father's worries about finances with the simple assertion that a rich alderman's daughter is about to be his "horse and foot" (1. 311), but the disquietingly pragmatic view he takes of the marriage seems, even for him, more callous than the situation warrants:

> If you will but tickle [Curtis] in the ear, look you,
> With a certain word, called a Jointure—
> Ha that same Jointure, and a proper man
> Withal, as I am, will draw you on a wench,
> As a squirril's skin will draw on a Spanish shoe.
>
> (11. 317-321)

And when he enlarges upon this statement shortly afterwards in an even more self-revealing fashion, we feel suddenly a satiric jolt more common to Jonsonian comedy than to the fledgling biographical drama:

> I have the wench's good will, and [Curtis] must yield
> Spite of his heart: she's worth forty thousand pound
> O father this is the right Philosophers stone!
> True multiplication! I have found it.
>
> (11. 327-330)

Again the dramatist reveals to us, by the simple accumulation of incidents, a noteworthy facet of his subject's personality that can appear either charming or cruel, ingratiating or satiric. The technique obviously has a particular appropriateness for a form of drama that is concerned first of all with human nature, and only secondarily with the effects of that nature upon human events.

The episodes which conclude the first act establish even further the many and diversified aspects of Stukeley's personality. We next see him, for instance, storming furiously from his own wedding reception to exchange heated words, and nearly blows, with one Captain Herbert, who has had the temerity to suggest that alderman Curtis "hath undone his daughter by the marriage" (1. 373). Stukeley is understandably outraged by the thinly-veiled allusion to his prodigality, yet he soon appears on stage doing precisely what his "disgraceful" (1. 374) accuser had foretold. In full view of his bewildered father-in-law he makes his entrance laden with bags of "marriage money" (1. 538), and proceeds to disperse it, in cavalier fashion, to "half the tradesmen in the town" (1. 542). But Stukeley's behavior, despite its insensitivity to his kinsman's feelings, has a strangely attractive side to it. There is something admirable about the loyal soldier who, while paying his debts, also gives unhesitatingly of his own resources to ransom from jail "a good sword and buckler man" (11. 619-620) who once fought alongside him. And as always in Stukeley's case, as in the case of the typical Marlovian hero, we are continually fascinated by his partly genuine, partly illusory sense of his own worth:

> [the money] is mine own, and Stukeley of his own
> Will be as frank as shall the Emperor.
> I scorn this trash, betrayer of mens souls;
> I'll spurn it with my foot; and with my hand
> Rain showers of plenty on this barren land.
> Were it my fortune could exceed the clouds
> Yet would I bear a mind surmounting that.
> Father you have enough for your, and for your store
> When mine is gone you must provide me more.

> (11. 632-640)

Yet no matter how inflated Stukeley's rhetoric may become, there is no disputing its appropriateness in regard to his military prowess. He is above all a soldier's soldier, "The foremost man that shall begin the fight" (1. 666), who "goes not to the wars / To make a gain of his poor soldiers spoil, / But spoil the foe to make his soldiers gain" (11. 677-679). It is, of course, largely as a result of the high esteem in which he is held by his men that Stukeley longs again for the world of bloody noses and cracked crowns. Like Hotspur, he is most at home on the battlefield; and also like his Shakespearean counterpart, he finds there the values that most profoundly shape his identity:

> It is not chambering
> Now I have beauty to be dallying with,
> Nor pampering of myself with belly-cheer
> Now I have got a little worldly pelf,
> That is the end or levels of my thought.
> I must have honour; honour is the thing
> Stukeley doth thirst for, and to climb the mount
> Where she is seated, gold shall be my footstool.

> (11. 701-708)

In King Cambises' vein, with Tamburlaine's ambitions, and with Hotspur's idealized sense of honor, Stukeley bids farewell to his wife of three days and sets sail for Ireland. The mode of departure is fully in keeping with the impulsive, willful, yet unquestionably valorous adventurer of Act I who seeks always to "purchase dignity" (1. 714) in a manner inimitably his own.

With the change of scene to Ireland in Act II we glean even further insights into the martial side of Stukeley's character. He first appears standing imperiously before a coastal city occupied by English troops, musing aloud "what Lord is governor of this town / That comes not forth to welcome Stukley in" (11. 943-944). Then he promptly displays some typically Stukelian pique over the fact that the "gallants" within "strain a further compliment / To see if I will vail my bonnet first" (11. 957-960). Naturally he does not; yet when the chief occupants of the city at last pay him due respect, he deigns to enquire about the progress of the wars. Now these are precisely the kind of heroical posturings in which the audience delights, but such behavior, as we have already seen, is often the herald of more sober things to come. When Stukeley quickly discovers to his surprise that Herbert (his near equal in arms if not in rhetoric) is leader of the English garrison, there follows a brief yet revealing glimpse of the man behind the Marlovian facade. Stukeley's instinctive response to the disquieting news comes, uncharacteristically, in an aside: "S'death, I am bewitched, mine enemy Governor!" (1. 985). The emotionalism of Stukeley's reaction belies for an instant the stoical histrionics he shows to the world, and although he quickly collects himself ("Well 'tis no matter, I'll about with him" [1. 986]) we have already seen the grimace behind the heroic mask. In fact, the dramatist's major concern in Act II is to establish unequivocally this intense emotionalism of his hero, and so to underscore in Stukeley a basic tension between the Marlovian abstraction and the real man. It is a "Rash, hare-brained Stukley" (1. 1046) indeed who violates "the discipline of war" (1. 1055) by drawing his sword heedlessly on the governor of the town he is bound by duty to defend. And there is more than a little of Hotspur's hasty temper in the man who in the thick of battle pays little heed to the orders of his more circumspect superiors:

> He is so eager to pursue the foe
> And flesh his soldiers that are new arrived
> That he forgot or heard not the retreat.

> (11. 1097-1099)

Despite the fact that Stukeley's refusal to retreat results in his troops gaining just the "lusty prey" (1. 1092) that an admiring soldier had earlier said it would, Herbert refuses to allow the captain or his men to re-enter the town after their successful plunder. What Herbert sees as a valuable lesson in warlike "discipline" Stukeley more bluntly regards as "a simple piece of small revenge" (1. 1137) which heaps disgrace both upon his soldiers and himself—and naturally he cannot endure it. After angrily shouting insults to Herbert from outside the walls of the city (yet in the midst of his outrage also seeing that his troops are rewarded properly for their valor) Stukeley ends his stay in Ireland as he began it, in a rush of Marlovian rhetoric:

Before the sun the morning doth salute
I'll see my hobbies safely set aboard
Then follow I, that scorn to be controlled
Of any man thats meaner than a king.
Farewell O'Neale; if Stukley here had stayed
Thy head for treason soon thou shouldst have paid.

(11. 1172-1177)

Such language is, of course, the standard poetic vehicle for any Elizabethan stage "hero" of the 1590's; yet what is so striking about its appearance in *Captain Thomas Stukeley* is its existence, side by side, with more realistic touches of personality that challenge the veracity of the stage type at the same time that they embroider it with a certain degree of psychological depth. It is this constant duality between the man and the poetic abstraction, the Tudor personality and Tudor stage practice, that is perhaps the most distinct feature of the biographical drama that emerges in Renaissance England.

Act III of *Captain Thomas Stukeley* deals with the hero's eventful sojourn in Spain, and begins by sounding many of the same thematic notes as the two acts which precede it. We see something of the charm that must have endeared Stukeley to Anne Curtis in his courtly behavior toward the wife of the governor of Cadiz—a lady so thoroughly captivated by his manner that she risks "honour and life" (1. 1410) to secure his freedom from captivity at her husband's hands. There is also, of course, the inevitable heroic rant, this time delivered by Stukeley before an appreciative King Philip, who is quick to reward such "knightly" (1. 1603) language with a hearty welcome "And favor too againe thine enemy" (1. 1638). We hear once more that Stukeley "bears a mind / That will not melt at any tyrants words" (11. 1824-1825), and see, as we have before, that he also bears a bitingly ironic wit to accompany it.[12]

All this reiteration, however, serves merely as a prelude to the most revealing—and tragic—aspect of Stukeley's personality. It is clear from King Philip's first appearance on stage that in his political dealings he is often "more deceitful than becomes a king" (1. 1570). Stukeley, however, always remains blissfully unaware of his royal patron's enormous capacity for evil. This blunt soldier who "holds his promise as religion" (1. 1647) swaggers joyfully through Philip's court, never fully sensitive to the Machiavellian intrigue that swirls everywhere about him and which draws him unwittingly yet inexorably into its midst. Stukeley sees in Philip a "royal Catholic King" (1. 1905) whose generosity merits unquestioned loyalty, while Philip merely regards his entertaining stranger as a "fond Englishman" (1. 2040) whose eccentricity (and egocentricity) can be exploited for political gain. There is thus a brilliant visual irony in the stage direction that shows the

Spanish king entering in state ("*leaning on* Stukley's *shoulder*" (1. 1901)[13]; for Philip here merely enacts a role that plays ingeniously upon Stukeley's compelling need to be regarded as a person of royal quality. It is flattery that Stukeley craves, and flattery that Philip gives him:

Heroic Stukley, on our royal word
We never did esteem a present more
Than those fair Irish horse of your frank gift,
. . . . .
How we esteem your present and yourself
Our instant favours shall advertise you.

(11. 1902-1913)

Philip's "instant favours", however, take the form of ruthless exploitation. He decides to send this credulous "agent of our guile" (1. 2028) on a seemingly important embassy to Rome to see if the Pope "doth hold it fit" (1. 1978) that Spain should join Sebastian of Portugal in the war against the Moors—a war that Philip has absolutely no intention of supporting. Thus Stukeley, Marlovian hero and figure of English folk legend, ironically becomes Philip's unwitting pawn in a game of international power politics; and it is the king himself, in a moment of reflective derision, who puts his finger on precisely the element of Stukeley's character that makes such exploitation possible:

Are not these English like their country fish
Called gudgeons that will bite at every bait?
How easily the credulous fools believe
The thing they fancy or would wish of chance,
Using no precepts of art prospective
To see what end each project sorteth to.

(11. 2010-2015)

There is a sense in which Philip here represents all those potentates, either secular or religious, for whom Stukeley labored diligently, yet for whom he was merely an efficient political tool to be discarded when the need required.[14] Like Shakespeare's Coriolanus, and again like Hotspur, he is noble and skilled in battle, but beneath the warrior's actual and psychological armor lies an astonishingly childlike approach to the practicalities of the world beyond the battlefield. His commitment to some abstract notion of what he should be, "the thing he fancies", so dominates his personality, that more pragmatic men have only to allow it freedom of scope and Stukeley becomes their agent.

It is thus Stukeley's purity and singleness of mind, the very aspect of his personality that makes him seem to his contemporaries like a Tamburlaine come to life, that also renders him vulnerable to the more subtle, psychological onslaughts of those who could never dare to brave him in the open field. Consider, for instance, the cast of mind that lies behind his triumphant assertion that:

If I had promised Philip all the world
Or any kingdom, England sole except,
I would have perished or perform'd my word,
And not reserved one cottage to myself
Nor so much ground as would have made my grave.

(ll. 2125-2129)

We recognize in these words the same dedication to the absolute that another deluded soldier, Othello, utters tormentedly when he begins to doubt the fidelity of his wife:

> I had rather be a toad
> And live upon the vapor of a dungeon
> Than keep a corner in the thing I love
> For others' uses.

(III.iii. 270-273)[15]

Although Othello speaks of love and Stukeley of honor, they nonetheless share the same unremitting idealism that makes them such easy prey for those pragmatists who do not. The curious presence of susceptibility in strength, and baseness in nobility, so masterfully explored in Shakespeare's play, obviously had a similar attraction for the anonymous dramatist who sought to depict the "life and death of Captain Thomas Stukeley" for the theatre-going public of his time. And with his attempt to portray something of the diversity that characterized one of the most popular figures of the age, the biographical drama, with its curious mixture of popular legend and popular stage practice, makes its first full-fledged appearance in Renaissance England.

Notes

1. *The English History Play in the Age of Shakespeare* (London: Methuen, 1965), p. 194; all subsequent references to this study will be indicated parenthetically in the text.

2. See Alfred Harbage and Samuel Schoenbaum, eds., *Annals of English Drama 975-1700* (Philadelphia: Univ. of Pennsylvania Press, 1964).

3. The remaining extant plays which deal with Tudor figures are somewhat later manifestations of the type: *Henry VIII* (1612-13), *The Duchess of Suffolk* (1623), and *Perkin Warbeck* (c. 1633).

4. I draw my information on Stukeley's life primarily from John Yoklavich's introduction to his edition of *The Battle of Alcazar* in *The Dramatic Works of George Peele,* II (New Haven: Yale Univ. Press, 1961), pp. 247-273; and from Richard Simpson's biography of Stukeley in *The School of Shakespeare* (New York: J. W. Bouton, 1878), pp. 1-156; all quotations relating to Stukeley's life which are noted parenthetically in the text are from Simpson's study.

5. Yoklavich, p. 252; all parenthetical references to *The Battle of Alcazar* are from this edition.

6. Although this character is designated simply as an "Irish Bishop" in the cast of characters, it seems quite likely from his demeanor that he is that "Goldwell [Bishop of St. Asaph]" who Simpson (p. 125) tells us was at Rome with Stukeley shortly before the invasion. It is also possible, however, that he is the Irish Archbishop Cashel, who at first ardently supported Stukeley's invasion, but later became jealous of the adventurer when he received most of the credit for the daring escapade; Simpson (pp. 70-74). In either case, whether the character is bishop of "St. Asaph" or "Cashel" (or a combination of both), Stukeley's pun would hold.

7. This colorful statement has ample foundation in the vast amount of anecdotal material that comprises the Stukeley myth. Simpson, (p. 32) tells us that tradition has it that Stukeley "determined to found a colony where he could 'play rex'; having the proverb often in his discourse 'I had rather be king of a molehill than subject to a mountain'".

8. Simpson, p. 140; all subsequent references to this introduction will be indicated by page numbers in parentheses; all subsequent references to *The Life and Death of Captain Thomas Stukeley* are from this edition and will be noted parenthetically by line number.

9. *"Captaine Thomas Stukeley", Journal of English and Germanic Philology,* 15 (1916), 107-129; see also Judith C. Levinson, "The Sources of *Captain Thomas Stukeley", English Language Notes,* 9 (1971), 85-90, who reiterates the arguments of Simpson and Adams.

10. Although Simpson claims to discern "traces of four different hands" in the play (p. 142), he notes that the first three acts are pretty much intact as the original playwright wrote them. The interpolations do not occur until Acts IV and V. See also Adams, p. 111.

11. As Simpson points out (p. 164), Stukeley was never a student of the Temple.

12. See especially Stukeley's sarcastic remarks to Hernando (ll. 1839-1840); and for earlier examples, his retorts to his father (ll. 252-330), and his punning language throughout the scene with his creditors (ll. 543-624).

13. Cf. the stage direction which opens I.ii of Shakespeare's *Henry VIII:* Henry enters "*leaning on the* Cardinal's *shoulder*", and also Samuel Rowley's *When You See Me, You Know Me* (I.ii.2) where Henry VIII also enters in precisely the same manner.

14. Stukeley was at various times employed and later neglected by such prominent international figures

as Elizabeth, Philip, Pope Pius V, and Pope Gregory XIII.

15. *The Riverside Shakespeare*, ed. G. Blakemore Evans, et al. (Boston: Houghton Mifflin, 1974), p. 1223.

Charles Edelman (essay date summer 2003)

SOURCE: Edelman, Charles. "Peele's *The Battle of Alcazar*." *The Explicator* 61, no. 4 (summer 2003): 196-97.

[*In the following essay, Edelman clarifies a textual problem at the beginning of Peele's* The Battle of Alcazar.]

One of the more vexing of the many textual problems in George Peele's **The Battle of Alcazar** is found in the lines that immediately follow the Presenter's prologue, as Abdelmelec, the deposed King of Morocco now returning to reclaim his throne, enters with his captains and soldiers. In the 1594 quarto, the sequence reads

(*Sound Drummes and trumpets, and enter Abdilmelec with Calsepius Bassa and his gard, and Zareo a Moore with souldiers.*)

ABDEL:

All haile Argerd Zareo and yee Moores,
Salute the frontires of your native home.

(*sig.* A2ʳ)

Zareo, as we soon learn, is Abdelmelec's chief lieutenant, but there seems no explanation for the word "Argerd." Elsewhere in the text he is simply "Zareo," a character Peele drew from his chief source, the Portuguese Friar Luis Nieto's account of the battle of Alcazar, published in a Latin translation entitled *Historia de Bello Africano* in 1581, and then given in English as part of John Polemon's *The Second part of the booke of Battailes, fought in our age*, printed in 1587. In Polemon, the left wing of Abdelmelec's army at Alcazar comprised "two thousand argolets, and tenne thousand horsemen with speare and sheeld. These did the Vizeroie Mahamet Zareo leade" (*sig.* X2ʳ).

Two nineteenth-century editors, Alexander Dyce and A. H. Bullen, give the lines as "All hail, Argerd Zareo; and, ye Moors. / Salute the frontires of your native home," their punctuation indicating that they consider Argerd Zareo to be one name. Neither, however, offers any explanatory note as to what "Argerd" might mean.

In a 1943 article,[1] Warner G. Rice observed that according to Polemon, Abdelmelec "came to Argier with mandates of the Turkish Emperour, in whome it was

conteined, that the Captaines in those parts, should supply unto him all things needefull for the warres" (*sig. S3ᵛ*). "Argerd" could then be a compositor's misreading of "Argere" [Argier],[2] hence "All hail, Argier Zareo [i.e. Zareo of Argier] and, ye Moors." Adding weight to this argument is the fact that this scene, in which Abdelmelec joins up with his "yonger brother Muly Mahamet Seth" to oust their usurping nephew Muly Mahamet, is later described as having taken place "neere to Argier" (*sig. B1ᵛ*).

However, another difficulty then becomes apparent: Abdelmelec is not greeting Zareo—the stage direction shows that he enters *with* him, along with Calsepius Bassa (another captain) and their soldiers. The welcoming party does not enter until thirty-three lines later: "*Enter Muly Mahamet Xeque [Seth], Rubin Arches, Abdil Rayes, with others*" (*sig. A3ᵛ*). Therefore "All hail, Argier Zareo" makes no more sense than "Argerd Zareo."

A possible solution presents itself if we remember that not only people, but places, can be greeted or saluted by the expression "all hail." In Chapman, Jonson and Marston's *Eastward Ho,* Slitgut arrives at Cuckold's Haven and proclaims

All haile, faire haven of married men onely, for there are none but married men Cuckolds

(*sig.* E3ᵛ)

while in the anonymous *Fair Maid of Bristow,* printed in 1605, King Richard arrives at Bristol with the words

All haile thou blessed bosome of my peace,
Richard findes instance of his home returne,
Bristow, thou hapie rode where first I land,
Doth welcome me now from the holy land

(*sig.* D3ᵛ)

Just as Richard salutes the town of Bristol, Abdelmelec may be expressing the same sentiments towards Argier:

All hail, Argier! Zareo, and ye Moors,
Salute the frontires of your native home.

Such a reading is consistent with early modern usage, with Peele's source text, and most importantly, with the narrative structure of **The Battle of Alcazar.**

Notes

1. W. G. Rice, "A Principal Source of *The Battle of Alcazar*," *Modern Language Notes* 58 (1943): 428-31.

2. "Argier" or "Argiers" in Peele, Marlowe, Shakespeare, and Heywood. "Algiers" was not common in English until the latter part of the seventeenth century.

Works Cited

Bullen, A. H., ed. *The Works of George Peele.* London: 1888.

Chapman, George, Ben Jonson, and John Marston. *Eastward Hoe: As it was played in the Blackfriers.* London: 1605.

Dyce, Alexander, ed. *The Works of George Peele.* 2d. ed. London: 1829.

The Faire Maide of Bristow. London: 1605.

Peele, George. *The Battell Of Alcazar, Fought in Barbarie, betweene Sebastian king of Portugall, and Abdelmelec king of Morocco.* London: 1594.

Polemon, John. *The Second part of the booke of Battailes, fought in our age.* London: 1587.

THE HUNTING OF CUPID (1591)

CRITICAL COMMENTARY

John P. Cutts (essay date 1958)

SOURCE: Cutts, John P. "Peele's *Hunting of Cupid.*" *Studies in the Renaissance* 5 (1958): 121-32.

[*In the following essay, Cutts investigates questions of form and genre regarding Peele's* The Hunting of Cupid.]

There appears in the Stationers' Register for 26 July 1591 the following entry:

> Rich[ard] Iones Entred vnto him for his copye vnder thandes of the B[ishop] of London and Mr Watkins a booke intituled the Huntinge of Cupid written by George Peele M^r of Artes of Oxford. / Provyded alwayes that yf yt be hurtfull to any other Copye before lycenced, then this to be voyde.
>
> vj^{d1}

from which it has been generally[2] assumed that a *play* by Peele called *The Hunting of Cupid* was licensed. Only E. K. Chambers[3] seems to have expressed any doubt whatsoever about its being a play. Certainly W. W. Greg, who carefully collected the known fragments of *The Hunting of Cupid,* was definitely of the opinion that they represented parts of a 'play of a pastoral or mythological nature', and thought it natural for fragments, the only part of the work extant, to be printed by the Malone Society in close succession to the society's printing of Peele's *Arraignment of Paris.* Throughout Greg's description of the fragments[4] *The Hunting of Cupid* is referred to several times as a play, and the suggestion is put forward that when William Drummond of Hawthornden was making his 'strangely muddled jottings' in his commonplace book, he was evidently noting down, 'in a very bad hand, any lines or phrases that struck his fancy as he read the play'.

The latest editor[5] of Peele has merely summarized the work done by Dyce, Bullen, and Greg and adds comments about the popularity[6] of the play. So far, therefore, there has been almost unanimous agreement that the fragments are parts of a play by Peele that has been lost.

Greg points out the established fact that *Englands Parnassus* contains extracts *only* from printed sources, and thus it would seem certain that some time between the licensing date 26 July 1591 and the printing of *Englands Parnassus* in 1600 *The Hunting of Cupid* was actually printed. Horne decides that the Stationers' entry indicates an older work and on this basis and on the basis of the similarity of mythological pastoral form which *The Hunting of Cupid* bears with the *Arraignment* suggests that 'Peele would be most interested in this type during his association with the poets and child players, 1581-85'.

There seems no evidence to contradict Greg's suggestion that *The Hunting of Cupid* was actually printed, but I see no reason, from the evidence at our disposal, why we must assume that what was printed was a *play*. Drummond includes *The Hunting of Cupid* in his list of 'Bookes read anno 1609 be me'[7] along with examples of poetical works that are not plays. Some significance may be attached to the fact that throughout the lists[8] of books given by Drummond every mention of a play is qualified with the nature of the play, comedy or tragedy, without exception.[9] This is particularly conspicuous in the list for 1609. I think it is fairly clear that *The Hunting of Cupid* was not thus qualified because it was a pastoral *poem* like several others which occur in Drummond's lists simply by title, as is the case with *The Hunting of Cupid.* Peele's poem may have had a greater tendency towards dramatization, and in this respect one could easily conceive of it as an entertainment[10] in something like masque form, but this is purely hypothetical. The point that is worth making is that there seems no real justification any longer for styling *The Hunting of Cupid* as a play and linking it with the *Arraignment.*

What is significant, also, is that where extracts of *The Hunting of Cupid* occur outside Drummond's manuscripts they are in every case the most lyrical sections and constitute 'songs'. These are certainly by Peele because they are all assigned to Peele in their different sources[11] by different people. Perhaps to these ought to be added the sections lines 73-77 and 79-92[12] as well as the opening lines which have some coherence about them. The rest seems to me to be odd jottings of Drummond's,[13] single lines and half lines which may or may not represent Drummond's own work or his modification, through faulty memory, of others' works. Greg, for instance, pointed out lines 10-11

> some v^t his suethart making false position putting
> a schort sillabe vher a long one should be.

as being 'clearly the origin of Drummond's own epigram "Of Nisa"', but need we attribute a source to Drummond's epigram here; may not the epigram be Drummond's own? May not a good many of the random jottings serve as Drummond's own comments on whatever material he was dealing with or Drummond's own spontaneous ideas interspersed between recognizable Peele?

Dyce, in printing from Drummond's manuscripts, attempted to show something of the nature of the sections presumably with a view to pointing out dramatic structure. The marginal '+cupid' opposite the fourth line from the end ('Those milkie mounts . . .') is printed in capitals by Dyce, allotted a full stop after it, and made to look like the name of the character intended to speak the lines. More blatant evidence of 'dramatization' forced onto the piece is Dyce's silent insertion in the margin of the word 'Love' in capitals, followed by a full stop, opposite the line 'What thing is loue' as if 'Love' were a character, presumably Venus, speaking these lines. It may be, too, that the capital letters 'Q' and 'R', after both of which Dyce adds a full stop, are part of this dramatization deception; Greg adds a full stop only after the 'Q'. 'Q' and 'R' surely stand only for Question and Reply and not for some hypothetical characters 'Queen' and '?'.

Where Dyce does seem to score, however, over Greg's much more accurate transcript is in his indication, by means of slight indention, of the more lyrical passages that portray some continuity of thought and expression. From Dyce's printing it is easy to see the songs[14] at a glance. It is the songs, above all, that suggest the pastoral element, couched as they are in terms that recall shepherds' dialogues.

One of the songs, 'What thing is love', besides being written down by Drummond and by the anonymous writer of the MS. Rawlinson Poet. 85, was printed in the anonymous play *The Wisdom of Doctor Dodypoll*, thereby presenting a very neat problem. Before discussing this, however, it may be well to recognize yet another source of the song which seems to have escaped the attention of all but the late Edmund Fellowes, whose note at the back of his *English Madrigal Verse*[15] has obviously gone unnoticed. John Bartlet included the song as number xiv in his collection

> A | Booke | of Ayres | With a Triplicitie of | Musick, | Whereof the First | Part is for
> the Lute or Orpharion, | and the Viole de Gambo, and 4. Partes | to sing, The second
> part is for 2. Trebles to sing | to the Lute and Viole, the third part is for | the Lute and
> one Voyce, and the | Viole de Gambo. | Composde by Iohn Bartlet | Gentleman and
> practitioner in this Arte. | London | Printed by Iohn Windet, for Iohn Browne and |
> are to bee solde at his shoppe in Saint Dun | stones Churchyeard in Fleetstreet. |
>
> 1606[16]

The song 'What thing is love' belongs to the first part of the collection; the text, taken from the treble line and including all the repeats, is as follows:

> What thing is loue, what thing is loue I pray thee tel
> it is a prickle it is a prickle
> it is a sting
> it is a prety prety thing
> it is a fire it is a coale
> whose flame creeps creeps in at euery hole
> and as my wits can best deuise,
> loues darling lies in Ladies eyes.

The canto is scored on sig. H^v to be sung with a lute accompaniment; alto, tenor, and basso voice parts are separately scored on sig. H2, the alto part being printed upside down at the top of the page, the basso following next but printed on its side beginning at the middle of the inner margin and facing the middle of the outer margin, the tenor being given at the foot of the page immediately readable at the opening of the book. With the book opened at sigs. H^v and H2 it would be possible for either a singer and a lutenist to attend only to sig. H^v and perform the solo song, or for four singers to read and sing from the book at once, the canto sitting at the front left of the table, the tenor at the front right, the alto at the back right, and the basso at the side right.[17]

The music is well worth attention. Fellowes has edited[18] the solo version and has provided a piano accompaniment based on the lute tablature, but has omitted giving the tablature itself. This, I think, would certainly be the version of the song sung in *The Wisdom of Doctor Dodypoll*. The four-part voice version, however, is fuller and richer and has so far gone unedited. I have endeavored in the transcript[19] accompanying this paper to present the complete song, as envisaged by John Bartlet, for the first time.

This song has elicited far more attention than any other section of *The Hunting of Cupid* already, and to present a rich contemporary musical setting adds even further to its popularity. It seems clear that a second verse is included in Drummond's manuscript beginning 'from vhence do glaunce loues pearcing darts' and ending 'since Mars & sche plaid euē & od'. The version in MS. Rawlinson Poet. 85, f. 13, preserves four lines of this extra verse.[20] I think it is fairly clear from a study of the second stanza in relation to the music that the first stanza should be printed with the repeats as given by Barlet[21] and not without them as Fellowes prints. It is curious to note that Drummond does not make allowance for the second repeat but does have something which makes up for the first, namely 'for (vel I vot)' instead of 'vhat thing is loue' again. His non-repetition of 'it is a pricke' is probably a slip.[22] From this consideration, therefore, it would seem that the only repetition in the first stanza which we can safely attribute to the musician is of the word 'creeps' in line 5.[23]

The first stanza alone is given in Bartlet's *Ayres* and in *The Wisdom of Doctor Dodypoll*. The inclusion of this lyric in the play presents an interesting problem. Fleay[24] was led by its inclusion to suggest that *The Wisdom of Doctor Dodypoll* was written by Peele.[25] His hypothesis received no support for two main reasons summed up by E. K. Chambers.[26] The inclusion of a song by Peele was not considered weighty enough evidence to prove anything other than the obvious fact that a song by Peele was printed (and presumably sung) in the play *The Wisdom of Doctor Dodypoll* published in 1600 with no author's name on the title page. The second objection arose from the observation, first put forward by Koeppel[27] and since taken over by Dover Wilson[28] and Herford & Simpson,[29] that a line in the play is a direct echo of a line in *Julius Caesar,* 1599, and since Peele died in 1596, the play *The Wisdom of Doctor Dodypoll* cannot possibly be his.

The first objection is based on the general belief that dramatists had no compunction about using other poets' songs in their plays and that they did this frequently. It is all part of the belief that the songs were 'extra' material to a play, could be supplied from sources exterior to the play itself, and were not an intrinsic part of the drama as a whole as conceived by the dramatist. This theory can no longer be held by any serious student of the use of song, masque, and music in drama. Pioneer investigations[30] into this field of dramatic song went unnoticed for the most part, possibly because of their tendency to be too sporadic and to treat only certain aspects, and because, too, of the fact that even the most renowned scholars of Elizabethan drama adopt an altogether unscholarly attitude to the use of music. Scholars have been content to consider every other detail appertaining to drama but what concerned music and its dramatic function. Bowden[31] has made an attempt at a comprehensive study of the use of song for dramatic purposes, and within the limitations of his scope he has shown convincingly that songs were overwhelmingly *part* of the dramatic scheme, were not extraneous to the drama's action, thought, and presenta-

tion, but were woven into the play's very fabric. For some years now I have been building up a catalogue of songs[32] used in English drama from its earliest beginnings until the closing of the theaters in 1642, and the conclusion forces itself on the attention that cases in which one dramatist employs another poet's lyric with no other purpose than pure annexation are so exceptional as to be good proof of the rule. In these cases the printing of another poet's lyric is often purely and simply due to the mistake of the printer, who, willing to supply the 'blank' songs, errs in his exact location of them, and in these cases the songs are often appended, *not* printed in their correct place in the text.[33]

We ought, therefore, to have no compunction about *entertaining* the idea that Peele's lyric was used in *The Wisdom of Doctor Dodypoll* because Peele also wrote the play. Certainly we cannot dismiss Fleay's suggestion offhand.

The second objection arises from the use in the play of the line

> Then reason's fled to animals I see[34]

which is termed by Koeppel an echo of the following lines from *Julius Caesar* (III.ii.114-115):

> O Iudgement! thou art fled to brutish Beasts,
> And Men haue lost their Reason.

This echo means nothing more for me than an echo of an Elizabethan commonplace, the distinction between men and animals, most familiar to us, perhaps, in Hamlet's words:

> O God! a beast, that wants discourse of reason.
>
>   (I.ii.150)

Koeppel notices that Jonson has similar words in *Every Man out of His Humour* (III.iv.32-33):

> Then comming to the pretty *Animall,* as
> *Reason long since is fled to animals,*

and hints, but does not go further than this, that Jonson's lines stem also from Shakespeare's. Herford and Simpson merely restate Koeppel's case without judgment. Dover Wilson takes over Koeppel's point but turns it to the effect that *The Wisdom of Doctor Dodypoll* is echoing Jonson, not Shakespeare. The three quotations taken side by side in conjunction with that from *Hamlet* are interesting exempla of the familiar Elizabethan idea, but need they be anything more? Scholars have grown more and more aware of the danger of reading too much into supposed echoes, especially since valuable studies such as Tilley's *Proverbs*[35] have made us realize how commonplace so many ideas were in roughly the same words. A complete review of *The Wisdom of Doctor Dodypoll* is necessary, and only one thoroughly familiar with all Peele's acknowledged works is really in a position to do this. He alone can say whether the play is Peele's or not.

If the arguments presented in this paper be in any way acceptable, then the logical results are twofold. Involved in the first place is the discarding of a 'lost' play from the Peele canon and its reinstatement as a pastoral poem of which various interesting fragments have survived in manuscript and printed sources, one of the fragments having received a delightful contemporary musical setting which is now presented for the first time in its entirety. In the second place, a complete reinvestigation is called for of the anonymous play *The Wisdom of Doctor Dodypoll* which was first attributed to Peele on then unacceptable evidence and was subsequently denied to Peele on evidence that now seems equally unacceptable.

Notes

1. W. W. Greg, *A Bibliography of the English Printed Drama* I (1939), 7.

2. Cf. *The Workes of George Peele*, ed. Alexander Dyce (London, 1828), II, 171-177; *The Works of George Peele*, ed. A. H. Bullen (London, 1888), II, 366-369; *A Collection of Old English Plays*, ed. A. H. Bullen (London, 1882-1885), III, 96; W. W. Greg, 'The Hunting of Cupid', *Malone Society Collections* I (1907-1911), 307-314.

3. 'Probably the play—I suppose it was a play—was printed . . .' (*The Elizabethan Stage,* Oxford, 1923, III, 462).

4. The fragments listed in Drummond's manuscripts comprise within themselves all the others found elsewhere, viz. 'At Venus intreatie for Cupid her sonne', under the heading of 'Loue' on sig. N of *Englands Parnassus* (1600) ascribed to 'G. Peele'; '*Melampus,* when will Loue be void of feares?', under the heading 'Coridon *and* Melampus *Song*' on sig. E3 of *Englands Helicon* (1600) ascribed to 'Geo. Peele'; 'What thinge is loue?', on f. 13 of Bodleian MS. Rawlinson Poet. 85 (circa 1600) ascribed to 'M^r G: Peelle', and the same song sung by Cornelia on sig. A4^v of the play of *The Wisdom of Doctor Dodypoll* (1600).

5. Cf. *The Life and Minor Works of George Peele*, ed. D. H. Horne (New Haven, 1952).

6. The popularity is deduced from the number of extracts in printed and manuscript sources.

7. Cf. F. R. Fogle, *A Critical Study of William Drummond of Hawthornden* (New York, 1952), p. 181.

8. *Ibid.,* pp. 179-184, covering the years 1606-1614.

9.

1606	1608
Orlando Furioso, comedie	*Comedies de la Riue*
Romeo and Julieta, tragedie	*Cinthia,* comedia, in Italien
Loues Labors Lost, comedie	1609
The Malcontent, comedie	*Deux Tragedies* de Jodelle
A Midsommers Nights Dreame, comedie	*No Body,* comedy
Doctor Dodipol, comedie	*Sir Gyles Gooscape,* comedie
Alphonsus historie, comed.	*A Mad World,* comedie
The Tragedie of Locrine	*The Ile of Gooles,* comedie
1607	*Liberalitie and Prodigalitie,* comedie
Tragedies Senic. Blacridii	*Parasitaster,* by Marston, comedie
	1611
	Menstries Workes, 4 Tragedies. Aurora

10. Entertainments and masques are not so styled in Drummond's lists; they are merely quoted by title: 1606 Dekkar's part of the Kings Entrance in London; 1609 Thetis Festiual, by Daniel.

11. Had Drummond not included *The Hunting of Cupid* in his list of books read in 1609 we might even have had to question whether the work was printed at all. Drummond could easily have taken the ascribed extracts from *Englands Helicon* and *Englands Parnassus*. Both collections, as well as *Doctor Dodypoll*, are mentioned in Drummond's lists.

12. All references to the text of *The Hunting of Cupid* are made to Greg's edition for the Malone Society.

13. It is relevant to point out the tendency for commonplace books to have interspersed comments and random jottings between recognizable quotations.

14. '*Melampus,* when will Loue be void of feares?' is designated 'Coridon *and* Melampus *Song*' in *Englands Helicon* (1600), and 'What thing is loue?' is sung by Cornelia in *The Wisdom of Doctor Dodypoll*, sig. A4^v:

    Enter Cornelia *sola, looking vpon the picture of* Alberdure *in a little Iewell, and singing.*

    Enter the Doctor and the Merchant following, and hearkning to her.

    The Song.

15. Oxford, 1920, p. 607. Fellowes refers only to Bullen's edition, apparently unaware of the more desirable, accurate Malone Society edition.

16. Only two copies of the book are listed by the *S.T.C.,* one in the British Museum and the other in the Huntington Library, San Marino, Calif. Through the kind offices of the Huntington Library, I have been provided with a complete microfilm and granted permission to reproduce any item.

17.

18. John Bartlet, *A Booke of Ayres 1606,* ed. E. H. Fellowes (The English School of Lutenist Song Writers, 2 ser., London, 1925), pp. 24-25.

19. I have scrupulously followed the original text of the song, adhering faithfully to the excellent precedent set by Fellowes. In a few respects, however, I have differed, not allowing myself the liberty of suggesting tempos or expressions, and I give the lute tablature valuation exactly as it is, not filling it out to even the bar measure.

20.   From whence he shootes his dayntye dartes
     In to the lusty gallunts hartes.
       And euer since was callde a god
       That Mars withe Venus playde euen and odd,
       Finis.

                     M^r G: Peelle

21. The second verse fits the musical setting admirably provided no word phrase is repeated as are 'What thing is loue' and 'it is a prickle' in the first. The concluding couplet makes a splendid finish to the whole song.

22. The version in MS. Rawlinson Poet. 85 is without repeats and just so does it omit lines.

23. This represents an effective use of the musician's license.

24. F. G. Fleay, *A Biographical Chronicle of the English Drama* (London, 1891), II, 155.

25. Dyce's and Bullen's editions of *The Hunting of Cupid* were available.

26. *Op. cit.,* IV, 54.

27. E. Koeppel, 'Shakespeare's *Julius Caesar* und die Entstehungszeit des anonymen Dramas *The Wisdome of Doctor Dodypoll*', *Shakespeare Jahrbuch* XLIII (1907), 210.

28. 'Ben Jonson and *Julius Caesar*', *Shakespeare Survey* II (1949), 36-43.

29. *Ben Jonson,* ed. C. H. Herford & P. Simpson (Oxford, 1925-1952), IX, 450.

30. Cf. E. B. Reed, *Songs from the British Drama* (New Haven, 1925); J. R. Moore, 'The Songs of the Public Theaters in the Time of Shakespeare', *J.E.G.P.* XXVIII (1929), 166-202; J. T. McCullen,

'The Functions of Songs Aroused by Madness in Elizabethan Drama', *A Tribute to George Coffin Taylor* (Chapel Hill, N.C., 1952), pp. 184-196.

31. W. R. Bowden, *The English Dramatic Lyric 1603-1642* (New Haven, 1951). The shortcomings of Bowden's work are pointed out by the present writer in 'Some Jacobean and Caroline Dramatic Lyrics', *Notes & Queries* n.s. II (1955), 106-109.

32. The music of the songs is also being assembled from music manuscripts scattered far afield, consulted personally where possible or by microfilm. In this latter respect I have been heavily indebted to the kindness of Professor Allardyce Nicoll, head of the Shakespeare Institute, Stratford-upon-Avon.

33. The case always cited is Blount's printing of twenty-one songs in his edition of Lyly's plays in 1632, songs which had been missing from the quarto editions of these plays. Scholars have argued about the authenticity of these lyrics (cf. Bowden, *op. cit.,* p. 105). Until it can be definitely proved that the lyrics are authentic or not, we can at least be grateful that Blount made an attempt to trace the originals and that the ones he printed do *seem* to fit the context. Webster disclaimed 'Armes, and Honors, decke thy story' (*The Duchesse of Malfy* III.iv) as being his, which was quite unnecessary unless the dramatist usually included only his own songs. The tendency to use another's lyric is late Caroline. Two of Suckling's lyrics from *The Goblins* (1637-1640) were utilized by Samuel Sheppard in *The Committee-man Curried* (1644), viz. 'A health to the nut-brown lass' (sig. B2) and 'Some drink! . . .' (sig. B^v).

34. Sig. E (ed. J. S. Farmer, *Tudor Facsimile Texts,* 1912).

35. M. P. Tilley, *A Dictionary of the Proverbs in England in the Sixteenth and Seventeenth Centuries* (Ann Arbor, 1950).

THE OLD WIVES TALE (C. 1593)

CRITICAL COMMENTARY

Robert H. Wilson (essay date June 1940)

SOURCE: Wilson, Robert H. "Reed and Warton on the *Old Wives Tale*." *PMLA* 55, no. 2 (June 1940): 605-08.

[In the following essay, Wilson briefly discusses the work of two early bibliographers of Peele's The Old Wives Tale.*]*

In the Introduction to his edition of the **Old Wives Tale,** Greg states:

> None of the early bibliographers of the drama had seen the play. In 1750 Chetwood invented the entry, 'An olde Wyfe her Tale, 1598,' which is sufficient evidence that neither had he. In 1782 the *Biographica* [sic] *Dramatica,* quoting his entry, added that of the Stationers' Register. Not till the edition of 1812 was any account of the play from actual inspection included. Meanwhile a fairly correct description had been given, and the identification of the initials as those of George Peele made, by Herbert in his *Typographical Antiquities* of 1785-90.[1]

As a matter of fact, two accounts of the play, ascribing it to Peele, antedate Herbert. In his edition of the Minor Poems of Milton in 1785 Thomas Warton provides, as is well known,[2] a summary of the similarities between the **Old Wives Tale** and *Comus.*[3] "I reserve a more distinct and particular view of Peele's play," he goes on, "with the use of which I have been politely favoured by Mr. Henderson of Covent-garden theatre, for an Appendix to the Notes on Comus."[4] In this Appendix are a more extended summary of the **Old Wives Tale,** a number of quotations from it, and a biographical sketch of Peele.[5]

A still earlier treatment is pointed out by Larsen:

> The first to ascribe this play to Peele in print was Reed: *Biogr. Dram.,* ii. (1782), p. 441. . . . The attribution occurs in the Appendix; the play is not added to the canon (i. p. 351, *s.v.* 'George Peele'), and in the body of the work (ii. p. 262) it is listed as anonymous. The statement of Dr. Greg . . . 'that [sic] the identification of the initials . . .' was first made by Herbert: *Typographical Antiquities,* ii. (1786), p. 1272, is evidently a slip. . . . The play was formally added to the canon by Egerton: *Theatrical Remembrancer* (1788), p. 8.[6]

The compression of Larsen's account probably does not make it sufficiently clear that Reed's appendix is one of "Additions and Corrections" after the body of the text had been set up[7]—hence the absence of references to Peele's authorship in the original accounts, written before Reed obtained his later information. It is this original description of the **Old Wives Tale** to which Greg refers correctly as quoting Chetwood.[8] His "slip" of failing to note in the appendix Reed's correction (which is reprinted in the body of the 1812 edition[9]) is easy enough to understand. Perhaps more difficult to follow is Larsen's failure to count Warton's references to the **Old Wives Tale** in his biographical sketch of Peele as a formal addition of the play to the canon, particularly when he so counts Warton's mention of *Polyhymnia* on the same page.[10]

Larsen has also indicated briefly that Reed's account represents material which he had obtained from George Steevens.[11] The source of Larsen's information, however, is worth quoting. It is a letter from Steevens to Warton, dated April 16, 1783, apparently replying to an inquiry:

> All I have learned relative to the original from which the idea of Milton's Comus might be borrowed, I communicated to Mr. Reed, and you will find it in the 2d vol. of his Biog. Dramatica, p. 441. Only a single copy of his *Old Wives Tale* has hitherto appeared, and even that is at present out of my reach. Your quotation, however, may give Reed's book a lift. My name is not worth mentioning.[12]

Now if one turns to the two accounts of the **Old Wives Tale** by Reed and Warton, he discovers that Warton, although he had read the play, and shows detailed knowledge of it in his "Appendix to the Notes on Comus," in his earlier summary not only makes the acknowledgment to Reed which Steevens had suggested, but lifts Reed's whole account nearly verbatim. The two passages are reprinted below, with the differences (except one in word order, and most of those in spelling, capitalization, and punctuation) in italics.[13]

Reed	*Warton*
P. 262. Nº 31. The Old Wife's Tale.] Dele *this article, and substitute the following.*	The ingenious and accurate Mr. Reed has *pointed out a rude outline, from which Milton seems partly to have sketched the plan of the fable of Comus. See Biograph. Dramat. ii. p. 441. It is an old play, with this title,*
The Old Wives tale, a pleasant conceited Comedie, plaied by the Queenes Majesties players. Written by G. P. [i.e. George Peele.] Printed at London by John Danter, and are to be sold by Ralph Hancocke and John Hardie, 1595.	"The Old Wives Tale, a pleasant conceited Comedie, plaied by the Queenes Ma*i*esties players. Written by G. P. [i.e. George Peele.] Printed at London by John Danter, and are to be sold by Ralph Hancocke and John Hardie, 1595." *In quarto.*
Perhaps the reader will join with me in supposing that Milton had read this very scarce *dramatic* piece, *which,* among other incidents, exhibits two Brothers wandering in quest of their Sister, whom an enchanter had *confined.* This *enchanter* had learned his art from his mother Merõe, as Comus had been instructed by his *parent* Circe. The Brothers call out on the Lady's name, and Echo replies *to them.* The Enchanter *has* given her a potion, which induces oblivion of herself. The Brothers afterwards meet with an Old Man, who is *likewise versed* in magic, and by listening to his *vaticinations, &c.* they recover their Sister; but not till the Enchanter's wreath had been torn from his head, his sword wrested from his hand, a glass broken, and a light extinguished.	This very scarce *and curious* piece exhibits among other *parallel* incidents, two Brothers wandering in quest of their Sister, whom an Enchanter had *imprisoned.* This *magician* had learned his art from his mother Meroe, as Comus had been instructed by his *mother* Circe. The Brothers call out on the Lady's name, and Echo replies. The Enchanter *had* given her a potion which *suspends the powers of reason, and super*induces oblivion of herself. The Brothers afterwards meet with an Old Man who is *also skilled* in magic; and by listening to his *soothsayings,* they recover their *lost* Sister. But not till the Enchanter's wreath had been torn from his head, his sword wrested from his hand, a glass broken, and a light extinguished.
Principiis quoties debemus grandia parvis! The names of some of the characters, as Sac*r*ipant, Corebus, *&c.* are *adopted* from the Orlando Furioso.	The names of some of the characters as Sacrapant, Chorebus, *and others,* are *taken* from the Orlando Furioso. *The history of Meroe a witch, may be seen in . . .*

That Warton's text is thoroughly unoriginal is obvious. Yet there are a relatively large number of alterations, falling into four classes: (a) the acknowledgment to Reed and resultant modification of the "Perhaps the reader will join with me" sentence; (b) a fairly consistent simplification of Reed's style, by the substitution of "mother" for "parent," "skilled" for "versed," "soothsayings" for "vaticinations," and so on, and the omission of the Latin verse; (c) a number of random alterations in wording, spelling, capitalization, and punctuation; and (d) a few changes which may derive from Warton's independent knowledge of the play. Of the statement that the volume is in quarto this is certainly true. The spelling Sacr*a*pant is that of the play, whereas Reed uses the "correct" *i* spelling from Ariosto;[14] hence it seems a little more likely than not that Warton's memory supplied him with the spelling he used, even while it was playing him false in introducing an unjustified *h* in Corebus.[15] But the spelling Ma*i*esties, although it is that of the title page (whereas Reed's is not), is probably the result of mere accident; for if Warton had gone to the trouble of collating the title page he would surely have corrected some of Reed's numerous other errors of transcription, all of which he reproduces.[16] The added statement that the potion "suspends the powers of reason" contributes so little definite information that it might well be classed with the merely verbal changes above; on the other hand, Warton may have been drawing on his memory of the play, perhaps even the lines:

> This vild inchanter
> Hath rauisht *Delya* of hir sences cleane,
> And she forgets that she is *Delya*.[17]

Both the introduction of these changes, and the way in which the derived material blends indistinguishably at beginning and end with remarks of Warton's own, make it impossible to think of the passage as merely a quotation without quotation marks. It must be described as plagiarism, however much the precise reference to Reed may testify to a lack of any feeling of wrongdoing, and however much one may doubt that an average eighteenth-century reader would have been disturbed had he followed up the page reference and discovered the identity.

Notes

1. W. W. Greg, ed., *The Old Wives Tale, 1595*, Malone Society (Oxford Univ. Press, 1908), pp. v-vi.

2. See A. H. Bullen, *The Works of George Peele* (London, 1888), I, 299; C. M. Gayley, *Representative English Comedies*, I (New York, 1930), 383; A. W. Verity, *Comus* (Cambridge, 1927), pp. xxix-xxx.

3. *Poems upon Several Occasions . . . by John Milton* (London, 1785), p. 126.

4. *Ibid.*, p. 127.

5. *Ibid.*, pp. 591-593.

6. T. Larsen, "The Growth of the Peele Canon," *The Library*, XI (1930), 305-306.

7. Isaac Reed, ed., David Erskine Baker, *Biographia Dramatica* (London, 1782), II, 436 ff.

8. *Ibid.*, p. 262.

9. *Biographia Dramatica*, ed. Stephen Jones (London, 1812), III, 97. The only change in wording is the substitution of "us" for "me" in the first sentence of the summary.

10. Warton, *op. cit.*, p. 593. Larsen, *op. cit.*, p. 306.

11. *Op. cit.*, p. 306.

12. Printed in John Wooll, *Biographical Memoirs of . . . Joseph Warton* (London, 1806), p. 398.

13. To avoid confusion, italics and small capitals in the originals have been suppressed. But the brackets are those of Reed and Warton.

14. Greg, *op. cit.*, p. vii and *passim*.

15. *Ibid.*, p. ix and *passim*.

16. *Ibid.*, facsimile title page opposite p. [x]. Correctly, "Wives" should be spelled with a *u*, "plaied" with a *y*, "John" (both appearances) with an *I*, "Ralph" without the *l;* "G. P." and the names of printer and booksellers should be italicized; there should be periods after "Tale" and "Hardie," and a comma after "Hancocke."

17. *Ibid.*, ll. 729-731.

Laurilyn J. Rockey (essay date October 1970)

SOURCE: Rockey, Laurilyn J. "*The Old Wives Tale* as Dramatic Satire." *Educational Theatre Journal* 22, no. 3 (October 1970): 268-75.

[*In the following essay, Rockey argues that Peele's* The Old Wives Tale *is one of the earliest satires in English drama.*]

George Peele's **The Old Wives Tale,** "A pleasant conceited Comedie"[1] printed in 1595, has been interpreted in a number of different ways. At various times during its critical history, the play has been condemned as an incoherent jumble of theatrical nonsense filled with "a disgusting quantity of trash and absurdity,"[2] patronized as a naive sentimental comedy in the *Mucedorus* tradition,[3] and praised as a charming fantasy play in which a unique atmosphere of dreamy enchantment is created.[4] Certain other critics—notably F. B. Gummere, Tucker Brooke, Felix Schelling, and G. P. Baker—have perceived the play as a burlesque, a travesty of the heroic-romantic genre which flourished during the early Elizabethan period.[5] Unfortunately, however, these critics have offered very little internal or external evidence to support their opinion, and as a result "the view that *The Old Wives' Tale* was satiric or burlesque is now fairly generally discarded."[6] I for one believe that this interpretation deserves further consideration. Therefore, at the risk of being considered hopelessly anachronistic, I propose to argue in support of the theory that the play was written as a dramatic satire, and that its structure is carefully designed to point up the absurdities of dramatic techniques which Peele regarded with amusement and contempt.

The outstanding characteristic of *The Old Wives Tale,* and the feature to which the play's detractors object most, is its confusing multiplicity of plots. The technique which Peele employs is the play within a play—the same technique used in Beaumont's early seventeenth-century comedy *The Knight of the Burning Pestle* (the play most often identified as the first mock-heroic burlesque written for the English stage[7]), and in later satires on the popular romantic drama such as Buckingham's *The Rehearsal* and Sheridan's *The Critic.* The basic plot structure of *The Old Wives Tale* involves a romantic fantasy set within a comparatively realistic framework. The induction (all in prose except for the songs) begins with the plight of Anticke, Frolicke, and Fantasticke, three pages[8] who have lost their way in the woods. They are rescued by Clunch, the local smith, who takes them to his cottage. There the three wanderers persuade Madge, Clunch's wife, to entertain them with "a merry winters tale" (l. 83).[9] After Madge has thoroughly bewildered her audience with several false starts, the characters of her tale enter to tell their own story. This play within the play, much of which is in outstandingly mediocre verse, is a bizarre fantasy involving an incongruous medley of stereotyped themes, actions, and characters from folklore and romance. The scenes in Madge's story are extremely brief, and often seem to possess no logical relation to one another. So abrupt are the transitions from scene to scene and plot to plot that several critics have assumed that the manuscript has somehow been mutilated.[10] Harold Jenkins complains that "repeatedly figures are brought before the spectator only to be speedily sent off the stage again before he has familiarized himself with them, making way for others who are dealt with in equally summary fashion."[11] Indeed, so many plot threads and characters are tangled up in underdeveloped scenes that it is no wonder that even Madge, the storyteller, is confused. The overall effect is one of "crowding and . . . haste."[12]

The first question which must be answered is whether certain distinctive features of the play such as the sense of confusion and abruptness, the muddled multiplicity of plot threads, the stereotyped characterizations, and the bad verse are the result of accident or intention. The view that the features in question are the result of manuscript mutilation has been convincingly refuted by Frank S. Hook in the introduction to his new edition of the play.[13] We must then look at Peele's other four plays, none of which is a comedy. For if the characteristics which are so noticeable in *The Old Wives Tale* are typical of Peele's playwriting style, they cannot be used as criteria in determining if this particular play is a satire. A brief examination soon reveals that there are significant differences between *The Old Wives Tale* and Peele's other dramatic works. For while it is true that the plots of his plays are loosely organized, and that his characters are seldom developed with as much skill as Shakespeare's, none of Peele's other four plays is remarkable for the abrupt jumble of incidents and the obviously stereotyped characterizations so conspicuous in *The Old Wives Tale.* In *The Araygnement of Paris* (1584), *The Battle of Alcazar* (1594), *Edward I* (1593), and *David and Bethsabe* (1599), the plots are coherent, the scenes usually long and well-developed, and the subplots all connected in some logical way with the main story line. Moreover, these plays clearly demonstrate that Peele had an ability for characterization and versification that goes far beyond anything found in *The Old Wives Tale.* Plot coherence, character consistency and originality, and versification are not merely careless or offhanded in *The Old Wives Tale,* they are made blatantly bad; and nothing in Peele's other work suggests that he could be so inept technically by accident, so unconscious of the most elementary principles of logic or art. But, most significantly, there is system in the ineptitude, a consistency of bad craftsmanship that a truly bad craftsman could not attain. This consistency can only be understood, I believe, in terms of a satirical intent.

When one attempts to determine what Peele was trying to satirize, it soon becomes apparent that *The Old Wives Tale* bears a distinct, if pointedly exaggerated, resemblance to early Elizabethan romances such as *Clyomon and Clamydes* and *Common Conditions.* These plays abound in plots and subplots which are not logically connected with one another. They are packed with improbable heroic adventures, multiple shipwrecks, numerous magical transformations, and, above all, the trials and tribulations of several pairs of lovers. The characterizations are serious treatments of the most basic stereotypes: knights are noble, maidens fair, and wizards wicked. The verse is stilted and clumsy, consistent with the inflated and elaborated conceits.

It is this type of play which Peele is burlesquing in *The Old Wives Tale.* The title itself states the play's satiric intent, for since at least 1388 the expression "old wives' tale" has meant "a foolish story such as is told by garrulous old women"[14]—a fact oddly overlooked by those critics who would make the play a serious attempt at the romantic genre. The play burlesques the most prominent characteristics of the romances. As usual, "hugie heapes of care"[15] are placed in the way of the lovers, but these obstacles, a mock-heroic mixture of wizards, amnesia, dragons, and shortness of funds, are thrown in so peremptorily and at such speed that the effect becomes comic instead of heroic. The almost-simultaneous presentation of all the plot strands adds to the comic confusion. No sooner have Delya's brothers arrived than Erestus tells them his woes, Venelia runs mad through the woods, Lampriscus comes to seek husbands for his daughters, Huanebango sets off to find the conjurer, and Jack's cronies try to get his body buried. Thus Peele achieves the effect of a comic summary of the "typical" romance by carrying the characteristic multiplicity of plots to an absurd extreme while at the same time shortening the scenes and leaving out the transitions. He simply puts in the basic ingredients—a maiden in distress, a conjurer, and a wandering knight—mixes in a number of sub-plots which have little if anything to do with the main action, and by his abrupt treatment of all these elements manages to parody the form he is ostensibly following. Peele was fully capable of writing a well-rounded scene when he chose. The "huddled"[16] effect of these scenes is intentional. In fact, the play is brilliantly constructed for its purpose on a single principle—a fact usually missed—that each one of the riddling prophecies which initiate the actions will fall out patly and in a hilariously literal way.

Just as in the early romantic plays, the characters in Madge's story never pass beyond the level of stereotypes. But in Peele's play, the crowded plot structure and the fast pace of the action both clarify and exaggerate the one-dimensional nature of such stereotypes. The scenes in the early romances often tend to be long and rambling, filled with lengthy speeches explaining the motivations and actions of the major characters. Peele's brief scenes barely give each character time to display his one distinctive trait before he is whisked off stage again, thus making the traditional stereotypes caricatures of themselves. Delya is an oversimplified prototype of all the beautiful, vacuous heroines of the romances: the Julianas, Clarisias, and Angelicas who exist only to be adored. Huanebango, like the noble warriors in *Clyomon and Clamydes,* expresses a proper knightly love of battles and "martiall play,"[17] but he carries this addiction to ridiculous extremes. For Peele allows him no chance to exhibit any other traditional knightly traits, and thus the chivalrous adventurer becomes the miles gloriosus, whose sole topic of conversation is his own warlike exploits. Likewise, Eumenides, the lovelorn wandering knight (a stock figure in the romances), is given little opportunity to do anything *but* wander, and gradually turns from a heroic into a comic figure. He spends most of the play straying vaguely about the periphery of the action, and is totally and comically ineffectual in moments of real crisis. For example, at the final confrontation with Sacrapant, Eumenides wanders around the stage with wool in his ears while his supernatural assistant, Jack, actually destroys the wizard. His major "heroic" decision—to cut his lady in half rather than break his word—pushes the chivalric code to its logical but absurd extreme and makes him even more ridiculous.

Peele also burlesques the clumsy techniques of verse and diction used in the romances. The romantic plays were usually written in heavily alliterated rhymed couplets or quatrains. Among the outstanding features of the verse were the deadly monotony of its metre and the labyrinthine complexity of its syntax. The language was patently artificial—the lines were long and unwieldy, and were crammed with overblown sentiments and every figure of speech the dramatist could command, as in this example from *Common Conditions:*

> Though deep despair doth drive, in doubt, due honour
>   to disgrace;
> Though dreadful dumps doth daunt the mind, being in
>   uncouth place;
> Though heart is harded to hazard forth, in lady's cause,
>   to try
> Against her cruel crabbed foe, and venture life to die:
> Yet, must he be advisedly, and in such kind of sort,
> That as well through wit as strength, it may deserve
>   report.[18]

Peele ridicules the bombastic rhetoric of such verses in Sacrapant's death speech:

> What hand invades the head of Sacrapant?
> What hatefull fury doth envy my happy state?
> Then Sacrapant these are thy latest dayes,
> Alas my vaines are numd, my sinews shrinke,
> My bloud is pearst, my breath fleeting away.
> And now my timelesse date is come to end:
> He in whose life his actions hath beene so foule,
> Now in his death to hell desends his soule.
>
> (ll. 809-816)

The long lines with their tortured syntax are parodied in Huanebango's hexameters:

> Wakte with a wench, pretty peat, pretty love, and my
>   sweet prettie pigsnie;
> Just by thy side shall sit surnamed great Huanebango,
> Safe in my armes will I keepe thee, threat Mars or
>   thunder Olympus.
>
> (ll. 648-650)

Peele was a noted lyricist whose subtly complex versification was highly acclaimed by his contemporaries and is still praised by critics today. Yet here he consciously reverts to an older, cruder poetic style for the play within the play. If he had wanted to make a serious attempt at writing a romance or a folk fantasy, he might have borrowed the traditional plot structure and characters, but he would hardly have endangered his reputation as a lyricist by deliberately writing bad poetry—unless he was making fun of the older techniques. Peele even borrows almost verbatim one of the more florid passages from Robert Greene's *Orlando Fvrioso,* a long-winded romance which seems to have been written just before *The Old Wives Tale.*[19] In *Orlando,* one of Greene's gallant knights tells the heroine:

> Come from the South, I furrowed Neptunes Seas,
> Northeast as far as is the frosen Rhene;
> Leauing faire Voya, crost vp Danuby,
> As hie as Saba, whose inhaunsing streames
> Cuts twixt the Tartares and the Russians.[20]

In Peele's play, Eumenides the wandering knight informs Delya:

> For thy sweet sake I have crost the frosen Rhine,
> Leaving faire Po, I saild up Danuby,
> As farre as Saba whose inhansing streames,
> Cuts twixt the Tartars and the Russians.

> (ll. 853-856)

Peele would hardly have plagiarized such a trivial set of lines from his fellow dramatist if he were seriously trying to rival Greene's romance. It seems much more likely that Peele was calling specific attention to the exaggerated, exotic descriptions so common in the romantic plays he was satirizing. Peele also makes fun of the over-use of verbal gingerbread—particularly alliteration—by giving Huanebango several nonsense speeches that are little *but* alliteration: "Phylyda phylerydos, Pamphylyda floryda flortos" (l. 646). Verbal repetition was another prominent characteristic of romantic diction. Any piece of information basic to the plot is stated again and again (Bryan Sans Foy in *Clyomon and Clamydes* announces at least four times that Clamydes will sleep ten days). Peele uses this device for comic effect by having various characters such as Delya's brothers, Eumenides, and Corebus constantly repeat Erestus's jangling riddle-rhymes over and over, word for word. In addition, Peele ridicules the heavy-handed classical allusions that fill the romances. Even in romantic plays supposedly set in Christian countries, everyone swears by Venus, Mars, or Jupiter, and Latin passages are quoted for no apparent reason. Peele goes the romantic playwrights one better by having Huanebango swear by every Olympian he can think of—"by Mars and Mercury, Jupiter and Janus, Sol and Saturnus, Venus and Vesta, Pallas and Proserpina" (ll. 257-258)—and decline Latin words at climactic moments—"Meus, mea, meum" (l. 281). Finally, Peele burlesques the arbitrary introduction of songs into the dramatic action at incongruous moments, as when Neronis sings as she is about to commit suicide in *Clyomon and Clamydes.* In *The Old Wives Tale,* the singing Harvesters have no connection with the plot at all, and they enter when least expected to interrupt the action with mowing songs after a somewhat offhanded introduction by

Madge: "O these are the harvest men; ten to one they sing a song of mowing" (ll. 248-249).

Peele also incorporates some literary parody into his play which is not directly related to the romances, but which underscores the satiric nature of *The Old Wives Tale.* For example, some of Huanebango's hexameters are a direct burlesque of the poetry of Gabriel Harvey. Harvey, a classicist and writer of Latin verse, had started a one-man campaign to introduce classical metres, particularly the hexameter, into English verse. His own poetry was pompous and long-winded, and his efforts were ridiculed by the playwrights Nashe and Greene in an acrimonious literary dispute. Apparently Peele took the side of his fellow dramatists, for the line "O that I might but I may not, woe to my destenie therefore" (l. 654) is taken directly from Harvey's "Encomium Lauri" (1580)[21] and put into the ludicrous context of Huanebango's bombastic love speech to Zantippa. Peele also parodies the work of Richard Stanyhurst, who, in an attempt to support Harvey's theories, translated the first four books of Vergil's *Aeneid* and other selected Latin poems and epigrams into English hexameters in 1582. In order to carry out the versification plan, Stanyhurst forced his translations to the point of absurdity, and came up with overstuffed lines such as "Thee whilst in the skye seat great bouncing rumbelo thundring/ Ratleth,"[22] "Lowd dub a dub tabering with frapping rip rap of Aetna,"[23] and "Linckt was in wedlock a loftye Thrasonical huf snuffe."[24] Peele simply makes whole hexameter lines out of the nonsense words which Stanyhurst used to pad his lines: "Dub dub a dub, bounce quoth the guns, with a sulpherous huffe snuffe" (l. 647). It makes little difference whether or not all the members of the audience can identify the specific authors being parodied. As Hook points out, "Peele is more concerned with ridiculous poetry than with particular authors."[25] By associating the poetry of the romantic dramas with the preposterously pompous verses of the Harvey and Stanyhurst type, Peele is making yet another derisive comment on the quality of the romantic poetry.

But it is the interplay of realistic and romantic elements that best reveals the essentially satiric purpose of the play, for the folk framework constantly undercuts the heroic tale even as it comments upon it. F. B. Gummere states that the dramatic irony of *The Old Wives Tale* springs from the "contrast of romantic plot and realistic diction."[26] Actually, the basic contrast involves far more. The world of Clunch and Madge is a very naturalistic one, where characters are primarily concerned with food and sleep, and speak earthy prose liberally sprinkled with obscenities. Madge garbles her story in a remarkably realistic manner, initially forgetting half of the essential details and inserting them later out of sequence: "O Lord I quite forgot, there was a Conjurer, and this Conjurer could doo anything" (ll. 119-120). On the other hand, the chief figures in her story are vague stereotypes who often speak in stilted, unnatural verse. Unconcerned with everyday realities, they exist on a plane of pure fantasy where magical spells are the rule rather than the exception, and where even homely maidens can find a husband at the nearest enchanted well. The constant juxtaposition of these two worlds, a juxtaposition which cannot help but accentuate the absurdity of the actions, characters, and language of the play within the play, seems far from accidental. Peele almost never uses low-life characters and realistic, rustic humor in his other plays. And such characters were certainly not part of the typical romance format—especially in the role of audience and chorus. As Gummere points out, the romantic plays had no humor at all "except the traditional humour of the Vice."[27] Indeed, the writers of the romantic dramas took great care not to use any realistic characters or diction at all in order to avoid the jarring contrast which Peele so deliberately sets up and maintains throughout *The Old Wives Tale.*

The interruptions of Madge, Frolicke, and Fantasticke constantly serve to remind the audience of this contrast. For even though Madge finally agrees to let the characters tell their own story, she and her audience persist in interpolating comments at climactic moments. They break into the action to introduce characters (sometimes twice), to discuss the behavior of the protagonists, or to clear up (somewhat belatedly) confusing points in the story:

FROLICKE:

> Why this goes rounde without a fiddling stick; but doo you heare Gammer, was this the man that was a Beare in the night, and a man in the day?

OLD WOMAN:

> I, this is hee; and this man that came to him was a beggar, and dwelt uppon a greene.

> (ll. 243-247)

It is difficult to see how the critics who believe that Peele was trying to create a fairy-tale mood of dreamy enchantment account for the fact that he purposely allows his induction characters to keep breaking in on the dream world this way, thereby shattering any "fairy-like atmosphere"[28] that has been built up. Hook is convinced that

> if the play were a satire, the author surely would have made his attitude clear in the commentary by the characters of the induction. Indeed, if Peele were writing satire, one would suppose that a primary function of the courtly pages would be to make the attack explicit in something like the manner of the courtly observers of the play of Pyramus and Thisbe in *Midsummer Night's Dream.* But far from making fun of the story unfolded before them, the pages are entranced, and their uncomplicated and sympathetic acceptance of the tale is an invitation to the audience to take the same point of view.[29]

However, while Frolicke and Fantasticke do indeed provide the audience with the proper perspective for viewing the play, their interpolations actually produce an effect totally opposite to the one which Hook describes. Madge's listeners are a pair of sophisticated city-dwellers who are wittily and ironically aware of the foolishness of the story, and they help to underscore it by asking (with gentle malice) pointed, logical questions just where the romantic play would require suspension of disbelief:

OLD WOMAN:

> . . . and hee [the King] sent all his men to seeke out his daughter, and hee sent so long, that he sent all his men out of his Land.

FROLICKE:

> Who drest his dinner then?

OLD WOMAN:

> Nay either heare my tale, or kisse my taile.

> (ll. 113-117)

They are amused by the absurdity of the tale, but their attitude is definitely not one of child-like acceptance. They function as fairly urbane images of the theatre audience, pointing out by means of their words and their very presence the unrealities and inconsistencies of the heroic action. Thus their criticism need not be explicit to get across the point that *The Old Wives Tale* is a satire. Just in case anyone is still in doubt by the end of the play, however, Peele makes one last devastating comment on the tale when Madge, as thoroughly confused as her audience, falls asleep during her own story.

In conclusion, I believe that George Peele's *The Old Wives Tale* is a satire, the earliest in English dramatic literature. The more-or-less measureable forms of evidence which I have cited indicate that the play is cleverly constructed to burlesque both individual poets and the romantic genre as a whole. However, the best reason for accepting this interpretation is demonstrable only to those who will read the play; that is, this interpretation not only accounts for all the features of the play, but also makes the play far more aesthetically satisfying.

Notes

1. From the title page of the first printed edition, reprinted by Frank S. Hook in his edition of George Peele's *The Old Wives Tale,* in *The Dramatic Works of George Peele,* Vol. III of *The Life and Works of George Peele,* ed. Charles T. Prouty (New Haven, 1970), p. 385.

2. J. Payne Collier, *The History of English Dramatic Poetry to the Time of Shakespeare: and Annals of the Stage to the Restoration,* III (London, 1831), 197.

3. Henry W. Wells, *Elizabethan and Jacobean Playwrights* (New York, 1939), pp. 214-215.

4. This is the most recent intrepretation. See M. C. Bradbrook, "Peele's *Old Wives' Tale:* A Play of Enchantment," *English Studies,* XLIII (1962), 323-330; A. K. McIlwraith, ed., in his "Introduction," *Five Elizabethan Comedies* (London, 1965), pp. xii-xiii; David H. Horne, *The Life and Minor Works of George Peele,* Vol. I of *The Life and Works of George Peele,* pp. 89-91; Frank S. Hook in his "Introduction" to *The Old Wives Tale.*

5. F. B. Gummere, "George Peele: Critical Essay," in *Representative English Comedies,* ed. Charles Gayley, I (New York, 1916), 341-347; Tucker Brooke, *The Tudor Drama* (Hamden, Conn., 1964), pp. 241-242; Felix Schelling, *Elizabethan Drama, 1558-1642,* I (Boston, 1908), 201-202; G. P. Baker, "The Plays of the University Wits," in *The Cambridge History of English Literature,* ed. A. W. Ward and A. R. Waller. V, Part I (Cambridge England, 1964), 128-132.

6. Bradbrook, 324.

7. Hazelton Spencer, *Elizabethan Plays* (Boston, 1933), p. 758.

8. The three are never explicitly identified as pages in the text, and there was no cast list in the Quarto. But the assumption is a logical one, and they are so labelled by W. W. Greg and Frank S. Hook in their respective editions of the play.

9. This and all subsequent quotations from *The Old Wives Tale* are from Frank S. Hook's edition of the play, and will be cited by line numbers in parentheses in the text of the article.

10. W. W. Greg, "Introduction" to his edition of George Peele's *The Old Wives Tale* (London, 1908), p. vii; Harold Jenkins, "Peele's 'Old Wive's Tale'," *The Modern Language Review,* XXXIV (April 1939), 177-185.

11. Jenkins., 178.

12. *Ibid.*

13. Hook, pp. 341-356.

14. *The Oxford English Dictionary,* VII (Oxford, 1961), 100.

15. Prologue to *Clyomon and Clamydes,* ed. W. W. Greg (London, 1913), 1. 9.

16. Jenkins, 178.

17. *Clyomon and Clamydes,* 1. 167.

18. *Common Conditions,* in *Five Anonymous Plays,* ed. John S. Farmer (London, 1908), pp. 236-237.

19. Greg, "Introduction," *The Old Wives Tale,* pp. vi-vii.

20. Robert Greene, *Orlando Fvrioso,* in *The Plays & Poems of Robert Greene,* ed. J. Churton Collins, I (Oxford, 1905), 225.

21. Greg, "Introduction," *The Old Wives Tale,* p. vi.

22. Vergil *Aeneid* 4, trans. Richard Stanyhurst, in *Translation of the first Four Books of the Aeneis of P. Virgilius Maro with other poetical Devices thereto annexed,* ed. Edward Arber (Westminster, 1895), p. 100.

23. "Thee description of Liparen" (from Vergil's *Aeneid* 8), trans. Richard Stanyhurst in *Translation of the first Four Books of the Aeneis,* p. 137.

24. "Of a Craking Cvtter" (from Sir Thomas More's *Epigrammata*), trans. Richard Stanyhurst, in *Translation of the first Four Books of the Aeneis,* p. 143.

25. Hook, p. 315.

26. Gummere, 342.

27. *Ibid.*

28. McIlwraith, p. xiii.

29. Hook, p. 359.

Thomas N. Grove (essay date 1979)

SOURCE: Grove, Thomas N. "Some Observations on the 'Marvellous' *Old Wives' Tale.*" *Studia Anglica Posnaniensia* 11 (1979): 201-02.

[*In the following essay, Grove gives a brief assessment of Peele's use of religious motifs in* The Old Wives Tale.]

The "marvellous" in English drama begins immediately and strikingly with the first known "play", the *Quemquaeritis* trope, as the human perception of the Marys is comically juxtaposed to spiritual perception of the angels. Christ becomes the first miracle-worker as he brings a humanly unintelligible event to pass: he comes alive after being dead—the supreme miracle. Only in a romantic frame can the same thing happen again as Jack seems to be resurrected in Sacrapant's world of ***The old wives' tale.***

And certainly Jack should recall Christ because both are the real centers of comedy in their particular worlds. Jack, through Eumenides' charity, can come back to life and offer himself *as a servant* to Eumenides, the wandering knight (compare everyman lost and wandering in the world). Sacrapant, a perverter of time and upsetter of the seasons, is quite similar to the Devil. Jack must finally kill this devil by simply taking away his source of power and enchantment—his sword and wreath. Without them, Sacrapant cannot maintain the illusion of youthful April and must die. He then hands the enchanter's sword to Eumenides as the ultimate source of the enchanted world is found (the Devil's creation is more powerful than the Devil himself) by turning the enchanter's own power against itself. The light which Eumenides seeks ironically contrasts with the true Light of the World and is closely associated with Lucifer. Jack, however, is not through. He has redeemed mankind—"all are restored to their former liberty"—but must make one final test of Eumenides in Old Testament form to determine the center of the knight's devotion and to demonstrate visually what is more important, the worldly love of Delia or devotion to the spiritual bond of Jack. As does Abraham with Isaac, Eumenides makes the right choice, and is therefore allowed to keep his worldly possession—having comprehended its proper place. Eumenides makes the order of importance clear to Delia: "Thanks, gentle madam, but here comes Jack; thank him, for he is the best friend we have". Both Fantastic and Frolic think that "this Jack bore a great sway" and Madge herself recognizes Jack as "a marvellous fellow! he was but a poor man, but very well beloved". So Christ: one faithful comes to bury His body.

Diccon and Idleness, as Sacrapant, are perversions of the truly marvellous—the Christian mystery. Idleness cannot even exert her superhuman powers until Wyt is tired of dancing with Honest Recreation and consciously decides: "among the dameselles now wyll I rest me". And her powers are, like Sacrapant's, finally superficial—Wyt may clean his face and take off Ignorance's cap and gown once he looks in the glass of Reason and decides he doesn't like Idleness' art. However, Lady Idleness does have the power to transform Wyt to a "starke foole". And Wyt is internally affected by Idleness. When he encounters Experience and Science with his besotted face, he immediately and uncouthly demands a kiss of Science; not getting it, he becomes even more surly, finally threatening blows and calling Experience a whore. So Sacrapant may give Delia the potion of forgetfulness so that she cannot recognize her brothers.

Diccon's enchantment in *Gammar Gurton's needle* is less elaborate and extensive than Sacrapant's as it hinges upon Hodge's fear of the Devil. Diccon tells Hodge the Devil said something between "cat" and "rat" and finally blurted out "chat". Hodge believes Diccon so much that he immediately thinks Chat has the needle when Gammar suggests so. Tyb says the cat Gyb has been acting sick and Hodge immediately suspects the "truth" as he grabs the cat to rake it. And when Gammar decides to send for Doctor *Rat* to bring Chat to justice, Hodge seconds the motion. Diccon also causes two physical beatings: Chat vs. Gammar and Chat vs. Rat. However, Diccon is not entirely an immoral force in *Gammar Gurton's needle*. He does reveal the ridiculousness of Gammar's devotion to her needle—certainly a worldly devotion (although we are not urged to condemn her for it). Also Diccon focuses upon our belief in rumor without proof—suspicious nature. Gammar and Chat must be brought before a third power to purge their differences: quite like Clem-

ent in *Everyman In*. Finally, Doctor Rat may deserve his desert—he complains about being a priest and having to be on call; he is only interested in the profits, a stray goose or a drink.

The marvellous may then be finally a moral function: Sacrapant, like Diccon, demonstrates how we may be deceived by immediate appearance in the world. Idleness' art is finally instructive—Wyt will learn by Experience.

Susan T. Viguers (essay date spring 1981)

SOURCE: Viguers, Susan T. "The Hearth and the Cell: Art in *The Old Wives Tale*." *Studies in English Literature, 1500-1900* 21, no. 2 (spring 1981): 209-21.

[*In the following essay, Viguers asserts that an understanding of the play's original staging is central to understanding Peele's* The Old Wives Tale.]

It is a commonplace that a play should be seen to be understood fully; directing an informal production of George Peele's **The Old Wives Tale**[1] (1595) convinced me that in that play, perhaps more than in most, the spatial dimension as it would have been defined by the original stage provides an essential key to the play's often misunderstood inner logic. Through my staging, the play's structure appears remarkably simple, in spite of the complex plot, and easy to diagram spatially. (This simplicity is by no means an accepted attribute of the play.[2]) Such staging not only helps make **The Old Wives Tale** accessible to a modern audience, but it reveals the play to be a rich and typically Renaissance exploration of the conflict between two fundamental kinds of art, represented by the two central figures in the play, Madge and Sacrapant. The stage diagram below, which includes three entrances[3] and five permanent locations or structures, represents the framework on which the discussion that follows will be built.

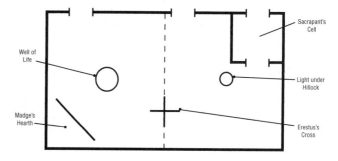

Although there is controversy about what the staging of the play would have been, there is agreement that the storyteller Madge and the sorcerer Sacrapant were each associated with a permanent location on stage. Sacrapant has a cell, which must be represented physically. Not only does his first entrance connect him to that mansion, but one stage direction indicates it is *his* cell even if he is not among the characters entering through it (after 629). The fire before which Madge sits and tells her tale at one point is tended, which suggests that there should be some structure representing the hearth. Whether there is a hearth is less important than that Madge, with her audience, Frolicke and Fantasticke, constitutes a permanent location for all but the opening of the play.

Where Madge tells her story (the hearth) and Sacrapant's cell are the features of the stage that take up the most space. They should be as far apart as possible. Necessities of blocking, as well as my interpretation of the play, dictate they be on opposite sides of the stage, dividing it vertically, and at opposite corners, creating a diagonal tension. The hearth and the cell set up the spatial tension for the stage.

Madge and Sacrapant each dominate the space and entrances nearest them. Thus one permanent structure, the Well of Life (in its fertility, associated with Madge's art), is near her, and another, the light under the hillock (an image of Sacrapant's art), is near Sacrapant. The three entrances, as I see them, are not symmetrically placed.[4] One is on Madge's side, one is Sacrapant's cell, and a third is near the center upstage, but in Sacrapant's domain. Those characters in Madge's tale on a journey to destroy Sacrapant and to rescue the princess Delya enter through the opening nearest Madge and exit on Sacrapant's side. All those under Sacrapant's control enter and exit through his cell or the other opening associated with his art. Characters on their way to the Well of Life enter on Madge's side[5] and, after their experience there, exit the same way. This blocking not only simplifies the immensely numerous entrances and exits, but helps focus our attention on Madge and Sacrapant as the two primary powers.

The final locus, positioned in the middle of the stage, is Erestus's Cross. Erestus, the young man made old by Sacrapant, nonetheless affirms Madge's definition of reality. He marks the crossroads between Madge's hearth and Sacrapant's cell, the confrontation at the center of the play.

The Old Wives Tale consists of a frame play and an inner play. Madge, in the frame, tells a story (the inner play) that includes Sacrapant. Spatially, however, Madge and Sacrapant are parallel; and that parallelism, necessary if Madge and Sacrapant are to function dramatically as opposing forces, is supported by the imagery of the text.

Both major characters are in a wood (Sacrapant's wood is a wood within a wood). As the frame play opens three Pages—Frolicke, Fantasticke, and Anticke, who will later be entertained by Madge and her husband Clunch—are lost in a forest; and in the inner play, two characters under Sacrapant's enchantment, Erestus and

his betrothed Venelia, are explicitly connected to the woods. The woods in both outer and inner tales, as is common in Renaissance literature, figures a realm of illusion and magic, both wonderful and fearful.

It is in a dwelling within her wood that the Pages meet the imaginative world of Madge's story. To the Pages at the beginning of the play, however, that wood is terrifying; it seems far from the rationality of daylight and the comfort of the everyday. In this world of "owlets, and Hobgoblins" (41), Anticke describes himself and his friends as making "faces for feare" (36). "Hush," cries his comrade Fantasticke on hearing the bark of a dog: "a dogge in the wood, or a wooden dogge" (23), "Wood" also means "mad," and the double meaning echoes through the play. Magic and the imaginative capacity are akin, in one way, to madness itself.

In Sacrapant's wood, full of marvels and strange magical beings, dwell prophecy, in the form of the Old Man, and madness, in the form of Venelia, each unfettered by "normal" rationality. His wood is even more obviously fraught with danger than Madge's. The young maiden Delya is imprisoned; her two brothers, who are searching for her, are enslaved; Huanebango and Booby, also engaged in that search, are struck deaf or blind; Erestus is transformed by day into the Old Man at the crossroads and by night into a bear; and Venelia is bewitched.

Not only Sacrapant, but the other master of a magical realm, Madge, as her name suggests, is a mage, a magician. Madge does not simply "tell" her story. Like a conjuror she seems more to summon than to create; her tale has a reality not wholly dependent on her. When, in Pirandellian fashion, the characters in her story take over their own tale, they are as much a surprise to the old woman as to her audience, Frolicke and Fantasticke (128). "Why this goes rounde without a fiddling sticke" (243), Frolicke exclaims later in the play; in other words, the tale moves by its own energy. Madge's story continues when she falls asleep, and, similarly, Sacrapant's death does not bring about the destruction of his art. That art has a reality of its own which must itself be confronted and destroyed; only when the light in the glass under the hillock is extinguished is his magic dispelled.

The autonomy of their illusions suggests that neither Madge nor Sacrapant is in complete control of what each creates. Madge's very introduction to her tale is disorganized and tentative. "Once upon a time," she begins, "there was a King or a Lord, or a Duke" (110-11). Later she amends the order of the tale and even confuses the sex of Sacrapant (125). Her erroneous introduction of the Harvesters, when they come on the stage the first time, is again striking evidence of her failure to be absolute mistress of her tale. "O these are the harvest men," she says with confidence; "ten to one they sing a song of mowing" (248-49). But the Harvesters sing of sowing, not mowing.

The limitation of Sacrapant's control is particularly evident when Sacrapant conjures for Delya "A Frier with a chine of Beefe and a pot of wine" (after 373). The scene proceeds as Sacrapant desires until the Friar, in response to Delya's question as to who is the "greediest Englishman" (390), implicates the magician himself, who angrily and abruptly dismisses him.[6] Sacrapant's own illusion defies him. Though Sacrapant is capable of changing Delya so that she does not know herself (572), he mournfully admits he cannot make her responsive in the ultimate way he would like (357-58). In the scene leading up to the conjuring of the Friar, the formality of Delya's speech, echoed visually by her failure to sit and relax when Sacrapant first requests that she do so (353-66), helps us understand Sacrapant's dissatisfaction.

As creators of illusion, both Sacrapant and Madge demand or even depend on audience perception and response. Sacrapant "was a miserable, old, and crooked man," explains the spirit Jack at the end of the play, "though to each mans eye he seemed young and fresh" (868-69). Like Susanne Langer's "virtual object," Sacrapant's art "exists only for perception."[7] Thus, when Sacrapant's art is destroyed, those entrapped in his magic suddenly see themselves and those about them as they truly are.

Sacrapant's art is, in fact, so completely dependent on his audience that a lack of response can destroy him. Like Odysseus, who blocks the ears of his sailors so that they will not hear the Sirens' song, Jack puts wool into the ears of Eumenides, Delya's rescuer, and positions him so that he will neither hear nor see Sacrapant. Eumenides sits there unmoving,[8] unaware of Sacrapant when he addresses him. When Sacrapant sees he is having no effect on Eumenides, he realizes his defeat (805-808).

Madge's art similarly requires her audience. Most obviously, she tells her story to entertain her guests. Thus she insists that the Pages stay awake and respond to the story (106-108), and their comments periodically interrupt her tale. Furthermore, unless they accept her conventions, she refuses to continue her story (116-17). But the relationship of audience to tale extends even further. The worlds of the audience and of the characters in Madge's tale mirror each other. Not only are both worlds defined as a wood inhabited by a mage or creator of illusion, but, as I shall discuss later, the movement of the tales within each wood is similar. Madge's work of art (the inner play) reflects her audience (the outer play). That audience, in more than one sense, is the *raison d'être* of her tale.

In defining Madge and Sacrapant as parallel characters, Peele delineates a typical Renaissance concept of the artist. Though as creators of illusion, Madge and Sacrapant are figures of power, they are not absolute masters of their creations; their art has a reality apart from them and a dependence on their audience. For Peele, as for others in the Renaissance, however, art has a potential for good *or* evil, and it is that difference between the art of Madge and of Sacrapant that creates the conflict in the play.

Nothing suggests both the parallel and the antithesis between Madge and Sacrapant more visually than the objects that symbolize their art. What the Pages lost in the woods first see of Madge's home is Clunch's lantern. The aura about Clunch is that of comforting familiarity, with which the Pages immediately identify, for Clunch's lantern embodies the reassurance of human order. The "Lanthorne and Candle," which the stage directions (after 27) tell us Clunch is carrying, were in fact words associated with the cry of the London night bellman.[9] Clunch's lantern soon expands to become the welcoming hearth of his home. "Well Masters it seemes to mee you have lost your waie in the wood," he says; "in consideration whereof, if you will goe with Clunch to his Cottage, you shall have house roome, and a good fire to sit by" (45-48). It is around that fire they gather for Madge's story. The fire associated with Clunch and Madge gives both light and warmth to the audience.

The image that represents Sacrapant's art, the flame in the glass under the turf, is an exact analogy to Clunch's lantern, yet diametrically opposed to it. Sacrapant's flame inverts the Christian parable of the candle which must not be covered up, but placed on a candlestick for all to see. That parable, as J. W. Lever remarks in his notes to *Measure for Measure,* was "a secular commonplace" in the Renaissance.[10] Sacrapant's hidden light is a perversion of the light that fights falsehood and despair, that is a spark of the heavenly flame. Sacrapant not only denies his audience guidance or protection, he endangers them.

How the two artists relate to space and how the structures with which they are associated are defined further delineate their differences. For Madge space is richly metamorphic: it is not static, but "becoming." The stage directions tell us that the entrance of Clunch and the three young men into the cottage is indicated by Madge's coming on stage. Instead of Clunch and his guests entering a limited place, the stage becomes the cottage. Later the stage as cottage becomes the world of her tale; the hearth before which she tells her tale opens out and embraces all. Critics have either assumed Madge has a mansion or that she does not necessarily *have* to have one.[11] I feel, however, that Madge *cannot* have a mansion: such a form would not reflect her art.

On the other hand, it is appropriate that Sacrapant have a mansion. In its position at the back of the stage, his cell both dominates and, at least for most of the audience, is distant—consistent with our feeling of Sacrapant's power and isolation. (Madge's hearth, in contrast, is downstage, close to the audience.) As a pavilion, the cell is a limited space, set apart from the rest of the stage. When the brothers are about to encounter Sacrapant, they speak of "enter[ing]" (414), as do Huanebango and Booby when they come to the same point (554), and that idea of entering accents the separateness of the structure confronting them. None of them successfully goes into that cell. At least for much of the play, it is actually sealed off with a curtain. In the end, after the sorcerer's death, it is that curtain behind which Eumenides discovers Delya as she "sitteth asleepe" (after 843): her location behind the curtain, as well as her sleep, figures her bondage. Significantly, there is no other such limited space, no other pavilion on stage.[12]

Typically in the Renaissance, as in such plays as *Doctor Faustus, The Jew of Malta,* and *Friar Bacon and Friar Bungay,* the kind of art that emerges from a cell, from a confined space, is profoundly sinister. Sacrapant's art presents illusion as though it were reality. That, contrary to appearance, Erestus is young and Sacrapant old is not something we see until Sacrapant's art is destroyed. Near the end of the play, Eumenides cannot believe the head Jack holds is Sacrapant's; and we, the play's audience, also need reassurance that the strange new head is the same as the very different one the magician previously possessed. For a similar reason, Erestus, when he enters at the end of the play as a young man,[13] must be welcomed by name (873). Through most of the play, illusion is visually more real to us than truth. That kind of confusion informs Sacrapant's world. The word "deceive," used again and again in connection with Sacrapant's art, acknowledges that illusion is presented and experienced as reality. Sacrapant, indeed, sets up his fiction as an alternate reality not only for others, but for himself as well. Through his art he creates a magical world, and at the center of it all he places himself, metamorphosed so that he can enjoy what he has created.

Madge presents and relates to illusion in a very different way. The fantastic and parodic quality of her tale so clearly points up its fictional character that the story is distanced from both us and the audience in the frame play. Madge's story is a fabulous one, a tale of strange creatures and enchantments. Its plot, characterizations, and language, moreover, parody the popular chivalric romances of the era.[14] The idiomatic, homely quality of Madge's remark as her story characters appear on stage, "gods me bones, who comes here?" (128), puts in high relief the rhetorical bombast with which the two brothers begin the dramatization of her tale. The farcelike quality of Madge's tale climaxes in the scene at the end of the play in which Eumenides reveals his willingness to cut his beloved Delya in half in order to keep his promise that his friend Jack would receive "halfe in al . . . [he] got" (884). Such monstrous foolishness outdoes even Valentine's willingness in *Two Gentlemen of Verona* to give his beloved Silvia to his friend Proteus.

The event in *The Old Wives Tale* is clearly a parody of such friendship stories. As a parody, Madge's tale calls attention to itself as an imitation of an imitation. It insists on its own unreality, on being a product of the imagination, and its humorous absurdity contrasts with the deadly earnestness of Sacrapant's art.

Nearly every time one of the characters in the frame play comments on the arrival of the characters within the tale, another immediately interjects, "Let them alone." The refusal of Frolicke, Fantasticke, and Madge to interfere in the play before them dramatizes their acceptance of the tale *as* a tale. For Peele, as for other Renaissance writers, a healthy artistic experience depends on understanding not only that a work of art is connected to the "real" world, but also that art, in consisting of shadows, of images, is different from that world. Indeed, it is only because art *is* different that it can point up the "real." Madge requires that her audience appreciate that fact; Sacrapant demands that his audience deny it.

For the Renaissance, the work of man must not be confused with the work of God (i.e., reality); but that is not to deny that above man's art stands Nature, the hand of God. Art is artificial because it is created by man; yet healthy art is also profoundly natural, for the artistic creation and audience experience are in keeping with the laws of Nature. Thus Pico della Mirandola in his *Oration on the Dignity of Man* describes the magus as one who "does not so much work wonders as diligently serve a wonder-working nature."[15] In *The Old Wives Tale* the confrontation between Sacrapant's art and Madge's art is that between art that seeks to subvert the natural movement of life and art that seeks to realize the ultimate end of that movement.

Sacrapant can be associated with the usurer (as the Friar conjured by the magician implies), because, like the usurer who breeds money out of money, Sacrapant's creations are fundamentally out of tune with organic processes. In the same tradition, Dante speaks of the usurer as one who "scorns Nature."[16] In turning himself into a young man and reversing the age of Erestus, Sacrapant is defying that instrument of nature, time. His is an art of transformations that bind and impair, of unnatural stasis and paralysis. Time, moreover, is inextricably connected to truth, as the Renaissance commonplace, Truth is the Daughter of Time, suggests. Sacrapant's artifice is empty of any significance that would tie it to the realm of reality beyond it; in manipulating appearances, undermining identities, he is denying truth. That, however, is Sacrapant's undoing. Evil spells "weare out with time, that treadeth all things down but truth," warns the magician Dipsas in John Lyly's *Endimion.*[17] As Eumenides comes on stage, he cries to Time to tell him the future; and quite clearly Time is represented by Erestus when, soon after, he prophesies the hero's success and Sacrapant's destruction.

Sacrapant's art is undone by time; Madge's art is realized by time. Moreover, in three episodes—the prologue and the two Harvester scenes—Madge defines time as a profoundly natural movement. These scenes are unusually important in setting up and ordering her tale. Before Madge is persuaded to begin her story, Frolicke and Clunch sing a song of late summer, harvest, and fertility, which serves as the prologue. The sexual overtones of the song's images of ripe cherries and strawberries are reinforced by the general import of the last lines: the "true love" in the song cannot live as a maiden because she is with child. Her child is symbolically the tale itself. The concept of time as organic and creative, introduced by the prologue, is developed and made structurally significant by the two Harvester episodes. Those two scenes, obvious lacunae in Madge's story, order the sequence of events in that tale;[18] the pattern of episodes and characters after the first of the two scenes is similar to that after the second. The first time the Harvesters come on stage they sing of sowing the fruits of love, and the second time, now joined by women who symbolize what has been fulfilled, they sing of reaping that fruit. The Harvester scenes, like the prologue, dramatize time as a process of fruition.

That definition of time is a key to Madge's art. Her art comprises both her tale and her effect on her audience, and the movement in both her tale and the world of her audience is natural and creative. Though both worlds begin in want and despair, they move to rewards and restoration.

The idea of a journey becomes for the audience an image of that movement. Most of the major characters within Madge's tale are on a quest, visually represented by their recurring movement across the stage. Lampriscus and the two daughters whom he despairs of marrying off are among the few not on a journey, but at the Well of Life his daughters' fates connect with those of Huanebango and Booby, who *are* among the travelers. The Well of Life, the importance of which is made obvious by its emblematic presence on the stage, and the journey become conflated. Life is figured as a journey. It is, moreover, a journey to appropriate rewards. The two Harvester episodes, we must remember, act out the adage that what one sows one reaps.

In the first part of Madge's tale the brothers, Lampriscus, Huanebango and Booby, and Eumenides, all meet the Old Man at the Cross as he is gathering "Hips and Hawes, and stickes and strawes" (143). The Old Man at the crossroads in the center of the stage is the touchstone and guide at the center of the play. All of the characters respond to him with kindness except for Huanebango: "Huanebango giveth no Cakes for Almes" (314), he says loftily. Eumenides is the last to meet Erestus; after that the Old Man disappears until the story's happy finale, and the spirit Jack (for whom Erestus, in

veiled terms, prepares Eumenides) takes over the Old Man's role. It is Eumenides' generosity to Jack—his giving all his money so that young man whom he has never known can be buried—that is the climactic act of kindness in Madge's story. That scene comes at the end of the "sowing" section fo the tale.

The Harvesters' reaping scene introduces what follows. The kind of people the characters in the tale have revealed themselves to be generates their rewards. At the beginning of the tale, Lampriscus receives directions on ridding himself of his two daughters, but it is not until after the Harvesters' second scene that the daughters do as their father bids. At the Well of Life the cursed daughter and the proud Huanebango find each other, and the union of the kind daughter and goodhearted Booby is blessed with gifts of corn and gold. But the culminating reward in the tale is Delya; and the play emphasizes that Eumenides has earned, not simply been given, that beautiful heroine (877-78, 905-909).

The paradox in the prologue and in the first Harvester episode is the same. The "true love" in the song looks ahead to the birth of her child and to becoming a maid again, and the Harvesters sing of planting. The fruits of autumn and the promise of spring co-exist. The movement of the story is not only to reward, but also from sorrow to restoration.

Most of the major characters in Madge's tale either begin in despair or are soon plunged into it. Erestus, Lampriscus, Eumenides, and Delya's two brothers all bewail their cruel fates. As the tale begins, we see love cut asunder (the separation of the betrothed Venelia and Erestus), love incomplete or frustrated (the searchers' unsuccessful efforts to find Delya, and also, perhaps, Delya's heart), and, most important, love perverted (Sacrapant's lust for Venelia and Delya). With the end of the tale, love transcends and is successful, and all but Sacrapant are made happy. When Erestus, the Old Man at the Cross, becomes a young man, age is even restored to youth. Delya herself, however, undergoes what is perhaps the most suggestive change. The "Castle . . . made of stone" (122), where Sacrapant keeps Delya, is an image of both a tomb and the hardness of the heart. When the hero Eumenides finally opens the curtains of the cell and awakes the maiden, he seems like the prince in "Sleeping Beauty" to have released her from a form of death.

That restoration in Madge's story is echoed by the frame play. The words of the Pages at the beginning of the play conjure despair and figurative death. "How nowe fellowe Frolicke, what all amort?" (1) asks Anticke; and Frolicke answers, "never in all my life was I so dead slain" (8). He proposes they sing to the tune of "O man in desperation" (16). "Desperately spoken fellow Frollicke in the darke" (17), responds Anticke. The very identities of Frolicke and Fantasticke seem threatened. Frolicke, whose name means "sportive mirth," is asked by Anticke. "Doth this sadness become thy madnes?" (1-2); and Fantasticke, whose name means one "having a lively imagination,"[19] shows unimaginative fatalism when he remarks to Frolicke that he should have anticipated their being lost, "seeing Cupid hath led our yong master to the faire Lady and she is the only Saint that he has sworne to serve" (11-13). The predicament in which the young men find themselves is somehow contingent on the loss of their master to love. As in the inner play, something about love has gone wrong. Cupid represents a power, as Frolicke puts it, "that hath cousned us all" (42).

Clunch and Madge, however, are themselves characters in the mythology of love. The smith Clunch is called "good Volcan" (41), making Madge a comic Venus. The kindness Clunch and Madge show the young men, moreover, is an example of a very different kind of love from the Pages' image of their master's love affair, which they find isolating and threatening. In Madge's tale itself the wandering knight does not divide his world in the process of rescuing the saint he has sworn to serve. He reunites it, destroying the evil that has held it in bondage.

The Pages' restoration begins when they are met by the kindly Clunch and brought to his cottage. Anticke goes off to bed with Clunch. They are to be renewed by sleep rather than by Madge's story; but those characters who witness the tale are similarly involved in a process connected with sleep. As has frequently been noted,[20] there is a dream-like quality to Madge's story. Fantasticke himself suggests the affinity of the story to sleep when he remarks, "a tale of an howre long were as good as an howres sleepe" (85-86). A few moments later he declares, "No better hay in Devonshire, a my word Gammer, Ile be one of your audience" (97-98): the tale is better than any bed.[21] Significantly, the ending of the tale coincides with the crow of the cock and dawn.

Madge's tale, moreover, is restorative in the way sleep is. The play ends with the two young men following Madge off the stage to have something to eat and drink before they depart, an event which contrasts to their turning away food when they arrive at the cottage. The weariness and negativity of the night before have vanished.

The artificial and elaborate divisions of the stage are dissolved in the resolution of Madge's tale. In the scene of Sacrapant's destruction, Jack positions Eumenides downstage and within Madge's part of the playing space. Not only does that blocking give room for the interaction between Sacrapant and Jack behind Eumenides, sitting deaf and blind to Sacrapant's art, but it

puts Eumenides symbolically within Madge's power. When Sacrapant goes to Madge's part of the stage to address Eumenides, he is destroyed. Soon after, when the light that represents his art is blown out, his cell is breached in a way not possible before. Earlier, when the brothers and Huanebango and Booby start to enter the cell, they are struck down; yet the words Eumenides and Delya exchange when they first see each other underscore the fact that Eumenides has entered the cell successfully and is standing by her (844-47). The space previously closed to all but Sacrapant and his slaves is integrated into the rest of the stage. Sacrapant, who pretends his art is not a fiction and creates an art profoundly unnatural, acknowledges the superiority of Madge, who presents her art as artifice and imbues it with the process and laws of nature. Her audience's experience affirms the same recreative and restorative movement that informs her story. In that victory of hearth over cell, Peele dramatizes a reaffirmation of art.

Notes

1. The edition of *The Old Wives Tale* used in this paper is Frank S. Hook's in *The Life and Works of George Peele*, gen. ed. Charles Tyler Prouty, 3 vols. (New Haven: Yale Univ. Press, 1970), vol. 3. Citations are given by line numbers.

2. See, for example, the Yale editor, Hook, who maintains that "there is not much point in trying to pretend that the play is really very clearly plotted" (p. 369), and Arthur M. Sampley, "Plot Structure in Peele's Play as a Test of Authorship," *PMLA* 51 (September 1936):697. Other critics, though none comes near making the demonstration I intend, are closer to my position. See John Doebler's review of the literature, "The Tone of George Peele's *The Old Wives' Tale*," *ES* 53 (October 1972):418, n. 18. Even John D. Cox, whose "Homely Matter and Multiple Plots in Peele's *Old Wives Tale*," *TSLL* 20 (Fall 1978):330-46, is very suggestive, does not come to grips with the dramatic (rather than literary) plot nor with the staging.

3. Textual evidence suggests the need for two entrances besides Sacrapant's cell: see especially after line 431. Moreover, throughout the play, blocking would be extremely awkward without a third entrance.

4. Little is known about stages at the time of *The Old Wives Tale*. It is possible to suggest a curtain at the back of the stage—either covering the tiring house, or, if the stage were a temporary, moveable playing booth, concealing the actors' dressing area—which allows flexibility: entrances through slits could occur anywhere along the curtain. The absence of a permanent inner stage (which would provide a center door) is reasonable since the play

would have been performed by the Queen's Men in first-generation London theaters and/or, more likely, in halls and innyards.

5. There is one appropriate exception: when the unconscious Huanebango is carted in by the Furies and laid by the Well of Life, they obviously enter through one of the entrances on Sacrapant's side.

6. Critics such as H. Jenkins, "Peele's 'Old Wive's Tale,'" *MLR* 34 (April 1939):178, and Hook, pp. 341-42, are disturbed by the Friar's abrupt dismissal, which does, however, work dramatically if we see Sacrapant as disconcerted by how Delya's question is answered: "The most miserable and most covetous Usurer" (391). Sacrapant has just recently called himself "miserable" (339); his coveting Venelia and Delya is the source of the evil in the play; and like a usurer his creations are unnatural.

7. Susanne Langer, *Feeling and Form: A Theory of Art* (New York: Charles Scribner's Sons, 1953), p. 47.

8. Laurilyn J. Rockey's statement, in "*The Old Wives Tale* as Dramatic Satire," *Educational Theatre Journal* 22 (October 1970):268-75, that "Eumenides wanders around the stage with wool in his ears" (p. 271) contradicts the text (line 804).

9. See *O.E.D.,* s.v. "lantern."

10. J. W. Lever, ed. *Measure for Measure,* Arden edn. (New York: Vintage Books, 1965), p. 6.

11. The following give Madge a pavilion: Robert Lee Blair, "An Edition of George Peele's *Old Wives' Tale*" (An Abstract of a Thesis, Univ. of Illinois, 1936), p. 14; M. C. Bradbrook, "Peele's *Old Wives' Tale:* A Play of Enchantment," *ES* 43 (October 1962):323; E. K. Chambers, *The Elizabethan Stage,* 4 vols. (Oxford: The Clarendon Press, 1923), 3: 48. Hook, pp. 375-76, feels that in some productions Madge's mansion could have been eliminated.

12. Both Blair, p. 14, and Chambers, p. 48, imply a mansion for the inn where Eumenides eats. Hook, while considering that structure superfluous (p. 375), nonsensically suggests (p. 374) that Erestus's Cross could be a mansion.

13. The text never mentions that Erestus is changed; but a careful reading makes it obvious.

14. See Doebler, Rockey, and F. G. Gummere, "Critical Essay on *The Old Wives Tale,*" in *Representative English Comedies,* ed. Charles Mills Gayley, 4 vols. (New York: Macmillan, 1903-1936), 1:335-48.

15. Giovanni Pico della Mirandola, *Oration,* trans. Elizabeth Livermore Forbes, in *The Renaissance Philosophy of Man,* ed. Ernst Cassirer et al. (Chicago: Univ. of Chicago Press, 1948), p. 248.

16. *The Divine Comedy,* trans. H. R. Huse (New York: Holt, Rinehart and Winston, 1954), *Inferno,* XI. 110.

17. *The Complete Works,* ed. R. Warwick Bond, 3 vols. (Oxford: The Clarendon Press, 1902). 3: I.iv.47.

18. Hook considers Erestus's exit after line 240 just before the Harvesters enter the first time as evidence of Peele's failure to think "through all the details" (p. 273) of the play, since Erestus is needed on the stage in the scene after the Harvesters. To the contrary, Erestus's exit, it seems to me, is necessary for it calls attention to the structural importance of the Harvester episode. Critics have not fully understood that importance. Hook maintains that "the only function [of the Harvesters and their women] is to add to the entertainment" (p. 372).

19. See *O.E.D.*

20. See, e.g., Bradbrook, p. 328; David H. Horne, *The Life and Works of George Peele,* gen. ed. Charles Tyler Prouty, 3 vols. (New Haven: Yale Univ. Press, 1952), 1:90; and Jenkins, p. 178.

21. Hook's note on this line (p. 424) misses the point: "Sounds proverbial, but I have not found it elsewhere. If Peele's family were from Devon (See Horne, p. 10), he might have preserved some local saying. McIlwaith notes: '"hay" may be either a country dance or an abbreviation of "have you," but I do not understand this in either case.'"

Roger deV. Renwick (essay date October-December 1981)

SOURCE: Renwick, Roger deV. "The Mummers' Play and *The Old Wives Tale.*" *Journal of American Folklore* 94, no. 374 (October-December 1981): 433-55.

[*In the following essay, Renwick analyses* The Old Wives Tale *from a folklorist's point of view.*]

The mummers' play, that seasonal part-celebration, part-drama, part-ritual, part-display of aggression, part-seeking for a handout, part many other things, was once a common traditional activity over most parts of the British Isles whose cultural heritage is chiefly Anglo-Saxon rather than Celtic. Like other substantive and relatively complex kinds of folklore, the mummers' play not only has been the subject of an impressive, though relatively small, body of scholarship but also has been analyzed from a variety of perspectives: typological, cultural evolutionary, functional, comparative, and semiotic, among others.[1]

Common to most of these studies is the identifying of motifs, characters, plot, and language that the mummers' play shares with cultivated literature; almost invariably, the aim is to answer questions about genetic connections between the two—to show, for instance, the influence of several folk play figures on the Vice figure in Tudor moralities, or, in the other direction, to reveal the mummers' borrowings of content from written literature.[2] While my essay carries on this tradition of interest in the folklore/literature relationship, I will be looking not for genetic links between the two, but for semantic ones. I shall apply the same interpretive method to the mummers' play (or, more precisely, to a hypothetical "ideal form" of it) and to a comparable sophisticated play in order to see just how their thematic structures and consequent meanings converge or diverge, as the case may be.[3] Such a comparison will, I hope, further stimulate our increasing interest in the nature of folk sensibility vis-à-vis literary sensibility.

The literary play I use for this comparison I do not choose at random. **The Old Wives Tale,** written sometime in the early 1590's by the late-Elizabethan dramatist and wit, George Peele, employs with full consciousness a plethora of folklore conventions, ranging from motifs, to tale types, to whole texts of shorter genres like proverbs and spells, to beyond: the play goes so far as to (re)create a folklore event. I use this phrase, "folklore event," because most of the plot of the wife's tale is not only clearly indebted to several international tale types, woven into a fairly coherent story, but is also framed by a performance context that includes an appropriate place (the woodland cottage of a village blacksmith, Clunch), time (from late at night until daybreak), performer (the smith's wife, Madge), audience (three merry servants of a gentleman whose romantic assignation has temporarily freed Antic, Frolic, and Fantastic from their duties), and even genre, as the play's title indicates. Clearly, Peele was not giving us simply an illustration of the use of folklore in literature but was taking inspiration from the more complex whole of an event.

Over and above the obvious similarity in genre, this very rare quality of Peele's play—the recreation of a folklore event rather than simply the employment of folklore elements—helps to justify a comparison of these two particular items. Peele was apparently attempting to capture the essential appeal or spirit of folklore, as his sympathetic, unself-conscious, nonparodying, nonartificially quaint treatment of traditional materials and of the rustic folk in the tale-telling session suggests. (Those who see **The Old Wives Tale** as parody have been convincingly refuted by Peele

scholars.)[4] It may be well also for me to counter here the argument that, since Peele based his plot on traditional folktales, then the folk genre comparable to **Old Wives Tale** might be folktale but is certainly not folk drama. Again, this argument misinterprets the spirit the playwright brought to his work in sympathetically recreating a *folklore* event. He uses folktale elements for his plot because, obviously, folktales are *the* folk genres with substantial plots. He also uses many other traditional items, like games and proverbs, but not for plot, of course. Indeed, were Peele attempting to recreate a folktale, then the wife's story would have obeyed the epic laws of folk narrative; but the framed tale consistently disobeys those laws.[5] In short, **The Old Wives Tale** attempts to be faithful to the spirit of folklore, as Peele saw it, expressed in dramatic form, just as each performance of the mummers' play is by definition faithful to the spirit of folklore expressed in dramatic form. A comparison which, through interpretation, shows the similarities and differences between the two should provide some ground for further generalizations between folk conceptions ("emic" meanings) and literary conceptions ("etic" meanings) of the same kind of imaginative materials.

Let me summarize Peele's play as cogently as I can. Lost in the forest at night, the three sophisticated young servant lads are discovered by the local smith, who agrees to shelter them in his cottage till daybreak.[6] His wife, Madge, welcomes the lads, feeds them, and at their request tells a "merry winters tale" for their entertainment. Soon after she has begun her introduction, "Once upon a time there was a King" (1.110), and sketched out the tale's background—an evil conjurer has bespelled two maidens, abducting one of them—the tale's personnel begin to appear on stage to act out their own story, Madge and her audience remaining in the background to pass occasional comments on the action as it progresses before their eyes.

This framed tale constitutes the major substance of Peele's little play. First to appear are the Two Brothers of the noble Delya, one of the abdubted maidens, seeking to rescue their bespelled sister from the conjurer. As do all other seekers yet to come, the Brothers first meet an old man at the crossroads who gathers alms and bestows, in allusive, paradoxical words, prophecy or advice on all who pass. We soon discover that this seer, Erestus, is a third victim of the conjurer villain, Sacrapant: he is in reality not old at all, but young and the husband of Sacrapant's other female victim, Venelia. The villain has stolen not only Erestus' wife but also his youthful appearance, in exchange for the conjurer's own aged countenance. Though puzzled by the old man's mysterious pronouncements, the Two Brothers both receive his advice and proffer their alms in good spirit before proceeding on their quest. The next seeker to arrive at the crossroads is a local resident, Lampriscus, whose quest is to marry off his two decidedly burdensome daughters; one, Zantippa, is fair in appearance but foul of tongue, the other, Celanta, fair-spoken but ugly. Lampriscus' alms are also rewarded with advice: "Send them to the Well for the water of life: there shall they finde their fortunes unlooked for" (11. 238-239).

After the main action has been momentarily broken by the entry of a chorus of Harvest Men who sing a quatrain about "sow[ing] sweete fruites of love" (1. 252), a third set of questers enters the crossroads: a braggart warrior, Huanebango, and his companion-cum-clown, Booby. They, like the Brothers, seek to rescue the fair maiden from the evil conjurer. Huanebango, a wildly extravagant boaster, refuses alms to Erestus; his companion, however, offers a piece of cake and receives the prophecy that his braggart master shall "be deafe," while Booby himself "shalt not see," though he will at least "have wealth to mend [his] wit" (1. 332).

At last we see the conjurer Sacrapant, in his "studie." We learn from his own lips what a rather sorry creature he is, fully cognizant of the unnaturalness of his stolen youth and wistfully saddened by the fact that, though he has enchanted her, gained a youthful appearance for her, and does all he can to please her, the heroine Delya loves him not. Soon the heroine's Two Brothers arrive at the conjurer's den, to be greeted first by a disembodied Eccho, which simply repeats the last word of each sentence they utter, and then by a blast of lightning and thunder, which fells them. Sacrapant orders his supernatural helpmates, two Furies, to carry off the stunned and helpless princes.

The action returns to the crossroads, at which arrives the fourth and final quester, the story's hero. He is the knight Eumenides, lover of the abducted heroine, Delya. Of his prophecy from the resident old man at the cross, our hero makes as little as had the Brothers of theirs: "Bestowe thy almes, give more than all, / Till dead mens bones come at thy call" (11. 445-446). Eumenides is soon to be tested, however, for he immediately comes across an altercation between church warden and sexton on the one hand and two villagers on the other. The latter want to bury the body of their dead friend, the pauper Jack, while the former won't permit it until the necessary fee is paid. As the dispute grows into blows, Eumenides intervenes; to bring peace, the noble stranger pays the burial fee himself, even though this altruism leaves him penniless. The action of the internal tale breaks again at this point, as the storyteller and her audience comment on the events so far and the chorus of Harvest Men enter once more, this time to sing a verse on reaping "harvest fruite."

The climaxes of the various subplots now begin. First, the braggart soldier Huanebango and his companion Booby arrive at their destination, the conjurer's den.

Like the Two Brothers before them, however, they too encounter the Eccho and are attacked with thunder and lightning. As Erestus had predicted, Booby is blinded, while Huanebango, struck down like the Brothers, is made deaf and is carried away by the Furies, who lay his body by the well. After a short interplay between the bespelled Delya and her now enslaved Brothers (whom she does not recognize), the fortunes of Lampriscus's foul-tongued daughter, Zantippa, are taken up. Arriving at the well, she lowers her pitcher, whereupon a Head emerges, asking to be combed. Instead, the girl berates and breaks her pitcher on the strange Head. Thunder and lightning again appear, resuscitating Huanebango, who proclaims that he will marry this girl at the well. As deaf as Erestus had predicted, the boastful warrior is accepted, even while ill-natured Zantippa heaps insults on him and promises to cuckold him, none of which, fortunately, he can hear.

The tale now picks up briefly the story of the hero, Eumenides, who is still en route to the villain's lair. Seeing little success in his quest, the knight is lamenting his circumstances when a boy appears, offers himself as a servant, and is accepted as a companion. The two repair to an inn, where the lad, Jack (who is, of course, the ghost of the villager whose burial fee Eumenides had paid), soon shows his worth by magically filling the knight's recently emptied purse. The hero readily agrees to Jack's suggestion that they share equally everything gained on the quest, which Eumenides now continues in renewed spirits. Meanwhile, Lampriscus' second daughter, the ill-favored but sweet-tongued Celanta, has been met, wooed, and won by Booby, the kind-hearted if witless servant to the ridiculous Huanebango; Booby, as prophesied, is now permanently blinded by Sacrapant's power. Celanta comes to the well for water, and like her sister before her, is greeted by the mysterious Head. Unlike her sister, however, Celanta obeys the Head's request to comb its hair of corn. A second Head then rises, also asking to be combed; the kind girl again obliges, and this time the hair is not of corn but of gold, which she combs into her lap as reward for her goodness.

The two subplots of Huanebango and Booby and of Lampriscus and his daughters concluded, the tale returns to the main plot, the quest of its hero, Eumenides, accompanied by his revenant servant-companion, Jack. They come to the villain's den, and Jack quickly brings about Sacrapant's physical death, again by magical means, while Erestus' enchanted lady, Venelia, mutely destroys the conjurer's external life token, a flame encased in glass. The Two Brothers, the heroine Delya, the formerly mad Venelia, and the old man/bear Erestus are now all unspelled, and reunite joyfully in their proper shapes and roles. Jack, however, is not quite through, and reminds Eumenides of his pledge to share equally with him all the hero has won, including his regained love. After a short protest, Eumenides, with no choice but to uphold his word and his honor, prepares to cut Delya in two. Satisfied that the knight has passed this final test, however, Jack stays his hand, reveals his own true identity and motives, and disappears. The others joyfully depart for their home in Thessaly. The "winters tale" over, we return to Madge and her audience. She offers the three lads breakfast before they leave, and all exit.

So much for the story of *The Old Wives Tale.* Fortunately, few readers of this journal will require as detailed a description of the British mummers' play. Traditionally, the play is performed by a small team of working-class men during such calendrical days and periods as Christmastime, New Year's, Plough Monday, Easter, and All Hallows. Usually composed of a shifting number—depending on availability, desire, and need—of kin, workmates, or close friends and neighbors, a team would visit mostly middle- and upper-class homes in their own and nearby communities to perform its piece in kitchen or hall (though in recent times the display has been confined to fewer and more public spots, such as public house or town square). Food, drink, and money would be (and often still are) expected from the audience at the end of the short but variable performance. The mummers' daylong enterprise was, in brief, a relatively full and complex amalgamation of several traditional activities, including music, song, dance, disguise, quête, and perambulation, as well as the most pronounced element, drama.

Like all folklore, the mummers' play resists classification into rigorous categories that will not leak or overlap, and for any generalization one may hazard about the play as a whole, examples that do not fit the generalization can always be offered. Quite rightly, however, we continue to search for regularities that will fit as much of the data as possible, and play scholars have found it useful to identify three main textual subtypes. The most widespread by far, found over most parts of predominantly Anglo-Saxon Britain, is the Hero Combat form. The essentials of its dramatic action (though the barest bones of the whole performance) consist of a battle between two warriors, such as St. George and the Turkish Knight; the felling of one by the other; the latter's cure by a comic Doctor, often assisted by his equally comical servant or apprentice, Jack; and then some semiautonomous cavorting by characters who play little if any part in the observed plot—characters like Beelzebub, Miss Funny, Big Head and Little Wit, Little Devil Doubt, Humpty Jack, and others.[7] A second type is the Wooing Play (sometimes called the Plough Play), found chiefly in the East Midland counties. Compared to the multitude of Hero Combat examples that have been recorded, data on the Wooing Play are slim, but in general the action entails a succession of courtings by different suitors of a most

independently minded Lady; the killing of the central figure, the Fool, by a warrior (such as St. George); his resurrection by a Doctor; a claim by an older woman, Dame Jane, that her bastard child has been fathered by the same Fool and his denial of the claim; and, finally, the Fool's successful courtship of the hitherto hard-to-win Lady. The third type, which has even more tenuous status as a distinct form of play than does the Wooing type, is the Sword Play, recovered versions of which are very scarce indeed and confined primarily to northeast England. In the Sword Play, a Fool is also slain, but by a group of dancers who are also characters in the slight drama but whose dance seems to be the chief matter in the performance. The Fool is then, as in the other types, revived by a Doctor. Finally, as is the case in most traditional performances of the mummers' play, whatever its type, the players accept contributions from the audience.

Whether the three main types of mummers' play, the Hero Combat, the Wooing, and the Sword, originated independently and have become similar by gradual cross-influencing; whether they represent different stages in the evolution of one custom; or whether they are but regional variations of a single model-play is not of great moment here. Without a doubt they all share a similar belief system and express it in a similar set of imaginative ideas, all of which, code and message, are about the interdependence of social Self and Other. In conveying this message, the mummers' play goes to great lengths to portray images of reciprocity, of egalitarianism, of mutuality, and even of likeness among the personnel of its social universe.

A discussion of a necessarily generalized, and thus hypothetical, type of Hero Combat play, the most common form of mumming, will show how this message about sociability is articulated. After its Presenter's opening call to the audience for playing room and his brief characterization of the action to come, the Hero Combat play sets up a confrontation between two combatants from the international realm of romance and legend. One warrior is usually an epitome of English Self, such as the patron saint, the Christian St. George, the other an epitome of strange Otherness, such as the heathen Turkish Knight. Other characters may fill these combatant slots, but they maintain their quality of national representativeness and their relationship of familiarity on the one hand, strangeness on the other, and of mutual threat. Each warrior boasts mightily of his own prowess and of the danger he presents to the other's wellbeing until the two come to blows. Most of the time, the familiar—St. George—slays the strange, but in many, many cases the opposite occurs.

That the apparent "hero" should be slain is not too surprising if we remember that we are not dealing with a homily about good and evil, but with the dramatic representation of an idea—social interdependence. Thus we often find, in this first section of the play, elements which reinforce the theme. For instance, an additional character like the King of Egypt may lament that his "only son" has been slain, thus foregrounding imaginatively a very important example of interdependence, a kin relationship. Or the slayer himself will call for—and, indeed, himself pay—someone to resuscitate the antagonist he has just slain. Or, more subtly, the idea may be communicated by the very similarity of the combatants' boasts and challenges, which are often little different from each other in rhetoric or content—sometimes, indeed, downright repetitive:

KING GEORGE:

> Battle, to battle with thee I call to
> see who on this ground shall fall

TURKISH KNIGHT:

> Battle, to battle with thee I pray to see
> who on this ground shall lay.[8]

Such elements as these—ascribed kin relationship, attempted restitution by paying for the victim's cure, and paralleled characterizations in speech and appearance, among others—minimize the disjunction between the antagonists that their primary designations, such as champion of Christendom and champion of Islam, and their fight to the death initially suggest.

After one champion has been slain and a healer requested, the ambience in the play shifts from the international domain of heroic legend, a realm remote from the phenomenal experience of players and audience, to a realm much closer to that experience; concomitantly, there is a shift in tone, as speech, actions, and appearances become decidedly more comic. The central figure in this second section is the Doctor who answers the call to revive the slain. Frequently, the principal dramatis personae are again two, for the Doctor may be accompanied by his man, often called Jack Finney; and like the warrior champions in the first section, the physician and his assistant are in conflict:

DOCTOR:

> Fetch my implements.

JACK:

> Fetch 'em thee-self.

DOCTOR:

> What's that, you saucy young beggar!

JACK:

> I'll fetch 'em meself.

DOCTOR:

> Fetch 'em then and quick about it.

(Jack brings the implements consisting of hammer, saw, files, pincers, etc., and throws them on the ground.)

DOCTOR:

> Well, what do'st want to throw 'em down there fur?

JACK:

> For thee to pick 'em up.

DOCTOR:

> What's that, you saucy young beggar?

JACK:

> For me to pick 'em up.

DOCTOR:

> Pick 'em up, then, and quick about it.[9]

In true Lévi-Straussian manner, however, this conflict is weaker than the one between the warrior heroes of the preceding section. The most important contribution to this weakening is that the phenomenal domain of physician-and-assistant was obviously much closer to the English country folk's actual experience than that of patron saint and Turkish champion—a regional as opposed to international domain. Similarly, the conflict not only is a more trivial one than the conflict between the warrior heroes, but also is conducted with high humor, as the above excerpt suggests. Like the Turkish Knight, the Doctor represents the Other; in real life a middle-class professional, a physician's contact with working-class folk was minimal, since they could not afford his services, for one, and for another, preferred to rely on traditional folk healing. The mummers' Doctor, however, goes to great lengths to demystify even his relatively weak degree of strangeness with humor: obvious hyperbole (his boasts of his skills are clearly those of a quack and thus far more benign than the Turkish Knight's boasts of martial prowess), inversion ("when I was up down under in York I cured old Mrs. Cork. She tumbled upstairs: empty teapot half full of barley-meal grazed her shin again[st] her elbow, made her stocking bleed and I set that"),[10] and oxymorons (in telling of his travels, for instance: he has been not only to such remote spots as Italy, France, and Spain but also to the most quotidian of places, such as his "grandmother's closet and back again").

The Doctor's antagonist is his assistant, Jack Finney, a representative of Self with whom country folk could more readily identify than St. George. However, just as the Doctor is only relatively strange, so is Finney only relatively familiar. He not only has the nerve to cheek his master, but he also is a putative gentleman: my

Saves His Sister and Brothers from the Dragon" (Type 312D).[14] The play is also replete with proverbs and proverbial phrases, beliefs, songs, rhymes, and charms, as well as with references to festivals, customs, and play.[15] Clearly, many of these items were considered folklore as much by our sixteenth-century playwright of London and Oxford as they are by us today.

At the simplest level of static, formal structure, we find a clear parallel between mummers' play and *Old Wives Tale*: the juxtaposition of three distinguishable realms of personnel. In Peele's play, these realms are the heroic (comparable to the mummers' international domain), the comic (comparable to the mummers' regional domain), and the emblematic (comparable to the mummers' fantastic domain). These three realms encompass the major dramatis personae of the internal story of *The Old Wives Tale*;[16] its frame story is analogous to the performance context of a folklore event.

The characters who occupy the heroic realm in *The Old Wives Tale* are, like St. George and the Turkish Knight, highborn in status and noble in manner, their arena of action an international one: they are the seer, Erestus; the hero, Eumenides; the heroine's Two Brothers; the heroine herself, Delya; the other enchanted maiden, Erestus' lost wife, Venelia; and the hero companion, Jack. All are figures of romance, expressive of few vernacular traits. Only Jack is significantly domesticated, but his status as a ghost, his extraordinary powers, and his dramatic role as hero companion and tester counterbalance his more everyday properties (in life, at least) as a local youth (though see 11. 485-486). The second domain of characters in *The Old Wives Tale,* the comic, is—like its analogue, the regional domain of the mummers' Doctor and assistant—closer to the phenomenal experience of its audience. These characters regularly exhibit the foibles and the stereotypical personality traits of everyday folk. Its personnel are Sacrapant, the villain; Huanebango, the braggart warrior; Lampriscus, father of the two unmarried girls; the girls themselves, ill-natured but beautiful Zantippa, good-natured but ugly Celanta; and Huanebango's clown companion, Booby. The third realm, analogous to the mummers' fantastics, is constituted of imaginary, semiautonomous "devices" rather than characters: the Furies, the Eccho, the Heads from the Well, and the chorus of Harvest Men.

Two of these characters whom I call "comic" and "everyday" require explanation: Sacrapant and Huanebango. European-born, a conjurer and shape shifter, Sacrapant would seem on the surface to belong to the heroic world of legend and romance. Peele brings the character repeatedly down to earth, however, by endowing practically all his onstage actions with a most prosaic quality. "Each thing rejoyseth underneathe the Skie," he complains, for instance, "But onely I whom

heaven hath in hate:/Wretched and miserable Sacrapant" (11. 337-339). In his lovesick complaints Sacrapant is not unlike the formerly henpecked husband and now beleaguered father, Lampriscus; the conjurer is acutely conscious of his stolen and false appearance and fawns over Delya, who, despite her enchantment, treats him with a combination of absolute obedience and personal disinterest that bears no resemblance to that which he really desires, love. Indeed, throughout the play Sacrapant is remarkably ineffectual in truly important matters, and his death is appositely enough an unusually quick and simply accomplished affair.

Similarly, the braggart warrior, Huanebango, despite his supposed aristocratic Spanish heritage, is familiarized—his sound and fury, like Sacrapant's, signifying little of substance. At one point he refers to himself as an Englishman (1. 546), and despite his putative nobility importunes his man, Booby, for a slice of cake, as does his equally aristocratic cousin, Bustegustecerydis, who possesses such an unseemly love of capon that he will "deceive[d] his boy of his dinner" (11. 298-299).

At a more sophisticated level of structure, each major figure in the heroic realm of *The Old Wives Tale,* as in the mummers' play, is paralleled by a similar but different character in the comic realm. Erestus' counterpart is Sacrapant, Eumenides' is Huanebango, Delya's Zantippa (the foul-tongued daughter), Venelia's Celanta, Jack's parallel is Booby, and the Two Brothers' double is Lampriscus. It is important to note, however, that the relationship between figures is not dialectical, as we saw to be the case in the mummers' play, but contrastive.

At the more abstract level of thematic structure—the articulation of concepts that informs the play with its meaning—*The Old Wives Tale* differs significantly from the folk drama's paradigmatic Self/Other opposition. The thematic opposition in Peele's play is between two metaphysical concepts: one is the idea of a rational control that is guided by wider rules of both human conduct and natural law; the other is the idea of lack of control, of personal whim and fancy, of egocentric, self-motivated, even willful behavior.

It is difficult, unless one is thoroughly versed in Elizabethan metaphysic and its associated language (which I am not), to hit upon two words which most aptly denote these two ideas. Let me instead identify their respective features. The characteristics of rational control are, first of all, an intellectual variable, *wit,* which is manifested in two ways: willingness to follow advice, and knowledge that one should not be influenced as much by appearances as by the truer essence of things, which may be hidden by false exteriors; second, an ethical variable, *charity;* and third, an ideological variable, *faith* in the cosmic principle that time and fate are parameters of the universe which operate according to laws beyond human power to question or manipulate. Contrasting with these three characteristics are the traits of the uncontrolled and irrational: lack of wit—in particular, a readiness to respond to surface appearances rather than to essences and an unwillingness to follow advice; selfish lack of charity toward others; and the belief that humans can manipulate time and fate. The precept that emerges as the principle thematic message in the play's moral universe is that the ratio of one's rewards to one's punishments will vary directly as the ratio of one's rational to irrational traits. Let me discuss each pair of counterpointed characters and their qualities in order.

Erestus possesses all three properties of control. His most prominent feature is his wit—as a seer he, above all others, knows that surface appearances are not the same as hidden reality. His very first piece of advice, given to the Two Brothers, is that "things that seeme are not the same" (1. 160). In fact, there is very little Erestus does not know; consequently, he not only is aware of just what is in store for all the questers he counsels, but also acknowledges the cosmic principle that fate rules mankind, urging the hero Eumenides to beseech fate to govern the hero's intellectual component, wit, if he wishes to succeed in the quest (11. 439-442). Erestus also possesses the third important variable, the ethical one of charity, though in this regard he functions more notably as the test case of others' charity; nevertheless, he gives freely of his prophecies, even to Huanebango, who refuses him alms. Erestus' parallel in the comic domain, the villain Sacrapant, possesses none of the rational virtues. Like all the heroic characters, Erestus' self-control makes him remarkably passive. He can do nothing to influence circumstances, despite his prophetic knowledge, but his shape-shifting counterpart, Sacrapant, like his comic brethren, though ineffectual, is remarkably active; yet this activeness is a sign of his flaws. Sacrapant attempts to manipulate the destiny of others as well as his own, but such matters should be left to fate. He also breaks cosmic law by manipulating time: he reverses it (by making himself young), speeds it up (by making Erestus old), and stops it altogether (by assuming that his supernatural properties, particularly his external soul, will keep him perpetually alive: "my timelesse date is come to end" [1. 814], he cries in horror and disbelief as he is killed). By definition, the conjurer deals with false appearances; in particular, when he steals Erestus' youth to aid his courtship of Delya, Sacrapant expects that appearance unrelated to reality will influence affairs. In addition, he is of course the very antithesis of charitable; and even his futile attempt to please Delya by conjuring up an illusion—a tableau scene containing "the best meate from the king of England's table, and the best wine in all France,

brought in by the veriest knave in all Spaine" (11. 363-364)—is but a false appearance, a chimera, as he himself is totally in his outward persona.

The hero, Eumenides, is appositely counterpointed by the comic false hero, the ruffler Huanebango. The heroic knight possesses the intellectual variable, wit, as the seer Erestus makes clear: "I do perceive that thou hast wit, / Beg of thy fate to governe it" (11. 441-442). Eumenides' wit is not as yet perfectly realized, however, and the narrative of his quest is a narrative of that realization. His most fully articulated weakness is his momentary lack of faith, as he laments at being "forlorne by Fate" (1. 688) and wishes to manipulate natural time by dying "in the spring, the Aprill of [his] age" (1. 690). His pessimism leads Jack at one point to exclaim, "why maister, your man can teach you more wit than this" (11. 752-753). And from that point on Eumenides' path leads upward to success, as he follows Jack's advice without question. He suffers through the various tests that all heroes must undergo in their quests, but his primary virtue of charity (remember that he surrenders all his money to pay for an unknown pauper's burial) and his basic acknowledgment of time's suzerainty ("Tell me Time, tell me just Time, / When shall I Delia see?" [11. 432-433]), along with his wit, allow him ultimately to triumph. Huanebango, in contrast, consistently displays the foolish and egocentric willfulness of the comic personality. His attitude toward fate is succinctly expressed: "I will followe my Fortune after mine owne fancie, and doo according to mine owne discretion" (11. 308-309), he proclaims in refusing to take notice of Erestus' wise words. And in following his "owne fancie" he also neglects the ethical virtue of charity: "Huanabango [*sic*] giveth no Cakes for Almes, aske of them that give giftes for poore Beggars" (11. 314-315), he tells the old man.

Delya's comic counterpart is Zantippa of the foul temper. Their outward behavior is similar: Zantippa insults and attacks her sister, breaking her pitcher, as Delya similarly attacks her brothers—whom Sacrapant has enslaved and who thus appear to be laborers—with abuse both verbal ("prating swaines" and "villaines") and physical (she prods them with a "gode" if they falter in their task of digging the rocky ground). The difference between the two is that Delya's lack of charity toward her kin is determined by external forces; when she is finally disenchanted, she displays the appropriate attitude toward her fate by courageously submitting herself to be cut in two so that Eumenides may fulfill his promise to Jack. Zantippa, on the other hand, always acting in full consciousness and with independent motives, refuses her father's advice to "give faire wordes" at the well, instead abusing not only her sister but also the mysterious Head, to whose hidden significance she is entirely blind.

A fourth parallel is between Venelia and the ugly but polite sister, Celanta. Venelia, more than anyone else it seems, is a pawn of external forces, as in her raging madness she speaks not a single word throughout the play. She also possesses by fate those artificial traits that help to bring about Sacrapant's downfall: stolen away from husband and home, she fits the paradoxical circumstances of one who is neither wife, widow, nor maid and thus the only one who can destroy the conjurer's life token. Like other comic characters, Celanta is far more self-motivated: she even lies to her blind wooer, Booby, assuring him of what he wants to hear—that she is as fair of face as she is of speech. To her credit, she follows the advice of her father to speak fair words at the well. A more subtle parallel between Venelia and Celanta is that they both display the proper attitude toward time: by destroying Sacrapant's life token, Venelia corrects the matter of stopped time, while Celanta, by harvesting the ripened corn from the magical head, assists the proper passage of nature's seasonal time, a passage which her sister, like Sacrapant of humanity's biological time, had retarded.

The substantive parallel between the fifth pair of characters, the Two Brothers from the heroic realm and Lampriscus from the comic, is their relationship to kin. In the idiosyncratic manner of most of the comic personnel, however, Lampriscus seeks to rid himself of his daughters, while the Two Brothers wish to restore their sister to her family home. Unique to this pair of contrasting characters is that the comic figure, Lampriscus, has no observable flaws (his part in the play is minimal, both in length and complexity), while the heroic Brothers do; they rail against "fortune cruell, cruell and unkind" (1. 137) and assume that their sister is a victim of "chance" (1. 139) rather than a subject of cosmic laws. Appropriately, like Eumenides they must suffer before they eventually triumph in their quest. But the Brothers do eventually succeed, for like Lampriscus they not only display charity to the old beggar but also follow his advice, which, in the Brothers' case, is to distrust appearances: "Things that seeme are not the same" (1. 160).

Finally, there is a parallel between the two young hero companions, Jack and Booby. Like Erestus, Jack possesses wisdom, a full knowledge of hidden realities; he goes further than Erestus, however, in his role as enabler, possessing the power to effect goals actively. Booby, on the other hand, has neither the genetic property of wit (as both Erestus [1. 332] and even Huanebango [11. 261-262] recognize) nor the properly deferential attitude toward fate: the ubiquitous comic qualities of willfulness and idiosyncratic fancy characterize his early behavior—"If it bee no more but running through a little lightning and thunder, and riddle me riddle me whats this, Ile have the wench from the Conjurer if he were ten Conjurers" (11. 274-277). He

soon learns that such tempting of fate and his not recognizing riddles, thunder, and lightning as but masks of a more malignant power are in error; he suffers for his witless lack of temperateness and control by being blinded. However, his ability to see through Huanebango's superficially imposing appearance ("superfantiall substance" [1. 322], he calls it) to the real foolishness within, and his kindness toward the old man at the cross, allow him tempered success: though permanently blinded, he does win a wife and gold.

All the characters from the heroic domain, then, ultimately attain grace, embracing the virtues and receiving their appropriate rewards, though all must first go through severe tests and the attendant ordeals. The comic characters are more heterogeneous in their share of punishments and rewards, ranging from the villain Sacrapant, who breaks all the rules and suffers totally; through Huanebango, who ends up deaf and with a wife both ill-spoken and adulterous; through Zantippa, who gets a husband in name only; through Booby, who finds a kindly and wealthy wife but who is permanently blinded; through Celanta; to Lampriscus, the only comic character whose quest is unqualifiedly successful (depending, of course, on how much contact he will have with his new son-in-law).

The third realm of characters in *The Old Wives Tale,* the emblematic, reveals another significant difference between Peele's play and the art of the mummers. The emblematic figures either constitute a sort of metacommentary on the human actions or function as agencies, which contrasts with the fantastics' integration into the dialectical structure of the mummers' play. In *The Old Wives Tale* the "supernumeraries" inhabiting the emblematic realm are the Eccho, the Furies, the Heads from the Well, and the Chorus of Harvest Men. The first two are uncomplicated signs of the ineffable force that is fate. The Eccho, for instance, simply repeats the last word of each sentence addressed to it, denoting the impossibility of man's questioning forces that govern his destiny. Similarly, the Furies are signs of an implacable "justice," though justice in its malignant aspect. (The beneficent side of what the Furies stand for is associated with the hero, whose name, Eumenides, betrays his Classical connotations; Venelia's raging madness is also reminiscent of the Furies' Classical characterization. Appropriately, both Eumenides and Venelia are integral in bringing "justice" to Sacrapant.)

The Heads in the Well and the chorus of Harvest Men are more metaphorical expressions of cosmic forces. The Heads represent a category of natural time—not the biological, with which Sacrapant has tampered, but the seasonal. The Heads have hair of corn, ripened and ready to be harvested. By refusing to comb the Head, Zantippa retards the passage of seasonal time, while her kindly sister, Celanta, respects time's demands and combs as requested; each girl reaps a commensurate reward. The Harvest Men are also emblematic of seasonal time, though they use words rather than visual imagery to express their significance: they first sing a song about sowing, later a song about reaping. As John D. Cox shows, these verses are resonant with the message of St. Paul's aphorism, "Whatsoever a man soweth, that shall he also reape."[17] Applied to the events in the framed story of *The Old Wives Tale,* St. Paul's principle can be illustrated thus: the more one behaves according to the requirements of wit (in following advice and in not confusing appearances with reality), of fate and time (in acknowledging their suzerainty rather than attempting to manipulate them), and of charity, then the more rewards one shall be heir to. The more one breaks these rules, the more one will suffer. The theme of *The Old Wives Tale* implies not just a humanistic and individual-centered conception, however, but also a cosmological principle, perhaps most closely matched by the precept of Ecclesiastes: "To every thing there is a season, and a time to every purpose under the heaven . . . a time to plant, and a time to pluck up that which is planted" (3: 1,2).

Just as the "new folkloristics" seeks to find a functional and semantic fit between text and context, so now may we look at the performance context in *The Old Wives Tale* in the light of the framed story's theme. The pages' names, Antic, Frolic, and Fantastic, imply character traits common in the tale's comic personnel: self-indulgent behavior that follows no higher rules of ideology or ethics. Their speech is laced with Latin tags and with puns, indicating that they do have "wit," but wit as yet uncontrolled: theirs is not the sort that produces wisdom. They use their wit to make fun of their benefactor, Clunch, with hyperbole and sarcasm: "good Vulcan . . . commaund us howsoever, wheresoever, whensoever, in whatsoever, for ever and ever" (11. 41-44), is the mock cry of Frolic, while all follow with "O blessed Smith, O bountifull Clunch" (1. 50). And while they are delighted at the chance to hear Madge tell a winter's tale, their pleasure is largely stimulated by the chance to make fun of her; no sooner has she launched into her introduction and told how the king sent all his men out of the kingdom to seek his stolen daughter, than Frolic interrupts with a quip—"Who drest his dinner then?" (1. 116). In short, as Cox has already shown, the jolly young lads are confusing the rustic appearance of Clunch and Madge with the couple's real essence, which is one of kindness and charity—rescuing the pages from the woods, sheltering them, and entertaining them—and even, indeed, of an unexpected "wit" of their own ("either heare my tale, or kisse my taile" [1.117] is Madge's response to the interruption). As the night and the tale progress, the pages adopt a proper attitude of respect and appreciation.[18]

These hedonistic youths also learn a lesson, it seems, about time. After entering the cottage, they seek some light and merry way to spend their visit, and break into song. The verses they sing are of a maid who cannot wait until harvesttime (and her marriage date, one infers) to lose her virginity:

> Then O, then O, then O my true love said,
> Till that time come againe,
> Shee could not live a maid.
>
> [11. 79-81]

This maiden, and the young sophisticates who sing her song, are not properly attuned to the ideology of respect toward seasonal time, it would seem. Rather, in their perception, the function of Madge's tale is to "drive away the time" (1. 83).[19] But the ancient formula with which she begins her story, "Once upon a time," should attune them to prepare, by night's end, to have their perception changed. Thus we have a final and most important difference between *The Old Wives Tale* and the mummers' play. In the literary artifact, the function of the folklore in its context of performance is didactic and theoretical, while the function of the traditional play in its context of performance is rhetorical and practical.

* * *

With the same kind of basic materials—a folklore event, traditional content, and a tripartite division of fictional characters into three phenomenally distinct but interrelated domains of experience—and with the same kind of serious-minded if light-hearted approach to their art, *The Old Wives Tale* and the mummers' play take quite different paths. Peele's ethos is dogmatic and universal, as his play dramatizes the rewards that follow from adhering to a specific code of values and beliefs and the punishments that follow from disregarding them. The mummers' play, on the other hand, is hortatory and particularistic, its aim an immediate and practical one. While *The Old Wives Tale* is thus essentially didactic, the mummers' play is rhetorical: by dramatizing an appropriate theme of commonality among its superficially quite diverse characters, the play seeks to persuade the audience to share its resources with the performers.[20]

At the same time, the literary vision and the folk vision differ interestingly in their view of humankind. In Peele's play, the operational unit, so to speak, is the individual, who has the responsibility for attaining the proper degrees and kinds of wit, charity, and faith as well as the accountability for failing to do so. In the context of these principles, each character is progressively individualized as the play unfolds, each proceeding on a different path of evolution or devolution as the case may be. Contrasting with this humanistic world view, the mummers' play proposes that the operational units of humankind are the relationships that obtain between people. As events proceed, the characters become not more but less individualized, as through analogy, homology, and dialectic each more familiar Self/Other relationship emerges as an organic extension of a less familiar one.

The folk product is, in short, less concerned with the kinds of abstractions that canonical religions foster in the world view of their flock than with the very real demands and constraints of day-to-day life, and less concerned with theories of personal advancement and decline that literary introspection and its attendant humanistic philosophy generate than with the nature of social relationships—which may, in fact, be the most influential variables in determining the form and quality of everyday life and of one's spiritual and material rise and fall. I would suggest that, for English folklore if for no other kind, these two interwoven properties of social theme and practical function may provide a way into a more fruitful conceptualization of that quintessentially relational construct of our own, "communal," a construct we have always felt to be important and as a result may have abused somewhat, but which may be due, I think, for rehabilitation.[21]

Notes

1. The classic typological work is E. C. Cawte, Alex Helm, and N. Peacock, *English Ritual Drama: A Geographical Index,* Publications of the Folk-Lore Society, vol. 127 (London: Folk-Lore Society, 1967). The fullest cultural evolutionary and comparative analyses may be found in E. K. Chambers, *The English Folk-Play* (Oxford: Oxford University Press, 1933) and Alan Brody, *The English Mummers and Their Plays: Traces of Ancient Mystery,* University of Pennsylvania Publications in Folklore and Folklife (Philadelphia: University of Pennsylvania Press, 1970). Functional questions are posed chiefly by Susan Pattison, "The Antrobus Soulcaking Play: An Alternative Approach to the Mummers' Play," *Folk-Life* 15 (1977), 5-11, functional and semiotic by Henry Glassie, *All Silver and No Brass: An Irish Christmas Mumming* (Bloomington: Indiana University Press, 1975). Strictly semiotic is Lorre Marie Weidlich's "The Mummers' Play: A Structural Analysis" (Master's Report, University of Texas at Austin 1979). All major perspectives may be found among the several essays in *Christmas Mumming in Newfoundland: Essays in Anthropology, Folklore, and History,* ed. Herbert Halpert and G. M. Story (Toronto: University of Toronto Press for Memorial University of Newfoundland, 1969); while primarily about a related custom of house visiting in disguise rather than about the mummers' play itself, the analyses in *Christmas Mumming in Newfoundland* are all relevant to the mother country's tradition.

2. For the first, see Francis Hugh Mares, "The Origin of the Figure Called 'the Vice' in Tudor Drama," *The Huntington Library Quarterly,* 22 (1958-59), 11-29, and P. Happé, "The Vice and the Folk-Drama," *Folklore,* 75 (1964), 161-193. For the second, see the citations throughout Charles Read Baskervill, "Mummers' Wooing Plays in England," *Modern Philology,* 21 (1924), 225-272. The most recent claim for mummers' play influence on a literary work is Thomas Pettitt, "The Folk-Play in Marlowe's *Doctor Faustus,*" *Folklore* 91 (1980), 72-77.

3. Of all the studies of the relationship between the mummers' play and sophisticated literature, Glassie's *All Silver and No Brass* is closest to my approach here.

4. See Frank S. Hook, ed., *The Old Wives Tale,* in *The Life and Works of George Peele,* gen. ed. Charles T. Prouty (New Haven: Yale University Press, 1970), III, 358-60.

5. Axel Olrik, "Epic Laws of Folk Narrative," in *The Study of Folklore,* ed. Alan Dundes (Englewood Cliffs, N.J.: Prentice-Hall, 1965), pp. 131-141.

6. For this study I use the Yale edition, to which all line numbers refer (see note 4 above).

7. Since my description and analysis are of an "ideal form" of the mummers' play, I will give bibliographical references to specific texts only when the example is an unusual or a lengthy one. The most readily available texts of mummers' plays may be found in R. J. E. Tiddy, *Mummers' Play* (Oxford: Oxford University Press, 1923); Cawte, Helm, and Peacock, *English Ritual Drama;* Brody, *English Mummers and Their Plays;* and Chambers, *English Folk-Play.* Many texts are scattered throughout the runs of *Journal of the English Folk Dance Society, Journal of the English Folk Dance and Song Society,* and *Folklore* (formerly *Folk-Lore*). For texts of Wooing Plays see especially Baskervill, "Mummers' Wooing Plays in England."

8. Tiddy, *Mummers' Play,* p. 186.

9. Tiddy, p. 177.

10. Tiddy, p. 239.

11. This felicitous phrase comes from an insightful review of Brody, *English Mummers and Their Plays,* by A. E. Green in *English Dance and Song,* 34 (1972), 119.

12. See "The Symondsbury Mumming Play," *Journal of the English Folk Dance and Song Society* 7 (1952), 1-12.

13. Motif numbers are from Stith Thompson, *Motif-Index of Folk-Literature,* rev. and enlarged ed., 6 vols. (Bloomington: Indiana University Press, 1955). The most extensive inventory (almost 100) of traditional motifs in *The Old Wives Tale* has been compiled by Sylvia Lyons-Render, "Folk Motifs in George Peele's *The Old Wives Tale,*" *Tennessee Folklore Society Bulletin,* 26 (1960), 62-71.

14. Tale-type numbers are from Antti Aarne, *The Types of the Folktale,* trans. and enlarged by Stith Thompson, Folklore Fellows Communication, No. 184 (Helsinki: Suomalainen Tiedakatemia, 1964). The most accurate study of traditional tale types that probably influenced Peele is Charles S. Adams, "The Tales in Peele's *Old Wives Tale,*" *Midwest Folklore,* 13 (1963), 13-20, in which may be found references to earlier studies on the same topic by Muriel C. Bradbrook and Sarah Lewis Carol Clapp. A more recent study arguing that Peele also borrowed from Type 425A, "The Monster (Animal) as Bridegroom," is James T. Bratcher, "Peele's *Old Wives Tale* and Tale-Type 425A," in *Studies in Medieval, Renaissance, American Literature,* ed. Betsy Feagan Colquitt (Fort Worth: Texas Christian University Press, 1971), pp. 95-102.

15. See Hook, "Introduction" (esp. pp. 317-341) and "Explanatory Notes" (pp. 422-443), *The Old Wives Tale,* for identification and discussion of the many folklore genres found in Peele's text. See also Lyons-Render, "Folk Motifs in George Peele's *The Old Wives Tale.*"

16. The characters whom I ignore in my analysis are all supporting figures whose function is to illuminate main characters. The ones I have excluded are the church warden and sexton; the two villagers, Corebus and Wiggen, who argue for Jack's burial; the hostess of the inn where the grateful dead man magically fills Eumenides' purse; and the vision of a Friar from Spain, conjured up by Sacrapant for Delya's entertainment.

17. In my discussion, I have drawn significantly upon Cox's insights to the characters' attitudes to charity and fortune (in Cox's conceptualization, related to but not the same as fate) in *The Old Wives Tale.* The role of these two variables, and the theme of the sowing-reaping function, are most elegantly worked out in his "Homely Matter and Multiple Plots in Peele's *Old Wives Tale,*" *Texas Studies in Literature and Language,* 20 (1978), 330-346.

18. See Cox, "Homely Matter," pp. 343-345. Cox's essay supersedes what had formerly been the most credible analysis of unity in *The Old Wives Tale,* Herbert Goldstone's "Interplay in Peele's *The Old Wives Tale,*" *Boston University Studies in English,* 4 (1960), 202-213.

19. Ironically, the internal tale does the same thing for the folk performer. Before the story begins, both she and her husband similarly think its function is to "passe away the time" (Clunch, 1. 65) and "drive away the time" (both Clunch, 1. 67, and Madge, 1. 95). But Peele makes much of the fact that the story-teller is as surprised by what transpires as her audience: "gods me bones, who comes here?" (1. 128), is her startled response to the entry of the Two Brothers as she is well into her introduction; when the Harvest Men first appear, she ventures they will sing a song of mowing, whereas they sing a song of sowing (1. 249); and it even appears that she falls asleep before the internal tale's denouement (1. 915).

20. While I cannot develop an argument here, I might at least mention that if my interpretation of the meaning the mummers' play projects is essentially correct, then the play may not be very old at all, and indeed, in the form that we know it, may not have been very widespread or common until the eighteenth century. For it is in that century, especially the latter half, that social and material disparity between classes, dependency on charity and on money as a medium of exchange, greater number of competing interests among a community's residents—in short, increasing heterogeneity—became widespread. Thus the mummers' play may have been an environmentally induced addition, transformation, or even more workable alternative to earlier house visiting and quête customs. For some stimulating suggestions along this line see Michael J. Preston, "The British Folk Play: An Elaborated Luck-Visit?" *Western Folklore,* 30 (1971), 45-48, and Martin J. Lovelace, "Christmas Mumming in England: The House-Visit," in *Folklore Studies in Honour of Herbert Halpert,* ed. Kenneth S. Goldstein and Neil V. Rosenberg (St. John's, Newfoundland: Memorial University of Newfoundland, 1980), pp. 271-281.

21. I don't posit this on the basis of the mummers' play only, of course. For further animadversions on the notion see my *English Folk Poetry: Structure and Meaning.* Publications of the American Folklore Society New Series vol. 2 (Philadelphia: University of Pennsylvania Press, 1980).

Frank A. Ardolino (essay date August 1983)

SOURCE: Ardolino, Frank A. "Severed and Brazen Heads: Headhunting in Elizabethan Drama." *Journal of Evolutionary Psychology* 4, nos. 3-4 (August 1983): 169-81.

[*In the following essay, Ardolino uses Peele's* The Old Wives Tale *to develop a theory about the significance of severed heads in Elizabethan drama.*]

THE HEAD AS ANIMA INTELLECTUALIS

Severing and displaying the heads of defeated antagonists or criminals has been practiced in primitive, biblical, and more advanced Christian societies such as Elizabethan England.[1] Decapitating any enemy provides an appropriate gesture of total victory and control because of the physical and symbolic significance of the head. Cutting the head off deprives the antagonist not only of his chief identifying appendage, the face, but also, in a more abstract and cumulative sense, of his soul.[2] The head contains the brain, the organ of man's rationality, which provides the impulses, thoughts, and plots that animate people and make them powerful opponents. When the head is severed and displayed on a pole, the victor is proclaiming that he has deprived his enemy of his life and his identity, and now exercises control over his soul as well.

Primitive headhunting societies believe that displaying the severed heads of their enemies brings them increased power and good fortune. Warriors are ranked by the number of heads they collect and the mounted trophies signal that they have destroyed rival warriors' bodies and captured their souls. Often the ghosts of the vanquished as represented by their heads are propitiated as apotropaic powers dispelling evil and vivifying crops.

Egyptian, Hebraic, Greek, and Christian societies have also used decapitation as the punishment for enemies and malefactors. One of the punishments in the Egyptian underworld is to have the head severed by Shesmu. The Bible contains numerous examples of beheading enemies and displaying their heads as trophies. The heads of Oreb and Zeeb were brought to Gideon. The Philistines cut off Saul's head and placed it on the ramparts of the city. Earlier when David had defeated Goliath, he decapitated the Philistine giant and brought the head to Saul who became jealous of the young warrior. This most celebrated of biblical decapitations was depicted in the Renaissance by Donatello's "David," which shows David standing on the severed head of the defeated giant as a type of Christ who slays the serpent which caused the Fall.[3]

In Greek mythology the most famous beheading and displaying of a severed head occurs in the story of Perseus and the Gorgon Medusa whose hair and girdle were entwined with snakes. Medusa's look could turn onlookers to stone, but Perseus nevertheless cut off her head and gave it to Athena, who set it in her shield as a charm against evil.[4] Like David, Perseus, in his defeat of the snaky-haired Gorgon, was conflated with Christ as the vanquisher of Satan (Doebler, p. 138). Erich Neumann refers to the attainment of consciousness in terms of the 'higher masculinity of the head.' "The higher masculinity is the masculinity of the 'higher phallus' with the head as the seat of creative realization."[5]

Renaissance England continued the tradition of decapitation as a punishment for evil. The heads of executed traitors were impaled on pikes and placed on Traitor's Gate of London Bridge. Seeing these grisly heads prominently displayed on the imposing bridge, English citizens would be given a grim reminder of the power of the state to punish its enemies. Elizabethan drama reflects the head-hunting propensities of Elizabethan society in its depiction of the beheading of evildoers. Such incidents occur most prominently in Peele's *Old Wives Tale,* Marlowe's *Edward II,* and Shakespeare's *Richard III,* and *Macbeth.* A variation on the motif of decapitation takes place in Greene's *Friar Bacon and Friar Bungay* in which Friar Bacon attempts to create a Brazen Head which will surround England with a wall of brass. The Brazen Head becomes a representation of Bacon's evil necromantic powers and its destruction helps Bacon to disavow the dark arts.

In this essay I would like to explore the similarities in the ways which these plays present the motif of the severed or Brazen Head. Other plays like Shakespeare's *Titus Andronicus, Cymbeline,* and *Measure for Measure* contain beheadings, but they are either done solely as executions without the subsequent display of the head or serve merely as causes of misidentification as in *Cymbeline* where Cloten's headless body is confused with that of Posthumous. In the five plays I will discuss, "heads" receive a range of related meanings as: the physical feature of identification; the mental power which creates evil plots; the site of the royal crown; and finally, the severed appendage held aloft or smashed at the conclusion. Once the heads of the evil tyrants and magicians are cut and displayed, the land is able to grow again, and people regain their identities and are free to develop their personalities within mature relationships. I will begin with the two romantic comedies which place the various concepts of "heads in mythological and folkloric contexts, and then I will treat Marlowe's and Shakespeare's plays which incorporate these motifs into more realistic political contexts.

THE STRUGGLE AGAINST NECROMANCY: RITES DE PASSAGE

In George Peele's *The Old Wives Tale,* "heads" play significant roles as both good and evil forces. For most of the play, the evil magician Sacrapant controls his victims by depriving them of their identities. The aged conjurer has exchanged his wizened physiognomy for Erestus' youthful face, transforming the young man into the Old Man at the Crossroads during the day and at night into an ugly white bear. In addition, Sacrapant has deprived Erestus' wife Venelia of her senses, driving her, so to speak, out of her head, and at the same time he has bewitched and enslaved the lovely Delia renaming her Berecynthia. From these characters Sacrapant has stolen a principle of identity, a face, a mind, and a name.

Sacrapant is opposed by a rival order of beneficial forces represented by the magical Harvesters who appear twice and promise the fulfillment of true love; by Erestus whose prophetic riddles prove to be auspicious for the lost pilgrims he encounters; by the Heads at the Well of Life who provide balanced marriages and natural riches; and finally by Jack, the Grateful Dead, who enables Eumenides to rescue Delia by overthrowing Sacrapant. These forces are allied with natural fulfillment, mature identity, and true love. As Susan Viguers has remarked: ". . . the movement in both her [Madge's] tale and the world of her audience is natural and creative. Though both worlds begin in want and despair, they move to rewards and restoration."[6]

The natural, artistic and timely forces which bring about the restoration of identity and love are set in motion by offerings made to the Old Man At the Crossroads, a theme similar to the classical motif of propitiating Hecate and Hermes at the Crossroads, which represents the crucial point in a character's life. By paying homage to the Old Man, the pilgrims insure a favorable outcome for their journeys. When Delia's two brothers encounter him, they give Erestus alms, and in return he predicts that their future will turn out happy "when one flame of fire goes out,"[7] an event brought about by Venelia who destroys Sacrapant's power by blowing out the light in the conjurer's magic glass.

The once-uxorious Lampriscus, now burdened by his shrewish and plain daughters gives Erestus a pot of honey—an image of sweetness and fruitfulness—and the Old Man counsels him to send his daughters to the Well of Life where they are respectively matched with the deaf Huanebango, and the blind Corebus or Booby. When these two pilgrims had met the Old Man earlier, Huanebango had refused to give him any of his cake, but Booby cheerfully gave him a piece. At the Well of Life, the foul-tempered Zantippa spitefully smashes her pitcher on the Head which promises her wealth if she "Stroke me smooth, and comb my head" (778), and for her violent refusal to propitiate the Head, she is given the nonsensical and deaf Huanebango as her husband. But Celanta, the plain daughter, does accede to the Head's wish and receives corn and gold in her lap. She and Booby are rewarded for giving offerings to Erestus

and serving the Head at the Well of Life. Their reception of wealth from the life-giving Head strongly contrasts with the slavery and loss of identity suffered by those under the spell of Sacrapant's evil head, which must be destroyed if his victims are to be liberated.

Sacrapant's overthrow occurs as the result of Eumenides, the Wandering Knight, paying for Jack's burial. Although Eumenides' offering is not made directly to the Old Man at the Cross, he does obey Erestus' counsel to "Bestow they alms, give more than all, / Till dead men's bones come at thy call" (548-49). After receiving Erestus' command, Eumenides falls asleep, but is awakened by the squabbling over Jack's burial in parish grounds. Eumenides pays his last shilling to bury Jack and realizes that his generosity fulfills Erestus' prophecy. The Harvesters enter and again promise fruitfulness, and then Jack, the analogue to the Harvesters, the Heads at the Well, and Erestus, arrives to serve his new master Eumenides. Jack magically fills Eumenides' purse with money to pay for his meal at the inn, providing direct repayment for Eumenides' charity and a promise of riches to come.

When he helps Eumenides to defeat Sacrapant, Jack's actions involve the extinction of the powers connected with Sacrapant's head. Jack stuffs wool into Eumenides' ears to prevent his being enchanted by Sacrapant's words. When the latter sees that Eumenides does not hear his questions, the magician realizes he has been betrayed, and at this point Jack steals in and removes the wreath from the conjurer's head and the sword from his hand. This action resembles the deposition of a king who is divested of his crown and sword of office. Sacrapant describes his approaching death in terms of a royal reign being ended:

> What hand invades the head of Sacrapant?
> What hateful Fury doth envy my happy state?
> Then, Sacrapant, these are thy latest days.
> Alas, my veins are numbed, my sinews shrink,
> My blood is pierced, my breath fleeting away,
> And now my timeless date is come to end!
>
> (996-1001)

But the magic glass with the light still exists. This folk motif of the Life Index represented by a light in a glass provides another parallel to Sacrapant's head; it is an extension of himself, an image of his evil mind which is hidden from sight under the hill, unearthed by Eumenides, who digs with Sacrapant's former sword, and snuffed out by Venelia who is "neither maid, wife, nor widow" (1030). As Jack says: "Master, without this the conjurer could do nothing; and so long as this light lasts, so long doth his art endure, and this being out, then doth his art decay" (1015-20).

Once the light of Sacrapant's baleful mind is extinguished, "all are restored to their former liberty" (1035-36). Eumenides enters Sacrapant's cell and releases Delia, the Sleeping Princess. Jack approaches with Sacrapant's head in his hand and by displaying the conjurer's real head, the aged face which Erestus was forced to bear, the truth is revealed, the state is released from tyranny, identities are restored, and fruitful unions established. Susan Viguers remarks about the severed head: "Sacrapant's art presents illusion as though it were reality. That, contrary to appearance, Erestus is young and Sacrapant old is not something we see until Sacrapant's art is destroyed. . . . Eumenides cannot believe the head Jack holds is Sacrapant's, and we, the play's audience, also need reassurance that the strange new head is the same as the very different one the magician previously possessed. . . . Erestus when he enters at the end of the play as a young man must be welcome [sic] by name" (pp. 215-16). The evil head which deprived the characters of their true identities is held aloft as the defeated icon which is now controlled by the magician's former victims.

Peele's *The Old Wives' Tale* establishes a number of important themes and motifs found in the other plays to be discussed: 1) the use of political, artistic, and psychological imagery to describe both the ascendancy of the evil conjurer or leader and his defeat by the rival orders; 2) the presence of omens and prophecies and a final sense of truth achieved in the unfolding of time; 3) the magic glass representing the conjurer's diseased imagination and art; 4) the severed head as the icon of evil defeated. Although Robert Greene's *The Honorable History of Friar Bacon and Friar Bungay* does not contain a severed head, it does follow the theme of a head serving as an icon of evil ideas and ambitions. Roger Bacon attempts to create a Brazen Head which serves as an extension of his overreaching mind. Bacon, like Sacrapant, has an enchanted glass which he uses to show scenes that provoke viewers to violence. Like Sacrapant's magic glass it is destroyed as the means of signalling the end of Bacon's devotion to necromancy. But unlike Sacrapant who is defeated by his victims, Bacon himself destroys his fatal glass and casts aside his necromantic ambitions.

The double plot in *Friar Bacon and Friar Bungay* involving Prince Edward's lust for Margaret of Fressingfield and Bacon's plan to surround England with a brass wall is connected, as Empson astutely noted, by the similarity in the themes of love and magic as dangerous forces capable of divesting people of their senses and identities.[8] Edward's lust encourages his fool and alter ego Rafe Simnell to devise the plot which is designed to command Margaret's favors: "Why, Ned, I have laid the plot in my head; thou shalt have her already" (i. 98-99). Rafe exchanges roles with Prince Edward when they journey to Oxford to enlist Bacon's aid in their plot. Rafe institutes a Feast of Fools during which he reigns as the Lord of Misrule, leading a riotous foray into town, cracking a vinter's head with a

pitcher, and finally being arrested.[9] These revels emanate from Rafe's lunatic mind and they reflect directly upon Edward's lust which has transformed the "frolic" Prince into a fool.

When Edward looks into Bacon's "prospective glass" he sees his companion Edmund Lacy proposing marriage to Margaret instead of advancing Edward's cause as he has been delegated to do. Edward hastens to Fressingfield to kill them, but when he sees that they truly love each other, he repents and regains his moral and royal identity. Edward renounces his lust and returns to Oxford to meet his betrothed Eleanor of Castile and to assume his rightful royal duties as heir to his father Henry III.

A similar restoration of identity through the renunciation of evil occurs in the plot concerning Friar Bacon's attempts to create a Brazen Head which will reveal to him the means of building a wall around England. Bacon, the overreaching scholar and necromancer, is, like Prince Edward, equated with his fool and alter ego, the hapless subsizar Miles. Bacon is both fool and evil magician determined to achieve personal eminence and national impregnability through the dark arts.

The references to the fashioning of the Brazen Head are couched in demonic terms and reveal the immorality of Bacon's aspirations.[10] The Oxford don Burden accuses the friar of "making . . . a brazen head by art, / . . . And by the help of devils and ghastly fiends, . . ." (ii.29,35). Bacon acknowledges his commerce with the devils, admitting that he "made Belcephon hammer out the stuff" (61), and later explaining to Miles how he created the Brazen Head:

> With seven years' tossing nigromantic charms,
> Poring upon dark Hecat's principles,
> I have framed out a monstrous head of brass,
> That, by the enchanting forces of the devil,
> Shall tell out strange and uncouth aphorisms,
> And girt fair England with a wall of brass.

(xi.17-22)

According to Albert Wertheim, "The accumulation of evidence . . . links the friar's art to sinfulness and brings both the friar and the audience . . . to a recognition of a destructive magic. . . ."[11]

On the night for which he has worked so painstakingly, Bacon leaves the incompetent subsizar Miles to monitor the Head's words. Bacon's action in allowing Miles to be in charge parallels Edward's permitting Rafe to assume his identity. Bacon sleeps heavily and Miles nods off while the Head speaks three times, moving backwards chronologically from "Time is" to "Time is past," when a hand appears which smashes the Head with a hammer. This scene has interesting similarities and contrasts with the episode at the Well of Life when Zantippa smashes the Head and as a result loses wealth and mature marital fulfillment. Bacon does not stay awake to hear the Brazen Head and it is destroyed along with his dreams of grandeur. However, this destruction is morally good and necessary. The Head is a demonic creation and it should be destroyed, but nevertheless Bacon's neglect is seen as slothful and foolish (Wertheim, p. 283). Just as Sacrapant's "timeless date is ended" when his head is severed, so too the Brazen Head loses its effectiveness when Bacon forfeits control over it.

Bacon takes the loss of the Brazen Head as a direct blow against his reputation as a necromancer, talking about the Head as if it were his own head: "For Bacon shall have never merry day, / To lose the fame and honor of His Head" (xi.153-54). But Bacon finally renounces the dark arts when his "prospective glass" causes four deaths among the two generations of Lamberts and Serlsbys. This glass, like Sacrapant's with the light in it, represents Bacon's dangerous arts and his ambition to control life through demonic means. Unlike Sacrapant, however, Bacon destroys his own glass and in so doing frees his mind and art from demonic control: "So fade the glass, and end with it the shows / That nigromancy did infuse the crystal with" (xiii.83-84). Black magic has been renounced, Bacon has been reintegrated into society, Edward is now the rightful heir about to marry Eleanor of Castile, and England, purged of the princely excesses of lust and the necromantic overreaching of its leading intellectual, is depicted as a great power which shall rule "over all the west" (xvi.76).

THE HEAD AS REPOSITORY OF DISEASED THOUGHTS

The next three plays to be considered are distinguished from the first two by the fact that they are historical tragedies based on the cruel realities of political turmoil. In *Edward II* and *Macbeth* the severed head motif involves the decapitation of a usurper who is oppressing the land and must be destroyed if the country is to be restored to order. In *Richard III* a variation on this theme is introduced involving the manipulation of public opinion by the vicious Duke of Gloucester, who beheads a scapegoat, Hastings, to convince the people that this victim was undermining political order when in actuality it is Richard who is the villain. In all three of the plays men murder to insert themselves into the line of succession, but with their success they discover that the crowns rest uneasily on their heads. The usurpers and their victims and antagonists see the crown as an extension of their identities in much the same manner as they consider their heads as their chief identification. Also, the societies presented are obsessed with heads as the prime trophies of war and political struggle;

when someone threatens his antagonist he promises to have his head and to display it as a trophy.

Edward II is filled with references to heads being cut off. Such threats appear so frequently as to become the common coinage of political exchange. Edmund, Earl of Kent, counsels his brother Edward to take strong action against the rebellious Barons: "Brother, revenge it, and let these their heads/ Preach upon poles, for trespass of their tongues" (i.116-17). Mortimer, Junior, angrily returns Edward's threat: ". . . our hands I hope shall fence our heads, / And strike off his that makes you threaten us" (122-23). The Duke of Lancaster concentrates his ire on Edward's recalling his minion Gaveston, whom the Barons had exiled from England:

> Adieu, my lord; and either change your mind,
> Or look to see the throne, where you should sit,
> To float in blood, and at thy wanton head
> The glozing head of thy base minion thrown.
>
> (129-132)

After Gaveston is captured by the obdurate Barons, Mortimer Junior, taunts Gaveston by promising to send his head to Edward:

> Thus we'll gratify the king:
> We'll send his head by thee [Lancaster]. Let him bestow
> His tears on that, for that is all he gets
> Of Gaveston, or else his senseless trunk.
>
> (ix.48-51)

Like the Earl of Kent at the outset of the play, Edward's new aide Spencer, Junior, counsels greater severity against the rebels, telling Edward to place their severed heads on poles as lessons that "will teach the rest / . . . to learn obedience to their lawful king" (xi.21,23). When Edward hears of Gaveston's beheading, he reaches new heights of gory invective:

> I will have heads and lives for him, as many
> As I have manors, castles, towns and towers! . . .
> If I be England's king in lakes of gore
> Your headless trunks, your bodies will I trail,
> That you may drink your fill. . . .
>
> (xi.132-33, 135-37)

As the fortunes of war point to Edward's overthrow, the references to heads now concentrate on the royal crown as the synecdoche for the kingship and as the parallel to the head, man's chief part. After Mortimer, Junior, defeats and imprisons Edward, the King puts a curse on his crown:

> But, if proud Mortimer do wear this crown,
> Heavens turn it to a blaze of quenchless fire,
> Or, like the snaky wrath of Tisiphon,
> Engirt the temples of his hateful head!
>
> (xviii. 43-46)

When Edward is pressed to relinquish his crown, he equates it with his head and his life:

> Here take my crown—the life of Edward too; . . .
> But stay awhile; let me be king till night,
> That I may gaze upon this glittering crown.
> So shall my eyes receive their last content,
> My head, the latest honor due to it,
> And jointly both yield up their wished night.
>
> (57, 59-63)

He grabs the crown again for its transitory comfort and royal identity only to relinquish it again to the ambitious Mortimer, Junior.

Mortimer, Junior, rises to power, having overthrown Edward, consorted with Isabella, and controlled the callow Edward III. He beheads Edmund, Earl of Kent, for his attempt to free his brother Edward, and now he has only to kill the King at Killingworth Castle to obtain full power. But Mortimer overreaches himself and his masterminding of Edward's murder by Lightborn and the latter's murder by Matrevis and Gurney is revealed to young Edward, who has gained a certain strength and independence through his discovery of his mother's collusion with the Lord Protector. Edward III, armed with proof of Mortimer's evil plotting, threatens him with beheading:

> My father murdered through thy treachery;
> And thou shalt die, and on his mournful hearse,
> Thy hateful and accursed head shall lie, . . .
>
> (xxiii.27-30)

Edward III concentrates on Mortimer's head as the repository of the Lord Protector's evil plots and control over his family. By severing his head, Edward III avenges his father's and uncle's deaths, and at the same time provides graphic proof that he has come of age in this brutal society as his father's lawful and worthy successor. Appropriately, Edward III addresses Mortimer's "Accursed head, / [which] could I have ruled thee then, as I do now, / Thou hadst not hatched this monstrous treachery!—" (95-97). And Edward concludes the obsequies for his father by offering to "thy murdered ghost / . . . this wicked traitor's head;" (99-100).

Unlike *The Old Wives Tale* and *Edward II* where the beheadings of Sacrapant and Mortimer, Junior, are viewed as necessary and beneficial for the kingdom, in *Richard III* the beheading of the innocent Hastings is a political ploy created by the evil Richard to gain sympathy for his kingship. Richard emerges as the manipulator of the severed head as an image of evil destroyed. However, although Richard does become King on the strength of this as well as other political murders, in the end he loses at Bosworth Field and has the crown removed from his lifeless head.

As in *Edward II* there are numerous references to chopping off the heads of political opponents. When Richard sends Catesby to determine Hasting's feelings about the Duke's becoming King, Richard threatens to "Chop off his head [Hastings'],"[12] if he does not support him. After Catesby broaches the idea of Richard's kingship, Hastings prophetically replies: "I'll have this crown of mine cut from my shoulders / Ere I will see the crown so foul misplaced" (III.ii.43-44). Catesby, realizing that Hastings unwittingly has sentenced himself to death with this remark, slyly retorts: "The princes both make high account of you; / [Aside] For they account his head upon the bridge" (71-72).

At the Tower council called by Richard, the Duke accuses the unsuspecting Hastings of having conspired with Mistress Shore to torment his body through witchcraft: "Thou art a traitor; / Off with his head! . . . / I will not dine until I see the same" (III.iv.77-79). Hastings finally realizes that Stanley's dream and the old Queen Margaret's curse have indeed been prophetic:

> Stanley did dream the boar did raze his helm, . . .
> O Margaret, Margaret, now thy heavy curse
> Is lighted on poor Hastings' wretched head!
>
> (84, 94-95)

After Hastings' execution, Lovel and Ratcliff bring "the head of that ignoble traitor, / The dangerous and unsuspected Hastings" (III.v.22-23) to Richard who uses the severed head as the object of his moralizing about Hastings' hidden vices. Buckingham and he create this scene on the Tower walls with the Lord Mayor of London to convince him to accept their version of Hastings' villainy. The beheading and display of Hastings' head is an integral part of their managed political meeting which will elevate Richard to the crown.

The decapitation imagery continues after Richard's coronation. When Richard proves to be unsympathetic to his demand for the promised earldom of Hereford, Buckingham exclaims "O let me think on Hastings, and be gone / To Brecknock, while my fearful head is on! (IV.ii.125-26). And Lord Stanley knows that if he revolts against Richard, his young son George will lose his head" (IV.v.4). Finally, when Richard is killed at Bosworth, Derby enters bearing the crown which he presents to Richmond: "Lo, here, this long-usurped royalty / From the dead temples of this bloody wretch / Have I pluck'd off, to grace thy brows withal" (V.v.4-6). The crown, the royal extension of the head, has been removed from the tyrant and order restored to the troubled land.

The final play *Macbeth* sums up the traditions connected with the "heads" motif. In this grisly play, "head," as John Doebler has shown, appear as the site of the royal crown, as the appendage severed when one antagonist loses the battle, as an apparition produced by the weird sisters, and primarily as the repository of diseased thoughts which when activated bring death into the country. Shakespeare endows the "heads" motif with a greater psychological import as Macbeth's diseased mind creates a sick kingdom which can be returned to health only with the death of the vicious King and the severing of his malevolent head (Doebler, pp. 137-40).

From the outset the society presented is brutal in its emphasis on bloody battles and the punishments engendered by war. The bloody man who reports the battle to Duncan says that brave Macbeth defeated the rebel Macdonwald "And fix'd his head upon our battlements" (I.i.23), a foreshadowing of Macduff's beheading of Macbeth. After Macbeth meets the witches and hears that he will become Thane of Cawdor and then King, his mind becomes a battlefield of hidden desires, qualms, and fears. His vaunted single-mindedness fostered by war is fragmented by the intrusion of these unnatural desires for the "golden round":

> Let not night see my black and deep desires:
> The eye wink at the hand; yet let that be,
> Which the eye fears, when it is done, to see.
>
> (I.iv.51-53)

As the result of his ambitions, Macbeth must hide his thoughts from the public scrutiny and his head becomes a seething cauldron of conflicting ideas.

At Inverness as they await Duncan's fatal entrance to their castle, Lady Macbeth counsels her wavering husband to pretend to be cheerful and she does so in fragmentary terms:

> To beguile the time,
> Look like the time; bear welcome in your eye,
> Your hand, your tongue: . . .
>
> (v.64-65)

A short time before the murder, Macbeth claims that now he is "settled, and [will] bend up / Each corporal agent to this terrible feat" (vii.79-80), but he immediately returns to fragmentation: "Away, and mock the time with fairest show: / False face must hide what the false heart doth know" (81-82). It is as if his head has been divorced from the rest of his body and it shelters festering plots which eventually are fearfully enacted.

After the murder of Duncan, Macbeth's mind is full of scorpions but not from remorse. He is worried about the witches' prediction that Banquo's line will produce kings:

> They hail'd him father to a line of kings:
> Upon my head they placed a fruitless crown, . . .

> If't be so,
> For Banquo's issue have I filed my mind; . . .
> Put rancours in the vessel of my peace
> Only for them; . . .
>
> (III.i.59-67)

Macbeth sends out the three murderers to kill Banquo and his son, but Fleance escapes and later that evening at the banquet in honor of Banquo, Banquo's ghost enters and unnerves Macbeth. But as a result of this confrontation with the ghost, Macbeth gains a new courage to face his fears and enemies. He regains a unity of mind and act but this oneness is now directed totally toward bloody deeds.

Macbeth decides to visit the Weird Sisters again to determine his future. The first apparition is an armed Head, another foreshadowing of Macbeth's severed head at the end of the play, which warns him of Macduff. However, Macbeth dismisses the first apparition's advice when the other two figures give him false hope. Armed with their equivocal promises of impregnability, Macbeth determines to make his thoughts and actions one:

> . . . from this moment
> The very firstlings of my heart shall be
> The firstlings of my hand. And even now,
> To crown my thoughts with acts, be it thought and
>   done:
>
> (IV.i.147-149)

However, as Macbeth has grown more obdurate and accomplished in committing evil deeds, his wife has suffered a reversal in which her mind plagues her for their murderous acts. Macbeth tells the physician:

> Cure her of that.
> Canst thou not minister to a mind diseased,
> Pluck from the memory a rooted sorrow,
> Raze out the written troubles of the brain. . . .
>
> (V.iii.39-42)

But the "perilous stuff" of the mind exerts too heavy a burden upon Lady Macbeth and she dies, reputedly the victim of her own hand.

After her death, Macbeth resolves "to die with harness on our back" (v.52). On the battlefield, Macduff threatens to make Macbeth an object of scorn by painting his picture on a board and suspending it on a pole as a sign of his tyranny. This threat immediately foreshadows Macduff's beheading of Macbeth. Malcolm is hailed as the King by the lords of his kingdom, the cursed head which held the land in thrall is destroyed, time is once more released into its natural succession, and the rightful order and health of the country are restored. As Macduff holds Macbeth's head aloft, he resembles Perseus holding the Gorgon's head, as Doebler has pointed out (p. 138). Earlier Macbeth had said that the murdered Duncan resembled "a new Gorgon" (II.iii.76), but Macbeth has been the true Gorgon's head whose thoughts resulted in men's deaths. Now, however, the head cannot destroy men because it is severed from his body and displayed by his conqueror.[13]

CONCLUSION

In this essay, I have traced the thematic, psychological, and ritualistic aspects of the severed head in representative Elizabethan dramas. George Peele's **The Old Wives Tale** uses the severed head of the evil conjurer Sacrapant to signal the end of his ascendancy over his enthralled subjects and the onset of a new order of natural and personal fulfillment. In *Friar Bacon and Friar Bungay* Robert Greene shows how a Faustian friar goes too far in his attempts to create a Brazen Head which will build a wall of brass around England. The chauvinistic insularity represented by such an ideal is dismissed by Greene in favor of an image of an open, united and circular Europe. Marlowe's *Edward II* emphasizes the political rites of passage involved in the rise to power of Edward III after the murder of his father by the ruthless and ambitious Mortimer, Jr. The new king executes Mortimer and then holds aloft the traitor's head as the talisman to cast off its evil plots and influence. In a related context, Shakespeare's deformed villain Richard III manipulates public opinion and facilitates his rise to the kingship by displaying the severed head of his unwitting enemy Hastings as an emblem of the putative forces arrayed against him. But in fact, Richard is the evil head who institutes a bloody reign that comes to an end at Bosworth Field when he is killed and the crown he murdered for is recovered from under a bush. And finally, *Macbeth* completes the cycle of "headhunting" plays by repeating the earlier emphasis on necromancy and politics and by expanding the depiction of madness resulting from an uneasy crown.

The literary emphasis on severed heads is paralleled by the Elizabethan government's use of beheading as a punishment for treason, by the practice of the headsman holding the head aloft by its hair immediately after the execution and ritually intoning "So perish all traitors,"[14] and by the conspicuous display of the traitors' heads on London Bridge and Tower Hill. Both in literature and society, Elizabethan England placed great value on the head as the double-edged faculty of "creative realization" and identity.

Notes

1. For the general background on the history and significance of "heads," I am indebted to *The Encyclopedia of Religion and Ethics,* ed. James Hastings (New York: Charles Scribner's Sons,

1925), VI, 532-40; Theodore Gaster, *Myth, Legend, and Custom in the Old Testament* (New York: Harper and Row, 1969), #131, p. 457; and C. G. Jung, "Transformation Symbolism in the Mass," in *The Mysteries: Papers from the Eranos Yearbook,* ed. Joseph Campbell (1955; Princeton Univ. Press, 1978), II, 306-11.

2. C. G. Jung aptly points to the head as the seat of the *anima intellectualis. The Collected Works,* Bollingen Series XX, vol. 12, (New York: Princeton Univ. Press, 1968), 87, passim.

3. John Doebler: *Shakespeare's Speaking Pictures: Studies in Iconic Imagery* (Univ. of New Mexico Press, 1974), p. 30.

4. Oscar Seffert: *A Dictionary of Classical Antiquities,* rev. and ed. Henry Nettleship and J. E. Sandys (1891; New York: Meridian Library, 1959), pp. 258-59.

5. Erich Neumann: *The Origins of Consciousness,* Bollingen Series XLII, Pantheon Books, (New York: Bollingen Foundation, 1964), p. 77.

6. Susan Viguers: "The Hearth and the Cell: Art in *The Old Wives Tale,*" *SEL,* 21 (1981), 218.

7. George Peele: *The Old Wives' Tale,* in *Elizabethan Plays,* ed. and rev. Arthur, H. Nethercot, C. R. Baskervill, and Virgil B. Hetzel (New York: Holt, Rinehart & Winston, 1971), line 208. I have also used this anthology for the editions of Greene's *The Honorable History of Friar Bacon and Friar Bungay* and Marlowe's *Edward II.*

8. William Empson: *Some Versions of Pastoral* (New York: New Directions, 1974), pp. 31-34.

9. Peter Mortenson: *"Friar Bacon and Friar Bungay:* Festive Comedy and 'Three-Formed Luna,'" *ELR,* 2 (1972), 194-207.

10. Vergil, Gerbert, who later became Pope Sylvester II, Albertus Magnus, and Robert Grosseteste, Bishop of Lincoln, were traditionally linked with the creation of oracular speaking heads. See: Domenic Comparetti, *Vergil in the Middle Ages,* trans. E. F. M. Benecke (New York: Macmillan, 1895), p. 272n. Greene's play *The Comical Historie of Alphonsus, King of Aragon* (IV.i.1195-1225) also contains an oracular Brazen Head, but here the Head serves merely as the mouthpiece of Mahomet. It is not created by a human being for divination.

11. Albert Wertheim: "The Presentation of Sin in 'Friar Bacon and Friar Bungay,'" *Criticism,* 16 (1974), 274.

12. For the text of *Richard III*—and *Macbeth*—I have used *The Complete Works of Shakespeare,* ed. Hardin Craig (Chicago: Scott, Foresman & Company), III.i.193.

13. In *Shakespeare's Typological Satire: A Study of the Falstaff-Oldcastle Problem* (Ohio Univ. Press, 1979), pp. 296 and 365n, Alice Scoufas relates the beheading of Macbeth to the decapitation of Thomas Percy, one of the chief conspirators against King James I in the Gunpowder Plot. Percy's head was impaled on a pole and placed above the Parliament Building where it remained for many years.

14. Norah Lofts: *Anne Boleyn* (New York: Coward, McCann & Geoghegan, Inc., 1979), p. 179.

Mary G. Free (essay date 1984)

SOURCE: Free, Mary G. "Audience within Audience in *The Old Wives Tale*." In *Renaissance Papers 1983*, edited by A. Leigh Deneef and M. Thomas Hester, pp. 53-61. Raleigh, N.C.: The Southeastern Renaissance Conference, 1984.

[*In the following essay, Free investigates Peele's communication with the audience in* The Old Wives Tale.]

The action which begins Peele's **The Old Wives Tale** is universally called an Induction; the term is somewhat inaccurate.[1] An Induction usually serves as a preface or prelude. Certainly, the dialogue of the jesters, Clunch, and Madge, gets things going; yet most Inductions in pre-seventeenth century drama have another characteristic—they end.[2] Once the play proper is underway, the characters of an Induction may disappear—as with those in the Christopher Sly Induction in *The Taming of the Shrew*—or become absorbed into the ensuing action—as with A and B in Medwall's *Fulgens and Lucrece* or Ralph in *The Knight of the Burning Pestle*. By contrast Madge and two of the jesters remain on stage observing and commenting on the action which follows as well as concluding the play. They neither vanish nor take up roles. They become instead an audience within an audience.

I use the phrase "audience within audience" deliberately. "Play within a play" limits attention to the intertextuality of the frame and the play within. What concerns me here depends upon that interrelationship but goes beyond the limitations it imposes. I wish to examine how Peele handles audience in **The Old Wives Tale.** Two audiences are present for this play. The first is the literal audience which has assembled in a Great Hall to view an evening's entertainment. This audience is external to the action within the play being presented. The second audience is the stage audience Peele has created to frame and comment on the action of the "old wives winters tale" which comes to life before their eyes.[3] It is this audience within audience which allows Peele to experiment.

If any play of the late Eighties or early Nineties demonstrates the attempt to maintain a sense of contact with the audience (a holdover from the Tudor Interludes) and at the same time create a self-contained play, it is Peele's **The Old Wives Tale.** The self-contained quality of this play is evident at the very beginning. Peele begins his play with three courtly clowns. The dialogue they exchange serves a basic expository function, and it arises naturally out of their situation. We learn that they are separated from the court and the master they serve and that they are lost in a wood. The dialogue establishes the comic tone as well. Such a natural beginning contrasts significantly with the cry to "make way" or the call for "room" which signaled the opening of the action of many Tudor Interludes. In fact, nothing in the first thirty lines of this play acknowledges the presence of an audience external to the action being performed. **The Old Wives Tale** thus opens as a self-contained play and appears to have moved beyond the need for extra-dramatic address.

Peele does not, however, ignore the audience; in fact, he cannot. As Anne Righter states, "Elizabethan dramatists were . . . obliged to associate their patrons with their characters, to define the relationship of the real world, represented by this ubiquitous audience with the illusory country of the play."[4] Peele establishes this obligatory sense of contact when the pages encounter Clunch and beg his hospitality. Clunch offers the pages "house roome, and a good fire to sit by," but far more significant is his next statement: "For your further intertainment, it shall be as it may be, so and so" (47-48, 51-52). In having the clowns accept Clunch's hospitality as graciously as they would from a more noble host, Peele creates a paradigm of the literal audience assembled in a Great Hall to observe an "entertainment" that their host will provide for their amusement. Clunch's "For your intertainment" works on two levels. It refers directly to his own "guests"—the three pages—and at the same time encompasses that greater assembled group—the audience external. Peele maintains this double view throughout.

Peele continues the paradigm when the pages enter the cottage. Madge extends the hospitality further by offering food which they refuse saying, "We come *to chat* and not *to eat*" (63, my italics). While this statement and Clunch's "take away"—to clear the table—naturally extend the dialogue, they also serve as comments on the activities going on in the Hall: that is, activities outside the context of the play world. I suggest an additional possibility as well. With the use of the infinitive "to chat" Peele may be alluding to the activity taking place within the play world. As the group on stage chats, someone must hear and attend to that chatter—that is, their performance.

Although the pages' names—Anticke, Fantasticke, Frolicke—along with the witty dialogue, the songs, and the emphasis on hospitality demonstrate that the external audience will not see a moral interlude, Peele makes his subject, romance, explicit with Anticke's request for a "merry winter's tale" (83). Fantasticke suggests a time limit of an hour—appropriate to a play this length—while Frolicke asks for a giant and a king's daughter in the plot. Peele also makes the audience within explicit as Fantasticke announces, "Ile be one of your audience," and Frolicke adds, "And I another thats flat" (98-99).

At this point the actors playing Anticke and Clunch depart the stage. They doubtless reappear to double and triple among the nineteen remaining named roles plus assorted furies, fiddlers, harvesters, and one friar. The significant point about their departure from the audience within is that they leave as the characters Anticke and Clunch. No crossover takes place between the audience within and the play world of the play within. Peele preserves the dramatic illusion he has created. He may, however, make a punning reference to the doubling. Earlier I suggested that "to chat" might be an overt reference on Peele's part to the play-acting. Here, as Anticke and Clunch leave, Clunch says, "Come on, my lad, thou shalt take thy unnatural rest with me" (102-03). As with "to chat" this bit of dialogue grows naturally from the action. Rather than Clunch lying with Madge or Anticke with his companions, these two will make strange bed-fellows. On another level, their rest will indeed be unnatural as they assume their various roles in the play within.

Once Anticke and Clunch depart the stage, the subject among the three characters remaining on stage turns to audience behavior. Madge insists that Frolicke and Fantasticke must "hum" and "ha" during her tale so that she will know they are awake. The pages agree to do so, thus setting up their later interruptions of the action and, at the same time, acknowledging the interruptions characteristic from the external audience, as Richard Southern has demonstrated.[5] Frolicke, in fact, complies almost immediately by interrupting Madge's story. His comment, however, is neither "hum" nor "ha"; instead it halts the plot and serves as a means for him to call attention to himself and possibly get a laugh. Madge's bawdy response, "Nay, either heare my tale or kisse my taile" (117), indicates that while *sotto voce* murmur serves its purpose, a good audience eschews such blatant intervention in the action.

The next interruption to Madge's tale is actually its continuation as the play within gets underway. All three members of the audience within acknowledge the players' arrival and thus alert the external audience to the beginning of the play within. Frolicke says that the players have come "to tell" the tale for Madge. As with "to chat" Peele again uses an infinitive associated with speaking to describe the performance taking place. Fantasticke follows with a command: "Let them alone, let us *heare* what they will say" (131, my italics), hearing

being appropriate attention to the telling of a tale. Yet this line raises two questions in regard to the audiences involved. First, to whom does Fantasticke address his command of "Let them alone," and second, who is the "us" of "let us heare"? He may be speaking to his companions on stage, the command carrying the idea of keeping quiet. If so, the "us" of the second question is Fantasticke himself, Peele having him use the royal plural. On the other hand, Peele may be reverting to the Interlude technique of direct audience address. In this case Fantasticke's command is for the audience external and carries the suggestion that the players enter through the Hall and therefore through the assembled crowd to get to the acting area. The "us" then becomes the audience within—Frolicke, Fantasticke, and Madge—who can no longer hear given the stir the players' arrival has created in the audience external. In either case Fantasticke's line becomes an extension of Madge's earlier guide to audience behavior.

Given the audience within audience Peele has constructed, I suggest that Fantasticke addresses both audiences simultaneously. Peele has given us an audience on stage, the audience within, which might interfere with the players' entrance. Such interference on stage serves as a parallel to any interference the audience external might engage in as the players move toward the acting area. In addressing the audience within as to its proper behavior, Peele addresses and controls his second audience, the audience external. Peele has no need to break the dramatic illusion by reverting to the Interlude technique of direct address. The paradigm obtains.

The next intrusion by the audience within occurs 112 lines into the play within. Employing a musical metaphor, an appropriate introduction for the Harvestmen's singing and dancing, Frolicke asserts that "this goes round without a fiddling stick" (243). The audience within introduces the harvestmen, thus providing information for the external audience. On the harvestmen's departure, they indicate the arrival of two new characters, Huanebango and Booby. Madge's answer to "Gammer, what is he" when Huanebango first appears is a simple "Let him alone; hear what he says" (254-56). In other words, let him speak for himself since the players have come to tell her tale. As before, the admonition applies to both audiences.

Two hundred and seventy-four lines pass between this interruption and the next. At this point, Peele uses the audience within to alert the audience external to Jack's importance and to the fact that he will appear again later in the play. Madge's "You shall see anon what this Jack will come to" (531-32) reinforces Fantasticke's observation that Jack held great sway in the community. It also strengthens Madge's position as a storyteller. These comments conclude the Jack-Eumenides episode for the moment, and Frolicke's "Soft, who have we heere" (533) introduces the second song and dance of the harvesters. Their departure occasions yet another interruption. Huanebango and Corebus reappear. Frolicke greets their second appearance with the same question he used for the harvesters, "Soft, who have we here?" (539). Madge offers a fuller reply than she gave when these two characters first appeared, a fact which has led Harold Jenkins to argue that the play as we have it is a mutilated text.[6] Jenkins argues that Madge's fuller assessment of Huanebango's nature should precede his first speech. Dramatically speaking, Jenkins' position will not work. To introduce Huanebango as a fool before he himself has a chance to reveal his own foolishness would destroy the comic effect of his first speech. Once he has so presented himself, however, Madge can mock his second entrance and ironically warn both audiences to "keepe out of the smell of his two handed sworde" (541-42). Fantasticke's observation—"Methinkes the Conjurer should put the foole into a Jugling boxe" (543-44)—supports the logic of having Madge make the fuller statement at Huanebango's second entrance. Having already witnessed the braggart's asinine behavior, Fantasticke draws his own conclusion and reinforces that of the audience external.

At this point Peele dispenses with the comments of the audience within until the play within concludes some 361 lines later. Ironically, it is Madge who has dozed off and the pages who must awaken her. Upon awakening, she finishes her tale; her last business pertaining to the play within is to sum up and clarify. She then turns to the pages: "But come, let us in, we will have a cup of ale and a tost this morning, and so depart" (922-24). As if her point is unclear, Fantasticke asks if the tale is indeed at an end. She replies with a variation of her previous conclusion: "When this was done I tooke a peece of bread and cheese, and came my way, and so shall you have too before you goe, to your breakefast" (926-28).

This double close raises two further questions about Peele's handling of his audiences. The pages entered Madge's cottage earlier. Where can they go "in" to partake of the ale and a toast? I suggest that with Madge's first ending, Peele begins to conclude his audience within audience paradigm. The "come let us in" starts to dissolve the illusion between the play world and the real world beyond. Fantasticke completes the dissolution with his question if the tale is over. While Madge's offer of hospitality again forms a parallel to the activity which would follow an entertainment in the Hall, the call for the actors to go "in" suggests their leaving the stage and returning the Hall to the control of the audience external.

Another question arises from the second conclusion. What purpose is there to this double close? In the second closing, Madge turns from offering the pages hospitality to enjoying that hospitality herself—"I tooke a peece of bread and cheese, and came my way." She then alludes to the presence of others—"so shall you

have"; but who is the "you"? The use of the past tense indicates that Madge has finished her toast with the pages and has left them, which would further indicate the dissolving of the illusion. On this second conclusion, Sidney Musgrove offers an interesting and, I believe, appropriate reading.[7] He suggests that with the second conclusion Madge has left the company of the pages and thus turns from the play and its self-contained world to the audience in the Hall. Her "so shall you have" becomes an extension of the host's hospitality. The "you" here at the end is specifically the audience external. To turn to direct address at this point does not violate the self-contained quality of the play. It serves as epilogue.

Peele had used this technique of turning to the audience earlier in **The Arraignment of Paris,** but there, as Righter notes, he "destroys the illusion. Diana . . . throws the play into confusion when she delivers [the golden ball] into the hands of the real Queen Elizabeth."[8] His use of the audience within audience in **The Old Wives Tale** shows an advancement in dramatic structure. Madge has dismissed her audience. The past tense of her "I tooke a peece of bread and cheese, and came my way" implies that she has been rewarded for her work, just as the audience external will be for its tolerance. Her turning outward and offering food has an interesting analogue as well. Richard Southern cites the stage direction near the opening of *The Coblers Prophesie* (ca. 1594).[9] In it we have a true Induction. Ceres ends the Induction by breaking the illusion between stage and audience. She orders Mercury to distribute sweetmeats to those assembled. The stage direction reads *"Cast Comfets."* What better way to achieve no interruption greater than a "hum" or "ha" than to keep the audience's mouth closed with comfets. Peele's comfet has been his play, and his means of controlling the spectators his audience within an audience.

Notes

1. The representative major studies of *The Old Wives Tale* which refer to the "Induction" are as follows: M. C. Bradbrook, "Peele's *Old Wives Tale:* A Play of Enchantment," *English Studies,* 43 (1962), 323-30; Herbert Goldstone, "Interplay in Peele's *The Old Wives Tale,*" *Boston University Studies in English,* 4 (1963), 202-13; F. B. Gummere, introd., *The Old Wives Tale,* by George Peele, in *Representative English Comedies,* Vol. I, ed. C. M. Gayley (London, 1903), pp. 340-48; Frank S. Hook, introd.. *The Old Wives Tale,* by George Peele, in *The Dramatic Works of George Peele* (New Haven, 1970), pp. 303-84; Harold Jenkins, "Peele's Old Wive's Tale," *MLR,* 34 (1939), 177-85; Gwenan Jones, "The Intention of Peele's 'Old Wives' Tale,'" *Aberystwyth Studies,* 7 (1925), 79-93; Thorlief Larson, "'The Old Wives Tale' by George Peele," *Transactions of the Royal Society of Canada,* 29 (1935), 157-70; Sidney Musgrove, "Peele's 'Old Wives Tale': An Afterpiece?" *Jour-*

nal of the Australasian Universities Language and Literature Association, 23 (1965), 86-95.

In these studies the major point of discussion centers upon the intention of the play within, that is whether or not it is a parody of heroical romance. As a result Peele's audience within audience receives attention only as a means of getting us to the action of the play within. These discussions then give but cursory note to the presence of the on-stage audience. The exception is Musgrove's study. He rightly perceives Peele's use of the audience within as a framing device although he refers to the action which precedes the play within as an "Induction."

2. The Induction to *The Spanish Tragedy* remains an exception. The Ghost of Andrea and Revenge begin and end that play. Their function remains choric, however, as Revenge states prior to the beginning of the play proper. As chorus they are more involved as actors within the overall play structure and function less as a pure audience. The on-stage audience in *The Old Wives Tale,* as I demonstrate, never loses its focus as audience. In the later *Pericles* (ca. 1607) and *Every Man Out of His Humour* (1600), the characters in the inductions remain throughout. Gower, as with the Ghost of Andrea and Revenge, serves as chorus rather than audience as I define it here. In *Every Man Out of His Humour* Asper and Mitis do form an audience within audience but one later than Peele's. Further, the question exists whether the Induction to Jonson's play was acted or added later for publication, whereas Peele's Induction is an integral part of the entire play structure. For a full discussion of the Induction in *Every Man Out of His Humour* see L. A. Beaurline, *Jonson and Elizabethan Comedy* (San Marino, 1978), pp. 110-20.

3. *The Old Wives Tale,* ed. Frank S. Hook, in *The Dramatic Works of George Peele* (New Haven, 1970), p. 391, l. 96. All subsequent references appear in the text and refer to this edition.

4. *Shakespeare and the Idea of Play* (New York, 1962), p. 60.

5. See *The Staging of Plays before Shakespeare* (London, 1973).

6. Jenkins, pp. 177-85.

7. Musgrove, pp. 86-95. Although I agree with Musgrove on this point, I disagree with his suggestion that Peele's play is an afterpiece. The play is too long and too self-contained to be an afterpiece.

8. Righter, p. 19.

9. Southern, p. 580.

Frank Ardolino (essay date winter 2004)

SOURCE: Ardolino, Frank. "Peele's Attack on Simony in *The Old Wives Tale.*" *ANQ* 17, no. 1 (winter 2004): 9-11.

[*In the following essay, Ardolino illuminates the significance of Simon's name in* The Old Wives Tale.]

The Old Wives Tale contains a longstanding crux in the scene dealing with the controversy over the burial of Jack in sanctified ground. In the first and only quarto edition, which was published in 1595 after the Queen's Men had performed the play, the churchwarden's first speech at line 459 has a speech prefix indicating that his name is Simon. But he is subsequently identified twice as the Churchwarden, and in lines 495-96 he refers to himself and is referred to as Stephen Loach. Frank Hook, the editor of the authoritative Yale edition of the play, conjectured that this crux may be part of the play's overall confusion of character names such as the appearance of the dual names of Corebus and Booby for the same clownish figure. Hook also mentioned H. M. Dowling's suggestion that Simon may indicate the actor playing the role, John Symons, who joined the Queen's Men in 1588 or 1589, but, finally, he concluded that perhaps Peele includes both names because he had not made up his mind (3: 349). More recently, McMillin and MacLean have suggested that Simon may refer to Simon Jewell, who was probably a member of the Queen's Men (111). Although it is true that actors' names were sometimes substituted in Elizabethan play quartos for the characters they played, it is more probable that by identifying the greedy churchwarden as Simon, Peele is directing his reader to understand this incident in the Protestant context of attacking simony.

In the play, Eumenides has come from Thessaly to rescue Delia from the evil magician Sacrapant. When he encounters Erestus, the old man at the crossroads whom he calls "just time" (432), the *senex* tells him that to rescue her he must achieve "wisdome govern'd by advise" (443) and must repent that he has given more money than he has as alms "Till dead mens bones come at thy call" (446).[1] This advice leaves him perplexed, and, as he stands there confused, a scene unfolds before him that is directly related to Erestus's prophecy. The sexton and the churchwarden are demanding more offerings for the proper burial in sanctified ground of Jack, who is described by Steven Loach as "not worth a halfepenny, and drunke out every penny" (489-90). Jack's brother Wiggen and his friend Corebus attack their venality vociferously, and Eumenides attempts to calm the explosive situation by paying the final fee of fifteen or sixteen shillings, which leaves him with only a three-half-pence, as Erestus had foretold.

The demand by the avaricious church officials that the exorbitant funerary dues of one hundred mourning gowns be paid for Jack's sanctified burial is directly connected with anticlerical satire and the Reformation attack on simony. Significantly, Peele changes the traditional folk motif of Jack's generalized debts in the "Grateful Dead" tales to funeral dues instead (Hook 3: 325). Simony, the buying and selling of ecclesiastical blessings, pardons, and offices, was named after Simon Magis, the magician who challenged St. Peter in Acts 8.20 by offering the apostles money to obtain their seemingly magical powers. The practice was the target of Luther's ninety-five theses, and, as Bowker has pointed out, simony was considered the greatest sin of the age because it served as the central part of the Roman Catholic financial system of mortuary endowments, indulgences, masses, and prayers, all of which were intended to lessen the time that sinners must spend in Purgatory before ascending to heaven (86).

English anticlericalism specifically directed its attack against the church's collection of tithes and mortuary dues and the sale of indulgences (Dickens 92). In his important treatise, *Supplication of Beggars* (1529), Simon Fish accused the clerics of stealing wealth that belonged to the poor people and of creating a vast system of financial pillaging. Similarly, Bishop Jewel in *An Apology of the Church of England* (1562) attacked simony as a crime against true spirituality: "[W]hat one is there of all the fathers which hath taught you to distribute Christ's blood and the holy martyr's merits, and to sell openly as merchandises your pardons and all the rooms and lodgings of purgatory?" (92). As a result of these attacks, Parliament put pressure on the church to regulate mortuary and probate fees according to the ability of the people to pay commensurate with their financial condition (Dickens 95).

Protestantism championed the giving of voluntary charitable acts in place of enforced payments (Russell 267). Good works freely tendered promote a good community; simony, however, implies a loss of honor for those forced to pay (Wall 158). In *The Old Wives Tale,* Peele shows the benefits of a voluntary system of charity as opposed to the coercion practiced by the churchwarden. Those characters who freely give Erestus offerings or, as in the case of Eumenides, bestow alms according to his bidding, receive favorable prophecies and beneficial results. Because Eumenides helped Jack receive a sanctified burial, Jack returns to life as his companion, who helps him rescue his beloved Delia and kill Sacrapant.

Thus, the use of the name *Simon* is not a mistake on Peele's part or a reference to the actor playing the role of the churchwarden. It is an indication by Peele of the simoniac practices of the Catholic Church authorities, as personified by Steven Loach, whose surname also meant *fool* in the sixteenth century (*OED* s.v. *loach,* def. 3).

Note

1. All quotations and line references are from Hook's edition.

Works Cited

Bowker, Margaret. "The Henrician Reformation and the Parish Clergy." *The English Reformation Revised.* Ed. Christopher Haigh. Cambridge: Cambridge UP, 1987. 75-93.

Dickens, A. G. *The English Reformation.* New York: Schocken, 1964.

Hook, Frank S., ed. *The Old Wives Tale. The Dramatic Works of George Peele.* Vol. 3. New Haven: Yale UP, 1970.

Jewel, John. *An Apology of the Church of England.* Ed. J. E. Booty. Ithaca: Cornell UP, 1963.

McMillin, Scott, and Sally-Beth MacLean. *The Queen's Men and Their Plays.* Cambridge: Cambridge UP, 1998.

Russell, Conrad. "The Reformation and the Creation of the Church of England, 1500-1640." *The Oxford Illustrated History of Tudor and Stuart Britain.* Ed. John Morrill. Oxford: Oxford UP, 1996. 258-92.

Wall, John. "Church of Rome." *The Spenser Encyclopedia.* Ed. A.C. Hamilton et al. Toronto: U of Toronto P, 1990. 153-60.

DAVID AND BETHSABE (C. 1594)

CRITICAL COMMENTARY

Inga-Stina Ewbank (essay date 1965)

SOURCE: Ewbank, Inga-Stina. "The House of David in Renaissance Drama: A Comparative Study." *Renaissance Drama* 8 (1965): 3-40.

[*In the following essay, Ewbank examines the genre of Peele's* David and Bethsabe, *comparing it to other plays handling the same material.*]

> Si j'avais à . . . [exposer sur le théâtre] . . . [l'histoire] de David et de Bethsabée, je ne décrirais pas comme il en devint amoureux en la voyant se baigner dans une fontaine, de peur que l'image de cette nudité ne fît une impression trop chatouilleuse dans l'esprit de l'auditeur; mais je me contenterais de le peindre avec de l'amour pour elle, sans parler aucunement de quelle manière cet amour se serait emparé de son cœur.[1]

It is highly unlikely that when Corneille wrote the above words, in his *Examen de Polyeucte,* he should have known of an English play, written some sixty or seventy years earlier, in which the episode of King David watching the bathing Bathsheba is not just described but actually put on the stage.[2] Corneille was discussing how to deal dramatically with religious, and especially biblical, material; and he was doing so at a time, well over a hundred years after Buchanan's *Jephthes,* when humanists all over Europe had proved the possibility of christianizing the Tragic Muse, of serving both the ancients (but more specifically the not-quite-so-ancient Seneca) and the Lord. French dramatists in particular had been quick to see that the Bible contained as much potentially tragic material as classical myth;[3] but at about the same time as Corneille was working on his play about Polyeucte, saint and martyr, Milton was pondering over biblical topics for tragedy and noting down as possibilities, among others, "David Adulterous," "Tamar," and "Achitophel." The House of David might be as fruitful as the House of Atreus when it came to furnishing a tragic plot, and there was always the advantage that scriptural authority would, by definition, make the argument not less but more heroic.

> L'execrable Inceste d'Amnon
> Dont tu peints si bien la vengeance,
> Plus que la mort d'Agamemnon
> Tesmoigne de Dieu la puissance,

we read in a commendatory ode on N. Chrestien's play about how David's son Amnon raped his sister Tamar and was, in revenge, slain by his brother Absalom.[4] Corneille, too, assumes that biblical story has the sanctity of divine inspiration about it, so that a dramatist using such material may not change anything in his source. But his second point, and the one that leads up to the quotation above, deals with the *omissions* which may be made—provided always that one does not obscure "ces verités dictées par le Saint-Esprit." In the cause of dramatic decorum and unity of impact, he says, one must be selective. It is here that Corneille becomes immediately relevant to my main theme in this essay, because he shows how, in neoclassic theory, the standards of the "well-made" play are already looming up. He is in fact anticipating the criteria by which George Peele's play, *The Love of King David and Fair Bethsabe, With the Tragedie of Absalon,* is still most frequently judged—and by which, inevitably, it is seen as the result of "shapeless unselectivity of incidents."[5]

There has always been disagreement as to what kind of a play *David and Bethsabe* really is. Peele's own title page shows a happy disregard of genres. Restoration play-lists call it a tragicomedy.[6] Thomas Warton places it in the medieval miracle tradition.[7] F. S. Boas veers between "revenge tragedy" and an almost Polonian labeling of the play as "Scriptural chronicle-history."[8] Lily B. Campbell is practically alone in taking it seriously as a new departure in drama, "a divine play conscious of its place in divine literature"; but even she finds the structure "cluttered with episodes."[9] Scholars

are, perhaps, no longer as anxious as they once were to father onto Peele every shapeless Elizabethan play of unknown authorship, but he still tends to be used as an example of someone who "cared little for structural consistency."[10] We might do well to listen to Wolfgang Clemen when he says that, in order to do justice to Peele's plays,

> dürfen wir sie nicht mit den üblichen Massstäben dramatischer Einheit und Komposition beurteilen, sondern müssen nach ihrer Eigengesetzlichkeit fragen.[11]

In this essay I propose to work toward a definition of that "Eigengesetzlichkeit" in *David and Bethsabe* and to do so by looking at other dramatic treatments of Peele's source (i.e., 2 Samuel XI-XIX.8), as well as at nondramatic versions of the story, wherever they illuminate points in the plays under consideration.

Peele's is the only Elizabethan play on the subject of the House of David: if the fourteenpence paid by Henslowe in October 1602 for "poleyes & worckmanshipp for to hange absalome" were spent on a play other than Peele's, that play is now lost. We therefore have to go abroad for comparative material, and rightly so, for—as scholars like F. S. Boas, and more recently Lily B. Campbell and Marvin T. Herrick, have shown—the Renaissance desire to turn Bible story into drama was a European, rather than a localized, phenomenon.[12] If anything, the English dramatists, academic as well as popular, seem to have been more wary of tackling this type of drama than, for example, their Dutch and French contemporaries. Comparisons for comparison's sake are odious, but in this case I hope that a comparative method, while incidentally throwing some light on the ways in which the same source material is shaped by different individuals in different dramatic traditions, will mainly prove helpful toward defining the nature of the play we have before our eyes.

At the outset, however, something must be said about the *text* we have before our eyes.[13] There is no doubt that the text of the quarto of *David and Bethsabe* printed in 1599 is garbled. There are such flagrant corruptions and problems as the three misplaced lines, 1660-1662, which belong nowhere in the play as it stands; the "5. Chorus" which is the second, and last, in the play; and the reference in this chorus to "a third discourse of Dauids life," with its never fulfilled promise of showing us "his most renowmed death" (ll. 1654-1655). I cannot deal here with the textual riddles of the play, but for the purposes of my argument they seem to have been solved satisfactorily by A. M. Sampley's theory, which is that Peele originally wrote a five-act play dealing with the love of David and Bathsheba and the tragedy of Absalom.[14] This version was cut for stage performances and gradually got so mutilated that in the end it had to be revised to be brought back to a more reasonable length. The play, then, in its present form represents a drastically cut stage version of the play as Peele first wrote it, plus an addition (the Solomon scene) made by Peele before sending it to the printer. The important point, to my argument, is that we can be fairly certain, because of the homogeneity of the style throughout, that the final revision was carried out by Peele himself. That being so, the present text—apart from such obvious errors as undeleted lines—represents what Peele himself deemed ready for the stage and for the reader. To Sampley it stands as a proof that Peele was not interested in "structural consistency." I shall argue, however, that the play has virtues—a kind of imaginative shape and thematic unity—which have not been allowed for; and I hope to bring these out by discussing what qualities there are in Peele's play that are not also in others dealing with the same subject, and vice versa.

David and Bethsabe opens with a Prologue which takes the form of an epic invocation—

> Of Israels sweetest singer now I sing,
> His holy stile and happie victories—

but, as the "Prologus" *"drawes a curtaine, and discouers Bethsabe with her maid bathing ouer a spring: she sings, and Dauid sits aboue vewing her,"* it is hardly one of the happy victories he presents. Peele's audience would have been conditioned toward two kinds of response to this scene, and in his treatment of the love of David and Bathsheba, Peele draws on both.

> Adam, Sansonem, Loth, David, sic Salomonem
> Femina decepit . . .

we read in the neo-Latin *Comedia Sancti Nicolai,*[15] and here we have in a nutshell the first attitude to David the lover, one which the sixteenth century had inherited from the Middle Ages. David's *sin* is emphasized and seen as another version of the Fall, with Bathsheba as another Eve. The David and Bathsheba story had become an *exemplum* to illustrate one of the great medieval moral-satirical themes. As late as 1581 there was printed in London a collection of the dialogues of Ravisius Textor, where in the *Dialogus* between "Troia," "Salomon," and "Sanson" we find the following well with three buckets:

TROIA:

> Quis generi humano Paradisi limina clausit?

SALOMON:

> Foemina. Quis lyrici cantus Davida peritum
> Fecit adulterium committere?

SANSON:

> Foemina. Sed quis
> Aeneam valido fecit confligere Turno?

TROIA:

> Foemina. Qui veteres fecit pugnare Sabinos
> Contra Romanes pastores?

SALOMON:

> Foemina . . .[16]

And so on, until the whole dialogue adds up to a flaming indictment of woman. Again, David's sin is linked with Adam's, as well as with that of the heroes of classical myth and history. David and Bathsheba form one of the examples of the Triumph of Love in Petrarch's *Trionfi* (together with such figures as Alexander the Great, Pyramus and Thisbe, and Hero and Leander), and of adultery ("true," historical, adultery as against the fictitious sins of classical myth) in Brant's *Narrenschiff.*[17]

To the less sophisticated members of the audience the image of David as the adulterous sinner would come from more familiar sources, fictional and homiletic. In a "pleasant fable" George Gascoigne showed how insidiously a would-be adulterer could use the example of David to argue his case;[18] and Vives, in his *Instruction of a Christen Woman,* used David as a warning example in his chapter "Of Loving."[19] In 1589 Henry Holland published a moral treatise called *Dauids Faith and Repentance,* in which is described how David saw Bathsheba washing herself,

> whereby his filthie lustes became so vehement, and kindled in him such a fire, that he could not, as in his former assaults, call for the presence of Gods spirit.[20]

Although the play entered on the Stationers' Register in 1561 as "an new interlude of the ii synnes of kynge David" is not extant, one can well imagine what it must have contained, especially as John Bale, in his *Tragedy or enterlude manyfestyng the chefe promyses of God unto men,* had shown the Lord rebuking David:

> Of late dayes thou hast, mysused Bersabe,
> The wyfe of Vrye, and slayne hym in the fyelde.[21]

But, as in Bale, David was not only the representative sinner but also the archpenitent. In his poem to the queen, "Of King Dauid," Harington stresses this side of the moral image:

> Thou, thou great Prince, with so rare gifts replenished
> Could'st not eschew blind Buzzard *Cupids* hookes,
> Lapt in the bayt of Bersabees sweet lookes:
> With which one fault, thy faultles life was blemished.
> Yet hence we learne a document most ample,
> That faln by fraillty we may rise by fayth,
> And that the sinne forgiuen, the penance staieth.[22]

Nathan's fable, as the Lord's method of rousing David's conscience, had attracted many; and both Harington and Sidney had seen in it the best mousetrap of all for catching the conscience of the king, and accordingly used it as a proof of the moral justification of fiction:

the applycation most diuinelye true, but the discourse it selfe fayned; which made *Dauid* (I speake of the second and instrumentall cause) as in a glasse to see his own filthines, as that heauenlye Psalme of mercie wel testifieth.[23]

As Sidney's words also suggest, it was natural to see David as an example of penitence when there were the Penitential Psalms as a constant reminder. The "miserere mei" of the Fifty-first Psalm had indeed become a universalized cry of confession and repentance; yet one also knew that it was "A Psalm of David, when Nathan the prophet came unto him, after he had gone in to Bathsheba." Many translators of, and commentators on, the Psalms had analyzed David's sin and repentance at great length, but perhaps the greatest literary expression of the connection between the Penitential Psalms and the love of David and Bathsheba is Wyatt's version, where his own links between the individual psalms describe the background story and David's progress in penance.

Indicative of the association of the Penitential Psalms with the love story behind them is the fact that in the late Middle Ages—and in France well into the Renaissance—a picture of Bathsheba bathing and David "above viewing her" would often be used in illustrating Books of Hours, as an introduction or frontispiece to the Penitential Psalms.[24] Here we are approaching the other form of response to the David and Bathsheba story—the delight in the sensuous beauty and sensual pleasure inherent in the scene as a human situation—for frequently the *Horae* illustrators seem to have taken more interest in the long, golden hair and other bodily charms of Bathsheba than in her representativeness as a vehicle of sin. In a typical Book of Hours, written in France in the early sixteenth century, we see David in contemplation of the carefully executed foreground figure of Bathsheba; she is standing in an ornate golden fountain, her equally golden hair falling over her shoulders, and with an arrow fired by a blind cupid heading straight for her breast (Figure 1). Bathsheba's bathing scene, we can see, was a natural meeting ground for Christian and pagan imagery. As Elizabeth Kunoth-Leifels has shown in her study of the David and Bathsheba motif in pictorial art, this motif—like its parallel, Susanna and the Elders—tended in the Renaissance to fuse with classical motifs, especially that of Venus and Adonis, into an image of earthly beauty.[25] The same tendency is obvious in verbal representations of the story: David appears torn between the Lord and Cupid, and Bathsheba's beauties are carefully catalogued. An English example of this is Francis Sabie's somewhat pedestrian epyllion, *Dauid and Beersheba* (1596), in which the poet, after entertaining us with Bathsheba's striptease act, cries out:

> O shut thine eies *Narcissus* come not neere,
> Least in the well a burning fire appeare.[26]

French poets were less restrained. In Remy Belleau's short epic, *Les Amours de David et de Bersabee* (1572), the emphasis is on the love story (for all that the poem ends with David's repentance) and above all on the bathing scene. The poet revels in Bathsheba's charms, and his lengthy catalogue of them becomes increasingly detailed and warmly sensual as he proceeds.[27] In Du Bartas, Bathsheba turns into an image of Venus:

> Elle oingt ses cheveux d'or: qu'elle plonge tantost
> De son corps bien formé l'albastre sous le flot,
> Telle qu'un lis qui tombe au creux d'une phiole,
> Telle qu'on peint Venus quand, lascivement molle,
> Elle naist dans la mer, et qu'avecques les thons
> Jà le feu de ses yeux embraze les Tritons.[28]

The same happens in the 1601 edition of Antoine de Montchrestien's play, *David ou l'adultère,* where David describes how he saw Bathsheba—

> . . . telle comme on dit qu'vne belle Déesse
> Poussa des flots feconds le thresor de sa tresse,
> Quand sur vne coquille à Cithere elle vint,
> Seiour plaisant & beau que depuis elle tint—

but a sense of decorum has made him remove these lines from the 1604 edition of the play.[29] Peele here shows more decorum than his French contemporaries, for, though his bathing scene is steeped in beauty, his imagery is taken from the Bible and especially from the Song of Songs, rather than from classical myth:

> Fairer then Isacs louer at the well,
> Brighter then inside barke of new hewen Cædar,
> Sweeter then flames of fine perfumed myrrhe.

> (ll. 81-83)

I have already tried to show elsewhere[30] how much the opening scene of *David and Bethsabe* is in the tradition of Ovidian sensual poetry of the fifteen-nineties. No doubt the boy acting Bathsheba would have had to be dressed rather the way Bathsheba is in those Dutch sixteenth-century pictures where she is depicted as modestly washing her feet, her skirt pulled up to barely reveal her knees;[31] but Peele's poetry provides all the erotic atmosphere that later Rubens, for example, was to give to the scene. It may not be altogether fanciful to suggest that the play on sense impressions in Bathsheba's song—

> Hot sunne, coole fire, temperd with sweet aire,
> Black shade, fair nurse, shadow my white haire
> Shine sun, burne fire, breath aire, and ease mee,
> Black shade, fair nurse, shroud me and please me—

stems from the same impulse as that which introduced into paintings of the scene either a colored handmaiden or a black messenger boy, to set off the white-skinned and blonde-haired beauty of the bathing figure. There is no moral condemnation within Peele's scene; it would be "placed" only by the audience's awareness of its traditional moral implications. When David says of Bathsheba,

> Faire Eua, plac'd in perfect happinesse,
>
> . . . . .
>
> Wrought not more pleasure to her husbands thoughts,
> Then this faire womans words and notes to mine,
>
> (ll. 57-61)

there is none of that irony in the image, placing the situation and anticipating its unhappy issue, which Marlowe uses so frequently—as when the Jew of Malta in Act I tells us that he holds his daughter as dear "As Agamemnon did his Iphigen." Like the illustrators of the Penitential Psalms, Peele is having his cake and eating it too: for, after using the first scene to celebrate the beauties of the flesh and the senses, he moves on to a strictly moral structure for the rest of the scenes dealing with the love story. Uriah is called home, and in a tragicomic scene (ll. 500-571) is made, ironically enough, to drink the health of "David's children"; and this is immediately followed by a chorus which underlines the sin of David—

> O prowd reuolt of a presumptious man,
> Laying his bridle in the necke of sin—

and goes on to point the general moral:

> If holy Dauid so shoke hands with sinne,
> What shall our baser spirits glorie in.
>
> (ll. 572-588)

The death of Uriah and the birth of the child, whether or not they had been enacted in an earlier version of the play, are summarized in the same chorus, leaving room for a scene of ritualistic lamentation of the sick child as a symbol of sin—

> The babe is sicke, and sad is Dauids heart,
> To see the guiltlesse beare the guilties paine;
>
> (ll. 625-626)

for Nathan's parable, which is taken almost verbatim from the Bible; and for David's penitence, with its echoes of the Psalms. Rapidly the rhythm of this scene brings David from penitence to purgation; as the child dies, retribution has been meted out, and David becomes the forgiven sinner:

> Let Dauids Harpe and Lute, his hand and voice,
> Giue laud to him that loueth Israel,
> And sing his praise, that shendeth Dauids fame,
> That put away his sinne from out his sight.
>
> (ll. 727-730)

The stage symbol of that forgiveness is the traditional *"Musike, and a banquet";* its spiritual symbol is the conception of another son—

> . . . decke faire Bersabe with ornaments,
> That she may beare to me another sonne,
> That may be loued of the Lord of hosts.
>
> (ll. 735-737)

And so, by his treatment of the subject, Peele ultimately turns the love of King David and Fair Bathsheba into a kind of divine comedy.

We can find a very similar pattern in Hans Sachs's play on the same subject. His *Comedia: Der Dauid mit Batseba im Ehbruch* (written some time before 1561) follows the rhythm of sin, forgiveness, and ultimate triumph: he takes us from the adultery, via the death of Uriah, Nathan's fable, and the death of the child, to the birth of a second son, Solomon,

> Herr König / Bathsheba ausserkorn
> Hat dir ein andern Sohn geborn
> Dich wider mit zu trösten thon.
>
> (fol. 89ᵛ)[32]

Sachs treats the story with the same concreteness as in his *Fastnachtsspiele* he treated secular material—"dry brevity" is Creizenach's description of his style[33]—and so the total effect is much like that of a medieval mystery. There is none of the nymph-in-fountain atmosphere round Bathsheba's ablutions; they have the same style of domestic realism as in the second *Horae* illustration reproduced here (Figure 2):

> Nun so hab ich gewaschen mich
> Von meinem schweiss / nun so will ich
> Mein hauss beschliessen.
>
> (fol. 85ʳ)

As always in Sachs's plays, all moralizing is kept away from the characters' speeches; it is left for the end, where the Epilogue warns against adultery but, above all, stresses that man must not despair, however great a sinner, but must trust to God's forgiveness. For, God

> . . . durchs heilig Evangelion
> Zeigt vergebung der sünden an
> Der Sünder wider thut begnaden
> Und wendet im ewigen schaden
> Dass auss verzweiflung im nit wachs
> Der ewig todt / das wünscht H. Sachs.
>
> (fol. 90ʳ)

The same material that was shaped by Sachs into a homiletic *comedia* was used, some forty years later, by Antoine de Montchrestien, writing in quite a different dramatic tradition,[34] for his neo-Senecan tragedy, *David ou l'adultère.*[35] His is also a play about sin and punishment, but with the stress on the sin and only a final gesture toward contrition in David. Where Sachs's five-act structure served him mainly to chop up the action into equal parts, Montchrestien's follows a formal pattern of exposition, development, and catastrophe. Act I, as we have already seen, is one long monologue by David, relating how he saw Bathsheba bathing, lusted for her, and satisfied his lust; at the end the news of her pregnancy is brought, and Uriah is sent for. Act II is virtually given over to Uriah, who returns with shrewd suspicions of what is going on; in Act III David debates with Nadab whether he should send Uriah to his death, and Uriah himself has a long speech in which he is shown as noble and loyal, as against the tyrannous king. In Act IV a messenger, in an elaborate account, relates the siege of Rabbah and Uriah's death. Act V opens with Bathsheba's lament over the death of Uriah and the sin of David, who "s'est montré trop homme et trop absolu Roy"; and David exhibits his hubris in sentences of extreme balance:

> On te rauit Vrie, et David t'est rendu;
> Tu gagnes beaucoup plus que tu n'auois perdu:
> Le Ciel t'oste vn soldat, vn Monarque il te donne.
>
> (p. 229)

But now the peripeteia occurs, as Nathan comes in and by his parable catches the conscience of David. The act and play end with Nathan's speech of absolution. A large proportion of the lines in each act is spoken by the chorus, which is significantly unspecified in nature and whose function is to provide lyrical-moralizing comments at the end of acts (or, in Act V, before the peripeteia). The subjects on which it meditates form, in order, a paradigm of the action. The chorus of Act I is on how *amor vincit omnia;* of Act II, on the sacredness of marriage; of Act III, on the terrible power of a tyrannical ruler; of Act IV, on the transitoriness of life; and of Act V, on how crimes will out and remorse will await the sinner.

As this will have indicated, in **David** the scriptural story has become purely a vehicle of moral generalizations. Nothing happens; all is said. Rhetoric is used to build the characters up into theoretically heroic positions. David in the first act, honor and love at war within him, has a lengthy, patterned sequence of lines, each starting "Suis-je ce grand Dauid qui . . . ?" which sets up the traditional figure of the Herculean hero conquered by love, and indeed the chorus comes in with the Hercules parallel:

> Hercvle auoit vaincu les monstres de la terre;
> Tout ce qui luy fist teste il le peut surmonter:
> Mais s'il fut indomptable au milieu de la guerre,
> Au milieu de la paix vn œil le sçeut donter.
> Amour n'est qu'vn enfant, mais sa puissance est grande.
> C'est vn aveugle Archer, mais il vise fort bien:
> C'est le plus grand des Rois puis qu'aux Rois il commande
> Et que de son seruage il ne s'exempte rien.
>
> (p. 207)

This is very much like the hubris of the David figure in one of Textor's dialogues, where David proudly declares his greatness and his scorn of any but divine love—

> Inter fatidicos prima est mihi gloria vates,
> Et mea prospiciunt praesagi verba prophetae,
> Ille ego sum David, tortae qui verbere fundae
> Magna Philistiae percussi membra gigantis.[36]

But there, too, Cupid shoots his arrow, and painfully David realizes, in the concluding words of the dialogue, that *Omnia vincit amor*. There is only one step from this image to the use of David in a *de casibus* tragedy; and thus we find him in Anthony Munday's *Mirrour of Mutabilitie* (1579), where he appears as a representative of the fall from high place through "Lecherye," warning the reader:

> You Princes great that rule in regall state,
> Beholde how I did blindly run astray:
> And brought my self unto destructions gate,
> But that my God redeemd me thence away.[37]

But Montchrestien does not seem to feel that the Fall of Princes is in itself a tragic enough subject, or that David is a satisfactory tragic hero, and so he places Uriah at the center of the tragic structure. He, even more than David, is allowed to build himself up to heroic stature:

> Mon cœur est grand et haut, mon ame ardente et pronte,
> Sensible au vitupere encor' plus qu'aux douleurs.
>
> (p. 218)

The play, then, works as a kind of debate on the nature of heroism and of kingship, epitomized in the interchanges of David and Uriah and in the stichomythia between Nadab and David in Act III. Montchrestien did not want merely to teach a moral lesson. The biblical story would have appealed to him, too, because it was rich in situations of a potentially antithetical kind—love versus honor in David, loyal soldier versus tyrannical ruler in Uriah's opposition to David, moral conscience versus exultant sinner in Nathan versus David.[38] The play becomes a pattern of antithetical positions, fine stuff for rhetorical monologues, sharp stichomythia, and choral meditations, but dramatically and spiritually stillborn.

What, in fact, we may see by comparing Montchrestien with Sachs, and with Peele, is something of the inherent weakness of a narrowly academic scriptural Seneca. The Senecan form was devised to accommodate the internal struggles of heroic minds, the stichomythic debates where such minds defined themselves more clearly, the violent physical actions which issued from them, and the remorse, torment, and punishment which followed. To achieve this out of the simple chronicle material of 2 Samuel would mean an inflation of figures, motives, and situations only possible if they were given a psychological depth which Montchrestien cannot master. (Later we shall see how another neo-Senecan, Honerdius, achieves this.)

What Montchrestien has also lost, because of his formal concentration on the single event, is the larger moral pattern which is implicit in the Bible and which is Peele's guiding idea: the effects of David's sin on his House. Seneca's is a drama of great individuals whose own tormented natures matter more than any hereditary curse over their House; and Montchrestien, as indeed his chosen structure forces him to do, treats David in isolation from his House. The play ends with Nathan's prophecy that the child of David and Bathsheba will die—thus not only before the first tangible occurrence of retribution but also well before the redemptory birth of Solomon which forms the "comic" conclusion of Sachs's play.

Montchrestien is here outside the main stream of sixteenth-century thought about David, for one of the fascinations his story held for the contemporary mind seems to have been its more extended moral perspective: the sin of the father being visited on the children and hence revisited onto the father himself. To some, David seemed the ideal hero of a moral tragedy; while on the one hand he was "a most mightie King, and . . . a most holie Prophet," the fortunes of his House, on the other hand, formed an unequaled "monument . . . of so many and heinous crimes proceeding out of one fact."[39] The connection between David's adultery, Amnon's rape of his sister Tamar, Absalom's murder of Amnon, and finally Absalom's rebellion and usurpation of the throne was used from the pulpit as a stock example of the subtle way in which the Lord arranges his retribution:

> Even as he had dishonoured another mans childe / so sawe he shame upon his owne children while he lyved / and that with greate wrechednesse. For Amnon defloured Thamar his awne naturall sister. And they both were Dauids children / yet Absalom did miserably slaye Amnon his brother / for comytting that wickednesse with his syster Thamar. Not long after / dyd the same Absalom dryve his own naturall father Dauid out of his realme / & shamefully lay with his fathers wifes. Whereupon there followed an horryble great slaughter / in the whych Absalom was slayne with many thousands mo of the comen people.[40]

Peele's structure shows that this connection between David's sins and the sexual disorders within his House, as well as civil strife within his realm, was his organizing principle. In the Bible the rape of Tamar is subsequent to the whole David and Bathsheba story, whereas in Peele's play it is fitted in between David's

adultery and the Lord's judgment, so that the thematic link is implicit. It is also made explicit by David's reaction to the rape:

> Sin with his seuenfold crowne and purple robe,
> Begins his triumphs in my guiltie throne.
>
> (ll. 402-403)

Again with a modification of scriptural chronology, the news that Absalom has murdered Amnon is brought to David just after the capture of Rabbah. This scene of victory is lamented by Sampley as a "digression,"[41] and so it is from the "well-made" point of view; but it seems to me obvious that Peele has here built up as effective a reversal—in visual and theatrical as well as moral terms—as possible. David, having taken Rabbah (at whose siege, we remember, Uriah was slain) and crowned himself with Hanun's crown, is at the height of his power and glory—

> Beauteous and bright is he among the Tribes,
> As when the sunne attir'd in glist'ring robe,
> Comes dauncing from his orientall gate,
> And bridegroome-like hurles through the gloomy aire—
>
> (ll. 863-866)

when suddenly the glories of this Sun King are dashed by the message that all his sons are dead. (A special poignancy is given here to that piece of misreporting.) Similar reversals, theatrical and moral, form a leading pattern in that part of the play which deals with Absalom's rebellion; and I shall deal with these later on.

For the moment we must turn to the story of Tamar, Amnon, and Absalom. Peele treats it concisely, with only two elaborations on the Bible account. The first is Jonadab's speech while the rape is being committed. It is out of character (as he had been the one to counsel Amnon to enjoy his sister) and entirely choric; it aims not only to raise sympathy for Tamar—

> Now Thamar ripened are the holy fruits
> That grew on plants of thy virginitie,
> And rotten is thy name in Israel,
> Poore Thamar, little did thy louely hands
> Foretell an action of such violence,
> As to contend with Ammons lusty armes,
> Sinnewd with vigor of his kindlesse loue—
>
> (ll. 303-309)

but also, by implication, to relate Amnon's sexual crime to David's:

> Why should a Prince, whose power may command,
> Obey the rebell passions of his loue,
> When they contend but gainst his conscience,
> And may be gouernd or suppress by will.
>
> (ll. 296-299)

The second is Tamar's *Klagerede* after the rape, when she sees herself

> Cast as was Eua from that glorious soile
> (Where al delights sat bating wingd with thoughts,
> Ready to nestle in her naked breasts)
> To bare and barraine vales with floods made wast,
> To desart woods, and hils with lightening scorcht,
> With death, with shame, with hell, with horrour sit.

(ll. 337-342)

The poetry here performs the function of realizing the emotional and moral state of a fall; and by the inversion of the Eden imagery from the bathing scene, the link with David's sin—as well as the sense that we are dealing with *all* sin—is kept.

Traditionally Amnon's rape was an *exemplum horrendum,* sometimes illustrating the Fall of Princes through lust,[42] sometimes a standard example of incest.[43] Peele, in concentrating on the plight of Tamar, shows more imagination. Dramatically his approach is a great deal more fruitful than that of Hans Sachs in his *Tragedia: Thamar die Tochter König Dauid mit irem Bruder Ammon vnd Absalom* (1556).[44] Sachs, too, connects the action with the David and Bathsheba story by giving David an opening speech about his guilt; and, as in Peele's play, the arrival of the news of the murder brings an ironic reversal into a scene where David muses on the happy and peaceful state of his kingdom. But his action leads up to an Epilogue which interprets the story typologically: David stands for God, who has two children; one—Tamar—is "die Christlich seel," the other—Amnon—is Satan. Absalom is God's vehicle of both retribution and consolation. The play is interesting to us chiefly, I think, as an indication that as late as 1556 a playwright could still ask his audience to keep together such (to us) disparate attitudes to a character as a cautionary and a typological one: David is, on the one hand, a human sinner and, on the other, a figure of God.

The story of David's children was obviously a subject which invited a Senecan treatment of passion, incest, revenge, and fratricide, while at the same time it had a built-in opportunity for combining "tragicos cum pietate modos."[45] In three plays first published within a few years of each other, it was thus used. N. Chrestien des Croix wrote in French a tragedy, *Amnon et Thamar* (Rouen, 1608); and from the Low Countries there are two neo-Latin tragedies on the subject: *Thamara* (Leyden, 1611) by Rochus Honerdius (Roch van den Honert, *c.* 1572-1638), and *Amnon* (Ghent, 1617), by Jacobus Cornelius Lummenaeus à Marca (Jaques-Corneille van Lummene van Marcke, 1570-1629).[46] A detailed analysis of all these plays is out of the question here; all I want to show is how a comparison of structure and thematic emphasis in the three plays may

bring out the different ways in which the same subject could be treated in what is, to a large extent, the same dramatic tradition. All three plays are neo-Senecan. They use a five-act structure with a chorus kept apart as commentator, a fairly unified action, and a relatively small number of characters. All are rhetorical rather than theatrical. In all, Amnon is given much scope to speak about the torments of his passion, Tamar to lament the outrage done to her, and Absalom to deliberate his revenge.

What initially distinguishes Chrestien's play from the two neo-Latin ones is that, while they put David at the moral center, Chrestien is writing a drama balanced between the two immoral individuals, Amnon and Absalom. David appears at the beginning of *Amnon et Thamar,* and is referred to throughout, as the godlike standard from which his two sons are aberrations. The pattern of concentration on villainy needs an ideal governor as a foil. Amnon wants his sister, Absalom wants the crown, to which Amnon is immediate heir; Amnon's rape gives Absalom the chance to combine moral revenge with the pursuit of political ambition:

> Dieu m'ouvre le moyen, & sans nul vitupere,
> De me deffaire en fin de ce pariure frere:
> Frere mon premier né, & qui doit deuant moy
> Succeder à l'Estat de Dauid nostre Roy.

(p. 87)

Chrestien, then, has built out of the Bible story at least the beginnings of an intrigue play; the plot has some complexity, and motives and actions are neatly intertwined. Both Amnon and Absalom are Senecan heroes, contemplating with fascinated horror the deeds they are about to perpetrate. Amnon can no longer be interesting after the rape, so he is dropped—only to be brought on for a brisk on-stage murder in Act V—and Absalom comes to the fore in the second half of the play. All of Acts I and II are taken up with Amnon's struggles with his "Meurtriere Passion,"

> Qui condamne mon ame, & destruit mon honneur;

and in Act III he even reads his confidant a love poem he has written about Tamar.[47] In Act I, with a slight reminiscence of morality technique, he has a dream where an angel and a "Megere" appear to him, respectively to persuade him to sin and dissuade him from it. This parallelism of contrasted counsel is made a structural principle for the whole play, which is exceedingly symmetrically built up. Amnon has a good counselor—Ithai—with whom he debates in Act I the problems of love versus honor, good versus evil; he also has a bad counselor—Jonadab—with whom there is much stichomythic debating in Act III on the subjects of suicide and freedom of the will. Parallel to these deliberations are Absalom's two sets of stichomythia in

Act II, with one good and one evil counselor. The dialogue between Absalom and Hushai becomes a debate on how to govern a state, with Absalom as the rebel and revolutionary and Hushai as the conservative speaker for king and country. In pointed contrast it is followed by the dialogue between Absalom and Ahitophel:

ABSALON:

> Mon Pere vit encor, & Amnon qui me passe.

ARCHITOPHEL:

> Il faut trouver moyen que ce frere trespasse.

ABSALON:

> Comment, tüer mon frere! ô forfait inhumain!

ARCHITOPHEL:

> Qui veut libre s'esbatre, oste le cruel frein.

ABSALON:

> Mais cest ébat, de Dieu le courroux nous attire.

ARCHITOPHEL:

> Ne desire donc point d'acquerir vn Empire.

ABSALON:

> Pourquoy, s'il est permis?

ARCHITOPHEL:

> Tu n'en as point de tel.

ABSALON:

> Mon Pere peut mourir, Amnon n'est immortel?

ARCHITOPHEL:

> La vie de ton frere est ta mort bien certaine.

(pp. 42-43)

This symmetry of contrasts is observed on the plane of sexual morality too. The first part of Act II presents Tamar as extremely pious, full of "l'amour vers Dieu" and ironically praying for her brothers' welfare, thus establishing a contrast with the ungodly passions of Amnon and also making the outrage on her more heinous; and we are also given a discussion between her and her women in which she appears as the mirror of chastity. The theme is taken up at the end of the act by the chorus of "Filles Iuifues," who sing the praises of chastity. Again, after the rape, there is a debate between her and her women about whether the violation of the body can also sully the spirit.

Altogether, then, *Amnon et Thamar* shows us a playwright interested in the Bible as Senecan raw material and (rather like Montchrestien) in this particular story

for its possibilities as a scaffold for antithetical arguments. It brings home to one the weaknesses of the post-Garnier Senecan tradition in France: A subject that could have lent itself to the psychological and moral tensions of a *Phèdre,* or the examinations of divine justice of an *Athalie,* never rises in its execution above a chess play of moral axioms and rhetorical posturing. Chrestien's chosen scope does not allow him to show justice done on Absalom and his rebellious ambitions; the play ends as David has reconciled himself to the death of Amnon. Thus it remains morally lopsided.

If one sets side by side with *Amnon et Thamar* the *Amnon* of Lummenaeus à Marca, the difference in moral structure becomes immediately apparent. Lummenaeus' scope is almost identical with Chrestien's: He starts with Amnon lamenting his infatuation and ends with David's reception of the news of Amnon's death at Absalom's hand. But his action is firmly held in relation to David's own guilt. Act IV is largely one long monologue of David's:

> Peccaui! & an diffitear? & crimen meum est,
> Quod fecit Amnon, publicum exemplum dedi,
> Et Bethsabea strauit incaesto viam;

(p. 29)

and the chorus which follows takes up the same idea. There is little theatrical interest in his structure. Everything happens offstage; the short acts are made up either entirely of monologues (Acts I and III) or of a combination of monologues and stichomythia; the choruses (by unidentified speakers) are very long and meditate upon the situation by giving examples—biblical and classical—of parallel situations. As in Montchrestien's *David,* each act is in fact a static tableau. But within the limits of a closet drama the play provides a dramatic tension between human and divine revenge, Absalom's and the Lord's, with David as the pivotal figure.

Also, Lummenaeus à Marca's stichomythia, unlike Chrestien's, grows from the situation rather than from theoretical concepts, and thus manages to communicate a human content. In the following exchange between Tamar and Absalom, the repetition of the words "frater" and "soror" is not just rhetorical patterning; it acquires a symbolical value as an index to the horror of the situation as it has to be spoken out by a sister and slowly dawn on a brother:

ABSALOMUS:

> Quid me occupas insaniis? rursum iacet.

THAMARA:

> Crudelis Amnon!

ABSALOMUS:

> Tetigit.

THAMARA:

Atrox, impie,

Incæste, abominabilis semper mihi!

Amnon! Iuuentæ carnifex turpis meæ!

ABSALOMUS:

Frater?

THAMARA:

Tacere liceat.

ABSALOMUS:

& rursum implicas.

THAMARA:

Frater pudorem rapuit incæstus meum.

ABSALOMUS:

Frater? Sorori Virgini?

THAMARA:

Parce obsecro.

ABSALOMUS:

Amnon Thamaræ noxiam? & potuit ferus,

Et potuit? Amnon Virgini stuprum intulit?

Amnon? Sorori Virgini? . . .

(p. 16)

This exchange is, too, an ironic echo of Amnon's words in Act I, while he still struggles with his passion:

O sancta probitas! Virginem vt stupro occupem?
Frater sororem?

(p. 8)

The repetition of the phrase "Absalom omnes tulit," when in Act V David has got the false news that Absalom has killed all his sons, has the same quality of expanding the Bible story not just into rhetoric but into fully realized human moments.

Honerdius, in *Thamara,* carries this psychological probing one step further—so that Leicester Bradner can, with some justification, speak of him as a forerunner of Racine.[48] With even less external action than Lummenaeus à Marca, he has concentrated on the tension inside his characters even more, humanizing them rather than merely making them vehicles of rhetoric. The difference in titles between the two plays is significant, and is reflected in the way identical material has been handled. In *Amnon* the rape takes place between Acts I and III—before Tamar has appeared on the stage—and the revenge is thus made the central element in the action. In *Thamara* the rape is delayed till between Acts

III and IV, and the action stops short of the retributive murder of Amnon. (The last speech is Absalom's vow to avenge the crime against "nobis, sorori, legibus, regi, deo.") The structure thus gives a different emphasis to the story: Amnon's act is one which he has fought hard against and which, when it comes, is seen as done on a girl who is innocent, tender, and sympathetic. Also, unlike the case in *Amnon,* David impresses his sense of sin on the reader *before* the crime has been committed. Act II consists of a six-and-a-half-page monologue in which he speaks of the expiation of his sin; ironically he fears a fate for Amnon similar to that of his firstborn child with Bathsheba:

Et morte pueri credidi falso scelus
Satis piatum. poena sic iuxta suum
Nefas stetisset . . .

(p. 21)

The play's emphasis, then, is thrown on Tamar, in herself innocent, expiating David's sin. This, together with the central position of David in the play, confirms the didactic purpose which Honerdius states in his preface "Ad Lectorem":

Tota namque haec actio nihil aliud est quam implexa disciplina. Quid enim? . . . Thamarae injuria, parentum libidinem, liberorum contumelia plerumque expiari?

Honerdius was not a professional divine, and, as far as I am aware,[49] he wrote only one other play, and that also a neo-Latin biblical one, *Moses nomoclastes* (Leyden, 1611). I have not seen this tragedy, but the title suggests that he may have chosen the subject for its moral, rather than inherently exciting, nature. On the other hand, Lummenaeus à Marca, who was first a Capuchin and then a Benedictine monk, was a prolific writer, especially of scriptural plays; and in the collection of his works published as *Musae Lacrymantes* (Douai, 1628), we find not only the almost inevitable *Jephtha* but also plays on such topics as *Bustum Sodomae* and *Samson.* He seems to have had a good eye for a sensational biblical subject. That, however, he combined this with an interest in moral themes can be seen from his *Dives Epulo*—one of his *Tragoedia Sacra* (Ghent, 1617)—in which, though presented in richly classical imagery, all the characters apart from Dives and Lazarus are personified abstractions: Voluptas, Desperatio, Poenitentia, and so on.

After Chrestien's *Amnon et Thamar,* the two neo-Latin plays from the Low Countries would seem to go some way toward justifying a Christian Seneca. The tight form makes for a solemn, almost ritualistic acting out of the doom on the House of David; moral emphasis grows out of the action itself and is, especially in the case of Honerdius, supported by psychological realization of the human problems involved.

In his lines "Ad Lectorem" Honerdius also speaks of Absalom's *ambitio* as another of David's punishments, and thereby he provides a link with the next, and last, group of plays I want to deal with—plays treating the rebellion of Absalom, his usurpation of David's throne, David's flight, and Absalom's death. (This is the story of 2 Samuel XIV-XIX.) Obviously these events contain much material that is naturally dramatic—from the hubris of Absalom to the pity and terror of David's lament over his son.

In Peele's play, as I have already said, it is made clear that Absalom's insurrection is part of a pattern of personal guilt and civil disorder evolving from David's adultery and his misuse of kingly power in having Uriah killed. The pattern is emphasized by the very abruptness—a structural flaw if we look at it from the viewpoint of the "well-made" play—with which we move from the scene where David forgives Absalom's fratricide (scene ix) to that which follows: *"Enter Dauid . . . with others, Dauid barefoot, with some lose couering ouer his head, and all mourning"* (S.D., ll. 1020-1022). It is one of the many sudden and morally effective reversals typical of the play. David's opening speech here is a confession of sins, in which the body politic and the individual conscience are fused into one image:

> And to inflict a plague on Dauids sinne,
> He makes his bowels traitors to his breast,
> Winding about his heart with mortall gripes.
>
> (ll. 1033-1035)

By the use of Gospel imagery, Absalom is seen as the type of an anti-Christ:

> Ah Absalon the wrath of heauen inflames
> Thy scorched bosome with ambitious heat,
> And Sathan sets thee on a lustie tower,
> Shewing thy thoughts the pride of Israel
> Of choice to cast thee on her ruthlesse stones.
>
> (ll. 1035-1040)

David's guilt, then, in all its aspects—personal, domestic, national, and moral-allegorical—is the thematic unifier which makes the Absalom scenes an essential part of Peele's play. It functions in the totality of the play somewhat as the usurpation of Henry IV functions in the three *Henry VI* plays.[50] As in Shakespeare's trilogy, the underlying moral-political cause may be lost sight of within the individual scenes, but it is brought up at key points and it forms the framework of the whole. Some of Peele's scenes, like Ithai's demonstration of faithfulness or the cursing of Shimei, are in themselves moral tableaux, but they are not "digressions." Shimei's cursing, in particular, is very effectively and cogently handled: Not only is Shimei himself made the voice of David's conscience (unlike the source passage in the Bible where he merely refers to vengeance for the blood of Saul)—

> Euen as thy sinne hath still importund heauen,
> So shall thy murthers and adulterie
> Be punisht in the sight of Israel,
> As thou deserust with bloud, with death, and hell—
>
> (ll. 1363-1366)

but he also gives the king the opportunity of appearing as David Penitens—

> The sinnes of Dauid, printed in his browes,
> With bloud that blusheth for his conscience guilt—
>
> (ll. 1374-1375)

and above all as the Christian figure of Patience. The various episodes of this part of the play are, in fact, devoted to bringing out David's patience, as a refusal to despair:

> I am not desperate Semei like thy selfe,
> But trust vnto the couenant of my God,
> Founded on mercie with repentance built,
> And finisht with the glorie of my soule.
>
> (ll. 1382-1385)

Most clearly the juxtaposition of despair with patience is brought out in the contrast, implied by the structure, between David and Ahitophel. In the Bible Ahitophel's suicide is dealt with very briefly:

> And when Ahitophel saw that his counsel was not followed, he saddled his ass, and arose, and gat him home to his house, to his city, and put his household in order, and hanged himself, and died.

In Peele he is given a scene to himself (xiii), in which he makes a speech of nihilistic despair, leading up to the climax,

> And now thou hellish instrument of heauen,
> Once execute th'arrest of Ioues iust doome,
> And stop his breast that curseth Israel. *Exit.*
>
> (ll. 1502-1504)

The "hellish instrument of heaven" is explained by the stage direction: *"Achitophel solus with a halter."* The halter, the instrument of Judas' self-destruction, was well known as a symbol of despair, from pictorial representations and from dramatic as well as nondramatic literature.[51] As Ahitophel exits, he is like Despayre in *The Faerie Queene,* who, from a collection of murderous instruments,

> . . . chose an halter from among the rest,
> And with it hong himself, unbid, unblest.
>
> (Bk. I, canto ix)

Another moral contrast theatrically pointed throughout these scenes is that between Absalom's pride and David's humility. We move, for example, from David's laudable *apatheia*—

Here lie I armed with an humble heart,
T'imbrace the paines that anger shall impose,
And kisse the sword my lord shall kill me with—

(ll. 1114-1116)

to the next scene: *"Absalon, Amasa, Achitophel, with the concubines of Dauid, and others in great state, Absalon crowned"* (S.D., ll. 1160-1161); and it becomes obvious that even without Absalom's proud and self-infatuated speeches this would have struck the audience with the force of a visual emblem—just as the sight of Absalom hanging by his hair hardly needs Joab's words to point the irony of moral retribution:

Rebell to nature, hate to heauen and earth,
. . . . .
Now see the Lord hath tangled in a tree
The health and glorie of thy stubborne heart,
And made thy pride curbd with a sencelesse plant.

(ll. 1579-1585)

Similar in many ways to the Absalom section of Peele's play is a *Tragedia Spirituale* by an Italian Franciscan friar, Pergiovanni Brunetto. *David Sconsolato* was first published in Florence in 1556 and appeared in several later editions.[52] In external shape it is a regular five-act tragedy, but its internal form is almost as episodic as the Bible story. Brunetto starts with Absalom's recall from banishment, expanding the scene of the widow from Tekoah; in Act II we see Absalom's growing rebelliousness; and only in Act III does the rebellion proper break out. Between David's flight from Jerusalem and his encounter with Shimei, the Bible has the episodes of Ittai, Zadok, Hushai, and Ziba. Out of these Peele has only included that of Ittai, the Gittite. He combines the others into the ritualized lamentation scene, ll. 1050-1071, where he gets the effect of a crowd of faithful followers round David, by lyrical rather than narrative or dramatic means. Brunetto, however, in a series of short scenes in Act III, includes and expands all the biblical episodes. In some ways, then, his structure is closer than Peele's to that of the mystery type of religious drama. But Brunetto's unifying theme, like Peele's—and as his title indicates—is that of David's sin; and here he makes effective use of a popular Senecan device. *David Sconsolato* opens with a prologue spoken by "Ombra del Figliuolo adulterino di Dauid," who expounds the whole tragic context in an atmosphere that is as much Senecan as biblical:

Da le dannate grotte vscit' à luce
Men vengo à voi presente ombra infelice,
Del figlio adulterin, del Gran Dauide;
Grande per certo per valor', & forte,
Temuto, & ammirato in ciascun' Clima:
Ma s'à le gent'indomite preualse,
Epost'ha'l freno à molte ampie prouincie;
Vinto si diede pur al van diletto,
De le brutte bellezze d'vna Donna,
Ne pote ritener in vita il figlio

Che egli contra'l mondo, e contra'l Cielo
Acquistò bruttamente, e chi puo mai
Il voler impedir del grande Dio?

(no sig.)

He also dwells on the intermediary tragedy—

Amnon Tamarre stupra sua sorella
Et Absalon l'vccide per vendetta—

and predicts "La morte d'Absalon ch'ambizioso." And the curse on David's House, and its origin in the adultery, is harked back to throughout the play—notably by Bathsheba on her first appearance (I.iii).

Despite the Senecan opening, the play does not develop into a horror tragedy: Absalom's death is reported; Ahitophel—though, Timon-fashion, he gives us his epitaph—hangs himself offstage. It is, though, a strongly emotional play, with a great deal of human interest gained out of the many episodes. Unlike the more formal French tragedies we have looked at, this play, with its wealth of characters and incidents, does create a strong sense of context—House and city—for David. Contributing to this effect is the chorus "di donne Gierosolimitane," which is used not only to provide meditative odes (like the "O' miseri mortali" at the end of Act II) but also to take part in the conversation and the action. Brunetto shows how effective, in relation to this material, is the tendency of Italian humanist tragedians of the sixteenth century to combine Senecan and Grecian dramatic techniques.[53] His moral theme also forces him toward a tragedy of double issue rather than a plain unhappy ending, in that the outcome is a fall for Absalom (and Ahitophel) but is at the same time ultimately happy—that is purgative—for David and his House. In the end David himself takes the place of the chorus:

Mal può letizia dar trafitto core
Dicesi, & è ben vero,
Spesso'n cibo soaue
Mosca noiosa, & importuna cade,
Dauid tropp'era liet'hor è beato,
Al Regno ritornato,
Se non moriua'l figlio,
Ma così'n questo esiglio
Il mal si purga, e illustrasi bontade.

Good has ultimately issued from evil, David disconsolate has become David consoled; and in Hans Sachs's terms the play would be a *Comedia*,[54] but like Peele's it remains formally the tragedy of Absalom. Yet its real nature is best indicated by the woodcut which, twice repeated, illustrates the play in the 1586 edition—one often used, too, to illustrate the Penitential Psalms in *Horae* (cf. Figure 2). It represents David kneeling in contrition, his crown laid humbly aside, with God's grace, symbolized by the sun, streaming down upon him. Brunetto could be used by either side in the debate about the possibility of a Christian tragedy.

Clearly the ambitious Absalom, rather than the contrite David, was the more stimulating figure to anyone wanting to pour this particular biblical story into a neoclassical mould. We see this exemplified in the Latin MS play *Absalon,* of unknown authorship and date.[55] Whether it is by Bishop Watson or not is immaterial here, though it seems to me that the careful metrical annotations on the autograph manuscript would fit in with an author "who to this day would never suffer yet his *Absalon* to go abroad, and that onelie because, in *locis paribus, Anapestus* is twise or thrise vsed in stede of *Iambus."*[56] Boas, who compares this play with Peele's, thinks that it "profits by comparison," for "in dexterous arrangement of material, in concentration of interest, and, above all, in psychological insight, *Absalon* is the work of an abler and more original playwright than Peele."[57] Boas' comparison, however, neglects the fact that Peele's whole intention and direction in this, the third, movement of his play were different from those of the classical scholar who penned *Absalon* into a neat five-act structure. Though the author of *Absalon* has not pressed his material into artificial conformity with the unities—like Brunetto he starts with Absalom's return from exile and ends with David's lament over Absalom's death—he has yet treated the Bible chronicle very selectively. According to the plan of a "well-made" play, he has subordinated the chosen events to an overall study of rebellion and of the casting out of a tyrant. Absalom emerges as a typical Senecan tyrant figure; Ahitophel, as the bad counselor hoist with his own petard, who wittily rationalizes his particular form of suicide:

> Ergo nocentis vinculo vocis viam
> Obstingere est equū. scelus cōcepit hec,
> Periat eadem. solū placeat suspendiū.

(fol. 24ᵛ)

We need only compare this situation to Peele's Ahitophel and his morally emblematic halter to see that the author's dramatic conception (as indeed Boas points out) is pagan rather than Christian. Although David is at one point (II.ii) made to recognize that what is happening is part of a retributive pattern, the structure itself does not bear out such a pattern. Although David is consoled at the end, he is so because Absalom deserved death rather than because Absalom's death was part of the ways of God to David. The author of *Absalon,* then, has admirably fulfilled his plan of constructing a classical tragedy out of biblical material; what he has not achieved, because he had no intention of doing so, is the creation of a spiritual pattern where, as in both Peele and Brunetto, divine comedy emerges out of tragedy. That this is the final direction of Peele's play becomes obvious when we turn to the scene which neither of the other Absalom plays dramatizes: that involving the accession of Solomon (xvii). To Boas and most other Peele critics, Peele's introduction of So-

lomon is particularly obnoxious; it "mars the emotional effect of Absalom's tragic fate and diverts the interest at a culminating point."[58] I would argue that, rather, it *directs* the interest—once we know what the interest is—*to* a culminating point.

Once we are clear—and I hope the preceding discussion has made that point—that it is not "the emotional effect of Absalom's tragic fate" Peele is primarily after, but the working out of moral and civil disorder within the House of David, then it also becomes clear that Solomon at the end of ***David and Bethsabe*** has a function that can be compared, however cautiously, with Richmond's at the end of *Richard III* or even Fortinbras' at the end of *Hamlet.* After the disorders in the House and the strife within the kingdom, here is the good son, figure of the future. Solomon's establishment in the succession of David means not merely the rooting out of evil from the House and realm of David but also the enthronement of good. Yet the use of Solomon, with the distortion of biblical chronology which it involves, has reverberations of a more general moral significance. Solomon is the son whom David begot on Bathsheba, with the Lord's blessing, after the child of adultery had died. We have already seen how his birth forms the resolution of Hans Sachs's *Comedia* on the adultery and how the conception of "another Sonne, That may be loued of the Lord of hosts" formed the happy resolution of the first movement of Peele's play. Nor would the audience have forgotten that this was the son who was to carry on the line of Jesse—the House of David—toward the Messiah. In Bale's interlude, *The chefe promyses of God unto men,* the Lord turns from rebuking David to his promise:

> A frute there shall come, forth yssuynge from thy
>   bodye,
> Whom I wyll aduance, vpon thy seate for euer.
> Hys trone shall become, a seate of heauenlye glorye,
> Hys worthy scepture, from ryght wyll not dysseuer,
> Hys happye kyngedome, of faythe, shall perysh neuer.
> Of heauen and of earthe, he was autor pryncypall,
> And wyll contynue, though they do perysh all.[59]

Of this fruit, Solomon is a prefiguration; the promise embodied in him reaches forward to the end of all sin. But we have also seen how, through the imagery of the play and through the traditional associations of the audience, David's sin reaches back to Adam's, to the beginning of all sin. At this point, the particular form of the Solomon scene becomes of interest. It has long been known that Peele here shamelessly incorporates a large number of lines almost literally translated from Du Bartas' *Les Artifices.*[60] In *Les Artifices* Du Bartas presents Adam in a state of poetic-prophetic "fureur secrete," in which he sees the future of his race and describes it to his son Seth. Now, Seth was the son of Adam and Eve who represented *their* special promise:

For God, said she, hath appointed me another seed
instead of Abel, whom Cain slew.

(Genesis IV.25)

And so Peele is not just plagiarizing when he modifies
Du Bartas' words into what he would see as a parallel
situation—for Adam showing the future of the world to
Seth is like David handing over to Solomon his House
and his vision,

Of all our actions now before thine eyes,
From Adam to the end of Adams seed.

(ll. 1821-1822)

He is using Du Bartas' material more organically than
Du Bartas himself had done, for the "fureur secrete"
which seizes Du Bartas' Adam is spiritually less
motivated than the fury that moves David to prayer—

Transforme me from this flesh, that I may liue
Before my death, regenerate with thee.
O thou great God, rauish my earthly sprite,
That for the time a more then humane skill
May feed the Organons of all my sence—

(ll. 1829-1833)

and that "ravisheth" the soul of Solomon. Peele has
given us the Psalmist, the inspired David of the Psalter,
and in so doing he has linked the scene up with the
invocation to the play:

And when his consecrated fingers strooke
The golden wiers of his rauishing harpe,
He gaue alarum to the host of heauen,
That wing'd with lightning, brake the clouds and cast
Their christall armor, at his conquering feet.

(ll. 10-14)

He has not simply improved on his source in using it;
he has also given us an indication, by the Adam-David
analogy, of the dramatic structure which his contemporary audience—whether they knew Du Bartas or not—
would, I think, have sensed in the "epic" drama on
"Israel's sweetest singer": the rhythm of God's promises, of Paradise lost and regained. It is at this point, I
think, that we can see why Peele inserted the succession of Solomon before the reception of the news of
Absalom's death: The final part of this scene gives in
an epitome the spiritual progress that the whole play
acts out.

With one of the sudden reversals which we have seen
as typical of the play, Absalom's death sends David
from the highest celestial communion to the lowest human despair, in which he sees his poetry, the link
between him and God, as shattered:

Then let them tosse my broken Lute to heauen,
Euen to his hands that beats me with the strings,

To shew how sadly his poore sheepeheard sings.
He goes to his pauillion, and sits close a while.

(ll. 1908-1911)

In the Bible, Nathan is not in this episode (2 Samuel
XIX), but in the play he is, to echo and complete his
role as a moral conscience. It is he who points out to
David that he is sinking into the sin of despair:

These violent passions come not from aboue,
Dauid and Bethsabe offend the highest,
To mourne in this immeasurable sort.

(ll. 1922-1924)

And after Joab's persuasion (which follows the Bible in
appealing on the point of national unity), in defiance of
psychological probability but in fulfillment of the
spiritual pattern, David "riseth up," to pronounce a
Lycidas-like apotheosis of Absalom. Boas finds this last
move on Peele's part "still more incongruous with the
general scheme and spirit of the play" and speaks of
"David's amazing final rhapsody upon Absalom's joy
in the beatific vision of the Triune Deity."[61] But David's
restoration to spiritual health, and his vision of a
forgiven and beatific Absalom, both summarize and
complete what I hope we have by now seen as the overall "scheme" of the play. Though infinitely more
inarticulate, intellectually and structurally, than Milton's
mighty edifice, Peele's *David and Bethsabe* yet
anticipates the epic on the Fall and the Redemption.

In the end the closest parallel to *David and Bethsabe*
among all the documents I have discussed here may be
the *Horae* illustration reproduced in Figure 2: Both
consist of fragments from the story of David, held
together under the one unifying vision of sin and grace.
By the standards of "well-made" structure, smooth-
flowing story, and consistent characters, Peele's play is
clearly inferior to the humanist tragedies on the same
biblical subject written in other languages. But by the
standards of its own elastic pattern—glorying in the sin
as much as in the redemption—it is not less but more
humanist. Perhaps his position in time and space, and
the freedom from the tyranny of external form which it
implied, gave Peele a better chance than any of the others who dramatized the story of the House of David—a
chance to embody in a dramatic structure, however
badly made, the glory that was the Renaissance.

Notes

1. *Oeuvres de P. Corneille,* nov. ed. (Paris, 1873), II,
   113.

2. Corneille presumably had in mind Montchrestien's *David,* which is discussed later in this essay.
   Cf. *Les Tragédies de Montchrestien,* ed. L. Petit
   de Julleville (Paris, 1891), p. 306.

3. Cf. the Introduction to *The Poetical Works of Sir
   William Alexander,* ed. L. E. Kastner and H. B.
   Charlton (Manchester, 1921), p. cxxxv. (This es-

say remains the best work in English on the Renaissance Senecan tradition in Europe.) Cf. also Lancaster E. Dabney, *French Dramatic Literature in the Reign of Henri IV* (Austin, 1952), Chap. I; and Gustave Lanson, *Esquisse d'une Histoire de la Tragédie Française* (New York, 1920), pp. 15 ff.

4. "Ode" by O. du Mont-Sacré in commendation of *Tragedie d'Amnon, et Thamar,* in *Les Tragedies de N. Chretien* (Rouen, 1608).—In the case of both Chrestien and Montchrestien, whose names appear variously with or without an "s," I follow the spelling used by Raymond Lebègue in *La Tragédie française de la Renaissance,* 2nd ed. (Brussels, 1954).—This argument for the superiority of a biblical subject over a similar classical one was a commonplace. See, e.g., Christopherson on his *Jephthah* as against Euripides' *Iphigenia in Aulis.* (Quoted in F. S. Boas, *University Drama in the Tudor Age* [Oxford, 1914], pp. 48-49.)

5. Madeleine Doran, *Endeavors of Art* (Madison, 1954), p. 102.

6. See Francis Kirkman, *A True, Perfect, and Exact Catalogue of all the Comedies, Tragedies, Tragi-Comedies . . .* (London, 1671), and William Winstanley, *The Lives of the Most Famous English Poets* (London, 1687), p. 97.

7. *The History of English Poetry,* rev. ed. (London, 1824), IV, 153, note e.

8. *An Introduction to Tudor Drama* (Oxford, 1933), p. 157, and *University Drama,* p. 363.

9. *Divine Poetry and Drama in Sixteenth Century England* (London, Berkeley, and Los Angeles, 1959), p. 260.

10. Arthus M. Sampley, "The Text of Peele's *David and Bethsabe,*" *PMLA,* XLVI (1931), 670.

11. *Die Tragödie vor Shakespeare* (Heidelberg, 1955), p. 146.—In his translation of Clemen's book, T. S. Dorsch renders this passage as follows: "To do justice to Peele's plays, we must not judge them according to the normally accepted standards of dramatic unity and structure; they must be judged by criteria that are appropriate to their special character" (*English Tragedy before Shakespeare* [London, 1961], p. 163).

12. See Boas, *University Drama;* Campbell, *Divine Poetry and Drama;* and Marvin T. Herrick, *Tragicomedy: Its Origin and Development in Italy, France and England* (Urbana, 1955). See also Herrick's essay, "Susanna and the Elders in Sixteenth-Century Drama," in *Studies in Honor of T. W. Baldwin,* ed. D. C. Allen (Urbana, 1958), pp. 125-135.—I have been helped in my search

for plays on the House of David by the bibliography in *Le Mistère du Viel Testament,* ed. James de Rothschild (Paris, 1882), IV, lvii ff.; and also by the list compiled by John McLaren McBryde, Jr., in his article, "A Study of Cowley's *Davideis,*" *JEGP,* II (1899), 454-527. Invaluable bibliographies of neo-Latin drama are Alfred Harbage's "Census of Anglo-Latin Plays," *PMLA,* LIII (1938), 624-629; and the two works by Leicester Bradner: "A Check-List of Original Neo-Latin Dramas by Continental Writers Printed before 1650," *PMLA,* LVIII (1943), 621-633, and "List of Original Neo-Latin Plays Published before 1650," *Studies in the Renaissance,* IV (1957), 31-70.

13. For the purpose of this essay I have used, and quoted from, the Malone Society reprint of the 1599 quarto of *David and Bethsabe* (ed. W. W. Greg, 1912).—To minimize the confusion which might arise from the fact that each author tends to use his own form of the biblical names (and that in Peele's play the spelling sometimes varies from scene to scene), I have in all cases, except in direct quotations, used the form and spelling to be found in the Authorized Version; thus "Bathsheba," "Hushai," "Absalom," "Ahitophel," etc.

14. See *PMLA,* XLVI (1931), 659-671.

15. This was written by a French Augustinian friar and printed about 1510. I have not seen this play but take my information about it, as well as the quotation, from Raymond Lebègue, *La Tragédie religieuse en France: les debuts (1514-1573),* (Paris, 1929), p. 121.

16. *Ioan. Ravisii Textoris Nivernen Dialogi aliquot festivissimi* (London, 1581), fol. Cc 5ᵛ. The dialogues of Textor, written for his pupils at the Collège de Navarre, were well known in England; they were performed in Latin at the universities and in translations and adaptations elsewhere. Some of them were translated by Thomas Heywood as late as 1637 (*Pleasant Dialogues and Dramas, Selected out of Lucian, Erasmus, Textor, Ovid. & c.*).

17. See *The Tryumphes of Fraunces Petrarcke, translated out of Italian into English by Henrye Parker knyght, Lorde Morley* (1565?), fol. D 1ᵛ; and *Narrenschiff* (Augsburg, 1498), fol. C 4ᵛ.

18. See *The Whole Woorkes of George Gascoigne* (London, 1587), pp. 195-196.

19. *A very Frutefull and Pleasant boke callyd the Instruction of a Christen woman* (London, 1541), fol. N 4ᵛ.

20. Henry Holland, *Dauids Faith and Repentance* (London, 1589), fol. C 3ʳ.

21. *A Tragedye or enterlude . . . manyfestyng the chefe promyses of God vnto man by all ages . . . Compyled by Johan Bale. Anno Domini 1538,* fol. D 1ᵛ.

22. *The Letters and Epigrams of Sir John Harington,* ed. N. E. McClure (Philadelphia and London, 1930), pp. 223-224. The epigram "Of King Dauid. Written to the Queene" is in both the 1600 and the 1603 MSS.

23. Sidney, *An Apologie for Poetrie,* in *Elizabethan Critical Essays,* ed. G. Gregory Smith (London, 1904), I, 174.—Cf. Harington's *Briefe Apologie of Poetrie* (1591), in which Nathan's parable is used to defend the poet's right to "lie" (*Elizabethan Critical Essays,* II, 205).

24. Cf. Louis Réau, *Iconographie de l'art chrétien* (Paris, 1956), II, 273 ff. I have also found much valuable information on this subject in M. R. James, *The Illustration of the Old Testament in Early Times* (The Sanders Lectures for 1924; typewritten copy in the British Museum, press-marked 03149.i.18).—In early printed books, a woodcut of the bathing scene was also extremely common. See Edward Hodnett, *English Woodcuts, 1480-1535* (London, 1935).

25. Elisabeth Kunoth-Leifels, *Über die Darstellungen der "Bathseba im Bade": Studien zur Geschichte des Bildthemas 4. bis 17. Jahrhundert* (Essen, 1962).—Cf. also Réau, *Iconographie.*

26. *Adams Complaint. The Olde Worldes Tragedie. Dauid and Bathsheba* (London, 1596), fol. F 1ᵛ.

27. See *La Bergerie de R. Belleau* (Paris, 1572), p. 103.

28. *The Works of Guillaume De Salluste Sieur Du Bartas,* ed. Holmes, Lyons, and Linker (Chapel Hill, 1940), III, 363 (*Les Trophées,* ll. 907 ff.).—Cf. the delight with which Sylvester, translating Du Bartas, elaborates on this description: "[Bathseba] Perfumes, and combes, and curls her golden hair; / Another-while vnder the Crystall brinks, / Her Alabastrine well-shap't Limbs she shrinks / Like to a Lilly sunk into a glasse: / Like soft loose *Venus* (as they paint the Lasse) / Born in the Seas, when with her eyes sweet-flames, / *Tonnies* and *Tritons* she at-once inflames." (Quoted from the 1613 ed. of Sylvester's translation, *Du Bartas His Deuine Weekes and Workes,* p. 542.)

29. I quote from *Les Tragedies d'Ant, de Montchrestien* (Rouen, 1601), fol. Q 2ᵛ. In the 1604 ed. (also Rouen), described on the title page as "edition nouvelle augmentée par l'auteur," the play has lost its subtitle and become just *David.*

30. I-S. Ekeblad, "The Love of King David and Fair Bethsabe," *English Studies,* XXXIX (1958), 57-62.

31. See, for example, Hans Bol's "The Handing of the Message to Bathseba" in the Amsterdam Rijksmuseum (1568); the same painter's drawing, under the same title, in the H. Reitlinger Collection, London; and Maerten van Heemskerck's "The Handing of the Message to Bathseba." All these are reproduced among the excellent illustrations to Elisabeth Kunoth-Leifels' study (see her figs. 41-43). For a colored messenger, see the Rubens painting, Dresden Gemäldegalerie, and for a colored handmaiden, see Cornelisz van Haarlem, "Bathseba Bathing" (1594), Amsterdam Rijksmuseum (Kunoth-Leifels, figs. 50 and 48).

32. *Das dritt vnd letzt Buch sehr Herrliche Schöne Tragedi / Komedi vnd schimpf Spil / Geistlich vnd Weltlich* (Nuremberg, 1561), I.

33. Wilhelm Creizenach, *Geschichte des Neueren Dramas* (Halle, 1903), III, 428.

34. A recent and valuable study of that tradition is *Les Tragédies de Sénèque et le théâtre de la Renaissance,* ed. Jean Jacquot (Paris, 1964). I am also indebted—apart from the studies of sixteenth-century French drama already cited—to H. C. Lancaster, *A History of French Dramatic Literature in the Seventeenth Century* (Baltimore, 1929) and Kosta Loukovitch, *L'Évolution de la tragédie religieuse classique en France* (Paris, 1933).

35. Cf. n. 29, above. In what follows, I quote from de Julleville's edition of Montchrestien (cf. n. 2, above).

36. *Dialogi* (cf. n. 16, above), fol. Bb 5ᵛ.

37. *The Mirrour of Mutabilitie, or the Principall Part of the Mirrour for Magistrates* (1579), fol. C 2ʳ.

38. It is interesting to note that all the plays in Montchrestien's 1601 collection have exemplary subtitles—such as *Aman, ou la vanité* or *Les Lacènes, ou la constance*—but that in the 1604 ed. these have been removed: perhaps an indication that he did not want to think of himself as writing in a plainly homiletic vein. The sensuous delight with which he elaborates the bathing scene in *David, ou l'adultère* rather obscures the moralistic purpose.

39. *The Psalmes of Dauid . . . set forth in Latine by that excellent learned man Theodore Beza. And faithfully translated into English, by Anthonie Gilbie* (London, 1581), p. 112.

40. Heinrich Bullinger, *The Christen State of Matrimonye,* trans. Myles Coverdale (London, 1541), fol. 3ʳ⁻ᵛ.—Cf. the same Bullinger's *Fiftie Godlie and Learned Sermons,* trans. "H. I." (London, 1587), p. 233, where the same point is made.

41. Arthur M. Sampley, "Plot Structure in Peele's Plays as a Test of Authorship," *PMLA,* LI (1936), 698.

42. Munday, *Mirrour of Mutabilitie,* fol. I 3ᵛ.

43. Vives, *Instruction of a Christen Woman,* fol. M 1ᵛ.

44. *Das dritt vnd letzt Buch . . .* (1561; though the *Thamar* is dated, at the end, 1556), I, fol. 90ᵛ ff.

45. See the epigram by Hugo Grotius, in commendation of Honerdius' *Thamara* (Leyden, 1611), no page ref. Cf. n. 4, above.

46. In discussing these three plays, I use, and quote from, the following editions: *Les Tragedies de N. Chretien, Sieur des Croix Argentenois* (Rouen, 1608); *Rochi Honerdii . . . Supremi in Hollandia Consistori Senatoris, Thamara Tragoedia* (Leyden, 1611); *Amnon Tragoedia Sacra. Autore Rdo. Domino D. Iacobo Cornelio Lvmmenaeo à Marca* (Ghent, 1617).

47. These "stances" use the image of Tamar as the sun and Amnon himself as an Icarus figure. Cf. the much more relevant use of this image in Peele's Prologue.

48. "Latin Drama of the Renaissance," *Studies in the Renaissance,* IV (1957), 42-43.

49. I take my information on Honerdius from the *Biographie Universelle* (Paris, 1857), XIX, 387.

50. Cf. E. M. W. Tillyard, *Shakespeare's History Plays* (London, Penguin, 1962), p. 147.

51. See S. C. Chew, "Time and Fortune," *ELH,* VI (1939), 83-113.

52. I have used, and quoted from, the 1586 edition. There were at least three separate editions: 1556 (though Rothschild, *Le Mistère du Viel Testament,* IV, lxxii, disputes its existence), 1586, and 1588; and the play was also published in Vol. III of *Raccolta di Rappresentazioni sacre* (Venice, 1605 and 1606). Despite the kind assistance of Professor Carlo Dionisotti, I have been able to find out very little about Brunetto. The title page of *David Sconsolato* describes him as "Frate di S. Francesco osseruante"; and Mazzuchelli, in *Scrittoria d'Italia,* II (1758 ed.), p. 2178, only adds that he flourished around the middle of the sixteenth century and wrote poetry in the vernacular. The bibliographical information above is also taken from Mazzuchelli, who lists no further works by Brunetto—whom, incidentally, he calls Brunetti.

53. Cf. Kastner and Charlton, *Works of Sir William Alexander,* pp. lxiii-xciv; and Herrick, *Tragicomedy,* pp. 93 ff.

54. Sachs himself did write a play on the Absalom story: *Ein Tragedi . . . der auffrhüriske Absalom mit seinem Vatter König David (Das ander Buch . . . [Nuremberg, 1560], I, fol. xviiʳ ff.). This is an allegorical morality about good fathers and bad children, good kings and rebellious subjects. The play itself is dated 1551.

55. There is a unique manuscript in the British Museum: MS Stowe 957. It is discussed most fully by G. R. Churchill and Wolfgang Keller, "Die lateinischen Universitäts-Dramen in der Zeit der Königin Elisabeth," *Shakespeare Jahrbuch,* XXXIV (1898), 229-232, and by Boas, *University Drama,* Appendix I.—Unfortunately, a recent critical edition and translation of the play came to my notice too late for me to use it for this essay: John Hazel Smith, *A Humanist's "Trew Imitation": Thomas Watson's "Absalon"* (Urbana, 1964).

56. Ascham, *Scholemaster,* in *Elizabethan Critical Essays,* I, 24.

57. *University Drama,* p. 365.

58. *Ibid.*

59. *The chefe promyses of God,* fol. D 2ʳ.

60. See P. H. Cheffaud, *George Peele* (Paris, 1913), esp. p. 131; and H. D. Sykes, "Peele's Borrowings from Du Bartas," *NQ,* CXLVII (1924), 349-351, 368-369.

61. *University Drama,* p. 365.—I should not like to conclude this essay without thanking all the friends and colleagues who, over the last few years, have helped me to collect David material—especially Mr. Bernard Harris, Professor G. K. Hunter, Miss Joan Grundy, and Mr. Brian Nellist. I should also like to thank Mr. David Cook for discussing *Horae* illustrations with me, and the staff of the Warburg Institute for letting me look at the Institute's collection of Renaissance biblical pictures.

Carolyn Whitney-Brown (essay date 1991)

SOURCE: Whitney-Brown, Carolyn. "'A Farre More Worthy Wombe': Reproduction Anxiety in Peele's *David and Bethsabe.*" In *In Another Country: Feminist Perspectives on Renaissance Drama,* edited by Dorothea Kehler and Susan Baker, pp. 181-204. Metuchen, N.J.: The Scarecrow Press, Inc., 1991.

[*In the following essay, Whitney-Brown argues that Peele's* David and Bethsabe *"is a play about reproduction."*]

ABSALON:

> What boots it Absalon, unhappie Absalon,
>   Sighing I say what boots it Absalon
> To have disclos'd a farre more worthy wombe.
>
> (1586-88)[1]

Absalon's mysterious lines are out of place in Peele's *David and Bethsabe*. The speaker, King David's beautiful, rebellious son, has been stabbed to death on stage as he hung in a tree, suspended by his hair. The lines quoted above occur after his staged death, somehow wandering into the text as an inconvenience and an interruption, signaling a dislocation where one need not be. The play could be read well without these wandering lines. We might recall the medical theory, popular in the sixteenth century, that a woman's womb moved through her body of its own volition, often wandering into the throat and causing suffocation, fainting fits, or erratic behavior. Our word *hysteria* derives from the notion of the wandering womb.[2]

Absalon's lines not only invoke the womb, but also function as a wandering womb, affecting discussions of the play, and suffocating a potentially coherent text. What can we say about this textual wandering womb?

Editors of Peele's play have been irritated by the mislocation of Absalon's lines. Unable to husband them into any more suitable place in the text, editors have resorted to three available treatments. Some coax the wayward lines into footnotes, with an apologetic explanation, such as A. H. Bullen's: "After the chorus in old ed. occurs the following passage which belonged to some lost or cancelled scene."[3] Others leave the lines in the text, seeking to draw their presence into rational discussion by means of brief notes. John Matthews Manly observes:

This fragment is printed in Isl. at the bottom of G4$_v$°. The word *then* is the catchword for the next page, and its presence indicates that more of the copy than has been preserved to us was in the printer's hands, if not actually set up—how much more is of course unknown.[4]

W. W. Greg's 1912 Malone Society Reprint, doubtless obliged by editorial constraint to leave the wandering lines in the text, warns the reader to resist entanglement—a marginal gloss diagnoses: *misplaced fragment.* These editorial responses engage the fact of the fragment's presence, but ignore the words themselves.

Absalon's words raise questions about what is "worthy" and what is "disclosed." In Peele's play, Absalon rebelliously discloses the faults of his father David that make David unworthy to rule. Though Absalon bases his own worthiness on his radiant beauty, the play discloses how that self-glorification becomes its own entanglement. Yet Absalon's lament asks, "What boots it . . . / To have disclos'd a farre more worthy wombe?" Why "wombe"?

I

David and Bethsabe is a play about reproduction. Four of King David's sons play key roles, paralleling the actions that constitute their father. After David forces

Bethsabe, the wife of one of his soldiers, to commit adultery with him, David's son Ammon unintentionally mirrors his father's sexual violence by incestuously "forcing" his half-sister Thamar. Further, the son adulterously conceived by David and Bethsabe is identified as the representation and scapegoat of David's sin. God's retribution for this sin is the sickness and death of that infant; after the son dies, David proclaims, "The child is dead, then ceaseth Davids shame" (l. 696). Solomon, David's second son by Bethsabe, is identified as God's anointed heir to David's kingdom. The boy reproduces David's passionate desire for God as well as David's authoritative vision of monarchy.

David's identification with another son, Absalon, is stressed even more strongly. Beginning with the opening invocation's promise to sing of "this sweet poet Joves Musition, / And of his beauteous sonne" (ll. 14-15), Absalon is associated with his father. David invokes his son as

> . . . Absalon the beautie of my bones,
> Faire Absalon the counterfeit of love,
> Sweet Absalon, the image of content,
> Must claime a portion in his fathers care,
> And be in life and death King Davids sonne.
>
> (ll. 1683-87)

Not only Absalon's life but his physical appearance echoes his father's aesthetic values:

> A beautifull and faire young man is he,
> In all his bodie is no blemish seene,
> His haire is like the wyer of Davids Harpe.
>
> (ll. 936-38; see also ll. 746-48)

Even Absalon's political rebellion is similar to David's adulterous rebellion: both are based in an ethic of beauty, specifically of beautiful hair that embodies desire—David's adulterous desire fixating upon Bethsabe's hair, and Absalon's political desire solipsistically focusing upon his own beauty radiating from his hair as an aesthetic legitimation of his claim to the throne.

The relation of the figures of David and his sons suggests the biblical adage that the sins of the fathers are visited upon their sons. By the time of the Renaissance, this adage was incorporated in a larger cultural fantasy of male preeminence in biological generation and reproduction. Some Renaissance writers adhered to the theories of Aristotle and his followers that the womb was like the earth into which a man casts seed. The seed determined all characteristics of the child, while the mother provided matter, nutriment, and incubation.[5] Even those who criticized Aristotle's construction believed that the sex of the child was determined by whether it had sufficient heat in its conception and gestation to extrude male genitals. Insufficient heat produced the interior genitals of a female; whether females were therefore imperfect males was a matter of discussion.[6]

Galen, writing in the second century A.D., held that both sexes had to ejaculate their seed for conception to occur. He agreed with Aristotle that the difference between the sexes was one of body heat. Although Galen's two-seed theory would seem to suggest that women and men played an equal role in conception, related beliefs and practices suggest that the male still assumed primary responsibility for the child's sex. A popular suggestion for conceiving a male child was that the male should tie off his left testicle, thereby begetting a son by the hotter seed of the right testicle.[7] Although the child's characteristics could be determined by either seed, the stronger or hotter seed was expected to dominate. Women's semen, however, was considered colder and less vigorous than men's semen.[8] One might assume therefore that a child would primarily resemble its father.[9] Aristotelian theorists understood that the father "perfected" the offspring, imparting living motion or the sensitive soul.[10] The material practices relating to conception and childbirth suggest that a variety of theories coexisted.[11] It is sufficient at present to note that all theories gave some sort of priority to male self-replication.

In Peele's play, then, one might expect a simple reproduction of David in his son Absalon. David's identification with Absalon, however, is not unidirectional. Absalon's rebellion is engendered in David himself when Absalon becomes a greater preoccupation for David than the responsibilities of his own kingship. This preoccupation sets the structure of father-son reproduction into a circuit whereby father and son each reproduce one another as rebel at the expense of other identities. The circular quality of this father-son relationship is most apparent toward the end of *David and Bethsabe,* when David is told of the "well-deserved" death of his rebellious son Absalon in language suiting the social relationship of subject and monarch:

> Happinesse and honour live with Davids soule,
> Whom God hath blest with conquest of his foes.
>   . . . . .
> The stubborne enemies to Davids peace,
> And all that cast their darts against his crowne,
> Fare ever like the young man Absalon.

> (ll. 1794-95, 1797-99)

Rather than responding with the appropriate expressions of kingly satisfaction and security, however, David breaks into an extravagant identification with Absalon, offering to reenact Absalon's fate:

> Die David for the death of Absalon,
> And make these cursed newes the bloudy darts,
> That through his bowels rip thy wretched breast.
> Hence David, walke the solitarie woods.

> (ll. 1806-9)

David continues his wild lament for eighteen lines, then collapses in grief. His behavior disgusts his general,

Joab, because he speaks not as a king, nor even as a loyal subject. A rebel, Joab notes, is a hate to heaven and earth; there is no reason ever to mourn a rebel's death. Nathan the prophet similarly finds David's grief excessive and offensive to God. To identify with the rebel is a rebellion within David: Joab threatens to lead his armies to another king. The figure of the monarch cannot be in rebellion against the ideology that constitutes it.

But David identifies with Absalon on aesthetic grounds. He had asked that Absalon's life be spared because of Absalon's beauty, an enticing beauty that subverts even kingly self-preservation and authority. David's blunt order to his assembled troops—"For my sake spare the young man Absalon" (l. 1396)—continues, not with urgent directions about the imminent battle, or even royal encouragement in battle, but with a seemingly irrelevant rhapsody:

> Friend him with deeds, and touch no haire of him,
> Not that fair haire with which the wanton winds
> Delight to play, and love to make it curle,
> Wherein the Nightingales would build their nests,
> And make sweet bowers in every golden tresse,
> To sing their lover every night asleepe.

> (ll. 1401-6)

Peele thus presents David's identity as aesthete or psalmist, set against his role as king. In response to Absalon's death, Peele's David extravagantly claims that he will break his lute and hang it in the tree where Absalon was caught by the hair and killed. His rebellious aesthetic yearnings represented by his lute will thus share the same fate as Absalon. In other words, Absalon's rebellion and demise beget similar rebellious desires and a kind of death wish in his father.

II

Critics have not questioned the centrality and self-sufficiency of the father-son relationships in *David and Bethsabe.* Accordingly, the play has been read around the unifying theme of David's guilt.[12] David's daughter, Thamar, is then read as the site that allows Ammon to mirror his father's sexual sin. Bethsabe and David's other concubines are seen to function as signals of "moral enervation" or figures of temptation that allow David to demonstrate his sins of lechery.[13] A. R. Braunmiller even suggests that "the audience's normal reaction with theater spectacle" associates "us" with David: "The King watches the beautiful bather in much the same way (and presumably with many of the same thoughts) as members of the audience."[14] This formulation implicates the audience in a specifically male gaze, and strangely occludes both the lack of any history of sixteenth-century performance of *David and Bethsabe* and the ambiguous gender-identification of female figures on the all-male Renaissance stage. It identifies the figure of Bethsabe primarily as a female object of male lust.

Peele's Bethsabe, however, is more than a sight or site of David's transgression, more than the silent object of desire. She is fully a speaking subject, exposing and criticizing the contradiction between David's lecherous behavior and the ideology of the godly king. "What is David," she asks bluntly early in the play, "that he should desire / For fickle beuties sake his servants wife?" (ll. 100-101). David's messenger responds that she has no need to question the purity of David's desire, reciting the ideology surrounding David. Since he is

> wise and just,
> Elected to the heart of Israels God,
> Then doe not thou expostulate with him.
>
> (ll.102-4)

Bethsabe's reply has an edge of sarcasm:

> My lord the king, elect to Gods owne heart,
> Should not his gracious jelousie incense,
> Whose thoughts are chast. I hate incontinence.
>
> (ll. 106-8)

The entrenched ideology of the godly king is not immediately dislocated by sarcasm, however, and David arranges the death of Bethsabe's husband. Bethsabe laments her position as female subject: "O what is it to serve the lust of Kings, / How Lyonlike they rage when we resist" (ll. 598-99).

Although Bethsabe's disgusted critique exposes David's inconsistent ideological position, she later enunciates a vision of the kingdom and David's kingship revived by David's poetic powers. As David waits despondently for news of Absalon's death, Bethsabe reminds him of what power he has to renew the kingdom:

> What meanes my lord, the lampse of Israel,
> From whose bright eyes all eyes receive their light,
> To dim the glory of his sweet aspects . . .
>
> . . . . .
>
> Take but your Lute, and make the mountaines dance,
> Retrive the sunnes sphere, and restraine the clouds,
> Give eares to trees, make savage Lyons tame,
> Impose still silence to the loudest winds,
> And fill the fairest day with foulest stormes:
> Then why should passions of much meaner power,
> Beare head against the heart of Israel?
>
> (ll. 1641-43, 1648-54)

One would think that David should be the head, not the heart, of Israel. Given what we have observed of how David's aesthetic yearnings interrupt and dislocate his authority as king, and how David the psalmist and lover of beauty forced Bethsabe to commit adultery, Bethsabe's invocation of the psalmist as the proper king is at

least surprising. She calls David to kingship by means of his lute, the lute that is identified with the father's reproduction in his sons, with Absalon's hair, and with the poetic desire for beauty that led to David's appropriation of Bethsabe's body. It would hardly seem in Bethsabe's best interests to recall in David aesthetic priorities that initially erupted in rebellious passions.

Calling the verbal response that Bethsabe inspires in David simply "aesthetic," however, is problematic. David's aesthetic language is crossed by aural pleasure, as well as lust and sexual manipulation. The utterances I have thus far grouped rather crudely under the category "aesthetic" take various significances from the location of their enunciation. This location has to do not only with the geographical space involved, but also with the social role and gender of the speaker. At the beginning of the play, an expression of erotic pleasure is enunciated in Bethsabe's private song:

> Shine sun, burne fire, breathe aire, and ease mee,
> Black shade, fair nurse, shroud me and please me.
> Shadow (my sweet nurse) keep me from burning,
> Make not my glad cause, cause of mourning.
> Let not my beauties fire.
> Enflame unstaied desire,
> Nor pierce any bright eye,
> That wandreth lightly.
> Come gentle Zephire trickt with those perfumes
> That erst in Eden sweetned Adams love,
> And stroke my bosome with thy silken fan . . .
>
> . . . . .
>
> Thou and thy sister, soft and sacred aire,
> Goddesse of life, and governesse of health,
> Keep every fountaine fresh and arbor sweet.
>
> (ll. 26-36, 41-43)

These words of pleasure are sung in seclusion; the stage directions read, "Bethsabe with her maid bathing over a spring." Bethsabe's lines should not be read as an invitation or license to rape the singer, but rather as the genuine voicing of pleasure in the female subject. Bethsabe's language here is that of erotic pleasure in her own body.

David's response to this language is complex. David violates Bethsabe's pleasure by subjecting her to his lust and adultery, but he also responds erotically and poetically to her. His violation is embedded in the hierarchical structure of monarch and subject. Bethsabe's blunt rebuke "I hate incontinence" (l. 108) is followed by a veiled threat from the king's messenger:

> Woman thou wrongst the King, and doubtst his ho-
> nour,
> Whose truth mainteines the crowne of Israel,
> Making him stay, that bad me bring thee strait.
>
> (ll. 109-11)

That Bethsabe hears the threat is apparent in her response, for she locates her own voice in relation to David's, saying, "The Kings poore handmaid will obey my lord" (l. 112). The messenger makes sure she understands the submission required: "Then come and doe thy dutie to his grace, / And doe what seemeth favour in his sight" (ll. 113-14). David, too, reminds Bethsabe that he is her King and Prince (ll. 143-44).

But David's response to Bethsabe is not simply a sovereign's urge to subject and violate the body he surveys. In fact, his initial response to Bethsabe's bathing is noteworthy for the relative unimportance of visual attention and description. David responds poetically to "tunes," "words," and "wonders" (l. 49):

> Faire Eva plac'd in perfect happinesse,
> Lending her praise-notes to the liberall heavens,
> Strooke with the accents of Arch-angels tunes,
> Wrought not more pleasure of her husbands thoughts,
> Then this faire womans words and notes to mine.
>
> (ll. 53-57)

Beyond the irony of David's invocation of Adam and Eve to image his adulterous urge for Urias's wife, one is struck by the verbal, aural focus of David's attraction. Words and notes bring pleasure to his thoughts. David's desire to be in Bethsabe's space is both a sexual urge to penetrate the body he lecherously views, and also a poetic desire to participate in Bethsabe's site of pleasurable enunciation.

Female pleasure is thus represented as a problem from the beginning of Peele's play. Bethsabe's poetic and erotic pleasure engenders in David both a desire for similar pleasure and a desire to rape Bethsabe as female object. Female pleasure is both affirmed and punished.

Such contradictory responses to female pleasure were a cultural problematic built into Galen's biology of reproduction. As we observed earlier, Renaissance writers following Galen believed that conception required that both partners ejaculate their seed. Thus, both men and women had to experience orgasm, unless the woman's womb was "so greedy, and lickerish that it doth euen come down to meet nature," engulfing the man's seed and ejaculating its own seed.[15] This greedy condition was rare, however. Female erotic pleasure was ordinarily required for conception. At the same time, attitudes from medieval theologians condemning sexual pleasure as sinful continued in the Renaissance: indeed the popular late medieval European text *Malleus Maleficarum,* reprinted throughout the Renaissance, insisted upon the demonic nature of female sexual pleasure. Medical historian Ilza Veith explains:

> [For the] authors of *Malleus,* any kind of sexual relations, even within the bond of matrimony, that evoked pleasure, were assumed to be the devil's doings. By torturous reasoning based on the works of Augustine, the ability to experience sexual pleasure derived from involvement with the devil. A woman's pleasures could

have only come from satanic copulation; the man in turn derived his gratification from the unholy wiles of his devil inspired partner.[16]

To sum up the paradox: dominant cultural teachings asserted that to engage in sexual activity without intention to conceive was sinful. Yet in order to conceive, the female partner must reach a climax. At the same time, female sexual pleasure was condemned as demonic.

The mixed messages that acknowledged female power were further complicated by the belief that a pregnant woman had an alarming capacity to subvert the male's "perfect" seed. Eating, walking, or imagination could affect the fetus. Birthmarks, deformities, or even surprising skin color could be produced by what a woman saw, sat upon, brooded upon, or feared. For example, it was asserted that a queen of Ethiopia

> bore a white child from thinking about a "marvellous white thing" when she lay with the king. Or the woman who, conversely, at the time of conception beholding the picture of a blackamoor, conceived and brought forth a black child. The case of the gentlewoman in Suffolk whose face was spotted with blood passing her butcher's, and had a child similarly marked was another example.[17]

Contradictory beliefs may disclose how mysterious and threatening female reproductive power was. Patricia Crawford, in her study of attitudes toward menstruation, suggests that patterns of taboo

> draw attention to the ambiguous position of women in the society. Women were dangerous, but they were dangerous because they were powerful. . . . After her childbearing was over a woman was no longer powerful and so less feared.[18]

Peele's Bethsabe embodies a mapping of these contradictions. Bethsabe is simultaneously the site of her own pleasure, and of David's pleasurable poetic desire, and also the sight of David's lust that ignites his adulterous, murderous sexual passion. Bethsabe is not only the site of discourses of lust and pleasure, but bears the king's heir. The female speaker of pleasure ultimately reproduces the kingship in Solomon: she is the agent of succession, disclosing her worthy womb.

In Peele's play, Bethsabe is the only mother of David's sons to be identified. David and Bethsabe's first son is recognized as "the babe is sicke, sweet babe, that Bersabe / With womans paine brought forth to Israel" (ll. 610-11). Bethsabe is the play's only recognized royal mother. Thus, when succession itself seems threatened, we may discern a displaced paternal anxiety about its necessary female agent. Just such an anxiety erupts in a strange scene at the height of David's military power, when after conquering a town, he is told that all his sons are dead. David responds:

Die David, for to thee is left no seed,
That may revive thy name in Israel.

(ll. 850—51)

David's sons, begotten by his seed, are now his seed, and his hope of future generation. To have no sons is to have no seed. The message, however, is false. Only one son, Ammon, is dead, killed by Absalon to avenge the rape of Absalon's sister Thamar. But the anxiety of succession is not forgotten with the corrected message. The Widow of Tecoa is sent by Joab to image David's banishment of Absalon as a loss of all possible heirs—a loss significantly figured by the barrenness implicitly represented by a widow:

So will they quench that sparkle that is left,
And leave nor name, nor issue on the earth,
To me, or to thy handmaids husband dead.
. . . . .
Call home the banished, that he may live,
And raise to thee some fruit in Israel.

(ll. 897-99, 915-16)

The scene reminds us that while David can easily recover from the death of one son, to have no sons left would be to have no seed, no name, nor issue. This curious sequence of events raises the anxiety of no succession, the anxiety of the monarch's, and indeed society's, dependence upon the worthy female womb.

III

While Absalon's wandering lines are not part of a unified text, they clearly belong to the text we have and the culture in which the text was produced. Although conception and birth were subject to intense cultural construction, the medical and political discourses legitimating male fantasies of being solely responsible for reproduction were limited by the necessity of the female agency of the womb. By the 1580s and early 1590s, in the particular case of royal reproduction, Elizabethan society was especially anxious about the sovereign womb and the succession of Queen Elizabeth I.

David and Bethsabe was written within seven years of a public enactment of the scene of Absalon and David played by women dressed as men. Queen Elizabeth, dressed in the heart and stomach of a king of England played David, and Mary, Queen of Scots, played her rebellious kin, Absalon. The scene had already been written by the parliaments of 1572 and 1586. At the parliament of 1572, the bishops urged Elizabeth to justly punish Mary, Queen of Scots, in the highest degree because the "late Scottish Queen hath heaped up together all the sins of the licentious sons of David." Neale then summarizes the bishop's point: "If she escape with slight or no punishment, the Queen and her subjects ought to fear that God will reserve her as an instrument to put the Queen from her royal seat of this Kingdom and to plague the people."[19] In 1586, the bishops were even more pressing: If Mary were not cut off by course of justice "the Queen's Majesty's most royal person cannot be continued with safety. They concluded solemnly, *'Ne pereat Israel, pereat Absolom'* (Absolom must perish lest Israel perish)."[20]

The queen was urged to play her part promptly, not only by direct address, but also obliquely, through public sermons. For instance, in a sermon on King David's psalm 4 "at what time a main treason was discovered," Bishop Sandys suppressed David's squalid family details and instead asserted:

God requireth as well the sacrifice of justice, as of mercy: yea, he sometimes accepteth justice for a sacrifice, and playgeth mercy as a grievous sin. If David had not spared his son for murder, his son had not troubled him with rebellion.[21]

By contrast, Peele's play demonstrates that if God had not spared David for the murder of Bethsabe's husband Urias, Absalon would not have needed to rebel: Absalon would have been king. But the bishops were not concerned to examine the complex relationships involved in the story of Absalon's rebellion.

Similarly, Archbishop Whitgift, who was involved in constructing the bishops' statement to the queen at the 1586 parliament, preached the Accession Day sermon at St. Paul's, London, in 1583 on the obedience the subject owes the monarch, invoking Absalon as an example of the fate of those who disobey a prince.[22] Elizabethan Accession Days continued to celebrate Elizabeth's lawful and peaceful accession, although by 1583 the next accession was becoming a topic of grave concern. The people's thwarted wish for the queen to produce an heir was a kind of backside to the queen's successful reign: indeed by 1583, the anxiety of succession focused on the queen's ability to bear children; she was fifty years old.[23] Of course, this side of the queen was not addressed by the Archbishop on Accession Day. On the same 1583 Accession Day, however, the English ambassador in Paris reported seeing the following representation of her majesty's other side:

a fowle picture of the Queen's majesty sett upp she being on horseback her left hand holding the brydell of the horse, with her right hande pullinge up her clothes shewing her hindparte.[24]

Under this portrait was a picture of the Duke of Anjou who had been trying to negotiate a marriage with Elizabeth.[25] The female hindpart was culturally perceived as directly reproductive: the scurrilous Parisian portrait illustrated a slur against the possibility of a reproductive French alliance with the English queen. When Peele's Bethsabe bares her hindpart, she immediately begins a reproduction of the king, and eventually gives birth to the heir. For Elizabeth I, having the heart and stomach of a king was not enough to produce an heir. This was clear enough to the Elizabethans, and to the unknown Parisian artist who graphically disclosed the reproductive hindpart that Elizabeth's subjects desired their queen to display.

The queen's body politic and mortal body converge in the question of reproduction.[26] The body politic requires the conditions of its reproduction: an heir. When the monarch is male as is Peele's David, queenly concubines can be employed to produce sons at little risk to the mortal body of the king. Though David may be in self-rebellion against the ideology of the king in whose name Joab fights, he has produced many possible successors, and can continue to produce more, if necessary. A queen, however, in order to give birth to an heir, must risk her mortal body on behalf of the body politic. The stakes are thus different when the monarch is female. The queen will be immanently expected to produce a child; she may die in childbirth, or once a male heir is produced, she may be expendable to the realm. Louis Montrose has observed how Elizabeth I was variously constructed by her subjects: "The collective discourse that we call 'Queen Elizabeth' was traversed by multiple and potentially antagonistic strategies."[27] Certainly, the efforts to construct Elizabeth as the fertile female monarch were relentless. In a characteristic maneuver, however, Elizabeth resisted this ideological construction by refusing to act or disclose the reproductive part.

Mary, Queen of Scots, in contrast, had a son and successor: James VI of Scotland. In other words, Mary, though identified as the rebel Absalon, disclosed a far more worthy womb, a womb that was biologically and politically reproductive.

IV

In Peele's play, Bethsabe gives birth to the royal heir, and thus discloses her worthy, politically reproductive womb. Yet Peele's rebel Absalon is the figure who claims to have disclosed a far more worthy womb. These two characters, Absalon and Bethsabe, are peculiarly congruent figures in Peele's text, both figures of pleasure and beauty. David demonstrates this congruence, invoking both Bethsabe and Absalon as sites of pleasure. We recall how Absalon's "fair haire with which the wanton winds / Delight to play, and love to make it curle" (ll. 1402-3) entangles and dislocates David's sovereign authority. At his first meeting with Bethsabe, David's description of her as the one who "brings my longings tangled in her haire" (l. 116) is like David's later description of Absalon's entangling power. David's longings for Bethsabe dislocate his ideology of the godly king, drawing him into an adulter-

ous self-rebellion. Bethsabe's beauty, her self-pleasure, and her own poetic capacities make her not simply an object of David's sovereign lust, however, but a figure who by the play's end engages David in a reciprocity of desire, pleasure, and poetic sympathies. Bethsabe and David become mutually entangled.

I have already considered how Bethsabe's opening song as she bathes pleasurably describes the sun on her body, and the breezes that stroke her bosom and gently penetrate her clothing. Absalon similarly enjoys himself, as "flowring in pleasant spring time of his youth" (l. 960). His self-appreciative language exceeds Bethsabe's, however, by claiming supernatural power in his beauty:

> Then shall the stars light earth with rich aspects,
> And heaven shall burne in love with Absalon,
> Whose beautie will suffice to chase all mists,
> And cloth the suns sphere with a triple fire. . . .
>
> 　　　　. . . . .
>
> Absalon, that in his face
> Carries the finall purpose of his God,
> That is, to worke him grace in Israel. . . .
>
> 　　　　. . . . .
>
> His thunder is intangled in my haire,
> And with my beautie is his lightning quencht,
> I am the man he made to glorie in.
>
> 　　　　　　(ll. 1117-20, 1163-65, 1168-70)

Whereas David initially projects upon Bethsabe the entanglement of his desire in her hair and beauty, Absalon claims for his own hair and beauty a power to entangle not only nature but even God. Furthermore, David's entanglement in Bethsabe's hair eventually produces an heir; significantly Absalon claims himself as the only worthy reproduction and heir of the kingship, most centrally because of the aesthetic authority of his beautiful hair.[28] Beyond imagining himself as an icon of divine radiance and authority, Absalon reproduces himself as king on the basis of an aesthetic politics that claims even God as subject, obediently entangled in his hair.

Yet Absalon's invitation to entanglement has an unexpected doubleness that eventually counters his claims to radiant authority. The play reveals how Absalon's entanglement with nature finally subjects him, and his hair—for of course, Absalon dies strung helpless in a tree that entwines and ravishes his hair while remaining oblivious to his radiant authority. Absalon exclaims in frustration:

> Hath Absalon no souldier neere his hand,
> Than may untwine me this unpleasant curle,
> Or wound this tree that ravisheth his lord?
> O God behold the glorie of thy hand,
> And choisest fruit of Natures workemanship,
> Hang like a rotten branch upon this tree. . . .
>
> 　　　　. . . . .

O let my beautie fill these sencelesse plants,
With sence and power to lose me from this plague.

(ll. 1473-78, 1482-83)

To Joab, Absalon's entanglement in the tree serves to condemn him decisively as a rebel. The tree reveals Absalon's self-preoccupation with his own beauty as a rebelliousness which ultimately entangles itself—at least this is how Joab and his soldiers interpret Absalon's demise. Joab declares: "Now see the Lord hath tangled in a tree / The health and glorie of thy stubborne heart, / And made thy pride curbd with a sencelesse plant" (ll. 1514-16). After Absalon's death, one soldier exclaims:

See where the rebell in his glorie hangs,
Where is the vertue of thy beautie Absalon,
Will any of us here now feare thy lookes?
Or be in love with that thy golden haire,
Wherein was wrapt rebellion gainst thy sire?

(ll. 1550-54)

Joab and his soldiers' reading of Absalon's hair and beauty as the essence of rebellion rather than legitimation follows the line of reason of the Elizabethan *Book of Homilies,* which identified Absalon as a rebel so contrary to God and nature as to be arrested by a tree:

[When] most men were afraid to lay their hands upon him, a great tree stretching out his arms, as it were for that purpose, caught him by the great and long bush of his goodly hair, lapping about it as he fled hastily bareheaded under the said tree and so hanged him up by the hair of his head in the air, to give an eternal document, that neither comeliness of personage, neither nobility, nor favour of the people, no nor the favour of the king himself, can save a rebel from due punishment: God, the King of kings, being so offended with him, that rather than he should lack due execution for his treason, every tree by the way will be a gallows or gibbet unto him . . . A fearful example of God's punishment, good people, to consider.[29]

Yet while Joab affirms an orthodox ideology of the godly king and the deserved punishment of the rebel, we have seen that King David himself is problematically attracted to the rebel and the rebellious entanglements of beauty. Likewise, the whole play interlocks contradictory claims of pleasure and authority, aesthetics and politics, poetry and reproduction, that all combine to dislocate the ideological orthodoxies of monarchy. Both Absalon and Bethsabe have the effect of inciting David's own rebellion against such orthodoxies, and both reproduce the kingship in their own fashions.

Absalon's complex congruence with Bethsabe should also be seen in his defense of another female victim of violation, his sister Thamar. Absalon is the only figure who protects and sympathizes with Thamar after her rape. He takes her home, and remembers her when all

the other characters, and perhaps even the audience or reader, have forgotten her. His revenge of stabbing Ammon is so extreme that he astonishes all the male figures present. This passionate expression of repressed sexual anger echoes Bethsabe's condemnation of royal sexual abuse. Here Bethsabe and Thamar could be read as gendered fragments of the same embarrassing family story of sexual violation. While Bethsabe is constrained to the patience of a handmaid, Absalon, on behalf of Thamar, stabs.

I do not wish, however, to oversimplify Absalon's figure: his sympathetic identification with female figures is not unproblematic. In order to publicize his father's shame and his own kingship, Absalon temporarily releases his father's concubines. Though his motive is to expose David's backside, so to speak, he expects that freedom from David will be desirable to the concubines. They refuse his authority, saying, "Thy fathers honour, gracelesse Absalon, / And ours thus beaten with thy violent armes, / Will crie for vengeance" (ll. 1123-25). Absalon's advisor Architophel recommends:

Let not my lord the King of Israel
Be angrie with a sillie womans threats,
But with the pleasure he hath erst enjoied,
Turne them into their cabinets againe.

(ll. 1138-41)

In what way have Absalon's violent "armes" beaten the concubines' honor? What pleasure has he enjoyed? Absalon releases the abusive concubines without punishing them "to recompence the shame they have sustained" (ll. 1155). Does he refer to the shame he supposed they experienced at his father's hands, or by being exposed publicly, or has he or his men shamed them? The concubines apparently do not regard Absalon as a sympathetic figure. Absalon uses the concubines' bodies as displays of his authority, to keep or release. In this identification of male power over female bodies, Absalon continues the hierarchical power relationships described by the prophet Nathan to David:

David, thus sayth the Lord thy God by me:
I thee annointed King in Israel,
And sav'd thee from the tyranny of Saul.
Thy maisters house I gave thee to possesse,
His Wives into thy bosome did I give . . .
. . . . .
Wherefore behold, I wil (saith Jacobs God)
In thine owne house stir evill up to thee,
Yea I before thy face will take thy Wives,
And give them to thy neighbor to possesse:
This shall be done to David in the day,
That Israel openly may see thy shame.

(ll. 635-39, 650-55)

Nathan's patriarchal claim is that God arranges for royal power to be represented by the exclusive possession of many female bodies; the public exposure and use of those same female bodies by a rival represents shame and a loss of authority. Absalon's appropriation of David's concubines makes such a rival challenge.

Absalon can thus be seen as a contradictory figure who both acts for female interests in the play yet at other times may seek to identify himself as sovereign by royal subjugation and violation of women. David himself is crossed by similar contradictions. Not only does David seek to penetrate Bethsabe first visually and then sexually, but he also desires to be penetrated himself. Upon first seeing Bethsabe, David declares, "What tunes, what words, what looks, what wonders pierce / My soule?" (ll. 49-50). Much later, when hearing of the death of Absalon he cries, "And make these cursed newes the bloudy darts, / That through his bowels rip thy wretched breast" (ll. 1807-8). This culturally "feminine" role of David as the penetrated one can be juxtaposed with the virgin and masculine roles of Elizabeth I. The queen is represented in portraits as impenetrable, iconographically defending the integrity of her body and her kingdom.[30] In contrast, no matter how many phallic towers David's men assault and assimilate, David's borders invite penetration. Although the borders and ideology of a monarch could be presented as a closed, self-cohesive system, David's borders are rebellious, and the discourses by which he enacts his kingship are partial and self-contradictory.[31] *David and Bethsabe* illustrates disclosure.

V

The multiple disclosures of Bethsabe's ambiguous reproductive power, Absalon's failed effort at dislocating sovereign power, and David's conflicting and fragmented discourses appear to be superseded by Joab's hierarchical model of kingship when David once again takes up his monarchy at the play's end, ostensibly to appease Joab. What then boots such disclosure? This final series of scenes begins with Bethsabe's plea to David that he not efface himself in his grief:

> What meanes my lord, the lampe of Israel,
> From whose bright eyes all eyes receive their light,
> To dim the glory of his sweet aspects,
> And paint his countenance with his hearts distresse?
>
> (ll. 1641-44)

David responds by offering to face Bethsabe:

> Faire Bersabe, thou mightst increase the strength,
> Of these thy arguments, drawne from my skill,
> By urging thy sweet sight to my conceits.
>
> (ll. 1655-57)

The disclosures of this scene take the form of countenancing and effacement. While waiting for news of Absalon, David is reluctant to instruct Salomon in succession, though he acknowledges that Salomon is God's

chosen heir. Upon hearing a description of Absalon's death, David refuses to face his own rule. It is Bethsabe who salvages his kingship. She articulates an ideology of a poet-king by reconstituting David through the means that first sighted her as a subject: she calls David to renew the kingdom with song. She then prevents Joab and his armies from leaving, giving David time and space to take up his authority again. Yet what Bethsabe has reproduced is, first, a political hegemony of father and son, David and Salomon, and second, an aesthetic and religious association of father and son, David and Absalon. David marks these reproductions by calling his sons into the same close relationship with the face of God that he has experienced. David teaches Salomon to pray and address God thus:

> O heaven protect my weaknesse with thy strength,
> So looke on me that I may view thy face,
> And see these secrets written in thy browes.
>
> (ll. 1742-44)

Later David prays that Absalon will behold God "face to face" (l. 1914). Both these father-son constructions would seem to exclude any female presence or agency and thus perpetuate the male fantasy with which I began this essay.

Joab insists that the king must face his troops. He is furious that David sits "daunted, frowning in the darke, / When his faire lookes, with Oyle and Wine refresht, / Should dart into their [the armies'] bosomes gladsome beames." (ll. 1883-85). As the disgruntled captains prepare to leave David's averted face, Bethsabe bids them stay, and David rises from his prostrate grief. His next words, an unexpected and mysterious hymn celebrating Absalon's transformation into God's subject, are remarkable enough to warrant quoting in full:

> Then happie art thou Davids fairest sonne,
> That freed from the yoke of earthly toiles,
> And sequestred from sence of humane sinnes,
> Thy soule shall joy the sacred cabinet
> Of those devine Ideas, that present
> Thy changed spirit with a heaven of blisse.
> Then thou art gone, ah thou art gone my sonne
> To heaven I hope my Absalon is gone.
> Thy soule there plac'd in honour of the Saints
> Or angels clad with immortalitie,
> Shall reape a sevenfold grace, for all thy greefes.
> Thy eyes now no more eyes but shining stars,
> Shall decke the flaming heavens with novell lampes.
> There shalt thou tast the drinke of Seraphins,
> And cheere thy feelings with archangels food.
> Thy day of rest, thy holy Sabboth day
> Shall be eternall, and the curtaine drawne,
> Thou shalt behold thy soveraigne face to face,
> With wonder knit in triple unitie,
> Unitie infinite and innumerable.
>
> (ll. 1897-1916)

I wish to consider who is reproduced here, and who is effaced. There are several possibilities.

When Mary, Queen of Scots, was executed, Queen Elizabeth proclaimed herself horrified, denied giving such an order, and grieved for her kinswoman. Most counselors at the time and historians since have been certain that Elizabeth's throne required the security of Mary's death and that Elizabeth wanted to maintain her throne, yet Elizabeth's strategy was to refuse to face the proceedings. She effaced herself by her absence from Mary's trial, and claimed not to countenance the execution.[32] In his "Murdering Peasants: Genre and the Representation of Rebellion," Stephen Greenblatt observes that Dürer's proposed "monument to celebrate a victory over rebellious peasants" reduces the rebel to "impotent absurdity, while the victor is entirely effaced."[33] How could the victor save face in vanquishing such an unworthy enemy as a rebel? In Peele's play, how could David save face in a victory over the impotent absurdity of his son hung by the hair, other than by self-effacement? Thus, like Elizabeth, David would necessarily appear to mourn the death of his close relative, musing on the face of Absalon while effacing himself. But this interpretation assumes controlled actions of political calculation on David's part that have no precedent in the play. Through his speeches of love for Absalon, his "favorite son," David has risked losing his crown: in fact, the play presents Bethsabe as the one who preserves David's monarchy.

Another reading could see the reestablishment of the hegemony of kingship in David's apparent gesture of effacement. While David momentarily denies his own face to his troops, the one who is permanently effaced is the rebel. The rebel has been changed, his face reduced to eyes turned into stars. The vision of Absalon subject to the "soveraigne" God effectively effaces the rebel Absalon who summoned God to be servant to his beauty. According to such a reading, David's eulogy actually shows Absalon not condemned but reappropriated by the generous power of his gracious monarch. Thus David saves face. In this formulation, Bethsabe is effaced with Absalon. She has restored the hegemony that Joab represents, a masculine kingdom of battles and "armes," bent on subduing heathen and women at the command of a relentlessly patriarchal God. Here any threatening reproductive power of the female is contained and effaced.

Yet I do not see how, in the context of the play, we have been prepared to see David's poetic ability so fully serving the requirements of the ideology of kingship. His aesthetic desires have thus far only entangled him, either in Bethsabe's hair or in sympathy for Absalon. His gesture of eulogizing Absalon has no single ideological function. It would rather appear that Bethsabe has dangerously summoned David to an ambiguous poet-king identity. The eulogy creates a space for an ungendered rebel, a space that might also be a site for the figure who is often paralleled with the rebel—Bethsabe. We have seen that Absalon's spaces are Bethsabe's spaces, sites that David wants to get into and be penetrated by, pleasurable sites of ambiguous gender identification. David's discourses do not merge here in a single sovereign reproduction, but rather fragment, dislocating Joab's patriarchal kingdom as well as Absalon's rebellion. The divine "triple unity" is not identified as masculine, nor is the subject after David's second reference to "sonne" (l. 1903). Is there a space invoked in which David, Bethsabe, and Absalon could get beyond the limiting positions of subject and monarch, feminized subjection and masculinized dominance? Could there be a space of a God who is not imaged as male, a space that transforms Elizabethan gender constructions of male and female into an aesthetically reproductive and verbally generative space?

There is not much space, no matter how one reads the discourses that traverse Peele's play. One cannot even suggest the play's possible theatrical effects: despite the quarto's claim, "As it has ben divers times plaied on the stage," we have no clear record that it was ever performed. Indeed, even an assertion of the necessary agency of the womb must be modified. Elizabeth I soon appropriated the fruit of her rebel's worthy womb to be her successor. James addressed Elizabeth as "Mother." Elizabeth thus reproduced herself politically, demonstrating that the fantasy of reproduction without a womb could be a political reality. James's subsequent embodiment of the body politic that had so reproduced itself continued to disclose a monarchy undergirded by patriarchal ideology.[34] Any disclosure of alternative space must be speculative.

Yet the fragmenting and dislocating effect of David's eulogy and lament for Absalon strike me as curiously in keeping with the unfixed fragment of Absalon's lament about having disclosed a far more worthy womb. I am not willing simply to edit out Absalon's inconvenient textual womb: I want to let it continue to vex us, because it provides an analogue to critical problems we are now seeking to address. The lines belong to the text and their cultural matrix, yet have no place in the play's unified structure. Similarly, early modern discourses about the material womb belong yet have no comfortable place in our formulation of the discourses that constituted Renaissance England. Reformulated on another scale, questions of gendered social positions and practices are often too easily marginalized in our critical discussions, like Bethsabe dismissed as the site of David's sin rather than recognized as the agent of royal succession. These gender-specific concerns cause uneasiness as they wander through our discussions and teaching, inviting fragmentary readings of fragmented plays, violently disrupting or suffocating complacent critical assumptions, and causing critical hysteria among those who would otherwise doctor and efface such matters. My study aims, midwifelike, at facilitating the occluded but irrepressible site of the "farre more worthy womb": spreading wives' tales beyond the margins of dominant patriarchy.

Notes

Many thanks to my friends who generously read this essay before I submitted it and to the Social Sciences and Humanities Research Council of Canada whose 1986-87 Fellowship was supporting me at the time. Geoffrey Whitney-Brown kindly enabled this essay in many ways; I am especially grateful to him.

1. All quotations are from Elmer Blistein's excellent edition of *David and Bethsabe*, in *The Life and Works of George Peele*, [Complete Works, 1952-70], gen. ed. Charles Proutty (New Haven: Yale Univ. Press, 1970), pp. 135-295.

2. The best remedy was a sexually attentive husband or the sweetly scented fingers of a midwife gently stroking the vagina in order to coax the willful womb back to its proper position. See Audrey Eccles, *Obstetrics and Gynecology in Tudor and Stuart England* (Kent, Ohio: Kent State Univ. Press, 1982), pp. 76-77; Ian Maclean, *The Renaissance Notion of Woman* (Cambridge: Cambridge Univ. Press, 1980), p. 41; and Ilze Veith, *Hysteria: The History of the Disease* (Chicago: Chicago Univ. Press, 1980), pp. 121-123, 126. Coppélia Kahn, "The Absent Mother in *King Lear*" (in *Rewriting the Renaissance*, Margaret W. Ferguson, Maureen Quilligan, and Nancy J. Vickers, eds. [Chicago: Chicago Univ. Press, 1986], pp. 33-49), provides a thoughtful consideration of how this belief is used as a metaphor in *King Lear.*

3. A. H. Bullen, ed., *The Works of George Peele* (London: J. C. Nimmo, 1888). Alexander Dyce's 1829 and 1861 editions of the play (*The Work of George Peele*, vol. 2 [New York: W. Pickering, 1829; Routledge, Warne and Routledge, 1861]), and the recent edition of Russell Frazer and Norman Rabkin (*Drama of the English Renaissance: The Tudor Period* [New York: Macmillan, 1976]), also suppress the lines into footnotes.

4. John Matthews Manly, ed., *Specimens of Pre-Shakespearean Drama* (Boston: Ginn and Co., 1897), p. 476. See also Blistein, pp. 178-79.

5. Maclean, p. 32; Joseph Needham, *A History of Embryology* (Cambridge: Cambridge Univ. Press, 1934), pp. 21-22.

6. Eccles, p. 26; Maclean, p. 8. For an especially lively discussion of some social implications of these beliefs, see Thomas Lacqueur's "Orgasm, Generation, and the Politics of Reproduction Biology," *Representations,* 14 (1986), 1-14.

7. Maclean, p. 37: "Another theory, influenced by or influencing Pythagoras' dualities attributes sexual difference to the position of the foetus in the uterus (left or right side), and the provenance of the semen from the left or right testicle."

8. Eccles, p. 26; Maclean, p. 36.

9. Even this was complicated, however, by the belief that the seed diminished in strength in older age.

10. Jay L. Halio ("'Perfection' and Elizabethan Ideas of Conception," *English Language Notes,* 1 [1964], 179-82) has used this sense of "perfect" to provide new meanings of familiar lines in Shakespeare.

11. Angus McLaren, *Reproductive Rituals: The Perception of Fertility in England from the Sixteenth Century to the Nineteenth Century* (London: Methuen, 1984), p. 55. In "*A Midsummer Night's Dream* and the Shaping Fantasies of Elizabethan Culture: Gender, Power, and Form," Louis Adrian Montrose posits that, although Galenic and Aristotelian ideas coexisted, Shakespeare inclined toward Aristotle's formulation (in *Rewriting the Renaissance,* pp. 75-76 and note 17).

12. Inga-Stina Ewbank, "The House of David in Renaissance Drama: A Comparative Study," *Renaissance Drama,* 8 (1965), 30.

13. See David Bevington, *Tudor Drama and Politics* (Cambridge: Harvard Univ. Press, 1968), pp. 219-20; Blistein, p. 183; Murray Roston, *Biblical Drama in England* (London: Faber, 1968), pp. 102-3.

14. A. R. Braunmiller, *George Peele: Criticism and Interpretation* (Boston: Twayne Publishers, 1983), p. 109.

15. See also Eccles, pp. 28-29; McLaren, p. 20. The language used to describe the activity of the womb is often startlingly energetic and emotional.

16. Veith, p. 62

17. Eccles, p. 46. See also Eccles, pp. 64-65, and McLaren, pp. 49-50.

18. Patricia Crawford, "Attitudes to Menstruation in Seventeenth-Century England," *Past and Present,* 91 (1981), 65.

19. J. E. Neale, *Elizabeth I and Her Parliaments, 1584-1601* (London: Jonathan Cape, 1953) 1: 270.

20. Neale, 2: 107.

21. Edwin Sandys, "A Sermon Preached at St. Paul's Cross, At What Time a Main Treason Was Discovered," in *The Sermons of Edwin Sandys,* ed. John Ayre (Cambridge: Cambridge Univ. Press, 1941), p. 413.

22. John Whitgift, "Contents of the Archbishop's Sermon Preached at the Cathedral of St. Paul's, London, Nov. the 17, 1583, being the Anniversary of Queen Elizabeth's Coming to the Crown," in *The Works of John Whitgift,* ed. John Ayre (Cambridge: Cambridge Univ. Press, 1853), p. 589.

23. Fifty was seen as nearing the end but not beyond childbearing age. Andrew Borde's popular book, *The Breviary of Health* (London: Wyllyam Powell, 1557), p. lxxvi, explains that women "brynge forth flowers" (menstruate) until the age of fifty give or take two years, and until the "flowers" cease "they maye brynge forth fruit and have chyldren."

24. Roy C. Strong, *Portraits of Queen Elizabeth I* (Oxford: Clarendon Press, 1963), p. 32.

25. According to Strong, p. 32, the English ambassador reported that "under" the portrait of Elizabeth was a picture of the Duke of Anjou, "in his best apparell havynge upon his fiste a hawke which continually bayted and koulde never make her sit still."

26. See Marie Axton, *The Queen's Two Bodies: Drama and Elizabethan Succession* (London: Royal Historical Society, 1977), for a fascinating and detailed account of the legal discourses concerning Queen Elizabeth's two bodies. Axton does not pursue the peculiar gender-specific situation of the body natural of the female monarch.

27. See Montrose, "Shaping Fantasies," p. 317.

28. The pun is obvious. The *OED* lists "heire" as an alternative spelling for "hair," and "haire" as an alternative spelling for "heire." See, for instance, Spenser's *Faerie Queene* I,ii,23: "The only haire of a mighty king."

29. *Certain Sermons Appointed by the Queen's Majesty, 1574,* ed. G. E. Corrie (London: John W. Parker, 1850), pp. 579-80.

30. Montrose, "The Elizabethan Subject and Spenserian Text," in *Literary Theory: Renaissance Texts,* ed. Patricia Parker and David Quint (Baltimore: Johns Hopkins Univ. Press, 1986), p. 315.

31. See Peter Stallybrass, "Patriarchal Territories: The Body Enclosed," in *Rewriting the Renaissance,* pp. 129-33. Stallybrass discusses the impenetrable integrity of the female body as an emblem for the integrity of the state—a figure that David's desire to be penetrated clearly inverts.

32. See Neale, 2: 137.

33. Stephen Greenblatt, "Murdering Peasants: Status, Genre, and the Representation of Rebellion," *Representations,* 1 (1983), 9, 13.

34. See Jonathan Goldberg's *James I and the Politics of Literature* (Baltimore: Johns Hopkins Univ. Press, 1983), for a thorough analysis of James's patriarchical ideology and government. James's use of "mother" and "alter-ego" in addressing Elizabeth is described on pp. 15-16.

FURTHER READING

Bibliography

Daves, Charles W. "George Peele." In *The Predecessors of Shakespeare,* edited by Terence P. Logan and Denzell S. Smith, pp. 143-52. Lincoln: University of Nebraska Press, 1973.

Provides annotated bibliographical information on Peele's biography, plays, general criticism, and criticism of specific plays.

Criticism

Berek, Peter. "*Tamburlaine*'s Weak Sons: Imitation and Interpretation before 1593." *Renaissance Drama,* no. 8 (1982): 55-82.

Traces the influence of Marlowe on a number of plays, including *The Battle of Alcazar.*

Craik, T. W. "The Reconstruction of Stage Action from Early Dramatic Texts." In *The Elizabethan Theatre V,* edited by G. R. Hibbard, pp. 76-91. Hamden, Conn.: Archon Books, 1975.

Suggests a method of reconstructing stage action in Elizabethan drama based on the text and other examples. Craik applies this technique to a couple of scenes in *David and Bethsabe.*

Ewbank, Inga-Stina. "'What Words, What Looks, What Wonders?': Language and Spectacle in the Theatre of George Peele." In *The Elizabethan Theatre V,* edited by G. R. Hibbard, pp. 124-54. Hamden, Conn.: Archon Books, 1975.

Examines Peele's *David and Bethsabe,* tying it in with the themes of Shakespeare's last plays.

Frontain, Raymond-Jean. "The Curious Frame on Chapman's *Ovids Banquet of Sence*: 2 Samuel 11." *Cahiers Élisabéthains* (30 April 1987): 37-43.

    Compares *David and Bethsabe* with George Chapman's *Ovid's Banquet of Sence.*

Moffett, A. S. "Process and Structure Shared: Similarities between the Commedia Dell'Arte and *The Old Wives Tale* of George Peele." *New England Theatre Journal* 4 (1993): 97-105.

    Discusses Peele's *The Old Wives Tale* from the viewpoint of a director rather than a critic.

Russell, W. M. S. "Folktales and the Theatre." *Folklore* 92, no. 1 (1981): 3-24.

    Explores the interrelationship between folktales and theater and discusses Peele's *The Old Wives Tale* as an example.

Additional coverage of Peele's life and career is contained in the following sources published by Thomson Gale: *British Writers,* **Vol. 1;** *Dictionary of Literary Biography,* **Vols. 62, 167;** *Literature Criticism from 1400 to 1800,* **Vol. 115;** *Literature Resource Center;* **and** *Reference Guide to English Literature,* **Ed. 2.**

How to Use This Index

CMW = *St. James Guide to Crime & Mystery Writers*
CN = *Contemporary Novelists*
CP = *Contemporary Poets*
CPW = *Contemporary Popular Writers*
CSW = *Contemporary Southern Writers*
CWD = *Contemporary Women Dramatists*
CWP = *Contemporary Women Poets*
CWRI = *St. James Guide to Children's Writers*
CWW = *Contemporary World Writers*
DA = *DISCovering Authors*
DA3 = *DISCovering Authors 3.0*
DAB = *DISCovering Authors: British Edition*
DAC = *DISCovering Authors: Canadian Edition*
DAM = *DISCovering Authors: Modules*
   DRAM: *Dramatists Module;* **MST:** *Most-studied Authors Module;*
   MULT: *Multicultural Authors Module;* **NOV:** *Novelists Module;*
   POET: *Poets Module;* **POP:** *Popular Fiction and Genre Authors Module*
DFS = *Drama for Students*
DLB = *Dictionary of Literary Biography*
DLBD = *Dictionary of Literary Biography Documentary Series*
DLBY = *Dictionary of Literary Biography Yearbook*
DNFS = *Literature of Developing Nations for Students*
EFS = *Epics for Students*
EXPN = *Exploring Novels*
EXPP = *Exploring Poetry*
EXPS = *Exploring Short Stories*
EW = *European Writers*
FANT = *St. James Guide to Fantasy Writers*
FW = *Feminist Writers*
GFL = *Guide to French Literature,* Beginnings to 1789, 1798 to the Present
GLL = *Gay and Lesbian Literature*
HGG = *St. James Guide to Horror, Ghost & Gothic Writers*
HW = *Hispanic Writers*
IDFW = *International Dictionary of Films and Filmmakers: Writers and Production Artists*
IDTP = *International Dictionary of Theatre: Playwrights*
LAIT = *Literature and Its Times*
LAW = *Latin American Writers*
JRDA = *Junior DISCovering Authors*
MAICYA = *Major Authors and Illustrators for Children and Young Adults*
MAICYAS = *Major Authors and Illustrators for Children and Young Adults Supplement*
MAWW = *Modern American Women Writers*
MJW = *Modern Japanese Writers*
MTCW = *Major 20th-Century Writers*
NCFS = *Nonfiction Classics for Students*
NFS = *Novels for Students*
PAB = *Poets: American and British*
PFS = *Poetry for Students*
RGAL = *Reference Guide to American Literature*
RGEL = *Reference Guide to English Literature*
RGSF = *Reference Guide to Short Fiction*
RGWL = *Reference Guide to World Literature*
RHW = *Twentieth-Century Romance and Historical Writers*
SAAS = *Something about the Author Autobiography Series*
SATA = *Something about the Author*
SFW = *St. James Guide to Science Fiction Writers*
SSFS = *Short Stories for Students*
TCWW = *Twentieth-Century Western Writers*
WLIT = *World Literature and Its Times*
WP = *World Poets*
YABC = *Yesterday's Authors of Books for Children*
YAW = *St. James Guide to Young Adult Writers*

Literary Criticism Series
Cumulative Author Index

Anderson, C. Farley
See Mencken, H(enry) L(ouis); Nathan, George Jean

Anderson, Jessica (Margaret) Queale
1916- .... **CLC 37**
See also CA 9-12R; CANR 4, 62; CN 4, 5, 6, 7

Anderson, Jon (Victor) 1940- .... **CLC 9**
See also CA 25-28R; CANR 20; CP 1, 3, 4; DAM POET

Anderson, Lindsay (Gordon)
1923-1994 .... **CLC 20**
See also CA 125; 128; 146; CANR 77

Anderson, Maxwell 1888-1959 .... **TCLC 2, 144**
See also CA 105; 152; DAM DRAM; DFS 16, 20; DLB 7, 228; MAL 5; MTCW 2; MTFW 2005; RGAL 4

Anderson, Poul (William)
1926-2001 .... **CLC 15**
See also AAYA 5, 34; BPFB 1; BYA 6, 8, 9; CA 1-4R, 181; 199; CAAE 181; CAAS 2; CANR 2, 15, 34, 64, 110; CLR 58; DLB 8; FANT; INT CANR-15; MTCW 1, 2; MTFW 2005; SATA 90; SATA-Brief 39; SATA-Essay 106; SCFW 1, 2; SFW 4; SUFW 1, 2

Anderson, Robert (Woodruff)
1917- .... **CLC 23**
See also AITN 1; CA 21-24R; CANR 32; CD 6; DAM DRAM; DLB 7; LAIT 5

Anderson, Roberta Joan
See Mitchell, Joni

Anderson, Sherwood 1876-1941 .. **SSC 1, 46; TCLC 1, 10, 24, 123; WLC**
See also AAYA 30; AMW; AMWC 2; BPFB 1; CA 104; 121; CANR 61; CDALB 1917-1929; DA; DA3; DAB; DAC; DAM MST, NOV; DLB 4, 9, 86; DLBD 1; EWL 3; EXPS; GLL 2; MAL 5; MTCW 1, 2; MTFW 2005; NFS 4; RGAL 4; RGSF 2; SSFS 4, 10, 11; TUS

Andier, Pierre
See Desnos, Robert

Andouard
See Giraudoux, Jean(-Hippolyte)

Andrade, Carlos Drummond de ..... **CLC 18**
See Drummond de Andrade, Carlos
See also EWL 3; RGWL 2, 3

Andrade, Mario de .... **TCLC 43**
See de Andrade, Mario
See also DLB 307; EWL 3; LAW; RGWL 2, 3; WLIT 1

Andreae, Johann V(alentin)
1586-1654 .... **LC 32**
See also DLB 164

Andreas Capellanus fl. c. 1185- .... **CMLC 45**
See also DLB 208

Andreas-Salome, Lou 1861-1937 ... **TCLC 56**
See also CA 178; DLB 66

Andreev, Leonid
See Andreyev, Leonid (Nikolaevich)
See also DLB 295; EWL 3

Andress, Lesley
See Sanders, Lawrence

Andrewes, Lancelot 1555-1626 .... **LC 5**
See also DLB 151, 172

Andrews, Cicily Fairfield
See West, Rebecca

Andrews, Elton V.
See Pohl, Frederik

Andreyev, Leonid (Nikolaevich)
1871-1919 .... **TCLC 3**
See Andreev, Leonid
See also CA 104; 185

Andric, Ivo 1892-1975 .... **CLC 8; SSC 36; TCLC 135**
See also CA 81-84; 57-60; CANR 43, 60; CDWLB 4; DLB 147; EW 11; EWL 3; MTCW 1; RGSF 2; RGWL 2, 3

Androvar
See Prado (Calvo), Pedro

Angela of Foligno 1248(?)-1309 .... **CMLC 76**

Angelique, Pierre
See Bataille, Georges

Angell, Roger 1920- .... **CLC 26**
See also CA 57-60; CANR 13, 44, 70, 144; DLB 171, 185

Angelou, Maya 1928- ... **BLC 1; CLC 12, 35, 64, 77, 155; PC 32; WLCS**
See also AAYA 7, 20; AMWS 4; BPFB 1; BW 2, 3; BYA 2; CA 65-68; CANR 19, 42, 65, 111, 133; CDALBS; CLR 53; CP 4, 5, 6, 7; CPW; CSW; CWP; DA; DA3; DAB; DAC; DAM MST, MULT, POET, POP; DLB 38; EWL 3; EXPN; EXPP; FL 1:5; LAIT 4; MAICYA 2; MAICYAS 1; MAL 5; MAWW; MTCW 1, 2; MTFW 2005; NCFS 4; NFS 2; PFS 2, 3; RGAL 4; SATA 49, 136; TCLE 1:1; WYA; YAW

Angouleme, Marguerite d'
See de Navarre, Marguerite

Anna Comnena 1083-1153 .... **CMLC 25**

Annensky, Innokentii Fedorovich
See Annensky, Innokenty (Fyodorovich)
See also DLB 295

Annensky, Innokenty (Fyodorovich)
1856-1909 .... **TCLC 14**
See also CA 110; 155; EWL 3

Annunzio, Gabriele d'
See D'Annunzio, Gabriele

Anodos
See Coleridge, Mary E(lizabeth)

Anon, Charles Robert
See Pessoa, Fernando (Antonio Nogueira)

Anouilh, Jean (Marie Lucien Pierre)
1910-1987 . **CLC 1, 3, 8, 13, 40, 50; DC 8, 21**
See also AAYA 67; CA 17-20R; 123; CANR 32; DAM DRAM; DFS 9, 10, 19; DLB 321; EW 13; EWL 3; GFL 1789 to the Present; MTCW 1, 2; MTFW 2005; RGWL 2, 3; TWA

Anselm of Canterbury
1033(?)-1109 .... **CMLC 67**
See also DLB 115

Anthony, Florence
See Ai

Anthony, John
See Ciardi, John (Anthony)

Anthony, Peter
See Shaffer, Anthony (Joshua); Shaffer, Peter (Levin)

Anthony, Piers 1934- .... **CLC 35**
See also AAYA 11, 48; BYA 7; CA 200; CAAE 200; CANR 28, 56, 73, 102, 133; CPW; DAM POP; DLB 8; FANT; MAICYA 2; MAICYAS 1; MTCW 1, 2; MTFW 2005; SAAS 22; SATA 84, 129; SATA-Essay 129; SFW 4; SUFW 1, 2; YAW

Anthony, Susan B(rownell)
1820-1906 .... **TCLC 84**
See also CA 211; FW

Antiphon c. 480B.C.-c. 411B.C. .... **CMLC 55**

Antoine, Marc
See Proust, (Valentin-Louis-George-Eugene) Marcel

Antoninus, Brother
See Everson, William (Oliver)
See also CP 1

Antonioni, Michelangelo 1912- .... **CLC 20, 144**
See also CA 73-76; CANR 45, 77

Antschel, Paul 1920-1970
See Celan, Paul
See also CA 85-88; CANR 33, 61; MTCW 1; PFS 21

Anwar, Chairil 1922-1949 .... **TCLC 22**
See Chairil Anwar
See also CA 121; 219; RGWL 3

Anzaldua, Gloria (Evanjelina)
1942-2004 .... **CLC 200; HLCS 1**
See also CA 175; 227; CSW; CWP; DLB 122; FW; LLW; RGAL 4; SATA-Obit 154

Apess, William 1798-1839(?) .... **NCLC 73; NNAL**
See also DAM MULT; DLB 175, 243

Apollinaire, Guillaume 1880-1918 .... **PC 7; TCLC 3, 8, 51**
See Kostrowitzki, Wilhelm Apollinaris de
See also CA 152; DAM POET; DLB 258, 321; EW 9; EWL 3; GFL 1789 to the Present; MTCW 2; RGWL 2, 3; TWA; WP

Apollonius of Rhodes
See Apollonius Rhodius
See also AW 1; RGWL 2, 3

Apollonius Rhodius c. 300B.C.-c.
220B.C. .... **CMLC 28**
See Apollonius of Rhodes
See also DLB 176

Appelfeld, Aharon 1932- ... **CLC 23, 47; SSC 42**
See also CA 112; 133; CANR 86; CWW 2; DLB 299; EWL 3; RGSF 2; WLIT 6

Apple, Max (Isaac) 1941- .... **CLC 9, 33; SSC 50**
See also CA 81-84; CANR 19, 54; DLB 130

Appleman, Philip (Dean) 1926- .... **CLC 51**
See also CA 13-16R; CAAS 18; CANR 6, 29, 56

Appleton, Lawrence
See Lovecraft, H(oward) P(hillips)

Apteryx
See Eliot, T(homas) S(tearns)

Apuleius, (Lucius Madaurensis)
125(?)-175(?) .... **CMLC 1**
See also AW 2; CDWLB 1; DLB 211; RGWL 2, 3; SUFW

Aquin, Hubert 1929-1977 .... **CLC 15**
See also CA 105; DLB 53; EWL 3

Aquinas, Thomas 1224(?)-1274 ..... **CMLC 33**
See also DLB 115; EW 1; TWA

Aragon, Louis 1897-1982 .... **CLC 3, 22; TCLC 123**
See also CA 69-72; 108; CANR 28, 71; DAM NOV, POET; DLB 72, 258; EW 11; EWL 3; GFL 1789 to the Present; GLL 2; LMFS 2; MTCW 1, 2; RGWL 2, 3

Arany, Janos 1817-1882 .... **NCLC 34**

Aranyos, Kakay 1847-1910
See Mikszath, Kalman

Aratus of Soli c. 315B.C.-c.
240B.C. .... **CMLC 64**
See also DLB 176

Arbuthnot, John 1667-1735 .... **LC 1**
See also DLB 101

Archer, Herbert Winslow
See Mencken, H(enry) L(ouis)

Archer, Jeffrey (Howard) 1940- .... **CLC 28**
See also AAYA 16; BEST 89:3; BPFB 1; CA 77-80; CANR 22, 52, 95, 136; CPW; DA3; DAM POP; INT CANR-22; MTFW 2005

Archer, Jules 1915- .... **CLC 12**
See also CA 9-12R; CANR 6, 69; SAAS 5; SATA 4, 85

Archer, Lee
See Ellison, Harlan (Jay)

Archilochus c. 7th cent. B.C.- .... **CMLC 44**
See also DLB 176

Bitov, Andrei (Georgievich) 1937- ... **CLC 57**
See also CA 142; DLB 302

Biyidi, Alexandre 1932-
See Beti, Mongo
See also BW 1, 3; CA 114; 124; CANR 81;
DA3; MTCW 1, 2

Bjarme, Brynjolf
See Ibsen, Henrik (Johan)

Bjoernson, Bjoernstjerne (Martinius)
1832-1910 .... **TCLC 7, 37**
See also CA 104

Black, Robert
See Holdstock, Robert P.

Blackburn, Paul 1926-1971 .... **CLC 9, 43**
See also BG 1:2; CA 81-84; 33-36R; CANR
34; CP 1; DLB 16; DLBY 1981

Black Elk 1863-1950 .... **NNAL; TCLC 33**
See also CA 144; DAM MULT; MTCW 2;
MTFW 2005; WP

Black Hawk 1767-1838 .... **NNAL**

Black Hobart
See Sanders, (James) Ed(ward)

Blacklin, Malcolm
See Chambers, Aidan

Blackmore, R(ichard) D(oddridge)
1825-1900 .... **TCLC 27**
See also CA 120; DLB 18; RGEL 2

Blackmur, R(ichard) P(almer)
1904-1965 .... **CLC 2, 24**
See also AMWS 2; CA 11-12; 25-28R;
CANR 71; CAP 1; DLB 63; EWL 3;
MAL 5

Black Tarantula
See Acker, Kathy

Blackwood, Algernon (Henry)
1869-1951 .... **TCLC 5**
See also CA 105; 150; DLB 153, 156, 178;
HGG; SUFW 1

Blackwood, Caroline (Maureen)
1931-1996 .... **CLC 6, 9, 100**
See also BRWS 9; CA 85-88; 151; CANR
32, 61, 65; CN 3, 4, 5, 6; DLB 14, 207;
HGG; MTCW 1

Blade, Alexander
See Hamilton, Edmond; Silverberg, Robert

Blaga, Lucian 1895-1961 .... **CLC 75**
See also CA 157; DLB 220; EWL 3

Blair, Eric (Arthur) 1903-1950 .... **TCLC 123**
See Orwell, George
See also CA 104; 132; DA; DA3; DAB;
DAC; DAM MST, NOV; MTCW 1, 2;
MTFW 2005; SATA 29

Blair, Hugh 1718-1800 .... **NCLC 75**

Blais, Marie-Claire 1939- .... **CLC 2, 4, 6, 13,
22**
See also CA 21-24R; CAAS 4; CANR 38,
75, 93; CWW 2; DAC; DAM MST; DLB
53; EWL 3; FW; MTCW 1, 2; MTFW
2005; TWA

Blaise, Clark 1940- .... **CLC 29**
See also AITN 2; CA 53-56, 231; CAAE
231; CAAS 3; CANR 5, 66, 106; CN 4,
5, 6, 7; DLB 53; RGSF 2

Blake, Fairley
See De Voto, Bernard (Augustine)

Blake, Nicholas
See Day Lewis, C(ecil)
See also DLB 77; MSW

Blake, Sterling
See Benford, Gregory (Albert)

Blake, William 1757-1827 . **NCLC 13, 37, 57,
127; PC 12, 63; WLC**
See also AAYA 47; BRW 3; BRWR 1; CD-
BLB 1789-1832; CLR 52; DA; DA3;
DAB; DAC; DAM MST, POET; DLB 93,
163; EXPP; LATS 1:1; LMFS 1; MAI-
CYA 1, 2; PAB; PFS 2, 12; SATA 30;
TEA; WCH; WLIT 3; WP

Blanchot, Maurice 1907-2003 .... **CLC 135**
See also CA 117; 144; 213; CANR 138;
DLB 72, 296; EWL 3

Blasco Ibanez, Vicente 1867-1928 . **TCLC 12**
See Ibanez, Vicente Blasco
See also BPFB 1; CA 110; 131; CANR 81;
DA3; DAM NOV; EW 8; EWL 3; HW 1,
2; MTCW 1

Blatty, William Peter 1928- .... **CLC 2**
See also CA 5-8R; CANR 9, 124; DAM
POP; HGG

Bleeck, Oliver
See Thomas, Ross (Elmore)

Blessing, Lee (Knowlton) 1949- .... **CLC 54**
See also CA 236; CAD; CD 5, 6

Blight, Rose
See Greer, Germaine

Blish, James (Benjamin) 1921-1975 . **CLC 14**
See also BPFB 1; CA 1-4R; 57-60; CANR
3; CN 2; DLB 8; MTCW 1; SATA 66;
SCFW 1, 2; SFW 4

Bliss, Frederick
See Card, Orson Scott

Bliss, Reginald
See Wells, H(erbert) G(eorge)

Blixen, Karen (Christentze Dinesen)
1885-1962
See Dinesen, Isak
See also CA 25-28; CANR 22, 50; CAP 2;
DA3; DLB 214; LMFS 1; MTCW 1, 2;
SATA 44; SSFS 20

Bloch, Robert (Albert) 1917-1994 .... **CLC 33**
See also AAYA 29; CA 5-8R, 179; 146;
CAAE 179; CAAS 20; CANR 5, 78;
DA3; DLB 44; HGG; INT CANR-5;
MTCW 2; SATA 12; SATA-Obit 82; SFW
4; SUFW 1, 2

Blok, Alexander (Alexandrovich)
1880-1921 .... **PC 21; TCLC 5**
See also CA 104; 183; DLB 295; EW 9;
EWL 3; LMFS 2; RGWL 2, 3

Blom, Jan
See Breytenbach, Breyten

Bloom, Harold 1930- .... **CLC 24, 103**
See also CA 13-16R; CANR 39, 75, 92,
133; DLB 67; EWL 3; MTCW 2; MTFW
2005; RGAL 4

Bloomfield, Aurelius
See Bourne, Randolph S(illiman)

Bloomfield, Robert 1766-1823 ..... **NCLC 145**
See also DLB 93

Blount, Roy (Alton), Jr. 1941- .... **CLC 38**
See also CA 53-56; CANR 10, 28, 61, 125;
CSW; INT CANR-28; MTCW 1, 2;
MTFW 2005

Blowsnake, Sam 1875-(?) .... **NNAL**

Bloy, Leon 1846-1917 .... **TCLC 22**
See also CA 121; 183; DLB 123; GFL 1789
to the Present

Blue Cloud, Peter (Aroniawenrate)
1933- .... **NNAL**
See also CA 117; CANR 40; DAM MULT

Bluggage, Oranthy
See Alcott, Louisa May

Blume, Judy (Sussman) 1938- .... **CLC 12, 30**
See also AAYA 3, 26; BYA 1, 8, 12; CA 29-
32R; CANR 13, 37, 66, 124; CLR 2, 15,
69; CPW; DA3; DAM NOV, POP; DLB
52; JRDA; MAICYA 1, 2; MAICYAS 1;
MTCW 1, 2; MTFW 2005; SATA 2, 31,
79, 142; WYA; YAW

Blunden, Edmund (Charles)
1896-1974 .... **CLC 2, 56; PC 66**
See also BRW 6; BRWS 11; CA 17-18; 45-
48; CANR 54; CAP 2; CP 1, 2; DLB 20,
100, 155; MTCW 1; PAB

Bly, Robert (Elwood) 1926- .... **CLC 1, 2, 5,
10, 15, 38, 128; PC 39**
See also AMWS 4; CA 5-8R; CANR 41,
73, 125; CP 1, 2, 3, 4, 5, 6, 7; DA3; DAM
POET; DLB 5; EWL 3; MAL 5; MTCW
1, 2; MTFW 2005; PFS 6, 17; RGAL 4

Boas, Franz 1858-1942 .... **TCLC 56**
See also CA 115; 181

Bobette
See Simenon, Georges (Jacques Christian)

Boccaccio, Giovanni 1313-1375 ... **CMLC 13,
57; SSC 10, 87**
See also EW 2; RGSF 2; RGWL 2, 3; TWA;
WLIT 7

Bochco, Steven 1943- .... **CLC 35**
See also AAYA 11; CA 124; 138

Bode, Sigmund
See O'Doherty, Brian

Bodel, Jean 1167(?)-1210 .... **CMLC 28**

Bodenheim, Maxwell 1892-1954 .... **TCLC 44**
See also CA 110; 187; DLB 9, 45; MAL 5;
RGAL 4

Bodenheimer, Maxwell
See Bodenheim, Maxwell

Bodker, Cecil 1927-
See Bodker, Cecil

Bodker, Cecil 1927- .... **CLC 21**
See also CA 73-76; CANR 13, 44, 111;
CLR 23; MAICYA 1, 2; SATA 14, 133

Boell, Heinrich (Theodor)
1917-1985 ..... **CLC 2, 3, 6, 9, 11, 15, 27,
32, 72; SSC 23; WLC**
See Boll, Heinrich (Theodor)
See also CA 21-24R; 116; CANR 24; DA;
DA3; DAB; DAC; DAM MST, NOV;
DLB 69; DLBY 1985; MTCW 1, 2;
MTFW 2005; SSFS 20; TWA

Boerne, Alfred
See Doeblin, Alfred

Boethius c. 480-c. 524 .... **CMLC 15**
See also DLB 115; RGWL 2, 3

Boff, Leonardo (Genezio Darci)
1938- .... **CLC 70; HLC 1**
See also CA 150; DAM MULT; HW 2

Bogan, Louise 1897-1970 .... **CLC 4, 39, 46,
93; PC 12**
See also AMWS 3; CA 73-76; 25-28R;
CANR 33, 82; CP 1; DAM POET; DLB
45, 169; EWL 3; MAL 5; MAWW;
MTCW 1, 2; PFS 21; RGAL 4

Bogarde, Dirk
See Van Den Bogarde, Derek Jules Gaspard
Ulric Niven
See also DLB 14

Bogosian, Eric 1953- .... **CLC 45, 141**
See also CA 138; CAD; CANR 102; CD 5,
6

Bograd, Larry 1953- .... **CLC 35**
See also CA 93-96; CANR 57; SAAS 21;
SATA 33, 89; WYA

Boiardo, Matteo Maria 1441-1494 .... **LC 6**

Boileau-Despreaux, Nicolas 1636-1711 . **LC 3**
See also DLB 268; EW 3; GFL Beginnings
to 1789; RGWL 2, 3

Boissard, Maurice
See Leautaud, Paul

Bojer, Johan 1872-1959 .... **TCLC 64**
See also CA 189; EWL 3

Bok, Edward W(illiam)
1863-1930 .... **TCLC 101**
See also CA 217; DLB 91; DLBD 16

Boker, George Henry 1823-1890 . **NCLC 125**
See also RGAL 4

Boland, Eavan (Aisling) 1944- .. **CLC 40, 67,
113; PC 58**
See also BRWS 5; CA 143, 207; CAAE
207; CANR 61; CP 1, 7; CWP; DAM
POET; DLB 40; FW; MTCW 2; MTFW
2005; PFS 12, 22

Boll, Heinrich (Theodor)
See Boell, Heinrich (Theodor)
See also BPFB 1; CDWLB 2; EW 13; EWL 3; RGSF 2; RGWL 2, 3

Bolt, Lee
See Faust, Frederick (Schiller)

Bolt, Robert (Oxton) 1924-1995 .... **CLC 14**
See also CA 17-20R; 147; CANR 35, 67; CBD; DAM DRAM; DFS 2; DLB 13, 233; EWL 3; LAIT 1; MTCW 1

Bombal, Maria Luisa 1910-1980 .... **HLCS 1; SSC 37**
See also CA 127; CANR 72; EWL 3; HW 1; LAW; RGSF 2

Bombet, Louis-Alexandre-Cesar
See Stendhal

Bomkauf
See Kaufman, Bob (Garnell)

Bonaventura .... **NCLC 35**
See also DLB 90

Bonaventure 1217(?)-1274 .... **CMLC 79**
See also DLB 115; LMFS 1

Bond, Edward 1934- .... **CLC 4, 6, 13, 23**
See also AAYA 50; BRWS 1; CA 25-28R; CANR 38, 67, 106; CBD; CD 5, 6; DAM DRAM; DFS 3, 8; DLB 13, 310; EWL 3; MTCW 1

Bonham, Frank 1914-1989 .... **CLC 12**
See also AAYA 1; BYA 1, 3; CA 9-12R; CANR 4, 36; JRDA; MAICYA 1, 2; SAAS 3; SATA 1, 49; SATA-Obit 62; TCWW 1, 2; YAW

Bonnefoy, Yves 1923- . **CLC 9, 15, 58; PC 58**
See also CA 85-88; CANR 33, 75, 97, 136; CWW 2; DAM MST, POET; DLB 258; EWL 3; GFL 1789 to the Present; MTCW 1, 2; MTFW 2005

Bonner, Marita .... **HR 1:2**
See Occomy, Marita (Odette) Bonner

Bonnin, Gertrude 1876-1938 .... **NNAL**
See Zitkala-Sa
See also CA 150; DAM MULT

Bontemps, Arna(ud Wendell)
1902-1973 .. **BLC 1; CLC 1, 18; HR 1:2**
See also BW 1; CA 1-4R; 41-44R; CANR 4, 35; CLR 6; CP 1; CWRI 5; DA3; DAM MULT, NOV, POET; DLB 48, 51; JRDA; MAICYA 1, 2; MAL 5; MTCW 1, 2; SATA 2, 44; SATA-Obit 24; WCH; WP

Boot, William
See Stoppard, Tom

Booth, Martin 1944-2004 .... **CLC 13**
See also CA 93-96, 188; 223; CAAE 188; CAAS 2; CANR 92; CP 1, 2, 3, 4

Booth, Philip 1925- .... **CLC 23**
See also CA 5-8R; CANR 5, 88; CP 1, 2, 3, 4, 5, 6, 7; DLBY 1982

Booth, Wayne C(layson) 1921-2005 . **CLC 24**
See also CA 1-4R; CAAS 5; CANR 3, 43, 117; DLB 67

Borchert, Wolfgang 1921-1947 .... **TCLC 5**
See also CA 104; 188; DLB 69, 124; EWL 3

Borel, Petrus 1809-1859 .... **NCLC 41**
See also DLB 119; GFL 1789 to the Present

Borges, Jorge Luis 1899-1986 ... **CLC 1, 2, 3, 4, 6, 8, 9, 10, 13, 19, 44, 48, 83; HLC 1; PC 22, 32; SSC 4, 41; TCLC 109; WLC**
See also AAYA 26; BPFB 1; CA 21-24R; CANR 19, 33, 75, 105, 133; CDWLB 3; DA; DA3; DAB; DAC; DAM MST, MULT; DLB 113, 283; DLBY 1986; DNFS 1, 2; EWL 3; HW 1, 2; LAW; LMFS 2; MSW; MTCW 1, 2; MTFW 2005; RGSF 2; RGWL 2, 3; SFW 4; SSFS 17; TWA; WLIT 1

Borowski, Tadeusz 1922-1951 .... **SSC 48; TCLC 9**
See also CA 106; 154; CDWLB 4; DLB 215; EWL 3; RGSF 2; RGWL 3; SSFS 13

Borrow, George (Henry)
1803-1881 .... **NCLC 9**
See also DLB 21, 55, 166

Bosch (Gavino), Juan 1909-2001 ..... **HLCS 1**
See also CA 151; 204; DAM MST, MULT; DLB 145; HW 1, 2

Bosman, Herman Charles
1905-1951 .... **TCLC 49**
See Malan, Herman
See also CA 160; DLB 225; RGSF 2

Bosschere, Jean de 1878(?)-1953 ... **TCLC 19**
See also CA 115; 186

Boswell, James 1740-1795 ... **LC 4, 50; WLC**
See also BRW 3; CDBLB 1660-1789; DA; DAB; DAC; DAM MST; DLB 104, 142; TEA; WLIT 3

Bottomley, Gordon 1874-1948 ..... **TCLC 107**
See also CA 120; 192; DLB 10

Bottoms, David 1949- .... **CLC 53**
See also CA 105; CANR 22; CSW; DLB 120; DLBY 1983

Boucicault, Dion 1820-1890 .... **NCLC 41**

Boucolon, Maryse
See Conde, Maryse

Bourdieu, Pierre 1930-2002 .... **CLC 198**
See also CA 130; 204

Bourget, Paul (Charles Joseph)
1852-1935 .... **TCLC 12**
See also CA 107; 196; DLB 123; GFL 1789 to the Present

Bourjaily, Vance (Nye) 1922- .... **CLC 8, 62**
See also CA 1-4R; CAAS 1; CANR 2, 72; CN 1, 2, 3, 4, 5, 6, 7; DLB 2, 143; MAL 5

Bourne, Randolph S(illiman)
1886-1918 .... **TCLC 16**
See also AMW; CA 117; 155; DLB 63; MAL 5

Bova, Ben(jamin William) 1932- ...... **CLC 45**
See also AAYA 16; CA 5-8R; CANR 11, 56, 94, 111; CLR 3, 96; DLBY 1981; INT CANR-11; MAICYA 1, 2; MTCW 1; SATA 6, 68, 133; SFW 4

Bowen, Elizabeth (Dorothea Cole)
1899-1973 . **CLC 1, 3, 6, 11, 15, 22, 118; SSC 3, 28, 66; TCLC 148**
See also BRWS 2; CA 17-18; 41-44R; CANR 35, 105; CAP 2; CDBLB 1945-1960; CN 1; DA3; DAM NOV; DLB 15, 162; EWL 3; EXPS; FW; HGG; MTCW 1, 2; MTFW 2005; NFS 13; RGSF 2; SSFS 5; SUFW 1; TEA; WLIT 4

Bowering, George 1935- .... **CLC 15, 47**
See also CA 21-24R; CAAS 16; CANR 10; CN 7; CP 1, 2, 3, 4, 5, 6, 7; DLB 53

Bowering, Marilyn R(uthe) 1949- .... **CLC 32**
See also CA 101; CANR 49; CP 4, 5, 6, 7; CWP

Bowers, Edgar 1924-2000 .... **CLC 9**
See also CA 5-8R; 188; CANR 24; CP 1, 2, 3, 4, 5, 6, 7; CSW; DLB 5

Bowers, Mrs. J. Milton 1842-1914
See Bierce, Ambrose (Gwinett)

Bowie, David .... **CLC 17**
See Jones, David Robert

Bowles, Jane (Sydney) 1917-1973 ..... **CLC 3, 68**
See Bowles, Jane Auer
See also CA 19-20; 41-44R; CAP 2; CN 1; MAL 5

Bowles, Jane Auer
See Bowles, Jane (Sydney)
See also EWL 3

Bowles, Paul (Frederick) 1910-1999 . **CLC 1, 2, 19, 53; SSC 3**
See also AMWS 4; CA 1-4R; 186; CAAS 1; CANR 1, 19, 50, 75; CN 1, 2, 3, 4, 5, 6; DA3; DLB 5, 6, 218; EWL 3; MAL 5; MTCW 1, 2; MTFW 2005; RGAL 4; SSFS 17

Bowles, William Lisle 1762-1850 . **NCLC 103**
See also DLB 93

Box, Edgar
See Vidal, (Eugene Luther) Gore
See also GLL 1

Boyd, James 1888-1944 .... **TCLC 115**
See also CA 186; DLB 9; DLBD 16; RGAL 4; RHW

Boyd, Nancy
See Millay, Edna St. Vincent
See also GLL 1

Boyd, Thomas (Alexander)
1898-1935 .... **TCLC 111**
See also CA 111; 183; DLB 9; DLBD 16, 316

Boyd, William (Andrew Murray)
1952- .... **CLC 28, 53, 70**
See also CA 114; 120; CANR 51, 71, 131; CN 4, 5, 6, 7; DLB 231

Boyesen, Hjalmar Hjorth
1848-1895 .... **NCLC 135**
See also DLB 12, 71; DLBD 13; RGAL 4

Boyle, Kay 1902-1992 .... **CLC 1, 5, 19, 58, 121; SSC 5**
See also CA 13-16R; 140; CAAS 1; CANR 29, 61, 110; CN 1, 2, 3, 4, 5; CP 1, 2, 3, 4; DLB 4, 9, 48, 86; DLBY 1993; EWL 3; MAL 5; MTCW 1, 2; MTFW 2005; RGAL 4; RGSF 2; SSFS 10, 13, 14

Boyle, Mark
See Kienzle, William X(avier)

Boyle, Patrick 1905-1982 .... **CLC 19**
See also CA 127

Boyle, T. C.
See Boyle, T(homas) Coraghessan
See also AMWS 8

Boyle, T(homas) Coraghessan
1948- .... **CLC 36, 55, 90; SSC 16**
See Boyle, T. C.
See also AAYA 47; BEST 90:4; BPFB 1; CA 120; CANR 44, 76, 89, 132; CN 6, 7; CPW; DA3; DAM POP; DLB 218, 278; DLBY 1986; EWL 3; MAL 5; MTCW 2; MTFW 2005; SSFS 13, 19

Boz
See Dickens, Charles (John Huffam)

Brackenridge, Hugh Henry
1748-1816 .... **NCLC 7**
See also DLB 11, 37; RGAL 4

Bradbury, Edward P.
See Moorcock, Michael (John)
See also MTCW 2

Bradbury, Malcolm (Stanley)
1932-2000 .... **CLC 32, 61**
See also CA 1-4R; CANR 1, 33, 91, 98, 137; CN 1, 2, 3, 4, 5, 6, 7; CP 1; DA3; DAM NOV; DLB 14, 207; EWL 3; MTCW 1, 2; MTFW 2005

Bradbury, Ray (Douglas) 1920- . **CLC 1, 3, 10, 15, 42, 98; SSC 29, 53; WLC**
See also AAYA 15; AITN 1, 2; AMWS 4; BPFB 1; BYA 4, 5, 11; CA 1-4R; CANR 2, 30, 75, 125; CDALB 1968-1988; CN 1, 2, 3, 4, 5, 6, 7; CPW; DA; DA3; DAB; DAC; DAM MST, NOV, POP; DLB 2, 8; EXPN; EXPS; HGG; LAIT 3, 5; LATS 1:2; LMFS 2; MAL 5; MTCW 1, 2; MTFW 2005; NFS 1, 22; RGAL 4; RGSF 2; SATA 11, 64, 123; SCFW 1, 2; SFW 4; SSFS 1, 20; SUFW 1, 2; TUS; YAW

Cankar, Ivan 1876-1918 .... **TCLC 105**
    See also CDWLB 4; DLB 147; EWL 3
Cannon, Curt
    See Hunter, Evan
Cao, Lan 1961- .... **CLC 109**
    See also CA 165
Cape, Judith
    See Page, P(atricia) K(athleen)
    See also CCA 1
Capek, Karel 1890-1938 .... **DC 1; SSC 36;**
    TCLC 6, 37; WLC
    See also CA 104; 140; CDWLB 4; DA;
    DA3; DAB; DAC; DAM DRAM, MST,
    NOV; DFS 7, 11; DLB 215; EW 10; EWL
    3; MTCW 2; MTFW 2005; RGSF 2;
    RGWL 2, 3; SCFW 1, 2; SFW 4
Capote, Truman 1924-1984 . **CLC 1, 3, 8, 13,**
    19, 34, 38, 58; SSC 2, 47; TCLC 164;
    WLC
    See also AAYA 61; AMWS 3; BPFB 1; CA
    5-8R; 113; CANR 18, 62; CDALB 1941-
    1968; CN 1, 2, 3; CPW; DA; DA3; DAB;
    DAC; DAM MST, NOV, POP; DLB 2,
    185, 227; DLBY 1980, 1984; EWL 3;
    EXPS; GLL 1; LAIT 3; MAL 5; MTCW
    1, 2; MTFW 2005; NCFS 2; RGAL 4;
    RGSF 2; SATA 91; SSFS 2; TUS
Capra, Frank 1897-1991 .... **CLC 16**
    See also AAYA 52; CA 61-64; 135
Caputo, Philip 1941- .... **CLC 32**
    See also AAYA 60; CA 73-76; CANR 40,
    135; YAW
Caragiale, Ion Luca 1852-1912 ...... **TCLC 76**
    See also CA 157
Card, Orson Scott 1951- .... **CLC 44, 47, 50**
    See also AAYA 11, 42; BPFB 1; BYA 5, 8;
    CA 102; CANR 27, 47, 73, 102, 106, 133;
    CPW; DA3; DAM POP; FANT; INT
    CANR-27; MTCW 1, 2; MTFW 2005;
    NFS 5; SATA 83, 127; SCFW 2; SFW 4;
    SUFW 2; YAW
Cardenal, Ernesto 1925- .... **CLC 31, 161;**
    HLC 1; PC 22
    See also CA 49-52; CANR 2, 32, 66, 138;
    CWW 2; DAM MULT, POET; DLB 290;
    EWL 3; HW 1, 2; LAWS 1; MTCW 1, 2;
    MTFW 2005; RGWL 2, 3
Cardinal, Marie 1929-2001 .... **CLC 189**
    See also CA 177; CWW 2; DLB 83; FW
Cardozo, Benjamin N(athan)
    1870-1938 .... **TCLC 65**
    See also CA 117; 164
Carducci, Giosue (Alessandro Giuseppe)
    1835-1907 .... **PC 46; TCLC 32**
    See also CA 163; EW 7; RGWL 2, 3
Carew, Thomas 1595(?)-1640 . **LC 13; PC 29**
    See also BRW 2; DLB 126; PAB; RGEL 2
Carey, Ernestine Gilbreth 1908- ...... **CLC 17**
    See also CA 5-8R; CANR 71; SATA 2
Carey, Peter 1943- .... **CLC 40, 55, 96, 183**
    See also CA 123; 127; CANR 53, 76, 117;
    CN 4, 5, 6, 7; DLB 289; EWL 3; INT CA-
    127; MTCW 1, 2; MTFW 2005; RGSF 2;
    SATA 94
Carleton, William 1794-1869 .... **NCLC 3**
    See also DLB 159; RGEL 2; RGSF 2
Carlisle, Henry (Coffin) 1926- .... **CLC 33**
    See also CA 13-16R; CANR 15, 85
Carlsen, Chris
    See Holdstock, Robert P.
Carlson, Ron(ald F.) 1947- .... **CLC 54**
    See also CA 105; 189; CAAE 189; CANR
    27; DLB 244
Carlyle, Thomas 1795-1881 ..... **NCLC 22, 70**
    See also BRW 4; CDBLB 1789-1832; DA;
    DAB; DAC; DAM MST; DLB 55, 144,
    254; RGEL 2; TEA

Carman, (William) Bliss 1861-1929 ... **PC 34;**
    TCLC 7
    See also CA 104; 152; DAC; DLB 92;
    RGEL 2
Carnegie, Dale 1888-1955 .... **TCLC 53**
    See also CA 218
Carossa, Hans 1878-1956 .... **TCLC 48**
    See also CA 170; DLB 66; EWL 3
Carpenter, Don(ald Richard)
    1931-1995 .... **CLC 41**
    See also CA 45-48; 149; CANR 1, 71
Carpenter, Edward 1844-1929 .... **TCLC 88**
    See also CA 163; GLL 1
Carpenter, John (Howard) 1948- ... **CLC 161**
    See also AAYA 2; CA 134; SATA 58
Carpenter, Johnny
    See Carpenter, John (Howard)
Carpentier (y Valmont), Alejo
    1904-1980 . **CLC 8, 11, 38, 110; HLC 1;**
    SSC 35
    See also CA 65-68; 97-100; CANR 11, 70;
    CDWLB 3; DAM MULT; DLB 113; EWL
    3; HW 1, 2; LAW; LMFS 2; RGSF 2;
    RGWL 2, 3; WLIT 1
Carr, Caleb 1955- .... **CLC 86**
    See also CA 147; CANR 73, 134; DA3
Carr, Emily 1871-1945 .... **TCLC 32**
    See also CA 159; DLB 68; FW; GLL 2
Carr, John Dickson 1906-1977 .... **CLC 3**
    See Fairbairn, Roger
    See also CA 49-52; 69-72; CANR 3, 33,
    60; CMW 4; DLB 306; MSW; MTCW 1,
    2
Carr, Philippa
    See Hibbert, Eleanor Alice Burford
Carr, Virginia Spencer 1929- .... **CLC 34**
    See also CA 61-64; DLB 111
Carrere, Emmanuel 1957- .... **CLC 89**
    See also CA 200
Carrier, Roch 1937- .... **CLC 13, 78**
    See also CA 130; CANR 61; CCA 1; DAC;
    DAM MST; DLB 53; SATA 105
Carroll, James Dennis
    See Carroll, Jim
Carroll, James P. 1943(?)- .... **CLC 38**
    See also CA 81-84; CANR 73, 139; MTCW
    2; MTFW 2005
Carroll, Jim 1951- .... **CLC 35, 143**
    See also AAYA 17; CA 45-48; CANR 42,
    115; NCFS 5
Carroll, Lewis ..... **NCLC 2, 53, 139; PC 18;**
    WLC
    See Dodgson, Charles L(utwidge)
    See also AAYA 39; BRW 5; BYA 5, 13; CD-
    BLB 1832-1890; CLR 2, 18; DLB 18,
    163, 178; DLBY 1998; EXPN; EXPP;
    FANT; JRDA; LAIT 1; NFS 7; PFS 11;
    RGEL 2; SUFW 1; TEA; WCH
Carroll, Paul Vincent 1900-1968 ...... **CLC 10**
    See also CA 9-12R; 25-28R; DLB 10; EWL
    3; RGEL 2
Carruth, Hayden 1921- ..... **CLC 4, 7, 10, 18,**
    84; PC 10
    See also CA 9-12R; CANR 4, 38, 59, 110;
    CP 1, 2, 3, 4, 5, 6, 7; DLB 5, 165; INT
    CANR-4; MTCW 1, 2; MTFW 2005;
    SATA 47
Carson, Anne 1950- .... **CLC 185; PC 64**
    See also AMWS 12; CA 203; DLB 193;
    PFS 18; TCLE 1:1
Carson, Ciaran 1948- .... **CLC 201**
    See also CA 112; 153; CANR 113; CP 7
Carson, Rachel
    See Carson, Rachel Louise
    See also AAYA 49; DLB 275

Carson, Rachel Louise 1907-1964 .... **CLC 71**
    See Carson, Rachel
    See also AMWS 9; ANW; CA 77-80; CANR
    35; DA3; DAM POP; FW; LAIT 4; MAL
    5; MTCW 1, 2; MTFW 2005; NCFS 1;
    SATA 23
Carter, Angela (Olive) 1940-1992 ...... **CLC 5,**
    41, 76; SSC 13, 85; TCLC 139
    See also BRWS 3; CA 53-56; 136; CANR
    12, 36, 61, 106; CN 3, 4, 5; DA3; DLB
    14, 207, 261, 319; EXPS; FANT; FW; GL
    2; MTCW 1, 2; MTFW 2005; RGSF 2;
    SATA 66; SATA-Obit 70; SFW 4; SSFS
    4, 12; SUFW 2; WLIT 4
Carter, Nick
    See Smith, Martin Cruz
Carver, Raymond 1938-1988 ..... **CLC 22, 36,**
    53, 55, 126; PC 54; SSC 8, 51
    See also AAYA 44; AMWS 3; BPFB 1; CA
    33-36R; 126; CANR 17, 34, 61, 103; CN
    4; CPW; DA3; DAM NOV; DLB 130;
    DLBY 1984, 1988; EWL 3; MAL 5;
    MTCW 1, 2; MTFW 2005; PFS 17;
    RGAL 4; RGSF 2; SSFS 3, 6, 12, 13;
    TCLE 1:1; TCWW 2; TUS
Cary, Elizabeth, Lady Falkland
    1585-1639 .... **LC 30**
Cary, (Arthur) Joyce (Lunel)
    1888-1957 .... **TCLC 1, 29**
    See also BRW 7; CA 104; 164; CDBLB
    1914-1945; DLB 15, 100; EWL 3; MTCW
    2; RGEL 2; TEA
Casal, Julian del 1863-1893 .... **NCLC 131**
    See also DLB 283; LAW
Casanova, Giacomo
    See Casanova de Seingalt, Giovanni Jacopo
    See also WLIT 7
Casanova de Seingalt, Giovanni Jacopo
    1725-1798 .... **LC 13**
    See Casanova, Giacomo
Casares, Adolfo Bioy
    See Bioy Casares, Adolfo
    See also RGSF 2
Casas, Bartolome de las 1474-1566
    See Las Casas, Bartolome de
    See also WLIT 1
Casely-Hayford, J(oseph) E(phraim)
    1866-1903 .... **BLC 1; TCLC 24**
    See also BW 2; CA 123; 152; DAM MULT
Casey, John (Dudley) 1939- .... **CLC 59**
    See also BEST 90:2; CA 69-72; CANR 23,
    100
Casey, Michael 1947- .... **CLC 2**
    See also CA 65-68; CANR 109; CP 2, 3;
    DLB 5
Casey, Patrick
    See Thurman, Wallace (Henry)
Casey, Warren (Peter) 1935-1988 .... **CLC 12**
    See also CA 101; 127; INT CA-101
Casona, Alejandro .... **CLC 49**
    See Alvarez, Alejandro Rodriguez
    See also EWL 3
Cassavetes, John 1929-1989 .... **CLC 20**
    See also CA 85-88; 127; CANR 82
Cassian, Nina 1924- .... **PC 17**
    See also CWP; CWW 2
Cassill, R(onald) V(erlin)
    1919-2002 .... **CLC 4, 23**
    See also CA 9-12R; 208; CAAS 1; CANR
    7, 45; CN 1, 2, 3, 4, 5, 6, 7; DLB 6, 218;
    DLBY 2002
Cassiodorus, Flavius Magnus c. 490(?)-c.
    583(?) .... **CMLC 43**
Cassirer, Ernst 1874-1945 .... **TCLC 61**
    See also CA 157
Cassity, (Allen) Turner 1929- .... **CLC 6, 42**
    See also CA 17-20R; 223; CAAE 223;
    CAAS 8; CANR 11; CSW; DLB 105

Clutha, Janet Paterson Frame 1924-2004
See Frame, Janet
See also CA 1-4R; 224; CANR 2, 36, 76, 135; MTCW 1, 2; SATA 119

Clyne, Terence
See Blatty, William Peter

Cobalt, Martin
See Mayne, William (James Carter)

Cobb, Irvin S(hrewsbury)
1876-1944 .... **TCLC 77**
See also CA 175; DLB 11, 25, 86

Cobbett, William 1763-1835 .... **NCLC 49**
See also DLB 43, 107, 158; RGEL 2

Coburn, D(onald) L(ee) 1938- .... **CLC 10**
See also CA 89-92

Cocteau, Jean (Maurice Eugene Clement)
1889-1963 ...... **CLC 1, 8, 15, 16, 43; DC 17; TCLC 119; WLC**
See also CA 25-28; CANR 40; CAP 2; DA; DA3; DAB; DAC; DAM DRAM, MST, NOV; DLB 65, 258, 321; EW 10; EWL 3; GFL 1789 to the Present; MTCW 1, 2; RGWL 2, 3; TWA

Codrescu, Andrei 1946- .... **CLC 46, 121**
See also CA 33-36R; CAAS 19; CANR 13, 34, 53, 76, 125; CN 7; DA3; DAM POET; MAL 5; MTCW 2; MTFW 2005

Coe, Max
See Bourne, Randolph S(illiman)

Coe, Tucker
See Westlake, Donald E(dwin)

Coen, Ethan 1958- .... **CLC 108**
See also AAYA 54; CA 126; CANR 85

Coen, Joel 1955- .... **CLC 108**
See also AAYA 54; CA 126; CANR 119

The Coen Brothers
See Coen, Ethan; Coen, Joel

Coetzee, J(ohn) M(axwell) 1940- ..... **CLC 23, 33, 66, 117, 161, 162**
See also AAYA 37; AFW; BRWS 6; CA 77-80; CANR 41, 54, 74, 114, 133; CN 4, 5, 6, 7; DA3; DAM NOV; DLB 225; EWL 3; LMFS 2; MTCW 1, 2; MTFW 2005; NFS 21; WLIT 2; WWE 1

Coffey, Brian
See Koontz, Dean R.

Coffin, Robert P(eter) Tristram
1892-1955 .... **TCLC 95**
See also CA 123; 169; DLB 45

Cohan, George M(ichael)
1878-1942 .... **TCLC 60**
See also CA 157; DLB 249; RGAL 4

Cohen, Arthur A(llen) 1928-1986 ...... **CLC 7, 31**
See also CA 1-4R; 120; CANR 1, 17, 42; DLB 28

Cohen, Leonard (Norman) 1934- ...... **CLC 3, 38**
See also CA 21-24R; CANR 14, 69; CN 1, 2, 3, 4, 5, 6; CP 1, 2, 3, 4, 5, 6, 7; DAC; DAM MST; DLB 53; EWL 3; MTCW 1

Cohen, Matt(hew) 1942-1999 .... **CLC 19**
See also CA 61-64; 187; CAAS 18; CANR 40; CN 1, 2, 3, 4, 5, 6; DAC; DLB 53

Cohen-Solal, Annie 1948- .... **CLC 50**
See also CA 239

Colegate, Isabel 1931- .... **CLC 36**
See also CA 17-20R; CANR 8, 22, 74; CN 4, 5, 6, 7; DLB 14, 231; INT CANR-22; MTCW 1

Coleman, Emmett
See Reed, Ishmael (Scott)

Coleridge, Hartley 1796-1849 .... **NCLC 90**
See also DLB 96

Coleridge, M. E.
See Coleridge, Mary E(lizabeth)

Coleridge, Mary E(lizabeth)
1861-1907 .... **TCLC 73**
See also CA 116; 166; DLB 19, 98

Coleridge, Samuel Taylor
1772-1834 ...... **NCLC 9, 54, 99, 111; PC 11, 39, 67; WLC**
See also AAYA 66; BRW 4; BRWR 2; BYA 4; CDBLB 1789-1832; DA; DA3; DAB; DAC; DAM MST, POET; DLB 93, 107; EXPP; LATS 1:1; LMFS 1; PAB; PFS 4, 5; RGEL 2; TEA; WLIT 3; WP

Coleridge, Sara 1802-1852 .... **NCLC 31**
See also DLB 199

Coles, Don 1928- .... **CLC 46**
See also CA 115; CANR 38; CP 7

Coles, Robert (Martin) 1929- .... **CLC 108**
See also CA 45-48; CANR 3, 32, 66, 70, 135; INT CANR-32; SATA 23

Colette, (Sidonie-Gabrielle)
1873-1954 .... **SSC 10; TCLC 1, 5, 16**
See Willy, Colette
See also CA 104; 131; DA3; DAM NOV; DLB 65; EW 9; EWL 3; GFL 1789 to the Present; MTCW 1, 2; MTFW 2005; RGWL 2, 3; TWA

Collett, (Jacobine) Camilla (Wergeland)
1813-1895 .... **NCLC 22**

Collier, Christopher 1930- .... **CLC 30**
See also AAYA 13; BYA 2; CA 33-36R; CANR 13, 33, 102; JRDA; MAICYA 1, 2; SATA 16, 70; WYA; YAW 1

Collier, James Lincoln 1928- .... **CLC 30**
See also AAYA 13; BYA 2; CA 9-12R; CANR 4, 33, 60, 102; CLR 3; DAM POP; JRDA; MAICYA 1, 2; SAAS 21; SATA 8, 70; WYA; YAW 1

Collier, Jeremy 1650-1726 .... **LC 6**

Collier, John 1901-1980 . **SSC 19; TCLC 127**
See also CA 65-68; 97-100; CANR 10; CN 1, 2; DLB 77, 255; FANT; SUFW 1

Collier, Mary 1690-1762 .... **LC 86**
See also DLB 95

Collingwood, R(obin) G(eorge)
1889(?)-1943 .... **TCLC 67**
See also CA 117; 155; DLB 262

Collins, Billy 1941- .... **PC 68**
See also AAYA 64; CA 151; CANR 92; MTFW 2005; PFS 18

Collins, Hunt
See Hunter, Evan

Collins, Linda 1931- .... **CLC 44**
See also CA 125

Collins, Tom
See Furphy, Joseph
See also RGEL 2

Collins, (William) Wilkie
1824-1889 .... **NCLC 1, 18, 93**
See also BRWS 6; CDBLB 1832-1890; CMW 4; DLB 18, 70, 159; GL 2; MSW; RGEL 2; RGSF 2; SUFW 1; WLIT 4

Collins, William 1721-1759 .... **LC 4, 40**
See also BRW 3; DAM POET; DLB 109; RGEL 2

Collodi, Carlo .... **NCLC 54**
See Lorenzini, Carlo
See also CLR 5; WCH; WLIT 7

Colman, George
See Glassco, John

Colman, George, the Elder
1732-1794 .... **LC 98**
See also RGEL 2

Colonna, Vittoria 1492-1547 .... **LC 71**
See also RGWL 2, 3

Colt, Winchester Remington
See Hubbard, L(afayette) Ron(ald)

Colter, Cyrus J. 1910-2002 .... **CLC 58**
See also BW 1; CA 65-68; 205; CANR 10, 66; CN 2, 3, 4, 5, 6; DLB 33

Colton, James
See Hansen, Joseph
See also GLL 1

Colum, Padraic 1881-1972 .... **CLC 28**
See also BYA 4; CA 73-76; 33-36R; CANR 35; CLR 36; CP 1; CWRI 5; DLB 19; MAICYA 1, 2; MTCW 1; RGEL 2; SATA 15; WCH

Colvin, James
See Moorcock, Michael (John)

Colwin, Laurie (E.) 1944-1992 .... **CLC 5, 13, 23, 84**
See also CA 89-92; 139; CANR 20, 46; DLB 218; DLBY 1980; MTCW 1

Comfort, Alex(ander) 1920-2000 .... **CLC 7**
See also CA 1-4R; 190; CANR 1, 45; CN 1, 2, 3, 4; CP 1, 2, 3, 4, 5, 6, 7; DAM POP; MTCW 2

Comfort, Montgomery
See Campbell, (John) Ramsey

Compton-Burnett, I(vy)
1892(?)-1969 .... **CLC 1, 3, 10, 15, 34**
See also BRW 7; CA 1-4R; 25-28R; CANR 4; DAM NOV; DLB 36; EWL 3; MTCW 1, 2; RGEL 2

Comstock, Anthony 1844-1915 ...... **TCLC 13**
See also CA 110; 169

Comte, Auguste 1798-1857 .... **NCLC 54**

Conan Doyle, Arthur
See Doyle, Sir Arthur Conan
See also BPFB 1; BYA 4, 5, 11

Conde (Abellan), Carmen
1901-1996 .... **HLCS 1**
See also CA 177; CWW 2; DLB 108; EWL 3; HW 2

Conde, Maryse 1937- ..... **BLCS; CLC 52, 92**
See also BW 2, 3; CA 110, 190; CAAE 190; CANR 30, 53, 76; CWW 2; DAM MULT; EWL 3; MTCW 2; MTFW 2005

Condillac, Etienne Bonnot de
1714-1780 .... **LC 26**
See also DLB 313

Condon, Richard (Thomas)
1915-1996 .... **CLC 4, 6, 8, 10, 45, 100**
See also BEST 90:3; BPFB 1; CA 1-4R; 151; CAAS 1; CANR 2, 23; CMW 4; CN 1, 2, 3, 4, 5, 6; DAM NOV; INT CANR-23; MAL 5; MTCW 1, 2

Condorcet .... **LC 104**
See Condorcet, marquis de Marie-Jean-Antoine-Nicolas Caritat
See also GFL Beginnings to 1789

Condorcet, marquis de
Marie-Jean-Antoine-Nicolas Caritat
1743-1794
See Condorcet
See also DLB 313

Confucius 551B.C.-479B.C. .... **CMLC 19, 65; WLCS**
See also DA; DA3; DAB; DAC; DAM MST

Congreve, William 1670-1729 ... **DC 2; LC 5, 21; WLC**
See also BRW 2; CDBLB 1660-1789; DA; DAB; DAC; DAM DRAM, MST, POET; DFS 15; DLB 39, 84; RGEL 2; WLIT 3

Conley, Robert J(ackson) 1940- .... **NNAL**
See also CA 41-44R; CANR 15, 34, 45, 96; DAM MULT; TCWW 2

Connell, Evan S(helby), Jr. 1924- . **CLC 4, 6, 45**
See also AAYA 7; AMWS 14; CA 1-4R; CAAS 2; CANR 2, 39, 76, 97, 140; CN 1, 2, 3, 4, 5, 6; DAM NOV; DLB 2; DLBY 1981; MAL 5; MTCW 1, 2; MTFW 2005

Connelly, Marc(us Cook) 1890-1980 . **CLC 7**
See also CA 85-88; 102; CAD; CANR 30; DFS 12; DLB 7; DLBY 1980; MAL 5; RGAL 4; SATA-Obit 25

Connor, Ralph .... **TCLC 31**
See Gordon, Charles William
See also DLB 92; TCWW 1, 2

Dimont, Penelope
See Mortimer, Penelope (Ruth)

Dinesen, Isak ..... **CLC 10, 29, 95; SSC 7, 75**
See Blixen, Karen (Christentze Dinesen)
See also EW 10; EWL 3; EXPS; FW; GL 2; HGG; LAIT 3; MTCW 1; NCFS 2; NFS 9; RGSF 2; RGWL 2, 3; SSFS 3, 6, 13; WLIT 2

Ding Ling .... **CLC 68**
See Chiang, Pin-chin
See also RGWL 3

Diphusa, Patty
See Almodovar, Pedro

Disch, Thomas M(ichael) 1940- ... **CLC 7, 36**
See Disch, Tom
See also AAYA 17; BPFB 1; CA 21-24R; CAAS 4; CANR 17, 36, 54, 89; CLR 18; CP 7; DA3; DLB 8; HGG; MAICYA 1, 2; MTCW 1, 2; MTFW 2005; SAAS 15; SATA 92; SCFW 1, 2; SFW 4; SUFW 2

Disch, Tom
See Disch, Thomas M(ichael)
See also DLB 282

d'Isly, Georges
See Simenon, Georges (Jacques Christian)

Disraeli, Benjamin 1804-1881 ... **NCLC 2, 39, 79**
See also BRW 4; DLB 21, 55; RGEL 2

Ditcum, Steve
See Crumb, R(obert)

Dixon, Paige
See Corcoran, Barbara (Asenath)

Dixon, Stephen 1936- .... **CLC 52; SSC 16**
See also AMWS 12; CA 89-92; CANR 17, 40, 54, 91; CN 4, 5, 6, 7; DLB 130; MAL 5

Dixon, Thomas, Jr. 1864-1946 ..... **TCLC 163**
See also RHW

Djebar, Assia 1936- .... **CLC 182**
See also CA 188; EWL 3; RGWL 3; WLIT 2

Doak, Annie
See Dillard, Annie

Dobell, Sydney Thompson
1824-1874 .... **NCLC 43**
See also DLB 32; RGEL 2

Doblin, Alfred .... **TCLC 13**
See Doeblin, Alfred
See also CDWLB 2; EWL 3; RGWL 2, 3

Dobroliubov, Nikolai Aleksandrovich
See Dobrolyubov, Nikolai Alexandrovich
See also DLB 277

Dobrolyubov, Nikolai Alexandrovich
1836-1861 .... **NCLC 5**
See Dobroliubov, Nikolai Aleksandrovich

Dobson, Austin 1840-1921 .... **TCLC 79**
See also DLB 35, 144

Dobyns, Stephen 1941- .... **CLC 37**
See also AMWS 13; CA 45-48; CANR 2, 18, 99; CMW 4; CP 4, 5, 6, 7; PFS 23

Doctorow, E(dgar) L(aurence)
1931- .... **CLC 6, 11, 15, 18, 37, 44, 65, 113, 214**
See also AAYA 22; AITN 2; AMWS 4; BEST 89:3; BPFB 1; CA 45-48; CANR 2, 33, 51, 76, 97, 133; CDALB 1968-1988; CN 3, 4, 5, 6, 7; CPW; DA3; DAM NOV, POP; DLB 2, 28, 173; DLBY 1980; EWL 3; LAIT 3; MAL 5; MTCW 1, 2; MTFW 2005; NFS 6; RGAL 4; RHW; TCLE 1:1; TCWW 1, 2; TUS

Dodgson, Charles L(utwidge) 1832-1898
See Carroll, Lewis
See also CLR 2; DA; DA3; DAB; DAC; DAM MST, NOV, POET; MAICYA 1, 2; SATA 100; YABC 2

Dodsley, Robert 1703-1764 .... **LC 97**
See also DLB 95; RGEL 2

Dodson, Owen (Vincent) 1914-1983 .. **BLC 1; CLC 79**
See also BW 1; CA 65-68; 110; CANR 24; DAM MULT; DLB 76

Doeblin, Alfred 1878-1957 .... **TCLC 13**
See Doblin, Alfred
See also CA 110; 141; DLB 66

Doerr, Harriet 1910-2002 .... **CLC 34**
See also CA 117; 122; 213; CANR 47; INT CA-122; LATS 1:2

Domecq, H(onorio Bustos)
See Bioy Casares, Adolfo

Domecq, H(onorio) Bustos
See Bioy Casares, Adolfo; Borges, Jorge Luis

Domini, Rey
See Lorde, Audre (Geraldine)
See also GLL 1

Dominique
See Proust, (Valentin-Louis-George-Eugene) Marcel

Don, A
See Stephen, Sir Leslie

Donaldson, Stephen R(eeder)
1947- .... **CLC 46, 138**
See also AAYA 36; BPFB 1; CA 89-92; CANR 13, 55, 99; CPW; DAM POP; FANT; INT CANR-13; SATA 121; SFW 4; SUFW 1, 2

Donleavy, J(ames) P(atrick) 1926- .... **CLC 1, 4, 6, 10, 45**
See also AITN 2; BPFB 1; CA 9-12R; CANR 24, 49, 62, 80, 124; CBD; CD 5, 6; CN 1, 2, 3, 4, 5, 6, 7; DLB 6, 173; INT CANR-24; MAL 5; MTCW 1, 2; MTFW 2005; RGAL 4

Donnadieu, Marguerite
See Duras, Marguerite

Donne, John 1572-1631 ... **LC 10, 24, 91; PC 1, 43; WLC**
See also AAYA 67; BRW 1; BRWC 1; BRWR 2; CDBLB Before 1660; DA; DAB; DAC; DAM MST, POET; DLB 121, 151; EXPP; PAB; PFS 2, 11; RGEL 3; TEA; WLIT 3; WP

Donnell, David 1939(?)- .... **CLC 34**
See also CA 197

Donoghue, Denis 1928- .... **CLC 209**
See also CA 17-20R; CANR 16, 102

Donoghue, P. S.
See Hunt, E(verette) Howard, (Jr.)

Donoso (Yanez), Jose 1924-1996 ... **CLC 4, 8, 11, 32, 99; HLC 1; SSC 34; TCLC 133**
See also CA 81-84; 155; CANR 32, 73; CD-WLB 3; CWW 2; DAM MULT; DLB 113; EWL 3; HW 1, 2; LAW; LAWS 1; MTCW 1, 2; MTFW 2005; RGSF 2; WLIT 1

Donovan, John 1928-1992 .... **CLC 35**
See also AAYA 20; CA 97-100; 137; CLR 3; MAICYA 1, 2; SATA 72; SATA-Brief 29; YAW

Don Roberto
See Cunninghame Graham, Robert (Gallnigad) Bontine

Doolittle, Hilda 1886-1961 . **CLC 3, 8, 14, 31, 34, 73; PC 5; WLC**
See H. D.
See also AAYA 66; AMWS 1; CA 97-100; CANR 35, 131; DA; DAC; DAM MST, POET; DLB 4, 45; EWL 3; FW; GLL 1; LMFS 2; MAL 5; MAWW; MTCW 1, 2; MTFW 2005; PFS 6; RGAL 4

Doppo, Kunikida .... **TCLC 99**
See Kunikida Doppo

Dorfman, Ariel 1942- .... **CLC 48, 77, 189; HLC 1**
See also CA 124; 130; CANR 67, 70, 135; CWW 2; DAM MULT; DFS 4; EWL 3; HW 1, 2; INT CA-130; WLIT 1

Dorn, Edward (Merton)
1929-1999 .... **CLC 10, 18**
See also CA 93-96; 187; CANR 42, 79; CP 1, 2, 3, 4, 5, 6, 7; DLB 5; INT CA-93-96; WP

Dor-Ner, Zvi .... **CLC 70**

Dorris, Michael (Anthony)
1945-1997 .... **CLC 109; NNAL**
See also AAYA 20; BEST 90:1; BYA 12; CA 102; 157; CANR 19, 46, 75; CLR 58; DA3; DAM MULT, NOV; DLB 175; LAIT 5; MTCW 2; MTFW 2005; NFS 3; RGAL 4; SATA 75; SATA-Obit 94; TCWW 2; YAW

Dorris, Michael A.
See Dorris, Michael (Anthony)

Dorsan, Luc
See Simenon, Georges (Jacques Christian)

Dorsange, Jean
See Simenon, Georges (Jacques Christian)

Dorset
See Sackville, Thomas

Dos Passos, John (Roderigo)
1896-1970 ... **CLC 1, 4, 8, 11, 15, 25, 34, 82; WLC**
See also AMW; BPFB 1; CA 1-4R; 29-32R; CANR 3; CDALB 1929-1941; DA; DA3; DAB; DAC; DAM MST, NOV; DLB 4, 9, 274, 316; DLBD 1, 15; DLBY 1996; EWL 3; MAL 5; MTCW 1, 2; MTFW 2005; NFS 14; RGAL 4; TUS

Dossage, Jean
See Simenon, Georges (Jacques Christian)

Dostoevsky, Fedor Mikhailovich
1821-1881 .. **NCLC 2, 7, 21, 33, 43, 119; SSC 2, 33, 44; WLC**
See Dostoevsky, Fyodor
See also AAYA 40; DA; DA3; DAB; DAC; DAM MST, NOV; EW 7; EXPN; NFS 3, 8; RGSF 2; RGWL 2, 3; SSFS 8; TWA

Dostoevsky, Fyodor
See Dostoevsky, Fedor Mikhailovich
See also DLB 238; LATS 1:1; LMFS 1, 2

Doty, M. R.
See Doty, Mark (Alan)

Doty, Mark
See Doty, Mark (Alan)

Doty, Mark (Alan) 1953(?)- .... **CLC 176; PC 53**
See also AMWS 11; CA 161, 183; CAAE 183; CANR 110

Doty, Mark A.
See Doty, Mark (Alan)

Doughty, Charles M(ontagu)
1843-1926 .... **TCLC 27**
See also CA 115; 178; DLB 19, 57, 174

Douglas, Ellen .... **CLC 73**
See Haxton, Josephine Ayres; Williamson, Ellen Douglas
See also CN 5, 6, 7; CSW; DLB 292

Douglas, Gavin 1475(?)-1522 .... **LC 20**
See also DLB 132; RGEL 2

Douglas, George
See Brown, George Douglas
See also RGEL 2

Douglas, Keith (Castellain)
1920-1944 .... **TCLC 40**
See also BRW 7; CA 160; DLB 27; EWL 3; PAB; RGEL 2

Douglas, Leonard
See Bradbury, Ray (Douglas)

Douglas, Michael
See Crichton, (John) Michael

Douglas, (George) Norman
1868-1952 .... **TCLC 68**
See also BRW 6; CA 119; 157; DLB 34, 195; RGEL 2

Douglas, William
See Brown, George Douglas

Douglass, Frederick 1817(?)-1895 ..... **BLC 1; NCLC 7, 55, 141; WLC**
    See also AAYA 48; AFAW 1, 2; AMWC 1; AMWS 3; CDALB 1640-1865; DA; DA3; DAC; DAM MST, MULT; DLB 1, 43, 50, 79, 243; FW; LAIT 2; NCFS 2; RGAL 4; SATA 29

Dourado, (Waldomiro Freitas) Autran 1926- .... **CLC 23, 60**
    See also CA 25-28R, 179; CANR 34, 81; DLB 145, 307; HW 2

Dourado, Waldomiro Freitas Autran
    See Dourado, (Waldomiro Freitas) Autran

Dove, Rita (Frances) 1952- . **BLCS; CLC 50, 81; PC 6**
    See also AAYA 46; AMWS 4; BW 2; CA 109; CAAS 19; CANR 27, 42, 68, 76, 97, 132; CDALBS; CP 7; CSW; CWP; DA3; DAM MULT; DLB 120; EWL 3; EXPP; MAL 5; MTCW 2; MTFW 2005; PFS 1, 15; RGAL 4

Doveglion
    See Villa, Jose Garcia

Dowell, Coleman 1925-1985 .... **CLC 60**
    See also CA 25-28R; 117; CANR 10; DLB 130; GLL 2

Dowson, Ernest (Christopher) 1867-1900 .... **TCLC 4**
    See also CA 105; 150; DLB 19, 135; RGEL 2

Doyle, A. Conan
    See Doyle, Sir Arthur Conan

Doyle, Sir Arthur Conan 1859-1930 . **SSC 12, 83; TCLC 7; WLC**
    See Conan Doyle, Arthur
    See also AAYA 14; BRWS 2; CA 104; 122; CANR 131; CDBLB 1890-1914; CMW 4; DA; DA3; DAB; DAC; DAM MST, NOV; DLB 18, 70, 156, 178; EXPS; HGG; LAIT 2; MSW; MTCW 1, 2; MTFW 2005; RGEL 2; RGSF 2; RHW; SATA 24; SCFW 1, 2; SFW 4; SSFS 2; TEA; WCH; WLIT 4; WYA; YAW

Doyle, Conan
    See Doyle, Sir Arthur Conan

Doyle, John
    See Graves, Robert (von Ranke)

Doyle, Roddy 1958- .... **CLC 81, 178**
    See also AAYA 14; BRWS 5; CA 143; CANR 73, 128; CN 6, 7; DA3; DLB 194; MTCW 2; MTFW 2005

Doyle, Sir A. Conan
    See Doyle, Sir Arthur Conan

Dr. A
    See Asimov, Isaac; Silverstein, Alvin; Silverstein, Virginia B(arbara Opshelor)

Drabble, Margaret 1939- ...... **CLC 2, 3, 5, 8, 10, 22, 53, 129**
    See also BRWS 4; CA 13-16R; CANR 18, 35, 63, 112, 131; CDBLB 1960 to Present; CN 1, 2, 3, 4, 5, 6, 7; CPW; DA3; DAB; DAC; DAM MST, NOV, POP; DLB 14, 155, 231; EWL 3; FW; MTCW 1, 2; MTFW 2005; RGEL 2; SATA 48; TEA

Drakulic, Slavenka 1949- .... **CLC 173**
    See also CA 144; CANR 92

Drakulic-Ilic, Slavenka
    See Drakulic, Slavenka

Drapier, M. B.
    See Swift, Jonathan

Drayham, James
    See Mencken, H(enry) L(ouis)

Drayton, Michael 1563-1631 .... **LC 8**
    See also DAM POET; DLB 121; RGEL 2

Dreadstone, Carl
    See Campbell, (John) Ramsey

Dreiser, Theodore (Herman Albert) 1871-1945 .... **SSC 30; TCLC 10, 18, 35, 83; WLC**
    See also AMW; AMWC 2; AMWR 2; BYA 15, 16; CA 106; 132; CDALB 1865-1917; DA; DA3; DAC; DAM MST, NOV; DLB 9, 12, 102, 137; DLBD 1; EWL 3; LAIT 2; LMFS 2; MAL 5; MTCW 1, 2; MTFW 2005; NFS 8, 17; RGAL 4; TUS

Drexler, Rosalyn 1926- .... **CLC 2, 6**
    See also CA 81-84; CAD; CANR 68, 124; CD 5, 6; CWD; MAL 5

Dreyer, Carl Theodor 1889-1968 ...... **CLC 16**
    See also CA 116

Drieu la Rochelle, Pierre(-Eugene) 1893-1945 .... **TCLC 21**
    See also CA 117; DLB 72; EWL 3; GFL 1789 to the Present

Drinkwater, John 1882-1937 .... **TCLC 57**
    See also CA 109; 149; DLB 10, 19, 149; RGEL 2

Drop Shot
    See Cable, George Washington

Droste-Hulshoff, Annette Freiin von 1797-1848 .... **NCLC 3, 133**
    See also CDWLB 2; DLB 133; RGSF 2; RGWL 2, 3

Drummond, Walter
    See Silverberg, Robert

Drummond, William Henry 1854-1907 .... **TCLC 25**
    See also CA 160; DLB 92

Drummond de Andrade, Carlos 1902-1987 .... **CLC 18; TCLC 139**
    See Andrade, Carlos Drummond de
    See also CA 132; 123; DLB 307; LAW

Drummond of Hawthornden, William 1585-1649 .... **LC 83**
    See also DLB 121, 213; RGEL 2

Drury, Allen (Stuart) 1918-1998 .... **CLC 37**
    See also CA 57-60; 170; CANR 18, 52; CN 1, 2, 3, 4, 5, 6; INT CANR-18

Druse, Eleanor
    See King, Stephen

Dryden, John 1631-1700 ..... **DC 3; LC 3, 21, 115; PC 25; WLC**
    See also BRW 2; CDBLB 1660-1789; DA; DAB; DAC; DAM DRAM, MST, POET; DLB 80, 101, 131; EXPP; IDTP; LMFS 1; RGEL 2; TEA; WLIT 3

du Bellay, Joachim 1524-1560 .... **LC 92**
    See also GFL Beginnings to 1789; RGWL 2, 3

Duberman, Martin (Bauml) 1930- ..... **CLC 8**
    See also CA 1-4R; CAD; CANR 2, 63, 137; CD 5, 6

Dubie, Norman (Evans) 1945- .... **CLC 36**
    See also CA 69-72; CANR 12, 115; CP 3, 4, 5, 6, 7; DLB 120; PFS 12

Du Bois, W(illiam) E(dward) B(urghardt) 1868-1963 ..... **BLC 1; CLC 1, 2, 13, 64, 96; HR 1:2; TCLC 169; WLC**
    See also AAYA 40; AFAW 1, 2; AMWC 1; AMWS 2; BW 1, 3; CA 85-88; CANR 34, 82, 132; CDALB 1865-1917; DA; DA3; DAC; DAM MST, MULT, NOV; DLB 47, 50, 91, 246, 284; EWL 3; EXPP; LAIT 2; LMFS 2; MAL 5; MTCW 1, 2; MTFW 2005; NCFS 1; PFS 13; RGAL 4; SATA 42

Dubus, Andre 1936-1999 ..... **CLC 13, 36, 97; SSC 15**
    See also AMWS 7; CA 21-24R; 177; CANR 17; CN 5, 6; CSW; DLB 130; INT CANR-17; RGAL 4; SSFS 10; TCLE 1:1

Duca Minimo
    See D'Annunzio, Gabriele

Ducharme, Rejean 1941- .... **CLC 74**
    See also CA 165; DLB 60

du Chatelet, Emilie 1706-1749 .... **LC 96**
    See Chatelet, Gabrielle-Emilie Du

Duchen, Claire .... **CLC 65**

Duclos, Charles Pinot- 1704-1772 .... **LC 1**
    See also GFL Beginnings to 1789

Dudek, Louis 1918-2001 .... **CLC 11, 19**
    See also CA 45-48; 215; CAAS 14; CANR 1; CP 1, 2, 3, 4, 5, 6, 7; DLB 88

Duerrenmatt, Friedrich 1921-1990 ... **CLC 1, 4, 8, 11, 15, 43, 102**
    See Durrenmatt, Friedrich
    See also CA 17-20R; CANR 33; CMW 4; DAM DRAM; DLB 69, 124; MTCW 1, 2

Duffy, Bruce 1953(?)- .... **CLC 50**
    See also CA 172

Duffy, Maureen (Patricia) 1933- ...... **CLC 37**
    See also CA 25-28R; CANR 33, 68; CBD; CN 1, 2, 3, 4, 5, 6, 7; CP 7; CWD; CWP; DFS 15; DLB 14, 310; FW; MTCW 1

Du Fu
    See Tu Fu
    See also RGWL 2, 3

Dugan, Alan 1923-2003 .... **CLC 2, 6**
    See also CA 81-84; 220; CANR 119; CP 1, 2, 3, 4, 5, 6, 7; DLB 5; MAL 5; PFS 10

du Gard, Roger Martin
    See Martin du Gard, Roger

Duhamel, Georges 1884-1966 .... **CLC 8**
    See also CA 81-84; 25-28R; CANR 35; DLB 65; EWL 3; GFL 1789 to the Present; MTCW 1

Dujardin, Edouard (Emile Louis) 1861-1949 .... **TCLC 13**
    See also CA 109; DLB 123

Duke, Raoul
    See Thompson, Hunter S(tockton)

Dulles, John Foster 1888-1959 .... **TCLC 72**
    See also CA 115; 149

Dumas, Alexandre (pere) 1802-1870 .... **NCLC 11, 71; WLC**
    See also AAYA 22; BYA 3; DA; DA3; DAB; DAC; DAM MST, NOV; DLB 119, 192; EW 6; GFL 1789 to the Present; LAIT 1, 2; NFS 14, 19; RGWL 2, 3; SATA 18; TWA; WCH

Dumas, Alexandre (fils) 1824-1895 ...... **DC 1; NCLC 9**
    See also DLB 192; GFL 1789 to the Present; RGWL 2, 3

Dumas, Claudine
    See Malzberg, Barry N(athaniel)

Dumas, Henry L. 1934-1968 .... **CLC 6, 62**
    See also BW 1; CA 85-88; DLB 41; RGAL 4

du Maurier, Daphne 1907-1989 .. **CLC 6, 11, 59; SSC 18**
    See also AAYA 37; BPFB 1; BRWS 3; CA 5-8R; 128; CANR 6, 55; CMW 4; CN 1, 2, 3, 4; CPW; DA3; DAB; DAC; DAM MST, POP; DLB 191; GL 2; HGG; LAIT 3; MSW; MTCW 1, 2; NFS 12; RGEL 2; RGSF 2; RHW; SATA 27; SATA-Obit 60; SSFS 14, 16; TEA

Du Maurier, George 1834-1896 ..... **NCLC 86**
    See also DLB 153, 178; RGEL 2

Dunbar, Paul Laurence 1872-1906 ... **BLC 1; PC 5; SSC 8; TCLC 2, 12; WLC**
    See also AFAW 1, 2; AMWS 2; BW 1, 3; CA 104; 124; CANR 79; CDALB 1865-1917; DA; DA3; DAC; DAM MST, MULT, POET; DLB 50, 54, 78; EXPP; MAL 5; RGAL 4; SATA 34

Dunbar, William 1460(?)-1520(?) .... **LC 20; PC 67**
    See also BRWS 8; DLB 132, 146; RGEL 2

Dunbar-Nelson, Alice .... **HR 1:2**
    See Nelson, Alice Ruth Moore Dunbar

Duncan, Dora Angela
    See Duncan, Isadora

Cumulative Author Index

Field, Andrew 1938- .... **CLC 44**
See also CA 97-100; CANR 25

Field, Eugene 1850-1895 .... **NCLC 3**
See also DLB 23, 42, 140; DLBD 13; MAI-CYA 1, 2; RGAL 4; SATA 16

Field, Gans T.
See Wellman, Manly Wade

Field, Michael 1915-1971 .... **TCLC 43**
See also CA 29-32R

Fielding, Helen 1958- .... **CLC 146**
See also AAYA 65; CA 172; CANR 127; DLB 231; MTFW 2005

Fielding, Henry 1707-1754 .... **LC 1, 46, 85; WLC**
See also BRW 3; BRWR 1; CDBLB 1660-1789; DA; DA3; DAB; DAC; DAM DRAM, MST, NOV; DLB 39, 84, 101; NFS 18; RGEL 2; TEA; WLIT 3

Fielding, Sarah 1710-1768 .... **LC 1, 44**
See also DLB 39; RGEL 2; TEA

Fields, W. C. 1880-1946 .... **TCLC 80**
See also DLB 44

Fierstein, Harvey (Forbes) 1954- ..... **CLC 33**
See also CA 123; 129; CAD; CD 5, 6; CPW; DA3; DAM DRAM, POP; DFS 6; DLB 266; GLL; MAL 5

Figes, Eva 1932- .... **CLC 31**
See also CA 53-56; CANR 4, 44, 83; CN 2, 3, 4, 5, 6, 7; DLB 14, 271; FW

Filippo, Eduardo de
See de Filippo, Eduardo

Finch, Anne 1661-1720 .... **LC 3; PC 21**
See also BRWS 9; DLB 95

Finch, Robert (Duer Claydon)
1900-1995 .... **CLC 18**
See also CA 57-60; CANR 9, 24, 49; CP 1, 2, 3, 4; DLB 88

Findley, Timothy (Irving Frederick)
1930-2002 .... **CLC 27, 102**
See also CA 25-28R; 206; CANR 12, 42, 69, 109; CCA 1; CN 4, 5, 6, 7; DAC; DAM MST; DLB 53; FANT; RHW

Fink, William
See Mencken, H(enry) L(ouis)

Firbank, Louis 1942-
See Reed, Lou
See also CA 117

Firbank, (Arthur Annesley) Ronald
1886-1926 .... **TCLC 1**
See also BRWS 2; CA 104; 177; DLB 36; EWL 3; RGEL 2

Firdawsi, Abu al-Qasim
See Ferdowsi, Abu'l Qasem
See also WLIT 6

Fish, Stanley
See Fish, Stanley Eugene

Fish, Stanley E.
See Fish, Stanley Eugene

Fish, Stanley Eugene 1938- .... **CLC 142**
See also CA 112; 132; CANR 90; DLB 67

Fisher, Dorothy (Frances) Canfield
1879-1958 .... **TCLC 87**
See also CA 114; 136; CANR 80; CLR 71; CWRI 5; DLB 9, 102, 284; MAICYA 1, 2; MAL 5; YABC 1

Fisher, M(ary) F(rances) K(ennedy)
1908-1992 .... **CLC 76, 87**
See also CA 77-80; 138; CANR 44; MTCW 2

Fisher, Roy 1930- .... **CLC 25**
See also CA 81-84; CAAS 10; CANR 16; CP 1, 2, 3, 4, 5, 6, 7; DLB 40

Fisher, Rudolph 1897-1934 . **BLC 2; HR 1:2; SSC 25; TCLC 11**
See also BW 1, 3; CA 107; 124; CANR 80; DAM MULT; DLB 51, 102

Fisher, Vardis (Alvero) 1895-1968 .... **CLC 7; TCLC 140**
See also CA 5-8R; 25-28R; CANR 68; DLB 9, 206; MAL 5; RGAL 4; TCWW 1, 2

Fiske, Tarleton
See Bloch, Robert (Albert)

Fitch, Clarke
See Sinclair, Upton (Beall)

Fitch, John IV
See Cormier, Robert (Edmund)

Fitzgerald, Captain Hugh
See Baum, L(yman) Frank

FitzGerald, Edward 1809-1883 ...... **NCLC 9, 153**
See also BRW 4; DLB 32; RGEL 2

Fitzgerald, F(rancis) Scott (Key)
1896-1940 ... **SSC 6, 31, 75; TCLC 1, 6, 14, 28, 55, 157; WLC**
See also AAYA 24; AITN 1; AMW; AMWC 2; AMWR 1; BPFB 1; CA 110; 123; CDALB 1917-1929; DA; DA3; DAB; DAC; DAM MST, NOV; DLB 4, 9, 86, 219, 273; DLBD 1, 15, 16; DLBY 1981, 1996; EWL 3; EXPN; EXPS; LAIT 3; MAL 5; MTCW 1, 2; MTFW 2005; NFS 2, 19, 20; RGAL 4; RGSF 2; SSFS 4, 15, 21; TUS

Fitzgerald, Penelope 1916-2000 . **CLC 19, 51, 61, 143**
See also BRWS 5; CA 85-88; 190; CAAS 10; CANR 56, 86, 131; CN 3, 4, 5, 6, 7; DLB 14, 194; EWL 3; MTCW 2; MTFW 2005

Fitzgerald, Robert (Stuart)
1910-1985 .... **CLC 39**
See also CA 1-4R; 114; CANR 1; CP 1, 2, 3, 4; DLBY 1980; MAL 5

FitzGerald, Robert D(avid)
1902-1987 .... **CLC 19**
See also CA 17-20R; CP 1, 2, 3, 4; DLB 260; RGEL 2

Fitzgerald, Zelda (Sayre)
1900-1948 .... **TCLC 52**
See also AMWS 9; CA 117; 126; DLBY 1984

Flanagan, Thomas (James Bonner)
1923-2002 .... **CLC 25, 52**
See also CA 108; 206; CANR 55; CN 3, 4, 5, 6, 7; DLBY 1980; INT CA-108; MTCW 1; RHW; TCLE 1:1

Flaubert, Gustave 1821-1880 .... **NCLC 2, 10, 19, 62, 66, 135; SSC 11, 60; WLC**
See also DA; DA3; DAB; DAC; DAM MST, NOV; DLB 119, 301; EW 7; EXPS; GFL 1789 to the Present; LAIT 2; LMFS 1; NFS 14; RGSF 2; RGWL 2, 3; SSFS 6; TWA

Flavius Josephus
See Josephus, Flavius

Flecker, Herman Elroy
See Flecker, (Herman) James Elroy

Flecker, (Herman) James Elroy
1884-1915 .... **TCLC 43**
See also CA 109; 150; DLB 10, 19; RGEL 2

Fleming, Ian (Lancaster) 1908-1964 . **CLC 3, 30**
See also AAYA 26; BPFB 1; CA 5-8R; CANR 59; CDBLB 1945-1960; CMW 4; CPW; DA3; DAM POP; DLB 87, 201; MSW; MTCW 1, 2; MTFW 2005; RGEL 2; SATA 9; TEA; YAW

Fleming, Thomas (James) 1927- ...... **CLC 37**
See also CA 5-8R; CANR 10, 102; INT CANR-10; SATA 8

Fletcher, John 1579-1625 .... **DC 6; LC 33**
See also BRW 2; CDBLB Before 1660; DLB 58; RGEL 2; TEA

Fletcher, John Gould 1886-1950 .... **TCLC 35**
See also CA 107; 167; DLB 4, 45; LMFS 2; MAL 5; RGAL 4

Fleur, Paul
See Pohl, Frederik

Flieg, Helmut
See Heym, Stefan

Flooglebuckle, Al
See Spiegelman, Art

Flora, Fletcher 1914-1969
See Queen, Ellery
See also CA 1-4R; CANR 3, 85

Flying Officer X
See Bates, H(erbert) E(rnest)

Fo, Dario 1926- .... **CLC 32, 109; DC 10**
See also CA 116; 128; CANR 68, 114, 134; CWW 2; DA3; DAM DRAM; DLBY 1997; EWL 3; MTCW 1, 2; MTFW 2005; WLIT 7

Fogarty, Jonathan Titulescu Esq.
See Farrell, James T(homas)

Follett, Ken(neth Martin) 1949- .... **CLC 18**
See also AAYA 6, 50; BEST 89:4; BPFB 1; CA 81-84; CANR 13, 33, 54, 102; CMW 4; CPW; DA3; DAM NOV, POP; DLB 87; DLBY 1981; INT CANR-33; MTCW 1

Fondane, Benjamin 1898-1944 ..... **TCLC 159**

Fontane, Theodor 1819-1898 .. **NCLC 26, 163**
See also CDWLB 2; DLB 129; EW 6; RGWL 2, 3; TWA

Fonte, Moderata 1555-1592 .... **LC 118**

Fontenot, Chester .... **CLC 65**

Fonvizin, Denis Ivanovich
1744(?)-1792 .... **LC 81**
See also DLB 150; RGWL 2, 3

Foote, Horton 1916- .... **CLC 51, 91**
See also CA 73-76; CAD; CANR 34, 51, 110; CD 5, 6; CSW; DA3; DAM DRAM; DFS 20; DLB 26, 266; EWL 3; INT CANR-34; MTFW 2005

Foote, Mary Hallock 1847-1938 .. **TCLC 108**
See also DLB 186, 188, 202, 221; TCWW 2

Foote, Samuel 1721-1777 .... **LC 106**
See also DLB 89; RGEL 2

Foote, Shelby 1916-2005 .... **CLC 75**
See also AAYA 40; CA 5-8R; 240; CANR 3, 45, 74, 131; CN 1, 2, 3, 4, 5, 6, 7; CPW; CSW; DA3; DAM NOV, POP; DLB 2, 17; MAL 5; MTCW 2; MTFW 2005; RHW

Forbes, Cosmo
See Lewton, Val

Forbes, Esther 1891-1967 .... **CLC 12**
See also AAYA 17; BYA 2; CA 13-14; 25-28R; CAP 1; CLR 27; DLB 22; JRDA; MAICYA 1, 2; RHW; SATA 2, 100; YAW

Forche, Carolyn (Louise) 1950- .... **CLC 25, 83, 86; PC 10**
See also CA 109; 117; CANR 50, 74, 138; CP 4, 5, 6, 7; CWP; DA3; DAM POET; DLB 5, 193; INT CA-117; MAL 5; MTCW 2; MTFW 2005; PFS 18; RGAL 4

Ford, Elbur
See Hibbert, Eleanor Alice Burford

Ford, Ford Madox 1873-1939 ... **TCLC 1, 15, 39, 57, 172**
See Chaucer, Daniel
See also BRW 6; CA 104; 132; CANR 74; CDBLB 1914-1945; DA3; DAM NOV; DLB 34, 98, 162; EWL 3; MTCW 1, 2; RGEL 2; TEA

Ford, Henry 1863-1947 .... **TCLC 73**
See also CA 115; 148

Ford, Jack
See Ford, John

French, Albert 1943- .... **CLC 86**
See also BW 3; CA 167

French, Antonia
See Kureishi, Hanif

French, Marilyn 1929- .. **CLC 10, 18, 60, 177**
See also BPFB 1; CA 69-72; CANR 3, 31, 134; CN 5, 6, 7; CPW; DAM DRAM, NOV, POP; FL 1:5; FW; INT CANR-31; MTCW 1, 2; MTFW 2005

French, Paul
See Asimov, Isaac

Freneau, Philip Morin 1752-1832 .. **NCLC 1, 111**
See also AMWS 2; DLB 37, 43; RGAL 4

Freud, Sigmund 1856-1939 .... **TCLC 52**
See also CA 115; 133; CANR 69; DLB 296; EW 8; EWL 3; LATS 1:1; MTCW 1, 2; MTFW 2005; NCFS 3; TWA

Freytag, Gustav 1816-1895 .... **NCLC 109**
See also DLB 129

Friedan, Betty (Naomi) 1921- .... **CLC 74**
See also CA 65-68; CANR 18, 45, 74; DLB 246; FW; MTCW 1, 2; MTFW 2005; NCFS 5

Friedlander, Saul 1932- .... **CLC 90**
See also CA 117; 130; CANR 72

Friedman, B(ernard) H(arper)
1926- .... **CLC 7**
See also CA 1-4R; CANR 3, 48

Friedman, Bruce Jay 1930- ...... **CLC 3, 5, 56**
See also CA 9-12R; CAD; CANR 25, 52, 101; CD 5, 6; CN 1, 2, 3, 4, 5, 6, 7; DLB 2, 28, 244; INT CANR-25; MAL 5; SSFS 18

Friel, Brian 1929- .... **CLC 5, 42, 59, 115; DC 8; SSC 76**
See also BRWS 5; CA 21-24R; CANR 33, 69, 131; CBD; CD 5, 6; DFS 11; DLB 13, 319; EWL 3; MTCW 1; RGEL 2; TEA

Friis-Baastad, Babbis Ellinor
1921-1970 .... **CLC 12**
See also CA 17-20R; 134; SATA 7

Frisch, Max (Rudolf) 1911-1991 ... **CLC 3, 9, 14, 18, 32, 44; TCLC 121**
See also CA 85-88; 134; CANR 32, 74; CD-WLB 2; DAM DRAM, NOV; DLB 69, 124; EW 13; EWL 3; MTCW 1, 2; MTFW 2005; RGWL 2, 3

Fromentin, Eugene (Samuel Auguste)
1820-1876 .... **NCLC 10, 125**
See also DLB 123; GFL 1789 to the Present

Frost, Frederick
See Faust, Frederick (Schiller)

Frost, Robert (Lee) 1874-1963 .. **CLC 1, 3, 4, 9, 10, 13, 15, 26, 34, 44; PC 1, 39; WLC**
See also AAYA 21; AMW; AMWR 1; CA 89-92; CANR 33; CDALB 1917-1929; CLR 67; DA; DA3; DAB; DAC; DAM MST, POET; DLB 54, 284; DLBD 7; EWL 3; EXPP; MAL 5; MTCW 1, 2; MTFW 2005; PAB; PFS 1, 2, 3, 4, 5, 6, 7, 10, 13; RGAL 4; SATA 14; TUS; WP; WYA

Froude, James Anthony
1818-1894 .... **NCLC 43**
See also DLB 18, 57, 144

Froy, Herald
See Waterhouse, Keith (Spencer)

Fry, Christopher 1907-2005 ... **CLC 2, 10, 14**
See also BRWS 3; CA 17-20R; 240; CAAS 23; CANR 9, 30, 74, 132; CBD; CD 5, 6; CP 1, 2, 3, 4, 5, 6, 7; DAM DRAM; DLB 13; EWL 3; MTCW 1, 2; MTFW 2005; RGEL 2; SATA 66; TEA

Frye, (Herman) Northrop
1912-1991 .... **CLC 24, 70; TCLC 165**
See also CA 5-8R; 133; CANR 8, 37; DLB 67, 68, 246; EWL 3; MTCW 1, 2; MTFW 2005; RGAL 4; TWA

Fuchs, Daniel 1909-1993 .... **CLC 8, 22**
See also CA 81-84; 142; CAAS 5; CANR 40; CN 1, 2, 3, 4, 5; DLB 9, 26, 28; DLBY 1993; MAL 5

Fuchs, Daniel 1934- .... **CLC 34**
See also CA 37-40R; CANR 14, 48

Fuentes, Carlos 1928- .. **CLC 3, 8, 10, 13, 22, 41, 60, 113; HLC 1; SSC 24; WLC**
See also AAYA 4, 45; AITN 2; BPFB 1; CA 69-72; CANR 10, 32, 68, 104, 138; CDWLB 3; CWW 2; DA; DA3; DAB; DAC; DAM MST, MULT, NOV; DLB 113; DNFS 2; EWL 3; HW 1, 2; LAIT 3; LATS 1:2; LAW; LAWS 1; LMFS 2; MTCW 1, 2; MTFW 2005; NFS 8; RGSF 2; RGWL 2, 3; TWA; WLIT 1

Fuentes, Gregorio Lopez y
See Lopez y Fuentes, Gregorio

Fuertes, Gloria 1918-1998 .... **PC 27**
See also CA 178, 180; DLB 108; HW 2; SATA 115

Fugard, (Harold) Athol 1932- . **CLC 5, 9, 14, 25, 40, 80, 211; DC 3**
See also AAYA 17; AFW; CA 85-88; CANR 32, 54, 118; CD 5, 6; DAM DRAM; DFS 3, 6, 10; DLB 225; DNFS 1, 2; EWL 3; LATS 1:2; MTCW 1; MTFW 2005; RGEL 2; WLIT 2

Fugard, Sheila 1932- .... **CLC 48**
See also CA 125

Fujiwara no Teika 1162-1241 .... **CMLC 73**
See also DLB 203

Fukuyama, Francis 1952- .... **CLC 131**
See also CA 140; CANR 72, 125

Fuller, Charles (H.), (Jr.) 1939- .... **BLC 2; CLC 25; DC 1**
See also BW 2; CA 108; 112; CAD; CANR 87; CD 5, 6; DAM DRAM, MULT; DFS 8; DLB 38, 266; EWL 3; INT CA-112; MAL 5; MTCW 1

Fuller, Henry Blake 1857-1929 .... **TCLC 103**
See also CA 108; 177; DLB 12; RGAL 4

Fuller, John (Leopold) 1937- .... **CLC 62**
See also CA 21-24R; CANR 9, 44; CP 1, 2, 3, 4, 5, 6, 7; DLB 40

Fuller, Margaret
See Ossoli, Sarah Margaret (Fuller)
See also AMWS 2; DLB 183, 223, 239; FL 1:3

Fuller, Roy (Broadbent) 1912-1991 ... **CLC 4, 28**
See also BRWS 7; CA 5-8R; 135; CAAS 10; CANR 53, 83; CN 1, 2, 3, 4, 5; CP 1, 2, 3, 4; CWRI 5; DLB 15, 20; EWL 3; RGEL 2; SATA 87

Fuller, Sarah Margaret
See Ossoli, Sarah Margaret (Fuller)

Fuller, Sarah Margaret
See Ossoli, Sarah Margaret (Fuller)
See also DLB 1, 59, 73

Fuller, Thomas 1608-1661 .... **LC 111**
See also DLB 151

Fulton, Alice 1952- .... **CLC 52**
See also CA 116; CANR 57, 88; CP 7; CWP; DLB 193

Furphy, Joseph 1843-1912 .... **TCLC 25**
See Collins, Tom
See also CA 163; DLB 230; EWL 3; RGEL 2

Fuson, Robert H(enderson) 1927- .... **CLC 70**
See also CA 89-92; CANR 103

Fussell, Paul 1924- .... **CLC 74**
See also BEST 90:1; CA 17-20R; CANR 8, 21, 35, 69, 135; INT CANR-21; MTCW 1, 2; MTFW 2005

Futabatei, Shimei 1864-1909 .... **TCLC 44**
See Futabatei Shimei
See also CA 162; MJW

Futabatei Shimei
See Futabatei, Shimei
See also DLB 180; EWL 3

Futrelle, Jacques 1875-1912 .... **TCLC 19**
See also CA 113; 155; CMW 4

Gaboriau, Emile 1835-1873 .... **NCLC 14**
See also CMW 4; MSW

Gadda, Carlo Emilio 1893-1973 ...... **CLC 11; TCLC 144**
See also CA 89-92; DLB 177; EWL 3; WLIT 7

Gaddis, William 1922-1998 ... **CLC 1, 3, 6, 8, 10, 19, 43, 86**
See also AMWS 4; BPFB 1; CA 17-20R; 172; CANR 21, 48; CN 1, 2, 3, 4, 5, 6; DLB 2, 278; EWL 3; MAL 5; MTCW 1, 2; MTFW 2005; RGAL 4

Gaelique, Moruen le
See Jacob, (Cyprien-)Max

Gage, Walter
See Inge, William (Motter)

Gaiman, Neil (Richard) 1960- .... **CLC 195**
See also AAYA 19, 42; CA 133; CANR 81, 129; DLB 261; HGG; MTFW 2005; SATA 85, 146; SFW 4; SUFW 2

Gaines, Ernest J(ames) 1933- .. **BLC 2; CLC 3, 11, 18, 86, 181; SSC 68**
See also AAYA 18; AFAW 1, 2; AITN 1; BPFB 2; BW 2, 3; BYA 6; CA 9-12R; CANR 6, 24, 42, 75, 126; CDALB 1968-1988; CLR 62; CN 1, 2, 3, 4, 5, 6, 7; CSW; DA3; DAM MULT; DLB 2, 33, 152; DLBY 1980; EWL 3; EXPN; LAIT 5; LATS 1:2; MAL 5; MTCW 1, 2; MTFW 2005; NFS 5, 7, 16; RGAL 4; RGSF 2; RHW; SATA 86; SSFS 5; YAW

Gaitskill, Mary (Lawrence) 1954- .... **CLC 69**
See also CA 128; CANR 61; DLB 244; TCLE 1:1

Gaius Suetonius Tranquillus
See Suetonius

Galdos, Benito Perez
See Perez Galdos, Benito
See also EW 7

Gale, Zona 1874-1938 .... **TCLC 7**
See also CA 105; 153; CANR 84; DAM DRAM; DFS 17; DLB 9, 78, 228; RGAL 4

Galeano, Eduardo (Hughes) 1940- . **CLC 72; HLCS 1**
See also CA 29-32R; CANR 13, 32, 100; HW 1

Galiano, Juan Valera y Alcala
See Valera y Alcala-Galiano, Juan

Galilei, Galileo 1564-1642 .... **LC 45**

Gallagher, Tess 1943- .... **CLC 18, 63; PC 9**
See also CA 106; CP 3, 4, 5, 6, 7; CWP; DAM POET; DLB 120, 212, 244; PFS 16

Gallant, Mavis 1922- ..... **CLC 7, 18, 38, 172; SSC 5, 78**
See also CA 69-72; CANR 29, 69, 117; CCA 1; CN 1, 2, 3, 4, 5, 6, 7; DAC; DAM MST; DLB 53; EWL 3; MTCW 1, 2; MTFW 2005; RGEL 2; RGSF 2

Gallant, Roy A(rthur) 1924- .... **CLC 17**
See also CA 5-8R; CANR 4, 29, 54, 117; CLR 30; MAICYA 1, 2; SATA 4, 68, 110

Gallico, Paul (William) 1897-1976 ..... **CLC 2**
See also AITN 1; CA 5-8R; 69-72; CANR 23; CN 1, 2; DLB 9, 171; FANT; MAICYA 1, 2; SATA 13

Gallo, Max Louis 1932- .... **CLC 95**
See also CA 85-88

Gallois, Lucien
See Desnos, Robert

Gallup, Ralph
See Whitemore, Hugh (John)

Gent, Peter 1942- .... **CLC 29**
See also AITN 1; CA 89-92; DLBY 1982

Gentile, Giovanni 1875-1944 .... **TCLC 96**
See also CA 119

Gentlewoman in New England, A
See Bradstreet, Anne

Gentlewoman in Those Parts, A
See Bradstreet, Anne

Geoffrey of Monmouth c.
1100-1155 .... **CMLC 44**
See also DLB 146; TEA

George, Jean
See George, Jean Craighead

George, Jean Craighead 1919- .... **CLC 35**
See also AAYA 8; BYA 2, 4; CA 5-8R;
CANR 25; CLR 1; 80; DLB 52; JRDA;
MAICYA 1, 2; SATA 2, 68, 124; WYA;
YAW

George, Stefan (Anton) 1868-1933 . **TCLC 2,
14**
See also CA 104; 193; EW 8; EWL 3

Georges, Georges Martin
See Simenon, Georges (Jacques Christian)

Gerald of Wales c. 1146-c. 1223 ... **CMLC 60**

Gerhardi, William Alexander
See Gerhardie, William Alexander

Gerhardie, William Alexander
1895-1977 .... **CLC 5**
See also CA 25-28R; 73-76; CANR 18; CN
1, 2; DLB 36; RGEL 2

Gerson, Jean 1363-1429 .... **LC 77**
See also DLB 208

Gersonides 1288-1344 .... **CMLC 49**
See also DLB 115

Gerstler, Amy 1956- .... **CLC 70**
See also CA 146; CANR 99

Gertler, T. .... **CLC 34**
See also CA 116; 121

Gertsen, Aleksandr Ivanovich
See Herzen, Aleksandr Ivanovich

Ghalib .... **NCLC 39, 78**
See Ghalib, Asadullah Khan

Ghalib, Asadullah Khan 1797-1869
See Ghalib
See also DAM POET; RGWL 2, 3

Ghelderode, Michel de 1898-1962 ..... **CLC 6,
11; DC 15**
See also CA 85-88; CANR 40, 77; DAM
DRAM; DLB 321; EW 11; EWL 3; TWA

Ghiselin, Brewster 1903-2001 .... **CLC 23**
See also CA 13-16R; CAAS 10; CANR 13;
CP 1, 2, 3, 4, 5, 6, 7

Ghose, Aurabinda 1872-1950 .... **TCLC 63**
See Ghose, Aurobindo
See also CA 163

Ghose, Aurobindo
See Ghose, Aurabinda
See also EWL 3

Ghose, Zulfikar 1935- .... **CLC 42, 200**
See also CA 65-68; CANR 67; CN 1, 2, 3,
4, 5, 6, 7; CP 1, 2, 3, 4, 5, 6, 7; EWL 3

Ghosh, Amitav 1956- .... **CLC 44, 153**
See also CA 147; CANR 80; CN 6, 7;
WWE 1

Giacosa, Giuseppe 1847-1906 .... **TCLC 7**
See also CA 104

Gibb, Lee
See Waterhouse, Keith (Spencer)

Gibbon, Edward 1737-1794 .... **LC 97**
See also BRW 3; DLB 104; RGEL 2

Gibbon, Lewis Grassic .... **TCLC 4**
See Mitchell, James Leslie
See also RGEL 2

Gibbons, Kaye 1960- .... **CLC 50, 88, 145**
See also AAYA 34; AMWS 10; CA 151;
CANR 75, 127; CN 7; CSW; DA3; DAM
POP; DLB 292; MTCW 2; MTFW 2005;
NFS 3; RGAL 4; SATA 117

Gibran, Kahlil 1883-1931 . **PC 9; TCLC 1, 9**
See also CA 104; 150; DA3; DAM POET,
POP; EWL 3; MTCW 2; WLIT 6

Gibran, Khalil
See Gibran, Kahlil

Gibson, Mel 1956- .... **CLC 215**

Gibson, William 1914- .... **CLC 23**
See also CA 9-12R; CAD; CANR 9, 42, 75,
125; CD 5, 6; DA; DAB; DAC; DAM
DRAM, MST; DFS 2; DLB 7; LAIT 2;
MAL 5; MTCW 2; MTFW 2005; SATA
66; YAW

Gibson, William (Ford) 1948- ... **CLC 39, 63,
186, 192; SSC 52**
See also AAYA 12, 59; BPFB 2; CA 126;
133; CANR 52, 90, 106; CN 6, 7; CPW;
DA3; DAM POP; DLB 251; MTCW 2;
MTFW 2005; SCFW 2; SFW 4

Gide, Andre (Paul Guillaume)
1869-1951 ..... **SSC 13; TCLC 5, 12, 36;
WLC**
See also CA 104; 124; DA; DA3; DAB;
DAC; DAM MST, NOV; DLB 65, 321;
EW 8; EWL 3; GFL 1789 to the Present;
MTCW 1, 2; MTFW 2005; NFS 21;
RGSF 2; RGWL 2, 3; TWA

Gifford, Barry (Colby) 1946- .... **CLC 34**
See also CA 65-68; CANR 9, 30, 40, 90

Gilbert, Frank
See De Voto, Bernard (Augustine)

Gilbert, W(illiam) S(chwenck)
1836-1911 .... **TCLC 3**
See also CA 104; 173; DAM DRAM, POET;
RGEL 2; SATA 36

Gilbreth, Frank B(unker), Jr.
1911-2001 .... **CLC 17**
See also CA 9-12R; SATA 2

Gilchrist, Ellen (Louise) 1935- .. **CLC 34, 48,
143; SSC 14, 63**
See also BPFB 2; CA 113; 116; CANR 41,
61, 104; CN 4, 5, 6, 7; CPW; CSW; DAM
POP; DLB 130; EWL 3; EXPS; MTCW
1, 2; MTFW 2005; RGAL 4; RGSF 2;
SSFS 9

Giles, Molly 1942- .... **CLC 39**
See also CA 126; CANR 98

Gill, Eric .... **TCLC 85**
See Gill, (Arthur) Eric (Rowton Peter
Joseph)

Gill, (Arthur) Eric (Rowton Peter Joseph)
1882-1940
See Gill, Eric
See also CA 120; DLB 98

Gill, Patrick
See Creasey, John

Gillette, Douglas .... **CLC 70**

Gilliam, Terry (Vance) 1940- .... **CLC 21, 141**
See Monty Python
See also AAYA 19, 59; CA 108; 113; CANR
35; INT CA-113

Gillian, Jerry
See Gilliam, Terry (Vance)

Gilliatt, Penelope (Ann Douglass)
1932-1993 .... **CLC 2, 10, 13, 53**
See also AITN 2; CA 13-16R; 141; CANR
49; CN 1, 2, 3, 4, 5; DLB 14

Gilligan, Carol 1936- .... **CLC 208**
See also CA 142; CANR 121; FW

Gilman, Charlotte (Anna) Perkins (Stetson)
1860-1935 ...... **SSC 13, 62; TCLC 9, 37,
117**
See also AMWS 11; BYA 11; CA 106; 150;
DLB 221; EXPS; FL 1:5; FW; HGG;
LAIT 2; MAWW; MTCW 2; MTFW
2005; RGAL 4; RGSF 2; SFW 4; SSFS 1,
18

Gilmour, David 1946- .... **CLC 35**

Gilpin, William 1724-1804 .... **NCLC 30**

Gilray, J. D.
See Mencken, H(enry) L(ouis)

Gilroy, Frank D(aniel) 1925- .... **CLC 2**
See also CA 81-84; CAD; CANR 32, 64,
86; CD 5, 6; DFS 17; DLB 7

Gilstrap, John 1957(?)- .... **CLC 99**
See also AAYA 67; CA 160; CANR 101

Ginsberg, Allen 1926-1997 .... **CLC 1, 2, 3, 4,
6, 13, 36, 69, 109; PC 4, 47; TCLC
120; WLC**
See also AAYA 33; AITN 1; AMWC 1;
AMWS 2; BG 1:2; CA 1-4R; 157; CANR
2, 41, 63, 95; CDALB 1941-1968; CP 1,
2, 3, 4, 5, 6; DA; DA3; DAB; DAC; DAM
MST, POET; DLB 5, 16, 169, 237; EWL
3; GLL 1; LMFS 2; MAL 5; MTCW 1, 2;
MTFW 2005; PAB; PFS 5; RGAL 4;
TUS; WP

Ginzburg, Eugenia .... **CLC 59**
See Ginzburg, Evgeniia

Ginzburg, Evgeniia 1904-1977
See Ginzburg, Eugenia
See also DLB 302

Ginzburg, Natalia 1916-1991 .... **CLC 5, 11,
54, 70; SSC 65; TCLC 156**
See also CA 85-88; 135; CANR 33; DFS
14; DLB 177; EW 13; EWL 3; MTCW 1,
2; MTFW 2005; RGWL 2, 3

Giono, Jean 1895-1970 .... **CLC 4, 11; TCLC
124**
See also CA 45-48; 29-32R; CANR 2, 35;
DLB 72, 321; EWL 3; GFL 1789 to the
Present; MTCW 1; RGWL 2, 3

Giovanni, Nikki 1943- ...... **BLC 2; CLC 2, 4,
19, 64, 117; PC 19; WLCS**
See also AAYA 22; AITN 1; BW 2, 3; CA
29-32R; CAAS 6; CANR 18, 41, 60, 91,
130; CDALBS; CLR 6, 73; CP 2, 3, 4, 5,
6, 7; CSW; CWP; CWRI 5; DA; DA3;
DAB; DAC; DAM MST, MULT, POET;
DLB 5, 41; EWL 3; EXPP; INT CANR-
18; MAICYA 1, 2; MAL 5; MTCW 1, 2;
MTFW 2005; PFS 17; RGAL 4; SATA
24, 107; TUS; YAW

Giovene, Andrea 1904-1998 .... **CLC 7**
See also CA 85-88

Gippius, Zinaida (Nikolaevna) 1869-1945
See Hippius, Zinaida (Nikolaevna)
See also CA 106; 212

Giraudoux, Jean(-Hippolyte)
1882-1944 .... **TCLC 2, 7**
See also CA 104; 196; DAM DRAM; DLB
65, 321; EW 9; EWL 3; GFL 1789 to the
Present; RGWL 2, 3; TWA

Gironella, Jose Maria (Pous)
1917-2003 .... **CLC 11**
See also CA 101; 212; EWL 3; RGWL 2, 3

Gissing, George (Robert)
1857-1903 .... **SSC 37; TCLC 3, 24, 47**
See also BRW 5; CA 105; 167; DLB 18,
135, 184; RGEL 2; TEA

Gitlin, Todd 1943- .... **CLC 201**
See also CA 29-32R; CANR 25, 50, 88

Giurlani, Aldo
See Palazzeschi, Aldo

Gladkov, Fedor Vasil'evich
See Gladkov, Fyodor (Vasilyevich)
See also DLB 272

Gladkov, Fyodor (Vasilyevich)
1883-1958 .... **TCLC 27**
See Gladkov, Fedor Vasil'evich
See also CA 170; EWL 3

Glancy, Diane 1941- .... **CLC 210; NNAL**
See also CA 136, 225; CAAE 225; CAAS
24; CANR 87; DLB 175

Gordone, Charles 1925-1995 .. **CLC 1, 4; DC 8**
See also BW 1, 3; CA 93-96; 180; 150; CAAE 180; CAD; CANR 55; DAM DRAM; DLB 7; INT CA-93-96; MTCW 1

Gore, Catherine 1800-1861 .... **NCLC 65**
See also DLB 116; RGEL 2

Gorenko, Anna Andreevna
See Akhmatova, Anna

Gorky, Maxim .... **SSC 28; TCLC 8; WLC**
See Peshkov, Alexei Maximovich
See also DAB; DFS 9; DLB 295; EW 8; EWL 3; TWA

Goryan, Sirak
See Saroyan, William

Gosse, Edmund (William)
1849-1928 .... **TCLC 28**
See also CA 117; DLB 57, 144, 184; RGEL 2

Gotlieb, Phyllis (Fay Bloom) 1926- .. **CLC 18**
See also CA 13-16R; CANR 7, 135; CN 7; CP 1, 2, 3, 4; DLB 88, 251; SFW 4

Gottesman, S. D.
See Kornbluth, C(yril) M.; Pohl, Frederik

Gottfried von Strassburg fl. c.
1170-1215 .... **CMLC 10**
See also CDWLB 2; DLB 138; EW 1; RGWL 2, 3

Gotthelf, Jeremias 1797-1854 .... **NCLC 117**
See also DLB 133; RGWL 2, 3

Gottschalk, Laura Riding
See Jackson, Laura (Riding)

Gould, Lois 1932(?)-2002 .... **CLC 4, 10**
See also CA 77-80; 208; CANR 29; MTCW 1

Gould, Stephen Jay 1941-2002 .... **CLC 163**
See also AAYA 26; BEST 90:2; CA 77-80; 205; CANR 10, 27, 56, 75, 125; CPW; INT CANR-27; MTCW 1, 2; MTFW 2005

Gourmont, Remy(-Marie-Charles) de
1858-1915 .... **TCLC 17**
See also CA 109; 150; GFL 1789 to the Present; MTCW 2

Gournay, Marie le Jars de
See de Gournay, Marie le Jars

Govier, Katherine 1948- .... **CLC 51**
See also CA 101; CANR 18, 40, 128; CCA 1

Gower, John c. 1330-1408 .... **LC 76; PC 59**
See also BRW 1; DLB 146; RGEL 2

Goyen, (Charles) William
1915-1983 .... **CLC 5, 8, 14, 40**
See also AITN 2; CA 5-8R; 110; CANR 6, 71; CN 1, 2, 3; DLB 2, 218; DLBY 1983; EWL 3; INT CANR-6; MAL 5

Goytisolo, Juan 1931- .... **CLC 5, 10, 23, 133; HLC 1**
See also CA 85-88; CANR 32, 61, 131; CWW 2; DAM MULT; DLB 322; EWL 3; GLL 2; HW 1, 2; MTCW 1, 2; MTFW 2005

Gozzano, Guido 1883-1916 .... **PC 10**
See also CA 154; DLB 114; EWL 3

Gozzi, (Conte) Carlo 1720-1806 .... **NCLC 23**

Grabbe, Christian Dietrich
1801-1836 .... **NCLC 2**
See also DLB 133; RGWL 2, 3

Grace, Patricia Frances 1937- .... **CLC 56**
See also CA 176; CANR 118; CN 4, 5, 6, 7; EWL 3; RGSF 2

Gracian y Morales, Baltasar
1601-1658 .... **LC 15**

Gracq, Julien .... **CLC 11, 48**
See Poirier, Louis
See also CWW 2; DLB 83; GFL 1789 to the Present

Grade, Chaim 1910-1982 .... **CLC 10**
See also CA 93-96; 107; EWL 3

Graduate of Oxford, A
See Ruskin, John

Grafton, Garth
See Duncan, Sara Jeannette

Grafton, Sue 1940- .... **CLC 163**
See also AAYA 11, 49; BEST 90:3; CA 108; CANR 31, 55, 111, 134; CMW 4; CPW; CSW; DA3; DAM POP; DLB 226; FW; MSW; MTFW 2005

Graham, John
See Phillips, David Graham

Graham, Jorie 1950- .... **CLC 48, 118; PC 59**
See also AAYA 67; CA 111; CANR 63, 118; CP 4, 5, 6, 7; CWP; DLB 120; EWL 3; MTFW 2005; PFS 10, 17; TCLE 1:1

Graham, R(obert) B(ontine) Cunninghame
See Cunninghame Graham, Robert (Gallnigad) Bontine
See also DLB 98, 135, 174; RGEL 2; RGSF 2

Graham, Robert
See Haldeman, Joe (William)

Graham, Tom
See Lewis, (Harry) Sinclair

Graham, W(illiam) S(idney)
1918-1986 .... **CLC 29**
See also BRWS 7; CA 73-76; 118; CP 1, 2, 3, 4; DLB 20; RGEL 2

Graham, Winston (Mawdsley)
1910-2003 .... **CLC 23**
See also CA 49-52; 218; CANR 2, 22, 45, 66; CMW 4; CN 1, 2, 3, 4, 5, 6, 7; DLB 77; RHW

Grahame, Kenneth 1859-1932 ...... **TCLC 64, 136**
See also BYA 5; CA 108; 136; CANR 80; CLR 5; CWRI 5; DA3; DAB; DLB 34, 141, 178; FANT; MAICYA 1, 2; MTCW 2; NFS 20; RGEL 2; SATA 100; TEA; WCH; YABC 1

Granger, Darius John
See Marlowe, Stephen

Granin, Daniil 1918- .... **CLC 59**
See also DLB 302

Granovsky, Timofei Nikolaevich
1813-1855 .... **NCLC 75**
See also DLB 198

Grant, Skeeter
See Spiegelman, Art

Granville-Barker, Harley
1877-1946 .... **TCLC 2**
See Barker, Harley Granville
See also CA 104; 204; DAM DRAM; RGEL 2

Granzotto, Gianni
See Granzotto, Giovanni Battista

Granzotto, Giovanni Battista
1914-1985 .... **CLC 70**
See also CA 166

Grass, Guenter (Wilhelm) 1927- ... **CLC 1, 2, 4, 6, 11, 15, 22, 32, 49, 88, 207; WLC**
See Grass, Gunter (Wilhelm)
See also BPFB 2; CA 13-16R; CANR 20, 75, 93, 133; CDWLB 2; DA; DA3; DAB; DAC; DAM MST, NOV; DLB 75, 124; EW 13; EWL 3; MTCW 1, 2; MTFW 2005; RGWL 2, 3; TWA

Grass, Gunter (Wilhelm)
See Grass, Guenter (Wilhelm)
See also CWW 2

Gratton, Thomas
See Hulme, T(homas) E(rnest)

Grau, Shirley Ann 1929- .... **CLC 4, 9, 146; SSC 15**
See also CA 89-92; CANR 22, 69; CN 1, 2, 3, 4, 5, 6, 7; CSW; DLB 2, 218; INT CA-89-92; CANR-22; MTCW 1

Gravel, Fern
See Hall, James Norman

Graver, Elizabeth 1964- .... **CLC 70**
See also CA 135; CANR 71, 129

Graves, Richard Perceval
1895-1985 .... **CLC 44**
See also CA 65-68; CANR 9, 26, 51

Graves, Robert (von Ranke)
1895-1985 .. **CLC 1, 2, 6, 11, 39, 44, 45; PC 6**
See also BPFB 2; BRW 7; BYA 4; CA 5-8R; 117; CANR 5, 36; CDBLB 1914-1945; CN 1, 2, 3; CP 1, 2, 3, 4; DA3; DAB; DAC; DAM MST, POET; DLB 20, 100, 191; DLBD 18; DLBY 1985; EWL 3; LATS 1:1; MTCW 1, 2; MTFW 2005; NCFS 2; NFS 21; RGEL 2; RHW; SATA 45; TEA

Graves, Valerie
See Bradley, Marion Zimmer

Gray, Alasdair (James) 1934- .... **CLC 41**
See also BRWS 9; CA 126; CANR 47, 69, 106, 140; CN 4, 5, 6, 7; DLB 194, 261, 319; HGG; INT CA-126; MTCW 1, 2; MTFW 2005; RGSF 2; SUFW 2

Gray, Amlin 1946- .... **CLC 29**
See also CA 138

Gray, Francine du Plessix 1930- ..... **CLC 22, 153**
See also BEST 90:3; CA 61-64; CAAS 2; CANR 11, 33, 75, 81; DAM NOV; INT CANR-11; MTCW 1, 2; MTFW 2005

Gray, John (Henry) 1866-1934 ...... **TCLC 19**
See also CA 119; 162; RGEL 2

Gray, John Lee
See Jakes, John (William)

Gray, Simon (James Holliday)
1936- .... **CLC 9, 14, 36**
See also AITN 1; CA 21-24R; CAAS 3; CANR 32, 69; CBD; CD 5, 6; CN 1, 2, 3; DLB 13; EWL 3; MTCW 1; RGEL 2

Gray, Spalding 1941-2004 .... **CLC 49, 112; DC 7**
See also AAYA 62; CA 128; 225; CAD; CANR 74, 138; CD 5, 6; CPW; DAM POP; MTCW 2; MTFW 2005

Gray, Thomas 1716-1771 .... **LC 4, 40; PC 2; WLC**
See also BRW 3; CDBLB 1660-1789; DA; DA3; DAB; DAC; DAM MST; DLB 109; EXPP; PAB; PFS 9; RGEL 2; TEA; WP

Grayson, David
See Baker, Ray Stannard

Grayson, Richard (A.) 1951- .... **CLC 38**
See also CA 85-88; 210; CAAE 210; CANR 14, 31, 57; DLB 234

Greeley, Andrew M(oran) 1928- ...... **CLC 28**
See also BPFB 2; CA 5-8R; CAAS 7; CANR 7, 43, 69, 104, 136; CMW 4; CPW; DA3; DAM POP; MTCW 1, 2; MTFW 2005

Green, Anna Katharine
1846-1935 .... **TCLC 63**
See also CA 112; 159; CMW 4; DLB 202, 221; MSW

Green, Brian
See Card, Orson Scott

Green, Hannah
See Greenberg, Joanne (Goldenberg)

Green, Hannah 1927(?)-1996 .... **CLC 3**
See also CA 73-76; CANR 59, 93; NFS 10

Green, Henry .... **CLC 2, 13, 97**
See Yorke, Henry Vincent
See also BRWS 2; CA 175; DLB 15; EWL 3; RGEL 2

Green, Julian .... **CLC 3, 11, 77**
See Green, Julien (Hartridge)
See also EWL 3; GFL 1789 to the Present; MTCW 2

Guillen, Nicolas (Cristobal)
1902-1989 .... **BLC 2; CLC 48, 79; HLC 1; PC 23**
See also BW 2; CA 116; 125; 129; CANR 84; DAM MST, MULT, POET; DLB 283; EWL 3; HW 1; LAW; RGWL 2, 3; WP

Guillen y Alvarez, Jorge
See Guillen, Jorge

Guillevic, (Eugene) 1907-1997 .... **CLC 33**
See also CA 93-96; CWW 2

Guillois
See Desnos, Robert

Guillois, Valentin
See Desnos, Robert

Guimaraes Rosa, Joao 1908-1967 .... **HLCS 2**
See Rosa, Joao Guimaraes
See also CA 175; LAW; RGSF 2; RGWL 2, 3

Guiney, Louise Imogen
1861-1920 .... **TCLC 41**
See also CA 160; DLB 54; RGAL 4

Guinizelli, Guido c. 1230-1276 ...... **CMLC 49**
See Guinizzelli, Guido

Guinizzelli, Guido
See Guinizelli, Guido
See also WLIT 7

Guiraldes, Ricardo (Guillermo)
1886-1927 .... **TCLC 39**
See also CA 131; EWL 3; HW 1; LAW; MTCW 1

Gumilev, Nikolai (Stepanovich)
1886-1921 .... **TCLC 60**
See Gumilyov, Nikolay Stepanovich
See also CA 165; DLB 295

Gumilyov, Nikolay Stepanovich
See Gumilev, Nikolai (Stepanovich)
See also EWL 3

Gump, P. Q.
See Card, Orson Scott

Gunesekera, Romesh 1954- .... **CLC 91**
See also BRWS 10; CA 159; CANR 140; CN 6, 7; DLB 267

Gunn, Bill .... **CLC 5**
See Gunn, William Harrison
See also DLB 38

Gunn, Thom(son William)
1929-2004 . **CLC 3, 6, 18, 32, 81; PC 26**
See also BRWS 4; CA 17-20R; 227; CANR 9, 33, 116; CDBLB 1960 to Present; CP 1, 2, 3, 4, 5, 6, 7; DAM POET; DLB 27; INT CANR-33; MTCW 1; PFS 9; RGEL 2

Gunn, William Harrison 1934(?)-1989
See Gunn, Bill
See also AITN 1; BW 1, 3; CA 13-16R; 128; CANR 12, 25, 76

Gunn Allen, Paula
See Allen, Paula Gunn

Gunnars, Kristjana 1948- .... **CLC 69**
See also CA 113; CCA 1; CP 7; CWP; DLB 60

Gunter, Erich
See Eich, Gunter

Gurdjieff, G(eorgei) I(vanovich)
1877(?)-1949 .... **TCLC 71**
See also CA 157

Gurganus, Allan 1947- .... **CLC 70**
See also BEST 90:1; CA 135; CANR 114; CN 6, 7; CPW; CSW; DAM POP; GLL 1

Gurney, A. R.
See Gurney, A(lbert) R(amsdell), Jr.
See also DLB 266

Gurney, A(lbert) R(amsdell), Jr.
1930- .... **CLC 32, 50, 54**
See Gurney, A. R.
See also AMWS 5; CA 77-80; CAD; CANR 32, 64, 121; CD 5, 6; DAM DRAM; EWL 3

Gurney, Ivor (Bertie) 1890-1937 ... **TCLC 33**
See also BRW 6; CA 167; DLBY 2002; PAB; RGEL 2

Gurney, Peter
See Gurney, A(lbert) R(amsdell), Jr.

Guro, Elena (Genrikhovna)
1877-1913 .... **TCLC 56**
See also DLB 295

Gustafson, James M(oody) 1925- ... **CLC 100**
See also CA 25-28R; CANR 37

Gustafson, Ralph (Barker)
1909-1995 .... **CLC 36**
See also CA 21-24R; CANR 8, 45, 84; CP 1, 2, 3, 4; DLB 88; RGEL 2

Gut, Gom
See Simenon, Georges (Jacques Christian)

Guterson, David 1956- .... **CLC 91**
See also CA 132; CANR 73, 126; CN 7; DLB 292; MTCW 2; MTFW 2005; NFS 13

Guthrie, A(lfred) B(ertram), Jr.
1901-1991 .... **CLC 23**
See also CA 57-60; 134; CANR 24; CN 1, 2, 3; DLB 6, 212; MAL 5; SATA 62; SATA-Obit 67; TCWW 1, 2

Guthrie, Isobel
See Grieve, C(hristopher) M(urray)

Guthrie, Woodrow Wilson 1912-1967
See Guthrie, Woody
See also CA 113; 93-96

Guthrie, Woody .... **CLC 35**
See Guthrie, Woodrow Wilson
See also DLB 303; LAIT 3

Gutierrez Najera, Manuel
1859-1895 .... **HLCS 2; NCLC 133**
See also DLB 290; LAW

Guy, Rosa (Cuthbert) 1925- .... **CLC 26**
See also AAYA 4, 37; BW 2; CA 17-20R; CANR 14, 34, 83; CLR 13; DLB 33; DNFS 1; JRDA; MAICYA 1, 2; SATA 14, 62, 122; YAW

Gwendolyn
See Bennett, (Enoch) Arnold

H. D. .... **CLC 3, 8, 14, 31, 34, 73; PC 5**
See Doolittle, Hilda
See also FL 1:5

H. de V.
See Buchan, John

Haavikko, Paavo Juhani 1931- .. **CLC 18, 34**
See also CA 106; CWW 2; EWL 3

Habbema, Koos
See Heijermans, Herman

Habermas, Juergen 1929- .... **CLC 104**
See also CA 109; CANR 85; DLB 242

Habermas, Jurgen
See Habermas, Juergen

Hacker, Marilyn 1942- ...... **CLC 5, 9, 23, 72, 91; PC 47**
See also CA 77-80; CANR 68, 129; CP 3, 4, 5, 6, 7; CWP; DAM POET; DLB 120, 282; FW; GLL 2; MAL 5; PFS 19

Hadewijch of Antwerp fl. 1250- ... **CMLC 61**
See also RGWL 3

Hadrian 76-138 .... **CMLC 52**

Haeckel, Ernst Heinrich (Philipp August)
1834-1919 .... **TCLC 83**
See also CA 157

Hafiz c. 1326-1389(?) .... **CMLC 34**
See also RGWL 2, 3; WLIT 6

Hagedorn, Jessica T(arahata)
1949- .... **CLC 185**
See also CA 139; CANR 69; CWP; DLB 312; RGAL 4

Haggard, H(enry) Rider
1856-1925 .... **TCLC 11**
See also BRWS 3; BYA 4, 5; CA 108; 148; CANR 112; DLB 70, 156, 174, 178; FANT; LMFS 1; MTCW 2; RGEL 2; RHW; SATA 16; SCFW 1, 2; SFW 4; SUFW 1; WLIT 4

Hagiosy, L.
See Larbaud, Valery (Nicolas)

Hagiwara, Sakutaro 1886-1942 .... **PC 18; TCLC 60**
See Hagiwara Sakutaro
See also CA 154; RGWL 3

Hagiwara Sakutaro
See Hagiwara, Sakutaro
See also EWL 3

Haig, Fenil
See Ford, Ford Madox

Haig-Brown, Roderick (Langmere)
1908-1976 .... **CLC 21**
See also CA 5-8R; 69-72; CANR 4, 38, 83; CLR 31; CWRI 5; DLB 88; MAICYA 1, 2; SATA 12; TCWW 2

Haight, Rip
See Carpenter, John (Howard)

Hailey, Arthur 1920-2004 .... **CLC 5**
See also AITN 2; BEST 90:3; BPFB 2; CA 1-4R; 233; CANR 2, 36, 75; CCA 1; CN 1, 2, 3, 4, 5, 6, 7; CPW; DAM NOV, POP; DLB 88; DLBY 1982; MTCW 1, 2; MTFW 2005

Hailey, Elizabeth Forsythe 1938- ..... **CLC 40**
See also CA 93-96, 188; CAAE 188; CAAS 1; CANR 15, 48; INT CANR-15

Haines, John (Meade) 1924- .... **CLC 58**
See also AMWS 12; CA 17-20R; CANR 13, 34; CP 1, 2, 3, 4; CSW; DLB 5, 212; TCLE 1:1

Hakluyt, Richard 1552-1616 .... **LC 31**
See also DLB 136; RGEL 2

Haldeman, Joe (William) 1943- .... **CLC 61**
See Graham, Robert
See also AAYA 38; CA 53-56, 179; CAAE 179; CAAS 25; CANR 6, 70, 72, 130; DLB 8; INT CANR-6; SCFW 2; SFW 4

Hale, Janet Campbell 1947- .... **NNAL**
See also CA 49-52; CANR 45, 75; DAM MULT; DLB 175; MTCW 2; MTFW 2005

Hale, Sarah Josepha (Buell)
1788-1879 .... **NCLC 75**
See also DLB 1, 42, 73, 243

Halevy, Elie 1870-1937 .... **TCLC 104**

Haley, Alex(ander Murray Palmer)
1921-1992 .... **BLC 2; CLC 8, 12, 76; TCLC 147**
See also AAYA 26; BPFB 2; BW 2, 3; CA 77-80; 136; CANR 61; CDALBS; CPW; CSW; DA; DA3; DAB; DAC; DAM MST, MULT, POP; DLB 38; LAIT 5; MTCW 1, 2; NFS 9

Haliburton, Thomas Chandler
1796-1865 .... **NCLC 15, 149**
See also DLB 11, 99; RGEL 2; RGSF 2

Hall, Donald (Andrew, Jr.) 1928- ...... **CLC 1, 13, 37, 59, 151**
See also AAYA 63; CA 5-8R; CAAS 7; CANR 2, 44, 64, 106, 133; CP 1, 2, 3, 4, 5, 6, 7; DAM POET; DLB 5; MAL 5; MTCW 1, 2; MTFW 2005; RGAL 4; SATA 23, 97

Hall, Frederic Sauser
See Sauser-Hall, Frederic

Hall, James
See Kuttner, Henry

Hall, James Norman 1887-1951 ..... **TCLC 23**
See also CA 123; 173; LAIT 1; RHW 1; SATA 21

Hall, Joseph 1574-1656 .... **LC 91**
See also DLB 121, 151; RGEL 2

Harrison, Elizabeth (Allen) Cavanna
1909-2001
See Cavanna, Betty
See also CA 9-12R; 200; CANR 6, 27, 85, 104, 121; MAICYA 2; SATA 142; YAW

Harrison, Harry (Max) 1925- .... **CLC 42**
See also CA 1-4R; CANR 5, 21, 84; DLB 8; SATA 4; SCFW 2; SFW 4

Harrison, James (Thomas) 1937- ...... **CLC 6, 14, 33, 66, 143; SSC 19**
See Harrison, Jim
See also CA 13-16R; CANR 8, 51, 79, 142; DLBY 1982; INT CANR-8

Harrison, Jim
See Harrison, James (Thomas)
See also AMWS 8; CN 5, 6; CP 1, 2, 3, 4, 5, 6, 7; RGAL 4; TCWW 2; TUS

Harrison, Kathryn 1961- .... **CLC 70, 151**
See also CA 144; CANR 68, 122

Harrison, Tony 1937- .... **CLC 43, 129**
See also BRWS 5; CA 65-68; CANR 44, 98; CBD; CD 5, 6; CP 2, 3, 4, 5, 6, 7; DLB 40, 245; MTCW 1; RGEL 2

Harriss, Will(ard Irvin) 1922- .... **CLC 34**
See also CA 111

Hart, Ellis
See Ellison, Harlan (Jay)

Hart, Josephine 1942(?)- .... **CLC 70**
See also CA 138; CANR 70; CPW; DAM POP

Hart, Moss 1904-1961 .... **CLC 66**
See also CA 109; 89-92; CANR 84; DAM DRAM; DFS 1; DLB 7, 266; RGAL 4

Harte, (Francis) Bret(t) 1836(?)-1902 ... **SSC 8, 59; TCLC 1, 25; WLC**
See also AMWS 2; CA 104; 140; CANR 80; CDALB 1865-1917; DA; DA3; DAC; DAM MST; DLB 12, 64, 74, 79, 186; EXPS; LAIT 2; RGAL 4; RGSF 2; SATA 26; SSFS 3; TUS

Hartley, L(eslie) P(oles) 1895-1972 ... **CLC 2, 22**
See also BRWS 7; CA 45-48; 37-40R; CANR 33; CN 1; DLB 15, 139; EWL 3; HGG; MTCW 1, 2; MTFW 2005; RGEL 2; RGSF 2; SUFW 1

Hartman, Geoffrey H. 1929- .... **CLC 27**
See also CA 117; 125; CANR 79; DLB 67

Hartmann, Sadakichi 1869-1944 ... **TCLC 73**
See also CA 157; DLB 54

Hartmann von Aue c. 1170-c. 1210 .... **CMLC 15**
See also CDWLB 2; DLB 138; RGWL 2, 3

Hartog, Jan de
See de Hartog, Jan

Haruf, Kent 1943- .... **CLC 34**
See also AAYA 44; CA 149; CANR 91, 131

Harvey, Caroline
See Trollope, Joanna

Harvey, Gabriel 1550(?)-1631 .... **LC 88**
See also DLB 167, 213, 281

Harwood, Ronald 1934- .... **CLC 32**
See also CA 1-4R; CANR 4, 55; CBD; CD 5, 6; DAM DRAM, MST; DLB 13

Hasegawa Tatsunosuke
See Futabatei, Shimei

Hasek, Jaroslav (Matej Frantisek)
1883-1923 .... **SSC 69; TCLC 4**
See also CA 104; 129; CDWLB 4; DLB 215; EW 9; EWL 3; MTCW 1, 2; RGSF 2; RGWL 2, 3

Hass, Robert 1941- ... **CLC 18, 39, 99; PC 16**
See also AMWS 6; CA 111; CANR 30, 50, 71; CP 3, 4, 5, 6, 7; DLB 105, 206; EWL 3; MAL 5; MTFW 2005; RGAL 4; SATA 94; TCLE 1:1

Hastings, Hudson
See Kuttner, Henry

Hastings, Selina .... **CLC 44**

Hathorne, John 1641-1717 .... **LC 38**

Hatteras, Amelia
See Mencken, H(enry) L(ouis)

Hatteras, Owen .... **TCLC 18**
See Mencken, H(enry) L(ouis); Nathan, George Jean

Hauptmann, Gerhart (Johann Robert)
1862-1946 .... **SSC 37; TCLC 4**
See also CA 104; 153; CDWLB 2; DAM DRAM; DLB 66, 118; EW 8; EWL 3; RGSF 2; RGWL 2, 3; TWA

Havel, Vaclav 1936- ..... **CLC 25, 58, 65, 123; DC 6**
See also CA 104; CANR 36, 63, 124; CDWLB 4; CWW 2; DA3; DAM DRAM; DFS 10; DLB 232; EWL 3; LMFS 2; MTCW 1, 2; MTFW 2005; RGWL 3

Haviaras, Stratis .... **CLC 33**
See Chaviaras, Strates

Hawes, Stephen 1475(?)-1529(?) .... **LC 17**
See also DLB 132; RGEL 2

Hawkes, John (Clendennin Burne, Jr.)
1925-1998 .. **CLC 1, 2, 3, 4, 7, 9, 14, 15, 27, 49**
See also BPFB 2; CA 1-4R; 167; CANR 2, 47, 64; CN 1, 2, 3, 4, 5, 6; DLB 2, 7, 227; DLBY 1980, 1998; EWL 3; MAL 5; MTCW 1, 2; MTFW 2005; RGAL 4

Hawking, S. W.
See Hawking, Stephen W(illiam)

Hawking, Stephen W(illiam) 1942- . **CLC 63, 105**
See also AAYA 13; BEST 89:1; CA 126; 129; CANR 48, 115; CPW; DA3; MTCW 2; MTFW 2005

Hawkins, Anthony Hope
See Hope, Anthony

Hawthorne, Julian 1846-1934 .... **TCLC 25**
See also CA 165; HGG

Hawthorne, Nathaniel 1804-1864 ... **NCLC 2, 10, 17, 23, 39, 79, 95, 158; SSC 3, 29, 39; WLC**
See also AAYA 18; AMW; AMWC 1; AMWR 1; BPFB 2; BYA 3; CDALB 1640-1865; CLR 103; DA; DA3; DAB; DAC; DAM MST, NOV; DLB 1, 74, 183, 223, 269; EXPN; EXPS; GL 2; HGG; LAIT 1; NFS 1, 20; RGAL 4; RGSF 2; SSFS 1, 7, 11, 15; SUFW 1; TUS; WCH; YABC 2

Hawthorne, Sophia Peabody
1809-1871 .... **NCLC 150**
See also DLB 183, 239

Haxton, Josephine Ayres 1921-
See Douglas, Ellen
See also CA 115; CANR 41, 83

Hayaseca y Eizaguirre, Jorge
See Echegaray (y Eizaguirre), Jose (Maria Waldo)

Hayashi, Fumiko 1904-1951 .... **TCLC 27**
See Hayashi Fumiko
See also CA 161

Hayashi Fumiko
See Hayashi, Fumiko
See also DLB 180; EWL 3

Haycraft, Anna (Margaret) 1932-2005
See Ellis, Alice Thomas
See also CA 122; 237; CANR 90, 141; MTCW 2; MTFW 2005

Hayden, Robert E(arl) 1913-1980 ..... **BLC 2; CLC 5, 9, 14, 37; PC 6**
See also AFAW 1, 2; AMWS 2; BW 1, 3; CA 69-72; 97-100; CABS 2; CANR 24, 75, 82; CDALB 1941-1968; CP 1, 2, 3; DA; DAC; DAM MST, MULT, POET; DLB 5, 76; EWL 3; EXPP; MAL 5; MTCW 1, 2; PFS 1; RGAL 4; SATA 19; SATA-Obit 26; WP

Haydon, Benjamin Robert
1786-1846 .... **NCLC 146**
See also DLB 110

Hayek, F(riedrich) A(ugust von)
1899-1992 .... **TCLC 109**
See also CA 93-96; 137; CANR 20; MTCW 1, 2

Hayford, J(oseph) E(phraim) Casely
See Casely-Hayford, J(oseph) E(phraim)

Hayman, Ronald 1932- .... **CLC 44**
See also CA 25-28R; CANR 18, 50, 88; CD 5, 6; DLB 155

Hayne, Paul Hamilton 1830-1886 . **NCLC 94**
See also DLB 3, 64, 79, 248; RGAL 4

Hays, Mary 1760-1843 .... **NCLC 114**
See also DLB 142, 158; RGEL 2

Haywood, Eliza (Fowler)
1693(?)-1756 .... **LC 1, 44**
See also DLB 39; RGEL 2

Hazlitt, William 1778-1830 ...... **NCLC 29, 82**
See also BRW 4; DLB 110, 158; RGEL 2; TEA

Hazzard, Shirley 1931- .... **CLC 18**
See also CA 9-12R; CANR 4, 70, 127; CN 1, 2, 3, 4, 5, 6, 7; DLB 289; DLBY 1982; MTCW 1

Head, Bessie 1937-1986 ...... **BLC 2; CLC 25, 67; SSC 52**
See also AFW; BW 2, 3; CA 29-32R; 119; CANR 25, 82; CDWLB 3; CN 1, 2, 3, 4; DA3; DAM MULT; DLB 117, 225; EWL 3; EXPS; FL 1:6; FW; MTCW 1, 2; MTFW 2005; RGSF 2; SSFS 5, 13; WLIT 2; WWE 1

Headon, (Nicky) Topper 1956(?)- ..... **CLC 30**

Heaney, Seamus (Justin) 1939- ..... **CLC 5, 7, 14, 25, 37, 74, 91, 171; PC 18; WLCS**
See also AAYA 61; BRWR 1; BRWS 2; CA 85-88; CANR 25, 48, 75, 91, 128; CD-BLB 1960 to Present; CP 1, 2, 3, 4, 5, 6, 7; DA3; DAB; DAM POET; DLB 40; DLBY 1995; EWL 3; EXPP; MTCW 1, 2; MTFW 2005; PAB; PFS 2, 5, 8, 17; RGEL 2; TEA; WLIT 4

Hearn, (Patricio) Lafcadio (Tessima Carlos)
1850-1904 .... **TCLC 9**
See also CA 105; 166; DLB 12, 78, 189; HGG; MAL 5; RGAL 4

Hearne, Samuel 1745-1792 .... **LC 95**
See also DLB 99

Hearne, Vicki 1946-2001 .... **CLC 56**
See also CA 139; 201

Hearon, Shelby 1931- .... **CLC 63**
See also AITN 2; AMWS 8; CA 25-28R; CANR 18, 48, 103, 146; CSW

Heat-Moon, William Least .... **CLC 29**
See Trogdon, William (Lewis)
See also AAYA 9

Hebbel, Friedrich 1813-1863 . **DC 21; NCLC 43**
See also CDWLB 2; DAM DRAM; DLB 129; EW 6; RGWL 2, 3

Hebert, Anne 1916-2000 .... **CLC 4, 13, 29**
See also CA 85-88; 187; CANR 69, 126; CCA 1; CWP; CWW 2; DA3; DAC; DAM MST, POET; DLB 68; EWL 3; GFL 1789 to the Present; MTCW 1, 2; MTFW 2005; PFS 20

Hecht, Anthony (Evan) 1923-2004 .... **CLC 8, 13, 19**
See also AMWS 10; CA 9-12R; 232; CANR 6, 108; CP 1, 2, 3, 4, 5, 6, 7; DAM POET; DLB 5, 169; EWL 3; PFS 6; WP

Hecht, Ben 1894-1964 ..... **CLC 8; TCLC 101**
See also CA 85-88; DFS 9; DLB 7, 9, 25, 26, 28, 86; FANT; IDFW 3, 4; RGAL 4

Hedayat, Sadeq 1903-1951 .... **TCLC 21**
See also CA 120; EWL 3; RGSF 2

Hewes, Cady
  See De Voto, Bernard (Augustine)
Heyen, William 1940- .... **CLC 13, 18**
  See also CA 33-36R, 220; CAAE 220;
  CAAS 9; CANR 98; CP 3, 4, 5, 6, 7; DLB
  5
Heyerdahl, Thor 1914-2002 .... **CLC 26**
  See also CA 5-8R; 207; CANR 5, 22, 66,
  73; LAIT 4; MTCW 1, 2; MTFW 2005;
  SATA 2, 52
Heym, Georg (Theodor Franz Arthur)
  1887-1912 .... **TCLC 9**
  See also CA 106; 181
Heym, Stefan 1913-2001 .... **CLC 41**
  See also CA 9-12R; 203; CANR 4; CWW
  2; DLB 69; EWL 3
Heyse, Paul (Johann Ludwig von)
  1830-1914 .... **TCLC 8**
  See also CA 104; 209; DLB 129
Heyward, (Edwin) DuBose
  1885-1940 .... **HR 1:2; TCLC 59**
  See also CA 108; 157; DLB 7, 9, 45, 249;
  MAL 5; SATA 21
Heywood, John 1497(?)-1580(?) .... **LC 65**
  See also DLB 136; RGEL 2
Heywood, Thomas 1573(?)-1641 .... **LC 111**
  See also DAM DRAM; DLB 62; LMFS 1;
  RGEL 2; TEA
Hibbert, Eleanor Alice Burford
  1906-1993 .... **CLC 7**
  See Holt, Victoria
  See also BEST 90:4; CA 17-20R; 140;
  CANR 9, 28, 59; CMW 4; CPW; DAM
  POP; MTCW 2; MTFW 2005; RHW;
  SATA 2; SATA-Obit 74
Hichens, Robert (Smythe)
  1864-1950 .... **TCLC 64**
  See also CA 162; DLB 153; HGG; RHW;
  SUFW
Higgins, Aidan 1927- .... **SSC 68**
  See also CA 9-12R; CANR 70, 115; CN 1,
  2, 3, 4, 5, 6, 7; DLB 14
Higgins, George V(incent)
  1939-1999 .... **CLC 4, 7, 10, 18**
  See also BPFB 2; CA 77-80; 186; CAAS 5;
  CANR 17, 51, 89, 96; CMW 4; CN 2, 3,
  4, 5, 6; DLB 2; DLBY 1981, 1998; INT
  CANR-17; MSW; MTCW 1
Higginson, Thomas Wentworth
  1823-1911 .... **TCLC 36**
  See also CA 162; DLB 1, 64, 243
Higgonet, Margaret ed. .... **CLC 65**
Highet, Helen
  See MacInnes, Helen (Clark)
Highsmith, (Mary) Patricia
  1921-1995 .... **CLC 2, 4, 14, 42, 102**
  See Morgan, Claire
  See also AAYA 48; BRWS 5; CA 1-4R; 147;
  CANR 1, 20, 48, 62, 108; CMW 4; CN 1,
  2, 3, 4, 5; CPW; DA3; DAM NOV, POP;
  DLB 306; MSW; MTCW 1, 2; MTFW
  2005
Highwater, Jamake (Mamake)
  1942(?)-2001 .... **CLC 12**
  See also AAYA 7; BPFB 2; BYA 4; CA 65-
  68; 199; CAAS 7; CANR 10, 34, 84; CLR
  17; CWRI 5; DLB 52; DLBY 1985;
  JRDA; MAICYA 1, 2; SATA 32, 69;
  SATA-Brief 30
Highway, Tomson 1951- ...... **CLC 92; NNAL**
  See also CA 151; CANR 75; CCA 1; CD 5,
  6; CN 7; DAC; DAM MULT; DFS 2;
  MTCW 2
Hijuelos, Oscar 1951- .... **CLC 65; HLC 1**
  See also AAYA 25; AMWS 8; BEST 90:1;
  CA 123; CANR 50, 75, 125; CPW; DA3;
  DAM MULT, POP; DLB 145; HW 1, 2;
  LLW; MAL 5; MTCW 2; MTFW 2005;
  NFS 17; RGAL 4; WLIT 1

Hikmet, Nazim 1902-1963 .... **CLC 40**
  See Nizami of Ganja
  See also CA 141; 93-96; EWL 3; WLIT 6
Hildegard von Bingen 1098-1179 . **CMLC 20**
  See also DLB 148
Hildesheimer, Wolfgang 1916-1991 .. **CLC 49**
  See also CA 101; 135; DLB 69, 124; EWL
  3
Hill, Geoffrey (William) 1932- ...... **CLC 5, 8,**
  18, 45
  See also BRWS 5; CA 81-84; CANR 21,
  89; CDBLB 1960 to Present; CP 1, 2, 3,
  4, 5, 6, 7; DAM POET; DLB 40; EWL 3;
  MTCW 1; RGEL 2
Hill, George Roy 1921-2002 .... **CLC 26**
  See also CA 110; 122; 213
Hill, John
  See Koontz, Dean R.
Hill, Susan (Elizabeth) 1942- ...... **CLC 4, 113**
  See also CA 33-36R; CANR 29, 69, 129;
  CN 2, 3, 4, 5, 6, 7; DAB; DAM MST,
  NOV; DLB 14, 139; HGG; MTCW 1;
  RHW
Hillard, Asa G. III .... **CLC 70**
Hillerman, Tony 1925- .... **CLC 62, 170**
  See also AAYA 40; BEST 89:1; BPFB 2;
  CA 29-32R; CANR 21, 42, 65, 97, 134;
  CMW 4; CPW; DA3; DAM POP; DLB
  206, 306; MAL 5; MSW; MTCW 2;
  MTFW 2005; RGAL 4; SATA 6; TCWW
  2; YAW
Hillesum, Etty 1914-1943 .... **TCLC 49**
  See also CA 137
Hilliard, Noel (Harvey) 1929-1996 ... **CLC 15**
  See also CA 9-12R; CANR 7, 69; CN 1, 2,
  3, 4, 5, 6
Hillis, Rick 1956- .... **CLC 66**
  See also CA 134
Hilton, James 1900-1954 .... **TCLC 21**
  See also CA 108; 169; DLB 34, 77; FANT;
  SATA 34
Hilton, Walter (?)-1396 .... **CMLC 58**
  See also DLB 146; RGEL 2
Himes, Chester (Bomar) 1909-1984 .. **BLC 2;**
  CLC 2, 4, 7, 18, 58, 108; TCLC 139
  See also AFAW 2; BPFB 2; BW 2; CA 25-
  28R; 114; CANR 22, 89; CMW 4; CN 1,
  2, 3; DAM MULT; DLB 2, 76, 143, 226;
  EWL 3; MAL 5; MSW; MTCW 1, 2;
  MTFW 2005; RGAL 4
Himmelfarb, Gertrude 1922- .... **CLC 202**
  See also CA 49-52; CANR 28, 66, 102
Hinde, Thomas .... **CLC 6, 11**
  See Chitty, Thomas Willes
  See also CN 1, 2, 3, 4, 5, 6; EWL 3
Hine, (William) Daryl 1936- .... **CLC 15**
  See also CA 1-4R; CAAS 15; CANR 1, 20;
  CP 1, 2, 3, 4, 5, 6, 7; DLB 60
Hinkson, Katharine Tynan
  See Tynan, Katharine
Hinojosa(-Smith), Rolando (R.)
  1929- .... **HLC 1**
  See Hinojosa-Smith, Rolando
  See also CA 131; CAAS 16; CANR 62;
  DAM MULT; DLB 82; HW 1, 2; LLW;
  MTCW 2; MTFW 2005; RGAL 4
Hinton, S(usan) E(loise) 1950- .. **CLC 30, 111**
  See also AAYA 2, 33; BPFB 2; BYA 2, 3;
  CA 81-84; CANR 32, 62, 92, 133;
  CDALBS; CLR 3, 23; CPW; DA; DA3;
  DAB; DAC; DAM MST, NOV; JRDA;
  LAIT 5; MAICYA 1, 2; MTCW 1, 2;
  MTFW 2005 !**; NFS 5, 9, 15, 16; SATA
  19, 58, 115, 160; WYA; YAW
Hippius, Zinaida (Nikolaevna) .... **TCLC 9**
  See Gippius, Zinaida (Nikolaevna)
  See also DLB 295; EWL 3

Hiraoka, Kimitake 1925-1970
  See Mishima, Yukio
  See also CA 97-100; 29-32R; DA3; DAM
  DRAM; GLL 1; MTCW 1, 2
Hirsch, E(ric) D(onald), Jr. 1928- .... **CLC 79**
  See also CA 25-28R; CANR 27, 51; DLB
  67; INT CANR-27; MTCW 1
Hirsch, Edward 1950- .... **CLC 31, 50**
  See also CA 104; CANR 20, 42, 102; CP 7;
  DLB 120; PFS 22
Hitchcock, Alfred (Joseph)
  1899-1980 .... **CLC 16**
  See also AAYA 22; CA 159; 97-100; SATA
  27; SATA-Obit 24
Hitchens, Christopher (Eric)
  1949- .... **CLC 157**
  See also CA 152; CANR 89
Hitler, Adolf 1889-1945 .... **TCLC 53**
  See also CA 117; 147
Hoagland, Edward (Morley) 1932- .. **CLC 28**
  See also ANW; CA 1-4R; CANR 2, 31, 57,
  107; CN 1, 2, 3, 4, 5, 6, 7; DLB 6; SATA
  51; TCWW 2
Hoban, Russell (Conwell) 1925- ... **CLC 7, 25**
  See also BPFB 2; CA 5-8R; CANR 23, 37,
  66, 114, 138; CLR 3, 69; CN 4, 5, 6, 7;
  CWRI 5; DAM NOV; DLB 52; FANT;
  MAICYA 1, 2; MTCW 1, 2; MTFW 2005;
  SATA 1, 40, 78, 136; SFW 4; SUFW 2;
  TCLE 1:1
Hobbes, Thomas 1588-1679 .... **LC 36**
  See also DLB 151, 252, 281; RGEL 2
Hobbs, Perry
  See Blackmur, R(ichard) P(almer)
Hobson, Laura Z(ametkin)
  1900-1986 .... **CLC 7, 25**
  See also BPFB 2; CA 17-20R; 118; CANR
  55; CN 1, 2, 3, 4; DLB 28; SATA 52
Hoccleve, Thomas c. 1368-c. 1437 ...... **LC 75**
  See also DLB 146; RGEL 2
Hoch, Edward D(entinger) 1930-
  See Queen, Ellery
  See also CA 29-32R; CANR 11, 27, 51, 97;
  CMW 4; DLB 306; SFW 4
Hochhuth, Rolf 1931- .... **CLC 4, 11, 18**
  See also CA 5-8R; CANR 33, 75, 136;
  CWW 2; DAM DRAM; DLB 124; EWL
  3; MTCW 1, 2; MTFW 2005
Hochman, Sandra 1936- .... **CLC 3, 8**
  See also CA 5-8R; CP 1, 2, 3, 4; DLB 5
Hochwaelder, Fritz 1911-1986 .... **CLC 36**
  See Hochwalder, Fritz
  See also CA 29-32R; 120; CANR 42; DAM
  DRAM; MTCW 1; RGWL 3
Hochwalder, Fritz
  See Hochwaelder, Fritz
  See also EWL 3; RGWL 2
Hocking, Mary (Eunice) 1921- .... **CLC 13**
  See also CA 101; CANR 18, 40
Hodgins, Jack 1938- .... **CLC 23**
  See also CA 93-96; CN 4, 5, 6, 7; DLB 60
Hodgson, William Hope
  1877(?)-1918 .... **TCLC 13**
  See also CA 111; 164; CMW 4; DLB 70,
  153, 156, 178; HGG; MTCW 2; SFW 4;
  SUFW 1
Hoeg, Peter 1957- .... **CLC 95, 156**
  See also CA 151; CANR 75; CMW 4; DA3;
  DLB 214; EWL 3; MTCW 2; MTFW
  2005; NFS 17; RGWL 3; SSFS 18
Hoffman, Alice 1952- .... **CLC 51**
  See also AAYA 37; AMWS 10; CA 77-80;
  CANR 34, 66, 100, 138; CN 4, 5, 6, 7;
  CPW; DAM NOV; DLB 292; MAL 5;
  MTCW 1, 2; MTFW 2005; TCLE 1:1
Hoffman, Daniel (Gerard) 1923- . **CLC 6, 13,**
  23
  See also CA 1-4R; CANR 4, 142; CP 1, 2,
  3, 4, 5, 6, 7; DLB 5; TCLE 1:1

Hoffman, Eva 1945- .... **CLC 182**
See also CA 132; CANR 146
Hoffman, Stanley 1944- .... **CLC 5**
See also CA 77-80
Hoffman, William 1925- .... **CLC 141**
See also CA 21-24R; CANR 9, 103; CSW;
DLB 234; TCLE 1:1
Hoffman, William M.
See Hoffman, William M(oses)
See also CAD; CD 5, 6
Hoffman, William M(oses) 1939- ..... **CLC 40**
See Hoffman, William M.
See also CA 57-60; CANR 11, 71
Hoffmann, E(rnst) T(heodor) A(madeus)
1776-1822 .... **NCLC 2; SSC 13**
See also CDWLB 2; DLB 90; EW 5; GL 2;
RGSF 2; RGWL 2, 3; SATA 27; SUFW
1; WCH
Hofmann, Gert 1931-1993 .... **CLC 54**
See also CA 128; CANR 145; EWL 3
Hofmannsthal, Hugo von 1874-1929 ... **DC 4;**
TCLC 11
See also CA 106; 153; CDWLB 2; DAM
DRAM; DFS 17; DLB 81, 118; EW 9;
EWL 3; RGWL 2, 3
Hogan, Linda 1947- ..... **CLC 73; NNAL; PC**
35
See also AMWS 4; ANW; BYA 12; CA 120,
226; CAAE 226; CANR 45, 73, 129;
CWP; DAM MULT; DLB 175; SATA
132; TCWW 2
Hogarth, Charles
See Creasey, John
Hogarth, Emmett
See Polonsky, Abraham (Lincoln)
Hogarth, William 1697-1764 .... **LC 112**
See also AAYA 56
Hogg, James 1770-1835 .... **NCLC 4, 109**
See also BRWS 10; DLB 93, 116, 159; GL
2; HGG; RGEL 2; SUFW 1
Holbach, Paul-Henri Thiry
1723-1789 .... **LC 14**
See also DLB 313
Holberg, Ludvig 1684-1754 .... **LC 6**
See also DLB 300; RGWL 2, 3
Holcroft, Thomas 1745-1809 .... **NCLC 85**
See also DLB 39, 89, 158; RGEL 2
Holden, Ursula 1921- .... **CLC 18**
See also CA 101; CAAS 8; CANR 22
Holderlin, (Johann Christian) Friedrich
1770-1843 .... **NCLC 16; PC 4**
See also CDWLB 2; DLB 90; EW 5; RGWL
2, 3
Holdstock, Robert
See Holdstock, Robert P.
Holdstock, Robert P. 1948- .... **CLC 39**
See also CA 131; CANR 81; DLB 261;
FANT; HGG; SFW 4; SUFW 2
Holinshed, Raphael fl. 1580- .... **LC 69**
See also DLB 167; RGEL 2
Holland, Isabelle (Christian)
1920-2002 .... **CLC 21**
See also AAYA 11, 64; CA 21-24R; 205;
CAAE 181; CANR 10, 25, 47; CLR 57;
CWRI 5; JRDA; LAIT 4; MAICYA 1, 2;
SATA 8, 70; SATA-Essay 103; SATA-Obit
132; WYA
Holland, Marcus
See Caldwell, (Janet Miriam) Taylor
(Holland)
Hollander, John 1929- .... **CLC 2, 5, 8, 14**
See also CA 1-4R; CANR 1, 52, 136; CP 1,
2, 3, 4, 5, 6, 7; DLB 5; MAL 5; SATA 13
Hollander, Paul
See Silverberg, Robert
Holleran, Andrew .... **CLC 38**
See Garber, Eric
See also CA 144; GLL 1

Holley, Marietta 1836(?)-1926 .... **TCLC 99**
See also CA 118; DLB 11; FL 1:3
Hollinghurst, Alan 1954- .... **CLC 55, 91**
See also BRWS 10; CA 114; CN 5, 6, 7;
DLB 207; GLL 1
Hollis, Jim
See Summers, Hollis (Spurgeon, Jr.)
Holly, Buddy 1936-1959 .... **TCLC 65**
See also CA 213
Holmes, Gordon
See Shiel, M(atthew) P(hipps)
Holmes, John
See Souster, (Holmes) Raymond
Holmes, John Clellon 1926-1988 ...... **CLC 56**
See also BG 1:2; CA 9-12R; 125; CANR 4;
CN 1, 2, 3, 4; DLB 16, 237
Holmes, Oliver Wendell, Jr.
1841-1935 .... **TCLC 77**
See also CA 114; 186
Holmes, Oliver Wendell
1809-1894 .... **NCLC 14, 81**
See also AMWS 1; CDALB 1640-1865;
DLB 1, 189, 235; EXPP; RGAL 4; SATA
34
Holmes, Raymond
See Souster, (Holmes) Raymond
Holt, Victoria
See Hibbert, Eleanor Alice Burford
See also BPFB 2
Holub, Miroslav 1923-1998 .... **CLC 4**
See also CA 21-24R; 169; CANR 10; CD-
WLB 4; CWW 2; DLB 232; EWL 3;
RGWL 3
Holz, Detlev
See Benjamin, Walter
Homer c. 8th cent. B.C.- .... **CMLC 1, 16, 61;**
PC 23; WLCS
See also AW 1; CDWLB 1; DA; DA3;
DAB; DAC; DAM MST, POET; DLB
176; EFS 1; LAIT 1; LMFS 1; RGWL 2,
3; TWA; WP
Hongo, Garrett Kaoru 1951- .... **PC 23**
See also CA 133; CAAS 22; CP 7; DLB
120, 312; EWL 3; EXPP; RGAL 4
Honig, Edwin 1919- .... **CLC 33**
See also CA 5-8R; CAAS 8; CANR 4, 45,
144; CP 1, 2, 3, 4, 5, 6, 7; DLB 5
Hood, Hugh (John Blagdon) 1928- . **CLC 15,**
28; SSC 42
See also CA 49-52; CAAS 17; CANR 1,
33, 87; CN 1, 2, 3, 4, 5, 6, 7; DLB 53;
RGSF 2
Hood, Thomas 1799-1845 .... **NCLC 16**
See also BRW 4; DLB 96; RGEL 2
Hooker, (Peter) Jeremy 1941- .... **CLC 43**
See also CA 77-80; CANR 22; CP 2, 3, 4,
5, 6, 7; DLB 40
Hooker, Richard 1554-1600 .... **LC 95**
See also BRW 1; DLB 132; RGEL 2
hooks, bell
See Watkins, Gloria Jean
Hope, A(lec) D(erwent) 1907-2000 .... **CLC 3,**
51; PC 56
See also BRWS 7; CA 21-24R; 188; CANR
33, 74; CP 1, 2, 3, 4; DLB 289; EWL 3;
MTCW 1, 2; MTFW 2005; PFS 8; RGEL
2
Hope, Anthony 1863-1933 .... **TCLC 83**
See also CA 157; DLB 153, 156; RGEL 2;
RHW
Hope, Brian
See Creasey, John
Hope, Christopher (David Tully)
1944- .... **CLC 52**
See also AFW; CA 106; CANR 47, 101;
CN 4, 5, 6, 7; DLB 225; SATA 62

Hopkins, Gerard Manley
1844-1889 .... **NCLC 17; PC 15; WLC**
See also BRW 5; BRWR 2; CDBLB 1890-
1914; DA; DA3; DAB; DAC; DAM MST,
POET; DLB 35, 57; EXPP; PAB; RGEL
2; TEA; WP
Hopkins, John (Richard) 1931-1998 .. **CLC 4**
See also CA 85-88; 169; CBD; CD 5, 6
Hopkins, Pauline Elizabeth
1859-1930 .... **BLC 2; TCLC 28**
See also AFAW 2; BW 2, 3; CA 141; CANR
82; DAM MULT; DLB 50
Hopkinson, Francis 1737-1791 .... **LC 25**
See also DLB 31; RGAL 4
Hopley-Woolrich, Cornell George 1903-1968
See Woolrich, Cornell
See also CA 13-14; CANR 58; CAP 1;
CMW 4; DLB 226; MTCW 2
Horace 65B.C.-8B.C. .... **CMLC 39; PC 46**
See also AW 2; CDWLB 1; DLB 211;
RGWL 2, 3
Horatio
See Proust, (Valentin-Louis-George-Eugene)
Marcel
Horgan, Paul (George Vincent
O'Shaughnessy) 1903-1995 .. **CLC 9, 53**
See also BPFB 2; CA 13-16R; 147; CANR
9, 35; CN 1, 2, 3, 4, 5; DAM NOV; DLB
102, 212; DLBY 1985; INT CANR-9;
MTCW 1, 2; MTFW 2005; SATA 13;
SATA-Obit 84; TCWW 1, 2
Horkheimer, Max 1895-1973 .... **TCLC 132**
See also CA 216; 41-44R; DLB 296
Horn, Peter
See Kuttner, Henry
Horne, Frank (Smith) 1899-1974 ...... **HR 1:2**
See also BW 1; CA 125; 53-56; DLB 51;
WP
Horne, Richard Henry Hengist
1802(?)-1884 .... **NCLC 127**
See also DLB 32; SATA 29
Hornem, Horace Esq.
See Byron, George Gordon (Noel)
Horney, Karen (Clementine Theodore
Danielsen) 1885-1952 .... **TCLC 71**
See also CA 114; 165; DLB 246; FW
Hornung, E(rnest) W(illiam)
1866-1921 .... **TCLC 59**
See also CA 108; 160; CMW 4; DLB 70
Horovitz, Israel (Arthur) 1939- .... **CLC 56**
See also CA 33-36R; CAD; CANR 46, 59;
CD 5, 6; DAM DRAM; DLB 7; MAL 5
Horton, George Moses
1797(?)-1883(?) .... **NCLC 87**
See also DLB 50
Horvath, odon von 1901-1938
See von Horvath, Odon
See also EWL 3
Horvath, Oedoen von -1938
See von Horvath, Odon
Horwitz, Julius 1920-1986 .... **CLC 14**
See also CA 9-12R; 119; CANR 12
Hospital, Janette Turner 1942- .... **CLC 42,**
145
See also CA 108; CANR 48; CN 5, 6, 7;
DLBY 2002; RGSF 2
Hostos, E. M. de
See Hostos (y Bonilla), Eugenio Maria de
Hostos, Eugenio M. de
See Hostos (y Bonilla), Eugenio Maria de
Hostos, Eugenio Maria
See Hostos (y Bonilla), Eugenio Maria de
Hostos (y Bonilla), Eugenio Maria de
1839-1903 .... **TCLC 24**
See also CA 123; 131; HW 1
Houdini
See Lovecraft, H(oward) P(hillips)
Houellebecq, Michel 1958- .... **CLC 179**
See also CA 185; CANR 140; MTFW 2005

Hrotsvit of Gandersheim c. 935-c.
1000 .... **CMLC 29**
See also DLB 148
Hsi, Chu 1130-1200 .... **CMLC 42**
Hsun, Lu
See Lu Hsun
Hubbard, L(afayette) Ron(ald)
1911-1986 .... **CLC 43**
See also AAYA 64; CA 77-80; 118; CANR
52; CPW; DA3; DAM POP; FANT;
MTCW 2; MTFW 2005; SFW 4
Huch, Ricarda (Octavia)
1864-1947 .... **TCLC 13**
See Hugo, Richard
See also CA 111; 189; DLB 66; EWL 3
Huddle, David 1942- .... **CLC 49**
See also CA 57-60; CAAS 20; CANR 89;
DLB 130
Hudson, Jeffrey
See Crichton, (John) Michael
Hudson, W(illiam) H(enry)
1841-1922 .... **TCLC 29**
See also CA 115; 190; DLB 98, 153, 174;
RGEL 2; SATA 35
Hueffer, Ford Madox
See Ford, Ford Madox
Hughart, Barry 1934- .... **CLC 39**
See also CA 137; FANT; SFW 4; SUFW 2
Hughes, Colin
See Creasey, John
Hughes, David (John) 1930-2005 ..... **CLC 48**
See also CA 116; 129; 238; CN 4, 5, 6, 7;
DLB 14
Hughes, Edward James
See Hughes, Ted
See also DA3; DAM MST, POET
Hughes, (James Mercer) Langston
1902-1967 ..... **BLC 2; CLC 1, 5, 10, 15,
35, 44, 108; DC 3; HR 1:2; PC 1, 53;
SSC 6; WLC**
See also AAYA 12; AFAW 1, 2; AMWR 1;
AMWS 1; BW 1, 3; CA 1-4R; 25-28R;
CANR 1, 34, 82; CDALB 1929-1941;
CLR 17; DA; DA3; DAB; DAC; DAM
DRAM, MST, MULT, POET; DFS 6, 18;
DLB 4, 7, 48, 51, 86, 228, 315; EWL 3;
EXPP; EXPS; JRDA; LAIT 3; LMFS 2;
MAICYA 1, 2; MAL 5; MTCW 1, 2;
MTFW 2005; NFS 21; PAB; PFS 1, 3, 6,
10, 15; RGAL 4; RGSF 2; SATA 4, 33;
SSFS 4, 7; TUS; WCH; WP; YAW
Hughes, Richard (Arthur Warren)
1900-1976 .... **CLC 1, 11**
See also CA 5-8R; 65-68; CANR 4; CN 1,
2; DAM NOV; DLB 15, 161; EWL 3;
MTCW 1; RGEL 2; SATA 8; SATA-Obit
25
Hughes, Ted 1930-1998 . **CLC 2, 4, 9, 14, 37,
119; PC 7**
See Hughes, Edward James
See also BRWC 2; BRWR 2; BRWS 1; CA
1-4R; 171; CANR 1, 33, 66, 108; CLR 3;
CP 1, 2, 3, 4, 5, 6; DAB; DAC; DLB 40,
161; EWL 3; EXPP; MAICYA 1, 2;
MTCW 1, 2; MTFW 2005; PAB; PFS 4,
19; RGEL 2; SATA 49; SATA-Brief 27;
SATA-Obit 107; TEA; YAW
Hugo, Richard
See Huch, Ricarda (Octavia)
See also MAL 5
Hugo, Richard F(ranklin)
1923-1982 .... **CLC 6, 18, 32; PC 68**
See also AMWS 6; CA 49-52; 108; CANR
3; CP 1, 2, 3; DAM POET; DLB 5, 206;
EWL 3; PFS 17; RGAL 4
Hugo, Victor (Marie) 1802-1885 .... **NCLC 3,
10, 21, 161; PC 17; WLC**
See also AAYA 28; DA; DA3; DAB; DAC;
DAM DRAM, MST, NOV, POET; DLB
119, 192, 217; EFS 2; EW 6; EXPN; GFL

1789 to the Present; LAIT 1, 2; NFS 5,
20; RGWL 2, 3; SATA 47; TWA
Huidobro, Vicente
See Huidobro Fernandez, Vicente Garcia
See also DLB 283; EWL 3; LAW
Huidobro Fernandez, Vicente Garcia
1893-1948 .... **TCLC 31**
See Huidobro, Vicente
See also CA 131; HW 1
Hulme, Keri 1947- .... **CLC 39, 130**
See also CA 125; CANR 69; CN 4, 5, 6, 7;
CP 7; CWP; EWL 3; FW; INT CA-125
Hulme, T(homas) E(rnest)
1883-1917 .... **TCLC 21**
See also BRWS 6; CA 117; 203; DLB 19
Humboldt, Wilhelm von
1767-1835 .... **NCLC 134**
See also DLB 90
Hume, David 1711-1776 .... **LC 7, 56**
See also BRWS 3; DLB 104, 252; LMFS 1;
TEA
Humphrey, William 1924-1997 .... **CLC 45**
See also AMWS 9; CA 77-80; 160; CANR
68; CN 1, 2, 3, 4, 5, 6; CSW; DLB 6, 212,
234, 278; TCWW 1, 2
Humphreys, Emyr Owen 1919- .... **CLC 47**
See also CA 5-8R; CANR 3, 24; CN 1, 2,
3, 4, 5, 6, 7; DLB 15
Humphreys, Josephine 1945- ..... **CLC 34, 57**
See also CA 121; 127; CANR 97; CSW;
DLB 292; INT CA-127
Huneker, James Gibbons
1860-1921 .... **TCLC 65**
See also CA 193; DLB 71; RGAL 4
Hungerford, Hesba Fay
See Brinsmead, H(esba) F(ay)
Hungerford, Pixie
See Brinsmead, H(esba) F(ay)
Hunt, E(verette) Howard, (Jr.)
1918- .... **CLC 3**
See also AITN 1; CA 45-48; CANR 2, 47,
103; CMW 4
Hunt, Francesca
See Holland, Isabelle (Christian)
Hunt, Howard
See Hunt, E(verette) Howard, (Jr.)
Hunt, Kyle
See Creasey, John
Hunt, (James Henry) Leigh
1784-1859 .... **NCLC 1, 70**
See also DAM POET; DLB 96, 110, 144;
RGEL 2; TEA
Hunt, Marsha 1946- .... **CLC 70**
See also BW 2, 3; CA 143; CANR 79
Hunt, Violet 1866(?)-1942 .... **TCLC 53**
See also CA 184; DLB 162, 197
Hunter, E. Waldo
See Sturgeon, Theodore (Hamilton)
Hunter, Evan 1926-2005 .... **CLC 11, 31**
See McBain, Ed
See also AAYA 39; BPFB 2; CA 5-8R; 241;
CANR 5, 38, 62, 97; CMW 4; CN 1, 2, 3,
4, 5, 6, 7; CPW; DAM POP; DLB 306;
DLBY 1982; INT CANR-5; MSW;
MTCW 1; SATA 25; SFW 4
Hunter, Kristin
See Lattany, Kristin (Elaine Eggleston)
Hunter
See also CN 1, 2, 3, 4, 5, 6
Hunter, Mary
See Austin, Mary (Hunter)
Hunter, Mollie 1922- .... **CLC 21**
See McIlwraith, Maureen Mollie Hunter
See also AAYA 13; BYA 6; CANR 37, 78;
CLR 25; DLB 161; JRDA; MAICYA 1,
2; SAAS 7; SATA 54, 106, 139; SATA-
Essay 139; WYA; YAW

Hunter, Robert (?)-1734 .... **LC 7**

Hurston, Zora Neale 1891-1960 .... **BLC 2;
CLC 7, 30, 61; DC 12; HR 1:2; SSC 4,
80; TCLC 121, 131; WLCS**
See also AAYA 15; AFAW 1, 2; AMWS 6;
BW 1, 3; BYA 12; CA 85-88; CANR 61;
CDALBS; DA; DA3; DAC; DAM MST,
MULT, NOV; DFS 6; DLB 51, 86; EWL
3; EXPN; EXPS; FL 1:6; FW; LAIT 3;
LATS 1:1; LMFS 2; MAL 5; MAWW;
MTCW 1, 2; MTFW 2005; NFS 3; RGAL
4; RGSF 2; SSFS 1, 6, 11, 19, 21; TUS;
YAW

Husserl, E. G.
See Husserl, Edmund (Gustav Albrecht)

Husserl, Edmund (Gustav Albrecht)
1859-1938 .... **TCLC 100**
See also CA 116; 133; DLB 296

Huston, John (Marcellus)
1906-1987 .... **CLC 20**
See also CA 73-76; 123; CANR 34; DLB
26

Hustvedt, Siri 1955- .... **CLC 76**
See also CA 137

Hutten, Ulrich von 1488-1523 .... **LC 16**
See also DLB 179

Huxley, Aldous (Leonard)
1894-1963 .... **CLC 1, 3, 4, 5, 8, 11, 18,
35, 79; SSC 39; WLC**
See also AAYA 11; BPFB 2; BRW 7; CA
85-88; CANR 44, 99; CDBLB 1914-1945;
DA; DA3; DAB; DAC; DAM MST, NOV;
DLB 36, 100, 162, 195, 255; EWL 3;
EXPN; LAIT 5; LMFS 2; MTCW 1, 2;
MTFW 2005; NFS 6; RGEL 2; SATA 63;
SCFW 1, 2; SFW 4; TEA; YAW

Huxley, T(homas) H(enry)
1825-1895 .... **NCLC 67**
See also DLB 57; TEA

Huygens, Constantijn 1596-1687 .... **LC 114**
See also RGWL 2, 3

Huysmans, Joris-Karl 1848-1907 ... **TCLC 7,
69**
See also CA 104; 165; DLB 123; EW 7;
GFL 1789 to the Present; LMFS 2; RGWL
2, 3

Hwang, David Henry 1957- .... **CLC 55, 196;
DC 4, 23**
See also CA 127; 132; CAD; CANR 76,
124; CD 5, 6; DA3; DAM DRAM; DFS
11, 18; DLB 212, 228, 312; INT CA-132;
MAL 5; MTCW 2; MTFW 2005; RGAL
4

Hyde, Anthony 1946- .... **CLC 42**
See Chase, Nicholas
See also CA 136; CCA 1

Hyde, Margaret O(ldroyd) 1917- ..... **CLC 21**
See also CA 1-4R; CANR 1, 36, 137; CLR
23; JRDA; MAICYA 1, 2; SAAS 8; SATA
1, 42, 76, 139

Hynes, James 1956(?)- .... **CLC 65**
See also CA 164; CANR 105

Hypatia c. 370-415 .... **CMLC 35**

Ian, Janis 1951- .... **CLC 21**
See also CA 105; 187

Ibanez, Vicente Blasco
See Blasco Ibanez, Vicente
See also DLB 322

Ibarbourou, Juana de
1895(?)-1979 .... **HLCS 2**
See also DLB 290; HW 1; LAW

Ibarguengoitia, Jorge 1928-1983 ..... **CLC 37;
TCLC 148**
See also CA 124; 113; EWL 3; HW 1

Ibn Battuta, Abu Abdalla
1304-1368(?) .... **CMLC 57**
See also WLIT 2

Ibn Hazm 994-1064 .... **CMLC 64**

Ibsen, Henrik (Johan) 1828-1906 .... **DC 2;
TCLC 2, 8, 16, 37, 52; WLC**
See also AAYA 46; CA 104; 141; DA; DA3;
DAB; DAC; DAM DRAM, MST; DFS 1,
6, 8, 10, 11, 15, 16; EW 7; LAIT 2; LATS
1:1; MTFW 2005; RGWL 2, 3

Ibuse, Masuji 1898-1993 .... **CLC 22**
See Ibuse Masuji
See also CA 127; 141; MJW; RGWL 3

Ibuse Masuji
See Ibuse, Masuji
See also CWW 2; DLB 180; EWL 3

Ichikawa, Kon 1915- .... **CLC 20**
See also CA 121

Ichiyo, Higuchi 1872-1896 .... **NCLC 49**
See also MJW

Idle, Eric 1943- .... **CLC 21**
See Monty Python
See also CA 116; CANR 35, 91

Idris, Yusuf 1927-1991 .... **SSC 74**
See also AFW; EWL 3; RGSF 2, 3; RGWL
3; WLIT 2

Ignatow, David 1914-1997 .... **CLC 4, 7, 14,
40; PC 34**
See also CA 9-12R; 162; CAAS 3; CANR
31, 57, 96; CP 1, 2, 3, 4, 5, 6; DLB 5;
EWL 3; MAL 5

Ignotus
See Strachey, (Giles) Lytton

Ihimaera, Witi (Tame) 1944- .... **CLC 46**
See also CA 77-80; CANR 130; CN 2, 3, 4,
5, 6, 7; RGSF 2; SATA 148

Ilf, Ilya .... **TCLC 21**
See Fainzilberg, Ilya Arnoldovich
See also EWL 3

Illyes, Gyula 1902-1983 .... **PC 16**
See also CA 114; 109; CDWLB 4; DLB
215; EWL 3; RGWL 2, 3

Imalayen, Fatima-Zohra
See Djebar, Assia

Immermann, Karl (Lebrecht)
1796-1840 .... **NCLC 4, 49**
See also DLB 133

Ince, Thomas H. 1882-1924 .... **TCLC 89**
See also IDFW 3, 4

Inchbald, Elizabeth 1753-1821 ...... **NCLC 62**
See also DLB 39, 89; RGEL 2

Inclan, Ramon (Maria) del Valle
See Valle-Inclan, Ramon (Maria) del

Infante, G(uillermo) Cabrera
See Cabrera Infante, G(uillermo)

Ingalls, Rachel (Holmes) 1940- .... **CLC 42**
See also CA 123; 127

Ingamells, Reginald Charles
See Ingamells, Rex

Ingamells, Rex 1913-1955 .... **TCLC 35**
See also CA 167; DLB 260

Inge, William (Motter) 1913-1973 ..... **CLC 1,
8, 19**
See also CA 9-12R; CAD; CDALB 1941-
1968; DA3; DAM DRAM; DFS 1, 3, 5,
8; DLB 7, 249; EWL 3; MAL 5; MTCW
1, 2; MTFW 2005; RGAL 4; TUS

Ingelow, Jean 1820-1897 .... **NCLC 39, 107**
See also DLB 35, 163; FANT; SATA 33

Ingram, Willis J.
See Harris, Mark

Innaurato, Albert (F.) 1948(?)- ... **CLC 21, 60**
See also CA 115; 122; CAD; CANR 78;
CD 5, 6; INT CA-122

Innes, Michael
See Stewart, J(ohn) I(nnes) M(ackintosh)
See also DLB 276; MSW

Innis, Harold Adams 1894-1952 .... **TCLC 77**
See also CA 181; DLB 88

Insluis, Alanus de
See Alain de Lille

Iola
See Wells-Barnett, Ida B

Ionesco, Eugene 1912-1994
11, 15, 41, 86; DC 12
See also CA 9-12R; 14
CWW 2; DA; DA3;
DRAM, MST; DFS 4,
13; EWL 3; GFL 178
LMFS 2; MTCW 1,
RGWL 2, 3; SATA
TWA

Iqbal, Muhammad 1877-19
See also CA 215; EWL 3

Ireland, Patrick
See O'Doherty, Brian

Irenaeus St. 130- ....

Irigaray, Luce 1930- ....
See also CA 154; CANR

Iron, Ralph
See Schreiner, Olive (Emi

Irving, John (Winslow) 194
38, 112, 175
See also AAYA 8, 62; A
89:3; BPFB 2; CA 25-28
112, 133; CN 3, 4, 5,
DAM NOV, POP; DL
1982; EWL 3; MAL
MTFW 2005; NFS 12, 1

Irving, Washington 1783-185
95; SSC 2, 37; WLC
See also AAYA 56; AMW
1865; CLR 97; DA; DA
DAM MST; DLB 3, 11,
183, 186, 250, 254; EXF
1; RGAL 4; RGSF 2;
SUFW 1; TUS; WCH; YA

Irwin, P. K.
See Page, P(atricia) K(athle

Isaacs, Jorge Ricardo 1837-18
See also LAW

Isaacs, Susan 1943- ....
See also BEST 89:1; BPFI
CANR 20, 41, 65, 112, 1
DAM POP; INT CANR-2
MTFW 2005

Isherwood, Christopher (Willi
1904-1986 .... **CLC 1, 9,
56**
See also AMWS 14; BRW
117; CANR 35, 97, 133; C
DAM DRAM, NOV; DLB
1986; EWL 3; IDTP; MTC
2005; RGAL 4; RGEL 2;

Ishiguro, Kazuo 1954- .. **CLC
**
See also AAYA 58; BEST
BRWS 4; CA 120; CANR
CN 5, 6, 7; DA3; DAM N
EWL 3; MTCW 1, 2; MTF
13; WLIT 4; WWE 1

Ishikawa, Hakuhin
See Ishikawa, Takuboku

Ishikawa, Takuboku 1886(?)-19
TCLC 15
See Ishikawa Takuboku
See also CA 113; 153; DAM

Iskander, Fazil (Abdulovich) 19
See Iskander, Fazil' Abdulevic
See also CA 102; EWL 3

Iskander, Fazil' Abdulevich
See Iskander, Fazil (Abdulovic
See also DLB 302

Isler, Alan (David) 1934- ....
See also CA 156; CANR 105

Ivan IV 1530-1584 ....

Ivanov, Vyacheslav Ivanovich
1866-1949 ....
See also CA 122; EWL 3

Ivask, Ivar Vidrik 1927-1992 ...
See also CA 37-40R; 139; CAN

Ives, Morgan
    See Bradley, Marion Zimmer
    See also GLL 1
Izumi Shikibu c. 973-c. 1034 .... **CMLC 33**
J. R. S.
    See Gogarty, Oliver St. John
Jabran, Kahlil
    See Gibran, Kahlil
Jabran, Khalil
    See Gibran, Kahlil
Jackson, Daniel
    See Wingrove, David (John)
Jackson, Helen Hunt 1830-1885 .... **NCLC 90**
    See also DLB 42, 47, 186, 189; RGAL 4
Jackson, Jesse 1908-1983 .... **CLC 12**
    See also BW 1; CA 25-28R; 109; CANR
    27; CLR 28; CWRI 5; MAICYA 1, 2;
    SATA 2, 29; SATA-Obit 48
Jackson, Laura (Riding) 1901-1991 .... **PC 44**
    See Riding, Laura
    See also CA 65-68; 135; CANR 28, 89;
    DLB 48
Jackson, Sam
    See Trumbo, Dalton
Jackson, Sara
    See Wingrove, David (John)
Jackson, Shirley 1919-1965 . **CLC 11, 60, 87;**
    SSC 9, 39; WLC
    See also AAYA 9; AMWS 9; BPFB 2; CA
    1-4R; 25-28R; CANR 4, 52; CDALB
    1941-1968; DA; DA3; DAC; DAM MST;
    DLB 6, 234; EXPS; HGG; LAIT 4; MAL
    5; MTCW 2; MTFW 2005; RGAL 4;
    RGSF 2; SATA 2; SSFS 1; SUFW 1, 2
Jacob, (Cyprien-)Max 1876-1944 .... **TCLC 6**
    See also CA 104; 193; DLB 258; EWL 3;
    GFL 1789 to the Present; GLL 2; RGWL
    2, 3
Jacobs, Harriet A(nn)
    1813(?)-1897 .... **NCLC 67, 162**
    See also AFAW 1, 2; DLB 239; FL 1:3; FW;
    LAIT 2; RGAL 4
Jacobs, Jim 1942- .... **CLC 12**
    See also CA 97-100; INT CA-97-100
Jacobs, W(illiam) W(ymark)
    1863-1943 .... **SSC 73; TCLC 22**
    See also CA 121; 167; DLB 135; EXPS;
    HGG; RGEL 2; RGSF 2; SSFS 2; SUFW
    1
Jacobsen, Jens Peter 1847-1885 .... **NCLC 34**
Jacobsen, Josephine (Winder)
    1908-2003 .... **CLC 48, 102; PC 62**
    See also CA 33-36R; 218; CAAS 18; CANR
    23, 48; CCA 1; CP 2, 3, 4, 5, 6, 7; DLB
    244; PFS 23; TCLE 1:1
Jacobson, Dan 1929- .... **CLC 4, 14**
    See also AFW; CA 1-4R; CANR 2, 25, 66;
    CN 1, 2, 3, 4, 5, 6, 7; DLB 14, 207, 225,
    319; EWL 3; MTCW 1; RGSF 2
Jacqueline
    See Carpentier (y Valmont), Alejo
Jacques de Vitry c. 1160-1240 ...... **CMLC 63**
    See also DLB 208
Jagger, Michael Philip
    See Jagger, Mick
Jagger, Mick 1943- .... **CLC 17**
    See also CA 239
Jahiz, al- c. 780-c. 869 .... **CMLC 25**
    See also DLB 311
Jakes, John (William) 1932- .... **CLC 29**
    See also AAYA 32; BEST 89:4; BPFB 2;
    CA 57-60, 214; CAAE 214; CANR 10,
    43, 66, 111, 142; CPW; CSW; DA3; DAM
    NOV, POP; DLB 278; DLBY 1983;
    FANT; INT CANR-10; MTCW 1, 2;
    MTFW 2005; RHW; SATA 62; SFW 4;
    TCWW 1, 2
James I 1394-1437 .... **LC 20**
    See also RGEL 2

James, Andrew
    See Kirkup, James
James, C(yril) L(ionel) R(obert)
    1901-1989 .... **BLCS; CLC 33**
    See also BW 2; CA 117; 125; 128; CANR
    62; CN 1, 2, 3, 4; DLB 125; MTCW 1
James, Daniel (Lewis) 1911-1988
    See Santiago, Danny
    See also CA 174; 125
James, Dynely
    See Mayne, William (James Carter)
James, Henry Sr. 1811-1882 .... **NCLC 53**
James, Henry 1843-1916 .... **SSC 8, 32, 47;**
    TCLC 2, 11, 24, 40, 47, 64, 171; WLC
    See also AMW; AMWC 1; AMWR 1; BPFB
    2; BRW 6; CA 104; 132; CDALB 1865-
    1917; DA; DA3; DAB; DAC; DAM MST,
    NOV; DLB 12, 71, 74, 189; DLBD 13;
    EWL 3; EXPS; GL 2; HGG; LAIT 2;
    MAL 5; MTCW 1, 2; MTFW 2005; NFS
    12, 16, 19; RGAL 4; RGEL 2; RGSF 2;
    SSFS 9; SUFW 1; TUS
James, M. R.
    See James, Montague (Rhodes)
    See also DLB 156, 201
James, Montague (Rhodes)
    1862-1936 .... **SSC 16; TCLC 6**
    See James, M. R.
    See also CA 104; 203; HGG; RGEL 2;
    RGSF 2; SUFW 1
James, P. D. .... **CLC 18, 46, 122**
    See White, Phyllis Dorothy James
    See also BEST 90:2; BPFB 2; BRWS 4;
    CDBLB 1960 to Present; CN 4, 5, 6; DLB
    87, 276; DLBD 17; MSW
James, Philip
    See Moorcock, Michael (John)
James, Samuel
    See Stephens, James
James, Seumas
    See Stephens, James
James, Stephen
    See Stephens, James
James, William 1842-1910 .... **TCLC 15, 32**
    See also AMW; CA 109; 193; DLB 270,
    284; MAL 5; NCFS 5; RGAL 4
Jameson, Anna 1794-1860 .... **NCLC 43**
    See also DLB 99, 166
Jameson, Fredric (R.) 1934- .... **CLC 142**
    See also CA 196; DLB 67; LMFS 2
James VI of Scotland 1566-1625 .... **LC 109**
    See also DLB 151, 172
Jami, Nur al-Din 'Abd al-Rahman
    1414-1492 .... **LC 9**
Jammes, Francis 1868-1938 .... **TCLC 75**
    See also CA 198; EWL 3; GFL 1789 to the
    Present
Jandl, Ernst 1925-2000 .... **CLC 34**
    See also CA 200; EWL 3
Janowitz, Tama 1957- .... **CLC 43, 145**
    See also CA 106; CANR 52, 89, 129; CN
    5, 6, 7; CPW; DAM POP; DLB 292;
    MTFW 2005
Japrisot, Sebastien 1931- .... **CLC 90**
    See Rossi, Jean-Baptiste
    See also CMW 4; NFS 18
Jarrell, Randall 1914-1965 .... **CLC 1, 2, 6, 9,**
    13, 49; PC 41
    See also AMW; BYA 5; CA 5-8R; 25-28R;
    CABS 2; CANR 6, 34; CDALB 1941-
    1968; CLR 6; CWRI 5; DAM POET;
    DLB 48, 52; EWL 3; EXPP; MAICYA 1,
    2; MAL 5; MTCW 1, 2; PAB; PFS 2;
    RGAL 4; SATA 7

Jarry, Alfred 1873-1907 .... **SSC 20; TCLC 2,**
    14, 147
    See also CA 104; 153; DA3; DAM DRAM;
    DFS 8; DLB 192, 258; EW 9; EWL 3;
    GFL 1789 to the Present; RGWL 2, 3;
    TWA
Jarvis, E. K.
    See Ellison, Harlan (Jay)
Jawien, Andrzej
    See John Paul II, Pope
Jaynes, Roderick
    See Coen, Ethan
Jeake, Samuel, Jr.
    See Aiken, Conrad (Potter)
Jean Paul 1763-1825 .... **NCLC 7**
Jefferies, (John) Richard
    1848-1887 .... **NCLC 47**
    See also DLB 98, 141; RGEL 2; SATA 16;
    SFW 4
Jeffers, (John) Robinson 1887-1962 .. **CLC 2,**
    3, 11, 15, 54; PC 17; WLC
    See also AMWS 2; CA 85-88; CANR 35;
    CDALB 1917-1929; DA; DAC; DAM
    MST, POET; DLB 45, 212; EWL 3; MAL
    5; MTCW 1, 2; MTFW 2005; PAB; PFS
    3, 4; RGAL 4
Jefferson, Janet
    See Mencken, H(enry) L(ouis)
Jefferson, Thomas 1743-1826 . **NCLC 11, 103**
    See also AAYA 54; ANW; CDALB 1640-
    1865; DA3; DLB 31, 183; LAIT 1; RGAL
    4
Jeffrey, Francis 1773-1850 .... **NCLC 33**
    See Francis, Lord Jeffrey
Jelakowitch, Ivan
    See Heijermans, Herman
Jelinek, Elfriede 1946- .... **CLC 169**
    See also AAYA 68; CA 154; DLB 85; FW
Jellicoe, (Patricia) Ann 1927- .... **CLC 27**
    See also CA 85-88; CBD; CD 5, 6; CWD;
    CWRI 5; DLB 13, 233; FW
Jelloun, Tahar ben 1944- .... **CLC 180**
    See Ben Jelloun, Tahar
    See also CA 162; CANR 100
Jemyma
    See Holley, Marietta
Jen, Gish .... **AAL; CLC 70, 198**
    See Jen, Lillian
    See also AMWC 2; CN 7; DLB 312
Jen, Lillian 1955-
    See Jen, Gish
    See also CA 135; CANR 89, 130
Jenkins, (John) Robin 1912- .... **CLC 52**
    See also CA 1-4R; CANR 1, 135; CN 1, 2,
    3, 4, 5, 6, 7; DLB 14, 271
Jennings, Elizabeth (Joan)
    1926-2001 .... **CLC 5, 14, 131**
    See also BRWS 5; CA 61-64; 200; CAAS
    5; CANR 8, 39, 66, 127; CP 1, 2, 3, 4, 5,
    6, 7; CWP; DLB 27; EWL 3; MTCW 1;
    SATA 66
Jennings, Waylon 1937-2002 .... **CLC 21**
Jensen, Johannes V(ilhelm)
    1873-1950 .... **TCLC 41**
    See also CA 170; DLB 214; EWL 3; RGWL
    3
Jensen, Laura (Linnea) 1948- .... **CLC 37**
    See also CA 103
Jerome, Saint 345-420 .... **CMLC 30**
    See also RGWL 3
Jerome, Jerome K(lapka)
    1859-1927 .... **TCLC 23**
    See also CA 119; 177; DLB 10, 34, 135;
    RGEL 2
Jerrold, Douglas William
    1803-1857 .... **NCLC 2**
    See also DLB 158, 159; RGEL 2

Jordan, June (Meyer)
1936-2002 .. **BLCS; CLC 5, 11, 23, 114; PC 38**
See also AAYA 2, 66; AFAW 1, 2; BW 2, 3; CA 33-36R; 206; CANR 25, 70, 114; CLR 10; CP 3, 4, 5, 6, 7; CWP; DAM MULT, POET; DLB 38; GLL 2; LAIT 5; MAICYA 1, 2; MTCW 1; SATA 4, 136; YAW

Jordan, Neil (Patrick) 1950- .... **CLC 110**
See also CA 124; 130; CANR 54; CN 4, 5, 6, 7; GLL 2; INT CA-130

Jordan, Pat(rick M.) 1941- .... **CLC 37**
See also CA 33-36R; CANR 121

Jorgensen, Ivar
See Ellison, Harlan (Jay)

Jorgenson, Ivar
See Silverberg, Robert

Joseph, George Ghevarughese .... **CLC 70**

Josephson, Mary
See O'Doherty, Brian

Josephus, Flavius c. 37-100 .... **CMLC 13**
See also AW 2; DLB 176

Josiah Allen's Wife
See Holley, Marietta

Josipovici, Gabriel (David) 1940- ...... **CLC 6, 43, 153**
See also CA 37-40R, 224; CAAE 224; CAAS 8; CANR 47, 84; CN 3, 4, 5, 6, 7; DLB 14, 319

Joubert, Joseph 1754-1824 .... **NCLC 9**

Jouve, Pierre Jean 1887-1976 .... **CLC 47**
See also CA 65-68; DLB 258; EWL 3

Jovine, Francesco 1902-1950 .... **TCLC 79**
See also DLB 264; EWL 3

Joyce, James (Augustine Aloysius)
1882-1941 .... **DC 16; PC 22; SSC 3, 26, 44, 64; TCLC 3, 8, 16, 35, 52, 159; WLC**
See also AAYA 42; BRW 7; BRWC 1; BRWR 1; BYA 11, 13; CA 104; 126; CD-BLB 1914-1945; DA; DA3; DAB; DAC; DAM MST, NOV, POET; DLB 10, 19, 36, 162, 247; EWL 3; EXPN; EXPS; LAIT 3; LMFS 1, 2; MTCW 1, 2; MTFW 2005; NFS 7; RGSF 2; SSFS 1, 19; TEA; WLIT 4

Jozsef, Attila 1905-1937 .... **TCLC 22**
See also CA 116; 230; CDWLB 4; DLB 215; EWL 3

Juana Ines de la Cruz, Sor
1651(?)-1695 ...... **HLCS 1; LC 5; PC 24**
See also DLB 305; FW; LAW; RGWL 2, 3; WLIT 1

Juana Inez de La Cruz, Sor
See Juana Ines de la Cruz, Sor

Judd, Cyril
See Kornbluth, C(yril) M.; Pohl, Frederik

Juenger, Ernst 1895-1998 .... **CLC 125**
See Junger, Ernst
See also CA 101; 167; CANR 21, 47, 106; DLB 56

Julian of Norwich 1342(?)-1416(?) . **LC 6, 52**
See also DLB 146; LMFS 1

Julius Caesar 100B.C.-44B.C.
See Caesar, Julius
See also CDWLB 1; DLB 211

Junger, Ernst
See Juenger, Ernst
See also CDWLB 2; EWL 3; RGWL 2, 3

Junger, Sebastian 1962- .... **CLC 109**
See also AAYA 28; CA 165; CANR 130; MTFW 2005

Juniper, Alex
See Hospital, Janette Turner

Junius
See Luxemburg, Rosa

Junzaburo, Nishiwaki
See Nishiwaki, Junzaburo
See also EWL 3

Just, Ward (Swift) 1935- .... **CLC 4, 27**
See also CA 25-28R; CANR 32, 87; CN 6, 7; INT CANR-32

Justice, Donald (Rodney)
1925-2004 .... **CLC 6, 19, 102; PC 64**
See also AMWS 7; CA 5-8R; 230; CANR 26, 54, 74, 121, 122; CP 1, 2, 3, 4, 5, 6, 7; CSW; DAM POET; DLBY 1983; EWL 3; INT CANR-26; MAL 5; MTCW 2; PFS 14; TCLE 1:1

Juvenal c. 60-c. 130 .... **CMLC 8**
See also AW 2; CDWLB 1; DLB 211; RGWL 2, 3

Juvenis
See Bourne, Randolph S(illiman)

K., Alice
See Knapp, Caroline

Kabakov, Sasha .... **CLC 59**

Kabir 1398(?)-1448(?) .... **LC 109; PC 56**
See also RGWL 2, 3

Kacew, Romain 1914-1980
See Gary, Romain
See also CA 108; 102

Kadare, Ismail 1936- .... **CLC 52, 190**
See also CA 161; EWL 3; RGWL 3

Kadohata, Cynthia (Lynn)
1956(?)- .... **CLC 59, 122**
See also CA 140; CANR 124; SATA 155

Kafka, Franz 1883-1924 ... **SSC 5, 29, 35, 60; TCLC 2, 6, 13, 29, 47, 53, 112; WLC**
See also AAYA 31; BPFB 2; CA 105; 126; CDWLB 2; DA; DA3; DAB; DAC; DAM MST, NOV; DLB 81; EW 9; EWL 3; EXPS; LATS 1:1; LMFS 2; MTCW 1, 2; MTFW 2005; NFS 7; RGSF 2; RGWL 2, 3; SFW 4; SSFS 3, 7, 12; TWA

Kahanovitsch, Pinkhes
See Der Nister

Kahn, Roger 1927- .... **CLC 30**
See also CA 25-28R; CANR 44, 69; DLB 171; SATA 37

Kain, Saul
See Sassoon, Siegfried (Lorraine)

Kaiser, Georg 1878-1945 .... **TCLC 9**
See also CA 106; 190; CDWLB 2; DLB 124; EWL 3; LMFS 2; RGWL 2, 3

Kaledin, Sergei .... **CLC 59**

Kaletski, Alexander 1946- .... **CLC 39**
See also CA 118; 143

Kalidasa fl. c. 400-455 .... **CMLC 9; PC 22**
See also RGWL 2, 3

Kallman, Chester (Simon)
1921-1975 .... **CLC 2**
See also CA 45-48; 53-56; CANR 3; CP 1, 2

Kaminsky, Melvin 1926-
See Brooks, Mel
See also CA 65-68; CANR 16; DFS 21

Kaminsky, Stuart M(elvin) 1934- ..... **CLC 59**
See also CA 73-76; CANR 29, 53, 89; CMW 4

Kamo no Chomei 1153(?)-1216 .... **CMLC 66**
See also DLB 203

Kamo no Nagaakira
See Kamo no Chomei

Kandinsky, Wassily 1866-1944 .... **TCLC 92**
See also AAYA 64; CA 118; 155

Kane, Francis
See Robbins, Harold

Kane, Henry 1918-
See Queen, Ellery
See also CA 156; CMW 4

Kane, Paul
See Simon, Paul (Frederick)

Kanin, Garson 1912-1999 .... **CLC 22**
See also AITN 1; CA 5-8R; 177; CAD; CANR 7, 78; DLB 7; IDFW 3, 4

Kaniuk, Yoram 1930- .... **CLC 19**
See also CA 134; DLB 299

Kant, Immanuel 1724-1804 ..... **NCLC 27, 67**
See also DLB 94

Kantor, MacKinlay 1904-1977 .... **CLC 7**
See also CA 61-64; 73-76; CANR 60, 63; CN 1, 2; DLB 9, 102; MAL 5; MTCW 2; RHW; TCWW 1, 2

Kanze Motokiyo
See Zeami

Kaplan, David Michael 1946- .... **CLC 50**
See also CA 187

Kaplan, James 1951- .... **CLC 59**
See also CA 135; CANR 121

Karadzic, Vuk Stefanovic
1787-1864 .... **NCLC 115**
See also CDWLB 4; DLB 147

Karageorge, Michael
See Anderson, Poul (William)

Karamzin, Nikolai Mikhailovich
1766-1826 .... **NCLC 3**
See also DLB 150; RGSF 2

Karapanou, Margarita 1946- .... **CLC 13**
See also CA 101

Karinthy, Frigyes 1887-1938 .... **TCLC 47**
See also CA 170; DLB 215; EWL 3

Karl, Frederick R(obert)
1927-2004 .... **CLC 34**
See also CA 5-8R; 226; CANR 3, 44, 143

Karr, Mary 1955- .... **CLC 188**
See also AMWS 11; CA 151; CANR 100; MTFW 2005; NCFS 5

Kastel, Warren
See Silverberg, Robert

Kataev, Evgeny Petrovich 1903-1942
See Petrov, Evgeny
See also CA 120

Kataphusin
See Ruskin, John

Katz, Steve 1935- .... **CLC 47**
See also CA 25-28R; CAAS 14, 64; CANR 12; CN 4, 5, 6, 7; DLBY 1983

Kauffman, Janet 1945- .... **CLC 42**
See also CA 117; CANR 43, 84; DLB 218; DLBY 1986

Kaufman, Bob (Garnell) 1925-1986 . **CLC 49**
See also BG 1:3; BW 1; CA 41-44R; 118; CANR 22; CP 1; DLB 16, 41

Kaufman, George S. 1889-1961 ...... **CLC 38; DC 17**
See also CA 108; 93-96; DAM DRAM; DFS 1, 10; DLB 7; INT CA-108; MTCW 2; MTFW 2005; RGAL 4; TUS

Kaufman, Moises 1964- .... **DC 26**
See also CA 211; DFS 22; MTFW 2005

Kaufman, Sue .... **CLC 3, 8**
See Barondess, Sue K(aufman)

Kavafis, Konstantinos Petrou 1863-1933
See Cavafy, C(onstantine) P(eter)
See also CA 104

Kavan, Anna 1901-1968 .... **CLC 5, 13, 82**
See also BRWS 7; CA 5-8R; CANR 6, 57; DLB 255; MTCW 1; RGEL 2; SFW 4

Kavanagh, Dan
See Barnes, Julian (Patrick)

Kavanagh, Julie 1952- .... **CLC 119**
See also CA 163

Kavanagh, Patrick (Joseph)
1904-1967 .... **CLC 22; PC 33**
See also BRWS 7; CA 123; 25-28R; DLB 15, 20; EWL 3; MTCW 1; RGEL 2

Keynes, John Maynard
1883-1946 .... **TCLC 64**
See also CA 114; 162, 163; DLBD 10;
MTCW 2; MTFW 2005

Khanshendel, Chiron
See Rose, Wendy

Khayyam, Omar 1048-1131 ... **CMLC 11; PC 8**
See Omar Khayyam
See also DA3; DAM POET; WLIT 6

Kherdian, David 1931- .... **CLC 6, 9**
See also AAYA 42; CA 21-24R, 192; CAAE 192; CAAS 2; CANR 39, 78; CLR 24; JRDA; LAIT 3; MAICYA 1, 2; SATA 16, 74; SATA-Essay 125

Khlebnikov, Velimir .... **TCLC 20**
See Khlebnikov, Viktor Vladimirovich
See also DLB 295; EW 10; EWL 3; RGWL 2, 3

Khlebnikov, Viktor Vladimirovich 1885-1922
See Khlebnikov, Velimir
See also CA 117; 217

Khodasevich, Vladislav (Felitsianovich)
1886-1939 .... **TCLC 15**
See also CA 115; DLB 317; EWL 3

Kielland, Alexander Lange
1849-1906 .... **TCLC 5**
See also CA 104

Kiely, Benedict 1919- ... **CLC 23, 43; SSC 58**
See also CA 1-4R; CANR 2, 84; CN 1, 2, 3, 4, 5, 6, 7; DLB 15, 319; TCLE 1:1

Kienzle, William X(avier)
1928-2001 .... **CLC 25**
See also CA 93-96; 203; CAAS 1; CANR 9, 31, 59, 111; CMW 4; DA3; DAM POP; INT CANR-31; MSW; MTCW 1, 2; MTFW 2005

Kierkegaard, Soren 1813-1855 ..... **NCLC 34, 78, 125**
See also DLB 300; EW 6; LMFS 2; RGWL 3; TWA

Kieslowski, Krzysztof 1941-1996 .... **CLC 120**
See also CA 147; 151

Killens, John Oliver 1916-1987 .... **CLC 10**
See also BW 2; CA 77-80; 123; CAAS 2; CANR 26; CN 1, 2, 3, 4; DLB 33; EWL 3

Killigrew, Anne 1660-1685 .... **LC 4, 73**
See also DLB 131

Killigrew, Thomas 1612-1683 .... **LC 57**
See also DLB 58; RGEL 2

Kim
See Simenon, Georges (Jacques Christian)

Kincaid, Jamaica 1949- ...... **BLC 2; CLC 43, 68, 137; SSC 72**
See also AAYA 13, 56; AFAW 2; AMWS 7; BRWS 7; BW 2, 3; CA 125; CANR 47, 59, 95, 133; CDALBS; CDWLB 3; CLR 63; CN 4, 5, 6, 7; DA3; DAM MULT, NOV; DLB 157, 227; DNFS 1; EWL 3; EXPS; FW; LATS 1:2; LMFS 2; MAL 5; MTCW 2; MTFW 2005; NCFS 1; NFS 3; SSFS 5, 7; TUS; WWE 1; YAW

King, Francis (Henry) 1923- .... **CLC 8, 53, 145**
See also CA 1-4R; CANR 1, 33, 86; CN 1, 2, 3, 4, 5, 6, 7; DAM NOV; DLB 15, 139; MTCW 1

King, Kennedy
See Brown, George Douglas

King, Martin Luther, Jr. 1929-1968 . **BLC 2; CLC 83; WLCS**
See also BW 2, 3; CA 25-28; CANR 27, 44; CAP 2; DA; DA3; DAB; DAC; DAM MST, MULT; LAIT 5; LATS 1:2; MTCW 1, 2; MTFW 2005; SATA 14

King, Stephen 1947- .... **CLC 12, 26, 37, 61, 113; SSC 17, 55**
See also AAYA 1, 17; AMWS 5; BEST 90:1; BPFB 2; CA 61-64; CANR 1, 30, 52, 76, 119, 134; CN 7; CPW; DA3; DAM NOV, POP; DLB 143; DLBY 1980; HGG; JRDA; LAIT 5; MTCW 1, 2; MTFW 2005; RGAL 4; SATA 9, 55, 161; SUFW 1, 2; WYAS 1; YAW

King, Stephen Edwin
See King, Stephen

King, Steve
See King, Stephen

King, Thomas 1943- .... **CLC 89, 171; NNAL**
See also CA 144; CANR 95; CCA 1; CN 6, 7; DAC; DAM MULT; DLB 175; SATA 96

Kingman, Lee .... **CLC 17**
See Natti, (Mary) Lee
See also CWRI 5; SAAS 3; SATA 1, 67

Kingsley, Charles 1819-1875 .... **NCLC 35**
See also CLR 77; DLB 21, 32, 163, 178, 190; FANT; MAICYA 2; MAICYAS 1; RGEL 2; WCH; YABC 2

Kingsley, Henry 1830-1876 .... **NCLC 107**
See also DLB 21, 230; RGEL 2

Kingsley, Sidney 1906-1995 .... **CLC 44**
See also CA 85-88; 147; CAD; DFS 14, 19; DLB 7; MAL 5; RGAL 4

Kingsolver, Barbara 1955- .... **CLC 55, 81, 130, 216**
See also AAYA 15; AMWS 7; CA 129; 134; CANR 60, 96, 133; CDALBS; CN 7; CPW; CSW; DA3; DAM POP; DLB 206; INT CA-134; LAIT 5; MTCW 2; MTFW 2005; NFS 5, 10, 12; RGAL 4; TCLE 1:1

Kingston, Maxine (Ting Ting) Hong
1940- .... **AAL; CLC 12, 19, 58, 121; WLCS**
See also AAYA 8, 55; AMWS 5; BPFB 2; CA 69-72; CANR 13, 38, 74, 87, 128; CDALBS; CN 6, 7; DA3; DAM MULT, NOV; DLB 173, 212, 312; DLBY 1980; EWL 3; FL 1:6; FW; INT CANR-13; LAIT 5; MAL 5; MAWW; MTCW 1, 2; MTFW 2005; NFS 6; RGAL 4; SATA 53; SSFS 3; TCWW 2

Kinnell, Galway 1927- ..... **CLC 1, 2, 3, 5, 13, 29, 129; PC 26**
See also AMWS 3; CA 9-12R; CANR 10, 34, 66, 116, 138; CP 1, 2, 3, 4, 5, 6, 7; DLB 5; DLBY 1987; EWL 3; INT CANR-34; MAL 5; MTCW 1, 2; MTFW 2005; PAB; PFS 9; RGAL 4; TCLE 1:1; WP

Kinsella, Thomas 1928- .... **CLC 4, 19, 138**
See also BRWS 5; CA 17-20R; CANR 15, 122; CP 1, 2, 3, 4, 5, 6, 7; DLB 27; EWL 3; MTCW 1, 2; MTFW 2005; RGEL 2; TEA

Kinsella, W(illiam) P(atrick) 1935- . **CLC 27, 43, 166**
See also AAYA 7, 60; BPFB 2; CA 97-100; 222; CAAE 222; CAAS 7; CANR 21, 35, 66, 75, 129; CN 4, 5, 6, 7; CPW; DAC; DAM NOV, POP; FANT; INT CANR-21; LAIT 5; MTCW 1, 2; MTFW 2005; NFS 15; RGSF 2

Kinsey, Alfred C(harles)
1894-1956 .... **TCLC 91**
See also CA 115; 170; MTCW 2

Kipling, (Joseph) Rudyard 1865-1936 . **PC 3; SSC 5, 54; TCLC 8, 17, 167; WLC**
See also AAYA 32; BRW 6; BRWC 1, 2; BYA 4; CA 105; 120; CANR 33; CDBLB 1890-1914; CLR 39, 65; CWRI 5; DA; DA3; DAB; DAC; DAM MST, POET; DLB 19, 34, 141, 156; EWL 3; EXPS; FANT; LAIT 3; LMFS 1; MAICYA 1, 2; MTCW 1, 2; MTFW 2005; NFS 21; PFS 22; RGEL 2; RGSF 2; SATA 100; SFW 4; SSFS 8, 21; SUFW 1; TEA; WCH; WLIT 4; YABC 2

Kircher, Athanasius 1602-1680 .... **LC 121**
See also DLB 164

Kirk, Russell (Amos) 1918-1994 .. **TCLC 119**
See also AITN 1; CA 1-4R; 145; CAAS 9; CANR 1, 20, 60; HGG; INT CANR-20; MTCW 1, 2

Kirkham, Dinah
See Card, Orson Scott

Kirkland, Caroline M. 1801-1864 . **NCLC 85**
See also DLB 3, 73, 74, 250, 254; DLBD 13

Kirkup, James 1918- .... **CLC 1**
See also CA 1-4R; CAAS 4; CANR 2; CP 1, 2, 3, 4, 5, 6, 7; DLB 27; SATA 12

Kirkwood, James 1930(?)-1989 .... **CLC 9**
See also AITN 2; CA 1-4R; 128; CANR 6, 40; GLL 2

Kirsch, Sarah 1935- .... **CLC 176**
See also CA 178; CWW 2; DLB 75; EWL 3

Kirshner, Sidney
See Kingsley, Sidney

Kis, Danilo 1935-1989 .... **CLC 57**
See also CA 109; 118; 129; CANR 61; CDWLB 4; DLB 181; EWL 3; MTCW 1; RGSF 2; RGWL 2, 3

Kissinger, Henry A(lfred) 1923- ..... **CLC 137**
See also CA 1-4R; CANR 2, 33, 66, 109; MTCW 1

Kivi, Aleksis 1834-1872 .... **NCLC 30**

Kizer, Carolyn (Ashley) 1925- ... **CLC 15, 39, 80; PC 66**
See also CA 65-68; CAAS 5; CANR 24, 70, 134; CP 1, 2, 3, 4, 5, 6, 7; CWP; DAM POET; DLB 5, 169; EWL 3; MAL 5; MTCW 2; MTFW 2005; PFS 18; TCLE 1:1

Klabund 1890-1928 .... **TCLC 44**
See also CA 162; DLB 66

Klappert, Peter 1942- .... **CLC 57**
See also CA 33-36R; CSW; DLB 5

Klein, A(braham) M(oses)
1909-1972 .... **CLC 19**
See also CA 101; 37-40R; CP 1; DAB; DAC; DAM MST; DLB 68; EWL 3; RGEL 2

Klein, Joe
See Klein, Joseph

Klein, Joseph 1946- .... **CLC 154**
See also CA 85-88; CANR 55

Klein, Norma 1938-1989 .... **CLC 30**
See also AAYA 2, 35; BPFB 2; BYA 6, 7, 8; CA 41-44R; 128; CANR 15, 37; CLR 2, 19; INT CANR-15; JRDA; MAICYA 1, 2; SAAS 1; SATA 7, 57; WYA; YAW

Klein, T(heodore) E(ibon) D(onald)
1947- .... **CLC 34**
See also CA 119; CANR 44, 75; HGG

Kleist, Heinrich von 1777-1811 ...... **NCLC 2, 37; SSC 22**
See also CDWLB 2; DAM DRAM; DLB 90; EW 5; RGSF 2; RGWL 2, 3

Klima, Ivan 1931- .... **CLC 56, 172**
See also CA 25-28R; CANR 17, 50, 91; CDWLB 4; CWW 2; DAM NOV; DLB 232; EWL 3; RGWL 3

Klimentov, Andrei Platonovich
See Klimentov, Andrei Platonovich

Klimentov, Andrei Platonovich
1899-1951 .... **SSC 42; TCLC 14**
See Platonov, Andrei Platonovich; Platonov, Andrey Platonovich
See also CA 108; 232

Kubrick, Stanley 1928-1999 .... **CLC 16;**
TCLC 112
See also AAYA 30; CA 81-84; 177; CANR
33; DLB 26

Kumin, Maxine (Winokur) 1925- ..... **CLC 5,**
13, 28, 164; PC 15
See also AITN 2; AMWS 4; ANW; CA
1-4R; CAAS 8; CANR 1, 21, 69, 115,
140; CP 2, 3, 4, 5, 6, 7; CWP; DA3; DAM
POET; DLB 5; EWL 3; EXPP; MTCW 1,
2; MTFW 2005; PAB; PFS 18; SATA 12

Kundera, Milan 1929- . **CLC 4, 9, 19, 32, 68,**
115, 135; SSC 24
See also AAYA 2, 62; BPFB 2; CA 85-88;
CANR 19, 52, 74, 144; CDWLB 4; CWW
2; DA3; DAM NOV; DLB 232; EW 13;
EWL 3; MTCW 1, 2; MTFW 2005; NFS
18; RGSF 2; RGWL 3; SSFS 18

Kunene, Mazisi (Raymond) 1930- ... **CLC 85**
See also BW 1, 3; CA 125; CANR 81; CP
1, 7; DLB 117

Kung, Hans .... **CLC 130**
See Kung, Hans

Kung, Hans 1928-
See Kung, Hans
See also CA 53-56; CANR 66, 134; MTCW
1, 2; MTFW 2005

Kunikida Doppo 1869(?)-1908
See Doppo, Kunikida
See also DLB 180; EWL 3

Kunitz, Stanley (Jasspon) 1905- .. **CLC 6, 11,**
14, 148; PC 19
See also AMWS 3; CA 41-44R; CANR 26,
57, 98; CP 1, 2, 3, 4, 5, 6, 7; DA3; DLB
48; INT CANR-26; MAL 5; MTCW 1, 2;
MTFW 2005; PFS 11; RGAL 4

Kunze, Reiner 1933- .... **CLC 10**
See also CA 93-96; CWW 2; DLB 75; EWL
3

Kuprin, Aleksander Ivanovich
1870-1938 .... **TCLC 5**
See Kuprin, Aleksandr Ivanovich; Kuprin,
Alexandr Ivanovich
See also CA 104; 182

Kuprin, Aleksandr Ivanovich
See Kuprin, Aleksander Ivanovich
See also DLB 295

Kuprin, Alexandr Ivanovich
See Kuprin, Aleksander Ivanovich
See also EWL 3

Kureishi, Hanif 1954- .. **CLC 64, 135; DC 26**
See also BRWS 11; CA 139; CANR 113;
CBD; CD 5, 6; CN 6, 7; DLB 194, 245;
GLL 2; IDFW 4; WLIT 4; WWE 1

Kurosawa, Akira 1910-1998 ..... **CLC 16, 119**
See also AAYA 11, 64; CA 101; 170; CANR
46; DAM MULT

Kushner, Tony 1956- .... **CLC 81, 203; DC 10**
See also AAYA 61; AMWS 9; CA 144;
CAD; CANR 74, 130; CD 5, 6; DA3;
DAM DRAM; DFS 5; DLB 228; EWL 3;
GLL 1; LAIT 5; MAL 5; MTCW 2;
MTFW 2005; RGAL 4; SATA 160

Kuttner, Henry 1915-1958 .... **TCLC 10**
See also CA 107; 157; DLB 8; FANT;
SCFW 1, 2; SFW 4

Kutty, Madhavi
See Das, Kamala

Kuzma, Greg 1944- .... **CLC 7**
See also CA 33-36R; CANR 70

Kuzmin, Mikhail (Alekseevich)
1872(?)-1936 .... **TCLC 40**
See also CA 170; DLB 295; EWL 3

Kyd, Thomas 1558-1594 .... **DC 3; LC 22**
See also BRW 1; DAM DRAM; DFS 21;
DLB 62; IDTP; LMFS 1; RGEL 2; TEA;
WLIT 3

Kyprianos, Iossif
See Samarakis, Antonis

L. S.
See Stephen, Sir Leslie

Laʒamon
See Layamon
See also DLB 146

Labe, Louise 1521-1566 .... **LC 120**

Labrunie, Gerard
See Nerval, Gerard de

La Bruyere, Jean de 1645-1696 .... **LC 17**
See also DLB 268; EW 3; GFL Beginnings
to 1789

Lacan, Jacques (Marie Emile)
1901-1981 .... **CLC 75**
See also CA 121; 104; DLB 296; EWL 3;
TWA

Laclos, Pierre-Ambroise Francois
1741-1803 .... **NCLC 4, 87**
See also DLB 313; EW 4; GFL Beginnings
to 1789; RGWL 2, 3

Lacolere, Francois
See Aragon, Louis

La Colere, Francois
See Aragon, Louis

La Deshabilleuse
See Simenon, Georges (Jacques Christian)

Lady Gregory
See Gregory, Lady Isabella Augusta (Persse)

Lady of Quality, A
See Bagnold, Enid

La Fayette, Marie-(Madelaine Pioche de la
Vergne) 1634-1693 .... **LC 2**
See Lafayette, Marie-Madeleine
See also GFL Beginnings to 1789; RGWL
2, 3

Lafayette, Marie-Madeleine
See La Fayette, Marie-(Madelaine Pioche
de la Vergne)
See also DLB 268

Lafayette, Rene
See Hubbard, L(afayette) Ron(ald)

La Flesche, Francis 1857(?)-1932 ...... **NNAL**
See also CA 144; CANR 83; DLB 175

La Fontaine, Jean de 1621-1695 .... **LC 50**
See also DLB 268; EW 3; GFL Beginnings
to 1789; MAICYA 1, 2; RGWL 2, 3;
SATA 18

Laforgue, Jules 1860-1887 . **NCLC 5, 53; PC**
14; SSC 20
See also DLB 217; EW 7; GFL 1789 to the
Present; RGWL 2, 3

Lagerkvist, Paer (Fabian)
1891-1974 ..... **CLC 7, 10, 13, 54; TCLC**
144
See Lagerkvist, Par
See also CA 85-88; 49-52; DA3; DAM
DRAM, NOV; MTCW 1, 2; MTFW 2005;
TWA

Lagerkvist, Par .... **SSC 12**
See Lagerkvist, Paer (Fabian)
See also DLB 259; EW 10; EWL 3; RGSF
2; RGWL 2, 3

Lagerloef, Selma (Ottiliana Lovisa)
.... **TCLC 4, 36**
See Lagerlof, Selma (Ottiliana Lovisa)
See also CA 108; MTCW 2

Lagerlof, Selma (Ottiliana Lovisa)
1858-1940
See Lagerloef, Selma (Ottiliana Lovisa)
See also CA 188; CLR 7; DLB 259; RGWL
2, 3; SATA 15; SSFS 18

La Guma, (Justin) Alex(ander)
1925-1985 . **BLCS; CLC 19; TCLC 140**
See also AFW; BW 1, 3; CA 49-52; 118;
CANR 25, 81; CDWLB 3; CN 1, 2, 3;
CP 1; DAM NOV; DLB 117, 225; EWL
3; MTCW 1, 2; MTFW 2005; WLIT 2;
WWE 1

Laidlaw, A. K.
See Grieve, C(hristopher) M(urray)

Lainez, Manuel Mujica
See Mujica Lainez, Manuel
See also HW 1

Laing, R(onald) D(avid) 1927-1989 . **CLC 95**
See also CA 107; 129; CANR 34; MTCW 1

Laishley, Alex
See Booth, Martin

Lamartine, Alphonse (Marie Louis Prat) de
1790-1869 .... **NCLC 11; PC 16**
See also DAM POET; DLB 217; GFL 1789
to the Present; RGWL 2, 3

Lamb, Charles 1775-1834 ..... **NCLC 10, 113;**
WLC
See also BRW 4; CDBLB 1789-1832; DA;
DAB; DAC; DAM MST; DLB 93, 107,
163; RGEL 2; SATA 17; TEA

Lamb, Lady Caroline 1785-1828 ... **NCLC 38**
See also DLB 116

Lamb, Mary Ann 1764-1847 .... **NCLC 125**
See also DLB 163; SATA 17

Lame Deer 1903(?)-1976 .... **NNAL**
See also CA 69-72

Lamming, George (William) 1927- ... **BLC 2;**
CLC 2, 4, 66, 144
See also BW 2, 3; CA 85-88; CANR 26,
76; CDWLB 3; CN 1, 2, 3, 4, 5, 6, 7; CP
1; DAM MULT; DLB 125; EWL 3;
MTCW 1, 2; MTFW 2005; NFS 15;
RGEL 2

L'Amour, Louis (Dearborn)
1908-1988 .... **CLC 25, 55**
See also AAYA 16; AITN 2; BEST 89:2;
BPFB 2; CA 1-4R; 125; CANR 3, 25, 40;
CPW; DA3; DAM NOV, POP; DLB 206;
DLBY 1980; MTCW 1, 2; MTFW 2005;
RGAL 4; TCWW 1, 2

Lampedusa, Giuseppe (Tomasi) di
.... **TCLC 13**
See Tomasi di Lampedusa, Giuseppe
See also CA 164; EW 11; MTCW 2; MTFW
2005; RGWL 2, 3

Lampman, Archibald 1861-1899 ... **NCLC 25**
See also DLB 92; RGEL 2; TWA

Lancaster, Bruce 1896-1963 .... **CLC 36**
See also CA 9-10; CANR 70; CAP 1; SATA
9

Lanchester, John 1962- .... **CLC 99**
See also CA 194; DLB 267

Landau, Mark Alexandrovich
See Aldanov, Mark (Alexandrovich)

Landau-Aldanov, Mark Alexandrovich
See Aldanov, Mark (Alexandrovich)

Landis, Jerry
See Simon, Paul (Frederick)

Landis, John 1950- .... **CLC 26**
See also CA 112; 122; CANR 128

Landolfi, Tommaso 1908-1979 .... **CLC 11, 49**
See also CA 127; 117; DLB 177; EWL 3

Landon, Letitia Elizabeth
1802-1838 .... **NCLC 15**
See also DLB 96

Landor, Walter Savage
1775-1864 .... **NCLC 14**
See also BRW 4; DLB 93, 107; RGEL 2

Landwirth, Heinz 1927-
See Lind, Jakov
See also CA 9-12R; CANR 7

Lane, Patrick 1939- .... **CLC 25**
See also CA 97-100; CANR 54; CP 3, 4, 5,
6, 7; DAM POET; DLB 53; INT CA-97-
100

Lang, Andrew 1844-1912 .... **TCLC 16**
See also CA 114; 137; CANR 85; CLR 101;
DLB 98, 141, 184; FANT; MAICYA 1, 2;
RGEL 2; SATA 16; WCH

Lang, Fritz 1890-1976 .... **CLC 20, 103**
See also AAYA 65; CA 77-80; 69-72;
CANR 30

Leblanc, Maurice (Marie Emile)
1864-1941 .... **TCLC 49**
See also CA 110; CMW 4

Lebowitz, Fran(ces Ann) 1951(?)- ... **CLC 11, 36**
See also CA 81-84; CANR 14, 60, 70; INT CANR-14; MTCW 1

Lebrecht, Peter
See Tieck, (Johann) Ludwig

le Carre, John .... **CLC 3, 5, 9, 15, 28**
See Cornwell, David (John Moore)
See also AAYA 42; BEST 89:4; BPFB 2; BRWS 2; CDBLB 1960 to Present; CMW 4; CN 1, 2, 3, 4, 5, 6, 7; CPW; DLB 87; EWL 3; MSW; MTCW 2; RGEL 2; TEA

Le Clezio, J(ean) M(arie) G(ustave)
1940- .... **CLC 31, 155**
See also CA 116; 128; CWW 2; DLB 83; EWL 3; GFL 1789 to the Present; RGSF 2

Leconte de Lisle, Charles-Marie-Rene
1818-1894 .... **NCLC 29**
See also DLB 217; EW 6; GFL 1789 to the Present

Le Coq, Monsieur
See Simenon, Georges (Jacques Christian)

Leduc, Violette 1907-1972 .... **CLC 22**
See also CA 13-14; 33-36R; CANR 69; CAP 1; EWL 3; GFL 1789 to the Present; GLL 1

Ledwidge, Francis 1887(?)-1917 .... **TCLC 23**
See also CA 123; 203; DLB 20

Lee, Andrea 1953- .... **BLC 2; CLC 36**
See also BW 1, 3; CA 125; CANR 82; DAM MULT

Lee, Andrew
See Auchincloss, Louis (Stanton)

Lee, Chang-rae 1965- .... **CLC 91**
See also CA 148; CANR 89; CN 7; DLB 312; LATS 1:2

Lee, Don L. .... **CLC 2**
See Madhubuti, Haki R.
See also CP 2, 3, 4

Lee, George W(ashington)
1894-1976 .... **BLC 2; CLC 52**
See also BW 1; CA 125; CANR 83; DAM MULT; DLB 51

Lee, (Nelle) Harper 1926- . **CLC 12, 60, 194; WLC**
See also AAYA 13; AMWS 8; BPFB 2; BYA 3; CA 13-16R; CANR 51, 128; CDALB 1941-1968; CSW; DA; DA3; DAB; DAC; DAM MST, NOV; DLB 6; EXPN; LAIT 3; MAL 5; MTCW 1, 2; MTFW 2005; NFS 2; SATA 11; WYA; YAW

Lee, Helen Elaine 1959(?)- .... **CLC 86**
See also CA 148

Lee, John .... **CLC 70**

Lee, Julian
See Latham, Jean Lee

Lee, Larry
See Lee, Lawrence

Lee, Laurie 1914-1997 .... **CLC 90**
See also CA 77-80; 158; CANR 33, 73; CP 1, 2, 3, 4; CPW; DAB; DAM POP; DLB 27; MTCW 1; RGEL 2

Lee, Lawrence 1941-1990 .... **CLC 34**
See also CA 131; CANR 43

Lee, Li-Young 1957- .... **CLC 164; PC 24**
See also AMWS 15; CA 153; CANR 118; CP 7; DLB 165, 312; LMFS 2; PFS 11, 15, 17

Lee, Manfred B(ennington)
1905-1971 .... **CLC 11**
See Queen, Ellery
See also CA 1-4R; 29-32R; CANR 2; CMW 4; DLB 137

Lee, Nathaniel 1645(?)-1692 .... **LC 103**
See also DLB 80; RGEL 2

Lee, Shelton Jackson 1957(?)- .. **BLCS; CLC 105**
See Lee, Spike
See also BW 2, 3; CA 125; CANR 42; DAM MULT

Lee, Spike
See Lee, Shelton Jackson
See also AAYA 4, 29

Lee, Stan 1922- .... **CLC 17**
See also AAYA 5, 49; CA 108; 111; CANR 129; INT CA-111; MTFW 2005

Lee, Tanith 1947- .... **CLC 46**
See also AAYA 15; CA 37-40R; CANR 53, 102, 145; DLB 261; FANT; SATA 8, 88, 134; SFW 4; SUFW 1, 2; YAW

Lee, Vernon .... **SSC 33; TCLC 5**
See Paget, Violet
See also DLB 57, 153, 156, 174, 178; GLL 1; SUFW 1

Lee, William
See Burroughs, William S(eward)
See also GLL 1

Lee, Willy
See Burroughs, William S(eward)
See also GLL 1

Lee-Hamilton, Eugene (Jacob)
1845-1907 .... **TCLC 22**
See also CA 117; 234

Leet, Judith 1935- .... **CLC 11**
See also CA 187

Le Fanu, Joseph Sheridan
1814-1873 .... **NCLC 9, 58; SSC 14, 84**
See also CMW 4; DA3; DAM POP; DLB 21, 70, 159, 178; GL 3; HGG; RGEL 2; RGSF 2; SUFW 1

Leffland, Ella 1931- .... **CLC 19**
See also CA 29-32R; CANR 35, 78, 82; DLBY 1984; INT CANR-35; SATA 65

Leger, Alexis
See Leger, (Marie-Rene Auguste) Alexis Saint-Leger

Leger, (Marie-Rene Auguste) Alexis Saint-Leger 1887-1975 .. **CLC 4, 11, 46; PC 23**
See Perse, Saint-John; Saint-John Perse
See also CA 13-16R; 61-64; CANR 43; DAM POET; MTCW 1

Leger, Saintleger
See Leger, (Marie-Rene Auguste) Alexis Saint-Leger

Le Guin, Ursula K(roeber) 1929- ..... **CLC 8, 13, 22, 45, 71, 136; SSC 12, 69**
See also AAYA 9, 27; AITN 1; BPFB 2; BYA 5, 8, 11, 14; CA 21-24R; CANR 9, 32, 52, 74, 132; CDALB 1968-1988; CLR 3, 28, 91; CN 2, 3, 4, 5, 6, 7; CPW; DA3; DAB; DAC; DAM MST, POP; DLB 8, 52, 256, 275; EXPS; FANT; FW; INT CANR-32; JRDA; LAIT 5; MAICYA 1, 2; MAL 5; MTCW 1, 2; MTFW 2005; NFS 6, 9; SATA 4, 52, 99, 149; SCFW 1, 2; SFW 4; SSFS 2; SUFW 1, 2; WYA; YAW

Lehmann, Rosamond (Nina)
1901-1990 .... **CLC 5**
See also CA 77-80; 131; CANR 8, 73; CN 1, 2, 3, 4; DLB 15; MTCW 2; RGEL 2; RHW

Leiber, Fritz (Reuter, Jr.)
1910-1992 .... **CLC 25**
See also AAYA 65; BPFB 2; CA 45-48; 139; CANR 2, 40, 86; CN 2, 3, 4, 5; DLB 8; FANT; HGG; MTCW 1, 2; MTFW 2005; SATA 45; SATA-Obit 73; SCFW 1, 2; SFW 4; SUFW 1, 2

Leibniz, Gottfried Wilhelm von
1646-1716 .... **LC 35**
See also DLB 168

Leimbach, Martha 1963-
See Leimbach, Marti
See also CA 130

Leimbach, Marti .... **CLC 65**
See Leimbach, Martha

Leino, Eino .... **TCLC 24**
See Lonnbohm, Armas Eino Leopold
See also EWL 3

Leiris, Michel (Julien) 1901-1990 ..... **CLC 61**
See also CA 119; 128; 132; EWL 3; GFL 1789 to the Present

Leithauser, Brad 1953- .... **CLC 27**
See also CA 107; CANR 27, 81; CP 7; DLB 120, 282

le Jars de Gournay, Marie
See de Gournay, Marie le Jars

Lelchuk, Alan 1938- .... **CLC 5**
See also CA 45-48; CAAS 20; CANR 1, 70; CN 3, 4, 5, 6, 7

Lem, Stanislaw 1921- ...... **CLC 8, 15, 40, 149**
See also CA 105; CAAS 1; CANR 32; CWW 2; MTCW 1; SCFW 1, 2; SFW 4

Lemann, Nancy (Elise) 1956- .... **CLC 39**
See also CA 118; 136; CANR 121

Lemonnier, (Antoine Louis) Camille
1844-1913 .... **TCLC 22**
See also CA 121

Lenau, Nikolaus 1802-1850 .... **NCLC 16**

L'Engle, Madeleine (Camp Franklin)
1918- .... **CLC 12**
See also AAYA 28; AITN 2; BPFB 2; BYA 2, 4, 5, 7; CA 1-4R; CANR 3, 21, 39, 66, 107; CLR 1, 14, 57; CPW; CWRI 5; DA3; DAM POP; DLB 52; JRDA; MAICYA 1, 2; MTCW 1, 2; MTFW 2005; SAAS 15; SATA 1, 27, 75, 128; SFW 4; WYA; YAW

Lengyel, Jozsef 1896-1975 .... **CLC 7**
See also CA 85-88; 57-60; CANR 71; RGSF 2

Lenin 1870-1924
See Lenin, V. I.
See also CA 121; 168

Lenin, V. I. .... **TCLC 67**
See Lenin

Lennon, John (Ono) 1940-1980 .. **CLC 12, 35**
See also CA 102; SATA 114

Lennox, Charlotte Ramsay
1729(?)-1804 .... **NCLC 23, 134**
See also DLB 39; RGEL 2

Lentricchia, Frank, (Jr.) 1940- .... **CLC 34**
See also CA 25-28R; CANR 19, 106; DLB 246

Lenz, Gunter .... **CLC 65**

Lenz, Jakob Michael Reinhold
1751-1792 .... **LC 100**
See also DLB 94; RGWL 2, 3

Lenz, Siegfried 1926- .... **CLC 27; SSC 33**
See also CA 89-92; CANR 80; CWW 2; DLB 75; EWL 3; RGSF 2; RGWL 2, 3

Leon, David
See Jacob, (Cyprien-)Max

Leonard, Elmore (John, Jr.) 1925- . **CLC 28, 34, 71, 120**
See also AAYA 22, 59; AITN 1; BEST 89:1, 90:4; BPFB 2; CA 81-84; CANR 12, 28, 53, 76, 96, 133; CMW 4; CN 5, 6, 7; CPW; DA3; DAM POP; DLB 173, 226; INT CANR-28; MSW; MTCW 1, 2; MTFW 2005; RGAL 4; SATA 163; TCWW 1, 2

Leonard, Hugh .... **CLC 19**
See Byrne, John Keyes
See also CBD; CD 5, 6; DFS 13; DLB 13

Leonov, Leonid (Maximovich)
1899-1994 .... **CLC 92**
See Leonov, Leonid Maksimovich
See also CA 129; CANR 76; DAM NOV; EWL 3; MTCW 1, 2; MTFW 2005

Limonov, Edward 1944- .... **CLC 67**
See Limonov, Eduard
See also CA 137

Lin, Frank
See Atherton, Gertrude (Franklin Horn)

Lin, Yutang 1895-1976 .... **TCLC 149**
See also CA 45-48; 65-68; CANR 2; RGAL
4

Lincoln, Abraham 1809-1865 .... **NCLC 18**
See also LAIT 2

Lind, Jakov .... **CLC 1, 2, 4, 27, 82**
See Landwirth, Heinz
See also CAAS 4; DLB 299; EWL 3

Lindbergh, Anne (Spencer) Morrow
1906-2001 .... **CLC 82**
See also BPFB 2; CA 17-20R; 193; CANR
16, 73; DAM NOV; MTCW 1, 2; MTFW
2005; SATA 33; SATA-Obit 125; TUS

Lindsay, David 1878(?)-1945 .... **TCLC 15**
See also CA 113; 187; DLB 255; FANT;
SFW 4; SUFW 1

Lindsay, (Nicholas) Vachel
1879-1931 .... **PC 23; TCLC 17; WLC**
See also AMWS 1; CA 114; 135; CANR
79; CDALB 1865-1917; DA; DA3; DAC;
DAM MST, POET; DLB 54; EWL 3;
EXPP; MAL 5; RGAL 4; SATA 40; WP

Linke-Poot
See Doeblin, Alfred

Linney, Romulus 1930- .... **CLC 51**
See also CA 1-4R; CAD; CANR 40, 44,
79; CD 5, 6; CSW; RGAL 4

Linton, Eliza Lynn 1822-1898 .... **NCLC 41**
See also DLB 18

Li Po 701-763 .... **CMLC 2; PC 29**
See also PFS 20; WP

Lipsius, Justus 1547-1606 .... **LC 16**

Lipsyte, Robert (Michael) 1938- ...... **CLC 21**
See also AAYA 7, 45; CA 17-20R; CANR
8, 57; CLR 23, 76; DA; DAC; DAM
MST, NOV; JRDA; LAIT 5; MAICYA 1,
2; SATA 5, 68, 113, 161; WYA; YAW

Lish, Gordon (Jay) 1934- .. **CLC 45; SSC 18**
See also CA 113; 117; CANR 79; DLB 130;
INT CA-117

Lispector, Clarice 1925(?)-1977 .... **CLC 43;**
HLCS 2; SSC 34
See also CA 139; 116; CANR 71; CDWLB
3; DLB 113, 307; DNFS 1; EWL 3; FW;
HW 2; LAW; RGSF 2; RGWL 2, 3; WLIT
1

Littell, Robert 1935(?)- .... **CLC 42**
See also CA 109; 112; CANR 64, 115;
CMW 4

Little, Malcolm 1925-1965
See Malcolm X
See also BW 1, 3; CA 125; 111; CANR 82;
DA; DA3; DAB; DAC; DAM MST,
MULT; MTCW 1, 2; MTFW 2005

Littlewit, Humphrey Gent.
See Lovecraft, H(oward) P(hillips)

Litwos
See Sienkiewicz, Henryk (Adam Alexander
Pius)

Liu, E. 1857-1909 .... **TCLC 15**
See also CA 115; 190

Lively, Penelope 1933- .... **CLC 32, 50**
See also BPFB 2; CA 41-44R; CANR 29,
67, 79, 131; CLR 7; CN 5, 6, 7; CWRI 5;
DAM NOV; DLB 14, 161, 207; FANT;
JRDA; MAICYA 1, 2; MTCW 1, 2;
MTFW 2005; SATA 7, 60, 101, 164; TEA

Lively, Penelope Margaret
See Lively, Penelope

Livesay, Dorothy (Kathleen)
1909-1996 .... **CLC 4, 15, 79**
See also AITN 2; CA 25-28R; CAAS 8;
CANR 36, 67; CP 1, 2, 3, 4; DAC; DAM
MST, POET; DLB 68; FW; MTCW 1;
RGEL 2; TWA

Livy c. 59B.C.-c. 12 .... **CMLC 11**
See also AW 2; CDWLB 1; DLB 211;
RGWL 2, 3

Lizardi, Jose Joaquin Fernandez de
1776-1827 .... **NCLC 30**
See also LAW

Llewellyn, Richard
See Llewellyn Lloyd, Richard Dafydd Viv-
ian
See also DLB 15

Llewellyn Lloyd, Richard Dafydd Vivian
1906-1983 .... **CLC 7, 80**
See Llewellyn, Richard
See also CA 53-56; 111; CANR 7, 71;
SATA 11; SATA-Obit 37

Llosa, (Jorge) Mario (Pedro) Vargas
See Vargas Llosa, (Jorge) Mario (Pedro)
See also RGWL 3

Llosa, Mario Vargas
See Vargas Llosa, (Jorge) Mario (Pedro)

Lloyd, Manda
See Mander, (Mary) Jane

Lloyd Webber, Andrew 1948-
See Webber, Andrew Lloyd
See also AAYA 1, 38; CA 116; 149; DAM
DRAM; SATA 56

Llull, Ramon c. 1235-c. 1316 .... **CMLC 12**

Lobb, Ebenezer
See Upward, Allen

Locke, Alain (Le Roy)
1886-1954 .... **BLCS; HR 1:3; TCLC 43**
See also AMWS 14; BW 1, 3; CA 106; 124;
CANR 79; DLB 51; LMFS 2; MAL 5;
RGAL 4

Locke, John 1632-1704 .... **LC 7, 35**
See also DLB 31, 101, 213, 252; RGEL 2;
WLIT 3

Locke-Elliott, Sumner
See Elliott, Sumner Locke

Lockhart, John Gibson 1794-1854 .. **NCLC 6**
See also DLB 110, 116, 144

Lockridge, Ross (Franklin), Jr.
1914-1948 .... **TCLC 111**
See also CA 108; 145; CANR 79; DLB 143;
DLBY 1980; MAL 5; RGAL 4; RHW

Lockwood, Robert
See Johnson, Robert

Lodge, David (John) 1935- .... **CLC 36, 141**
See also BEST 90:1; BRWS 4; CA 17-20R;
CANR 19, 53, 92, 139; CN 1, 2, 3, 4, 5,
6, 7; CPW; DAM POP; DLB 14, 194;
EWL 3; INT CANR-19; MTCW 1, 2;
MTFW 2005

Lodge, Thomas 1558-1625 .... **LC 41**
See also DLB 172; RGEL 2

Loewinsohn, Ron(ald William)
1937- .... **CLC 52**
See also CA 25-28R; CANR 71; CP 1, 2, 3,
4

Logan, Jake
See Smith, Martin Cruz

Logan, John (Burton) 1923-1987 .... **CLC 5**
See also CA 77-80; 124; CANR 45; CP 1,
2, 3, 4; DLB 5

Lo Kuan-chung 1330(?)-1400(?) .... **LC 12**

Lombard, Nap
See Johnson, Pamela Hansford

Lombard, Peter 1100(?)-1160(?) ... **CMLC 72**

London, Jack 1876-1916 .. **SSC 4, 49; TCLC**
9, 15, 39; WLC
See London, John Griffith
See also AAYA 13; AITN 2; AMW; BPFB
2; BYA 4, 13; CDALB 1865-1917; DLB

8, 12, 78, 212; EWL 3; EXPS; LAIT 3;
MAL 5; NFS 8; RGAL 4; RGSF 2; SATA
18; SFW 4; SSFS 7; TCWW 1, 2; TUS;
WYA; YAW

London, John Griffith 1876-1916
See London, Jack
See also CA 110; 119; CANR 73; DA; DA3;
DAB; DAC; DAM MST, NOV; JRDA;
MAICYA 1, 2; MTCW 1, 2; MTFW 2005;
NFS 19

Long, Emmett
See Leonard, Elmore (John, Jr.)

Longbaugh, Harry
See Goldman, William (W.)

Longfellow, Henry Wadsworth
1807-1882 .... **NCLC 2, 45, 101, 103; PC**
30; WLCS
See also AMW; AMWR 2; CDALB 1640-
1865; CLR 99; DA; DA3; DAB; DAC;
DAM MST, POET; DLB 1, 59, 235;
EXPP; PAB; PFS 2, 7, 17; RGAL 4;
SATA 19; TUS; WP

Longinus c. 1st cent. - .... **CMLC 27**
See also AW 2; DLB 176

Longley, Michael 1939- .... **CLC 29**
See also BRWS 8; CA 102; CP 1, 2, 3, 4, 5,
6, 7; DLB 40

Longstreet, Augustus Baldwin
1790-1870 .... **NCLC 159**
See also DLB 3, 11, 74, 248; RGAL 4

Longus fl. c. 2nd cent. - .... **CMLC 7**

Longway, A. Hugh
See Lang, Andrew

Lonnbohm, Armas Eino Leopold 1878-1926
See Leino, Eino
See also CA 123

Lonnrot, Elias 1802-1884 .... **NCLC 53**
See also EFS 1

Lonsdale, Roger ed. .... **CLC 65**

Lopate, Phillip 1943- .... **CLC 29**
See also CA 97-100; CANR 88; DLBY
1980; INT CA-97-100

Lopez, Barry (Holstun) 1945- .... **CLC 70**
See also AAYA 9, 63; ANW; CA 65-68;
CANR 7, 23, 47, 68, 92; DLB 256, 275;
INT CANR-7, -23; MTCW 1; RGAL 4;
SATA 67

Lopez de Mendoza, Inigo
See Santillana, Inigo Lopez de Mendoza,
Marques de

Lopez Portillo (y Pacheco), Jose
1920-2004 .... **CLC 46**
See also CA 129; 224; HW 1

Lopez y Fuentes, Gregorio
1897(?)-1966 .... **CLC 32**
See also CA 131; EWL 3; HW 1

Lorca, Federico Garcia
See Garcia Lorca, Federico
See also DFS 4; EW 11; PFS 20; RGWL 2,
3; WP

Lord, Audre
See Lorde, Audre (Geraldine)
See also EWL 3

Lord, Bette Bao 1938- .... **AAL; CLC 23**
See also BEST 90:3; BPFB 2; CA 107;
CANR 41, 79; INT CA-107; SATA 58

Lord Auch
See Bataille, Georges

Lord Brooke
See Greville, Fulke

Lord Byron
See Byron, George Gordon (Noel)

Lorde, Audre (Geraldine)
1934-1992 .... **BLC 2; CLC 18, 71; PC**
12; TCLC 173
See Domini, Rey; Lord, Audre
See also AFAW 1, 2; BW 1, 3; CA 25-28R;
142; CANR 16, 26, 46, 82; CP 2, 3, 4;
DA3; DAM MULT, POET; DLB 41; FW;
MAL 5; MTCW 1, 2; MTFW 2005; PFS
16; RGAL 4

MacDonald, John D(ann)
1916-1986 .... **CLC 3, 27, 44**
See also BPFB 2; CA 1-4R; 121; CANR 1, 19, 60; CMW 4; CPW; DAM NOV, POP; DLB 8, 306; DLBY 1986; MSW; MTCW 1, 2; MTFW 2005; SFW 4

Macdonald, John Ross
See Millar, Kenneth

Macdonald, Ross ..... **CLC 1, 2, 3, 14, 34, 41**
See Millar, Kenneth
See also AMWS 4; BPFB 2; CN 1, 2, 3; DLBD 6; MSW; RGAL 4

MacDougal, John
See Blish, James (Benjamin)

MacDougal, John
See Blish, James (Benjamin)

MacDowell, John
See Parks, Tim(othy Harold)

MacEwen, Gwendolyn (Margaret)
1941-1987 .... **CLC 13, 55**
See also CA 9-12R; 124; CANR 7, 22; CP 1, 2, 3, 4; DLB 53, 251; SATA 50; SATA-Obit 55

Macha, Karel Hynek 1810-1846 .... **NCLC 46**

Machado (y Ruiz), Antonio
1875-1939 .... **TCLC 3**
See also CA 104; 174; DLB 108; EW 9; EWL 3; HW 2; PFS 23; RGWL 2, 3

Machado de Assis, Joaquim Maria
1839-1908 .... **BLC 2; HLCS 2; SSC 24; TCLC 10**
See also CA 107; 153; CANR 91; DLB 307; LAW; RGSF 2; RGWL 2, 3; TWA; WLIT 1

Machaut, Guillaume de c.
1300-1377 .... **CMLC 64**
See also DLB 208

Machen, Arthur .... **SSC 20; TCLC 4**
See Jones, Arthur Llewellyn
See also CA 179; DLB 156, 178; RGEL 2; SUFW 1

Machiavelli, Niccolo 1469-1527 ... **DC 16; LC 8, 36; WLCS**
See also AAYA 58; DA; DAB; DAC; DAM MST; EW 2; LAIT 1; LMFS 1; NFS 9; RGWL 2, 3; TWA; WLIT 7

MacInnes, Colin 1914-1976 .... **CLC 4, 23**
See also CA 69-72; 65-68; CANR 21; CN 1, 2; DLB 14; MTCW 1, 2; RGEL 2; RHW

MacInnes, Helen (Clark)
1907-1985 .... **CLC 27, 39**
See also BPFB 2; CA 1-4R; 117; CANR 1, 28, 58; CMW 4; CN 1, 2; CPW; DAM POP; DLB 87; MTCW 1, 2; MTFW 2005; SATA 22; SATA-Obit 44

Mackay, Mary 1855-1924
See Corelli, Marie
See also CA 118; 177; FANT; RHW

Mackay, Shena 1944- .... **CLC 195**
See also CA 104; CANR 88, 139; DLB 231, 319; MTFW 2005

Mackenzie, Compton (Edward Montague)
1883-1972 .... **CLC 18; TCLC 116**
See also CA 21-22; 37-40R; CAP 2; CN 1; DLB 34, 100; RGEL 2

Mackenzie, Henry 1745-1831 .... **NCLC 41**
See also DLB 39; RGEL 2

Mackey, Nathaniel (Ernest) 1947- .... **PC 49**
See also CA 153; CANR 114; CP 7; DLB 169

MacKinnon, Catharine A. 1946- .... **CLC 181**
See also CA 128; 132; CANR 73, 140; FW; MTCW 2; MTFW 2005

Mackintosh, Elizabeth 1896(?)-1952
See Tey, Josephine
See also CA 110; CMW 4

MacLaren, James
See Grieve, C(hristopher) M(urray)

MacLaverty, Bernard 1942- .... **CLC 31**
See also CA 116; 118; CANR 43, 88; CN 5, 6, 7; DLB 267; INT CA-118; RGSF 2

MacLean, Alistair (Stuart)
1922(?)-1987 .... **CLC 3, 13, 50, 63**
See also CA 57-60; 121; CANR 28, 61; CMW 4; CP 2, 3, 4, 5, 6, 7; CPW; DAM POP; DLB 276; MTCW 1; SATA 23; SATA-Obit 50; TCWW 2

Maclean, Norman (Fitzroy)
1902-1990 .... **CLC 78; SSC 13**
See also AMWS 14; CA 102; 132; CANR 49; CPW; DAM POP; DLB 206; TCWW 2

MacLeish, Archibald 1892-1982 ... **CLC 3, 8, 14, 68; PC 47**
See also AMW; CA 9-12R; 106; CAD; CANR 33, 63; CDALBS; CP 1, 2; DAM POET; DFS 15; DLB 4, 7, 45; DLBY 1982; EWL 3; EXPP; MAL 5; MTCW 1, 2; MTFW 2005; PAB; PFS 5; RGAL 4; TUS

MacLennan, (John) Hugh
1907-1990 .... **CLC 2, 14, 92**
See also CA 5-8R; 142; CANR 33; CN 1, 2, 3, 4; DAC; DAM MST; DLB 68; EWL 3; MTCW 1, 2; MTFW 2005; RGEL 2; TWA

MacLeod, Alistair 1936- .... **CLC 56, 165**
See also CA 123; CCA 1; DAC; DAM MST; DLB 60; MTCW 2; MTFW 2005; RGSF 2; TCLE 1:2

Macleod, Fiona
See Sharp, William
See also RGEL 2; SUFW

MacNeice, (Frederick) Louis
1907-1963 .... **CLC 1, 4, 10, 53; PC 61**
See also BRW 7; CA 85-88; CANR 61; DAB; DAM POET; DLB 10, 20; EWL 3; MTCW 1, 2; MTFW 2005; RGEL 2

MacNeill, Dand
See Fraser, George MacDonald

Macpherson, James 1736-1796 .... **LC 29**
See Ossian
See also BRWS 8; DLB 109; RGEL 2

Macpherson, (Jean) Jay 1931- .... **CLC 14**
See also CA 5-8R; CANR 90; CP 1, 2, 3, 4, 5, 6, 7; CWP; DLB 53

Macrobius fl. 430- .... **CMLC 48**

MacShane, Frank 1927-1999 .... **CLC 39**
See also CA 9-12R; 186; CANR 3, 33; DLB 111

Macumber, Mari
See Sandoz, Mari(e Susette)

Madach, Imre 1823-1864 .... **NCLC 19**

Madden, (Jerry) David 1933- .... **CLC 5, 15**
See also CA 1-4R; CAAS 3; CANR 4, 45; CN 3, 4, 5, 6, 7; CSW; DLB 6; MTCW 1

Maddern, Al(an)
See Ellison, Harlan (Jay)

Madhubuti, Haki R. 1942- ... **BLC 2; CLC 6, 73; PC 5**
See Lee, Don L.
See also BW 2, 3; CA 73-76; CANR 24, 51, 73, 139; CP 5, 6, 7; CSW; DAM MULT, POET; DLB 5, 41; DLBD 8; EWL 3; MAL 5; MTCW 2; MTFW 2005; RGAL 4

Madison, James 1751-1836 .... **NCLC 126**
See also DLB 37

Maepenn, Hugh
See Kuttner, Henry

Maepenn, K. H.
See Kuttner, Henry

Maeterlinck, Maurice 1862-1949 ..... **TCLC 3**
See also CA 104; 136; CANR 80; DAM DRAM; DLB 192; EW 8; EWL 3; GFL 1789 to the Present; LMFS 2; RGWL 2, 3; SATA 66; TWA

Maginn, William 1794-1842 .... **NCLC 8**
See also DLB 110, 159

Mahapatra, Jayanta 1928- .... **CLC 33**
See also CA 73-76; CAAS 9; CANR 15, 33, 66, 87; CP 4, 5, 6, 7; DAM POET

Mahfouz, Naguib (Abdel Aziz Al-Sabilgi)
1911(?)- .... **CLC 153; SSC 66**
See Mahfuz, Najib (Abdel Aziz al-Sabilgi)
See also AAYA 49; BEST 89:2; CA 128; CANR 55, 101; DA3; DAM NOV; MTCW 1, 2; MTFW 2005; RGWL 2, 3; SSFS 9

Mahfuz, Najib (Abdel Aziz al-Sabilgi)
.... **CLC 52, 55**
See Mahfouz, Naguib (Abdel Aziz Al-Sabilgi)
See also AFW; CWW 2; DLBY 1988; EWL 3; RGSF 2; WLIT 6

Mahon, Derek 1941- .... **CLC 27; PC 60**
See also BRWS 6; CA 113; 128; CANR 88; CP 1, 2, 3, 4, 5, 6, 7; DLB 40; EWL 3

Maiakovskii, Vladimir
See Mayakovski, Vladimir (Vladimirovich)
See also IDTP; RGWL 2, 3

Mailer, Norman (Kingsley) 1923- . **CLC 1, 2, 3, 4, 5, 8, 11, 14, 28, 39, 74, 111**
See also AAYA 31; AITN 2; AMW; AMWC 2; AMWR 2; BPFB 2; CA 9-12R; CABS 1; CANR 28, 74, 77, 130; CDALB 1968-1988; CN 1, 2, 3, 4, 5, 6, 7; CPW; DA; DA3; DAB; DAC; DAM MST, NOV, POP; DLB 2, 16, 28, 185, 278; DLBD 3; DLBY 1980, 1983; EWL 3; MAL 5; MTCW 1, 2; MTFW 2005; NFS 10; RGAL 4; TUS

Maillet, Antonine 1929- .... **CLC 54, 118**
See also CA 115; 120; CANR 46, 74, 77, 134; CCA 1; CWW 2; DAC; DLB 60; INT CA-120; MTCW 2; MTFW 2005

Maimonides, Moses 1135-1204 ..... **CMLC 76**
See also DLB 115

Mais, Roger 1905-1955 .... **TCLC 8**
See also BW 1, 3; CA 105; 124; CANR 82; CDWLB 3; DLB 125; EWL 3; MTCW 1; RGEL 2

Maistre, Joseph 1753-1821 .... **NCLC 37**
See also GFL 1789 to the Present

Maitland, Frederic William
1850-1906 .... **TCLC 65**

Maitland, Sara (Louise) 1950- .... **CLC 49**
See also BRWS 11; CA 69-72; CANR 13, 59; DLB 271; FW

Major, Clarence 1936- ... **BLC 2; CLC 3, 19, 48**
See also AFAW 2; BW 2, 3; CA 21-24R; CAAS 6; CANR 13, 25, 53, 82; CN 3, 4, 5, 6, 7; CP 2, 3, 4, 5, 6, 7; CSW; DAM MULT; DLB 33; EWL 3; MAL 5; MSW

Major, Kevin (Gerald) 1949- .... **CLC 26**
See also AAYA 16; CA 97-100; CANR 21, 38, 112; CLR 11; DAC; DLB 60; INT CANR-21; JRDA; MAICYA 1, 2; MAIC-YAS 1; SATA 32, 82, 134; WYA; YAW

Maki, James
See Ozu, Yasujiro

Makine, Andrei 1957- .... **CLC 198**
See also CA 176; CANR 103; MTFW 2005

Malabaila, Damiano
See Levi, Primo

Malamud, Bernard 1914-1986 .. **CLC 1, 2, 3, 5, 8, 9, 11, 18, 27, 44, 78, 85; SSC 15; TCLC 129; WLC**
See also AAYA 16; AMWS 1; BPFB 2; BYA 15; CA 5-8R; 118; CABS 1; CANR 28, 62, 114; CDALB 1941-1968; CN 1, 2, 3, 4; CPW; DA; DA3; DAB; DAC; DAM MST, NOV, POP; DLB 2, 28, 152; DLBY

Marley, Bob .... **CLC 17**
See Marley, Robert Nesta
Marley, Robert Nesta 1945-1981
See Marley, Bob
See also CA 107; 103
Marlowe, Christopher 1564-1593 . **DC 1; LC 22, 47, 117; PC 57; WLC**
See also BRW 1; BRWR 1; CDBLB Before 1660; DA; DA3; DAB; DAC; DAM DRAM, MST; DFS 1, 5, 13, 21; DLB 62; EXPP; LMFS 1; PFS 22; RGEL 2; TEA; WLIT 3
Marlowe, Stephen 1928- .... **CLC 70**
See Queen, Ellery
See also CA 13-16R; CANR 6, 55; CMW 4; SFW 4
Marmion, Shakerley 1603-1639 .... **LC 89**
See also DLB 58; RGEL 2
Marmontel, Jean-Francois 1723-1799 .. **LC 2**
See also DLB 314
Maron, Monika 1941- .... **CLC 165**
See also CA 201
Marquand, John P(hillips)
1893-1960 .... **CLC 2, 10**
See also AMW; BPFB 2; CA 85-88; CANR 73; CMW 4; DLB 9, 102; EWL 3; MAL 5; MTCW 2; RGAL 4
Marques, Rene 1919-1979 .. **CLC 96; HLC 2**
See also CA 97-100; 85-88; CANR 78; DAM MULT; DLB 305; EWL 3; HW 1, 2; LAW; RGSF 2
Marquez, Gabriel (Jose) Garcia
See Garcia Marquez, Gabriel (Jose)
Marquis, Don(ald Robert Perry)
1878-1937 .... **TCLC 7**
See also CA 104; 166; DLB 11, 25; MAL 5; RGAL 4
Marquis de Sade
See Sade, Donatien Alphonse Francois
Marric, J. J.
See Creasey, John
See also MSW
Marryat, Frederick 1792-1848 .... **NCLC 3**
See also DLB 21, 163; RGEL 2; WCH
Marsden, James
See Creasey, John
Marsh, Edward 1872-1953 .... **TCLC 99**
Marsh, (Edith) Ngaio 1895-1982 .. **CLC 7, 53**
See also CA 9-12R; CANR 6, 58; CMW 4; CN 1, 2, 3; CPW; DAM POP; DLB 77; MSW; MTCW 1, 2; RGEL 2; TEA
Marshall, Allen
See Westlake, Donald E(dwin)
Marshall, Garry 1934- .... **CLC 17**
See also AAYA 3; CA 111; SATA 60
Marshall, Paule 1929- .. **BLC 3; CLC 27, 72; SSC 3**
See also AFAW 1, 2; AMWS 11; BPFB 2; BW 2, 3; CA 77-80; CANR 25, 73, 129; CN 1, 2, 3, 4, 5, 6, 7; DA3; DAM MULT; DLB 33, 157, 227; EWL 3; LATS 1:2; MAL 5; MTCW 1, 2; MTFW 2005; RGAL 4; SSFS 15
Marshallik
See Zangwill, Israel
Marsten, Richard
See Hunter, Evan
Marston, John 1576-1634 .... **LC 33**
See also BRW 2; DAM DRAM; DLB 58, 172; RGEL 2
Martel, Yann 1963- .... **CLC 192**
See also AAYA 67; CA 146; CANR 114; MTFW 2005
Martens, Adolphe-Adhemar
See Ghelderode, Michel de
Martha, Henry
See Harris, Mark

Marti, Jose
See Marti (y Perez), Jose (Julian)
See also DLB 290
Marti (y Perez), Jose (Julian)
1853-1895 .... **HLC 2; NCLC 63**
See Marti, Jose
See also DAM MULT; HW 2; LAW; RGWL 2, 3; WLIT 1
Martial c. 40-c. 104 .... **CMLC 35; PC 10**
See also AW 2; CDWLB 1; DLB 211; RGWL 2, 3
Martin, Ken
See Hubbard, L(afayette) Ron(ald)
Martin, Richard
See Creasey, John
Martin, Steve 1945- .... **CLC 30**
See also AAYA 53; CA 97-100; CANR 30, 100, 140; DFS 19; MTCW 1; MTFW 2005
Martin, Valerie 1948- .... **CLC 89**
See also BEST 90:2; CA 85-88; CANR 49, 89
Martin, Violet Florence 1862-1915 .. **SSC 56; TCLC 51**
Martin, Webber
See Silverberg, Robert
Martindale, Patrick Victor
See White, Patrick (Victor Martindale)
Martin du Gard, Roger
1881-1958 .... **TCLC 24**
See also CA 118; CANR 94; DLB 65; EWL 3; GFL 1789 to the Present; RGWL 2, 3
Martineau, Harriet 1802-1876 ...... **NCLC 26, 137**
See also DLB 21, 55, 159, 163, 166, 190; FW; RGEL 2; YABC 2
Martines, Julia
See O'Faolain, Julia
Martinez, Enrique Gonzalez
See Gonzalez Martinez, Enrique
Martinez, Jacinto Benavente y
See Benavente (y Martinez), Jacinto
Martinez de la Rosa, Francisco de Paula
1787-1862 .... **NCLC 102**
See also TWA
Martinez Ruiz, Jose 1873-1967
See Azorin; Ruiz, Jose Martinez
See also CA 93-96; HW 1
Martinez Sierra, Gregorio
1881-1947 .... **TCLC 6**
See also CA 115; EWL 3
Martinez Sierra, Maria (de la O'LeJarraga)
1874-1974 .... **TCLC 6**
See also CA 115; EWL 3
Martinsen, Martin
See Follett, Ken(neth Martin)
Martinson, Harry (Edmund)
1904-1978 .... **CLC 14**
See also CA 77-80; CANR 34, 130; DLB 259; EWL 3
Martyn, Edward 1859-1923 .... **TCLC 131**
See also CA 179; DLB 10; RGEL 2
Marut, Ret
See Traven, B.
Marut, Robert
See Traven, B.
Marvell, Andrew 1621-1678 .... **LC 4, 43; PC 10; WLC**
See also BRW 2; BRWR 2; CDBLB 1660-1789; DA; DAB; DAC; DAM MST, POET; DLB 131; EXPP; PFS 5; RGEL 2; TEA; WP
Marx, Karl (Heinrich)
1818-1883 .... **NCLC 17, 114**
See also DLB 129; LATS 1:1; TWA
Masaoka, Shiki -1902 .... **TCLC 18**
See Masaoka, Tsunenori
See also RGWL 3

Masaoka, Tsunenori 1867-1902
See Masaoka, Shiki
See also CA 117; 191; TWA
Masefield, John (Edward)
1878-1967 .... **CLC 11, 47**
See also CA 19-20; 25-28R; CANR 33; CAP 2; CDBLB 1890-1914; DAM POET; DLB 10, 19, 153, 160; EWL 3; EXPP; FANT; MTCW 1, 2; PFS 5; RGEL 2; SATA 19
Maso, Carole (?)- .... **CLC 44**
See also CA 170; CN 7; GLL 2; RGAL 4
Mason, Bobbie Ann 1940- ... **CLC 28, 43, 82, 154; SSC 4**
See also AAYA 5, 42; AMWS 8; BPFB 2; CA 53-56; CANR 11, 31, 58, 83, 125; CDALBS; CN 5, 6, 7; CSW; DA3; DLB 173; DLBY 1987; EWL 3; EXPS; INT CANR-31; MAL 5; MTCW 1, 2; MTFW 2005; NFS 4; RGAL 4; RGSF 2; SSFS 3, 8, 20; TCLE 1:2; YAW
Mason, Ernst
See Pohl, Frederik
Mason, Hunni B.
See Sternheim, (William Adolf) Carl
Mason, Lee W.
See Malzberg, Barry N(athaniel)
Mason, Nick 1945- .... **CLC 35**
Mason, Tally
See Derleth, August (William)
Mass, Anna .... **CLC 59**
Mass, William
See Gibson, William
Massinger, Philip 1583-1640 .... **LC 70**
See also BRWS 11; DLB 58; RGEL 2
Master Lao
See Lao Tzu
Masters, Edgar Lee 1868-1950 ...... **PC 1, 36; TCLC 2, 25; WLCS**
See also AMWS 1; CA 104; 133; CDALB 1865-1917; DA; DAC; DAM MST, POET; DLB 54; EWL 3; EXPP; MAL 5; MTCW 1, 2; MTFW 2005; RGAL 4; TUS; WP
Masters, Hilary 1928- .... **CLC 48**
See also CA 25-28R; CAAE 217; CANR 13, 47, 97; CN 6, 7; DLB 244
Mastrosimone, William 1947- .... **CLC 36**
See also CA 186; CAD; CD 5, 6
Mathe, Albert
See Camus, Albert
Mather, Cotton 1663-1728 .... **LC 38**
See also AMWS 2; CDALB 1640-1865; DLB 24, 30, 140; RGAL 4; TUS
Mather, Increase 1639-1723 .... **LC 38**
See also DLB 24
Matheson, Richard (Burton) 1926- .. **CLC 37**
See also AAYA 31; CA 97-100; CANR 88, 99; DLB 8, 44; HGG; INT CA-97-100; SCFW 1, 2; SFW 4; SUFW 2
Mathews, Harry (Burchell) 1930- ..... **CLC 6, 52**
See also CA 21-24R; CAAS 6; CANR 18, 40, 98; CN 5, 6, 7
Mathews, John Joseph 1894-1979 .. **CLC 84; NNAL**
See also CA 19-20; 142; CANR 45; CAP 2; DAM MULT; DLB 175; TCWW 1, 2
Mathias, Roland (Glyn) 1915- .... **CLC 45**
See also CA 97-100; CANR 19, 41; CP 1, 2, 3, 4, 5, 6, 7; DLB 27
Matsuo Basho 1644(?)-1694 ...... **LC 62; PC 3**
See Basho, Matsuo
See also DAM POET; PFS 2, 7, 18
Mattheson, Rodney
See Creasey, John
Matthews, (James) Brander
1852-1929 .... **TCLC 95**
See also CA 181; DLB 71, 78; DLBD 13

McGinley, Patrick (Anthony) 1937- . **CLC 41**
See also CA 120; 127; CANR 56; INT CA-127

McGinley, Phyllis 1905-1978 .... **CLC 14**
See also CA 9-12R; 77-80; CANR 19; CP 1, 2; CWRI 5; DLB 11, 48; MAL 5; PFS 9, 13; SATA 2, 44; SATA-Obit 24

McGinniss, Joe 1942- .... **CLC 32**
See also AITN 2; BEST 89:2; CA 25-28R; CANR 26, 70; CPW; DLB 185; INT CANR-26

McGivern, Maureen Daly
See Daly, Maureen

McGrath, Patrick 1950- .... **CLC 55**
See also CA 136; CANR 65; CN 5, 6, 7; DLB 231; HGG; SUFW 2

McGrath, Thomas (Matthew)
1916-1990 .... **CLC 28, 59**
See also AMWS 10; CA 9-12R; 132; CANR 6, 33, 95; CP 1, 2, 3, 4; DAM POET; MAL 5; MTCW 1; SATA 41; SATA-Obit 66

McGuane, Thomas (Francis III)
1939- .... **CLC 3, 7, 18, 45, 127**
See also AITN 2; BPFB 2; CA 49-52; CANR 5, 24, 49, 94; CN 2, 3, 4, 5, 6, 7; DLB 2, 212; DLBY 1980; EWL 3; INT CANR-24; MAL 5; MTCW 1; MTFW 2005; TCWW 1, 2

McGuckian, Medbh 1950- .... **CLC 48, 174; PC 27**
See also BRWS 5; CA 143; CP 4, 5, 6, 7; CWP; DAM POET; DLB 40

McHale, Tom 1942(?)-1982 .... **CLC 3, 5**
See also AITN 1; CA 77-80; 106; CN 1, 2, 3

McHugh, Heather 1948- .... **PC 61**
See also CA 69-72; CANR 11, 28, 55, 92; CP 4, 5, 6, 7; CWP

McIlvanney, William 1936- .... **CLC 42**
See also CA 25-28R; CANR 61; CMW 4; DLB 14, 207

McIlwraith, Maureen Mollie Hunter
See Hunter, Mollie
See also SATA 2

McInerney, Jay 1955- .... **CLC 34, 112**
See also AAYA 18; BPFB 2; CA 116; 123; CANR 45, 68, 116; CN 5, 6, 7; CPW; DA3; DAM POP; DLB 292; INT CA-123; MAL 5; MTCW 2; MTFW 2005

McIntyre, Vonda N(eel) 1948- .... **CLC 18**
See also CA 81-84; CANR 17, 34, 69; MTCW 1; SFW 4; YAW

McKay, Claude .... **BLC 3; HR 1:3; PC 2; TCLC 7, 41; WLC**
See McKay, Festus Claudius
See also AFAW 1, 2; AMWS 10; DAB; DLB 4, 45, 51, 117; EWL 3; EXPP; GLL 2; LAIT 3; LMFS 2; MAL 5; PAB; PFS 4; RGAL 4; WP

McKay, Festus Claudius 1889-1948
See McKay, Claude
See also BW 1, 3; CA 104; 124; CANR 73; DA; DAC; DAM MST, MULT, NOV, POET; MTCW 1, 2; MTFW 2005; TUS

McKuen, Rod 1933- .... **CLC 1, 3**
See also AITN 1; CA 41-44R; CANR 40; CP 1

McLoughlin, R. B.
See Mencken, H(enry) L(ouis)

McLuhan, (Herbert) Marshall
1911-1980 .... **CLC 37, 83**
See also CA 9-12R; 102; CANR 12, 34, 61; DLB 88; INT CANR-12; MTCW 1, 2; MTFW 2005

McManus, Declan Patrick Aloysius
See Costello, Elvis

McMillan, Terry (L.) 1951- . **BLCS; CLC 50, 61, 112**
See also AAYA 21; AMWS 13; BPFB 2; BW 2, 3; CA 140; CANR 60, 104, 131; CN 7; CPW; DA3; DAM MULT, NOV, POP; MAL 5; MTCW 2; MTFW 2005; RGAL 4; YAW

McMurtry, Larry 1936- .... **CLC 2, 3, 7, 11, 27, 44, 127**
See also AAYA 15; AITN 2; AMWS 5; BEST 89:2; BPFB 2; CA 5-8R; CANR 19, 43, 64, 103; CDALB 1968-1988; CN 2, 3, 4, 5, 6, 7; CPW; CSW; DA3; DAM NOV, POP; DLB 2, 143, 256; DLBY 1980, 1987; EWL 3; MAL 5; MTCW 1, 2; MTFW 2005; RGAL 4; TCWW 1, 2

McNally, T. M. 1961- .... **CLC 82**

McNally, Terrence 1939- .... **CLC 4, 7, 41, 91**
See also AAYA 62; AMWS 13; CA 45-48; CAD; CANR 2, 56, 116; CD 5, 6; DA3; DAM DRAM; DFS 16, 19; DLB 7, 249; EWL 3; GLL 1; MTCW 2; MTFW 2005

McNamer, Deirdre 1950- .... **CLC 70**

McNeal, Tom .... **CLC 119**

McNeile, Herman Cyril 1888-1937
See Sapper
See also CA 184; CMW 4; DLB 77

McNickle, (William) D'Arcy
1904-1977 .... **CLC 89; NNAL**
See also CA 9-12R; 85-88; CANR 5, 45; DAM MULT; DLB 175, 212; RGAL 4; SATA-Obit 22; TCWW 1, 2

McPhee, John (Angus) 1931- .... **CLC 36**
See also AAYA 61; AMWS 3; ANW; BEST 90:1; CA 65-68; CANR 20, 46, 64, 69, 121; CPW; DLB 185, 275; MTCW 1, 2; MTFW 2005; TUS

McPherson, James Alan 1943- . **BLCS; CLC 19, 77**
See also BW 1, 3; CA 25-28R; CAAS 17; CANR 24, 74, 140; CN 3, 4, 5, 6; CSW; DLB 38, 244; EWL 3; MTCW 1, 2; MTFW 2005; RGAL 4; RGSF 2

McPherson, William (Alexander)
1933- .... **CLC 34**
See also CA 69-72; CANR 28; INT CANR-28

McTaggart, J. McT. Ellis
See McTaggart, John McTaggart Ellis

McTaggart, John McTaggart Ellis
1866-1925 .... **TCLC 105**
See also CA 120; DLB 262

Mead, George Herbert 1863-1931 . **TCLC 89**
See also CA 212; DLB 270

Mead, Margaret 1901-1978 .... **CLC 37**
See also AITN 1; CA 1-4R; 81-84; CANR 4; DA3; FW; MTCW 1, 2; SATA-Obit 20

Meaker, Marijane (Agnes) 1927-
See Kerr, M. E.
See also CA 107; CANR 37, 63, 145; INT CA-107; JRDA; MAICYA 1, 2; MAIC-YAS 1; MTCW 1; SATA 20, 61, 99, 160; SATA-Essay 111; YAW

Medoff, Mark (Howard) 1940- .... **CLC 6, 23**
See also AITN 1; CA 53-56; CAD; CANR 5; CD 5, 6; DAM DRAM; DFS 4; DLB 7; INT CANR-5

Medvedev, P. N.
See Bakhtin, Mikhail Mikhailovich

Meged, Aharon
See Megged, Aharon

Meged, Aron
See Megged, Aharon

Megged, Aharon 1920- .... **CLC 9**
See also CA 49-52; CAAS 13; CANR 1, 140; EWL 3

Mehta, Deepa 1950- .... **CLC 208**

Mehta, Gita 1943- .... **CLC 179**
See also CA 225; CN 7; DNFS 2

Mehta, Ved (Parkash) 1934- .... **CLC 37**
See also CA 1-4R; 212; CAAE 212; CANR 2, 23, 69; MTCW 1; MTFW 2005

Melanchthon, Philipp 1497-1560 .... **LC 90**
See also DLB 179

Melanter
See Blackmore, R(ichard) D(oddridge)

Meleager c. 140B.C.-c. 70B.C. ...... **CMLC 53**

Melies, Georges 1861-1938 .... **TCLC 81**

Melikow, Loris
See Hofmannsthal, Hugo von

Melmoth, Sebastian
See Wilde, Oscar (Fingal O'Flahertie Wills)

Melo Neto, Joao Cabral de
See Cabral de Melo Neto, Joao
See also CWW 2; EWL 3

Meltzer, Milton 1915- .... **CLC 26**
See also AAYA 8, 45; BYA 2, 6; CA 13-16R; CANR 38, 92, 107; CLR 13; DLB 61; JRDA; MAICYA 1, 2; SAAS 1; SATA 1, 50, 80, 128; SATA-Essay 124; WYA; YAW

Melville, Herman 1819-1891 ..... **NCLC 3, 12, 29, 45, 49, 91, 93, 123, 157; SSC 1, 17, 46; WLC**
See also AAYA 25; AMW; AMWR 1; CDALB 1640-1865; DA; DA3; DAB; DAC; DAM MST, NOV; DLB 3, 74, 250, 254; EXPN; EXPS; GL 3; LAIT 1, 2; NFS 7, 9; RGAL 4; RGSF 2; SATA 59; SSFS 3; TUS

Members, Mark
See Powell, Anthony (Dymoke)

Membreno, Alejandro .... **CLC 59**

Menand, Louis 1952- .... **CLC 208**
See also CA 200

Menander c. 342B.C.-c. 293B.C. .... **CMLC 9, 51; DC 3**
See also AW 1; CDWLB 1; DAM DRAM; DLB 176; LMFS 1; RGWL 2, 3

Menchu, Rigoberta 1959- .. **CLC 160; HLCS 2**
See also CA 175; CANR 135; DNFS 1; WLIT 1

Mencken, H(enry) L(ouis)
1880-1956 .... **TCLC 13**
See also AMW; CA 105; CDALB 1917-1929; DLB 11, 29, 63, 137, 222; EWL 3; MAL 5; MTCW 1, 2; MTFW 2005; NCFS 4; RGAL 4; TUS

Mendelsohn, Jane 1965- .... **CLC 99**
See also CA 154; CANR 94

Mendoza, Inigo Lopez de
See Santillana, Inigo Lopez de Mendoza, Marques de

Menton, Francisco de
See Chin, Frank (Chew, Jr.)

Mercer, David 1928-1980 .... **CLC 5**
See also CA 9-12R; 102; CANR 23; CBD; DAM DRAM; DLB 13, 310; MTCW 1; RGEL 2

Merchant, Paul
See Ellison, Harlan (Jay)

Meredith, George 1828-1909 .. **PC 60; TCLC 17, 43**
See also CA 117; 153; CANR 80; CDBLB 1832-1890; DAM POET; DLB 18, 35, 57, 159; RGEL 2; TEA

Meredith, William (Morris) 1919- .... **CLC 4, 13, 22, 55; PC 28**
See also CA 9-12R; CAAS 14; CANR 6, 40, 129; CP 1, 2, 3, 4, 5, 6, 7; DAM POET; DLB 5; MAL 5

Merezhkovsky, Dmitrii Sergeevich
See Merezhkovsky, Dmitry Sergeyevich
See also DLB 295

Merezhkovsky, Dmitry Sergeevich
See Merezhkovsky, Dmitry Sergeyevich
See also EWL 3

Merezhkovsky, Dmitry Sergeyevich
1865-1941 .... **TCLC 29**
See Merezhkovsky, Dmitrii Sergeevich;
Merezhkovsky, Dmitry Sergeyevich
See also CA 169

Merimee, Prosper 1803-1870 ... **NCLC 6, 65;
SSC 7, 77**
See also DLB 119, 192; EW 6; EXPS; GFL
1789 to the Present; RGSF 2; RGWL 2,
3; SSFS 8; SUFW

Merkin, Daphne 1954- .... **CLC 44**
See also CA 123

Merleau-Ponty, Maurice
1908-1961 .... **TCLC 156**
See also CA 114; 89-92; DLB 296; GFL
1789 to the Present

Merlin, Arthur
See Blish, James (Benjamin)

Mernissi, Fatima 1940- .... **CLC 171**
See also CA 152; FW

Merrill, James (Ingram) 1926-1995 .. **CLC 2,
3, 6, 8, 13, 18, 34, 91; PC 28; TCLC
173**
See also AMWS 3; CA 13-16R; 147; CANR
10, 49, 63, 108; CP 1, 2, 3, 4; DA3; DAM
POET; DLB 5, 165; DLBY 1985; EWL 3;
INT CANR-10; MAL 5; MTCW 1, 2;
MTFW 2005; PAB; PFS 23; RGAL 4

Merriman, Alex
See Silverberg, Robert

Merriman, Brian 1747-1805 .... **NCLC 70**

Merritt, E. B.
See Waddington, Miriam

Merton, Thomas (James)
1915-1968 . **CLC 1, 3, 11, 34, 83; PC 10**
See also AAYA 61; AMWS 8; CA 5-8R;
25-28R; CANR 22, 53, 111, 131; DA3;
DLB 48; DLBY 1981; MAL 5; MTCW 1,
2; MTFW 2005

Merwin, W(illiam) S(tanley) 1927- ... **CLC 1,
2, 3, 5, 8, 13, 18, 45, 88; PC 45**
See also AMWS 3; CA 13-16R; CANR 15,
51, 112, 140; CP 1, 2, 3, 4, 5, 6, 7; DA3;
DAM POET; DLB 5, 169; EWL 3; INT
CANR-15; MAL 5; MTCW 1, 2; MTFW
2005; PAB; PFS 5, 15; RGAL 4

Metastasio, Pietro 1698-1782 .... **LC 115**
See also RGWL 2, 3

Metcalf, John 1938- .... **CLC 37; SSC 43**
See also CA 113; CN 4, 5, 6, 7; DLB 60;
RGSF 2; TWA

Metcalf, Suzanne
See Baum, L(yman) Frank

Mew, Charlotte (Mary) 1870-1928 .. **TCLC 8**
See also CA 105; 189; DLB 19, 135; RGEL
2

Mewshaw, Michael 1943- .... **CLC 9**
See also CA 53-56; CANR 7, 47; DLBY
1980

Meyer, Conrad Ferdinand
1825-1898 .... **NCLC 81; SSC 30**
See also DLB 129; EW; RGWL 2, 3

Meyer, Gustav 1868-1932
See Meyrink, Gustav
See also CA 117; 190

Meyer, June
See Jordan, June (Meyer)

Meyer, Lynn
See Slavitt, David R(ytman)

Meyers, Jeffrey 1939- .... **CLC 39**
See also CA 73-76, 186; CAAE 186; CANR
54, 102; DLB 111

**Meynell, Alice (Christina Gertrude
Thompson)** 1847-1922 .... **TCLC 6**
See also CA 104; 177; DLB 19, 98; RGEL
2

Meyrink, Gustav .... **TCLC 21**
See Meyer, Gustav
See also DLB 81; EWL 3

Michaels, Leonard 1933-2003 ..... **CLC 6, 25;
SSC 16**
See also CA 61-64; 216; CANR 21, 62, 119;
CN 3, 45, 6, 7; DLB 130; MTCW 1;
TCLE 1:2

Michaux, Henri 1899-1984 .... **CLC 8, 19**
See also CA 85-88; 114; DLB 258; EWL 3;
GFL 1789 to the Present; RGWL 2, 3

Micheaux, Oscar (Devereaux)
1884-1951 .... **TCLC 76**
See also BW 3; CA 174; DLB 50; TCWW
2

Michelangelo 1475-1564 .... **LC 12**
See also AAYA 43

Michelet, Jules 1798-1874 .... **NCLC 31**
See also EW 5; GFL 1789 to the Present

Michels, Robert 1876-1936 .... **TCLC 88**
See also CA 212

Michener, James A(lbert)
1907(?)-1997 .. **CLC 1, 5, 11, 29, 60, 109**
See also AAYA 27; AITN 1; BEST 90:1;
BPFB 2; CA 5-8R; 161; CANR 21, 45,
68; CN 1, 2, 3, 4, 5, 6; CPW; DA3; DAM
NOV, POP; DLB 6; MAL 5; MTCW 1, 2;
MTFW 2005; RHW; TCWW 1, 2

Mickiewicz, Adam 1798-1855 . **NCLC 3, 101;
PC 38**
See also EW 5; RGWL 2, 3

Middleton, (John) Christopher
1926- .... **CLC 13**
See also CA 13-16R; CANR 29, 54, 117;
CP 1, 2, 3, 4, 5, 6, 7; DLB 40

Middleton, Richard (Barham)
1882-1911 .... **TCLC 56**
See also CA 187; DLB 156; HGG

Middleton, Stanley 1919- .... **CLC 7, 38**
See also CA 25-28R; CAAS 23; CANR 21,
46, 81; CN 1, 2, 3, 4, 5, 6, 7; DLB 14

Middleton, Thomas 1580-1627 ...... **DC 5; LC
33**
See also BRW 2; DAM DRAM, MST; DFS
18, 22; DLB 58; RGEL 2

Migueis, Jose Rodrigues 1901-1980 . **CLC 10**
See also DLB 287

Mikszath, Kalman 1847-1910 .... **TCLC 31**
See also CA 170

Miles, Jack .... **CLC 100**
See also CA 200

Miles, John Russiano
See Miles, Jack

Miles, Josephine (Louise)
1911-1985 .... **CLC 1, 2, 14, 34, 39**
See also CA 1-4R; 116; CANR 2, 55; CP 1,
2, 3, 4; DAM POET; DLB 48; MAL 5;
TCLE 1:2

Militant
See Sandburg, Carl (August)

Mill, Harriet (Hardy) Taylor
1807-1858 .... **NCLC 102**
See also FW

Mill, John Stuart 1806-1873 .... **NCLC 11, 58**
See also CDBLB 1832-1890; DLB 55, 190,
262; FW 1; RGEL 2; TEA

Millar, Kenneth 1915-1983 .... **CLC 14**
See Macdonald, Ross
See also CA 9-12R; 110; CANR 16, 63,
107; CMW 4; CPW; DA3; DAM POP;
DLB 2, 226; DLBD 6; DLBY 1983;
MTCW 1, 2; MTFW 2005

Millay, E. Vincent
See Millay, Edna St. Vincent

Millay, Edna St. Vincent 1892-1950 ..... **PC 6,
61; TCLC 4, 49, 169; WLCS**
See Boyd, Nancy
See also AMW; CA 104; 130; CDALB
1917-1929; DA; DA3; DAB; DAC; DAM
MST, POET; DLB 45, 249; EWL 3;
EXPP; FL 1:6; MAL 5; MAWW; MTCW
1, 2; MTFW 2005; PAB; PFS 3, 17;
RGAL 4; TUS; WP

Miller, Arthur 1915-2005 ..... **CLC 1, 2, 6, 10,
15, 26, 47, 78, 179; DC 1; WLC**
See also AAYA 15; AITN 1; AMW; AMWC
1; CA 1-4R; 236; CABS 3; CAD; CANR
2, 30, 54, 76, 132; CD 5, 6; CDALB
1941-1968; DA; DA3; DAB; DAC; DAM
DRAM, MST; DFS 1, 3, 8; DLB 7, 266;
EWL 3; LAIT 1, 4; LATS 1:2; MAL 5;
MTCW 1, 2; MTFW 2005; RGAL 4;
TUS; WYAS 1

Miller, Henry (Valentine)
1891-1980 .... **CLC 1, 2, 4, 9, 14, 43, 84;
WLC**
See also AMW; BPFB 2; CA 9-12R; 97-
100; CANR 33, 64; CDALB 1929-1941;
CN 1, 2; DA; DA3; DAB; DAC; DAM
MST, NOV; DLB 4, 9; DLBY 1980; EWL
3; MAL 5; MTCW 1, 2; MTFW 2005;
RGAL 4; TUS

Miller, Hugh 1802-1856 .... **NCLC 143**
See also DLB 190

Miller, Jason 1939(?)-2001 .... **CLC 2**
See also AITN 1; CA 73-76; 197; CAD;
CANR 130; DFS 12; DLB 7

Miller, Sue 1943- .... **CLC 44**
See also AMWS 12; BEST 90:3; CA 139;
CANR 59, 91, 128; DA3; DAM POP;
DLB 143

Miller, Walter M(ichael, Jr.)
1923-1996 .... **CLC 4, 30**
See also BPFB 2; CA 85-88; CANR 108;
DLB 8; SCFW 1, 2; SFW 4

Millett, Kate 1934- .... **CLC 67**
See also AITN 1; CA 73-76; CANR 32, 53,
76, 110; DA3; DLB 246; FW; GLL 1;
MTCW 1, 2; MTFW 2005

Millhauser, Steven (Lewis) 1943- .... **CLC 21,
54, 109; SSC 57**
See also CA 110; 111; CANR 63, 114, 133;
CN 6, 7; DA3; DLB 2; FANT; INT CA-
111; MAL 5; MTCW 2; MTFW 2005

Millin, Sarah Gertrude 1889-1968 ... **CLC 49**
See also CA 102; 93-96; DLB 225; EWL 3

Milne, A(lan) A(lexander)
1882-1956 .... **TCLC 6, 88**
See also BRWS 5; CA 104; 133; CLR 1,
26; CMW 4; CWRI 5; DA3; DAB; DAC;
DAM MST; DLB 10, 77, 100, 160; FANT;
MAICYA 1, 2; MTCW 1, 2; MTFW 2005;
RGEL 2; SATA 100; WCH; YABC 1

Milner, Ron(ald) 1938-2004 ..... **BLC 3; CLC
56**
See also AITN 1; BW 1; CA 73-76; 230;
CAD; CANR 24, 81; CD 5, 6; DAM
MULT; DLB 38; MAL 5; MTCW 1

Milnes, Richard Monckton
1809-1885 .... **NCLC 61**
See also DLB 32, 184

Milosz, Czeslaw 1911-2004 .... **CLC 5, 11, 22,
31, 56, 82; PC 8; WLCS**
See also AAYA 62; CA 81-84; 230; CANR
23, 51, 91, 126; CDWLB 4; CWW 2;
DA3; DAM MST, POET; DLB 215; EW
13; EWL 3; MTCW 1, 2; MTFW 2005;
PFS 16; RGWL 2, 3

Milton, John 1608-1674 ..... **LC 9, 43, 92; PC
19, 29; WLC**
See also AAYA 65; BRW 2; BRWR 2; CD-
BLB 1660-1789; DA; DA3; DAB; DAC;
DAM MST, POET; DLB 131, 151, 281;
EFS 1; EXPP; LAIT 1; PAB; PFS 3, 17;
RGEL 2; TEA; WLIT 3; WP

Min, Anchee 1957- .... **CLC 86**
See also CA 146; CANR 94, 137; MTFW
2005

Minehaha, Cornelius
See Wedekind, (Benjamin) Frank(lin)

Miner, Valerie 1947- .... **CLC 40**
See also CA 97-100; CANR 59; FW; GLL
2

Minimo, Duca
  See D'Annunzio, Gabriele
Minot, Susan (Anderson) 1956- ...... **CLC 44, 159**
  See also AMWS 6; CA 134; CANR 118; CN 6, 7
Minus, Ed 1938- .... **CLC 39**
  See also CA 185
Mirabai 1498(?)-1550(?) .... **PC 48**
Miranda, Javier
  See Bioy Casares, Adolfo
  See also CWW 2
Mirbeau, Octave 1848-1917 .... **TCLC 55**
  See also CA 216; DLB 123, 192; GFL 1789 to the Present
Mirikitani, Janice 1942- .... **AAL**
  See also CA 211; DLB 312; RGAL 4
Mirk, John (?)-c. 1414 .... **LC 105**
  See also DLB 146
Miro (Ferrer), Gabriel (Francisco Victor)
  1879-1930 .... **TCLC 5**
  See also CA 104; 185; DLB 322; EWL 3
Misharin, Alexandr .... **CLC 59**
Mishima, Yukio ... **CLC 2, 4, 6, 9, 27; DC 1; SSC 4; TCLC 161**
  See Hiraoka, Kimitake
  See also AAYA 50; BPFB 2; GLL 1; MJW; RGSF 2; RGWL 2, 3; SSFS 5, 12
Mistral, Frederic 1830-1914 .... **TCLC 51**
  See also CA 122; 213; GFL 1789 to the Present
Mistral, Gabriela
  See Godoy Alcayaga, Lucila
  See also DLB 283; DNFS 1; EWL 3; LAW; RGWL 2, 3; WP
Mistry, Rohinton 1952- ... **CLC 71, 196; SSC 73**
  See also BRWS 10; CA 141; CANR 86, 114; CCA 1; CN 6, 7; DAC; SSFS 6
Mitchell, Clyde
  See Ellison, Harlan (Jay)
Mitchell, Emerson Blackhorse Barney
  1945- .... **NNAL**
  See also CA 45-48
Mitchell, James Leslie 1901-1935
  See Gibbon, Lewis Grassic
  See also CA 104; 188; DLB 15
Mitchell, Joni 1943- .... **CLC 12**
  See also CA 112; CCA 1
Mitchell, Joseph (Quincy)
  1908-1996 .... **CLC 98**
  See also CA 77-80; 152; CANR 69; CN 1, 2, 3, 4, 5, 6; CSW; DLB 185; DLBY 1996
Mitchell, Margaret (Munnerlyn)
  1900-1949 .... **TCLC 11, 170**
  See also AAYA 23; BPFB 2; BYA 1; CA 109; 125; CANR 55, 94; CDALBS; DA3; DAM NOV, POP; DLB 9; LAIT 2; MAL 5; MTCW 1, 2; MTFW 2005; NFS 9; RGAL 4; RHW; TUS; WYAS 1; YAW
Mitchell, Peggy
  See Mitchell, Margaret (Munnerlyn)
Mitchell, S(ilas) Weir 1829-1914 .... **TCLC 36**
  See also CA 165; DLB 202; RGAL 4
Mitchell, W(illiam) O(rmond)
  1914-1998 .... **CLC 25**
  See also CA 77-80; 165; CANR 15, 43; CN 1, 2, 3, 4, 5, 6; DAC; DAM MST; DLB 88; TCLE 1:2
Mitchell, William (Lendrum)
  1879-1936 .... **TCLC 81**
  See also CA 213
Mitford, Mary Russell 1787-1855 ... **NCLC 4**
  See also DLB 110, 116; RGEL 2
Mitford, Nancy 1904-1973 .... **CLC 44**
  See also BRWS 10; CA 9-12R; CN 1; DLB 191; RGEL 2

Miyamoto, (Chujo) Yuriko
  1899-1951 .... **TCLC 37**
  See Miyamoto Yuriko
  See also CA 170, 174
Miyamoto Yuriko
  See Miyamoto, (Chujo) Yuriko
  See also DLB 180
Miyazawa, Kenji 1896-1933 .... **TCLC 76**
  See Miyazawa Kenji
  See also CA 157; RGWL 3
Miyazawa Kenji
  See Miyazawa, Kenji
  See also EWL 3
Mizoguchi, Kenji 1898-1956 .... **TCLC 72**
  See also CA 167
Mo, Timothy (Peter) 1950- .... **CLC 46, 134**
  See also CA 117; CANR 128; CN 5, 6, 7; DLB 194; MTCW 1; WLIT 4; WWE 1
Modarressi, Taghi (M.) 1931-1997 ... **CLC 44**
  See also CA 121; 134; INT CA-134
Modiano, Patrick (Jean) 1945- .... **CLC 18**
  See also CA 85-88; CANR 17, 40, 115; CWW 2; DLB 83, 299; EWL 3
Mofolo, Thomas (Mokopu)
  1875(?)-1948 .... **BLC 3; TCLC 22**
  See also AFW; CA 121; 153; CANR 83; DAM MULT; DLB 225; EWL 3; MTCW 2; MTFW 2005; WLIT 2
Mohr, Nicholasa 1938- .... **CLC 12; HLC 2**
  See also AAYA 8, 46; CA 49-52; CANR 1, 32, 64; CLR 22; DAM MULT; DLB 145; HW 1, 2; JRDA; LAIT 5; LLW; MAICYA 2; MAICYAS 1; RGAL 4; SAAS 8; SATA 8, 97; SATA-Essay 113; WYA; YAW
Moi, Toril 1953- .... **CLC 172**
  See also CA 154; CANR 102; FW
Mojtabai, A(nn) G(race) 1938- ..... **CLC 5, 9, 15, 29**
  See also CA 85-88; CANR 88
Moliere 1622-1673 ..... **DC 13; LC 10, 28, 64; WLC**
  See also DA; DA3; DAB; DAC; DAM DRAM, MST; DFS 13, 18, 20; DLB 268; EW 3; GFL Beginnings to 1789; LATS 1:1; RGWL 2, 3; TWA
Molin, Charles
  See Mayne, William (James Carter)
Molnar, Ferenc 1878-1952 .... **TCLC 20**
  See also CA 109; 153; CANR 83; CDWLB 4; DAM DRAM; DLB 215; EWL 3; RGWL 2, 3
Momaday, N(avarre) Scott 1934- ...... **CLC 2, 19, 85, 95, 160; NNAL; PC 25; WLCS**
  See also AAYA 11, 64; AMWS 4; ANW; BPFB 2; BYA 12; CA 25-28R; CANR 14, 34, 68, 134; CDALBS; CN 2, 3, 4, 5, 6, 7; CPW; DA; DA3; DAB; DAC; DAM MST, MULT, NOV, POP; DLB 143, 175, 256; EWL 3; EXPP; INT CANR-14; LAIT 4; LATS 1:2; MAL 5; MTCW 1, 2; MTFW 2005; NFS 10; PFS 2, 11; RGAL 4; SATA 48; SATA-Brief 30; TCWW 1, 2; WP; YAW
Monette, Paul 1945-1995 .... **CLC 82**
  See also AMWS 10; CA 139; 147; CN 6; GLL 1
Monroe, Harriet 1860-1936 .... **TCLC 12**
  See also CA 109; 204; DLB 54, 91
Monroe, Lyle
  See Heinlein, Robert A(nson)
Montagu, Elizabeth 1720-1800 .... **NCLC 7, 117**
  See also FW
Montagu, Mary (Pierrepont) Wortley
  1689-1762 .... **LC 9, 57; PC 16**
  See also DLB 95, 101; FL 1:1; RGEL 2
Montagu, W. H.
  See Coleridge, Samuel Taylor

Montague, John (Patrick) 1929- ..... **CLC 13, 46**
  See also CA 9-12R; CANR 9, 69, 121; CP 1, 2, 3, 4, 5, 6, 7; DLB 40; EWL 3; MTCW 1; PFS 12; RGEL 2; TCLE 1:2
Montaigne, Michel (Eyquem) de
  1533-1592 .... **LC 8, 105; WLC**
  See also DA; DAB; DAC; DAM MST; EW 2; GFL Beginnings to 1789; LMFS 1; RGWL 2, 3; TWA
Montale, Eugenio 1896-1981 ... **CLC 7, 9, 18; PC 13**
  See also CA 17-20R; 104; CANR 30; DLB 114; EW 11; EWL 3; MTCW 1; PFS 22; RGWL 2, 3; TWA; WLIT 7
Montesquieu, Charles-Louis de Secondat
  1689-1755 .... **LC 7, 69**
  See also DLB 314; EW 3; GFL Beginnings to 1789; TWA
Montessori, Maria 1870-1952 ...... **TCLC 103**
  See also CA 115; 147
Montgomery, (Robert) Bruce 1921(?)-1978
  See Crispin, Edmund
  See also CA 179; 104; CMW 4
Montgomery, L(ucy) M(aud)
  1874-1942 .... **TCLC 51, 140**
  See also AAYA 12; BYA 1; CA 108; 137; CLR 8, 91; DA3; DAC; DAM MST; DLB 92; DLBD 14; JRDA; MAICYA 1, 2; MTCW 2; MTFW 2005; RGEL 2; SATA 100; TWA; WCH; WYA; YABC 1
Montgomery, Marion H., Jr. 1925- .... **CLC 7**
  See also AITN 1; CA 1-4R; CANR 3, 48; CSW; DLB 6
Montgomery, Max
  See Davenport, Guy (Mattison, Jr.)
Montherlant, Henry (Milon) de
  1896-1972 .... **CLC 8, 19**
  See also CA 85-88; 37-40R; DAM DRAM; DLB 72, 321; EW 11; EWL 3; GFL 1789 to the Present; MTCW 1
Monty Python
  See Chapman, Graham; Cleese, John (Marwood); Gilliam, Terry (Vance); Idle, Eric; Jones, Terence Graham Parry; Palin, Michael (Edward)
  See also AAYA 7
Moodie, Susanna (Strickland)
  1803-1885 .... **NCLC 14, 113**
  See also DLB 99
Moody, Hiram (F. III) 1961-
  See Moody, Rick
  See also CA 138; CANR 64, 112; MTFW 2005
Moody, Minerva
  See Alcott, Louisa May
Moody, Rick .... **CLC 147**
  See Moody, Hiram (F. III)
Moody, William Vaughan
  1869-1910 .... **TCLC 105**
  See also CA 110; 178; DLB 7, 54; MAL 5; RGAL 4
Mooney, Edward 1951-
  See Mooney, Ted
  See also CA 130
Mooney, Ted .... **CLC 25**
  See Mooney, Edward
Moorcock, Michael (John) 1939- ...... **CLC 5, 27, 58**
  See Bradbury, Edward P.
  See also AAYA 26; CA 45-48; CAAS 5; CANR 2, 17, 38, 64, 122; CN 5, 6, 7; DLB 14, 231, 261, 319; FANT; MTCW 1, 2; MTFW 2005; SATA 93; SCFW 1, 2; SFW 4; SUFW 1, 2
Moore, Brian 1921-1999 ... **CLC 1, 3, 5, 7, 8, 19, 32, 90**
  See Bryan, Michael
  See also BRWS 9; CA 1-4R; 174; CANR 1, 25, 42, 63; CCA 1; CN 1, 2, 3, 4, 5, 6;

Mphahlele, Es'kia
See Mphahlele, Ezekiel
See also AFW; CDWLB 3; CN 4, 5, 6; DLB 125, 225; RGSF 2; SSFS 11

Mphahlele, Ezekiel 1919- ... **BLC 3; CLC 25, 133**
See Mphahlele, Es'kia
See also BW 2, 3; CA 81-84; CANR 26, 76; CN 1, 2, 3; DA3; DAM MULT; EWL 3; MTCW 2; MTFW 2005; SATA 119

Mqhayi, S(amuel) E(dward) K(rune Loliwe) 1875-1945 .... **BLC 3; TCLC 25**
See also CA 153; CANR 87; DAM MULT

Mrozek, Slawomir 1930- .... **CLC 3, 13**
See also CA 13-16R; CAAS 10; CANR 29; CDWLB 4; CWW 2; DLB 232; EWL 3; MTCW 1

Mrs. Belloc-Lowndes
See Lowndes, Marie Adelaide (Belloc)

Mrs. Fairstar
See Horne, Richard Henry Hengist

M'Taggart, John M'Taggart Ellis
See McTaggart, John McTaggart Ellis

Mtwa, Percy (?)- .... **CLC 47**
See also CD 6

Mueller, Lisel 1924- .... **CLC 13, 51; PC 33**
See also CA 93-96; CP 7; DLB 105; PFS 9, 13

Muggeridge, Malcolm (Thomas) 1903-1990 .... **TCLC 120**
See also AITN 1; CA 101; CANR 33, 63; MTCW 1, 2

Muhammad 570-632 .... **WLCS**
See also DA; DAB; DAC; DAM MST; DLB 311

Muir, Edwin 1887-1959 . **PC 49; TCLC 2, 87**
See Moore, Edward
See also BRWS 6; CA 104; 193; DLB 20, 100, 191; EWL 3; RGEL 2

Muir, John 1838-1914 .... **TCLC 28**
See also AMWS 9; ANW; CA 165; DLB 186, 275

Mujica Lainez, Manuel 1910-1984 ... **CLC 31**
See Lainez, Manuel Mujica
See also CA 81-84; 112; CANR 32; EWL 3; HW 1

Mukherjee, Bharati 1940- ..... **AAL; CLC 53, 115; SSC 38**
See also AAYA 46; BEST 89:2; CA 107, 232; CAAE 232; CANR 45, 72, 128; CN 5, 6, 7; DAM NOV; DLB 60, 218; DNFS 1, 2; EWL 3; FW; MAL 5; MTCW 1, 2; MTFW 2005; RGAL 4; RGSF 2; SSFS 7; TUS; WWE 1

Muldoon, Paul 1951- .... **CLC 32, 72, 166**
See also BRWS 4; CA 113; 129; CANR 52, 91; CP 2, 3, 4, 5, 6, 7; DAM POET; DLB 40; INT CA-129; PFS 7, 22; TCLE 1:2

Mulisch, Harry (Kurt Victor) 1927- .... **CLC 42**
See also CA 9-12R; CANR 6, 26, 56, 110; CWW 2; DLB 299; EWL 3

Mull, Martin 1943- .... **CLC 17**
See also CA 105

Muller, Wilhelm .... **NCLC 73**

Mulock, Dinah Maria
See Craik, Dinah Maria (Mulock)
See also RGEL 2

Munday, Anthony 1560-1633 .... **LC 87**
See also DLB 62, 172; RGEL 2

Munford, Robert 1737(?)-1783 .... **LC 5**
See also DLB 31

Mungo, Raymond 1946- .... **CLC 72**
See also CA 49-52; CANR 2

Munro, Alice (Anne) 1931- ... **CLC 6, 10, 19, 50, 95; SSC 3; WLCS**
See also AITN 2; BPFB 2; CA 33-36R; CANR 33, 53, 75, 114; CCA 1; CN 1, 2, 3, 4, 5, 6, 7; DA3; DAC; DAM MST, NOV; DLB 53; EWL 3; MTCW 1, 2; MTFW 2005; RGEL 2; RGSF 2; SATA 29; SSFS 5, 13, 19; TCLE 1:2; WWE 1

Munro, H(ector) H(ugh) 1870-1916 .... **WLC**
See Saki
See also AAYA 56; CA 104; 130; CANR 104; CDBLB 1890-1914; DA; DA3; DAB; DAC; DAM MST, NOV; DLB 34, 162; EXPS; MTCW 1, 2; MTFW 2005; RGEL 2; SSFS 15

Murakami, Haruki 1949- .... **CLC 150**
See Murakami Haruki
See also CA 165; CANR 102, 146; MJW; RGWL 3; SFW 4

Murakami Haruki
See Murakami, Haruki
See also CWW 2; DLB 182; EWL 3

Murasaki, Lady
See Murasaki Shikibu

Murasaki Shikibu 978(?)-1026(?) .. **CMLC 1, 79**
See also EFS 2; LATS 1:1; RGWL 2, 3

Murdoch, (Jean) Iris 1919-1999 ... **CLC 1, 2, 3, 4, 6, 8, 11, 15, 22, 31, 51; TCLC 171**
See also BRWS 1; CA 13-16R; 179; CANR 8, 43, 68, 103, 142; CBD; CDBLB 1960 to Present; CN 1, 2, 3, 4, 5, 6; CWD; DA3; DAB; DAC; DAM MST, NOV; DLB 14, 194, 233; EWL 3; INT CANR-8; MTCW 1, 2; MTFW 2005; NFS 18; RGEL 2; TCLE 1:2; TEA; WLIT 4

Murfree, Mary Noailles 1850-1922 .. **SSC 22; TCLC 135**
See also CA 122; 176; DLB 12, 74; RGAL 4

Murnau, Friedrich Wilhelm
See Plumpe, Friedrich Wilhelm

Murphy, Richard 1927- .... **CLC 41**
See also BRWS 5; CA 29-32R; CP 1, 2, 3, 4, 5, 6, 7; DLB 40; EWL 3

Murphy, Sylvia 1937- .... **CLC 34**
See also CA 121

Murphy, Thomas (Bernard) 1935- ... **CLC 51**
See Murphy, Tom
See also CA 101

Murphy, Tom
See Murphy, Thomas (Bernard)
See also DLB 310

Murray, Albert L. 1916- .... **CLC 73**
See also BW 2; CA 49-52; CANR 26, 52, 78; CN 7; CSW; DLB 38; MTFW 2005

Murray, James Augustus Henry 1837-1915 .... **TCLC 117**

Murray, Judith Sargent 1751-1820 .... **NCLC 63**
See also DLB 37, 200

Murray, Les(lie Allan) 1938- .... **CLC 40**
See also BRWS 7; CA 21-24R; CANR 11, 27, 56, 103; CP 1, 2, 3, 4, 5, 6, 7; DAM POET; DLB 289; DLBY 2001; EWL 3; RGEL 2

Murry, J. Middleton
See Murry, John Middleton

Murry, John Middleton 1889-1957 .... **TCLC 16**
See also CA 118; 217; DLB 149

Musgrave, Susan 1951- .... **CLC 13, 54**
See also CA 69-72; CANR 45, 84; CCA 1; CP 2, 3, 4, 5, 6, 7; CWP

Musil, Robert (Edler von) 1880-1942 .... **SSC 18; TCLC 12, 68**
See also CA 109; CANR 55, 84; CDWLB 2; DLB 81, 124; EW 9; EWL 3; MTCW 2; RGSF 2; RGWL 2, 3

Muske, Carol .... **CLC 90**
See Muske-Dukes, Carol (Anne)

Muske-Dukes, Carol (Anne) 1945-
See Muske, Carol
See also CA 65-68, 203; CAAE 203; CANR 32, 70; CWP

Musset, (Louis Charles) Alfred de 1810-1857 .... **NCLC 7, 150**
See also DLB 192, 217; EW 6; GFL 1789 to the Present; RGWL 2, 3; TWA

Mussolini, Benito (Amilcare Andrea) 1883-1945 .... **TCLC 96**
See also CA 116

Mutanabbi, Al-
See al-Mutanabbi, Ahmad ibn al-Husayn Abu al-Tayyib al-Jufi al-Kindi
See also WLIT 6

My Brother's Brother
See Chekhov, Anton (Pavlovich)

Myers, L(eopold) H(amilton) 1881-1944 .... **TCLC 59**
See also CA 157; DLB 15; EWL 3; RGEL 2

Myers, Walter Dean 1937- .. **BLC 3; CLC 35**
See also AAYA 4, 23; BW 2; BYA 6, 8, 11; CA 33-36R; CANR 20, 42, 67, 108; CLR 4, 16, 35; DAM MULT, NOV; DLB 33; INT CANR-20; JRDA; LAIT 5; MAICYA 1, 2; MAICYAS 1; MTCW 2; MTFW 2005; SAAS 2; SATA 41, 71, 109, 157; SATA-Brief 27; WYA; YAW

Myers, Walter M.
See Myers, Walter Dean

Myles, Symon
See Follett, Ken(neth Martin)

Nabokov, Vladimir (Vladimirovich) 1899-1977 .... **CLC 1, 2, 3, 6, 8, 11, 15, 23, 44, 46, 64; SSC 11, 86; TCLC 108; WLC**
See also AAYA 45; AMW; AMWC 1; AMWR 1; BPFB 2; CA 5-8R; 69-72; CANR 20, 102; CDALB 1941-1968; CN 1, 2; CP 2; DA; DA3; DAB; DAC; DAM MST, NOV; DLB 2, 244, 278, 317; DLBD 3; DLBY 1980, 1991; EWL 3; EXPS; LATS 1:2; MAL 5; MTCW 1, 2; MTFW 2005; NCFS 4; NFS 9; RGAL 4; RGSF 2; SSFS 6, 15; TUS

Naevius c. 265B.C.-201B.C. .... **CMLC 37**
See also DLB 211

Nagai, Kafu .... **TCLC 51**
See Nagai, Sokichi
See also DLB 180

Nagai, Sokichi 1879-1959
See Nagai, Kafu
See also CA 117

Nagy, Laszlo 1925-1978 .... **CLC 7**
See also CA 129; 112

Naidu, Sarojini 1879-1949 .... **TCLC 80**
See also EWL 3; RGEL 2

Naipaul, Shiva(dhar Srinivasa) 1945-1985 .... **CLC 32, 39; TCLC 153**
See also CA 110; 112; 116; CANR 33; CN 2, 3; DA3; DAM NOV; DLB 157; DLBY 1985; EWL 3; MTCW 1, 2; MTFW 2005

Naipaul, V(idiadhar) S(urajprasad) 1932- .... **CLC 4, 7, 9, 13, 18, 37, 105, 199; SSC 38**
See also BPFB 2; BRWS 1; CA 1-4R; CANR 1, 33, 51, 91, 126; CDBLB 1960 to Present; CDWLB 3; CN 1, 2, 3, 4, 5, 6, 7; DA3; DAB; DAC; DAM MST, NOV; DLB 125, 204, 207; DLBY 1985, 2001; EWL 3; LATS 1:2; MTCW 1, 2; MTFW 2005; RGEL 2; RGSF 2; TWA; WLIT 4; WWE 1

Nakos, Lilika 1903(?)-1989 .... **CLC 29**

Napoleon
See Yamamoto, Hisaye

Niven, Laurence Van Cott 1938-
See Niven, Larry
See also CA 21-24R, 207; CAAE 207;
CAAS 12; CANR 14, 44, 66, 113; CPW;
DAM POP; MTCW 1, 2; SATA 95; SFW
4

Nixon, Agnes Eckhardt 1927- .... **CLC 21**
See also CA 110

Nizan, Paul 1905-1940 .... **TCLC 40**
See also CA 161; DLB 72; EWL 3; GFL
1789 to the Present

Nkosi, Lewis 1936- .... **BLC 3; CLC 45**
See also BW 1, 3; CA 65-68; CANR 27,
81; CBD; CD 5, 6; DAM MULT; DLB
157, 225; WWE 1

Nodier, (Jean) Charles (Emmanuel)
1780-1844 .... **NCLC 19**
See also DLB 119; GFL 1789 to the Present

Noguchi, Yone 1875-1947 .... **TCLC 80**

Nolan, Christopher 1965- .... **CLC 58**
See also CA 111; CANR 88

Noon, Jeff 1957- .... **CLC 91**
See also CA 148; CANR 83; DLB 267;
SFW 4

Norden, Charles
See Durrell, Lawrence (George)

Nordhoff, Charles Bernard
1887-1947 .... **TCLC 23**
See also CA 108; 211; DLB 9; LAIT 1;
RHW 1; SATA 23

Norfolk, Lawrence 1963- .... **CLC 76**
See also CA 144; CANR 85; CN 6, 7; DLB
267

Norman, Marsha (Williams) 1947- . **CLC 28,
186; DC 8**
See also CA 105; CABS 3; CAD; CANR
41, 131; CD 5, 6; CSW; CWD; DAM
DRAM; DFS 2; DLB 266; DLBY 1984;
FW; MAL 5

Normyx
See Douglas, (George) Norman

Norris, (Benjamin) Frank(lin, Jr.)
1870-1902 .... **SSC 28; TCLC 24, 155**
See also AAYA 57; AMW; AMWC 2; BPFB
2; CA 110; 160; CDALB 1865-1917; DLB
12, 71, 186; LMFS 2; NFS 12; RGAL 4;
TCWW 1, 2; TUS

Norris, Leslie 1921- .... **CLC 14**
See also CA 11-12; CANR 14, 117; CAP 1;
CP 1, 2, 3, 4, 5, 6, 7; DLB 27, 256

North, Andrew
See Norton, Andre

North, Anthony
See Koontz, Dean R.

North, Captain George
See Stevenson, Robert Louis (Balfour)

North, Captain George
See Stevenson, Robert Louis (Balfour)

North, Milou
See Erdrich, (Karen) Louise

Northrup, B. A.
See Hubbard, L(afayette) Ron(ald)

North Staffs
See Hulme, T(homas) E(rnest)

Northup, Solomon 1808-1863 ...... **NCLC 105**

Norton, Alice Mary
See Norton, Andre
See also MAICYA 1; SATA 1, 43

Norton, Andre 1912-2005 .... **CLC 12**
See Norton, Alice Mary
See also AAYA 14; BPFB 2; BYA 4, 10,
12; CA 1-4R; 237; CANR 68; CLR 50;
DLB 8, 52; JRDA; MAICYA 2; MTCW
1; SATA 91; SUFW 1, 2; YAW

Norton, Caroline 1808-1877 .... **NCLC 47**
See also DLB 21, 159, 199

Norway, Nevil Shute 1899-1960
See Shute, Nevil
See also CA 102; 93-96; CANR 85; MTCW
2

Norwid, Cyprian Kamil
1821-1883 .... **NCLC 17**
See also RGWL 3

Nosille, Nabrah
See Ellison, Harlan (Jay)

Nossack, Hans Erich 1901-1978 .... **CLC 6**
See also CA 93-96; 85-88; DLB 69; EWL 3

Nostradamus 1503-1566 .... **LC 27**

Nosu, Chuji
See Ozu, Yasujiro

Notenburg, Eleanora (Genrikhovna) von
See Guro, Elena (Genrikhovna)

Nova, Craig 1945- .... **CLC 7, 31**
See also CA 45-48; CANR 2, 53, 127

Novak, Joseph
See Kosinski, Jerzy (Nikodem)

Novalis 1772-1801 .... **NCLC 13**
See also CDWLB 2; DLB 90; EW 5; RGWL
2, 3

Novick, Peter 1934- .... **CLC 164**
See also CA 188

Novis, Emile
See Weil, Simone (Adolphine)

Nowlan, Alden (Albert) 1933-1983 ... **CLC 15**
See also CA 9-12R; CANR 5; CP 1, 2, 3;
DAC; DAM MST; DLB 53; PFS 12

Noyes, Alfred 1880-1958 ...... **PC 27; TCLC 7**
See also CA 104; 188; DLB 20; EXPP;
FANT; PFS 4; RGEL 2

Nugent, Richard Bruce
1906(?)-1987 .... **HR 1:3**
See also BW 1; CA 125; DLB 51; GLL 2

Nunn, Kem .... **CLC 34**
See also CA 159

Nussbaum, Martha Craven 1947- .. **CLC 203**
See also CA 134; CANR 102

Nwapa, Flora (Nwanzuruaha)
1931-1993 .... **BLCS; CLC 133**
See also BW 2; CA 143; CANR 83; CD-
WLB 3; CWRI 5; DLB 125; EWL 3;
WLIT 2

Nye, Robert 1939- .... **CLC 13, 42**
See also BRWS 10; CA 33-36R; CANR 29,
67, 107; CN 1, 2, 3, 4, 5, 6, 7; CP 1, 2, 3,
4, 5, 6, 7; CWRI 5; DAM NOV; DLB 14,
271; FANT; HGG; MTCW 1; RHW;
SATA 6

Nyro, Laura 1947-1997 .... **CLC 17**
See also CA 194

Oates, Joyce Carol 1938- .. **CLC 1, 2, 3, 6, 9,
11, 15, 19, 33, 52, 108, 134; SSC 6, 70;
WLC**
See also AAYA 15, 52; AITN 1; AMWS 2;
BEST 89:2; BPFB 2; BYA 11; CA 5-8R;
CANR 25, 45, 74, 113, 129; CDALB
1968-1988; CN 1, 2, 3, 4, 5, 6, 7; CP 7;
CPW; CWP; DA; DA3; DAB; DAC;
DAM MST, NOV, POP; DLB 2, 5, 130;
DLBY 1981; EWL 3; EXPS; FL 1:6; FW;
GL 3; HGG; INT CANR-25; LAIT 4;
MAL 5; MAWW; MTCW 1, 2; MTFW
2005; NFS 8; RGAL 4; RGSF 2; SATA
159; SSFS 1, 8, 17; SUFW 2; TUS

O'Brian, E. G.
See Clarke, Arthur C(harles)

O'Brian, Patrick 1914-2000 .... **CLC 152**
See also AAYA 55; CA 144; 187; CANR
74; CPW; MTCW 2; MTFW 2005; RHW

O'Brien, Darcy 1939-1998 .... **CLC 11**
See also CA 21-24R; 167; CANR 8, 59

O'Brien, Edna 1932- ..... **CLC 3, 5, 8, 13, 36,
65, 116; SSC 10, 77**
See also BRWS 5; CA 1-4R; CANR 6, 41,
65, 102; CDBLB 1960 to Present; CN 1,
2, 3, 4, 5, 6, 7; DA3; DAM NOV; DLB
14, 231, 319; EWL 3; FW; MTCW 1, 2;
MTFW 2005; RGSF 2; WLIT 4

O'Brien, Fitz-James 1828-1862 ..... **NCLC 21**
See also DLB 74; RGAL 4; SUFW

O'Brien, Flann .... **CLC 1, 4, 5, 7, 10, 47**
See O Nuallain, Brian
See also BRWS 2; DLB 231; EWL 3;
RGEL 2

O'Brien, Richard 1942- .... **CLC 17**
See also CA 124

O'Brien, (William) Tim(othy) 1946- . **CLC 7,
19, 40, 103, 211; SSC 74**
See also AAYA 16; AMWS 5; CA 85-88;
CANR 40, 58, 133; CDALBS; CN 5, 6,
7; CPW; DA3; DAM POP; DLB 152;
DLBD 9; LATS 1:2; MAL 5; MTCW 2;
MTFW 2005; RGAL 4; SSFS 5, 15; TCLE 1:2

Obstfelder, Sigbjoern 1866-1900 .... **TCLC 23**
See also CA 123

O'Casey, Sean 1880-1964 .... **CLC 1, 5, 9, 11,
15, 88; DC 12; WLCS**
See also BRW 7; CA 89-92; CANR 62;
CBD; CDBLB 1914-1945; DA3; DAB;
DAC; DAM DRAM, MST; DFS 19; DLB
10; EWL 3; MTCW 1, 2; MTFW 2005;
RGEL 2; TEA; WLIT 4

O'Cathasaigh, Sean
See O'Casey, Sean

Occom, Samson 1723-1792 .... **LC 60; NNAL**
See also DLB 175

Ochs, Phil(ip David) 1940-1976 .... **CLC 17**
See also CA 185; 65-68

O'Connor, Edwin (Greene)
1918-1968 .... **CLC 14**
See also CA 93-96; 25-28R; MAL 5

O'Connor, (Mary) Flannery
1925-1964 .... **CLC 1, 2, 3, 6, 10, 13, 15,
21, 66, 104; SSC 1, 23, 61, 82; TCLC
132; WLC**
See also AAYA 7; AMW; AMWR 2; BPFB
3; BYA 16; CA 1-4R; CANR 3, 41;
CDALB 1941-1968; DA; DA3; DAB;
DAC; DAM MST, NOV; DLB 2, 152;
DLBD 12; DLBY 1980; EWL 3; EXPS;
LAIT 5; MAL 5; MAWW; MTCW 1, 2;
MTFW 2005; NFS 3, 21; RGAL 4; RGSF
2; SSFS 2, 7, 10, 19; TUS

O'Connor, Frank .... **CLC 23; SSC 5**
See O'Donovan, Michael Francis
See also DLB 162; EWL 3; RGSF 2; SSFS
5

O'Dell, Scott 1898-1989 .... **CLC 30**
See also AAYA 3, 44; BPFB 3; BYA 1, 2,
3, 5; CA 61-64; 129; CANR 12, 30, 112;
CLR 1, 16; DLB 52; JRDA; MAICYA 1,
2; SATA 12, 60, 134; WYA; YAW

Odets, Clifford 1906-1963 ..... **CLC 2, 28, 98;
DC 6**
See also AMWS 2; CA 85-88; CAD; CANR
62; DAM DRAM; DFS 3, 17, 20; DLB 7,
26; EWL 3; MAL 5; MTCW 1, 2; MTFW
2005; RGAL 4; TUS

O'Doherty, Brian 1928- .... **CLC 76**
See also CA 105; CANR 108

O'Donnell, K. M.
See Malzberg, Barry N(athaniel)

O'Donnell, Lawrence
See Kuttner, Henry

O'Donovan, Michael Francis
1903-1966 .... **CLC 14**
See O'Connor, Frank
See also CA 93-96; CANR 84

Parks, Suzan-Lori 1964(?)- .... **DC 23**
See also AAYA 55; CA 201; CAD; CD 5,
6; CWD; DFS 22; RGAL 4

Parks, Tim(othy Harold) 1954- ...... **CLC 147**
See also CA 126; 131; CANR 77, 144; CN
7; DLB 231; INT CA-131

Parmenides c. 515B.C.-c.
450B.C. .... **CMLC 22**
See also DLB 176

Parnell, Thomas 1679-1718 .... **LC 3**
See also DLB 95; RGEL 2

Parr, Catherine c. 1513(?)-1548 .... **LC 86**
See also DLB 136

Parra, Nicanor 1914- ... **CLC 2, 102; HLC 2;
PC 39**
See also CA 85-88; CANR 32; CWW 2;
DAM MULT; DLB 283; EWL 3; HW 1;
LAW; MTCW 1

Parra Sanojo, Ana Teresa de la
1890-1936 .... **HLCS 2**
See de la Parra, (Ana) Teresa (Sonojo)
See also LAW

Parrish, Mary Frances
See Fisher, M(ary) F(rances) K(ennedy)

Parshchikov, Aleksei 1954- .... **CLC 59**
See Parshchikov, Aleksei Maksimovich

Parshchikov, Aleksei Maksimovich
See Parshchikov, Aleksei
See also DLB 285

Parson, Professor
See Coleridge, Samuel Taylor

Parson Lot
See Kingsley, Charles

Parton, Sara Payson Willis
1811-1872 .... **NCLC 86**
See also DLB 43, 74, 239

Partridge, Anthony
See Oppenheim, E(dward) Phillips

Pascal, Blaise 1623-1662 .... **LC 35**
See also DLB 268; EW 3; GFL Beginnings
to 1789; RGWL 2, 3; TWA

Pascoli, Giovanni 1855-1912 .... **TCLC 45**
See also CA 170; EW 7; EWL 3

Pasolini, Pier Paolo 1922-1975 .. **CLC 20, 37,
106; PC 17**
See also CA 93-96; 61-64; CANR 63; DLB
128, 177; EWL 3; MTCW 1; RGWL 2, 3

Pasquini
See Silone, Ignazio

Pastan, Linda (Olenik) 1932- .... **CLC 27**
See also CA 61-64; CANR 18, 40, 61, 113;
CP 3, 4, 5, 6, 7; CSW; CWP; DAM
POET; DLB 5; PFS 8

Pasternak, Boris (Leonidovich)
1890-1960 ...... **CLC 7, 10, 18, 63; PC 6;
SSC 31; WLC**
See also BPFB 3; CA 127; 116; DA; DA3;
DAB; DAC; DAM MST, NOV, POET;
DLB 302; EW 10; MTCW 1, 2; MTFW
2005; RGSF 2; RGWL 2, 3; TWA; WP

Patchen, Kenneth 1911-1972 .... **CLC 1, 2, 18**
See also BG 1:3; CA 1-4R; 33-36R; CANR
3, 35; CN 1; CP 1; DAM POET; DLB 16,
48; EWL 3; MAL 5; MTCW 1; RGAL 4

Pater, Walter (Horatio) 1839-1894 . **NCLC 7,
90, 159**
See also BRW 5; CDBLB 1832-1890; DLB
57, 156; RGEL 2; TEA

Paterson, A(ndrew) B(arton)
1864-1941 .... **TCLC 32**
See also CA 155; DLB 230; RGEL 2; SATA
97

Paterson, Banjo
See Paterson, A(ndrew) B(arton)

Paterson, Katherine (Womeldorf)
1932- .... **CLC 12, 30**
See also AAYA 1, 31; BYA 1, 2, 7; CA 21-
24R; CANR 28, 59, 111; CLR 7, 50;
CWRI 5; DLB 52; JRDA; LAIT 4; MAI-
CYA 1, 2; MAICYAS 1; MTCW 1; SATA
13, 53, 92, 133; WYA; YAW

Patmore, Coventry Kersey Dighton
1823-1896 .... **NCLC 9; PC 59**
See also DLB 35, 98; RGEL 2; TEA

Paton, Alan (Stewart) 1903-1988 ...... **CLC 4,
10, 25, 55, 106; TCLC 165; WLC**
See also AAYA 26; AFW; BPFB 3; BRWS
2; BYA 1; CA 13-16; 125; CANR 22;
CAP 1; CN 1, 2, 3, 4; DA; DA3; DAB;
DAC; DAM MST, NOV; DLB 225;
DLBD 17; EWL 3; EXPN; LAIT 4;
MTCW 1, 2; MTFW 2005; NFS 3, 12;
RGEL 2; SATA 11; SATA-Obit 56; TWA;
WLIT 2; WWE 1

Paton Walsh, Gillian 1937- .... **CLC 35**
See Paton Walsh, Jill; Walsh, Jill Paton
See also AAYA 11; CANR 38, 83; CLR 2,
65; DLB 161; JRDA; MAICYA 1, 2;
SAAS 3; SATA 4, 72, 109; YAW

Paton Walsh, Jill
See Paton Walsh, Gillian
See also AAYA 47; BYA 1, 8

Patterson, (Horace) Orlando (Lloyd)
1940- .... **BLCS**
See also BW 1; CA 65-68; CANR 27, 84;
CN 1, 2, 3, 4, 5, 6

Patton, George S(mith), Jr.
1885-1945 .... **TCLC 79**
See also CA 189

Paulding, James Kirke 1778-1860 ... **NCLC 2**
See also DLB 3, 59, 74, 250; RGAL 4

Paulin, Thomas Neilson 1949-
See Paulin, Tom
See also CA 123; 128; CANR 98

Paulin, Tom .... **CLC 37, 177**
See Paulin, Thomas Neilson
See also CP 3, 4, 5, 6, 7; DLB 40

Pausanias c. 1st cent. - .... **CMLC 36**

Paustovsky, Konstantin (Georgievich)
1892-1968 .... **CLC 40**
See also CA 93-96; 25-28R; DLB 272;
EWL 3

Pavese, Cesare 1908-1950 .... **PC 13; SSC 19;
TCLC 3**
See also CA 104; 169; DLB 128, 177; EW
12; EWL 3; PFS 20; RGSF 2; RGWL 2,
3; TWA; WLIT 7

Pavic, Milorad 1929- .... **CLC 60**
See also CA 136; CDWLB 4; CWW 2; DLB
181; EWL 3; RGWL 3

Pavlov, Ivan Petrovich 1849-1936 . **TCLC 91**
See also CA 118; 180

Pavlova, Karolina Karlovna
1807-1893 .... **NCLC 138**
See also DLB 205

Payne, Alan
See Jakes, John (William)

Payne, Rachel Ann
See Jakes, John (William)

Paz, Gil
See Lugones, Leopoldo

Paz, Octavio 1914-1998 . **CLC 3, 4, 6, 10, 19,
51, 65, 119; HLC 2; PC 1, 48; WLC**
See also AAYA 50; CA 73-76; 165; CANR
32, 65, 104; CWW 2; DA; DA3; DAB;
DAC; DAM MST, MULT, POET; DLB
290; DLBY 1990, 1998; DNFS 1; EWL
3; HW 1, 2; LAW; LAWS 1; MTCW 1, 2;
MTFW 2005; PFS 18; RGWL 2, 3; SSFS
13; TWA; WLIT 1

p'Bitek, Okot 1931-1982 .... **BLC 3; CLC 96;
TCLC 149**
See also AFW; BW 2, 3; CA 124; 107;
CANR 82; CP 1, 2, 3; DAM MULT; DLB
125; EWL 3; MTCW 1, 2; MTFW 2005;
RGEL 2; WLIT 2

Peacham, Henry 1578-1644(?) .... **LC 119**
See also DLB 151

Peacock, Molly 1947- .... **CLC 60**
See also CA 103; CAAS 21; CANR 52, 84;
CP 7; CWP; DLB 120, 282

Peacock, Thomas Love
1785-1866 .... **NCLC 22**
See also BRW 4; DLB 96, 116; RGEL 2;
RGSF 2

Peake, Mervyn 1911-1968 .... **CLC 7, 54**
See also CA 5-8R; 25-28R; CANR 3; DLB
15, 160, 255; FANT; MTCW 1; RGEL 2;
SATA 23; SFW 4

Pearce, Philippa
See Christie, Philippa
See also CA 5-8R; CANR 4, 109; CWRI 5;
FANT; MAICYA 2

Pearl, Eric
See Elman, Richard (Martin)

Pearson, T(homas) R(eid) 1956- .... **CLC 39**
See also CA 120; 130; CANR 97; CSW;
INT CA-130

Peck, Dale 1967- .... **CLC 81**
See also CA 146; CANR 72, 127; GLL 2

Peck, John (Frederick) 1941- .... **CLC 3**
See also CA 49-52; CANR 3, 100; CP 4, 5,
6, 7

Peck, Richard (Wayne) 1934- .... **CLC 21**
See also AAYA 1, 24; BYA 1, 6, 8, 11; CA
85-88; CANR 19, 38, 129; CLR 15; INT
CANR-19; JRDA; MAICYA 1, 2; SAAS
2; SATA 18, 55, 97, 110, 158; SATA-
Essay 110; WYA; YAW

Peck, Robert Newton 1928- .... **CLC 17**
See also AAYA 3, 43; BYA 1, 6; CA 81-84,
182; CAAE 182; CANR 31, 63, 127; CLR
45; DA; DAC; DAM MST; JRDA; LAIT
3; MAICYA 1, 2; SAAS 1; SATA 21, 62,
111, 156; SATA-Essay 108; WYA; YAW

Peckinpah, (David) Sam(uel)
1925-1984 .... **CLC 20**
See also CA 109; 114; CANR 82

Pedersen, Knut 1859-1952
See Hamsun, Knut
See also CA 104; 119; CANR 63; MTCW
1, 2

Peele, George 1556-1596 .... **LC 115**
See also BRW 1; DLB 62, 167; RGEL 2

Peeslake, Gaffer
See Durrell, Lawrence (George)

Peguy, Charles (Pierre)
1873-1914 .... **TCLC 10**
See also CA 107; 193; DLB 258; EWL 3;
GFL 1789 to the Present

Peirce, Charles Sanders
1839-1914 .... **TCLC 81**
See also CA 194; DLB 270

Pellicer, Carlos 1897(?)-1977 .... **HLCS 2**
See also CA 153; 69-72; DLB 290; EWL 3;
HW 1

Pena, Ramon del Valle y
See Valle-Inclan, Ramon (Maria) del

Pendennis, Arthur Esquir
See Thackeray, William Makepeace

Penn, Arthur
See Matthews, (James) Brander

Penn, William 1644-1718 .... **LC 25**
See also DLB 24

PEPECE
See Prado (Calvo), Pedro

MAL 5; MAWW; MTCW 1, 2; MTFW 2005; NFS 14; RGAL 4; RGSF 2; SATA 39; SATA-Obit 23; SSFS 1, 8, 11, 16; TCWW 2; TUS

Porter, Peter (Neville Frederick)
1929- .... **CLC 5, 13, 33**
See also CA 85-88; CP 1, 2, 3, 4, 5, 6, 7; DLB 40, 289; WWE 1

Porter, William Sydney 1862-1910
See Henry, O.
See also CA 104; 131; CDALB 1865-1917; DA; DA3; DAB; DAC; DAM MST; DLB 12, 78, 79; MAL 5; MTCW 1, 2; MTFW 2005; TUS; YABC 2

Portillo (y Pacheco), Jose Lopez
See Lopez Portillo (y Pacheco), Jose

Portillo Trambley, Estela 1927-1998 .. **HLC 2**
See Trambley, Estela Portillo
See also CANR 32; DAM MULT; DLB 209; HW 1

Posey, Alexander (Lawrence)
1873-1908 .... **NNAL**
See also CA 144; CANR 80; DAM MULT; DLB 175

Posse, Abel .... **CLC 70**

Post, Melville Davisson
1869-1930 .... **TCLC 39**
See also CA 110; 202; CMW 4

Potok, Chaim 1929-2002 ... **CLC 2, 7, 14, 26, 112**
See also AAYA 15, 50; AITN 1, 2; BPFB 3; BYA 1; CA 17-20R; 208; CANR 19, 35, 64, 98; CLR 92; CN 4, 5, 6; DA3; DAM NOV; DLB 28, 152; EXPN; INT CANR-19; LAIT 4; MTCW 1, 2; MTFW 2005; NFS 4; SATA 33, 106; SATA-Obit 134; TUS; YAW

Potok, Herbert Harold -2002
See Potok, Chaim

Potok, Herman Harold
See Potok, Chaim

Potter, Dennis (Christopher George)
1935-1994 .... **CLC 58, 86, 123**
See also BRWS 10; CA 107; 145; CANR 33, 61; CBD; DLB 233; MTCW 1

Pound, Ezra (Weston Loomis)
1885-1972 .. **CLC 1, 2, 3, 4, 5, 7, 10, 13, 18, 34, 48, 50, 112; PC 4; WLC**
See also AAYA 47; AMW; AMWR 1; CA 5-8R; 37-40R; CANR 40; CDALB 1917-1929; CP 1; DA; DA3; DAB; DAC; DAM MST, POET; DLB 4, 45, 63; DLBD 15; EFS 2; EWL 3; EXPP; LMFS 2; MAL 5; MTCW 1, 2; MTFW 2005; PAB; PFS 2, 8, 16; RGAL 4; TUS; WP

Povod, Reinaldo 1959-1994 .... **CLC 44**
See also CA 136; 146; CANR 83

Powell, Adam Clayton, Jr.
1908-1972 .... **BLC 3; CLC 89**
See also BW 1, 3; CA 102; 33-36R; CANR 86; DAM MULT

Powell, Anthony (Dymoke)
1905-2000 .... **CLC 1, 3, 7, 9, 10, 31**
See also BRW 7; CA 1-4R; 189; CANR 1, 32, 62, 107; CDBLB 1945-1960; CN 1, 2, 3, 4, 5, 6; DLB 15; EWL 3; MTCW 1, 2; MTFW 2005; RGEL 2; TEA

Powell, Dawn 1896(?)-1965 .... **CLC 66**
See also CA 5-8R; CANR 121; DLBY 1997

Powell, Padgett 1952- .... **CLC 34**
See also CA 126; CANR 63, 101; CSW; DLB 234; DLBY 01

Powell, (Oval) Talmage 1920-2000
See Queen, Ellery
See also CA 5-8R; CANR 2, 80

Power, Susan 1961- .... **CLC 91**
See also BYA 14; CA 160; CANR 135; NFS 11

Powers, J(ames) F(arl) 1917-1999 ..... **CLC 1, 4, 8, 57; SSC 4**
See also CA 1-4R; 181; CANR 2, 61; CN 1, 2, 3, 4, 5, 6; DLB 130; MTCW 1; RGAL 4; RGSF 2

Powers, John J(ames) 1945-
See Powers, John R.
See also CA 69-72

Powers, John R. .... **CLC 66**
See Powers, John J(ames)

Powers, Richard (S.) 1957- .... **CLC 93**
See also AMWS 9; BPFB 3; CA 148; CANR 80; CN 6, 7; MTFW 2005; TCLE 1:2

Pownall, David 1938- .... **CLC 10**
See also CA 89-92, 180; CAAS 18; CANR 49, 101; CBD; CD 5, 6; CN 4, 5, 6, 7; DLB 14

Powys, John Cowper 1872-1963 ... **CLC 7, 9, 15, 46, 125**
See also CA 85-88; CANR 106; DLB 15, 255; EWL 3; FANT; MTCW 1, 2; MTFW 2005; RGEL 2; SUFW

Powys, T(heodore) F(rancis)
1875-1953 .... **TCLC 9**
See also BRWS 8; CA 106; 189; DLB 36, 162; EWL 3; FANT; RGEL 2; SUFW

Pozzo, Modesta
See Fonte, Moderata

Prado (Calvo), Pedro 1886-1952 ... **TCLC 75**
See also CA 131; DLB 283; HW 1; LAW

Prager, Emily 1952- .... **CLC 56**
See also CA 204

Pratchett, Terry 1948- .... **CLC 197**
See also AAYA 19, 54; BPFB 3; CA 143; CANR 87, 126; CLR 64; CN 6, 7; CPW; CWRI 5; FANT; MTFW 2005; SATA 82, 139; SFW 4; SUFW 2

Pratolini, Vasco 1913-1991 .... **TCLC 124**
See also CA 211; DLB 177; EWL 3; RGWL 2, 3

Pratt, E(dwin) J(ohn) 1883(?)-1964 . **CLC 19**
See also CA 141; 93-96; CANR 77; DAC; DAM POET; DLB 92; EWL 3; RGEL 2; TWA

Premchand .... **TCLC 21**
See Srivastava, Dhanpat Rai
See also EWL 3

Prescott, William Hickling
1796-1859 .... **NCLC 163**
See also DLB 1, 30, 59, 235

Preseren, France 1800-1849 .... **NCLC 127**
See also CDWLB 4; DLB 147

Preussler, Otfried 1923- .... **CLC 17**
See also CA 77-80; SATA 24

Prevert, Jacques (Henri Marie)
1900-1977 .... **CLC 15**
See also CA 77-80; 69-72; CANR 29, 61; DLB 258; EWL 3; GFL 1789 to the Present; IDFW 3, 4; MTCW 1; RGWL 2, 3; SATA-Obit 30

Prevost, (Antoine Francois)
1697-1763 .... **LC 1**
See also DLB 314; EW 4; GFL Beginnings to 1789; RGWL 2, 3

Price, (Edward) Reynolds 1933- ... **CLC 3, 6, 13, 43, 50, 63, 212; SSC 22**
See also AMWS 6; CA 1-4R; CANR 1, 37, 57, 87, 128; CN 1, 2, 3, 4, 5, 6, 7; CSW; DAM NOV; DLB 2, 218, 278; EWL 3; INT CANR-37; MAL 5; MTFW 2005; NFS 18

Price, Richard 1949- .... **CLC 6, 12**
See also CA 49-52; CANR 3; CN 7; DLBY 1981

Prichard, Katharine Susannah
1883-1969 .... **CLC 46**
See also CA 11-12; CANR 33; CAP 1; DLB 260; MTCW 1; RGEL 2; RGSF 2; SATA 66

Priestley, J(ohn) B(oynton)
1894-1984 .... **CLC 2, 5, 9, 34**
See also BRW 7; CA 9-12R; 113; CANR 33; CDBLB 1914-1945; CN 1, 2, 3; DA3; DAM DRAM, NOV; DLB 10, 34, 77, 100, 139; DLBY 1984; EWL 3; MTCW 1, 2; MTFW 2005; RGEL 2; SFW 4

Prince 1958- .... **CLC 35**
See also CA 213

Prince, F(rank) T(empleton)
1912-2003 .... **CLC 22**
See also CA 101; 219; CANR 43, 79; CP 1, 2, 3, 4, 5, 6, 7; DLB 20

Prince Kropotkin
See Kropotkin, Peter (Aleksieevich)

Prior, Matthew 1664-1721 .... **LC 4**
See also DLB 95; RGEL 2

Prishvin, Mikhail 1873-1954 .... **TCLC 75**
See Prishvin, Mikhail Mikhailovich

Prishvin, Mikhail Mikhailovich
See Prishvin, Mikhail
See also DLB 272; EWL 3

Pritchard, William H(arrison)
1932- .... **CLC 34**
See also CA 65-68; CANR 23, 95; DLB 111

Pritchett, V(ictor) S(awdon)
1900-1997 ... **CLC 5, 13, 15, 41; SSC 14**
See also BPFB 3; BRWS 3; CA 61-64; 157; CANR 31, 63; CN 1, 2, 3, 4, 5, 6; DA3; DAM NOV; DLB 15, 139; EWL 3; MTCW 1, 2; MTFW 2005; RGEL 2; RGSF 2; TEA

Private 19022
See Manning, Frederic

Probst, Mark 1925- .... **CLC 59**
See also CA 130

Procaccino, Michael
See Cristofer, Michael

Prokosch, Frederic 1908-1989 ...... **CLC 4, 48**
See also CA 73-76; 128; CANR 82; CN 1, 2, 3, 4; CP 1, 2, 3, 4; DLB 48; MTCW 2

Propertius, Sextus c. 50B.C.-c. 16B.C. .... **CMLC 32**
See also AW 2; CDWLB 1; DLB 211; RGWL 2, 3

Prophet, The
See Dreiser, Theodore (Herman Albert)

Prose, Francine 1947- .... **CLC 45**
See also CA 109; 112; CANR 46, 95, 132; DLB 234; MTFW 2005; SATA 101, 149

Proudhon
See Cunha, Euclides (Rodrigues Pimenta) da

Proulx, Annie
See Proulx, E. Annie

Proulx, E. Annie 1935- .... **CLC 81, 158**
See also AMWS 7; BPFB 3; CA 145; CANR 65, 110; CN 6, 7; CPW 1; DA3; DAM POP; MAL 5; MTCW 2; MTFW 2005; SSFS 18

Proulx, Edna Annie
See Proulx, E. Annie

Proust, (Valentin-Louis-George-Eugene) Marcel 1871-1922 ..... **SSC 75; TCLC 7, 13, 33; WLC**
See also AAYA 58; BPFB 3; CA 104; 120; CANR 110; DA; DA3; DAB; DAC; DAM MST, NOV; DLB 65; EW 8; EWL 3; GFL 1789 to the Present; MTCW 1, 2; MTFW 2005; RGWL 2, 3; TWA

Prowler, Harley
See Masters, Edgar Lee

Ralegh, Sir Walter
See Raleigh, Sir Walter
See also BRW 1; RGEL 2; WP

Raleigh, Richard
See Lovecraft, H(oward) P(hillips)

Raleigh, Sir Walter 1554(?)-1618 .... **LC 31, 39; PC 31**
See Ralegh, Sir Walter
See also CDBLB Before 1660; DLB 172; EXPP; PFS 14; TEA

Rallentando, H. P.
See Sayers, Dorothy L(eigh)

Ramal, Walter
See de la Mare, Walter (John)

Ramana Maharshi 1879-1950 .... **TCLC 84**

Ramoacn y Cajal, Santiago 1852-1934 .... **TCLC 93**

Ramon, Juan
See Jimenez (Mantecon), Juan Ramon

Ramos, Graciliano 1892-1953 .... **TCLC 32**
See also CA 167; DLB 307; EWL 3; HW 2; LAW; WLIT 1

Rampersad, Arnold 1941- .... **CLC 44**
See also BW 2, 3; CA 127; 133; CANR 81; DLB 111; INT CA-133

Rampling, Anne
See Rice, Anne
See also GLL 2

Ramsay, Allan 1686(?)-1758 .... **LC 29**
See also DLB 95; RGEL 2

Ramsay, Jay
See Campbell, (John) Ramsey

Ramuz, Charles-Ferdinand 1878-1947 .... **TCLC 33**
See also CA 165; EWL 3

Rand, Ayn 1905-1982 ...... **CLC 3, 30, 44, 79; WLC**
See also AAYA 10; AMWS 4; BPFB 3; BYA 12; CA 13-16R; 105; CANR 27, 73; CDALBS; CN 1, 2, 3; CPW; DA; DA3; DAC; DAM MST, NOV, POP; DLB 227, 279; MTCW 1, 2; MTFW 2005; NFS 10, 16; RGAL 4; SFW 4; TUS; YAW

Randall, Dudley (Felker) 1914-2000 . **BLC 3; CLC 1, 135**
See also BW 1, 3; CA 25-28R; 189; CANR 23, 82; CP 1, 2, 3, 4; DAM MULT; DLB 41; PFS 5

Randall, Robert
See Silverberg, Robert

Ranger, Ken
See Creasey, John

Rank, Otto 1884-1939 .... **TCLC 115**

Ransom, John Crowe 1888-1974 .. **CLC 2, 4, 5, 11, 24; PC 61**
See also AMW; CA 5-8R; 49-52; CANR 6, 34; CDALBS; CP 1, 2; DA3; DAM POET; DLB 45, 63; EWL 3; EXPP; MAL 5; MTCW 1, 2; MTFW 2005; RGAL 4; TUS

Rao, Raja 1909- .... **CLC 25, 56**
See also CA 73-76; CANR 51; CN 1, 2, 3, 4, 5, 6; DAM NOV; EWL 3; MTCW 1, 2; MTFW 2005; RGEL 2; RGSF 2

Raphael, Frederic (Michael) 1931- ... **CLC 2, 14**
See also CA 1-4R; CANR 1, 86; CN 1, 2, 3, 4, 5, 6, 7; DLB 14, 319; TCLE 1:2

Ratcliffe, James P.
See Mencken, H(enry) L(ouis)

Rathbone, Julian 1935- .... **CLC 41**
See also CA 101; CANR 34, 73

Rattigan, Terence (Mervyn) 1911-1977 .... **CLC 7; DC 18**
See also BRWS 7; CA 85-88; 73-76; CBD; CDBLB 1945-1960; DAM DRAM; DFS 8; DLB 13; IDFW 3, 4; MTCW 1, 2; MTFW 2005; RGEL 2

Ratushinskaya, Irina 1954- .... **CLC 54**
See also CA 129; CANR 68; CWW 2

Raven, Simon (Arthur Noel) 1927-2001 .... **CLC 14**
See also CA 81-84; 197; CANR 86; CN 1, 2, 3, 4, 5, 6; DLB 271

Ravenna, Michael
See Welty, Eudora (Alice)

Rawley, Callman 1903-2004
See Rakosi, Carl
See also CA 21-24R; 228; CANR 12, 32, 91

Rawlings, Marjorie Kinnan 1896-1953 .... **TCLC 4**
See also AAYA 20; AMWS 10; ANW; BPFB 3; BYA 3; CA 104; 137; CANR 74; CLR 63; DLB 9, 22, 102; DLBD 17; JRDA; MAICYA 1, 2; MAL 5; MTCW 2; MTFW 2005; RGAL 4; SATA 100; WCH; YABC 1; YAW

Ray, Satyajit 1921-1992 .... **CLC 16, 76**
See also CA 114; 137; DAM MULT

Read, Herbert Edward 1893-1968 ..... **CLC 4**
See also BRW 6; CA 85-88; 25-28R; DLB 20, 149; EWL 3; PAB; RGEL 2

Read, Piers Paul 1941- .... **CLC 4, 10, 25**
See also CA 21-24R; CANR 38, 86; CN 2, 3, 4, 5, 6, 7; DLB 14; SATA 21

Reade, Charles 1814-1884 .... **NCLC 2, 74**
See also DLB 21; RGEL 2

Reade, Hamish
See Gray, Simon (James Holliday)

Reading, Peter 1946- .... **CLC 47**
See also BRWS 8; CA 103; CANR 46, 96; CP 7; DLB 40

Reaney, James 1926- .... **CLC 13**
See also CA 41-44R; CAAS 15; CANR 42; CD 5, 6; CP 1, 2, 3, 4, 5, 6, 7; DAC; DAM MST; DLB 68; RGEL 2; SATA 43

Rebreanu, Liviu 1885-1944 .... **TCLC 28**
See also CA 165; DLB 220; EWL 3

Rechy, John (Francisco) 1934- ...... **CLC 1, 7, 14, 18, 107; HLC 2**
See also CA 5-8R, 195; CAAE 195; CAAS 4; CANR 6, 32, 64; CN 1, 2, 3, 4, 5, 6, 7; DAM MULT; DLB 122, 278; DLBY 1982; HW 1, 2; INT CANR-6; LLW; MAL 5; RGAL 4

Redcam, Tom 1870-1933 .... **TCLC 25**

Reddin, Keith 1956- .... **CLC 67**
See also CAD; CD 6

Redgrove, Peter (William) 1932-2003 .... **CLC 6, 41**
See also BRWS 6; CA 1-4R; 217; CANR 3, 39, 77; CP 1, 2, 3, 4, 5, 6, 7; DLB 40; TCLE 1:2

Redmon, Anne .... **CLC 22**
See Nightingale, Anne Redmon
See also DLBY 1986

Reed, Eliot
See Ambler, Eric

Reed, Ishmael (Scott) 1938- . **BLC 3; CLC 2, 3, 5, 6, 13, 32, 60, 174; PC 68**
See also AFAW 1, 2; AMWS 10; BPFB 3; BW 2, 3; CA 21-24R; CANR 25, 48, 74, 128; CN 1, 2, 3, 4, 5, 6, 7; CP 1, 2, 3, 4, 5, 6, 7; CSW; DA3; DAM MULT; DLB 2, 5, 33, 169, 227; DLBD 8; EWL 3; LMFS 2; MAL 5; MSW; MTCW 1, 2; MTFW 2005; PFS 6; RGAL 4; TCWW 2

Reed, John (Silas) 1887-1920 .... **TCLC 9**
See also CA 106; 195; MAL 5; TUS

Reed, Lou .... **CLC 21**
See Firbank, Louis

Reese, Lizette Woodworth 1856-1935 . **PC 29**
See also CA 180; DLB 54

Reeve, Clara 1729-1807 .... **NCLC 19**
See also DLB 39; RGEL 2

Reich, Wilhelm 1897-1957 .... **TCLC 57**
See also CA 199

Reid, Christopher (John) 1949- .... **CLC 33**
See also CA 140; CANR 89; CP 4, 5, 6, 7; DLB 40; EWL 3

Reid, Desmond
See Moorcock, Michael (John)

Reid Banks, Lynne 1929-
See Banks, Lynne Reid
See also AAYA 49; CA 1-4R; CANR 6, 22, 38, 87; CLR 24; CN 1, 2, 3, 7; JRDA; MAICYA 1, 2; SATA 22, 75, 111, 165; YAW

Reilly, William K.
See Creasey, John

Reiner, Max
See Caldwell, (Janet Miriam) Taylor (Holland)

Reis, Ricardo
See Pessoa, Fernando (Antonio Nogueira)

Reizenstein, Elmer Leopold
See Rice, Elmer (Leopold)
See also EWL 3

Remarque, Erich Maria 1898-1970 . **CLC 21**
See also AAYA 27; BPFB 3; CA 77-80; 29-32R; CDWLB 2; DA; DA3; DAB; DAC; DAM MST, NOV; DLB 56; EWL 3; EXPN; LAIT 3; MTCW 1, 2; MTFW 2005; NFS 4; RGWL 2, 3

Remington, Frederic S(ackrider) 1861-1909 .... **TCLC 89**
See also CA 108; 169; DLB 12, 186, 188; SATA 41; TCWW 2

Remizov, A.
See Remizov, Aleksei (Mikhailovich)

Remizov, A. M.
See Remizov, Aleksei (Mikhailovich)

Remizov, Aleksei (Mikhailovich) 1877-1957 .... **TCLC 27**
See Remizov, Alexey Mikhaylovich
See also CA 125; 133; DLB 295

Remizov, Alexey Mikhaylovich
See Remizov, Aleksei (Mikhailovich)
See also EWL 3

Renan, Joseph Ernest 1823-1892 . **NCLC 26, 145**
See also GFL 1789 to the Present

Renard, Jules(-Pierre) 1864-1910 .. **TCLC 17**
See also CA 117; 202; GFL 1789 to the Present

Renault, Mary .... **CLC 3, 11, 17**
See Challans, Mary
See also BPFB 3; BYA 2; CN 1, 2, 3; DLBY 1983; EWL 3; GLL 1; LAIT 1; RGEL 2; RHW

Rendell, Ruth (Barbara) 1930- .. **CLC 28, 48**
See Vine, Barbara
See also BPFB 3; BRWS 9; CA 109; CANR 32, 52, 74, 127; CN 5, 6, 7; CPW; DAM POP; DLB 87, 276; INT CANR-32; MSW; MTCW 1, 2; MTFW 2005

Renoir, Jean 1894-1979 .... **CLC 20**
See also CA 129; 85-88

Resnais, Alain 1922- .... **CLC 16**

Revard, Carter (Curtis) 1931- .... **NNAL**
See also CA 144; CANR 81; PFS 5

Reverdy, Pierre 1889-1960 .... **CLC 53**
See also CA 97-100; 89-92; DLB 258; EWL 3; GFL 1789 to the Present

Rexroth, Kenneth 1905-1982 .... **CLC 1, 2, 6, 11, 22, 49, 112; PC 20**
See also BG 1:3; CA 5-8R; 107; CANR 14, 34, 63; CDALB 1941-1968; CP 1, 2, 3; DAM POET; DLB 16, 48, 165, 212; DLBY 1982; EWL 3; INT CANR-14; MAL 5; MTCW 1, 2; MTFW 2005; RGAL 4

Reyes, Alfonso 1889-1959 .... **HLCS 2; TCLC 33**
See also CA 131; EWL 3; HW 1; LAW

Ross, Martin 1862-1915
See Martin, Violet Florence
See also DLB 135; GLL 2; RGEL 2; RGSF 2

Ross, (James) Sinclair 1908-1996 ... **CLC 13; SSC 24**
See also CA 73-76; CANR 81; CN 1, 2, 3, 4, 5, 6; DAC; DAM MST; DLB 88; RGEL 2; RGSF 2; TCWW 1, 2

Rossetti, Christina 1830-1894 ... **NCLC 2, 50, 66; PC 7; WLC**
See also AAYA 51; BRW 5; BYA 4; DA; DA3; DAB; DAC; DAM MST, POET; DLB 35, 163, 240; EXPP; FL 1:3; LATS 1:1; MAICYA 1, 2; PFS 10, 14; RGEL 2; SATA 20; TEA; WCH

Rossetti, Christina Georgina
See Rossetti, Christina

Rossetti, Dante Gabriel 1828-1882 . **NCLC 4, 77; PC 44; WLC**
See also AAYA 51; BRW 5; CDBLB 1832-1890; DA; DAB; DAC; DAM MST, POET; DLB 35; EXPP; RGEL 2; TEA

Rossi, Cristina Peri
See Peri Rossi, Cristina

Rossi, Jean-Baptiste 1931-2003
See Japrisot, Sebastien
See also CA 201; 215

Rossner, Judith (Perelman) 1935- . **CLC 6, 9, 29**
See also AITN 2; BEST 90:3; BPFB 3; CA 17-20R; CANR 18, 51, 73; CN 4, 5, 6, 7; DLB 6; INT CANR-18; MAL 5; MTCW 1, 2; MTFW 2005

Rostand, Edmond (Eugene Alexis)
1868-1918 .... **DC 10; TCLC 6, 37**
See also CA 104; 126; DA; DA3; DAB; DAC; DAM DRAM, MST; DFS 1; DLB 192; LAIT 1; MTCW 1; RGWL 2, 3; TWA

Roth, Henry 1906-1995 ..... **CLC 2, 6, 11, 104**
See also AMWS 9; CA 11-12; 149; CANR 38, 63; CAP 1; CN 1, 2, 3, 4, 5, 6; DA3; DLB 28; EWL 3; MAL 5; MTCW 1, 2; MTFW 2005; RGAL 4

Roth, (Moses) Joseph 1894-1939 ... **TCLC 33**
See also CA 160; DLB 85; EWL 3; RGWL 2, 3

Roth, Philip (Milton) 1933- ... **CLC 1, 2, 3, 4, 6, 9, 15, 22, 31, 47, 66, 86, 119, 201; SSC 26; WLC**
See also AAYA 67; AMWR 2; AMWS 3; BEST 90:3; BPFB 3; CA 1-4R; CANR 1, 22, 36, 55, 89, 132; CDALB 1968-1988; CN 3, 4, 5, 6, 7; CPW 1; DA; DA3; DAB; DAC; DAM MST, NOV, POP; DLB 2, 28, 173; DLBY 1982; EWL 3; MAL 5; MTCW 1, 2; MTFW 2005; RGAL 4; RGSF 2; SSFS 12, 18; TUS

Rothenberg, Jerome 1931- .... **CLC 6, 57**
See also CA 45-48; CANR 1, 106; CP 1, 2, 3, 4, 5, 6, 7; DLB 5, 193

Rotter, Pat ed. .... **CLC 65**

Roumain, Jacques (Jean Baptiste)
1907-1944 .... **BLC 3; TCLC 19**
See also BW 1; CA 117; 125; DAM MULT; EWL 3

Rourke, Constance Mayfield
1885-1941 .... **TCLC 12**
See also CA 107; 200; MAL 5; YABC 1

Rousseau, Jean-Baptiste 1671-1741 ...... **LC 9**

Rousseau, Jean-Jacques 1712-1778 .... **LC 14, 36; WLC**
See also DA; DA3; DAB; DAC; DAM MST; DLB 314; EW 4; GFL Beginnings to 1789; LMFS 1; RGWL 2, 3; TWA

Roussel, Raymond 1877-1933 .... **TCLC 20**
See also CA 117; 201; EWL 3; GFL 1789 to the Present

Rovit, Earl (Herbert) 1927- .... **CLC 7**
See also CA 5-8R; CANR 12

Rowe, Elizabeth Singer 1674-1737 ..... **LC 44**
See also DLB 39, 95

Rowe, Nicholas 1674-1718 .... **LC 8**
See also DLB 84; RGEL 2

Rowlandson, Mary 1637(?)-1678 .... **LC 66**
See also DLB 24, 200; RGAL 4

Rowley, Ames Dorrance
See Lovecraft, H(oward) P(hillips)

Rowley, William 1585(?)-1626 .... **LC 100**
See also DFS 22; DLB 58; RGEL 2

Rowling, J.K. 1966- .... **CLC 137**
See also AAYA 34; BYA 11, 13, 14; CA 173; CANR 128; CLR 66, 80; MAICYA 2; MTFW 2005; SATA 109; SUFW 2

Rowling, Joanne Kathleen
See Rowling, J.K.

Rowson, Susanna Haswell
1762(?)-1824 .... **NCLC 5, 69**
See also AMWS 15; DLB 37, 200; RGAL 4

Roy, Arundhati 1960(?)- .... **CLC 109, 210**
See also CA 163; CANR 90, 126; CN 7; DLBY 1997; EWL 3; LATS 1:2; MTFW 2005; NFS 22; WWE 1

Roy, Gabrielle 1909-1983 .... **CLC 10, 14**
See also CA 53-56; 110; CANR 5, 61; CCA 1; DAB; DAC; DAM MST; DLB 68; EWL 3; MTCW 1; RGWL 2, 3; SATA 104; TCLE 1:2

Royko, Mike 1932-1997 .... **CLC 109**
See also CA 89-92; 157; CANR 26, 111; CPW

Rozanov, Vasilii Vasil'evich
See Rozanov, Vassili
See also DLB 295

Rozanov, Vasily Vasilyevich
See Rozanov, Vassili
See also EWL 3

Rozanov, Vassili 1856-1919 .... **TCLC 104**
See Rozanov, Vasilii Vasil'evich; Rozanov, Vasily Vasilyevich

Rozewicz, Tadeusz 1921- ...... **CLC 9, 23, 139**
See also CA 108; CANR 36, 66; CWW 2; DA3; DAM POET; DLB 232; EWL 3; MTCW 1, 2; MTFW 2005; RGWL 3

Ruark, Gibbons 1941- .... **CLC 3**
See also CA 33-36R; CAAS 23; CANR 14, 31, 57; DLB 120

Rubens, Bernice (Ruth) 1923-2004 . **CLC 19, 31**
See also CA 25-28R; 232; CANR 33, 65, 128; CN 1, 2, 3, 4, 5, 6, 7; DLB 14, 207; MTCW 1

Rubin, Harold
See Robbins, Harold

Rudkin, (James) David 1936- .... **CLC 14**
See also CA 89-92; CBD; CD 5, 6; DLB 13

Rudnik, Raphael 1933- .... **CLC 7**
See also CA 29-32R

Ruffian, M.
See Hasek, Jaroslav (Matej Frantisek)

Ruiz, Jose Martinez .... **CLC 11**
See Martinez Ruiz, Jose

Ruiz, Juan c. 1283-c. 1350 .... **CMLC 66**

Rukeyser, Muriel 1913-1980 . **CLC 6, 10, 15, 27; PC 12**
See also AMWS 6; CA 5-8R; 93-96; CANR 26, 60; CP 1, 2, 3; DA3; DAM POET; DLB 48; EWL 3; FW; GLL 2; MAL 5; MTCW 1, 2; PFS 10; RGAL 4; SATA-Obit 22

Rule, Jane (Vance) 1931- .... **CLC 27**
See also CA 25-28R; CAAS 18; CANR 12, 87; CN 4, 5, 6, 7; DLB 60; FW

Rulfo, Juan 1918-1986 .. **CLC 8, 80; HLC 2; SSC 25**
See also CA 85-88; 118; CANR 26; CD-WLB 3; DAM MULT; DLB 113; EWL 3; HW 1, 2; LAW; MTCW 1, 2; RGSF 2; RGWL 2, 3; WLIT 1

Rumi, Jalal al-Din 1207-1273 ...... **CMLC 20; PC 45**
See also AAYA 64; RGWL 2, 3; WLIT 6; WP

Runeberg, Johan 1804-1877 .... **NCLC 41**

Runyon, (Alfred) Damon
1884(?)-1946 .... **TCLC 10**
See also CA 107; 165; DLB 11, 86, 171; MAL 5; MTCW 2; RGAL 4

Rush, Norman 1933- .... **CLC 44**
See also CA 121; 126; CANR 130; INT CA-126

Rushdie, (Ahmed) Salman 1947- .... **CLC 23, 31, 55, 100, 191; SSC 83; WLCS**
See also AAYA 65; BEST 89:3; BPFB 3; BRWS 4; CA 108; 111; CANR 33, 56, 108, 133; CN 4, 5, 6, 7; CPW 1; DA3; DAB; DAC; DAM MST, NOV, POP; DLB 194; EWL 3; FANT; INT CA-111; LATS 1:2; LMFS 2; MTCW 1, 2; MTFW 2005; NFS 22; RGEL 2; RGSF 2; TEA; WLIT 4

Rushforth, Peter (Scott) 1945- .... **CLC 19**
See also CA 101

Ruskin, John 1819-1900 .... **TCLC 63**
See also BRW 5; BYA 5; CA 114; 129; CD-BLB 1832-1890; DLB 55, 163, 190; RGEL 2; SATA 24; TEA; WCH

Russ, Joanna 1937- .... **CLC 15**
See also BPFB 3; CA 25-28; CANR 11, 31, 65; CN 4, 5, 6, 7; DLB 8; FW; GLL 1; MTCW 1; SCFW 1, 2; SFW 4

Russ, Richard Patrick
See O'Brian, Patrick

Russell, George William 1867-1935
See A.E.; Baker, Jean H.
See also BRWS 8; CA 104; 153; CDBLB 1890-1914; DAM POET; EWL 3; RGEL 2

Russell, Jeffrey Burton 1934- .... **CLC 70**
See also CA 25-28R; CANR 11, 28, 52

Russell, (Henry) Ken(neth Alfred)
1927- .... **CLC 16**
See also CA 105

Russell, William Martin 1947-
See Russell, Willy
See also CA 164; CANR 107

Russell, Willy .... **CLC 60**
See Russell, William Martin
See also CBD; CD 5, 6; DLB 233

Russo, Richard 1949- .... **CLC 181**
See also AMWS 12; CA 127; 133; CANR 87, 114

Rutherford, Mark .... **TCLC 25**
See White, William Hale
See also DLB 18; RGEL 2

Ruyslinck, Ward .... **CLC 14**
See Belser, Reimond Karel Maria de

Ryan, Cornelius (John) 1920-1974 ..... **CLC 7**
See also CA 69-72; 53-56; CANR 38

Ryan, Michael 1946- .... **CLC 65**
See also CA 49-52; CANR 109; DLBY 1982

Ryan, Tim
See Dent, Lester

Rybakov, Anatoli (Naumovich)
1911-1998 .... **CLC 23, 53**
See Rybakov, Anatolii (Naumovich)
See also CA 126; 135; 172; SATA 79; SATA-Obit 108

Rybakov, Anatolii (Naumovich)
See Rybakov, Anatoli (Naumovich)
See also DLB 302

Schnitzler, Arthur 1862-1931 ..... **DC 17; SSC 15, 61; TCLC 4**
See also CA 104; CDWLB 2; DLB 81, 118; EW 8; EWL 3; RGSF 2; RGWL 2, 3

Schoenberg, Arnold Franz Walter 1874-1951 .... **TCLC 75**
See also CA 109; 188

Schonberg, Arnold
See Schoenberg, Arnold Franz Walter

Schopenhauer, Arthur 1788-1860 . **NCLC 51, 157**
See also DLB 90; EW 5

Schor, Sandra (M.) 1932(?)-1990 ..... **CLC 65**
See also CA 132

Schorer, Mark 1908-1977 .... **CLC 9**
See also CA 5-8R; 73-76; CANR 7; CN 1, 2; DLB 103

Schrader, Paul (Joseph) 1946- . **CLC 26, 212**
See also CA 37-40R; CANR 41; DLB 44

Schreber, Daniel 1842-1911 .... **TCLC 123**

Schreiner, Olive (Emilie Albertina) 1855-1920 .... **TCLC 9**
See also AFW; BRWS 2; CA 105; 154; DLB 18, 156, 190, 225; EWL 3; FW; RGEL 2; TWA; WLIT 2; WWE 1

Schulberg, Budd (Wilson) 1914- .. **CLC 7, 48**
See also BPFB 3; CA 25-28R; CANR 19, 87; CN 1, 2, 3, 4, 5, 6, 7; DLB 6, 26, 28; DLBY 1981, 2001; MAL 5

Schulman, Arnold
See Trumbo, Dalton

Schulz, Bruno 1892-1942 .. **SSC 13; TCLC 5, 51**
See also CA 115; 123; CANR 86; CDWLB 4; DLB 215; EWL 3; MTCW 2; MTFW 2005; RGSF 2; RGWL 2, 3

Schulz, Charles M. 1922-2000 .... **CLC 12**
See also AAYA 39; CA 9-12R; 187; CANR 6, 132; INT CANR-6; MTFW 2005; SATA 10; SATA-Obit 118

Schulz, Charles Monroe
See Schulz, Charles M.

Schumacher, E(rnst) F(riedrich) 1911-1977 .... **CLC 80**
See also CA 81-84; 73-76; CANR 34, 85

Schumann, Robert 1810-1856 ...... **NCLC 143**

Schuyler, George Samuel 1895-1977 . **HR 1:3**
See also BW 2; CA 81-84; 73-76; CANR 42; DLB 29, 51

Schuyler, James Marcus 1923-1991 .. **CLC 5, 23**
See also CA 101; 134; CP 1, 2, 3, 4; DAM POET; DLB 5, 169; EWL 3; INT CA-101; MAL 5; WP

Schwartz, Delmore (David) 1913-1966 ... **CLC 2, 4, 10, 45, 87; PC 8**
See also AMWS 2; CA 17-18; 25-28R; CANR 35; CAP 2; DLB 28, 48; EWL 3; MAL 5; MTCW 1, 2; MTFW 2005; PAB; RGAL 4; TUS

Schwartz, Ernst
See Ozu, Yasujiro

Schwartz, John Burnham 1965- .... **CLC 59**
See also CA 132; CANR 116

Schwartz, Lynne Sharon 1939- .... **CLC 31**
See also CA 103; CANR 44, 89; DLB 218; MTCW 2; MTFW 2005

Schwartz, Muriel A.
See Eliot, T(homas) S(tearns)

Schwarz-Bart, Andre 1928- .... **CLC 2, 4**
See also CA 89-92; CANR 109; DLB 299

Schwarz-Bart, Simone 1938- . **BLCS; CLC 7**
See also BW 2; CA 97-100; CANR 117; EWL 3

Schwerner, Armand 1927-1999 .... **PC 42**
See also CA 9-12R; 179; CANR 50, 85; CP 2, 3, 4; DLB 165

Schwitters, Kurt (Hermann Edward Karl Julius) 1887-1948 .... **TCLC 95**
See also CA 158

Schwob, Marcel (Mayer Andre) 1867-1905 .... **TCLC 20**
See also CA 117; 168; DLB 123; GFL 1789 to the Present

Sciascia, Leonardo 1921-1989 .. **CLC 8, 9, 41**
See also CA 85-88; 130; CANR 35; DLB 177; EWL 3; MTCW 1; RGWL 2, 3

Scoppettone, Sandra 1936- .... **CLC 26**
See Early, Jack
See also AAYA 11, 65; BYA 8; CA 5-8R; CANR 41, 73; GLL 1; MAICYA 2; MAICYAS 1; SATA 9, 92; WYA; YAW

Scorsese, Martin 1942- .... **CLC 20, 89, 207**
See also AAYA 38; CA 110; 114; CANR 46, 85

Scotland, Jay
See Jakes, John (William)

Scott, Duncan Campbell 1862-1947 .... **TCLC 6**
See also CA 104; 153; DAC; DLB 92; RGEL 2

Scott, Evelyn 1893-1963 .... **CLC 43**
See also CA 104; 112; CANR 64; DLB 9, 48; RHW

Scott, F(rancis) R(eginald) 1899-1985 .... **CLC 22**
See also CA 101; 114; CANR 87; CP 1, 2, 3, 4; DLB 88; INT CA-101; RGEL 2

Scott, Frank
See Scott, F(rancis) R(eginald)

Scott, Joan .... **CLC 65**

Scott, Joanna 1960- .... **CLC 50**
See also CA 126; CANR 53, 92

Scott, Paul (Mark) 1920-1978 ...... **CLC 9, 60**
See also BRWS 1; CA 81-84; 77-80; CANR 33; CN 1, 2; DLB 14, 207; EWL 3; MTCW 1; RGEL 2; RHW; WWE 1

Scott, Ridley 1937- .... **CLC 183**
See also AAYA 13, 43

Scott, Sarah 1723-1795 .... **LC 44**
See also DLB 39

Scott, Sir Walter 1771-1832 .... **NCLC 15, 69, 110; PC 13; SSC 32; WLC**
See also AAYA 22; BRW 4; BYA 2; CD-BLB 1789-1832; DA; DAB; DAC; DAM MST, NOV, POET; DLB 93, 107, 116, 144, 159; GL 3; HGG; LAIT 1; RGEL 2; RGSF 2; SSFS 10; SUFW 1; TEA; WLIT 3; YABC 2

Scribe, (Augustin) Eugene 1791-1861 . **DC 5; NCLC 16**
See also DAM DRAM; DLB 192; GFL 1789 to the Present; RGWL 2, 3

Scrum, R.
See Crumb, R(obert)

Scudery, Georges de 1601-1667 .... **LC 75**
See also GFL Beginnings to 1789

Scudery, Madeleine de 1607-1701 .. **LC 2, 58**
See also DLB 268; GFL Beginnings to 1789

Scum
See Crumb, R(obert)

Scumbag, Little Bobby
See Crumb, R(obert)

Seabrook, John
See Hubbard, L(afayette) Ron(ald)

Seacole, Mary Jane Grant 1805-1881 .... **NCLC 147**
See also DLB 166

Sealy, I(rwin) Allan 1951- .... **CLC 55**
See also CA 136; CN 6, 7

Search, Alexander
See Pessoa, Fernando (Antonio Nogueira)

Sebald, W(infried) G(eorg) 1944-2001 .... **CLC 194**
See also BRWS 8; CA 159; 202; CANR 98; MTFW 2005

Sebastian, Lee
See Silverberg, Robert

Sebastian Owl
See Thompson, Hunter S(tockton)

Sebestyen, Igen
See Sebestyen, Ouida

Sebestyen, Ouida 1924- .... **CLC 30**
See also AAYA 8; BYA 7; CA 107; CANR 40, 114; CLR 17; JRDA; MAICYA 1, 2; SAAS 10; SATA 39, 140; WYA; YAW

Sebold, Alice 1963(?)- .... **CLC 193**
See also AAYA 56; CA 203; MTFW 2005

Second Duke of Buckingham
See Villiers, George

Secundus, H. Scriblerus
See Fielding, Henry

Sedges, John
See Buck, Pearl S(ydenstricker)

Sedgwick, Catharine Maria 1789-1867 .... **NCLC 19, 98**
See also DLB 1, 74, 183, 239, 243, 254; FL 1:3; RGAL 4

Seelye, John (Douglas) 1931- .... **CLC 7**
See also CA 97-100; CANR 70; INT CA-97-100; TCWW 1, 2

Seferiades, Giorgos Stylianou 1900-1971
See Seferis, George
See also CA 5-8R; 33-36R; CANR 5, 36; MTCW 1

Seferis, George .... **CLC 5, 11; PC 66**
See Seferiades, Giorgos Stylianou
See also EW 12; EWL 3; RGWL 2, 3

Segal, Erich (Wolf) 1937- .... **CLC 3, 10**
See also BEST 89:1; BPFB 3; CA 25-28R; CANR 20, 36, 65, 113; CPW; DAM POP; DLBY 1986; INT CANR-20; MTCW 1

Seger, Bob 1945- .... **CLC 35**

Seghers, Anna .... **CLC 7**
See Radvanyi, Netty
See also CDWLB 2; DLB 69; EWL 3

Seidel, Frederick (Lewis) 1936- .... **CLC 18**
See also CA 13-16R; CANR 8, 99; CP 1, 2, 3, 4, 5, 6, 7; DLBY 1984

Seifert, Jaroslav 1901-1986 . **CLC 34, 44, 93; PC 47**
See also CA 127; CDWLB 4; DLB 215; EWL 3; MTCW 1, 2

Sei Shonagon c. 966-1017(?) .... **CMLC 6**

Sejour, Victor 1817-1874 .... **DC 10**
See also DLB 50

Sejour Marcou et Ferrand, Juan Victor
See Sejour, Victor

Selby, Hubert, Jr. 1928-2004 ..... **CLC 1, 2, 4, 8; SSC 20**
See also CA 13-16R; 226; CANR 33, 85; CN 1, 2, 3, 4, 5, 6, 7; DLB 2, 227; MAL 5

Selzer, Richard 1928- .... **CLC 74**
See also CA 65-68; CANR 14, 106

Sembene, Ousmane
See Ousmane, Sembene
See also AFW; EWL 3; WLIT 2

Senancour, Etienne Pivert de 1770-1846 .... **NCLC 16**
See also DLB 119; GFL 1789 to the Present

Sender, Ramon (Jose) 1902-1982 ...... **CLC 8; HLC 2; TCLC 136**
See also CA 5-8R; 105; CANR 8; DAM MULT; DLB 322; EWL 3; HW 1; MTCW 1; RGWL 2, 3

Seneca, Lucius Annaeus c. 4B.C.-c. 65 .... **CMLC 6; DC 5**
See also AW 2; CDWLB 1; DAM DRAM; DLB 211; RGWL 2, 3; TWA

Shepherd, Michael
  See Ludlum, Robert
Sherburne, Zoa (Lillian Morin)
  1912-1995 .... **CLC 30**
  See also AAYA 13; CA 1-4R; 176; CANR
  3, 37; MAICYA 1, 2; SAAS 18; SATA 3;
  YAW
Sheridan, Frances 1724-1766 .... **LC 7**
  See also DLB 39, 84
Sheridan, Richard Brinsley
  1751-1816 .... **DC 1; NCLC 5, 91; WLC**
  See also BRW 3; CDBLB 1660-1789; DA;
  DAB; DAC; DAM DRAM, MST; DFS
  15; DLB 89; WLIT 3
Sherman, Jonathan Marc 1968- .... **CLC 55**
  See also CA 230
Sherman, Martin 1941(?)- .... **CLC 19**
  See also CA 116; 123; CAD; CANR 86;
  CD 5, 6; DFS 20; DLB 228; GLL 1; IDTP
Sherwin, Judith Johnson
  See Johnson, Judith (Emlyn)
  See also CANR 85; CP 2, 3, 4; CWP
Sherwood, Frances 1940- .... **CLC 81**
  See also CA 146, 220; CAAE 220
Sherwood, Robert E(mmet)
  1896-1955 .... **TCLC 3**
  See also CA 104; 153; CANR 86; DAM
  DRAM; DFS 11, 15, 17; DLB 7, 26, 249;
  IDFW 3, 4; MAL 5; RGAL 4
Shestov, Lev 1866-1938 .... **TCLC 56**
Shevchenko, Taras 1814-1861 .... **NCLC 54**
Shiel, M(atthew) P(hipps)
  1865-1947 .... **TCLC 8**
  See Holmes, Gordon
  See also CA 106; 160; DLB 153; HGG;
  MTCW 2; MTFW 2005; SCFW 1, 2;
  SFW 4; SUFW
Shields, Carol (Ann) 1935-2003 ...... **CLC 91,**
  113, 193
  See also AMWS 7; CA 81-84; 218; CANR
  51, 74, 98, 133; CCA 1; CN 6, 7; CPW;
  DA3; DAC; MTCW 2; MTFW 2005
Shields, David (Jonathan) 1956- .... **CLC 97**
  See also CA 124; CANR 48, 99, 112
Shiga, Naoya 1883-1971 .... **CLC 33; SSC 23;**
  TCLC 172
  See Shiga Naoya
  See also CA 101; 33-36R; MJW; RGWL 3
Shiga Naoya
  See Shiga, Naoya
  See also DLB 180; EWL 3; RGWL 3
Shilts, Randy 1951-1994 .... **CLC 85**
  See also AAYA 19; CA 115; 127; 144;
  CANR 45; DA3; GLL 1; INT CA-127;
  MTCW 2; MTFW 2005
Shimazaki, Haruki 1872-1943
  See Shimazaki Toson
  See also CA 105; 134; CANR 84; RGWL 3
Shimazaki Toson .... **TCLC 5**
  See Shimazaki, Haruki
  See also DLB 180; EWL 3
Shirley, James 1596-1666 .... **DC 25; LC 96**
  See also DLB 58; RGEL 2
Sholokhov, Mikhail (Aleksandrovich)
  1905-1984 .... **CLC 7, 15**
  See also CA 101; 112; DLB 272; EWL 3;
  MTCW 1, 2; MTFW 2005; RGWL 2, 3;
  SATA-Obit 36
Shone, Patric
  See Hanley, James
Showalter, Elaine 1941- .... **CLC 169**
  See also CA 57-60; CANR 58, 106; DLB
  67; FW; GLL 2
Shreve, Susan
  See Shreve, Susan Richards
Shreve, Susan Richards 1939- .... **CLC 23**
  See also CA 49-52; CAAS 5; CANR 5, 38,
  69, 100; MAICYA 1, 2; SATA 46, 95, 152;
  SATA-Brief 41

Shue, Larry 1946-1985 .... **CLC 52**
  See also CA 145; 117; DAM DRAM; DFS
  7
Shu-Jen, Chou 1881-1936
  See Lu Hsun
  See also CA 104
Shulman, Alix Kates 1932- .... **CLC 2, 10**
  See also CA 29-32R; CANR 43; FW; SATA
  7
Shuster, Joe 1914-1992 .... **CLC 21**
  See also AAYA 50
Shute, Nevil .... **CLC 30**
  See Norway, Nevil Shute
  See also BPFB 3; DLB 255; NFS 9; RHW;
  SFW 4
Shuttle, Penelope (Diane) 1947- .... **CLC 7**
  See also CA 93-96; CANR 39, 84, 92, 108;
  CP 3, 4, 5, 6, 7; CWP; DLB 14, 40
Shvarts, Elena 1948- .... **PC 50**
  See also CA 147
Sidhwa, Bapsi
  See Sidhwa, Bapsy (N.)
  See also CN 6, 7
Sidhwa, Bapsy (N.) 1938- .... **CLC 168**
  See Sidhwa, Bapsi
  See also CA 108; CANR 25, 57; FW
Sidney, Mary 1561-1621 .... **LC 19, 39**
  See Sidney Herbert, Mary
Sidney, Sir Philip 1554-1586 . **LC 19, 39; PC**
  32
  See also BRW 1; BRWR 2; CDBLB Before
  1660; DA; DA3; DAB; DAC; DAM MST,
  POET; DLB 167; EXPP; PAB; RGEL 2;
  TEA; WP
Sidney Herbert, Mary
  See Sidney, Mary
  See also DLB 167
Siegel, Jerome 1914-1996 .... **CLC 21**
  See Siegel, Jerry
  See also CA 116; 169; 151
Siegel, Jerry
  See Siegel, Jerome
  See also AAYA 50
Sienkiewicz, Henryk (Adam Alexander Pius)
  1846-1916 .... **TCLC 3**
  See also CA 104; 134; CANR 84; EWL 3;
  RGSF 2; RGWL 2, 3
Sierra, Gregorio Martinez
  See Martinez Sierra, Gregorio
Sierra, Maria (de la O'LeJarraga) Martinez
  See Martinez Sierra, Maria (de la
  O'LeJarraga)
Sigal, Clancy 1926- .... **CLC 7**
  See also CA 1-4R; CANR 85; CN 1, 2, 3,
  4, 5, 6, 7
Siger of Brabant 1240(?)-1284(?) . **CMLC 69**
  See also DLB 115
Sigourney, Lydia H.
  See Sigourney, Lydia Howard (Huntley)
  See also DLB 73, 183
Sigourney, Lydia Howard (Huntley)
  1791-1865 .... **NCLC 21, 87**
  See Sigourney, Lydia H.; Sigourney, Lydia
  Huntley
  See also DLB 1
Sigourney, Lydia Huntley
  See Sigourney, Lydia Howard (Huntley)
  See also DLB 42, 239, 243
Siguenza y Gongora, Carlos de
  1645-1700 .... **HLCS 2; LC 8**
  See also LAW
Sigurjonsson, Johann
  See Sigurjonsson, Johann
Sigurjonsson, Johann 1880-1919 ... **TCLC 27**
  See also CA 170; DLB 293; EWL 3
Sikelianos, Angelos 1884-1951 .... **PC 29;**
  TCLC 39
  See also EWL 3; RGWL 2, 3

Silkin, Jon 1930-1997 .... **CLC 2, 6, 43**
  See also CA 5-8R; CAAS 5; CANR 89; CP
  1, 2, 3, 4, 5, 6; DLB 27
Silko, Leslie (Marmon) 1948- .... **CLC 23, 74,**
  114, 211; NNAL; SSC 37, 66; WLCS
  See also AAYA 14; AMWS 4; ANW; BYA
  12; CA 115; 122; CANR 45, 65, 118; CN
  4, 5, 6, 7; CP 4, 5, 6, 7; CPW 1; CWP;
  DA; DA3; DAC; DAM MST, MULT,
  POP; DLB 143, 175, 256, 275; EWL 3;
  EXPP; EXPS; LAIT 4; MAL 5; MTCW
  2; MTFW 2005; NFS 4; PFS 9, 16; RGAL
  4; RGSF 2; SSFS 4, 8, 10, 11; TCWW 1,
  2
Sillanpaa, Frans Eemil 1888-1964 ... **CLC 19**
  See also CA 129; 93-96; EWL 3; MTCW 1
Sillitoe, Alan 1928- .. **CLC 1, 3, 6, 10, 19, 57,**
  148
  See also AITN 1; BRWS 5; CA 9-12R, 191;
  CAAE 191; CAAS 2; CANR 8, 26, 55,
  139; CDBLB 1960 to Present; CN 1, 2, 3,
  4, 5, 6; CP 1, 2, 3, 4; DLB 14, 139; EWL
  3; MTCW 1, 2; MTFW 2005; RGEL 2;
  RGSF 2; SATA 61
Silone, Ignazio 1900-1978 .... **CLC 4**
  See also CA 25-28; 81-84; CANR 34; CAP
  2; DLB 264; EW 12; EWL 3; MTCW 1;
  RGSF 2; RGWL 2, 3
Silone, Ignazione
  See Silone, Ignazio
Silver, Joan Micklin 1935- .... **CLC 20**
  See also CA 114; 121; INT CA-121
Silver, Nicholas
  See Faust, Frederick (Schiller)
Silverberg, Robert 1935- .... **CLC 7, 140**
  See also AAYA 24; BPFB 3; BYA 7, 9; CA
  1-4R, 186; CAAE 186; CAAS 3; CANR
  1, 20, 36, 85, 140; CLR 59; CN 6, 7;
  CPW; DAM POP; DLB 8; INT CANR-
  20; MAICYA 1, 2; MTCW 1, 2; MTFW
  2005; SATA 13, 91; SATA-Essay 104;
  SCFW 1, 2; SFW 4; SUFW 2
Silverstein, Alvin 1933- .... **CLC 17**
  See also CA 49-52; CANR 2; CLR 25;
  JRDA; MAICYA 1, 2; SATA 8, 69, 124
Silverstein, Shel(don Allan)
  1932-1999 .... **PC 49**
  See also AAYA 40; BW 3; CA 107; 179;
  CANR 47, 74, 81; CLR 5, 96; CWRI 5;
  JRDA; MAICYA 1, 2; MTCW 2; MTFW
  2005; SATA 33, 92; SATA-Brief 27;
  SATA-Obit 116
Silverstein, Virginia B(arbara Opshelor)
  1937- .... **CLC 17**
  See also CA 49-52; CANR 2; CLR 25;
  JRDA; MAICYA 1, 2; SATA 8, 69, 124
Sim, Georges
  See Simenon, Georges (Jacques Christian)
Simak, Clifford D(onald) 1904-1988 . **CLC 1,**
  55
  See also CA 1-4R; 125; CANR 1, 35; DLB
  8; MTCW 1; SATA-Obit 56; SCFW 1, 2;
  SFW 4
Simenon, Georges (Jacques Christian)
  1903-1989 .... **CLC 1, 2, 3, 8, 18, 47**
  See also BPFB 3; CA 85-88; 129; CANR
  35; CMW 4; DA3; DAM POP; DLB 72;
  DLBY 1989; EW 12; EWL 3; GFL 1789
  to the Present; MSW; MTCW 1, 2; MTFW
  2005; RGWL 2, 3
Simic, Charles 1938- .... **CLC 6, 9, 22, 49, 68,**
  130
  See also AMWS 8; CA 29-32R; CAAS 4;
  CANR 12, 33, 52, 61, 96, 140; CP 2, 3, 4,
  5, 6, 7; DA3; DAM POET; DLB 105;
  MAL 5; MTCW 2; MTFW 2005; PFS 7;
  RGAL 4; WP
Simmel, Georg 1858-1918 .... **TCLC 64**
  See also CA 157; DLB 296

Smith, Iain Crichton 1928-1998 .... **CLC 64**
See also BRWS 9; CA 21-24R; 171; CN 1,
2, 3, 4, 5, 6; CP 1, 2, 3, 4; DLB 40, 139,
319; RGSF 2
Smith, John 1580(?)-1631 .... **LC 9**
See also DLB 24, 30; TUS
Smith, Johnston
See Crane, Stephen (Townley)
Smith, Joseph, Jr. 1805-1844 .... **NCLC 53**
Smith, Lee 1944- .... **CLC 25, 73**
See also CA 114; 119; CANR 46, 118; CN
7; CSW; DLB 143; DLBY 1983; EWL 3;
INT CA-119; RGAL 4
Smith, Martin
See Smith, Martin Cruz
Smith, Martin Cruz 1942- .. **CLC 25; NNAL**
See also BEST 89:4; BPFB 3; CA 85-88;
CANR 6, 23, 43, 65, 119; CMW 4; CPW;
DAM MULT, POP; HGG; INT CANR-
23; MTCW 2; MTFW 2005; RGAL 4
Smith, Patti 1946- .... **CLC 12**
See also CA 93-96; CANR 63
Smith, Pauline (Urmson)
1882-1959 .... **TCLC 25**
See also DLB 225; EWL 3
Smith, Rosamond
See Oates, Joyce Carol
Smith, Sheila Kaye
See Kaye-Smith, Sheila
Smith, Stevie .... **CLC 3, 8, 25, 44; PC 12**
See Smith, Florence Margaret
See also BRWS 2; CP 1; DLB 20; EWL 3;
PAB; PFS 3; RGEL 2
Smith, Wilbur (Addison) 1933- .... **CLC 33**
See also CA 13-16R; CANR 7, 46, 66, 134;
CPW; MTCW 1, 2; MTFW 2005
Smith, William Jay 1918- .... **CLC 6**
See also AMWS 13; CA 5-8R; CANR 44,
106; CP 1, 2, 3, 4, 5, 6, 7; CSW; CWRI
5; DLB 5; MAICYA 1, 2; SAAS 22;
SATA 2, 68, 154; SATA-Essay 154; TCLE
1:2
Smith, Woodrow Wilson
See Kuttner, Henry
Smith, Zadie 1976- .... **CLC 158**
See also AAYA 50; CA 193; MTFW 2005
Smolenskin, Peretz 1842-1885 .... **NCLC 30**
Smollett, Tobias (George) 1721-1771 ... **LC 2,
46**
See also BRW 3; CDBLB 1660-1789; DLB
39, 104; RGEL 2; TEA
Snodgrass, W(illiam) D(e Witt)
1926- .... **CLC 2, 6, 10, 18, 68**
See also AMWS 6; CA 1-4R; CANR 6, 36,
65, 85; CP 1, 2, 3, 4, 5, 6, 7; DAM POET;
DLB 5; MAL 5; MTCW 1, 2; MTFW
2005; RGAL 4; TCLE 1:2
Snorri Sturluson 1179-1241 .... **CMLC 56**
See also RGWL 2, 3
Snow, C(harles) P(ercy) 1905-1980 ... **CLC 1,
4, 6, 9, 13, 19**
See also BRW 7; CA 5-8R; 101; CANR 28;
CDBLB 1945-1960; CN 1, 2; DAM NOV;
DLB 15; 77; DLBD 17; EWL 3; MTCW
1, 2; MTFW 2005; RGEL 2; TEA
Snow, Frances Compton
See Adams, Henry (Brooks)
Snyder, Gary (Sherman) 1930- . **CLC 1, 2, 5,
9, 32, 120; PC 21**
See also AMWS 8; ANW; BG 1:3; CA 17-
20R; CANR 30, 60, 125; CP 1, 2, 3, 4, 5,
6, 7; DA3; DAM POET; DLB 5, 16, 165,
212, 237, 275; EWL 3; MAL 5; MTCW
2; MTFW 2005; PFS 9, 19; RGAL 4; WP
Snyder, Zilpha Keatley 1927- .... **CLC 17**
See also AAYA 15; BYA 1; CA 9-12R;
CANR 38; CLR 31; JRDA; MAICYA 1,
2; SAAS 2; SATA 1, 28, 75, 110, 163;
SATA-Essay 112, 163; YAW

Soares, Bernardo
See Pessoa, Fernando (Antonio Nogueira)
Sobh, A.
See Shamlu, Ahmad
Sobh, Alef
See Shamlu, Ahmad
Sobol, Joshua 1939- .... **CLC 60**
See Sobol, Yehoshua
See also CA 200
Sobol, Yehoshua 1939-
See Sobol, Joshua
See also CWW 2
Socrates 470B.C.-399B.C. .... **CMLC 27**
Soderberg, Hjalmar 1869-1941 ...... **TCLC 39**
See also DLB 259; EWL 3; RGSF 2
Soderbergh, Steven 1963- .... **CLC 154**
See also AAYA 43
Sodergran, Edith (Irene) 1892-1923
See Soedergran, Edith (Irene)
See also CA 202; DLB 259; EW 11; EWL
3; RGWL 2, 3
Soedergran, Edith (Irene)
1892-1923 .... **TCLC 31**
See Sodergran, Edith (Irene)
Softly, Edgar
See Lovecraft, H(oward) P(hillips)
Softly, Edward
See Lovecraft, H(oward) P(hillips)
Sokolov, Alexander V(sevolodovich) 1943-
See Sokolov, Sasha
See also CA 73-76
Sokolov, Raymond 1941- .... **CLC 7**
See also CA 85-88
Sokolov, Sasha .... **CLC 59**
See Sokolov, Alexander V(sevolodovich)
See also CWW 2; DLB 285; EWL 3; RGWL
2, 3
Solo, Jay
See Ellison, Harlan (Jay)
Sologub, Fyodor .... **TCLC 9**
See Teternikov, Fyodor Kuzmich
See also EWL 3
Solomons, Ikey Esquir
See Thackeray, William Makepeace
Solomos, Dionysios 1798-1857 .... **NCLC 15**
Solwoska, Mara
See French, Marilyn
Solzhenitsyn, Aleksandr I(sayevich)
1918- .. **CLC 1, 2, 4, 7, 9, 10, 18, 26, 34,
78, 134; SSC 32; WLC**
See Solzhenitsyn, Aleksandr Isaevich
See also AAYA 49; AITN 1; BPFB 3; CA
69-72; CANR 40, 65, 116; DA; DA3;
DAB; DAC; DAM MST, NOV; DLB 302;
EW 13; EXPS; LAIT 4; MTCW 1, 2;
MTFW 2005; NFS 6; RGSF 2; RGWL 2,
3; SSFS 9; TWA
Solzhenitsyn, Aleksandr Isaevich
See Solzhenitsyn, Aleksandr I(sayevich)
See also CWW 2; EWL 3
Somers, Jane
See Lessing, Doris (May)
Somerville, Edith Oenone
1858-1949 .... **SSC 56; TCLC 51**
See also CA 196; DLB 135; RGEL 2; RGSF
2
Somerville & Ross
See Martin, Violet Florence; Somerville,
Edith Oenone
Sommer, Scott 1951- .... **CLC 25**
See also CA 106
Sommers, Christina Hoff 1950- ...... **CLC 197**
See also CA 153; CANR 95
Sondheim, Stephen (Joshua) 1930- . **CLC 30,
39, 147; DC 22**
See also AAYA 11, 66; CA 103; CANR 47,
67, 125; DAM DRAM; LAIT 4
Sone, Monica 1919- .... **AAL**
See also DLB 312

Song, Cathy 1955- .... **AAL; PC 21**
See also CA 154; CANR 118; CWP; DLB
169, 312; EXPP; FW; PFS 5
Sontag, Susan 1933-2004 ... **CLC 1, 2, 10, 13,
31, 105, 195**
See also AMWS 3; CA 17-20R; 234; CANR
25, 51, 74, 97; CN 1, 2, 3, 4, 5, 6, 7;
CPW; DA3; DAM POP; DLB 2, 67; EWL
3; MAL 5; MAWW; MTCW 1, 2; MTFW
2005; RGAL 4; RHW; SSFS 10
Sophocles 496(?)B.C.-406(?)B.C. .... **CMLC 2,
47, 51; DC 1; WLCS**
See also AW 1; CDWLB 1; DA; DA3;
DAB; DAC; DAM DRAM, MST; DFS 1,
4, 8; DLB 176; LAIT 1; LATS 1:1; LMFS
1; RGWL 2, 3; TWA
Sordello 1189-1269 .... **CMLC 15**
Sorel, Georges 1847-1922 .... **TCLC 91**
See also CA 118; 188
Sorel, Julia
See Drexler, Rosalyn
Sorokin, Vladimir .... **CLC 59**
See Sorokin, Vladimir Georgievich
Sorokin, Vladimir Georgievich
See Sorokin, Vladimir
See also DLB 285
Sorrentino, Gilbert 1929- .. **CLC 3, 7, 14, 22,
40**
See also CA 77-80; CANR 14, 33, 115; CN
3, 4, 5, 6, 7; CP 1, 2, 3, 4, 5, 6, 7; DLB 5,
173; DLBY 1980; INT CANR-14
Soseki
See Natsume, Soseki
See also MJW
Soto, Gary 1952- ... **CLC 32, 80; HLC 2; PC
28**
See also AAYA 10, 37; BYA 11; CA 119;
125; CANR 50, 74, 107; CLR 38; CP 4,
5, 6, 7; DAM MULT; DLB 82; EWL 3;
EXPP; HW 1, 2; INT CA-125; JRDA;
LLW; MAICYA 2; MAICYAS 1; MAL 5;
MTCW 2; MTFW 2005; PFS 7; RGAL 4;
SATA 80, 120; WYA; YAW
Soupault, Philippe 1897-1990 .... **CLC 68**
See also CA 116; 147; 131; EWL 3; GFL
1789 to the Present; LMFS 2
Souster, (Holmes) Raymond 1921- .... **CLC 5,
14**
See also CA 13-16R; CAAS 14; CANR 13,
29, 53; CP 1, 2, 3, 4, 5, 6, 7; DA3; DAC;
DAM POET; DLB 88; RGEL 2; SATA 63
Southern, Terry 1924(?)-1995 .... **CLC 7**
See also AMWS 11; BPFB 3; CA 1-4R;
150; CANR 1, 55, 107; CN 1, 2, 3, 4, 5,
6; DLB 2; IDFW 3, 4
Southerne, Thomas 1660-1746 .... **LC 99**
See also DLB 80; RGEL 2
Southey, Robert 1774-1843 .... **NCLC 8, 97**
See also BRW 4; DLB 93, 107, 142; RGEL
2; SATA 54
Southwell, Robert 1561(?)-1595 .... **LC 108**
See also DLB 167; RGEL 2; TEA
Southworth, Emma Dorothy Eliza Nevitte
1819-1899 .... **NCLC 26**
See also DLB 239
Souza, Ernest
See Scott, Evelyn
Soyinka, Wole 1934- .. **BLC 3; CLC 3, 5, 14,
36, 44, 179; DC 2; WLC**
See also AFW; BW 2, 3; CA 13-16R;
CANR 27, 39, 82, 136; CD 5, 6; CDWLB
3; CN 6, 7; CP 1, 2, 3, 4, 5, 6, 7; DA;
DA3; DAB; DAC; DAM DRAM, MST,
MULT; DFS 10; DLB 125; EWL 3;
MTCW 1, 2; MTFW 2005; RGEL 2;
TWA; WLIT 2; WWE 1
Spackman, W(illiam) M(ode)
1905-1990 .... **CLC 46**
See also CA 81-84; 132

Szirtes, George 1948- .... **CLC 46; PC 51**
See also CA 109; CANR 27, 61, 117; CP 4, 5, 6, 7

Szymborska, Wislawa 1923- ... **CLC 99, 190; PC 44**
See also CA 154; CANR 91, 133; CDWLB 4; CWP; CWW 2; DA3; DLB 232; DLBY 1996; EWL 3; MTCW 2; MTFW 2005; PFS 15; RGWL 3

T. O., Nik
See Annensky, Innokenty (Fyodorovich)

Tabori, George 1914- .... **CLC 19**
See also CA 49-52; CANR 4, 69; CBD; CD 5, 6; DLB 245

Tacitus c. 55-c. 117 .... **CMLC 56**
See also AW 2; CDWLB 1; DLB 211; RGWL 2, 3

Tagore, Rabindranath 1861-1941 .... **PC 8; SSC 48; TCLC 3, 53**
See also CA 104; 120; DA3; DAM DRAM, POET; EWL 3; MTCW 1, 2; MTFW 2005; PFS 18; RGEL 2; RGSF 2; RGWL 2, 3; TWA

Taine, Hippolyte Adolphe
1828-1893 .... **NCLC 15**
See also EW 7; GFL 1789 to the Present

Talayesva, Don C. 1890-(?) .... **NNAL**

Talese, Gay 1932- .... **CLC 37**
See also AITN 1; CA 1-4R; CANR 9, 58, 137; DLB 185; INT CANR-9; MTCW 1, 2; MTFW 2005

Tallent, Elizabeth (Ann) 1954- .... **CLC 45**
See also CA 117; CANR 72; DLB 130

Tallmountain, Mary 1918-1997 .... **NNAL**
See also CA 146; 161; DLB 193

Tally, Ted 1952- .... **CLC 42**
See also CA 120; 124; CAD; CANR 125; CD 5, 6; INT CA-124

Talvik, Heiti 1904-1947 .... **TCLC 87**
See also EWL 3

Tamayo y Baus, Manuel
1829-1898 .... **NCLC 1**

Tammsaare, A(nton) H(ansen)
1878-1940 .... **TCLC 27**
See also CA 164; CDWLB 4; DLB 220; EWL 3

Tam'si, Tchicaya U
See Tchicaya, Gerald Felix

Tan, Amy (Ruth) 1952- . **AAL; CLC 59, 120, 151**
See also AAYA 9, 48; AMWS 10; BEST 89:3; BPFB 3; CA 136; CANR 54, 105, 132; CDALBS; CN 6, 7; CPW 1; DA3; DAM MULT, NOV, POP; DLB 173, 312; EXPN; FL 1:6; FW; LAIT 3, 5; MAL 5; MTCW 2; MTFW 2005; NFS 1, 13, 16; RGAL 4; SATA 75; SSFS 9; YAW

Tandem, Felix
See Spitteler, Carl (Friedrich Georg)

Tanizaki, Jun'ichiro 1886-1965 ... **CLC 8, 14, 28; SSC 21**
See Tanizaki Jun'ichiro
See also CA 93-96; 25-28R; MJW; MTCW 2; MTFW 2005; RGSF 2; RGWL 2

Tanizaki Jun'ichiro
See Tanizaki, Jun'ichiro
See also DLB 180; EWL 3

Tannen, Deborah F(rances) 1945- .. **CLC 206**
See also CA 118; CANR 95

Tanner, William
See Amis, Kingsley (William)

Tao Lao
See Storni, Alfonsina

Tapahonso, Luci 1953- .... **NNAL; PC 65**
See also CA 145; CANR 72, 127; DLB 175

Tarantino, Quentin (Jerome)
1963- .... **CLC 125**
See also AAYA 58; CA 171; CANR 125

Tarassoff, Lev
See Troyat, Henri

Tarbell, Ida M(inerva) 1857-1944 . **TCLC 40**
See also CA 122; 181; DLB 47

Tarkington, (Newton) Booth
1869-1946 .... **TCLC 9**
See also BPFB 3; BYA 3; CA 110; 143; CWRI 5; DLB 9, 102; MAL 5; MTCW 2; RGAL 4; SATA 17

Tarkovskii, Andrei Arsen'evich
See Tarkovsky, Andrei (Arsenyevich)

Tarkovsky, Andrei (Arsenyevich)
1932-1986 .... **CLC 75**
See also CA 127

Tartt, Donna 1964(?)- .... **CLC 76**
See also AAYA 56; CA 142; CANR 135; MTFW 2005

Tasso, Torquato 1544-1595 .... **LC 5, 94**
See also EFS 2; EW 2; RGWL 2, 3; WLIT 7

Tate, (John Orley) Allen 1899-1979 .. **CLC 2, 4, 6, 9, 11, 14, 24; PC 50**
See also AMW; CA 5-8R; 85-88; CANR 32, 108; CN 1, 2; CP 1, 2; DLB 4, 45, 63; DLBD 17; EWL 3; MAL 5; MTCW 1, 2; MTFW 2005; RGAL 4; RHW

Tate, Ellalice
See Hibbert, Eleanor Alice Burford

Tate, James (Vincent) 1943- ..... **CLC 2, 6, 25**
See also CA 21-24R; CANR 29, 57, 114; CP 1, 2, 3, 4, 5, 6, 7; DLB 5, 169; EWL 3; PFS 10, 15; RGAL 4; WP

Tate, Nahum 1652(?)-1715 .... **LC 109**
See also DLB 80; RGEL 2

Tauler, Johannes c. 1300-1361 ...... **CMLC 37**
See also DLB 179; LMFS 1

Tavel, Ronald 1940- .... **CLC 6**
See also CA 21-24R; CAD; CANR 33; CD 5, 6

Taviani, Paolo 1931- .... **CLC 70**
See also CA 153

Taylor, Bayard 1825-1878 .... **NCLC 89**
See also DLB 3, 189, 250, 254; RGAL 4

Taylor, C(ecil) P(hilip) 1929-1981 .... **CLC 27**
See also CA 25-28R; 105; CANR 47; CBD

Taylor, Edward 1642(?)-1729 . **LC 11; PC 63**
See also AMW; DA; DAB; DAC; DAM MST, POET; DLB 24; EXPP; RGAL 4; TUS

Taylor, Eleanor Ross 1920- .... **CLC 5**
See also CA 81-84; CANR 70

Taylor, Elizabeth 1912-1975 ..... **CLC 2, 4, 29**
See also CA 13-16R; CANR 9, 70; CN 1, 2; DLB 139; MTCW 1; RGEL 2; SATA 13

Taylor, Frederick Winslow
1856-1915 .... **TCLC 76**
See also CA 188

Taylor, Henry (Splawn) 1942- .... **CLC 44**
See also CA 33-36R; CAAS 7; CANR 31; CP 7; DLB 5; PFS 10

Taylor, Kamala (Purnaiya) 1924-2004
See Markandaya, Kamala
See also CA 77-80; 227; MTFW 2005; NFS 13

Taylor, Mildred D(elois) 1943- .... **CLC 21**
See also AAYA 10, 47; BW 1; BYA 3, 8; CA 85-88; CANR 25, 115, 136; CLR 9, 59, 90; CSW; DLB 52; JRDA; LAIT 3; MAICYA 1, 2; MTFW 2005; SAAS 5; SATA 135; WYA; YAW

Taylor, Peter (Hillsman) 1917-1994 .. **CLC 1, 4, 18, 37, 44, 50, 71; SSC 10, 84**
See also AMWS 5; BPFB 3; CA 13-16R; 147; CANR 9, 50; CN 1, 2, 3, 4, 5; CSW; DLB 218, 278; DLBY 1981, 1994; EWL 3; EXPS; INT CANR-9; MAL 5; MTCW 1, 2; MTFW 2005; RGSF 2; SSFS 9; TUS

Taylor, Robert Lewis 1912-1998 .... **CLC 14**
See also CA 1-4R; 170; CANR 3, 64; CN 1, 2; SATA 10; TCWW 1, 2

Tchekhov, Anton
See Chekhov, Anton (Pavlovich)

Tchicaya, Gerald Felix 1931-1988 .. **CLC 101**
See Tchicaya U Tam'si
See also CA 129; 125; CANR 81

Tchicaya U Tam'si
See Tchicaya, Gerald Felix
See also EWL 3

Teasdale, Sara 1884-1933 .... **PC 31; TCLC 4**
See also CA 104; 163; DLB 45; GLL 1; PFS 14; RGAL 4; SATA 32; TUS

Tecumseh 1768-1813 .... **NNAL**
See also DAM MULT

Tegner, Esaias 1782-1846 .... **NCLC 2**

Teilhard de Chardin, (Marie Joseph) Pierre
1881-1955 .... **TCLC 9**
See also CA 105; 210; GFL 1789 to the Present

Temple, Ann
See Mortimer, Penelope (Ruth)

Tennant, Emma (Christina) 1937- .. **CLC 13, 52**
See also BRWS 9; CA 65-68; CAAS 9; CANR 10, 38, 59, 88; CN 3, 4, 5, 6, 7; DLB 14; EWL 3; SFW 4

Tenneshaw, S. M.
See Silverberg, Robert

Tenney, Tabitha Gilman
1762-1837 .... **NCLC 122**
See also DLB 37, 200

Tennyson, Alfred 1809-1892 ... **NCLC 30, 65, 115; PC 6; WLC**
See also AAYA 50; BRW 4; CDBLB 1832-1890; DA; DA3; DAB; DAC; DAM MST, POET; DLB 32; EXPP; PAB; PFS 1, 2, 4, 11, 15, 19; RGEL 2; TEA; WLIT 4; WP

Teran, Lisa St. Aubin de .... **CLC 36**
See St. Aubin de Teran, Lisa

Terence c. 184B.C.-c. 159B.C. ...... **CMLC 14; DC 7**
See also AW 1; CDWLB 1; DLB 211; RGWL 2, 3; TWA

Teresa de Jesus, St. 1515-1582 .... **LC 18**

Teresa of Avila, St.
See Teresa de Jesus, St.

Terkel, Louis 1912-
See Terkel, Studs
See also CA 57-60; CANR 18, 45, 67, 132; DA3; MTCW 1, 2; MTFW 2005

Terkel, Studs .... **CLC 38**
See Terkel, Louis
See also AAYA 32; AITN 1; MTCW 2; TUS

Terry, C. V.
See Slaughter, Frank G(ill)

Terry, Megan 1932- .... **CLC 19; DC 13**
See also CA 77-80; CABS 3; CAD; CANR 43; CD 5, 6; CWD; DFS 18; DLB 7, 249; GLL 2

Tertullian c. 155-c. 245 .... **CMLC 29**

Tertz, Abram
See Sinyavsky, Andrei (Donatevich)
See also RGSF 2

Tesich, Steve 1943(?)-1996 .... **CLC 40, 69**
See also CA 105; 152; CAD; DLBY 1983

Tesla, Nikola 1856-1943 .... **TCLC 88**

Teternikov, Fyodor Kuzmich 1863-1927
See Sologub, Fyodor
See also CA 104

Tevis, Walter 1928-1984 .... **CLC 42**
See also CA 113; SFW 4

Tey, Josephine .... **TCLC 14**
See Mackintosh, Elizabeth
See also DLB 77; MSW

Thackeray, William Makepeace
1811-1863 .... NCLC **5, 14, 22, 43; WLC**
See also BRW 5; BRWC 2; CDBLB 1832-
1890; DA; DA3; DAB; DAC; DAM MST,
NOV; DLB 21, 55, 159, 163; NFS 13;
RGEL 2; SATA 23; TEA; WLIT 3

Thakura, Ravindranatha
See Tagore, Rabindranath

Thames, C. H.
See Marlowe, Stephen

Tharoor, Shashi 1956- .... CLC **70**
See also CA 141; CANR 91; CN 6, 7

Thelwall, John 1764-1834 .... NCLC **162**
See also DLB 93, 158

Thelwell, Michael Miles 1939- .... CLC **22**
See also BW 2; CA 101

Theobald, Lewis, Jr.
See Lovecraft, H(oward) P(hillips)

Theocritus c. 310B.C.- .... CMLC **45**
See also AW 1; DLB 176; RGWL 2, 3

Theodorescu, Ion N. 1880-1967
See Arghezi, Tudor
See also CA 116

Theriault, Yves 1915-1983 .... CLC **79**
See also CA 102; CCA 1; DAC; DAM
MST; DLB 88; EWL 3

Theroux, Alexander (Louis) 1939- .... CLC **2,
25**
See also CA 85-88; CANR 20, 63; CN 4, 5,
6, 7

Theroux, Paul (Edward) 1941- ..... CLC **5, 8,
11, 15, 28, 46**
See also AAYA 28; AMWS 8; BEST 89:4;
BPFB 3; CA 33-36R; CANR 20, 45, 74,
133; CDALBS; CN 1, 2, 3, 4, 5, 6, 7; CP
1; CPW 1; DA3; DAM POP; DLB 2, 218;
EWL 3; HGG; MAL 5; MTCW 1, 2;
MTFW 2005; RGAL 4; SATA 44, 109;
TUS

Thesen, Sharon 1946- .... CLC **56**
See also CA 163; CANR 125; CP 7; CWP

Thespis fl. 6th cent. B.C.- .... CMLC **51**
See also LMFS 1

Thevenin, Denis
See Duhamel, Georges

Thibault, Jacques Anatole Francois
1844-1924
See France, Anatole
See also CA 106; 127; DA3; DAM NOV;
MTCW 1, 2; TWA

Thiele, Colin (Milton) 1920- .... CLC **17**
See also CA 29-32R; CANR 12, 28, 53,
105; CLR 27; CP 1, 2; DLB 289; MAI-
CYA 1, 2; SAAS 2; SATA 14, 72, 125;
YAW

Thistlethwaite, Bel
See Wetherald, Agnes Ethelwyn

Thomas, Audrey (Callahan) 1935- .... CLC **7,
13, 37, 107; SSC 20**
See also AITN 2; CA 21-24R; 237; CAAE
237; CAAS 19; CANR 36, 58; CN 2, 3,
4, 5, 6, 7; DLB 60; MTCW 1; RGSF 2

Thomas, Augustus 1857-1934 .... TCLC **97**
See also MAL 5

Thomas, D(onald) M(ichael) 1935- . CLC **13,
22, 31, 132**
See also BPFB 3; BRWS 4; CA 61-64;
CAAS 11; CANR 17, 45, 75; CDBLB
1960 to Present; CN 4, 5, 6, 7; CP 1, 2, 3,
4, 5, 6, 7; DA3; DLB 40, 207, 299; HGG;
INT CANR-17; MTCW 1, 2; MTFW
2005; SFW 4

Thomas, Dylan (Marlais) 1914-1953 .... PC **2,
52; SSC 3, 44; TCLC 1, 8, 45, 105;
WLC**
See also AAYA 45; BRWS 1; CA 104; 120;
CANR 65; CDBLB 1945-1960; DA; DA3;
DAB; DAC; DAM DRAM, MST, POET;
DLB 13, 20, 139; EWL 3; EXPP; LAIT
3; MTCW 1, 2; MTFW 2005; PAB; PFS
1, 3, 8; RGEL 2; RGSF 2; SATA 60; TEA;
WLIT 4; WP

Thomas, (Philip) Edward 1878-1917 . PC **53;
TCLC 10**
See also BRW 6; BRWS 3; CA 106; 153;
DAM POET; DLB 19, 98, 156, 216; EWL
3; PAB; RGEL 2

Thomas, Joyce Carol 1938- .... CLC **35**
See also AAYA 12, 54; BW 2, 3; CA 113;
116; CANR 48, 114, 135; CLR 19; DLB
33; INT CA-116; JRDA; MAICYA 1, 2;
MTCW 1, 2; MTFW 2005; SAAS 7;
SATA 40, 78, 123, 137; SATA-Essay 137;
WYA; YAW

Thomas, Lewis 1913-1993 .... CLC **35**
See also ANW; CA 85-88; 143; CANR 38,
60; DLB 275; MTCW 1, 2

Thomas, M. Carey 1857-1935 .... TCLC **89**
See also FW

Thomas, Paul
See Mann, (Paul) Thomas

Thomas, Piri 1928- .... CLC **17; HLCS 2**
See also CA 73-76; HW 1; LLW

Thomas, R(onald) S(tuart)
1913-2000 .... CLC **6, 13, 48**
See also CA 89-92; 189; CAAS 4; CANR
30; CDBLB 1960 to Present; CP 1, 2, 3,
4, 5, 6, 7; DAB; DAM POET; DLB 27;
EWL 3; MTCW 1; RGEL 2

Thomas, Ross (Elmore) 1926-1995 .. CLC **39**
See also CA 33-36R; 150; CANR 22, 63;
CMW 4

Thompson, Francis (Joseph)
1859-1907 .... TCLC **4**
See also BRW 5; CA 104; 189; CDBLB
1890-1914; DLB 19; RGEL 2; TEA

Thompson, Francis Clegg
See Mencken, H(enry) L(ouis)

Thompson, Hunter S(tockton)
1937(?)-2005 .... CLC **9, 17, 40, 104**
See also AAYA 45; BEST 89:1; BPFB 3;
CA 17-20R; 236; CANR 23, 46, 74, 77,
111, 133; CPW; CSW; DA3; DAM POP;
DLB 185; MTCW 1, 2; MTFW 2005;
TUS

Thompson, James Myers
See Thompson, Jim (Myers)

Thompson, Jim (Myers)
1906-1977(?) .... CLC **69**
See also BPFB 3; CA 140; CMW 4; CPW;
DLB 226; MSW

Thompson, Judith (Clare Francesca)
1954- .... CLC **39**
See also CA 143; CD 5, 6; CWD; DFS 22

Thomson, James 1700-1748 .... LC **16, 29, 40**
See also BRWS 3; DAM POET; DLB 95;
RGEL 2

Thomson, James 1834-1882 .... NCLC **18**
See also DAM POET; DLB 35; RGEL 2

Thoreau, Henry David 1817-1862 .. NCLC **7,
21, 61, 138; PC 30; WLC**
See also AAYA 42; AMW; ANW; BYA 3;
CDALB 1640-1865; DA; DA3; DAB;
DAC; DAM MST; DLB 1, 183, 223, 270,
298; LAIT 2; LMFS 1; NCFS 3; RGAL
4; TUS

Thorndike, E. L.
See Thorndike, Edward L(ee)

Thorndike, Edward L(ee)
1874-1949 .... TCLC **107**
See also CA 121

Thornton, Hall
See Silverberg, Robert

Thorpe, Adam 1956- .... CLC **176**
See also CA 129; CANR 92; DLB 231

Thubron, Colin (Gerald Dryden)
1939- .... CLC **163**
See also CA 25-28R; CANR 12, 29, 59, 95;
CN 5, 6, 7; DLB 204, 231

Thucydides c. 455B.C.-c. 395B.C. . CMLC **17**
See also AW 1; DLB 176; RGWL 2, 3

Thumboo, Edwin Nadason 1933- .... PC **30**
See also CA 194; CP 1

Thurber, James (Grover)
1894-1961 .. CLC **5, 11, 25, 125; SSC 1,
47**
See also AAYA 56; AMWS 1; BPFB 3;
BYA 5; CA 73-76; CANR 17, 39; CDALB
1929-1941; CWRI 5; DA; DA3; DAB;
DAC; DAM DRAM, MST, NOV; DLB 4,
11, 22, 102; EWL 3; EXPS; FANT; LAIT
3; MAICYA 1, 2; MAL 5; MTCW 1, 2;
MTFW 2005; RGAL 4; RGSF 2; SATA
13; SSFS 1, 10, 19; SUFW; TUS

Thurman, Wallace (Henry)
1902-1934 ..... BLC **3; HR 1:3; TCLC 6**
See also BW 1, 3; CA 104; 124; CANR 81;
DAM MULT; DLB 51

Tibullus c. 54B.C.-c. 18B.C. .... CMLC **36**
See also AW 2; DLB 211; RGWL 2, 3

Ticheburn, Cheviot
See Ainsworth, William Harrison

Tieck, (Johann) Ludwig
1773-1853 .... NCLC **5, 46; SSC 31**
See also CDWLB 2; DLB 90; EW 5; IDTP;
RGSF 2; RGWL 2, 3; SUFW

Tiger, Derry
See Ellison, Harlan (Jay)

Tilghman, Christopher 1946- .... CLC **65**
See also CA 159; CANR 135; CSW; DLB
244

Tillich, Paul (Johannes)
1886-1965 .... CLC **131**
See also CA 5-8R; 25-28R; CANR 33;
MTCW 1, 2

Tillinghast, Richard (Williford)
1940- .... CLC **29**
See also CA 29-32R; CAAS 23; CANR 26,
51, 96; CP 2, 3, 4, 5, 6, 7; CSW

Timrod, Henry 1828-1867 .... NCLC **25**
See also DLB 3, 248; RGAL 4

Tindall, Gillian (Elizabeth) 1938- ...... CLC **7**
See also CA 21-24R; CANR 11, 65, 107;
CN 1, 2, 3, 4, 5, 6, 7

Tiptree, James, Jr. .... CLC **48, 50**
See Sheldon, Alice Hastings Bradley
See also DLB 8; SCFW 1, 2; SFW 4

Tirone Smith, Mary-Ann 1944- .... CLC **39**
See also CA 118; 136; CANR 113; SATA
143

Tirso de Molina 1580(?)-1648 .... DC **13;
HLCS 2; LC 73**
See also RGWL 2, 3

Titmarsh, Michael Angelo
See Thackeray, William Makepeace

**Tocqueville, Alexis (Charles Henri Maurice
Clerel Comte) de** 1805-1859 .. NCLC **7,
63**
See also EW 6; GFL 1789 to the Present;
TWA

Toer, Pramoedya Ananta 1925- ...... CLC **186**
See also CA 197; RGWL 3

Toffler, Alvin 1928- .... CLC **168**
See also CA 13-16R; CANR 15, 46, 67;
CPW; DAM POP; MTCW 1, 2

Toibin, Colm 1955- .... CLC **162**
See also CA 142; CANR 81; CN 7; DLB
271

Tolkien, J(ohn) R(onald) R(euel)
1892-1973 .... CLC **1, 2, 3, 8, 12, 38;
TCLC 137; WLC**
See also AAYA 10; AITN 1; BPFB 3;
BRWC 2; BRWS 2; CA 17-18; 45-48;
CANR 36, 134; CAP 2; CDBLB 1914-

1945; CLR 56; CN 1; CPW 1; CWRI 5;
DA; DA3; DAB; DAC; DAM MST, NOV,
POP; DLB 15, 160, 255; EFS 2; EWL 3;
FANT; JRDA; LAIT 1; LATS 1:2; LMFS
2; MAICYA 1, 2; MTCW 1, 2; MTFW
2005; NFS 8; RGEL 2; SATA 2, 32, 100;
SATA-Obit 24; SFW 4; SUFW; TEA;
WCH; WYA; YAW

Toller, Ernst 1893-1939 .... **TCLC 10**
See also CA 107; 186; DLB 124; EWL 3;
RGWL 2, 3

Tolson, M. B.
See Tolson, Melvin B(eaunorus)

Tolson, Melvin B(eaunorus)
1898(?)-1966 .... **BLC 3; CLC 36, 105**
See also AFAW 1, 2; BW 1, 3; CA 124; 89-
92; CANR 80; DAM MULT, POET; DLB
48, 76; MAL 5; RGAL 4

Tolstoi, Aleksei Nikolaevich
See Tolstoy, Alexey Nikolaevich

Tolstoi, Lev
See Tolstoy, Leo (Nikolaevich)
See also RGSF 2; RGWL 2, 3

Tolstoy, Aleksei Nikolaevich
See Tolstoy, Alexey Nikolaevich
See also DLB 272

Tolstoy, Alexey Nikolaevich
1882-1945 .... **TCLC 18**
See Tolstoy, Aleksei Nikolaevich
See also CA 107; 158; EWL 3; SFW 4

Tolstoy, Leo (Nikolaevich)
1828-1910 . **SSC 9, 30, 45, 54; TCLC 4,
11, 17, 28, 44, 79, 173; WLC**
See Tolstoi, Lev
See also AAYA 56; CA 104; 123; DA; DA3;
DAB; DAC; DAM MST, NOV; DLB 238;
EFS 2; EW 7; EXPS; IDTP; LAIT 2;
LATS 1:1; LMFS 1; NFS 10; SATA 26;
SSFS 5; TWA

Tolstoy, Count Leo
See Tolstoy, Leo (Nikolaevich)

Tomalin, Claire 1933- .... **CLC 166**
See also CA 89-92; CANR 52, 88; DLB
155

Tomasi di Lampedusa, Giuseppe 1896-1957
See Lampedusa, Giuseppe (Tomasi) di
See also CA 111; DLB 177; EWL 3; WLIT
7

Tomlin, Lily .... **CLC 17**
See Tomlin, Mary Jean

Tomlin, Mary Jean 1939(?)-
See Tomlin, Lily
See also CA 117

Tomline, F. Latour
See Gilbert, W(illiam) S(chwenck)

Tomlinson, (Alfred) Charles 1927- .... **CLC 2,
4, 6, 13, 45; PC 17**
See also CA 5-8R; CANR 33; CP 1, 2, 3, 4,
5, 6, 7; DAM POET; DLB 40; TCLE 1:2

Tomlinson, H(enry) M(ajor)
1873-1958 .... **TCLC 71**
See also CA 118; 161; DLB 36, 100, 195

Tonna, Charlotte Elizabeth
1790-1846 .... **NCLC 135**
See also DLB 163

Tonson, Jacob fl. 1655(?)-1736 .... **LC 86**
See also DLB 170

Toole, John Kennedy 1937-1969 ..... **CLC 19,
64**
See also BPFB 3; CA 104; DLBY 1981;
MTCW 2; MTFW 2005

Toomer, Eugene
See Toomer, Jean

Toomer, Eugene Pinchback
See Toomer, Jean

Toomer, Jean 1894-1967 .. **BLC 3; CLC 1, 4,
13, 22; HR 1:3; PC 7; SSC 1, 45;
TCLC 172; WLCS**
See also AFAW 1, 2; AMWS 3, 9; BW 1;
CA 85-88; CDALB 1917-1929; DA3;
DAM MULT; DLB 45, 51; EWL 3; EXPP;
EXPS; LMFS 2; MAL 5; MTCW 1, 2;
MTFW 2005; NFS 11; RGAL 4; RGSF 2;
SSFS 5

Toomer, Nathan Jean
See Toomer, Jean

Toomer, Nathan Pinchback
See Toomer, Jean

Torley, Luke
See Blish, James (Benjamin)

Tornimparte, Alessandra
See Ginzburg, Natalia

Torre, Raoul della
See Mencken, H(enry) L(ouis)

Torrence, Ridgely 1874-1950 .... **TCLC 97**
See also DLB 54, 249; MAL 5

Torrey, E(dwin) Fuller 1937- .... **CLC 34**
See also CA 119; CANR 71

Torsvan, Ben Traven
See Traven, B.

Torsvan, Benno Traven
See Traven, B.

Torsvan, Berick Traven
See Traven, B.

Torsvan, Berwick Traven
See Traven, B.

Torsvan, Bruno Traven
See Traven, B.

Torsvan, Traven
See Traven, B.

Tourneur, Cyril 1575(?)-1626 .... **LC 66**
See also BRW 2; DAM DRAM; DLB 58;
RGEL 2

Tournier, Michel (Edouard) 1924- .... **CLC 6,
23, 36, 95**
See also CA 49-52; CANR 3, 36, 74; CWW
2; DLB 83; EWL 3; GFL 1789 to the
Present; MTCW 1, 2; SATA 23

Tournimparte, Alessandra
See Ginzburg, Natalia

Towers, Ivar
See Kornbluth, C(yril) M.

Towne, Robert (Burton) 1936(?)- ..... **CLC 87**
See also CA 108; DLB 44; IDFW 3, 4

Townsend, Sue .... **CLC 61**
See Townsend, Susan Lilian
See also AAYA 28; CA 119; 127; CANR
65, 107; CBD; CD 5, 6; CPW; CWD;
DAB; DAC; DAM MST; DLB 271; INT
CA-127; SATA 55, 93; SATA-Brief 48;
YAW

Townsend, Susan Lilian 1946-
See Townsend, Sue

Townshend, Pete
See Townshend, Peter (Dennis Blandford)

Townshend, Peter (Dennis Blandford)
1945- .... **CLC 17, 42**
See also CA 107

Tozzi, Federigo 1883-1920 .... **TCLC 31**
See also CA 160; CANR 110; DLB 264;
EWL 3; WLIT 7

Tracy, Don(ald Fiske) 1905-1970(?)
See Queen, Ellery
See also CA 1-4R; 176; CANR 2

Trafford, F. G.
See Riddell, Charlotte

Traherne, Thomas 1637(?)-1674 .... **LC 99**
See also BRW 2; BRWS 11; DLB 131;
PAB; RGEL 2

Traill, Catharine Parr 1802-1899 .. **NCLC 31**
See also DLB 99

Trakl, Georg 1887-1914 .... **PC 20; TCLC 5**
See also CA 104; 165; EW 10; EWL 3;
LMFS 2; MTCW 2; RGWL 2, 3

Trambley, Estela Portillo .... **TCLC 163**
See Portillo Trambley, Estela
See also CA 77-80; RGAL 4

Tranquilli, Secondino
See Silone, Ignazio

Transtroemer, Tomas Gosta
See Transtromer, Tomas (Goesta)

Transtromer, Tomas (Gosta)
See Transtromer, Tomas (Goesta)
See also CWW 2

Transtromer, Tomas (Goesta)
1931- .... **CLC 52, 65**
See Transtromer, Tomas (Gosta)
See also CA 117; 129; CAAS 17; CANR
115; DAM POET; DLB 257; EWL 3; PFS
21

Transtromer, Tomas Gosta
See Transtromer, Tomas (Goesta)

Traven, B. 1882(?)-1969 .... **CLC 8, 11**
See also CA 19-20; 25-28R; CAP 2; DLB
9, 56; EWL 3; MTCW 1; RGAL 4

Trediakovsky, Vasilii Kirillovich
1703-1769 .... **LC 68**
See also DLB 150

Treitel, Jonathan 1959- .... **CLC 70**
See also CA 210; DLB 267

Trelawny, Edward John
1792-1881 .... **NCLC 85**
See also DLB 110, 116, 144

Tremain, Rose 1943- .... **CLC 42**
See also CA 97-100; CANR 44, 95; CN 4,
5, 6, 7; DLB 14, 271; RGSF 2; RHW

Tremblay, Michel 1942- .... **CLC 29, 102**
See also CA 116; 128; CCA 1; CWW 2;
DAC; DAM MST; DLB 60; EWL 3; GLL
1; MTCW 1, 2; MTFW 2005

Trevanian .... **CLC 29**
See Whitaker, Rod(ney)

Trevor, Glen
See Hilton, James

Trevor, William .. **CLC 7, 9, 14, 25, 71, 116;
SSC 21, 58**
See Cox, William Trevor
See also BRWS 4; CBD; CD 5, 6; CN 1, 2,
3, 4, 5, 6, 7; DLB 14, 139; EWL 3; LATS
1:2; RGEL 2; RGSF 2; SSFS 10; TCLE
1:2

Trifonov, Iurii (Valentinovich)
See Trifonov, Yuri (Valentinovich)
See also DLB 302; RGWL 2, 3

Trifonov, Yuri (Valentinovich)
1925-1981 .... **CLC 45**
See Trifonov, Iurii (Valentinovich); Trifonov, Yury Valentinovich
See also CA 126; 103; MTCW 1

Trifonov, Yury Valentinovich
See Trifonov, Yuri (Valentinovich)
See also EWL 3

Trilling, Diana (Rubin) 1905-1996 . **CLC 129**
See also CA 5-8R; 154; CANR 10, 46; INT
CANR-10; MTCW 1, 2

Trilling, Lionel 1905-1975 ..... **CLC 9, 11, 24;
SSC 75**
See also AMWS 3; CA 9-12R; 61-64;
CANR 10, 105; CN 1, 2; DLB 28, 63;
EWL 3; INT CANR-10; MAL 5; MTCW
1, 2; RGAL 4; TUS

Trimball, W. H.
See Mencken, H(enry) L(ouis)

Tristan
See Gomez de la Serna, Ramon

Tristram
See Housman, A(lfred) E(dward)

Trogdon, William (Lewis) 1939-
See Heat-Moon, William Least
See also AAYA 66; CA 115; 119; CANR
47, 89; CPW; INT CA-119

Trollope, Anthony 1815-1882 .... **NCLC 6, 33, 101; SSC 28; WLC**
See also BRW 5; CDBLB 1832-1890; DA; DA3; DAB; DAC; DAM MST, NOV; DLB 21, 57, 159; RGEL 2; RGSF 2; SATA 22

Trollope, Frances 1779-1863 .... **NCLC 30**
See also DLB 21, 166

Trollope, Joanna 1943- .... **CLC 186**
See also CA 101; CANR 58, 95; CN 7; CPW; DLB 207; RHW

Trotsky, Leon 1879-1940 .... **TCLC 22**
See also CA 118; 167

Trotter (Cockburn), Catharine 1679-1749 .... **LC 8**
See also DLB 84, 252

Trotter, Wilfred 1872-1939 .... **TCLC 97**

Trout, Kilgore
See Farmer, Philip Jose

Trow, George W. S. 1943- .... **CLC 52**
See also CA 126; CANR 91

Troyat, Henri 1911- .... **CLC 23**
See also CA 45-48; CANR 2, 33, 67, 117; GFL 1789 to the Present; MTCW 1

Trudeau, G(arretson) B(eekman) 1948-
See Trudeau, Garry B.
See also AAYA 60; CA 81-84; CANR 31; SATA 35

Trudeau, Garry B. .... **CLC 12**
See Trudeau, G(arretson) B(eekman)
See also AAYA 10; AITN 2

Truffaut, Francois 1932-1984 ... **CLC 20, 101**
See also CA 81-84; 113; CANR 34

Trumbo, Dalton 1905-1976 .... **CLC 19**
See also CA 21-24R; 69-72; CANR 10; CN 1, 2; DLB 26; IDFW 3, 4; YAW

Trumbull, John 1750-1831 .... **NCLC 30**
See also DLB 31; RGAL 4

Trundlett, Helen B.
See Eliot, T(homas) S(tearns)

Truth, Sojourner 1797(?)-1883 ...... **NCLC 94**
See also DLB 239; FW; LAIT 2

Tryon, Thomas 1926-1991 .... **CLC 3, 11**
See also AITN 1; BPFB 3; CA 29-32R; 135; CANR 32, 77; CPW; DA3; DAM POP; HGG; MTCW 1

Tryon, Tom
See Tryon, Thomas

Ts'ao Hsueh-ch'in 1715(?)-1763 .... **LC 1**

Tsushima, Shuji 1909-1948
See Dazai Osamu
See also CA 107

Tsvetaeva (Efron), Marina (Ivanovna) 1892-1941 .... **PC 14; TCLC 7, 35**
See also CA 104; 128; CANR 73; DLB 295; EW 11; MTCW 1, 2; RGWL 2, 3

Tuck, Lily 1938- .... **CLC 70**
See also CA 139; CANR 90

Tu Fu 712-770 .... **PC 9**
See Du Fu
See also DAM MULT; TWA; WP

Tunis, John R(oberts) 1889-1975 ..... **CLC 12**
See also BYA 1; CA 61-64; CANR 62; DLB 22, 171; JRDA; MAICYA 1; SATA 37; SATA-Brief 30; YAW

Tuohy, Frank .... **CLC 37**
See Tuohy, John Francis
See also CN 1, 2, 3, 4, 5, 6, 7; DLB 14, 139

Tuohy, John Francis 1925-
See Tuohy, Frank
See also CA 5-8R; 178; CANR 3, 47

Turco, Lewis (Putnam) 1934- ..... **CLC 11, 63**
See also CA 13-16R; CAAS 22; CANR 24, 51; CP 1, 2, 3, 4, 5, 6, 7; DLBY 1984; TCLE 1:2

Turgenev, Ivan (Sergeevich) 1818-1883 ..... **DC 7; NCLC 21, 37, 122; SSC 7, 57; WLC**
See also AAYA 58; DA; DAB; DAC; DAM MST, NOV; DFS 6; DLB 238, 284; EW 6; LATS 1:1; NFS 16; RGSF 2; RGWL 2, 3; TWA

Turgot, Anne-Robert-Jacques 1727-1781 .... **LC 26**
See also DLB 314

Turner, Frederick 1943- .... **CLC 48**
See also CA 73-76, 227; CAAE 227; CAAS 10; CANR 12, 30, 56; DLB 40, 282

Turton, James
See Crace, Jim

Tutu, Desmond M(pilo) 1931- .. **BLC 3; CLC 80**
See also BW 1, 3; CA 125; CANR 67, 81; DAM MULT

Tutuola, Amos 1920-1997 ..... **BLC 3; CLC 5, 14, 29**
See also AFW; BW 2, 3; CA 9-12R; 159; CANR 27, 66; CDWLB 3; CN 1, 2, 3, 4, 5, 6; DA3; DAM MULT; DLB 125; DNFS 2; EWL 3; MTCW 1, 2; MTFW 2005; RGEL 2; WLIT 2

Twain, Mark .... **SSC 6, 26, 34, 87; TCLC 6, 12, 19, 36, 48, 59, 161; WLC**
See Clemens, Samuel Langhorne
See also AAYA 20; AMW; AMWC 1; BPFB 3; BYA 2, 3, 11, 14; CLR 58, 60, 66; DLB 11; EXPN; EXPS; FANT; LAIT 2; MAL 5; NCFS 4; NFS 1, 6; RGAL 4; RGSF 2; SFW 4; SSFS 1, 7, 16, 21; SUFW; TUS; WCH; WYA; YAW

Tyler, Anne 1941- . **CLC 7, 11, 18, 28, 44, 59, 103, 205**
See also AAYA 18, 60; AMWS 4; BEST 89:1; BPFB 3; BYA 12; CA 9-12R; CANR 11, 33, 53, 109, 132; CDALBS; CN 1, 2, 3, 4, 5, 6, 7; CPW; CSW; DAM NOV, POP; DLB 6, 143; DLBY 1982; EWL 3; EXPN; LATS 1:2; MAL 5; MAWW; MTCW 1, 2; MTFW 2005; NFS 2, 7, 10; RGAL 4; SATA 7, 90; SSFS 17; TCLE 1:2; TUS; YAW

Tyler, Royall 1757-1826 .... **NCLC 3**
See also DLB 37; RGAL 4

Tynan, Katharine 1861-1931 .... **TCLC 3**
See also CA 104; 167; DLB 153, 240; FW

Tyndale, William c. 1484-1536 .... **LC 103**
See also DLB 132

Tyutchev, Fyodor 1803-1873 .... **NCLC 34**

Tzara, Tristan 1896-1963 .... **CLC 47; PC 27; TCLC 168**
See also CA 153; 89-92; DAM POET; EWL 3; MTCW 2

Uchida, Yoshiko 1921-1992 .... **AAL**
See also AAYA 16; BYA 2, 3; CA 13-16R; 139; CANR 6, 22, 47, 61; CDALBS; CLR 6, 56; CWRI 5; DLB 312; JRDA; MAICYA 1, 2; MTCW 1, 2; MTFW 2005; SAAS 1; SATA 1, 53; SATA-Obit 72

Udall, Nicholas 1504-1556 .... **LC 84**
See also DLB 62; RGEL 2

Ueda Akinari 1734-1809 .... **NCLC 131**

Uhry, Alfred 1936- .... **CLC 55**
See also CA 127; 133; CAD; CANR 112; CD 5, 6; CSW; DA3; DAM DRAM, POP; DFS 11, 15; INT CA-133; MTFW 2005

Ulf, Haerved
See Strindberg, (Johan) August

Ulf, Harved
See Strindberg, (Johan) August

Ulibarri, Sabine R(eyes) 1919-2003 .... **CLC 83; HLCS 2**
See also CA 131; 214; CANR 81; DAM MULT; DLB 82; HW 1, 2; RGSF 2

Unamuno (y Jugo), Miguel de 1864-1936 .. **HLC 2; SSC 11, 69; TCLC 2, 9, 148**
See also CA 104; 131; CANR 81; DAM MULT, NOV; DLB 108, 322; EW 8; EWL 3; HW 1, 2; MTCW 1, 2; MTFW 2005; RGSF 2; RGWL 2, 3; SSFS 20; TWA

Uncle Shelby
See Silverstein, Shel(don Allan)

Undercliffe, Errol
See Campbell, (John) Ramsey

Underwood, Miles
See Glassco, John

Undset, Sigrid 1882-1949 ..... **TCLC 3; WLC**
See also CA 104; 129; DA; DA3; DAB; DAC; DAM MST, NOV; DLB 293; EW 9; EWL 3; FW; MTCW 1, 2; MTFW 2005; RGWL 2, 3

Ungaretti, Giuseppe 1888-1970 ... **CLC 7, 11, 15; PC 57**
See also CA 19-20; 25-28R; CAP 2; DLB 114; EW 10; EWL 3; PFS 20; RGWL 2, 3; WLIT 7

Unger, Douglas 1952- .... **CLC 34**
See also CA 130; CANR 94

Unsworth, Barry (Forster) 1930- .... **CLC 76, 127**
See also BRWS 7; CA 25-28R; CANR 30, 54, 125; CN 6, 7; DLB 194

Updike, John (Hoyer) 1932- . **CLC 1, 2, 3, 5, 7, 9, 13, 15, 23, 34, 43, 70, 139, 214; SSC 13, 27; WLC**
See also AAYA 36; AMW; AMWC 1; AMWR 1; BPFB 3; BYA 12; CA 1-4R; CABS 1; CANR 4, 33, 51, 94, 133; CDALB 1968-1988; CN 1, 2, 3, 4, 5, 6, 7; CP 1, 2, 3, 4, 5, 6, 7; CPW 1; DA; DA3; DAB; DAC; DAM MST, NOV, POET, POP; DLB 2, 5, 143, 218, 227; DLBD 3; DLBY 1980, 1982, 1997; EWL 3; EXPP; HGG; MAL 5; MTCW 1, 2; MTFW 2005; NFS 12; RGAL 4; RGSF 2; SSFS 3, 19; TUS

Upshaw, Margaret Mitchell
See Mitchell, Margaret (Munnerlyn)

Upton, Mark
See Sanders, Lawrence

Upward, Allen 1863-1926 .... **TCLC 85**
See also CA 117; 187; DLB 36

Urdang, Constance (Henriette) 1922-1996 .... **CLC 47**
See also CA 21-24R; CANR 9, 24; CP 1, 2, 3, 4; CWP

Uriel, Henry
See Faust, Frederick (Schiller)

Uris, Leon (Marcus) 1924-2003 ... **CLC 7, 32**
See also AITN 1, 2; BEST 89:2; BPFB 3; CA 1-4R; 217; CANR 1, 40, 65, 123; CN 1, 2, 3, 4, 5, 6; CPW 1; DA3; DAM NOV, POP; MTCW 1, 2; MTFW 2005; SATA 49; SATA-Obit 146

Urista (Heredia), Alberto (Baltazar) 1947- .... **HLCS 1**
See Alurista
See also CA 182; CANR 2, 32; HW 1

Urmuz
See Codrescu, Andrei

Urquhart, Guy
See McAlmon, Robert (Menzies)

Urquhart, Jane 1949- .... **CLC 90**
See also CA 113; CANR 32, 68, 116; CCA 1; DAC

Usigli, Rodolfo 1905-1979 .... **HLCS 1**
See also CA 131; DLB 305; EWL 3; HW 1; LAW

Usk, Thomas (?)-1388 .... **CMLC 76**
See also DLB 146

West, Dorothy 1907-1998 ...... **HR 1:3; TCLC 108**
See also BW 2; CA 143; 169; DLB 76

West, (Mary) Jessamyn 1902-1984 ... **CLC 7, 17**
See also CA 9-12R; 112; CANR 27; CN 1, 2, 3; DLB 6; DLBY 1984; MTCW 1, 2; RGAL 4; RHW; SATA-Obit 37; TCWW 2; TUS; YAW

West, Morris L(anglo) 1916-1999 ..... **CLC 6, 33**
See also BPFB 3; CA 5-8R; 187; CANR 24, 49, 64; CN 1, 2, 3, 4, 5, 6; CPW; DLB 289; MTCW 1, 2; MTFW 2005

West, Nathanael 1903-1940 .. **SSC 16; TCLC 1, 14, 44**
See also AMW; AMWR 2; BPFB 3; CA 104; 125; CDALB 1929-1941; DA3; DLB 4, 9, 28; EWL 3; MAL 5; MTCW 1, 2; MTFW 2005; NFS 16; RGAL 4; TUS

West, Owen
See Koontz, Dean R.

West, Paul 1930- .... **CLC 7, 14, 96**
See also CA 13-16R; CAAS 7; CANR 22, 53, 76, 89, 136; CN 1, 2, 3, 4, 5, 6, 7; DLB 14; INT CANR-22; MTCW 2; MTFW 2005

West, Rebecca 1892-1983 ... **CLC 7, 9, 31, 50**
See also BPFB 3; BRWS 3; CA 5-8R; 109; CANR 19; CN 1, 2, 3; DLB 36; DLBY 1983; EWL 3; FW; MTCW 1, 2; MTFW 2005; NCFS 4; RGEL 2; TEA

Westall, Robert (Atkinson)
1929-1993 .... **CLC 17**
See also AAYA 12; BYA 2, 6, 7, 8, 9, 15; CA 69-72; 141; CANR 18, 68; CLR 13; FANT; JRDA; MAICYA 1, 2; MAICYAS 1; SAAS 2; SATA 23, 69; SATA-Obit 75; WYA; YAW

Westermarck, Edward 1862-1939 . **TCLC 87**

Westlake, Donald E(dwin) 1933- .. **CLC 7, 33**
See also BPFB 3; CA 17-20R; CAAS 13; CANR 16, 44, 65, 94, 137; CMW 4; CPW; DAM POP; INT CANR-16; MSW; MTCW 2; MTFW 2005

Westmacott, Mary
See Christie, Agatha (Mary Clarissa)

Weston, Allen
See Norton, Andre

Wetcheek, J. L.
See Feuchtwanger, Lion

Wetering, Janwillem van de
See van de Wetering, Janwillem

Wetherald, Agnes Ethelwyn
1857-1940 .... **TCLC 81**
See also CA 202; DLB 99

Wetherell, Elizabeth
See Warner, Susan (Bogert)

Whale, James 1889-1957 .... **TCLC 63**

Whalen, Philip (Glenn) 1923-2002 .... **CLC 6, 29**
See also BG 1:3; CA 9-12R; 209; CANR 5, 39; CP 1, 2, 3, 4, 5, 6, 7; DLB 16; WP

Wharton, Edith (Newbold Jones)
1862-1937 ... **SSC 6, 84; TCLC 3, 9, 27, 53, 129, 149; WLC**
See also AAYA 25; AMW; AMWC 2; AMWR 1; BPFB 3; CA 104; 132; CDALB 1865-1917; DA; DA3; DAB; DAC; DAM MST, NOV; DLB 4, 9, 12, 78, 189; DLBD 13; EWL 3; EXPS; FL 1:6; GL 3; HGG; LAIT 2, 3; LATS 1:1; MAL 5; MAWW; MTCW 1, 2; MTFW 2005; NFS 5, 11, 15, 20; RGAL 4; RGSF 2; RHW; SSFS 6, 7; SUFW; TUS

Wharton, James
See Mencken, H(enry) L(ouis)

Wharton, William (a pseudonym)
1925- .... **CLC 18, 37**
See also CA 93-96; CN 4, 5, 6, 7; DLBY 1980; INT CA-93-96

Wheatley (Peters), Phillis
1753(?)-1784 ... **BLC 3; LC 3, 50; PC 3; WLC**
See also AFAW 1, 2; CDALB 1640-1865; DA; DA3; DAC; DAM MST, MULT, POET; DLB 31, 50; EXPP; FL 1:1; PFS 13; RGAL 4

Wheelock, John Hall 1886-1978 .... **CLC 14**
See also CA 13-16R; 77-80; CANR 14; CP 1, 2; DLB 45; MAL 5

Whim-Wham
See Curnow, (Thomas) Allen (Monro)

White, Babington
See Braddon, Mary Elizabeth

White, E(lwyn) B(rooks)
1899-1985 .... **CLC 10, 34, 39**
See also AAYA 62; AITN 2; AMWS 1; CA 13-16R; 116; CANR 16, 37; CDALBS; CLR 1, 21; CPW; DA3; DAM POP; DLB 11, 22; EWL 3; FANT; MAICYA 1, 2; MAL 5; MTCW 1, 2; MTFW 2005; NCFS 5; RGAL 4; SATA 2, 29, 100; SATA-Obit 44; TUS

White, Edmund (Valentine III)
1940- .... **CLC 27, 110**
See also AAYA 7; CA 45-48; CANR 3, 19, 36, 62, 107, 133; CN 5, 6, 7; DA3; DAM POP; DLB 227; MTCW 1, 2; MTFW 2005

White, Hayden V. 1928- .... **CLC 148**
See also CA 128; CANR 135; DLB 246

White, Patrick (Victor Martindale)
1912-1990 ...... **CLC 3, 4, 5, 7, 9, 18, 65, 69; SSC 39**
See also BRWS 1; CA 81-84; 132; CANR 43; CN 1, 2, 3, 4; DLB 260; EWL 3; MTCW 1; RGEL 2; RGSF 2; RHW; TWA; WWE 1

White, Phyllis Dorothy James 1920-
See James, P. D.
See also CA 21-24R; CANR 17, 43, 65, 112; CMW 4; CN 7; CPW; DA3; DAM POP; MTCW 1, 2; MTFW 2005; TEA

White, T(erence) H(anbury)
1906-1964 .... **CLC 30**
See also AAYA 22; BPFB 3; BYA 4, 5; CA 73-76; CANR 37; DLB 160; FANT; JRDA; LAIT 1; MAICYA 1, 2; RGEL 2; SATA 12; SUFW 1; YAW

White, Terence de Vere 1912-1994 ... **CLC 49**
See also CA 49-52; 145; CANR 3

White, Walter
See White, Walter F(rancis)

White, Walter F(rancis) 1893-1955 ... **BLC 3; HR 1:3; TCLC 15**
See also BW 1; CA 115; 124; DAM MULT; DLB 51

White, William Hale 1831-1913
See Rutherford, Mark
See also CA 121; 189

Whitehead, Alfred North
1861-1947 .... **TCLC 97**
See also CA 117; 165; DLB 100, 262

Whitehead, E(dward) A(nthony)
1933- .... **CLC 5**
See Whitehead, Ted
See also CA 65-68; CANR 58, 118; CBD; CD 5; DLB 310

Whitehead, Ted
See Whitehead, E(dward) A(nthony)
See also CD 6

Whiteman, Roberta J. Hill 1947- ...... **NNAL**
See also CA 146

Whitemore, Hugh (John) 1936- .... **CLC 37**
See also CA 132; CANR 77; CBD; CD 5, 6; INT CA-132

Whitman, Sarah Helen (Power)
1803-1878 .... **NCLC 19**
See also DLB 1, 243

Whitman, Walt(er) 1819-1892 .. **NCLC 4, 31, 81; PC 3; WLC**
See also AAYA 42; AMW; AMWR 1; CDALB 1640-1865; DA; DA3; DAB; DAC; DAM MST, POET; DLB 3, 64, 224, 250; EXPP; LAIT 2; LMFS 1; PAB; PFS 2, 3, 13, 22; RGAL 4; SATA 20; TUS; WP; WYAS 1

Whitney, Phyllis A(yame) 1903- .... **CLC 42**
See also AAYA 36; AITN 2; BEST 90:3; CA 1-4R; CANR 3, 25, 38, 60; CLR 59; CMW 4; CPW; DA3; DAM POP; JRDA; MAICYA 1, 2; MTCW 2; RHW; SATA 1, 30; YAW

Whittemore, (Edward) Reed, Jr.
1919- .... **CLC 4**
See also CA 9-12R; 219; CAAE 219; CAAS 8; CANR 4, 119; CP 1, 2, 3, 4, 5, 6, 7; DLB 5; MAL 5

Whittier, John Greenleaf
1807-1892 .... **NCLC 8, 59**
See also AMWS 1; DLB 1, 243; RGAL 4

Whittlebot, Hernia
See Coward, Noel (Peirce)

Wicker, Thomas Grey 1926-
See Wicker, Tom
See also CA 65-68; CANR 21, 46, 141

Wicker, Tom .... **CLC 7**
See Wicker, Thomas Grey

Wideman, John Edgar 1941- ... **BLC 3; CLC 5, 34, 36, 67, 122; SSC 62**
See also AFAW 1, 2; AMWS 10; BPFB 4; BW 2, 3; CA 85-88; CANR 14, 42, 67, 109, 140; CN 4, 5, 6, 7; DAM MULT; DLB 33, 143; MAL 5; MTCW 2; MTFW 2005; RGAL 4; RGSF 2; SSFS 6, 12; TCLE 1:2

Wiebe, Rudy (Henry) 1934- .. **CLC 6, 11, 14, 138**
See also CA 37-40R; CANR 42, 67, 123; CN 1, 2, 3, 4, 5, 6, 7; DAC; DAM MST; DLB 60; RHW; SATA 156

Wieland, Christoph Martin
1733-1813 .... **NCLC 17**
See also DLB 97; EW 4; LMFS 1; RGWL 2, 3

Wiene, Robert 1881-1938 .... **TCLC 56**

Wieners, John 1934- .... **CLC 7**
See also BG 1:3; CA 13-16R; CP 1, 2, 3, 4, 5, 6, 7; DLB 16; WP

Wiesel, Elie(zer) 1928- .... **CLC 3, 5, 11, 37, 165; WLCS**
See also AAYA 7, 54; AITN 1; CA 5-8R; CAAS 4; CANR 8, 40, 65, 125; CDALBS; CWW 2; DA; DA3; DAB; DAC; DAM MST, NOV; DLB 83, 299; DLBY 1987; EWL 3; INT CANR-8; LAIT 4; MTCW 1, 2; MTFW 2005; NCFS 4; NFS 4; RGWL 3; SATA 56; YAW

Wiggins, Marianne 1947- .... **CLC 57**
See also BEST 89:3; CA 130; CANR 60, 139; CN 7

Wigglesworth, Michael 1631-1705 .... **LC 106**
See also DLB 24; RGAL 4

Wiggs, Susan .... **CLC 70**
See also CA 201

Wight, James Alfred 1916-1995
See Herriot, James
See also CA 77-80; SATA 55; SATA-Brief 44

Wilbur, Richard (Purdy) 1921- ..... **CLC 3, 6, 9, 14, 53, 110; PC 51**
See also AMWS 3; CA 1-4R; CABS 2; CANR 2, 29, 76, 93, 139; CDALBS; CP 1, 2, 3, 4, 5, 6, 7; DA; DAB; DAC; DAM MST, POET; DLB 5, 169; EWL 3; EXPP;

Cumulative Author Index

Literary Criticism Series
Cumulative Topic Index

This index lists all topic entries in Gale's *Children's Literature Review* (CLR), *Classical and Medieval Literature Criticism* (CMLC), *Contemporary Literary Criticism* (CLC), *Drama Criticism* (DC), *Literature Criticism from 1400 to 1800* (LC), *Nineteenth-Century Literature Criticism* (NCLC), *Short Story Criticism* (SSC), and *Twentieth-Century Literary Criticism* (TCLC). The index also lists topic entries in the Gale Critical Companion Collection, which includes the following publications: *The Beat Generation* (BG), and *Harlem Renaissance* (HR).

DC Cumulative Nationality Index

ALGERIAN
Camus, Albert **2**

AMERICAN
Albee, Edward (Franklin III) **11**
Baldwin, James (Arthur) **1**
Baraka, Amiri **6**
Brown, William Wells **1**
Bullins, Ed **6**
Chase, Mary (Coyle) **1**
Childress, Alice **4**
Chin, Frank (Chew Jr.) **7**
Elder, Lonne III **8**
Edson, Margaret **24**
Fornés, Mariá Irene **10**
Fuller, Charles (H. Jr.) **1**
Glaspell, Susan **10**
Gordone, Charles **8**
Gray, Spalding **7**
Guare, John **20**
Hansberry, Lorraine (Vivian) **2**
Hellman, Lillian (Florence) **1**
Henley, Beth **6, 14**
Hughes, (James) Langston **3**
Hurston, Zora Neale **12**
Hwang, David Henry **4, 23**
Kaufman, George S. **17**
Kaufman, Moises **26**
Kennedy, Adrienne (Lita) **5**
Kramer, Larry **8**
Kushner, Tony **10**
Mamet, David (Alan) **4, 24**
Mann, Emily **7**
McNally, Terrence **27**
Miller, Arthur **1**
Moraga, Cherríe **22**
Norman, Marsha **8**
Odets, Clifford **6**
O'Neill, Eugene **20**
Parks, Suzan-Lori **23**
Rabe, David (William) **16**
Shange, Ntozake **3**
Shepard, Sam **5**
Simon, (Marvin) Neil **14**
Sondheim, Stephen **22**
Stein, Gertrude **19**
Terry, Megan **13**
Valdez, Luis (Miguel) **10**
Vogel, Paula **19**
Wasserstein, Wendy **4**
Wilder, Thornton (Niven) **1, 24**
Williams, Tennessee **4**
Wilson, August **2**
Wilson, Lanford **19**
Zindel, Paul **5**

AUSTRIAN
Bernhard, Thomas **14**
Grillparzer, Franz **14**
Handke, Peter **17**
Hofmannsthal, Hugo von **4**
Schnitzler, Arthur **17**

BARBADIAN
Kennedy, Adrienne (Lita) **5**

BELGIAN
Ghelderode, Michel de **15**

CANADIAN
Pollock, Sharon **20**

CUBAN
Fornés, Mariá Irene **10**

CZECH
Chapek, Karel **1**
Havel, Václav **6**

DUTCH
Bernhard, Thomas **14**

ENGLISH
Ayckbourn, Alan **13**
Beaumont, Francis **6**
Beddoes, Thomas Lovell **15**
Behn, Aphra **4**
Byron, Lord (George Gordon Noel) **24**
Centlivre, Susanna **25**
Chapman, George **19**
Churchill, Caryl **5**
Congreve, William **2**
Dekker, Thomas **12**
Dryden, John **3**
Etherege, George **23**
Fletcher, John **6**
Ford, John **8**
Frayn, Michael **27**
Hare, David **26**
Jonson, Ben(jamin) **4**
Kureishi, Hanif **26**
Kyd, Thomas **3**
Lyly, John **7**
Marlowe, Christopher **1**
Middleton, Thomas **5**
Orton, Joe **3**
Otway, Thomas **24**
Peele, George **27**
Pinter, Harold **15**
Rattigan, Terence (Mervyn) **18**
Shaffer, Peter (Levin) **7**
Shaw, George Bernard **23**
Sheridan, Richard Brinsley **1**

Shirley, James **25**
Stoppard, Tom **6**
Webster, John **2**
Wilde, Oscar **17**

FRENCH
Anouilh, Jean (Marie Lucien Pierre) **8, 21**
Artaud, Antonin (Marie Joseph) **14**
Beaumarchais, Pierre-Augustin Caron de **4**
Beckett, Samuel **22**
Becque, Henri **21**
Camus, Albert **2**
Cocteau, Jean **17**
Corneille, Pierre **21**
Dumas, Alexandre (fils) **1**
Genet, Jean **25**
Ionesco, Eugène **12**
Joyce, James (Augustine Aloysius) **16**
Marivaux, Pierre Carlet de Chamblain de **7**
Molière **13**
Musset, Alfred de **27**
Rostand, Edmond (Eugene Alexis) **10**
Séjour, Victor **10**
Sartre, Jean-Paul **3**
Scribe, (Augustin) Eugène **5**

GERMAN
Brecht, (Eugen) Bertolt (Friedrich) **3**
Goethe, Johann Wolfgang von **20**
Hebbel, Friedrich **21**
Lessing, G. E. **26**
Schiller, Friedrich von **12**

GREEK
Aeschylus **8**
Aristophanes **2**
Euripides **4**
Menander **3**
Sophocles **1**

IRISH
Friel, Brian **8**
Goldsmith, Oliver **8**
O'Casey, Sean **12**
Sheridan, Richard Brinsley **1**
Synge, (Edmund) J(ohn) M(illington) **2**

ITALIAN
Fo, Dario **10**
Machiavelli, Niccolò **16**
Pirandello, Luigi **5**
Plautus **6**

JAPANESE
Mishima, Yukio **1**
Zeami **7**

475

DC Cumulative Title Index

503

Title Index

ISBN 0-7876-8111-3

90000